The Dasam Granth
ਸ੍ਰੀ ਦਸਮ ਗ੍ਰੰਥ ਸਾਹਿਬ

The *Dasam Granth* connotes "The Book of the Tenth Guru" of the Sikhs, Sri Guru Gobind Singh, a great reformer, littérateur, spiritual leader and unparalleled warrior, who traced his lineage to Lord Rama. After the compilation of the *Dasam Granth* by the Tenth Guru, it was called *Chhotta Granth* (the Younger Book) as compared to the *Adi Granth* (Guru Granth Sahib) which was called *Wadda Granth* (the Elder Book). *Dasam Granth* consists of religious compositions in the first part and the other part mostly comprises of mythological compositions. The work has an original, forceful and fearless expression and a social and political consciousness as the Guru wants to instill such noble qualities in man, which can make him individually great and also a very healthy constituent of the society.

Dr. Surindar Singh Kohli (1920-2003) was the very first Professor of Punjabi literature in the world. He became Professor and Head of the Department of Punjabi at Punjab University, Chandigarh in 1962 and retired in 1979. During this period he created forty-nine successful Ph.D. research scholars under his guidance. He has not only made a significant contribution to the field of Punjabi literature, research and guidance, but has done an outstanding service in the realm of comparative religion in general and Sikh religion in particular. He was an authority on Sikh scriptures and has made their analytical and thorough study in a dispassionate and scholarly manner. His works are marked by clarity, brevity and profound scholarship.

The Dasam Granth
ਸ੍ਰੀ ਦਸਮ ਗ੍ਰੰਥ ਸਾਹਿਬ
The Second Scripture of the Sikhs
written by
Sri Guru Gobind Singh

Translated into English by
Surindar Singh Kohli

Munshiram Manoharlal
Publishers Pvt. Ltd.

ISBN 978-81-215-1044-8
Reprinted **2016**
First published 2005

© Munshiram Manoharlal Publishers Pvt. Ltd.

All rights reserved, including those of translation into other languages.
No part of this book may be reproduced, stored in a retrieval system,
or transmitted in any form, or by any means, electronic,
mechanical, photocopying, recording, or otherwise,
without the written permission of the publisher.

PRINTED IN INDIA
Published by **Vikram Jain** *for*
Munshiram Manoharlal Publishers Pvt. Ltd.
PO Box 5715, 54 Rani Jhansi Road, New Delhi 110 055, INDIA

www.mrmlbooks.com

Contents

Preface — vii
Introduction — ix
   Life and Footprints of Guru Gobind Singh — ix
   Autobiograghy of Guru in Bachittar Natak (AD 1666-96) — xiv
   A Glimpse of Sri Guru Sobha of Sainapat — xxiv
   Chronology of the Main Events — xxvii
   Literary Contributions of Guru Gobind Singh—A View — xxviii

JAAPU — **1**

GYAN PRABODH — **12**

AKAL USTAT — **38**

ATH CHANDI CHARITRA UKATI BILAS — **64**

CHANDI CHARITRA II — **86**

VAR SRI BHAGAUTI JI KI — **103**

BACHITTAR NATAK — **111**
   Apni Katha (Autobiography) — 118
   Chaubis Avatar (Vishnu's Twenty-four Incarnations) — 140
   Hymns of the Tenth Guru — 537
   Thirty-three Swayyas — 539
   The Swayyas in Praise of the Khalsa — 542

SHRI SHASTAR NAAM-MAALA PURANA — **544**

ZAFARNAMAH — **596**

Preface

For several years I had been thinking of translating into English the *Dasam Granth*, the Second Sikh Scripture. The First Scripture i.e., the *Adi Granth* or *Guru Granth Sahib* had been translated earlier. The Professor and Head of the Department of Punjabi Literary Studies of Punjabi University, Patiala, had assured me that he would get my translation published by the university itself. But to my great surprise I received a letter from the Secretary of the Sikh National Heritage Trust, Birmingham (U.K.) in the second half of 1993, that their Trust wanted to get the *Dasam Granth* translated into English and since they considered me the appropriate person for this work, they requested me to spell out my conditions for this work. Since I had retired from the Punjab University, Chandigarh as Professor and Head of the Department of Punjabi several years earlier, I was in need of some financial support for this work of great magnitude. I had already translated a few smaller portions of the work of Guru Gobind Singh and published the same in my book *The Life and Ideals of Guru Gobind Singh* in 1986. At that time I was staying with my younger son at Vancouver (Canada), when the letter of the Trust was received at home in Chandigarh. An agreement was executed with the Trust, by which they had to pay me a fixed amount every month for three years, when the work was to be completed. The Trust wanted to publish this work in several volumes like the English translation of *Guru Granth Sahib*. Since my elder son lived at home in Chandigarh and my daughter in England, the Trust had to make payment of the monthly amount to me in India, Canada or England, wherever I lived as a roving ambassador of Sikhism.

I began the work of translation in Canada, where I was staying at that time. From Canada, I came to meet my daughter for a month in Coventry (U.K.) in the beginning of 1994, from where I went to my home in Chandigarh in March 1994. But the providence had destined me for a long stay in England, because of some serious problems of my daughter. I reached England again by the end of July 1994, where I am still staying. According to the agreement, the work of translation had begun by the end of 1993 and had to be delivered completely by the end of 1996 after three years. The work was done in full swing and by May 1995, more than half the work was done. Since the Trust wanted to begin publishing side by side, the Secretary received from me on May 27, 1995 the translated work from the beginning upto the nineteenth Rudra incarnation. They had arranged the publication with Messrs Singh Brothers, Bazar Mai Sewan, Amritsar (India), but because of some reasons, this could not be accomplished. The work was of such magnitude that it could not be finished in three years. It took me at least three and a half years to complete it. The Secretary received the remaining portion of the translation on May 7, 1997, beginning from the twentieth incarnation of Rama upto the end of the *Dasam Granth*. I had to do the complete translation, although I had told verbally the Trust that they cannot publish *Charitropakhyan Hikayats* (minus *Zafarnama*) and *Asphotak Kabit* without the permission by SGPC, the central Sikh organisation, to which they agreed.

It is from May 1995 upto this day, i.e., for more than seven years, the Trust has not been able to publish the translation. The manuscript is with them and whenever they like, they can publish it in several volumes alongwith the original. In the meantime the present expressed their desire to publish only the translation itself. There has been various queries why the work is not being published. Therefore, I have decided that only the translation be published, so that the world may be able to know the contents of this Second Sikh Scripture and also know that it contains only a few works of the Guru alongwith the compositions of the court-poets and some works of poetic exercise by the Guru.

It was Guru Gobind Singh himself who bestowed the position of Guruship on the *Adi Granth*, ending the line of personal Guruship for all times.

Before the publication of the translation, as an Introduction I have given the brief life of the Guru alongwith my Introductory Note on the *Dasam Granth*.

I am confident that the long-standing need of this publication will be welcomed by the Sikhs as well as the scholars of other religions.

SURINDAR SINGH KOHLI

Manchester, U.K.
26 January 2001

Introduction

LIFE AND FOOTPRINTS OF GURU GOBIND SINGH

In his autobiography named Bachittar Natak, Guru Gobind Singh has traced his lineage to Lord Rama. In his previous birth, as "Dusht Daman," he was absorbed in deep meditation in the vicinity of seven-pinnacled Hemkunt. This sacred mount had been hallowed by the footprints of Guru Nanak, the founder of Sikhism. The sage of Hemkunt was destined to be the tenth and last successor of the Great Guru and give final touches to his mission in the world. The Lord appeared to him and said, "I have appointed thee as my son and have created thee to propagate the *panth* (the path), spread *dharma* (righteousness), and forbid the people from unwise acts." The sage bowed his head, standing with folded hands and replied, "The *panth* (the path) will spread in the world only with Thine assistance." The Guru proceeds to record in his autobiography: "For this reason, the Lord sent me and I was born in the world. Whatever the Lord has spoken to me, I am saying the same to you. I have no enmity with anyone. Whosoever will speak of me as the supreme *Ishvara*, fie upon all of them. Consider me as His slave, there is not an iota of doubt about it. I am the slave of the supreme *Purusha* and have come to see the play of the world. Whatever the Lord of the World hath said, I, repeat the same. I shall not keep aloof from the *jivas* of this world."

Guru Gobind Singh was born at Patna in the State of Bihar on December 22, 1666, when his father Guru Tegh Bahadur, the ninth Sikh Guru was touring through Kamarup, the region of sorcery, touching the areas already visited by Guru Nanak and preaching his mission. The ninth Guru had left his family at Patna and [went] deeper into Assam in view of his mission and also at the request of his disciple Rai[...] had been sent by Aurangzeb at the head of Imperial forces in order to invade [...] The news of the birth of Govind Rai were conveyed to the Guru, when thr[...] [agreeme]nt had been reached between the king of Assam and the envoy of [...] [G]reat soul had descended on the earth in order to give final shape [...] and aggression.

[...] Singh during his short life-span of forty-two years are [...] accomplished marvels as a spiritual teacher, as a leader of [...] [lit]erary artist. His life was a life of struggle and strife. "As [...] [ne]w contributions and procured followers from all parts [...] [kn]own as "Manjha," as the splendid physique of the [...] [ma]terial which could be effectively exploited to be [...] but as a leader he perceived the necessity of a [...] the value of a secure retreat."

[...] main divisions:

The dates of the above-mentioned periods are approximate dates. A short detail of these periods is given in the following pages. Each period is marked by some significant developments in the life of the great Guru.

At Patna (1661-70)

It is recorded that of the first six or seven years of his life, the young Govind remained at Patna, while his father returned from the east and journeyed homewards in early 1668. It was probably considered necessary to keep the child at a safe distance from the jealous Sodhis, who felt very sore about the denial of Guruship to them at the instance of Guru Tegh Bahadur. The early schooling of young Govind was, therefore, done at Patna. The language of the area had a great impact on him. His poetic compositions are mainly written in the literary language of the area. He studied not only the Bihari language, but also Sanskrit, Persian and Arabic.

At the age of four and five, Govind Rai, led a group of young children and used to play on the bank of the Ganges. Sometimes, as a sport, two parties were formed and battles were fought. The courage, bravery and material trend of the child manifested itself in his various movements. Before he left Patna, he was noted as a great marksman, whose arrows never missed the targets. Many elderly and saintly people saw in him a great spiritual force and a would-be leader of humanity.

At Anandpur (1670-82)

At the call of his father, the young Govind left Patna for Anandpur in 1670 with the members of his family. The ninth Guru was highly pleased to meet his son. He had made arrangements not only for his further schooling in Sanskrit, Persian, and Arabic, but also in archery and swordsmanship. Though he himself had passed several years of his life in seclusion and had led a saintly life, he wanted his son to wield the dual authority like his grandfather Guru Hargovind (the sixth Guru), the temporal grandeur (*miri*) and the spiritual power (*piri*). This was the requirement of the times.

It is recorded in Sikh chronicles that Kashmiri Brahmins, fearing a forceful on-slaught on their religion, approached the ninth Sikh Guru for his assistance and advice. The Guru became very pensive and wanted to save *dharma* at all costs. On seeing his father immersed in deep thoughts, the young son enquired from him about the reason. The Guru replied that the country was subjected to a rule of tyranny, which demanded the sacrifice of a great soul. The young Gobind, who was only nine, immediately said, "I do not see a worthier soul than yours for the purpose." The father was highly satisfied because such words could only come from the mouth of a worthy successor. Thereafter the Guru is said to have started on a tour in order to exhort the people to become fearless and to face the tyranny. He openly declared: "Frighten not and Fear not." His words and his following were considered a danger to the state. He was arrested and finally beheaded under orders from the emperor on November 11, 1675. He was succeeded by his son as the tenth and the last Guru of the Sikhs at the tender age of nine.

After the martyrdom of his father, Guru Gobind Singh began to consolidate his position as the spiritual head of the community. The Sikhs came from all directions to meet their new spiritual g... and brought splendid gifts for him. The Guru asked the Sikhs to bring in future war-material... Within a couple of years, the Guru raised a contingent of brave and selfless Sikh... shortage of arms and ammunition, horses and swords. Such activities in the h... ...ised great fears in the minds of the hill-chiefs, who became antagonisti... ...veral skirmishes here and there.

...ta (1682-86)

...vitation of the Raja of Nahan, the Guru h...
...ave stayed here for about four ye...
...fought including the fa...

literary pursuits. Several Sanskrit and Persian classics were translated by various poets, who had gathered at Paonta and enjoyed the munificence of the great Guru. Sometimes poetical symposiums were held and the Guru distributed the awards. Most of the compositions of the Guru were written at Paonta.

Baba Ajit Singh, the eldest son of the Guru was born to Mata Sundari, at Paonta.

The number of court-poets of Guru Gobind Singh has been fixed at fifty-two. Most of them were present at Paonta and helped in rendering the classical literature into Brajbhasha, especially from Sanskrit. The poets whose renderings from Sanskrit are available, are Alam, Amrit Rai, Sainapat, Hans Ram, Kuvresh, Tehkan, Mangal, and Lakhan.

At Anandpur Again (1686-1704)

Anandpur was strategically most important base for the Guru, where he returned in 1686. The hill-chiefs becoming more jealous with the increasing popularity of the Guru and finding in his religious reforms a grave danger for their traditional religion, misinterpreted the activities of the Guru to the Mughal Emperor and sought his help. They depicted him as a very dangerous revolutionary for the State and Society. The bigot Muslim Emperor willingly agreed. Therefore, Anandpur was besieged on one side by the hill-chiefs and on the other side by the Imperial forces. The Guru was pressed to vacate Anandpur.

Before the siege, on the Baisakhi day of 1699, the Khalsa was born. The "Five Beloved Ones" presented themselves for sacrifice. They were administered "the nectar of double-edged sword" (*khande ki pahul*) and were named as the Khalsa or the Pure. The Guru vested himself in the Khalsa. In the words of Indubhushan Banerjee, "the introduction of *pahul* and the simultaneous abolition of the pontifical Guruship formed the cornerstone of the edifice built by Guru Gobind Singh. Militarism was now adopted finally as an article of creed and the leadership of the community was left to the community itself, thus bringing into existence a military commonwealth with the fullest of democratic freedom."[1] In the words of Gokul Chand Narang, "Abolition of caste-prejudices, equality of privileges with one another and with the Guru, common worship, common place of pilgrimage, common baptism for all classes, and lastly, common external appearance—these were the means besides common leadership and the community of aspirations, which Govind employed to bring about unity among his followers, and by which he bound them together into a compact mass before they were hurled against the legions of the great Mughals."[2]

During this period three sons where born to Mata Jito, Jujhar Singh in 1690, Zorawar Singh in 1696 and Fateh Singh in 1699.

When Anandpur was besieged the Guru and the Khalsa fought against the enemy with full fury. One fiery Khalsa could stand against a lakh and a quarter of the enemy—such was the spirit infused into the Khalsa by the Guru. The enemy wanted the Guru to leave the strategic town of Anandpur. "The sight of the suffering Khalsa and the solemn promises of the enemy for a safe exit moved him to leave the town, which he did in the winter of 1704."[3] When the Guru came out with his followers, he was attacked by the enemy on the banks of the Sarsa. In the ensuing confusion, the Guru was separated from his family members except his two elder sons Ajit Singh and Jujhar Singh. His two younger sons alongwith his mother took shelter with an old servant who betrayed them and handed them over to the officials of the Governor of Sarhind. The children were bricked alive and their grandmother could not survive the shock. The Guru himself proceeded to Chamkaur with only forty brave Sikhs, when he was besieged in the dilapidated fortress.

---

[1] *Evolution of the Khalsa*, vol. II, p. 118.
[2] *The Transformation of Sikhism*, p. 83.
[3] Teja Singh and Ganda Singh, *A Short History of the Sikhs*, vol. I, p. 72.

The warriors went out of the fortress in small groups and gave a tough flight to the enemy. Both the elder sons of the Guru and three "Beloved Ones" fell in the battlefield. When only five Sikhs were left to defend the fortress, they requested the Guru to leave in order to fulfil his mission. The Guru obeyed "The Five" and left the fortress in the darkness.

At Damdama (1704-5)

Passing through the thorny wilds of Machhiwara without any food and shelter for days, the Guru met Nabbi Khan and Ghani Khan who carried him in a litter declaring him as "Uchch ka Pir," evading the pursuing army. With the help of the friendly Muslims, the Guru reached Ferozepore district, where he collected his men again and the last, battle was fought at Muktsar, where the revolting, forty Sikhs also laid down their lives for his mission. They are still remembered as the "Forty Saved Ones" with great reverence. The Guru ultimately reached Talwandi Sabo, which is now known as Damdama Sahib. Here the Guru stayed for nine and a half months. The recension of the *Adi Granth*, known as the "Damdama Wali Bir" was prepared here. The Guru is said to have dictated the whole of the *Adi Granth* from memory. He added the hymns of his father, giving the scripture a final form. The Guru made Damdama Sahib a great seat of learning therefore, it is often called "Guru ki Kashi".

At Nander (1707-8)

Aurangzeb died in March 1707. A war of succession ensued between his sons Bahadur Shah and Tara Azam. In this war Bahadur Shah was victorious. He had earlier approached the Guru for help through Bhai Nand Lal and the Guru acceded to his request. After his victory, the new Emperor presented the Guru a robe of honour. For sometime the Guru accompanied the emperor to Deccan at the royal request, but later on broke off and encamped at Nander, where Madho Das Bairagi was converted to Sikhism and given the name of Banda Singh. This new convert was sent by the Guru to Punjab and the Sikhs were instructed to cooperate with him in his objective of ending the unjust and tyrannical rule. The Guru stayed at Nander till his death.

While at Nander, the Guru was stabbed by a Pathan, who had come to wreck vengeance due to old animosity. The Guru was attacked while he was asleep. But the assailant was immediately despatched by the Guru's sabre. The wound was sewn up and within a few days, it healed. But one day when the Guru tried to bend a stiff bow, the wound opened up again and there was good deal of bleeding. The Guru knew that he was going to cast off his earthly body, therefore, on October 7, 1708, he called all his Sikhs, who could be gathered on the occasion. In the words of Macauliffe, "He opened the *Granth Sahib* and placing five paise and a cocoanut before it, solemnly bowed to it as his successor. Then uttering 'Waheguru ji ka Khalsa, Waheguru ji ki Fateh,' he circumambulated the sacred volume and said, "O Beloved Khalsa! Let him who desire to behold me, behold the *Guru Granth*, Obey the *Granth Sahib*. It is the visible body of the Guru. And let him who desireth to meet me diligently, search its hymn."[1] The Guru then breathed his last.

The Guru had led the Sikhs from generation to generation in the practice and qualities which make a great nation; and now that the task was over, the last of them merged his personality in the ranks of his disciples. All Sikhs history had been moving towards this divine event. There was to be no personal Guru in future. The whole Sikh community, in its organised form called the "Panth," was to guide itself by the teachings of the Guru as incorporated in the *Holy Granth*, and also by the collective sense of the Community.[2]

A short sketch of the life of the Guru has been presented above. There are, however, two different significant facets of his life. Like his grandfather Guru Hargobind, the sixth Guru, besides being a spiritual preceptor, he led a princely life. Guru Hargobind was called a True King (*Sachcha Patshah*)

---

[1] M.A. Macauliffe, *The Sikh Religion*, vol. V, p. 244.
[2] Teja Singh and Ganda Singh, *A Short History of the Sikhs*, vol. I, pp. 78-79.

by his Sikhs, likewise the tenth Guru was called *Kalgian Wala* (crest-worn), *Chitian Bajan Wala* (white falcon carrier) and *Neele Ghore Wala* (blue-horse-rider).

The Kingly Life of Guru Gobind Singh: The Guru used to hold a court, sit on a throne and wear crest on his head like a king. He used to carry falcon on his hand, ride a swift-footed horse and used to go hunting like a king. Every word from his mouth was like an order for his Sikhs. His kingly demeanour has been described by Bhai Sukha Singh in his *Guru Bilas Patshahi Daswin* in the following words: "The Guru wore costly dress and valuable ornaments on his body. The sword hung from his left side. . . . There was a shining girdle round his waist. . . . The studded crest was worn on the head. . . . In his one hand he had a bow and in the other an arrow. In this way, the Gracious Lord came on the throne. Like kings, he had poets in his court."

The Guru was a great general and commander of his forces. He fixed a special uniform for his army, on account of which even a single Sikh could be recognised among lakhs of people. The spirit that the ambrosia (*amrit*) filled in the Khalsa, could enable one to withstand a quarter and a lakh of hordes. In *Prachin Panth Prakash*, Bhangoo Rattan Singh has given the following description: "The True Guru gave arms to the Khalsa alongwith various types of dresses. The Guru would sit in the centre on a cot and around him the Singhs would stand completely armed. Among his Singhs, the Guru appeared like Krishna among his *gopis*. He would order the Singhs to march, run or stand. On his orders the Singhs would sit, get up or run. On his orders some Singhs would march in turns catching hold of mighty clubs. The True Guru would stand in the ploughed field, the Singhs would fight with the clods."

The major part of the life of the Guru passed in fighting battles. He has depicted these battles in Bachittar Natak. On one side there were Mughal forces and on the other the army of the hill-chiefs. On this account, he had to erect several forts like Anandgarh, Kesgarh, Lohgarh and Holgarh. He instructed his Sikhs to wear long hair and to arm themselves. This fact is mentioned in *Parchi Patshahi Daswin* by Bhai Sewa Das in the following manner. "Once the Guru was encamped in Lakhi forest. A Sikh approached him and said that a batch of Sikhs coming to meet the Guru had been plundered on the way by a Subedar. The Guru remained calm and gave no reply. The very next day another Sikh came and said that another batch of Sikhs had been looted by some other Subedar. The Guru said why it is not voiced that the Sangat had plundered the Subedar. . . . And now I shall cause the Sangat to catch hold of *bhagauti* (the sword) and cause the sparrows to tear away the falcons. The Guru said further, whosoever will be my Sikhs, they will not remain without long hair (*keshas*) and arms. The human being is incomplete without them. He becomes a complete person when he adopts both of them. Then following the instructions of the Guru, the Sikhs wore long hair and armed themselves. Then the Guru said that the Sangat would be trained then in warfare. . . . "

Guru Gobind Singh as a Spiritual Preceptor: The spirit of the First Guru manifested itself in the Tenth Guru, who being one with omnipotent. Lord, was the master of all powers. But having been embodied as a human being, he had to face several odds and obstacles. Howsoever, he did not use any spiritual power. If Guru Nanak, as is often claimed by *Janamsakhis*, had flown from one place to another in order to reform the world, he would have accomplished his task within days and months. But he had been marching on foot for about twenty-two years of his life and reached distant lands. In a similar manner, the Tenth Guru being master of all the powers, he did not use any of them. It is recorded in the forty-first Sakhi of *Sau Sakhi:* ". . . then the Guru stretched his bow and all the mountains trembled. There were supplications: O Kind Guru! Protect us! Protect us! . . ." Then the Guru said, ". . . I would destroy the whole world with an arrow, but I am embodied as a human being. I shall act according to the limitations."

The ideal of the Guru was the propagation of *dharma* in all directions. He himself has written in Bachittar Natak:

I have come into the world for this task

I have been sent by the Guru for the sake of *dharma*
He instructed me to spread *dharma* everywhere
And subdue all the evil-minded ones and tyrants.

Where as the Guru had to spread *dharma*, his objective was also to destroy and eradicate *adharma*. His message is contained in his hymns. He has elucidated the views of the earlier Gurus. His primary teaching concerns the attunement of the human being with the ever-awakening Lord. He rejected the worship of gods and goddesses and the practice of *karmakanda*. He said,

(The Khalsa) should always remember the Ever-Awakening Lord. And should not bring any other in his mind.

He should devote himself with perfect! love and faith.
And should not believe in fasts, graves and tombs at all.

For higher spiritual life the adoption, and observance of good qualities in life is essential. The Guru said, "O Primal Power! Give me this boon, that I may not deter from good actions. I should not fear an enemy when I go to the battlefield and with full determination, I may gain victory. And I give this advice to my mind that I may always be ready to utter Thy Praises. When the end of my life draws near, I may die as a warrior in the battlefield."

The following words of the Guru are very significant: "I have to take the Panth to higher planes, therefore, we have not to imitate the unworthy and debased." (*Sau Sakhi.*) The Guru preached the equality of all the humanity. None can be lowly because of caste and birth. He said,

The temple and the mosque are the same
The worship (of the Hindus) and prayer (of the Muslims) are the same
Though seemingly diverse, the human being is the same everywhere.
The Gods, the Demons, the Yakshas, the Gandharvas, the Turks and the Hindus,
All are the manifestations according to the nature of various countries.
The same eyes, the same ears, the same body, the same nature,
There is the same combination of earth, air, fire, and water.

Just as God and Guru are one, likewise the Guru and the Sikh are one. When the Sikh, following the discipline enunciated by the Guru, becomes pure, he attains attunement with the Guru. This is the reason, that the Guru is within the Khalsa (The Pure) and the Khalsa is within the Guru. The Guru belongs to God, therefore, the Khalsa belongs to God. The victory of the Khalsa is the victory of the Guru and God, therefore, it is said, "Waheguru ji ka Khalsa, Waheguru ji ki Fateh."

AUTOBIOGRAPHY OF GURU IN BACHITTAR NATAK (AD 1666-96)

Section II

Ancestry

Now, I narrate my own story and the origin of the Sodhi clan. In the beginning, when the world was created, it was brought into being by the One Lord, Kal Sain was the first king, who was of immeasurable strength and supreme beauty. Kalket became the second king and Karurabaras, the third. Kaldhuj was the fourth king, from whom the whole world originated. He had a thousand eyes and a thousand feet. He slept on Sheshanaga, therefore, he was called the master of Shesha. Out of the secretion from one of his ears, Madhu and Kaitabh came into being. And from the secretion of the other ear, the whole world materialised. After some period; the Lord killed the demons (Madhu and Kaitabh), when their marrow flowed into the ocean. The greasy substance floated thereon. Because of that *med* (marrow), the earth was called *medha* (or *medani*). Because of virtuous actions; a *Purusha* (person) is known as *devata* (godly) and because of evil actions, he is known as *asura* (demoniac). If everything is described

INTRODUCTION   XV

in detail, it is feared that the description will become voluminous. There were many kings after Kaldhuj like Daksha Prajapati, etc. Ten thousand daughters were born to them, whose beauty was not matched by others. In due course all these daughters were married with the kings. Kadru, Diti and Aditi became the wives of sages (*rishis*) and Nagas, their enemies (like Garuda); the gods and demons were born to them.

In this way, the sun was born, from whom Surajvansh (the Dynasty of Sun clan) originated. If I describe the names of the kings of this clan, I fear a great extension of the story. In this clan, there was a king named Raghu, who was the originator of Raghuvansh (the clan of Raghu) in the world. He had a great son Aja, a mighty warrior and superb archer. When he renounced the world as a Yogi, he passed on his kingdom to his son Dasharatha, who had been a great archer. He had three wives, the eldest one gave birth to Rama. The others gave birth to Bharat, Lakshman and Shatrughan. They ruled over their kingdom for a long time after which they left for their heavenly abode. After that the two sons of Sita (and Rama) became the kings. They married the Punjabi princesses and performed various types of sacrifices. There they founded two cities. Lav founded Lahore and Kush Kasur. Both the cities surpassed in beauty to that of Lanka and Amravati. For a long time both the brothers ruled over their kingdom and ultimately they were bound down by the noose of death. After them their sons and grandsons ruled over the world. They were innumerable, therefore, it is difficult to describe all. It is not possible to count the names and castes of all those who ruled their kingdoms in all the four *yugas* (ages). If now you shower your grace upon me, I shall describe (a few) names, as I know them. Kal Ket and Kal Rai had innumerable descendents. Kal Ket was a mighty warrior, who drove out Kal Rai from his city. Kal Rai settled in the country named Sanaudh and married the king's daughter. A son was born to him, who was named Sodhi Rai. Sodhi Rai was the founder of Sanaudh dynasty by the will of the supreme *Purusha*. His sons and grandsons were called Sodhis. They became very famous in the world and gradually prospered in wealth. They ruled over the country in various ways and subdued kings of many countries. They extended their *dharma* everywhere and had the royal canopy over their heads. They performed Rajsu sacrifice several times declaring themselves as supreme rulers, after conquering kings of various countries. They performed Bajmedh sacrifice (horse-sacrifice) several times, clearing their dynasty of all the blemishes. After that there arose quarrels and differences within the dynasty and none could set the things right. The great warriors and archers moved towards the battlefield for a fight. The world has perished after quarrels on wealth and property from very olden times. The attachment, ego and infights spread widely and the world was conquered by lust and anger. The whole world was slave of the mammon and went in search for it and bowed before it.

Section III

This sections describes the battles between the descendants of Lav and Kush. Ultimately the descendants of Lav were the conquerors and descendants of Kush were defeated. Those who survived, ran away to safety. They settled at Kashi and studied the four Vedas. They remained therefor several years.

Section IV

Those who studied Vedas, were called Vedis (Bedis). They absorbed themselves in good acts of righteousness. The Sodhi King of Madra Desha (Punjab) sent letters to them entreating them to forget the past enmities. The messenger sent by the king came to Kashi and gave the message to all the Bedis. All the reciters of the Vedas came to Madra Desha and made obeissance to the king. The king caused them to recite the Vedas in the traditional manner and all the brethren (both Sodhis and Bedis) sat together. *Samaveda*, *Yajurveda*, and *Rigveda* were recited. The essence of the sayings was imbibed (by the king and his clan). The sin-remover *Atharvaveda* was recited. The king was highly pleased and he bequeathed his kingdom to Bedis. He himself adopted the sin-destroyer Vanaprastha ashrama.

He put on the grab of a sage (*rishi*) and gave his kingdom to the reciter (Amrit Rai). Other people, forgetting all sorrows and leaving their wealth and property, absorbed themselves in divine love.

Having been bestowed the kingdom, the Bedi was very much pleased. With happy heart, he predicted this boon: "When in the Iron Age, I shall be called Nanak, you will attain the Supreme State and be worshipped by the world."

The descendants of Lav, after handing over the kingdom, went to the forest and the Bedis (descendants of Kush) began to rule. They enjoyed all comforts of the earth in various ways.

You have listened to the recitation of three Vedas and while listening to the fourth, you gave away your kingdom. When I shall have taken three births, you will be made the Guru in the fourth birth. That king left for the forest and this one absorbed himself in royal pleasures. To what extent I should narrate the story? It is feared that this book will become voluminous.

Section V

Guru Nanak to Guru Tegh Bahadur

There arose again quarrels and enmities. There was none to defuse the situation. In due course of time it actually happened that the Bedi clan lost its kingdom. The Brahmins acted like Shudras and Kshatriyas like Vaishyas. The Vaishyas acted like Kshatriyas and Shudras like Brahmins. Only twenty villages were left with the Bedis, where they became agriculturists. A long time passed like this till the birth of Nanak. Nanak Rai took birth in that Bedi clan. He brought comfort to all his disciples and helped them at all times.

Guru Nanak spread *dharma* in the Iron Age and put the seekers on the path. Those who followed the Path propagated by him, were never haunted by the vices. All those who came within his fold they were absolved of all their sins and troubles, their sorrows, their wants and even transmigration. Nanak transformed himself to Angad and spread *dharma* in the world. He was called Amar Das in the next transformation. A lamp was lighted from the lamp. When the opportune time came for the boon, then the Guru was called Ramdas. He was bestowed upon the old boon, when Amar Das departed for the heavens. Sri Nanak was recognised in Angad and Angad in Amar Das. Amar Das was called Ram Das; only the saints knew it and the fools did not. The people on the whole considered them as separate ones, but there were a few who recognised them as one and the same. Those who recognised them as One, they were successful on the spiritual plane. Without recognition there was no success. When Ram Das merged in the Lord, the Guruship was bestowed upon Arjan. When Arjan left for the abode of the Lord, Hargobind was seated on his throne. When Hargobind left for the abode of the Lord, Har Rai was seated in his place. Har Krishan (the next Guru) was his son. After him, Tegh Bahadur became the Guru. He protected the forehead mark and sacred thread (of the Hindus) which marked a great event in the Iron Age. For the sake of saints, he laid down his head without even a sigh. For the sake of *dharma*, he sacrificed himself; he laid down his head, but not his creed. The saints of the Lord abhor the performance of miracles and malpractices. Breaking the pot of his body on the head of the king of Delhi (Aurangzeb), he left for the abode of the Lord. None could perform such a feat. The whole world bemoaned the departure of Tegh Bahadur. While the world lamented, the gods hailed his arrival in heavens.

Section VI

The Lord and the Guru (before birth)

Now I relate my own story as to how I was brought here, while I was absorbed in deep meditation. The mountain named Hemkunt, with seven peaks, where the Pandavas practised yoga, was the site, where I was absorbed in deep meditation on the Primal Power. My meditation reached its zenith and I became one with the Omnipotent Lord. My parents also meditated for the union with the Lord. Their efforts pleased the Lord, whose orders caused my birth in this Iron Age (Kaliyuga). I had no desire to

INTRODUCTION

come, because I was totally absorbed in devotion for the Holy feet of the Lord. But the Lord made me understand His Will and sent me in this world with these words:

> When I created the world in the beginning, I created the ignominious and dreadful Daityas, who became mad with power and abandoned the worship of supreme *Purusha*. I destroyed them in no time and created gods in their place. They were also absorbed in the worship of Power and called themselves omnipotent. Mahadeo (Shiva) was called *Achyuta* (blotless), Vishnu considered himself the Supreme, Brahma called himself *Para Brahman*. None could comprehend the Lord. Then I created eight *sakshis*, in order to give evidence of my entity, but they considered themselves all in all and asked the people to worship them. Those who did not comprehend the Lord, they were considered as *Ishwara*. Several people worshipped the Sun and the Moon and several others worshipped Fire and Air. Several of them considered God as stone and several others bathed considering the Lordship of Water. Several bore fear of *Dharmaraj* in their actions considering him as the supreme representative of *dharma*. All those whom God established for the revelation of His Supremacy, they themselves were called Supreme. They forgot the Lord in their race for Supremacy. When they did not comprehend the Lord, then I established human beings in their place. They also were overpowered by "mineness" and exhibited the Lord in statues. I created Siddhas and Sadhs, who also could not realise the Lord. On whomsoever wisdom dawned, he started his own path; none could realise the Supreme Lord, but instead spread enmity, strife and ego. The tree and the leaves began to burn because of inner fire. None followed the path of the Lord. Whosoever attained spiritual power, he started his own path. None could comprehend the Lord, but instead became mad with "I-ness." Nobody recognised the Supreme Essence, but was entangled within himself. All the great *rishis* (seers), who were then created, produced their own Smritis. All those who became followers of these Smritis, they abandoned the path of the Lord. Those who devoted themselves to the Feet of the Lord, they did not adopt the path of the Smritis. Brahma composed all the four Vedas. All the people followed the injunctions contained in them.

Those who were devoted to the Feet of the Lord, they abandoned the Vedas. Those who abandoned the path of the Vedas and Katebas, they became the devotees of the Lord. Whosoever follows their path, he crushes various types of sufferings. Those who consider the castes illusory, they do not abandon the love of the Lord. When they leave the world, they go to the abode of the Lord and there is no difference between them and the Lord. Those who fear the castes and follow their path, abandoning the Supreme Lord, they fall into hell and transmigrate again and again.

Then I created Dutt, who also started his own path. His followers have long nails in their hands and matted hair on their heads. They do not understand the ways of the Lord. Then I created Gorakh, who made great kings his disciples. His disciples wear rings in their ears and do not know the love of the Lord. Then I created Ramanand, who put on the grab of a *bairagi*. Around his neck he wore a necklace of wooden beads and did not comprehend the ways of the Lord. All the great *Purushas* created by me started their own paths. Then I created Muhammad, who was made the Master of Arabia. He started a religion and circumcised all the kings. He caused all to utter his name and not the True Name. Everyone placed his own interest first and foremost and did not comprehend the Supreme Brahman.

While I was busy in austere devotion, the Lord called me and sent me to this world with these words, "I have adopted you as my son and created you for the propagation of the path (Panth). You go therefore for the spread of *dharma* (righteousness) and cause people to retrace their steps from evil actions." I stood up with folded hands and bowing down my head, I said, "The path shall prevail in the world only with your assistance." For this reason the Lord sent me and I was born in this world. I do not have enmity with anyone. Whosoever shall call me the Lord, shall fall into hell. Consider me as his servant and do not think of any difference between me and the Lord. I am the servant of the supreme *Purusha* and has come to see the sport of the world. Whatever the Lord of the world said, I say the same unto you. I cannot remain silent in this abode of death.

I say only that, while the Lord hath said. I do not yield to anyone else. I do not feel pleased with any particular garb. I sow the seed of God's Name. I do not worship tones, nor I have any liking for a particular guise. I sing infinite names (of the Lord) and meet the supreme *Purusha*. I do not wear matted hair on my head, nor do I put rings in my ears. I do not pay attention to anyone else. All my actions are at the bidding of the Lord. I recite only the name of the Lord, which is useful at all places. I do not meditate on anyone else, nor do I seek assistance from any other quarter. I recite infinite names and attain the Supreme Light. I do not meditate on anyone else, nor do I repeat the name of anyone else. I am absorbed only in the name of the Lord and honour none else. By meditating on the Supreme, I am absolved of infinite sins. I am absorbed only in His sight and do not attend to any other charitable action. By uttering only His name, I am absolved of infinite sorrows.

Those who mediated on the name of the Lord, none of the sorrows and sins came near them. Those who meditated on any other entity, they ended themselves in futile discussions and quarrels. I have been sent into this world by the Lord to propagate *dharma* (righteousness). The Lord has asked me to spread *dharma* and vanquish the tyrants and evil-minded persons. The saints should comprehend this in their minds that I have taken birth to spread *dharma*, protect saints and root out tyrants and evil-minded persons. All the earlier incarnations proclaimed their own authority. They did not strike the tyrants and did not make them follow the path of *dharma*. All the earlier prophets ended themselves in ego and did not comprehend the supreme *Purusha*. They did not care for the righteous actions. Have no hopes on others, rely only on the One Lord. The hopes on others are never fruitful, therefore, keep in your mind the hopes on the One Lord.

Someone studies *Quran* and someone studies Puranas. Mere reading cannot save one from death. Millions of people recite *Quran* and many study Puranas without understanding the crux. It will be of no use at the time of death and none will be saved. Why do you not meditate on Him, who will help you at the time of death? Consider the religions as illusory, because they do not serve our purpose (of life). For this reason, the Lord created me and sent me in this world, telling me the secret. Whatever He told me, I say unto you. There is no heresy in it. I neither wear matted hair nor ear-rings. I meditate on the name of the Lord, which helps me in all my errands. Neither I close my eyes, nor exhibit heresy, nor perform evil actions, nor cause others to call me a person in disguise. Those persons who adopt different guises are never liked by the men of God. All of you may understand this that God is absent from all these guises. Those who exhibit various garbs through various actions, they never get release in the next world. While alive, their worldly desires may be fulfilled and the king may be pleased on seeing their mimicry. You may search anywhere, God is absent from all such shows. Only those who controlled their minds, recognised the Supreme Brahman.

Those who exhibit various guises in the world and win people on their side, they will reside in hell, when the sword of death falls on them. Those who exhibit different guises, find disciples and enjoy great comforts, Those who close their nostrils and practise *pranayama*, their path (without the name) is useless. All the followers of the futile paths, fall into hell from within. They cannot go to heavens with the movement of the hands, because they could not control their minds in any way. Whatever my Lord said to me, I say the same in the world. Those who have meditated on the Lord, ultimately go to heaven. The Lord and His devotees are one; there is no difference between them, just as the wave of water merges in water. Those who quarrel in ego, they are far removed from the Lord. O men of God, understand this that the Lord does not reside in Vedas and Katebs He who exhibits his guise by closing his eyes, attains blindness. By closing the eyes one cannot know the path, how can, then, he meet Infinite Lord? To what extent the details be given? When one understands, he feels tired. If one is blessed with million of tongues, even then he feels them short in number while (singing the praises of the Lord).

When the Lord willed, I was born on this earth. Now I shall narrate briefly my own story.

SECTION VII

Birth and Childhood of the Guru

"My father proceeded towards the east and visited several places of pilgrimage. When he went to Triveni (Prayag) he passed his days in acts of charity. I was conceived there and took birth at Patna, whence I was brought to Madra Desha (Punjab). I was caressed by various nurses—I was given physical protection in various ways and given various types of education. When I began to perform the acts of *dharma* (righteousness), my father departed for his heavenly abode."

SECTION VIII

Battle of Bhangani

When I obtained the position of responsibility, I performed religious acts to the best of my ability. I went hunting various kinds of animals in the forest and killed bears, nilgais and elks. Then I left my home and went to a place named Paonta. I enjoyed my stay on the banks of Kalindri (Yamuna) and saw amusements of various kinds. There I killed many lions, nilgais and bears. On this the king Fateh Shah became angry and fought with me without any reason.

There Sri Shah (Sango Shah) became enraged and all the five warriors stood firmly in the battlefield, including the tenacious. Jit Mal and the desperate hero Gulab, whose faces were red with ire, in the field, the persistent Mahari Chand and Ganga Ram who had defeated lot of forces; Lal Chand was red with anger, who had shattered the pride of several lion-like heroes. Maharu got enraged and with frightening expression killed brave Khans in the battlefield. The godly Daya Ram, filled with great ire, fought very heroically in the field like Dronacharya. Kripal, in rage, rushed with his mace and struck it on the head of the tenacious Hayat Khan.

Then Nand Chand, in fierce rage, wielding his sword, struck it with force, but it broke. Then he drew his dagger. The tenacious warrior saved the honour of the Sodhi clan. Then the maternal uncle Kripal, in great ire, manifested the war-feats like a true Kshatriya. The great hero was struck by an arrow, but he caused the brave Khan fall from his saddle.

Sahib Chand, the valiant Kshatriya, killed a bloody Khan of Khorasan. He slew several graceful warriors with full force. The soldiers who survived, fled away in order to save their lives. There (Sango) Shah exhibited his acts of bravery in the battlefield and trampled under feet many bloody Khans. Gopal, the king of Guleris, stood firmly in the field and roared like a lion amidst a herd of deer. There is great fury a warrior Hari Chand very skilfully took position in the battlefield. He discharged sharp arrows in great rage and whosoever was struck, left for the other world.

Hari Chand (Handooria) in great fury, killed significant heroes. He shot skilfully a volley of arrows and killed a lot of forces. He was absorbed in dreadful feat of arms. Armed warriors were being killed and great kings were falling on the ground. Then Jit Mal aimed at and struck Hari Chand down to the ground with his spear. The warriors struck with arrows became red with blood. Their horses fell and they left for heavens.

In the hands of blood-thirsty Khans there were the Khorasan swords, whose sharp edges flashed like fire. The bows shooting out volleys of arrows twanged. The splendid horses fell because of the heavy blows. The trumpets sounded and the musical pipes were played. The brave warriors thundered from both sides and with their strong arms struck (the enemy). The witches drank blood to their fill and produced dreadful sounds. How far should I describe the great battle? Those who fought attained martyrdom; thousands fled away. The hill chief spurred his horse and fled. The warriors went away without discharging their arrows. The chiefs of Jaswal and Dadhwal who were fighting (in the field) left with all their soldiers. The Raja of Chandel was perplexed when the tenacious Hari Chand caught hold of the spear in his hand. He was filled with great fury, fulfilling his duty as a general. Those who came in front, were cut into pieces and fell (into the field). Then Najabat Khan came forward and struck Sango Shah with his weapons. Several skilful Khans fell on him with their arms and sent Shah

Sangram to heaven. The brave warrior Sango Shah fell down after killing Najabat Khan. There were lamentations in this world and rejoicings in heaven.

When this lowly person saw Shah Sangram falling (while fighting bravely), he held aloft his bows and arrows. He fixing his gaze on a Khan, shot an arrow which stung the enemy like a black cobra, who (the Khan) fell down. He drew out another arrow and aimed and shot it on the face of Bhikhan Khan. The bloody Khan fled away leaving his horse in the field, who was killed with the third arrow. After regaining consciousness from the swoon Hari Chand shot his arrows with unerring aim. Whosoever was struck, fell down unconscious and leaving his body, went to the heavenly abode. He aimed and shot two arrows at the same time and did not care for the selection of his target. Whosoever was struck and pierced by his arrows, went straight to the other world. The warriors remained true to their duty in the field. The witches and ghosts drank blood to their fill and raised shrill voices. The Birs, Baitals and Siddhs (legendary creatures) laughed. The witches were talking and huge kites were flying (for meat).

Hari Chand, filled with rage, drew out his bow. He aimed and shot his arrow, which struck my horse. He aimed and shot the second arrow to me. The Lord protected me. His arrow grazed my ear. His third arrow penetrated the buckle of my waist-belt and its edge touched the body, but did not cause a wound. The Lord saved His servant. When the edge of the arrow touched my body, it kindled my resentment. I took the bow in my hand and aimed and shot the arrow. All the warriors fled, when a volley of arrows was showered. Then I aimed the arrow on a warrior and killed him. Hari Chand was killed and his brave soldiers were trampled. The Chief of Kot Lehar was seized by death. The hill-men fled from the battlefield. All were filled with fear. I gained victory through the favour of the Eternal Lord. We returned after victory and sang songs of triumph. I showered wealth on the warriors, who were full of rejoicings.

When I returned after victory, I did not remain at Paonta. I came to Kahlur and established the village of Anandpur. Those who did not join the forces, were turned out from the town and those who fought bravely were patronised by me. Many days passed in this way. The saints were protected and the wicked were killed.

Section IX

The Battle of Nadaun

Much time passed in this way. Mian Khan came (from Delhi) to Jammu (for collection of revenue). He sent Alif Khan to Nadaun, who developed enmity towards Bhim Chand (the Chief of Kahlur). Bhim Chand called me for assistance and himself went to face (the enemy). Alif Khan prepared a wooden fort on the hill of Navras. The Hill Chiefs also prepared their arrows and guns. With brave Bhim Chand there were Raj Singh, illustrious Ram Singh and Sukhdev Gaji of Jasrot. They were full of fury and managed their affairs with enthusiasm. There came also the brave Prithi Chand of Dadhwar after having made arrangements regarding the affairs of his state. Kripal Chand (of Kangra) arrived with ammunition and drove back and killed many of the warriors (of Bhim Chand). When for the second time the forces of Bhim Chand advanced, they were beaten back downwards to the great sorrow of (the allies of Bhim Chand). The warriors on the hill sounded trumpets, while the Chiefs below were filled with remorse. Then Bhim Chand was filled with great ire and began to recite the incantations of Hanuman. He called all his warriors and also called me. Then all assembled and advanced like a flame over a fence of dry weeds. Then on the other side the valiant Raja Dayal of Bijharwal advanced with Raja Kripal, alongwith all his army.

Kripal Chand was in great fury. The horses danced and the pipes were played, which presented a dreadful scene. The warriors fought and struck their spears. With rage they showered volley of arrows. The fighting soldiers fell in the field and breathed their last. They fell like thundering clouds. Kripal Chand in great anger stood firmly in the field. With his volleys of arrows, he killed great warriors. He killed the chiefs, who lay dead on the ground. The trumpets sounded and the warriors thundered.

INTRODUCTION xxi

Kripal Chand, in great fury, made a great fight. Great heroes thundered, while using dreadful weapons. Such a heroic battle was fought that all the people of the world (living in nine quarters) knew it. His weapons wrought havoc and he exhibited himself as a true Rajput.

All the chiefs of the allies, in great anger, entered the fray and besieged the army of Katoch. The Rajputs of the tribes of Nanglu and Panglu advanced in group alongwith the soldiers of Jaswar and Guler. The great warrior Dayal also joined and saved the honour of the people of Bijharwal. Then this lowly person (the Guru himself) took up his gun and aimed unerringly at one of the chiefs, who reeled and fell down on the ground in the battlefield, but even then he thundered in anger. I then threw away the gun and took the arrows in my hand. I shot four of them. Another three I discharged with my left hand. Whether they struck anybody, I do not know. Then the Lord brought the end of the fight and the enemy was driven out into the river. From the hill, the bullets and arrows were showered. It seemed that the gun set down after playing a good Holi. Pierced by arrows and spears the warriors fell in the battlefield. Their clothes were dyed with blood. It seemed that they played Holi. After conquering the enemy, they came for rest at their place of encampment, on the other side of the river. Sometime after midnight they left while beating the drums. When the whole night ended and the sun arose, the warriors on our side marched hastily, brandishing their spears.

Alif Khan fled away, leaving back his belongings. All the other warriors fled away and did not stay anywhere. I remained thereon the bank of the river for eight more days and visited the palaces of all the chiefs. Then I took leave and came home. They went thereto settle the terms of peace. Both the parties made an agreement, therefore, the story ends here.

I came to this side after plundering Alsun on my way and enjoyed in various ways after reaching Anandpur.

Section X

The Expedition of the Khanzada

Many years elapsed in this way. All the wicked persons (thieves) were spotted, caught and killed. Some of them fled away from the city but came back after starvation. Then Dilawar Khan (Governor of Lahore) sent his son against me. A few hours after nightfall the Khans assembled and advanced for attack. When their forces crossed the river, Alam (Singh) came and woke me up. There was a great consternation and all the people got up. They took up their arms with valour and zeal. The discharge of the volleys of shots from guns began immediately. Everyone was in rage, holding the arms in hand. They raised various dreadful shouts. The noise was heard on the other side of the river. The bugles blew, the trumpets resounded, the great heroes entered the fray shouting loudly. From both sides the arms clattered with force and the horses danced. It seemed that the dreadful Goddess Kali thundered in the battlefield. The river appeared like the night of death. The severe chill cramped the soldiers. The heroes from this (my) side thundered and the bloody Khans fled away without using their weapons.

The shameless Khans fled away and none of them wore the arms. They left battlefield though they pretended to be the valiant heroes. They left on galloping horses and could not use the weapons. They did not shout loudly like valiant heroes and felt ashamed on seeing ladies.

On their way, they plundered the village Barwa and halted at Bhallon. They could not touch me because of the Grace of the Lord and fled away ultimately. Because of Thy Favour, O Lord, they could not do any harm here, but plundered the village Barwa. . . .

Section XI

The Expedition of Hussain Khan

The Khanzada fled to his father and being ashamed of his conduct he could not speak. Then Hussain thundered, striking his arms and prepared for attack with all his brave warriors. Hussain assembled all his forces and advanced. At first, he plundered the houses of the hill-people. Then he conquered the

Raja of Dadhwal and brought him under submission. The sons of the Raja were made slaves. Then he plundered the Doon thoroughly. None could face the barbarian. He took away forcibly the foodgrains and distributed them (among the soldiers). The big fool thus committed a very bad act.

Some days passed in such acts. The turn of meeting the Raja of Guler came. If he had not met (Hussain) for two days more, the enemy would have come here (towards me), but the providence had thrown a device of discord towards his house. The Raja of Guler came to meet Hussain and with him came Ram Singh. They met Hussain after the four quarters of the day had passed. The slave Hussain became blind in vanity, just as the sand becomes heated by the heat of the sun, but the wretched does not know the night of the sun and become proud of itself. Similarly, this slave Hussain was puffed up with ego. He did not care to notice them. With the Rajas of Kahlur and Katoch on his side, he considered himself peerless. (The Raja of Guler and Ram Singh) offered money to Hussain, which they had brought with them. A dispute arose in giving and taking, therefore, the Rajas returned to their places with the money.

Then Hussain was enraged and lost the power of discriminating between good and bad. He made no other consideration and ordered the beating of the drum against the Raja of Guler. He did not think of any tactical consideration. The hare surrounded the lion for frightening him. He besieged him for fifteen *pahars* (about 45 hours) and did not allow the items of food and drink to reach the state. Being without food and drink, the warriors were filled with ire. The Raja sent the messengers for the purpose of making peace. Seeing the Pathan forces around him, the slave Hussain lost his balance and did not consider the request of the Raja. He said, "Either give me ten thousand rupees immediately or take death on your head." I had sent Sangtia Singh there (for making peace among the chiefs). He brought Dayal on oath of God, but he could not reconcile with them. Then Kripal thought within his mind that such an opportunity would not be available again because the circle of Time deceives everybody. He decided to catch hold to Gopal immediately, either to imprison him or kill him. When Gopal got scent of the conspiracy, he escaped to his people. When Gopal was gone, Kripal was filled with anger. Himmat and Hussain rushed for fighting in the field.

Then the Raja of Kangra and Katoch were filled with rage. His face and eyes became red with anger and he freed himself from all other thoughts. From another side the Khans entered with arrows in their hands. It seemed that leopards were roaming in search of flesh. A warrior named Hari Singh rushed into the field. He received many arrows in his body. In great rage he killed many soldiers and after a great fight departed for the heavenly abode. The tenacious Himmat and Kimmat drew out the spears. Jalal Khan joined with a mace. The determined warriors fought, seemingly intoxicated. There were blows after blows and the sparks fell when the weapons struck each other. The Raja of Jaswal rushed forward on the galloping horse. He surrounded Hussain and struck his sharp lance at him. . . .

The Hussain himself entered the fray. All (the warriors) took up bows and arrows. The bloody Khans stood firmly and began to fight with faces and eyes and with ire. The terrible battle of valiant warriors began. The arrows, spears and double-edged swords were used by the heroes. . . . The warriors met warriors.... The fight was most terrible. The armies were exhausted. The great hero Hussain stood firmly in the field. The heroes of Jaswal ran towards him. The horsemen were cut in the manner the cloth is cut (by the tailor). There Hussain stood quite alone like the pole of a flag fixed in the ground. Wherever that tenacious warrior shot his arrow, it pierced through the body and went out. The warriors who were struck by arrows came together against him. From all the four sides, they shouted "kill, kill." They carried and struck their weapons very ably. At last Hussain fell down and left for heaven. When Hussain was killed, the warriors were in great fury. All the others fled but the forces of Katoch felt excited. All the soldiers of Katoch rushed with great anger together with Himmat and Kimmat. Then Hari Singh also came forward and killed many brave horsemen. Then the Raja of Katoch became furious and stood firmly in the field. He used his weapons unerringly shouting death

INTRODUCTION

(for the enemy). (From the other side) the Raja of Chandel raged and all attacked in a body with indignation. Those who faced him were killed and those who remained behind, ran away. Sangat Rai (Sangtia Singh) died with his seven companions. When Darsho came to know of it, he also came in the field and died. Then Himmat came in the battlefield. He received several wounds and struck his weapons on several others. His horse was killed there, but Himmat fled. The warriors of Katoch came with great rage in order to take away the dead body of their Raja Kripal. . . .

When Kripal died in the battlefield, Gopal rejoiced. All the army fled in disorder, when their leaders (Hussain and Kripal) were killed. After the death of Hussain and Kripal and fall of Himmat all the warriors fled just as people go away after giving authority to the Mahant.

In this way all the enemies were aimed and killed. After that they took care of their dead. Then on seeing Himmat lying wounded, Ram Singh said to Gopal, "That Himmat who had been the root-cause of all the quarrels, has now fallen wounded in our hands." When Gopal heard these words, he killed Himmat and did not allow him to get up alive. The victory was gained and the battle ended. While remembering homes, all went there. The Lord protected me from the cloud of battle, which rained elsewhere.

Section XII

The Expedition of Jujhar Singh

In this way, the battle was fought, when the leader of the Turks (Mohammedans) was killed. On this Dilawar became very angry and sent a contingent of horsemen in this direction. From the other side Jujhar Singh was sent who drove out the enemy from Bhallan immediately. On this side Gaj Singh and Pamma (Parmanand) assembled their forces and fell upon them early in the morning. On the other side Jujhar Singh stood firmly like a flagpost planted in the battlefield. Even the flagpost might be loosened, but the brave Rajput did not waver. He received the blows (without flinching). The warriors of both the armies moved in detachments, Raja of Chandel on that side and Raja of Jaswar on this side. All the warriors were in great rage and the fight began in the battlefield. The brave heroes of both the armies were in great anger, warriors of Chandel on this side and the warriors of Jaswar on the other. . . .

The battle continued on both sides (with great vigour). Chandan Rai was killed. Then Jujhar Singh continued the fight quite alone. He was surrounded from all the sides. He rushed into the army of the enemy without any hesitation and killed many soldiers, wielding his weapons very skilfully. In this way, he destroyed many homes using various kinds of weapons. He aimed and killed the brave horsemen, but at last he left for the heavenly abode himself.

Section XIII

The Arrival of Shahzada in Madra Desha (Punjab)

In this way when Jujhar Singh was killed, the soldiers returned to their homes. Then Aurangzeb became very angry and sent his son to Madra Desha (Punjab). On his arrival all were frightened and hid themselves in big hills. The people tried to frighten me also, because they did not understand the ways of Almighty. Some people left me and took refuge in the big hills. The cowards were so much frightened that they did not consider their safety with me. The son of Aurangzeb grew very angry and sent a subordinate in this direction. Those who had left me in distrust, their homes were demolished by him. . . .

The successors of both Baba (Nanak) and Babur were created by God Himself. Recognise the former as the spiritual king and the later as the temporal king. Those who do not deliver the Guru's money, the successors of Babur shall seize and take away from them forcibly. They will be greatly punished and their houses will be plundered. . . .

Mirza Beg was the name of the officer, who demolished the houses of the apostates. Those who remained faithful, were protected by the Guru; not even a little harm was done to them.

There (the son of) Aurangzeb grew most angry. He sent four other officers. Those apostates who had escaped (the punishment) earlier, their houses were demolished by the officers. ...

In this way, the apostates received foul treatment. All the saints saw this spectacle. No harm was done to them. The Lord saved them Himself. To whosoever the Lord protects, the enemy can do nothing to him. None can touch his shadow. The fool makes useless effort. Those who have taken refuge with the saints, what can be said about them? God saves them from the inimical and wicked person by destroying them, just as the tongue is protected within the teeth.

A GLIMPSE OF SRI GUR SOBHA OF SAINAPAT

Guru Gobind Singh passed away in AD 1708, in the first decade of the eighteenth century. His autobiography given in the previous chapter is incomplete and ends with the arrival of the prince (Bahadur Shah) in the Punjab in order to chastise the rebels. In order to get a glimpse of the complete life of the Guru, we have to rely upon the biographies of the Guru written in the eighteenth century. These biographies are as follows:

1. *Sri Gur Sobha* of Sainapat completed in AD 1711, three years after the passing away of the Guru
2. *Gur Bilas Patshahi Das* of Kuir Singh completed in AD 1751
3. *Bansavali Nama* of Kesar Singh Chhibbar, completed in AD 1769
4. *Gur Bilas Patshahi Daswin* of Sukha Singh, completed in AD 1797

Out of the above four works, *Bansavali Nama* of Kesar Singh Chhibbar contains an account of Sikh history from Guru Nanak Dev upto Banda Bahadur. All the other works are the biographies of Guru Gobind Singh. All these works are written in poetry.

The author of *Sri Gur Sobha* was one of the court-poets of the Guru and completed his work in AD 1711, three years after the passing away of the Guru. He seems to have studied the autobiography of the Guru given in the previous chapter, therefore, in order to get a fuller view of the life of the Guru we ought to make a short survey of his work.

The original name of Sainapat was Chandar Sain. He was a Jat Sikh of Wazirabad (Gujranwala distt.). After baptism, he was named Saina Singh. Sainapat was his *nom-de-plume*. Since he knew the Guru very closely, he is considered to be a very reliable biographer of the Guru. Though very brief, his is the first complete biography of the Guru. The sequence of the events given by him is authentic, though his knowledge regarding the martyrdom of the sons of the Guru, seems to be defective. He has recorded the name of the eldest son of the Guru as Jit Singh or Ranjit Singh instead of Ajit Singh. According to him the body of Baba Ajit Singh could not be found after the martyrdom in the battle of Chamkaur. Baba Jujhar Singh was caught alive and martyred alongwith Baba Fateh Singh at Sirhind. Baba Zorawar Singh steered clear through the enemy ranks and later on met the Guru in Rajputana. Sainapat also wrongly refers to a marriage of the Guru in the country of the Rajputs. He has given a correct interpretation of the Sikh doctrines. His work contains twenty chapters. The events narrated by the Guru in his autobiography have been given by Sainapat in the first four chapters of his work.

A brief account of the twenty chapters of *Sri Gur Sobha* is given below. This chapter is entitled "Panth Pragas Barnana (Description of the manifestation of the Panth)."

CHAPTER I

It is mainly a reproduction of the sixth section of Bachittar Natak. The invocation is for God only and none of the gods and goddesses as has been done by some other biographers.

CHAPTER II

This chapter is entitled "Tegh Pragas—Shah Sangram Judh" (The Appearance of the Sword. ... The

Battle of Shah Sangram). This chapter deals with the battle of Bhangani, which has been described in the eighth section of the autobiography of the Guru, given in the previous chapter.

Chapter III

This chapter is entitled "Rajan Het Sangram" (The Battle with the Hill-Chiefs). It deals with the battle of Nadaun, which has been narrated in the ninth section of the autobiography of the Guru, given in the previous chapter.

Chapter IV

This chapter is entitled "Khanzade ate Hussaini nal Judh" (The Battle with the Khanzade and Hussain Khan). The description of these battles is found in the tenth and eleventh sections of the autobiography of the Guru, given in the pervious chapter.

Chapter V

This chapter is entitled "Bachan Pragas" (The Sermon of the Guru). It deals with the creation of the Khalsa very briefly and lays emphasis mainly on the injunctions delivered to the Khalsa at the time of its creation.

Chapter VI

This chapter is entitled "Bachan Bichar" (Consultations about the saying of the Guru). It deals with the mutual understanding and practice of the injunctions of the Guru.

Chapter VII

This chapter is entitled "Rahat Pragas" (Manifestation of the discipline). It describes the opposition to the new discipline and ultimate victory of the discipline.

Chapter VIII

This chapter is entitled "Sangram Anandpur ka Pahla" (The First Battle of Anandpur). It deals with the battle of the hill chiefs with the Guru. After the death of Raja Bhim Chand, his son Ajmer Chand became the chief of Kahlur. He threatened the Guru with war, if he did not pay the rental for the usage of his territory or did not leave the territory. The Guru told him that the land of Anandpur was purchased by his father, therefore, there was no question of the payment of rental. Raja Ajmer Chand with the help of other hill-chiefs attacked the Guru, but he was defeated in the battle.

Chapter IX

This chapter is entitled "Judh Nirmoh ka" (The Battle of Nirmoh). The hill chiefs besieged Anandpur and promised to vacate the siege if the Guru left Anandpur for some time. They swore that no harm would come and everything would remain, as it was. Though the Guru did not have faith in their oath, he left Anandpur and went to Nirmoh. But the hill chiefs broke their oath and indulged in loot and violence. The Guru retaliated with his forces and defeated the enemies, who then sought the help of the Mughals. The Nawab of Sarhind sent his forces to assist the hill-chiefs, but the spirited Sikhs of the Guru repulsed the attack of the combined forces.

Chapter X

This chapter is entitled "Judh Basali Kalmot ka" (The Battle of Basali and Kalmot). The Guru had gone to Basali on the request of its Raja, where after a week from the battle of Nirmoh, he was intercepted during a hunting expedition by the hill-forces coming from Kalmot. In the skirmishes that ensued, the hill-forces were repulsed.

Chapter XI

This chapter is entitled "Anandgarh da doosra Judh" [The Second Battle of Anandgarh (Anandpur)]. The poet has covered in this chapter all the remaining skirmishes and battles of Anandpur. The hill-chiefs wanted to capture Anandgarh and on their request the Mughal forces sided with them. There was a long siege of Anandpur. The food stocks dwindled away. There was a general request to the Guru to leave the fort. The Guru acceded to their request and ordered his people to vacate Anandpur.

Chapter XII

This chapter is entitled "Chamkaur da Judh" (The Battle of Chamkaur). When the Guru left Anandpur with his forces, there was a severe battle on Shahi Tibbi and on the banks of Sirsa. Due to sudden attack, there was a great confusion. The members of the family of the Guru were segregated and the invaluable manuscripts were destroyed in Sirsa. The Guru, alongwith about forty Sikhs stayed in a dilapidated fortress at Chamkaur. In an unequal battle the Sikhs alongwith the two sons of the Guru, fought very bravely, but they could not face it for long. After the death of Bhai Sant Singh, the Guru came out of the fortress and showering volleys of arrows went out safely from the battlefield. Two of the sons of the Guru had been captured earlier and sent to Sarhind, where they attained martyrdom. The knowledge of poet regarding the martyrdom, of the two sons of the Guru is defective.

Chapter XIII

This chapter is entitled "Kala Pragas" (Manifestation of Power). From Chamkaur, the Guru went to the country of Brars. There is mention of a battle, most probably the battle of Muktsar. The Guru wrote a letter (Zafarnama) to the Emperor Aurangzeb and sent Bhai Daya Singh to deliver it. The letter could not be delivered for several months. Bhai Daya Singh sought the blessings for the Guru for the success in his errand. After that there were no tidings from Bhai Daya Singh. In the meantime, the letter was delivered and Aurangzeb after reading it sent his men in the company of Bhai Daya Singh to request the Guru to come and meet him.

Chapter XIV

This chapter is entitled "Keechak Mar" (A visit to the place where Keechak was killed). The Guru decided to go towards the south through Marwar. When he reached the country of the Rajputs. Several chiefs and warriors came to meet him. There is a mention of the marriage of the Guru here, but this information of the poet does not seem to be correct. Bhai Daya Singh came back and met the Guru, the messengers sent by Aurangzeb had proceeded to Delhi. The news of the death of Aurangzeb also reached, therefore, the Guru instead of proceeding towards the south halted at Bagharu. He visited Keechak Bhoomi. The people in the area were terrified on seeing the armed followers of the Guru. There were small skirmishes. A few camels of the Guru's camp devastated a garden, which led to a fight with the inhabitants of the area. In a pitched fight that ensued, two chiefs were killed.

Chapter XV

This chapter is entitled "Zikar Badshahi" (Description about the Rulers). After the death of Aurangzeb, his sons fought with each other for supremacy. The prince Tara Azam declared himself king. Bahadur Shah requested the Guru for help. With the assistance of the Guru he defeated Tara Azam in the battle of Jajau. After ascending the throne, he spent four months at Agra. The Guru came directly to Delhi.

Chapter XVI

This chapter is entitled "Mulakat Badshah ki" (Meeting with the King). From Delhi, the Guru went to Mathura and Vrindavan. After that he went to Agra, where he met the king. He was received with great respect. The king presented a robe of honour to him. The king then left Agra for Rajputana. The

Chapter XVII

This chapter is entitled "Judh Sahibzada ka Hor Mazkur Rah ka" (The Battle of the Sahibzada and the Description regarding the Way). The king and the Guru met in the way and proceeded together through Ajmer, Jodhpur, Udaipur, and Chittor. Sahibzada Zorawar Singh is said to have been killed in a skirmish at Chittor, which seems to be incorrect and based on wrong information. Then the Guru crossed the Narbada river. In a quarrel with the local people Bhai Man Singh was killed in the way. Then the Guru reached Burhanpur.

Chapter XVIII

This chapter in entitled "Joti Jot Samavana" (The passing away of the Guru). The king and the Guru met again after crossing the Tapti river. They proceeded together and reached Nanded. Here a Pathan attacked the Guru with his sword and wounded him. The wounds were sewn. After some days, the Guru attended the congregation. But the end was near and the Guru merged in the Supreme Lord on the night of Kartik Sudi Panchmi, Sammat Bikrami 1765. One day before his passing away, the Sikhs asked him about his next form. The Guru said, "My next form shall be Khalsa. I shall reside in the Khalsa."

Chapter XIX

It contains an eulogy of the Guru. It is entitled "Agaman Pragas" (The Manifestation of Future Greatness).

Chapter XX

It also contains an eulogy of the Guru. It is entitled "Sarab Upama" (All Praise).

CHRONOLOGY OF THE MAIN EVENTS

Birth at Patna	December 22, 1666
Arrival at Anandpur	May 1673
Marriage with Jeeto Ji	July 1677
Repulsing the attack of Bhim Chand on Anandpur	1682
Marriage with Sundari Ji	May 1685
Leaves Anandpur for Paonta	July 1685
Birth of Ajit Singh to Mata Sundari Ji	November 1686
Battle of Bhangani	1687
Back of Anandpur	November 1688
Battle of Nadaun	1689
Birth of Jujhar Singh to Mata Jeeto Ji	March 1690
Khanzada attacks Anandpur	1694
Battle with Hussain Khan	1695
Birth of Zorawar Singh to Mata Jeeto Ji	1697
Birth of Fateh Singh to Mata Jeeto Ji	1699
Creation of the Khalsa	March 30, 1699
Skirmishes with Bhim Chand	September 1699
Attacked by the combined forces of hill-chiefs	December 1700
Leaves Anandpur for Nirmoh	January 1701
Battle of Nirmoh	1702

Goes to Basoli	April 1702
Occupation of Kalmot	June 1702
Back to Anandpur	August 1702
Repulsing the attack of hill-chiefs	February 1703
Repulsing the combined attack of hill-chiefs and Mughals	June 1704
Evacuates Anandpur	December 1704
Battle of Chamkaur and martyrdom of Ajit Singh and Jujhar Singh	December 1704
Martyrdom of Zorawar Singh and Fateh Singh	December 1704
Battle of Khidrana	May 1705
Battle of Muktsar	June 1705
Reaches Talwandi Sabo (Damdama)	1705
Starts from Talwandi Sabo to meet Aurangzeb	November 1705
Death of Aurangzeb	February 20, 1706
The Guru receives the news of the death of Aurangzeb	March 1706
Meets Bahadur Shah at Agra	July 23, 1707
Moves towards South	November 1707
Reaches Nanded	September 1708
Wounded by the Pathan	September 19, 1708
Passed away at Nanded	October 7, 1708

LITERARY CONTRIBUTION OF GURU GOBIND SINGH—A VIEW

Introductory: The Birth of Dasam Granth

The conjunctive of two words i.e., *Dasam+Granth* means the Book of the Tenth Guru, *Dasam* meaning the Tenth and *Granth* meaning the Book. *Dasam* here conveys the sense of the Tenth Guru, i.e., Guru Gobind Singh. From this name it appears that this Book contains only the compositions of only the Tenth Guru. In the very beginning, when the Tenth Master prepared this volume, its name was *Chhota Granth* (Smaller Book), because *Adi Granth* was then *Wadda Granth* (Bigger Book). Kesar Singh Chhibbar writes in his composition *Bansavali Nama*:

> *Chhota Granth* took its birth in the house of the Tenth Master,
> It was the year 1755, the author made it play with this name,
> He loved it after writing it with his own hands and made it playful;
> And he himself composed it after uttering it with his holy tongue.
> The Sikhs prayed to him to combine it with the other one,
> The Master said, "that one is the real *Granth*, this one is my poetic exercise;"
> This beloved one was not combined, who knows the mystery?

After the passing away of Guru Gobind Singh in AD 1708, for some time, in the earlier phases, the names of this *Granth* had been *Bachittar Natak* and *Daswen Patshah ka Granth*. This recension, which the Guru prepared himself, was lost for ever alongwith the treasure of the compositions of the court-poets of the Guru, weighing nine maunds and named *Vidya Sagar* or *Vidya Saar*, when he left Anandpur for good. It was submerged in the Sutlej river. It is said that Mata Sundari, the wife of Guru Gobind Singh asked Bhai Mani Singh to prepare another compilation of the compositions of the Guru, because the copies of these compositions lay scattered at several places with the Sikhs. Bhai Mani Singh was a very famous Sikh scholar at that time and was also the scribe of the Damdama recension of the *Adi Granth*. It is probable that he might have seen the earlier compilation of the Guru's compositions, therefore for this very work, he was the most appropriate compiler. But in those days of chaos and unrest, he could only finish this work after the passing away of the Guru, when he was the high-priest of Darbar Sahib, Amritsar.

INTRODUCTION

The Preparation of the First Recension of the Dasam Granth

The first recension of the *Dasam Granth* was prepared by Bhai Mani Singh. We cannot say with full confidence that this recension was the exact copy of the *Granth* prepared under the supervision of the Guru. That letter, which was brought to light by Harnam Singh Ballabh, and which was written by Bhai Mani Singh to Mata Sundari, in which he made a mention of his search of the scattered compositions of the Guru, does not appear to be an authentic document. There is mention of 303 Charitropakhyan and also of Krishnavatara in that letter, but there being 404 Charitropakhyan in the *Dasam Granth*, that letter becomes suspicious. Some scholars have called it fake. The compilation of the *Adi Granth* was prepared by Guru Arjan Dev keeping in view a significant assumption, but this compilation of the *Dasam Granth* was not prepared by Guru Gobind Singh himself. This work was completed by one of his Sikhs. Moreover, there seems to be no significant assumption in its preparation. Most of the compositions are Pauranic and are related to Hindu Trinity and Goddess Durga. The Guru had no faith in these gods and goddesses, whom he considered fatal. He has written in Akal Ustat: "Brahma, Shiva, Vishnu and Indra will ultimately fall into the noose of Yama and only those will be saved, who will touch the Holy Feet of the Lord." This shows that some of the compositions of the Guru were his literary exercise or the same had been composed by his court poets. Despite the Pauranic compositions, there are the *charitras* of the sexual and voluptuous women, which are not in consonance with the ordained discipline of the Guru, therefore, they cannot be the work of the Guru and can only be considered as the work of the court-poets.

The recension of the *Dasam Granth*, which was prepared by Bhai Mani Singh, that is the part and parcel of a bigger volume, in which both the Scriptures i.e., the *Adi Granth,* and the *Dasam Granth* have been combined at one place. In this work, the hymns of each Guru in every raga of the *Adi Granth,* have been put separately. In this bigger volume, there are the following compositions of the *Dasam Granth*:

1. Jaapu
2. Bachittar Natak (in which in addition to the Apni Katha of the Guru, both Chandi Charitras, Chaubis Avataras, Brahm Avatar, Rudra Avatar, 32 Swayyas and the hymns of the nine ragas are included).
3. Shastar Naam-Maala
4. Gyan Prabodh
5. Akal Ustat
6. Var Durga di
7. Charitropakhyan
8. Zafarnama
9. Hikayats
10. Sadd

Asphotak Kabit and the stanzas eulogising Khalsa are not therein this recension. They are found in other recensions. This recension is said to have been completed in AD 1725-26. The following five recensions are considered significant:

1. The recension of Bhai Mani Singh
2. The recension of Baba Deep Singh
3. The recension of Gurdwara Moti Bagh
4. The recension of Diwan Khana, Sangrur
5. The recension of Patna Sahib

There are minor differences at some places in these recensions. There is also difference in their order and sequence. Some specially signed leaves are appended with the first and the third recensions. It is said that these leaves were written by the Guru himself with his holy hands.

The order of the compositions in the recension of Diwan Khana, Sangrur is as follows:

1. Jaapu
2. (Shastar) Naam-Maala Purana
3. Akal Purkh di Ustat
4. Bachittar Natak Granth
5. Gyan Prabodh Granth
6. Charitropakhyan
7. Sahansar Sukhmana
8. Var Malkaus ki
9. Var Bhagauti ki
10. Shabad Sri Mukhbaak
11. Jang (Zafar) nama
12. Sri Mukhbaak Swayye 33
13. Asphotak Kabit Swayye 56

The Chandi Charitra II and Var Durga (Chandi) are not included in this recension. Although this recension is an old one, it is undated. The order of the compositions in the recension of Patna Sahib is as follows:

1. Jaapu
2. Shastar Naam-Maala
3. Ustat Sri Akal Ji ki
4. Sri Bachittar Natak (in which in addition to Apni Katha, Chandi Charitra Ukat Bilas, Chandi Charitra II, Vishnu Avatar, Brahma Avatar, and Rudra Avatar are included).
5. Gyan Prabodh
6. Var Durga ki
7. Sri Charitropakhyan Granth
8. Photak Kabit Swayye
9. Shabad Ragan ki
10. Jang (Zafar) nama

The date of copying this recension is AD 1765, from which it appears that after the recension of Bhai Mani Singh, this is also an old recension. The recension of Baba Deep Singh, which was prepared in AD 1747, is not available now. The recension of Moti Bagh, which was edited by Bhai Charhat Singh son of Bhai Sukha Singh, was completed in AD 1775. Somewhere in other Gurdwaras the manuscripts of the *Dasam Granth* are also found. The research scholar Bhai Randhir Singh consider the recensions of Bhai Mani Singh and Patna Sahib as the old ones and also authentic.

The Origin and Growth of the Controversy about the Dasam Granth

The controversy about the authorship of the compositions of the *Dasam Granth* began immediately after the compilation of the recension of Bhai Mani Singh. Bhai Mani Singh was martyred in AD 1737. According to *Gurshabad Ratnakar Mahan Kosh* after the passing away of Bhai Mani Singh, his compilation of the *Dasam Granth* was sent to Damdama Sahib (which was famous with the name of Kashi of the Sikhs), so that the Sikh scholars may make its critical study. The Sikh savants held a discussions about the various parts of this recension. According to some of them, all its parts may be allowed to remain together, but the others presented the idea that all its parts may remain separate, so that the readers may study them according to their will. But still the majority was in favour of dividing it into two parts. In one of the parts only those compositions were to be included, which were in consonance with the views of *Guru Granth Sahib* and in the second the other compositions including the Pauranic ones. Another idea was also presented, according to which all other compositions be left to remain in the same volume except the Charitropakhyan and Hikayats. This controversy continued for some time, but no clear-cut decision could be taken. In AD 1740, listening to the sacrilege of Darbar Singh, Amritsar by Massa Ranghar, Bhai Mehtab Singh decided to chastise him. While going from Bikaner to Amritsar, he stayed at Damdama Sahib in the way. The Sikh savants also sought his advice, when he said, "If I come back safe and sound after killing Massa Ranghar, then the recension of Bhai Mani Singh be allowed to remain as it is and if I receive martyrdom at Amritsar, then the compositions of the *Dasam Granth* be divided into different parts." Bhai Mehtab Singh was successful in his errand and the recension of Bhai Mani Singh was allowed to remain as it was. In this connection, the controversy came to a close for sometime.

The above-mentioned controversy raised its head again, when with the birth of Singh Sabha Movement the zeal for reformation manifested itself. The traditionalists believed that all the compositions of the *Dasam Granth* were prepared by the Guru himself. These traditionalists included Dr. Trilochan Singh, Bhai Randhir Singh, research scholars, Dr. Dharampal Ashta, Dr. Harbhajan Singh, Dr. Kimari Prasinni Sehgal, Dr. Mahip Singh, etc. But those scholars who believe that amongst the compositions of the *Dasam Granth*, some were composed by the Guru himself and some were composed by the Court-poets of the Guru, they included the scholars of Panch Khalsa, Bhasaur, Giani Lal Singh, Shamsher Singh Ashok, Harnam Singh Vallabh, Rattan Singh Jaggi, etc., both the sides are adamant of their views.

Dr. Mahip Singh presents his views regarding the compositions according to the internal evidence. He has bought forward these points:

1. In some of the compositions of the *Dasam Granth*, no name of any poet has been mentioned e.g., in Jaapu Sahib, Akal Ustat, Apni Katha in Bachittar Natak, both the parts of Chandi Charitra, Chandi di Var, Shastar Naam-Maala, Asphotak Kabit Swayye, and Shabad Hazare. These compositions do not raise any suspicion in our minds about their authorship.
2. But there are some compositions, in which the names of more than one poets are found, e.g., in Avataras and Charitropakhyan. The names of the poets are Shyam, Ram and Kal. The style and order bring forward this fact that only one poet has used all these names. Inspite of this, at several places, the similarity of diction also creates this impression.
3. In some compositions, the signs of autobiography are found, e.g., in stanza nos. 231 and 2479 of Krishnavatar and in stanza nos.16, 21, 22, 23, 49, and 71 of Charitropakhyan and Kal. The style and order bring forward this fact that only one poet has used all these names. Inspite of this, at several places, the similarity of diction also creates this impression. In some compositions, the signs of autobiography are found, e.g., in stanza nos. 231 and 2479 of Krishnavatar and in stanza nos.16, 21, 22, 23, 49, and 71 of Charitropakhyan.
4. The court-poets, in their compositions, have expressed their indebtedness to the Guru, but in the compositions of the *Dasam Granth*, we get no impression like this.

In his research work entitled *The Poetry of Dasam Granth*, Dr. Dharampal Ashta has written about Charitropakhyan: "The objective of writing Charitropakhyan is ethical and by giving good or bad instances for the readers it appears that he wants to raise their moral standard, so that they may be inspired to become better-character people or they may be warned against the vagaries of the characterless women."

Dr Rattan Singh Jaggi, in his appreciative work *Dasam Granth ki Pauranic Prashtbhoomi* (The Pauranic background of the *Dasam Granth*), making a comparative study critically has come to this outcome that all the Pauranic compositions of the *Dasam Granth* are the work of only the court-poets of the Guru. The Guru himself could not compose them. According to him, the inspiration for producing such literature is not in consonance with the personality of the Guru and the Sikh traditions. Inspite of this, these compositions are full of poetic flaws and the editors and cimpilers have been making changes at several places. The courtly tendencies of the poets appear with sufficient clarity. From the list of the fifty-two court-poets of the Guru, the names of Ram and Shyam are found several times in the Pauranic compositions.

The discipline earmarked for the Sikhs by Guru Gobind Singh falls completely in line with the thoughts of the earlier Gurus. His compositions could not be according to the spirit of the previous Gurus. There could be the eulogy of the Transcendent Lord, the True Guru, Gurmukh and the Name of the Lord in their works, which is therein their hymns in the *Adi Granth*. Therefore, it will be a big mistake to append the vagaries of voluptuous women, as in Charitropakhyan, with their names. It does not look proper to mention the reason of raising the moral standard of the people. Such like tales of the sexy women can cause the fall in the character of the young people instead of raising it and can become detrimental for the nation.

The following episodes give us the knowledge of the moral greatness of Guru Gobind Singh:

1. When the Guru was busy in fighting with the Turks, some Sikhs came before him and supplicated: "O true king! The Turks rape the Hindu women; it will be better if the Sikhs retaliate on this issue. Why the Guru has forbidden us about it?" Then the Guru replied, "O Sikh brethren! I have to take this Panth, much higher and not downgrade it, therefore we have not to imitate the disgraceful people."

2. On the occasion of the fair of Rawalsar, Padmini, the daughter of the king of Chamba, went to have the sight of the Guru with full faith and bowed at the feet of the Guru, the Guru patted her shoulder with his bow. At this Padmini said, "O great Guru, I am your Sikh, why did you not pat me with your lotus-hands?" The Guru replied, "I have not touched anyone else except my wives with my own hands."

3. Once, when the hill chiefs and Mughal forces besieged Anandpur, the Sikhs fought very heroically. The fighting continued for fifteen days. There was deficiency of corn. The Guru, in order to test the faith of the Khalsa, taking out the treasure, began to throw it in river Sutlej. Because of the deficiency of corn, the Sikhs also began to remain hungry. There was hue and cry from all sides, "O Guru, protect us, protect us." One day the mother came and said to the Guru, "Why have you taken this step of killing your Sikhs? The Sikhs fight and thunder over the head of the enemy and then there is hunger all around and you are getting your treasures thrown in the river. What sin the Sikhs have committed? They got only a quarter of seer of corn for eating, how will they be able to fight in the battlefield? The Guru then replied, "This Panth has been created with the command of the Creator. I have to increase the Panth and not to destroy it. The day on which, they will look greedily towards the treasures of worship, then undoubtedly there will be only declination. The alms of worship is poison, whosoever will eat it, he will be destroyed. I have created the Panth for fighting, it is good to have it hungry and naked, but I shall not throw it into hell and put it to loss. Just as I am your son, if you as mother want to poison me, can you poison me?" Then the mother said, "The mother can never give poison to her son." Then the Guru retorted, "I also cannot give poison to the Sikhs, who are my sons."

Such a Guru can never be the author of Charitropakhyan, which contains only the vagaries of crafty and wily women.

Guru Granth Sahib, The Real Touchstone

Guru Gobind Singh himself bestowed Guruship on *Granth Sahib* or the *Adi Granth*. He called his own compositions only a poetic exercise. But it is not known, which of his own compositions he included in his *Granth*. It is not correct to say that Bhai Mani Singh could include all the works of the Guru in his compilation. He included only those compositions, which he could get at that time. If his close contemporaries doubted about the authenticity of some of the works in his compilation, then this suspicion was appropriate. They had a very glaring touchstone and that touchstone was *Gurbani* (the Scripture), from which the Guru himself speaks. This was *Guru Granth Sahib*, which is at present and in future for all times will be the touchstone for testing the authenticity of the recorded events of the lives of the Gurus or the instructions given by them. The Guru is ever infallible and the Sikh is prone to error. Therefore, it will be appropriate to test everything according to the spirit of *Guru Granth Sahib*, which is called the "voice of the Lord."

The light of Guru Nanak Dev illuminated all his successors. This fact has been very aptly conveyed in the Var of Satta Balwand included in the Ramkali raga of *Guru Granth Sahib*. This fact has even been conveyed by Guru Gobind Singh in Bachittar Natak. If the spirit of Guru Nanak Dev pervaded in all his successors, there can be no doubt in the unity of all the Sikh thought. The same spirit is working in the compositions of all the Gurus. If any composition of the *Dasam Granth* is not in accordance with the spirit of *Guru Granth Sahib,* that cannot be the work of the tenth Guru. The compositions of the court-poets manifest a vast and varied literary exercise. Out of them, some names are found in the *Dasam Granth*. Several compositions of the *Dasam Granth* are related to Hindu Trinity, their incarnations and the Goddess Durga.

At the very outset we should know the views of *Guru Granth Sahib* about these gods and goddesses:

1. Brahma, Vishnu and Shiva, the Trinity, has strayed in the illusion of three modes. (Ramkali M.3, p. 909)
2. Brahma, Vishnu and Shiva are in the service of that Lord, whose end they cannot trace and Who is Imperceptible and Indivisible. (Maru M.3, p. 1053)
3. The Vedas do not know His Eulogy. Brahma does not know His Secrets, Shiva does not know His Mysteries, all the gods have become tired in His Search. The goddesses do not know His Mystification, that Imperceptible Transcendent Lord is above all. (Ramkali M.5, p. 894)
4. We worship gods and goddesses, O brother! what should we beg from them and what can they give? if we bathe the stones in water, O brother! they sink down therein. (Sorath M.1, p. 637)

Guru Gobind Singh has himself written in *Shabad Hazare*:

1. Do not search the other one except the One Lord.
2. Do not have faith in the created one, only worship the Creator, consider Him as the Supreme *Ishvara*, Who is Primal, Unborn, Unconquerable and Eternal.

From the above quotations, this fact becomes clear that the Gurus had no faith in the gods and goddesses. They never worshipped them. It can be said about the Chaubis avatars of Vishnu, Brahma avatars and Rudra (Shiva) avatars that they were only the poetic exercise of Guru Gobind Singh. In the beginning of Bachittar Natak, in Apni Katha, he has clearly written:

In whatever way, I became conscious of the births,
In that respect, I composed my works;
In the first place, in whatever way I wrote about Satyuga,
Primarily I wrote about the memoirs of gods,
Firstly I composed Chandi Charitra,
I have spoken about the order from top to toe.

From the above views it appears that Guru Gobind Singh wanted to take his Sikhs towards ethical and spiritual greatness. He did not like the retaliation from the Sikhs for the tyrannical and characterless actions of others. He wanted them to followed the prescribed discipline very closely. He himself has written:

1. He should not bring in his mind the lust, anger, ego, greed, doggedness and attachment, Only then he can visualise the soul-essence and realise the Supreme Reality. (*Shabad Hazare*)

2. Have the matted hair of self-control and bath of yoga and extend the nails of observance,
   With knowledge as preceptor, instruct yourself, and rub the ashes of the Name. (*Shabad Hazare*)

This discipline has been mentioned several times in *Guru Granth Sahib*. We give some quotations down below in this regard:

1. Five thieves abide in this body, lust, anger, greed, attachment and ego. They loot the nectar, but the self-willed does not comprehend it and none listens to the cries. (Sorath M.3, p. 300)
2. O lust! the place-giver in hell and marking us stray in many species. The stealer of mind and goer to the three worlds, and also destroyer of the remembrance of Name, austerity and character. (Sahaskriti Sloks M.5, p. 1358)
3. For one moment of the pleasure of lust, you suffer for million of days.... The house of another person is like the company of a snake. (Asa M.5, p. 403)
4. Closing the door behind many curtains, you rape another's wife. When you are asked to render the account by Chitra and Gupta, who will help you to cover your guilt? (Sorath M.5, p. 616)
5. He should not see the beauty of another's wife with lustful eyes. (Gauri Sukhmani M.5, p. 274)
6. They only feel ashamed, who go to another's home for lust. (Phunhe M.5, p. 1362)

Other such like examples can be added. The views of the Gurus are very clear about the raping of another's wife. This is the significant aspect of the character of a Sikh. Bhai Gurdas, the first Sikh theologian, has described the woman as the better half and the gate of salvation. He has laid emphasis on the golden principle of becoming a celibate with only one woman. According to him, a woman older in years may be considered a mother, a woman of nearly the same age a sister and a younger woman a daughter. In the *Rahtnamas*, that person is considered a very great sinner, who inflicts an attack on the chastity of another's wife.

In Charitropakhyan, there are many such episodes, which contain very naked description of the sexy behaviour of voluptuous women with other men. At several places, there is great nakedness in the language and no attempt seems to have been made for reformation. The scholars, who believe that these episodes will create hatred in the minds of the young people against the sexual hunger, they are a prey to deception. They can become prone towards evil action instead of hatred. These episodes can create a society of evil persons. They are quite against the Sikh concepts and therefore are strongly refutable. Therefore Charitropakhyan cannot be the composition of the Guru and also not his literary exercise. The subject of several Hikayats in nearly the same of the Charitropakhyan. They are in Persian language. Therefore, this view of the old Sikh savants seems to be correct that Charitropakhyan and Hikayats should not be a part of the *Dasam Granth*.

A Look on the Compositions of the Dasam Granth

Jaap Sahib

Just as Jaapu is the first composition in *Guru Granth Sahib*, similarly Jaap Sahib is the first composition in the *Dasam Granth*. The words "Sri Mukhvak Patshahi 10" have been written in the beginning, therefore this is the work of the Tenth Guru. This composition, as ordained, is to be recited alongwith Japu in the morning by every Sikh. Ten forms of versifications have been used in this work viz., Chhappai Bhujang Prayaat, Chaachari, Charpat, Rooaal, Madhubhaar, Bhagvati, Ramaval, Harbolmana, and Ek Achhari. There are 199 stanzas. In the first stanza, the words *neti neti*, occur. Just as we go on reciting the poem, some new and fresh words of God's praise are found. In this respect, this peom can be called a "Brahm Astotar" (A Eulogy of God). In various Bhakti cults, *Sahasranamas* of the worshipped god are prepared. Keeping this in view this peom is also a *Naama*

INTRODUCTION

or *Naam-Maala*. The Guru has used the words of praise mostly with negative suffixes and prefixes. The description of the nature of God can be done more strongly with negative signs. For this objective, the Guru has combined the following negative prefixes and suffixes, which are as follow:

Prefixes: ˙,ਨਹ,ਨਹਿਨ,ਨਿ; ਅ,ਆਂ; ਅਨ; ਨਿ,ਬਿ.
Suffixes: ਹੀਨ; ਬਿਹੀਨ; ਹਰਿਤ.

While eulogising the Transcendent Brahman, the Guru has repeated several words in divine love. He has used the same ideas again and again with different prefixes and suffixes. The significant facts about the philosophy of Transcendent Brahman, which come before us, they are given hereunder:

1. There is none equal to Transcendent Brahman (ਨਿਸਰੀਕ,ਅਨੂਪ,ਅਥੇ,ਅਨਥੇ)
2. He is Eternal and non-Temporal (ਅਕਾਲ,ਅੰਮਿਜ,ਅਨਾਦਿ,ਅਸੇਖ,ਅਭੰਗ,ਅਲੇ,ਨਿਭੰਗੀ,ਅਨਾਸ,ਆਛਿਦ,ਨਿਘਾਤੇ,ਅਨੰਤ)
3. He is without form, colour, and mark (ਅਰੂਪ,ਅਰੰਗ,ਅਭਹਨ,ਅਨੀਲ,ਅਨੰਗ,ਅਲੀਕ)
4. He is Unborn (ਅਜੋਨਿ,ਅਸ੍ਰਤ)
5. He is Omnipotent (ਅਜੀਤੇ,ਅਮੰਡ,ਨਿਭਾਕੇ,ਅਡੇ,ਅਛੇਦੇ)
6. He is Infinite (ਨਿਭਾਏ,ਅਸਿਤੇ,ਅਪਹ,ਅਪਾਨ)
7. He does not transmigrate (ਅਜਾਏ,ਅਸੰਭ,ਅਸੀਪ,ਅਭੂ,ਅਨਭਵ,ਅਜੂ,ਅਜੂ,ਅਜਾ,ਅਪਹਨੇ)
8. He is not a god (ਅਦੇਵ)
9. He is without relation and without company (ਅਨੰਗ,ਨਿਸਾਕ,ਨ ਤਾਤੈ,ਨ ਮਾਤੈ,ਨ ਪੋਤੈ,ਨ ਪੁਤੈ,ਨ ਪੁਤੈ, ਨ ਪਿਤੈ ਨਿਬਾਮੇ, ਨਿਸੰਗੀ)
10. He is Pure (ਅਪੂਤ,ਅਛੂਤ,ਅਭੇਡ,ਅਕਲੰਕ੍ਰਿਤ,ਨਿਤਾਪੇ)
11. He is without the impact of *maya* (ਅਜਾਲ,ਅਧੰਧ,ਅਬੰਧ,ਅਜਾਦਿ,ਅੜੰਤ)
12. He is devoid of time and place (ਅਕਾਲ,ਅਜਾਹ,ਨਿਪਾਸੇ,ਅਦੇਸ)
13. He is devoid of elements (ਅਤਤੇ,ਨਿਘਾਤੇ,ਅਭੂਤੇ,ਅਕਾਏ)
14. He is far away from the discrimination of religions (ਅਮਜਥੇ,ਅਧਰਮੇ)
15. He is Self-existent (ਅਕ੍ਰਿਤਾ,ਅਨਿਤ,ਅਬਾਧੇ)
16. He is without any *karma*-bondage (ਨਿਕਰਮ,ਨਿਭੇਸ,ਅਭੇਖ, ਅਸੋਗ,ਅਕਰਮੰ,ਅਲਿਪ)
17. He is changeless (ਅਥੈ)
18. He is desireless (ਨਿਕਾਮੇ,ਅਕਾਮੇ)
19. He is Imperceptible (ਅਰੀਮ,ਅਰੀਡ,ਨਿਭੁਡ,ਅਸ੍ਰਭ,ਅਡੀਠ,ਅਡੀਠ,ਟਦਿਖ,ਆਦੀਸ,ਅਖੰਡ,ਨਿਨਾਮੇ)

In the above-mentioned thoughts, there is one significant and a very new thought regarding the Transcendent Brahman and that is of ਅਮਜਥੇ (*amajbe*) = devoid of religion. The religions of the world are the limited boundaries for the Guru, therefore, he has risen much above it and take the whole of humanity in hid grasp. Though he is religious *in toto*, but he is the devotee of that Lord God, who rises above the boundaries of all religions.

In Jaap Sahib, the Guru appears before us as a great linguist. He has composed most of his works in Brajbhasha, but he has made Jaap Sahib a queer combination of Persian, Arabic and Brajbhasha. With the suffix 'ul' of Arabic, he has coined several queer compound words, viz., ਅਗੰਜੁਲ ਅਨਮ,ਅਗੰਜੁਲ ਗਨੀਮ,ਅਜੀਜੁਲ ਨਿਵਾਜ,ਅਦਸੁਲ ਅਲੇਖ,ਅਨੇਕੁਲ ਤਰੰਗ,ਅਮੀਕੁਲ ਇਮਾ,ਸਮਸਤੁਲ ਨਿਵਾਸੀ,ਸਮਸਤੁਲ ਸਲਾਮ,ਸਮਸਤੁਲ ਕਲਾਮ,ਸਮਸਤੁਲ ਜੁਬਾ,ਸਮਸਤੁਲ ਅਜੀਜ,ਸਮਸਤਲ ਅਦੀਸ,ਸਮਸਤੁਲ ਪਟਸ਼ੇ,ਸਮਵਡੁਲ ਸਰੂਪ,ਸਦੇਵੁਲ ਅਕਾਮ,ਸਰਬੁਲ ਗਵੰਨ,ਹਮੇਸੁਲ ਹਵੰਨ,ਹਮੇਸੁਲ ਅਥੇਖ,ਹਮੇਸੁਲ ਸਲਾਮ,ਹਰੀਫੁਲ ਅਜੀਮੈ,ਹਰੀਫੁਲ ਸਿਕੰਨ,ਹਿਰਾਸੁਲ ਫਿਕੰਨ,ਰਸਨੁਲ ਚਿਰਾਗ,ਕਰੀਮੁਲ ਕਮਾਲ, ਗਨੀਮੁਲ ਸ਼ਿਕਸਤੈ,ਗਨੀਮੁਲ ਖਿਰਾਜ, ਗਰੀਬੁਲ ਨਿਵਾਜ,ਗਰੀਬੁਲ ਪਰਸਤੇ,ਤਮਾਮੁਲ ਰੂਜ,ਤਮੀਜੁਲ ਤਮਾਮੇ,ਤਮਾਮੁਲ ਤਮੀਜ,ਨਮਸਤੁਲ ਪ੍ਰਨਾਮੇ, and ਬਿਲੰਦੁਲ ਮਕਾਨੇ

Instead of the diction of Persian and Arabic, it was natural that with Brajbhasha, the diction of Sanskrit and Prakrit should also be there. Regarding this we quote below one of the examples from Jaap Sahib:

ਚਕ੍ਰ ਚਿਹਨ ਅਰ ਬਰਨ ਜਾਤਿ ਅਰੁ ਪਾਤਿ ਨਹਿਨ ਜਿਹ,
ਰੂਪ ਰੰਗ ਅਰੁ ਰੇਖ ਭੇਖ ਕੋਊ ਨ ਸਕਤ ਕਿਧੁ,
ਅਚਲ ਮੁਰਤਿ ਅਨਭਉ ਪ੍ਰਕਾਸ ਅਮਿਤੋਜ ਕਹਿਜੈ,

ਕੋਟਿ ਇਦ੍ਰਾ ਸਾਹੁ ਸਾਹਾਨਿ ਗਨਿਜੈ,
ਤ੍ਰਿਭਵਣ ਮਹੀਪ ਸੁਹ ਨਹ ਅਸੁਹ ਨਤਿ ਨੇਤ ਥਨ ਤ੍ਰਿਣ ਕਹਤ,
ਤਵ ਸਹਬ ਨਾਮ ਕਬੈ ਕਵਨ ਕਹਮ-ਨਾਮ ਬਹਤ ਸੁਮਤਿ ॥੧॥

Akaal Ustat

The first 271 stanzas of this composition are complete, but the stanza 272 is unfinished, therefore the scholars consider it an incomplete composition. Except these stanzas, the following words are therein the beginning:

੧ਓ ਸਤਿਗੁਰ ਪਸਾਦਿ
ਸ੍ਰੀ ਭਗਉਤੀ ਜੀ ਸਹਾਇ
ਸ੍ਰੀ ਅਕਾਲ ਜੀ ਕੀ ਉਸਤਤਿ
ਓਹਾ ਖਾਸੇ ਦਸਤਖਤ ਕਾ ॥ ਪਾਤਸ਼ਾਹੀ੧੦॥
ਅਕਲਿ ਪੁਰਖ ਕੀ ਹਛਾ ਹਮਨੈ ॥ ਸਹਬ ਲੋਹ ਕੀ ਹਛਿਆ ਹਮਨੈ ॥
ਸਹਬ ਕਾਲ ਜੀ ਕੀ ਹਛਿਆ ਹਮਨੈ ॥ ਸਹਬ ਲੋਹ ਜੀ ਦੀ ਹਛਿਆ ਹਮਨੈ ॥
ਆਗੇ ਲਿਖਾਹੀ ਕੇ ਦਸਤਖਤ

In the book entitled *Shabdarath Dasam Granth*, edited by Bhai Randhir Singh, Research Scholar for Punjabi University, Patiala, a footnote is found regarding the abovementioned scribe, whose translation is given below:

"The manuscript from which the scribe of the volume is copying this composition, in that the four underlined verses have been written by the Guru with his lotus hands. After that there was the writing of the scribe." In the above-mentioned four verses, the following significant views come before us:

1. The symbol of the Transcendent Lord for the Guru is *Sarab-Loh* (All Steel).
2. The Guru also calls the Transcendent Lord *Sarab-Kaal* (Death for All).
3. In his verses he has hailed *Sarab-Loh* double-edged sword or spear.
4. He has talked about *Sarab-Kaal* in his verses several times. Whereas God is the Creator and Sustainer, He is also the Destroyer. As *Sarab-Kaal* God destroyed the demons, fiends etc. He has written:

ਛਜ਼ਓ ਕਟਾਖ ਜ਼ਖਰਟਜ਼ ਜ਼ਖਟਜ਼ੋ ॥ ਛਜ਼ਓ ਧੋਜ਼ ਥੈ ਡਕੰਕਜ਼ ਓਟਜੋ ॥ (The All-Death Lord is my Protector, O All-See Lord, I am Thy slave.)

The peom Akaal Ustat is a eulogy of the Transcendent Lord. In this way, this composition is a Brahm-Stotar like Jaap Sahib. But besides this, there are some other points, which demand out attention. The Ten Swayyas, which are recited daily by the Sikhs, they are also the part of this composition. Shamsher Singh Ashok in his article on "Akaal Ustat de Dohare te Unhan de Uttar" published in his book *Dasam Granth Bare* writes: From nos. 221 to 230, there are Dohiras (couplets) in the form of questions, whose answers are not given in the composition. It is thought that the answers were there, but Bhai Mani Singh etc., could not obtain them. According to the research of Pandit Kartar Singh Dakha, the answers to these Dohiras lie with themselves. He has even written a small tract on this subject. On making a research study of the *Dasam Granth*, I have found the answers to these Dohiras, which I present to the readers. According to the manuscript no. p. 205, it is generally thought that these answers are the work of the Guru himself. At the time of the preparation of the recension of the *Dasam Granth*, they could not be found, therefore, they could not be included. . . . According to the noteworthy scholar Bhai Kahn Singh of Nabha, these answers were written by the sectarian scholars and not by the Guru. In *Gurshabad Ratnakar Mahan Kosh*, while explaining the verses 'ਏਕ ਸਮੇ ਸ੍ਰੀ ਆਤਮ,' Bhai Kahn Singh recorded 25 Dohiras, which look much different and do not resemble these Dohiras." Out of these Dohiras, the first one is reproduced below:

INTRODUCTION

ਏਕ ਸਮੇ ਸ੍ਰੀ ਆਤਮਾ ਉਚਰਿਓ ਮਤਿ ਸਿਉ ਬੈਨ॥
ਸਭ ਪ੍ਰਤਾਪ ਜਗਦੀਸ ਕੇ ਕਹੁ ਸਕਲ ਬਿਧਿ ਤੈਨ॥੨੭੧॥

According to Piara Singh Padam: "There are 271 and a half stanzas in Akaal Ustat. I think, the twenty Tribhangi stanzas praising Chandi, they should have been in the beginning of Chandi Charittar II and not here. Like this the ten questioning Dohiras are perhaps the part of Gyan Prabodh and not the part of Akaal Ustat. The eulogy of the Transcendent Lord has been generally presented in ten or twenty stanzas." (*Dasam Granth Darshan*)

Another important part of Akaal Ustat, besides the ten Swayyas are the Kabits, which also demand our attention. In Swayyas and Kabits both, there is criticism of ritualism. In Swayyas the rituals have been described as Koor Kriya (false actions), while inspiring for the love of God and humanity:

ਸਾਚ ਕਹੂੰ ਸੁਨਿ ਲੇਹੁ ਸਭੈ ਜਿਨ ਪ੍ਰੇਮ ਕੀਓ ਤਿਨ ਹੀ ਪ੍ਰਭੁ ਪਾਇਓ॥

In Kabits, while telling the people of the world to utter Praises of the Lord, the Guru has pointed towards the unity of all humanity by saying "*Manas ki jaat sabhai ekai pehchanbo.*" He has written:

ਦੇਹੁਰਾ ਮਸੀਤ ਸੋਈ ਪੂਜਾ ਨਿਵਾਜ ਓਈ, ਮਨਿਸ ਸਭੈ ਏਕ ਪੈ ਅਨੇਕ ਕੋ ਭ੍ਰਮਾਉ ਹੈ॥
ਦੇਵਤਾ ਅਦੇਵ ਜਛ ਗੰਧ੍ਰਬ ਤੁਰਕ ਹਿੰਦੂ, ਨਿਆਰੇ ਨਿਆਰੇ ਦੇਸਨ ਕੇ ਭੇਸ ਕੋ ਪ੍ਰਭਾਉ ਹੈ॥
ਏਕੈ ਨੈਨ ਏਕੈ ਕਾਨ ਏਕੈ ਦੇਹ ਏਕੈ ਬਾਨ, ਖਾਕ ਬਾਦ ਆਤਸ਼ ਔ ਆਬ ਕੋ ਰਲਾਉ ਹੈ॥
ਅਲਹ ਅਭੇਖ ਸੋਈ, ਪੁਰਾਨ ਔ ਕੁਰਾਨ ਓਈ, ਏਕ ਹੀ ਸਰੂਪ ਸਭੈ ਏਕ ਹੀ ਬਨਾਉ ਹੈ॥

Bachittar Natak

There are two longer poems in the *Dasam Granth:* Bachittar Natak and Charitropakhyan. There are three parts of Bachittar Natak. In the first part, there is Apni Katha (autobiography) of the Guru, in which he has introduced us to his clan, his previous birth, his birth in this world and the events of his life upto AD 1696. The second part is about the wars between gods and demons. Three compositions are included in it; Chandi Charittar Ukat Bilas, Chandi Charittar II and Var Durga ki. In the third part of Bachittar Natak there is description of the twenty-four incarnations of Vishnu, seven incarnations of Brahma and two incarnations of Shiva. Hereunder a brief description of the second part of given:

Chandi Charittar Ukat Bilas

This composition has eight chapters totalling 233 stanzas. It has been written on the basis of the mythological story of Durga Saptshati in *Markandeya Purana*. It inspires one to fight bravely for the sake of *dharma*. It ends with the following verses:

ਦੇਹ ਸਿਵਾ ਬਰ ਮੋਹਿ ਇਹੈ ਸੁਭ ਕਰਮਨ ਤੇ ਕਬਹੂੰ ਨ ਟਰੋਂ॥
ਨ ਡਰੋਂ ਅਰਿ ਸੋ ਜਬ ਜਾਇ ਲਰੋਂ ਨਿਸਚੈ ਕਰ ਅਪਨੀ ਜੀਤ ਕਰੋਂ॥
ਅਰੁ ਸਿਖ ਹੋਂ ਆਪਨੇ ਹੀ ਮਨ ਕੋ, ਇਹ ਲਾਲਚ ਹਉ ਗੁਨ ਤਉ ਉਚਰੋਂ॥
ਜਬ ਆਵ ਕੀ ਅਉਧ ਨਿਦਾਨ ਬਨੈ, ਅਤਿ ਹੀ ਰਨ ਮੈ ਤਬ ਜੂਝ ਮਰੋਂ॥

In this composition Dohiras, Kabits and mostly Swayyas have been used.

Chandi Charittar II

This composition has also eight chapters. The stanzas are 262. The forms of versification used in it are Naraaj, Rasaaval, Dohira, Bhujang Prayaat, Totak, Chaupai, Madhubhaar, Rooaamal, Kulk, Rooaal, Bije, Manohar, Beli Biddaram and Birdh Naraaj. The sentiment of heroism overflows in it. It ends with the following Dohira:

ਜੇ ਜੇ ਤੁਮਰੇ ਧਿਆਨ ਕੋ ਨਿਤ ਉਠਿ ਧਿਐਹੈ ਸੰਤ॥
ਅਮ੍ਰਿਤ ਲਹੈਗੇ ਮੁਕਤਿ ਫਲ ਪਾਵਹਿਗੇ ਭਗਵੰਤ॥

Var Durga di

This composition is also called Chandi di Var and Var Bhagauti Ji ki. It contains only 55 Pauris, in which the story of *Durga Saptshati* has been repeated very briefly. This is the only composition of the Guru in Punjabi language and moreover, it is the model Var of Punjabi literature. It has cast a great influence on Punjabi Var literature. The languages contains a good number of words of western Punjabi (Lehndi) and overflows with sentiment of heroism. Very apt similes have been used. Such an atmosphere is created that the war seems to be enacted before our eyes. The horns and trumpets are sounding and the warriors are angrily fighting against one another. The brave fighters are stringed in lances. Two examples are given hereunder from this Var:

(੧) ਜੰਗ ਮੁਸਾਫਾ ਬਜਿਆ ਹਣ ਘੁਹੇ ਨਗਾਰੇ ਚਾਵਲੇ॥
ਝਲਨ ਨੇਜੇ ਬੈਹਕਾਂ ਨੀਸਾਨ ਲਸਇ ਲਸਾਵਲੇ॥
ਢੋਲ ਨਗਾਰੇ ਪਉਣ ਦੇ ਉਂਘਨ ਜਾਣ ਜਟਾਵਲੇ॥
ਦੁਰਗਾ ਦਾਨੋ ਭੇ ਹਣ ਨਾਦ ਵਜਤ ਖੇਤ ਭਹਿਵਲੇ॥
ਬੀਹ ਪਹੋਤੇ ਬਹਛੀਏ ਜਣ ਡਾਲ ਚਮੁਟੇ ਆਚਲੇ॥
ਇਕ ਚਢੇ ਤੇਗੀਂ ਤਤਫੀਆਂ ਤੀਹ ਵਚੋ ਸੁਇਨਾ ਡਾਵਲੇ॥
ਜਣ ਡਸੇ ਭੁੜੰਗਮ ਸਾਵਲੇ॥
ਮਹ ਜਾਵਣ ਬੀਹ ਹੁਹਾਵਲੇ॥

(੨) ਸਟ ਪਈ ਜਮਧਾਵੀ ਦਲਾਂ ਮੁਕਾਬਲਾ॥
ਧੂਹ ਲਈ ਕ੍ਰਿਪਾਣੀ ਦੁਰਗਾ ਘਮਾਨ ਤੇ॥
ਚੰਡੀ ਹਾਖਸ਼ ਖਾਣੀ ਵਾਹੀ ਦੈਂਤ ਨੂੰ॥
ਕੋਪਰ ਚੂਰ ਚਵਾਣੀ ਲਥੀ ਕਰਗ ਲੈ॥
ਪਾਖਰ ਤੁਰਾ ਪਲਾਣੀ ਸਿੰਗਾਂ ਵਉਲ ਦਿਆਂ॥
ਕੂਹਮ ਸਿਹ ਲਹਿਲਾਵੀ ਦਾਝਮਨ ਮਾਹ ਕੇ॥
ਵਢੇ ਗਣ ਤਿਖਾਣੀ ਮੂਏ ਖੇਤ ਸਿਰ॥
ਹਣ ਵਿਚ ਅਤੀ ਘਾਣੀ ਲੋਹੂ ਮਿਟੀ ਲੋਹੂ ਮਿਝ ਦੀ॥

The second name of Durga is Chandi, but the word "Bhagauti" has not been used for any goddess. It has been used for the sword. Its meaning becomes clear from the Vars of Bhai Gurdas, wherein he has written: "Naun Bhagauti Loh Gharaya" (Var 25). (Its name is Bhagati and it has been made from steel.)

The Guru has himself used this word for the sword in his Var:

Lai Bhagauti Durg Shah Varjagan Bhaari (Durga took up her sword—greatly blessed one.)

In fact the Guru wanted to manifest the greatness of the sword or weapons, because they were the symbols of the "Primal Power" for him. We have already made clear the views of the Guru about the gods and goddesses. Even the goddess has been created by God. This fact has been conveyed by him in his Var:

Tain hi Durga saaj ke Daintaan da naas karaya (You have created Durga and caused the destruction of the demons.)

Twenty-four Incarnations and other Incarnations

This is the third part of Bachittar Natak. The incarnation of the Trinity, who have been dealt within this part are as follows:

The incarnations of Vishnu: Machh (Matsya), Kachh (Tortoise), Nara, Narayan, Mohini, Bairah (Boar), Narasingh, Bawan (Vaman), Parashurama, Brahma, Rudra, Jalandhar, Arhant, Manu,

INTRODUCTION

Dhanwantar, Suraj, Chandra, Rama, Krishna, Nara (Arjan), Buddha, and Kalki (Nihkalanki). The incarnations of Rudra: Dattatreya, Parasnath.

The incarnations of Brahma: Balmeek (Valmiki), Kashyap, Shukracharya, Vaches (Brihaspati), Byas (Vyas), Khat Shastarkar Rish, and Kalidas.

At the end of this part, the story of Mir Mehdi and Kalki has been related. This is of course surprising that Brahma and Rudra have also been shown as the incarnations of Vishnu, whereas they have their own separate incarnations.

Of all the above-mentioned incarnations, the episode of Krishnavatar is the longest. After that there is Ramavatar. The total stanzas of Krishnavatar are 2492 and of Ramavatar 864. The best stanzas of the poetry of the Guru are found in the description of these incarnations. We have told in the preceding pages that the Guru has rejected the idea of the incarnation of these gods and goddesses. He had not composed his poetry about them with any faith in them, But it was only a poetic exercise. In Chandi di Var (or Durga di Var) he has addressed the Lord God thus:

> Rama, taking his strength from you, killed Ravana with his arrows, Krishna, taking his strength from you, overthrew Kansa by catching hold of his hair.

All of the gods and goddesses and their incarnations take their strength from God, they are powerless themselves. The Guru composed the description of the incarnation in poetry, because he wanted to raise the zeal of people for fighting for *dharma*. He writes in Krishnavatar:

> I have composed the episode of the tenth part of Bhagavata in the folk-language,
> I have no other desire except raising the heroism of the people for fighting for *dharma*.

There is one special thing to be noted that while writing the poetry of these incarnations, he has clearly expressed his own views. He writes in Ramavatar:

"Since the day, I touched Thy Feet, I did not bring any other in my sight: Ram, Rahim, Purana, and *Quran* speak of many others, but I do not believe in anyone the Smritis, Shastras and Vedas tell of many aspects, but I do not know anyone. O Lord! because of Thy Grace, I did not say anything, but you said everything." Similarly, he has written in Krishnavatar:

> I do not initially appease Ganesha,
> I never worship Krishna and Vishnu,
> I have heard about then, but do not recognise them,
> I have fallen in love with Lord's Feet,
> The Supreme Destroyer is my Protector
> O Supreme Steel, I am Thy slave.

In order to clarify this fact further, Piara Singh Padam writes:

"Therefore, there is no basis for this suspicion that the Guru was the worshipper of the incarnation. For the redress of this suspicion, at the end of the Bachittar Natak he has included the hymns in nine ragas and 32 Swayyas, in which he has rejected the worship of incarnation, idol-worship and other actions."

In the description of the episode of Krishnavatar, Ramavatar, and Kalkiavatar we find several excellent examples of heroic poetry:

In Ramavatar: ਭੁਜੰਗ ਪ੍ਰਯਾਤ ਛਮਕ:

ਗਿਰੇ ਹੁੰਡ ਮੁੰਡੇ ਭਸੁੰਡੇ ਗਜਾਨੰ॥
ਧਿਰੇ ਹੁੰਡ ਮੁੰਡੇ ਸੁ ਡੁੰਡੇ ਨਿਸਾਨੰ॥
ਹਤੇ ਕੰਕ ਬੰਕੰ ਸਸੰ ਕੰਤ ਜੋਧੰ॥
ਉਠੀ ਕੂਹ ਜੂਹੰ ਮਿਲੇ ਸੈਨ ਕ੍ਰੋਧੰ॥੪੨੦॥

ਝਿਮੀ ਤੇਗ ਤੇਜੰ ਸਹੰਸੰ ਪ੍ਰਹਾ ॥
ਖਿਮੀ ਦਾਮਨੀ ਜਾਣ ਭਾਦੋਂ ਮੜਾਹੈਂ ॥
ਹਸੇ ਹੱਕ ਬੰਕੇ ਕਸੇ ਸੂਹ ਵੀਰੰ ॥
ਢਲੀ ਢਾਲ ਮਾਲੰ ਸੁਭੇ ਤੱਛ ਤੀਰੰ ॥੪੨੧॥

Wherever Sirkhandi stanza has been used, firstly, the language is Punjabi and secondly, it appears like the language of Chandi di Var:

ਸਿਹਖੰਡੀ ਛੰਦ: ਜੁਟੇ ਵੀਹ ਜੁਝਾਰੇ ਧਗਾਂ ਵਜੀਆਂ ॥
ਬਜੇ ਨਾਦ ਕਲਾ ਦਲਾਂ ਮੁਸਹਿਦਾ ॥
ਲੁਝੇ ਕਾਹਨ ਝਾਰੇ ਸੰਘਰ ਸੂਹਮੇ ॥
ਵੂਠੇ ਜਾਣ ਡਾਹੇ ਅਣੀਅਹ ਕੈਬਰੀ ॥੪੬੧॥
ਵਜੇ ਸੰਗਲੀਆਲੇ ਹਾਠਾਂ ਜੁਟੀਆਂ ॥
ਖੇਤ ਬਹੇ ਮੁਛਾਲੇ ਕਹਤ ਤਾਹਰੇ ॥
ਡਿਗੇ ਵੀਹ ਜੁਝਾਰੇ ਹੂਗਾਂ ਫੁਟੀਆਂ ॥
ਬਕੇ ਜਾਣ ਮਤਵਾਰੇ ਭੰਗਾਂ ਖਾਇਕੈ ॥੪੬੯॥

From Krishnavatara

ਸਵੈਯਾ: ਜੁਧ ਬਿਧੈ ਅਤਿ ਤੀਹ ਲਰੇ, ਬਹੁ ਬੀਹਨ ਕੇ ਤਨ ਸੋਣਤ ਭਨੀ ॥
ਕਾਇਹ ਭਾਜ ਗਏ ਹਨ ਤੇ ਅਤਿ ਹੀ ਡਹ ਸਿਉ ਜਿਹ ਗਾਤ ਪਸੀਨੇ ॥
ਭੂਤ ਪਿਸਾਚ ਕਹੇ ਕਿਲਕਾਹ, ਫਿਹੇ ਹਨ ਜੋਗਿਨ ਖਪ ਲੀਨੇ ॥
ਆਨ ਫਿਹੋਏ ਤਹ ਸੀ ਤ੍ਰਿਪੁਰਾਹ, ਸੁ ਆਧੇ ਈ ਅਮਗ ਸਿਵਾ ਤਨ ਕੀਨੇ ॥੧੨੩੧॥

Several other sentiments have been seen used in the compositions of the Guru. Specially look at the use of amorous sentiment:

ਸਵੈਯਾ: ਏ ਸਮੇ ਖਿਜ ਕੁੰਜਨ ਪੈ ਸੁਹਿ ਕਾਨਨ ਸਖਾਮ ਟਟਕ ਧਹਾਏ ॥
ਕੰਚਨ ਕੇ ਬਹੁ ਮੇਲ ਜਹੇ ਨਗ ਬੂਹਮ ਸਕੈ ਉਪਮਾ ਨ ਗਨਾਏ ॥
ਬਜ੍ਰ ਲਗੀ ਜਿਨ ਬੀਚ ਛਟਾ ਚਨਕੇ ਚਰੂੰ ਵਹ ਧਹ ਛਬਿ ਪਾਏ ॥
ਤਰੁਣ ਸਮੈ ਹਹਿ ਵੈ ਦਏ ਉਧਵ ਦੈ ਅਬ ਹਾਵਲ ਭੇਖ ਪਠਾਏ ॥੯੦੧॥…
ਤੋਹਿ ਹੀ ਧਟਾਨ ਧਹੈ ਹਹਿ ਜੁ ਅਹ ਤੋਹਿ ਹੀ ਲੈ ਕਹ ਨਾਮ ਪੁਕਰਹੈ ॥
ਮਾਤ ਪਿਤਾ ਕੀ ਨ ਲਾਜ ਕਹੈ ਹਹਿ ਸਾਇਤ ਸਖਾਮ ਹੀ ਸਖਾਮ ਚਿਤਰਹੈ ॥
ਨਾਮ ਅਦਾਹ ਤੇ ਜੀਵਤ ਹੈ ਬਿਨ ਨਾਮ ਕਹੋਏ ਛਿਨ ਮੈ ਕਸ ਟਾਰੈ ॥
ਯਾ ਬਿਧਿ ਦੇਖ ਦਸਾ ਉਨ ਕੀ ਅਤਿ ਬੀਚ ਬਢਏ ਜੀਅ ਸੋਕ ਹਮਾਰੈ ॥੯੧੯॥

Example of heroic poetry from Kalki incarnation:

ਸਿਹਖੰਡੀ ਛੰਦ: ਵਜੇ ਨਾਦ ਸੁਹਾਵਗੀ ਧਗਾਂ ਘੇਹੀਆਂ ॥
ਨਚੇ ਜਾਣ ਫਿਹਗੀ ਵਜੇ ਘੁੰਘ੍ਰੂ ॥
ਗਦਾ ਤ੍ਰਿਸੂਲ ਨਿਖੰਗੀ ਝੁਲਨ ਬੇਰਖਾਂ ॥
ਸਾਵਣ ਜਾਣ ਉਮੰਗੀ ਘਟਾ ਢਹਾਵਹੀ ॥੧੭੯॥
ਬਾਣੇ ਅਮਗ ਭੁਜੰਗੀ ਸਾਵਲ ਸੋਹਣੇ ॥
ਤ੍ਰੈ ਸੈ ਹਬ ਉਤਰਗੀ ਖੰਡਾ ਧੁਹਿਆ ॥

ਤਾਜੀ ਭਉਹ ਪਿਲੰਗੀ   ਛਾਲਾਂ ਪਾਈਆਂ ॥
ਭੰਗੀ ਜਾਣ ਭਿਤੰਗੀ   ਨਚੇ ਦਾਇਨੀ ॥੧੯੦॥
ਬਜੇ ਨਾਦ ਸੁਹੰਗੀ   ਅਟੀਆਂ ਜੁਟੀਆਂ ॥
ਪੈਹੈ ਧਾਧ ਪਵੰਗੀ   ਫਉਜਾਂ ਚੀਹ ਕੈ ॥
ਉਠੇ ਛੈਲ ਛਲੰਗੀ   ਛਾਲਾਂ ਪਾਈਆਂ ॥
ਝਾਤ ਝਵਾਕ ਝਤੰਗੀ   ਤੇਗਾਂ ਵਜੀਆਂ ॥੧੯੧॥

With the use of middle rhyme, the above form of versification becomes more impressive and powerful.

Gyan Prabodh

According to Piara Singh Padam "Just as Bachittar Natak presents the Pauranic history of Indian religions, Gyan Prabodh presents the Indian ideology, but it is not available as a complete composition. We have got 336 stanzas only." Several forms of versification have been used in this composition also viz., Bhujang Prayaat, Tribhangi, Rasaaval, Chhappai, Kalas, Naraaj, Bahr Taveel, Paadhari, Rooaal, Tomar, Totak, etc. It is thought, that the answers to the questions, which are not available in Akaal Ustat, we get them in this composition from the stanzas 126 to 136. . . . If this thing may not be correct, even then there seems to be some connection between Akaal Ustat and Gyan Prabodh.

In the beginning of this composition, there is the eulogy of Transcendent Brahman. After that there are questions and answers of the soul and God. The soul questions and God answers. But the composition being incomplete, we get answer to only one question. The subject about which we get the knowledge in this composition is about the four types of disciplines, i.e.,

1. *Raj Dharam* or Political discipline,
2. *Daan Dharam* or Religious discipline,
3. *Bhog Dharam* or Householder's discipline, and
4. *Moksha Dharma* or Ascetic's discipline

The curious soul makes the following enquiry from Lord God:

The Soul said to the Higher Soul,
The Germinating Entity, Unmanifested and Invincible,
"What is the Soul-Entity?
Which hath indelible glory and which is of queer substance."
The Higher Soul answers thus:
The Higher Soul said:
"This Soul is itself Brahman,
Who is of Everlasting glory and is Unmanifested and Desireless,
Who is indiscriminate, actionless and deathless,
Who hath no enemy and friend and is merciful towards all."

This answer continues further. If this composition had been completed, then we could have got the answers regarding all the four disciplines. The discussion of the religious discipline has been given priority over the political discipline. In the religious disciplines there is mention of the charities made at the time of sacrifices (*yajnas*) by the kings. The narration is decorated with short anecdotes. The kings arrange sacrifices and the Brahmins perform them according to Vedic rites. While composing the Eulogy of God, the Guru has strongly rejected ritualism.

Shastar Naam-Maala

This composition is a dictionary of weapons. It is completed in five chapters and has 1318 stanzas. The detail of the chapters is as follows:

- First Chapter: It has 27 stanzas, in which the Guru bows down before the weapons considering them as the symbols of the Primal Power.
- Second Chapter: It begins from 28th stanza and ends at 74th. In these 47 stanzas various names of the sword and disc have been mentioned. The names of the sword are from 28th to 56th stanza and of the disc from 57th to 74th.
- Third Chapter: This chapter is spread from 75th stanza to 252nd stanza. Various names of the arrow are given in it.
- Fourth Chapter: This chapter is spread from 253rd stanza to 460th stanza. Various names of the noose are given in it.
- Fifth Chapter: This is the last chapter, which is spread from the 461st stanza to 1318th stanza. Various names of the gun are given in it.

Charitropakhyan

It is also known as Triya Charittar. This part of the *Dasam Granth* is the second longest part after Bachittar Natak. There are 404 Charitras in this part in which the conduct of malicious, fraudulent and deceitful women has been depicted. These Charitras are mostly related to the sexual nature of women. The total number of stanzas are 7558. The sources of these Charitras are *Mahabharata*, *Ramayana*, Puranas, *Panchatantra, Hitopadesh, Bagh-O-Bahar, Chahar Darvesh*, and the folk literature of Punjab. Their classification is thus the religious, the Pauranic, the historical, the social and the Romantic, etc. Dr. Dharampal Ashta, Dr. Harbhajan Singh, Dr. Mahip Singh, Dr. Taran Singh, Dr. Trilochan Singh, Piara Singh Padam, and Dr. Kumari Prasinni Sehgal consider these Charitras as the composition of the Guru. Dr. Kumari Prasinni Sehgal in her Ph.D. thesis entitled "Guru Gobind Singh Aur Unka Kavya" has presented this view: "There was an objective before the Guru in the preparation of this composition that he may be able to depict the low character of his contemporaries and thus establish the higher ethical values. He has tried to turn towards a successful higher life, by giving a realisic picture of the conduct of the characterless and lustful persons. In the last Charittar he has clarified his stand that after listening to these Charitras even the dumb will enjoy them and the imbecile will become intelligent. In that period the kidnappings, misconduct, immorality and rapes were ordinary events, by depicting which the Guru, by making known to various classes of men and women their weaknesses, he inspired them towards the ideal path of ethical life, good character and restraint. By giving a detailed description of he gave the consciousness of moral degeneration to men and women both." Several other scholars have presented such like views. Giani Lal Singh of Sangrur has written in his *Sri Dasam Granth Sahib Kosh* about these Charitras: "By continuously studying these Charitras or by listening to them attentively, there arises moral degeneration in the mind. Moreover, the Charitras, which contain the slander of women, they should not be considered as the part of the *Dasam Granth*. As written above, these Charitras violate the rules of the Sikh character, it will definitely be improper to associate them with the Guru. The Guru had clearly said, "I have to take the Panth much higher." He wanted to see the Panth with higher and purely moral and spiritual standards.

The majority of Charitras in Charitropakhyan are Triya Charitras. Though there are Purusha Charitras also, but very less in number. Though the number of Charitras are 404, but there is also a 405th Charittar, which contains Chaupai, which is recited daily by the Sikhs. According to Dr. Rattan Singh Jaggi, "In order to justify the number of Charitras as 405, the word *satarvin* (seventeenth) has been dishonestly written instead of *solvin* (sixteenth). . . . I do not agree with the view of Giani Harnam Singh Vallabh that originally there were only 303 Charitras. According to Piara Singh Padam, It is generally believed that there are 404 Charitras in the *Granth*, but this is not correct. The very first thing we find is that there are not 404 episodes. At some places, one story has been split into several Charitras.... On the whole, it may be said that there are not 404 episodes, but there are 404 chapters. Moreover, the total number is given as 405, but the 325th Charittar is not there." It seems that the 405th Charittar has been wrongly appended with Charitropakhyan by the compiler. It does not seem to be well-connected there. It could have been appended with Chandi Charitras, because it depicts the war of Durga and Maha Kaal with the demons.

Just as we have written earlier that according to Sikh doctrines, the position of woman is much higher, but some Sikh scholars are deliberately associating Charitropakhyan with the *Dasam Granth* and showing it as the composition of the Guru. Piara Singh Padam writes in this connection: "It is quite clear the position of woman before the Guru was much higher. Despite such tradition and faith why the Guru wanted to write such Charitras of women? The answer to it very clear. By writing such stories, the Guru did not condemn the womanhood, but he has definitely censured characterless women and the raping of another's wife.... If we see a little carefully, because of the feudal administration in the Mughal rule, the prostitution was common, there was no legal restricton on it. Therefore, the Guru wanted that the householder, saint-soldier Sikh should be saved from the deceitful net of the immoral women. He did not like the Sikh soldiers to become apostates, being enmeshed into the net of these immoral women. With this not only they will become irreligious, but it will also be a great blow to the independence movement...."

According to Shamsher Singh Ashok, Charitropakhyan is the composition of three poets: Ram, Shyam and Kali(das), which is considered correct by Mr. G.B. Singh, but he differs in this respect that the name Shyam is the poetic nom de plume of the Guru himself, but I do not agree with him.... The detail of different portions written by the poets is as under:

1. The poet Ram: From the first Charittar to 108th Charittar
2. The poet Shyam: From 109th Charittar to 194th Charittar and also from 227th Charittar to 404th Charittar
3. The poet Kali(das): From 195th Charittar to 226th Charittar

We cannot say with certainly whether some other poets also worked with them. Mr. G.B. Singh had written that the need for composing Charitropakhyan was felt by the Guru for the personal incident (the Charittar of Anup Kaur) experienced by him, which induced the Guru for composing this fifth Veda. This supposition for me is quite wrong. He himself says that these things are not historical but only the imaginary episodes. Then is the incident of Anup Kaur not imaginary Apni Katha of Bachittar Natak is considered as the autobiography of the Guru by Mr. G.B. Singh, but there is no mention of this incident of Anup Kaur in that composition. Secondly the poet Sainapat, the court-poet of the Guru makes no mention of this incident in his work entitled *Gur-Shobha Granth*. The other works like *Gur-Bilas*, *Suraj Prakash* and *Prachin Panth Prakash* are also silent about this incident. Sardar Kahn Singh and other noteworthy writers even deny the existence of this incident. Then why the Guru needed to compose this incident for this unhappened incident?

We restrain to give here the obscene sexual instances from Charitropakhyan.

Zafarnama (The Epistle of Victory)

This composition is an historical letter, which is written in Persian and was sent by the Guru to Emperor Aurangzeb. After leaving the fortress of Chamkaur, the Guru sent it from Dina Kangar. It contains only 115 couplets and is given as the first Hikayat at the end of the *Dasam Granth*. We give below the translation of a few couplets:

1. How could forty famished persons fight in the battlefield, on whom ten lakh soldiers made a sudden attack.—19
2. When all other methods fail, it is proper to hold the sword in hand.—22

3. They were neither men of Faith, nor true followers of Islam; they did not know the Lord, nor had faith in their Prophet.—46
4. The true Lord is known as Protector of the lowly. He is carefree and free from want.—74
5. With the help of your intelligence and the sword, you have become the master of Degh and Tegh.—90
6. If God is friendly, no enemy can do anything; the generous actions proceed from the Merciful Lord—98
7. Just as your hopes lie in your wealth; I depend on the Grace of the Lord.—105
8. You are proud of your kingdom and wealth, but I take refuge in the Non-temporal Lord.—106
9. Do not be careless about this fact that this *sarai* (resting place) in not the permanent abode.—107

In this letter the Guru has warned Aurangzeb about his tyranny and cruelty. The Guru has clearly said that when all the other efforts bear no fruit, then it will be proper to hold the sword in hand.

Hikayats

These Persian compositions are eleven in number. We have seen that the first Hikayat is Zafarnama. The compiler has appended these Hikayats with Zafarnama, although their subject is quite different. They are the compositions like Triya-Charittars and they have been rejected like Charitropakhyan. There total number of stanzas are 756.

Shabad Ragan de

These hymns are also entitled Shabad Hazare. The hymns are nine in number and are written in ragas like the hymns of the *Adi Granth*. Three hymns are Ramkali raga, two in Devgandhari and one each in Sorath, Kalyan, Tilang and Bilawal. Though the nom de plume of Nanak has not been used in these hymns, even then, as tradition says, they are the hymns of Guru Gobind Singh. There is one other hymn entitled Khyal Patshahi 10, which is not included in nine hymns. Another hymn Sun ke Sadd Mahi di is also available separately.

An example of the hymn:

ਹੇ ਮਨ ਇਹ ਬਿਧਿ ਜੋਗੁ ਕਮਾਓ॥
ਸਿੰਡ ਸਾਚ ਅਕਪਟ ਕੰਠਲਾ ਧਿਆਾਨ ਬਿਭੂਤ ਚੜ੍ਹਾਓ॥੧॥ਰਹਾਸੁ॥
ਤਾਂਤੀ ਗਹੁ ਆਤਮ ਬਸਿ ਕਹਕੀ ਬਿਛਾ ਨਾਮ ਅਧਾਰੰ॥
ਬਾਜੇ ਪਰਮ ਤਾਰ ਤਤ ਹਰਿ ਕੋ ਉਪਜੈ ਰਾਗ ਹਸਾਰੰ॥੧॥
ਉਘਟੇ ਤਾਨ ਤਰੰਗ ਰੰਗ ਅਤਿ ਗਿਆਨ ਗੀਤ ਬੰਧਾਨੰ॥
ਚਕਿ ਚਕਿ ਰਹੇ ਦੇਵ ਦਾਨਵ ਮੁਨਿ ਛਕਿ ਛਕਿ ਬਿਓਮ ਬਿਬਾਨੰ॥੨॥
ਆਤਮ ਉਪਦੇਸ ਭੇਸੁ ਸੰਜਮ ਕੋ ਜਾਪੁ ਸੁ ਅਜਪਾ ਜਾਪੈ॥
ਸਗਲ ਹੋ ਕੰਚਨ ਸੀ ਕਾਇਆ ਕਾਨ ਨ ਕਬਹੂੰ ਬਿਆਪੈ॥੩॥

This hymn has three *padas*. All the nine hymns of the Guru have three *padas*. In the beginning there is a *pada* of the pause (Rahaao), which is followed by other three *padas*. There is only the difference of the language from the hymns of *Guru Granth Sahib*. The language of *Guru Granth Sahib* is the saint-language (*sant bhaasha*), but Guru Gobind Singh has used Brajbhasha in his compositions. As in Jaapu of Guru Nanak Dev, the words *dhyan ki karah bibhoot* and *dhyan bibhoot charhao* have been inserted in the above hymn.

Swayye

All the Swayyas either eulogise God or condemn ritualism and hypocrisy. There are ten Sudha Swayye and also ten Tav Prasad Swayye in Akaal Ustat. Teti Swayye (Thirty-three Swayyas) is a

INTRODUCTION

separate composition, in which the first Swayya "Jaagat Jot Japai Nisbaasar..." was written after the ceremony of baptism and the other thirty-two were written earlier. All these Swayyas are considered the composition of the Guru "Three Swayyas," which contain two Swayyas in the praise of the Khalsa, are also the composition of the Guru.

An example from Sudha Swayye:

ਕਾਹੂੰ ਲੈ ਪਾਹਨ ਪੂਜ ਧਰਿਓ ਸਿਰ ਕਾਹੂੰ ਲੈ ਗਰੇ ਲਟਕਾਇਓ।।
ਕਾਹੂੰ ਲਖਿਓ ਹਰਿ ਅਵਾਚੀ ਦਿਸਾ ਮਹਿ ਕਾਹੂੰ ਪਛਾਹ ਕੋ ਸੀਸੁ ਨਿਵਾਇਓ।।
ਕੋਊ ਬੁਤਾਨ ਕੋ ਪੂਜਤ ਹੈ ਪਸੁ ਕੋਊ ਮਿਹਤਾਨ ਕੋ ਪੂਜਨ ਧਾਇਓ।।
ਕੂਰ ਕਿਰਿਆ ਉਰਝਿਓ ਸਭ ਹੀ ਜਗ ਸ੍ਰੀ ਭਗਵਾਨ ਕੋ ਭੇਦ ਨ ਪਾਇਓ।।

An example from Teti Swayye (Thirty-three Swayyas):

ਜਾਗਤ ਜੋਤ ਜਪੈ ਨਿਸਬਾਸਰ ਏਕ ਬਿਨਾ ਮਨ ਨੈਕ ਨ ਆਨੈ।।
ਪੂਰਨ ਪ੍ਰੇਮ ਪ੍ਰਤੀਤ ਸਜੈ ਬ੍ਰਤ ਗੋਰ ਮੜ੍ਹੀ ਮਠ ਭੂਲ ਨ ਮਾਨੈ।।
ਤੀਰਥ ਦਾਨ ਦਇਆ ਤਪ ਸੰਜਮ ਏਕ ਬਿਨਾ ਨਹਿ ਏਕ ਪਛਾਨੈ।।
ਪੂਰਨ ਜੋਤ ਜਗੈ ਘਟ ਮਹਿ ਤਬ ਖਾਲਸ ਤਾਹਿ ਨਖਾਲਸ ਜਾਨੈ।।

The Swayya written in praise of the Khalsa:

ਸੇਵ ਕਰੀ ਇਨ ਹੀ ਕੀ ਭਾਵਤ ਅਉਰ ਕੀ ਸੇਵ ਸੁਹਾਤ ਨ ਜੀਅ ਕੋ।।
ਦਾਨ ਦੀਓ ਇਨਹੀ ਕੋ ਭਲੋ ਅਰੁ ਆਨ ਕੋ ਦਾਨ ਨ ਲਾਗਤ ਨੀਕੋ।।
ਆਗੈ ਫਲੈ ਇਨਹੀ ਕੋ ਦੀਓ ਜਗ ਮਹਿ ਜਸ ਅਉਰ ਦੀਓ ਸਭ ਫੀਕੋ।।
ਮੋ ਗ੍ਰਹਿ ਮਹਿ ਤਨ ਤੇ ਮਨ ਤੇ ਸਿਰ ਲਉ ਧਨ ਹੈ ਸਭ ਹੀ ਇਨਹੀ ਕੋ।।

Asphotak Kabit

Under this title the Kabits, Swayyas and Dohiras have been appended together. They are about 50 and are written on different subjects. Most of them have been written in praise of Krishna and Radha. It seems that some compiler found them later on and he included them in his recension. This is an incoherent material. According to Piara Singh Padam, "Within them there are some such stanzas, which we get in Bachittar Natak and Charitropakhyan. Two Kabits exhibits the heroism of Sango Shah, the son of the aunt of the Guru, who fell a martyr, while fighting in the battle of Bhangani."

Sadd

It is a three-verse composition, which is said to have been uttered by the Guru in Lakhi Jangal. It has been composed in folk-metre.

The Compositions of the Guru in the Dasam Granth

The scholars, who believe that there are also the compositions of the court-poets in the *Dasam Granth*, they have kept before them the touchsone of *Gurbani*. Dr. Rattan Singh Jaggi writes in the appendix of his work entitled *Dasam Granth da Kartritav*: "This is my view in brief that the Tenth Guru is not the author of the whole of the *Dasam Granth*, which contains several compositions of the court-poets of the Guru. The authentic compositions in the name of the Guru are Jaapu, Akal Ustat (leaving the part of the stanzas from 201 to 230, Swayye, Zafarnama, etc." According to Shamsher Singh Ashok the compositions of the Guru are Jaapu, Akal Ustat (except Devi-Stotar), Thirty-two Swayyas, Swayyas in praise of the Khalsa, Zafarnama (except the Hikayats). I think that the following are the compositions of the Guru:

1. Jaapu Sahib
2. Akal Ustat

3. Apni Katha in Bachittar Natak
4. Gyan Prabodh
5. Zafarnama
6. 33 Swayyas
7. Shabad Ragan de

The following compositions can be considered as his poetic exercise:

(a) Chandi Charittar Ukat Bilas
(b) Chandi Charittar II
(c) Var Durga ki
(d) Twenty-four incarnations of Vishnu
(e) The incarnations of Brahma
(f) The incarnations of Rudra (Shiva)
(g) Shastar Naam-Maala
(h) 405th Charittar of Charitropakhyan

The following cannot be the compositions of the Guru, because they are not in consonance with the spirit of *Guru Granth Sahib* and violate the Sikh descipline:

1. Charitropakhyan (404 Charitras)
2. Hikayats
3. Asphotak Kabit

JAAPU
The Sacred Utterance of the Tenth Sovereign

CHHAPPAI STANZA   **BY THY GRACE**

He who is without mark or sign,
He who is without caste or line,
He who is without colour or form,
And without any distinctive norm,
He who is without limit and motion,
All-effulgence, non-descript ocean,
The Lord of millions of Indras and kings,
The master of all worlds and beings,
Each twig of the foliage proclaims: "Not this Thou art."
All Thy names cannot be told. One doth impart Thy action-name with benign heart. —1

BHUJANG PRAYAAT STANZA

Salutation to Thee O timeless Lord!
Salutation to Thee O beneficent Lord!
Salutation to Thee O formless Lord!
Salutation to Thee O wonderful Lord! —2

Salutation to Thee O garbless Lord!
Salutation to Thee O accountless Lord!
Salutation to Thee O bodyless Lord!
Salutation to Thee O unborn Lord! —3

Salutation to Thee O indestructible Lord!
Salutation to Thee O indivisible Lord!
Salutation to Thee O nameless Lord!
Salutation to Thee O non-spatial Lord! —4

Salutation to Thee O deedless Lord!
Salutation to Thee O non-religious Lord!
Salutation to Thee O nameless Lord!
Salutation to Thee O abodeless Lord! —5

Salutation to Thee O unconquerable Lord!
Salutation to Thee O fearless Lord!
Salutation to Thee O vehicleless Lord!
Salutation to Thee O unfallen Lord! —6

Salutation to Thee O colourless Lord!
Salutation to Thee O beginningless Lord!
Salutation to Thee O blemishless Lord!
Salutation to Thee O infinite Lord! —7

Salutation to Thee O cleaveless Lord!
Salutation to Thee O partless Lord!
Salutation to Thee O generous Lord!
Salutation to Thee O limitless Lord! —8

Salutation to Thee O the only one Lord!
Salutation to Thee O the multiform Lord!
Salutation to Thee O non-elemental Lord!
Salutation to Thee O bondless Lord! —9

Salutation to Thee O deedless Lord!
Salutation to Thee O doubtless Lord!
Salutation to Thee O homeless Lord!
Salutation to Thee O garbless Lord! —10

Salutation to Thee O nameless Lord!
Salutation to Thee O desireless Lord!
Salutation to Thee O non-elemental Lord!
Salutation to Thee O invincible Lord! —11

Salutation to Thee O motionless Lord!
Salutation to Thee O elementless Lord!
Salutation to Thee O invisible Lord!
Salutation to Thee O griefless Lord! —12

Salutation to Thee O woeless Lord!
Salutation to Thee O non-established Lord!
Salutation to Thee O universally honoured Lord!
Salutation to Thee O treasure Lord! —13

Salutation to Thee O bottomless Lord!
Salutation to Thee O motionless Lord!
Salutation to Thee O virtueful Lord!
Salutation to Thee O unborn Lord! —14

Salutation to Thee O enjoyer Lord!
Salutation to Thee O well-united Lord!
Salutation to Thee O colourless Lord!
Salutation to Thee O immortal Lord! —15

Salutation to Thee O unfathomable Lord!
Salutation to Thee O all-pervasive Lord!
Salutation to Thee O waters-sustainer Lord!
Salutation to Thee O propless Lord! —16

Salutation to Thee O casteless Lord!
Salutation to Thee O lineless Lord!
Salutation to Thee O religionless Lord!
Salutation to Thee O wonderful Lord! —17

Salutation to Thee O homeless Lord!
Salutation to Thee O garbless Lord!
Salutation to Thee O abodeless Lord!
Salutation to Thee O spouseless Lord! —18

Salutation to Thee O all-destroyer Lord!
Salutation to Thee O entirely generous Lord!
Salutation to Thee O multiform Lord!
Salutation to Thee O universal king Lord! —19

Salutation to Thee O destroyer Lord!
Salutation to Thee O establisher Lord!
Salutation to Thee O annihilator Lord!
Salutation to Thee O all-sustainer Lord! —20

Salutation to Thee O divine Lord!
Salutation to Thee O mysterious Lord!
Salutation to Thee O unborn Lord!
Salutation to Thee O loveliest Lord! —21

Salutation to Thee O all-pervasive Lord!
Salutation to Thee O all-permeator Lord!
Salutation to Thee O all-loving Lord!
Salutation to Thee O all-destroying Lord! —22

Salutation to Thee O death-destroyer Lord!
Salutation to Thee O beneficent Lord!
Salutation to Thee O colourless Lord!
Salutation to Thee O deathless Lord! —23

Salutation to Thee O omnipotent Lord!
Salutation to Thee O doer Lord!
Salutation to Thee O involved Lord!
Salutation to Thee O detached Lord! —24

Salutation to Thee O kindredless Lord!
Salutation to Thee O fearless Lord!
Salutation to Thee O generous Lord!
Salutation to Thee O merciful Lord! —25

Salutation to Thee O infinite Lord!
Salutation to Thee O greatest Lord!
Salutation to Thee O lover Lord!
Salutation to Thee O universal master Lord! —26

Salutation to Thee O destroyer Lord!
Salutation to Thee O sustainer Lord!
Salutation to Thee O creator Lord!
Salutation to Thee O all-vanquisher Lord! —27

Salutation to Thee O greatest yogi Lord!
Salutation to Thee O great indulger Lord!
Salutation to Thee O gracious Lord!
Salutation to Thee O sustainer Lord! —28

CHACHARI STANZA   BY THY GRACE

Thou art formless Lord!
Thou art unparalleled Lord!
Thou art unborn Lord!
Thou art non-being Lord! —29

Thou art unaccountable Lord!
Thou art garbless Lord!
Thou art nameless Lord!
Thou art desireless Lord! —30

Thou art propless Lord!
Thou art non-discriminating Lord!
Thou art fearless Lord!
Thou art unconquerable Lord! —31

Thou art universally-honoured Lord!
Thou art the treasure Lord!
Thou art master of attributes Lord!
Thou art unborn Lord! —32

Thou art colourless Lord!
Thou art beginningless Lord!
Thou art unborn Lord!
Thou art independent Lord! —33

Thou art unborn Lord!
Thou art colourless Lord!
Thou art elementless Lord!
Thou art perfect Lord! —34

Thou art invincible Lord!
Thou art unbreakable Lord!
Thou art unconquerable Lord!
Thou art tensionless Lord! —35

Thou art deepest Lord!
Thou art friendliest Lord!
Thou art strifeless Lord!
Thou art bondless Lord! —36

Thou art unthinkable Lord!
Thou art unknowable Lord!
Thou art immortal Lord!
Thou art unbound Lord! —37

Thou art unbound Lord!
Thou art placeless Lord!
Thou art infinite Lord!
Thou art greatest Lord! —38

Thou art limitless Lord!
Thou art unparalleled Lord!
Thou art propless Lord!

Thou art unborn Lord! —39
Thou art unfathomable Lord!
Thou art unborn Lord!
Thou art elementless Lord!
Thou art uncontaminated Lord! —40
Thou art all-pervasive Lord!
Thou art woeless Lord!
Thou art deedless Lord!
Thou art illusionless Lord! —41
Thou art unconquerable Lord!
Thou art fearless Lord!
Thou art motionless Lord!
Thou art unfathomable Lord! —42
Thou art immeasurable Lord!
Thou art the treasure Lord!
Thou art manifold Lord!
Thou art the only one Lord! —43

BHUJANG PRAYAAT STANZA

Salutation to Thee O universally honoured Lord!
Salutation to Thee O the treasure Lord!
Salutation to Thee O greatest Lord!
Salutation to Thee O garbless Lord! —44
Salutation to Thee O death-destroyer Lord!
Salutation to Thee O sustainer Lord!
Salutation to Thee O all-pervasive Lord!
Salutation to Thee O universal Lord! —45
Salutation to Thee O limitless Lord!
Salutation to Thee O masterless Lord!
Salutation to Thee O omnipotent Lord!
Salutation to Thee O the greatest sun Lord! —46
Salutation to Thee O moon-sovereign Lord!
Salutation to Thee O sun-sovereign Lord!
Salutation to Thee O supreme song Lord!
Salutation to Thee O supreme tune Lord! —47
Salutation to Thee O supreme dance Lord!
Salutation to Thee O supreme sound Lord!
Salutation to Thee O water-essence Lord!
Salutation to Thee O air-essence Lord! —48
Salutation to Thee O bodyless Lord!
Salutation to Thee O nameless Lord!
Salutation to Thee O all-form Lord!
Salutation to Thee O destroyer Lord!
Salutation to Thee O omnipotent Lord!
Salutation to Thee O greatest of all Lord! —49
Salutation to Thee O blotless Lord!
Salutation to Thee O pure form Lord!
Salutation to Thee O supreme sovereign Lord!
Salutation to Thee O most beautiful Lord! —50
Salutation to Thee O supreme yogi Lord!
Salutation to Thee O supreme adept Lord!
Salutation to Thee O supreme emperor Lord!
Salutation to Thee O supreme entity Lord! —51
Salutation to Thee O weapon-wielder Lord!
Salutation to Thee O weapon-user Lord!
Salutation to Thee O supreme knower Lord!
Salutation to Thee O universal mother Lord! —52
Salutation to Thee O garbless Lord!
Salutation to Thee O illusionless Lord!
Salutation to Thee O temptationless Lord!
Salutation to Thee O supreme yogi Lord!
Salutation to Thee O supremely disciplined Lord! —53
Salutation to Thee O benign protector Lord!
Salutation to Thee O heinous-actions-performer Lord!
Salutation to Thee O virtuous-sustainer Lord!
Salutation to Thee O evil-sustainer Lord! —54
Salutation to Thee O ailments-remover Lord!
Salutation to Thee O love-incarnate Lord!
Salutation to Thee O supreme emperor Lord!
Salutation to Thee O supreme sovereign Lord! —55
Salutation to Thee O greatest donor Lord!
Salutation to Thee O greatest-honours-recipient Lord!
Salutation to Thee O ailments-destroyer Lord!
Salutation to Thee O health-restorer Lord! —56
Salutation to Thee O supreme *mantra* Lord!
Salutation to Thee O supreme *yantra* Lord!
Salutation to Thee O supreme *tantra* Lord!
Salutation to Thee O highest-worship-entity Lord! —57

Thou art ever O Lord truth, consciousness and bliss,
Unique, formless, all-pervading and all-destroyer. —58
Thou art ever the giver of riches and wisdom and promoter,
Thou pervadest netherworld, heaven and space and destroyer of innumerable sins. —59
Thou art the supreme master and sustain all without being seen,

Thou art ever the donor of riches and merciful. —60

Thou art invincible, unbreakable, nameless and lustless,
Thou art victorious over all and art present every where. —61

ALL THY MIGHT   CHACHARI STANZA

Thou art in water,   Thou art on land,
Thou art fearless,   Thou art indiscriminate. —62

Thou art the master of all,   Thou art unborn,
Thou art countryless,   Thou art garbless. —63

BHUJANG PRAYAAT STANZA   BY THY GRACE

Salutation to Thee O impenetrable Lord!
Salutation to Thee O unbound Lord!
Salutation to Thee O all-bliss-entity Lord!
Salutation to Thee O universally-honoured Lord!
Salutation to Thee O all-treasure Lord! —64
Salutation to Thee O masterless Lord!
Salutation to Thee O destroyer Lord!
Salutation to Thee O unconquerable Lord!
Salutation to Thee O invincible Lord! —65
Salutation to Thee O deathless Lord!
Salutation to Thee O patronless Lord!
Salutation to Thee O all-pervasive Lord!
Salutation to Thee O all-garb Lord! —66
Salutation to Thee O supreme sovereign Lord!
Salutation to Thee O best musical equipment Lord!
Salutation to Thee O supreme emperor Lord!
Salutation to Thee O supreme moon Lord! —67
Salutation to Thee O supreme song Lord!
Salutation to Thee O supreme love Lord!
Salutation to Thee O supreme zeal Lord!
Salutation to Thee O brightest Lord! —68
Salutation to Thee O universal-ailment Lord!
Salutation to Thee O universal-enjoyer Lord!
Salutation to Thee O all-conquering Lord!
Salutation to Thee O universal fear Lord! —69
Salutation to Thee O omniscient Lord!
Salutation to Thee O omnipotent Lord!
Salutation to Thee O entire-*mantras*-knower Lord!
Salutation to Thee O entire-*yantra*-knower Lord! —70

Salutation to Thee O all-beholder Lord!
Salutation to Thee O universal attraction Lord!
Salutation to Thee O all-colour Lord!
Salutation to Thee O three-world destroyer Lord! —71
Salutation to Thee O universal-life Lord!
Salutation to Thee O primal-seed Lord!
Salutation to Thee O harmless Lord!
Salutation to Thee O non-appeaser Lord!
Salutation to Thee O universal boon-bestower Lord! —72
Salutation to Thee O generosity-embodiment Lord!
Salutation to Thee O sins-destroyer Lord!
Salutation to Thee O ever-universal riches denizen Lord!
Salutation to Thee O ever-universal powers denizen Lord! —73

CHARPAT STANZA   BY THY GRACE

Thy actions are permanent,   Thy laws are permanent,
Thou art united with all,   Thou art their permanent enjoyer. —74

Thy kingdom is permanent,   Thy adornment is permanent,
Thy laws are complete,   Thy works are beyond comprehension. —75

Thou art the universal donor,   Thou art omniscient,
Thou art the enlightener of all,   Thou art the enjoyers of all. —76

Thou art the life of all,   Thou art the strength of all,
Thou art the enjoyer of all,   Thou art united with all. —77

Thou art worshipped by all,   Thou art a mystery for all,
Thou art the destroyer of all,   Thou art the sustainer of all. —78

ROOAAL STANZA   BY THY GRACE

Thou art the supreme *Purusha,* an eternal entity in the beginning and free from birth,
Worshipped by all and venerated by three gods, Thou art without difference and art generous from the very beginning,
Thou art the sustainer, inspirer and destroyer of all,

Thou art present everywhere like an ascetic with a generous disposition. —79

Thou art nameless, placeless, casteless, formless, colourless and lineless,
Thou, the primal *Purusha*, art unborn, generous entity and perfect from the very beginning,
Thou art countryless, garbless, formless, lineless and non-attached,
Thou art present in all directions and corners and pervadest the universe as love. —80

Thou appearest without name and desire, thou hast no particular abode,
Thou, being worshipped by all, art the enjoyer of all,
To, the one entity, appearest as many creating innumerable forms,
After playing the world-drama, when Thou wilt stop the play, Thou wilt be the same once again. —81

The gods and the scriptures of Hindus and Muslims do not know Thy secret,
How to know Thee when Thou art formless, colourless, casteless and without lineage?
Thou art without father and mother and art casteless, Thou art without births and deaths,
Thou movest fast like the disc in all the four directions and art worshipped by the three worlds. —82

Thy name is recited in the fourteen divisions of the universe,
Thou, the primal God, art eternal entity and hast created the entire universe,
Thou, the holiest entity, art of supreme form, Thou art bondless, perfect *Purusha*.
Thou, the self-existent, creator and destroyer, hast created the whole, universe. —83

Thou art deathless, almighty, timeless *Purusha* and countryless,
Thou art the abode of righteousness; Thou art illusionless, garbless, incomprehensible and devoid of five elements,
Thou art without body, without attachment, without colour, caste, lineage and name,
Thou art the destroyer of ego, the vanquisher of tyrants and performer of works leading to salvation. —84

Thou art the deepest and indescribable entity, the one unique ascetic *Purusha*,
Thou, the unborn primal entity, art the destroyer of all egocentric people,
Thou, the boundless *Purusha*, art limbless, indestructible and without mind-self,
Thou art capable of doing everything; Thou destroyest all and sustainest all. —85

Thou knowest all, destroyest all and art beyond all the guises,
Thy form, colour and marks are not known to all the scriptures,
The Vedas and the Puranas always declare Thee the supreme and the greatest,
None can comprehend Thee completely through millions of Smritis, Puranas and Shastras. —86

MADHUBHAAR STANZA   BY THY GRACE

Thy virtues like generosity and Thy praises are unbounded,
Thy seat is eternal, Thy eminence is perfect. —87

Thou art self-luminous and remainest the same during day and night,
Thy arms stretch upto Thy knees and Thou art king of kings. —88

Thou art King of kings, Sun of suns, God of gods and of greatest eminence. —89

Thou art Indra of Indras, smallest of the small, poorest of the poor and the death of deaths. —90

Thy limbs are not of five elements, Thy glow is eternal,
Thou art immesurable and Thy virtues like generosity are countless. —91

Thou art fearless and desireless and all the sages bow before Thee,
Thou, of the brightest effulgence, art perfect in Thy doings. —92

Thy works are spontaneous and Thy laws are ideal,
Thou Thyself art wholly ornamented and none can chastise Thee. —93

CHACHARI STANZA   BY THY GRACE

O the preserver Lord!   O salvation giver Lord!
O most generous Lord!   O boundless Lord! —94

O the destroyer Lord! O the creator Lord!
O the nameless Lord! O the desireless Lord!
—95

BHUJANG PRAYAAT STANZA

O the creator Lord of all the four directions,
O the destroyer Lord of all the four directions,
O the donor Lord of all the four directions,
O the known Lord of all the four directions.
—96

O the pervading Lord of all the four directions,
O the permeator Lord of all the four directions,
O the sustainer Lord of all the four directions,
O the destroyer Lord of all the four directions.
—97

O the Lord present in all the four directions,
O the dweller Lord in all the four directions,
O the Lord worshipped in all the four directions,
O the donor Lord of all the four directions.
—98

CHACHARI STANZA

Thou art the foeless Lord,
Thou art the friendless Lord,
Thou art the illusionsless Lord,
Thou art the fearless Lord. —99

Thou art the actionless Lord,
Thou art the bodyless Lord,
Thou art the birthless Lord,
Thou art the abodeless Lord. —100

Thou art the portraitless Lord,
Thou art the friendless Lord,
Thou art the attachment-free Lord,
Thou art the most pure Lord. —101

Thou art the worldmaster Lord,
Thou art the primal Lord,
Thou art the invisible Lord,
Thou art the almighty Lord. —102

BHAGVATI STANZA   UTTERED WITH THY GRACE

That Thy abode is unconquerable,
That Thy garb is unimpaired,
That Thou art beyond impact of *karmas,*
That Thou art free from doubts. —103

That Thy abode is unimpaired,
That Thou canst dry up the sun,
That Thy demeanour is saintly,
That Thou art the source of wealth. —104

That Thou art the glory of kingdom,
That Thou art the ensign of righteousness,
That Thou hast no worries,
That Thou art the ornamentation of all. —105

That Thou art the creator of the universe,
That Thou art the bravest of the brave,
That Thou art all-pervading entity,
That Thou art the source of divine knowledge.
—106

That Thou art the primal entity without a master,
That Thou art self-illumined,
That Thou art without any portrait,
That Thou art master of Thyself. —107

That Thou art the sustainer and generous,
That Thou art the redeemer and pure,
That Thou art flawless,
That Thou art most mysterious. —108

That Thou forgivest sins,
That Thou art the emperor of emperors,
That Thou art the doer of everything,
That Thou art the giver of the means of sustenance.
—109

That Thou art the generous sustainer,
That Thou art the most compassionate,
That Thou art omnipotent,
That Thou art the destroyer of all. —110

That Thou art worshipped by all,
That Thou art the donor of all,
That Thou goest everywhere,
That Thou residest everywhere. —111

That Thou art in every country,
That Thou art in every garb,
That Thou art the king of all,
That Thou art the creator of all. —112

That Thou belongest to all religions,
That Thou art within every one,
That Thou livest everywhere,
That Thou art the glory of all. —113

That Thou art in all the countries,
That Thou art in all the garbs,
That Thou art the destroyer of all,
That Thou art the sustainer of all. —114

That Thou destroyest all,
That Thou goest to all the places,
That Thou wearest all the garbs,
That Thou seest all. —115

That Thou art the cause of all,
That Thou art the glory of all,
That Thou driest up all,
That Thou fillest up all. —116
That Thou art the strength of all,
That Thou art the life of all,
That Thou art in all countries,
That Thou art in all garbs. —117
That Thou art worshipped everywhere,
That Thou art the supreme controller of all,
That Thou art remembered everywhere,
That Thou art established everywhere. —118
That Thou illuminest everything,
That Thou art honoured by all,
That Thou art Indra (king) of all,
That Thou art the moon (light) of all. —119
That Thou art master of all powers,
That Thou art most intelligent,
That Thou art most wise and learned,
That Thou art the master of languages. —120
That Thou art the embodiment of beauty,
That all look towards Thee,
That Thou abidest forever,
That Thou hast perpetual offspring. —121
That Thou art the conqueror of mighty enemies,
That Thou art the protector of the lowly,
That Thy abode is the highest,
That Thou pervadest on Earth and in Heavens. —122
That Thou discriminatest all,
That Thou art most considerate,
That Thou art the greatest friend,
That Thou art certainly the giver of food. —123
That Thou, as ocean, hast innumerable waves,
That Thou art immortal and none can know Thy secrets,
That Thou protectest the devotees,
That Thou punishest the evil-doers. —124
That Thy entity is inexpressible,
That Thy glory is beyond the three modes,
That Thine is the most powerful glow,
That Thou art ever united with all. —125
That Thou art eternal entity,
That Thou art undivided and unparalleled,
That Thou art the creator of all,
That Thou art ever the ornamentation of all. —126

That Thou art saluted by all,
That Thou art ever the desireless Lord,
That Thou art invincible,
That Thou art impenetrable and unparalleled entity. —127
That Thou art *Om*, the primal entity,
That Thou art also without beginning,
That Thou art bodyless and nameless,
That Thou art the destroyer and restorer of three modes. —128
That Thou art the destroyer of three gods and modes,
That Thou art immortal and impenetrable,
That Thy writ of destiny is for all,
That Thou lovest all. —129
That Thou art the enjoyer entity of three world,
That Thou art unbreakable and untouched,
That Thou art the destroyer of hell,
That Thou pervadest the Earth. —130
That Thy glory is inexpressible,
That Thou art eternal,
That Thou abidest in innumerable diverse guises,
That Thou art wonderfully united with all. —131
That Thou art ever inexpressible,
That Thy glory appears in diverse guises,
That Thou form is indescribable,
That Thou art wonderfully united with all. —132

CHACHARI STANZA

Thou art indestructible, Thou art limbless,
Thou art dressless, Thou art indescribable. —133

Thou art illusionless, Thou art actionless,
Thou art beginningless, Thou art from the beginning of the ages. —134

Thou art unconquerable, Thou art indestructible,
Thou art elementless, Thou art fearless. —135

Thou art eternal, Thou art non-attached,
Thou art non-involved, Thou art unbound. —136

Thou art indivisible, Thou art non-attached,
Thou art eternal, Thou art supreme light. —137

Thou art carefree, Thou canst restrain the senses,

Thou canst control the mind,
Thou art accountless,
Thou art coastless,
Thou art invisible. —138
Thou art garbless,
Thou art bottomless. —139

Thou art unborn,
Thou art countless,
Thou art bottomless,
Thou art beginningless. —140

Thou art causeless,
Thou art unborn,
Thou art the listener,
Thou art free. —141

CHARPAT STANZA   BY THY GRACE

Thou art the destroyer of all,
Thou art the goer to all,
Thou art well-known to all,
Thou art the knower of all. —142

Thou killest all,
Thou createst all,
Thou art the life of all,
Thou art the strength of all. —143

Thou art in all works,
Thou art in all religions,
Thou art united with all,
Thou art free from all. —144

RASAAVAL STANZA   BY THY GRACE

Salutation to Thee O destroyer of hell Lord!
Salutation to Thee O ever-illumined Lord!
Salutation to Thee O bodyless entity Lord!
Salutation to Thee O eternal and effulgent Lord! —145

Salutation to Thee O destroyer of tyrants Lord!
Salutation to Thee O companion of all Lord!
Salutation to Thee O impenetrable entity Lord!
Salutation to Thee O non-annoying glorious Lord! —146

Salutation to Thee O limbless and nameless Lord!
Salutation to Thee O destroyer and restorer of three modes Lord!
Salutation to Thee O eternal entity Lord!
Salutation to Thee O unique in all respects Lord! —147

O Lord! Thou art sonless and grandsonless,
O Lord! Thou art enemyless and friendless,
O Lord! Thou art fatherless and motherless,
O Lord! Thou art casteless and lineageless. —148

O Lord! Thou art relativeless,
O Lord! Thou art limitless and profound,
O Lord! Thou art ever glorious,
O Lord! Thou art unconquerable and unborn. —149

BHAGVATI STANZA   BY THY GRACE

That Thou art visible illumination,
That Thou art all-pervading,
That Thou art receiver of eternal compliments,
That Thou art venerated by all. —150

That Thou art most intelligent,
That Thou art the lamp of beauty,
That Thou art completely generous,
That Thou art sustainer and merciful. —151

That Thou art giver of sustenance,
That Thou art ever the sustainer,
That Thou art the perfection of generosity,
That Thou art most beautiful. —152

That Thou art the panaliser of enemies,
That Thou art the supporter of the poor,
That Thou art destroyer of enemies,
That Thou art remover of fear. —153

That Thou art destroyer of blemishes,
That Thou art the dweller in all,
That Thou art invincible by enemies,
That Thou art the sustainer and gracious. —154

That Thou art the master of all languages,
That Thou art most glorious,
That Thou art destroyer of hell,
That Thou art the dweller in heaven. —155

That Thou art the goer to all,
That Thou art ever blissful,
That Thou art the knower of all,
That Thou art dearest to all. —156

That Thou art the Lord of lords,
That Thou art hidden from all,
That Thou art countryless and accountless,
That Thou art ever garbless. —157

That Thou art in Earth and Heaven,
That Thou art most profound in signs,
That Thou art most generous,
That Thou art embodiment of courage and beauty. —158

That Thou art perpetual illimitation,
That Thou art limitless fragrance,
That Thou art wonderful entity,

That Thou art limitless grandeur. —159
That Thou art limitless expanse,
That Thou art self-luminous,
That Thou art steady and limbless,
That Thou art infinite and indestructible. —160

MADHUBHAAR STANZA   BY THY GRACE

O Lord! the sages bow before Thee in their mind,
O Lord! Thou art ever the treasure of virtues,
O Lord! Thou canst not be destroyed by great enemies,
O Lord! Thou art the destroyer of all. —161
O Lord! innumerable beings bow before Thee,
O Lord! the sages salute Thee in their mind,
O Lord! Thou art complete controller of men,
O Lord! Thou canst not be installed by the chiefs. —162
O Lord! Thou art eternal knowledge,
O Lord! Thou art illumined in the hearts of the sages,
O Lord! The art assemblies of virtuous bow before Thee,
O Lord! Thou pervadest in water and on land. —163
O Lord! Thy body is unbreakable,
O Lord! Thy seat is perpetual,
O Lord! Thy praises are boundless,
O Lord! Thy nature is most generous. —164
O Lord! Thou art most glorious in water and on land,
O Lord! Thou art free from slander at all places,
O Lord! Thou art supreme in water and on land,
O Lord! Thou art endless in all directions. —165
O Lord! Thou art eternal knowledge,
O Lord! Thou art supreme among the contented ones,
O Lord! Thou art the arm of gods,
O Lord! Thou art ever the only one. —166
O Lord! Thou art *Om*, the origin of creation,
O Lord! Thou art stated to be without beginning,
O Lord! Thou destroyest the tyrants instantly,
O Lord! Thou art supreme and immortal. —167
O Lord! Thou art honoured in every house,
O Lord! Thy feet and Thy name are meditated in every heart,
O Lord! Thy body never becomes old,
O Lord! Thou art never subservient to anybody. —168

O Lord! Thy body is ever steady,
O Lord! Thou art free from rage,
O Lord! Thy store is inexhaustible,
O Lord! Thou art uninstalled and boundless. —169
O Lord! Thy law is imperceptible,
O Lord! Thy actions are most fearless,
O Lord! Thou art invincible and infinite,
O Lord! Thou art the supreme donor. —170

HARBOLMANA STANZA   BY THY GRACE

O Lord! Thou art the house of mercy,
O Lord! Thou art the destroyer of enemies,
O Lord! Thou art the killer of evil persons,
O Lord! Thou art the ornamentation of Earth. —171
O Lord! Thou art the master of the universe,
O Lord! Thou art the supreme *Ishvara*,
O Lord! Thou art the cause of strife,
O Lord! Thou art the saviour of all. —172
O Lord! Thou art the support of the Earth,
O Lord! Thou art the creator of the universe,
O Lord! Thou art worshipped in the heart,
O Lord! Thou art known throughout the world. —173
O Lord! Thou art the sustainer of all,
O Lord! Thou art the creator of all,
O Lord! Thou pervadest all,
O Lord! Thou destroyest all. —174
O Lord! Thou art the fountain of mercy,
O Lord! Thou art the nourisher of the universe,
O Lord! Thou art the master of all,
O Lord! Thou art the master of the universe. —175
O Lord! Thou art the life of the universe,
O Lord! Thou art the destroyer of evil-doers,
O Lord! Thou art beyond everything,
O Lord! Thou art the fountain of mercy. —176
O Lord! Thou art the unmuttered *mantra*,
O Lord! Thou canst be installed by none,
O Lord! Thy image canst not be fashioned,
O Lord! Thou art immortal. —177
O Lord! Thou art immortal,
O Lord! Thou art the merciful entity,
O Lord! Thy image canst not be fashioned,
O Lord! Thou art the support of the Earth. —178
O Lord! Thou art the master of nectar,
O Lord! Thou art supreme *Ishvara*,

O Lord! Thy image canst not be fashioned,
O Lord! Thou art immortal. —179

O Lord! Thou art of wonderful form,
O Lord! Thou art immortal,
O Lord! Thou art the master of men,
O Lord! Thou art the destroyer of evil persons. —180

O Lord! Thou art the nourisher of the world,
O Lord! Thou art the house of mercy,
O Lord! Thou art the Lord of the kings,
O Lord! Thou art the protector of all. —181

O Lord! Thou art the destroyer of the cycle of transmigration,
O Lord! Thou art the conqueror of enemies,
O Lord! Thou causest suffering to the enemies,
O Lord! Thou makest others to repeat Thy name. —182

O Lord! Thou art free from blemishes,
O Lord! all are Thy forms,
O Lord! Thou art the creator of the creators,
O Lord! Thou art the destroyer of the destroyers. —183

O Lord! Thou art the supreme soul,
O Lord! Thou art the origin of all the souls,
O Lord! Thou art controlled by Thyself,
O Lord! Thou art not subject to change. —184

BHUJANG PRAYAAT STANZA

Salutation to Thee O Sun of suns,
Salutation to Thee O Moon of moons,
Salutation to Thee O King of kings,
Salutation to Thee O Indra of Indras,
Salutation to Thee O creator of pitch darkness,
Salutation to Thee O Light of lights,
Salutation to Thee O greatest of the great (multitudes),
Salutation to Thee O subtlest of the subtle. —185

Salutation to Thee O entity bearing three modes,
Salutation to Thee O supreme essence and elementless entity,
Salutation to Thee O fountain of all yogas,
Salutation to Thee O fountain of all knowledge,
Salutation to Thee O supreme *Mantra,*
Salutation to Thee O highest meditation. —186

Salutation to Thee O conqueror of wars,
Salutation to Thee O fountain of all knowledge,
Salutation to Thee O essence of food,

Salutation to Thee O essence of water,
Salutation to Thee O originator of strife,
Salutation to Thee O embodiment of peace,
Salutation to Thee O Indra of Indras,
Salutation to Thee O beginningless effulgence. —187

Salutation to Thee O entity inimical to blemishes,
Salutation to Thee O ornamentation of the ornaments,
Salutation to Thee O fulfiller of hopes,
Salutation to Thee O most beautiful,
Salutation to Thee O eternal entity, limbless and nameless,
Salutation to Thee O destroyer of three worlds in three tenses,
Salutation to Thee O limbless and desireless Lord! —188

EK ACHHARI STANZA

O unconquerable Lord!   O indestructible Lord!
O fearless Lord!   O ageless Lord! —189
O unborn Lord!   O perpetual Lord!
O indestructible Lord!   O all-pervasive Lord! —190

O eternal Lord!   O indivisible Lord!
O unknowable Lord!   O uninflammable Lord! —191

O non-temporal Lord!   O merciful Lord!
O accountless Lord!   O guiseless Lord! —192

O nameless Lord!   O desireless Lord!
O unfathomable Lord!   O unfaltering Lord! —193

O masterless Lord!   O greatest-glorious Lord!
O birthless Lord!   O silenceless Lord! —194

O unattached Lord!   O colourless Lord!
O formless Lord!   O lineless Lord! —195
O actionless Lord!   O illusionless Lord!
O indestructible Lord!   O accountless Lord! —196

BHUJANG PRAYAAT STANZA

O most venerated and destroyer of all Lord! Salutation to Thee,
O indestructible, nameless and all-pervading Lord! Salutation to Thee,

O desireless, glorious and all-pervading Lord! Salutation to Thee,
O destroyer of evil and illuminator of supreme piety Lord! Salutation to Thee! —197
O perpetual embodiment of truth, consciousness and bliss and destroyer of enemies Lord! Salutation to Thee,
O gracious creator and all-pervading Lord! Salutation to Thee,
O wonderful, glorious and calamity for enemies Lord! Salutation to Thee,
O destroyer, creator, gracious and merciful Lord! Salutation to Thee. —198
O pervader and enjoyer in all the four directions Lord! Salutation to Thee,
O self-existent, most beautiful and united with all Lord! Salutation to Thee,
O destroyer of hard times and embodiment of mercy Lord! Salutation to Thee,
O ever present with all, indestructible and glorious Lord! Salutation to Thee. —199

THE LORD IS ONE. HE CAN BE REALISED BY THE GRACE OF THE TRUE GURU
LET THE LORD (THE PRIMAL LORD, ALSO KNOWN AS SRI BHAGAUTI JI—THE PRIMAL MOTHER)
BE HELPFUL
THUS THE BOOK NAMED *GYAN PRABODH* (UNFOLDMENT OF KNOWLEDGE) IS BEING WRITTEN

GYAN PRABODH
The Unfoldment of Knowledge by the Tenth Sovereign (Guru)

BHUJANG PRAYAAT STANZA   BY THY GRACE

Salutation to Thee, O perfect Lord! Thou art the doer of perfect *karmas* (actions),
Thou art unassailable, indiscriminate and ever of one discipline,
Thou art without blemishes, O unblemished entity!
Invincible, unmysterious, unharmed and unequalled Lord. —1

Salutation to Thee, O the Lord of people and master of all,
Thou art ever the comrade and Lord of the patronless,
Salutation to Thee, O one Lord pervading in many forms,
Always the king of all and always the monarch of all. —2

Thou art unassailable, indiscriminate, without name and place,
Thou art the master of all powers and the home of intellect,
Thou art neither in *yantras*, nor in *mantras*, nor in other activities nor in any religious discipline,
Thou art without suffering, without mystery, without destruction and without action. —3

Thou art unfathomable, unattached, inaccessible and endless,
Thou art accountless, guiseless, elementless and innumerable,
Thou art without colour, form, caste and lineage,
Thou art without enemy, friend, son and mother. —4

Thou art elementless, indivisible, wantless and only Thyself,
Thou art beyond everything, Thou art holy, immaculate and supreme,
Thou art invincible, indivisible, without desires and actions,
Thou art endless, boundless, all-pervasive and illusionless. —5

His form and mark cannot be comprehended at all,
Where doth He live? and in what guise He moves?
What is His name? and how is He called?
What should I say? I lack expression. —6

He is unborn, unconquerable, most beautiful and supreme,
He is unassailable, indiscriminate, formless and unmatchable,
He is incorrigible, unfathomable, and indestructible by enemies,
He, who rememberest Thee, Thou makest him griefless, He is the deliverer and merciful Lord. —7

He is ever the giver of power and intellect to all,
Salutations to Him, the knower of the secrets of the people and their Lord,
He is unassailable, fearless, the Primal entity and boundless,
He is unassailable, invincible, Primal, non-dual and very difficult to realise. —8

NARAAJ STANZA

He is boundless and Primal Lord; He is endless and indiscriminate from illusion,
He is unfathomable and destroyer of ailments; He is always with every one. —1-9

His painting is marvellous; He is indivisible and destroyer of tyrants,
He is indiscriminate from the very beginning and always sustains all. —2-10

He is indivisible and hast terrible form; His powerful entity manifests all,
He is the death of death and is also always the protector. —3-11

He is the kind and merciful entity and is ever the sovereign of all,
He is boundless and fulfiller of the hopes of all; He is very far away and also very near. —4-12

He is invisible but abides in inner meditation; He is always honoured by all,
He is merciful and eternal and is always honoured by all. —5-13

Therefore I meditate on Thee, I meditate on Thee ...

He is unfathomable and destroyer of ailment; He is far beyond and supremely adorable,
He is worshipped by all in the past, present and future; He is always the supreme *Purusha*. —6-14

Thou art of such attributes; Thou art of such attributes ...

He, the merciful Lord performs actions of kindness, He is invincible and destroys illusions,
He is the sustainer of people in past, present and future and is always compassionate towards all. —7-15

Therefore I repeat Thy name, I repeat Thy name ...

He is supreme in remaining peaceful; He is far beyond, superb and supreme,
He is the destroyer of ghosts since ancient times and always abides with all. —8-16

Thy assembly is mighty and indivisible, Thy rule is fearless, Thy flame of Thy fire is illumined like the row of lamps. —9-17

The eyes of the merciful and kind Lord humiliate the arrows of Cupid,
Thou art wearing such crown on Thy head that debases the pride of the sun. —10-18

Thy wide and red eyes destroy the pride of Cupid,
The brilliance of Thy head gear astounds even the elegant moonlight. —11-19

The illumination of the flame of Thy fire puzzles brightness of Thy kingdom,
Even Durga praises the brilliance of that conquering light. —12-20

TRIBHANGI STANZA   BY THY GRACE

He is without distress from the very beginning, master of unlimited wealth, an immovable entity and creator of the universe,
There is illumination of His light in the world, He is indestructible from the very beginning, He, of boundless heaven, is the sustainer of all,
He is invincible, deathless, sustainer of the universe, merciful Lord of the lowly and performer of good actions,
He is blissful entity, an unlimited entity of boundless wealth, I am in Thy refuge. —1-21

Thou art the sustainer of the universe, the creator of the world, the support of the helpless and the author of macrocosm,
Thou art blissful and unlimited entity, of unlimited wealth and of supreme magnificence,
Thy glory is indivisible, Thou art the establisher of the whole world, incomprehensible, without suffering and creator of the world,
Thou art non-dual, indestructible, illuminator of Thy light, detached from all and the only Lord. —2-22

Thou art indivisible, unestablished, of supreme splendour and light, and of boundless intellect,
Thou art fearless, unfathomable, incomprehensible, unattached, keeper of the universe under discipline and of infinite movement,
Thou art blissful and unlimited entity, of stable wealth and the causer of swimming across the dreadful world-ocean,
Thou art the unfathomable, unattached, keeper of the world under discipline and meditated upon by all; I am in Thy refuge. —3-23

Thou art unblemished, unattached, keeper of the universe under discipline, remembered by the world and destroyer of fear,
Thou art the sustainer of the universe, destroyer of sins, redeemer of the sinners and the comrade of all,
Thou art the master of the masterless, uncreated, undescribed, unlimited, patronless and remover of sufferings,

Thou art invincible, indestructible, illuminator of light, the destroyer of the world, I am in Thy refuge. —4-24

KALAS STANZA

Thou art of unlimited brilliance and Thy light hath illumined the world,
Thou art primal, unassailable, fearless and indestructible,
Thou art the supreme essence and enlightener of the path of subtle truth,
Thou art primal entity, indivisible and unattached. —5-25

TRIBHANGI STANZA

Thou art indivisible, unattached, the supreme enlightener, primal, indestructible and creator of the universe,
Thou art the creator, destroyer and sustainer of the world and the treasure of powers,
Thou art unassailable, indestructible, illuminator of the light, and the outlay of beauty of all the earth,
Thou art blissful and unlimited entity, incomprehensible wealth and of unlimited movement. —6-26

KALAS STANZA

Thou art primal, fearless and unfathomable entity,
Thou art without affection, colour, mark and form,
Somewhere Thou art pauper, somewhere chieftain and somewhere king,
Somewhere Thou art ocean, somewhere stream and somewhere a well. —7-27

TRIBHANGI STANZA

Somewhere Thou art in the form of stream, somewhere well and somewhere ocean; Thou art of incomprehensible wealth and unlimited movement,
Thou art non-dual, indestructible, illuminator of Thy light, the outlay of splendour and creator of the uncreated,
Thou art without form and mark, Thou art incomprehensible, guiseless, unlimited, unblemished, manifesting all forms,
Thou art the remover of sins, the redeemer of sinners and is the only motivator of keeping the patronless under refuge. —8-28

KALAS STANZA

Thou hast long arms uptil Thy knees, Thou holdest the bow in Thy hand,
Thou hast unlimited light, Thou art the illuminator of light in the world,
Thou art the bearer of sword in Thy hand and remover of the strength of the forces of foolish tyrants,
Thou art the most powerful and sustainer of the universe. —9-29

TRIBHANGI STANZA

Thou art the remover of the strength of the forces of foolish tyrants and causest fear amongest them, Thou art the keeper of patronless under Thy refuge and hast unlimited movement,
Thy mercurial eyes even undo the movement of the fishes; Thou art the destroyer of sins and hast unlimited intellect,
Thou hast long arms upto the knees and art the king of kings, Thy praise pervades all likewise,
Thou abidest in waters, on lands and in forests, Thou art praised by forests and blades of grass; O supreme *Purusha*! Thou art the consumer of the forces of foolish tyrants. —10-30

KALAS STANZA

Thou art most powerful and destroyer of the forces of the tyrants,
Thy glory is unlimited and all the world bows before Thee,
The beautiful painting appears good-looking like the moon,
Thou art the destroyer of sins and punisher of the forces of the tyrants. —11-31

CHHAPPAI STANZA

The Vedas and even Brahma do not know the secret of Brahman,
Vyas, Parashar, Sukhdev, Sanak, etc., and Shiva do not know His limits,
Sanat Kumar, Sanak, etc., all of them do not comprehend the time,
Lakhs of Lakshmis and Vishnus and many Krishnas call Him *neti*,
He is an unborn entity, His glory is manifested through knowledge, He is most powerful and cause of the creation of water and land,
He is imperishable, boundless, non-dual, unlimited and the transcendent Lord, I am in Thy refuge. —1-32

He is imperishable, fearless, indiscriminate, unlimited, indivisible and hath unweighable strength,
He is eternal, infinite, beginningless, indivisible, and master of mighty forces,
He is limitless, boundless, unweighable, elementless, indiscriminate and invincible,
He is spiritual entity without vices, pleasing to gods, men and sages,
He is an entity without vices, always fearless, the assemblies of sages and men bow at His feet,
He pervades the world, removes the sufferings and blemishes,
Supremely glorious and effacer of illusions and fears. —2-33

CHHAPPAI STANZA   BY THY GRACE

On His facial sphere glistens the brilliant light of infinite movement,
Such is the setting and illumination of that light that lakhs and millions of moon feel shy before it,
He carries the four corners of the world on His hand and thus the universal monarchs are amazed,
The ever-new Lord of lotus with lotus-eyes, He is the Lord of men,
Remover of darkness and destroyer of sins, all the gods, men and sages bow at His feet,
He is breaker of the unbreakable, He is the establisher on the fearless position, salutation to Thee, O Lord, the remover of fear. —3-34

CHHAPPAI STANZA

Salutation to Him the merciful donor Lord! Salutation to Him the transcendent and modest Lord!
The destroyer of indestructible, invincible, indiscriminate and imperishable Lord,
Unassailable, incorruptible, devoid of vices, fearless, unattached and undistinguishable, Lord,
Affliction of the unafflicted, blissful without blemish and unassailable,
The Lord with long arms upto knees, wearer of the bow and the sword for vanquishing the enemies,
The sovereign of good people, hero and master of armies; salutation to Him who pervades waters and lands. —4-35

He is the merciful Lord of the lowly, destroyer of suffering, and vicious intellect and the refuter of suffering,
He is greatly peaceful, captivator of the heart, alluring like Cupid and creator of the world,
He is the Lord of limitless glory, without vices, indestructible, invincible having boundless power,
He is unbreakable, without fear and enmity, without malice and the monarch of waters and lands,
He is unassailable entity, untouchable, eternal, imperishable, unhidden and without deception,
He is non-dual-entity, unique, immortal and is deeply adored by gods, men and demons. —5-36

He is the ocean and source of mercy and remover of blemishes from all,
He is the cause of causes, powerful, merciful entity and prop of creation,
He is the destroyer of the actions of death and none knows His doing,
What doth he say and do? What facts doth reveal Him?
His eyes are like lotus, neck like conchshell, waist like lion and gait like elephant,
Legs like banana, swiftness like deer and fragrance like camphor, O non-temporal Lord! Who else can be without Thee with such attributes? —6-37

CHHAPPAI STANZA

He is an incomprehensible entity, accountless, valueless, elementless and unbreakable,
He is the Primal *Purusha*, without vices, unconquerable, unfathomable and invincible,
He is without vices, unmalicious entity, unblemished and transcendent,
He is the breaker of the unbreakable, indiscriminate, elementless and infrangible,
He is the king of kings, beautiful, of propitious intellect, of handsome countenance and most fortunate,
He is seated on His throne with the effulgence of millions of earthly suns. —7-38

CHHAPPAI STANZA   BY THY GRACE

Visualising the beauty of the universal monarch all the four directions seem stunned,

He hath the light of million suns, nay, even the light is two to four times,
A million moons are astonished to find their light dim as compared to His light,
Vyas, Parashar, Brahma, and Vedas can nay describe His mystery,
He is the king of kings, the Lord of wisdom, supremely glorious, beautiful and powerful,
He is the monarch of monarchs, the Lord of the mighty having unlimited splendour, unassailable and without deception. —8-39

KABIT   BY THY GRACE

He, who cannot be grasped, He is called inaccessible and He, who cannot be assailed is recognised as unassailable,
He, who cannot be destroyed is known as indestructible and He, who cannot be divided is considered as indivisible,
He, who cannot be desciplined, may be called incorrigible and He, who cannot be deceived is considered as undeceivable,
He, who is without the impact of *mantras* (incantations) may be considered as unspellable and He, who is without the impact of *yantras* (mystical diagrams) may be known as unmagical. —1-40

KABIT   BY THY GRACE

Consider Him as casteless in Thy mind, who is devoid of caste, call Him lineageless who is devoid of lineage,
He may be called as indiscriminate, who is devoid of discrimination, He, who cannot be assailed, may be spoken as unassailable,
He, who cannot be divided, may be considered as indivisible, He who cannot be grasped in thought, always makes us sorrowful,
He, who is without the impact of mystical diagrams, may be muttered as unmagical, He who doth not come in contemplation, may be contemplated upon and meditated. —2-41

KABIT   BY THY GRACE

He is sung as the canopied monarch, the Lord of canopies, a winsome entity, the master and creator of the earth and the superb support,
He is the Lord sustainer of the universe, master of Vedas and lofty *karmas* (actions), juggler, bearer of shafts and depicted as Lord having discipline,
The yogis performing Neoli *karma* (cleansing of intestines), those subsisting only on milk, learned and celebates all meditate upon Him, but without an iota of getting His comprehension,
He is the king of kings and emperor of emperors, who else should be meditated upon, forsaking such a supreme monarch? —3-42

KABIT   BY THY GRACE

His name is sung in all the three worlds, who is the conqueror of ways, the mover on the stage and the effacer of the burden of earth
He hath neither a son, nor mother nor brother, He is the support of the earth, forsaking such Lord whom shoud we love?
We should always meditate upon Him, who is instrumental in all accomplishments, establisher of the earth and support of these,
Whom should we meditate upon forsaking the Lord who prolongs the age of our life, who causes the name to be repeated and all other works to be done? —4-43

KABIT   BY THY GRACE

He is called the creator, who completes all the errands, who gives the comfort and honour and who is the destroyer of warriors stout like elephants,
He is the wielder of bow, the protector from all types of afflictions, deceiver of the universal monarchs and donor of everything without asking, He should be worshipped with diligence,
He is the giver of wealth, knower of life and honour and sorter of light and reputation. His praises should be sung.
He is the effacer of blemishes, the giver of religious discipline and wisdom and the destroyer of vicious people, whom else should we remember? —5-44

KABIT   BY THY GRACE

He endures everything peacefully, He is engrossed in attainment of perfection, and He is the only Lord who pervades in all limbs,
He is the remover of darkness, the masher of the

Pathans of Khorasan, perisher of the egoists and idlers, He is described as the destroyer of people full of vices,
Whom should we worship except the Lord who is the vanquisher of the conquerors, giver of the glory of conquest and who shoots the miraculous arrows from His bow,
Whom else should we adore except Him who is the giver of truth and driver of falsehood and performer of graceful acts? —6-45

KABIT   BY THY GRACE

He is the enlightener of the lights, giver of the victory in wars and is known as the destroyer of the murderer of friends,
He is the sustainer, giver of shelter, far-sighted and knower; He is considered as listener of entertaining modes of music and full of blissful splendour,
He is the cause of the repetition of His name and giver of peace and honour; He is the forgiver of the blemishes and is considered as unattached,
He is the prolonger of life, the promoter of the entertainments of music and the masher of tyrants and malevolent. Whom else should we then Adore? —7-46

KABIT   BY THY GRACE

His self is supreme, He is power-incarnate, His wealth is His intellect and His nature is that of a redeemer,
He is without affection, colour, form and mark, still He hath beautiful limbs and His nature is that of love,
His painting of the universe is wonderful and supremely spotless; He is friend of friends and supreme donor of wealth,
He is the god of gods and monarch of monarchs; He is the king of kings and chieftain of the chiefs. —8-47

TAVEEL STANZA PASCHAMI   BY THY GRACE

That Lord is indestructible,
That Lord is indivisible,
That Lord is formless,
That Lord is griefless. —1-48
That Lord is unassailable,
That Lord is indiscriminate,
That Lord is nameless,
That Lord is desireless. —2-49
That Lord is guiseless,
That Lord is accountless,
That Lord is beginningless,
That Lord is unfathomable. —3-50
That Lord is formless,
That Lord is elementless,
That Lord is stainless,
That Lord is affectionless. —4-51
That Lord is indiscriminate,
That Lord is unassailable,
That Lord is unveiled,
That Lord is unfathomable. —5-52
That Lord is indestructible,
That Lord is unbreakable,
That Lord is indiscriminate,
That Lord is unassailable. —6-53
That Lord is devoid of service,
That Lord is devoid of contemplation,
That Lord is indestructible,
That Lord is supreme essence. —7-54
That Lord is immanent,
That Lord is transcendent,
That Lord is unannoyable,
That Lord is unbreakable. —8-55
That Lord is without deception,
That Lord is the sustainer,
That Lord is motionless,
That Lord is fraudless. —9-56
That Lord is unborn,
That Lord is invisible,
That Lord is fraudless,
That Lord is eternal. —10-57

BEHR TAVEEL PASCHAMI   BY THY GRACE

That Lord is not crooked,
That Lord is not admonishable,
That Lord cannot be stung,
That Lord is limbless. —11-58
That Lord is not affected by might (or musical tunes),
That Lord is not affected by site,
That Lord is not affected by strife,
That Lord is not affected by senses. —12-59

That Lord is infinite,
That Lord is supreme,
That Lord cannot be chopped,
That Lord is fearless. —13-60

That Lord is without ego,
That Lord is without loss,
That Lord cannot be absorbed in senses,
That Lord is unaffected by the waves. —14-61

That Lord is peaceful,
That Lord is perfect in learning,
That Lord is not affected by the potent warriors,
That Lord is unconquerable. —15-62

PASCHAMI

That Lord is full of all above-mentioned attributes,
That Lord is fearless (or garbless),
That Lord is in male body,
That Lord is also in female body. —16-63

That Lord is *Omkar* (the one and only one),
That Lord is *Akar* i.e., pervasive in all forms,
That Lord is indivisible,
That Lord is beyond all devices. —17-64

That Lord is without suffering,
That Lord cannot be established,
That Lord is not affected by strife,
That Lord is formless. —18-65

That Lord is without ailments,
That Lord cannot be established,
That Lord cannot be enumerated,
That Lord reckons everything Himself. —19-66

ARDH NARAAJ STANZA   BY THY GRACE

O Lord! Thou art praiseworthy,
Thou art the banner of honour,
Thou art all-pervading,
Thou art the only one. —1-67

Thou art in water,
Thou art on land,
Thou art in the city,
Thou art in the forest. —2-68

Thou art the Guru,
Thou art in caves,
Thou art without sap,
Thou art indescribable. —3-69

Thou art the sun,
Thou art the moon,
Thou art activity,
Thou art morbidity. —4-70

Thou art the wealth,
Thou art the mind,
Thou art the tree,
Thou art the vegetation. —5-71

Thou art the intellect
Thou art salvation,
Thou art the fast,
Thou art the consciousness. —6-72

Thou art the father,
Thou art the son,
Thou art the mother,
Thou art the liberation. —7-73

Thou art the man,
Thou art woman,
Thou art the beloved,
Thou art the *dharma* (piety). —8-74

Thou art the destroyer,
Thou art the doer,
Thou art the deception,
Thou art the power. —9-75

Thou art the stars,
Thou art the sky,
Thou art the mountain,
Thou art the ocean. —10-76

Thou art the sun,
Thou art the sunshine,
Thou art the pride,
Thou art the wealth. —11-77

Thou art the conqueror,
Thou art the destroyer,
Thou art the semen,
Thou art the woman. —12-78

NARAAJ STANZA   BY THY GRACE

Thy winsome lustre astonishes the moonlight,
Thy royal glory looks splendid,
The clique of tyrants is suppressed,
Such is the glamour of Thy metropolis (world).
   —1-79

Moving like Chandika (Goddess) in the battle-field,
Thou destroyest in an instant seemingly imperishable warriors,
Thou movest like the fire of lightening,
O infinite Lord! Thy throne is visualised in all directions. —2-80

Thy pure emotions gleam,
And destroy the forces of suffering,
The row of Thy horses looks graceful,
Seeing which the horse of the ocean gets angry.
—3-81

Thou art radiant like the great ball of the Sun,
Beyond the tunes of worldly joys,
Thou art everlasting like the Banyan-seed,
And art blissful ever perfectly. —4-82

The treasure of Thy wealth is inexhaustible,
O immaculate Lord! Thou art not united with any one,
Thy seat is eternal,
Thou art accountless, guiseless and imperishable.
—5-83

The row of Thy teeth looks graceful,
Seeing which the dark clouds feel jealous,
The small bells look elegant in the string round Thy waist,
Seeing Thy effulgence the splendour of the sun feels jealous. —6-84

The crest on Thy head seems splendid
Like the shaft high up in the clouds,
The crown on Thy head looks elegant,
Seeing which the moon feels shy. —7-85

The rows of demons are moving,
And both the armies are running,
When Thou usest Thy arms and weapons,
And Thy disc moves in all the four directions.
—8-86

Thy inaccessible glory looks elegant,
Therefore the great sages and Shiva are covetous to have Thy sight,
They remember Thy Name many times,
Even then they have not been able to know Thy limits. —9-87

Many with faces upside down light the fire,
Many ascetics roam forsaking their sleep,
Many perform austerity of five fires,
Even they have not been able to know Thy limits.
—10-88

The performance of Neoli *karmas* (cleansing of intestines),
The innumerable religious acts of giving charities,
Abiding at pilgrim stations for numberless times,
All these acts do not equal the merit of the remembrance of the name of one Lord. —11-89

The performance of innumerable acts of sacrifices,
The performance of the religious act of giving elephant etc., in charity,
Wandering in many countries,
All these acts do not equal the merit of the remembrance of the name of one Lord. —12-90

Dwelling in solitary confinement,
Wandering in millions of forests,
Becoming unattached many recite *mantras*,
Many roam like hermits. —13-91

Many move in various guises adopt several postures,
Millions hold million types of fasts,
One may roam in many directions,
He may observe many types of guises. —14-92

One may perform millions of types of charities,
He may perform many types of sacrifices and actions,
One may adopt the religious garb of a mendicant,
He may perform many rituals of a hermit.
—15-93

One may read the religious texts continuously,
He may perform many ostentations,
None of them equals the name of one Lord,
They are all an illusion like the world. —16-94

One may perform the religious acts of the ancient ages,
He may perform the ascetic and monastic works,
He may perform the works of mercy etc., and magic,
They are all works of great restraint, prevalent from times immemorial. —17-95

One may wander in many countries,
He may adopt the discipline of giving millions of charities,
Many songs of knowledge are sung,
He may be proficient in innumerable types of knowledge and contemplation. —18-96

Those who are superb by achieving millions of types of knowledge,
They are also observing many good actions like Vyas, Narad, etc.,
They even have not been able to know the secret of Brahman. —19-97

Though millions of *yantras* and *mantras* may be practised,

Innumerable *tantras* may be made,
One may even sit on the seat of Vyas,
And forsake many types of food. —20-98

All the gods and demons remember Him,
All the Yakshas and Gandharvas worship Him,
The Vidyadhars sing His praises,
The remaining categories including Nagas remember His name. —21-99

He is remembered by all in this and the other worlds,
He hath put the seven oceans at their places,
He is known in all the four directions,
The wheel of His discipline keeps moving. —22-100

He is remembered by serpents and octopus,
The vegetation narrates His praises,
The beings of sky, earth and water remember Him,
The beings in water and on land repeat His name. —23-101

Millions of four-headed Brahmas
Recite the four Vedas,
Millions of Shivas worship that wonderful entity,
Millions of Vishnus adore Him. —24-102

Innumerable Saraswatis (goddess) and Satis (Parvati—goddess) and Lakshmis (goddess) sing His praises,
Innumerable Sheshanagas eulogize Him,
That Lord is comprehended as infinite ultimately. —25-103

BRIDH NARAAJ STANZA

He is beginningless, unfathomable and source of all beings; that beginningless Lord be worshipped,
He is indestructible, unbreakable, griefless and inexhaustible treasure, He should be meditated upon,
He is accountless, guiseless, without blemish, without mark and without a remainder, He should be recognised,
Even by mistake He should not be considered in *yantras*, *tantras*, *mantras*, illusions and guises. —1-104

The name of that Lord be uttered who is merciful, beloved, deathless, patronless and compassionate,
We should reflect upon Him in all works whether irreligious, religious or fallacious,
We should visualise Him in infinite charities, in contemplation, in knowledge and in those who contemplate,
Forsaking the irreligious *karmas*, we should comprehend the *karmas* that are religious and spiritual. —2-105

The *karmas* which come in the categories of fasts etc., charities, restraints etc., bathing at pilgrim stations and worship of gods,
Which are to be performed without illusion including the horse-sacrifice elephant-sacrifice and Rajsu sacrifice performed, by a universal monarch,
And the Neoli *karma* of yogis (cleansing of intestines) etc., may all be considered as *karmas* of various sects and guises,
In the absence of the pure *karmas* related to the invisible Lord, all the other *karmas* be considered as illusion and hypocrisy. —3-106

He is without caste and lineage, without mother and father; He is unborn and ever perfect,
He is without enemy and friend, without son and grandson and He is always everywhere,
He is supremely glorious and is called the crusher and breaker of the unbreakable,
He cannot be placed in the garb of form colour, mark and calculation. —4-107

Bathing at innumerable pilgrim stations etc., adopting various postures etc., following the discipline of worship according to *Narada Pancharatra*,
Adoption of *vairagya* (monasticism and asceticism) and *sannyas* (renunciation) and observing yogic discipline of olden times,
Visiting ancient pilgrim stations and observing restraints etc., fasts and other rules,
Without the beginningless and unfathomable Lord all the above *karmas* be considered as illusion. —5-108

RASAAVAL STANZA

The religious discipline like mercy etc.,
The *karmas* like *sannyas* (renunciation) etc.,
The charities of elephants etc.,
The places of sacrifice of horses etc. —1-109

The charities like gold etc.,
The baths in the sea etc.,
Wanderings in the universe etc.,

The works of austerities etc. —2-110
The *karmas* like Neoli (cleansing of intestines) etc.,
Wearing of blue clothes etc.,
Contemplation of colourless etc.,
The supreme essence is the remembrance of the Name. —3-111
O Lord! The types of Thy devotion are unlimited
Thy affection is unmanifested,
Thou becomest apparent to the seeker,
Thou art unestablished by devotions. —4-112
Thou art the doer of all the works of Thy devotees,
Thou art the destroyer of the sinners,
Thou art the illuminator of detachment,
Thou art the destroyer of tyranny. —5-113
Thou art the supreme authority over all,
Thou art the axle of the banner,
Thou art ever unassailable,
Thou art the only one formless Lord. —6-114
Thou Thyself manifestest Thy forms,
Thou art merciful to the deserving,
Thou pervadest the earth indivisibly,
Thou canst not be attached with anything. —7-115
Thou art the superb abode among abodes,
Thou art the householder among householders,
Thou art conscious entity devoid of ailments,
Thou art there on the earth but hidden. —8-116
Thou art conqueror and without affect of muttering,
Thou art fearless and invisible,
Thou art the only one amongst many,
Thou art ever indivisible. —9-117
Thou art beyond all ostentations,
Thou art far away from all pressures,
Thou canst not be vanquished by anyone,
Thy limits canst not be measured by anyone. —10-118
Thou art beyond all ailments and agonies,
Thou canst not be established,
Thou art the masher of all blemishes from the beginning,
There is none other so extraordinary as Thou. —11-119
Thou art most Holy,
Thou promotest the flourishing of the world,
Distinctively Thou art supporting,
O guiseless Lord! Thou art worshipped by all. —12-120
Thou art the sap in flowers and fruits,
Thou art the inspirer in the hearts,
Thou art the one to resist among the resistant,
Thou art the destroyer of the three worlds (or modes). —13-121
Thou art the colour as well as devoid of colour,
Thou art the beauty as well as the lover of beauty,
Thou art the only one and only one like Thyself,
Thou art the only one now and shall be the only one in future. —14-122
Thou art described as the donor of boons,
Thou art the only one, the only one,
Thou art affectionate and accountless,
Thou art depicted as markless. —15-123
Thou art in the three worlds and also the destroyer of three modes,
O Lord! Thou art in every colour,
Thou art the earth and also the Lord of the earth,
O guiseless Lord! all adore Thee. —16-124
Thou art the superb of the eminent ones,
Thou art the giver of reward in an instant,
Thou art the sovereign of men,
Thou art the destroyer of the masters of the armies. —17-125

PAADHARI STANZA   BY THY GRACE

On a day the curious soul (asked),
The infinite and desireless Lord, the intuitive entity
Of everlasting glory and long-armed,
The king of kings and emperor of emperors. —1-126
The soul said to the higher soul,
The germinating entity, unmanifested and invincible:
"What is this soul entity?
Which hath indelible glory and which is of queer substance." —2-127
The higher soul said, "This soul is itself Brahman,
Who is of everlasting glory and is unmanifested and desireless,
Who is indiscriminate, actionless and deathless,
Who hath no enemy and friend and is merciful towards all. —3-128
It is neither drowned nor soaked,
It can neither be chopped nor burnt,

It can not be assailed by the blow of weapon,
It hath neither an enemy nor a friend, neither caste nor lineage. —4-129
By the blows of thousands of enemies,
It is neither wasted away nor fragmented,
It is not burnt even in the fire,
It is neither drowned in the sea nor soaked by the air. —5-130
Then the soul questioned the Lord thus:
"O Lord! Thou art invincible, intuitive and indiscriminate entity,
This world mentions four categories of charities,
Which are these categories, tell me graciously." —6-131
One is political discipline, one is religious discipline,
One is householder's discipline, one is ascetic's discipline,
All the world knows this one of four categories,
That soul makes enquiries from the Lord. —7-132
One is political discipline one is religious discipline,
One is householder's discipline, one is ascetic's discipline,
Tell me graciously Thy thoughts about all the four,
And also tell me their originators in long ages in three epochs. —8-133
Describe to me the first discipline,
How this religious discipline was observed by the kings,
In Satyuga charities were given by performing virtuous actions,
Indescribable charities of lands etc., were given. —9-134
It is difficult to describe the kings of three ages,
Their story is endless and the praise indescribable,
By performing sacrifices, the religious discipline that was observed,
Cannot be narrated; they performed unlimited actions. —10-135
The kings that reigned before Kaliyuga,
In the Jambudvipa in the Bharatkhand,
I describe them with Thy strength and glory,
The king Yudhishtra was the unblemished sustainer of the earth. —11-136
He (Yudhishtra) broke the unbreakable ones in the four *khands* (regions),
He destroyed the Kauravas with great might in the war of Kurukshetra,
He conquered twice all the four directions,
The mighty warriors like Arjuna and Bhim were his brothers. —12-137
He sent Arjuna towards the North for conquest,
Bhim went for conquest to the East,
Sahdev was sent to the country in the South,
Nakul was sent to the West. —13-138
The Kshatriya kings were mashed and destroyed,
In the great war the unconquerable were conquered,
The Khorasan country in the North was destroyed,
The kings of the South and East were conquered. —14-139
The kings of all the regions were defeated with might of sword,
In this Jambudvipa the trumpet (of Yudhishtra) sounded,
He gathered together the kings of various countries at one place,
He expressed his wish for the performance of Rajsu sacrifice. —15-140
He sent letters to all countries,
All the qualified Brahmins were gathered together,
The performance of Rajsu sacrifice was started,
Many of the conquered kings was called. —16-141

ROOAAL STANZA

Millions of ritual-conscious Brahmins were called,
Millions of different foods were prepared which were enjoyed with relish,
Many chief sovereigns were busy in collecting required materials,
Thus, the Rajsu sacrifice began to be performed with religious zeal. —1-142
The orders were given for giving one load of gold to each Brahmin,
One hundred elephants, one hundred chariots and two thousand horses,
And also four thousand cows with gilded horns and innumerable buffaloes in charity,
Listen O chief of the kings, give these gifts to each Brahmin. —2-143
Innumerable articles like gold, silver and copper were given in charity,

Innumerable alms of grain were given to many gathered poor people,
Other items given in charity were the common clothes, silken cloth and weapons,
The beggars from many countries became well-off. —3-144
The fire-altar extended upto four *kos* and had one thousand drains,
One thousand Brahmins, considered incarnations of Vedavyas, began the performance of sacrifice,
The continuous current of clarified butter of the size of elephant's trunk fell in the pit,
Many materials were reduced to ashes by the dreadful flame. —4-145
The earth and water of all the pilgrim stations was brought,
Also the fuel-wood and food-materials from all countries,
Various kinds of tasteful foods were burnt in the altar,
Seeing which the superb Brahmins were astonished and the kings were pleased. —5-146
Many and various types of foods were burnt in the altar,
On all the four sides the learned Brahmins were reciting the four Vedas, like Vyas,
Many kings were giving innumerable types of gifts in charity,
Here, there and everywhere on the earth infinite strain of victory was sounded. —6-147
Conquering the rebel kings and seizing the unaccountable wealth and precious things,
(Yudhishtra) the king of Kuru country brought that wealth and distributed among the Brahmins,
Many types of fragrant materials were ignited there,
Here, there and everywhere in all directions many types of the strains of victory were sounded. —7-148
After slaying Jarasandh and then conquering the Kauravas,
Yudhishtra performed the great Rajsu sacrifice in consultation with Krishna,
Conquering innumerable enemies, for many days, he performed the Rajsu sacrifice,
Then, with the advice of Vedavyas, he began the performance of horse-sacrifice. —8-149

Here ends the First Sacrifice.

The Slaying of Sri Baran

(The sacrificial horse) is of white colour, black ears having golden tail,
With eyes high and wide and lofty neck like Uchchishravas,
He walks on the earth with dancing pose, glorious in beauty like Cupid,
On seeing him all the kings are pleased and also (Yudhishtra) the king of kings. —9-150
Vina, ven, mridang, bansuri, and *bheri* are being played,
Innumerable *muj, toor, murchang, mandal, changbeg,* and *sarnaaee,*
Dhol, dholak, khanjari, daph, and *jhaanjh* are also being played,
Big bell and small bells resound and innumerable modes of music are created. —10-151
Kettledrums when played produce unlimited sound and innumerable horses neigh,
Wherever the horse named Sri Baran goes, the army chiefs follow him,
Whosoever chains the horse, they fight with him and conquer him,
He who receives them, he is saved, otherwise one who confronts, is violently killed. —11-152
All the kings were conquered by sending the horse in all the four directions,
The horse-sacrifice was thus completed; it is very great and marvellous in the world,
Various types of materials were given to the Brahmins in charity,
Also many types of silken clothes, horses and great elephants. —12-153
Many gifts and unaccountable wealth was given in charity to innumerable Brahmins,
Including diamonds, common clothes, silken clothes and many loads of gold,
All the great enemies were horrified and even Sumeru, the king of mountains trembled on listening to the details of charity,
Fearing that the chief sovereign may not cut him into bits and then distribute the bits. —13-154
Moving it throughout the country, the horse was ultimately killed in the sacrificial place,
Then it was cut into four pieces (parts),
One part was given to the Brahmins, one to Kshatriyas and one to women.

The remaining fourth part was burnt in the fire-altar. —14-155

After ruling this Dvipa for five hundred years,

These sons of king Pandu ultimately fell in the Himalayas (nether-world),

After them Parikshat, who was most beautiful and mighty, (their grandson, the son of Abhimanyu) became the king of Bharat,

He was man of boundless charm, a generous donor and a treasure of invincible glory. —15-156

This is the end of the Second Sacrifice in the book entitled Sri Gyan Prabodh.

Description of the Rule of King Parikshat

ROOAAL STANZA

One day the king Parikshat consulted his ministers,

As to how the elephant sacrifice be performed methodically?

The friends and the ministers who spoke gave the idea,

That abandoning all other thoughts, the elephant of white teeth be sent for. —1-157

The sacrificial altar was constructed within eight *kos*,

Eight thousand ritual-performing and eight lakh other Brahmins,

Eight thousand drains of various types were, prepared,

Through which the continuous current of the clarified butter of the size of the elephant-trunk flowed. —2-158

Various types of kings from various countries were called,

They were given many gifts of various types with honour,

Including diamonds, silken clothes etc., horses and big elephants,

The great sovereign gave all the things highly decorated to the kings. —3-159

In this way he ruled there for many years,

Many eminent enemies like the king Karan were conquered alongwith many of their precious belongings,

On one day the king went on a merry-making trip and hunting,

He saw and pursued a deer and met a great sage. —4-160

(He said to the sage) O great sage! Please speak, did the deer go this way?

The sage did not open his eye nor gave any answer to the king,

Seeing a dead snake, (the king) raised it with the tip of his bow,

Put it around the neck of the sage; then the great sovereign went away. —5-161

What did the sage see on opening his eyes? He was frightened to see the snake (around his neck),

There he became very angry and the blood oozed out from the eyes of the Brahmin,

(He said) "He, who hath put this snake around my neck, he will be bitten by the king of snakes,

He will die within seven days. This curse of mine will ever be true." —6-162

Coming to know about the curse, the king was frightened. He got an abode constructed,

That palace was constructed within the Ganges, which could not even be touched by air,

How could the snake reach there and bite the king?

But within the due time, the king of snakes came there and bit (the king). —7-163

(The king Parikshat) ruled for sixty years two months and four days,

Then the light of the soul of the king Parikshat merged in the light of the creator,

Then the great king Janmeja became the sustainer of the earth,

He was a great hero, headstrong, ascetic and adept in eighteen learnings. —8-164

The end of the episode of king Parikshat.

The Rule of King Janmeja begins

ROOAAL STANZA

Born in the house of a king, the great king Janmeja,

Was a great hero, headstrong, ascetic and adept in eighteen learnings,

Being enraged at the death of his father, he called all the Brahmins,

And engaged himself in the performance of the snake-sacrifice in the zest of his mind for *dharma*. —1-165

GYAN PRABODH

The sacrificial pit was constructed within one *kos*,
After preparing the fire-altar, the Brahmins began to recite *mantras* methodically,
Millions and innumerable serpents came to fall there in the fire,
Here, there and everywhere resounded the strain of victory of the pious king. —2-166

The snakes measuring one arm's length, two arms length, and three, four and five arms length,
Twenty arms length, twenty-one arms length and twenty-five arms length,
Thirty arms length, thirty-two arms length and thirty-six arms length fell,
And began to fall there all and reduced to ashes. —3-167

Those measuring one hundred arms length and two hundred arms length,
Three hundred arms length and four hundred arms length,
Five hundred and six hundred arms length began to fall there within the fire-pit,
Even upto one thousand arms length and all innumerable ones were burnt and (thus reduced to ashes). —4-168

BHUJANG PRAYAAT STANZA

Sovereign (Janmeja) is performing the serpent sacrifice,
The Brahmins are busy in performing *homa* ritual whose merit is setting everything right,
Innumerable types of snakes are being burnt in the pit,
Innumerable cobras, drawn by the *mantras* at the gate of the king have been burnt. —1-169

Many snakes of about eight arms length and about seven arms length, with necks,
Many weighty serpents of twelve arms length,
Many of two thousand arms length and many of one *yojana* length,
They all fell in the fire-altar pit unconsciously. —2-170.

Many serpents of two *yojanas* length and many of three *yojanas*,
Many of four *yojanas* length, all these serpents of the earth were burnt,
Many of the size of a fist and a thumb and the length of a span,
And many of the length of one and a half span and many of the size of half a thumb were burnt. —3-171

Many serpents from the length of four *yojanas* upto four *kos*,
Were burnt in the altar-fire, as though the fire was touching the clarified butter,
While burning the snakes fluttered their hoods, frothed and hissed,
When they fell in the fire, the flame flared up. —4-172

Many serpents from the length of seven *yojanas* upto eight *kos*,
Many of the length of eight *yojanas* and very fat,
Millions of snakes were thus burnt and there was great killing,
Takshak, the king of snakes ran away like the crow from the falcon for fear of being eaten. —5-173

Millions of serpents of his clan were burnt in the fire-altar,
Those who were saved, were bound down and collectively thrown in the fire-pit,
The king of Nagas ran away and took shelter in the world of Indra,
With the power of Vedic *mantras*, the abode of Indra also began to broil and with this Indra was in great agony. —6-174

Bound by *mantras* and *yantras*, (Takshak) ultimately fell on the earth,
At that time the great adept Brahmin Aasteek resisted the orders of the king,
He quarrelled with the king and in the strife felt offended,
And rose in great anger, breaking the strings of his clothes. —7-175

He asked the king to forsake the serpent sacrifice and meditate on the one Lord,
With whose grace all the *mantras* and materials of the world come to our mind,
O the Lion-like monarch and the treasure of learning,
Thy glory will shine like sun and blaze like fire. —8-176

Thy beauty on the earth shall be moonlike and Thy splendour sunlike,
Thou shall be treasure of fourteen learnings,

Listen, O wielder of the bow and the monarch with knowledge of the Shastras,
Bestow on me this gift on abandoning the serpent-sacrifice. —9-177
If Thou dost not abandon this serpent-sacrifice, I shall burn myself in the fire,
Or by giving such curse I shall reduce Thee to ashes,
Or I shall pierce my belly with the sharp dagger,
Listen! O king! Thou shalt be causing a great sin for Thyself of Brahmin-killing. —10-178
Hearing these words of the Brahmin, the king stood up,
He abandoned the serpent-sacrifice and enmity for the death of his father,
He called Vyas near him and began consultations,
Vyas was the great scholar of Vedas and the learning of grammar. —11-179
The king had heard that the king of Kashi had two daughters,
Who were most beautiful and splendour of society,
He wanted to go there in order to conquer them after killing the mighty tyrants,
He then left (for that city) with loaded camels. —12-180
The army moved towards the east like swift wind,
With many heroes, enduring and resolute and weapon-wielders,
The king of Kashi concealed himself in his citadel,
Which was besieged by the army of Janmeja; he meditated only on Shiva. —13-181
The war began in full swing; there were many slaying with weapons,
And the heroes, cut into bits, fell in the field,
The warriors experienced bloodbath and fell with their clothes filled with blood,
They were chopped into halves; the contemplation of Shiva was interrupted. —14-182
Many Kshatriyas of reputation fell in the battlefield,
The dreadful sound of kettledrums and trumpets resounded,
The heroic warriors were shouting and making pledges, and also striking blows,
The trunks and heads and bodies pierced by arrows were roaming. —15-183
The shafts were penetrating into the steel-armour,
And the heroic warriors were destroying the pride of others,
The bodies and armour were being cut and the flywhisks were being trampled,
And with the blows of weapons, the bold warriors were falling. —16-184
The king of Kashi was conquered and all his forces were destroyed,
Both his daughters were wedded by Janmeja, seeing which Shiva, the three-eyed god, trembled,
Both the kings then became friendly; the conquered kingdom was returned,
Friendship developed between both the kings and all their works were settled appropriately. —17-185
The king Janmeja received a unique maid-servant in his dowry,
Who was very learned and supremely beautiful,
He also received diamonds, garments and horses of black ears,
He also got many wanton white-coloured elephants with tusks. —18-186
On his marriage, the king became very happy,
All the Brahmins were satisfied with the grant of all types of corn,
The king gave in charity various types of elephants,
From both his wives two very beautiful sons were born. —19-187
(One day) the king saw the winsome maid-servant,
He felt as if the moonlight hath penetrated out of the moon,
He considered her as beautiful lightening and as creeper of learning,
Or the inner glory of the lotus hath manifested itself. —20-188
It seemed as if she was a garland of flowers or the moon itself,
It may be the flower of *malti* or it may be *padmini*,
Or it may be Rati (the wife of god of love) or it may be the superb creeper of flowers,
The fragrance of the flowers of *champa* (*Michelia chapacca*) was emanating from her limbs. —21-189
It seemed as if a heavenly damsel was roaming on the earth,

Or a Yaksha or Kinnar woman was busy in her frolics,
Or the semen of god Shiva had strayed in the form of young damsel,
Or the drops of water were dancing on the lotus leaf. —22-190
It seemed as if a wreath of musical modes was presenting itself in colour and form,
Or the Lord, king of kings, had created her as the sovereign of beautiful women,
Or she was the daughter of a Naga or Bavasi, the wife of Sheshanaga,
Or she was the charming replica of Sankhani, Chitrani or Padmini (the types of women). —23-191
Her wonderful and infinite beauty glistened like a painting,
She was most elegant and most youthful,
She was most knowledgeable and adept in scientific works,
She had all learning at her fingers ends and was thus she was an adept in the discipline of learning. —24-192
The king considered her more winsome than the king's daughters,
The light of her face shone enormously than the light of fire,
The king Janmeja himself considered her like this,
Therefore he ardently copulated with her and gave her all the royal paraphernalia. —25-193
The king was greatly in love with her; he abandoned the king's daughters (queens),
Who were considered eminent and fortunate in the sight of the world,
A son, a great weapon-wielder was born to him,
He became adept in fourteen learnings. —26-194
The king named his first son as Asumedh,
And named his second son as Asmedhara,
The maid-servant's son was named Ajai Singh,
Who was a great hero, a great warrior and greatly renowned. —27-195
He was a person of healthy body and great strength,
He was a great warrior in the battlefield and adept in warfare,
He killed prominent tyrants with his sharp-edged weapons,
He conquered many enemies like Lord Rama, the killer of Ravana. —28-196
One day the king Janmeja went hunting,
Seeing a deer, he pursued him and went to another country,
After the long and arduous journey, the king was tired, when he saw a tank,
He ran there quickly to drink water. —29-197
Then the king went to sleep, (the destiny) caused a horse to come out of water,
He saw the beautiful royal mare,
He copulated with her and made her pregnant,
From her an invaluable horse of black ears was born. —30-198
The king Janmeja began his great horse-sacrifice,
He conquered all the kings and all his errands were set right,
The columns of the sacrificial place were fixed and the sacrificial altar was constructed,
He satisfied nicely the assembly of the Brahmins giving wealth in charity. —31-199
Millions of gifts were given in charity and pure foods were served,
The king performed a great event of *dharma* in the Kaliyuga,
As the queen began to scan all this,
She, the most beautiful and abode of supreme glory. —32-200
The frontal garment of the queen flew away by the gust of wind,
The Brahmins and Kshatriyas (in the assembly) seeing the nakedness of the queen laughed,
The king in great fury caught hold of all the Brahmins,
All the highly proud great pundits were burnt with hot mixture of milk and sugar. —33-201
Firstly all the Brahmins were bound down and their heads were shaved,
Then the pads were placed on the top of their heads,
Then the boiling milk was poured (within the pads),
And thus all the Brahmins were burnt and killed. —34-202
Many Brahmins were entombed in the walls,
Many eminent Brahmins were hanged,
Many were drowned in water and many were burnt in fire,

Many were sawed into halves and many were bound and their bellies were torn. —35-203

The king then suffered from the blemish of Brahmin-killing and his body was inflicted by leprosy,

He called all other Brahmins and treated them with love,

He asked them to sit and contemplate as to how

The suffering of the body and the great sin can be removed? —36-204

All the invited Brahmins came to the royal court,

The eminent like Vyas and others were called,

After scanning the Shastras, all the Brahmins said,

"The ego of the king hath increased and because of this conceit, he mashed the Brahmins." —37-205

"Listen! O supreme monarch, the treasure of learning,

"Thou didst mash the Brahmins during the sacrifice,

"All this happened suddenly, no one directed thee for this,

"All this hath been got done by the Providence, such happening had been recorded earlier." —38-206

"O king! Listen from Vyas the eighteen parvas (parts) of *Mahabharata*,

"Then all the ailment of leprosy will be removed from thy body,"

The eminent Brahmin Vyas was then called and the king began to listen to the parvas (of *Mahabharata*),

The king fell at the feet of Vyas forsaking all pride. —39-207

(Vyas said): Listen, O supreme monarch! the treasure of learning,

"In the lineage of Bharat, there was a king named Raghu,

"In his line, there was the king Rama,

"Who gave the gift of life to the Kshatriyas from the wrath of Parasurama and also the treasures and comfortable living." —40-208

"In his clan, there was a king named Yadu,

"Who was erudite in all fourteen learnings,

"In his family, there was a king named Santanu,

"In his line, there were then the Kauravas and Pandavas." —41-209

"In his family, there was Dhritrashtra,

"Who was a great hero in wars and a teacher of great enemies,

"In his house there were Kauravas of vicious *karmas*,

Who worked as chisel (destroyer) for the clan of Kshatriyas." —42-210

"They made Bhishama the general of their forces,

"In great fury they waged their war against the sons of Pandu,

"In that war, the supreme hero Arjuna roared,

"He was an adept in archery and shot his shafts superbly." —43-211

The great hero Arjuna shot his chain of arrows in the field with such skill,

That he killed Bhishama and destroyed all his forces,

He gave Bhishama the bed of arrows, on which he lay down,

The great Pandava (Arjuna) attained the victory comfortably. —44-212

The second general of Kauravas and master of their forces was Daronacharya,

There at that time a horrible war was waged,

Dhrishtadyumna killed Dronacharya, who breathed his last,

Dying in the battlefield, he went to heaven. —45-213

Karan became the third general of the Kaurava army,

Who in great fury waged a terrible war,

He was killed by Partha (Arjuna) and immediately cut off his head,

After his fall (death), the rule of Yudhishtra was firmly established. —46-214

Then the brave warrior Salaya became the general of Kauravas,

He beat the Pandava forces fiercely,

And wounded the elephant of Yudhishtra with his dagger,

Because of this Yudhishtra fell down, but he killed the brave Salaya. —47-215

CHAUPAI (QUATRAIN)

The day on which the king Salaya died in fighting,

The Kauravas felt their impending defeat,

When Salaya died, Ashvathama became the general,

He beat violently millions of forces for one watch. —1-216

He killed the expert charioteer Dharishtadyumna,
And mashed the Pandava forces nicely,
He also killed the five sons of Pandavas,
He fought very great war in Dvapar age. —2-217

Then Duryodhana, the king of Kauravas waged the war,
Against Bhim in great fury,
He was never defeated while fighting,
But the mighty death came and killed him. —3-218

BHUJANG PRAYAAT STANZA

There the fierce war of Duryodhana began with Bhim,
Because of which the meditation of Shiva was shattered and that great god began to dance,
Because of the blows of warriors terrible sound arose,
The bodies were pierced by arrows and the heads were separated from the trunks. —1-219

Fighting in various ways many warriors fell in the field,
Many had fallen in halves who had been hungry of the sharp edges of weapons,
The intoxicated elephants of Kauravas had been chopped in the field,
Seeing the brave warriors wielding weapons in the field, the vultures were feeling pleased. —2-220

The warriors were fighting in the battlefield in enclosures,
They laughed, roared and patted their arms, they challenged from both sides,
They were standing and showing feats of bravery in enclosures,
They swayed their arms and were producing terrible sounds with the blows of their maces. —3-221

The sheets of gold covering the maces looked splendid,
Their glory exhibited the blaze of fire at their tops,
The warriors moved in the field and rotated their discs,
They appreciated those on their sides who inflicted deep wounds. —4-222

There the great warrior Bhim used his weapon with his arms,
He was trampling armies nicely,
On the other side Yudhishtra was bound by Kshatriya discipline,
And was performing wonderful and holy *karmas*. —5-223

All of them looked elegant with ornaments like armlets,
Their necklaces of gems glistened and their turbans looked graceful on the heads of both the warriors of the same age,
Both the chiefs were men of great strength and composure,
Both were either king Mandhata or king Bhoj. —6-224

Both the warriors had tightened their tearing shafts,
Both the weapon-wielding warriors began to wage war in great fury,
Both the heroes of violent actions had long arms like gods,
Both were great kings with extraordinary knowledge of Hinduism. —7-225

Both were weapon-wielders and supreme donors,
Both were Indians and capable of protecting themselves with their shields,
Both were the users of their arms and were kings with canopies,
Both were supreme warriors and great fighters. —8-226

Both were the destroyers of their enemies.
Both were the terrible conquerors of the great heroes,
Both the warriors were adept in shooting arrows and had mighty arms,
Both the heroes were the Sun and Moon of their forces. —9-227

Both were the universal monarchs and had knowledge of warfare,
Both were the warriors of war and conquerors of war,
Both were marvellously beautiful carrying beautiful bows,
Both were clad in armour and were the destroyers of enemies. —10-228

Both were the destroyers of the enemies with their

double-edged swords and were also their establishers,
Both were glory-incarnate and mighty heroes,
Both were like intoxicated elephants and like king Vikrama,
Both were adepts in warfare and had weapons in their hands. —11-229
Both were supreme warriors full of rage,
Both were adepts in warfare and were the source of beauty,
Both were sustainers of Kshatriyas and followed the discipline of Kshatriyas,
Both were the heroes of war and men of violent actions. —12-230
Both were standing and fighting in enclosures,
Both struck their arms with their hands and shouted loudly,
Both had Kshatriya discipline but both were the destroyers of Kshatriyas,
Both had swords in their hands and both were the adornment of the battlefield. —13-231
Both were beauty-incarnate and had lofty thoughts,
Both were operating their double-edged swords in their enclosures,
Both had their swords smeared with blood and both worked against Kshatriya discipline,
Both were capable of risking their life in the battlefield. —14-232
Both the heroes had their weapons in their hands,
It seemed as if the spirits of the dead kings moving in the sky were calling them,
They were shouting seeing their heroism, they were praising them with the words "Well done, bravo!"
The king of Yakshas seeing their bravery was astonished and the earth was trembling. —15-233
(Ultimately) the king Duryodhana was killed in the battlefield,
All the noisy warriors ran helter-skelter,
(After that) Pandavas ruled over the family of Kauravas unconcerned,
Then they went to Himalaya mountains. —16-234
At that time a war was waged with a Gandharva,
There that Gandharva adopted a wonderful garb,
Bhima threw there the elephants of the enemy upwards,
Which are still moving in the shy and have not returned as yet. —17-235
Hearing these words, the king Janmeja turned his nose in such a manner,
And laughed contemptuously as though the utterance about the elephants was not true,
With this disbelief the thirty-sixth part of leprosy remained in his nose,
And with this ailment, the king passed away. —18-236

CHAUPAI

In this way for eighty-four years,
Seven months and twenty-four days,
The king Janmeja remained the ruler,
Then, the trumpet of death sounded over his head. —1-237

Thus the king Janmeja breathed his last.

CHAUPAI

Asumedh and Asmedhara (the sons of Janmeja),
Were great heroes and truthful (princes),
They were very brave, mighty and archers,
Their praises were sung in every home in the country. —1-238
They were supreme warriors and supreme archers,
Because of their fear, the three worlds trembled,
They were great kings of indivisible glory,
They were persons of unlimited splendour and the whole world remembered them. —2-239
On the other hand, Ajai Singh was a superb hero,
Who was a great monarch and adept in fourteen learnings,
He was without any vices, he was incomparable and of unweighable might,
Who conquered many enemies and mashed them. —3-240
He was the conqueror of many wars,
None of the weapon-wielders could escape him,
He was a great hero, possessing great qualities,
And all the world venerated him. —4-241
At the time of death, the king Janmeja,
Consulted his council of ministers,
As to whom should the kingship be awarded?
They looked for the mark of kingship. —5-242
(Out of these three) who should be given the kingship?

Which son of the king should be made the king?
The son of the maid-servant is not entitled to be the king,
The enjoyments of kingship are not meant for him. —6-243
(The eldest son) Asumedh was made the king,
And all the people cheered him as king,
The funeral rites of Janmeja were performed,
There were great rejoicings in the house of Asumedh. —7-244
Another one brother that the king had,
Was given enormous wealth and precious articles,
He was also made one of the ministers,
And placed him at another position. —8-245
The third one, who was the son of maid-servant,
He was given the position of army-general,
He was made the *Bakhshi*,
And he administered all the work of the forces. —9-246
(All the brothers) were happy on getting their positions in kingdom,
The king felt great pleasure in seeing dances,
There were thirteen hundred and sixty-four *mridangs*,
And millions of other musical instruments resounded in his presence. —10-247
The second brother took to heavy drinking,
He was fond of applying perfumes and seeing-dances,
Both the brothers forgot to perform the royal responsibilities,
And the canopy of royalty was held on the head of the third one. —11-248
After the passage of many days in the kingdom like this,
Both the brothers forgot the royal responsibilities,
Both the brothers became blind with heavy drinking,
And forgot everything about kingdom. —12-249

DOHIRA

Whomsoever (Ajai Singh) wants, he kills him; whatever he desires, he gets,
Whomsoever he protects, he remains safe and whomsoever he considers protagonist, he bestows on him the desired position. —13-250

CHAUPAI

When he began such a treatment,
All the subjects, with this, came under his control,
And the chieftains and other prominent persons came under his control,
Who had earlier owed allegiance to the king. —1-251
One day all the three sagacious brothers,
Began to play chess,
When the dice was thrown, (one of the two real brothers) thought in indignation,
And uttered these words, while Ajai listened. —2-252

DOHIRA

Let us see, what he does? How doth he throw the dice? How shalt he keep the propriety of conduct?
How shalt the enemy be killed by him, who himself is the son of maid-servant? —3-253

CHAUPAI

We have thought about this game today,
That we utter apparently,
One of them took the gems of the kingdom,
The second one took horses, camels and elephants. —1-254
The princes distributed all the forces,
They divided the army in three parts,
They thought, how the die be cast and the ruse be played?
How the game and trick be played? —2-255
The game of dice was begun, amongst the princes,
The high and low all began to watch the play,
The fire of jealousy increased in their hearts,
Which is said to be the destroyer of the kings. —3-256
The game was played thus amongst them,
That they reached the stage of destroying one another and it was difficult to pacify them,
In the beginning the princes put the gems and wealth to stake,
Then they bet the clothes, horses and elephants, they lost all. —4-257
The wrangling increased on both the sides,
On both the sides, the warriors drew their swords,
The sharp edges of the swords glistened,
And many corpses lay scattered there. —5-258

The vamps and demons wandered with pleasure,
The vultures and ganas of Shiva manifested their pride through their gay voices,
The ghosts and goblins danced and sang,
Somewhere the Baitals raised their voice. —6-259

Somewhere the sharp edges of the swords gleamed,
The heads of warriors and trunks of elephants lay scattered on the earth,
Somewhere the intoxicated elephants were trumpeting after having fallen,
Somewhere the furious warriors in the battlefield rolled down. —7-260

Somewhere the wounded horses have fallen and are neighing,
Somewhere the terrible warriors are lying down; they have been sent,
Someone's armour was cut down and someone's was broken,
Somewhere the armours of elephants and horses were cut down. —8-261

Somewhere the vamps were raising joyful shrieks,
Somewhere the ghosts were dancing, while clapping their hands,
The fifty-two heroic spirits were wandering in all the four directions,
Maru musical mode was being played. —9-262

The war was waged so violently as if the ocean was thundering,
The gathering of ghosts and goblins ran away in great fear,
The Maru raga was played from this side,
Which made even the cowards so courageous that they did not run away from the battlefield. —10-263

The support of the sword remained only with the warriors,
The trunks of many elephants were chopped off,
Somewhere the vamp and Baitals danced,
Somewhere the terrible ghosts and goblins were running here and there. —11-264

Many trunks cut into halves were running,
The princes were fighting and were stabilising their positions,
The musical modes were played with such intensity,
That even the cowards did not run away from the field. —12-265

Millions of drums and musical instruments sounded,
The elephants also joined this music with their trumpets,
The swords gleamed like lightening,
And the shafts came like rain from clouds. —13-266

The wounded warriors with dripping blood revolved,
As if the intoxicated persons are playing Holi,
Somewhere the armour and the warriors had fallen,
Somewhere the vultures shrieked and the dogs barked. —14-267

The forces of both the brothers ran helter and skelter,
No pauper and king could stand there (before Ajai Singh),
The running kings with their forces entered the beautiful country of Orissa,
Whose king Tilak was a person of good qualities. —15-268

The kings who get intoxicated with wine,
All their errands are destroyed like this;
(Ajai Singh) seized the kingdom and held the canopy on his head,
He caused himself to be called Maharaja. —16-269

The defeated Asumedh was running in front,
And the great army was pursuing him;
Asumedh went to the kingdom of Maharaja Tilak,
Who was a most appropriate king. —17-270

There lived a Sanaudhi Brahmin,
He was a very great Pundit and had many great qualities,
He was the preceptor of the king and all worshipped him,
None other was adored there. —18-271

BHUJANG PRAYAAT

Somewhere there was the recitation of Upanishads and somewhere there was discussion about the Vedas,
Somewhere the Brahmins were seated together and worshipping Brahman,
There the Sanaudh Brahmin lived with such qualifications,
He wore the clothes of the leaves and bark of birch

tree and moved around subsisting only on air. —1-272

Somewhere the hymns of *Samaveda* were sung melodiously,

Somewhere the *Yajurveda* was being recited and honours were received,

Somewhere the *Rigveda* was being read and somewhere the *Atharvaveda*,

Somewhere there was the discourse about Brahmsutras and somewhere there was discussion about the mysteries of Vishnu. —2-273

Somewhere the discourse about the ten incarnations was being delivered,

There were persons adept in fourteen learnings,

There were three very learned Brahmins,

Who were unattached with the world and had faith only in one Lord. —3-274

Somewhere Koksar and somewhere Dharma-*niti* was being read,

Somewhere the Nyayashastra and somewhere Kshatriya-*dharma* was being studied,

Somewhere Theology and somewhere Astronomy was being studied,

Somewhere the Eulogy of war-goddess was being sung with devotion. —4-275

Somewhere the Prakrit language and somewhere the Naga language was being studied,

Somewhere Sahaskriti and somewhere Sanskrit (or Astrology) was being discussed,

Somewhere songs were sung from Sangeetshastra,

Somewhere the differences in the learnings of Yakshas and Gandharvas were being elucidated. —5-276

Somewhere Nyayashastra, somewhere Mimansashastra and somewhere Tarkashastra (Logic) were studied,

Somewhere the *mantras* of fire-shafts and Brahmastras were recited,

Somewhere Yogashastra and somewhere Samkhyashastra was read,

The cycle of the treasure of fourteen learnings was studied. —6-277

Somewhere *Mahabhashya* of Patanjali and somewhere the *Kaumudi* of Panini was studied,

Somewhere *Siddhantakaumudi* somewhere *Chandrika* and somewhere *Sushrut* were read,

Somewhere other grammatical works including that of Vaisheshika were discussed,

Somewhere *Kashika* commentaries on Panini grammar *Prakriya* were being churned. —7-278

Somewhere someone studied the book *Manorama*,

Somewhere someone sang in musical mode and danced,

Somewhere someone ruminated on the learning of all weapons,

Somewhere someone was removing anxiety by studying the science of warfare. —8-279

Somewhere someone exhibited the war-fighting of maces,

Somewhere someone received the award in sword-fighting,

Somewhere mature scholars held discourses on rhetorics,

Somewhere the art of swimming and syntax were discussed. —9-280

Somewhere *Garudapurana* was being studied,

Somewhere the eulogies of Shiva were being composed in Prakrit,

Somewhere Greek, Arabic and language of heroic spirits was being learnt,

Somewhere Persian and new art of warfare were being studied. —10-281

Somewhere someone was elucidating the treatment of weapon-wounds,

Somewhere the targets were being shot at with arms,

Somewhere the skilful use of the shield was being described,

Somewhere someone was delivering discourse on Vedanta and receiving monetary award. —11-282

Somewhere the art of dancing and the mystery of sound was being described,

Somewhere the discourses were being held on Puranas and Semitic texts,

Somewhere alphabets and languages of various countries were being taught,

Somewhere the significance was being attached to the worship practised in various countries. —12-283

Somewhere the lioness was causing her milk to be sucked by the calves,

Somewhere the lion was grazing a herd of cows,
At that place the snake was creeping without ire,
Somewhere the learned Pundit was praising the enemy in his discourse. —13-284

The enemy and the friend and the friend and the enemy are alike,
An ordinary Kshatriya and a universal monarch are alike,
In that place (of Sanaudhi Brahmin) went the warrior Ajai Singh in great rage,
Who wanted to kill Asumedh in a fierce war. —14-285

Both the brothers were frightened on seeing the son of the maid-servant,
They took shelter of the Brahmin and said,
"Save our life, thou shalt receive the gifts of cows and gold from the Lord,
O Guru! we are in thy shelter we are in thy shelter we are in thy shelter. —15-286

CHAUPAI

The king (Ajai Singh) sent his messengers (to king Tilak and Sanaudhi Brahmin),
Who satisfied all the incoming Brahmins,
(These messengers said:) "Asumedh and Asumedhara,
Have run and hid themselves in thy home." —1-287

"O Brahmin either bind and deliver them to us,
"Or thou shalt be considered like them,
"Thou shalt neither be worshipped nor any gift be given to thee,
Thou shalt then be given various types of sufferings." —2-288

"Why hast thou hugged these two dead ones to thy bosom?
"Give them back to us; why art thou hesitating?
"If thou dost not return both of them to me,
"Then we shall not be thy disciples." —3-289

Then the Sanaudhi Brahmin got up early in the morning and took bath,
He worshipped in various ways the gods and manes,
Then he put the frontal marks of sandal and saffron on his forehead,
After that he walked upto his court. —4-290

The Brahmin said:
"Neither have I seen both of them,
"Nor have they taken shelter,
"Whosoever has given thee the news about them, he hath told a lie,
"O emperor, the king of kings." —1-291

"O emperor, the king of kings,
"O the hero of all the universe and master of the earth,
"While sitting here, I am giving blessing to thee,
"Thou O monarch, art the Lord of the kings." —2-292

The King said:
"If thou art thy own well-wisher,
"Bind both of them and give them immediately to me,
"I shall make all of them the food of fire,
"And worship thee as my father." —3-293

"If they have not run and concealed themselves in thy house,
"Then thou obeyest me today,
"I shall prepare very tasteful food for thee,
"Which they, thou and me, all shall eat together." —4-294

Hearing these words of the king, all the Brahmins went to their homes,
And asked their brothers sons and elders:
"If they are bound and given then we lose our *dharma*"
"If we eat their food, then we pollute our *karmas*." —5-295

This son of the maid-servant is a mighty warrior,
Who hath conquered and mashed the Kshatriya forces,
He hath acquired his kingdom with his own might,
And hath ousted them from his boundaries. —6-296

TOTAK STANZA

When they heard the king saying in this manner,
All the Brahmins sat in their houses and decided,
That this son of maid-servant is unconquerable hero and his army is unconquerable,
He is very stern and a man of vicious intellect and actions. —7-297

If we eat in his company then we lose our birth in the world,
If we do not eat, then we will have to go in the jaws of death,

After assembling we should take such decision,
With which we keep up our honour in the world.
—8-298
After taking decision, they said to king, "O king of great intellect, listen,
"Thou art fearless and unconquerable monarch on the whole earth,
"Thou art unfathomable, bottomless and master of innumerable forces,
"Thou art invincible, unassailable and sovereign of supreme might." —9-299
"There is not even one Kshatriya in this place,
"O great and superb monarch, listen to this truth,"
Uttering these words, the Brahmins got up and went away,
But the spies gave the news of the presence of his brothers there. —10-300
Then the anger increased in the mind of Ajai Singh,
In great rage, he ordered his forces of four types to move forward,
The army reached there where both the superb Kshatriyas were stationed,
They jumped from the roof of the house into the abode of Sanaudh Brahmin to take shelter. —11-301
The assembly of Brahmins met and reflected on the issue,
The whole assembly affectionately kept the two in their midst,
They ruminated over the issue as to what measures be taken?
So that they may not offend the king and also save the two refugees. —12-302
When they said these words, then all of them desired:
"Break the sacred threads immediately,"
Those who accepted it, they became without the thread,
They became Vaishyas and took trade as their occupation. —13-303
Those who did not dare to break the thread doggedly,
The two refugee kings dined together with them,
Then the spies went and told (the king Ajai Singh),
There is one difference between the former and the latter. —14-304

Then the king (Ajai Singh) addressed all his Brahmins:
"If there is no Kshatriya amongst them, then give your daughters in marriage to them,"
Hearing these words none replied as though they were dead,
Then they got up and went away to their homes. —15-305
Then all gathered to take a decision,
All of them seemed to have been drowned in the ocean of sorrow,
He (Ajai Singh) wants to bind his brothers and the Brahmins were full of persistence,
We shall all side together with the brothers. —16-306
The Sanaudh Brahmin persisted in not returning the refugee brothers, then the king Ajai Singh married his daughter,
She was very beautiful, winsome and glorious,
The sons born of that Sanaudh woman, were called Sanaudh. —17-307
The sons of other Kshatriyas, who lived at that place,
They became Kshatriyas of many junior castes,
Those Brahmins who ate together with the king, they were called Rajputs. —18-308
After conquering them, the king (Ajai Singh) moved to gain further conquests,
His glory and magnificence increased enormously,
Those who surrendered before him and married their daughters to him, they were also called Rajputs. —19-309
Those who did not marry their daughters, the wrangle increased with them,
He (the king) completely uprooted them,
Their armies, might and wealth were finished,
And they adopted the occupation of traders. —20-310
Those who did not surrender and fought violently,
Their bodies were bound and reduced to ashes in big fires,
They were burnt in the fire-altar-pit, uninformed,
Thus there was a very great sacrifice of Kshatriyas. —21-311

Here ends the complete description of the rule of Ajai Singh. —6-4

The King Jag

TOMAR STANZA   BY THY GRACE

For eighty-two years,
Ruled very prosperously,
Eight months and two days,
The king of kings (Ajai Singh).—1-312
Listen, the king of great kingdom,
Who recited the *mantra* of twelve letters,
Who was treasure of fourteen learnings,
And was the supreme sovereign on the earth. —2-313
Then the great king Jag took birth,
Who was highly lustrous was than the sun,
Who was very beautiful and affectionate,
His great effulgence indestructible. —3-314
He called all the great Brahmins,
He called very learned Brahmins,
In order to perform the animal sacrifice,
Who called themselves very beautiful like Cupid. —4-315
Many Brahmins beautiful like Cupid,
Innumerable animals of the world,
Were especially invited by the king,
Were caught and burnt in altar-pit thoughtlessly. —5-316
Ten times on one animal,
The animal was burnt in the altar-pit,
The Vedic mantras was recited thoughtlessly,
For which much wealth was received from the king. —6-317
By performing animal-sacrifice,
For eighty-eight years,
The kingdom prospered in many ways,
And two months, the monarch ruled the kingdom. —7-318
Then the terrible sword of death,
Broke the unbreakable king,
Whose flame hath burnt the world,
Whose rule was entirely glorious. —8-319

Here ends the description of the benign rule of the fifth king.

The King Muni

TOMAR STANZA   BY THY GRACE

Then Muni became the king of the earth,
The Lion-king of this world,
By conquering the unbreakable enemies,
He ruled gloriously over the earth. —1-320
He killed many enemies,
And did not leave even one of them alive,
He then ruled uninterrupted,
He seized other lands and held the canopy over his head. —2-321
He was person of superb and perfect beauty,
An impetuous warrior-king,
Glory-incarnate and devoid of vices,
The sovereign of undivided and imperishable kingdom. —3-322
Conquering many kings,
And shooting many arrows,
Killing innumerable enemies,
He established immeasurable kingdom on the earth. —4-323
Ruling the prosperous kingdom for a long time,
The king of kings said thus:
"Prepare an altar for sacrifice,
"And call the Brahmins quickly." —5-324
Many Brahmins were then invited,
None of them was left at his home,
The consultation with ministers and Brahmins began,
The sagacious friends and ministers began to recite *mantras*. —6-325
Then the king of kings said,
"There is incentive in my mind for a sacrifice,
"What type of sacrificial altar be prepared?
"O my friends, tell me quickly." —7-326
Then the friends consulted one another,
They told the king like this:
"O generous monarch, listen,
"Thou art very sagacious in all the fourteen worlds." —8-327
"Listen, O king, in Satyuga,
"The goddess Chandi had performed the sacrifice,
"By killing the enemy, the demon Mahishasura,
"She had pleased Shiva greatly." —9-328

After killing Mahishasura in the battlefield,
The canopy was held over the head of Indra,
She had pleased all the vamps,
And effaced the pride of the demons. —10-329

After conquering Mahishasura in the battlefield,
She had made the Brahmins and gods fearless,
She called the god Indra,
And seizing the earth from Mahishasura, she held the canopy over his head. —11-330

She called the four-headed Brahma,
With her heart's desire, she (the Mother of the world),
Began the performance of the sacrifice,
She had indivisible and powerful glory. —12-331

Then the four-headed Brahma spoke,
"Listen, O Chandi, I bow in obeisance to thee,
"Just as thou hast asked me,
"In the same way, I advise thee." —13-332.

The innumerable beings and creatures of the world,
The goddess herself called them to come,
And within her enemies, she cut them in an instant,
With her loud voice she recited the Vedic mantras and performed the sacrifice. —14-333

ROOAAL STANZA   BY THY GRACE

The Brahmins began the performance of the sacrifice by the recitation of auspicious *mantras*,
Brahma, Indra and other gods were also invited,
"In what way, the sacrifice be begun now?" the king asked again,
"O friends, give me today thy advice in this impossible errand." —1-334

The friends advised that the flesh chopped into bits alongwith the recitation of mantras,
Be burnt in the sacrificial fire; the king was asked to listen and act without any other thoughts,
The goddess had killed the demons named Chithar and Biraal and destroyed Dhoolkaran,
After killing the demons, she performed the demon-sacrifice. —2-335

"Listen, O most glorious sovereign, thou shouldst perform the sacrifice in that way,
"O mighty and perfect Lord, therefore conquer all the demons of the country,
"Just as the goddess having killed the demons, held the canopy over the head of Indra,
"And made all the gods happy, similarly Thou mayst help the saints." —3-336

THE LORD IS ONE AND HE CAN BE ATTAINED THROUGH THE GRACE OF THE GURU

AKAL USTAT
Eulogy of the Non-Temporal Lord

The non-temporal *Purusha* (All-Pervading Lord) is my protector,
The all-steel Lord is my protector,
The all-destroying Lord is my protector,
The all-steel Lord is ever my protector.
Then the signatures of the author (Guru Gobind Singh).

CHAUPAI (QUATRAIN)   BY THY GRACE

I salute the one Primal Lord,
Who pervades the watery, earthly and heavenly expanse,
That primal *Purusha* is unmanifested and immortal,
His light illumines the fourteen worlds. —1

He hath merged himself within the elephant and the worm,
The king and the beggar are equal before him,
That non-dual and imperceptible *Purusha* is inseparable,
He reaches the inner core of every heart. —2

He is an inconceivable entity, eternal and garbless,
He is without attachment, colour, form and mark,
He is distinct from all others of various colours and signs,
He is the primal *Purusha*, unique and changeless. —3

He is without colour, mark, caste and lineage,
He is without enemy, friend, father and mother,
He is far away from all and closest to all,
His dwelling is within water, on earth and in heavens. —4

He is limitless entity and hath infinite celestial strain,
The goddess Durga takes refuge at His feet and abides there,

Brahma and Vishnu could not know His end,
The four-headed god Brahma described Him as *neti*, *neti* (not this, not this). —5

He hath created millions of Indras and Upendras (smaller Indras),
He hath created and destroyed Brahmas and Rudras (Shivas),
He hath created the play of fourteen worlds,
And then Himself merges it within Himself. —6

Infinite demons, gods and Seshanagas,
He hath created Gandharvas, Yakshas and beings of high character,
The story of past, future and present,
Regarding the inward recesses of every heart are known to Him. —7

He who hath no father, mother, caste and lineage,
He is not imbued with undivided love for any one of them,
He is merged in all lights (souls),
I have recognised Him within all and visualised Him at all places. —8

He is deathless and a non-temporal entity
He is imperceptible *Purusha*, unmanifested and unscathed,
He who is without caste, lineage, mark and colour,
The unmanifest Lord is indestructible and ever stable. —9

He is the destroyer of all and creator of all,
He is the remover of maladies, sufferings and blemishes,
He who meditates upon Him with single mind even for an instant,
He doth not come within the trap of death. —10

KABIT   BY THY GRACE

O Lord! somewhere becoming conscious, Thou

AKAL USTAT

adornest consciousness somewhere becoming carefree Thou sleepest unconsciously,

Somewhere becoming a beggar Thou beggest alms and somewhere becoming a supreme donor Thou bestowest the begged wealth,

Somewhere Thou givest inexhaustible gifts to emperors and somewhere Thou deprivest the emperors of their kingdoms,

Somewhere Thou workest in accordance with Vedic rites and somewhere Thou art quite opposed to it; somewhere Thou art without three modes of maya and somewhere Thou hast all godly attributes. —1-11

O Lord! somewhere Thou art Yaksha, Gandharva, Seshanaga and Vidyadhar and somewhere Thou becomest Kinnar, Pishacha and Preta,

Somewhere Thou becomest a Hindu and repeatest Gayatri secretly; somewhere becoming a Turk Thou callest Muslims to worship,

Somewhere being a poet Thou recitest the Pauranic wisdom and somewhere Thou comprehendest the essence of *Quran*,

Somewhere Thou workest in accordance with Vedic rites and somewhere Thou art quite opposed to it; somewhere Thou art without three modes of *maya* and somewhere Thou hast all godly attributes. —2-12

O Lord! somewhere Thou art seated in the Court of gods and somewhere Thou givest the egoistic intellect to demons,

Somewhere Thou bestowest the position of the king of gods to Indra and somewhere Thou deprivest Indra of this position,

Somewhere Thou discriminatest between good and bad intellect, somewhere Thou art with Thy own spouse and somewhere with another's wife,

Somewhere Thou workest in accordance with Vedic rites and somewhere Thou art quite opposed to it; somewhere Thou art without three modes of *maya* and somewhere Thou hast all godly attributes. —3-13

O Lord! somewhere Thou art an armed warrior, somewhere a learned thinker, somewhere a hunter and somewhere an enjoyer of woman,

Somewhere Thou art the divine speech, somewhere Sarada and Bhavani, somewhere Durga, the trampler of corpses, somewhere in black colour and somewhere in white colour,

Somewhere Thou art abode of *dharma* (righteousness), somewhere all-pervading, somewhere a celibate, somewhere a lustful person, somewhere a donor and somewhere a taker,

Somewhere Thou workest in accordance with Vedic rites and somewhere Thou art quite opposed to it; somewhere Thou art without three modes of *maya* and somewhere Thou hast all godly attributes. —4-14

O Lord! somewhere Thou art a sage wearing matted hair, somewhere Thou art a rosary-wearing celibate,

Somewhere Thou hast practised yoga and somewhere Thou art practising yoga; somewhere Thou art a Kanphata yogi and somewhere Thou roamest like a Dandi saint,

Somewhere Thou steppest on the earth very cautiously; somewhere becoming a soldier, Thou practisest arms and somewhere becoming a Kshatriya, Thou slayest the enemy or be slayed Thyself;

Somewhere Thou removest the burden of the earth, O supreme sovereign! and somewhere Thou fulfillest the wishes of the worldly beings. —5-15

O Lord! somewhere Thou elucidatest the traits of song and sound and somewhere Thou art the treasure of dancing and painting,

Somewhere Thou art ambrosia which Thou drinkest and causest to drink somewhere Thou art honey and sugarcane-juice and somewhere Thou seemest intoxicated with wine,

Somewhere, becoming a great warrior Thou slayest the enemies and somewhere Thou art like the chief gods,

Somewhere Thou art very humble, somewhere Thou art full of ego, somewhere Thou art an adept in learning, somewhere Thou art earth and somewhere Thou art the sun. —6-16

O Lord! somewhere Thou art without any blemish, somewhere Thou smitest the moon, somewhere Thou art completely engrossed in enjoyment on Thy couch and somewhere Thou art the essence of purity,

Somewhere Thou performest godly rituals, somewhere Thou art the abode of religious discipline, somewhere Thou art the vicious actions and somewhere Thou appearest in variety of virtuous acts,

Somewhere Thou subsistest on air, somewhere Thou art a learned thinker and somewhere Thou art a yogi, a celibate, a *Brahmachari* (disciplined student), a man and a woman,

Somewhere Thou art a mighty sovereign, somewhere Thou art a great preceptor sitting on a deer-skin, somewhere Thou art prone to be deceived and somewhere Thou art various types of deception Thyself. —7-17

O Lord! somewhere Thou art singer of song, somewhere Thou art player of flute, somewhere Thou art a dancer and somewhere in the form of a man,

Somewhere Thou art the Vedic hymns and somewhere the story of the elucidator of the mystery of love; somewhere Thou art Thyself the king, the queen and also various types of women,

Somewhere Thou art the player of flute, somewhere the grazier of cows and somewhere Thou art the beautiful youth, enticer of lakhs (of lovely maids),

Somewhere Thou art the splendour of purity, the life the saints, the donor of great charities and the immaculate formless Lord. —8-18

O Lord! Thou art the invisible cataract, the most beautiful entity, the king of kings and the donor of great charities,

Thou art the saviour of life, the giver of milk and offspring, the remover of ailments and sufferings and somewhere Thou art the Lord of highest honour,

Thou art the essence of all learning, the embodiment of monism, the being of all-powers and the glory of sanctification,

Thou art the snare of youth, the death of death, the anguish of enemies and the life of the friends. —9-19

O Lord! somewhere Thou art lofty in deific conduct, somewhere Thou appearest as contention in learning, somewhere Thou art the tune of sound and somewhere a perfect saint (attuned with celestial strain),

Somewhere Thou art Vedic ritual, somewhere the love for learning, somewhere ethical and unethical and somewhere appearest as the glow of fire,

Somewhere Thou art perfectly glorious, somewhere engrossed in solitary recitation, somewhere remover of suffering in great agony and somewhere Thou appearest as a fallen yogi,

Somewhere Thou bestowest the boon and somewhere withdrawest it with deceit, Thou art all times and at all the places Thou comest into view as the same. —10-20

SWAYYAS   BY THY GRACE

I have seen during my tours pure Sravaks (Jaina and Buddhist monks), groups of adepts and abodes of ascetics and yogis,

Valiant heroes, demons killing gods, gods drinking nectar and assemblies of saints of various sects,

I have seen the disciplines of the religious systems of all the countries, but seen none of the Lord, the master of my life,

They are worth nothing without an iota of the grace of the Lord. —1-21

With intoxicated elephants, studded with gold, incomparable and huge, painted in bright colours,

With millions of horses galloping deer, moving faster than the wind,

With many kings indescribable, having long arms (of heavy allied forces), bowing their heads in fine array,

What matters if such mighty emperors were there, because they had to leave the world with bare feet. —2-22

With the beat of drums and trumpets if the emperor conquers all the countries,

Alongwith many beautiful roaring elephants and thousands of neighing horses of best breed,

Such like emperors of the past, present and future cannot be counted and ascertained,

But without remembring the name of the Lord, they ultimately leave for their final abode. —3-23

Taking bath at holy places, exercising mercy, controlling passions, performing acts of charity, practising austerity and many special rituals,

Studying of Vedas, Puranas and holy *Quran* and scanning all this world and the next world,

Subsisting only on air, practising continence and meeting thousands of persons of all good thoughts,

But O king! Without the remembrance of the name of the Lord, all this is of no account, being without an iota of the grace of the Lord. —4-24

The trained soldiers, mighty and invincible, clad in coat of mail, who would be able to crush the enemies,
With great ego in their mind that they would not be vanquished even if the mountains move with wings,
They would destroy the enemies, twist the rebels and smash the pride or intoxicated elephants,
But without the grace of the Lord-God, they would ultimately leave the world. —5-25

Innumerable brave and mighty heroes, fearlessly facing the edge of the sword,
Conquering the countries, subjugating the rebels and crushing the pride of the intoxicated elephants,
Capturing the strong forts and conquering all sides with mere threats,
The Lord-God is the commander of all and is the only donor, the beggars are many. —6-26

Demons, gods, huge serpents, ghosts, past, present and future would repeat His name,
All the creatures in the sea and on land would instantly establish Him (in their hearts),
The praises of the glories of virtues would increase and the heaps of sins would be destroyed,
All the saints would wander in the world with bliss and the enemies would be annoyed on seeing them. —7-27

Kings of men and elephants, emperors who would rule over the three worlds,
Who would perform millions of ablutions, give elephants and other animals in charity and arrange many *svayamvaras* (self-marriage functions) for weddings and,
Brahma, Shiva, Vishnu and consort of Sachi (Indra) would ultimately fall in the noose of death,
But those who fall at the feet of Lord-God, they would not appear again in physical form. —8-28

Of what use it is if one sits and meditates like a crane with his eyes closed,
If he takes bath at holy places upto the seventh sea, he loses this world and also the next world,
He spends his life in performing evil actions and wastes his life in such pursuits,
I speak truth, all should turn their ears towards it: he, who is absorbed in true love, he would realise the Lord. —9-29

Someone worshipped stone and placed it on his head, someone hung the phallus (*lingam*) from his neck,
Someone visualised God in the south and someone bowed his head towards the west,
Some fool worships the idols and someone goes to worship the dead,
The whole world is entangled in false rituals and has not known the secret of Lord-God. —10-30

TOMAR STANZA   BY THY GRACE

The Lord is sans birth and death,
He is skilful in all eighteen sciences,
That unblemished entity is infinite,
His benevolent glory is everlasting. —1-31

His unaffected entity is all-pervasive,
He is the supreme Lord of the saints of all the world,
He is the frontal-mark of glory and life-giver sun of the earth,
He is the treasure of eighteen sciences. —2-32

He, the unblemished entity is infinite,
He is the destroyer of sufferings of all the worlds,
He is without the rituals of iron age,
He is an adept in all religious works. —3-33

His glory is indivisible and in-estimable,
He is the establisher of all the institutions,
He is indestructible with imperishable mysteries,
All the four-headed Brahmas sing the Vedas. —4-34

To Him, the Nigam (Vedas) call *neti* (not this),
The four headed-Brahma speaks of Him as unlimited,
His glory is unaffected and in-estimable,
He is undivided, unlimited and un-established. —5-35

He, who hath created the expanse of the world,
He hath created it in full consciousness,
His infinite form is indivisible,
His immeasurable glory is powerful. —6-36

He, who hath created the universe from the cosmic egg,

He hath created the fourteen regions,
He hath created all the expanse of the world,
That benevolent Lord is unmanifested. —7-37

He, who hath created millions of king Indras,
He hath created many Brahmas and Vishnus after consideration,
He hath created many Ramas, Krishnas and Rasuls (Prophets),
None of them is approved by the Lord without devotion. —8-38

He created many oceans and mountains like Vindhyachal,
Many fish incarnations, tortoise incarnations and Seshanagas,
Many gods, and Adikumars, sons of Brahma (Sanak, Sanandan, Sanatan, and Sant Kumar),
Many Krishnas and incarnations of Vishnu. —9-39

Many Indras sweep at His door,
Many Vedas and four-headed Brahmas are there,
Many Rudras (Shivas) of ghastly appearance are there,
Many unique Ramas and Krishnas are there. —10-40

Many poets compose poetry there,
Many speak of the distinction of the knowledge of Vedas,
Many elucidate Shastras and Smritis,
Many hold discourses of Puranas. —11-41

Many perform *agnihotras* (fire-worship),
Many perform arduous austerities while standing,
Many are ascetics with raised arms and many are anchorites,
Somewhere many are in the garbs of yogis and *udasis* (stoics). —12-42

Somewhere many perform Neoli ritual of yogis of purging intestines,
Somewhere they are innumerable who subsist on air,
Somewhere many offer great charities at pilgrim stations,
Somewhere benevolent sacrificial rituals are performed. —13-43

Somewhere exquisite fire-worship is arranged,
Somewhere justice is done with emblem of royalty,
Somewhere ceremonies are performed in accordance with Shastras and Smritis,
Somewhere the performance is antagonistic to Vedic injunctions. —14-44

Many wander in various countries,
Many stay only at one place,
Somewhere the meditation is performed in water,
Somewhere heat is endured on the body. —15-45

Somewhere some reside in the forest,
Somewhere heat is endured on the body,
Somewhere many follow the householder's path,
Somewhere the benevolent kingly rites are being followed. —16-46

Somewhere people are without ailment and illusion,
Somewhere forbidden actions are being done,
Somewhere there are Sheikhs, somewhere there are Brahmins,
Somewhere there is the prevalence of unique politics. —17-47

Somewhere someone is without suffering and ailment,
Somewhere someone follows the path of devotion closely,
Somewhere someone is poor and someone a prince,
Somewhere someone is incarnation of Vedavyas. —18-48

Some Brahmins recite vedas,
Some Sheikhs repeat the name of the Lord,
Somewhere there is a follower of the path of *bairag* (detachment) and somewhere one follows the path of *sannyas* (asceticism),
Somewhere someone wanders as an *udasi* (stoic). —19-49

Know all the *karmas* (actions) as useless,
Consider all the religious paths of no value,
Without the prop of the only name of the Lord,
All the *karmas* be considered as illusion. —20-50

LAGHU NIRAAJ STANZA   BY THY GRACE

The Lord is in water, The Lord is on land,
The Lord is in the heart, The Lord is in the forests. —1-51
The Lord is in the mountains, The Lord is in the caves,

The Lord is in the earth, The Lord is in the sky. —2-52

The Lord is here, The Lord is there,
The Lord is in the earth, The Lord is in the sky. —3-53

The Lord is accountless, The Lord is guiseless,
The Lord is blemishless, The Lord is sans duality. —4-54

The Lord is non-temporal, The Lord cannot be reared,
The Lord is Indestructible, The Lord's secrets can not be known.—5-55

The Lord is not in mystical diagrams,
The Lord is not in incantations,
The Lord is of bright effulgence,
The Lord is not in *tantras* (magical formulas). —6-56

The Lord does not take birth,
The Lord does not experience death,
The Lord is without any friend,
The Lord is without mother. —7-57

The Lord is without any ailment,
The Lord is without grief,
The Lord is illusionless,
The Lord is actionless. —8-58

The Lord is unconquerable,
The Lord is fearless,
The Lord's secrets cannot be known,
The Lord is unassailable. —9-59

The Lord is indivisible,
The Lord cannot be slandered,
The Lord cannot be punished,
The Lord is supremely glorious. —10-60

The Lord is extremely great,
The Lord's mystery cannot be known,
The Lord needs no food,
The Lord is invincible. —11-61

Meditate on the Lord,
Worship the Lord,
Perform devotion for the Lord,
Repeat the name of the Lord. —12-62

O Lord! Thou art water,
O Lord! Thou art dry land,
O Lord! Thou art the stream,
O Lord! Thou art the ocean. —13-63

O Lord! Thou art the tree,
O Lord! Thou art the leaf,
O Lord! Thou art the earth,
O Lord! Thou art the sky. —14-64

O Lord! I meditate on Thee,
O Lord! I meditate on Thee,
O Lord! I repeat Thy name,
O Lord! I worship Thee. —15-65

O Lord! Thou art the earth,
O Lord! Thou art the sky,
O Lord! Thou art the owner of the house,
O Lord! Thou art the house Thyself. —16-66

O Lord! Thou art birthless,
O Lord! Thou art fearless,
O Lord! Thou art untouchable,
O Lord! Thou art invincible. —17-67

O Lord! Thou art the celibacy,
O Lord! Thou art the means for a virtuous deed,
O Lord! Thou art the salvation,
O Lord! Thou art the redemption. —18-68

O Lord! everything art Thou, everything Thou art,
O Lord! everything art Thou, everything Thou art,
O Lord! everything art Thou, everything Thou art,
O Lord! everything art Thou, everything Thou art. —19-69

O Lord! everything art Thou, everything Thou art,
O Lord! everything art Thou, everything Thou art,
O Lord! everything art Thou, everything Thou art,
O Lord! everything art Thou, everything Thou art. —20-70

KABIT   **BY THY GRACE**

If the Lord is realised by eating filth, by besmearing the body with ashes and by residing in the cremation ground, then the hog eats filth, the elephant and ass get their bodies filled with ashes and the badger resides in the cremation ground,

If the Lord meets in the cloister of mendicants, by wandering like a stoic and abiding in silence, then the owl lives in the cloister of mendicants, the deer wanders like a stoic and the tree abides in silence till death,

If the Lord is realised by restraining the emission of semen and by wandering with bare feet, then a eunuch may be eulogised for restraining the emission of semen and the monkey always wanders with bare feet,

One who is under the control of a woman and who is active in lust and anger and also who is ignorant of the Knowledge of the one Lord, how can such person ferry across the world-ocean? —1-71

If the Lord is realised by wandering in the forest, by drinking only the milk and by subsisting on air, then the ghost wanders in the forest, all the infants live on milk and the serpents subsist on air,

If the Lord meets by eating grass and forsaking the greed of wealth then the Bulls, the young ones of cows, do that,

If the Lord is realised by flying in the sky and by closing the eyes in meditation, then the birds fly in the sky and those who close their eyes in meditation are considered like crane, cat and wolf,

All the knowers of Brahman know the reality of these imposters, but have related it; never bring in your mind such deceitful thoughts even by mistake. —2-72

He who lives on the earth should be called the young one of white ant and those who fly in the sky may be called sparrows,

They, who eat fruit may be called young ones of monkeys, those who wander invisibly, may be considered as ghosts,

One, who swims in water is called water-fly by the world, one, who eats fire, may be considered like *chakor* (red-legged partridge),

One, who worships the sun, may be symbolised as lotus and one, who worships the moon may be recognised as water-lily (The lotus blooms on seeing the sun and the water-lily blossoms on seeing the moon). —3-73

If the name of the Lord is Narayana (one whose house is in water) then Kachh (tortoise), Macha (fish), and Tandooaa (octopus) will be called Narayana and if the name of the Lord is Kaul-naabh (Navel-lotus), then the tank in which the lotus has grown, its name is also Kaul-naabh,

If the name of the Lord is Gopi Nath, then the Lord of *gopi* is a cowherd, if the name of the Lord is Gopal, the sustainer of cows, then all the cowherds are *Dhen-charis* (the graziers of cows), if the name of the Lord is Rikhikes, then there are several chieftains of this name,

If the name of the Lord is Madhva, then the black bee is also called Madhva, if the name of the Lord is Kanhaiya, then the spider is also called Kanhaiya, if the name of the Lord is the "slayer of Kansa," then the messenger of Yama, who slayed Kansa, may be called the "slayer of Kansa."

The foolish people wail and weep, but do not know the profound secret, therefore they do not worship Him, who protects our life. —4-74

The sustainer and destroyer of the universe is benevolent towards the poor, tortures the enemies, preserves ever and is without the snare of death,

The yogis, hermits with matted locks, true donors and great celibates for a Sight of Him, endure hunger and thirst on their bodies,

For a sight of Him, the intestines are purged, offerings are made to water, fire and air, austerities are performed with face upside down standing on a single foot,

The men, Seshanaga, gods and demons have not been able to know His secret and the Vedas and *Katebs* (Semitic Scriptures) speak of Him as *neti, neti* (not this, not this) and infinite. —5-75

If the Lord is realised by devotional dancing, then the peacocks dance with the thundering of the clouds and if the Lord gets pleased on seeing the devotion through friendliness, then the lightening performs it by various flashes,

If the Lord meets by adopting coolness and serenity, then there is none cooler than the moon, if the Lord meets by the endurance of heat, then none is hotter than the sun and if the Lord is realised by the munificence, then none is more munificent than Indra, the king of gods, who as rain-god fills the world and the earth with abundance of wherewithals,

If the Lord is realised by the practice of austerities, then none is more austere than god Shiva, if the Lord meets by the recitation of Vedas, then none is more conversant with the Vedas than the god Brahma; there is also no great performer of asceticism than Sanat Kumar (the son of Brahma),

The persons without the knowledge of the Lord, entrapped in the snare of death always transmigrate in all the four Ages. —6-76

There was one Shiva, who passed away and another one came into being, there are many incarnations of Ramchandra and Krishna,

There are many Brahmas and Vishnus, there are many Vedas and Puranas, there have been the authors of all the Smritis, who created the works and passed away,

Many religious leaders, many chieftains of clans, many Ashwani Kumars and many degrees of incarnations, they had all been subject to death,

Many Muslim preceptors (*pirs*) and Prophets, who cannot be counted, they were born out of the earth, ultimately, merged in the earth. —7-77

The Yogis, celibates and students observing celibacy, many great sovereigns, who walk several miles under the shade of canopy,

Who conquer the countries of many great kings and bruise their ego,

The sovereign like Mandhata and the canopied sovereign like Dalip, who were proud of their mighty forces,

The emperor like Darius and the great egoist like Duryodhana, after enjoying the earthly pleasures, finally merged in the earth. —8-78

If the Lord is pleased by prostrating before Him, then the gunner full of deceit bows his head several times while igniting the gun and the addict acts in the same manner in intoxication,

What, then, If the wrestler bends his body several times during his rehearsal of exercises, but that is not the prostration, of eight parts of the body,

What, then, if the patient lies down with his face upwards, he has not bowed his head before the primal Lord with single-mindedness,

But one always subservient to desire and active in telling the beads of the rosary, and also without faith, how can he realise the Lord of the world? —9-79

If the Lord is realised by knocking the head, then that person repeatedly knocks his head, in whose ear the centipede enters and if the Lord meets by beating the head, then one beats his head in grief over the death of friends or sons,

If the Lord is realised by wandering in the forest, then there is none other like the he-goat, who grazes the *akk* (*Calotropis procera*), eats the flowers and fruit and always wanders in the forest,

If the Lord meets by rubbing the head with the trees in order to remove drowsiness, then the sheep always rubs its head with the trees and if the Lord meets by eating the earth, then you can and ask the leech,

How can one meet the Lord in the next world, who is subservient to desire, active in lust and anger and without faith? —10-80

If the Lord is realised by dancing and shouting, then peacock dances, the frog croaks and the clouds thunder,

If the Lord meets by standing on one leg, then the tree stands on one foot in the forest, and if the Lord meets on observing non-violence then the Sravak (Jaina monk) places his feet very cautiously on the earth,

If the Lord is realised by not moving from one place or by wandering then the stone remains at one place for many ages and the crow and kite continue wandering in several countries,

When a person without knowledge cannot merge in the Supreme Lord, then how can these devoid of trust and faith ferry across the world-ocean? —11-81

Just as an actor sometimes becomes a Yogi, sometimes a *bairagi* (recluse) and sometimes shows himself in the guise of a *sannyasi* (mendicant),

Sometimes he becomes a person subsisting on air, sometimes sits observing abstract meditation and sometimes under the intoxication greed, sings praises of many kinds,

Sometimes he becomes a *brahmachari* (student observing celibacy), sometimes shows his promptness and sometimes becoming a staff bearing hermit deludes the people,

He dances becoming subordinate to passions; how will he be able to attain an entry into Lord's abode without knowledge? —12-82

If the jackal howls for five times, then either the winter sets in or there is famine, but nothing happens if the elephant trumpets and ass brays many times. (Similarly the actions of a knowledgeable person are fruitful and those of an ignorant one are fruitless),

If one observes the ritual of sawing at Kashi, nothing will happen, because a thief is slayed and sawed several times with axes,

If a fool, with a noose around his neck, is drowned in the current of Ganges, nothing will happen, because several times the dacoits kill the wayfarer by putting the noose, around his neck,

The fools have drowned in the current of hell without deliberations of knowledge, because how can a faithless person comprehend the concepts of knowledge? —13-83

If the blissful Lord is realised by the endurance of sufferings, then a wounded person endures several types of sufferings on his body,

If the unmutterable Lord can be realised by the repetition of His name, then a small bird called Pudana repeats "Tuhi, Tuhi" (Thou art everything) all the time,

If the Lord can be realised by flying in the sky, then the phoenix always flies in the sky,

If the salvation is attained by burning oneself in fire, then the woman burning herself on the funeral pyre of her husband (*sati*) should get salvation; and if one achieves liberation by residing in a cave, then why the serpents residing in the nether-world do not attain liberation? —14-84

Somebody became a *bairagi* (recluse), somebody a *sannyasi* (mendicant), somebody a Yogi, somebody a *brahmachari* (student obsering celibacy) and someone is considered a celibate,

Someone is Hindu and someone Muslim, then someone is Shia, and someone a Sunni, but all the human beings, as a species, are all recognised as one and the same,

Karta (the creator) and *Karim* (merciful) is the same Lord, *Razak* (the sustainer) and *Rahim* (compassionate) is the same Lord, there is no other second, therefore consider this verbal distinguishing feature of Hinduism and Islam as an error and an illusion,

Thus worship the one Lord, who is the common enlightener of all; all have been created in His image and amongst all comprehend the same one light. —15-85

The temple and the mosque are the same, there is no difference between a Hindu worship and Muslim prayer; all the human beings are the same, but the illusion is of various types,

The gods, demons, Yakshas, Gandharvas, Turks and Hindus—all these are due to the differences of the various garbs of different countries,

The eyes are the same, the ears are the same, the bodies are the same, structures and the habits are the same, all the creation is the amalgam of earth air, fire and water,

Allah of Muslims and *Abhekh* (guiseless) of Hindus are the same, the Puranas of Hindus and the holy *Quran* of the Muslims depict the same reality; all have been created in the image of the same Lord and have the same formation. —16-86

Just as millions of sparks are created from the same fire; although they are different entities, they merge in the same fire,

Just as from the same dust many dust-particles emanate and then all the particles merge in the same dust,

Just as millions of waves are created on the surface of the big river and all the waves are called water.

Similarly the animate and inanimate objects come out of the supreme Lord; having been created from the same Lord, they merge in the same Lord. —17-87

There are many a tortoise and fish and there are many who devour them; there are many a winged phoenix, who always continue flying,

There are many who devour even the phoenix in the sky and there are many, who even eat and digest the materialised devourers,

Not only to speak of the residents of water, earth and wanderers of the sky, all those created by god of death will ultimately be devoured (destroyed) by him,

Just as the light merges in darkness and the darkness merges in the light, all the created beings generated by the Lord will ultimately merge in Him. —18-88

Many cry out while wandering, many weep and many die; many are drowned in water and many are burnt in fire,

Many live on the banks of Ganges and many reside in Mecca and Medina, many becoming hermits, indulge in wanderings,

Many endure the agony of sawing, many get buried in the earth, many are hanged on the gallows and many undergo great anguish,

Many fly in the sky, many live in water and many without knowledge, in their waywardness burn themselves to death. —19-89

The gods got weary of making offerings of fragrances, the antagonistic demons have got weary, the knowledgeable sages have got weary and worshippers of good understanding have also got weary,

Those who rub sandalwood have got tired, the appliers of fine scent (otto) have got tired, the image-worshippers have got tired and those making offerings of sweet curry, have also got tired,

The visitors of graveyards have got tired, the worshippers of hermitage and monuments have got tired; those who besmear the walls images have got tired and those who print with embossing seal have also got tired,

Gandharvas, the musicians of gods have got tired, Kinnars, the players of musical instruments have got tired, The Pundits have got highly weary and the ascetics observing austerities have also got tired. None of the above-mentioned people have been able to know the secret of the Supreme Lord. —20-90

BHUJANG PRAYAAT STANZA   BY THY GRACE

The Lord is without affection, without colour, without form and without line,

He is without attachment, without anger, without deceit and without malice,

He is actionless, illusionless, birthless and casteless,

He is sans friend, sans enemy, sans father and sans mother. —1-91

He is without love, without home, without lust and without home,

He is without son, without friend, without enemy and without wife,

He is accountless, guiseless, and unborn entity,

He is ever the giver of power and intellect, He is is most beautiful. —2-92

Nothing can be known about His form and mark,

Where doth He live? In what garb He moves?

What is His name? Of what place He is told?

How should He be described? Nothing can be said. —3-93

He is without ailment, without sorrow, without attachment and without mother,

He is without work, without illusion, without birth and without caste,

He is without malice, without guise, and unborn entity,

Salutation to Him of one form, salutation to Him of one form. —4-94

Yonder and Yonder is He, the Supreme Lord, He is the illuminator of intellect,

He is invincible, indestructible, the primal, non-dual and eternal,

He is without caste, without line, without form and without colour,

Salutation to Him, who is primal and immortal, salutation to Him, who is primal and immortal. —5-95

He hath created millions of Krishnas like worms,

He created them, annihilated them, again created them, again destroyed them, still again created them,

He is unfathomable, fearless, primal, non-dual and indestructible,

Yonder and Yonder is He, the supreme Lord, He is the perfect illuminator. —6-96

He, the unfathomable entity is without the ailments of the mind and body,

He is the Lord of indivisible glory and master of eternal wealth from the very beginning,

He is without birth, without death, without colour and without ailment,

He is partless, mighty, unpunishable and incorrigible. —7-97

He is without love, without home, without affection and without company, unpunishable, non-thrustable, mighty and omnipotent,

He is without caste, without line, without enemy and without friend,

That imageless Lord was in the past, is in the present and will be in the future. —8-98

He is neither the king, nor the poor He is without form and without mark,

He is without greed, without jealousy, without body and without guise,

He is without enemy, without friend, without love and without home,

He always has love for all at all times. —9-99

He is without lust, without anger, without greed and without attachment,

He is unborn, invincible, the primal, non-dual and imperceptible,

He is without birth, without death, without colour and without ailment,
He is without malady, without sorrow, without fear and without hatred. —10-100
He is invincible, indiscriminate, actionless and timeless,
He is indivisible, indefamable, mighty and patronless,
He is without father, without mother, without birth and without body,
He is without love, without home, without illusion and without affection. —11-101
He is without form, without hunger, without body and without action,
He is without suffering, without strife, without discrimination and without illusion,
He is eternal, He is the perfect and oldest Entity,
Salutation to the Lord of one form, salutation to the Lord of one form. —12-102
His glory is inexpressible; His excellence from the very beginning cannot be described,
Non-aligned, unassailable and from the very beginning unmanifested and unestablished,
He is the enjoyer in diverse guises, invincible from the very beginning and an unassailable entity,
Salutation to the Lord of one form; salutation to the Lord of one form. —13-103
He is without love, without home, without sorrow and without relations,
He is in the yond, He is holy and immaculate and He is independent,
He is without caste, without line, without friend and without adviser,
Salutation to the one Lord in warp and woof; salutation to the one Lord in warp and woof. —14-104
He is without religion, without illusion, without shyness and without relations,
He is without coat of mail, without shield, without steps and without speech,
He is without enemy, without friends and without countenance of a son,
Salutation to the primal entity; salutation to that primal entity. —15-105
Somewhere as a black bee Thou art engaged in the delusion of getting the fragrance of the lotus,
Somewhere Thou art describing the characteristics of a king and the poor,
Somewhere Thou art the abode of virtues of various guises of the country,
Somewhere Thou art manifesting the mode of *tamas* in a kingly mood. —16-106
Somewhere Thou art practising for the realisation of powers through the medium of learning and science,
Somewhere Thou art searching the secrets of powers and intellect,
Somewhere Thou art seen in excitement of warfare. —17-107
Somewhere Thou art considered as the abode of the acts of piety,
Somewhere Thou acceptest the ritualistic discipline as illusion,
Somewhere Thou makest grand efforts and somewhere Thou lookest like a picture,
Somewhere Thou art embodiment of fine intellect and somewhere Thou art the sovereign of all. —18-108
Somewhere Thou art an eclipse of love and somewhere Thou art physical ailment,
Somewhere Thou art the medicine, drying up the grief of malady,
Somewhere Thou art the learning of gods and Somewhere Thou art the speech of demons,
Somewhere Thou art the episode of Yaksha, Gandharva and Kinnar. —19-109
Somewhere Thou art Rajasic (full of activity), Sattvic (rhythmic) and Tamasic (full of morbidity),
Somewhere Thou art an ascetic, practising the learning of Yoga,
Somewhere Thou art the remover of malady and somewhere Thou art cohesive with Yoga,
Somewhere Thou art deluded in enjoying the earthly victuals. —20-110
Somewhere Thou art a daughter of gods and somewhere a daughter of demons,
Somewhere a daughter of Yakshas, Vidyadhars and men,
Somewhere Thou art the queen and somewhere Thou art the princess,
Somewhere Thou art the superb daughter of the Nagas of nether-world. —21-111

Somewhere Thou art the learning of Vedas and somewhere the voice of heaven,
Somewhere Thou art the discourse and story of general poets,
Somewhere Thou art iron and somewhere Thou art splendid gold,
Somewhere Thou art sweet speech and somewhere Thou art critical and fault-finding. —22-112

Somewhere Thou art the learning of the Vedas and Somewhere Thou art literature,
Somewhere Thou makest superb effort and somewhere Thou lookest like a picture,
Somewhere Thou comprehendest the tenets of holy Puranas and somewhere Thou singest the songs of sacred *Quran*. —23-113

Somewhere Thou art a true Muslim and somewhere the adherent of the religion of Brahmins,
Somewhere Thou art in old age and somewhere actest as a child,
Somewhere Thou art a youth sans an old body,
Somewhere Thou lovest the body and somewhere Thou forsakest Thy home. —24-114

Somewhere Thou art engrossed in Yoga and enjoyment and Somewhere Thou art experiencing ailment and attachment,
Somewhere Thou art the remover of ailment and somewhere Thou forsakest enjoyment,
Somewhere Thou art in pomp of royalty and somewhere Thou art without kingship,
Somewhere Thou art perfect intellectual and somewhere Thou art embodiment of supreme Love. —25-115

Somewhere Thou art Arabic, somewhere Turkish, somewhere Persian,
Somewhere Thou art Pahlavi, somewhere Pushtu, somewhere Sanskrit,
Somewhere Thou, art the country's language, somewhere the language of gods (Sanskrit),
Somewhere Thou art the State-learning and somewhere Thou art State-Capital. —26-116

Somewhere Thou art the instruction of *mantras* (spells) and somewhere Thou art the essence of *tantras*,
Somewhere Thou art the instruction of the method of *yantras* and somewhere Thou art the wielder of arms,
Somewhere Thou art the learning of *homa* (fire)-worship, somewhere Thou art the instruction about offerings to gods,
Somewhere Thou art the instruction about Prosody, somewhere Thou art the instruction about the discussion regarding the songs on minstrels. —27-117

Somewhere Thou art the learning about lyre, somewhere about singing song,
Somewhere Thou art the language of Malechhas (barbarians), somewhere about the Vedic rituals,
Somewhere Thou art the learning of dancing, somewhere Thou art the language of Nagas (serpents),
Somewhere Thou art Gararoo *mantra* (that *mantra*, which effaces the snake-poison) and somewhere Thou tellest the mysterious story (through astrology). —28-118

Somewhere Thou art the belle of this world, somewhere the *apsara* (nymph of heaven) and somewhere the handsome maid of netherworld,
Somewhere Thou art the learning about the art of warfare and somewhere Thou art the non-elemental beauty,
Somewhere Thou art the gallant youth, somewhere the ascetic on the deer-skin, somewhere a king under the canopy,
Somewhere Thou art the ruling sovereign authority. —29-119

I bow before Thee, O perfect Lord! the donor ever of miraculous powers,
Invisible, unassailable, the primal, non-dual Providence,
Thou art fearless, free from any bondage and Thou manifestest in all beings,
I bow before Thee, I bow before Thee, O wonderful non-elemental Lord. —30-120

PAADHARI STANZA   BY THY GRACE

O Lord!
Thou art unmanifested glory and light of knowledge,
Thou art unassailable entity, non-dual indestructible,
Thou art indivisible glory and an inexhaustible store,
Thou art the infinite donor of all kinds. —1-121

Thine is the wonderful glory and indestructible body,
Thou art ever the creator and remover of meanness,
Thy seat is stable and Thy actions are non-elemental,
Thou art the beneficent donor and Thy religious discipline is beyond the working of elements. —2-122
Thou art that ultimate reality,
Which is without enemy, friend, birth and caste,
Which is without son, brother, friend and mother,
Which is actionless, illusionless and without any consideration of religious disciplines,
Which is without love, home and beyond any thought-system. —3-123
Which is without caste, line, enemy and friend,
Which is without love, home, mark and picture,
Which is without colour, form, affection and line,
Which is without birth, caste, illusion and guise. —4-124
Which is without action, delusion, caste and lineage,
Which is without love, home, father and mother,
Which is without name, place and also without species of maladies,
Which is without ailment, sorrow, enemy and a saintly friend. —5-125
Which never remains in fear and whose body is indestructible,
Which has no beginning, no end, no form and no outlay,
Which has no ailment, sorrow and no device of Yoga,
Which has no fear, no hope and no earthly enjoyment. —6-126
Thou art That whose bodily limb hath never been stung by the serpent of death,
Who is unassailable entity and who is indestructible and imperishable,
Whom the Vedas call *neti, neti* (not this, not this) and infinite,
Whom the semitic scriptures call incomprehensible. —7-127
Whose form is unknowable and whose seat is stable,
Whose light is unlimited and who is invincible and unweighable,
For whose meditation and sight infinite sages

Perform hard yoga practices for many *kalpas* (ages). —8-128
For Thy realisation they endure cold, heat and rain on their body,
For many ages they remain in the same posture,
They make many efforts and ruminate over the learning of yoga,
They practise yoga, but still they cannot know Thy end. —9-129
Many wander in several countries with raised arms,
Many burn their bodies upside down,
Many recite Smritis, Shastras and Vedas,
Many go through *Kokshastra* (pertaining to sex), other poetry books and semitic scripture. —10-130
Many perform *havan* (fire-worship) and many subsist on air,
Many a million eat clay,
Many people eat green leaves,
Still the Lord does not manifest Himself to them. —11-131
There are many song-tunes and observances of Gandharvas,
There are many who are absorbed in the learning of Vedas and Shastras,
Somewhere *yajnas* (sacrifices) are performed according to the Vedic injunctions,
Somewhere *havans* are performed and somewhere at pilgrim stations the befitting rituals are being followed. —12-132
Many speak languages of different countries,
Many study the learning of various countries,
Many ruminate over several types of philosophies,
Still they can not comprehend even a little of the Lord. —13-133
Many wander away on various pilgrim stations, in delusion,
Some perform *havans* and some perform rituals to please gods,
Some pay consideration to the learning of warfare,
Sill they cannot comprehend the limits of the Lord. —14-134
Somewhere royal discipline is being followed and somewhere the discipline of Yoga,
Many perform the recitation of Smritis and Shastras,

Somewhere Yogic *karmas* including Neoli (purgation of intestines) are being practised and somewhere elephants are being given as gifts,
Somewhere the horse-sacrifices are being performed and their merits are being related. —15-135
Somewhere the Brahmins are holding discussions about theology,
Somewhere the yogic methods are being practised and somewhere the four stages of life are being followed,
Somewhere the Yakshas and Gandharvas sing,
Somewhere the offerings of incense, earthen lamps and libations are made. —16-136
Somewhere *karmas* are performed for the manes and somewhere the Vedic injunctions are followed,
Somewhere the dances are accomplished and somewhere songs are sung,
Somewhere the Shastras and Smritis are recited,
Many pray standing on a single foot. —17-137
Many are attached to their bodies and many reside in their homes,
Many wander in various countries as hermits,
Many live in water and many endure the heat of fire,
Many worship the Lord with face upside down. —18-138
Many practise yoga for various *kalpas* (ages),
Still they cannot know the Lord's end,
Many millions indulge in the study of sciences, still they cannot behold the sight of the Lord. —19-139
Without the power of devotion they cannot realise the Lord,
Though they perform *havans*, hold *yajnas* (sacrifices) and offer charities,
With the single-minded absorption in the Lord's name all the religious rituals are useless. —20-140

TOTAK STANZA   BY THY GRACE

Gather ye together and shout victory to that Lord,
In whose fear tremble the heaven, nether-world and the earth,
For whose realisation all the ascetics of water and land perform austerities,
To whom Indra, Kuber and king Bal hail. —1-141

He is griefless entity indiscriminate and fearless,
He is indivisible, elementless, invincible and indestructible,
He is deathless, patronless, beneficent and self-existent,
Who hath established Sumeru, heaven and earth. —2-142
He is non-divisible, non-stable and mighty *Purusha*,
Who hath created great gods and demons,
Who hath created both earth and sky,
Who hath created all the universe and the objects of the universe. —3-143
He has no affection for any form, sign or face,
He is without any effect of heat and curse and without grief and comfort,
He is without ailment, sorrow, enjoyment and fear,
He is without pain, without contrast, without jealousy, without thirst. —4-144
He is without caste, wthout lineage, without mother and father,
He hast created the Kshatriya warriors under royal canopies on the earth,
He is said to be without affection, without lineage and ailment,
He is considered without blemish, stain and malice. —5-145
He hath created the universe out of the cosmic egg,
He hath created fourteen worlds and nine regions,
He hath created *rajas* (activity), *tamas* (morbidity), light and darkness,
And He Himself manifested His mighty resplendent form. —6-146
He created the ocean, Vindhyachal mountain and Sumeru mountain,
He created Yakshas, Gandharvas, Seshanagas and serpents,
He created the indiscriminate gods, demons and men,
He created kings and the great crawling and dreadful beings. —7-147
He created many worms, moths, serpents and men,
He created many beings of the divisions of creation including *andaja*, *svedaja* and *udbhijja*,
He created the gods, demons, *shradha* (funeral rites) and manes,

His glory is unassailable and His gait is supremely speedy. —8-148

He is without caste and lineage, and as light He is united with all,
He is without father, mother, brother and son,
He is without ailment and sorrow, He is not absorbed in enjoyments,
To him, the Yakshas and Kinnars unitedly meditate. —9-149

He hath created men, women and eunuchs,
He hath created Yakshas, Kinnars, Ganas and serpents,
He hath created elephants, horses, chariots etc., including footmen,
O Lord! Thou hast also created the past, present and future. —10-150

He hath created all the beings of the divisions of creation including *andaja*, *svedaja* and *jeruja*,
He hath created the earth, sky, nether-world and water,
He hath created the powerful elements like fire and air,
He hath created the forest, fruit, flower and bud. —11-151

He hath created the earth, Sumeru mountain and the sky, the earth hath been made the abode for living,
The Muslim fasts and the Ekadashi fast hath been associated with the moon,
The lamps of moon and sun have been created,
And the powerful elements of fire and air have been created. —12-152

He hath created the indivisible sky with sun within it,
He hath created the stars and concealed them within sun's light,
He hath created the fourteen beautiful worlds,
He hath also created Ganas, Gandharvas, gods and demons. —13-153

He is immaculate, elementless with unpolluted intellect,
He is unfathomable, without malady and is active from eternity,
He is without anguish, without difference, and unassailable *Purusha*,
His discus rotates over all the fourteen worlds. —14-154

He is without affection, colour and without any mark,
He is without sorrow, enjoyment and association with Yoga,
He is the destroyer of the earth and the primal creator,
The gods, demons and men all make obeisance to Him. —15-155

He created Ganas, Kinnars, Yakshas and serpents,
He created the gems, rubies, pearls and jewels,
His glory is unassailable and His account is eternal,
No one of perfect wisdom could know His limits. —16-156

He is the invincible entity and His glory is unpunishable,
All the Vedas and Puranas hail Him,
The Vedas and Katebs (Semitic scriptures) call Him infinite,
The gross and subtle both could not know his secret. —17-157

The Vedas, Puranas and Katebs pray to Him,
The son of ocean i.e. Moon, with face upside down performs austerities for His realisation,
He performs austerities for many *kalpas* (ages),
Still the merciful Lord is not realised by him even for a short while. —18-158

Those who forsake all the fake religions,
And meditate on the merciful Lord single-mindedly,
They ferry across this dreadful world-ocean,
And never come again in human body even by mistake. —19-159

Without one Lord's name, one cannot be saved even by millions of fasts,
The superb *Shrutis* (Vedas) declare thus,
Those, who are absorbed with the ambrosia of the name,
Even by mistake, they will not be entrapped in the snare of death. —20-160

NARAAJ STANZA   BY THY GRACE

The primal Lord is eternal, He may be comprehended as the breaker of the unbreakable,
He is ever both gross and subtle, He assails the unassailable,
He is both god and demon, He is the Lord of both covert and overt,
He is the donor of all powers and ever accompanies all. —1-161

AKAL USTAT

He is the patron of patronless and breaker of the unbreakable,
He is the donor of treasure to treasureless and also giver of power,
His form is unique and His glory be considered invincible,
He is the chastiser of powers and is the splendour-incarnate. —2-162
He is without affection, colour and form and without the ailment, attachment and sign,
He is devoid of blemish stain and fraud, He is without element, illusion and guise,
He is without father, mother and caste and He is without lineage, mark and colour,
He is imperceptible, perfect and guiseless and is always the sustainer of the universe. —3-163
He is the creator and master of the universe and especially its sustainer,
Within the earth and the universe, He is always engaged in actions,
He is without malice, without guise, and is known as the accountless master,
He may especially be considered abiding for ever in all the places. —4-164
He is not within *yantras* and *tantras*, He cannot be brought under control through *mantras*,
The Puranas and the *Quran* speak of Him as *neti, neti* (infinite),
He cannot be told within any *karmas*, religions and illusions,
The primal Lord is indestructible, say, how can He be realised? —5-165
Within all the earth and sky, there is only one light,
Which neither decreases nor increases in any being, it never decreases or increases,
It is without decadence and without habit, it is known to have the same form,
In all houses and places its unlimited brilliance is acknowledged. —6-166
He hath no body, no home, no caste and no lineage,
He hath no minister, no friend, no father and no mother,
He hath no limb, no colour, and hath no affection for a companion,
He hath no blemish, no stain, no malice and no body. —7-167
He is neither a lion, nor a jackal, nor a king nor a poor,
He is egoless, deathless, kinless and doubtless,
He is neither a Yaksha, nor a Gandharva, nor a man nor a woman,
He is neither a thief, nor a moneylender nor a prince. —8-168
He is without attachment, without home and without the formation of the body,
He is without deceit, without blemish and without the blend of deceit,
He is neither a *tantra*, nor a *mantra* nor the form of *yantra*,
He is without affection, without colour, without lineage and without form. —9-169
He is niether a *yantra*, nor a *mantra* nor the formation of a *tantra*,
He is without deceit, without blemish and without the blend of ignorance,
He is without affection, without colour, without form and without like,
He is actionless, religionless, girthless and guiseless. —10-170
He is without father, without mother, beyond thought and indivisible entity,
He is invincible and indiscriminate; He is neither a pauper nor a king,
He is in the yond, He is holy, immaculate and ancient,
He is indestructible, invincible, merciful and holy like *Quran*. —11.171
He is non-temporal, patronless, a concept and indivisible,
He is without ailment, without sorrow, without contrast and without slander,
He is limbless, colourless, comradeless and companionless,
He is beloved, sacred, immaculate and the subtle truth. —12-172
He is neither chilly nor sorrowful, nor shade nor sunshine,
He is without greed, without attachment, without anger and without lust,
He is neither god nor demon nor in the form of a human being,
He is neither deceit nor blemish nor the substance of slander. —13-173
He is without lust, anger, greed and attachment,
He is without malice, garb, duality and deception,

He is deathless, childless and always merciful entity,
He is indestructible, invincible, illusionless and elementless. —14-174
He always assails the unassailable, He is the destroyer of the indestructible,
His elementless garb is powerful, He is the original form of sound and colour,
He is without malice, garb, lust, anger and action,
He is without caste, lineage, picture, mark and colour. —15-175
He is limitless, endless and be comprehended as consisting of endless glory,
He is unearthly and unappeasable and be considered as consisting of unassailable glory,
He is without the ailments of body and mind and be known as the Lord of unfathomable form,
He is without blemish and stain and be visualised as consisting of indestructible glory. —16-176
He is beyond the impact of action, illusion and religion,
He is neither *yantra*, nor *tantra* nor blend of *mantra*,
He is neither deceit, nor malice nor a form of slander,
He is indivisible, limbless and treasure of unending equipment. —17-177
He is without the activity of lust, anger, greed and attachment,
He, the unfathomable Lord, is without the concepts of the ailments of the body and mind,
He is without affection for colour and form, He is without the dispute of beauty and line,
He is without gesticulation and charm and any kind of deception. —18-178
Indra and Kuber are always at Thy service,
The Moon, Sun and Varuna ever repeat Thy name,
All the distinctive and great ascetics—including Agastya etc.,
See them reciting the praises of the infinite and limitless Lord. —19-179
The discourse of that profound and primal Lord is without beginning,
He hath no caste, lineage, adviser, friend, enemy and love,
I may always remain absorbed in the beneficent Lord of all the worlds,
That Lord removes immediately all the infinite agonies of the body. —20-180

ROOAAMAL STANZA   BY THY GRACE

He is without form, affection, mark and colour and also without birth and death,
He is the primal master, unfathomable and all-pervading Lord and also adept in pious actions,
He is the Primal and Infinite *Purusha* without any *yantra*, *mantra* and *tantra*,
He abides in both the elephant and the ant, and be considered living at all the places. —1-181
He is without caste, lineage, father, mother adviser and friend,
He is all-pervading, and without mark, sign and picture,
He is the primal Lord, beneficent entity, unfathomable and infinite Lord,
His beginning and end are unknown and He is far away from conflicts. —2-182
His secrets are not known to gods and also the Vedas and Semitic texts,
Sanak, Sanandan etc., the sons of Brahma could not know his secret inspite of their service, and also Yakshas, Kinnars, fishes, men, and many beings and serpents of the nether-world,
The gods Shiva, Indra and Brahma repeat *neti, neti* about him. —3-183
All the beings of the seven nether-worlds down below repeat His name,
He is the primal Lord of unfathomable glory, the beginningless and anguishless entity,
He cannot be overpowered by *yantras* and *mantras*, he never yielded before *tantras* and *mantras*,
That superb sovereign is all-pervading and scans all. —4-184
He is neither in Yakshas, Gandharvas, gods and demons, nor in Brahmins and Kshatriyas,
He is neither in Vaishnavas nor in Shudras,
He is neither in Rajputs, Gaurs and Bhils, nor in Brahmins and Sheikhs,
He is neither within night and day, He, the unique Lord is also not within earth, sky and nether-world. —5-185
He is without caste, birth, death and action and also without the impact of religious rituals,

He is beyond the impact of pilgrimage, worship of deities and the sacrament of creation,
His light pervades in all the beings of the seven nether-worlds down below,
The Sheshanaga with his thousand hoods repeats His names, but still short of his efforts. —6-186

All the gods and demons have grown tired in His search,
The ego of Gandharvas and Kinnars has been shattered by singing his praises continuously,
The great poets have become weary of reading and composing their innumerable epics,
All have ultimately declared that the meditation on the name of the Lord is a very hard task. —7-187

The Vedas have not been able to know His mystery and the Semitic scriptures could nor comprehend His service,
The gods, demons and men are foolish and the Yakshas do not know His glory,
He is the king of past, present and future and primal master of the masterless,
He abides at all the places including fire, air, water and earth. —8-188

He hath no affection for body or love for home, he is invincible and unconquerable Lord,
He is the destroyer and defacer of all and hath no fear from anyone,
He is the creator and destroyer of all, He is without malice and merciful to all,
He is without mark, sign and colour, He is without caste, lineage and guise. —9-189

He is without form, line and colour, and hath no affection for sound and beauty,
He is capable to do everything, he is the destroyer of all and cannot be vanquished by anyone,
He is the donor, knower and sustainer of all,
He is the friend of the poor, He is the beneficent Lord and patronless primal deity. —10-190

He, the adept Lord of *maya*, is the friend of the lowly and creator of all,
He is without colour, mark and sign, he is without mark, sign and form,
He is without caste, lineage and story of descent, he is without form, lineage and colour,
He is the donor and knower of all and the sustainer of all the universe. —11-191

He is the destroyer of the tyrants and vanquisher of the enemies, and the omnipotent Supreme *Purusha*,
He is vanquisher of the tyrants and the creator of the universe and His story is being narrated in the whole world,
He, the invincible Lord, is the same in the past, present and future,
He the Lord of *maya*, the immortal and unassailable Supreme *Purusha*, was there in the beginning and will be there at the end. —12-192

He hath spread all the other religious practices,
He hath created innumerable gods, demons, Gandharvas, Kinnars, fish-incarnations and tortoise-incarnations,
His name is reverently repeated by the beings on earth, in sky, in water and on land,
His works include the decimation of tyrants, giver of strength (to the saints) and support to the world. —13-193

The beloved merciful Lord is the vanquisher of the tyrants and the creator of the universe,
He is the sustainer of the friends and the slayer of the enemies, He, the merciful Lord of the lowly,
He is the punisher of the sinners and destroyer of the tyrants, He is the decimater even of death,
He is the vanquisher of the tyrants, giver of strength (to the saints) and the sustainer of all. —14-194

He is the creator and destroyer of all and the fulfiller of the desires of all,
He is the destroyer and punisher of all and also their personal abode,
He is the enjoyer of all and is united with all, He is also an adept in all *karmas* (actions),
He is the destroyer and punisher of all and keeps all the works under his control. —15-195

He is not within the contemplation of all the Smritis, all the Shastras and all the Vedas,
He, the infinite primal entity is the vanquisher of the tyrants and the sustainer of the universe,
He, the primal indivisible Lord is the punisher of the tyrants and breaker of the ego of the mighty,
The name of that uninstalled Lord is being repeated by the beings of earth, sky, water and land. —16-196

All the pious thoughts of the world know through the medium of knowledge,

They are all within that infinite Primal Lord of *maya*, the destroyer of mighty tyrants,
He is the donor of sustenance, the knower of knowledge and the sovereign revered by all,
He hath created many Vedavyas and millions of Indras and other gods. —17-197

He is the cause of birth and knower of actions and notions of beauteous religious discipline,
But the Vedas, Shiva, Rudra and Brahma could not know His mystery and the secret of His notions,
Millions of Indras and other subordinate gods, Vyas, Sanak and Santkumar,
They and Brahma have got tired of singing his praises in state of astonishment. —18-198

He is devoid of beginning, middle and end and also of past, present and future,
He is supremely pervasive in the four ages of Satyuga, Treta, Dvapara and Kaliyuga,
The great sages have got tired of meditating upon Him and also infinite Gandharvas singing His praises continuously,
All have gone weary and accepted defeat, but none could know His end. —19-199

The sage Narada and others, Vedavyas and others and innumerable great sages,
Practising millions of arduous hardships and meditations all have got tired,
Gandharvas have got tired by singing and countless Apsaras (heavenly damsels) by dancing,
The great gods have got tired in their continuous search, but they could not know His end. —20-200

DOHIRA (COUPLET) BY THY GRACE

Once the soul spoke these words to intellect:
"Describe to me in every way all the glory of the Lord of the world. —1-201

What is the nature of the soul? What is the concept of the world?
What is the object of *dharma*? Tell me all in detail. —2-202

What are birth and death? What are heaven and hell?
What are wisdom and foolishness? what are logical and illogical? —3-203

What are slander and praise? What are sin and rectitude?
What are enjoyment and ecstasy? What are virtue and vice? —4-204

What is called effort? And what should endurance be called?
Who is hero? And who is donor? Tell me what are *tantra* and *mantra*? —5-205

What are the pauper and the king? what are joy and sorrow?
Who is ailing? and who is attached? Tell me their substance. —6-206

Who are hale and hearty? What is the object of the creation of the world?
Who is superb? And who is defiled? Tell me all in detail. —7-207

How an action is recompensed: How an illusion is destroyed?
What are the cravings of the mind? And what is the carefree illumination? —8-208

What are the observance and restraint? What are the knowledge and nescience?
Who is ailing? And who is sorrowful? And where does the downfall of *dharma* occur? —9-209

Who is hero? And who is beautiful? What is the essence of yoga?
Who is the donor? And who is the knower? Tell me the judicious and injudicious." —10-210

DIRAGH TRIBHANGI STANZA BY THY GRACE

Thy nature from the very beginning is to punish the multitudes of vicious people, to destroy the demons and to uproot the tyrants,
Thou hast profound discipline of killing the demon named Chachhyar, of liberating the sinners and saving them from hell,
Thy intellect is incomperhensible, Thou art immortal, indivisible, supremely glorious and unpunishable entity,
Hail, hail, the canopy of the world, the slayer of Mahishasura, wearing the knot of elegant long hair on Thy head. —1-211

O supremely beautiful goddess! the slayer of demons, destroyer of tyrants and chastiser of the mighty,
Punisher of the demon Chand, slayer of the demon

Mund, the killer of Dhumar Lochan and trampler of Mahishasura,
Destroyer of demons, saviour from hell, and liberator of the sinners of upper and nether regions,
Hail, hail, O slayer of Mahishasura, the primal power with elegant knots of long hair on Thy head. —2-212

Thy tabor is played in the battlefield and Thy lion roars and with Thy strength and glory, Thy arms quiver,
Furnished with armour Thy soldiers take strides over the field, Thou art the slayer of armies and the death of the demons,
The eight weapons glisten in Thy hands like ornaments; Thou art gleaming like lightning and hissing like snakes,
Hail, hail, O slayer of Mahishasura, O conquerors of demons with elegant knot of long hair on Thy head. —3-213

Punisher of the demon Chand, slayer of the demon Mund and, breaker into pieces of the unbreakable in the battlefield,
O goddess! Thou flashest like lightning, Thy flags oscillate, Thy serpents hiss, O conqueror of the warriors,
Thou causest the rain of the arrows and makest the tyrants trampled in the battlefield; Thou givest great delight to the Yogini Pusit who drank the blood of Raktavija demon and destroyest the scoundrels,
Hail, hail, O slayer of Mahishasura, pervading the earth, sky and nether-worlds, both above and below. —4-214

Thou laughest like the flash of lightning, Thou abidest in winsome elegance, Thou givest birth to the world, O deity of profound principles,
O pious-natured goddess! Thou art the devourer of the demon Raktavija, enhancer of the zeal for warfare and fearless dancer,
Thou art the drinker of blood, emitter of fire (from the mouth), the conqueror of Yoga and wielder of the sword,
Hail, hail, O slayer of Mahishasura, the destroyer of sin and originator of *dharma*. —5-215
Thou art the effacer of all the sins, the burner of the tyrants, protector of the world and possessor of pure intellect,

The snakes hiss (on Thy neck), Thy vehicle, the lion roars, Thou operatest arms, but art of saintly disposition,
Thou carriest arms like "saihathi" in Thy eight long arms, Thou art true to Thy words and Thy glory is immeasurable,
Hail, hail, O slayer of Mahishasura, pervading in earth, sky, nether-world and water. —6-216

Thou art the brandisher of the sword, vanquisher of the demon Chichhur, carder of Dhumar Lochan like cotton and masher of ego,
Thy teeth are like grains of pomegranate, Thou art the conqueror of the yoga, masher of men and deity of profound principles,
O the goddess of eight long arms! Thou art the destroyer of sinful actions with moonlike light and sunlike glory,
Hail, hail, O slayer of Mahishasura, Thou art the destroyer of illusion and the protection banner of *dharma* (righteousness). —7-217

O goddess of the banner of *dharma*! The bells of Thy anklets clink, Thy arms gleam and Thy serpents hiss,
O deity of loud laughter! Thou abidest in the world, destroyest the tryants and movest in all directions,
Thou hast the lion as Thy vehicle and art clad in pure armour, Thou art unapproachable and unfathomable and the power of one transcendent Lord,
Hail, hail, O slayer of Mahishasura, the primal virgin of inscrutable reflection. —8-218

All the gods, men and sages bow before Thee, O the masher of tyrants, destroyer of the vicious and even the ruinous of death,
O virgin deity of Kamrup! Thou art the liberator of the lowly, protector from death and called the primal entity,
Thou hast a very beautiful ornamental string round Thy waist, Thou hast bewitched gods and men, Thou mountest the lion and also prevadest the nether-world,
Hail, hail, O all pervading deity! Thou art there in air, nether-world sky and fire. —9-219

Thou art the remover of sufferings, liberator of the lowly, supremely, glorious and hast irate disposition,
Thou burnest the sufferings and blemishes, Thou

art the conqueror of fire, Thou art the primal, without beginning, unfathomable and unassailable,
Thou blessest with purity, remover of reasonings, and giver of glory to ascetics engaged in meditation,
Hail, hail, O operator of arms, the primal, stainless, unfathomable and fearless deity! —10-220
Thou hast agile eyes and limbs, Thy hair are like snakes, Thou hast sharp and pointed arrows and Thou art like a nimble mare,
Thou art holding an axe in Thy hand, Thou O long-armed deity! protectest from hell and liberatest the sinners,
Thou gleamest like lightning seated on the back of Thy lion, Thy frightful discourses create a sense of horror,
Hail, hail, O goddess! the slayer of Raktavija demon, ripper of the demon-king Sumbh and masher of the demon-king Nisumbh. —11-221
Thou hast lotus-eyes, Thou art, O wearer of armour! the remover of sufferings, griefs and anxieties,
Thou hast laughter like lightning, and nostrils like parrot; Thou hast superb conduct, and beautiful dress; Thou seizest the tyrants,
Thou hast a winsome body like lightning, Thou art associated thematically with Vedas, O demon-destroying deity! Thou hast very swift horses to ride upon,
Hail, hail, O slayer of Mahishasura, the primal, beginningless, unfathomable, the uppermost deity. —12-222
Listening to the tune of the harmonious resounding of the bell (in Thy camp), all the fears and illusions vanish away,
The nightingale, listening to the tune, feels inferior; the sins are effaced and joy wells up in the heart,
The forces of the enemies are scorched, their minds and bodies experience great suffering; when Thou showest Thy anger, in the battlefield, the forces cannot even run out of fear,
Hail, hail, O slayer of Mahishasura, masher of the demon Chand and worshipped from the very beginning. —13-223
Thou hast superb arms and armour including sword, Thou art the final enemy of tyrants, O deity of frightful temperament, Thou stoppest only in great anger,
Thou art the destroyer of the demon Dhumar Lochan, Thou causest the final destruction and the devastation of the world, Thou art the deity of pure intellect,
Thou art the conqueror of Jalpa, the masher of enemies and thrower of tyrants in blaze, O deity of profound intellect,
Hail, hail, O slayer of Mahishasura, Thou art the primal and from the beginning of the ages, Thy discipline is unfathomable. —14-224
O destroyer of Kshatriyas! Thou art fearless, unassailable, primal, bodyless, the deity of unfathomable glory,
Thou art the primal power, the killer of the demon Bridal and punisher of the demon Chichhar, and intensely glorious,
Thou art the sustainer of gods and men, saviour of sinners, vanquisher of tyrants and destroyer of blemishes,
Hail, hail, O slayer of Mahishasura, Thou art the destroyer of the universe and creator of the world. —15-225
Thou art lustrous like lightning, destroyer of the bodies (of demons), O deity of immeasurable strength! Thy light pervades,
Thou art the masher of the forces of demons, with the rain of sharp arrows, Thou causest the tyrants to swoon and pervadest also in the nether-world,
Thou operatest all Thy eight weapons, Thou art true to Thy words, Thou art the support of the saints and hast profound discipline,
Hail, hail, O slayer of Mahishasura, the primal, beginningless deity! Thou art of unfathomable disposition. —16-226
Thou art the consumer of sufferings and blemishes, protector of Thy servants, giver of Thy glimpse to Thy saints, Thy shafts are very sharp,
Thou art the wearer of sword and armour, Thou causest the tyrants to blaze and treadest on the forces of the enemies, Thou removest the blemishes,
Thou art worshipped by saints from beginning to end, Thou destroyest the egoists and hast immeasurable authority,

Hail, hail, O slayer of Mahishasura, Thou manifestest Thyself to Thy saints and killest the tyrants. —17-227

Thou art the cause of all causes, Thou art the chastiser of the egoists, Thou art the light-incarnate having sharp intellect,

All of Thy eight weapons gleam, when they wink, they glisten like lightning, O primal power!,

Thy tambourine is being struck, Thy lion is roarling, Thy arms are quivering, O the deity of pure discipline!

Hail, hail, O slayer of Mahishasura, O Intellect-incarnate deity from the very beginning, beginning of the ages and even without any beginning. —18-228

Thou art the killer of the demon Chichhar, O unique warrior, Thou art the protector from hell and the liberator of the sinners,

Thou art the destroyer of the sins, punisher of the tyrants, breaker of the unbreakable and even the chopper of death,

Thy face is more winsome than moon, Thou art the protector from hell and liberator of the sinners, O the masher of the demon Mund,

Hail, hail, O slayer of Mahishasura, O destroyer of Dhumar Lochan, Thou hast been described as the primal deity. —19-229

O slayer of the demon Raktavija, O the masher of the demon Chand, O the destroyer of the demons and the killer of the demon Bridal,

Thou causest the rain of shafts and also makest the vicious people to swoon, Thou art the deity of immeasurable ire and protector of the banner of *dharma*,

O destroyer of the demon Dhumar Lochan, O the blood-drinker of Raktavija, O the killer and masher of the demon-king Nisumbh,

Hail, hail, O slayer of Mahishasura, described as primal, stainless and unfathomable. —20-230

PAADHARI STANZA   BY THY GRACE

I relate to Thee all the thoughts, O Gurudeva! (or O Gurudeva! Tell me all the musings) how the creator created the expanse of the world?

Although the Lord is elementless, fearless and infinite, then how did he extend the texture of this world? —1-231

He is the doer, beneficent, mighty and merciful. He is non-dual, non-elemental, fearless and benign. He is the donor, endless and devoid of sufferings and blemishes. All the Vedas call Him *neti*, *neti* (not this, not this—infinite). —2-232

He hath created many beings in upper and lower regions, His glory is spread in all places here and there. All the beings and creatures know Him. O foolish mind! Why dost thou not remember Him? —3-233

Many fools worship the leaves (of *tulsi* plant). Many adepts and saints adore the Sun, many prostrate towards the west (opposite side of sunrise). They consider the Lord as dual, who is actually one. —4-234

His glory is unassailable and His illumination is devoid of fear.

He is infinite donor, non-dual and indestructible. He is an entity devoid of all ailments and sorrows. He is fearless, immortal and invincible entity. —5-235

He is treasure of sympathy and perfectly merciful, He, the donor and merciful Lord removes all sufferings and blemishes. He is without the impact of *maya* and is an infrangible Lord. His glory pervades in water and on land and is the companion of all. —6-236

He is without caste, lineage, contrast and illusion. He is without colour, form and special religious discipline. For Him the enemies and friends are the same. His invincible form is everlasting and infinite. —7-237

His form and mark cannot be known. Where doth He live? And what is His garb? What is His name? and what is His caste? He is without any enemy, friend, son and brother. —8-238

He is the treasure of mercy and the cause of all causes. He hath no mark, sign, colour and form. He is without suffering, contrast, action and death. He is the sustainer of all the beings and creatures. —9-239

He is the loftiest, biggest and perfect entity. His intellect is boundless and is unique in warfare. He is without form, line, colour and affection. His glory is unassailable, unappeasable and stainless. —10-240

He is the king of waters and lands, He, the infinite

Lord pervades the forests and the blades of grass. He is called *neti, neti* (not this, not this—infinite) night and day. His limits cannot be known. He, the generous Lord, burns the blemishes of the lowly. —11-241

Millions of Indras are at His service. Millions of the Yogi Rudras (Shivas) stand at His gate.

Many Vedavyas and innumerable Brahmas utter the words *neti, neti* about Him, night and day. —12-242

SWAYYAS   BY THY GRACE

He always sustains the lowly, protects the saints and destroys the enemies,

At all times He sustains all, animals, birds, mountains (or trees), serpents and men (kings of men),

He sustains in an instant all the beings living in water and on land and doth not ponder over their actions,

The merciful Lord of the lowly and the treasure of mercy sees their blemishes, but doth not fail in His bounty. —1-243

He burns the sufferings and blemishes and in an instant mashes the forces of the vicious people,

He even destroys them who are mighty and glorious and assail the unassailable and responds the devotion of perfect love,

Even Vishnu cannot know His end, the Vedas and Katebs (Semitic scriptures) call Him indiscriminate,

The Provider-Lord always sees our secrets, even then in anger He doth not stop His munificence. —2-244

He created in the past, creates in the present and shall create in the future the beings including insects, moths, deer and snakes,

The gods and demons have been consumed in ego, but could not know the mystery of the Lord, being engrossed in delusion,

The Vedas, Puranas, Katebs and the *Quran* have tired of giving His account, but the Lord could not be comprehended,

Without the impact of perfect love, who hath realised Lord-God with grace? —3-245

The primal, infinite, unfathomable Lord is without malice and is fearless in the past, present and future,

He is endless, Himself selfless, stainless, blemishless, flawless and invincible,

He is the creator and destroyer of all in water and on land and also their sustainer—Lord,

He, the Lord of *maya*, is compassionate to the lowly, source of mercy and most beautiful. —4-246

He is without lust, anger, greed, attachment, ailment, sorrow, enjoyment and fear,

He is bodyless, loving everybody but without worldly attachment, invincible and cannot be held in grasp,

He provides sustenance to all animate and inanimate beings and all those living on the earth and in the sky,

Why dost thou waver, O creature! The beautiful Lord of *maya* will take care of Thee. —5-247

He protects in many ways from the diseases, sorrows and water-spirits,

The enemy strikes many blows, but none doth inflict Thy body,

When the Lord protects with his own hands, none of the sins even come near Thee,

What else should I say unto you, He protects (the infant) even in the membranes of the womb. —6-248

The Yakshas, serpents, demons and gods meditate on Thee considering Thee as indiscriminate,

All the beings of the earth, Yakshas of the sky and the serpents of the nether-world bow their heads before Thee,

None could comprehend the limits of Thy glory and even the Vedas declare Thee as *neti, neti*,

All the searchers have got tired in their search and none of them could realise the Lord. —7-249

Narada, Brahma and the sage Rumna all have together sung Thy praises,

The Vedas and Ketebs could not know His secret; all have got tired, but the Lord could not be realised,

Shiva also could not know His limits; the adepts (Siddhas) alongwith Naths and Sanak etc., meditated upon Him,

Concentrate upon Him in Thy mind, whose unlimited glory is spread all the world. —8-250

The Vedas, Puranas, Katebs and the *Quran* and kings—all are tired and greatly afflicted by not knowing the Lord's mystery,

They could not comprehend the mystery of the indiscriminate Lord, Being greatly aggrieved, they recite the name of the unassailable Lord,

The Lord who is without affection, form, mark, colour, relative and sorrow, abides with Thee,

Those who have remembered that primal, beginningless, guiseless and blemishless Lord, they have ferried across their whole clan. —9-251

Having taken bath at millions of pilgrim stations, having given many gifts in charity and having observed important fasts,

Having wandered in the garb of an ascetic in many countries and having worn matted hair, the beloved Lord could not be realised,

Adopting millions of postures and observing the eight steps of Yoga, touching the limbs while reciting the *mantras* and blackening the face,

But without the remembrance of the Nontemporal and merciful Lord of the lowly, one will ultimately go to the abode of Yama. —10-252

KABITS   BY THY GRACE

He operates the weapons, beguiles the sovereign of the earth having canopies over their heads and mashes the mighty enemies,

He is the donor of gifts, He causes to enhance the great honour, He is the giver of encouragement for greater effort and is the cutter of the snare of death,

He is the conqueror of war and, effacer of the opposition, He is giver of great intellect and the honour of the illustrious,

He is the knower of the knowledge, the giver-god of the supreme intellect; He is the death of death and also the death of the supreme death (Maha Kal). —1-253

The inhabitants of the east could not know Thy end, the people of Hingala and Himalaya mountains remember Thee, the resident of Gor and Gardez sing the praises of Thy name,

The Yogis perform Yoga, many are absorbed in doing Pranayama and residents of Arabia remember Thy name,

The people of France and England revere the inhabitants of Kandhahar and Quraishis know Thee: the people of the western side recognise their duty towards Thee,

The inhabitants of Maharashtra and Magadha perform austerities with profound affection; the residents of Darawar and Tilang countries recognise Thee as the abode of *dharma*. —2-254

The Bengalis of Bengal, the Farangis of Farangistan and Dilwalis of Delhi are the followers of Thy command,

The Rohelas of Rohu mountain, the Maghelas of Magadha, the heroic Bangasis of Bangas and the Bundhelas of Bundhelkhand destroy their sins in Thy devotion,

Gurkhas sing Thy praises, the residents of China and Manchuria bow their heads before Thee and the Tibetans destroy the sufferings of their bodies by remembering Thee,

Those who meditated on Thee, they obtained perfect glory, they prosper greatly with wealth, fruit and flowers in their homes. —3-255

Thou art called Indra among gods, Shiva among the donors and also garbless, though thou wearest the Ganges,

Thou art the brightness in colour, adept in sound and beauty, and not bow before anybody, but obedient to the saint,

None can know Thy limit, O infinitely glorious Lord! Thou art the giver of all learning, therefore Thou art called boundless,

The prayer of an elephant reaches Thee after some time, but the trumpet of an ant is heard by Thee before it. —4-256

There are many Indras, many four-headed Brahmas, many incarnations of Krishna and many called Ram at His gate,

There are many moons, many signs of Zodiac and many illuminating suns, there are many ascetics, stoics and Yogis consuming, there bodies with austerity at His gate,

There are many Muhammads, many adepts like Vyas, many Kumars (Kubers) and many belonging to high clans and many are called Yakshas,

All of them reflect upon Him, but none can know

His limits, therefore they consider the infinite Lord supportless. —5-257

He is perfect entity, supportless and without limits, His end is unknown, therefore He is described as infinite,

He is non-dual, immortal, supreme, perfectly lustrous, treasure of supreme beauty and deemed eternal,

He is without *yantra* (mystical diagram) and caste, without father and mother and presumed as the splash of perfect beauty,

It cannot be said whether He is the abode of splendour or political mechanism or the incantation of an enchantress or the inspiration of all of them. —6-258

Is He the tree of splendour? Is He the tank of activities? Is He the abode of purity? Is He the essence of powers?

Is He the treasure of the fulfilment of desires? Is He the glory of discipline? Is He the dignity of asceticism? Is He the master of generous intellect?

Doth He contain beautiful form? Is He the king of kings? Is He the beauty of beauty? Is He the destroyer of bad intellect?

Is He the donor of the poor? Is He the perisher of the enemies? Is He the protector of the saints? Is He the mountain of qualities? —7-259

He is the salvation-incarnate, He is the wealth of intellect, He is the destroyer of anger. He is unassailable and eternal,

He is the doer of errand and the giver of qualities; He is the perisher of enemies and igniter of fire,

He is the death of death and smasher of enemies; He is the protector of friends and subduer of excellence,

He is the mystical diagram of gaining control over Yoga, He is the mystical formula of overpowering glory; He is the incantation of bewitching the enchantress and perfect enlightener. —8-260

He is the abode of beauty and enlightener of intellect; He is the home of salvation and the dwelling of intelligence,

He is the god of gods and the indiscriminate transcendent Lord; He is the deity of the demons and the tank of purity,

He is the saviour of life and giver of faith; He is the chopper of the god of death and the fulfiller of desires,

He is the intensifier of glory and breaker of the unbreakable; He is the establisher of kings, but Himself He is neither male nor female. —9-261

He is the sustainer of the universe and remover of the trouble; He is the giver of comfort and igniter of the fire,

His limits and bounds cannot be known; If we reflect on Him, He is the abode of all thoughts,

The beings of Hingala and Himalaya sing His praises; the people of Habash country and Halab city meditate on Him. The residents of the East do not know His end and losing all hope they have become disappointed,

He is the God of gods and God of supreme gods, He is transcendent, indiscriminate, non-dual and immortal Lord. —10-262

He is without the impact of *maya*, He is adept and transcendent Lord, He is obedient to his servant and is the chopper of the snare of Yama (god of death),

He is the God of gods and the Lord God of the supreme gods, He is enjoyer of the earth and the provider of the great power,

He is the king of kings and the Decoration of the supreme decoration, He is the supreme Yogi of the Yogis wearing the bark of trees,

He is the fulfiller of desire and remover of vicious intellect; He is the comrade of perfection and the destroyer of bad conduct. —11-263

Awadh is like milk and the town of Chhatraner is like buttermilk; the banks of Yamuna are beautiful like the brilliance of the moon,

The country of Ram is like the beautiful *hansani* (damsel), the town of Husainabad is like a diamond; the winsome current of the Ganges makes the seven seas diffident,

Palayugarh is like mercury and Rampur is like silver; Surangabad is like nitre (swinging elegantly),

Kot Chanderi is like *champa* flower (*Michelia champacca*), Chandagarh is like moonlight; but Thy glory, O Lord! is like the beautiful flower of *malti* (a creeper). —12-264

The places like Kailasa, Kumaoun and Kashipur are clear like crystal and Surangabad looks graceful like glass,

Himalaya bewitches the mind with whiteness of snow, Halbaner like milkyway and Hajipur like swan,
Champawati looks like sandalwood, Chandragiri moon and Chandagarh town like moonlight, Gangdhar (Gandhar) seems like the Ganges and Bulandabad like a crane; all of them are the symbols of the splendour of Thy praise. —13-265

The Persians and the residents of Firangistan and France, people of two different colours and the Mridangis (inhabitants) of Makran sing the songs of Thy praise,
The people of Bhakkar, Kandhahar, Gakkhar and Arabia and others living only on air remember Thy name,
At all the places including Palayu in the East, Kamrup and Kumaoun, wherever we go, Thou art there,
Thou art perfectly glorious, without any impact of *yantras* and *mantras*, O Lord! the limits of Thy praise cannot be known. —14-266

PAADHARI STANZA   BY THY GRACE

He is non-dual, indestructible, and hath steady seat,
He is non-dual, endless and of immeasurable (unweighable) praise,
He is unassailable entity and unmanifested Lord,
He is the motivator of gods and destroyer of all.
—1-267

He is the sovereign here, there, everywhere, He blossoms in forests and blades of grass,
Like the splendour of the spring He is scattered here and there,
He, the infinite and supreme Lord is within the forest, blade of grass, bird and deer,
He blossoms here, there and everywhere, the beautiful and all-knowing. —2-268

The peacocks are delighted to see the blossoming flowers,
With bowed heads they are accepting the impact of Cupid,
O sustainer and merciful Lord! Thy nature is marvellous,
O the treasure of mercy, perfect and gracious Lord! —3-269

Wherever I see, I feel Thy touch there,
O motivator of gods, Thy unlimited glory is bewitching the mind,
Thou art devoid of anger, O treasure of mercy!
Thou blossomest here, there and everywhere, O beautiful and all-knowing Lord!. —4-270

Thou art the king of forests and blades of grass, O supreme Lord of waters and land!
O the treasure of mercy, I feel Thy touch everywhere,
Thy light is glittering, O perfectly glorious Lord!
The heaven and earth are repeating Thy name.
—5-271

In all the seven heavens and seven nether-worlds His net of *karmas* (actions) is invisibly spread.

The Eulogy is complete.

THE LORD IS ONE AND VICTORY IS OF THE LORD
NOW BEGIN THE EXTRAORDINARY FEATS FROM THE LIFE OF CHANDI

ATH CHANDI CHARITRA UKATI BILAS

SWAYYA

The Lord is primal, infinite, accountless, boundless, deathless, garbless, incompre-hensible and eternal,
He created Shiva-Shakti, four Vedas and three modes of *maya* and pervades in three worlds,
He created day and night, the lamps of Sun and Moon and the whole world with five elements,
He extended enmity and fight between the gods and demons and Himself seated (on His throne) scans it. —1

DOHIRA

O ocean of mercy! if Thy grace is bestowed upon me, I may compose the story of Chandika and my poetry be all good. —2
Thy light is shining in the world, O powerful Chand-Chamunda,
Thou art the punisher of the demons with Thy strong arms and art the creator of the nine regions. —3

SWAYYA

Thou art the same Chandika, who ferries across the people, Thou art the redeemer of the earth and destroyer of the demons,
Thou art the cause of the Shakti of Shiva, Lakshmi of Vishnu and Parvati, the daughter of Himavan, wherever we see. Thou art there,
Thou art Tamas, the quality of morbidity, mineness and modesty, Thou art poetry, latent in the mind of the poet,
Thou art the philosopher's stone in the world, which transforms the iron into gold that it touches. —4

DOHIRA

She whose name is Chandika delights and removes fear of all, illumine me with good intellect, so that I may compose Thy wonderful deeds. —5

PARHA

If I am permitted now, I shall compose my *Granth* (book),
I shall find and set the delight-giving gem-like words,
In this composition, I shall use the beautiful language,
And whatever I have thought in my mind, I shall narrate that wonderful story. —6

SWAYYA

Dejected on account of the tragic happening in the family he deserted his home and came to live in the forest,
His name was Surath and adopting the garb of sages, he engaged himself in contemplation,
The goddess Chandika of perfect brilliance is there before. She is the destroyer of demons and protector of gods,
The sage Surath told his companion sage, "O hermit, try to comprehend now, what this marvellous story it is?" —7

TOTAK STANZA

The great sage said:
The Lord was sleeping on an adorned bed,
Within the terrible and vast expanse of water,
From His navel-lotus Brahma was born,
With some device, the demons were created from the dross of His ear. —8

They were named as Madhu and Kaitabh,
Their bodies were enormously great,
Seeing them, Brahma became fearful,
He contemplated in his mind on the universal mother. —9

DOHIRA

When the Lord Vishnu awoke from sleep, he made preparations for war,
So that the demons may decrease in number and the rule of gods be increased. —10

SWAYYA

The Lord waged the war against the demons, but He could not kill them because they were very brave,
It took five thousand years in fighting, but they were not tired,
Having been pleased with the power of the Lord the demons asked the Lord to request for a boon; the Lord asked them to surrender their bodies,
Putting them in his lap, the Lord cut their heads and assimilated their strength within Himself. —11

SORATHA

The Lord established rule of gods after killing Madhu and Kaitabh,
He gave all the paraphernalia to them and Himself went to heaven. —12

End of the first chapter of the killing of "Madhu and Kaitabh" as described in Ath Chandi Charitra Ukati Bilas of *Markandeya Purana*.

PARHA

Then there appeared Mahishasura and whatever he did is as follows:
With his armed strength, he conquered the whole world,
He challenged all the gods in the battlefield,
And with his weapons he chopped them all. —13

SWAYYA

The demon-king Mahishasura waged the war and killed all the forces of gods,
He cut the mighty warriors into halves and threw them in the field, he waged such a terrible and fierce war,
Seeing him besmeared with the blood, it seems thus in the mind of the poet,
As if killing the Kshatriyas, Parashuram has bathed himself in their blood. —14

SWAYYA

With his arms and weapons, Mahishasura sawed and threw the warriors as in a saw,
The corpse fell on the corpse and the big horses have fallen in flocks like mountains,
The black elephants have fallen in the field alongwith white fat and red blood,
They all are lying dead as if the tailor, cutting the clothes makes their heaps. —15

SWAYYA

Indra taking all the gods with him, invaded the forces of the enemy,
Covering the face with shield and holding the sword in hand, they attacked with loud shouts,
The demons are dyed with blood and it seems to the poet,
As if Rama after conquering the war is bestowing (the red-coloured) robes of honour to all bears. —16

SWAYYA

Many wounded warriors are rolling in the battlefield and many of them are writhing and crying on the ground,
The trunks are also twirling there, seeing which the cowards are frightened,
Mahishasura waged such a war that the jackals and vultures are highly pleased,
And the heroes being intoxicated are lying prostrate in the stream of blood. —17

SWAYYA

Seeing the fighting in the war of the demon Mahishasura, the sun is not-moving on its orbit,
Brahma has also forgotten his texts on beholding the stream of blood,
Seeing the flesh, the vultures are seated in such a way, as if the children are learning their lessons in school,
The jackals are pulling the corpses in the field in such a way as the Yogis, sitting on the banks of Saraswati are mending their patched quilts. —18

DOHIRA

Innumerable gods were killed and innumerable ran away in fear,
All (the remaining) gods meditating on Shiva went towards Kailasa mountain. —19

DOHIRA

The demons seized all the abodes and wealth of gods,
They drove them out of the city of gods; the gods then came to live in the city of Shiva. —20

DOHIRA

After several days the goddess came to take a bath,
All the gods, according to the prescribed method, made obeisance to her. —21

REKHATA

The gods told the goddess all their occurrences, stating the demon-king Mahishasura had seized all their abode,
They said, "O mother! Thou mayst do whatever pleasest Thee, we have all come to seek Thy refuge,
"Please get us back our abodes, remove our sufferings and make those demons garbless and wealthless; This is a very great task which can only be accomplished by Thee.
"No one beats or talks ill to the dog, only his master is rebuked and censured." —22

DOHIRA

Hearing these words, Chandika was filled with great rage in her mind,
She said, "I shall destroy all the demons, go and abide in the city of Shiva." —23

When the idea of destroying the demons was given by Chandi,
The lion, conch and all other weapons and arms came themselves to her. —24

It seemed that death itself had taken the birth to destroy the demons,
The lion, who causes great suffering to the enemies, became the vehicle of the goddess Chandi. —25

SWAYYA

The terrible form of the lion is like an elephant, he is mighty like a big lion,
The hair of the lion are like arrows and appear as trees growing on a yellow mountain,
The back-line of the lion looks like the current of Yamuna on the mountain, and the black hair on his body appear like the black bees on the flower of *ketki*,
Various sinewy limbs seem like the action of king Prithu of segregating the mountains from the earth by raising his bow and shooting with all his might. —26

DOHIRA

The gong, mace, trident, sword, conch, bow and arrows,
Alongwith the terrible disc—the goddess took all these weapons in her hands; they have created the atmosphere like summer's sun. —27

In fierce rage, Chandika took the weapons in her hands,
And near the city of demons, raised the horrible sound of her gong. —28

DOHIRA

Hearing the loud voice of the gong and the lion holding their swords entered the battlefield,
They came furiously in great numbers and began to wage the war. —29

Forty-five *padam* army of the demons adorned with their four divisions,
Some on the left and some on the right and some warriors with the king. —30

All the army of forty-five *padam* was divided into ten, fifteen and twenty,
Fifteen on the right, ten on the left, followed by twenty. —31

SWAYYA

All those black demons ran and stood before Chandika,
Taking arrows with extended bows, many enemies in great fury attack the lion,
Protecting Herself from all attacks and challenging all the enemies dispelled them,
Just as Arjuna had dispelled the clouds, which came to protect the Khandav forest being burnt by fire. —32

DOHIRA

One of the demons went on a galloping horse with rage before the goddess like the moth before the lamp. —33

SWAYYA

That mighty chieftain of the demons took out his sword from the sheath in great ire,

He gave one blow to Chandi and the second on the head of the lion,
Chandi protecting Herself from all the blows caught hold of the demon in Her mighty arms and threw him on the ground,
Just as the washerman beats the clothes in washing against a wooden plank on the bank of the stream. —34

DOHIRA

In this way, the goddess killed the demon, who came and fought before her,
Then she penetrated into the army of the enemies by blowing her conch. —35

SWAYYA

The mighty Chandika, taking the bow in her hand, in great rage, did this,
She scanned once all the army of the enemy and with terrible shout destroyed it,
Seeing a large number of chopped and bleeding demons, the poet feel in his mind,
That Garuda had chopped the snakes into bits and thrown them helter-skelter. —36

DOHIRA

The goddess killed many demons and made the strong ones weak,
Holding the weapons in her hands, she made the forces of the enemy run away. —37
The army of Mahishasura ran away and sought the shelter of its king,
It told him after running that twenty *padam* of the forces had been killed. —38
Hearing this, the foolish Mahishasura was highly enraged,
He ordered that the goddess be besieged. —39

SWAYYA

Listening to the words of their king, all the warriors together took this decision,
That with firm determination in the mind, the goddess be attacked from all the four directions,
With swords in their hands and uttering loud shouts of "kill, kill" the army of demons swarmed from all directions,
They all besieged Chandi from all the four sides, like the moon encircled amongst clouds. —40

SWAYYA

Scanning the army of Mahishasura, Chandika caught hold of her fierce bow,
With anger, She waged the terrible war by showering the rain of her innumerable shafts,
By chopping the forces of the enemy, such a great quantity of blood fell on the ground,
As though the Lord God hath created the eighth ocean alongwith already created seven oceans. —41

DOHIRA

Chandi in great anger, holding up her disc, within the enemy's army,
She cut off the warriors into halves and quarters. —42

SWAYYA

Such a terrible war was waged that the profound contemplation of Shiva was infringed,
Chandi then held up her mace and raised a violent sound by blowing her conch,
The disc fell on the heads of the enemies; that disc went in such a way with the might of her hand, that it seemed that the children were throwing the potsherd so as to swim on the surface of the water. —43

DOHIRA

Scanning the forces of Mahishasura the goddess pulling up Her strength,
She destroyed all killing some through her lion and some with her disc. —44
One of the demons ran to the king and told him about the destruction of all the army,
Hearing this, Mahishasura became furious and marched towards the battlefield. —45

SWAYYA

Knowing about the destruction of all his forces in the war Mahishasura held up his sword,
And going before the fierce Chandi, he began to roar like a dreadful bear,
Taking his heavy mace in his hand, he threw it on the body of the goddess like an arrow,
It seemed that Hanuman carrying a hillock, threw it on the chest of Ravana. —46
Then he held up bows and arrows in his hands,

killed the warriors who could not ask for water before dying,

The wounded warriors were moving in the field like lame elephants,

The bodies of the warriors alongwith their armours were lying fried up on the ground,

As if the forest is on fire and the snakes are running to feed themselves on the fast moving worms. —47

SWAYYA

Chandi in great ire penetrated into the war-arena with her lion,

Holding her sword in her hand, she dyed the battlefield in red as if the forest is on fire,

When the demons besieged the goddess from all the four sides, the poet felt like this in his mind,

That the body of the mother of the world moved swifter than her mind, she appeared as lightning moving in the clouds. —48

When the goddess held her sword in her hand all the army of the demons cracked,

The demons were also very powerful, they did not die and instead were fighting in transformed forms,

Chandi segregated the heads of the enemies by throwing her disc with her hands,

Consequently, the current of blood flowed as if Rama was offering water to the Sun. —49

SWAYYA

When that mighty goddess killed all the chivalrous demons with her power,

Then so much mass of blood fell on the earth that it become a sea of blood,

The mother of the world, with her power, removed the suffering of gods and the demons went to the abode of Yama,

Then, the goddess Durga glistened like lightning amongst the army of elephants. —50

DOHIRA

When Mahishasura, the king of all demons, was killed,

Then all the cowards ran away leaving behind all paraphernalia. —51

KABIT

Supremely heroic goddess, with the magnificence of the Sun at noon killed the demon-king for the well-being of gods,

The remaining demon-army ran helter-skelter in such a way as the clouds speed away before the wind; the goddess with her prowess bestowed the kingdom on Indra,

She caused sovereigns of many countries to bow in obeisance to Indra and his coronation ceremony was thoughtfully performed by the assembly of gods,

In this way, the goddess disappeared from here and manifested herself there, where the god Shiva was seated on the lion-skin. —52

End of the second chapter entitled "The Killing of Mahishasura" as recorded in Ath Chandi Charitra Ukati Bilas of *Markandeya Purana*.

DOHIRA

In this way Chandika disappeared after bestowing the kingship on Indra,

She killed the demons and destroyed them for the well-being of the saints. —53

SWAYYA

The great sages became pleased and received comfort in meditating on the gods,

The sacrifices are being performed, the Vedas are being recited and for the removal of suffering, contemplation is being done together,

The tunes of various musical instruments like cymbals, big and small trumpet, kettledrum and *rabab* area being made harmonious,

Somewhere the Kinnars and Gandharvas are singing and somewhere the Ganas, Yakshas and Apsaras are dancing. —54

With the sound of conches and gongs, they are causing the rain of flowers,

Millions of gods fully decorated are performing *arati* (circumambulation) and seeing Indra, they show intense devotion,

Giving gifts and performing circumambulation around Indra, they are applying the frontal-mark of saffron and rice on their foreheads,

In all the city of gods, there is much excitement and the families of gods are singing songs of felicitations. —55

DOHIRA

In this way through the glory of Chandi, the splendour of gods increased,

ATH CHANDI CHARITRA UKATI BILAS

All the three worlds are rejoicing and the sound of the recitation of true name is being heard. —56

The gods ruled comfortably like this,

But after some time, two mighty demons named Sumbh and Nisumbh appeared. —57

For conquering the kingdom of Indra, the king Sumbh came forward,

With his four types of army containing soldiers on foot, in chariots and on elephants. —58

SWAYYA

Hearing the sound of the war-trumpets and getting dubious in mind, Indra closed the portals of his citadal,

Considering the hesitation of the warriors to come forward for fight all the demons gathered together at one place,

Seeing their gathering the oceans trembled and the movement of the earth changed with heavy burden,

Seeing the forces of Sumbh and Nisumbh running, Sumeru mountain moved and the world of gods became agitated. —59

DOHIRA

All the gods then went running to Indra,

They asked him to take some steps because of the conquest of powerful demons. —60

Hearing this, the king of gods got furious and began to take steps for waging war,

He called also all the remaining gods. —61

SWAYYA

The Lord of the world in order to lighten the burden of the earth brought about this war,

The intoxicated elephants began to trumpet like the clouds and their tusks appeared like the queues of cranes,

Wearing their armour and holding daggers in their hands, the warriors seemed like the lustre of lightning,

The forces of the demons were gushing out on the inimical gods like the dark clouds. —62

DOHIRA

All the demons gathered together and prepared for the war,

They went to the city of gods and besieged Indra, the king of gods. —63

SWAYYA

Opening all the gates and portals of the citadel, the army of Indra, the enemy of demons, marched outside,

All of them assembled in the battlefield and the army of the enemy, seeing the army of Indra, trembled like a leaf,

The elephants and horses tall like trees and the warriors on foot and on chariots moved like fruit, flowers and bud,

In order to destroy the clouds-like forces of Sumbh, Indra came forward like mighty wind-god. —64

Indra came forward in great rage from this side and from the other side Sumbh marched forward for war,

There are bows, arrows, swords, maces etc., in the hands of the warriors and they are wearing armour on their bodies,

Undoubtedly horrible slayings began from both sides,

The jackals and vultures began to pour into the battlefield on hearing the terrible sounds and the joy increased amongst the Ganas of Shiva. —65

On this side, Indra is getting very furious and on the other side, all the army of the demons hath assembled,

The army of demons appears like the sun-chariot of the Lord encircled by the dark thundering clouds,

The sharp edges of thy arrows shot from the bow of Indra, piercing the hearts of the enemies glisten,

Like the beaks of the young ones of storks spread in the caves of the mountains. —66

Seeing the king Sumbh pierced by the arrows, the demon-forces jumped into the battlefield, drawing out their swords,

They slayed many enemies in the field and in this way good deal of the blood of gods flowed,

Various types of ganas, jackals, vultures, ghosts etc., appearing in the battlefield, produced various sounds in such a way,

As though the warriors, at the time of taking bath in Saraswati river are removing various types of their sins. —67

Nisumbh then waged such a terrible war as none of the demons had waged earlier,

The corpses are amassed on corpses and their flesh is being eaten by jackals and vultures,
The white current of fat coming out of the heads is falling on the ground in this way,
As if the current of Ganges hath gushed out of the hair of Shiva. —68
The hair of the heads are floating on water like scum and the canopies of the kings like froth,
The fingers of hands are writhings like fish and the chopped arms seem like serpents,
Within the blood the horses, chariots and wheels of chariots are rotating as in whirlpool of water,
Sumbh and Nisumbh waged such a furious war together which hath caused the flow of the stream of blood in the field. —69

DOHIRA

The gods were defeated and the demons were victorious who captured all the paraphernalia,
With the help of very powerful army, they caused the flight of Indra. —70

SWAYYA

The demons seized away the wealth from Kuber and the necklace of jewels from Seshanaga,
They conquered Brahma, Sun, Moon, Ganesh Varuna etc., and caused them to run away,
They established their own kingdom after conquering all the three worlds,
All the demons went to abide in the cities of gods and proclamations were made in the names of Sumbh and Nisumbh. —71

DOHIRA

The demons conquered the war and the gods ran away,
The gods then ruminated in their mind that Shiva be propitiated for re-establishment of their rule. —72

SWAYYA

Indra, the king of gods Sun and Moon all went to abide in the city of Shiva,
They were in bad shape and because of the fear of war, the hair on their heads became matted and enlarged,
They had not been able to control themselves and in straitened circumstances, they appeared to be seized by death,
They seemed to be repeatedly calling for help and in great suffering lay concealed in caves. —73
When the most powerful Chandika heard the cries of gods with her own ears, she avowed to kill all the demons,
The mighty goddess manifested Herself and in great rage, she engrossed Her mind in thoughts of war,
At that juncture, the goddess Kali appeared by bursting her forehead visualising this it appeared to the poet's mind,
That in order to destroy all the demons, the death had incarnated in the form of Kali. —74
That powerful goddess, taking the sword in her hand, in great ire, thundered like lightning,
Hearing her thunder, the great mountains like Sumeru shook and the earth resting on the hood of Seshanaga, trembled,
Brahma, Kuber, Sun etc., were frightened and the chest of Shiva throbbed,
Highly glorious Chandi, in her balanced state creating Kalika like death, spoke thus. —75

DOHIRA

Chandika, seeing Her, thus spoke to Her,
"O my daughter Kalika, merge in Me." —76
Hearing these words of Chandi, she merged in Her,
Like Yamuna falling into the current of Ganges. —77

SWAYYA

Then the goddess Parvati together with the gods, reflected thus in their mind,
That the demons are considering the earth as their own, it is futile to get it back without the war,
Indra said, "O mother, listen to my supplication, we should not delay any more,"
Then the mighty Chandi like a terrible black she-serpent, moved into the battlefield in order to kill the demons. —78
The body of the goddess is like gold, and her eyes are like the eyes of *mamola* (wagtail), before which the beauty of lotus is feeling shy,
It seems that the creator, taking ambrosia in His hand, hath created an entity, saturated with nectar in every limb,

The Moon doth not present an appropriate comparison for the face of goddess, nothing else also cannot be compared,
The goddess sitting on the summit of Sumeru appears like the queen of Indra (Sachi) seated on her throne. —79

DOHIRA

The powerful Chandi looks splendid on the summit of Sumeru thus,
With the sword in her hand, she seems like Yama carrying his club. —80
For unknown reason, one of the demons came to that side,
When he saw the horrible form of Kali, he fell down unconscious. —81
When he came to his senses, that demon, pulling himself up, said to the goddess,
"I am the brother of King Sumbh," then he added with some hesitation. —82
"He hath brought under his control all the three worlds with his mighty armed-strength,
"Such is the king Sumbh, O superb Chandi, marry him." —83
Hearing the words of the demon, the goddess replied thus:
"O foolish demon, I cannot marry him without waging the war." —84
Hearing this, that demon went to king Sumbh very swiftly,
And with folded hands, falling at his feet, he supplicated thus. —85
"O king, Thou hast all other gems except the gem of wife,
"One beautiful woman lives in the forest, O adept one, marry her." —86

SORATHA

When the king hears these bewitching words, he said,
"O brother, tell me, how she looks like?" —87

SWAYYA

Her face is like the Moon, seeing which all the sufferings are effaced; her curly hair even steal the beauty of snakes,
Her eyes are like the blossomed lotus, her eyebrows are like bow and her eyelashes are like arrows,
Her waist is slim like that of a lion, her gait is like that of an elephant and makes shyful the glory of the wife of Cupid,
She hath a sword in her hand and rides a lion; she is most magnificent like the sun and she is the wife of god Shiva. —88

KABIT

Seeing the playfulness of the eyes, the big fish becomes shy, the tenderness makes the lotus shyful and the beauty makes the wagtail coy; considering the face as lotus, the black bees in their madness wander hither and thither in the forest,
Seeing the nose, the parrots and looking at the neck, the pigeons and hearing the voice, the nightingale consider themselves robbed, their mind feels comfort nowhere,
Seeing the row of teeth, the heart of pomegranate hath burst; the lust of her beauty is spreading like moonshine in the world,
That most beautiful damsel hath manifested herself as the ocean of such like qualities; she hath captivated my mind with the sharpness of her eyes. —89

DOHIRA

Hearing the words of the demon, the king Sumbh said smilingly,
"Some expert spy be sent there in order to know her ingenuity." —90
That demon said again, "It may now be considered,"
To send the most efficient warrior in the army giving him authority. —91

SWAYYA

The king was seated in his court and there with folded hands (Dhumar Lochan) said, "I will go,"
"Firstly, I shall please her with talk, otherwise, I shall bring her, seizing her by her hair,
"If she makes me furious, I shall wage the war with her and cause the streams of blood to flow in the battlefield,"
"I have so much strength that I can make the mountains fly with the blowing of my breaths," said Dhumar Lochan. —92

DOHIRA

Seeing that warrior getting up, Sumbh told him to go,

"Bring her if she is pleased to come, if she is furious, then wage the war." —93

Then Dhumar Lochan went there after arranging the four parts of his army,

Like dark clouds, he besieged the mountain (of the goddess), thundering like the king of elephants. —94

Dhumar Lochan then shouted loudly, standing on the base of the mountain:

"O Chandi, either marry the king Sumbh or wage the war." —95

Hearing the words of the enemy, the goddess mounted her lion,

She descended the mountain swiftly, holding the weapons in her hands. —96

SWAYYA

From that side, the powerful Chandi marched forward in great fury and from this side, the army of Dhumar Lochan moved forward,

There were great slayings with shafts and swords; the goddess held up the sharp dagger in her hand,

She ran forward and struck on the face of the enemy and cut his lips just as the chisel cuts the iron,

The demon had black body and the teeth like Ganges and Yamuna; together with red blood all the three colours have taken the form of Tribeni. —97

Seeing himself wounded Dhumar Lochan with great strength took control of his sword,

The demon struck twenty to twenty-five blows, but the lion did not take even one foot backward,

Holding her mace, the goddess splitting the army of the enemy struck such a blow on the head of the demon Dhumar Lochan,

Just as Indra, in great fury, hath attacked a mountainous citadel with his weapon Vajra. —98

Dhumar Lochan shouting loudly and taking his forces with him,

Holding his sword in his hand, suddenly struck a blow on lion's body,

Chandi, on the other hand, with Her hand's sword cut off the head of Dhumar Lochan, hurled it on the demons,

Just as in a violent storm the dates falls far away, after breaking from the palm-tree. —99

DOHIRA

When the goddess killed Dhumar Lochan in this way,

The army of the demons, being confounded, greatly lamented. —100

End of the third chapter entitled "Slaying of Dhumar Lochan" in Ath Chandi Charitra Ukati Bilas of *Markandeya Purana*.

SWAYYA

When the powerful Chandi heard the furore of the demons, her eyes became red with anger,

The contemplation of Shiva was broken by the noise and being perturbed slackened the winged flight,

With the fire from the eyes of the goddess, the army of the demons was reduced to ashes, the poet imagined this analogy,

All the demon-army was reduced to ashes just as the bees are destroyed by the poisonous smoke. —101

DOHIRA

All the other army was burnt except the single demon,

Chandi had deliberately saved him in order to kill others. —102

The foolish demon ran away and told the king Sumbh,

"Chandi hath destroyed Dhumar Lochan alongwith his army." —103

"All the warriors of the army, those on foot, on chariots, horses and elephants have been killed,"

Hearing these words and in astonishment, the king Sumbh became furious. —104

Then the king called two demons Chand and Mund,

Who came in the king's court, holding sword and shield in their hands. —105

Both of them bowed in obeisance to the king, who asked them to sit near him,

And presenting them the seasoned and folded betel leaf, he uttered thus from his mouth.

"Both of you are great heroes." —106

The king gave them his waist-girdle, dagger and sword (and said):

"Arrest and bring Chandi, otherwise kill her." —107

SWAYYA

Chand and Mund, with great ire, marched towards the battlefield, alongwith four types of fine army,

At that time, the earth shook on the head of Seshanaga like the boat in the stream,

The dust which rose towards the sky with the hooves of the horses, the poet firmly imagined in his mind,

That the earth is going towards the city of god in order to supplicate for the removal of its enormous burden. —108

DOHIRA

Both the demons Chand and Mund took a great army of warriors with them,

On reaching near the mountain, they besieged it and raised great furore. —109

SWAYYA

When the goddess heard the tumult of demons, she was filled with great rage in her mind,

She moved immediately, riding on her lion, blowing her conch and carrying all the weapons on her body,

She descended from the mountain on the forces of the enemy and the poet felt,

That the falcon hath swooped down from the sky on the flock of cranes and sparrows. —110

One arrow shot from the bow of Chandi increases in number to ten, one hundred and one thousand,

Then becomes one lakh and pierces its target of demons, bodies and remains fixed there,

Without extracting those arows, which poet can praise them and make an appropriate comparison,

It appears that with the blowing of the wind of Phalgun, the trees are standing without the leaves. —111

The demon Mund held his sword and shouting loudly, he struck many blows on the limbs of the lion,

Then very swiftly he gave a blow on the body of the goddess, wounding it and then drew the sword out,

Covered with blood, the sword in the hand of the demon is vibrating what comparison the poet can give except,

Yama, the god of death, after eating the betel leaf to his satisfaction is proudly watching his protruded tongue. —112

When the demon returned after wounding the goddess, she took out a shaft from her quiver,

She pulled the bow upto her ear and let go the arrow, which increases enormously in numbers,

The demon Mund put his shield before his face and the arrows are fixed in the shield,

It seemed that seated on the back of the Tortoise, the hoods of Seshanaga are standing erect. —113

Caressing the lion, the goddess moved forward and holding the sword in hand she sustained herself,

And began a terrible war, killing, rolling in dust and mashing innumerable warriors of the enemy,

Taking back the lion, she encircled the enemy from the front and gave such a blow that the head of Mund was separated from his body,

Which fell on the ground, like the pumpkin cut off from the creeper. —114

The goddess riding on the lion and blowing the conch with her mouth seems like the lightning glistening among dark clouds,

She killed the running superb mighty warriors with her disc,

The ghosts and goblins are eating the flesh of the dead, raising loud shouts,

Removing the head of Mund, now Chandi is preparing to deal with Chand. —115

Killing Mund in the battlefield, the dagger of Chandi then did this—

She killed and destroyed all the forces of the enemy, confronting Chand in the war,

Taking her dagger in her hand, she struck it with great force on the head of the enemy and separated it from the body,

It seemed that god Shiva hath separated the trunk of Ganesh from his head with his trident. —116

End of the fourth chapter entitled "Slaying of Chand and Mund" in Ath Chandi Charitra Ukati Bilas of *Markandeya Purana*.

SORATHA

Millions of demons, wounded and writhing went to supplicate before the king Sumbh,
That the goddess hath killed very great heroes, difficult to kill. —117

DOHIRA

The king said at the same place these words:
"I am saying nothing else except the truth that I shall not let him live." —118
These words were uttered by Chandika Herself, seated on the tongue of Sumbh,
It seemed that the demon had invited himself his own death. —119
Both Sumbh and Nisumbh sat together and decided,
That the whole army be called and a superb hero be selected for war with Chandi. —120
The ministers advised that Raktavija be sent (for the purpose),
He will kill Chandi by throwing her from the mountain like a stone after challenging her. —121

SORATHA

Some messenger may be sent to call him from his home,
He had conquered Indra with his unlimited strength of arms. —122

DOHIRA

A demon went to the house of Raktavija and requested,
"Thou hast been summoned in the royal court, appear before it very quickly." —123
Raktavija came and bowed in obeisance before the king,
With due veneration he said in the court, "Tell me, what can I do?" —124

SWAYYA

Sumbh and Nisumbh called Raktavija in their presence and offered him a seat with respect,
He was given the crown for his head and presented with elephants and horses, which he accepted with pleasure,
After taking the betel leaf, Raktavija said, "I shall immediately separate the head of Chandika from her trunk,"
When he said these words before the assembly, the king was pleased to award him a dreadful thundering trumpet and a canopy. —125
Sumbh and Nisumbh said, "Now go and take a huge army with you,
Reduce the great mountain of the goddess to dust and with all your strength challenge and kill her,"
Hearing the words of the king with his own ears, Raktavija riding on his elephant and in great fury, marched away,
It seemed that the Yama, manifesting himself is taking the demon to his destruction by fighting in the battlefield. —126
The trumpet was sounded by Raktavija who sent forward his forces on elephants, horses and chariots,
All those demons are very powerful, who can even crush Sumeru with their feet,
Their bodies and limbs look very strong and large on which they are wearing the armour, with quivers tied with their waists,
Raktavija is going with his companions wearing their weapons like bows, arrows, swords etc., alongwith all other paraphernalia. —127

DOHIRA

Raktavija, keeping his army in array, encamped at the base of Sumeru,
Hearing their tumult with her ears, the goddess prepared for war. —128

SORATHA

Riding on her lion, Chandika, shouting loudly,
Marched, holding her mighty sword, in order to kill Raktavija. —129

SWAYYA

Raktavija was very much pleased on seeing the powerful Chandi coming,
He moved forward and penetrated into the forces of the enemy and in anger moved further to fight,
He gushed forward with his army like clouds, the poet hath imagined this comparison for his demeanour,

The arrows of the warriors move as though enormous clouds are raining heavily. —130

The arrows shot by the hands of the warriors, piercing the bodies of the enemies cross to the other side,

Leaving the bows and piercing the armours, these arrows stand fixed like cranes, the enemies of fish,

Many wounds were inflicted on the body of Chandi, from which the blood flowed like a stream,

It seemed that (instead of arrows), the snakes (sons of Takshak) have come out changing their garbs. —131

When the arrows were shot by the hands of the warriors, Chandika roared like a lioness,

She held arrows, bow, sword, mace, disc, carver and dagger in her hands,

She destroyed the canopies, separated the palanquins from the elephants,

It seemed that Hanuman after setting Lanka on fire, has thrown down the loft of the palace of the citadel. —132

Chandi, taking her superb sword, twisted the faces of the demons with her blows,

She destroyed those demons, who had obstructed her advance with their strength being arrayed in rows,

Eroding the demons by creating fear, she ultimately crushed their bones,

She drank the blood as Krishna quaffed fire and the sage Agastya drank the water of ocean. —133

Chandi began the war very swiftly, holding the bow in her hand; she killed the unaccountable number of demons,

She killed all the army of the demon Raktavija and with their blood, the jackals and vultures satisfied their hunger,

Seeing the dreadful face of the goddess, the demons ran away from the field like this,

Just as with the blowing of swift and forceful wing the leaves of the fig tree (*peepal*) fly away. —134

With great ire the mighty Chandika holding the sword in her hand, destroyed the horses and the enemies,

Many were killed with arrows, disc and mace and the bodies of many were torn by the lion,

She killed forces on horses, elephants and on foot and wounding those on chariots hath rendered them without chariots,

The elements lying on the ground at that place seem to have fallen like mountains during the earthquake. —135

DOHIRA

All the army of Raktavija ran away in fear of the goddess,

The demon brought them back and said, "I shall destroy Chandi." —136

SWAYYA

Hearing these words with their ears, the warriors returned and holding their swords in their hands,

And with great rage in their minds with great force and swiftness, they began the war with the goddess,

The blood flowed out from their wounds and falls on the ground like the water in the cataract,

The sound of the arrows appears like the cracking sound produced by the fire burning the reeds. —137

Hearing the command of Raktavija the army of the demons came and resisted before the goddess,

The warriors began to wage war holding their shields, swords and daggers in their hands,

They did not hesitate to come and have plucked up their hearts firmly,

They withheld Chandi from all the four sides like the sun encircled by clouds from all directions. —138

The powerful Chandi, in great rage hath caught hold of her mighty bow with great force,

Penetrating like lightning amongst the clouds-like enemy, she hath cut asunder the army of demons,

She hath destroyed the enemy with her arrows the poet hath imagined it in this manner,

It seems that the arrows are moving like the radiant rays of the sun and the bits of the flesh of the demons are flying here and there like dust. —139

After killing the enormous army of the demons Chandi hath swiftly held up her bow,

She hath torn the forces with her arrows and the mighty lion hath also roared loudly,

Many chieftains have been killed and the blood is flowing on the ground in this great war,
The head of one demon hath been kicked by the bow and thrown away like the lightning desecrating a palace. —140

DOHIRA

Chandi destroyed all the army of the demons in this way,
Just as Hanuman, the son of wind-god, uprooted the garden of Lanka. —141

SWAYYA

Very powerful Chandi, thundering like clouds, hath showered her arrows on the enemy like rain-drops,
Taking the lightning-like sword in her hand, she hath cut into halves the trunks of the warriors and thrown them on the ground,
The wounded revolve and fall like this according to the imagination of the poet,
Within the flowing stream of blood are drowned the corpses formulating the banks (of the stream). —142

In this way, the warriors cut into havles by Chandi, are lying on the ground,
The corpse hath fallen on the corpses and the blood is flowing enormously as if millions of spouts are feeding the flow,
The elephants are bumped against the elephants and the poet imagines it like this,
That with blowing of the wind of great doomsday, the great mountains are colliding with each other. —143

Holding her terrible sword in her hand, Chandi hath begun her function with powerful movement in the battlefield,
With great force she hath killed many warriors and their flowing blood seems like Vaitarni stream,
The arm like the trunk of the elephant hath been cut in the middle and the poet hath depicted it like this,
That fighting with each other two she-serpents have dropped down. —144

DOHIRA

Chandi hath caused all the mighty army of the demons to run away,
Just as with the remembrance of the name of the Lord, the sins and sufferings are removed. —145

SWAYYA

The demons were frightened from the goddess like the darkness from sun, like the clouds from the wind and the snake from the peacock,
Just like the cowards from the heroes, falsehood from the truth and the deer from the lion become fearful immediately,
Just as the praise from the miser, bliss from separation and the family from a bad son are destroyed,
Just as the *dharma* is destroyed with anger and intellect with illusion, similarly the war with Chandi hath driven the demons away. —146

The demons returned again for war and in great anger ran forward,
Some of them run their swift horses, pulling their bows fitted with arrows,
The dust which hath been created by horse's hooves and hath gone upwards, hath covered the sun's sphere,
It seemed that Brahma hath created the fourteen worlds again with six nether-worlds and eight skies because the sphere of dust hath become the eighth sky. —147

Chandi, taking her terrific bow, hath carded like cotton the bodies of the demons with her arrows,
She hath killed the elephants with her sword, because of which the pride of the demons hath flown away like the flakes of *akk*-plant,
The white turbans of the heads of warriors flowed in the blood-stream,
It seemed that in the current of Sarasvati, the bubbles of heroe's praises are flowing. —148

The goddess, taking her mace in her hand, waged a ferocious war against the demons in great anger,
Holding her sword in her hand, she, the mighty Chandika killed and reduced the army of demons to dust,
Seeing one head falling with turban, the poet imagined,
That with the end of the merit of virtuous actions, a star hath fallen down on earth from the sky. —149

ATH CHANDI CHARITRA UKATI BILAS

Then the goddess, with her great strength, throwing the big elephants far away like clouds, did this,
Holding the arrows in her hand she pulled the bow, destroying the demons and drank the blood with great interest,
Seeing this and shrivelling, some of the demons, being perturbed have run away with great heart-beat,
Are the arrows of Chandi like the rays of the sun? seeing which the light of the demon-lamp hath become dim. —150

Holding her sword in her hand, she grew furious and with great force waged a terrible war,
Moving swiftly from her place, she killed many demons and destroyed a very big elephant in the battlefield,
Seeing that elegant event in the battlefield, the poet imagines,
That in order to construct the bridge on the sea Nal and Neel have thrown the mountain after uprooting it. —151

DOHIRA

When his army was killed by Chandi, Raktavija did this—
He equipped himself with his weapons and thought of killing the goddess in his mind. —152

SWAYYA

Seeing the dreadful form of Chandi (whose vehicle is the lion), all the demons were filled with awe,
She manifested Herself in queer form, holding the conch, disc and bow in her hand,
Raktavija moved forward and knowing his superb strength he challenged the goddess for a fight,
And said, "Thou has named Thyself as Chandika come forward to fight with me." —153

When the army of Raktavija was destroyed or ran away then in great fury, he himself came forward to fight,
He fought a very fierce battle with Chandika and (while fighting) his sword fell down from his hand, but he did not lose heart,
Taking the bow in hand and recouping his strength he is swimming in the ocean of blood like this,
As though he was the Sumeru mountain like the one used at the time of churning of ocean by the gods and demons. —154

The powerful demon waged the war with great anger and swam over and crossed the ocean of blood,
Holding his sword and controlling his shield, he ran forward and challengd the lion,
Seeing him coming, Chandi shot an arrow from Her bow, which caused the demon to become unconscious and fall down,
It seemed that the brother of Rama (Bharat) had caused Hanuman to fall down with the mountain. —155

The demon got up and holding the sword in his hand he waged the war with powerful Chandi,
He wounded the lion, whose blood flowed enormously and fell upon the earth,
The poet hath described this scene in a very attractive manner,
According to him the colour of the ochre-mountain is melting and falling on earth in the rainy season. —156

Filled with rage, Chandika waged a fierce war with Raktavija in the battlefield,
She pressed the army of the demons in an instant, just as the oilman presses the oil from the sesame seed,
The blood is dripping on the earth just as the dyer's colour-vessel cracks and the colour spreads,
The wounds of the demons glitter like the lamps in the containers. —157

Wherever the blood of Raktavija fell, many Raktavija rose up there,
Chandi caught hold of her ferocious bow and killed all of them with her arrows,
Though all the new born Raktavija were killed, still more Raktavija rose up, Chandi killed all of them,
They all die and are re-born like bubbles produced by rain and then immediately becoming extinct. —158

As many drops of blood of Raktavija fall on the ground, so many Raktavija come into being,
Shouting loudly "kill her, kill her," those demons run before Chandi,

Seeing this scene at that very moment, the poet imagined this comparison,
That in the glass-palace only one figure multiplies itself and appears like this. —159

Many Raktavija rise and in fury wage the war,
The arrows are shot from the ferocious bow of Chandi like the rays of the sun,
Chandi killed and destroyed them but they rose up again; the goddess continued killing them like the paddy thrashed by the wooden pestle,
Chandi hath separated their heads with her double-edged sword just as the fruit of marmelos breaks away from the tree. —160

Many Raktavija rising up, with swords in their hands move towards Chandi like this,
Such demons rising from the drops of blood in great numbers, shower the arrows like rain,
Chandi again took her ferocious bow in her hand shooting volley of arrows killed all of them,
The demons rise from the blood like the hair rising in cold season. —161

Many Raktavija have gathered together and with force and swiftness they have besieged Chandi,
Both the goddess and the lion together have killed all these forces of demons,
The demons rose up again and produced such a loud voice, which broke the contemplation of the sages,
All the efforts of the goddess were lost, but the pride of Raktavija was not decreased. —162

DOHIRA

In this way Chandika fought with Raktavija,
The demons became innumerable and the ire of the goddess was fruitless. —163

SWAYYA

The eyes of powerful Chandi became red with rage on seeing many demons in all the ten directions,
She chopped with her sword all the enemies like the petals of roses,
One drop of blood fell on the body of the goddess, the poet hath imagined its comparison in this way,
In the temple of gold, the jeweller has got studded the red jewel in decoration. —164

With anger Chandi fought a long war, the like of which had earlier been fought by Vishnu with the demon Madhu,
In order to destroy the demons, the goddess hath drawn forth the flame of fire from her forehead,
From that flame, Kali manifested herself and her glory spread like fear amongst cowards,
It seemed that breaking the peak of Sumeru, the current of Yamuna hath fallen down. —165

The Sumeru shook and the heaven was terrified and the big mountains began to move speedily in all the ten directions,
In all the fourteen worlds there was great commotion and a great illusion was created in the mind of Brahma,
The meditative state of Shiva was broken and the earth burst when with great force Kali shouted loudly,
In order to kill the demons Kali hath taken the deathlike sword in her hand. —166

DOHIRA

Chandi and Kali both together took this decision,
"I shall kill the demons and thou drinkest their blood; in this way we shall kill all the enemies." —167

SWAYYA

Taking Kali and the lion with her, Chandi besieged all the Raktavija like the forest by the fire,
With the power of the arrows of Chandi, the demons were burnt like bricks in the kiln,
Kali drank their blood and the poet hath created this image regarding Kali,
She accomplished the feat like the grand mythological opening in which the water of all the oceans merges. —168

The demons were killed by Chandi and Kali in great rage treated the Raktavija in this way,
She held her sword and challenging the demons and shouting loudly, she destroyed all the army,
Kali ate and drank enormous quantity of flesh and blood, the poet hath depicted her glory like this—
As though afflicted with hunger the human being hath eaten the salted curry and drank the soup abundantly. —169

ATH CHANDI CHARITRA UKATI BILAS

The war that Raktavija waged on the earth, it was seen by all the gods,
As many drops of blood fall, so many demons manifest and come forward,
The vamps have reached from all sides; they have matted locks on their heads and bows in their hands,
They drink that drop of blood which falls in their bowls and taking the sword Chandi goes on killing very swiftly. —170
Kali and Chandi, holding the bow have begun the war unhesitatingly with the demons,
There was great killing in the battlefield; for one watch of the day the steel rattled with the steel,
Raktavija hath fallen on the ground and in this way the head of the enemy hath broken—
It seemed that the rich person hath detached himself from the riches and hath forsaken all his wealth. —171

SORATHA

Chandi hath destroyed (the demons) and Kali hath drunk their blood,
In this way, both of them together, have killed the chief demon Raktavija in an instant. —172

End of the fifth chapter entitled "Killing of Raktavija" in Ath Chandi Charitra Ukati Bilas of *Markandeya Purana*.

SWAYYA

A small number of demons were saved by running away; they went to Sumbh and Nisumbh and requested them:
"Both of them together have killed Raktavija and also have killed and destroyed many others,"
Hearing these words from their mouth the king Sumbh spoke thus holding his sword,
"I shall kill the fierce Chandi thus going in front of her just as the lion knocks down a goat in the forest. —173

DOHIRA

He gave the material of war to all the warriors,
He himself wore his arms and armour and said this: "I shall kill Chandi today." —174

SWAYYA

In great rage, both Sumbh and Nisumbh marched forward for war; the trumpets sounded in all the ten directions,
In front there were warriors on foot, in the middle the warriors on horses and behind them, the charioteers have arranged the chariots in rows,
On the palanquins of the intoxicated elephants, beautiful and lofty banners are flying,
It seems that in order to wage a war with Indra, the large mountains are flying from the earth. —175

DOHIRA

Gathering their forces Sumbh and Nisumbh have besieged the mountain,
On their bodies they have tightened their armour and in rage they are roaring like lions. —176

SWAYYA

The mighty demons Sumbh and Nisumbh, filled with rage, have entered the battlefield,
They, whose limbs are winsome and lofty, they are driving their swift horses on the earth,
The dust rose at that time, whose particles are embracing their feet,
It seems that in order to conquer the invisible place, the mind in the form of particles hath come to learn about swiftness from the hooves. —177

DOHIRA

Chandi and Kali both heard slight rumour with their ears,
They came down from the top of Sumeru and raised a great furore. —178

SWAYYA

Seeing the powerful Chandika coming towards him, the demon-king Sumbh became very furious,
He wanted to kill her in an instant, therefore he fitted the arrows in the bow and pulled it,
Seeing the face of Kali, misapprehension was created in his mind, the face of Kali seemed to him as the face of Yama,
Still he shot all his arrows and thundered like the clouds of doomsday. —179

Entering the clouds-like army of the enemies, Chandi caught hold of his bows and arrows in his hand,

She killed the black-mountains-like demons, just as the sun-rays destroy the darkness,
The army ran away out of fear, which hath been imagined by the poet like this,
As though seeing the mouth of Bhim filled with blood, Kauravas have run away from the battlefield. —180

KABIT
On receiving orders from king Sumbh, the warriors of great strength and composure, marched towards Chandi in great rage,
Chandika taking her bow and arrow and Kali her sword, with great force destroyed the army in an instant,
Many left the battlefield out of fear, many of them became corpses with arrows; routed from its place the army hath fled helter-skelter like this—
Just as in the desert, millions of the particles of dust, fly away before the violent wind. —181

SWAYYA
Kali, taking the double-edged sword and Chandi her bow, have threatened the forces of the enemy like this—
Many have been chewed by Kali with her mouth, many have been beheaded by Chandi,
A sea of blood hath appeared on the earth; many warriors have left this battlefield and many are lying wounded,
Those who have fled, they have told Sumbh like this: "Many heroes are lying (dead) in that place." —182

DOHIRA
Seeing such a violent war, Vishnu thought,
And sent the powers for the help of the goddess in the battlefield. —183

SWAYYA
As commanded by Vishnu, the powers of all the gods came for help for powerful Chandi,
The goddess, in reverence, said to them: "Welcome you have come as though I have called you,"
The poet hath imagined well in his mind the glory of that occasion,
It seemed that the stream of Sawan (the rainy month) hath come and merged in the sea. —184

Seeing the great army of the demons, the warriors of the powers of gods went in front of them for war,
With great force they killed many with their arrows and caused the confronting warriors to lie dead in the battlefield,
Kali chewed many with her molars, and had thrown asunder many of them in all the four directions,
It seemed that while fighting with Ravana, in great fury, Jamwant has picked up and destroyed the great mountains. —185

Then taking the sword in her hand, Kali hath waged a ferocious war with the demons,
She hath destroyed many, who are lying dead on the earth and the blood is oozing out of the corpses,
The marrow, which is flowing from the heads of the enemies, the poet hath thought about it in this way,
It seemed that slipping down from the peak of the mountain, the snow hath fallen on the earth. —186

DOHIRA
When no other remedy was left, all the forces of the demons fled away,
At that time Sumbh said to Nisumbh, "Take the army and go to fight." —187

SWAYYA
Obeying the orders of Sumbh, the mighty Nisumbh hath arrayed and moved forward like this—
Just as in the war of Mahabharata, Arjuna, filled with anger, had fought with Karan,
The arrows of Chandi struck the demon in great quantity, which pierced and crossed the body, how?
Just as the young shoots of paddy in the field of a farmer in the rainy month of Sawan. —188

At first She caused the warriors to fall with Her arrows, then taking Her sword in Her hand She waged the war like this—
She killed and destroyed the whole army, which resulted in the depletion of the strength of the demons,
At that place there is blood everywhere, the poet hath imagined its comparison like this—

ATH CHANDI CHARITRA UKATI BILAS

After creating the seven oceans, Brahma hath created this eighth ocean of blood. —189

The powerful Chandi, taking the sword in her hand is fighting in the battlefield with great ire,

She hath destroyed four types of army and Kalika hath also killed many with great force,

Showing her frightening form, Kalika hath effaced the glory of the face of Nisumbh,

The earth hath become red with blood; it seems that the earth is wearing the red *sari*. —190

All the demons, recouping their strength, are resisting Chandi again in war,

Equipping themselves with their weapons they are fighting in the battlefield like the moths surrounding the lamps,

Holding her ferocious bow, she hath chopped the warriors into halves in the battlefield,

It seems that in the dense forest, the carpenter hath cut the forest-trees and placed them separately. —191

When some army was killed and some fled away then Nisumbh became very furious in his mind,

He stood firmly before Chandi and waged a violent war, he did not recede even one step,

The arrows of Chandi struck the faces of demons and great deal of blood hath flown on the earth,

It seems that Rahu hath caught hold of Sun in the sky, resulting in the great carving of blood by the Sun. —192

Holding the spear in her hand, Chandi with great force, thrust it into the forehead of the enemy like this,

That it pierced the helmet like the cloth,

The current of blood flowing out upwards, what comparison the poet hath imagined about it?

With the opening of the third eye of Shiva, the light appeared like this current. —193

The demon, with his strength, took out that spear and with the same swiftness struck Chandi with it,

The spear struck the face of the goddess resulting in the flow of blood from her face, which created a splendid scene,

The comparison which hath emerged in the mind of the poet, can be told like this,

It seemed that in the throat of the most beautiful woman of Lanka, the saliva of the chewed betel leaf is being visualised. —194

Nisumbh hath waged a very fierce war, which poet can describe its splendour?

Such a war hath not been fought by Bhishma, Dronacharya, Kripacharya, Bhim, Arjuna, and Karan,

The current of blood is flowing from the bodies of many demons, because they have been pierced by the arrow,

It seems that in order to end the night, the sun-rays are scattering at dawn from all the ten directions. —195

Chandi penetrated in the battlefield with her disc and with anger in her heart she killed many demons,

Then she caught hold of the mace and revolved it; it glistened; then shouting loudly, she killed with it the army of the enemy,

Taking her glittering sword in her hand, she hath thrown and scattered the heads of great demons on the earth,

It seems that in the war fought by Ram Chandra, the mighty Hanuman hath thrown down the great mountains. —196

One very powerful demon, holding his sword in his hand and shouting loudly came running,

Chandi, taking out her double-edged sword from the sheath, with great force struck the body of the demon,

His head broke and fell on the earth, the poet hath imagined thus this comparison—

It seemed that a crow eaten by a dreadful snake hath fallen on the earth from the lofty mountain. —197

One powerful demon-warrior of Nisumbh, speeding his horse, went in front of the battlefield,

On seeing him, one loses his composure, who is then so powerful as to try to go before this demon?

Chandi, taking her sword in her hand, hath killed many enemies, and at the same time, she struck it on the head of this demon,

This sword piercing the head, the face, the trunk, the saddle and the horse hath thrust into the earth. —198

When the powerful Chandi killed that demon in this way, then another demon shouting loudly came forward in the battlefield,

Going in front of the lion and running in anger, he inflicted on him two-three wounds,
Chandi held up her sword and shouting loudly with great force, she struck it on the head of the demon,
His head fell far away like the mangoes by the violent wind. —199

Consider the war at its peak, all the divisions of the army of demons are running towards the battlefield,
The steel collided with steel and the cowards fled away and left the battlefield,
With the blows of the sword and mace of Chandi, the bodies of demons have fallen in fragments
It seems that the gardener hath shaken and even thrashed with wooden pestles the mulberry tree and caused the fall of its fruit. —200

Seeing still a large remaining army of the demons, Chandi held up her weapons,
She ripped the sandalwood-like bodies of the warriors and challenging them, she knocked down and killed them,
They have been wounded in the battlefield and many have fallen with their heads severed from their trunks,
It seems that at the time of the war, Saturn hath chopped all the limit of the Moon and thrown them. —201

At that time, the powerful Chandi, pulling up her strength, held fast her sword in her hand,
In anger, She struck it on the head of Nisumbh; it struck in such a way that it crossed to the other end,
Who can appreciate such a blow? At the same instant that demon hath fallen on the earth in two halves,
It seems that the soap-maker, taking the steel-wire in his hand, hath struck the soap with it. —202

End of the sixth chapter entitled "Slaying of Nisumbh" in Ath Chandi Charitra Ukati Bilas of *Markandeya Purana*.

DOHIRA

When the goddess killed Nisumbh in this way in the battlefield,
Then one of the demons went to Sumbh speedily on the horse. —203

He told Sumbh all that had happened in the war,
Telling him "When the goddess killed thy brother, then all the demons fled away." —204

SWAYYA

When Sumbh heard about the death of Nisumbh, the anger of that mighty warrior knew no bounds,
Filled with great fury, he bedecked all the paraphernalia of elephants and horses, and taking the divisions of his army, he entered the battlefield,
In that frightening field, seeing the corpses and the blood, he was greatly astonished,
It seemed that the surging Saraswati is running to meet the ocean. —205

The fierce Chandi, lion, Kalika and other powers have waged a violent war together,
"They have killed all the army of the demons," saying this the mind of Sumbh was filled with rage,
Seeing the trunk of his brother on one side, and in deep sorrow, he could not move a step forward,
He was so much frightened that he could not speedily go forward; it seemed that the leopard had become lame. —206

When Sumbh commanded his army, many demons marched forward obeying the orders,
Who could count the riders of great elephants and horses, the chariot warriors on chariots and warriors on foot?
They, of very huge bodies, besieged Chandi from all the four sides,
It seemed that the overflowing, proud and thundering dark clouds have enshrouded the sun. —207

DOHIRA

When Chandi was besieged from all the four sides. she did this;
She laughed and said to Kali, also hinting with her eyes. —208

KABIT

When Chandi hinted to Kali, she killed many, chewed many and threw many far away, in great rage,
She ripped with her nails many big elephants and horses; such a war was waged that had not been waged before,

ATH CHANDI CHARITRA UKATI BILAS

Many warriors ran away, none of them remained conscious about his body, there was so much uproar, and many of them died by mutual pressing,

Seeing the demons being killed, Indra, the king of gods, was very much pleased in his mind and calling all the group of gods he hailed the victory. —209

The king Sumbh became very furious and told all the demons, "That Kali, hath waged the war in which she hath killed and thrown down my warriors,"

Recouping his power, Sumbh held his sword and shield in his hands and shouting "kill, kill" he entered the battlefield,

The great heroes and warriors of great composure took their weapons and sustaining their power, accompained Sumbh,

The demons marched like the flying locust swarms in order to enshroud the Sun. —210

SWAYYA

Seeing the powerful forces of the demons, Chandi revolved the lion's face swiftly,

Even the disc, spindle, wind, canopy and grind-stone cannot revolve so swiftly,

The lion hath revolved in that battlefield in such a way that even the whirlwind cannot compete with it,

There can be no other comparison except that the the face of the lion may be considered on both the sides of his body. —211

At that time the powerful Chandi had fought a great war with a huge gathering of demons,

Challenging the unaccountable army, chastening and awakening it, Kali had destroyed it in the battlefield,

The war was fought there upto four hundred *kos* and the poet hath imagined it like this:

Only one *ghari* (small duration of time) was not complete when the demons had fallen on the earth like the leaves (of trees) in autumn. —212

When all the four divisions of army were killed, Sumbh marched forward to obstruct the advance of Chandi,

At that time the whole earth shook and Shiva rose and ran from his seat of contemplation,

The necklace of (snake of) Shiva had withered because of fear, it trembled because of great fear in his heart,

That snake clinging to Shiva's throat appears like the string of the wreath of skulls. —213

Coming in front of Chandi, the demon Sumbh uttered from his mouth, "I have come to know all this,"

"Alongwith Kali and other powers Thou hast destroyed all the parts of my army,"

At that time Chandi uttered these words from her mouth to Kali and other powers: "Merge in Me" and at the same instant they all merged in Chandi,

Like the rain-water in the current of the stream. —214

In the war, Chandi taking the dagger, struck it with great force on the demon,

It penetrated into the breast of the enemy; the vamps were fully satisfied with his blood,

Seeing that horrible war, the poet hath imagined it like this—

The corpses falling on one another seem like a ladder of heaven made by the warriors in the war. —215

Chandi, with great rage, hath waged war several times with the forces of Sumbh,

The jackals, vamps and vultures are like labourers and the dancer standing in the mud of flesh and blood is Shiva Himself,

The corpses upon corpses have become a wall and the fat and marrow are the plaster (on that wall),

(This is not the battlefield) it appears that Vishwa-karma, the builder of beatiful mansions, hath created this wonderful portrait. —216

Ultimately there was battle only between the two, Sumbh from that side and Chandi from this side, sustained their power,

Several wounds were inflicted on the bodies of both, but the demon lost all his power,

The arms of the powerless demon tremble for which the poet hath imagined this comparison,

It seemed that they are the black serpents of five-mouths, which are hanging unconsciously with the power of snake-spell. —217

Very powerful Chandi became furious in the battlefield and with great force she fought the battle,

Very powerful Chandi, taking her sword and shouting loudly she struck it on Sumbh,

The sword's edge collided with the sword's edge from which there arose tinkling sound and sparks,

It seemed that during the night of Bhadon (month), there are the glow-worms. —218

Much blood flowed out of the wounds of Sumbh, therefore he lost his power, how doth he look like?

The glory of his face and the power of his body have depleted like the decrease in the light of the Moon from full-moon to the new-moon,

Chandi picked up Sumbh in her hand, the poet hath imagined the comparison of this scene like this—

It seemed that in order to protect the flock of cows, Krishna had lifted the Govardhana mountain. —219

DOHIRA

Sumbh fell from the hand of Chandi on the earth and from the earth it flew to the sky,

In order to kill Sumbh, Chandi approached him. —220

SWAYYA

Such a war was waged by Chandi in the sky as had never been waged before,

The Sun, Moon, stars, Indra and all other gods saw that war,

The goddess pulled out her sword and struck it on the neck of Sumbh, cutting his body into two parts,

The body of Sumbh cut into two fell in such a way on the earth as the same had been ripped by the saw. —221

DOHIRA

After killing Sumbh, Chandika rose to blow her conch,

Then she sounded the gong as a mark of victory, with great delight in her mind. —222

The goddess killed the king of demons in this way in an instant,

Holding her weapons in her eight hands, she destroyed the army of demons. —223

SWAYYA

When Chandi appeared with her sword in the battlefield, none of the demons could withstand her ire,

She killed and destroyed all; who can then wage a war without the king?

The enemies trembled with fear in their hearts, they abandoned the pride of their heroism,

Then the demons, leaving the battlefield, ran away like the good qualities from the avarice. —224

End of the seventh chapter entitled "Slaying of Sumbh" in Ath Chandi Charitra Ukati Bilas of *Markandeya Purana*.

SWAYYA

With whose fear Indra had fled from heaven and Brahma and all other gods had been filled with fear,

The same demons, seeing their defeat in the battlefield being devoid of their power had run away,

The jackals and vultures, having been dejected, have returned to the forest, even the two watches of the day have not elapsed,

The mother of the world (goddess), ever the protector of saints, hath conquered the great enemies Sumbh and Nisumbh. —225

All the gods gathering at one place and taking rice, saffron and sandalwood,

Lakhs of gods, circumambulating the goddess immediately applied the frontal mark (of victory) on her forehead,

The glory of that event hath been imagined by the poet in his mind like this—

It seemed that in the sphere of the Moon, the period of "propitious rejoicings" hath penetrated. —226

KABIT

All the gods gathered and sang this eulogy in praise of the goddess "O universal mother, Thou hast effaced a very great sin,

"Thou hast bestowed on Indra the kingdom of heaven by killing the demons, Thou hast earned great reputation and Thy glory hath spread in the world,

"All the sages, spiritual as well as royal bless Thee again and again, they have recited there the *mantra* called 'Brahm-Kavach' (the spiritual coat of mail),"

The praise of Chandika pervades thus in all the three worlds like the merging of pure water of the Ganges in the current of the ocean. —227

SWAYYA

All the women of the gods bless the goddess and performing the *arati* (the religious ceremony performed around the image of the deity) they have lighted the lamp,
They offer flowers, fragrance and rice and the women of Yakshas sing songs of victory,
They burn the incense and blow the conch and supplicate bowing the heads,
"O universal mother, ever giver of the comfort, by killing Sumbh, Thou hast earned a great approbation." —228

Giving all the royal paraphernalia to Indra, Chandi is very much pleased in Her mind,
Stabilising the Sun and Moon in the sky and making them glorious, she herself hath disappeared,
The light of Sun and Moon hath increased in the sky, the poet hath not forgotten its comparison from his mind,
It seemed that the sun had become filthy with dust and the goddess Chandi hath given him the splendour. —229

KABIT

She who is the destroyer of the pride of Madhu and Kaitabh and then the ego of Mahishasura and who is very active in granting the boon,
She who dashed the tumultuous Dhumar Lochan against the earth and sliced the heads of Chand and Mund,
She who is the killer of Raktavija and drinker of his blood, masher of the enemies and beginner of the war with Nisumbh with great ire in the battlefield,
She who is the destroyer of the powerful Sumbh, with sword in her hand and is the conqueror of all the forces of foolish demons, hail, hail to that Chandi. —230

SWAYYA

O goddess, grant me this boon that I may not hesitate to perform good actions,
I may not fear the enemy, when I go to fight and assuredly I may become victorious,
And I may give this instruction to my mind and have this temptation that I may ever utter Thy praise,
When the end of my life comes, then I may die fighting in the battlefield. —231

I have narrated this Chandi Charitra in poetry, which is all full of Raudra *rasa* (sentiment of rage),
The stanzas, one and all, are beautifully composed, which contain new similes from beginning to end,
The poet hath composed it for the pleasure of his mind, and the discourse of seven hundred *shlokas* is completed here,
For whatever purpose a person reads it or listens to it, the goddess will assuredly grant him that. —232

DOHIRA

I have translated the book named *Satsayya* (a poem of seven hundred *shlokas*), which hath nothing to equal it.
The purpose for which the poet hath composed it, Chandi may grant him the same. —233

End of the eighth chapter entitled "Words Hailing the Victory of the Goddess and Indra" in Ath Chandi Charitra Ukati Bilas of *Markandeya Purana*.

THE LORD IS ONE AND THE VICTORY IS OF THE LORD

CHANDI CHARITRA II
The Euology of Chandi Charitra by Tenth Guru

NARAAJ STANZA

The demon-warrior Mahishasura,
That steel-clad hero extended (his dominions),
He conquered Indra, the king of gods,
And ruled over the three worlds. —1

At that time the gods ran away,
And all of them gathered together,
They inhabited the Kailasa mountain,
With great fear in their mind. —2

They disguised themselves as great Yogis,
And throwing their weapons, they all ran away,
Crying in great distress they walked,
The fine heroes were in great agony. —3

They lived there for many years,
And endured many sufferings on their bodies,
They meditated on the mother of the universe,
For conquering the demon Mahishasura. —4

The gods were pleased,
And sped to worship the feet of the goddess,
They stood before her,
And recited her eulogy. —5

RASAAVAL STANZA

Then the gods ran towards the goddess with bowed heads,
The followers were showered and all the saints (gods) were pleased. —6

The goddess was worshipped with the recitation of Vedas manifested by Brahma,
When they fell at the feet of the goddess, all their sufferings ended. —7

They made their supplication and pleased the goddess,
Who wore all her weapons and mounted the lion. —8

The gongs resounded without interruption,
The sound was heard by the demon-king, who made preparations for the war. —9

The demon-king marched forward and appointed four generals,
One was Chamar, the second was Chichhur, both brave and persistent. —10

The third was the brave Biralachh, they were all mighty warriors and most tenacious,
They were great archers and marched forward like dark clouds. —11

DOHIRA

The arrows showered by all the demons together in great numbers,
Became a garland around the neck of the goddess (the universal mother), bedecking it. —12

BHUJANG PRAYAAT STANZA

All the shafts shot by the demons with their hands,
Were intercepted by the goddess to protect herself,
Many were thrown on the ground with her shield and many were entrapped within the baited trap,
The clothes saturated with blood created an illusion of Holi. —13

The trumpets sounded and Durga began to wage war,
She had *pattas*, axes and baits in her hands,
She caught hold of pellet bow, mace and pellets;
The persistent warriors were shouting "kill, kill." —14

The goddess held eight weapons in her eight hands,
And hit them on the heads of chief demons,
The demon-king roared like a lion in the battlefield,
And chopped into bits many great warriors. —15

TOTAK STANZA

All the demons were filled with anger,
When they were pierced by the arrows of the mother of the world,
Those brave warriors caught hold of their weapons with pleasure,
And began to shoot arrows like the rain-drops. —16

Like the roaring and advancing dark clouds,
The forces of the demon-king marched forward,
The mother of the world, penetrating into the armies of the enemy,
She caught hold of the bow and arrows smilingly. —17

She overthrew in the battlefield the herds of elephants,
And chopped into halves some of them,
On the heads of some of them she struck such a mighty blow,
That the bodies were pierced from the head to the foot-palm. —18

The decayed bodies fell in the battlefield,
Some ran away and did not return,
Some have caught hold of weapons and entered the battlefield,
And after fighting have died and fallen in the field. —19

NARAAJ STANZA

Then the demon-king gathered all the war-paraphernalia,
He drove his horse forward and wanted to kill the Mother (goddess). —20

Then the goddess Durga challenged him, taking up her bow and arrows,
She wounded (one of) the general named Chamar and threw him down on the ground from his elephant. —21

BHUJANG PRAYAAT STANZA

Then the hero named Biralachh was filled with ire,
He bedecked himself with weapons and walked towards the battlefield,
He struck his weapon on the head of the lion and wounded him,
But the brave lion killed him with his hands. —22

When Biralachh was killed, Pingachh ran forward,
Going in front of Durga, he uttered some ironical words,
Roaring like a cloud, he showered a volley of arrows,
That great hero was filled with pleasure in the battlefield. —23

Then the goddess caught hold of her bow and arrows,
She wounded the tyrant on his head with her shaft,
Who swayed, fell down on the ground and breathed his last,
It seemed that the seventh peak of Sumeru mountain had fallen down. —24

When the warriors like Pingachh fell in the field,
Other warriors holding their weapons marched forward,
Then the goddess in great ire shot many arrows,
Which laid to rest many warriors in the battlefield. —25

CHAUPAI

The enemies who came before the goddess,
They were all killed by her,
When all the army was thus effaced,
Then the egoistic demon-king was filled with rage. —26

Then the goddess Durga herself waged the war,
And picked up and killed the warriors wearing armour,
The flame of ire manifested itself from her forehead,
Which appeared in the form of goddess Kalka. —27

MADHUBHAAR STANZA

The flames of fire came from her mouth and she herself came out from the forehead (of Durga),
She killed the great elephants and the warriors on horseback. —28

The arrows are being shot and the swords are glistening,
The daggers are being struck and it appears that the festival of Holi is being celebrated. —29

The weapons are being used unhesitatingly, which create clattering sounds,
The guns boom and produce roaring sounds. —30

The Mother (goddess) challenges and the wounds burst,

The youthful warriors fight and the horses dance. —31

ROOAAMAL STANZA

With increased anger, the demon-king sped forward,
He had four kinds of forces with him, who caused dance of sharp weapons,
Whosoever was struck by the weapons of the goddess, those fighting warriors fell in the field,
Somewhere the elephants and somewhere horses are roaming without riders in the battlefield. —32

Somewhere clothes, turbans and fly-whisks are lying scattered and somewhere elephants, horses and chieftains are lying dead,
Somewhere generals and warriors with weapons and armours are lying down,
Somewhere the sound of arrows, swords, gun, axes and special shafts is being heard,
Somewhere the heroes pierced by the daggers have fallen gracefully. —33

Large-sized vultures are flying there, the dogs are barking and the jackals are howling,
The intoxicated elephants look like the winged-mountains and the crows, flying down eat the flesh,
The swords on the bodies of the demons appear like small fish and the shields look like tortoises,
On their bodies, the steel-armour looks elegant and the blood is flowing down like flood. —34

The new young warriors appear like boats and the charioteers look like ships,
All this appears as if the traders loading their commodities are coyly running out of the battlefield,
The arrows of the battlefield are like the agents, who are busy in settling the account of the transaction,
The armies are fastly moving in the field for settlement and emptying their treasure of quivers. —35

Somewhere multi-coloured garments and chopped limbs are lying,
Somewhere there are shields and armours and somewehre there are only weapons,
Somewhere there are heads, flags and ensigns scattered here and there,
In the battlefield all the enemies have fallen down while fighting and none has been left alive. —36

Then in great ire, the demon, Mahishasura marched forward,
He appeared in a frightful form and held up all his weapons and arms,
The goddess Kalka took her sword in her hand and killed him instantly,
His soul left Brahmrandhra (the life-channel of Dasam Dvar) and merged in Divine Light. —37

DOHIRA

After killing Mahishasura, the Mother of the world was greatly pleased,
And from that day the whole world gives the sacrifice of the animals for the attainment of peace. —38

Here ends the first chapter entitled "Killing of Mahishasura" of Chandi Charitra II in Bachittar Natak.

Here begins the Description of the War with Dhumar Nain

KULAK STANZA

Then the goddess roared and there was continuous intonation,
All were delighted and felt comfortable. —1-39
The trumpets sounded and all the gods shouted,
They eulogise the goddess and shower flowers on her. —2-40
They worshipped the goddess in various ways and sang her praises,
They have touched her feet and all their sorrows have ended. —3-41
They sang the songs of victory and showered flowers,
They bowed their heads and obtained great comfort. —4-42

DOHIRA

The goddess Chandi disappeared after bestowing kingdom on the gods,
Then after some time, both the demon kings came to power. —5-43

CHAUPAI

Both Sumbh and Nisumbh marched with their forces,
They conquered many enemies in water and on land,
They seized the kingdom of Indra, the king of gods,
Seshanaga sent his head-jewel as a gift. —6-44

They snatched the treasure of Kuber and conquered the kings of various countries,
Wherever they sent their forces, they returned after conquering many countries. —7-45

DOHIRA

All the gods were filled with fear and thought in their mind,
Being helpless, they all ran to come under the refuge of the goddess. —8-46

NARAAJ STANZA

The gods ran in great fear and felt ashamed with particular self-abasement,
They had fitted poisonous shafts in their bows and in this way they went to reside in the city of goddess. —9-47

Then the goddess was filled with great rage and marched towards the battlefield with her weapons and arms,
She drank the nectar in her delight and roared while taking the sword in her hand. —10-48

RASAAVAL STANZA

Listening to the talk of the gods, the queen (goddess) mounted the lion,
She had worn all her auspicious weapons and she is the one who effaces all the sins. —11-49

The goddess commanded that highly inebriating trumpets be sounded,
Then the conches created great noise, which was heard in all the four directions. —12-50

The demons marched forward and brought great forces,
Their faces and eyes were red like blood and they shouted pricking words. —13-51

Four types of forces rushed and shouted from their mouths: "kill, kill,"
They took up in their hands the arrows, daggers and swords. —14-52

They are all active in warfare and shoot arrows,
The weapons like swords and daggers glisten. —15-53

The great heroes rushed forward and many of them shot arrows,
They strike blows on the enemy with such swiftness like the water-bird. —16-54

BHUJANG PRAYAAT STANZA

With elevated tail and full of rage the lion ran forward,
There the goddess holding the conch in her hand blew it,
Its sound reverberated in all the fourteen regions,
The face of the goddess was filled with brightness in the battlefield. —17-55

Then Dhumar Nain, the weapon-wielder, was greatly excited,
He took many brave warriors with him,
They besieged the mountain and began to shout at the top of their voice,
Which when heard could destroy the pregnancy of women. —18-56

When the goddess heard the voice the demon-chief, she was greatly enraged,
She bedecked herself with shield and armour and wore the steel-helmet on her head,
She mounted the lion and shouted loudly,
Hearing her shouts, the pride of the demons was destroyed. —19-57

In great ire, the goddess penetrated into the demon-army,
She chopped into halves the great heroes,
On whomsoever the goddess struck her blow with her trident and the destructive weapon Saihathi,
He could not hold again his bow and arrows in his hands. —20-58

RASAAVAL STANZA

Whosoever was shot with the arrows, he was killed instantly,
Wherever the lion rushed forward he destroyed the army. —21-59

All those who were killed, they were thrown into caves,
The enemies who confronted could not return alive. —22-60

Those who were active in the battlefield, they were all decimated,
Those who caught hold of weapons, they were all killed. —23-61
Then the mother Kali flared up like the flaming fire,
To whomsoever she struck, he departed for heaven. —24-62
The whole army was destroyed within a very short time,
Dhumar Nain was killed and the gods heard it in heaven. —25-63

DOHIRA

The demon forces ran towards their king,
Intimating him that Kali had killed Dhumar Nain and the forces had fled in disappointment. —26-64

Here ends the second chapter entitled "Killing of Dhumar Nain" of Chandi Charitra II in Bachittar Natak.

Now the Battle with Chand and Mund is described

DOHIRA

In this way, killing the demons, the goddess Durga went to her abode,
He who reads or listens to this discourse, he will attain in his house wealth and miraculous powers. —1-65

CHAUPAI

When it was learnt that Dhumar Nain had been killed,
The demon-king then called Chand and Mund,
They were sent after bestowing many honours on them,
And also many gifts like horses, elephants and chariots. —2-66
Those who had earlier seen the goddess, they were sent towards Kailasa mountain (as spies),
When the goddess heard some rumour about them,
She then promptly came down with her weapons and armour. —3-67

ROOAAL STANZA

Decorating their forces many demon-generals marched towards the battlefield,
Many warriors are with half-shaven heads, many with full-shaven heads and many are with matted hair,
All of them, in great fury, are causing the dance of their weapons and armour,
They are running and striking blows, causing their sharp swords to shake and glitter. —4-68
All the blows of weapons and arms, which struck the goddess, they appeared as garlands of flowers around her neck,
Seeing this all the demons were filled with anger and astonishment,
Many of them running ahead repeatedly strike blows with their weapons,
And with shouts of "kill, kill," they are fighting and falling down. —5-69
The horse-riding, generals are driving forward the horses and the elephant-riding generals are goading their elephants,
Facing unlimited weapons, the enemy, generals, enduring the blows are still making an assault,
The armies crushing the warriors are marching forward and showering their arrows,
Many heroic fighters, became limbless, have fallen down in the battlefield. —6-70
Somewhere the shafts are falling like rain-showers and somewhere the swords are striking blows collectively,
The elephants seen together are like stony rocks and the heads of the warriors appear like stones,
The crooked arms appear like octopus and the chariot-wheels are like tortoises,
The hair seem like noose and scum and the crushed bones like sand. —7-71
The warriors have bedecked themselves with weapons and the elephants are roaring while moving forward,
The horse-riding warriors are speedily moving with the sounds of various types of musical instruments,
Holding their weapons in their hands, the heroes are shouting "kill, kill,"
Blowing many conches, the demons are running in the battlefield. —8-72
The conches and horns are being blown loudly and the generals of the enemy are ready for war,
Somewhere the cowards, forsaking their shame, are running away,

CHANDI CHARITRA II

The sound of large-sized drums is being heard and the flags are fluttering,
The forces are roaming and striking their maces. —9-73
The heavenly maids are bedecking themselves and offering ornaments to the warriors,
Selecting their heroes, the heavenly ladies are being bound with them in wedlock by showering the oil impregnated with the essence of flowers,
They have taken away the warriors with them in their vehicles,
The heroes inebriated for fighting in the war, jump from the vehicles and being shot with arrows, fall down below. —10-74
Delightfully shouting in the battlefield, the heroic generals have waged war,
Who had several times conquered the king and other chieftains of gods,
Whom Durga (Kapali) chopped and thrown in various directions,
And dealt with those who had ground the mountains with the strength of their hands and feet. —11-75
The enemies speedily marching ahead are killing countless horses,
And in the battlefield, the terrible stream of blood is flowing,
The weapons like bow and arrows, sword, trident and sharp axe are being used,
The goddess Kali, in great rage, struck down and killed both Chand and Mund. —12-76

DOHIRA

Kali in great rage, struck down both Chand and Mund and killed them,
And all the army, that was there, was destroyed in an instant. —13-77

Here ends the third chapter entitled "Killing of Chand and Mund" of Chandi Charitra II in Bachittar Natak.

Now the War with Raktavija is described

SORATHA

Then the demon-king heard this news that Kali had killed Chand and Mund,
Then the brothers sat and decided in this manner. —1-78

CHAUPAI

Then the king called Raktavija and sent him after giving him enormous wealth,
He was also given various types of forces, which were fourfold: on horses, on elephants, on chariots and on foot. —2-79
Raktavija marched after sounding his trumpet, which was heard even in the habitation of gods,
The earth trembled and the sky vibrated, all the gods including the king were filled with fear. —3-80
When they came near the Kailasa mountain, they sounded trumpets, drums and tabors,
When the gods heard the noises with their ears, the goddess Durga descended the mountain, taking many weapons and arms. —4-81
The goddess showered arrows like incessant rain, which caused the horses and their riders fall down,
Many warriors and their chieftains fell, it seemed as if the trees had been sawed. —5-82
Those enemies who came in front of her, they could not again return to their homes alive,
Those who were struck by the sword, they fell down in two halves or four quarters. —6-83

BHUJANG PRAYAAT STANZA

The sword which she has struck in ire, it hath glistened like lightning in the month of Bhadon,
The jingling sound of bows appears like the sound of flowing stream,
And the steel-weapons have been struck in great anger, which appear unique and frightening. —7-84
The sound of drums rises in the battle and the warriors glisten their weapons,
There is a great rush of blows and the men of endurance are experiencing shocks,
The vultures shriek and the clarionets are being played,
It appears that the terrible tigers are roaring and roaming. —8-85
On the other side the demon warrior Raktavija was infuriated,
He shot his arrows very dextrously,

The goddess then speedily struck her sword,
Which caused the demon to fall senseless, it seemed that he has passed away. —9-86

When he came to senses, the mighty hero roared,
For four *gharis* the steel clashed with steel,
With the infliction of the arrow of the goddess, the blood of Raktavija began to fall on the ground,
With innumerable drops of blood arose innumerable Raktavija, who began to shout with rage. —10-87

All the warriors who arose, were destroyed by Kali,
Somewhere their shields, armour and wounded bodies are lying scattered,
With all the drops of blood that fall on the ground, the same number of warriors arise shouting "kill, kill." —11-88

There were struck blows after blows and the warriors being chopped are rolling in dust,
Their heads, faces and pieces of flesh are lying scattered,
For four hundred *kos*, the battlefield was occupied by warriors,
Most of whom are lying dead or senseless. —12-89

RASAAVAL STANZA

From all the four sides, the warriors are marching forward, and are shouting "kill, kill" from their mouths,
They have fixed firmly their banners and in excitement their rage is increasing. —13-90

The warriors filled with delight are showering their arrows,
All the four types of forces are moving forward and staying in their arena. —14-91

With the use of all the weapons, the stream of blood began to flow,
The most honoured warriors arose with bow and arrows in their hands. —15-92

They are roaring in great anger, and the clarionets and drums are being played,
Filled with great fury, the wielders of canopies are much excited. —16-93

There are shouts after shouts and the forces are running hither and thither,
With great ire, the steel is being used, and the inebriated warriors look glorious. —17-94

The warriors with chopped limbs have fallen and the red blood appears like flaming fire,
The jingling and the twanging sounds of weapons are being heard. —18-95

The weapons are being struck with clinking sound and both sides want their victory,
Many are intoxicated with wine and in great fury, they appear highly inflamed. —19-96

They are flushed with rage and are absorbed in waging war,
They offer arrows and are discussing archery. —20-97

The heroes are absorbed in heroic feats and are raining the shafts,
They are penetrating into the warrior-stronghold and do not turn away their eyes from it —21-98

They are striking their weapons, facing the enemy and are pulling their bow-strings,
They are showering the arrows and striking the sharp steel-arms. —22-99

The stream of blood has become full and the *houris* are roaming in the sky,
The goddess Kali is roaring in the firmament and the female demon of the begging bowl is laughing. —23-100

Somewhere there are dead horses and somewhere the fallen mighty warriors,
Somewhere there are broken shields and somewhere the wounded elephants are roaming. —24-101

Somewhere the armour is penetrated and the inflicted skin is being seen,
Somewhere there are chopped elephants and somewhere the saddles of horses are seen cut down. —25-102

The brave warriors are engaged in inimical acts, all of them are fighting with their weapons,
Realising the presence of warriors in the battlefield, the ghosts and evil spirits are dancing. —26-103

The meat-eaters are dancing, those who roam in the sky, are laughing,
The crows are cawing and the elegant warriors are intoxicated. —27-104

The wearers of canopies are full of fury and from their bows shoot their arrows,

They are desirous of their victory and thus are shooting their sharp shafts. —28-105

Ganas, Gandharvas, spies, minstrels and the Siddhas with miraculous powers, all of them laugh and the warriors are inebriated with rage. —29-106

The vampires are belching and the egoist warriors are shouting,

The drums are creating loud sound and there are clanging noises. —30-107

The mighty warriors are roaring and the new instruments are being sounded,

The trumpets are resounding and the forces of Durga and the demons are fighting. —31-108

BIJAI STANZA

All the arrows shot by the enemy bedeck as garlands of flowers around the neck of the goddess,

Seeing this wonder the forces of the enemy have run away from the battlefield and none could stay there,

Many elephants have fallen at that place alongwith many healthy steeds, all are smeared with blood,

It appears that running away out of the fear of Indra, the mountains have hidden themselves in the sea. —32-109

MANOHAR STANZA

When the Mother of the Universe waged the war, holding her bow in her hand and blowing her conch,

Her lion walked roaring in the field in great ire, crushing and destroying the forces of the enemy,

He goes on tearing with his nails the armours on the bodies of the warriors and the torn limbs appear like

The rising flames of fire extended in midst of the ocean. —33-110

BIJAY STANZA

The sound of the bow permeates the whole universe and the flying dust of the battlefield hath spread over the whole firmament,

The brightened faces have fallen after receiving blows and seeing them, the hearts of the vampires have been pleased,

The forces of the extremely infuriated enemies are elegantly stationed in the whole battlefield,

And winsome and youthful warriors are falling in bits in this manner as though the apothecary after grinding the earth, hath prepared the digestive medicine (*churan*). —34-111

SANGEET BHUJANG PRAYAAT STANZA

The sounds of the blows of the daggers and swords are being heard,

The sounds of the shafts and gunshots are being heard,

Various sounds of musical instruments are resounding,

The warriors are roaring and shouting loudly. —35-112

The great heroes have been infuriated,

With the jingling of their weapons they are standing firmly on their feet,

The weapons are being struck and the brave fighters are belching. —36-113

The warriors seem pleased on shooting sharp arrows on the bodies,

There are loud shouts with profound resoundings,

And the poets describe them in their verses. —37-114

The demons are running away and the heroes are shouting loudly,

The sounds are produced by the striking axes and daggers,

The arrows and the guns are creating their own noises. —38-115

The loud noise of drums and the resounding of conches and trumpets is being heard in the battlefield,

The musical instruments of the warriors are being played and the ghosts and goblins are dancing. —39-116

The noises of the arrows and shafts, daggers and swords are being heard,

The music of the musical instruments and the drumming of the trumpets resounds and the warriors and chieftains are doing their job amidst such resonance. —40-117

The conches, clarionets and the drums resounded. The trumpets and musical instruments produced their sounds and alongwith their resonance, the warriors thundered. — 41-118

NARAAJ STANZA

All the forms of demons created with the spilling of the blood of Raktavija on the ground, were killed by the goddess,

All the forms that are going to materialise, will also be destroyed by Durga. —42-119

With the showering of weapons (on Raktavija), the currents of blood oozed out (from the body of Raktavija),

All the drops that fell (on the ground), the goddess Kali drank them all. —43-120

RASAAVAL STANZA

The demon-chief Raktavija became bloodless and his limbs became very weak,

Ultimately he fell down on the ground wavering like the cloud on the earth. —44-121

All the gods were pleased (to see this) and they showered the flowers,

Raktavija was killed and in this way the goddess saved the saints. —45-122

Here ends the fourth chapter entitled "The killing of Raktavija" of Chandi Charitra II in Bachittar Natak.

Now the Battle with Nisumbh is described

DOHIRA

When Sumbh and Nisumbh heard about the destruction of Raktavija,

They marched forward themselves gathering their forces and bedecking themselves with axes and nooses. —1-123

BHUJANG PRAYAAT STANZA

The mighty warriors Sumbh and Nisumbh began the invasion,

The sound of musical instruments and trumpets resounded,

The shade of canopies spread over eight hundred *kos*,

And the sun and moon sped away and Indra, the king of gods was frightened. —2-124

The drum and the tabor reverberated,

The earth splitted because of the roar of the lion and the attack of his nails,

The sound of the trumpets and the tabors is being heard,

And the huge vultures and crows are shrieking and flying. —3-125

The sky is filled with the dust risen by the hooves of the animals,

And these animals have broken into pieces Vindhyachal mountain and other small mounts,

The goddess Kali hearing the din, held her weapons in her hands,

While roaring she ate up the limbs of the killed youthful warriors. —4-126

RASAAVAL STANZA

The brave warriors are thundering and the horses are speedily moving,

The bows are being pulled and the shafts are raining. —5-127

From this side the lion hath roared and the conch hath been blown,

Its sound is filling the atmosphere,

The sky is filled with the dust risen from the battlefield. —6-128

The warriors have bedecked themselves with weapons and are thundering like clouds,

They are furiously moving, carrying countless weapons. —7-129

From all four sides the warriors are closing their ranks, shouting "kill, kill,"

The mighty warriors are thundering and countless weapons are striking blows. —8-130

Carrying the powerful weapons in their hands, their faces and eyes are becoming blood-red,

In great fury, they are marching and showering their arrows. —9-131

Many of the tyrants have been killed and consequently countless weapons are lying scattered hither and thither,

The goddess hath been pleased and is showering arrows. —10-132

BELI BIDDARAM STANZA

The crows are uttering "caw, caw" and the blood of mighty heroes is flowing,

The arrows and swords are waving in the wind and the ghosts and evil spirits are catching the dead. —11-33

The tabors are resounding and the swords are glistening,

The sounds of striking daggers and the thundering of the warriors are being heard. —12-134

The arrows shot from the bows create surprises in the minds of the warriors,
The vampires are fearing from the sound of the tabor and the female evil spirits are wandering and laughing. —13-135
Because of the rain of sharp arrows, the blood is splashing,
Many warriors are roaring and the jackals, in particular, being pleased are howling. —14-136
The immortal Durga, the dyer with blood, is moving, pleased with her task,
The roaring lion is running and such is the continuous situation in the battlefield. —15-137
The drums are resounding and the daggers are clanking,
The fighting warriors, in great fury, are striking their swords. —16-138

DOHIRA

Seeing with his own eyes the running demon-army,
Sumbh spoke to the mighty warriors standing near him. —17-139

NARAAJ STANZA

Striking his foot on the earth Sumbh sent Nisumbh saying:
"Go immediately and bring Durga after binding her. —18-140
Thundering and in great fury, he marched forward alongwith his arms,
The trumpets were sounded, hearing which caused the king of gods run away. —19-141
Beating his drums, he marched forward taking countless warriors with him,
He called and gathered so many brave fighters, seeing whom the gods were frightened. —20-142

MADHUBHAAR STANZA

The king of gods trembled and related all his painful circumstances to God Shiva,
When he gave out all his reflections, Shiva asked him about the number of his warriors. —21-143
(He further asked him) to make friends with all others through all possible means,
So that the victory of the mother of the world is assured. —22-144
Bring out all your powers and send them in the war,
So that they may go before enemies and in great rage destroy them. —23-145
The wise gods did as advised,
And sent their boundless powers from amongst themselves to the battlefield. —24-146

BIRADH NIRAAJ STANZA

Immediately the powers wore the swords and went towards the arena of war,
And with them ran the great vultures and belching vampires,
The terrible crows smiled and the blind headless bodies also moved,
From this side, the gods and other heroes began to shower shafts. —25-147

RASAAVAL STANZA

All the powers came and went back paying their obeisance,
They wore terrible arms and killed many great warriors. —26-148
Their faces and eyes are reddened with blood and they are uttering challenging words from their mouths,
They are holding arms, daggers and swords in their hands. —27-149
From the other side, the demons are thundering, and the trumpets are resounding,
They are wearing cruel armour, holding winsome shields in their hands. —28-150
They began to roar from all the four sides and hearing their voices, all the gods trembled,
The sharp arrows were shot and the garments and fly whisks were torn. —29-151
Inebriated with extreme ferocity, the warriors are seen with brightened faces,
The goddess Durga, being very much pleased, hath begun showering the rain of arrows. —30-152
On this side, the goddess is busy in killing and the other side the lion is tearing up all,
Hearing the roars of the Ganas (attendants) of Shiva, the demons have become frightened. —31-153

There was rain of arrows and with this the goddess became victorious,
All the tyrants were killed by the goddess and the mother saved the saints. —32-154

The goddess killed Nisumbh and destroyed the army of demons,
On this side the lion roared and from the other side all the demons fled. —33-155

On the victory of the army of gods, there was rain of flowers,
The saints hailed it and the demons trembled with fear. —34-156

Here ends the fifth chapter entitled "The killing of Nisumbh" of Chandi Charitra II in Bachittar Natak.

Now the War with Sumbh is described

BHUJANG PRAYAAT STANZA

When Sumbh heard about the death of his younger brother,
He, in fury and excitement, marched forward to wage war, bedecking himself with arms and armour,
There was terrible sound which permeated in the firmament,
Hearing this sound, the gods, demons and Shiva all trembled. —1-157

Brahma was frightened and the throne of Indra, the king of gods, wavered,
Seeing the bedecked form of the demon-king, the mountains also began to fall,
Shrieking and screaming in great ire the demons appear,
Like the seventh peak of Sumeru mountain. —2-158

Bedecking himself, Sumbh raised a terrible sound,
Hearing which the pregnancy of women was miscarried,
The furious warriors made continuous use of steel arms and the weapons began to rain,
The voices of vultures and vampires were heard in the battlefield. —3-159

With the use of weapons and arms, the winsome armours were being cut,
And the warriors performed their religious duties in a nice manner,
There was consternation in the whole battlefield and the canopies and garments began to fall,
The chopped bodies were being trodden in the dust and because of the infliction of arrows, the warriors were becoming senseless. —4-160

The warriors fell in the battlefield alongwith the elephants and goads,
The headless trunks began to dance senselessly,
The large-sized vultures began to fly and the crows with curved beaks began to caw,
The frightful sound of drums and the clatter of tabors was heard. —5-161

There was knocking of helmets and the sound of blows on the shields,
The swords began to chop the bodies with terrible noises,
The warriors were attacked continuously and the clatter of daggers was being heard,
There was such consternation that its noise was heard in the nether-world by the Nagas. —6-162

The vampires, female evil spirits, ghosts, headless trunks and the Kapalikas are dancing in the battlefield,
All the gods appear pleased and the demon-king is getting furious,
It appears that the flame of fire is blazing. —7-163

DOHIRA

All those demons, sent by Sumbh, in great fury,
Were destroyed by the goddess like the water-drops on the hot iron-griddle. —8-164

NARAAJ STANZA

He (demon-king) marched forward, in great fury, bedecking himself with an army of warriors,
He moved, wearing his weapons, with shouts of "kill, kill." —9-165

SANGEET MADHUBHAAR STANZA

There were sounds of clattering and twanging,
The warriors were shouting loudly and thundering profoundly. —10-166

The resonance of trumpets was precipitating the youthful warriors,
Those brave men were jumping and engaged in chivalrous acts. —11-167

In great rage, the warriors showed signs of anger on their faces,

CHANDI CHARITRA II

They were striking their swords. —12-168

The arrows shot by the warriors were blowing away and throwing down those coming in front of them . —13-169

The winsome brave horse-riders were fighting courageously. —14-170

Several types of noises were spreading in the battlefield. —15-171

The arms were being swung in the battlefield and the stream of blood was flowing,

Manifesting her frighful form Kapali Durga was dancing. —16-172

NARAAJ STANZA

Killing the countless tyrants, Durga effaced many sufferings,

The blind trunks were rising and moving and they were being felled on the ground with the shower of arrows. —17-173

The sounds of working bows and striking daggers are being heard,

In this continuous shower of arrows the significantly honoured heroes have been tested. —18-174

SANGEET NARAAJ STANZA

Alongwith the clattering of swords, the youthful warriors are busy in hand-fight,

The heroic warriors have been inspired to face the fighters. —19-175

RASAAVAL STANZA

The striking swords are glistening and the daggers are striking fastly,

The brave warriors are giving blows of maces on the back of the lion. —20-176

Somewhere the blood is being drunk, somewhere the head lying broken,

Somewhere there is din and somewhere the heroes are rising again. —21-177

Somewhere the warriors are lying in the dust, somewhere there is repetition of the shouts of "kill, kill,"

Somewhere the minstrels are eulogising the warriors and somewhere warriors with wounded bellies are lying down. —22-178

The bearers of canopies are running away and somewhere the blood is being flown,

Somewhere the tyrants are being destroyed and the warriors are running hither and thither like the Persian wheel. —23-179

All the warriors are bedecked with the bows,

And all of them are holding their swords like the dreadful saw. —24-180

They are verily of dark complexion like the saltish sea,

Though they have been destroyed several times, but still they are shouting "kill, kill."—25-181

Bhavani (Durga) hath destroyed all like the *jawahan* plant destroyed by the continuous rain,

Many other brave demons have been crushed under her feet. —26-182

The enemies have been destroyed in the first round and thrown away. They have been struck on their bodies with weapons and made cool (by death),

Many mighty warriors have been killed and the sound of the drums is continuously being heard. —27-183

Wonderful type of arrows have been shot and because of them many fighters have expired,

When the demon-warriors of great might saw the goddess in person, they became senseless. —28-184

Many brave fighters were torn by the lion and thrown on the ground,

And many huge demons were personally killed and destroyed by the goddess. —29-185

Many real heroes who stuck fast before the goddess and who were extemely hard-hearted and renowned for their mercilessness ultimately ran away. —30-186

The egoist warriors with brightened faces who ran forward, and also the mighty and furious heroes were killed by the dreadful death. —31-187

DOHIRA

In this way, destroying the tyrants, Durga again wore her weapons and armour,

At first she showered her arrows and then her lion roared heavily. —32-188

RASAAVAL STANZA

When the demon-king Sumbh heard all that had happened, he marched forward in great excitement,

His soldiers bedecked with weapons came forward to wage war. —33-189

The sounds created by drums, blows and trumpets were continuously heard. —34-190

The swords of the persistent and renowned fighters glistened,

The great heroes raised loud shouts and the trumpets sounded. —35-191

The demons thundered from all the four sides and the gods collectively trembled,

Showering her arrows Durga herself is testing the strength of all. —36-192

CHAUPAI

All those demons, carrying their weapons, came in front of the goddess,

Were all subjected to death,

The edges of the swords are glistening and the headless trunks, in dreadful forms are raising their voices. —37-193

DOHIRA

The elephants, horses and warriors on foot were all chopped and none could survive,

Then the king Sumbh himself marched forward for war and on seeing him it appears that whatever he will desire, he will achieve. —38-194

CHAUPAI

On this side, Durga after reflecting called a female messenger of Shiva and making her conscious gave this message in her ear, "Send Lord Shiva to the place where the demon-king is standing." —39-195

When the female messenger of Shiva heard this, she sent Shiva as a messenger there. Since that day, the name of Durga became "Shiv-Duti" (the messenger of Shiva), all men and women know this. —40-196

Shiva said to the demon-king, "Listen to my words, the mother of the universe hath said this that either you return the kingdom to gods or wage the war with me." —41-197

The demon-king Sumbh did not accept this proposal and in his pride, marched forward for war. The place where Kali like death was thundering, that demon-king reached there. —42-198

There the edges of swords glistened and the ghosts, goblins and evil spirits began to dance, there the blind headless trunks came into motion senselessly. There many Bhairavas and Bhimas began to roam. —43-199

The clarionets, drums and trumpets sounded and many types of warriors thundered in the battlefield; the tambourines, tabors etc., were played loudly and the musical instruments like shehnai etc., were being played in such numbers that they cannot be counted.— 44-200

MADHUBHAAR STANZA

The horses are neighing and the trumpets are resounding,

The bedecked warriors are roaring profoundly. —45-201

The heroes coming near unhesitatingly are striking blows and jumping,

The smart warriors fight each other and the beautiful heroes are bedecking themselves. The heavenly demsels (Apsaras) are feeling inspired. —46-202

The horses are being chopped and the faces are being torn,

The sounds created by tridents are being heard. —47-203

The trumpets are resounding and the youthful warriors are thundering,

The kings and chieftains are bedecked and the elephants are screeching. —48-204

BHUJANG PRAYAAT STANZA

The beautiful horses are roaming hither and thither,

The elephants of the princes are roaring dreadfully,

The sound of conches and drum is rising,

The clarionets are being played continuously. —49-205

The swords and daggers are producing their sounds,

There is vehement run in the whole battlefield,

The bodies having been chopped and the garments and fly whisks having been torn have fallen down,

Somewhere the hands, somewhere the foreheads and somewhere the armours are lying scattered. —50-206

RASAAVAL STANZA

The mighty enemies are busy in fighting with all their weapons,

CHANDI CHARITRA II

Holding their arms, they are shouting "kill, kill." —51-207

Being completely dressed with their weapons the brave fighters are roaring,
There has been a volley of arrows producing hissing sounds. —52-208

Various types of musical instruments are being played and the Gandharvas are laughing,
The warriors after fixing their banners firmly are busy in fighting and their armours are being torn with arrows. —53-209

From all the four sides, the arrows are being showered,
The fierce and frightful warriors are busy in various types of prattle. —54-210

BHUJANG PRAYAAT STANZA

Somewhere the brave fighters are being chopped and somewhere the arrows are being showered,
The horses without saddless are lying in dust in the battlefield,
The warriors of gods and demons both are fighting against one another,
It appears that the dreadful warriors are Bhishma Pitamahas. —55-211

The decorated horses and elephants are thundering,
And the arrows of brave warriors are being shot,
The clatter of swords and the resounding of trumpets,
Alongwith the sounds of daggers and drums are being heard. —56-212

The sounds of drums and shields resound continuously,
And the horses running hither and thither have caused consternation,
The daggers are being struck violently and the swords are besmeared with blood,
The armours on the bodies of the warriors are breaking and the limbs are coming out with them. —57-213

The blows of swords on the helmets create flames of fire,
And in the utter darkness that has spread, the ghosts and goblins considering it night, have awakened,
The vampires are belching and the tabors are being played,
And in accompaniment with their sound, the ghosts and evil spirits are dancing. —58-214

BELI BIDDARAM STANZA

All the blows struck by the weapons have been annulled by the goddess Durga,
Besides these all other blows, that are being struck, are being annulled and the weapons are thrown on the ground by the goddess. —59-215

Kali herself made use of her weapons and made all the weapons of the demons ineffective,
When the gods saw Sumbh without weapons they began to hail the goddess. —60-216

The musical instruments were played in the firmament and now the gods also began to roar,
The gods began to view repeatedly and raise shouts of victory. —61-217

Now in great rage in the battlefield, the dreadful Kali raised her six hands of her arms powerfully and struck them on the head of Sumbh and with one blow she destroyed the tyrant. —62-218

DOHIRA

The manner in which, with extreme fury, Kali destroyed the demon-king Sumbh,
All the enemies of the saints are destroyed in the same manner. —63-219

Here ends the sixth chapter entitled "The killing of Sumbh" of Chandi Charitra II in Bachittar Natak.

Now the Words of Victory are related

BELI BIDDARAM STANZA

All the gods are hailing the victory of the goddess and showering the flowers,
They brought the saffron and with great delight they applied the mark on their foreheads. —1-220

CHAUPAI

All of them extremely eulogised the goddess and repeated the mantra known as "Brahm-kavach,"
All the saints were pleased because the tyrants have been destroyed. —2-221

The comfort of the saints increased in many ways and not even one demon could survive,

The mother of the universe ever helps the saints and is helpful to them everywhere. —3-222

Eulogy of the Goddess

BHUJANG PRAYAAT STANZA

O Yoga-fire, O enlightener of the earth! I salute Thee,
O the destroyer of Sumbh and dreadful manifestation of Death!
O the destroyer of Dhumar Nain, O the destroyer of Raktavija!
O blazing like fire Kalika! I salute Thee. —4-223

O Ambika! O Jambhaha (the killer of the demon Jambh)!
O manifestation of light! I salute Thee,
O the killer of Chand and Mund and O the sovereign of sovereigns! I salute Thee,
O the sawer of the demon Chamar! O the one looking a portrait! I salute Thee. —5-224

O the supreme manifestation of the doer of dreadful actions! I salute Thee,
O the bearer of the three modes of *rajas, sattva* and *tamas*!
O the manifestation of supreme steel armour! O the destroyer of Mahishasura, destroyer of all, the killer of all! I salute Thee. —6-225

O the killer of Biralachh! the destroyer of Karurachh! O the one showing mercy on Brahma in her delight! O Yogamaya! I salute Thee; O Bhairavi, Bhavani, Jalandhari and the destiny through all! I salute Thee. —7-226

Thou art seated everywhere, up and below, Thou art Lakshmi, Kamakhya and Kumar-kanya, Thou art Bhavani and manifestation of Bhairavi and Bhim, Thou art seated at Hinglaj and Pinglaj, Thou art unique, I salute Thee. —8-227

Thou art the performer of dreadful acts, while infuriated in the battlefield, Thou art most wise, master of powers and doer of pure deeds, Thou art most beautiful like an Apsara (heavenly damsel), Padmini and the goddess Parbati, Thou art the source of the power of Shiva, the power of Indra and the power of Brahma. I salute Thee. —9-228

O the maker of the dead ones as thy vehicles! the enchantress the ghosts and goblins! Thou art the greatest Apsara, Parbati and the killer of tyrants, performer of gentle acts like children at the places Hinglaj and Pinglaj! Thou art the power of Kartikeya and Shiva etc.! I salute Thee. —10-229

O the power of Yama! O the power of Bhrigu and the wielder of weapons in Thy hands! I salute Thee. Thou art the wearer of arms, most glorious, unconquerable for ever and conqueror of all, bearer of elegant shield and performer of justice at all times, the Merciful Kalika! I salute Thee. —11-230

O the wielder of bow, sword, shield and mace, the user of the disc and of the honoured portrait! I salute Thee. Thou art the mother of the universe and wielder of trident and dagger! Thou art the knower of all the knowledge of all sciences! I salute Thee. —12-231

Thou art the preserver and destroyer of all, Thou art the rider of the dead, Thou art the destroyer of tyrants in the manifestation of Kali! I salute Thee. O Yoga-fire! the power of Kartikeya! O Ambika! O Bhavani! I salute Thee. —13-232

O the effacer and destroyer of sorrows! O the wager of war with weapons and arms! O most healthy! O supreme fire! O the supreme manifestation of young and old women! I salute Thee. —14-233

O the one with dreadful teeth! the rider of the lion! I salute Thee. Thou art the glistening sword, annulling the daggers, Thou art most profound, omnipresent, eternal and destroyer of tyrants, I salute Thee. —15-234

O the bestower of powers! preserver of all and destroyer of all! the one of the pure form like silver and dreadful like the dark night! Thou art the Yoga-fire and the sickle for the tyrants, I salute Thee. —16-235

O the power of righteousness of the Supreme Lord! Thou art ever new, the destroyer of tyrants, the deceiver of all, the Yoga-fire of Shiva, the steel-armour for the saints and the dreadful Kali for the saints! I salute Thee. —17-236

Thou art the breath-moving process and the early morning worship,

Thou art Anjani (mother of Hanuman), the crusher of the pride of all and the wielder and user of all the weapons, I salute Thee. —18-237

O Anjani! the masher of the pride of tyrants, the sustainer and bestower of pleasure to all the saints! I salute Thee. O the manifestation of trident, wielder of sword in Thy hand, the deliverer of all, the cause and the manifestation of the sword! I salute Thee. —19-238

O Kali, with the begging bowl, and the bestower of bliss! I salute Thee. O one of the most beautiful form like sun-rays and moon-beams! the destroyer of the tyrants, the sustainer of the world and the cause of all causes! I salute Thee. —20-239

O the one who showers her weapons in her pleasure! Thou art the deliverer of all, I salute Thee. O goddess Durga! Thou art most wise, a Yogini, a goddess and a demoness! I salute Thee. —21-240

O the one of the dreadful form and winsome eyes! Thou are the wielder of trident and dagger and speaker of harsh words, I salute Thee. O the blazer of Yoga-fire, the manifestation of supreme wisdom, the destroyer of Chand and Mund and performer of the heinous action of crushing their dead bodies! I salute Thee. —22-241

Thou art the bestower of bliss by destroying the great sinners,

Thou art the remover of the anguish of saints by destroying the tyrants with Thy dreadful teeth, Thou art the knower of Shastras, knower of the use of weapons, perfect in the knowledge of Yaksha and the fulfiller of the desires, I salute Thee. —23-242

O the giver of suffering to the enemies! all the people worship, Thee,

Thou art the creator of all interests and also their destroyer, Thou art the power of Hanuman, Thou art Kalika and manifestation of the sword and wielder of the power in Thy own hands, I salute Thee. —24-243

O the masterly power of Hanuman! Thou art the goddess of Nagark (Kangra), Thou art the manifestation of Kama (love), Thou art Kamakhya, the goddess and the bestower of bliss on all like Kalratri (Kali), O the bestower of the great miraculous powers and wealth and wielder of the sword! I salute Thee. —25-244

O goddess! Thou art four-armed, eight-armed and sustainer of the whole world, O Ambika! Thou art the killer of the demon Jambh, the power of Kartikeya and the crusher of the dead, O Bhavani! I salute Thee. —26-245

O the destroyer of the enemies of the gods! white, black and red coloured, O fire! the enhancer of bliss by conquering illusion, Thou art the *maya* of Unmanifested Brahman and the Shakti of Shiva, I salute Thee. —27-246

Thou art the bestower of cheerfulness to all, the conqueror of all and the manifestation of Kal (death), O Kapali! (the goddess carrying begging bowl), Shiva-Shakti! (the power of Shiva) and Bhadarkali! Thou obtainest satisfaction by piercing Durga, Thou art pure fire-manifestation and also cold-incarnate, I salute Thee. —28-247

O the masticater of the demons! the manifestation of the banners of all religions, the source of the power of Hinglaj and Pinglaj, I salute Thee, O the one of dreadful teeth, Anjani of black colour and the masher of demons! I salute Thee. —28-248

O the adopter of half-moon and wearer of the moon as an ornament!

Thou hast the power of clouds and hast dreadful jaws, Thy forehead is like the moon, O Bhavani! Thou art also Bhairavi and Bhutani, Thou art the wielder of the sword, I salute Thee. —30-249

O Kamakhya and Durga! Thou art the cause and deed of Kaliyuga (the Iron Age), like Apsaras (heavenly damsels) and the Padmini women, Thou art the fulfiller of all desires, Thou art the conqueror Yogini of all and performer of *yajnas* (sacrifices), Thou art the nature of all substances, Thou art the creator of the world and the destroyer of the enemies. —31-250

Thou art pure, holy, ancient, greatness, perfection, maya and unconquerable, Thou art formless, unique, nameless and abodeless, Thou art fearless, unconquerable and treasure of the great *dharma*.—32-251

Thou art indestructible, indistinguishable, deedless and *dharma*-incarnate, O the holder of the arrow in Thy hand and wearer of the armour! I salute Thee. Thou art unconquerable, indistinguishable, formless, eternal, shapeless and the cause of *nirvana* (salvation) and all the works. —33-252

Thou art Parbati, fulfiller of the wishes, the power of Krishna, most powerful, the power of Vamana and art like the fire of the *yajna* (sacrifice), O the chewer of the enemies and masher of their pride, sustainer and destroyer in Thy pleasure! I salute Thee. —34-253

O the rider of the steed like lion! O Bhavani of beautiful limbs! Thou art the destroyer of all engaged in the war, O the mother of the universe having large body! Thou art the power of Yama, the giver of the fruit of actions performed in the world, Thou art also the power of Brahma, I salute Thee. —35-254

O the most pure power of God! Thou art the *maya* and Gayatri, sustaining all, Thou art Chamunda, the wearer of the necklace of heads, Thou art also the fire of the matted locks of Shiva, Thou art the donor of boons and destroyer of tyrants, but Thou Thyself ever remain indivisible. —36-255

O the Saviour of all the saints and the donor of boons to all, the one who ferries across all over the terrible sea of life, the primary cause of all causes, O Bhavani the mother of the universe! I salute Thee again and again. O the manifestation of the sword! Protect me ever with Thy grace. —37-256

Here ends the seventh chapter entitled "The Eulogy of the Goddess" of Chandi Charitra II in Bachittar Natak.

Description of the Praise of Chandi Charitra

BHUJANG PRAYAAT STANZA

The Yoginis have filled their beautiful vessels (with blood) and are moving at various places here and there belching thereby, the comely crows and vultures having liking for that place have also departed for their homes and the warriors have been left to decay in the battlefield uncoubtedly. —1-257

Narada is moving with *vina* in his hand and Shiva, the rider of the bull, playing his tabor, is looking elegant. In the battlefield, the thundering heroes have fallen alongwith the elephants and horses and seeing the chopped heroes rolling in dust, the ghosts and goblins are dancing. —2-258

The blind trunks and the brave Baital are dancing and the fighting warriors alongwith the dancers with the small bells tied around their waists have also been killed. All the resolute assemblies of saints have become fearless, O the mother of the people; Thou hast performed a nice task by conquering the enemies! I salute Thee.—3-259

If any foolish person recites this (poem), his wealth and property will increase here. If any one, not participating in the war, listens to it, he will be bestowed with the power of fighting (in battle) and that yogi, who repeats it, keeping awake throughout the night, he will attain supreme Yoga and miraculous powers. —4-260

Any student, who reads it for the attainment of knowledge, he will become knowledgeable of all the Shastras. Any one either a yogi or a *sannyasi* or a *vairagi*, whosoever reads it, he will be blessed with all the virtues. —5-261

DOHIRA

All those saints, who will ever meditate on Thee, They will attain salvation at the end and will realise the Lord. —6-262

Here ends the eighth chapter entitled "Description of the Praise of Chandi Charitra" of Chandi Charitra II in Bachittar Natak.

THE LORD IS ONE AND THE VICTORY IS OF THE LORD
MAY SRI BHAGAUTI JI (THE SWORD) BE HELPFUL

VAR SRI BHAGAUTI JI KI
The Heroic Poem of Sri Bhagauti Ji (Goddess Durga) by the Tenth King (Guru)

In the beginning I remember Bhagauti, the Lord (whose symbol is the sword) and then I remember Guru Nanak,
Then I remember Guru Angad, Guru Amar Das and Guru Ram Das, may they be helpful to me.
Then I remember Guru Arjan, Guru Hargobind and Guru Har Rai, (After them) I remember Guru Har Krishan, by whose sight all the sufferings vanish,
Then I do remember Guru Tegh Bahadur, through whose grace the nine treasures come running to my house,
May they be helpful to me everwhere. —1
At first the Lord created the double-edged sword and then He created the whole world,
He created Brahma, Vishnu and Shiva and then created the play of nature,
He created the oceans, mountains and the earth and made the sky stable without columns,
He created the demons and gods and caused strife between them,
O Lord! By creating Durga, Thou hast caused the destruction of demons,
Rama received power from Thee and he killed Ravana with arrows,
Krishna received power from Thee and he threw down Kansa by catching his hair.
The great sages and gods, even practising great austerities for several ages, could not know Thy end. —2
The saintly Satyuga (the age of truth) passed away and the treta age of semi-righteousness came,
The discord danced over all the heads and Kal and Narad sounded their tabor,
Mahishasura and Sumbh were created for removing the pride of the gods,
They conquered the gods and ruled over the three worlds,
He was called a great hero and had a canopy moving over his head,
Indra was turned out of his kingdom and he looked towards the Kailasa mountain,
Frightened by the demons, the elements of fear grew enormously in his heart,
He came, therefore to Durga. —3

PAURI

One day Durga came for a bath,
Indra related to her the story of his agony,
The demons have seized from us our kingdom,
They have proclaimed their authority over all the three worlds,
They have played musical instruments in their rejoicings in Amaravati, the city of gods,
All the demons have caused the flight of the gods,
None hath gone and conquered Mahikha (Mahishasura), the demon,
O goddess Durga, I have come under Thy refuge. —4

PAURI

Listening to these words (of Indra), Durga laughed heartily,
She sent for that lion, who was the devourer of demons,
She said to gods, "Do not worry any more,"
For killing the demons, the great mother exhibited great fury. —5

DOHIRA

The infuriated demons came with the desire of fighting in the battlefield,
The swords and daggers glisten with such brilliance that the sun cannot be seen. —6

PAURI

Both the armies faced each other and the drums, conches and trumpets sounded,
The demons came in great rage, decorated with swords and armour,
The warriors were facing the war-front and none of them knows to retrace his step,
The brave fighters were roaring in the battlefield. —7

PAURI

The war-trumpet sounded and the enthusiastic drums thundered in the battlefield,
The lances swung and the lustrous tassels of the banners glistened.
The drum and trumpets echoed and the warriors were dozing like the drunkard with matted hair,
Durga and demons waged war in the battlefield where dreadful music is being played,
The brave fighters were pierced by daggers like the *Phyllanthus emblica* sticking with the bough,
Some writhe being chopped by the sword like the rolling mad drunkards,
Some are picked up from the bushes like the process of panning out gold from the sand,
The maces, tridents, daggers and arrows are being struck with real hurry,
It appears that the black snakes are stinging and the furious heroes are dying. —8

PAURI

Seeing the intense glory of Chandi, the trumpets sounded in the battlefield,
The highly furious demons ran on all four sides,
Holding their swords in their hands they fought very bravely in the battlefield,
These militant fighters never ran away from war-arena,
Highly infuriated they shouted "kill, kill" in their ranks,
The intensely glorious Chandi killed the warriors and threw them in the field,
It appeared that the lightning had eradicated the minarets and thrown them headlong. —9

PAURI

The drum was beaten and the armies attacked each other,
The goddess caused the dancing of the lioness of steel (sword),
And gave a blow to the demon Mahikha who was rubbing his belly (the sword) pierced the kidneys, intestines and the ribs,
Whatever hath come in my mind, I have related that,
It appears that Dhumketu (the shooting star) had displayed its top-knot. —10

PAURI

The drums are being beaten and the armies are engaged in close fight with each other,
The gods and demons have drawn their swords,
And strike them again and again killing warriors,
The blood flows like waterfall in the same manner as the red ochre colour is washed off from clothes,
The ladies of demons see the fight, while sitting in their lofts,
The carriage of the goddess Durga hath raised a tumult amongst the demons. —11

PAURI

A hundred thousand trumpets resound facing one another,
The highly infuriated demons do not flee from the battlefield,
All the warriors roar like lions,
They stretch their bows and shoot the arrows in front of Durga. —12

PAURI

The dualistically chained trumpets sounded in the battlefield,
The demon chieftains having matted locks are enveloped in dust,
Their nostrils are like mortars and the mouths seem like niches,
The brave fighters bearings long moustaches ran in front of the goddess,
The warriors like the king of gods (Indra) had become tired of fighting, but the brave fighters could not be averted from their stand,

They roared, on besieging Durga, like dark clouds. —13

The drum, wrapped in donkey's skin, was beaten and the armies attacked each other,
The brave demon-warriors besieged Durga,
They are greatly knowledgable in warfare and do not know running back,
They ultimately went to heaven on being killed by the goddess. —14

PAURI

With the flaring up of fight between the armies, innumerable trumpets sounded,
The gods and demons both have raised great tumult like male buffaloes.
The infuriated demons strike strong blows causing wounds,
It appears that the swords pulled from the scabbards are like saws,
The warriors look like high minarets in the battlefield,
The goddess herself killed these mountains-like demons,
They never uttered the word "defeat" and ran in front of the goddess,
Durga, holding her sword, killed all the demons. —15

PAURI

The fatal martial music sounded and the warriors came in the battlefield with enthusiasm,
Mahishasura thundered in the field like the cloud:
"The warrior like Indra fled from me,
"Who is this wretched Durga, who hath come to start war with me?" —16

PAURI

The drums and trumpets have sounded and the armies have attacked each other,
The arrows move opposite to each other guidingly,
With the infliction of arrows countless warriors have been killed,
Falling like the minarets smote by lightning,
All the demon-fighters with untied hair shouted in agony,
It seems that the hermits with matted locks are sleeping after eating the intoxicating hemp. —17

PAURI

Both the armies are facing each other alongwith the resounding big trumpet,
The highly egoist warrior of the army thundered,
He is moving towards the war-arena with thousands of mighty warriors,
Mahishasura pulled out his huge double-edged sword from his scabbard,
The fighters entered the field enthusiastically and there occurred formidable fighting,
It appears that the blood like the water (of Ganges) flowed from the tangled hair of Shiva. —18

PAURI

When the trumpet, enveloped by the skin of the male buffalo, the vehicle of Yama, sounded, the armies attacked each other,
Durga pulled her sword from the scabbard,
She struck the demon with that Chandi, the devourer of demons (that is the sword),
It broke the skull and face into pieces and pierced through the skeleton,
And it further pierced through the saddle and caparison of the horse, and struck on the earth supported by the bull (Dhaul),
It moved further and struck the horns of the bull,
Then it struck on the tortoise supporting the bull and thus killing the enemy,
The demons are lying dead in the battlefield like the pieces of wood sawed by the carpenter,
The press of blood and marrow has been set in motion in the battlefield,
The story of the sword will be related in all the four ages,
On the demon Mahisha the period of agony occurred in the battlefield. —19

In this way the demon Mahishasura was killed on the arrival of Durga,
The queen caused the lion to dance in the fourteen worlds,
She killed a great number of brave demons with matted locks in the battlefield,
Challenging the armies, these warriors do not even ask for water,
It seems that listening to the music, the Pathans have realised the state of ecstasy,
The flood of the blood of the fighters is flowing,
The brave warriors are roaming as if they have ignorantly consumed the intoxicating poppy-flower. —20

Bhavani (Durga) disappeared after bestowing kingdom on the gods,

The day for which Shiva granted the boon,
The proud warriors Sumbh and Nisumbh were born,
They planned to conquer the capital of Indra. —21
The great fighters decided to rush towards the kingdom of Indra,
They began to prepare the war-material consisting of armour with belts and saddle-gear,
An army of lakhs of warriors gathered and the dust rose to the sky,
Sumbh and Nisumbh, full of rage, have marched forward. —22

PAURI

Sumbh and Nisumbh ordered the great warriors to sound the bugle of war,
Great fury was visualised and the brave fighters caused the horses to dance,
The double-trumpets sounded like the loud voice of the male buffalo, the vehicle of Yama,
The gods and demons have gathered to fight. —23

PAURI

The demons and gods have started a continuous war,
The garments of the warriors appear like flowers in the garden,
The ghosts, vultures and crows have eaten the flesh,
The brave fighters have begun to run about. —24
The trumpet was beaten and the armies attack each other,
The demons have gathered together and have caused the gods to flee,
They exhibited their authority in the three worlds,
The gods, having been frightened went under the refuge of Durga,
They caused the goddess Chandi to wage war with demons. —25

PAURI

The demons heard the news that the goddess Bhavani has come again,
The highly egoist demons gathered together,
The king Sumbh sent for the egoist Lochan Dhum,
He caused himself to be called the great demon,
The drum, enveloped by the skin of donkey, was struck and it was proclaimed that Durga would be brought. —26

PAURI

Seeing the armies in the battlefield, Chandi shouted loudly,
She pulled her double-edged sword from her scabbard and came before the enemy,
She killed all the warriors of Dhumar Nain,
It seems that the carpenters have chopped the trees with the saw. —27

PAURI

The drummer sounded the drum and the armies attacked each other,
The infuriated Bhavani lodged the attack over the demons,
With her left hand, she caused the dance of the lioness of steel (sword),
She struck it on the bodies of many warriors and made them colourful,
The brothers kill brothers mistaking them for Durga,
Having been infuriated, she struck it on the king of the demons,
Lochan Dhum was sent to the city of Yama.
It seems that she gave the advance money for the killing of Sumbh. —28

PAURI

The demons ran to their king Sumbh and beseeched:
"Lochan Dhum has been killed alongwith his soldiers,
"She hath selected the warriors and killed them in the battlefield,
"It seems that the warriors have fallen like the stars from the sky,
"The huge mountains have fallen, having been smote by the lightning,
"The forces of the demons have been defeated on becoming panicky,
"Those who were left have also been killed and the remaining have come to the king." —29

PAURI

Highly enraged, the king called the demons,
They decided to capture Durga,
Chand and Mund were sent with huge forces,

It seemed that the swords coming together were like the thatched roofs.
All those who were called marched for war,
It appears that they were all caught and sent to the city of Yama after killing. —30

PAURI

The drums and trumpets were sounded and the armies attacked each other,
The enraged warriors marched against the demons,
All of them, holding their daggers, caused their horses to dance,
Many were killed and thrown in the battlefield,
The arrows shot by the goddess came in showers. —31

The drums and conches were sounded and the war began,
Durga, taking her bow, stretched it again and again for shooting arrows,
Those who raised their hands against the goddess, did not survive,
She destroyed both Chand and Mund. —32

Sumbh and Nisumbh were highly enraged on hearing this killing,
They called all the brave fighters, who were their advisers,
Those who had caused the gods like Indra run away.
The goddess killed them in an instant,
Keeping Chand and Mund in their mind, they rubbed their hands in sorrow,
Then Saranwatvija was prepared and sent by the king
He wore the armour with belts and the helmet which glistened,
The infuriated demons shouted loudly for war,
After waging war, none could get their retreat,
Such demons have gathered together and come now to see the ensuing war. —33

PAURI

On coming near, the demons raised the din,
Hearing this clamour, Durga mounted her lion,
She twirled her mace, raising it with her left hand,
She killed all the army of Saranwatvija,
It appears that the warriors were roaming like the drug-addicts taking drugs,
Innumerable warriors are lying neglected in the battlefield, stretching their legs,
It seems that the revellers, playing Holi are sleeping. —34

Saranwatvija called all the remaining warriors,
They seem like minarets in the battlefield,
All of them pulling their swords, raised their hands,
They came in front shouting "kill, kill,"
With the striking of swords on the armour, the clatter arises,
It seems that the tinkers are fashioning the vessels with the blows of hammer. —35

When the trumpet enveloped by the skin of the male buffalo, the vehicle of Yama, sounded the armies attacked each other,
(The goddess) was the cause the flight and consternation in the battlefield,
The warriors fall alongwith their horses and saddles,
The wounded ones arise and ask for water while roaming,
Such a great calamity fell on the demons,
From this side the goddess rose like thundering lightning. —36

PAURI

The drummer sounded the trumpet and the armies attacked each other,
All the army of the demons was killed in an instant,
Highly infuriated, Durga killed the demons,
She struck the sword on the head of Saranwatvija. —37

Innumerable mighty demons were steeped in blood,
Those minarets-like demons in the battlefield,
They challenged Durga and come in front of her,
Durga killed all the coming demons,
From their bodies the drains of blood fell on the ground,
Some of the active demons arise out of them laughingly. —38

The enchained trumpets and bugles sounded,
The warriors fought with daggers bedecked with tassels,
The war of bravery was waged between Durga and demons,
There had been extreme destruction in the battlefield,
It appears that the actors, sounding their drum, have jumped into the war-arena,

The dagger penetrated in the corpse seems like a blood-stained fish entrapped in the net,
The swords glistened like the lightning in the clouds,
The swords have covered (the battlefield) like the winter-fog. —39
The trumpets were sounded with the beating of drum-stick and the armies attacked each other,
The youthful warriors pulled out their swords from their scabbards,
Saranwatvija increased himself into innumerable forms,
Which came in front of Durga, highly enraged,
All of them pulled out their swords and struck,
Durga saved herself from all, holding her shield carefully,
The goddess herself then struck her swords looking carefully towards the demons,
She steeped her naked swords in blood,
It appeared that the goddess gathering together, took their bath in river Saraswati,
The goddess hath killed and thrown on the ground in the battlefield (all the forms of Saranwatvija),
Immediately then the forms again increased greatly. —40

PAURI
Sounding their drums, conches and trumpets, the warriors have begun the war,
Chandi, being highly enraged, remembered Kali in her mind,
She came out shattering the forehead of Chandi, sounding the trumpet and flying flag of victory,
On manifesting herself she marched for war, like Bir Bhadra manifesting from Shiva,
The battlefield was surrounded by her and she seemed moving like a roaring lion,
(The demon-king) himself was in great anguish, while exhibiting his anger over the three worlds,
Durga, being enraged, hath marched, holding her disc in her hand and raising her sword,
There before her there were infuriated demons, showering their arrows and blows of swords,
Going within the forces of demons, she caught and knocked down the demons,
She threw down many by catching them from their hair and raising a tumult among their forces,
She picked up mighty fighters by catching them with the corner of her bow and throwing them,
In her fury, Kali hath done this in the battlefield. —41

PAURI
Both the armies are facing each other and the blood is dripping from the tips of arrows,
Pulling the sharp swords, they have been washed with blood,
The heavenly damsels (*houris*), surrounding Saranwatvija are standing,
Like the brides surrounding the bridegroom in order to see him. —42
The drummer beat the trumpet and the armies attacked each other,
With their hands they pulled the naked swords and caused their dance,
These devourers of meat were struck on the bodies of the warriors,
The nights of agony have come for the men and horses,
The Yoginis have came together speedily in order to drink the blood,
The goddess hath repulsed the demon-forces with her blows,
They told the story of their repulsion before the king Sumbh,
The drop of blood (of Saranwatvija) could not fall on the earth,
Kali destroyed all the manifestations of (Saranwatvija) in the battlefield,
The last moments of death came over the heads of many fighters
The brave fighters could not even be recognised by their mothers, who gave birth to them. —43
Sumbh heard the bad news about the death of Saranwatvija,
And that none could withstand the marching Durga in the battlefield,
Many brave fighters with matted hair got up saying,
That drummers should sound the drums because they would go for war,
When the armies marched, the earth trembled,
Like the shaking boat, which is still in the river,
The dust arose with the hooves of the horses,
And it seemed that the earth is going to Indra for a complaint. —44

PAURI

The willing workers got engaged in work and as warriors they equipped the army,
They marched in front of Durga like the pilgrims going for Haj to Kaabah (in Mecca),
They are inviting the warriors in the battlefield through the medium of arrows, swords and daggers,
Some wounded warriors are swinging like the Qadis in the school, reciting the holy *Quran*,
Some brave fighters are pierced by daggers and learning like a devout Muslim performing prayer,
Some go in front of Durga in great fury by inciting their malicious horses,
Some run in front of Durga like the hungry scoundrels,
Who had never been satisfied in the war, but now they are satiated and pleased. —45

The enchained doublet trumpets sounded,
Gathering together in ranks, the warriors with matted hair are engaged in war in the battlefield,
The lances bedecked with tassels seem leaning,
Like the hermits with matted locks going towards the Ganges for taking a bath. —46

The forces of Durga and demons are piercing each other like sharp thorns,
The warriors showered arrows in the battlefield,
Pulling their sharp swords, they chop the limbs,
When the forces met, at first there was war with swords. —47

The forces came in great numbers and the ranks of warriors marched forward,
They pulled their sharp swords from their scabbards,
With the blazing of the war, the great egoist warriors shouted loudly,
The pieces of head, trunk and arms look like garden-flowers,
And (the bodies) appear like the trees of sandal-wood cut and sawed by the carpenters. —48

When the trumpet, enveloped by the skin of a donkey, was beaten, both the forces faced each other,
Looking at the warriors, Durga pointedly shot her arrows on the brave fighters,
The warriors on foot were killed, the elephants were killed alongwith the fall of the chariots and horse-riders,
The tips of arrows penetrated in the armour like the flowers on pomegranate-plants,
The goddess Kali got enraged, holding her sword in her right hand,
She destoryed several thousand demons (Hiranayakashipus) from this end of the field to the other end,
The only one is conquering the army,
O goddess; hail, hail to Thy blow. —49

PAURI

The trumpet, enveloped by the skin of the male buffalo, the vehicle of Yama, was beaten and both the armies faced each other,
Then Nisumbh caused the horse to dance, putting on his back the saddle-armour,
She held the big bow, which was caused to be brought on order from Multan,
In fury she then came in front in order to fill the battlefield with the mud and fat,
She flashed her sword and struck it cutting the demon and piercing through the saddle,
It went further and struck the earth after cutting the saddle-armour and the horse,
The great hero (Nisumbh) fell down from the horse-saddle,
Offering salutation to the wise Sumbh,
Hail, hail, to the winsome chieftain (Khan),
Hail, hail, ever to thy strength,
Praises are offered for the chewing of betel,
Hail, hail, to thy addiction,
Hail, hail, to thy horse-control. —50

PAURI

Durga and demons sounded their trumpets, in the remarkable war,
The warriors arose in great numbers and have come to fight,
They have come to tread through the forces in order to destroy (the enemy) with guns and arrows,
The angels have come down (to the earth) from the sky in order to see the war. —51

PAURI

The trumpets have sounded in the army and both the forces face each other,

The chief and brave warriors swayed in the field,
They raised their weapons including the swords and daggers,
They have bedecked themselves with helmets on their heads, and armour around their necks alongwith their horses-saddles with belts,
Durga holding her dagger, killed many demons,
She killed and threw those on the ground, who were riding chariots, elephants and horses,
It appears that the confectioner has cooked small round cakes of grounded pulse, piercing them with a spike. —52

PAURI

Alongwith the sounding of the large trumpet, both the forces faced each other,
Durga held out her sword, appearing like great lustrous fire,
She struck it on the king Sumbh and this lovely weapon drinks blood,
Sumbh fell down from the saddle for which the following simile hath been thought,
That the double-edged dagger, smeared with blood, which hath come out (from the body of Sumbh),
Seems like a princess coming down from her loft, wearing the red sari. —53

PAURI

The war between Durga and the demons started early in the morning,
Durga held her weapons firmly in all her arms,
She killed both Sumbh and Nisumbh, who were the masters of all the materials,
Seeing this, the helpless forces of the demons, weep bitterly,
Accepting their defeat (by putting the straws of grass in their mouth) and leaving their horses in the way,
They are being killed, while fleeing, without looking back. —54

PAURI

Sumbh and Nisumbh were despatched to the abode of Yama,
And Indra was called for crowning him,
The canopy was held up over the head of king Indra,
The praise of the mother of the universe spread over all the fourteen worlds,
All the *pauris* (stanzas) of this Durga Path (The text about the exploits of Durga) have been composed,
And that person who sings it, will not take birth again. —55

BACHITTAR NATAK
The Granth (Book) Entitled Bachittar Natak is Composed by Thy Grace from the Holy Mouth of the Tenth King (Guru)

DOHIRA

I salute the glorious sword with all my heart's affection,
I shall complete this Granth only if Thou helpest me. —1

The Eulogy of the Revered Death (Kal)

TRIBHANGI STANZA

The sword chops well, chops the forces of fools and this mighty one bedecks and glorifies the battlefield,
It is the unbreakable staff of the arm, it has the powerful lustre and its light even bedims the radiance of the sun,
It brings happiness to the saints, mashing the vicious ones, it is the destroyer of sins and I am under its refuge,
Hail, hail to the cause of the world, saviour of the universe, it is my preserver, I hail its victory. —2

BHUJANG PRAYAAT STANZA

He, who is ever light-incarnate and birthless entity,
Who is the god of chief gods, the king of chief kings,
Who is formless, eternal, amorphous and ultimate bliss,
Who is the cause of all the powers, I salute the wielder of the sword. —3

He is formless, flawless, eternal and non-aligned,
He is neither distinctively old, nor young nor immature,
He is neither poor, nor rich; He is formless and markless,
He is colourless, non-attached, limitless and guiseless. — 4

He is formless, signless, colourless and non-attached,
He is nameless, placeless and a radiating great effulgence,
He is blemishless, guiseless, formless and eternal,
He is a superb practising Yogi and a supremely holy entity. —5

He is unconquerable, indistinguishable, nameless and placeless,
He is a superb practising Yogi, He is the supreme ravisher,
He is accountless, garbless, stainless and without beginning,
He is in the yond, immaculate and ever without contention. —6

He is the primal, originless, stainless and endless,
He is blemishless, guiseless, master of the earth and the destroyer of pride,
He is ireless, ever fresh, deceitless and non-attached,
He is lustless, angerless, birthless and sightless. —7

He is in the yond, immaculate, most holy and ancient,
He is unconquerable, indistinguishable, will be in future and is always present,
He is without ailment and sorrow and is ever new,
He is birthless, he is the supporter and is supremely dexterous. —8

He pervades in the past, future and present,
I salute him, who is without vices and without ailments,
I salute him, who is the God of gods and King of kings,
He is supportless, eternal and greatest of emperors. —9

He is accountless, guiseless, elementless and blemishless,
He is without attachment, colour, form and mark,

He is the greatest of gods and the supreme Yogi,
He is the greatest of the rapturous and the greatest of the ravishing. —10

Somewhere He bears the quality of *rajas* (activity), somewhere *tamas* (morbidity) and somewhere *sattva* (rhythm),
Somewhere He takes the form of a woman and somewhere man,
Somewhere He manifests Himself as a goddess, god and demon,
Somewhere He appears in several unique forms. —11

Somewhere He, taking the form of a flower, is rightly puffed up,
Somewhere becoming a black bee, seems inebriated (for the flower),
Somewhere becoming the wind, moves with such speed,
Which is indescribable, how can I elucidate it? —12

Somewhere He becomes a musical instrument, which is played appropriately,
Somewhere He becomes a hunter who looks glorious with His arrow (in His bow),
Somewhere He becomes a deer and allures exquisitely,
Somewhere He manifests Himself as Cupid's wife, with impressive beauty. —13

His form and mark cannot be comprehended,
Where doth He live? And what guise doth He adopt?
What is His name? and how He is called?
How can I describe? He is indescribable. —14

He hath no father, mother and brother,
He hath no son, no grandson, and no male and female nurses,
He hath no attachment, no home, no army and no companion,
He is the great king of kings and great Lord of lords. —15

He is supreme, ancient, immaculate and in the yond,
He is beginningless, stainless, non-existant and unconquerable,
He is indistinguishable, indestructible, holy and paramount,
He is the most humble of the meek and great Lord of lords. —16

He is stainless, imperishable, accountless and guiseless,
He is limitless, blemishless, formless and maliceless,
He is the most effulgent of all lights and supreme conflagration of all fires,
He is the supreme spell of all incantations and supreme embodiment of death over all such powers. —17

He holds the bow in His left hand and the terrible sword (in the right),
He is the supreme effulgence of all lights and sits in his great glory,
He, of infinite splendour, is the masher of the boar-incarnation with great grinder tooth,
He crushed and devoured thousands of the creatures of the world. —18

The tabor [in the hand of great death (Kal)] resounds and the black and white canopy swings,
Loud laughter emanates from his mouth and the weapons (in his hands) glisten,
His conch produces such a terrible sound,
That appears like the blazing fire of the death on doomsday. —19

RASAAVAL STANZA

Many gongs resound and hearing their sound the clouds feel ashamed,
Such a sound is produced that it appears like the sound of the surging waves of the sea. —20

The small bells of the feet jingle, and the anklets rattle,
Such sounds are peaceful sounds against the great resounding (of gongs). —21

The rosary of heads glorifies his neck, seeing which the god Shiva feels abashed,
Such a beautiful image appears magnificent and it is greatly holy. —22

He produces the very loud roar, hearing which the messengers (of Yama) tremble,
The blood oozes (from his rosary of skulls) glorifying his neck and it is fascinating his great honour. —23

BHUJANG PRAYAAT STANZA

Thou hast created the *svedajia*, *jerajju* and *udbhijja* divisions of creation,
Like this Thou hast created the *andajja* divison and also the regions and universe,

Thou hast also created the directions, the indications, the earth and the sky,
Thou hast also related the four Vedas, the *Quran* and the Puranas. —24
Thou hast created night and day, established the sun and moon,
Thou hast created gods and demons and also the warriors and old learned people,
Thou hast created the pen to write on the tablet and hast recorded the writ on the forehead,
The hand of the mighty death hath subdued all. —25
He hath effaced many and then made (created) others,
He destroys the created ones and then creates after effacing,
None could comprehend the working of death (Kal),
Many have experienced it and many will experience it. —26
Somewhere He hath created millions of the servants like Krishna,
Somewhere he hath effaced and then created (many) like Rama,
Many Muhammads had been born on the earth,
They were born and then died in their own times. —27
All the prophets and saints of the past,
Were conquered by death (Kal), but none could conquer it (him),
All the incarnations of Vishnu like Rama and Krishna,
Were destroyed by Kal, but they could not destroy him. —28
All the Indras and Chandras (moons) who came into being,
Were destroyed by Kal, but they could not destroy him,
All those prophets, saints and hermits, who came into being,
Were all ultimately crushed under the grinder tooth of Kal. —29
All the glorious kings like Mandhata,
Were all bound down and thrown in the noose of Kal,
Those who have remembered the name of the Lord, have been saved,
Without coming under His refuge, millions are considered as having been killed by Kal. —30

RASAAVAL STANZA   BY THY GRACE

The sword of Kal glistens, which is non-elemental and terrible,
While moving, his anklets rattle and the small bells jingle. —31
He hath four winsome arms and on His head, his long hair have been bound in a lovely knot,
The mace with Him appears splendid, which fascinates the honour of Yama. —32
His tongue red like fire seems magnificent and His grinder teeth are very frightening,
His conches and drums resound,
Like the thundering sound of the sea. —33
His dark form looks elegant and is the abode of great glory,
On His face there are lovely delineations, which are superbly holy. —34

BHUJANG PRAYAAT STANZA

On His head there swings the beautiful, lustrous and white canopy,
Seeing whose shadow and considering it winsome, the light feels abashed,
The fleshy and red eyes of God seem magnificent,
Before whose light millions of suns appear irritated. —35
Somewhere He appears impressive in the semblance of a great king,
Somewhere He allures the minds of Apsaras or the daughters of gods,
Somewhere as a warrior He holds the bow in his hand,
Somewhere as king He causes the resounding of his trumpets. —36

RASAAVAL STANZA

He seems bedecked beautiful, wielding his bow and arrows,
He holds the sword like a great warrior. —37
He is forcefully enagaged in war, fighting frightening battles,
He is the treasure of mercy and ever kind. —38
He is always the same (Kind Lord) and the monarch of all,

He is unconquerable and birthless and helps those who come under His refuge. —39

The sword shines in His hand and He is a great donor for the people,
I salute the supreme Kal, who is unique in the present and shall be unique in future. —40

He is the effacer of the pride of the demon Madhu and the destroyer of the demon Sumbh,
He hath white canopy over His head and the weapons glisten in His hands. —41

Hearing His loud voice, the great monarchs are frightened,
He wears elegantly the garments of directions and listening to His voice, the sorrows run away. —42

Hearing His call, the infinite happines is attained,
He is Shyam in the form of clouds and appears beautiful and impressive. —43

He hath four beautiful arms and is wearing crown on the head,
The mace, conch and disc glisten and seem frightful and resplendent. —44

NARAAJ STANZA

The unique beauty appears graceful and on seeing it the Cupid seems ashamed,
In the worlds it has supernatural radiance, seeing which all the people are fascinated. —45

The moon is beaming on his head, seeing which the god Shiva feels shy,
The ornaments of Nagas bedeck his neck, which have the power of destruction for the tyrants. —46

He, who wields the sword in his hand, he is the remover of millions of sins,
He hath caught hold of the big mace and hath fitted the arrow in his stretched bow. —47

There is sound of the blowing conch and jingling of many small bells,
O Lord, I have come under Thy refuge, protect my honour. —48

Thou appearest impressive in various forms and allurest the great gods,
Thou art the worshipping temple of the demons and gods and art the treasure of the grace alone. —49

He remains uniform from the beginning to end and hath adopted various forms,
The sword appears impressive in his hand, seeing which the sins run away. —50

His body is bedecked with ornaments, which allures both body and mind,
The arrow is fitted in the bow, which causes many enemies to flee away. —51

There is the jingling sound of the small bells and a new sound emantes from the anklets,
There is light like the blazing fire and lightning, which is highly holy and pure. —52

TOTAK STANZA   BY THY GRACE

Various kinds of pure tunes emanate from the anklets,
The face appears like the blaze of lightning in the dark clouds,
His gait is like that of an intoxicated elephant with wine,
His loud thunder appears like the roar of a cub in the forest. —53

Thou art in the world in the past, future and present,
Thou art the only one saviour in the iron age,
Thou art ever new continuously at all places,
Thou appearest impressive and sweet in Thy blissful form. —54

Thou hast two grinder teeth, terrible, white and high,
Seeing which the tyrants run away from the battlefield,
Thou art inebriated, holding the terrible sword in Thy hand,
Both the gods and demons sing the eulogy of Thy victory. —55

When the united sound of the girdle bells and the anklets emanates,
Then all the mountains become restless like mercury and the earth trembles,
When the constant jingling loud sound is heard,
Then all the movable and immovable objects become restless. —56

Thy weapons are in use in all the fourteen worlds alongwith Thy command,
With which Thou causest deficiency in the augmented ones and fill to the brim, the empty ones,
All the creatures of the world on land and in water,
Who is he amongst them, who hath the audacity to refuse Thy command? —57

Just as the dark clouds seem impressive in the month of Bhadon,
In the same manner Thy dark body hath its glow,
The chain of thy teeth glisters like lightning,
The melody of the small bells and gongs is like the thunder of the clouds. —58.

BHUJANG PRAYAAT STANZA

Thy beauty appears elegant like the dark clouds of the month of Sawan,
Comprehending Thy beautiful form, the mountain of blue gems hath bent its head,
The most beautiful black colour highly fascinates the mind,
Thou art the most beautiful of the beautiful ones and the most passionate of the passionate ones. —59

The order of Kal is prevalent in all the fourteen worlds,
Who is the other one who hath the audacity to refuse His order?
Tell me, in which direction you can flee and remain safe?
Since the Kal dances over the heads of all. —60

Though one may erect millions of forts and may remain under their protection,
Even then, in the case of a blow of Kal, he will not be saved in any way,
Though one may write many *yantras* and recite millions of *mantras* even then he cannot be saved,
No other shelter can save one without coming under His refuge. —61

The writers of *yantras* have grown weary and the reciters of *mantras* have accepted defeat,
But ultimetly, they all have been destroyed by Kal,
Many *tantras* have been tamed and in such endeavours one hath wasted his birth,
All have become useless and none hath proved useful. —62

Many have becomes *brahmacharis* and have closed their nostrils (in their process of contemplation),
Many have worn *kanthi* (necklace) on their necks and have matted hair on their heads,
Many have got their ears perforated and caused others to call them great yogis,
All such religious observances were useless and none of them became useful. —63

There had been mighty demon-kings like Madhu and Kaitabh,
The Kal crushed them on their turn,
Then there were Sumbh, Nisumbh and Saranwatvija.
They were also chopped into bits by Kal. —64

The mighty king Prithu and the great sovereign like Mandhata,
Who had demarcated seven continents with his chariot-wheel,
The king Bhim and king Bharat, who had conquered and brought the world under their control with the strength of arms,
They were all destroyed by Kal, when they were nearing their end. —65

He, who hath created the frightening dominance of His name,
He, who had snatched the earth from the Kshatriyas with the strength of staff-like arms,
He, who had performed millions of *yajnas* (sacrifices) and earned multi-faceted approbation,
Even that winsome warrior (Parashuram) hath been conquered by Kal. —66

Those who had conquered millions of forts and razed them,
Those who had treaded the forces of innumerable warriors,
Those who had indulged in many wars, events and disputes,
I have seen them subdued and killed by Kal. —67

Those who had ruled for millions of ages,
And had enjoyed nicely the pleasure and vicious tastes,
They had ultimetly gone with naked feet,
I have seen them having been subdued, fallen and killed by the persistant Kal. —68

He, who had destroyed many kings,
He, who had enslaved the moon and the sun in his house,
He (as Ravana) had conquered the god Indra in war and later released him,
I have seen (him and Meghnad) being subdued fallen and killed by Kal. —69

RASAAVAL STANZA

All the Ramas who incarnated ultimetly passed away,

All the Krishnas, who had incarnated, have all passed away. —70
All the gods who will come into being in future they will all ultimately expire,
All the demon-kings, who came into being they were all destroyed by Kal. —71
The incarnation Narsingh was also killed by Kal,
The incarnation with grinder teeth (i.e., Boar) was killed by mighty Kal. —72
Vaman, the Brahmin incarnation, was killed by Kal,
The fish incarnation of spacious mouth, was entrapped by Kal. —73
All those who had come into being they were all conquered by Kal,
Those who will go under His (God's) refuge they will all be saved by him. —74

BHUJANG PRAYAAT STANZA

Without coming under His refuge, there is no other measure for protection,
May be a god, a demon, a pauper or a king,
May be the sovereign and may be the courtiers,
Without coming under His shelter, millions of measures for protection will be useless. —75
All the creatures created by Him in the world,
Will ultimetely be killed the mighty Kal,
There is no other protection without coming under His shelter,
Even though many *yantras* be written and millions of *mantras* be recited. —76

NARAAJ STANZA

All the kings and paupers who have come into being are sure to be killed by Kal,
All the Lokpals, who have come into being will ultimately be mashed by Kal. —77
Those who meditate on the supreme Kal, the wielder of the sword they firmly adopt innumerable measures for protection,
Those who remember Kal, they conquer the world and depart. —78
That supreme Kal is supremely pure, whose image is supernatural and winsome,
He is bedecked with supernatural beauty, all the sins flee on hearing His name. —79
He, who hath wide and red eyes, and who is the destroyer of innumerable sins,
The glitter on his face is more beautiful than that of the moon and who hath caused many sinners to ferry across. —80

RASAAVAL STANZA

All the Lokpals are subservient to Kal,
All the suns and moons and even Indra and Vaman (are subservient to Kal). —81

BHUJANG PRAYAAT STANZA

All the fourteen worlds are under the command of Kal,
He hath stringed all the Naths by turning about the slanting eyebrows,
May be Rama and Krishna, may be the moon and sun,
All are standing with folded hands in the presence of Kal. —82

SWAYYA

At the instance of Kal, Vishnu appeared, whose power is manifested through the world,
At the instance of Kal Brahma appeared and also at the instance of Kal Yogi Shiva appeared,
At the instance of Kal, the gods, demons, Gandharvas, Yakshas, Bhujang, directions and indications have appeared,
All the other prevalent objects are within Kal, only one supreme Kal is ever timeless and eternal. —83

BHUJANG PRAYAAT STANZA

Salutation to the god of gods and salutation to the wielder of sword,
Who is ever monomorphic and ever without vices,
Salutation to Him, who manifests the qualities of activity (*rajas*), rhythm (*sattva*) and morbidity (*tamas*),
Salutation to Him who is without vices and who is without ailments. —84

RASAAVAL STANZA

Salutation to Him, who wields the bow in His hands,
Salutation to Him, who is fearless,
Salutation to Him, who is god of gods,
Salutation to Him, who shall ever be within the world. —85

BHUJANG PRAYAAT STANZA

Salutation to the spear, double-edged sword, sword and dagger,

BACHITTAR NATAK

Who is ever monomorphic and ever without vices,
Salutation to Him, who is the wielder of bow in His hands and who also carries the staff,
Who hath spread His light in all the fourteen worlds. —86

I salute the arrow and the gun,
I salute the lustrous sword, which is impenetrable and indestructible,
I salute the great mace and lance, which have no equal or second in bravery. —87

RASAAVAL STANZA

Salutation to Him, who holds the disc in His hand,
He hath manifested Himself without elements,
Salutation to Him, who hath sharp grinder teeth,
Which are thick and string. —88

Salutation to Him, who hath the arrows and the cannon,
Who hath destroyed the enemies,
Salutation to Him, who holds the straight sword and the bayonet,
Who hath reprimanded the tyrants. —89

I salute all the weapons of various names,
I salute all kinds of armour. —90

SWAYYA

There is no other support for the poor except Thee, who hath made me a mountain from a straw,
O Lord! Forgive me for my mistake, because who is there so much blunder-head like me?
Those who have served Thee, there seems wealth and self-confidence in all their homes,
In this iron age, the supreme trust is only for Kal, who is the sword-incarnate and hath mighty arms. —91

He, who hath destroyed millions of demons like Sumbh and Nisumbh in an instant,
Who hath annihilated in an instant the demons like Dhumar Lochan, Chand, Mund, and Mahishasura,
Who hath immediately thrashed and thrown down far away the demons like Chamar, Ranchichhar and Raktavija,
On realising the Lord like Thee, this servant of yours doth not care for anyone else. —92

He, who hath mashed millions of demons like Mundakasura, Madhu, Kaitabh, Mur, and Aghasura,

And such heroes who had never asked anyone for support in the battlefield and had never turned even two feet,
And such demons, who could not be drowned even in the sea and there was no impact on them of the fire-shafts,
On seeing Thy sword and forsaking their shyness, they are fleeing away. —93

Thou hast destroyed in an instant the warriors like Ravana, Kumbhakarana and Chatkasura,
And like Meghanad, who could defeat even Yama in the war,
And the demons like Kumbh and Akumbh, who conquering all, washed away the blood from their weapons in seven seas, etc.,
All of them died with the terrible sword of the mighty Kal. —94

If one tries to flee and escape from Kal, then tell in which direction shall he flee?
Wherever one may go, even there he will perceive the well-seated thundering sword of Kal,
None hath been able to tell uptil now the measure, which may be adopted to save himself from the blow of Kal,
O foolish mind! The one from whom Thou canst not escape in any manner, why doth Thee not go under His refuge. —95

Thou hast meditated on millions of Krishnas, Vishnus, Ramas ond Rahims,
Thou hast recited the name of Brahma and established Shiva-lingam, even none could save Thee,
Thou hast observed millions of austerities for millions of days, but Thou couldst not be recompensed even for the value of a cowrie,
The *mantra* recited for fulfilment of worldly desires doth not even bring least gain and none of such *mantras* canst save from the blow of Kal. —96

Why doth thou indulge in false austerities? because they will not bring in gain of even one cowrie,
Those who cannot save themselves from the blow (of Kal), how can they protect thee?
They are all hanging in the blazing fire of anger, therefore they will cause thy hanging similarly,
O fool! ruminate now in thy mind; none will be of any use to thee except the grace of Kal. —97

O foolish beast! Thou doth not recognise Him, whose glory hath spread over all the three worlds,
Thou worshippest those as God, by whose touch thou shalt be driven far away from the next world,
Thou art committing such sins in the name of *parmarath* (the subtle truth) that by committing them the great sins may feel shy,
O fool! fall at the feets of Lord God, the Lord is not within the stone-idols. —98

The Lord cannot be realised by observing silence, by forsaking pride, by adopting guises and by shaving the head,
He cannot be realised by wearing *kanthi* (a short necklace of small beads of different kinds made of wood or seeds worn by mendicants or ascetics) for severe austerities or by making a knot of matted hair on the head,
Listen attentively, I speak truth, Thou shalt not achieve the target without going under the refuge of the Lord, who is ever merciful to the lowly,
God can only be realised with love, He is not pleased by circumcision. —99

If all the continents are transformed into paper and all the seven seas into ink,
By chopping all the vegetation the pen may be made for the sake of writing,
If the goddess Saraswati be made the speaker (of eulogies) and Ganesha be there to write with hands for millions of ages,
Even then, O God! O sword-incarnate Kal; without supplication, none can make Thee pleased even a little one. —100

Here ends the first chapter entitled "The Eulogy of the Revered Death (Kal)" of Bachittar Natak.

APNI KATHA (AUTOBIOGRAPHY)
The Description of Ancestry

CHAUPAI

O Lord! Thy praise is supreme and infinite,
None could comprehend its limits,
O god of gods and king of kings,
The merciful Lord is the protector of the humble. —1

DOHIRA

The dumb utters the six Shastras and the crippled climbs the mountain,
The blind one sees and the deaf listens, if the Kal becomes gracious. —2

CHAUPAI

O God! My intellect is trifling,
How can it narrate Thy praise?
I cannot (have sufficient words to) praise Thee,
Thou mayst Thyself improve this narration. —3

Upto what limit this insect can depict (Thy praises)?
Thou only knowest Thy greatness,
Just as the son cannot say anything about the birth of his father,
Then how can one unfold Thy mystery. —4

Thy greatness is only Thine,
It cannot be described by others,
O Lord! only Thou knowest Thy doings,
Who hast the power to elucidate Thy high or low acts? —5

Thou hast made one thousand hoods of Seshanaga,
Which contain two thousand tongues,
He is reciting till now Thy infinite names,
Even then he hath not known the end of Thy names. —6

What can one say about Thy doings?
One gets puzzled while understanding it,
Thy subtle form is indescribable,
(Therefore) I speak about Thy immanent form. —7

When I shall observe Thy loving devotion,
I shall then describe all Thy anecdotes from the beginning,
Now I narrate my own life-story,
How the Sodhi clan came into being (in this world). —8

DOHIRA

With the concentration of my mind, I narrate in brief my earlier story,
Then after that, I shall relate all in great detail. —9

CHAUPAI

In the beginning, when Kal created the world,
It was brought into being by *Omkara* (the one Lord),
Kal Sain was the first king, who was of immeasurable strength and supreme beauty. —10

Kalket became the second king and Karurabaras, the third,
Kaldhuj was the fourth king, from whom the whole world originated. —11

He had a thousand eyes and a thousand feet,
He slept on Sheshanaga, therefore he was called the master of Shesha. —12

Out of the secretion from one of his ears, Madhu and Kaitabh came into being,
And from the secretion of the other ear, the whole world materialised. —13

After some period, the Lord killed the demons (Madhu and Kaitabh), their marrow flowed into the ocean,
The greasy substance floated thereon, because of that *med* (marrow), the earth was called *medha* (or *medani*). —14

Because of virtuous actions, a *Purusha* (person) is known as *devata* (god),
And because of evil actions, he is known as *asura* (demon). —15

If everything is described in detail, it is feared that the description will become voluminous,
There were many kings after Kaldhuj like Daksha, Prajapati etc. —16

Ten thousand daughters were born to them, whose beauty was not matched by others,
In due course all these daughters were married with the kings. —17

DOHIRA

Banita and Aditi became the wives of sages (*rishis*) and Nagas,
Their enemies (like Garuda), the gods and demons were born to them. —18

CHAUPAI

From that (Aditi), the sun was born, from whom Suraj *vansh* (the Sun dynasty) originated,
If I describe the names of the kings of this clan, I fear a great extension of the story. —19

In this clan, there was a king named Raghu, who was the originator of Raghu *vansh* (the clan of Raghu) in the world,
He had a great son Aja, a mighty warrior and superb archer. —20

When he renouced the world as a yogi, he passed on his kingdom to his son Dasratha,
Who had been a great archer and had married three wives with pleasure. —21

The eldest one gave birth to Rama, the others gave birth to Bharat, Lakshman and Shatrughan,
They ruled over their kingdom for a long time, after which they left for their heavenly abode. —22

After that the two sons of Sita (and Rama) became the kings,
They married the Punjabi princesses and performed various types of sacrifices. —23

There they founded two cities, the one Kasur and the other Lahore,
Both the cities surpassed in beauty to that of Lanka and Amravati. —24

For a long time, both the brothers ruled over their kingdom and ultimately they were bound down by the noose of death,
After them their sons and grandsons ruled over the world. —25

They were innumerable, therefore it is difficult to describe all,
It is not possible to count the names of all those who ruled over their kingdoms in all the four ages. —26

If now you shower your grace upon me, I shall describe (a few) names, as I know them,
Kalket and Kal Rai had innumerable descendents. —27

Kalket was a mighty warrior, who drove out Kal Rai from his city,
Kal Rai settled in the country named Sanaudh and married the king's daughters. —28

A son was born to him, who was named Sodhi Rai,
Sodhi Rai was the founder of Sanaudh dynasty by the will of the supreme *Purusha*. —29

His sons and grandsons were called Sodhis,
They became very famous in the world and gradually prospered in wealth. —30

They ruled over the country in various ways and subdued kings of many countries,
They extended their *dharma* everywhere and had the royal canopy over their heads. —31

They performed Rajsu sacrifice several times declaring themselves as supreme rulers, after conquering kings of various countries,
They performed Bajmedh sacrifice (horse-

sacrifice) several times, clearing their dynasty of all the blemishes. —32

After that there arose quarrels and differences within the dynasty and none could set the things right,

The great warriors and archers moved towards the battlefield for a fight. —33

The world hath perished after quarrels on wealth and prosperity from very olden times,

The attachments, ego and infights spread widely and the world was conquered by lust and anger. —34

DOHIRA

The mammon may be hailed, who hath the whole world as her slave,

All the world goes in search for her and all go to salute her. —35

CHAUPAI

None could remember Kal and there was only extension of enmity, strife and ego,

Only greed became the base of the world,

Because of which every one wants the other to die. —36

End of the second chapter entitled "The Description of Ancestry" of Bachittar Natak.

The Description of the War of the Descendents of Lava and Kusha

BHUJANG PRAYAAT STANZA

The Providence created the great vices of enmity and strife, which could not be controlled by any reformer,

Which warriors could save himself from the blows of mighty king lust and the great courtiers greed and attachment? —1

There the youthful warriors are busy in challenging shouts amongst themselves,

They stand up with their weapons and are engaged in tough fight,

In this fight, somewhere there are innumerable shafts, helmets and double-edged swords in use,

The evil spirits and ghosts are dancing and the tabors are resounding. —2

Somewhere the god Shiva is striking the skulls in his rosary of skulls,

Somewhere the vampires and ghosts are shrieking joyfully,

Somewhere the terrible goddess Chamunda is shouting and somewhere the vultures are shrieking,

Somewhere the corpses of youthful warriors are lying inter-locked. —3

There had been tough battle, because of which the chopped corpses are rolling in dust,

Somewhere the dead warriors are lying uncared with their hands on their whiskers,

Somewhere the skulls, helmets, bows and arrows are lying scattered,

Somewhere the swords and quivers of the warriors are there in the battlefield. —4

Somewhere the vultures shriek and somewhere the vampire is belching,

Somewhere Bhairo, Bhairavi and ghosts are roaring,

Somewhere the evil spirits and ghosts are walking slantingly,

Somewhere the ghosts, fiends and meat-eaters are laughing. —5

RASAAVAL STANZA

Hearing the thunder of mighty warriors, the clouds felt shy,

Strong banners have been fixed and highly infuriated the heroes are engaged in war. —6

Holding their swords and daggers, they are fighting in great anger,

The winsome great heroes, with their fighting, make the earth tremble. —7

The warriors are fighting with their weapons in great excitment; the weapons as well as the armour are glistening,

There is the great steel-killing with weapons like swords and daggers. —8

BHUJANG PRAYAAT STANZA

Various types of swords, the swords from Halab and Junab, Sarohi sword and the double-edged sword, knife, spear and dagger were struck wth great ire,

Somewhere the lancet and somewhere the pike only were used,

Somewhere the lance and the dagger were being used violently. —9

NARAAJ STANZA

The warriors are fiercely adorned with weapons, with which they fight forsaking all doubts,
Without hesitation they strike the weapons and chop the limbs. —10

They do not care at all and shout "kill, kill,"
They challenge and drive with force and endure the blows of many weapons. —11

Thousands of *houris* (beautiful heavenly damsels) move in the sky,
They move forward to marry the martyrs,
The warriors move in the battlefield in a frightful manner, and utter "kill, kill." —12

The limbs of some warrior have been chopped and the hair of some have been uprooted,
The flesh of some one has been peeled and some one hath fallen after being chopped. —13

There is knocking sound of drums and shields,
The frontline army hath been uprooted,
The warriors strike their weapons very quickly and trample over the heroic army. —14

New trumpets resound and the mighty warriors with quality of forbearance, roar,
They strike the swords and shoot the arrows and suddenly chop away the limbs. —15

Filled with anger, they move forward and do not go back even four feet,
They hold the weapons and challenge and hearing their thunder, the clouds feel shy. —16

They raise their heart-rending shouts and strike their weapon violently,
They fight, forgetting all sorrows and several of them move towards heaven. —17

The warriors filled with ire and moving forward shoot a volley of arrows,
The conch is blown and in such a terrible time, the warriors get adorned with patience. —18

RASAAVAL STANZA

The trumpet and conch resound and the great warriors look impressive,
The swift-running horses dance and the brave warriors are excited. —19

The glistening sharp swords flash like lightning,
The sound of drums arises and is heard continuously. —20

Somewhere the double-edged swords and helmets lie broken,
Somewhere the warriors shout "kill, kill,"
Somewhere the warriors are forcefully knocked about and,
Somewhere, being puzzled, they have fallen down. —21

The great army is being trembled and limbs are being chopped into halves,
The long steel maces are struck and the shouts of "kill, kill" are raised. —22

The stream of blood is full and the *houris* walk over the sky,
The goddess Kali is thundering in the sky and the vamps are laughing. —23

The great warriors equipped with steel and filled with ire look impressive,
They roar with great pride and hearing them, the clouds feel shy. —24

The warriors are adorned with steel-weapons and shout "kill, kill,"
They have slanting whiskers on their faces and fight without caring for their life. —25

There are shouts after shouts and the army hath laid the siege,
In great anger the warriors rush from all sides shouting "kill, kill." —26

The warriors are meeting with their lances like the Ganges with the sea,
Many of them under cover of their shields even break the striking swords with cracking sound. —27

There are shouts after shouts and the swift-running horses dance,
The warriors are highly ferocious and are fighting with the awakening of anger. —28

The sharp lances have fallen down and there is great knocking,
The eaters of flesh are dancing and the warriors are engaged in hot war. —29

The flesh-eating creatures are laughing and the gang of ghosts are dancing,
The persistant warriors are moving forward and shouting "kill, kill." —30

That goddess hath roared in the sky, who hath been brought into being by supreme Kal,
The ghosts are dancing excitedly and are saturated with great anger. —31

The warriors are fighting with each other because

of enmity and the great heroes are falling as martyrs,
Fixing their strong banner and with increased enmity they are shouting. —32
They have adorned their head with the ornament and have stretched their bows in their hands,
They shoot their arrows confronting the opponents, some of them fall down, having been chopped into halves. —33
The elephants and horses are lying dead and the warriors are engaged in enmity and,
Fearlessly strike their weapons; both sides wish for their victory. —34
The warriors are roaring and the swiftly-running heroes dance,
There are shouts after shouts and in this way the army is running about. —35
The warriors are intoxicated with wine and are absorbed in great rage,
The groups of elephants are adorned and the warriors are fighting with increased anger. —36
The sharp sword glistens like the flash of lightning in the clouds,
The blows are struck on the enemy like the swift-moving water-insect. —37
They strike weapons confronting each other; both sides wish for their victory,
They are absorbed in violent rage and are highly intoxicated. —38

BHUJANG PRAYAAT STANZA

The warriors fighting with warriors are looking wonderfully frightening,
The clattering sound of kettle-drums is heard and there is also the thunder of trumpets,
The serious note of the new trumpets resounds,
Somewhere the trunk, somewhere the head, somewhere the bodies hewed by arows are seen moving. —39
The warriors strike their swords and care for their arrows in the battlefield,
The great heroes, chopped in the war are rolling in dust,
The greatly proud warriors, having tied their quivers and equipped with armour,
Move in the battlefield like the drunkards. —40

The weapons were struck and there was confusion all around,
It seemed that the clouds of doomsday were thundering,
Hearing the cracking sound of bows, the warriors of great endurance are becoming cowards,
The steel clatters in rage, with steel and the great war is in progress. —41
The youthful warriors are moving in this great war,
With naked swords the fighters look wonderfully terrible,
Absorbed in violent rage the brave warriors are engaged in war,
The heroes with upmost enthusiasm are catching hold the waists of opponents in order to throw them down. —42.
The sharp swords glisten and are struck with great rage,
Somewhere the trunks and heads are rolling in dust and with the collision of weapons the fire-sparks arise,
Somewhere the warriors are shouting and somewhere the blood is emerging out of the wounds,
It appears that Indra and Britrasura are engaged in war. —43
The terrible war is in progress, in which the great heroes are thundering,
The weapons collide with the confronting weapons,
The sparks of fire come out of the striking spears and in violent rage the steel reigns supreme,
It seems that good persons, looking impressive, are playing Holi. —44

RASAAVAL STANZA

All the fighters engaged in war against their enemies, ultimately fell as martyrs,
All those who have run away from the battlefield, they all feel ashamed at the end. —45
The armours of the bodies are broken and the shields have fallen from the hands,
Somewhere there are helmets scattered in the battlefield and somewhere the groups of warriors have fallen. —46
Somewhere the faces with whiskers have fallen,
Somewhere only weapons are lying,
Somewhere there are scabbards and swords and

Somewhere there are only feet lying in the field. —47

Holding their winsome whiskers, the proud warriors are somewhere engaged in fighting,
Somewhere the weapons are being struck with great knocking on the shield,
A great commotion has arisen (in the field). —48

BHUJANG PRAYAAT STANZA

The brave warriors are moving in the battlefield with naked swords, smeared with blood,
Evil spirits, ghosts, fiends and goblins are dancing,
The tabor and small drum resound and the sound of conches arises,
It appears that the wrestlers, holding with their hands the waists of their opponents are trying to throw them down. —49

CHAUPAI

Those warriors who had begun the war and confronted their opponents with great strength,
Out of those warriors the Kal had left any one alive,
All the warriors had gathered in the battlefield holding their swords,
Enduring the smokeless fire of the steel-edge, they have saved themselves from the bondages,
They have all been chopped and fallen as martyrs and none of them hath retraced his steps,
Those who have gone like this to the abode of Indra, they are hailed with utmost reverence in the world. —50

Such like horrible war blazed and the brave warriors left for their (heavenly) abode,
Upto which limit should I describe that war?
I cannot describe it with my own understanding. —51

BHUJANG PRAYAAT STANZA

(The descendents of Lava) have all been victorious and the (descendents of Kusha) were all defeated,
The descendents of Kusha who remained alive, saved themselves by fleeing away,
They went to Kashi and read all the four Vedas,
They lived there for many years. —52

End of the third chapter entitled "The Description of the War of the Descendents of Lava and Kusha" of Bachittar Natak.

The Recitation of the Vedas and the Offering of Kingdom

BHUJANG PRAYAAT STANZA

Those who studied the Vedas, were called Vedis (Bedis),
They absorbed themselves in good acts of righteousness,
The Sodhi king of Madra Desha (Punjab) sent letters to them,
Entreating them to forget the past enmities. —1

The messengers sent by the king came to Kashi,
And gave the message to all the Bedis,
All the reciters of the Vedas came to Madra Desha,
And made obeissance to the king. —2

The king caused them to recite the Vedas in the traditional manner,
And all the brethren (both Sodhis and Bedis) sat together,
Samaveda, *Yajurveda* and *Rigveda* were recited,
The essence of the sayings was imbibed (by the king and his clan). —3

RASAAVAL STANZA

The sin-remover *Atharvaveda* was recited,
The king was highly pleased and he bequeathed his kindom to Bedis. —4

He himself adopted the sin-destroyer Vanaprastha *ashrama*,
He put on the garb of a sage (*rishi*),
And gave his kingdom to the reciter (Amrit Rai). —5

Other people, forgetting all sorrows,
And leaving their wealth and property, absorbed themselves in divine love. —6

ARIL

Having been bestowed the kingdom, the Bedis was very much pleased,
With happy heart, he predicated this boon:
"When in the iron age, I shall be called Nanak,
"You will attain the supreme state and be worshipped by the world." —7

DOHIRA

The descendents of Lava, after handing over the kingdom, went to the forest,
And the Bedis (descendents of Kusha) began to rule; they enjoyed all comforts of the earth in various ways. —8

CHAUPAI

"O Sodhi king! You have listened to the recitation of three Vedas,
"And while listening to the fourth, you gave away your kingdom,
"When I shall have taken three births,
"You will be made the Guru in the fourth birth." —9

That (Sodhi) king left for the forest,
And this (Bedi) king absorbed himself in royal pleasures,
To what extent, I should narrate the story?
It is feared that this book will become voluminous. —10

End of the fourth chapter entitled "The Recitation of the Vedas and the Offering of Kingdom" of Bachittar Natak.

The Description of the Gurus

NARAAJ STANZA

There arose again quarrels and enmities,
There was none to defuse the situation,
In due course of time it actually happened,
That the Bedi clan lost its kingdom. —1

DOHIRA

The Brahmins acted like Shudras and Kshatriyas like Vaishyas,
The Vaishyas acted like Kshatriyas and Shudras like Brahmins. —2

CHAUPAI

Only twenty villages were left with the Bedis,
Where they became agriculturists,
A long time passed like this,
Till the birth of Nanak. —3

DOHIRA

Nanak Rai took birth in the Bedi clan,
He brought comfort to all his disciples and helped them at all times. —4

CHAUPAI

Guru Nanak spread *dharma* in the iron age,
And put the seekers on the path,
Those who followed the path propagated by him,
Were never haunted by the vices. —5

All those who came within his fold,
They were absolved of all other sins and troubles,
Their sorrows, their wants,
And even their transmigration. —6

Nanak transformed himself to Angad,
And spread *dharma* in the world,
He was called Amar Das in the next transformation,
A lamp was lighted from the lamp. —7

When the opportune time came for the boon,
Then the Guru was called Ramdas,
The old boon was bestowed upon him,
When Amar Das departed for the heavens. —8

Sri Nanak was recognised in Angad,
And Angad in Amar Das,
Amar Das was called Ramdas,
Only the saints know it and the fools did not. —9

The people on the whole considered them as separate ones,
But there were few who recognised them one and same,
Those who recognised them as one,
They were successful on the spiritual plane,
Without recognition there was no success. —10

When Ramdas merged in the Lord,
The Guruship was bestowed upon Arjan,
When Arjan left for the abode of the Lord,
Hargobind was seated on his throne. —11

When Hargobind left for the abode of the Lord,
Har Rai was seated in his place,
Har Krishan (the next Guru) was his son,
After him, Tegh Bahadur became the Guru. —12

He protected the forehead mark and sacred thread (of the Hindus),
Which marked a great event in the iron age,
For the sake of saints, he laid down his head without even a sigh. —13

For the sake of *dharma*, he sacrificed himself,
He laid down his head but not his creed,
The saints of the Lord abhor the performance of miracles and malpractices. —14

DOHIRA

Breaking the potsherd of his body on the head of the king of Delhi (Aurangzeb),
He left for the abode of the Lord,
None could perform such a feat as that of Tegh Bahadur. —15

The whole world bemoaned the departure of Tegh Bahadur,
While the world lamented, the gods hailed his arrival in heavens. —16

End of the fifth chapter entitled "The Description of the Gurus" of Bachittar Natak.

The Call of the Supreme Kal to Me for Coming into the World

CHAUPAI

Now I relate my own story,
As to how I was brought here, while I was absorbed in deep meditation,
The site was, the mountain named Hemkunt, with seven peaks and looks there very impressive. —1

That mountain is called Sapt Shring (seven-peaked mountain),
Where the Pandavas practised yoga,
There I was absorbed in deep meditation on the primal power, the supreme Kal. —2

In this way, my meditation reached its zenith
And I became one with the omnipotent Lord,
My parents also meditated for the union with the incomprehensible Lord,
And performed many types of disciplines for union. —3

The service that they rendered the incomprehensible Lord,
Caused the pleasure of the supreme Guru (i.e. Lord),
When the Lord ordered me,
I was born in this Iron Age. —4

I had no desire to come,
Because I was totally absorbed in devotion for the holy feet of the Lord,
But the Lord made me understand His will,
And sent me in this world with the following words. —5

The Words of the Non-temporal Lord to This Insect

CHAUPAI

When I created the world in the beginning,
I created the ignominious and dreadful *daityas*,
Who became mad with power,
And abandoned the worship of supreme *Purusha*. —6

I destroyed them in no time,
And created gods in their place,
They were also absorbed in the worship of power,
And called themselves omnipotent. —7

Mahadeo (Shiva) was called *achyute* (blotless),
Vishnu considered himself the supreme,
Brahma called himself *Para Brahman*,
None could comprehend the Lord. —8

Then I created eight *sakshis*,
In order to give evidence of my entity,
But they considered themselves all in all,
And asked the people to worship them. — 9

Those who did not comprehend the Lord,
They were considered as *Ishvara*,
Several people worshipped the sun and the moon,
And several others worshipped fire and air. —10

Several of them considered god as stone,
And several others bathed considering the Lordship of water,
Considering Dharmaraja as the supreme representative of *dharma*,
Several bore fear of him in their actions. —11

All those whom god established for the revelation of His supremacy,
They themselves were called supreme,
They forgot the Lord in their race for supremacy. —12

When they did not comprehend the Lord,
Then I established human beings in their place,
They also were overpowered by mineness,
And exhibited the Lord in statues. —13

Then I created Siddhas and Sadhus,
Who also could not realise the Lord,
On whomsoever wisdom dawned,
He started his own path. —14

None could realise the supreme Lord,
But instead spread, strife, enmity and ego,
The tree and the leaves began to burn, because of the inner fire,
None followed the path of the Lord. —15

Whosoever attained a little spiritual power,
He started his own path,

None could comprehend the Lord,
But instead became mad with "I-ness." —16
Nobody recognised the supreme essence,
But was entangled within himself,
All the great *rishis* (sages), who were then created,
Produced their own Smritis. —17
All those who became followers of these Smritis,
They abandoned the path of the Lord,
Those who devoted themselves to the feet of the Lord,
They did not adopt the path of the Smritis. —18
Brahma composed all the four Vedas,
All the people followed the injunctions contained in them,
Those who were devoted to the feet of the Lord,
They abandoned the Vedas. —19
Those who abandoned the path of the Vedas and Katebs,
They became the devotees of the Lord,
Whosoever follows their path,
He crushes various types of sufferings. —20
Those who consider the castes illusory,
They do not abandon the love of the Lord,
When they leave the world, they go to the abode of the Lord,
And there is no difference between them and the Lord. —21
Those who fear the castes and follow their path, abandoning the supreme Lord,
They fall into hell,
And transmigrate again and again. —22
Then I created Dutt,
Who also started his own path,
His followers have long nails in their hands,
And matted hair on their heads,
They did not understand the ways of the Lord. —23
Then I created Gorakh,
Who made great kings his disciples,
His disciples wear rings in their ears,
And do not know the love of the Lord. —24
Then I created Ramanand,
Who adopted the garb of a *bairagi*,
Around his neck he wore a necklace of wooden beads,
And did not comprehend the ways of the Lord. —25

All the great *purushas* created by me,
Started their own paths,
Then I created Muhammad,
Who was made the master of Arabia. —26
He started a religion,
And circumcised all the kings,
He caused all to utter his name,
And did not give the true name of the Lord with firmness to any one. —27
Everyone placed his own interest first and foremost,
And did not comprehend the supreme Brahman,
When I was busy in austere devotion,
The Lord called me and sent me to this world with these words. —28

The Words of the Non-temporal Lord

CHAUPAI

"I have adopted you as my son,
And hath created you for the propagation of the path (Panth),
You go therefore for the spread of *dharma* (righteouness),
And cause people to retrace their steps from evil actions." —29

The Words of the Poet

DOHIRA

I stood up with folded hands and bowing down my head, I said,
"The path (Panth) shall prevail only in the world, with Thy assistance." —30

CHAUPAI

For this reason the Lord sent me,
And I was born in this world,
Whatever the Lord said, I am repeating the same upto you,
I do not bear enmity with any one. —31
Whosoever shall call me the Lord,
Shall fall into hell,
Consider me as His servant,
And do not think of any difference between me and the Lord. —32
I am the servant of the supreme *Purushá*
And hath come to see the sport of the world,
Whatever the Lord of the world said, I say the same unto you,

I cannot remain silent in this abode of death. —33

NARAAJ STANZA

I say only that which the Lord hath said,
I do not yield to anyone else,
I do not feel pleased with any particular garb,
I sow the seed of God's name. —34

I do not worship stones,
Nor I have any liking for a particular guise,
I sing infinite names (of the Lord),
And meet the supreme *Purusha*. —35

I do not wear matted hair on my head,
Nor do I put rings in my ears,
I do not pay attention to anyone else,
All my actions are at the bidding of the Lord. —36

I recite only the name of the Lord,
Which is useful at all places,
I do not meditate on anyone else,
Nor did I seek assistance from any other quarter. —37

I recite infinite names,
And attain the supreme light,
I do not meditate on anyone else,
Nor do I repeat the name of anyone else. —38

I am absorbed only in the name of the Lord,
And honour none else,
By meditating on the supreme,
I am absolved of infinite sins. —39

I am absorbed only in His sight,
And do not attend to any other charitable action,
By uttering only His name,
I am absolved of infinite sorrows. —40

CHAUPAI

Those who meditate on the name of the Lord,
None of the sorrows and sins came near them,
Those who meditated on any other entity,
They ended themselves in futile discussions and quarrels. —41

I have been sent into this world,
By the preceptor-Lord to propagate *dharma* (righteousness),
The Lord asked me to spread *dharma*,
And vanquish the tyrants and evil-minded persons. —42

I have taken birth for this purpose,
The saints should comprehend this in their minds,
(I have been born) to spread *dharma*, and protect saints,
And root out tyrants and evil-minded persons. —43

All the earlier incarnations,
Caused only their names to be remembered,
They did not strike the tyrants,
And did not make them follow the path of *dharma*. —44

All the earlier prophets,
Ended themselves in ego,
And did not comprehend the supreme *Purusha*,
They did not care for the righteous actions. —45

Have no hopes on others,
Rely only on the one Lord,
The hopes on others are never fruitful,
Therefore, keep in your mind the hopes on the one Lord. —46

DOHIRA

Someone studies the *Quran* and someone studies the Puranas,
Mere reading cannot save one from death, therefore such works are vain and do not help at the time of death. —47

CHAUPAI

Millions of people recite the *Quran*,
And many study Puranas without understanding the crux,
It will be of no use at the time of death,
And none will be saved. —48

O brother! Why do you not meditate on Him,
Who will help you at the time of death?
Consider the vain religions as illusory,
Because they do not serve our purpose (of life). —49

For this reason the Lord created me,
And sent me in this world, telling me the secret,
Whatever He told me, I say unto you,
There is not even a litle heresy in it. —50

RASAAVAL STANZA

I neither wear matted hair on the head nor bedeck myself with ear-rings,
I meditate on the name of the Lord, which helps me in all my errands. —51

Neither I close my eyes, nor exhibit heresy,
Nor perform evil actions, nor cause others to call me a person in disguise. —52

CHAUPAI

Those persons who adopt different guises are never liked by the men of God,
All of you may understand this that God is absent from all these guises. —53
Those who exhibit various garbs through various actions,
They never get release in the next world,
While alive, their worldly desires may be fulfilled,
And the king may be pleased on seeing their mimicry. —54
The Lord-God is not present in such mimics,
Even all the places be searched by all,
Only those who controlled their minds,
Recognised the supreme Brahman. —55

DOHIRA

Those who exhibit various guises in the world and win people on their side,
They will reside in hell, when the sword of death chops them. —56

CHAUPAI

Those who exhibit different guises, find disciples and enjoy great comforts,
Those who close their nostrils and perform prostrations, their religious discipline is vain and useless. —57
All the followers of the futile paths fall into hell from within,
They cannot go to heaven with the movement of the hands, because they could not control their minds in any way. —58

The Words of the Poet

DOHIRA

Whatever my Lord said to me, I say the same in the world,
Those who have meditated on the Lord, ultimately go to heaven. —59

DOHIRA

The Lord and His devotees are one, there is no difference between them,
Just as the wave of water, arising in water, merges in water. —60

CHAUPAI

Those who quarrel in ego, they are far removed from the Lord,
O men of God! understand this that the Lord doth not reside in Vedas and Katebs. —61
He, who exhibits heresy in closing his eyes, attains the state of blindness,
By closing the eyes one cannot know the path, how can then, O brother! He meets the infinite Lord? —62
To what extent the details be given?
When one understands, he feels tired,
If one is blessed with millions of tongues,
Even then he feels them short in number (while singing the praises of the Lord). —63

DOHIRA

When the Lord willed, I was born on this earth,
Now I shall narrate briefly my own story. —64

End of the sixth chapter entitled "The Command of Supreme Kal to Me for coming into the World" of Bachittar Natak.

The Description of the Birth

CHAUPAI

My father proceeded towards the east and visited several places of pilgrimage,
When he went to Triveni (Prayag), he passed his days in acts of charity. —1
I was conceived there and took birth at Patna,
When I was brought to Madra Desha (Punjab), I was caressed by various nurses. —2
I was given physical protection in various ways and given various types of education,
When I began to perform the acts of *dharma* (righteousness), my father departed for his heavenly abode. —3

End of the seventh chapter entitled of "Description of the Birth of the Poet" of Bachittar Natak.

Descriptin of the Battle of Bhangani

CHAUPAI

When I obtained the position of responsibility, I performed the religious acts to the best of my ability,

I went hunting various kinds of animals in the forest and killed bears, *nilgais* (blue bulls) and elks. —1

Then I left my home and went to a place named Paonta,

I enjoyed my stay on the banks of Kalindri (Yamuna) and saw amusements of various kinds. —2

There I killed many lions, *nilgais* and bears,

On this the King Fateh Shah became angry and fought with me without any reason. —3

BHUJANG PRAYAAT STANZA

There Sri Shah (Sango Shah) became enraged and all the five warriors stood firmly in the battlefield,

Including the tenacious Jit Mal and the desperate hero Gulab, whose faces were red with ire, in the field. —4

The persistent Mahari Chand and Ganga Ram, who had defeated lot of forces,

Lal Chand was red with anger, who had shattered the pride of several lion-like heroes. —5

Maharu got enraged and with frightening expression killed brave Khans in the battlefield,

The godly Daya Ram, filled with great ire, fought very heroically in the field like Dronacharya. —6

Kirpal in rage, rushed with his mace and struck it on the head of the tenacious Hayat Khan,

With all his might, he caused the marrow flow out of his head, which splashed like the butter spattering out of the pitcher of butter broken by Lord Krishna. —7

Then Nand Chand, in fierce rage, wielding his sword struck it with force, but it broke,

Then he drew his dagger and the tenacious warrior saved the honour of the Sodhi clan. —8

Then the maternal uncle Kirpal, in great ire, manifested the war-feats like a true Kshatriya,

The great hero was struck by an arrow, but he caused the brave Khan to fall from the saddle. —9

Sahib Chand, the valiant Kshatriya, killed a bloody Khan of Khorasan,

He slew several graceful warriors, with full force, the soldiers who survived, fled away in order to save their lives. —10

There (Sango) Shah exhibited his acts of bravery in the battlefield and trampled under feet many bloody Khans,

Gopal, the king of Guleri, stood firmly in the field and roared like a lion amidst a herd of deer. —11

There in great fury, a warrior Hari Chand, very skilfully took position in the battlefield,

He discharged sharp arrows in great rage and whosoever was struck left for the other world. —12

RASAAVAL STANZA

Hari Chand (Handooria) in great fury, killed significant heroes,

He shot skilfully a volley of arrows and killed a lot of forces. —13

He was absorbed in dreadful feat of arms,

Armed warriors were being killed and great kings were falling on the ground. —14

Then Jit Mal aimed at and struck Hari Chand down to the ground with his spear. —15

The warriors struck with arrows became red with blood,

Their horses fell and they left for heavens. —16

BHUJANG PRAYAAT STANZA

In the hands of blood-thirsty Khans, there were the Khorasan swords, whose sharp edges flashed like fire,

The bows shooting out volleys of arrows twanged, the splendid horses fell because of the heavy blows. —17

The trumpets sounded and the musical pipes were played, the brave warriors thundered from both sides,

And with their strong arms struck (the enemy), the witches drank blood to their fill and produced dreadful sounds. —18

DOHIRA

How far should I describe the great battle?

Those who fought attained martyrdom; thousands fled away. —19

BHUJANG PRAYAAT STANZA

The hill-chief spurred his horse and fled, the warriors went away without discharging their arrows,

The chiefs of Jaswal and Dadhwal, who were fighting (in the field) left with all their soldiers. —20

The Raja of Chandel was perplexed and filled with great fury, fulfilling his duty as a general, those who come in front, were cut into pieces and fell (in the field). —21

Then Najabat Khan came forward and struck Sango Shah with his weapons,

Several skilful Khans fell on him with their arms and sent Shah Sangram to heaven. —22

DOHIRA

The brave warrior Sango Shah fell down after killing Najbat Khan,

There were lamentations in this world and rejoicings in heaven. —23

BHUJANG PRAYAAT STANZA

When this lowly person saw Shah falling (while fighting bravely) he held aloft his bow and arrows,

He, fixing his gaze on a Khan, shot an arrow, which stung the enemy like a black cobra, who (the Khan) fell down. —24

He drew out another arrow and aimed and shot it on the face of Bhikhan Khan,

The bloody Khan fled away leaving his horse in the field, who was killed with the third arrow. —25

After regaining consciousness from the swoon, Hari Chand shot his arrows with unerring aim,

Whosoever was struck, fell down unconscious, and leaving his body, went to the heavenly abode. —26

He aimed and shot two arrows at the same time and and did not care for the selection of his target,

Whosoever was struck and pierced by his arrows, went straight to the other world. —27

The warriors remained true to their duty in the field, the witches and ghosts drank blood to their fill and raised shrill voices,

The Birs (heroic spirits), Baitals (ghosts) and Siddhas (adepts) laughed, the witches were talking and huge kites were flying (for meat). —28

Hari Chand, filled with rage, drew out his bow, he aimed and shot his arrow, which struck my horse,

He aimed and shot the second arrow towards me, the Lord protected me, his arrow only grazed my ear. —29

His third arrow penetrated the buckle of my waist-belt and its edge touched the body, but did not cause a wound, the Lord saved his servant. —30

RASAAVAL STANZA

When the edge of the arrow touch my body, it kindled my resentment,

I took the bow in my hand and aimed and shot the arrow. —31

All the warriors fled, when a volley of arrows was showered,

Then I aimed the arrow on a warrior and killed him. —32

Hari Chand was killed and his brave soldiers were trampled,

The chief of Kot Lehar was seized by death. —33

The hill-men fled from the battlefield, all were filled with fear,

I gained victory through the favour of the eternal Lord (Kal). —34

We returned after victory and sang songs of triumph,

I showered wealth on the warriors, who were full of rejoicings. —35

DOHIRA

When I returned after victory, I did not remain at Paonta,

I came to Kahlur and established the village of Anandpur. —36

Those, who did not join the forces, were turned out from the town,

And those who fought bravely were patronised by me. —37

CHAUPAI

Many days passed in this way,

The saints were protected and the wicked persons were killed,

The tyrants were hanged and ultimately killed, They breathed their last like dogs. —38

End of the eighth chapter entitled "Description of the Battle of Bhangani" of Bachittar Natak.

The Description of the Battle of Nadaun

CHAUPAI

Much time passed in this way,
Mian Khan came (from Delhi) to Jammu (for collection of revenue),
He sent Alif Khan to Nadaun,
Who developed enmity towards Bhim Chand (the Chief of Kahlur). —1

Bhim Chand called me for assistance and himself went to face (the enemy),
Alif Khan prepared a wooden fort on the hills of Navras,
The hill-chiefs also prepared their arrows and guns. —2

BHUJANG PRAYAAT STANZA

With brave Bhim Chand, there were Raj Singh, illustrious Ram Singh and Sukhdev Gaji of Jasrot,
They were full of fury and managed their affairs with enthusiam. —3

There came also the brave Prithi Chand of Dadhwar after having made arrangements regarding the affairs of his state,
Kirpal Chand (of Kangra) arrived with ammunition and drove back and killed many of the warriors (of Bhim Chand). —4

When for the second time, the forces of Bhim Chand advanced, they were beaten back downwards to the great sorrows of (the allies of Bhim Chand),
The warriors on the hill sounded trumpets, while the chiefts below were filled with remorse. —5

Then Bhim Chand was filled with great ire and began to recite the incantations of Hanuman,
He called all his warriors and also called me,
Then all assembled and advanced for attack. —6

All the great warriors marched forward with great ire like a flame over a fence of dry weeds,
Then on the other side, the valiant, Raja Dayal of Bijharwal advanced with Raja Kirpal, alongwith all his army. —7

MADHUBHAAR STANZA

Kirpal Chand was in great fury,
The horses denced and the pipes were played, which presented a dreadful scene. —8

The warriors fought and struck their spears,
With rage, they showered volley of arrows. —9
The fighting soldiers fell in the field and breathed their last,
They fell like thundering clouds on the earth. —10

RASAAVAL STANZA

Kirpal Chand, in great anger, stood firmly in the field,
With his volleys of arrows, he killed great warriors. —11
He killed the chiefs, who lay dead on the ground,
The trumpets sounded and the warriors thundered. —12
Kirpal Chand, in great fury, made a great fight,
Great heroes thundered, while using dreadful weapons. —13
Such a heroic battle was fought that all the people of the world, living in nine quarters, knew it,
His weapons wrought havoc and he exhibited himself as a true Rajput. —14

DOHIRA

All the chiefs of the allies, in great anger, entered the fray,
And besieged the army of Kotoch. —15

BHUJANG PRAYAAT STANZA

The Rajputs of the tribes Nanglu and Panglu advanced in group alongwith the soldiers of Jaswar and Guler,
The great warrior Dayal also joined and saved the honour of the people of Bijharwal. —16

Then this lowly person (the Guru himself) took up his gun and aimed unerringly at one of the chiefs,
Who reeled and fell down on the ground in the battlefield, but even then he thundered in anger. —17

I then threw away the gun and took the arrows in my hand, I shot four of them,
Another three I discharged with my left hand,
Whether they struck anybody, I do not know. —18

Then the Lord brought the end of the fight and the enemy was driven out into the river,
From the hill the bullets and arrows were showered,

It seemed that the sun set down after playing a good Holi. —19

Pierced by arrows and spears, the warriors fell in the battlefield,

Their clothes were dyed with blood, it seemed that they played Holi,

After conquering the enemy, they came for rest at their place of the encampment, on the other side of the river. —20

Sometime after midnight they left, while beating the drums,

When the whole night ended and the sun arose,

The warriors on our side marched hastily, brandishing their spears. —21

Alif Khan fled away leaving back his belongings,

All the other warriors fled away and did not stay anywhere,

I remained there on the bank of the river for eight more days,

And visited the palaces of all the chiefs. —22

CHAUPAI

Then I took leave and came home,

They went there to settle the terms of peace,

Both the parties made an agreement, therefore the story ends here. —23

DOHIRA

I came to this side after destroying Alsun on my way,

And enjoyed in various ways after reaching Anandpur. —24

End of the ninth chapter entitled "Description of the Battle of Nadaun" of Bachittar Natak.

Description of the Expedition of Khanzada and His Flight out of Fear

CHAUPAI

Many years elasped in this way, all the wicked persons (thieves) were spotted, caught and killed,

Some of them fled from the city, but came back on account of starvation. —1

Then Dilawar Khan (Governer of Lahore) sent his son against me,

A few hours after nightfall, the Khans assembled and advanced for attack. —2

When their forces crossed the river, Alam (Singh) came and woke me up,

There was a great consternation and all the people got up,

They took up their arms with valour and zeal. —3

The discharge of the volleys of shots from guns began immediately,

Everyone was in rage, holding the arms in hand,

They raised various dreadful shouts,

The noise was heard on the other side of the river. —4

BHUJANG PRAYAAT STANZA

The bugles and the trumpets resounded, the great heroes entered the fray, shouting loudly,

From both sides, the arms clattered with force and horses danced,

It seemed that the dreadful goddess Kali thundered in the battlefield. —5

The river appeared like the night of death; the severe chill cramped the soldiers,

The heroes from (my) side thundered and the bloody Khans fled away without using their weapons. —6

NARAAJ STANZA

The shameless Khans fled away and none of them wore the arms,

They left the battlefield though they pretended to be the valiant heroes. —7

They left on galloping horses and could not use the weapons,

They did not shout loudly like valiant heroes and felt ashamed on seeing ladies. —8

DOHIRA

On the way they plundered the village Barwa and halted at Bhallon,

They could not touch me because of the grace of the Lord and fled away ultimately. —9

Because of Thy favour, O Lord! They could not do any harm here, but filled with great anger, they destroyed the village Barwa,

Just as a Vaishya (Bania), though desirous of tasting meat, cannot actually have its relish, but instead prepares and eats the salted soup of parched wheat. —10

End of the tenth chapter entitled "Description of the Expedition of Khanzada and His Flight out of Fear" of Bachittar Natak.

Description of the Killing of Hussain and also Kirpal, Himmat and Sangita

BHUJANG PRAYAAT STANZA

The Khanzada fled to his father and being ashamed of his conduct, he could not speak,
Then Hussain thundered, striking his arms and prepared for attack with all his brave warriors. —1

Hussain assembled all his forces and advanced,
At first he plundered the houses of the hill-people,
Then he conquered the Raja of Dadhwal and brought him under submission,
The sons of the Raja were made slaves. —2

Then he plundered the Doon thoroughly, none could face the barbarian,
He took away forcibly the food grains and distributed them (amongst the soldiers), the big fool thus committed a very bad act. —3

DOHIRA

Some days passed in such acts,
The turn of meeting the Raja of Guler came. —4

If he had not met (Hussain) for two days more,
The enemy would have come here (towards me), but the Providence had thrown a device of discord towards his house. —5

CHAUPAI

The Raja of Guler came to meet Hussain and with him came Ram Singh,
They met Hussain after the four quarters of the day had passed,
The slave Hussain became blind in vanity. —6

DOHIRA

Just as the sand becomes heated by the heat of the sun,
The wretched sand doth not know the might of the sun and becomes proud of itself. —7

CHAUPAI

Similarly the slave Hussain was puffed up with ego, he did not care to notice them,
With the Raja of Kahlur and Katoch on his side he considered himself peerless. —8
(The Raja of Guler and Ram Singh) offered money to Hussain, which they had brought with them,
A dispute arose in giving and taking,
Therefore the Rajas returned to their places with the money. —9

Then Hussain was enraged and lost the power of discriminating between good and bad,
He made no other consideration and ordered the beating of the drum against the Raja of Guler. —10

He did not think of any tactical consideration,
The hare surrounded the lion for frightening him,
He besieged him for fifteen *pahars* (about 45 hours) and did not allow the items of food and drink to reach the state. —11

Being without food and drink, the warriors were filled with ire,
The Raja sent the messengers for the purpose of making peace,
Seeing the Pathan forces around him, the slave Hussain lost his balance and did not consider the request of the Raja. —12

He said, "Either give me ten thousand rupees immediately or take death on your head,"
I had sent Sangita Singh there for making peace (among the chiefs), he brought Gopal on oath of God. —13

But he could not reconcile with them; then Kirpal thought within his mind,
That such an opportunity will not be available again, because the circle of time deceives everybody. —14

He decided to catch hold of Gopal immediately, either to imprison him or kill him,
When Gopal got scent of the conspiracy, he escaped to his people (forces). —15

MADHUBHAAR STANZA

When Gopal was gone, Kirpal was filled with anger,
Himmat and Hussain rushed for fighting in the field. —16

With great pride, more warriors followed; the drums and trumpets resounded. —17

On the other side, the trumpets also resounded and the horses danced in the battlefield,
The warriors enthusiastically strike their weapons, creating clattering sound. —18

The fearless warriors blow their horns and shout loudly,

The swords are struck and the warriors are lying on the ground. —19

The guns, arrows, lances and axes create noises. —20

The warriors shout, the heroes who stand firmly in the field thunder, the fighters move in the field like leopards. —21

The horses neigh and the trumpets resound, the warriors strike their weapons enthusiastically and also endure the blows. —22

The warriors falling as martyrs appear like the carefree intoxicated person lying down on the ground,

Their dishevelled hair appear like the matted hair (of hermits). —23

The huge elephants are decorated their bows, thunder in the field. —24

TRIBHANGI STANZA

Kirpal Chand, in great ire decorated his horse and he, the long-armed warrior held his shield,

All the dreadful-looking warriors, with red and radiant faces are moving,

Holding their swords and decorated with bow and arrows, the youthful warriors, full of heat,

Are engaged in frolics in the battlefield and shouting "kill, kill" appear like intoxicated elephants in the forest. —25

BHUJANG PRAYAAT STANZA

Then the Raja of Kangra (Kirpal Chand Katoch) was filled with anger,

His face and eyes became red with rage and he freed himself from all other thoughts,

From another side, the Khans entered with arrows in their hands,

It seemed that the leopards were roaming in search of flesh. —26

The kettle-drums, the arrows and swords in action create their particular sounds, the hands move towards the wounded waist,

The trumpets resound in the field and the minstrels sing their heroic ballads, the bodies are pierced by arrows and the headless trunks are moving in the field. —27

The blows of maces on helmets create knocking sounds, the bodies of killed warriors are rolling in dust,

The swords are inflicting wounds on the bodies of heroes; the bodies pierced by arrows and headless trunks are moving in the field. —28

The armies are engaged in continuosly shooting arrows, the striking swords are creating grave clattering sounds,

The warriors, in great fury, are showering volleys of arrows; some arrows miss the targets and on account of some arrows, the horses are; seen roaming without the riders. —29

The brave warriors fighting with each other appear like the elephants with tusks fighting mutually or the tiger confronting the tiger,

In a similar manner, Gopal Chand Guleria is fighting with Kirpal Chand, (the ally of Hussain). —30

Then another warrior Hari Singh (an ally of Hussain) rushed into the field; he received many arrows in his body,

In great rage, he killed many soldiers and after a great fight departed for the heavenly abode. —31

The tenacious Himmat and Kimmat drew out their spears and Jalal Khan joined with a mace,

The determined warriors fought, seemingly intoxicated; there were blows after blows and the sparks fell, when the weapons struck each other. —32

RASAAVAL STANZA

The Raja of Jaswal rushed forward on the galloping horse,

He surrounded Hussain and struck his sharp lance at him. —33

He (Hussain) discharged arrows and destroyed much of the army,

He, who is struck by the arrows on his chest, he breathes his last. —34

Whenever one is wounded, he gets highly infuriated,

Then, holding his bow, he kills the warriors with arrows. —35

The warriors advance from all the four sides and shout "kill, kill,"

They strike their weapons fearlessly, both the sides wish for their victory. —36

The sons of Khans, in great ire and puffed up with great ego, shower the rain of arrows; all the warriors are filled with anger. —37

There is spattering of arrows (in worship) and the bows seem engaged in Vedic discussion, wherever the warrior wants to strike the blow, he strikes it. —38

The brave fighters are busy in this task; they are engaged in war with all their weapons; the warriors, with the quality of forbearance, are knocking forcefully and their swords are clattering. —39

The bows crackle and the swords clatter; the arrows, when discharged, produce knocking sounds, and the weapons when struck, produce jingling sounds. —40

The warriors are striking their weapons, they do not think of the impending death; the arrows are being discharged and the swords are being struck. —41

The stream of blood is full, the *houris* (the heavenly damsels) are moving in, the sky; on both sides, the warriors utter dreadful shouts. —42

PAADHARI STANZA

The ghosts are laughing loudly in the battlefield, the elephants are rolling in dust and the horses are roaming without riders,

The warriors are fighting with one another and their weapons are creating knocking sounds,

The swords are being struck and the arrows are being showered. —43

The vampires are shouting and the hags are shrieking,

The crows are cawing loudly and the double-edged swords are clattering,

The helmets are being knocked at and the guns are booming,

The daggers are clattering and there is violent pushing. —44

BHUJANG PRAYAAT STANZA

Then Hussain himself entered the fray, all the warriors took up bows and arrows,

The bloody Khans stood firmly and began to fight with faces and eyes red with ire. —45

The terrible battle of valiant warriors began,

The arrows, spears and double-edged swords were used by the heroes,

The warriors met warriors, elegant and most enduring,

The spears are being pushed forward and the swords are jingling. —46

The drums and the pipes are resounding, the arms rise to strike blows and the brave fighters are roaring,

The new trumpets resound in great numbers,

The chopped heroes are rolling in dust and the sparks arise with the collision of weapons. —47

The helmets and shields have been broken into bits and the great heroes shooting arrows look terrible and not elegant,

The heroic spirits, ghosts, fiends and goblins are dancing,

The vampires, female demons and Shiva also are dancing. —48

The supreme Rudra hath awakened on coming out of the yogic contemplation,

The meditation of Brahma hath been interrupted and all the Siddhas (adepts) in great fear have run away from their abodes,

The Kinnars, Yakshas and Vidyadhars are laughing and the fairies and the wives of bards are dancing. —49

The fight was most terrible and the army fled away,

The great hero Hussain stood firmly in the field,

The heroes of Jaswal ran towards him,

The horsemen were cut in the manner the cloth is cut (by the tailor). —50

There Hussain stood quite alone like the pole of a flag fixed in the ground,

Wherever that tenacious warrior shot his arrow, it pierced through the body and went out. —51

The warriors who were struck by arrows came together against him,

From all the four sides, they shouted "kill, kill," They carried and struck their weapons very ably,

At last Hussain fell down and left for heaven. —52

DOHIRA

When Hussain was killed, the warriors were in great fury,

All the others fled, but the forces of Katoch felt excited. —53

CHAUPAI

All the soldiers of Katoch rushed with great anger together with Himmat and Kimmat,

Then Hari Singh, who came forward, killed many brave horsemen. —54

NARAAJ STANZA

Then the Raja of Katoch became furious and stood firmly in the field,
He used his weapons unerringly shouting death (for the enemy). —55
(From the other side) the Raja of Chandel got enraged And attacked all in a body with indignation,
Those who faced him were killed and those who remained behind, ran away. —56

DOHIRA

(Sangita Singh) died with his seven companions,
When Darsho came to know of it, he also came in the field and died. —57
Then Himmat came in the battlefield; he received several wounds and struck his weapons on several others. —58
His horse was killed there, but Himmat fled,
The warriors of Katoch came with great rage in order to take away the dead body of their Raja Kirpal. —59

RASAAVAL STANZA

The warriors are busy in wreaking vengeance, they become martyrs facing the sword,
The warrior Kirpal Ram fought so severely that all the army seems running away. —60
He tramples the big army and strikes his weapons fearlessly,
After destroying many and receiving approbation, he hath left. —61
The conches and trumpets resound and their sound is heard constantly,
The tabors and drums resound and the warriors are taking out their weapons. —62
There is overcrowding and the kings have fallen as martyrs; the warrior,
On whose faces there are winsome whiskers, they are shouting very loudly. —63
From their mouths, they are shouting "kill, kill," and roam in the battlefield; they hold the weapons and cause the horses of both sides to flee. —64

DOHIRA

When Kirpal died in the battlefield, Gopal rejoiced,
All the army fled in disorder,
When their leaders, Hussain and Kirpal were killed. —65
After the death of Hussain and Kirpal and the fall of Himmat,
All the warriors fled, just as people go away after giving authority to the Mahant. —66

CHAUPAI

In this way, all the enemies were aimed and killed,
After that they took care of their dead,
Then on seeing Himmat lying wounded, Ram Singh said to Gopal. —67
Himmat, who had been the root-cause of all the quarrels, hath now fallen wounded in our hands,
When Gopal heard these words, he killed Himmat and did not allow him to get alive. —68
The victory was gained and the battle ended,
While remembring homes, all went there,
The Lord protected me from the cloud of battle, which rained elsewhere. —69

End of the eleventh chapter entitled "Description of the Killing of Hussain and also Kirpal, Himmat and Sangita" of Bachittar Natak.

Description of the Battle with Jujhar Singh

CHAUPAI

In this way, the great battle was fought, when the leader of the Turks (Muhammedans) was killed,
On this Dilawar became very angry and sent a contingent of horsemen in this direction. —1
From the other side, Jujhar Singh was sent, who drove out the enemy from Bhallan immediately,
On this side, Gaj Singh and Pamma (Parmanand) assembled their forces and fell upon them early in the morning. —2
On the other side Jujhar Singh stood firmly like a flagpost planted in the battlefield,
Even the flagpost might be loosened, but the brave Rajput did not waver, he received the blows without flinching. —3
The warriors of both the armies moved in detachments, Raja of Chandel on that side and Raja of Jaswar on this side,

All the warriors were in great rage and the fight began in the battlefield. —4

The brave heroes of both the armies were in great anger, warriors of Chandel on this side and warriors of Jaswar on the other,

Many drums and trumpets resounded, the terrible Bhairo (the god of war) shouted. —5

RASAAVAL STANZA

Listening to the resounding voice of the drums, the warriors thunder,

They inflict wounds with weapons, their minds filled with great zest. —6

Fearlessly, they cause their horses to run and strike the blows of axes,

Many inflict wounds with their swords and the minds of all are very enthusiastic. —7

From their mouths, they shout "kill, kill," without any doubts,

The chopped warriors are rolling in dust and wish to go to heaven. —8

DOHIRA

They do not retrace their steps from the battlefield and inflict wounds fearlessly,

Those who fall from their horses, the heavenly damsels go to wed them. —9

CHAUPAI

In this way, the battle continued on both sides (with great vigour),

Chandan Rai was killed; then Jujhar Singh continued the fight quite alone,

He was surrounded from all the sides. —10

DOHIRA

He rushed into the army of the enemy without any hesitation

And killed many soldiers, wielding his weapons very skilfully. —11

CHAUPAI

In this way, he destroyed many homes, using various kinds of weapons,

He aimed and killed the brave horsemen, but at last he left for the hevenly abode himself. —12

End of the twelfth chapter entitled "Description of the Battle with Jujhar Singh" of Bachittar Natak.

Description of the Arrival of Shahzada and the Officers

CHAUPAI

In this way, when Jujhar Singh was killed, the soldiers returned to their homes,

Then Aurangzeb became very angry and sent his son to Madra Desha (Punjab). —1

On his arrival, all were frightened and hide themselves in big hills,

The people tried to frighten me also, because they did not understand the ways of Almighty. —2

Some people left me and took refuge in the big hills,

The cowards were so much frightened that they did not consider their safety with me. —3

The son of Aurangzeb grew very angry and sent a subordinate in this direction,

Those who had left me in distrust, their homes were demolished by him. —4

Those who turn away their faces from the Guru, their houses are demolished in this and the next world,

They are ridiculed here and also do not get an abode in heaven,

They also remain disappointed in all things. —5

They are always inflicted by hunger and sorrow,

Those, who have forsaken the service of the saints,

None of their wish is fulfilled in the world,

And also ultimately fall in the world. —6

They are always ridiculed in the world and in the end, they abide in the fire of the abyss of hell,

Those, who turn away their face from the feet of the Guru, their faces are blackened in this and the next world. —7

Their sons and grandsons do not prosper and they die, creating great agony for their parents,

The one, who hath malice of the Guru in his heart, dies the death of a dog,

He repents, when he is thrown in the abyss of hell. —8

The successors of both, Baba (Nanak) and Babur were created by god Himself,

Recognise the former as the spiritual king and the later as the temporal king. —9

Those who do not deliver the Guru's money, the successors of Babur shall seize and take away forcibly, from them,
They will be greatly punished and their houses will be plundered. —10

When those impertinent persons will be without money, they will beg for it from the Sikhs,
And those Sikhs, who will give them money, their houses will be plundered by the Malechhas (barbarians). —11

When their wealth will be destroyed, then they will keep hopes on their Guru,
They will all come then to have a sight of the Guru, But the Guru will not receive them. —12

Then without seeking the permission of the Guru, they will return to their homes,
Therefore none of their work will be fruitful,
He, who doth not get the refuge at the house of the Guru, he doth not get an abode in the Court of the Lord,
He ramains disappointed at both the places, in this world as well as the next world. —13

Those, who are the devotees of Guru feet, the sufferings cannot touch them,
The wealth and prosperity always abide in their house and the sins and ailments cannot even come near their shadow. —14

The Malechha (barbarian) cannot touch their shadow, the eight miraculous powers live in their house,
Even if they endeavour to reap gains by way of fun, the nine treasures come to their abode by themselves. —15

Mirza Beg was the name of the officer, who demolished the houses of the apostates,
Those who remained faithful, were protected by the Guru,
Not even a little harm was done to them. —16

There the son of Aurangzeb grew most angry, he sent four other officers,
Those apostates who had escaped (the punishment) earlier, their houses were demolished by the officers. —17

Those who had fled from Anandpur forsaking the refuge of the Guru and considered the officers as their Guru,
Who have put the urine on their heads and shaved them,
It appears that they have come and brought to their homes such a nectar from their new Guru. —18

Those who had fled from Anandpur without the permission of their Guru, these officers enquired about their address from others,
They have got their heads shaved and caused them to move throughout the city,
It appears that they have been sent to collect the offerings by the officers. —19

The boys who are following them and jeering them, appear like their disciples and servants,
The nose-bags containing turf of the horses, tied on their faces,
Make them appear to have received for eating the sweet-meat from their homes. —20

The marks of the wounds on their foreheads, caused by the beating with shoes, look like the frontal marks put by the officers (as Guru),
The wounds on the heads caused by the brick-hittings, appears like the previous offering given to them. —21

DOHIRA

Those who have never participated in the war in the battlefield and also have got earned approbation by offering bribe,
Who are not known anybody as the resident of the village,
It is, indeed, wonderful as to who hath given their address to Yama (the god of death)? —22

CHAUPAI

In this way, the apostates received foul treatment,
All the saints saw this spectacle,
No harm was done to them,
The Lord saved them Himself. —23

Chaarni
DOHIRA

To whomsoever the Lord protects, the enemy can do nothing to him,
None can touch his shadow, the fool makes useless effort. —24

Those who have taken refuge with the saints, what can be said about them?
God saves them from the inimical and wicked persons by destroying them, just as the tongue is protected within the teeth. —25

End of the thirteenth chapter entitled "Description of the Arrival of Shahzada (the Prince) and the Officers" of Bachittar Natak.

Description of the Supplication to the Lord, Destroyer of All

CHAUPAI

At all times, the Lord protected all the saints and hath (killed all the malicious persons, subjecting them to great agony,
He hath exhibited His marvellous state to the saints,
And hath saved them from all sufferings. —1
He hath saved His saints from all sufferings,
He hath destroyed all the malevolent persons like the thorns,
Considering me as His servant, He hath helped me,
And hath protected me with His own hands. —2
All those spectacles which have been visualised by me,
I dedicate all of them to Thee,
If Thou castest Thy merciful glance at me,
Then Thy servant shall utter all about them. —3
The kinds of spectacles that I have seen,
I want to enlighten (the world) about them,
All the past lives that I have peeped into,
I shall speak about them with Thy power. —4
He, my Lord, the father and destroyer of all,
The goddess Kalika is my mother,
The mind is my Guru and the discriminating intellect, the Guru's wife is my mother,
Who hath taught me all about good deeds. —5
When I (as mind) reflected on the kindness of the discriminating intellect,
The Guru-mind uttered his refined statement,
All the wonderful things that were comprehended by the ancient sages,
I want to speak about all of them. —6
Then my Lord, destroyer of all, was filled with kindless,
And considering me as His servnt, He was gracefully pleased,
The births of all the incarnations in the previous ages,
He hath caused me to remember all of them. —7
How could I have all this information?,
The Lord mercifully gave such intellect,
My Lord, the destroyer of all, then became Benevolent,
At all times, I have the protection of that steel-incarnated Lord. —8
At all times, the Lord, destroyer of all protects me,
That all-pervading Lord is my protector like steel,
Comprehending Thy kindness I have become fearless,
And in my pride, I consider myself as the king of all. —9
The way in which I came to know about the births of incarnations,
In the same manner, I have rendered them in books,
The way, in which I came to know about Satyuga,
I have narrated it in the first poem of the miraculous feats of the goddess. —10
The miraculous feats of goddess Chandi have been composed earlier,
I have composed (the same) in strict order from top to toe,
In the beginning I composed a comprehensive discourse,
But now I want again to compose a Eulogy. —11

End of the fourteenth chapter entitled "Description of the Supplication to the Lord, Destroyer of all," of Bachittar Natak.

*　　*　　*

IK OMKAR SRI WAHAGURU JI KI FATEH, PATSHAH
THE LORD IS ONE AND THE VICTORY IS OF THE LORD

CHAUBIS AVATAR (VISHNU'S TWENTY-FOUR INCARNATIONS)

MACHH (FISH INCARNATION)

CHAUPAI

Now I describe the wonderful performances of twenty-four incarnations,
In the way I visualised the same,
O saints; listen to it attentively,
The poet Shyam is narrating it according to his own understanding. —1

Whenever numerous tyrants take birth,
Then the Lord manifests Himself in physical form,
The Kal (destroyer Lord) scans the plays of all,
And ultimately destroys all. —2

The Kal (destroyer Lord) causes the expansion of all,
The same temporal Lord ultimately destroys all,
He manifests Himself in innumerable forms,
And Himself merges all within Himself. —3

In this creation is included the world and the ten incarnation,
Within them pervades our Lord,
Besides ten, other fourteen incarnation are also reckoned,
And I describe the performance of all of them. —4

The Kal (temporal Lord) conceals His name,
And imposes the villainy over the heads of others,
He Himself remains detached from the world,
I know this fact from the very beginning (ancient times). —5

He creates Himself and destroys Himself,
But he imposes the responsibility on the heads of others,
He Himself remains detached and Beyond Everything,
Therefore, He is called "infinite." —6

Those who are called twenty-four incarnations,
O Lord; they even could not realise Thee in a small measure,
They became kings of the world and got deluded,
Therefore they were called by innumerable names. —7

O Lord; Thou hast been deluding others, but could not be deluded by others,
Therefore Thou art called *crafty*,
Thou becomest agitated on seeing the saints in agony,
Therefore Thou art also called "the friend of the humble."—8

At times Thou destroyest the universe,
Therefore the world hath named you Kal (the destroyer Lord),
Thou hast been helping all the saints,
Therefore the saints have reckoned Thy incarnations. —9

Seeing Thy mercifulness towards the lowly,
Thy name *Deenbandhu* (the helper of the lowly) hath been thought out,
Thou art compassionate towards the saints,
Therefore the world calls Thee *Karuna-nidhi* (the treasure of mercy). —10

Thou ever removest the distress of the saints,
Therefore Thou art named *Sankat-haran* the remover of the distresses,
Thou hast been art called *Dukh-dahan* (the destroyer of sufferings. —11

Thou art infinite and none could know Thy limits,
Therefore Thou art called *Beant* (the boundless Lord),
Thou createst the forms of all in the world,
Therefore Thou art called the Creator. —12

None hath been able to comprehend Thee,
Therefore Thou hast called *Alakh* (incomprehensible),
Thou dost not take birth in the world,
Therefore all called Thee *Ajoni* (Unborn). —13

Brahma and others have got tired in knowing Thy end,
What are the helpless gods Vishnu and Shiva?
The sun and moon also meditate on Thee,
Therefore Thou art known as the Creator. —14

Thou art ever guiseless and shall be guiseless,
Therefore the world calls Thee *Abhekhi* (guiseless),
None knows Thy invisible form,
Therefore Thou art described as *Alakh* (Incomprehensible). —15

Thy beauty is unique and Thy forms are innumerable,
Thou art distinctly separate from all guises and not committed to any faith or idea,
Thou art the universal donor and Thou Thyself dost not beg,
Therefore I have known Thee as the Creator. —16.

Thou art not influenced by any omen or auspicious time,
This fact is known to all the world,
None of the *yantras*, *mantras* and *tantras* please Thee,
And none could realise Thee by adopting different guises. —17

All the world is engaged in its own interests,
And none comprehends the transcendental Brahman,
For Thy realisation many go to the cremation grounds and graveyards,
But the Lord is not there in both of them. —18

Both of them (the Hindus and Muslims) are destroying themselves in attachment and in vain discussions and disputes,
But O Lord; Thou art distinct separate from both of them,
He, with whose realisation, the illusion of the mind is removed,
Before that Lord, none is a Hindu or a Muslim. —19

One of them wears a *tasbih* (the rosary of Muslims) and the other one wears *mala* (the rosary of a Hindu),
One of them recites the *Quran* and the other one reads Puranas,
The adherents of both the religions are foolishly dying in opposing each other,
And none of them is dyed in the love of the Lord. —20

Those who are imbued in the love of the Lord,
They forsake their shyness and dance in ecstasy,
Those who have recognised that Primal *Purusha*,
The duality is destroyed from their hearts. —21

Those who are absorbed in duality,
They are far away from the union of the Lord, their supreme friend,
They have recognised the Supreme *Purusha* even a little,
They have comprehended Him as the supreme essence. —22

All the yogis and *sannyasis*,
All the ascetics and monks with shaven heads and Muslims,
They are all plundering the world in different guises,
The real saint, whose prop is the name of the Lord, they hide themselves. —23

The people of the world, exhibit heresies in order to fill their bellies,
Because without heresy, they do not gain money,
The person, who hath meditated only on the Supreme *Purusha*,
He hath never exhibited an act of heresy to any one. —24

One's interest remains unfulfilled without heresy,
And none bows down his head before any one without interest,
If the belly had not been attached with any one,
Then there would not have been any king or pauper in this world. —25

Those who have recognised only God as the Lord of all,
They have never exhibited any heresy to any one,
Such a person get his head chopped off but never his creed,
And such person considers his body equivalent only to a particle of dust. —26

One is called a yogi on perforating his ears,
And goes to the forest, performing many deceitful acts,
But the person, who hath not absorbed the essence of the name in his heart,
He neither belongs to the forest nor his home. —27

Upto what extent this poor poet can describe?
Because one person cannot know the mystery of the infinte Lord,
Undoubtedly, if one may have millions of tongues,
Even then the ocean of Thy attributes cannot be fathomed. —28

First of all, the Lord as Kal is the Primal father of the whole universe,
And from Him emanated the powerful lustre,
The same Lord was considered as Bhavani,
Who created the whole world. —29

First of all, He uttered *Omkar*,
And the sound of *Omkar* pervaded the whole world,
From the union of *Purusha* and *Prakriti*,
There was expansion of the whole world. —30

The world was created and from that time, every one knows it as world,
Four divisions of creation became manifest and as such they were described,
I have no power to give their description,
And tell their names separately. —31

That Lord created both the powerful and the weak,
They were shown distinctly as high and low,
The powerful Kal, adopting the physical form,
Manifested Himself in numerous forms. —32

According as the Lord adopted different forms,
In the same manner, He became renown as different incarnations,
But whatever is the supreme form of the Lord,
Ultimately all merged in Him. —33

Consider all the beings in the world,
As the illumination of the same light,
The Lord, who is known as Kal,
All the world will merge in Him. —34

Whatever appears inconceivable to us,
The mind gives it the name *maya*,
Only one Lord pervades all,
But appears to every one as distinctly separate according to his discernment. —35

That inconceivable Lord pervades all,
And all the beings beg from Him according to their writ,
He, who hath comprehended the Lord as one,
Only he hath realised the supreme essence. —36

That one Lord hath a unique beauty and form,
And He Himself is somewhere a king and somewhere a pauper,
He hath involved all through various means,
But He Himself is separate from all and none could know His mystery. —37

He hath created all in separate forms,
And He Himself destroys all,
He doth not take any blame on His own head,
And fixes the responsibility of vicious acts on others. —38

Once there was born a demon named Shankhasura,
Who, in many ways, distressed the world,
Then the Lord manifested Himself as *Machh* (Fish) incarnation,
Who repeated his own name himself. —39

At first the Lord manifested Himself as small fish
And shook the ocean violently,
Then he enlarged His body,
Seeing which Shankhasura got greatly enraged. —40

BHUJANG PRAYAAT STANZA

Then in great anger, the mighty Shankhasura thundered, and wore his armour bedecking himself with weapons and arms,
He threw the four Vedas in the ocean, which frightened the eight-eyed Brahma and caused him to remember the Lord. — 41

Then the Lord, the well-wisher of both (the Vedas as well as Brahma) was filled with kindness and highly enraged, He wore His steel-armour,
The blows of weapons were struck alongwith arms causing destruction, all the gods in groups moved away from their seats and the seven worlds trembled because of this horrible war. —42

With the blows of arms, the fly whisks and the garments began to fall and with the volley of arrows, the chopped bodies began to fall on the ground,
The chopped trunks and heads of huge elephants began to fall; it appeared that the group of persistent youths was playing Holi. —43

The swords and daggers of the warriors with the power of endurance have been struck and the brave fighters are bedecked with weapons and armours,
The mighty heroes have fallen down with empty hands and seeing all this spectacle, the god Shiva is busy in another dance and on the other side, the *Machh* incarnation, being pleased, is stirring the ocean. —44

RASAAVAL STANZA

Bedecked with auspicious weapons, the brave fighters are thundering and seeing the killing of huge and mighty warriors like elephants, the heavenly damsels beings pleased with their feats, are waiting in heaven, in order to wed them. —45

The noises of the knockings on the shields and the blows of the swords are being heard, the daggers are being struck with chattering sounds, and both the sides are desirous of their victory. —46

The whiskers on the faces and terrible swords in the hands of the warriors look impressive, the mighty warriors are wandering in the battlefield and supremely swift horses are dancing. —47

BHUJANG PRAYAAT STANZA

On seeing the army, Shankhasura was highly enraged, other heroes also blazing with anger began to shout loudly, with their eyes reddened with blood,

The king Shankhasura, knocking his arms, raised a terrible thunder and hearing his frightening sound, the pregnancy of women was miscarried. —48

All resisted at their places and the trumpets began to resound violently, the bloody daggers coming out (from the scabbards) glistened in the battlefield,

The voices of the cracking of the cruel bows were heard and the ghosts and goblins began to dance furiously. —49

The warriors began to fall in the battlefield alongwith their weapons, and the headless trunks began to dance unconsciously in the war,

The bloody daggers and sharp arrows were struck, the trumpets began to resound violently and the warriors began to run hither and thither. —50

The armours and bodies of the enemies were chopped and the weapons began to fall; the ghosts began to wander fearfully on the ground,

All were dyed in the dye of war and the mighty warriors began to fall in the battlefield swinging and reeling. —51

Such a horrible battle was fought between Shankhasura and *Machh*, it appeared clearly that two mountains were waging war with each other,

The bits of flesh began to fall, which were devoured by huge vultures, and the sixty-four vampires (Yoginis) began to laugh on seeing this terrible war. —52

After killing Shankhasura, the *Machh* (Fish) incarnation redeemed the Vedas and Lord, forsaking the fish-form, bedecked himself with winsome garments,

After destroying the tyrants the Lord, established again all the gods and the demons frightening the creatures were destroyed. —53

TRIBHANGI STANZA

The Lord received great approbation on killing the demon Shankhasura, redeeming the Vedas and destroying the enemies,

He called Indra, the king of gods and blessed him with royalty and its comforts,

Millions of musical instruments began to resound, the gods began to play the tune of bliss and the sorrows of every house were destroyed,

All the gods bowed in respect at the feet of Fish incarnation presenting various types of gifts and making millions of circumambulations. —54

End of "The Description of the First *Machh* (Fish) Incarnation and Killing of Shankhasura" in Bachittar Natak.

KACHH (TORTOISE) INCARNATION

BHUJANG PRAYAAT STANZA

Indra, the king of gods, ruled for a long time and his palaces were full of all materials of comfort,

But once Vishnu reflected upon a unique idea in his mind that this king is without elephants, horses and jewels (therefore something should be done in this direction). —1

Indra gathered together all the gods including Chandra, Surya and Upendra,

Considering this gathering as some stratagem against them, the proud demons also gathered together. —2

Now both the groups decided that whatever shall be attained, the same shall be distributed equally,

All of them agreed on this proposal and the work was begun,

Both the gods and demons settled the programme of churning the milk-ocean, making the churning-stick of the Mandrachal mountain. —3

The serpent Vasuki was made the rope of the churning-stick and dividing the participants equally, both the ends of the rope were held tightly,

The demons caught hold of the side of the head and the gods the tail, they began to churn the ocean like the curd in a vessel. —4

Now they reflected on this idea as to who can be the mighty hero, who can endure the load of the mountain (because a base was required for the purpose)?

Hearing this Ditya, Aditya etc., all the heroes shuddered, faltering in absurd prattle,

Then observing this difficulty of both the gods and demons, Vishnu himself thought about it and transforming Himself in the form of *Kachh* (Tortoise), seated himself at the base of the mountain. —5

End of "The Description of the Second *Kachh* (Tortoise) Incarnation" in Bachittar Natak.

Now begins the Description of the Churning of the Milk-ocean and the Fourteen Jewels. Let Shri Bhagauti (the Primal Power) be Helpful

TOTAK STANZA

Both the gods and demons unitedly churned the ocean, which hath been narrated in verse by the poet Shyam,

Then the fourteen jewels, in their splendour emanated from the sea, just as the moon looks elegant during the night. —1

The demons caught Vasuki from the side of the head and the gods from the side of the tail,

On seeing the jewels emanating from the sea, they became pleased as though they had drunk ambrosia. —2

The bow and arrow of purely white colour came out, and those intoxicated ones brought out from the ocean a pitcher of honey,

The elephant, horse, nectar and Laxmi came out and looked splendid like the flash of lightning from the clouds. —3

After *kalpadrum* (lysian, wish-fulfilling tree) and poison, the heavenly damsel Rambha came out, seeing whom, the people of Indra's court were allured,

The *kaustubh* jewel and the Moon also came out, which are remembered by the demons in the battlefield. —4

Kamadhenu (the wish-fulfilling cow) also came out, which was seized by the mighty Sahasrarjun,

After reckoning the jewels, now I mention the minor jewels, O saints! listen to me attentively. —5

These minor jewels are: leech, myrobalan, honey, conch (Panchjanya), *ruta*, hemp, discus and mace; the later two look impressive in the hands of princes always. —6

The bow and arrow, the bull Nandi and the dagger (which had destroyed the demons) came out of the ocean,

The trident of Shiva, Barvanal (the fire), Kapil Muni and Dhanwantari came out as the fourteenth jewel. —7

After counting the greater and minor jewels, now I count the metals and afterwards I shall count the lesser metals,

All these names have been reckoned by the poet Shyam according to his own understanding, considering them in small number, the poets are requested not to slander me. —8

First of all I reckon iron, lead and gold alongwith the fourth white metal silver,

Then mentioning copper, tin and brass, I consider the eighth metal as zinc, which is found within the earth. —9

Now I describe the minor metals; they are: antimony, cinnabar, yellow orpiment, bombax, potash, conchshell, mica, artemesia and calomal. —10

DOHIRA

These metals and minor metals have been described by me according to my own understanding and they are all found in the mines of the earth also,

He, who desires to have them, can get them. —11

CHAUPAI

As the major and minor jewels, the major and minor matels came out, they were taken away by Vishnu and distributed the remaining thing amongst all. —12

He took away Himself the bow and arrows, the sword, the discus, the mace and the (Panchjanya) conch etc.,

And taking the trident, the bow named Pinak and poison in his hands, gave them to Shiva. —13

BHUJANG PRAYAAT STANZA

The elephant named Airavat was given to Indra

Nara and Narayana Incarnation

BHUJANG PRAYAAT STANZA

and the horse to the sun, seeing which the demons, in great fury, marched to wage war,
Seeing the advancing army of the demons, Vishnu thought in his mind. —14

Nara and Narayana Incarnation

BHUJANG PRAYAAT STANZA

Manifesting himself as Nara and Narayan, Vishnu, managing his weapons and arms, came in front of the demon forces,
The warriors tied their garments tightly and the kings beat their arms, in that war, the tridents and the spears began to collide with each other. —15
In great anger, the blows of the steel-arms began to rain and at this juncture Vishnu manifested his third incarnation,
Nara and Narayan both had similar forms and their effulgence assumed unparallel lusture. —16
Wearing their helmets the warriors are striking their blows with maces and the mighty heroes are engrossed in the war,
The dust hath flown and spread in such a great measure in the sky that both the gods and demons, having gone astray, were falling and even the three-eyed god Shiva trembled. —17
Many types of warriors fell in the field and the great fighters looked impressive in the war,
The brave fighters, being chopped into bits, began to fall and it appeared that the wrestlers are lying intoxicated after drinking hemp. —18
More forces of demons came from another direction, seeing which the gods, leaving all paraphernalia, ran away,
The limbs began to fall in great numbers and the arrows looked auspicious in the manner of the flowers of capparis in the month of Chaitra. —19
The gods were defeated in the war and Vishnu, thinking over it, disappeared, with the help of his Tantric science,
Then He manifested Himself in the unique form of Maha-Mohini, seeing whom, the chief of both the demons and gods were highly pleased. —20

End of "The Description of the Third Incarnation of Nara and the Fourth Incarnation of Narayana" in Bachittar Natak.

Maha-Mohini Incarnation

BHUJANG PRAYAAT STANZA

Vishnu transformed himself into the form of Maha-Mohini,
Seeing which both the gods and the demons were allured, both of them wanted to please her and thought of sharing her love, abandoned their weapons and arms and also their pride. —1
All of them, having been entrapped in her noose of love forsook their anger,
And rushed towards her in order to relish the wantonness of her eyes and the sweetness of her words,
All of them, while swinging, fell on the earth as though they were lifeless,
All became without consciousness as though they were hit by the arrows. — 2
Seeing all of them without consciousness, the weapons and arms were discharged by the gods,
The demons began to die and felt that they were considered worthy of love for Mohini,
They appeared like the lion entrapped in a snare. —3
You know the story of the distribution of the jewels,
Therefore, for fear of the increase in narration, I relate it only in brief,
All the warriors, loosening the waist-garments and forsaking the sword, sat in a line. —4

CHAUPAI

Dhanwantri was given for the world and the wish-fulfilling tree and Lakshmi were given to gods,
Shiva was given the poison and Rambha, the heavenly damsel, was given to all other people; she was the giver of all comforts and the destroyer of the sufferings. —5

DOHIRA

Maha-Mohini took the moon in her own hand for giving it to some one and also the gem and Lakshmi for keeping it with herself, She concealed the gem in her own heart, but its lustre could be seen clearly. —6
The wish-fulfilling cow was given to the sages; how far can I describe all these things?

You may improve (their description) by reflecting on the Shastras and asking the poets. —7

BHUJANG PRAYAAT STANZA

Both the gods and demons were swinging like the king of deer, who gets absorbed in the sound of music,

All the jewels were distributed and the dispute ended; in this way, the fifth incarnation of Vishnu became apparent. —8

End of "The Description of the Fifth Incarnation Maha-Mohini" in Bachittar Natak.

VARAHA (BOAR) INCARNATION

BHUJANG PRAYAAT STANZA

In this way, the god Vishnu distributed the honey and ambrosia and all the gods and demons went away to their places,

Again the enmity grew between both of them and the war was waged, in which the gods fled and could not withstand the demons. —1

Hiranayaksha and Hiranayakashipu, both the demon brothers conquered the treasures of all the worlds,

They ruled over the places in water and on land, And seeing their own great physical strength their pride knew no bounds. —2

They wanted that some brave warrior may come forward to fight with them,

But only he could march against them, who could be greatly stronger than them,

They climbed to the top of the Sumeru mountain and with the blows of their maces,

They took away the Vedas and the earth forcibly and caused the destruction of all natural principles. —3

The earth went deep into the nether-world,

Then Vishnu manifested himself in the form of a Boar of terrible and cruel teeth,

He penetrated into water and raised a thunderous shout,

Which spread equally throughout the universe. —4

Hearing this terrible shout and the resounding of the trumpets both the brave demons awakened,

Listening to their thundering voice, the cowards ran away,

The war began and the clattering of the glistening swords and the sound of the furious blows was heard,

The lustre of the swords looked like the flash of lightening in the month of Bhadon. —5

The warriors of winsome whiskers are shouting and the sounds of the blows of the swords and arrows are being heard,

With the knocking of the daggers and swords, the helmets are breaking and falling and the sparks are coming out from them. —6

With the resounding of trumpets and drums and the knocking sound on the shields, the utterance of "kill, kill" coming from the mouths is being heard,

The bloody daggers of the warriors have come out in the battlefield and the headless trunks are dancing in an unconscious state. —7

The sixty-four female evil spirits (Yoginis) have filled their bowls with blood,

And loosening their matted hair, they are raising their terrible sounds,

Most awful ghosts and fiends are laughing and the shrieking sound of the hideous vampires is being heard. —8

The warriors are giving the blows of their fists and feet in this way,

As if the thundering lions have furiously attacked one another,

Hearing the terrible sound of the war, the attention of gods Shiva and Brahma hath distracted,

The moon also trembled and the noonday sun also fled in fear. —9

There was water everywhere upward and downward and in this atmosphere Vishnu took aim of his arrows on his targets,

The demons were collectively giving terrible blows of their fists in the way,

Like a crocodile aiming his blows on another crocodile. —10

The trumpets resounded and the mighty and terrible warriors fought with each other in this way,

As if the elephants with long tusks are fighting with each other,

The sound of the drums and horns was being heard and there was also the clattering of the daggers and the crackling of the arrows. —11

The war was waged for eight days and nights, in which the earth and the sky trembled,
All the warriors appeared absorbed in warfare in the battlefield
And Vishnu caused the death and fall of the enemy. —12

Then he placed all the four Vedas on the protruding part of his teeth and caused the death and fall of the persistent inimical demons,
Vishnu commanded Brahma and he created the Dhanur-veda for the happiness of all the saints. —13

In this way, the sixth partial incarnation of Vishnu manifested himself,
Who destroyed the enemies and protected the Vedas,
There was the victory of *dharma* (righteousness) and the gods collectively were victorious,
And they caused to remove the pride of all in a right way. —14

End of "The Description of the Sixth Boar Incarnation" in Bachittar Natak.

Narasingh (Man-lion) Incarnation

Let Shri Bhagauti Ji (The Primal Lord) be Helpful

PAADHARI STANZA

In this way, Indra, the king of gods ruled and filled the granaries of materials through all modes,
When the pride of the gods grew enormously, then in order to shelve their pride, the hard-hearted mighty demons rose again. —1

The kingdoms of Indra was seized and this proclamation was made on all sides with the accompaniment of many musical instruments,
That Hiranayakashipu is the emperor at all the places. —2

One day, this mighty ruler bedecking himself went to his wife and absorbed himself with her so intensely that at the time of his intercourse, his semen was discharged. —3

From that semen Prahlad was born in order to help and protect the saints,
When the king sent him to school for education, he asked his father to write the name of Lord-God on his tablet. —4

TOTAK STANZA

One day the king went to the school and seeing his son, he was startled,
When the king asked, the child told whatever he had learnt and fearlessly began to read the name of Lord-God. —5

On hearing the name of Lord-God, the demon became furious and said, "who else is there except me on whom you are meditating?"
He decided to kill this student and said, "O fool! Why are you repeating the name of Lord-God?" —6

"Only Hiranayakashipu is considered the mighty-one in water and on land, then why are you repeating the name of Lord-God"
Then, as commanded by the king, the demons tied him with the column. —7

When those foolish persons advanced to kill this student, the Lord manifested Himself at the same time in order to protect His disciple,
All those who saw the Lord at that time were astonished, the Lord had manifested Himself by tearing off the doors. —8

Seeing Him, all the gods and demons trembled and all the animate and inanimate objects became fearful in their hearts,
The Lord in the form of Narasingh (Man-lion), with red eyes and the mouth filled with blood, thundered dreadfully. —9

Seeing this and hearing the thunder of Narasingh all the demons fled,
Only the emperor, fearlessly holding his mace in his hand, stood firmly in that battlefield. —10

When the emperor roared loudly, then all the brave warriors trembled and all those warriors came forward in groups before that lion,
All those who went in front of Narasingh, He caught hold of all those warriors like a juggler and knocked them down on the ground. —11

The warriors shouted loudly at one another and saturated with blood began to fall,
The enemies advanced from all the four sides with such intensity like the clouds in the rainy season. —12

Advancing from all the ten directions the warriors began to shower the arrows and stones,

The swords and arrows glistened in the war-field and the brave fighters began to flutter their flags. —13

The persistent warrior with loud shouts are showering a volley of arrows in this way,
As if it is the second cloud burst in the month of Sawan,
The flags are fluttering and the horses are neighing
And seeing all this scene, the heart of the demon-king was filled with fear. —14

The horses are neighing and the elephants are roaring,
The chopped long arms of the warriors look like the flag of Indra,
The warriors are writhing and the elephant are roaring in such a way,
That the clouds of the month of Sawan are feeling shy. —15

As soon as the horse of Hiranayakashipu turned a little, he himself deviated and retraced two steps,
But still he was infuriated in the manner of the snake who gets infuriated when its tail is crushed by a foot.
His face was shining in the battlefield like the blossoming of the lotus on seeing the sun. —16

The forces are moving in so much intoxication and creating noise that the attention of Shiva was dissolved,
And it seemed that the universe had been displaced,
The arrows, daggers and stones were flying and filling both the earth and the sky. —17

The Ganas and Gandharvas, seeing both were pleased and the gods showered flowers,
Two warriors were fighting with each other like the children competing with one another in their play during the night. —18

BELI BIDDARAM STANZA

The warriors are thundering in the war and seeing them both the gods and demons are feeling shy,
The brave fighters, who have been wounded, are roaming and it appears that the smoke is flying upwards. —19

The brave fighters of many types are fighting bravely with one another,
The lances and arrows are being hurled and the horses of the warriors are advancing hesitantly. —20

TOMAR STANZA

Millions of horses are neighing and the warriors are showering arrows,
The bows have slipped and fallen from the hands and in this way the terrible and unique war is being waged. —21

Many types of warriors and innumerable horsemen are fighting with one another,
They are striking their sword without any suspicion and in this way, a unique war is going on. —22

DODHAK STANZA

After striking their swords and arrows the fighters ultimately fell down during that great war,
The wounded warriors are swinging like the blossomed spring at the end of the month of Phagun. —23

Somewhere the chopped arms of the warriors appear like the trunks of the elephants,
The brave fighters appear beautiful like the flowers blooming in the garden. —24

The enemies were dyed with blood like many types of blooming flowers,
After having been wounded with swords the brave soldiers were roaming like the manifestation of anger itself. —25

TOTAK STANZA

Many enemies fell down fighting and Narasingh, the incarnation of Vishnu also received many wounds,
The chopped bits of the warriors were flowing in the stream of blood like the bubbles of foam. —26

The fighting soldiers, having been cut into bits, fell down, but none of them did not put to disrepute the dignity of their master,
Showering the blows of the swords and arrows, the warriors fled away ultimately in great fear. —27

CHAUPAI

All the warriors, abandoning their shyness and getting impatient left the battlefield and ran away,
Seeing this, Hiranayakashipu himself in great ire, moved forward for waging war. —28

Seeing the emperor coming towards him, Narasingh also got infuriated,
He did not care for his wounds, beacause he was in extreme agony on seeing the suffering of his devotees. —29

BHUJANG PRAYAAT STANZA

Giving a jerk to his neck, Narasingh raised a terrible thunder and listening to his thunder, the faces of the heroes turned pale,
Because of that dreadful sound, the earth trembled and its dust touched the sky,
All the gods began to smile and the heads of the demons bowed down with shame. —30

The dreadful war of both the heroic fighters got ablazed, and the clattering sound of the swords and the crackling sound of the bows was heard,
The demon-king fought in great fury and there was flood of blood in the battlefield. —31

With the clattering of swords and the crackling noise of the arrows, the mighty and the enduring heroes were chopped into bits,
The conches, clarionets and drums resounded and the wanton soldiers, riding on the sharp horses stood firmly in the battlefield. —32

Many a warrior riding on the horses and elephants fled away and none of the chiefs could stand against Narasingh,
That terrible and dreadful Narasingh moved in the battlefield and began to stir his neck and wag his tail. —33

DOHIRA

Many warriors fled hearing the thunder of Narasingh and none could stand in the battlefield except Hiranayakashipu. —34

CHAUPAI

The war with fists of both the warriors began and none other except those two could be seen in the battlefield,
The eyes of both had become red and all the groups of gods were seeing this performance from the sky. —35

For eight days and eight nights both these brave heroes, furiously, waged the dreadful war,
After this, the demon-king felt weakness and fell down on the earth like an old tree. —36

Narasingh sprinkled ambrosia and woke him up from the unconscious state and he became alert after coming out of the state of unconsciousness,
Both the heroes began to fight again furiously and a dreadful war began again. —37

BHUJANG PRAYAAT STANZA

After challenging each other, both the heroes began to fight again, and a dreadful war ensured between them for gaining victory over the other,
Both of them were giving destructive blows to one another with their nails,
And appeared like two intoxicated elephants fighting each other in the forest. —38

Narasingh again threw Hiranayakashipu on the earth just as the old *palash* tree (*Butea frondosa*) falls down on the earth with a gust of wind
Seeing that the tyrant hath died, there was a rain of flowers and the gods, coming there, sang many types of the songs of victory. —39

PAADHARI STANZA

Narasingh destroyed the tyrant and in this way Vishnu manifested his seventh incarnation,
He protected his devotee and spread righteousness on the earth. —40

The canopy was swung over the head of Prahlad and he was made a king, and in this way, the demons, who were darkness-incarnate, were destroyed,
Destroying all the tyrants and vicious people Narasingh merged his light in the supreme light. —41

PAADHARI STANZA

By killing them, all the tyrants were put to shame,
And that imperceptible Lord God merged again in His Ownself,
The poet, according to his own understanding, after reflection hath uttered the above-mentioned saying,
That in this way, Vishnu manifested himself in his seventh incarnation. —42

End of "The Description of the Seventh Incarnation of Narasingh."

Vaman (Dwarf) Incarnation

Let Shri Bhagauti Ji (The Primal Lord) be Helpful

BHUJANG PRAYAAT STANZA

After passing away of the epoch of Narasingh incarnation, the sins began to grow in intensity on the earth again,
The demons to perform *yajnas* (sacrificial rituals) again and the king Bali became proud of his greatness. —1

There was no position of gods in the *yajnas* of king Bali and the capital of Indra was also destroyed,
In great agony, all the gods meditated on the Lord, by which the supreme destroyer *Purusha* was pleased. —2

The Non-temporal Lord asked Vishnu out of all gods to assume his eighth manifestation in the form of Vaman incarnation,
Vishnu after seeking permission of the Lord, moved like a servant at the command of a king. —3

NARAAJ STANZA

He transformed himself as a dwarf and after some reflection, he moved towards the court of the king Bali, where, on reaching, he stood firmly. —4

This Brahmin recited all the four Vedas, which the king listened to attentively,
The king Bali then called the Brahmin and got him seated respectfully on a seat of sandal-wood. —5

The king quaffed the water, with which the feet of the Brahmin had been washed and offered charities,
Then he circumambulated around the Brahmin several times; after that the king offered millions of charities, but the Brahmin did not touch anything with his hand. —6

The Brahmin said that all those things were of no use to him and all the ostentations offered by the king were false,
He then asked him to give only two and a half steps of the earth and accept the special eulogy. —7

CHAUPAI

Then the Brahmin uttered these words, the king alongwith the queen could not understand its import,
That Brahmin again said the same thing with determination that he had asked only for two and a half steps of the earth. —8

Shukracharya, the preceptor of the king was with him at that time, and he alongwith all the ministers comprehended the mystery of asking only for earth,
Many times the king orders for the donation of the earth, for many times the preceptor Shukracharya asks him not to agree to that. —9

When the king made up his mind firmly to give the required earth as alms, then Shukracharya giving his reply said this to the king,
"O king! do not consider him a small-sized Brahmin, consider him only as an incarnation of Vishnu." —10

Hearing this, all the demons laughed and said, "Shukracharya is only thinking of useless things,"
"The Brahmin, whose body doth not contain the flesh more than a rabbit, how can be destroy the world?" —11

DOHIRA

Shukracharya said,
"The manner in which only a spark of fire, falling down, grows immensely in stature, likewise this small-sized Brahmin is not a man." —12

CHAUPAI

The king Bali, laughingly said these words to Shukracharya, "O Shukracharya you are not comprehending it, I shall not regain such an occasion, because I shall not be able to get such a God-like beggar again." —13

The king decided this general notion in his mind, but perceptibly he did not divulge it to anyone,
He asked the mendicant to give his pot, in order to enact such a base deed. —14

Shukracharya understood the notion of the mind of the king, but the ignorant king could not comprehend it,
Shukracharya transformed into a small fish and seated himself in the mendicant's pot. —15

The king took the mendicant's pot in his hand

and the time for giving alms to the Brahmin arrived,
When the king in order to give alms took some water in his hand, no water came out of the pot. —16

TOMAR STANZA

Then the Brahmin became furious and told the king to check up the pot,
The pipe of the pot was searched with a straw and with this search one eye of Shukracharya was lost. —17
The king took the straw in his hand revolved it within the pot,
It pierced the eye of Shukracharya and thus one eye of the preceptor Shukracharya was lost. —18
The water that oozed out from the eye of Shukracharya the king took it in his hand,
Shukracharya did not allow the water to leak and in this way, he tried to protect his master from destruction. —19

CHAUPAI

When the water (from the eye) oozed out on the hand of the king, he gave it as alms, notionally, on the hand of the Brahmin,
After this the dwarf expanded his body, which became so huge that it touched the heavens after penetrating through this world. —20
Seeing this, all the people were wonder-struck and visualising such a huge form of Vishnu, the demons became unconscious,
The feet of Vishnu touched the nether-worlds and the head touched the heavens; all were nonplussed on seeing this. —21
With one step, he measured the nether-world and with second step he measured the heavens,
In this way, Vishnu touched the whole universe and the current of Ganges began to flow down from the whole universe. —22
In this way, the king was also astonished and remained puzzled in mind, words and deeds, whatever Shukracharya had said, the same had happened and he himself had seen all this with his own eyes on that day. —23
For the remaining half a step, the king got measured his own body and earned approbation,
As long as there is water in the Ganges and Yamuna, till that time, the story of this enduring king will be narrated. —24
Vishnu was then pleased and manifesting himself said, "O king! I shall be a watchman and servant at your gate myself,
And as long as there will be water in the Ganges and Yamuna, the story of your charity will be narrated." —25

DOHIRA

Wherever the saints are in distress, the non-temporal Lord comes there for help,
The Lord, coming under the control of his devotee, became his gate-keeper. —26

CHAUPAI

In this way, Vishnu, manifesting himself as the eighth incarnation, gratified all the saints,
Now I describe the ninth incarnation, which may please be listened to and understood correctly by all the saints. —27

End of "The Description of Vaman, the Eighth Incarnation of Vishnu and the Deception of the king Bali" in Bachittar Natak.

PARASHURAM INCARNATION

Let Sri Bhagauti Ji (The Primal Lord) be Helpful

CHAUPAI

Then a long period of time elapsed and the Kshatriyas conquered all the earth,
They considered themselves as the most high and their strength became unlimited. —1
Realising this all the gods were worried and went to Indra and said,
"All the demons have transformed themselves as Kshatriyas, O king! now tell us your view about it." —2
All the gods together reflected on this issue and went towards the milk-ocean,
There they eulogised Kal, the destroyer Lord and received the following message. —3
The destroyer Lord said, "A sage named Yamadagni abides on the earth, who always gets up to destroy the sins by his virtuous deeds,

O Vishnu, manifest yourself in the his house and destroy the enemies of Indra." —4

BHUJANG PRAYAAT STANZA

Hail, hail to the incarnation-like sage Yamadagni, through whose wife Renuka was born the wearer of armour and carrier of axe (that is Parashurama),

He manifested himself as death for the Kshatriyas and destroyed the king named Sahasrabahu. —5

I have not the requisite wisdom to describe the whole story, therefore fearing lest it may not become voluminous, I say it very briefly,

The Kshatriya kings had been intoxicated with pride and in order to destroy them Parashurama held up the axe in his hand. —6

Nandini, the wish-fulfilling cow was like the daughter of Yamadagni and the Kshatriya king Sahasrabahu had got tired in begging it from the sage,

Ultimately, he snatched away the cow and killed Yamadagni and in order to wreak his vengeance, Parashurama destroyed all the Kshatriya kings. —7

From the very childhood Parashurama had been quite inquisitive in his mind about the identity of the killer of his father and when he came to know that it was the king Sahasrabahu, he moved towards his palace with his arms and weapons. —8

Parashurama said to the king, "O king! How hast thou killed my father? Now I want to wage war with you in order to kill you," he also said, "O fool! Hold your weapons, otherwise forsaking them, run away from this palace." —9

Hearing these ironical words, the king was filled with fury and holding his weapons in his hands, got up like a lion, He came to the arena of battle with determination knowing that the Brahmin Parashurama was desirous of fighting with him on the same day. —10

Hearing the furious words of the king, his warriors in great ire, decorating themselves (with their weapons) marched forward,

Holding firmly their tridents, lances, maces etc., the great canopied kings moved forward for waging war. —11

NARAAJ STANZA

Holding their swords in their hands, the mighty warriors marched forward with loud shouts,

They uttered "kill, kill" and their arrows were drinking blood. —12

Wearing their armour and holding their daggers, the warriors in great ire moved forward,

The blows of whips on horses produced knocking sounds and thousands of arrows flew out (from the bows). —13

RASAAVAL STANZA

All the warriors ran and gathered at one place,

And they besieged Parashurama, just as the clouds besiege the sun. —14

With the crackling of bows a queer sound was produced,

And the army swarmed like the dark clouds. —15

With the clattering of the daggers, a queer sound was produced,

The elephants began to roar in groups and bedecked with armour the warriors seemed impressive. —16

Gathering from all the four sides, the groups of elephants began a fight,

The volleys of arrows were shot and the heads of the kings were shattered. —17

The frightful sound emanated and all the kings got infuriated,

Parashurama was besieged by the army like Shiva encircled by the forces of Cupid. —18

All being absorbed and dyed with the dye of war, feared the glory of others,

So much dust arose by (the movements of the) army that the sky was filled with dust. —19

The drums resounded violently and the mighty warriors began to roar,

The warriors were fighting each other like the freely roaming lions. —20

With the shouts of "kill, kill," the warriors were uttering dreadful voice,

The chopped limbs of the warriors are falling and it appeared that there is fire on all the four sides. —21

The weapons began to fall from the hands and the warriors began to run away empty-handed,

The horses were neighing and were running hither and thither with swiftness. —22

The warriors are wounding the enemy by showering their arrows, they were also patting their arms,

The warriors, by planting their daggers and increasing their inimical intentions, are waging a terrible war. —23

Many wounds are being inflicted and the wounded warriors appear to be playing Holi,

Showering their arrows, all are desirous of the victory. —24

The warriors were roaming and falling like the swinging trees,

After the breaking of their weapons and becoming armless, the warriors sped away. —25

All the enemies who came in front of him, Parashurama killed them all,

Ultimately all of them ran away and their pride was shattered. —26

BHUJANG PRAYAAT STANZA

Wearing his important weapons, the king himself, taking the mighty warriors with him, marched forward to wage the war,

Forsaking his innumerable weapons, he waged a terrible war,

The king himself seemed like the rising sun at dawn. —27

Patting his arms, the king firmly waged the war, like the war waged by Vrittasura with Indra,

Parashurama made him armless by chopping away all his arms, and shattered his pride by destroying all his army. —28

Parashurama held up his dreadful axe in his hand chopped the arms of the king like the trunk of the elephant,

In this way becoming limbless, the whole army of the king was destroyed and his ego was shattered. —29

Ultimately, becoming unconscious the king fell down in the battlefield, and all his warriors, who remained alive, fled away to their own countries,

Parashurama seized his capital and destroyed the Kshatriyas and for a long time, the people worshipped him. —30

End of "The Description of the Killing of the King Sahasrabahu" in Bachittar Natak.

Let Sri Bhagauti Ji (The Primal Lord) be Helpful

BHUJANG PRAYAAT STANZA

After seizing the capital, Parashurama made a Brahmin the king, but again the Kshatriyas, conquering all the Brahmins, snatched their city,

The Brahmins, in great agony called Parashurama, who holding his axe, moved, with great fury. —31

When all the kings heard that taking a vow of killing Kshatriyas, the persistent Parashurama had arrived,

Then all of them prepared for war, taking all their weapons, ,

In great ire, all of them came to wage the war like Rama and Ravana in Sri Lanka. —32

When Parashurama saw that he was being attacked with arms and weapons, then he took the arrows in his hand and killed his enemies,

Many warriors became armless and many became headless,

All those warriors who went in front of Parashurama, he killed all of them. —33

He caused the earth to become without Kshatriyas for twenty-one times and in this way, he destroyed all the kings and their base,

And if I describe the complete story from one end to the other, then I fear that the book will become very voluminous. —34

CHAUPAI

In this way, Vishnu manifested for the ninth time in order to enact the wonderful play,

Now I describe the tenth incarnation, who is the support of the life-breath of the saints. —35

End of "The Description of the Ninth Incarnation Parashurama" in Bachittar Natak.

BRAHMA INCARNATION

Let Sri Bhagauti Ji (The Primal Lord) be Helpful

CHAUPAI

Now I describe that ancient story as to how the knowledgeable Brahma was born,

The four-headed Brahma was born as the destroyer of sins and the creator of all the universe. —1

Whenever the knowledge of Vedas is destroyed, Brahma is then manifested,

For this purpose Vishnu manifested himself as Brahma and he was known as "Chaturanan" (four-faced) in the world. —2

When Vishnu manifested himself as Brahma, he propagated the doctrines of the Vedas in the world,

He composed Shastras and Smritis and gave a life-discipline to the beings of the world. —3

Those people who were there to perform sinful actions, after getting the knowledge from the Vedas, they became the remover of sins,

The sinful actions were explained and all the beings became absorbed in the actions of *dharma* (righteousness). —4

In this way, the Brahma incarnation manifested, who is the remover of all sins,

All the subjects began to tread the path of *dharma* and abandoned the sinful actions. —5

DOHIRA

In this way, the Brahma incarnation manifested for purifying the subjects,

And all the beings began to perform the righteous actions, forsaking the sinful actions. —6

CHAUPAI

The tenth incarnation of Vishnu is Brahma, who established the righteous actions in the world,

It hath been said in Shastras and Smritis that there is no difference between Brahma and Vishnu. —7

End of "The Description of the Tenth Incarnation Brahma" in Bachittar Natak.

RUDRA INCARNATION

Let Sri Bhagauti Ji (The Primal Lord) be Helpful

TOTAK STANZA

All the people absorbed themselves in the works of *dharma*,

But the time came when the discipline of Yoga and Bhakti (devotion) was abandoned,

When the path of *dharma* is adopted, all the souls get pleased and practising equality, they visualise one Brahman within all. —1

This earth was pressed under the load of sufferings of the people of the world and it was impossible to describe its anguish and agony,

Then the earth transformed itself into a cow and weeping bitterly, she reached the milk-ocean before the non-temporal Lord. —2

When the Lord heard with His own ears the sufferings of the earth, then the destroyer Lord was pleased and laughed,

He called Vishnu in His presence and said to him in this way. —3

The destroyer Lord asked Vishnu to manifest himself as Rudra in order to destroy the beings of the world,

Then Vishnu manifested himself as Rudra and destroying the beings of the world, he established Yoga. —4

I shall describe now as to how Shiva waged wars and gave comfort to saints,

I shall also tell how he wedded Parbati after conquering her in the *swayamvara* (self-selection of a husband from amongst the suitors). —5

How Shiva waged a war against Andhakasura? How he effaced the pride of Cupid? and getting furious, how he mashed the gathering of demons? I shall describe all these anecdotes. —6

PAADHARI STANZA

When the earth is pressed by the load of sins, then she cannot have peace in her heart,

Then she goes and shouts loudly in the milk-ocean and the Rudra incarnation of Vishnu is manifested. —7

After manifestation, Rudra destroys the demons and crushing them, he protects the saints,

In this way, destroying all the tyrants, he then abides in the heart of his devotees. —8

TOTAK STANZA

In Tripura state lived a three-eyed demon, whose glory was equal to the glory of the Sun, which spread over the three worlds,

After receiving the boon, that demon became so powerful that he conquered all the fourteen regions of the universe. —9

(That demon had this boon) that any one who had the power to kill him with one arrow, he only could kill that terrible demon,

The poet now wants to describe that mighty warrior who could kill that three-eyed demon with one arrow. —10

For the protection of the beings of the world and the killing of that demon, the God Shiva moved forward,

In great fury, he shot one arrow and only with that arrow, he destroyed that demon of Tripura, named Tripura. —11

Seeing this performance, all the saints were pleased and gods showered flowers from heaven,

The sound of "hail, hail" resounded, there was consternation on Himalaya mountain and the earth trembled. —12

After a long time, another demon named Andhakasura came on the scene,

Mounting his bull and holding his trident, Shiva moved forward (to chastise him),

Seeing his terrible form, the gods were also startled. —13

Shiva marched forward alongwith Ganges, Gandharvas, Yakshas and Nagas and Durga also granted boon to him,

The gods began to see that Shiva would kill Andhakasura in the same way as he had killed the demon Tripura. —14

From the other side that demon of vicious intellect started,

From this side in great fury and holding the trident in his hand Shiva moved,

Intoxicated with war-tactics the mighty warriors presented the scene like the blazing flames of fire in the forest. —15

Both the demons and gods became absorbed in the war and bedecking themselves with weapons all the warriors enjoyed the relish of anger,

The warriors of both the side, enjoyed the shooting of arrows and the arrows are being showered like the raining of clouds on the doomsday. —16

ROOAAMAL STANZA

The demons being wounded and becoming weak began to run away and at that time, Andhakasura, resounding his drums turned and moved towards the battlefield,

The blows were struck with tridents, swords, arrows and other weapons and arms and the warriors swung and fell, it seemed that there was a programme of dance and amorous pastime. —17

With the blows of swords and arrows, there was consternation in the battlefield and striking their weapons the warriors were stirring up the armies,

Somewhere the limbless fighters and somewhere the complete bodies are immersed in blood; the warriors who had attained martyrdom, are wedding the heavenly damsels, after making search for them. —18

The garments, chariot-riders and many horses are lying hither and thither and a dreadful stream of blood is flowing in the battlefield,

Somewhere the bedecked horses and elephants are lying chopped and somewhere there are heaps of warriors lying down; not a single enemy hath remained alive. —19

The kings have abandoned their bedecked horses and elephants and gone away and the god Shiva, shouting very loudly, hath destroyed the mighty warriors,

The brave fighters have also abandoned their weapons and gone away, after leaving behind their bows and arrows and steel-armours. —20

NARAAJ STANZA

All the warriors who go in front of him, Rudra destroys them all,

Those who will advance, will also be destroyed by Shiva. —21

The blind (headless) trunks are rising in the battlefield and casting special showers of arrows,

Innumerable warriors, shooting arrows from their bows are exhibiting proof of their bravery. —22

RASAAVAL STANZA

Bedecked with the steel-armour, the warriors are thundering, on all the four sides,

The wanton mighty heroes are irresistible. —23

The horrible sound of musical instruments is being

heard and the bedecked warriors are being seen,
The bows are crackling like the thundering of the clouds. —24

The gods, holding their bows, are also moving and all the brave fighters being pleased, are showering their arrows. —25

Holding their bows in their hands, excessively glorious and proud warriors have marched forward and with the clattering of their weapons, the bodies of the enemies are being chopped into two parts. —26

Seeing the fury of Rudra, the weak demons are running away,
Bedecked with their armour, the mighty warriors are thundering. —27

Holding the Shakti (his power) in his hands, the supremely glorious Shiva, thundering dreadfully, is absorbed in war, and is looking impressive. —28

The blood is oozing out of the wounds and all the fighters are fighting with enthusiasm,
The vampires are pleased and the horses etc., are rolling in dust. —29

Rudra, in great fury, hath destroyed the demons and hath chopped their bodies into bits and killed the army. —30

Shiva, the holder of the trident, is in extreme anger and he hath destroyed the demons,
The arrows are being showered like the raining clouds. —31

When Rudra thundered in the battlefield, then all the demons ran away,
All of them abandoned their weapons and the pride of all was shattered. —32

CHAUPAI

At that time, the mighty Andhakasura, alongwith the army of demons, sped towards the front,
He discharged many arrows on Nandi, which penetrated through his limbs. —33

When the god Shiva saw the infliction of the arrows on his vehicle, then he became violently furious,
With great ire, he discharged his poisonous arrows, which spread over the earth and sky in an instant. —34

When Rudra shot his arrows, the army of demons sped away,
Then Andhakasura came in front of Shiva, a dreadful war ensued. —35

ARIL

The demon, highly infuriated, discharged twenty arrows on Shiva, which struck the body of Shiva and wounded it,
Shiva also ran forward, holding his bow in his hand and a fearful war began between them. —36

Then Shiva took out two arrows from his quiver, and aiming them at the tyrant, he discharged them in great anger,
The arrow struck the head of the enemy and he fell down on the earth; he fell like a column falling flat on the ground having been hit by lightening. —37

TOTAK

After one *ghari* (about 24 minutes), the enemy (Andhakasura) regained his senses and that mighty warrior again took bow and arrows in his hands,
The bow was pulled in his hands in great anger and a volley of arrow were showered like rain. —38

In great ire, that mighty warrior began to discharge and shower his distinctively powerful arrows, which struck on one side and came out from the other side,
Then greatly infuriated, Shiva took the trident in his hand, and cut the head of the enemy into two parts. —39

End of "The Description of the Killing of the Demon Andhak and the Eulogy of Shiva" in Bachittar Natak.

**Killing of Parbati
Let Sri Bhagauti Ji (The Primal Lord)
be Helpful**

TOTAK STANZA

When Indra heard about the destruction of Andhakasura, he was very much pleased,
In this way, many days elapsed and Shiva also went to Indra's place. —1

Then Rudra manifested himself in a dreadful form,
Seeing Shiva, Indra discharged his weapon,
Then Shiva, was highly infuriated and blazed like live charcoal. —2
With that blaze, all the beings of the world began to burn,
Then Shiva in order to pacify his anger threw his weapon and anger into the sea,
But it could not be drowned and manifested itself in the form of the demon Jalandhar. —3

CHAUPAI

In this way, this demon grew in strength excessively and he also looted the treasure of Kuber,
He caught Brahma and caused him to weep, and conquering Indra, he seized his canopy and swung over his head. —4
After conquering the gods, he caused them to fall at his feet and faced Vishnu and Shiva to abide only within their own cities,
He gathered all the fourteen jewels in his own house and fixed the places of nine planets at his will. —5

DOHIRA

The demon-king, conquering all, caused them to live in his own territory,
The gods went to Kailasa mountain and worshipped him. —6

CHAUPAI

They performed various types of meditation, worship and service day and night for a long time,
Now everything depended on the support of Shiva. —7
All the enemies on water and land trembled, seeing the innumerable forces of Shiva, the Lord of ghosts,
Out of all the kings, the king Daksha was most respected, who had ten thousand daughters in his home. —8
Once that king held a *swayamvara* at his place and permitted his ten thousand daughters to wed according to their interest forsaking all thought of high and low in society. —9
Each one of them wed whomsoever she liked, but all such anecdotes cannot be described, if all of them are narrated in detail, then there will always be the fear of increasing the volume. —10
Four daughters were given to the sage Kashyap, and many of the daughters married the god Chandrama (Moon),
Many of them went to foreign countries, but Gauri (Parvati) named and married Shiva. —11
When, after wedding, Parvati reached the home of Shiva (Rudra), many types of narratives became prevalent,
The king called all his daughters and all of them came to their father's home alongwith their husbands. —12
All the kings within and outside the country began to reach at the house of their father-in-law,
Considering the queer dressing habits of Rudra, no one could think of him. —13
The king Daksha did not invite Gauri, when Gauri heard about it from the mouth of Narad, she got extremely angry in her mind,
She went to her father's house without telling anybody, and her body and mind were emotionally blazing. —14
Being extremely infuriated, she plunged into the sacrificial pit, and because of her dignified demeanour, the fire cooled down,
But Sati (Parvati) lighted her Yoga-fire and with that fire, her body was destroyed. —15
Narad, on the other side, came to Shiva and said, "Why art thou sitting here, having been intoxicated with hemp (and there Gauri hath burnt herself alive)?"
Hearing this, Shiva's meditation was shattered and his heart was filled with rage; he held up his trident and ran towards that side. —16
When Shiva reached the place where Sati had burnt herself, he caught his trident also very firmly,
With blows of various types, he destroyed the merit of the whole *yajna* (sacrifice). —17
He destroyed many kings and chopped their bodies into bits,
On whomsoever the blow of the trident struck, he died there and then. —18
When Shiva looked into the sacrificial pit and saw the burnt body of Gauri, he began to pluck his matted hair,

At that time, Virbhadra manifested himself there and after his manifestation, he began to destroy the kings. —19

He chopped several kings into two parts and sent several of them to the abode of Yama,

Just as with the flooding of the stream, the banks are eroded further, likewise many terrible warriors began to fall on the earth. —20

At that time, Shiva regained his senses and fell on the enemy with his bow in his hand,

Whomsoever Shiva struck his arrow by pulling his bow, he breathed his last there and then. —21

The tabors began to resound and in all the ten directions, the ghosts and fiends began to roar,

The swords glittered and their blows were showered and the headless trunks began to dance on all the four sides. —22

The trumpets and drums resounded and their sound was heard; the warriors fought bravely in the war,

They collided with one another, being filled with great anger, and they were never seen again, riding on their horses. —23

On whomsoever, there was the blow of the trident, held in the fist of Shiva, he was killed there and then,

Virbhadra fought such a fierce fight, that in great confusion, the ghosts and fiends were awakened. —24

DOHIRA

The arrows, daggers, lances and other types of weapons were showered,

And all the warriors fell as martyrs and none remained alive. —25

CHAUPAI

The kings, chopped into bits, were lying like the cluster of trees fallen down by the blows of wind,

When Rudra, holding his trident wrought the destruction, then the scene of that place looked very queer. —26

Then the kings, forgetting the *yajna*, began to run away to their countries,

When Rudra pursued them as fury-incarnate, then none of the running kings could survive. —27

Then all the kings, becoming alert, were highly activated and the musical instruments resounded from all the sides,

Then the war became more intense and the house of Yama began to be filled with the dead. —28

The kings returned with several kinds of arrows and weapons for waging the war,

They began to strike blows speedily like the strokes on the gong. —29

The mighty warriors began to fall as bits and all the nine regions of the world trembled,

Forsaking their swords, the kings began to fall down and there was a dreadful scene in the battlefield. —30

NARAAJ STANZA

The warriors riding on the horses, coming down, began to roam, holding their weapons,

The arrows were discharged and the bows crackled. —31

The swords began to fall and the dust rose from the earth upwards,

On one side, the sharp arrows are being discharged and on the other side people are repeating request for water. —32

The vultures are swooping down and the warriors equal in strength are fighting,

Durga is laughing and the glittering swords are being showered. —33

BRAHAD NARAAJ STANZA

The brave fighters marched forward with their shouts of "kill, kill" and from this side, the Ganas of Rudra destroyed innumerable warriors,

The furious arrows are being showered like the drops from the visible rising dark thundering clouds in the month of Sawan. —34

NARAAJ STANZA

Many warriors are running forward and with their blows are wounding the enemies,

Many warriors, being wounded, are roaming and showering arrows. —35

Bedecked with several arms, the warriors are marching forward and thundering,

And striking their blows fearlessly, they are shouting "kill, kill." —36

Preparing themselves like the thundering dark clouds, the brave fighters are marching forward,

Bedecked with weapons, they are looking so beautiful that the daughters of the gods are getting allured by them. —37

They are very selective in wedding the warriors and all the heroes are moving about and looking impressive in the battlefield like Indra, the king of gods,

All those kings, who are frightened, they have been abandoned by the daughters of the gods. —38

BRAHAD NARAAJ STANZA

The warriors thundering dreadfully and bedecked with arms and weapons fell (on the enemy) and seeing, the anger of Rudra they gethered all the forces,

They gathered quickly like the rising and thundering clouds of Sawan and gathering the glory of heaven in themselves, began to dance, being highly intoxicated. —39

BRAHAD NARAAJ STANZA

Holding their swords in their hands and galloping their horses, the mighty youthful warriors stopped there, where Rudra was standing,

The brave fighters began to inflict blows with many types of arrows and weapons and forcibly move forward, without retracing their steps. —40

The clattering of daggers and swords is being heard, the warriors are wounding one another, roaring like lions,

On getting wounded the warriors are falling down, but are not retracing their steps. —41

CHAUPAI

In this way, all his companions fell down and Daksha was only left behind,

He called again his remaining fighters and wearing his armour, he caused the resounding of the musical instrument. —42

The king Daksha, moved forward, with the strength of the innumerable warriors,

Innumerable arrows were discharged from his bow and such a scene was created that there was darkness during the day. —43

The ghosts and fiends began to shout and the tabors resounded from both the sides,

A fierce fighting ensued and it appeared that the war was going on between Rama and Ravana in Sri Lanka. —44

BHUJANG PRAYAAT STANZA

In great ire, Rudra held his trident in his hand and vacating the saddles of many horses, he killed many warriors,

On the other side, Daksha was alone and on this side, Rudra was also alone; both of them highly infuriated, waged the war in many ways. —45

Rudra chopped the head of Daksha with his trident and he fell down like an uprooted tree,

Daksha the king of kings, fell down after his head was cut and he looked like the fallen mountain, whose wings had been cut by Indra with his weapon *vajra*. —46

All the pride of Daksha was shattered and the mighty Rudra destroyed him completely,

Then Rudra, getting impatient, speedily came to Antaipura, where every one came with the cloth around his neck and falling at his feet said, "O Rudra! Be merciful to us, protect and help us." —47

CHAUPAI

"O Shiva! We have not recognised thee, you are supremely mighty and an ascetic,"

Hearing these words, Rudra became gracious and he caused Daksha to become alive again and get up. —48

Then Rudra, meditated upon the Lord and restored the life of all other kings,

He restored the life of the husbands of all the princesses and seeing this wonderful performance, all the saints were extremely pleased. —49

The god of love troubled greatly the god Shiva, who was without his consort, without which Shiva remained in great agony,

Being extremely vexed, once in great fury, Shiva reduced Kamdev (the god of love) to ashes and from that day this god was called *Anang* (bodyless). —50

End of "The Description of the Killing of Daksha, the Greatness of Rudra and the Killing of Gauri (Parbati) in the Eleventh Incarnation Rudra" in Bachittar Natak.

JALANDHAR INCARNATION

Let Sri Bhagauti Ji (The Primal Lord) be Helpful

CHAUPAI

After having been burnt and died, the wife of Rudra was born in the house of Himalaya,
After the end of her childhood, when she attained the age of puberty, She was again united with her Lord Shiva. —1

Just as Sita, on meeting Rama, became one with him, just as *Gita* and Vedic ideology are one, just as, on meeting the sea, the Ganges becomes one with the sea, in the same manner, Parvati and Shiva bacame one. —2

When, after wedding, Rudra brought her to his home, the demon Jalandhar was allured on seeing her,
He sent a messenger, saying this: "Go and bring that woman, after seizing her from Rudra." —3

DOHIRA

Jalandhar told his messenger to say this to Shiva, "Shiva! Either send your bedecked wife to me, or hold up your trident and wage war with me."—4

CHAUPAI

How this story occurred? In this context, now I relate the story of the wife of Vishnu,
One day, she cooked the brinjals in her home and at the same time, Vishnu was called by the assembly of demons, where he went. —5

At the same time, the great sage Narada reached the house of Vishnu and he was very hungry,
Seeing the cooked vegetable of brinjals, his mind was tempted, but he did not get it, even on asking for it. —6

The wife of Vishnu said that she had prepared that food for her Lord, therefore it was not possible for her to give it to him,
(She also said): "I have sent a messenger to call him and he may be coming", the wife of Vishnu thought that if Narada partook it the food would become impure and her Lord would be angry with her. — 7

Narada said,
"The sage had been repeatedly asking for the food, but you did not give it to him,"
The sage flew into rage and said, "You will live in the house of the demon Jalandhar as his wife named Varinda, after getting her body." —8

No sooner than the sage departed after cursing her, Vishnu reached his home; hearing about the curse, he was greatly agonised and his wife smilingly confirmed (what the sage had said). —9

DOHIRA

Then Vishnu created Varinda from the shadow of his wife;
She took birth on the earth in the house of the demon Dhumarkesh. —10

CHAUPAI

Just as the lotus-leaf in water remains unaffected by the drops of water, in the same manner, Varinda lived in the house of Jalandhar as his wife,
And for Vishnu manifested himself as Jalandhar and in this way, Vishnu assumed a unique form. —11

In this way, the story hath taken a new turn and now it hath halted on Rudra,
The demon Jalandhar asked for his wife from Rudra and Rudra did not oblige him, therefore the king of demons flew into rage instantly. —12

The trumpets and drums resounded on all the four sides and the knocking sound of tabors was heard from all the four directions,
The steel collided with the steel dreadfully and the daggers glittered with infinite beauty. —13

The warriors began to fall in the battlefield and the ghosts and fiends began to run on all the four sides,
The innumerable riders of elephants, chariots and horses began to fall as martyrs in the battle-field. —14

TOTAK STANZA

The warriors moved in the battlefield in great anger and a dreadful war began,

Hearing the neighing of horses and the trumpeting of the elephants, the clouds of Sawan felt shy. —15

The arrows and the swords were showered in the war and in this way, this war a dreadful and horrible war,
The warriors fall, but in their persistence, they raise dreadful sound,
In this way, the forces of the enemy, gathered quickly from all the four sides in the battlefield. —16

Having been besieged from all the four sides, Shiva held his arrow and flew into rage over the demons,
The arrows were showered so intensely from both the sides, that there was shade on the earth and over the sky. —17

The helmets broke and fell in the battlefield like the flowers saturated with blood,
The unapproachable and unique Shiva thought over in this way in his mind. —18

And perplexed in his heart, Shiva, shouting loudly, jumped into the forces of the demons,
Holding his trident, he began to strike blows and hearing the sound of his blows, both gods and demons were all filled with fear. —19

When Shiva meditated in his mind on the non-temporal Lord, the Lord was pleased at the same time,
Vishnu was ordered to manifest himself as Jalandhar and in this way, destroy the king of enemies. —20

BHUJANG PRAYAAT STANZA

The destroyer Lord commanded and Vishnu manifested himself in the form of Jalandhar, and bedecked in all manner, he appeared as a king,
Vishnu manifested himself in this form in order to protect his wife, and in this way, he defiled the chastity of the extremely chaste Varinda. —21

Abandoning the body of demons, Varinda again manifested herself as Lakshmi, the wife of Vishnu and in this way Vishnu assumed the twelfth incarnation in the form of a demon,
The war continued again and the warriors held their weapons in their hands, the brave fighters began to fall in the battlefield and also the air-vehicles came down in order to take away the dead warriors from the battlefield. —22

On this side, the chastity of woman was defiled and on that side all the army was chopped; by this the pride of Jalandhar was shattered; but still the weak king continued the fight and all his companions and subordinates ran away from the battlefield. —23

CHAUPAI

Both Shiva and Jalandhar fought and there was none other in the battlefield,
The war continued for several months and Jalandhar was filled with great fury for (the actions of) Shiva. —24

Then Shiva meditated upon the Shakti (power) and the power (Shakti) was gracious towards him,
Now, Rudra getting mightier than before began to wage war. —25

On that side, Vishnu had defiled the chastity of woman and on this side, Shiva also, having received the effulgence from the goddess became more powerful,
Therefore he destroyed the demon Jalandhar in an instant; seeing this scene all were pleased. —26

Those who repeat the name of Chandika, they know that from that day, Chandika came to be known as Jalandhari,
By repeating her name, the body becomes pure like taking bath in the Ganges. —27

Keeping in mind the fear of making the book voluminous, I have not narrated the complete story of Rudra,
This story has only been narrated in brief; on knowing this, kindly do not jeer at me. —28

End of "The Description of the Twelfth i.e. Jalandhar Incarnation" in Bachittar Natak.

VISHNU INCARNATION

Let Sri Bhagauti Ji (The Primal Power) be Helpful

CHAUPAI

Now I enumerate the incarnations of Vishnu as to what type of incarnations he adopted?

When the earth is distempered with the load of sins, then she manifests her anguish before the destroyer Lord. —1
When the demons cause the gods to run away and seize their kingdom from them,
Then the earth, pressed under the load of sins, calls for help,
And then the destroyer Lord becomes kind. —2

DOHIRA

Then taking the elements of all the gods and principally merging himself in it, Vishnu manifests himself in different forms and takes birth in the clan of Aditi. —3

CHAUPAI

In this way, incarnating himself, he removes the load of the earth and destroys the demons in various ways,
After removing the load of the earth, he goes again to the abode of gods and merges Himself in the destroyer Lord. —4
If I relate all these stories in detail, then it may delusively be called Vishnu-system,
Therefore, I narrate it in brief and O Lord; protect me from ailment and suffering. —5

* * *

DOHIRA

In the body of the immanent Lord, millions of Vishnus and Shivas abide,
Millions of Indras, Brahmas, Suryas, Chandras and Varunas are present there in His divine body. —1

CHAUPAI

Fatigued by His work, Vishnu remains merged in Him and within that immanent Lord, there are unaccountable oceans and worlds,
The bed of great serpent, on which that immanent Lord sleeps,
Millions of Seshanagas appear graceful near it. —2
He hath thousands of heads, trunks and legs; He hath thousands of hands and feet, He, the invincible Lord,
He hath thousands of eyes and all types of excellences kiss His feet. —3

DOHIRA

The day on which Vishnu manifested Himself for the killing of Madhu and Kaitabh, the poet Shyam knows him as the fourteenth, incarnation. —4

CHAUPAI

From the dross of the ear, the demons were born and were considered glorious like Chandra and Surya,
With the orders of the immanent Lord, Vishnu abandoned *maya* and manifested himself at that time, when demons indulged in riots. —5
Vishnu waged ferocious war with them for five thousand years,
The immanent Lord then helped Vishnu and in great fury he destroyed the demons. —6

DOHIRA

In this way, Vishnu manifested himself as the fourteenth incarnation,
And in order to give comfort to the saints, he destroyed both these demons. —7

End of "The Description of the Thirteenth and Fourteenth Incarnations i.e., Vishnu" in Bachittar Natak.

ARHANT DEV INCARNATION

Let Sri Bhagauti Ji (The Primal Lord) be Helpful

CHAUPAI

Whenever the demons extend their rule,
Then Vishnu comes to destroy them,
Once all the demons gathered together,
(Seeing them) the gods and their preceptors went to their abodes. —1
All the demons gathered together thought out (over this issue),
That Vishnu always destroys the demons,
And now they should devise some plan,
To settle the issue. —2
The preceptor of the demons (Shukracharya) said,
"O demons, you have not understood this mystery till now,
The gods gather together and perform *yajnas* (sacrifices),
Therefore they always remain happy." —3
"You should also perform sacrifices,

BACHITTAR NATAK

And then you will be victorious in battlefield,"
The demons then began the performance of a *yajna*,
And hearing about it, the people of the region of gods became fearful. —4

All the gods went to meet Vishnu and said,
"O destroyer of demons! Take some steps now,"
Vishnu said, "I shall manifest myself in a new body,
And destroy the *yajna* of the demons." —5

Vishnu then took bath at various pilgrim-stations,
And distributed unlimited alms to the Brahmins,
Brahma, born out of the navel-lotus of Vishnu, propagated the divine knowledge,
And Vishnu meditated on the immanent Lord. —6

The immanent Lord, then became merciful and addressed his servant Vishnu with sweet words,
"O Vishnu, manifest yourself in the form of Arhant,
"And destroy the kings of the demons." —7

Vishnu, after receiving the orders of the immanent Lord, eulogised Him,
He manifested himself as Arhant Dev on the earth and started a new religion. —8

When he became the preceptor of the demons, he started different kinds of sects,
One of the sects he started was Shravak sect (Jainism) and bestowed supreme comfort to the saints. —9

He caused all to hold the forceps for plucking hair and in this way he made many demons devoid of the lock of hair on the crown of the head.

Those without hair or without the lock of hair on the crown of their heads could not remember any *mantras* and if anyone repeated the *mantras*, there was negative influence of the *mantras* on him. —10

Then he ended the performance of *yajnas* and made all indifferent to the idea of violence on beings,
There can be no *yajna* without the violence on beings, therefore no one performed *yajna* now. —11

In this way, the practice of performing *yajnas* was destroyed and any one who used to kill beings, he was ridiculed,
There could be no *yajna* without the killing of beings and if one performed a *yajna*, he availed no merit. —12

The Arhant incarnation, instructed all in this way; that no king could perform a *yajna*,
Every one was put on a wrong path and no one was performing the action of *dharma*. —13

DOHIRA

Just as corn is produced from corn, grass from grass, in the same way the man from man (thus there is no creator—*Ishvara*). —14

CHAUPAI

Such a knowledge was given to all that none performed the action of *dharma*,
Every one's mind was absorbed in such things and in this way, the clan of demons became weak. —15

Such rules were propagated, that no demon could take a bath now, and without taking bath no one could become pure,
Without becoming pure no *mantra* could be recited and in this way, all the actions became fruitness. —16

In this way, Arhant ruled for ten thousand years and propagated his religion throughout the world,
The actions of *dharma* ended in the world and in this way, the clan of demons became weak. —17

Indra, the king of gods, liked all this very much in his mind that Vishnu had done such a great thing for them,
All of them, forsaking grief, were filled with joy and the songs of happiness were sung in every home. —18

DOHIRA

Instructing in this way, Vishnu caused all to abandon the actions of *dharma* and went back again to heavens. —19

Assuming the status of supreme preceptor of Shravaks and engrossing the demons on the wrong path, Vishnu manifested himself as the fifteenth incarnation in this way. —20

End of "The Description of Arhant, the Fifteenth Incarnation" in Bachittar Natak.

King Manu Incarnation

Let Sri Bhagauti Ji (The Primal Lord) be Helpful

CHAUPAI

All the people were absorbed in Shravak religion (Jainism) and all abandoned the actions of *dharma*,
All of them forsook the service of the Lord and none worshipped the supreme preceptor (The immanent Lord). —1

The saints became devoid of saintliness and all abandoned the actions of *dharma*,
Then the immanent Lord ordered Vishnu, who did as commanded. —2

Vishnu manifested himself as king Manu and propagated *Manusmriti* in the world,
He brought all the corrupt persons on the right path and caused the people to become devoid of sinful actions. —3

Vishnu incarnated himself as the king Manu and established all the actions of *dharma*,
If any one committed a sin, he was now killed and in this way, the king made all his subjects to tread on the right path. —4

The sinner was killed instantly and all the subjects were given instructions of *dharma*,
Now all attained the instructions about the name of the Lord and about virtuous actions like charity etc.,
And in this way, the king got abandoned the discipline of Shravaks. —5

The people who had run away from the kingdom of the king Manu, they only remained adherents of Shravak religion,
All the remaining subjects followed the path of *dharma* and abandoning the wrong path acquired the path of *dharma*. —6

The king Manu was the incarnation of Vishnu and he propagated in the right manner the actions of *dharma*,
He put all the followers of wrong values on the right path and brought the people towards *dharma*, who were absorbed then in sinful actions. —7

DOHIRA

All those who tread on the wrong paths, began to follow the right path and in this way, the Shravak religion receded far away,
For this work, the king Manu was highly venerated in all the world. —8

End of "The Description of King Manu, the Sixteenth Incarnation" in Bachittar Natak.

Dhanwantar Vaid Incarnation

Let Sri Bhagauti Ji (The Primal Lord) be Helpful

CHAUPAI

The people of all the world grew wealthy and there remained no anxiety on their body and mind,
They began to eat various kinds of foods and consequently they suffered from various kinds of ailments. —1

All the people got worried about their ailment and the subjects became extremely distressed,
All of them sang the praises of the immanent Lord and he became gracious towards all. —2

Vishnu was called by the supreme Lord and ordered Him to manifest Himself in the form of Dhanwantar,
He also told him to spread Ayurveda and destroy the ailments of the subjects. —3

DOHIRA

Then all the gods gathered and churned the ocean and for the welfare of the subjects and destruction of their ailments, they acquired Dhanwantar from the ocean. —4

CHAUPAI

He spread Ayurveda and destroyed the ailments from the whole world,
He disclosed the Vedic Shastra and brought it before the people and described various medicines. —5

DOHIRA

Administering the medicine to all the world, he made the world devoid of ailments,
And departed for heaven after having been stung by Takshak (the king of snakes). —6

End of "The Description of the Seventeenth Incarnation named Dhanwantar" in Bachittar Natak.

Suraj (Sun) Incarnation

Let Sri Bhagauti Ji (The Primal Lord) be Helpful

CHAUPAI

The might of demons, the sons of Diti, increased very much and they conquered many enemies in water and on land,
Receiving the command of the immanent Lord, Vishnu manifested himself as Suraj incarnation. —1

Wherever the demons become powerful, the Suraj incarnation kills them in different ways,
The Sun destroyed the darkness from the earth and in order to give comfort to the subjects, he used to roam hither and thither. —2

NARAAJ STANZA

(Seeing the Sun) all the people abandoned idleness and woke up at dawn and meditating on the Omnipresent Lord, used to repeat His name in various ways,
Working on difficult jobs, they used to stabilise in their mind the uninstallable Lord and used to recite the Gayatri and *sandhya*. —3

All the people, repeating the name of the Lord, used to perform godly deeds and also reflected on the Vedas and Vyakarna etc., alongwith the burning of incense, lighting the earthen lamps and performing *yajna*.
They used to perform rituals for the manes according to their power and used to concentrate on virtuous actions alongwith the recitation of Shastras, Smritis, etc. —4

ARDH NARAAJ STANZA

The smoke of *yajna* was visible on all the four sides and all the people slept on the earth,
Performing meditation and worship in many ways, they used to work for the growth of distant places. —5
Reciting many *mantras*, the people performed Yogic discipline and repeated the name,
They meditated on the detached Supreme *Purusha* and ultimately they acquired the air-vehicles for transportation to heaven. —6

DOHIRA

In this way, a good deal of time elapsed in performing religious and charitable actions and then a powerful demon named Dooraghkaya was born. —7

CHAUPAI

His body increased in length every day by the length of an arrow and he destroyed the gods and twice-born night and day,
On the birth of the enemy like Dooraghkaya, even the chariot of the sun hesitated to move. —8

ARIL

When the chariot of the sun stopped moving, the sun, then in great fury marched forward alongwith his arms, weapons and forces,
He started various types of war, seeing which both gods and demons, experienced a dilemma.—9
Holding their swords in their hands, the warriors of both the sides, fought with one another in the battlefield,
They fell, having been chopped into bits, but still they did not retrace their steps,
Having been wounded their glory increased still further and they appeared like the member of the marriage party walking and exhibiting their dresses. —10

ANBHAV STANZA

Hearing the resounding of the trumpets the clouds are feeling shy,
The army is swelling forward like the clouds, from all the four sides,
And it appears that there is a large gathering of peacocks in the forest. —11

MADHUR DHUN STANZA

The lustre of the shields appears like the red roses,
The movement of warriors and the shooting of arrows are creating different distinct sounds. —12
Such a sound is being heard in the battlefield as if the clouds are thundering,
The resounding of the drums and the sound of the empty quivers is also being heard. —13
The warriors are baffled and seeing the dreadful war, they are meditating upon the Lord God,

All are absorbed in the war and are submerged in the thoughts of war. —14

The brave fighters are moving hither and thither and the heavenly damsels are looking at them,

The heroes have abandoned everything and having been chopped, several warriors have played with their lives. —15

The arrows are glittering and the flags are flying; the warriors are fighting face to face very quickly and the blood is oozing out of their chests. —16

Bedecked with the arrows, the brave warriors are roaring, they are ornamented with steel armours and are moving towards heaven. —17

When the superior arrows are discharged, the chests of the enemies are wounded,

The shields being cut are producing knocking sound and the armours are being torn. —18

NARAAJ STANZA

Taking his arrow in his hand, Suraj ran towards the enemy Dooraghkaya and in great ire began a dreadful war,

Many people came running under the refuge of gods and Suraj, who ends the night conquered many warriors. —19

The warriors are striking the daggers, holding them tightly and coming face to face and the brave fighters are challenging one another, roaring like the lions,

The firm limbs of the warriors swinging continuously, are falling down and the brave fighters, fearlessly coming face to face with others are clashing. —20

ARDH NARAAJ STANZA

Listening to the resonance of the trumpets, the clouds are feeling shy,

The fastened trumpets have resounded and hearing their sound the warriors are thundering. —21

Fighting ferociously, the gods and their kings are moving (here and there), they are roaming by mounting on air-vehicles and the hearts of the gods and demons both are feeling envious. —22

BELI BIDDARAM STANZA

The sound of the tabors of vampires and the cries of the Yoginis are being heard,

The daggers are glistening and glittering and the elephants and horses are jumping in the battlefield. —23

The resonance of drum is being heard and the lustre of swords is glimmering,

Rudra is also dancing there with his loosened matted hair and a dreadful war is being waged there. —24

TOTAK STANZA

The winsome horses of the warriors are jumping in the war and the swords are glistening in their hands like the flash of lightening in the clouds,

The arrows are seen penetrated in the waists of the warriors and they are taking out the blood of one another. —25

The flags are fluttering and the brave fighters have become fearful,

Seeing the glitter of the arrows and the swords the lightening in the dark clouds is also feeling shy,

And this scene looks like the flash of lightning in the thundering clouds of the month of Sawan. —26

DOHIRA

How far should I narrate the story for fear of lengthening the same;

Ultimately the arrow of Suraj became the reason for the end of that demon. —27

End of "The Description of the Eighteenth Incarnation Suraj" in Bachittar Natak.

CHANDRA INCARNATION

Let Sri Bhagauti Ji (The Primal Lord) be Helpful

DODHAK STANZA

Now I think about Chandrama, how did Vishnu manifest Himself as Chandra incarnation?

I am narrating a very ancient story, hearing which the poets will be pleased. —1

There was not even a little farming anywhere and the people were dying with hunger,

The nights were full of darkness and during the

day the sun blazed, therefore nothing grew anywhere. —2

For this reason all the beings were agitated and they were destroyed like the old leaves,

Everyone worshipped, adored and served in warious ways and the supreme preceptor (i.e. the Lord) was pleased. —3

(This was the situation at that time) that the wife did no service to her husband and ever remained displeased with him,

The lust did not overpower the wives and in the absence of sexual instinct, all the works for the growth of the world had ended. —4

TOMAR STANZA

No wife worshipped her husband and always remained in her pride,

She had no grief and did not suffer because of the sexual instinct,

Therefore there was no desire for supplication in them. —5

Neither she served her husband, nor worshipped and adored the preceptors; neither she meditated on Lord God nor she ever took bath. —6

Then the immanent Lord called Vishnu and giving instruction to him, told him that without taking any other thing into consideration, he should manifest himself as Chandra incarnation. —7

Then Vishnu bowing his head said with folded hands, "I shall assume the form of Chandra incarnation, so that the beauty may prosper in the world." —8

Then the extremely glorious Vishnu manifested Himself as Chandra (incarnation), and he shot continuously the arrows of the god of love towards women. —9

Because of this the women became modest and all their pride was shattered; they again began to perform service to their husbands and by this all the gods were pleased. —10

Seeing Chandra, people began to do farming to a large extent; in this way all the thought-out works were accomplished, in this manner, Chandra incarnation came into being. —11

CHAUPAI

In this way, Vishnu manifested himself as Chandra (incarnation), but Chandra also became egoistic about his own beauty; he also abandoned the meditation of any other, therefore he was also blemished. —12

He was engrossed with the wife of the sage (Gautama), which made the sage highly infuriated in his mind; the sage struck him with his deer-skin, which created a mark on his body and he was thus blemished. —13

With the curse of the sage he keeps on decreasing and increasing,

Because of this event, he felt extremely ashamed and his pride was extremely shattered. —14

He then performed austerities for a long time, by which the immanent Lord became merciful towards him; his destructive ailment decayed and by the grace of the supreme immanent Lord, he attained a higher status than the sun. —15

End of "The Description of the Nineteenth Incarnation i.e., Chandra" in Bachittar Natak.

THE LORD IS ONE AND THE VICTORY IS OF THE LORD

RAM, THE TWENTIETH INCARNATION

CHAUPAI

Now I describe the incarnation of Ram,

Now He exhibited his performance in the world,

After a long time the family of demons raised its head again. —1

The demons began to perform vicious actions,

And no one could chastise them,

Then all the gods assembled and went to the milk-ocean. —2

There they stayed for a long time with Vishnu and Brahma,

They cried out in anguish many times,

And ultimately their consternation was heard by the Lord. —3

TOTAK STANZA

When the immanent Lord saw the air-vehicles of Vishnu and other gods,

He raised sound and smiled and addressed Vishnu thus: "Manifest yourself as Raghunath (Ram) and rule over Oudh for a long time." —4

Vishnu heard this command from the mouth of the Lord (and did as ordered),
Now begins the story of Raghu clan,
If the poet describes the whole story, another complete book will be prepared with all the narration. —5

Therefore, O Lord! I compose in brief this significant story according to the intellect given to me by Thee,
If there is any lapse on my part, for that I am answerable,
Therefore, O Lord! Grant me strength to compose this poem in appropriate language. —6

"The king Raghu looked very impressive as a gem in the necklace of Raghu clan,
He ruled over Oudh for a long time,
Then the death (Ram) ultimately brought his end,
Then the king Aja ruled over the earth." —7

When the king Aja was destroyed by the mighty destroyer Lord,
Then the story of Raghu clan moved forward through king Dasrath,
He also ruled over Oudh with comfort and passed his comfortable days in the forest killing the deer. —8

When Dasrath, the Lord of Sumitra became the king,
Then the *dharma* of sacrifice was extensively propagated,
The king moved in the forest day and night and hunted the tigers, elephants and deer. —9

In this wary, the story advanced in Oudh and now the part of the mother of Ram comes before us,
There was a brave king in the city of Kuhram, which was known as the kingdom of Kaushal. —10

In his home was born an extremely beautiful daughter Kaushalya, who conquered all the beauty of the moon,
When she grew of age, she selected Dasrath, the king of Oudh, in the ceremony of *swayamvara* and married him. —11

The mighty and glorious king Sumitra, who was the conqueror of Madra Desha had a daughter named Sumitra in his home,
That virgin was so winsome and radiant that she seemed to have conquered the lustre of the sun and moon. —12

When she grew of age, she also married the king of Oudh,
The same thing happened with the king of Kaikeya, who had a glorious daughter named Kaikeyi. —13

The king reflected (in his mind) about the son to be born to his daughter,
Kaikeyi also thought about it; she was extremely beautiful like the sun and moon. —14

On being married she asked for two boons from the king, which ultimately resulted in his death,
At that time, the king could not understand the mystery (of the boons) and gave his consent for them. —15

Then once a war was waged between the gods and demons, in which the king gave a tough fight from the side of gods,
In that war the charioteer of the king was killed, and instead Kaikeyi drove the chariot; on seeing this, the king was nonplussed. —16

The king was pleased and gave her two boons, he did not have any distrust in his mind,
Now the king cooperated for the victory of Indra, the king of gods, this story has been told in the drama. —17

The king fulfils his heart's desires by conquering many enemies, he passed his time mostly in the forests,
Once a Brahmin named Shravan Kumar was roaming there in search of water. —18

Leaving his blind parents at some spot, the son had come for water, holding the pitcher in his hand,
That Brahmin sage was sent there by death, where the king was resting in a tent. —19

There was sound of filling the pitcher with water, which was heard by the king,
The king fitted the arrow in the bow and pulled it and considering the Brahmin as a deer, he shot the arrow on him and killed him. —20

On being struck by the arrow, the ascetic fell down and there was sound of lamentation from his mouth,
For seeing the spot, where the deer had died, the king went there, but on seeing that Brahmin he pressed his finger under his teeth in distress. —21

Speech of Shravan

There were still some life-breaths in the body of Shravan,
In his final life-breaths, the Brahmin said to the king, "My mother and father are blind and are lying on that side,
"You go there and make them drink water, so that I may die peacefully." —22

PAADHARI STANZA

O king! Both my parents are without sight, listen to me and give them water,
Do not say anything about me to them, otherwise they will die in extreme agony. —23
When Shravan Kumar said these words to the king about giving water to his blind parents, then tears gushed out of his eyes,
The king said, "It is a disgrace for me that I have done such a deed, my royal merit hath been destroyed and I am now devoid of *dharma*." —24
When the king pulled out Shravan from the pool, then that ascetic breathed his last,
Then the king became very sad and abandoned the idea of returning to his home. —25
He thought in his mind that he may wear the garb of a yogi and abide in the forest forsaking his royal duties,
My royal duties are now meaningless for me, when I have committed a bad deed by killing a Brahmin. —26
The king then uttered these words, "I have brought under my control the situations of all the world, but now what hath been committed by me?"
"Now I should take such measures, that may cause his parents to survive." —27
The king filled the pitcher with water and lifted it on his head and reached at the spot, where the parents of Shravan had been lying,
When the king reached near them with very slow steps, then they heard the voice of the moving footsteps. —28

The Speech of the Brahmin
Addressed to the King

"O son! Tell us the reason for so much delay." Hearing these words the large-hearted king remained silent,
They again said, "O son! Why do you not speak?" The king, fearing his reply to be unfavourable, again remained silent. —29
Coming near them, the king gave them water, then on touching his hand those blind persons, getting bewildered asked angrily about his identity,
Hearing these words, the king began to weep. —30

The Speech of the King
Addressed to the Brahmin

"O eminent Brahmin! I am the killer of your son, I am the one who has killed your son, I am Dasrath, seeking your refuge, "O Brahmin! Do to me whatever you wish." —31
"If you want, you may protect me, otherwise kill me, I am under your shelter, I am here before you."
Then the king Dasrath on their bidding asked some attendant to bring good deal of wood for burning. —32
A great load of wood was brought, and they (the blind parents) got prepared the funeral pyres and sat on them,
The fire was lighted on all the four sides and in this way those Brahmins caused the end of their lives. —33
They created the fire of yoga from their bodies and wanted to be reduced to ashes,
Both of them reduced themselves to ashes and in their final hour cursed the king in great anger. —34

The Speech of the Brahmin
Addressed to the King

"O king! The manner in which we are breathing our last, you will also experience the same situation."
Saying this, the Brahmin was burnt to ashes alongwith his wife and went to heaven. —35

The Speech of the King

Then the king expressed this wish that either he would burn himself that day or forsaking his kingdom, he would go to the forest,
"What will I say at home? That I am coming back after killing the Brahmin with my own hand." —36

Speech of Gods

Then there was an utterance from heaven: "O Dasrath! Do not be sad, Vishnu will take birth as son in your home and through him, the impact of the sinful deed of this day will end." —37

"He will be famous by the name of Ramavatar and he will redeem the whole world,

"He will destroy the tyrants in an instant and in this way his fame will spread on all the four sides." —38

NARAAJ STANZA

"O King! Forsake all anxiety and go to your home, the king Ram will come to your home, on conquering the tyrants, he will obtain the deed of victory from all; he will shatter the pride of egoists; having royal canopy over his head, he will sustain all. —39

"He will repudiate the mighty ones and punish those, whom none has been able to punish upto this day,

"He will extend his domains by conquering the unconquerable and removing all the blemishes, he will definitely conquer Lanka and conquering Ravana, he will shatter his pride." —40

"O king! Go to your home, forsaking the anxiety and begin the *yajna* by calling the Brahmins." Hearing these words, the king came to his capital and calling the sage Vashistha, he determined to perform the Rajsuya *yajna*. —41

He invited the kings of many countries and also the Brahmins of different garbs reached there,

The king honoured all in many ways and the Rajsuya *yajna* began. —42

Washing the feet of Brahmins and giving them their seats and burning the incenses and earthen lamps, the king circumambulated the Brahmins in a special manner,

He gave millions of coins to each Brahmin as religious gift and in this way, the Rajsuya *yajna* began. —43

The comedians and minstrels from various countries began to sing songs and obtaining various kinds of honours they were well-seated in a special manner,

The pleasure of the people is indescribable and there were so many air-vehicles in the sky that they could not be recognised. —44

The heavenly damsels, leaving the heaven, were turning their limbs in special postures and dancing,

Many kings, in their pleasure were giving charities and seeing their beautiful queens, the heavenly damsels were feeling shy. —45

Bestowing various types of gifts and honours, the king called many mighty heroes and sent them in all the ten directions alongwith the tough forces,

They conquered the kings of many countries and made them subservient to Dasrath and in this way, conquering the kings of the whole world, brought them before the sovereign Dasrath. —46

ROOAAMAL STANZA

After conquering the kings, the king Dasrath called together the enemies as well as friends, the sages like Vashistha and the Brahmins,

Those who did not accept his supremacy, in great fury, he destroyed them and in this way the kings of all the earth became subservient to the king of Oudh. —47

All the kings were honoured in various ways; they were given the wealth, elephants and horses equivalent to millions and billions of gold coins,

The garments studded with diamonds and the saddles of horses studded with gems cannot be enumerated and even Brahma cannot describe the grandeur of the ornaments. —48

The woollen and silken garments were given by the king and seeing the beauty of all the people it seemed that even Indra was ugly before them,

All the tyrants were frightened and even the Sumeru mountain tremble with fear that the king may not chop him and distribute his bits to the participants. —49

All the Brahmins started the *yajna* by reciting the Vedic *mantras* and uttering various kinds of sounds, they performed the *havan* (fire-worship) in accordance with the *mantras*,

When many sages and hermits performed the *havan* in appropriate manner, then from the sacrificial-pit arose the agitated sacrificial *Purushas*. —50

They had a milkpot in their hands, which they gave to the king,
The king Dasrath was so much pleased on obtaining it, just as a pauper is pleased on receiving a gift,
The king divided it into four parts with his own hands and gave one part each to two queens and two parts to the third one. —51

The queens on drinking that milk, became pregnant and remained as such for twelve months,
At the beginning of the thirteenth month Ram, the enemy of Ravana incarnate for the protection of the saints. —52

Then the three princes named Bharat, Lakshman and Shatrughan were born and various kinds of musical instruments were played at the gate of Dasrath's palace,
Bowing at the feet of Brahmins, he gave them innumerable gifts and all the people felt that now the enemies will be destroyed and the saints will attain peace and comfort. —53

Wearing the necklaces of diamonds and jewels, the sages are extending the royal glory and the king is presenting documents to the twice-born (*dvijas*) for gold and silver,
The chieftains of various places, are exhibiting their delight and all the people are dancing like the frolicsome people in the spring season. —54

The network of bells is seen decorated on the elephants and horses and such like elephants and horses have been presented by the kings to Dasrath, the husband of Kaushalya,
There has been such a grand festival in Ayodhya on the birth of Ram that the beggars laden with gifts have become king-like. —55

The tunes of drums and clarionets are being heard alongwith the sound of flutes and lyres,
The sounds of bells, walrus and kettledrums are audible and these sounds are so attractive that the air-vehicles of gods, being impressed are coming down to the earth. —56

Here, there and everywhere the songs of praise are being sung and the Brahmins have begun the discussion on Vedas,
Because of the incense and earthen lamps, the palace of the king has become so impressive that Indra alongwith gods are moving hither and thither in their delight. —57

All the people are saying that on that day all their wishes have been fulfilled,
The earth is filled with shouts of victory and the musical instruments are being played in the sky,
There are small air flags at all the places, there are greetings on all the paths and all shops and bazars have been plastered with sandalwood. —58

The poor people are being given the horses decorated with gold, and many intoxicated elephants like Airavat (the elephant of Indra) are being given in charity,
The horses studded with bells and being given as gifts; it appears that in the city of singers, the prudence is coming itself. —59

The innumerable horses and elephants were given as gifts by the king on one hand and I am began to grow day by day on the other hand,
He was taught all the required wisdom of the arms and religious texts and Ram learnt everything within eight days (i.e., a very short period). —60

They began to roam on the banks of the Saryu river and all the four brothers collected the yellow leaves and butterflies,
Seeing all the princes moving together, the waves of Saryu exhibited many coloured garments. —61

All this was going on this side and on the other side Vishwamitra began a *yajna* for the worship of his manes,
Attracted by the incense of fire-worship (*havan*), the demons would come to the sacrificial pit and would eat the materials of *yajna*, snatching it from the performer. —62

Seeing the loot of the materials of the fire-worship and feeling himself helpless, the great sage Vishwamitra came to Ayodhya in great anger,
On reaching (Ayodhya) he said to the king, "Give me your son Ram for a few days, otherwise I shall reduce you to ashes on this very spot." —63

Visualising the fury of the sage, the king asked his son to accompany him and the sage accompanied by Ram went to begin the *yajna* again,
The sage said, "O Ram! Listen, there are two routes, on the one the *yajna*-spot is far away

and on the other it is quite near, but on the later route there lives a demoness named Taraka, who kills the wayfarers. —64

Ram said, "let us go by the small-distance-route, abandoning the anxiety, this work of killing the demons is the work of the gods,"

They began to move on that route and at the same time the demons came and laid obstruction on the path saying "O Ram! How will you proceed and save yourself." —65

On seeing the demoness Taraka, Ram held his bow and arrows in his hand, and pulling the bow discharged the arrow on her head,

On being struck by the arrow, the heavy body of the demoness fell down and in this way, the end of the sinner came at the hands of Ram. —66

In this way, after killing the demoness, when the *yajna* was started, two large-sized demons, Marich and Subahu, appeared there,

Seeing them, all the sages ran away and only Ram persistently stood there and the war of those three was waged continuously for sixteen watches. —67

Holding firmly their arms and weapons, the demons began to shout "kill, kill;" they caught hold of their axes, bows and arrows in their hands,

From all the ten directions, the demon warriors rushed forth for fighting only with Ram. —68

RASAAVAL STANZA

Seeing Ram, the *dharma*-incarnate, in the battlefield and uttering various shouts from their mouth, the demons rushed forth from all the four directions and gathered together. —69

The musical instruments resounded violently and hearing their sounds, the clouds felt shy,

Fixing their banners on the earth, the demons, filled with enmity, began to wage war. —70

The bows clattered and the swords struck, there was great knocking on the shields and the swords falling on them performed the rite of love. —71

All the warriors were absorbed in the war so much like the wrestlers in the wrestling arena,

The arrows were showered and there was the crackling of the bows. —72

Wishing for their victory, the demons showered their arrows,

Subahu and Marich, knocking their teeth in fury, marched forward. —73

Both of them together pounced upon Ram like a falcon, They surrounded Ram like the Cupid (Kamdev) surrounding the Moon. —74

Ram was surrounded by the forces of demons like Shiva by the forces of Cupid (Kamdev),

Ram tarried there for war like Ganges on meeting the ocean. —75

Ram shouted so loudly in the war that the clouds felt shy,

The warriors rolled in dust and mighty heroes fell on the earth. —76

Subahu and Marich began to search for Ram, while twisting their whiskers,

And said, "Where will he go and save himself, we will catch him just now." —77

Seeing the enemies Ram became persistent and serious and the eyes of that knower of the science of archery, reddened. —78

The bow of Ram raised a terrible sound and showered a volley of arrows,

The armies of the enemies were being destroyed, seeing which the gods smiled in heaven. —79

Marich saw his army running away, and challenged his forces in great ire like the rage of a snake. —80

Ram discharged his arrow towards Marich, who ran towards the sea,

He adopted the grab of a yogi, abandoning his kingdom and country. —81

He wore the garments of a yogi on forsaking the beautiful royal dress,

And abandoning all inimical ideas, he began to live in a cottage in Lanka. —82

Subahu marched forward alongwith his soldiers in great rage,

And in the war of arrows, he also heard the terrible sound. —83

In the bedecked forces, very swift horses began to run,

The elephants roared in all the four directions and infront of their roars, the thunder of clouds appeared very dull. —84

The knocking on the shields was audible and the yellow and red shields looked impressive,

BACHITTAR NATAK

The warriors began to rise holding their weapons in their hands, and there was a continuous flow of shafts. —85

The fire-shifts were discharged and the weapons, began to fall from the hands of the warriors,

The brave fighter saturated with blood appeared like the participants in a marriage party wearing red garments. —86

Many wounded people are roaming like a drunkard swinging in intoxication,

The warriors have caught hold of each other like a flower meeting the other flower joyfully. —87

The demon-king was killed and he attained his real form,

The musical instruments were played and listening to their sound, the clouds felt shy. —88

Many charioteers were killed and the horses began to roam in the battlefield unclaimed,

This war was so dreadful that even the meditation of Shiva was ruptured. —89

The resounding of the gongs, drums and tabors began,

The trumpets were sounded and the horses neighed. —90

Various sounds arose in the battlefield and there were knocking on the helmets,

The armours on the bodies were chopped and the heroes followed the discipline of Kshatriyas. —91

Ram was highly infuriated on seeing the continuance of the terrible war,

He chopped the arms of Subahu and killed him. —92

On seeing this, the frightened demons ran away and Ram thundered in the battlefield,

Ram lightened the burden of the earth and protected the sages. —93

All the saints were pleased over the victory,

The gods were worshipped and the discussion of Vedas began. —94

The *yajna* (of Vishwamitra) was complete and all the sins were destroyed,

On seeing this, the gods were pleased and began to shower flowers. —95

End of "The Description of the Story of the Killing of Marich and Subahu and also the Completion of yajna" in Ramavatar in Bachittar Natak.

Now begins the Description of the Swayamvara of Sita

RASAAVAL STANZA

The day of the *swayamvara* of Sita was fixed, who was extremely pure like *Gita*,

Her words were winsome like those of the nightingale, She had eyes like the eyes of the king of deer. —96

The chief sage Vishwamitra had heard about it,

He took with him Ram, the wise and beautiful young man of the country,

And went (to Janakpuri), the abode of righteousness. —97

"O dear Ram, listen accompany me there,

"The *swayamvara* of Sita has been fixed and the king (Janak) has called us." —98

"We may go there at day-dawn and conquer Sita,

"Obey my saying, now it is upto you." —99

"With your beautiful and strong hands, break the bow,

"Conquer and bring Sita and destroy all the demons." —100

He (the sage) went with Ram and the quiver (of Ram) seemed impressive,

They went and stood there, their delight extended extremely. —101

The women of the city look (towards Ram), they considered him Kamdev (Cupid) in reality,

The inimical participants comprehend him as an enemy and the saintly persons consider him a saint. —102

For children he is a boy, the kings consider him a king,

The ascetics look towards him as Shiva, with sustenance of air, and the bard considers him a weapon-wielder,

For the night he is the moon and for day he is the sun. —103

The Ganas marked him as Rudra and the gods saw him as Indra. —104

The Vedas comprehended him as Brahmin, the Brahmins considered him as Vyas,

Vishnu visualised him as the immanent Lord and Sita sees him as Ram. —105

Sita looks towards him as Ram, being pierced by Cupid's arrow,

She fell down swinging on the earth like a roaming drunkard. —106

She gained consciousness and arose like a great warrior,
She kept her eyes concentrated like that of a *chakori* (a hill bird) on the moon. —107

Both were attached to each other and none of them faltered,
They stood firmly like the warrior in the battlefield. —108

The messengers were sent in the fort who went swiftly like Hanuman, the son of wind god,
The bow was placed after showing it to the gathered kings. —109

Ram took it in his hand, the hero (Ram) was filled with pride,
He pulled it smilingly and broke it into two parts. —110

All the gods were pleased and a lot of flowers were showered,
Other kings felt shy and went back to their countries. —111

Then the princess, the most fortunate in three worlds, garlanded Ram and wedded him as her spouse. —112

BHUJANG PRAYAAT STANZA

Sita appeared like the daughter of a god or Indra, daughter of a Naga, daughter of a Yaksha or daughter of a Kinnar,
She looked like the daughter of a Gandharva, daughter of a demon or goddess,
She appeared like the daughter of sun or also like the ambrosial light of the moon. —113

She appeared like a Gandharva woman, having obtained the learning of Yakshas or a complete creation of *ragini* (musical mode),
She looked like a Golden puppet or the glory of a beautiful lady, full of passion. —114

She appeared like a puppet exquisite as a portrait,
She was either Sankhani, Chitrani or Padmini (different gradations of a woman),
She looked like Ragmala, studded completely with Ragas (musical modes),
And Ram wedded such a beautiful Sita. —115

Having been absorbed in love both are staring at each other like the deer bound in love for each other,
Sita of sweet speech and slim waist and visually absorbed with Ram, is looking exquisitely beautiful. —116

When Parashuram heard this that Ram hath conquered Sita,
He at that time in great ire held up his arms and weapons,
He asked Ram to stop there and challenged him saying, "I shall now see, what type of hero thou art." —117

Bhasha Pingal ki (The Language of Prosody)

SUNDARI STANZA

The warriors raised loud shouts and the terrible trumpets resound,
There were war cries in the battlefield and the warriors, being pleased began to hurl their shields up and down. —118

The warriors with twined whiskers gathered together for war and fought with each other discharging dreadful shower of arrows,
The fighters drenched with blood began to fall and the horses were being crushed in the battlefield. —119

The sound of the drums of yogins was being heard, and the double-edged dagger glistened,
The warriors were mumbling and falling as martyrs and the heroes, wearing armours were rolling in dust. —120

The brave fighters thundered and the warriors wearing steel armours, being intoxicated began to dance,
The terrible trumpets resounded and the warriors with dreadful whiskers began to fight in the war. —121

The chopping heroes were jumping like the winged mountains the warriors were fighting with each other while twisting their whiskers,
The brave soldiers wearing armours and lying down on the earth. —122

The trumpets resounded upto distant places and the heroes began to run hither and thither,
The heavenly damsels began to roam in the sky and bedecking themselves and putting collyrium in their eyes, they began to see the war. —123

The thundering musical instruments were played in the war and the brave soldiers roared,
The warriors holding their spears in their hands began to strike them, the arms and weapons of the warriors were put to use. —124
The wounded warriors fell down and their bodies were chopped,
The armies thundered and the trumpets resounded; the restless horses neighed in the battlefield. —125
The vultures shrieked on all the four sides and they began to reduce already chopped bodies into bits,
In the jungle of that battlefield they began to play with the bits of flesh and the adepts and yogins wished for victory. —126
Just as the flowers blossom in the spring, in the same manner are seen the mighty warriors fighting in the war,
The trunks of the elephants began to fall in the battlefield and the whole earth was filled with hecked heads. —127

MADHUR DHUN STANZA

Parashuram, who had abandoned his desires created a sensation in all the four direction and began to discharge arrows like the brave fighters. —128
Observing his fury, the man of wisdom, meditated on the Lord and began to repeat the name of Lord, trembling with fear. —129
Agonised by extreme rage, the intellect was destroyed,
A stream of arrows flowered from his hands and with them the life-breath of opponents was removed. —130

MADHUR DHUN STANZA

Holding their arrows in their hands and filled with pride, the warriors are imposing them in the hearts of the enemies like the hoeing of the earth by the gardener. —131
All trembled on account of the fury by the warriors and because of their activities in respect of warfare, the masters of the horses were being destroyed. —132
Every limb of the warriors was pierced by arrows and Parashuram began to shower a volley of his arms. —133
He who advances to that side goes straight to the feet of the Lord (i.e., he is killed),
Hearing the knocks on the shields, the god of death came down. —134
The superb enemies were killed and the eminent arrows were destroyed on the bodies of the enduring warriors. —135
The eminent persons were destroyed and the remaining sped away, they respected Shiva's name and created confusion. —136
Parashuram, the wielder of axe had power to destroy all in the war, his arms were long. —137
The brave fighters struck blows and the rosary of skulls on the neck of Shiva looked impressive,
Ram stood firmly and within the whole palace, there was turmoil. —138

CHARPAT CHHIGA KE ADIKRIT STANZA

In the use of the sword the noteworthy and greatly wise persons are being seen; those with beautiful bodies are wearing armours which seem like portraits. —139
Those who are specialists in arms and scholars of Shastras and also the famous warriors are busy in warfare in great rage. —140
The eminent warriors are filling others with fear; wearing their armours they are destroying the enemies. —141
The brave fighters, piercing the armours are boring the bodies with the use of arms, the canopies of the kings are being destroyed. —142
Those who know the secrets of arms and weapons, they marched towards the battlefield. —143
The warriors wandered in the battlefields like the gardeners of the forest who prune the plants, they began to destroy the reputation of the heroes,
In that battlefield the beautiful Ram, who is the abode of righteousness is looking glorious. —144
He is a hero with the quality of forbearance, he is the destroyer of warriors, conqueror of war and eminently specialist in the use of weapons. —145
He has the giant of an elephant and an abode of *dharma*,

He is the master of yoga-fire and protector of the supreme light. —146

The Speech of Parashuram

Wearing his bow and quiver, the Brahmin Parashuram in great rage said to Ram, "O the breakers of the bow of Shiva and the conqueror of Sita, who are you? Tell me the truth otherwise you will not be able to save yourself and you will have to bear the blow of the sharp edge of my axe on your neck. It will be appropriate, if you leave the war-arena and run away to your home, otherwise if you stay here for another instant, you will have to die." —147

SWAYYA

You know that no mighty warrior can stay here firmly on seeing me; those whose fathers and grandfathers held the blades of grass within their teeth on seeing me (i.e., they accepted defeat) what type of war will they wage with me now? Even if there is wage a terrible war now, how can they be bold enough now to march forward for war by taking hold of their weapons again? —148

Speech of Poet

Hearing these words of the enemy (Parashuram), Ram looked like a mighty hero, visualising the serene posture of Ram, exhibiting the serenity of seven seas the mountains, sky and the whole world trembled. The Yakshas, Nagas, gods and demons of all the four directions were frightened. Getting hold of his bow in his hand Ram said to Parashuram, "On whom you have stretched this arrow in anger?" —149

Speech of Parashuram Addressed to Ram

O Ram! Whatever you have said, you have said and now if you say anything further, then you will not remain alive, the weapon that you had to wield, you have wielded and if you try to wield anything more, your effort will be of no avail. Then getting furious Parashuram said to Ram, "Say, where will you run away now from war and how will you save your life? O Ram! breaking the bow of Shiva and now wedding Sita, you will not be able to reach your home." —150

Speech of Ram Addressed to Parashuram

SWAYYA

"O Brahmin! You have also said, whatever you wanted to say and if you say anything more now, you will have to risk your life. O fool! Why do you speak with such pride, you will have to go now to your home after getting your teeth broken and after receiving good threshing, I am seeing you with patience. If I consider it necessary, then I shall have to discharge only one arrow. Therefore, talk with restraint, otherwise you will receive the reward for such talk just now." —151

Speech of Parashuram

SWAYYA

You should then dream it true that if you are called Ramavatar, then the way you have broken the bow of Shiva, show me your strength in the same way. Show me your mace, discus, bow and also the mark of the stroke of the foot of sage Bhrigu. Alongwith this dismount my mighty bow and pull its string. —152

Speech of Poet

SWAYYA

Ram, the supreme hero took the bow in his hand smilingly, pulled its string and tightening the arrow, broke it into two pieces. On breaking, the bow produced such a dreadful sound as if the arrow had struck the chest of the sky which had burst. The manner in which the dancer jumps on the rope, in the same way the whole universe shook on the breaking of the bow and remained entangled, within the two pieces of the bow. —153

End of "The Description of Ram's Victory in War" in Ramavatar in Bachittar Natak.

Now begins the Description of the Entry in Oudh

SWAYYA

With tears of joy in both his eyes and meeting affectionately with his people Ram entered Ayodhya,

The black bees were humming on the cheeks and the braids of long hair of Sita were hanging like the Nagas looking towards her face,
The lotus, deer, moon, lioness and nightingale were perplexed in their minds on seeing her (eyes, agility, beauty, courage and sweet voice respectively),
The children, seeing her beauty also were falling unconscious and the travelling abandoning their path, were looking at her. —154

Sita was getting worried or reflecting whether Ram will agree with her sayings or not and also whether it can happen that Ram may wed another woman like wedding me on breaking the bow of Shiva,
If he thinks of another marriage in his mind, then her Lord on forgetting her, will fill her life definitely with unrest,
Let us see what is recorded in my fate and what he will do in future? —155

At the same time, the groups of Brahmins came forward and began to sing songs of felicitations,
Hearing about the victory of Ram in the war, all the people ran hither and thither in joy,
When Dasrath came to know that after conquering Sita. Ram has also conquered the war, then his delight know no bounds and he showered the wealth like the rain of clouds. —156

The door of all the subjects were bedecked with greetings and the sandalwood was sprinkled over all the houses,
Saffron was sprinkled over all the companions (of Ram) and it seemed that Indra was entering his city,
The drums and other musical instruments resounded and the dances of various kinds were arranged,
All the people advanced to meet Ram as the father Dasrath took his son with him reached Oudhpuri (in his palaces). —157

CHAUPAI

With great enthusiasm the marriage of the three remaining sons was fixed,
After the marriage of Ram and Sita, the congratulating messages were received from various countries, when they returned to their home. —158

There was atmosphere of zest on all sides and the arrangements were being made for the celebration of the marriage of three sons,
On all sides the drums resounded in various tunes and many companies of dances began to dance. —159

The warriors decorated with armours and the youthful soldiers marched forward,
All these great charioteers and archers come and stood at the gate of the king Dasrath. —160

Many types of musical instruments sounded and the melodious sounds of the drums were heard.
The energetic women began to sing and reveal their joy by dancing their eyes and clapping their hands. —161

The beggars had no more desire for wealth because the gifts of gold flow like a stream,
Anyone who asked for one thing, he would return to his home with twenty things. —162

The sons of king Dasrath playing in the forest appeared like the flowers bloomed in spring season,
The saffron sprinkled on the hands appeared like the bliss gushing forth from the heart. —163

They are gathering their limitless fourfold army like the gushing forth of the Ganges,
With their armed forces the princes appear glorious like millions of suns in the sky. —164

All the brothers alongwith Bharat seem in such splendour what cannot be described,
The beautiful princes are alluring the minds of their mothers and appear like the sun and moon born in the house of Diti, increasing its magnificence. —165

In this way the beautiful wedding-parties were embellished, which are indescribable.
By saying all this the volume of the book will be increased,
And all these children moved towards the palace of their father for getting his permission to depart. —166

They all came and bowed before their father and stood there with folded hands,
The king was filled with joy on seeing his sons and he gave many things in charity to the Brahmins. —167

Hugging their children to their bosom the parents felt great pleasure like a poor man on acquiring the gems,
After taking permission for departure they reached the palace of Ram and bowed their heads on his feet. —168

KABIT

Ram kissed the heads of all and placed his hand on their back with love,
He presented with betel leaf etc., and affectionately bade them farewell,
Playing on the drums and the musical instruments all the people moved as if millions of suns and moons have manifested on the earth,
The garments saturated with saffron are looking splendid as if the beauty itself has materialised,
The princes of Dasrath the king of Oudh, appear splendid like the god of love alongwith his arts. —169

KABIT

All have moved out of Oudhpuri and all of them taken alongwith them the winsome warriors, who never retrace their steps in war,
They are beautiful princes, bedecked with necklaces around their necks,
They are all going to bring their wedded women,
They are all the mashers of the tyrants, capable of conquering the three worlds, lovers of the name of the Lord and brothers of Ram. They are magnanimous in wisdom, the incarnation of embellishment, the mountain of magnificence and are just like Ram. —170

The Description of Horses

KABIT

The horses, restless like the eyes of a woman, swift like the swift utterances of a shrewd person and mercurial like the crane rising up in the sky, are vibrating hither and thither,
They are swift like the feeling of a dancer, they are the tactics of throwing the dice or even some hallucination,
These brave horses are swift like arrow and gunshot, shrewd and mighty like Hanuman, the son of Anjani, they are roaming like the fluttering banners,

These horses are like the intense emotions of the god of love, or the swift waves of the Ganges,
They have beautiful limbs like the limbs of Cupid and are not stay at anyone place. —171
All the princes are being considered as moon by the night and sun by the day, they are known as great donors for the beggars, the ailments consider them as medicine,
When they consisting of endless beauty are nearly, then there is suspicion about their impending separation,
They are all most honourable like Shiva,
They are famous swordsmen, childlike for their mothers, the supreme knowledgeable for great sages, they appear apparently like providence,
All the Ganas consider them Ganesh and all the gods as Indra,
The Sun and substance is this that they manifest themselves in the same form as one thinks about them. —172
Having bathed in ambrosia and the manifestation of beauty and glory, these very winsome princes appear as having been created in special mould,
It seems that in order to allure some most beautiful damsel, the Providence created these great heroes in a special way,
They appear as having been taken out as gems by churning the ocean by the gods and demons on abandoning their disputes, or it seems that the Lord of the universe made improvement in the creation of their faces Himself for having their continuous sight. —173
Crossing the frontier of their kingdom and passing through other countries, all these princes reached the abode of king Janak of Mithila,
On reaching there they caused the high-pitch resonance of the drums and other musical instruments,
The king came forward and hugged all the three to his bosom,
All the Vedic rites were performed and there was continuous charitable flow of wealth and on acquiring the alms, the beggars become king like. —174
The banners were unfurled and the drums resounded, the brave heroes began to shout loudly on reaching Janakpuri,

Somewhere the wishes are being swung, somewhere the minstrels are singing eulogies and somewhere the poets are reciting their beautiful stanzas,
Somewhere the lyre is being played, somewhere flute, drum and other musical instruments,
On seeing all this the god of love is feeling shy and so much charity was donated that the beggars feel satisfy, the poor became king-like and began to give blessings,
After receiving alms, no tendency for begging was left. —175
Janak came and hugged all the three to his bosom and honoured them in various ways,
The Vedic discipline was observed and the Brahmins recited the congratulatory Vedic *mantras*,
The king gave the gift of gold to each Brahmin, The princes were given presents and there shower of gems,
The white elephants and the brisk horses of Sindhu were presented to the princes,
In this way all the three princes moved back after their wedding. —176

DODHAK STANZA

After marrying the daughters of king Janak the princes soon asked for permission to depart,
The group of kings accompanied by elephants and horses, having many desires in their mind, started (for back journey). —177
The dowry was given in such a great measure that even the Brahmins could not keep the same collectings,
Many types of horses and the thundering elephants in many garbs started moving. —178
The sound of fifes resounded and the mighty warriors thundered,
When Oudhpuri, was nearby, then all were welcomed by Ram. —179
The mothers drank water after its propitiatory offering to princes and the king Dasrath was highly pleased in his mind on seeing this splendour,
On seeing the princess, the king hugged them to his bosom and all the people entered the city while dancing and singing. —180
When the princes came home after their marriage, then many kinds of congratulatory songs were sung,
Dasrath called Vashistha and Sumanta and with them came several, other sages. —181
At that time the clouds gathered on all the four sides and all saw apparently the flames of fire in all the four directions,
On seeing this all the ministers and friends became worried and requested the king in the following manner. —182
"O king! There are many cases of providingly wrath (tumult) on all the four sides, therefore give thought to them by calling all the sages and advisers,
Call the Brahmins without delay and begin Krit *yajna*." —183
"O king! In view of the great wisdom of friends and ministers give instant orders for starting the Krit *yajna* without delay." —184
The king called the eminent sage and great friends soon,
The sacrificial pit was dug up there and a pillar of righteousness was established. —185
A horse was let off from the stable so that ending the glory of other kings they may be conquered,
The king of several countries were sent alongwith the horses and all of them were persons of beauteous limbs and the enhancer of glory. —186

SAMANKA STANZA

The king Dasrath made selection of other efficient kings and sent them with the horse and they went having been completely embellished,
These brave man were of very gently demeanour. —187
They roamed in several countries both inland and foreign and at all the places they destroyed (the pride of) all with the blaze of their glory,
They caused their horse to revolve on all the four sides and in this way they enhanced the royal prestige of king Dasrath. —188
Many kings bowed at his feet and he removed all their agonies, He completed his *yajna* and in this way destroyed the anguish of his subjects. —189
Receiving the gifts of many kinds and giving the blessings of various kinds and singing the Vedic *mantras*, the Brahmins pleased and

satisfied in their mind, they moved back to their places. —190

The kings of the inland and foreign countries decorated themselves in various garbs and noticing the significant glory of the warriors the beautiful and enlightened women were allured towards them. —191

Millions of musical instruments were played and all the bedecked persons were full of love,

The idols of gods were established and all were bowing with respect to the gods, expressing their gratitude. —192

All the people prostrated and bowed at the feet of gods and were assuming significant emotions in their minds,

There was recitation of *mantras* and *yantras* and idols of Ganas were being fixed. —193

Beautiful women and heavenly damsels began to dance,

In this way there was the sway of Ram-rajya and there was no dearth of anything. —194

SARASWATI STANZA

On one side the Brahmins are teaching about the activities of various countries,

And on the other side the methods of archery an being revealed,

Instructions are being given about various types of the embellishment of women,

The art of love, poeting, grammar and Vedic learning are being taught side by side. —195

The incarnation of Ram of the clan of Raghu is extremely pure,

He is the destroyer of tyrants and demons and is thus the support of the life breath of the saints,

He has subordinated the kings of various countries by conquering them, and his banners of victory are fluttering here, there and everywhere. —196

After discussing for a long time with Vashistha, the king gave his three sons the kingdoms of three directions and gave Ram the kingdom of his capital Ayodhya,

There lived a demoness in the house of Dasrath in disguise who had asked for all this activity the fructifying mango dust, pure water of the stream and many flowers. —197

Four adorned salvers containing saffron, sandalwood etc., were kept with the king for the fulfilment of this function,

At the same time Brahmin sent a Gandharva, woman named Manthra to the palace who embellished with all kinds of arts and wearing white garments started very quickly. —198

She was surprised to listen to the sound of lyre, drum and other musical instruments and also saw on that wide plain the sound having the victory of Ram-rajya was being heard,

Going near Kaikeyi she addressed her in this way: "When the opportunity will go out of hand, then for whom you will ask for the boons." —199

When Kaikeyi heard all the account, she was completely full of anguish and fell down unconscious on the earth like the one pierced by an arrow,

Going in the presence of the king of Oudh, she said this, "O king! You had promised to grant me two boons, grant them to me just now." —200

"Give exile to Ram and your kingdom to my son, give him (Bharat) the kingdom, wealth, whisk and canopy—everything, when you will grant me the ruling power over the inland and foreign countries, then I shall consider you the observer of truthfulness and recognisor of righteousness." —201

The king replied, "O sinful woman! What approbation you will gain by sending Ram to the forest,

By such surpassing utterance of yours the ash of magnificence on my forehead has flown down with the upcoming perspiration,"

The king taking his bow in his hand said this angrily, "I would have chopped and thrown you just now and destroyed you, but I let you go because you are a woman." —202

NAGSWAROOPI STANZA

"The superb god amongst men is Ram who is containing the abode of *dharma*, O foolish woman! Why are you uttering such contrary words."—203

"He is unfathomable and infinite god and is highly seated beyond all elements,

He is merciful and kind towards all and mercifully gives support to helpless and ferries them across." —204

"He is the saviour of many saints and is the basic cause of the gods and demons, He is also the king of gods and is the story of all powers." —205

The queen said, "O king! Grant me the boons and fulfil thy saying,

"Abandon the position of duality from your mind and do not fail in your promise." —206

NAGSWAROOP ARDH STANZA

"O king! Do not hesitate and run away from your promise, give exile to Ram." —207

"Bid farewell to Ram and take back the proposed rule from him,

"Do not run away from your promise and be seated peacefully." —208

"O king! Call Vashistha and the royal priest and send Ram to the forest." —209

The king heaved a long sigh, moved hither and thither and then fell down. —210

The king again came to his senses from the stupor and grievously heaved a long breath. —211

UGAADH STANZA

With tears in his eyes and anguish in his utterance, the king said Kaikeyi, "You are a mean and evil woman." —212

"You are a blemish on womenkind and a store of vices, you have no shame in your eyes and your words are ignominious. —213

"You are evil woman and are the destroyer of enhancement,

"You are performer of evil deeds and shamelessness in your *dharma*. —214

"You are the abode of Shamelessness and a woman forsaking hesitation (shyness),

"You are the performer of misdeeds and destroyer of glory." —215

"O shameless woman! You are the doer of evil acts, impiety incarnate and store of vicious works. —216

"O the baskets of sins! Evil doer, you do not die even we wish you to die, you are the performer of misdeeds." —217

The Speech of Kaikeyi

"O king! Accept my saying and remember your words, 'whatever you have promised, grant me two boons according to that'." —218

"Remember rightly and give whatever you have said, 'do not forsake your *dharma* and do not shatter my trust.' —219

"Call Vashistha, your unique spiritual head, order the husband of Sita for his exile." —220

"Do not cause any delay in this task and accept my saying, 'Making Ram a sage, turn him out of the house'." —221

(The poet says) she was stubborn like a child and verged on madness,

She did not keep silent and was continuously speaking. —222

She was worthy of reproach and store of mean acts,

She was evil tongued queen and the cause of weakening the strength of the king. —223

She got the ouster of Ram, who was the pillar (support) of the house,

And in this way she performed the evil act of killing her husband. —224

UGAATHA STANZA

(The poet says that the woman) conquered the unconquerable, destroyed this indestructible, broke the unbreakable and (with her blaze) reduced to ashes the indeclinable, she has slandered him who cannot be columniated, she has given a blow to him who cannot be harmed, she has deceived him who is beyond deception and disjoined the compact one. —225

She has engrossed the detached one in actions and her vision is so sharp that she can see providence, She can caused the unpunishable to be punished and uneatable to be eaten, She has fathomed the unfathomable and has destroyed the indestructible; She has broken the unbreakable and has made the immovable as her vehicles. —226

She has dyed the dried one, blazed the incombustible,

She has destroyed the indestructible and has moved the immovable,

She has disjoined the compact one and has punished the unpunishable,

She can do whatever is not to be done and can corroborate the irrefortable. —227

She has blemished the unblemishable and has stained the pure one, she has made thieves and thugs the persons who are never deceptive, She has discriminated the indiscriminate and has broken the unbreakable, she has covered the nacked ones and united the disjoined. —228

She has burnt the incombustible and can bend the unbendable,

She has pulled the unpullable and has united the disjointed, she has taken out those which can never be taken out and fashioned the unfashionable, she has wounded the unconquerable and has entrapped those who cannot be entrapped. —229

She preforms all forbidden works and she protects all vicious acts, she create, the sense of friendship in detached ones and the stable ones run away when they face her, she tease the peaceful person and reveals a very mysterious one, she conquers the unconquerable and kills those cannot be killed. —230

She rips and breaks the hardest one, she establishes the unestablished and tears that which cannot be torn, she drives the immovable and makes a leper of a healthy person, she engages herself in battle with the mighty ones and with whomsoever suppressed strong person, she fights, she lays obstruction in their art of war and finishes them. —231

She has defeated the mighty ones and injures the invincible, she crushes those who cannot be crushed, she deceives the undeceivable, she frightens the fearless and destroys the indestructible, she breaks the unbreakable and turns into those of healthy bodies. —232

She routes those who take a stand and pulls down those who are firm and stable, she breaks the unbreakable and ride, over many, making them her slaves, she deceives those who are undeceivable and makes the chaste ones licencious; the house in which the woman has the upper hand, how can there be peace? —233

DOHIRA

In this way Kaikeyi persisted in her demand for boons from the king, the king became greatly agitated, but because of the attachment with the winsome wife and under the impact of the god of love (Kamdev), he could not say anything. —234

The king in many ways, holding the feet of the queen, tried to back out from his promise, but that woman, showing her weakness (if fair sex), persisted in her demand and did not accept any request of the king. —235

"I shall not leave you without getting the boons, though you may make millions of efforts. Give the kingdom to my son and exile Ram." —236

Hearing these words of his wife the king became unconscious and fell down on the earth like a lion pierced by arrow in the forest. —237

Hearing about the exile of Ram the king writhed and fell down on the earth like the spinning of the fish out of water and breathing her last. —238

Hearing again the name of Ram the king came to his senses and stood up like a warrior becoming unconscious and falling in war and standing up again holding his hand after becoming conscious. —239

The king accepted death rather, than the abandonment of his *dharma* and the boons, which he had promised he granted them and exiled Ram. —240

The Speech of Kaikeyi and the King Addressed to Vashistha

DOHIRA

Exile Ram and give the kingdom to Bharat, After fourteen years Ram will again become the king. —241

Vashistha said the same thing to Ram in an improved way that for fourteen years Bharat shall rule and after that you will be the king. —242

Listening to the words of Vashistha, Ram (Raghuvir) left with a sad heart,

And on this side, the king not enduring the separation of Ram, breathed his last. —243

SORATHA

On reaching his palace Ram gave all his wealth in charity and binding his quiver to his waist he said to Sita. —244

O wise Sita! You stay with Kaushalya and I shall rule again alongwith you after exile. —245

Speech of Sita Addressed to Ram
SORATHA

I cannot forsake the company of my beloved even if I have to undergo a great suffering,
For this undoubtedly if my limbs are chopped, I shall not turn back a little and shall not deem it an anguish. —246

Speech of Ram Addressed to Sita
MANOHAR STANZA

O lady of slim waist! If you do not like to stay with your in-law then I shall send you to your father's house,
And I shell make the arrangements that you like, there shall be no objection in my heart,
If you want to have some wealth, then tell me clearly,
I shell give you wealth according to your wishes,
O lady of beautiful eyes! There is only a time factor, if you agree, I shall give in charity to the poor a city full of riches like the city of Lanka. —247

O Sita! The forest life is full of troubles and you are a princess you may tell me, how will you carry on there,
The lions roar there, there are dreadful Kauls, Bhils, seeing whom one is frightened,
The serpents hiss there, the tigers thunder and there are also extremely agonising ghosts and fiends,
The Lord has made you a delicate one, think for a little while why should you go to the forest? —248

Speech of Sita Addressed to Ram
MANOHAR STANZA

If the thorns sting and the body pinched away, I shall endure the hardship of the thorn on my head,
If the tigers and serpents fell on my head, even then I shall not utter "oh or alas,"
For me the exile in the forest is good than the palace,
O beloved! I bow at your feet, do not joke with me at this sad hour, I shall have hope to return to our home if I shall be with you, but I shall not live here without you. —249

Speech of Ram Addressed to Sita

O Sita! I am telling you the truth that you will be able to serve your mother-in-law nicely while living in your home,
O doe-eyed! The time will pass away quickly, I shall, alongwith you,
If indeed, your mind does not feel at home in Oudh,
O winsome faced! You go to your father's house,
In my mind the instruction of my father abides, therefore you permit me to go to the forest. —250

Speech of Lakshman

This talk was going on when hearing it, Lakshman came with his bow in his hand said, "Who can be that undutiful son in our clan who has asked for exile of Ram? This foolish person (king pierced by the arrows of the god of love) entrapped in cruel misconduct, under the impact of a foolish woman is dancing like a monkey, understanding the signs of stick." —251

"Taking the stick of lust in her hand Kaikeyi is causing the king to dance like a monkey; that proud woman has caught hold of the king and sitting with him she is teaching him lessons like a parrot, this woman is riding over the heads of her co-wives like a god of gods and for a short while is making currency the coins of leather like the kings (she is behaving to her liking). This cruel, inferior, ill-disciplined, and ill-mouthed woman has not only caused resentment of the people here but has also lost any merit in the next world." —252

The people began to talk ill of both the king and the queen, "How can I live by forsaking the feet of Ram, therefore, I shall also go to the forests; the whole time has passed in seeking an opportunity to serve Ram and in this way the time will deceive all, I am telling the truth that I shall not stay at home and if this opportunity of service is lost, then I cannot avoid it." —253

Holding the bow in one hand and tightening the quiver and holding three-four arrows in the other hand both the brothers are looking impressive; the side on where the queens of the king of Oudh are residing, both these brothers went to that side, they bow before the mothers who hugging them with their bosoms said, "O son! You come with great hesitation when you are called, but now you have come today yourself."—254

Speech of Ram Addressed to the Mother

"The father has exiled me and now you permit us to depart for the forest, I shall come back on the fourteenth year after roaming in the forest stuffed with thorns for thirteen years, O mother! if I live, we shall meet again and if I die then for that purpose I have came to request you for forgiveness of my mistakes, on account of the boons granted by the king after residing in the forest, I shall rule again." —255

Speech of Mother Addressed to Ram

MANOHAR STANZA

When the mother heard these words, she clung to the neck of her son and said, "Alas, O Ram, the superb person of Raghu clan! Why are you going to the forest, leaving me here? The position which is felt by the fish on forsaking, water, she was in the same condition and all her hunger and thirst ended, she fell unconscious with a jerk and her heart felt scorching blaze. —256

"O son! I live only on seeing your face and Sita also remains pleased on visualising your divinity, on seeing the beauty of Lakshman, Sumitra remains pleased, forgetting all her sorrows," these queens seeing Kaikeyi and other co-wives and expressing their contempt felt pride on account of their self-respect, but see, today their sons are going to the forest, leaving them weeping like orphans. —257

There were many other people also who collectively laid emphasis on not allowing Ram to leave for the forest, but he did not agree with anyone. Lakshman also went to the palace of his mother in order to bid farewell to her, He said to his mother, "the earth is full of sinful acts and this is the opportune time to live with Ram. After hearing such words his mother fell down like the great and proud warrior who falls down with the blow of the spear and sleeps." —258

Which mean person her done this deed and said such things to Ram? He has lost his merit in this and the next world and who killing the king has thought about the acquisition of supreme comfort, the trust and rightful acts have flown away from the world and authentically there remains only the impiety, this demoness has put the clan to disgrace and she does not feel sorrow as the death of her husband. —259

Speech of Sumitra Addressed to Lakshman

"O son! Always like him a servant (with your brother) and consider Sita as your mother and her husband Ram as your father and always keep these rightful facts in your mind, endure all the troubles of the forest as comfort-like, think always of the feet of Ram and consider the forest as home and the home as forest." —260

The lotus-eyed Ram moved alongwith his brother to the forest,
On seeing this the gods were startled and the demons wondered,
And visualising the end of demons, Indra felt highly pleased,
The moon also being pleased began to spread his reflect on less the earth and being a resident within the sky, he became famous with the name of "Mayank." —261

DOHIRA

With the permission of his father Ram left his home for the forest,
And with him the doe-eyed Sita of infinite glory went. —262

End of "The Description of the Exile of Ram" in Ramavatar in Bachittar Natak.

Now begins the Description of the Exile

Speech about the Charm of Sita

BIJAI STANZA

She was looking like moon to *chakors* and lightning in clouds to the peacocks,
She appeared as Power-incarnate and the beauty of the sun at dawn to the intoxicated elephants,
To the gods she seemed like the destroyer of suffering and the performer of the religious activities of all kinds,

She appeared as the ocean to the earth, all pervading of all the directions and pure like Ganges to the Yogis. —263

DOHIRA

On that side leaving home alongwith Sita, Ram went to the forest and on this side in Ayodhyapuri whatever happened, the saints may listen to that. —264

Speech of the Mother
KABIT

They had taken all the comforts with them and giving us great agony, they have left us to see also the agony of the death of king Dasrath,

The king Ram, seeing and listening of all this, is not softening,

O Ram! Accept now whatever we say please tell, who is the survivor Lord, O Ram! Take the reins of kingdom and do all the work,

Tell us, why are you going now,

O exiled Ram in the garb of an ascetic and taking Janaki (Sita) with you, why are you giving me sadness? —265

I shall also put on the black garb leaving the country of the king, and becoming an ascetic, I shall accompany you,

I shall lower the family practice and abandon the royal splendour, but shall not turn my face away from you,

I shall wear the rings in the ear and smear the ashes over my body, I shall live in persistence, O my son! I shall forsake all the royal paraphernalia

I shall adopt the garb of a yogi, and leaving Kaushal (country), I shall go with the king Ram. —266

APOORAV STANZA

Ram, the abode of religious actions, went to the forest alongwith Lakshman and Janaki (Sita). —267

On that side, the father breathed his last and left for heaven in an air-vehicle of gods,

On this side, the ministers reflected on the situation. —268

The advice of Vashistha, the eminent Brahmin amongst all the Brahmins, was accepted,

A letter was written and sent to Magadh. —269

A very brief discussion was held and several fast-moving messages like Hanuman were sent. —270

Ten messengers, who were specialists in their work, were searched and sent to the place where Bharat resided. —271

Those messengers delivered the message and told that the king Dasrath had died, Bharat read the letter and accompanied them. —272

The anger blazed in his mind and the sense of *dharma* and respect disappeared from it,

They left Kashmir (and started on return journey) and began to remember the Lord. —273

The brave hero Bharat reached Oudh and saw the king Dasrath as dead. —274

Speech of Bharat Addressed to Kaikeyi

O mother! When you saw that the worst had happened and then you called your son,

You must be reproached, I feel ashamed. —275

How is it that you lost all sense of shame, that you have done such a bad deed,

I shall go now where Ram has gone. —276

KUSAM VACHITRA STANZA

The people residing in the forest know Raghuvir Ram and consider his suffering and comfort as their own,

Now I shall wear the rind of the tree and go to the forest and shall eat the forest fruit with Ram. —277

Saying this Bharat left his home and breaking the ornaments he threw them away and wear the bark-peel,

He performed the death ceremony of king Dasrath and left Oudh and concentrated in abiding at the face of Ram. —278

The forest dwellers seeing the strong army of Bharat, came alongwith the sages and reached, the place where Ram was staying,

Seeing the strong force Ram thought that some tyrants had come to attack, therefore he held the bow and arrows in his hands. —279

Ram taking his bow in has hand began to discharge arrows and seeing this Indra, sun etc., trembled with fear,

Seeing this the forest dwellers felt pleased in their dwelling places, but the gods of Amarpuri seeing this battle become anxious. —280

Then Bharat reflected in his mind that Ram was thinking of starting the battle, therefore he left all his forces, went forward alone and seeing Ram all his suffering ended. —281

When Bharat saw with his own eyes the mighty Ram, then abandoning all his desires, Bharat before him,

Seeing this, Ram realised that it was Bharat who had come leaving his capital. —282

Seeing Shatrughan and Bharat, Ram recognised them and it came into the mind of Ram and Lakshman that king Dasrath had left the world,

They abandoned their arrows and effacing their displeasure and came down from the mountain. —283

Leaving the army aside they hugged each other and wept,

The Providence had given them such agony that they had lost all comforts; Bharat said, "O Raghubir, abandon your persistence and return to your home, because for this very reason all the people had fallen at your feet." —284

Speech of Ram Addressed to Bharat
KANTH AABHUSHAN STANZA

O Bharat! Do not be obstinate, go to your home, do not give me more anguish by staying here; whatever permission has been given to me, I am acting according to that and accordingly I shell remain in the forest for thirteen years (and return in the fourteenth year). —285

I shall return after thirteen years and sit on the throne under a canopy, listen to my instruction and return home, your mothers must be weeping there. —286

Speech of Bharat Addressed to Ram
KANTH AABHUSHAN STANZA

O Ram! Where should I go now after touching your feet? Shall I not be ashamed I am extremely low, dirty and motionless, O Ram! Manage your kingdom and glorify it with your ambrosial feet. —287

Just as a bird became sightless fells down, in the same way Bharat fell down before Ram, At the same time Ram hugged him to his bosom and there Lakshman and all the brothers wept. —288

The brave Bharat was brought to his senses by giving water Ram again said smilingly, "After the elapse of thirteen years we shell return, now you go back because I have to fulfil some tasks in the forest." —289

When Ram said this, then all the people understood its substance (that he had to kill the demons in the forest). Submitting serviency to the instruction of Ram and with pleased mind Bharat took the sandals of Ram and forgetting the recognition of Ayodhya, he began to live out of its limits. —290

Wearing matted hair on his head he dedicated all the royal task, to these sandals. During the day he used to fulfil his royal duties with the support of those sandals and during the night, he protected them. —291

The body of Bharat withered and became decrepit but still he always kept the memory of Ram in his mind. Alongwith this he destroyed the groups of enemies and instead of ornaments he wore rosaries as necklaces. —292

JHOOTA STANZA

On this side the king Ram is doing the duties of gods by killing the demons, he looks like a mighty hero by taking the bow in his hand. —293

Where there were the tree of *saal* in the forest alongwith other trees and tanks etc., its glory seemed heaven-like and was the destroyer of all sorrows. —294

Ram stayed at that spot and looked like a mighty warrior, Sita was with him who was like a divine song. —295

She was a lady of sweat speech and her eyes were like the queen of deer,

She had a slim waist and she looked like a fairy, a Padmini (amongst women). —296.

JHOOLANA STANZA

Ram looks glorious with the sharp arrows in his hand and Sita, the queen of Ram appears elegant with the beautiful arrows of her eyes,

She roams, with Ram, being absorbed with such thought as if having been ousted from his capital Indra was staggering hither and thither,

The loose hair of her braids, causing shyness to the glory of Nagas, are becoming a sacrifice to Ram,

The deer looking at her are allowed by her, the fishes looking at her beauty are feeling jealous of her,

He, whoever has seen her, he has sacrificed himself for her. —297

The nightingale, listening to her speech is getting angry on account of jealousy and the moon looking at her face is feeling shy like women, the fish is allured by seeing her eyes and her beauty seems like the extension of sunlight,

Seeing her eyes they appear like the blossomed lotus and all the people in the forest are extremely enchanted by her beauty, O Sita! Seeing your intoxicated eyes Ram himself seems pierced by them. —298

Yours eyes are intoxicated, having been dyed in your love and it seems that they are the lovely roses. The narcissus flowers are expressing contempt with jealousy and the does on seeing her are feeling blows at their self-respect, the swine inspite of all its strength is feeling itself equivalent to the ardent passion of Sita in the whole world, her eyebrows are lovely like the bow and from those eyebrows she is discharging the arrows at her eyes. —299

KABIT

Where there are high *saal* trees and Banyan trees and the large tanks, who is the person who performs austerities and seeing whose beauty, the beauty of Pandavas seems devoid of radiance and the forests of heaven feel it better to keep silent on observing his beauty,

There is so much dense shade there that not to speak of the stars, the sky is also not seen there, the light of the sun and moon does not reach there, no god or demon lives there and the birds and even an ant has no access there. —300

APOORAV STANZA

Seeing the ignorant persons (Ram-Lakshman) as good food, a demon named Vivadh came forward and in this way there came a calamitous situation in their peaceful lives. —301

Ram saw him and holding his weapons, he went towards him keeping control of their weapons, both the warriors began their bath. —302

The vultures shrieked and the warriors faced each other, they were bedecked nicely and there was unending zeal in them. —303

There were horses and intoxicated elephants bedecked with armours, the shrieks of the vultures were heard and the warriors were seen entangled with each other. —304

The elephants serene like Sindhu were there and the trumpets were resounding, the long-armed warriors with unparalleled enthusiasm looked impressive. —305

The warriors who never fall, began to fall and also regain their control, there were egoistic attacks from all the four sides and the warriors blazed like embers. —306

The warriors were keeping their control and the weapons began to slip away from their hands like serpents. —307

ANOOP NARAAJ STANZA

The horses began to move and elephants roared, there was confusion on all the four sides, the musical instruments resounded and the harmonious sounds of the discharge of arrows was heard, the horses vied with one another in speed and the pure blood gushed out of the wounds. In the turmoil of the war, the corpses rolling in dust, scattered hither and thither. —308

Because of the blows of the sword being struck in the waists, the corpses were scattered and the warriors, turning with difficulty, began to strike blows with double-edged daggers, the Yogins while shrieking and taking the blood in their hands began to drink it, the Bhairavas roamed themselves in the fields and the fires of war blazed. —309

The jackals and big vultures roamed in the battlefield hither and thither, the vampires bellowed and the Baitals (ghosts) raised their shrill voice,

The white edged dagger in the hands of the Kshatriyas (Ram and Lakshman) was well placed in their hands like the lightning in the dark clouds. —310

The Yogins with the bowls were drinking blood and the kites were eating flesh, the warriors keeping control of their double-edged spears were fighting, while shouting at their composures they were shouting "kill, kill" and bearing the burden of their weapons, some warriors were there in the cities of gods (i.e., they had died) and some are chopping other warriors. —311

The warriors, hurling their blows, were roaming in intoxication like the ascetics performing austerities and swinging with their faces bent downward over the smoke, there is flow of arms and the broken limbs were falling down, the waves of the desire of victory are rising and the chopped flesh is falling. —312

The Aghori (Sadhus) seen pleased in eating the chopped limbs and the Siddhas and Rawalpanthis the demoness of flesh and blood have taken seats with postures, shouting "kill, kill" the warriors are falling with broken limbs and because of their bravery, they are being greeted. —313

The special sound of obstructing the blows on the shields is being heard, the mixed sound of the harp flute, drum, kettledrum etc., is creating a dreadful atmosphere, the beautiful sounds also tearing the tunes of the blows of different kinds of weapons are arising in the battlefield, somewhere the servitors are busy in prayers and somewhere the poets are reciting their compositions. —314

The sound of obstructing the shields and the sound of the striking swords and being heard and the sharp arrows destroying innumerable people are being discharged, the daggers and spears are producing rustling sound and the chopped dead heads, having rolled in dust, are scattered here and there. —315

The peculiar type of arrows, drawing pictures, are being discharged in the battlefield and the knocking of the spears in the shields is being heard, The armies are being mashed and the earth is getting hot (because of the hot blood), the dreadful sound is being heard continuously from all the four sides. —316

Sixty-four Yogins, shouting loudly, are filling their pots with colour and the heavenly damsels are moving on the earth in order to wed the great heroes, the heroes, bedecking themselves are wearing armours on their hands and the vampires are roaming in the battlefield, eating flesh and bellowing. —317

The loud voice of the goddess Kali, who drinks blood, and the sound of tabor are being heard, the dreadful laughter is being heard in the battlefield and the dust settled on armours is also being seen, the elephants and horses are creating noise on being struck with the blows of swords and abandoning their shyness and being helpless, they are running away from the war. —318

Having been bedecked with arms and weapons the warriors are busy in war and not being stick in the mud of shyness they are waging war, being filled with ire, the limbs and the bits of flesh of the warriors are falling on the earth like Krishna playing amongst *gopis* by throwing up the ball from this to that side. —319

The tabors and famous gestures of the vampires are being seen saw the dreaded sound of drums and fifes in being heard,

The terrible sound of big drums is being heard in the ears, the jingling of anklets and the sweet voice of flutes are also being heard in the battlefield. —320

The swift horses, are dancing and moving swiftly and with their gait they are creating coiled mars on the earth,

Because of the sound of their hoofs the dust is rising upto the sky and seems like the whirlpool in water. —321

The enduring warriors are fleeing with their honour and life-break and the lines of the elephants have been destroyed, the demons inimical to Ram, taking the blades of grass in their teeth, have uttered the words "Protect us" and in this way the demons named Vivadh has been killed. —322.

End of "The Description of Killing of the Demon Viradh" in Ramavatar in Bachittar Natak.

Now begins the Description regarding Entry in the Forest

DOHIRA

In this way killing Viradh, Ram and Lakshman, penetrated into the forest,

The poet Shyam has described this incident in the above mentioned way. —323

BACHITTAR NATAK

SUKHDA STANZA

The king Ram went to the hermitage of the sage Agastya and Sita was with him, who is the abode of *dharma*. —324

Seeing the great hero Ram, the sage advised him to kill all the enemies and remove the anguish of all the people. —325

In this way giving his blessings, the sage recognising the beauty and power of Ram dexterously in his mind, bade him farewell. —326

Ram, alongwith his winsome wife Sita and his brother moved fearlessly in the dense forest, forsaking all his anxieties. —327

With his sword tied by the waist and holding the arrows in his hand, the long armed heroes started for the bath at pilgrim station. —328

He reached on the bank of Godavari alongwith his heroic brother and there Ram put off his clothes and took a bath, thus cleansing his body. —329

Ram had a marvellous body, when he came out after bath, on seeing his beauty the officials of the place went to the royal lady Surapanakha. —330

They said to her, "Please listen to us O royal lady! Two strangers of unique bodies have came to our kingdom." —331

SUNDARI STANZA

When Surapanakha heard these words, she immediately started and reaching there, she considered all of them as Cupid incarnate and believed in her mind that no one equalled them in beauty. —332

Coming before Ram, without feeling ashamed, She said, "I have halted here because of your beauty and my mind is dyed with the dye of your intoxicated eyes." —333

Speech of Ram
SUNDARI STANZA

"You go to the place of my brother who will be bewitched on seeing your beautiful eyes, you can see that with me there is Sita of beautiful waist and in such situation how can I keep you in my house." —334

"She has abandoned the attachment towards her parents and is roaming with me in the forest, O beautiful lady! How can I forgive her, you go there where my brother is sitting." —335

Hearing these words of Ram, that lady, Surapanakha went there when Lakshman was sitting, when he also refused to wed her, then she was filled with great rage and went to her home after getting her nose chopped. —336

End of the chapter regarding "The Chopping of the Nose of Surapanakha" in Ramavatar in Bachittar Natak.

The beginning of the Description of the Battle with the Demons Khar and Dushan

SUNDARI STANZA

When Surapanakha went weeping near Ravana, then the whole demon-clan was filled with furry, the king of Lanka called his ministers for consultations and sent two demons Khar and Dushan for killing Ram etc. —337

Wearing their armours all the long-armed warriors marched forwards with the resounding of musical instruments and the roaring of elephants,

There was noise of "kill, kill" from all the four sides and the army gushed forward like the clouds of the month of Sawan. —338

The mighty warriors thundered and stood firmly on the ground,

The pools of blood flourished and the warriors raised terrible shrieks. —339

TAARAKA STANZA

When the princes will begin the battle, there will be the dance of lances and shafts,

The warriors will roar on seeing the opposing forces, and Ram will be absorbed in the fighting mood. —340

There will be showers of arrows and the fighters will roam in the battlefield fearlessly, the tridents and arrows will be struck and the sons of demons will roll in dust. —341

They will discharge arrows, undoubtedly and destroy the forces of the enemy, the corpses will be scattered on the earth and the great warriors will uproot the trees. —342

The musical notes of fifes were played and the

persistent warrior began to roar like lions and roam in the fields,
The shafts were being taken out from quivers and the serpent like arrows were struck-like the messenger of death. —343

The warriors are spraying arrows fearlessly and are challenging one another,
They are discharging shafts and stones and are drinking in the hearts the poison of indignation. —344

The conquering warriors have fought with one another in the battle and are fighting furiously,
Both the god and demons are viewing the battle and are raising the sound of victory. —345

The Ganas and large vultures are roaming in the sky and the vampires are shrieking violently,
The ghosts are laughing fearlessly and both the brothers Ram and Lakshman are looking at this continued fight. —346

Ram caused both Khar and Dushan flow down in the stream of death after killing them,
The victory was greatly hailed from all the four sides, The gods showered the flowers and enjoyed the sight of both the victorious warriors Ram and Lakshman. —347

End of "The Story of the Killing of Khar and Dushan" in Ramavatar in Bachittar Natak.

Now begins the Description of the Abduction of Sita

MANOHAR STANZA

Hearing about the killing of Khar and Dushan the vile Ravana went to the house of Marich,
He held his weapons in all his twenty hands and was furiously muzzling his ten heads,
He said, "Those who have chopped the nose of Surapanakha, their such action has agonised me, I shall steal their wife in the garb of a yogi form the forest in your company." —348

Speech of Marich
MANOHAR STANZA

O my Lord! You had been very kind to come to my place,
My stores are overflowing in your arrival,
O my Lord! My house has become elegant, but with folded hands I request and kindly do not mind, this is my supplication that Ram is in reality an incarnation, do not consider him as a man like yourself. —349

Hearing these words, Ravana was filled with anger and his limbs began to burn, his face turned red and his eyes exhausted with anger,
He said, "O fool! What are you speaking before me and considering those two men as incarnations, their mother spike only once and their father indignantly sent them to the forest, Both of them are lowly and helpless. —350

"O fool! If I had not come to ask you for going there, I would have uprooted and thrown your matted hair and from the top of the golden citadel I would have thrown you in the sea and got you drowned," hearing these words and pinning in his mind and in anger, realising the gravity of the occasion, Marich left that place, he felt that the death and decadence of the vile Ravana is certain at the hands of Ram. —351

He transformed himself into a golden deer and reached at the abode of Ram, On the other side Ravana put on the garb of a yogi and went to abduct Sita, it seemed that the death was driving him there; seeing the beauty of the golden deer Sita came near Ram and said, "O the king of Oudh and the destroyer of demons! Go and bring that deer for me." —352

Speech of Ram

O Sita! No one has heard about the golden deer and even the Lord hath not created it, this is certainly the deceit of some demon who has caused this deception in you; seeing the affliction of Sita, Ram could not turned down her wish, he tied his quiver and left for bringing the golden deer, leaving behind Lakshman for Sita's protection. —353

The demon Marich tried to put Ram in uncertainty by running away at a high speed, but ultimately he was tired and Ram killed him, but at the time of death he shouted loudly in the voice of Ram, "O brother, save me when Sita heard this frightening voice, she sent the mighty Lakshman to that side, who before leaving drew a line and there as then Ravana came in." —354

Wearing the garb of a yogi and uttering the traditional invocation for alms, Ravana went near Sita like a *thug* visiting a wealthy person and said, "O doe-eyed! Cross this line and give me some alms" and when Ravana saw Sita crossing the line, he seized her and began to fly towards the sky. —355

End of the chapter entitled "Abduction of Sita" in Ramavatar in Bachittar Natak.

Now begins the Description about the Search for Sita

TOTAK STANZA

When Ram visualised in his mind about the abduction of Sita, he caught hold of his bow and arrows in his hands and sat down on a white rock,

He saw once again on all the four sides, but ultimately he fell down on the earth in disappointment. —356

His younger brother clasped him and raised him and said while cleansing his face, "O my Lord! Do not be impatient, keep your composure, ruminate on the fact where Sita has gone. —357

Ram got up but again swooned and came to consciousness again after sometime, He got up from the earth like a warrior slowly regaining consciousness in the battlefield. —358

He grew tired on shouting on all the four sides and experienced great anguish alongwith his younger brother,

He went to take bath early in the morning and with the impact of the heat of agony, all the creatures in the water were burnt down and reduced to ashes. —359

The direction to which Ram saw in his state of separation from his beloved, all the flowers and fruit as well as the trees of *palash* and the sky burnt with the heat of his vision, Whenever he touched the earth with his hands and the earth cracked like a brittle vessel with his touch. —360

The ground on which Ram rested, the *palash* trees (on that ground) were burnt down and reduced to ashes like the grass, the continuous flow of his tears evaporated on falling down on the earth like the drops of water falling on the hot plate. —361

Even the cold wind burnt when it touched his body and controlling its coolness and forsaking its patience, it merged into the pool of water, even there the leaves of lotus could not survive and the creatures of water, grass, leaves, etc., all were reduced to ashes with the heat of the state of separation of Ram. —362

On this side Ram was roaming in the forest in search of Sita, on the other side Ravana was surrounded by Jatayu, the persistent Jatayu did not yield in its fierce fighting even though its wings were chopped. —363

GEETA MATI STANZA

Ravana took away Sita after killing Jatayu, this message was communicated by Jatayu, when Ram saw towards the sky, on meeting Jatayu Ram came to know for certain that Ravana had abducted Sita roaming on the paths (of the forest) Ram met Hanuman and they both became friends. —364

Hanuman brought Sugriva; the king of monkeys to fall at the feet of Ram and all of them unitedly held consultation amongst themselves, all the ministers sat down and gave their personal views, Ram killed Bali, the king of monkeys and made Sugriva his permanent ally. —365

End of the chapter entitled "Killing of Bali" in Ramavatar in Bachittar Natak.

Now begins the Description of Sending of Hanuman in Search of Sita

GEETA MALTI STANZA

The army of monkeys was divided into four parts and sent in all the four directions and Hanuman was sent to Lanka,

Hanuman took the ring (of Rama) and immediately went crossed the sea, he reached the place where Sita was kept (by Ravana),

Destroying Lanka, killing Akshay Kumar and devastating Ashok Vatika, Hanuman came back and presented before Ram, the creation of Ravana, the enemy of gods. —366

Now combining all the forces they all proceeded (with millions of fighters) and there were mighty warriors like Ram, Sugriva, Lakshman, Sushen, Neel, Hanuman, Angad, etc., in their army,

The swarms of troops of the sons of monkeys gushed forward like clouds from all the four directions. —367

When after splitting the sea and forming a passage they all crossed the sea, then the messengers of Ravana fled towards him to convey the news, they requested him to get ready for war and protect the beautiful city of Lanka from the entry of Ram. —368

Ravana called Dhumraksha and Jambumali and sent them for war. Both of them shouting terribly reached near Ram,

Hanuman in great rage firmly stood on the earth on one foot and attacked violently with his second foot with which the mighty Dhumraksha fell down and died. —369

Then Jambumali fought in the war but he was killed in the same manner, the demons accompanying him sped towards Lanka to give the news to Ravana that both Dhumraksha and Jambumali had been killed at the hands of Rama, They requested him "O Lord! Now whatever please you, take any other measure." —370

Seeing Akampan near him, Ravana sent him alongwith the forces. On his departure, many kind of musical instruments were played, which resounded in the whole city of Lanka, The ministers including Prahasta held consultations and thought that Ravana should return Sita to Ram and not offend him more. —371

CHHAPPAI STANZA

The sound of musical instruments and the striking sound of the swords resounded and maditation of the ascetic was distracted by the horrible voices of the battlefield,

The warriors came forward after one another and began to fight one to one, there was such a terrible destruction that nothing could be recognised, the mighty forces alongwith Angad are being seen and the hails of victory began to resound in the sky. —372

On this side the crown prince Angad and on that side the mighty Akampan are not feeling tired of showering their arrows,

The hands are meeting hands and the corpses are lying scattered, the brave fighters are roaming and killing one another after challenging them, the gods are hailing them while sitting in their air-vehicles. They are saying that they have never seen such like horrible war earlier. —373

Somewhere the heads are being seen and somewhere the headless trunks are visible, somewhere the legs are withering and jumping and somewhere the vampires are filling their vessels with blood, somewhere the shrieks of vultures are being heard, somewhere the ghosts are shouting violently and somewhere the Bhairavas are laughing, in the way there was victory of Angad as he killed Akampan, the son of Ravana, on his death the frightened demons fled with the blades of grass in their mouths. —374

On that side the messengers gave the news of the death of Akampan to Ravana and on this side Angad the lord of monkeys was sent as envoy of Ram to Ravana, he was sent to tell Ravana all the facts and also advising him to return Sita in order to stall his death,

Angad the son of Bali went on his errand after touching the feet of Ram, who bade him farewell by patting on his back and expressing many types of benedictions. —375

Responsive Dialogue

CHHAPPAI STANZA

Angad says, "O ten-headed Ravana! Return Sita, you will not be able to see her shadow (i.e., you will be killed)," Ravana says, "None can conquer me even after the seizure of Lanka." Angad says again, "Your intellect has been spoiled by your rage, how will you be able to wage the war,"

Ravana replies, "I shall cause even today all the army of monkeys alongwith Ram to be devoured by the animals as jackals."

Angad says, "O Ravana do not be egoistic, this ego has destroyed many houses."

Ravana replies, "I am proud because I have brought under control all with my own power, then what power there two human beings Ram and Lakshman can wield." —376

Speech of Ravana Addressed to Angad
CHHAPPAI

The god of fire is my cook and the god of wind is my sweeper, the moon-god swings the fly whisk over my head and the sun-god wields the canopy over my head, Lakshmi the goddess of wealth serves drinks to me and Brahma recites the Vedic *mantras* for me, Varun is my water-carrier and pays obeisance in front of my family-god, this is my whole power-formation, besides them all the demon-forces are with me, for which reason the Yakshas etc., gladly present all types of their wealth to me, the person about whom you are talking both of them are very low and helpless men, how shell then they win the war. —377

Angad the monkey-chief advised Ravana several times, but he did not accept his advice,

When he got up, he firmly planted his foot in the assembly and moving his foot he challenged them to remove his foot (from the floor); none of the demons could do that and accepted defeat; many of them fell down unconscious because of their spent-up strength, that earthen-coloured Angad left the court of Ravana alongwith Vibhishana. When the demons tried to obstruct him, he routed and destroyed them and winning the battle in favour of Ram, he came to him. —378

Angad said on reaching, "O lotus-eyed Ram! The king of Lanka has called you for war at that time some curly looks of hair were waving and looking at the beauty of his anguished face, the monkeys who had been victorious over Ravana earlier, were highly enraged on listening to the words of Angad about Ravana, they marched towards the south in order to advance towards Lanka, when on this side Mandodari the wife of Ravana learnt about the scheme of Ram for making Vibhishana the king of Lanka, she fell down unconscious on the earth. —379

The Speech of Mandodari
UTANGAN STANZA

"The warriors are decorating themselves and the horrible battle drums are resounding, O my husband! You may flee for your safety because Ram has arrived, he, who had killed Bali, who has splitted the sea and create the passage, why have you created enmity with him, he, who has killed Viradh and Jambasura, it is the same power, which has manifested itself as Ram, return Sita to him and see him, this is the only wise thing do not try to introduce the coins of leather. —380

Speech of Ravana

Even if there is siege of army on all the four side and there may be the resonance of horrible sound of war-drums and millions of warriors may roar near me, even then I shell, on wearing my armour, destroy them within your sight, I shall conquer Indra and loot all the treasure of Yaksha and after winning the war, I shell wed Sita, if with the fire of my furry, when the sky, netherworld and heaven burn, then how Ram will remain safe before me? —381

Speech of Mandodari

He who has killed Taraka, Subahu and Marich and also killed Viradh, and Khar-Dushan and killed Bali with one arrow, he who has destroyed Dhumraksha and Jambumali in the war, he will conquer you by challenging you and kill you like a lion killing a jackal. —382

Speech of Ravana

The moon waves the fly whisk over my head, the sun catches hold of my canopy and Brahma recites Vedas at my gate, the god of fire prepares my food, the god Varuna brings water for me and the Yakshas teach various sciences, I have enjoyed the comforts of millions of heavens, you may see how I kill the warriors, I shell wage such as horrible war that the vultures will became happy, the vampires will roam and the ghosts and fiends will dance. —383

Speech of Mandodari

Look there, the swinging lances are visible, the terrible instruments are resounding and Ram has arrived with his mighty forces the sound of "kill, kill" is emanating from the army of monkeys from all the four sides, O Ravana! Till the time when the war-drums resound and the thundering warriors discharge their arrows, recognising the opportunity before that, accept my saying for the protection of your body (and leave the idea of war). —384

Obstruct the movement of the armies on the seashore and other routes, because now Ram has arrived, do all the work by removing the veil of heresy from your eyes and do not become self-willed. If your remain in distress, your family will be destroyed you can feel yourself protected till the army of monkeys does not begin its violent thunderings, after that all the sons of demons will flee, after jumping over the walls of the citadel and pressing the blades of grass in their mouths. —385

Speech of Ravana

O foolish prostitute! Why do you prattle? Stop the praises of Ram, He will only discharge very small arrows like incense-stick towards me, I shall see this sport today, I have twenty arms and ten heads and all the forces are with me, Ram will not even get a passage for running away, wherever I shall find him, I shall kill him there like a falcon killing a quail. —386

I shall search for each one and kill him and all of them will fall down on listening to my challenge wherever they will run to, I shall pursue them and reach there, they shall not be able to conceal themselves, after bedecking myself, I shell catch them today and my whole work will be accomplished by my men, I shall destroy the army of monkeys, I shall kill Ram and Lakshman and after conquering them, I shall break to pieces your arrogance. —387

Many things were said but Ravana paid a deaf ear to them and highly infuriated, he sent his sons to war-arena one of them was Narantak and the other Devantak, they were mighty warriors, on seeing whom the earth trembled the steel struck with steel and with the shower of arrows, there was splash of blood, the headless trunks writhed, the blood gushed out of the wounds and the corpses were scattered here and there. —388

The Yogins filled their bowls with blood and began to call out for the goddess Kali; Bhairvas began to sing songs with terrible sounds, the ghosts, fiend and other flesh-eaters clapped their hands, the Yakshas, Gandharvas, and Gods specialist in all sciences moved in the sky, the corpses were, scattered and on all the four sides the atmosphere was filled terrible din and in this way the terrible war made unique advancement. —389

SANGEET CHHAPPAI STANZA

The army of monkeys got infuriated and the terrible war-instruments resounded, there was the glitter of the swords and the warriors thundered like lions, seeing the warriors fighting with each other the sage Narada danced with joy, the stampede of the brave fiends became violent and alongwith it the war also grew in intensity, the warriors danced in the battlefield and the blood flowed from their bodies like the flow of poison from, the thousands of hoods of Seshanaga and they began to play Holi, the warriors sometimes recede like the hoods of serpents and sometimes strike while advancing forward. —390

There are splashes of blood on all the four sides and there seems to be a show of Holi, the vultures are seen in the battlefield, the corpses are lying scattered and the blood is gushing out of the bodies of the warriors, there is shower of the arrows and the glimmer of the swords is visible, the elephants are thundering and the horses are running amuck, the heads of the warriors are flowing in the stream of blood and there is glitter of the swords which are falling with sound like the lightning from the sky. —391

When Narantak fell down, Devantak ran forward and fighting bravely left for heaven, on seeing this the gods were filled with joy and there was anguish in the army of demons, the Siddhas (adepts) and saints, forsaking their yoga contemplated, began to dance, there was destruction of the army of demons and the gods showered flowers and the males and females of the city of gods hailed the victory. —392

Ravana also heard that both his sons and many other warriors had died while fighting, the corpses lie scattered in the battlefield and the vultures, while tearing away the flesh, are shrieking the streams of blood have flowed in the battlefield and the goddess Kali is raising horrible shouts, there has been a frightening war and the Yogins, having gathered for drinking blood, and having filled their bowls, they are shrieking violently. —393

End of the chapter entitled "The Killing of Devantak-Narantak" in Ramavatar in Bachittar Natak.

Now begins the Description of the War with Prahasta

SANGEET CHHAPPAI STANZA

Then Ravana sent innumerable soldiers with Prahasta for waging the war and the earth trembled under the impact of horses, hoofs, Neel entangled himself with him and threw him on the ground and there was great lamentation in the demon forces, the wounds were inflicted from which the blood oozed out and flowed, the gatherings of Yogins began to recite (their *mantras*) and the cowing of the crows was heard. —394

Fighting very bravely alongwith his forces, Prahasta advanced forward and with his movements the earth and the water felt a sensation, there was dreadful sound and the dreadful resonance of drums was heard, the lances glittered and the shining arrows were discharged, there was rattling of spears and with their blows on the shields the sparks arose such a knocking sound was heard as though a tinker was fashioning a utensil. —395

The shields sprang up and the warriors began to shout at each other, with one tone the weapons were struck and they rose high and then fell down, it appeared that the strange musical instruments and lyres were played in one tune the sound of the conches thundered all around, the heart of the earth beat and seeing the dreadfulness of war the gods also wondered and the Yakshas, Gandharvas, etc., began to shower flowers. —396

The warriors even falling down began to shout "kill, kill" from their mouths wearing their gauzy armours they appeared like the waving dark clouds, there was shower of maces and arrows and the heavenly damsels began to recite *mantras* in order to wed their deer warriors, the heroes remembered Shiva and died while fighting and on their falling down the heavenly damsels advanced to wed them. —397

BHUJANG PRAYAAT STANZA

On this side, there is dialogue between Ram and Ravana and on the other side the gods mounted on their chariots in the sky, are looking at this scene, all those warriors who are fighting in the battlefield, they can be described one by one in various ways. —398

Speech of Vibhishan Addressed to Ram

He, who has the spherical bow and on whose head the white canopy is rotating like a letter of victory and who is sitting on the lion-skin fearlessly in the chariot, O Lord, he is the persistent Indarjit (Meghnad). —399

He, with whose chariot there are brown horse and seeing whose broad body even the gods become fearful and who has mashed the pride of all the gods, he is known as broad-bodied Kumbhakaran. —400

The chariot with which the peacock-coloured horses are harnessed and who is showering arrows alongwith his shouts of "kill, kill," O Ram! His name is Mahodar and should he considered a very great warrior. —401

The chariot with which the white horses like the face are harnessed, and who in gait, put the wind to shame, and who seems like death (*kal*), catching hold of his arrows in his hand, O Ram! Consider him as Ravana, the king of demons. —402

He, on whom the fly whisk of the feathers of a peacock is being waved and before whom many people are standing in the position of salutation, and in whose chariot the smell bells of gold seem impressive and seeing whom the daughters of gods are getting enamoured. —403

In the centre of whose banner there is the sign of a lion, he is Ravana, the king of demons and has ill-will for the Ram in his mind, he on whose crown there are the Moon and the Sun, O all-filling Lord! Recognise him, he is the ten headed Ravana. —404

Many instruments began to resound from both sides and the warriors began to shower the current of great weapons, the arms were struck and the warriors fell and in this war this terrible headless trunks arose and moved. —405

The trunks, the heads and the trunks of elephants began to fell, and the chopped limbs of the groups of warriors rolled in dust, there were terrible noises and shouts in the battlefield and it appeared that having been intoxicated the warriors were swinging. —406

The wounded groups of warriors are swinging and being bewildered are falling on the earth and with double zeal they are getting up and striking with their maces, the warriors have begun the war in many ways, the chopped limbs are falling even then the warriors are shouting "kill, kill." —407

A dreadful sound is created with the discharge of arrows and the large-bodied warriors fall on the ground while swinging, all are dancing to the tune of music in the fighting and many are roaming hither and thither, becoming empty handed with the discharge of arrows. —408

The lances destroying the warriors are falling down and the unconscious headless trunks are dancing in the battlefield, the sixty-four Yogins have filled their bowls with blood and all the flesh-eaters are roaming with great joy. —409

The foppish warriors and beautiful horses are falling and on the other side the drivers of elephants are lying down with their dishevelled hair, the brave fighters are striking blows on their enemy with full strength, on account of which there is continuous flow of the blood. —410

Queer type of arrows, making beautiful paintings, are moving fastly while piercing the bodies and alongwith it the warriors are flying away in the air-vehicles of death, because of the falling arrows, the cluster of corpses are lying scattered and the gates of heaven have opened for the brave warriors. —411

DOHIRA

In this way, the army opposing Ram was killed and Ravana, sitting in the beautiful citadel of Lanka got highly infuriated. —412

BHUJANG PRAYAAT STANZA

Then, remembering the name of Shiva through his mind, speech and action, Ravana, the king of Lanka, sent his messengers to Kumbhakaran, all of them were without the strength of *mantra* and knowing about their impending end, they were remembering the one Beneficent Immanent Lord. —413

The warriors on foot, on horses, on elephants and in the chariots, wearing their armours, marched forward, they all penetrated into the nose and ears of Kumbhakaran and began to play their tabors and other musical instruments. —414

The warriors played their musical instruments which resounded at high pitch, all of them, like children fled in a state of perplexity, but even then the mighty Kumbhakaran did not awake. —415

Finding themselves helpless in not being able to awaken Kumbhakaran, all of them felt disappointed and started going away and became anxious on becoming unsuccessful in their endeavour, then the daughters of god began to sing songs, hearing which the enemy of gods i.e., Kumbhakaran awoke and took his mace in his hand. —416

That mighty warrior entered Lanka, where there was the mighty hero Ravana of twenty arms, bedecked with great weapons, they all held consultations together and talked to one another about the war. —417.

Kumbhakaran used seven thousand metallic pitchers of water to cleanse his face; he ate flesh to his fill and drank wine excessively, after all this that proud warrior got up with his mace and marched forward. —418

Seeing him the innumerable army of monkey fled away and many groups of gods became frightful, the terrible shouts of the warriors were heard and the truncated bodies paved by the arrows were seen moving. —419

BHUJANG PRAYAAT STANZA

The chopped trunk of the elephants is falling down

and the torn banners are swinging hither and thither; the beautiful horses are rolling down and the warriors are robbing in the battlefield, there is terrible lamentation in the whole field. —420

There are fast knocking of the blows, exhibiting the glitter of swords and it seems that the lightening is flashing in the month of Bhadon, the beautiful horses carrying warriors are neighing and the rosary of shields alongwith the sharp shafts look impressive. —421

VIRAAJ STANZA

A terrible war began in order to appease the goddess Kali and the Bhairavas began to shout; the vultures shrieked and the vampires beheld. —422

The bowls of Yogins were being filled and the corpses scattered; the clusters were destroyed and there was tumult all around. —423

The heavenly damsels began to dance and the bangles sounded, the shouts of "kill, kill" and the rustling of arrows were heard. —424

VIRAAJ STANZA

The warriors got entangled with one another and the fighters gushed forward; the tabors and other musical instruments were played in the battlefield. —425

RASAAVAL STANZA

There were blows of arms and the edges of the weapons were sharpened; the warriors repeated the shouts of "kill, kill" and the edges of the spears began to break. —426

There was continuous flow of the blood and it also spattered, the flesh-eaters smiled and the jackals drank blood. —427

The beautiful fly whiskers fell and on one side the defeated warriors ran away; there were repetitions of the shouts of "kill, kill" on the other side and the horse-riders fell. —428

On one side the horse-riders started moving and altogether made an attack, they drew out their weapons and began to wage a terrible war. —429

The striking sharp edges of the swords look impressive, the knockings on the shields and the collision of the swords create sparks, which are being seen by the gods from the sky. —430

He, on whom the warriors attack, they thrust on him the sharp edges of their arms; the shout of "kill, kill" is being raised and the warriors trembling with rage look impressive. —431

The great warriors have fought with one another and the armours are being torn by the arrows the arrows are being discharged with crackling sound and the tinkling sound is being heard. —432

There is shower of arrows and it appears that the whole world is absorbed in the war; the warriors are knocking their blows in fury over one another and are chopping (the limbs). —433

The fallen shields are being picked up and the forces of the enemy are being torn asunder; of the lances are overturning and being used miraculously. —434

Many people are lying down on the earth and many of those fallen down are getting up and being absorbed in the war, are excessively knocking and breaking their swords. —435

The warriors are fighting with warriors and are ripping them with their weapons; they are causing the weapons to fell down and inflicting wounds with their arms. —436

On this side the arrows are being discharged and on that side Kumbhakaran is doing his job of destroying the army, but in the end that brother of Ravana fell down like the tree of *saal*. —437

Both his legs cracked and form there came out the continuous flow of blood, Ram saw that mighty tyrant fallen down. —438

Ram showered the arrows and the army of the monkeys was filled with joy he stretched his bow and shot an arrow, which killed Kumbhakaran. —439

In their joy the gods showered flowers, when Ravana, the king of Lanka heard this news, he, in great anguish, threw his head on the earth. —440

End of the chapter entitled "The Killing of Kumbhakaran" in Ramavatar in Bachittar Natak.

Now begins the Description of the War with Trimund

RASAAVAL STANZA

Now Ravana sent the demon Trimund who marched at the head of the army, that warrior was unique like a portrait and a demon of supreme furry. —441

He shouted "kill, kill" and discharged a current of arrows, with great rage Hanuman stood with a firm fort in the battlefield. —442

Hanuman seized the sword of that demon and with the same he gave a blow on his neck. That six-eyed demon was killed, seeing whom the gods smiled in the sky. —443

End of the chapter entitled "The Killing of Trimund" in Ramavatar in Bachittar Natak.

Now begins the Description of the War with the Minister Mahodar

RASAAVAL STANZA

When Ravana heard the news about the destruction of his warriors, he held his forehead in extreme anguish, (in order to forget his agony), he in his pride drank wine. —444

There was sound of the pulling of bows and the arrows were being showered, the persistent warriors like Mahodar held their swords and stood firmly with forbearance. —445

MOHINI STANZA

The shields sounded like drums and there was being heard the agitated atmosphere of the war; the sound of fifes filled all the four directions and small symbols of different colours rang. —446

The kettledrums sounded like the resonance of the group of peacocks on seeing the clouds in the months of Sawan; the armoured horses jumped and the warriors were absorbed in war. —447

The elephants having trunks and tusks got intoxicated and the warriors of frightful whiskers danced; there was movement of all the forces and the gods saw them from the sky. —448

The blows of very stern warriors are being endured; the fighters are falling in the battlefield and are flowing in the stream of blood, the wounded warriors are wandering circularly and are falling on the earth with downward faces. —449

In great fury they are killing others and are going on killing; the persistent warriors are tightening their weapons smilingly and being enraged are churning the fighters and are raising the ire of others. —450

The warriors bedecked with weapons in the war are thundering and the arrows are being showered by repeatedly pulling their bows, the brave heroes are destroying the forces by striking their weapons and are engaged in continuous fighting. —451

The warriors are being faced and killed and they are falling on the ground with armours and fly-whisks; the brave fighters are moving with their long lances like the yogis of Ravel Panth wearing matted locks. —452

The egoist sword-bearers are showing persistence and the armoured warriors are fighting; the magnificent heroes are exhibiting pride and on their bodies the armours of steel-strips look impressive. —453

NAV NAAMAK STANZA

The brave fighters are seen writhing to whom all the gods and men are looking; it seems that the abode of Indra, filled with ghosts, fiends and Ganas, has become the dwelling place of Shiva; all the people are looking at this scene. —454

There is shower of arrows and the bows are being pulled, people are leaving the city and this scene is being viewed by all. —455

The people are leaving the city very quickly, they are testing their own endurance and are leaving keeping their desires within their hearts. —456

The warriors are entangled among themselves and all are fighting with one another, some people are getting delighted and showering their arrows. —457

People who are afraid in their minds, are meditating on Shiva and remembering Shiva for their protection, they are trembling. —458

As soon as the sound rises, people go into their houses and the warriors here are falling on the earth, moving like man-lion incarnation. —459

TILKARIYA STANZA

The blows of the swords are causing knocking sounds on the shields and the warriors are saving themselves from the shields, the weapons are being struck and (the warriors) are being killed by making them targets. —460

The heavenly damsels are moving in the battlefield and wedding the warriors; they are seeing the war and the warriors who are desirous of obtaining them, are getting immensely infuriated. —461

The bowls are being filled with blood, the arms are breaking, the spark of fire are looking like glowworms. —462

The warriors are fighting, the armours are breaking, the spears are falling on the shields and the sparks are rising. —463

With the discharge of arrows, the directions have turned, there are blows and counter-blows with weapons. —464

The Kshatriyas, getting hold of arms in their hands, are fighting, they are discharging arrows and striking with swords. —465

DOHIRA

In this war between Ram and Ravana the clusters of corpses scattered here and there and seeing Mahodar being killed, Indarjit (Meghnad) marched forward. —466

End of the chapter entitled "The Killing of Mahodar Mantri" in Ramavatar in Bachittar Natak.

Now begins the Description of War with Indarjit

SIRKHAND STANZA

The trumpets sounded and the warriors faced one another and both the armies, prepared for war while thundering; they who performed very difficult tasks, fought with one another and the arrows were discharged like the frightful flying serpents. —467

The big chained trumpets sounded and the rows of soldiers began to fight with one another, the long-whiskered and tyrannical warriors marched forward and alongwith them the powerful fighters began to sob on falling in the battlefield, the warriors being intoxicated are shouting like someone shrieking in inebriation after eating hemp. —468

The proud warriors marched forward after causing the resonance of big trumpets and began to strike blows with their swords, with the shower of arrows a continuous stream of blood flowed and this war of Ram and Ravana became famous on all the four sides. —469

With the sounding of trumpets a terrible war began and the enemies wandered here and there on the fast-moving steeds, and there on the sky the heavenly damsels gathered together with the zeal of wedding the brave warriors and came nearer in order to see them waging the war. —470

PAADHARI STANZA

Inderjit in great fury, holding his wide bow, began to discharge arrows, the corpses writhed and the arms of the warriors fluttered; the warriors began to fight and the heavenly damsels were filled with joy. —471

The discus glittered, the lances moved and the fighters with matted hair sped up to fight as if they are going to take a bath in the Ganges, the wounded warriors were killed and on the other hand the warriors began to shower arrows with fourfold zeal. —472

The frightful warriors entangled in war are showering arrows like poisonous serpents; with the shower of arrows the sky is not visible and there is no differentiation between high and low. —473

All the warriors specialise in the science of weaponary and locating the generals they are showering arrows on them; even Ram, the king of Raghu clan was beguiled and fell on the earth alongwith his army. —474

Then the messengers went to give the news to Ravana that the forces of monkeys have been defeated and he could certainly wed Sita on that day because Indarjit has killed Ram in the war. —475

Then Ravana called the demoness named Trijatha and asked him to show the dead Ram to Sita; she took away Sita from that place with her *tantric* power to the place where Ram was sleeping in unconscious state like a lion after killing the deer. —476

Seeing Ram in such a state, the mind of Sita was filled with extreme agony because Ram was the storehouse of fourteen arts and it was impossible to make her believe in such an event; Sita went near Ram reciting Nag *mantra* and reviving both Ram and Lakshman her mind was filled with joy. —477

When Sita went back, Ram woke up alongwith his brother and forces, on getting up Ram, the abode of *dharma*, the brave fighters thundered bedecking themselves with weapons and the great warriors with power of endurance began to run away from the battlefield. —478

The warriors with frightful prowess began to shower arrows in the war and being highly infuriated began to destroy even the trees; at this time Indarjit Meghnad forsook the war-arena and returned to perform the *hom yajna* (sacrifice). —479

Coming near the younger brother Vibhishan said that at that time his supreme enemy and the mighty warrior Indarjit is within your ambush. —480

He is performing *havana* (sacrifice) by chopping his flesh, with which the whole earth is trembling and the sky is wandering, hearing this Lakshman went there fearlessly with his bow in his hand and quiver tied to his back. —481

Inderjit began to recite *mantras* for the manifestation of the goddess and Lakshman discharged his arrow and killed Indarjit into two halves, Lakshman returned with his forces, playing on the drum and on the other side the demons ran away on seeing their general dead. —482

End of the chapter entitled "Killing of Indrajit" in Ramavatar in Bachittar Natak.

Now begins the Description of the War with the Demon Atkaaya

SANGEET PADHISTAKA STANZA

The demon-king in great fury, began the war, calling his innumerable warriors. —483

Very swift moving horses were brought, Who jumped hither and thither like an actor taking out their frightening weapons, the warriors began to fight with one another. —484

On this side, the warriors in the army of Ram, started fighting in great rage; the foolish Makradh thundered, carrying his new banner. —485

There was one demon named Atkaaya in the demon forces who rushed with serious fury, many warriors confronted him and began to fight with discriminating intellect. —486

There was a huge shower of arrows which fell like raindrops; the army looked like locusts and army of ants. —487

The warriors reached near Atkaaya in order to see him fighting; the gods hailed him and the king uttered "Bravo, Bravo!"—488

The terrible goddess Kali began to shout and great number of Yogins roamed in the battlefield; innumerable Bhairavas and ghosts began to drink blood. —489

The tabors of vampires sounded and the in-auspicious crows began to caw; on all the four sides there were hand and seen shrieks of vultures and leapings, and hoppings of ghosts and fiends. —490

HOHA STANZA

The warriors felt weakness as then regained strength and in rage caught hold of their swords. —491

Seeing the discharge of arrows the clouds wondered; because of the arrows all the sides were hindered. —492

The arrows are being discharged in fury as the warriors are falling in the earth like the effacement of the thorough ones. —493

The frightened warriors, while wandering, are being wounded and great heroes are flying fast. —494

BACHITTAR NATAK

They are reciting the name of Shiva in order to kill the enemies with jealously in their mind and they are fighting in the field wandering with fear. —495

The people are getting delighted with the falling of demons on the earth; the arrows are penetrating, into the demons and the warriors are being crushed. —496

The wounded warriors are wandering and writhing in the battlefield; they are feeling shy in being entrapped, having been girdled. —497

The throbbing of the heart continues, the arrows are being discharged intermittently, and the directions are being hindered. —498

CHHAPPAI STANZA

The warriors excelling one another are coming and looking at each other one by one; they are moving with each one and are being startled by each one, on one side they are discharging arrows and on the other, they are pulling their bows in rage on one side the fighters are writing and on the other side, the dead ones are ferrying across the world ocean; the warriors excelling one another have fought and died, all the warriors are alike, but the weapons are many and these weapons are striking blows on the soldiers like rain. —499

On one side, the warriors have fallen and on the other they are shouting; on one side they have entered the city of gods and on the other, having been wounded, they have sped away some are fighting in the war fiercely and on the other, side they are falling down having been chopped like trees; on one side many wounds are being endured and on the other, the arrows are being discharged with full strength; Divaghkaya and Lakshman have wandered and created such a situation in the battlefield as if they are large trees in a forest or eternal and immorable pole-stars in the north. —500

AJBA STANZA

The warriors fought, the arrows were discharged, there was knocking on the shields and the death-like warriors were infuriated. —501

The drums sounded, the blows of the swords were heard, and the weapons and arms were struck. —502

Highly infuriated and with great understanding, the forces are being mashed, the warriors are thundering and showering arrows. —503

The warriors with red eyes are shouting, having been intoxicated; they are fighting and the heavenly damsels are looking at them. —504

Having been pierced by arrows, the warriors are fleeing and (some) are fighting with arms, being highly enraged. —505

The warriors are swinging and the heavenly damsels, while wandering are looking at them and are wondering on listening to their shouts of "kill, kill." —506

The weapons, coming into contact with armours are piercing the bodies, the spears are breaking and the sparks of fire are coming out from them. —507

The horses are dancing and the warriors are thundering; they are falling while discharging the arrows. —508

Seeing the heavenly damsels moving the warriors are swinging and, being intoxicated, are discharging arrows. —509

PAADHARI STANZA

In this way; the war ensured and many warriors fell in the field; on one side, there is Lakshman; brother of Ram and on the other there is the demon Atkaaya and both these princes are fighting with each other. —510

There Lakshman became highly infuriated and increased it with zeal like the fire blazing fiercely when the *ghee* is poured over it, he discharged the scorching arrows like the terrible sunrays of the month of Jyestha. —511

Getting himself wounded he discharged so many arrows which are indescribable; these brave fighters are absorbed in fight and on the other hand the gods are raising the sound of victory. —512

Ultimately Lakshman deprived, Atkaaya the specialist in many sciences of weapons and arms of his weapons and arms; he was deprived of his horse; crown all garments and he tried to conceal himself like a thief mustering his strength. —513

He discharged arrows causing destruction like Indra's *vajra* and they were stricking like the advancing fire of death; the hero Atkaaya became highly infuriated like the clouds of domsday. —514

He began to prattle like a man without the energy of an youth, clinging to a woman without satisfying her or like a teethless dog on catching a rabbit whom he can do no harm, or like a libertine without the seman. —515

Atkaaya was in such a situation which is experienced by a trader without money or a warrior without weapons, he looked like an ugly prostitute or a chariot without horses. —516

Then the benevolent Lakshman struck his sharp-edged sword and chopped the demon into two halves, that warrior named Atkaaya fell in the battlefield and on seeing him (felling) many warriors fled away. —517

End of the chapter entitled "Killing of Atkaaya" in Ramavatar in Bachittar Natak.

Now begins the Description of the War with Makrachh

PAADHARI STANZA

After that Makrachh joined the army and said. "O Ram! You cannot save yourself now; he who has killed my father that mighty warrior should come forward and wage war with me." —518

Ram heard these crooked words and in great rage he held his weapons and arms in his hand; he pulled (his bow) discharged his arrows, and fearlessly killed Makrachh. —519

When this hero and his army were killed, then all the warriors, becoming weaponless, ran away (from the field); after that Kumbh and Ankumbh came forward and obstructed the army of Ram. —520

AJBA STANZA

The horses jumped, the warriors thundered and began to strike blows, being bedecked with weapons and arms. —521

The bows broke, the arrows were discharged, the warriors became firm and the shafts were showered. —522

The warriors wandered after getting wounded and their zeal grew, with fury, they began to lose their senses. —523

The warriors covered with armours, began to fight in the battlefield and fell down unconscious —524

The foppish warriors besieged Lanka; the demons army sped away feeling ashamed. —525

The brave fighters fell and their faces shone, they wedded the heavenly damsels and fulfilled their wishes. —526

End of the chapter entitled "Killing of Makrachh, Kumbh and Ankumbh" in Ramavatar in Bachittar Natak.

Now begins the Description of the War with Ravana

HOHA STANZA

Ravana heard about the victory (of Ram), he being highly infuriated in his mind, began to shout violently. —527

Seeing his citadel besieged; his ire grew more and he saw the women running away in fear. —528

All the women are running away in illusion and Ravana obstructed them by catching their hair. —529

They were lamenting profusely and praying to god and were asking for forgiveness for their sins. —530

That persistent Ravana got up on listening to such sounds and it seemed that a fire-cauldron was blazing. —531

He began to kill the human army and with his arrows all the directions were obstructed. —532

TRINANINE STANZA

The arrows were discharged and the warriors were wounded, the shields were slipping down and the fires blazed. —533

The helmets were knocked and the wounds were caused, the warriors were infuriated and their zeal grew. —534

The fast moving horses began to run and the warriors obtained salvation after severe fighting. —535

The elephants ran like deer and the warriors took refuge with their comrades, the enemies ran and felt shy of fighting. —536

The bodies and the armours were cut, the ears and eyes were amputated. —537

The warriors breathed their last and ferried across the world-ocean, some were burnt in the fire of ire and took refuge. —538

The gods moved in their air-vehicles and saw the scene the heavenly damsels wandered and began to wed the warriors. —539

Various types of musical instruments resounded and the elephants thundered; the warriors took refuge while some began to fight. —540

TRIGATHA STANZA

The arrows began to kill warriors and the fires came out of the shields. —541

The horses began to run and the warriors began to roar; they began to kill one another and ferry across the world-ocean. —542

After gaining victory in war, the enemies were being made allies, the cleavage was caused amongst the warriors and they were also being forsaken. —543

The king Ravana thundered violently and with great zeal marched forward. —544

The warriors began to fell after being saturated with blood, and the blood was flowing like water. —545

There is lot of discipline and lot of obstruction; the limbs are being chopped in the war. —546

The warriors, being infuriated are inflicting wounds in the war, and are fleeing away. —547

The sky is becoming full of heavenly damsels. —548

The warriors are pulling bows and discharging arrows. —549

The musical instruments are resounding, the warriors are thundering and are falling in the ground after swinging. —550

ANAAD STANZA

The sky is torn with arrows and the eyes of the warriors are getting red, the knocking on the shields is being heard and the rising flames are being seen. —551

The warriors saturated with blood are falling down on the earth and the heavenly damsels are roaming; the sky is filled with the sounds of conches, other tunes and drums. —552

The armours of the warriors have been torn and they are fighting in the war; the brave fighters are confronting one another and the heavenly damsels are dancing; there is talk of war on the earth. —553

The headless trunks arose in the war and were opening their gauzy armours; with garbs like lions the warriors are highly infuriated and their hair have loosened. —554.

The helmets have broken and the kings have fled away; the warriors, having been wounded are felling on the earth after swinging and with a bang they are falling. —555

The large trumpets have resounded and the bedecked warriors are being seen; they are dying in the war being chopped in bits and being intoxicated in war frenzy, they are becoming unconscious. —556

Innumerable weapons and arms are being used and the earth is coloured with blood upto a great distance; the weapons are being struck indiscretely and the terrible warriors are shouting. —557

The clusters of corpses are lying scattered; the warriors are engrossed in a horrible war on one side and on the other some of them are running away, the ghosts and fiends are laughing in the cementries and here the brave fighters are fighting after receiving blows of swords. —558

BAHARA STANZA

The demon warriors wearing armours, march forward in great fury, but on reaching within the forces of Ram, they become like followers of Ram and begin to shout the name of Ram; while fighting they fall down on the earth in a dreadful posture and ferrying across the world-ocean at the hands of Ram. —559

After revolving and holding the lance the warriors come forward and fight and fall down on being chopped into bits; on receiving only the small blows of the edge of swords the brave fighters fell down in numerous parts. —560

SANGEET BAHARA STANZA

Holding the lances the warriors are causing them to dance in the war and after swinging and felling on the earth, they are leaving for the abode of gods; the brave fighters are falling with chopped limbs in the battlefield and their dreadful bodies are saturated with blood. —561

The enemy king Ravana fell in great fury on Lakshman and went towards him with wind, speed and great ire, he inflicted a wound on the heart of Lakshman and in this way wreaking vengeance on him for the killing of his son, he caused the fall of Lakshman. —562

The vultures shrieked and the vampires belched; burning in this fire of fury in the battlefield the ghosts and others were filled with joy; Lakshman while fighting in the field became unconscious and Ram, the king of Raghava clan, considering him dead, became pale. —563

End of the chapter entitled "Lakshman becoming Unconscious" in Ramavatar in Bachittar Natak.

SANGEET BAHARA STANZA

The force of monkeys ran halter-skelter when Lakshman fall down and catching hold of his weapons and arms in his hands Ram was highly infuriated; with the clattering sound of the weapons of Ram the bull, the support of earth trembled and the earth shook as if the doomsday had arrived. —564

ARDH-NARAAJ STANZA

The double-edged swords came out and Ram seemed greatly impressive, the sound of kettledrums was heard and the imprisoned people began to cry. —565

A queer scene was created and the forces of men and monkeys fell on the demon forces with sharp nails like the rising clouds of the month of Savan. —566

The warriors are roaming on all the four sides for the destruction of sins and are challenging one another; the brave fighters are leaving their bodies and the gods are shouting "bravo, bravo." —567

The sharp arrows are being discharged and the terrible kettledrums are resounding; the intoxicating sounds are being heard from all the four sides. —568

Shiva and his Ganas (attendants) are seen dancing and it seems that the female ghosts are laughing and bowing their heads before Parvati. —569

ANOOP NARAAJ STANZA

The vampires are roaming and the horses are moving creating a circular spectacle; the warriors are being made prisoners and are hailing. —570

There are knockings of the blows of the swords on the shields and with the arrows being discharged by the kings the humans and monkeys are falling on the earth. —571

On the other side the monkeys are shrieking, on account of which the demons are fleeing; the sounds of arrows and other weapons are creating the terrible and tumultuous resonance. —572

The groups of ghosts are feeling frightened and perplexed; the armoured horses and roaring elephants are moving in the battlefield. —573

The gods are also becoming fearful on seeing the terrible war of the warriors; the white swords and sharp arrows are being showered. —574

SANGEET BHUJANG PRAYAAT STANZA

Ram saw his brother Lakshman fighting and he discharged the arrows touching the sky. —575

These arrows chopped the riders on chariots and horses, but still the warriors stood firmly in the field; Ram killed the brave fighters who were wedded by the heavenly damsels. —576

In this way, the war was conquered and in this war many warriors fled away; wherever the brave fighters saw one another, they cleared the account only on sacrificing their lives. —577

BACHITTAR NATAK

The army felt ashamed on remembering the defeat; Sugriva and others got highly enraged. —578

Hanuman was also greatly infuriated and he stood firmly in the battlefield; all those who fought with him suffered defeat and for this reason Hanuman is called the "killer of all." —579

Hanuman said to Ram, "kindly stretch your hand towards me and bless me by patting me on my back and I shall conquer all the abodes of gods today." —580

Uttering these words Hanuman flew and it seemed that he had became one with the sky, Ram sat down disappointed, keeping the hope in his mind. —581

Whosoever came in front of Hanuman, he killed him and thus killing (the forces) he reached on the bank of tank. —582

There a terrible-looking demon was hiding and at the same place Hanuman saw many herbs clustered with one another. —583

The highly radiant Hanuman, seeing this, was perturbed and felt confused about the herb, to be taken away; he uprooted the whole mountain and returned with the medicinal herbs. —584

He reached that battlefield with the mountain where Lakshman was lying unconscious, the apothecary Sushen, put the required herb in the mouth of Lakshman. —585

The mighty warrior Lakshman regained his senses and the roaming heavenly damsels went back; the great trumpets resounded in the battlefield. —586

The arrows were discharged and the warriors began to fight again with one another, the brave fighters dying in the battlefield became true martyrs. —587

KALAS

The terrible warriors were absorbed in fighting; the ghosts, fiends and baitals began to dance; the blows were struck with many hands creating knocking sounds and the white edges of the swords glittered. —588

TRIBHANGI STANZA

The white edges of the swords, increasing splendour, looked impressive; these swords are the destroyers of the enemies and appear like saws; they frighten the enemy by granting victory, by bathing in the blood, by destroying the intoxicated tyrants and by perishing all the vices. —589

KALAS

There was consternation, the warriors ran and their bodies wearing armours trembled; the trumpets resounded violently in the war and seeing the mighty warriors the heavenly damsels advanced towards them again. —590

TRIBHANGI STANZA

Returning form heaven the damsels moved towards the warriors and enchanted their mind; their bodies were red like the arrows saturated with blood and their beauty was unparalleled; seeing the beauty of these heavenly damsels, who were wearing elegantly coloured raisments, the Cupid was feeling shy and there were the intelligent heavenly damsels, doe-eyed, destroyer of bad intellect and wedders of mighty warriors. —591

KALAS

Their faces were like lotus, eyes like deer and utterance like nightingale, these heavenly damsels were stores of elegance, with gait of elephants, with slim waists of lions and were captivators of mind with the side glances of their eyes. —592

TRIBHANGI STANZA

They have splendid eyes, their utterance is sweat like nightingale and they captivate the mind like the gait of the elephant; they are all-pervading, have charming faces, with elegance of the god of love, they are the storehouse of good intellect, the destroyer of evil intellect, have godly limbs; they stand slantingly on one side, wear anklets in their feet, ivory-ornament in their nose and have black curly hair. —593

KALAS

These heavenly damsels of elegant cheecks and unique beauty; have wreaths of gems on various parts of their bodies, the bracelets of their hands are spreading brightness and seeing such elegance the beauty of the god of love is getting dim. —594

TRIBHANGI STANZA

With black hair and sweet speech they appear very impressive and moving freely they are roaming within the jostling of the elephants, with antimony in their eyes and dyed in various colours they look splendid with their beautiful eyes, in this way, their eyes, assaulting like poisonous serpents, but innocent like deer, they are winsome like lotus and moon. —595

KALAS

The foolish Ravana was highly infuriated in the war, when the terrible war began amidst violent resonance, all the warriors began to fight and roam shouting violently among the enemy forces. —596

TRIBHANGI STANZA

That demon of vicious intellect, holding arrows in his hand and highly enraged marched forward to wage a war, he fought a terrible war and amidst the pulled up bows in the battlefield, the headless trunks began to dance; the king moved forward while challenging and inflicting wounds on the warriors they were in great ire, the wounds were inflicted on the bodies of the fighters, but still they are not fleeing and thundering like clouds they are firmly standing and fighting in the battlefield. —597

KALAS

With the increase of indignation the warriors attached each other and the armours and helmets were shattered; the arrows were discharged from bows and the bits of flesh fell on being chopped from the bodies of the enemies. —598

TRIBHANGI STANZA

As soon as the arrows are discharged, the enemies in still greater numbers gather and prepare to fight even with the shattered armours; they move forward and run like a hungry person here and there; they are roaming hither and thither, striking their weapons, they fight face to face and do not run away; seeing them waging war even the gods feel shy, the gods seeing this terrible war shower flowers with the sound of "hail, hail," they also hail the fight in the war-arena. —599

KALAS

There is betel in the mouth of Ravana and the colour of his body is red, he is moving fearlessly in the battlefield and has plastered his body with sandalwood, he is bright like the sun and is moving with a superior gait. —600

TRIBHANGI STANZA

Seeing his winsome body and elegant limbs, the god of love is feeling shy, he has black curly hair and sweat speech; his face is fragranced and appears shining like sun and glorifying like moon, on seeing him all feel delighted and the people of the abode of gods also do not hesitate to see him. —601

KALAS

In one of his hands there was the sword named Chandrahaas, in the second hand there another arm named *dhop* and in the third hand there was a spear; in his fourth hand there was a weapon named *saihathi* having sharp glimmer in his fifth and sixth hands there was a glittering mace and a weapon named *gophan*. —602

TRIBHANGI STANZA

In his seventh hand there was another heavy and swollen mace and in other hands there were trident, pineers, arrows, bow etc., as weapons and arms, in his fifteenth hand there were an arrow like pellet bow and a weapon named *pharsa*, he had worn in his hands steel hooked weapons shaped like tigers, claws and he was roaming like dreadful Yama. —603

KALAS

He was repeating the name of Shiva from one face, from the second he was looking at the beauty of Sita, from the third he was seeing his own warriors and from the fourth he was shouting "kill. kill." —604

TRIBHANGI STANZA

From his fifth face he was looking at Hanuman and repeating the *mantra* at great speed and was trying to pull his strength, from his sixth head he was seeing his fallen brother Kumbhakaran and his heart was burning from his seventh head he was seeing Ram and the army of monkeys and other mighty warriors, he was shaking his eighth head and surveying everything form his ninth head and he was getting highly infuriated with rage. —605

CHABOLA STANZA

Setling their white arrows the mighty warriors moved with beautiful dress on their bodies; their horses were very swift moving and were exhibiting complete quickness in the battlefield; sometimes they fight on this side and challenge on the other and wherever they strike the blows, the enemies flee, they appear like one intoxicated on eating hemp and roaming hither and thither. —606

The warriors roared and the heavenly damsels roamed in the sky in order to see this unique war, they prayed that this warrior waging the dreadful war should live for eyes and should firmly enjoy his rule, O warriors! Forsake their Lanka and come to wed us and depart for heaven. —607

SWAYYA (OF INNUMERABLE VERSES)

Ravana, abandoning his senses, became very furious and attacked Ramchander, the king of Raghu clan, on this side Ram intercepted midway his arrows; then he began to destroy collectively the army of monkeys and struck various types of terrible arms. —608

CHABOLE SWAYYA

Ram took his bow in his hand and in great ire, discharged many arrows which killed the warriors and penetrating, on the other side, came in showers again from the sky, innumerable elephants, horses and chariots fell in the battlefield and it appeared that with the flow of the violent wound the leaves are seen flying. —609

SWAYYA STANZA

On being enraged, Ram discharged many arrows on Ravana and those arrows saturated slightly with blood, penetrated through the body to the other side; the elephants, horses, chariots and charioteers fell down in the battlefield after having been chopped like the trees of banana uprooted and thrown, around by the violent land at the end of spring. —610

The forces of monkeys also fell on the enemy, having been gently enraged in the heart and gushed forward from all the four sides, shouting violently without retreating from its position, from the other side, the army of Ravana rushed forward taking its weapons and arms like arrows, bows, maces, spears etc., and the warriors fighting with one another fell in such a way that the moon taking its curse got illusioned and the contemplation of Shiva was obstructed. —611

After receiving wounds on the body, the warriors swung and began to fall and the jackals, vultures, ghosts and fiends were delighted in mind; all the directions trembled on seeing the terrible war and the *dikpals* (supervision and directions) guessed the arrival of doomsday the earth and sky became anxious and seeing the dreadfulness of the war, the gods and demons were both bewildered. —612

Being highly infuriated in mind Ravana began to discharge arrows collectively and with his arrows the earth, sky and all directions were torn asunder; on this side, Ram was enraged, for an instant and destroyed the collective discharging of all these arrows and the darkness that had spread on account of arrows, got cleaned by the spread of the sunshine again on all the four sides. —613

Filled with anger Ram discharged many arrows and caused the elephants, horses and charioteers to fly away; the way in which the anguish of Sita could be removed and she could be set free, Ram made today all such efforts and that lotus-eyed one caused the destruction of many homes with his terrible warfare. —614

Ravana thundered in rage and causing his army to rush forward, shouting loudly and holding his weapons in his hands, he came straight towards Ram and forget with him; he caused his horses to gallop fearlessly by whipping them, he left his chariot in order to kill Ram with his arrows and came forward. —615

When the arrows were discharged from the hands of Ram, the earth, sky, netherworld and the four directions could hardly be recognised those arrows, piercing things, armours of warriors and killing them without the utterance of a sign, they penetrated to the other side; when the arrows fell after piercing, the steel-armours, Sita realised by that these arrows were discharged by Ram. —616

He, who was struck by one arrow by Ram, that warrior could neither run away from that place nor could fight but fell dead on the ground, the arrows of Ram pierced through the armours of warriors and then mighty fighters fell down on the earth without uttering a sign. —617

Ravana called all his warriors, but those remaining fighters fled away; Ravana, then killed millions of gods and demons, but it made no difference in the battlefield, seeing the power of Ram all the illustrious persons were perturbed and jumping over the wells of the citadel, they ran away. —618

In great fury Ravana attacked with weapons from all the twenty army and with his blows the earth, sky and all the four directions, become invisible; Ram threw away the enemies from the war-arena, chopping them easily like a fruit, Ram chopped and threw all the canopies banners, horses and charioteers belonging to Ravana. —619

When Ravana saw his chariot deprived of the horses, he marched forward quickly and holding his shield, trident, mace and spear in his hands he fought with Ram; the persistent Ravana, without any fear of the forces of the monkeys, moved forward fearlessly, shouting violently, there were many warriors there like Angad, Hanuman etc., but he did not fear any one. —620

When the king of Raghava clan, saw Ravana coming forward, he (Ram) attacked him by discharging his twenty arrows like slabs on his chest, these arrows penetrated through his vital parts and he bathed in the stream of blood; Ravana fell down and crawled forward, he forget even the location of his house. —621

Ram, the king of Raghava clan, in great fury, taking his bow in his hand and taking five steps backward, chopped all his twenty arms; with ten arrows, he chopped his ten heads for despatching them to the abode of Shiva; after the war Ram wedded Sita again as if he had conquered her in the ceremony of *swayamvara*. —622

End of the chapter entitled "Killing of Ten-headed (Ravana)," in Ramavatar in Bachittar Natak.

Now begins the Description of Contemporaneous Knowledge to Mandodari, and then bestowed the Kingdom of Lanka to Vibhishana; Description of the Union with Sita

SWAYYA STANZA

He, from whom Indra, Moon and Sun felt baffled, he who had plundered the stores of Kuber and he before whom Brahma kept silent; he with whom many beings Indra fought, but who could not be conquered, conquering him toady in the battlefield, Ram also conquered Sita as in the ceremony of *swayamvara*. —623

ALKA STANZA

The forces ran quickly and began to fight, the warriors ran speedily and they forgot their thoughts about the heavenly damsels. —624

The warriors abandoning the field and the arrows entered Lanka seeing Ram with their own eyes they raised utterances of lamentation. —625

The superb Ram killed all of them and chopped their arms; then all (others) saving themselves; fled away and Ram showered arrows on those running fighters. —626

All the queens ran weeping instantly and came to fell at the feet of Ram; Ram saw all the spectacle. —627

The queens rolled on the earth and began to weep and lament in various ways; they pulled, their hair and garments and cried and shrieked in various ways. —628

They began to tear their garments and put the dust on their heads; they in great sorrow cried threw themselves, down and rolled. —629

RASAAVAL STANZA

When all of them saw the most beautiful Ram, they bowed their heads and stood before him. —630

They were allured to see the beauty of Ram; there was talk about Ram on all four sides and they all gave Ram the kingdom of Lanka like the taxpayer setting tax with the authority. —631

Ram bowed down his eyes filled with grace; seeing him, the tears of joy flowed down from the eyes of people like the rain falling from the clouds. —632

The women allured by lust, were delighted to see Ram and they all ended their identity in Ram, the abode of *dharma*. —633

They all absorbed their minds in Ram, forsaking the love of their husbands and looking towards him resoluting, they began to talk with one another. —634

Ram, the lord of Sita, is winsome and abductor of the mind; he is stealing the conscious mind like a thing. —635.

All the wives of Ravana were told to abandon the sorrow of their husband and touch the feet of Ram; all of them came forward and fell on his feet. —636

The most beautiful Ram recognised their feelings; he absorbed himself in the minds of all and all of them pursued him like shadow. —637

Ram appeared to them in golden hue, and looked like king of all kings; the eyes of all were dyed in his love and the gods were delighted to see him from the sky. —638

He, who saw Ram even trace, she was completely allured. —639

She forget the consciousness of all else seeing the beauty of Ram and began to talk to supremely mighty Ram. —640

The Speech of Ram Addressed to Mandodari
RASAAVAL STANZA

O queen! I have not committed a mistake in killing your husband, think rightly in your mind about it and then blame me. —641

I should get my Sita back, so that the work of righteousness may move forward; (saying in this way) Ram sent Hanuman, the son of Wind-god like an envoy (in advance). —642

Searching for Sita, he reached there where she was sitting in the garden under a tree. —643

Hanuman, falling at the feet of Sita, said, "O mother Sita! Ram has killed the enemy (Ravana) and now he is standing at your door." —644

"O mother Sita! Go to the place of Ram quickly, he has lightened the burden of the earth by killing all the enemies." —645

Being highly pleased Sita accompanied Hanuman, she saw Ram and found Ram retaining his previous beauty. —646

Sita fell at the feet of Ram who saw towards her and addressed to that lady of lotus eyes and sweat speed. —647

"O Sita! Enter the fire, so that you may become pure," she agreed and prepared a pyre of fire. —648

She merged in the fire like the lightning seen in the clouds; she became one with fire like *Gita* with *shrutis* (recorded texts). —649

She entered the fire and came out like pure gold; Ram held her to his bosom and the poets sang in praise about this fact. —650

All the saints accepted this type of fire-test and the beings of the three world accepted this fact, the musical instruments of victory were played and Ram also thundered in great joy. —651

The pure Sita was conquered like a superbly auspicious song all the gods began to shower flowers from the sky. —652

End of the chapter entitled "The Bestowed of Kingdom on Vibhishana, Imparting of Contemporaneous Knowledge to Mandodari and the Union with Sita" in Ramavatar in Bachittar Natak.

Now begins the Description of the Entry into Ayodhya

RASAAVAL STANZA

Gaining victory in war, then Ram mounted on the air-vehicle Pushpak, all the warriors roared in great joy and the musical instruments of victory resounded. —653

The monkeys in great delight caused the air-vehicle to fly and they saw Avadhpuri, beautiful like heaven. —654

MAKRA STANZA

Ram has came and brought Sita with him and there are rejoicing in the city; the joy is growing in the heart of Oudh. —655

The women are coming at speed, there is endless crowd, all are standing amazed and asking "where is our Lord Ram?" —656

"He, whose hair are unique and black like serpents; he whose thinking is wonderful, where is that deer Ram?" —657

"He, who is ever in blossom like garden and ever thoughtful about his kingdom; he, who hath stolen our mind, where is that Ram." —658

"He, who hath stolen our heart and given us serperation from him, where is that flower-faced and alluring Ram." —659

"Someone may tell us and take whatever he wants from us, but he should tell us where is that alluring Ram?" —660

"He accepted the orders of his father like a drunkard accepting every word of the giver of intoxicant and he left his country, where is he, the beauty incarnate of the world and rose-faced?" —661

"The wagtail (birds) were envious of his cruel gestures; he who hath allured our mind, where is that Ram of blossomed face?" —662

"His gestures were the gestures of an intoxicated person; all the world is obedient to his personality; some one may tell where is that flower-faced Ram?" —663

"The splendour of this face was significant and he was perfect in intellect; he, who is a vessel full of the wine of heart's love, where is that flower-faced Ram?" —664

"After conquering the tyrants the beloved Ram has come back from distant lands where is he, the perfect one in all arts and who hath flower like face?" —665

"His qualities are known all over the world and he is famous in the seven regions of the world; he whose light hath spread throughout the world, where is that flower-faced Ram?" —666

"He who conquered the tyrants with the blows of his arrows; where is he who mounts the air-vehicle Pushpak and accompanies Sita?" —667

"He, who sacrificed thousands of his joys in order to please his mother, where is he, the mother-Sita may also be congratulated toady, but someone may tell us where is that flower-faced Ram?" —668

End of the chapter entitled "The entry of Sita in Ayodhya" in Ramavatar in Bachittar Natak.

Now begins the Description of the Meeting with the Mothers

RASAAVAL STANZA

When the people heard that Ram had returned, then all the people ran and fell at his feet; Ram met all of them. —669

Someone swung the fly whisk, someone offered the betel; Ram fell at the feet of his mother and his mother hugged him to their bosom. —670

On being hugged he was weeping in order to wash away all his suffering; the brave Ram began to talk and all the mothers listened. —671

Then he met the mother of Lakshman and the brothers Bharat and Shatrughan touched his feet; on account of the joy of union unaccountable charity was given. —672

Then Ram met the mother of Bharat and told her all that happened with him; Ram said, "O mother, I am thankful to you because you have made me free from indebtedness." —673

"You are not to be blamed for this, because it was recorded in many desting, whatever happens, has to happen, none can describe it." —674

He pacified his mothers in this way and then he met his brother Bharat, Bharat on hearing his arrival ran towards him and touched his head with the feet of Ram. —675

Ram hugged him to his bosom and cleared all the doubts, then he met Shatrughan, who had expert knowledge of weapons and Shastras. —676

The brothers cleansed the dust form the feet and matted hair of Ram, they worshipped him in royal way and the Brahmins recited the Vedas. —677

All the brothers sang songs full of love, Ram was made the king and all the works were completed in this way. —678

The Brahmins were called in and with the recitation of Vedic *mantras* Ram was enthroned; on all the four sides resounded the musical instruments denoting victory. —679

BHUJANG PRAYAAT STANZA

The sovereigns were called from all the four directions and they all reached Ouadhpuri; they all fell at the feet of Ram, exhibiting their supreme love and met him with great presents. —680

The kings presented gifts from various and beautiful maidens of elegant hair; they also present rare gems, jewels and garments. —681

They presented winsome horses, jewels, gems, pearls as well as elephants, the chariots, diamonds, raiments and invaluable precious stones were also presented. —682

Somewhere the white elephants bedecked with gems are being presented and somewhere the horses tightened with brocaded thick cloth are dancing exhibiting a spectacle of war. —683

Somewhere the elephant-drivers are seen wearing armours and somewhere royal horses are being presented; the kings; who presented multi-coloured red and blue gems, had a sight of Ram, the wielder of weapons and arms. —684

Somewhere the kings are meeting Ram with golden coloured silken raiment and various types of ornaments; somewhere the garments shining like Sun are being sent to the abode of Sita. —685

Somewhere the ornaments shining like Sun are being sent to Sita; many ornaments; and garments were sent to the mothers of Ram, seeing which many became covetous in their hearts. —686

On all the four sides, revolving the canopies, declaration were made regarding Ram and Sita also looked splendid like a decorated garden, the kings were sent to far off places with the canopy of Ram, they smashed the pride of all and arranged festivities. —687

In this way sufficient time elapsed in Ram's kingdom and Ram began to rule magnificently; letters of victory were sent to all sides and under a white canopy and commanding Ram looked greatly impressive. —688

Everyone was given wealth in various ways and the people saw the real personality of Ram, he was known on all four directions as the destroyer of the rebels of Vishnu and the Lord of Sita. —689

Everyone considered him as an incarnation of Vishnu and he was famous among the people as the Lord, in all the four directions the current of Ram's praise flowed and he, the enemy of Ravana, was known as the supreme sovereign. —690

He looked like a supreme yogi amongst yogis, great god amongst gods and a supreme sovereign amongst kings; he was considered the great enemy of enemies and supreme saint amongst saints; he was extremely elegant personality who was the destroyer of all ailments. —691

He was like god for women and like a sovereign for men; he was a supreme warrior amongst warriors and a great wielder of weapons amongst the weapon-wielders. —692

He was the giver of salvation, blissful, adept-like, giver of intellect and the storehouse of wealth of powers; with whatever feeling one looked towards him, he saw him in that form. —693

All the weapon-wielders saw him as a specialist in weapon-warfare and all the demons who were spiteful towards gods, visualising him as destroyer of life, hid themselves; with whatever feeling one thought of him, Ram seemed to him in the same colour. —694

ANANT-TUKA BHUJANG PRAYAAT STANZA

A good deal of time passed during the reign of Ram and all the enemies were conquered after great; wars Ram's influence spread in all the four directions and he became the supreme sovereign. —695

All the sages including Agastya, Bhring, Vyas, Vashistha, Vishwamitra, Valmiki, and Atri came to him. —696

When Ram saw all the Brahmins coming to him, then Ram, the Lord of Sita and the world ran to touch their feet; he gave them seats, washed their feet and all the great sages blessed him with delight. —697

Great discussions pertaining to drive knowledge were held between the sages and Ram and if all of it is desireless, this *Granth* (book) will became voluminous, all the sages were bestowed with suitable presents on bidding farewell to them who went away to their places happily. —698

During this period a sage came with the corpse of his dead son and said to Ram, "If my child is not revived, I shell curse you," Ram ruminated about it in his mind and started towards the westerly direction in his air-vehicle. —699

In the northwestern direction, a Shudra was hanging overturned in a well and was performing a penance; Ram killed him with his own hand. —700

The son of Brahmin regained his life and his agony ended; the praises of Ram spread in all the four direction, in this way Ram was eulogised all over and he ruled over his kingdom for ten thousand years. —701

Ram conquered the kings of various countries and he was considered a great conqueror in the three worlds, he made Bharat his minister and made Lakshman and Shatrughan, the sons of Sumitra, his generals. —702

MRITGAT STANZA

The drum is resounding on the door of the great sage Raghuvir (Ram) and in the whole world, in all houses and in the abode of gods, he was hailed. —703

Being known with the name of Raghunandan, Ram is the Lord of the world and is worshipped by the sages, he identified the people on the earth and comforted them, removing their agony. —704

All the people considered him as the destroyer of enemies, remover of sufferings and the giver of comforts; all the city of Ayodhya is living in comfort because of his unique personality and the fearless blessings. —705

ANKA STANZA

That Ram is god, infinite, unconquerable and fearless. —706

He is the Lord of nature, he is *Purusha*, he is the whole world and higher Brahmin. —707

BHUJANG PRAYAAT STANZA

One day Ram sent for the son of Sumitra and said to him, "In a distant land there lives a huge demon named Lavan who has got the trident of Shiva." —708

Ram gave him an arrow after reciting a *mantra* which was a great weapon from Ram, the abode of *dharma*, Ram said to him, "When you see the enemy without the trident of Shiva, then wage a war with him." —709

Shatrughan taking that charmed arrow and bowing his head started for his errand and it seemed that he was going as conqueror of the three world; when he saw the enemy without the trident of Shiva, then finding an opportunity, he furiously began to wage war with him. —710

After getting wounded the warriors began to run away and the crows began to caw on seeing the corpses, the heavenly damsels began to wander in the sky, the helmets broke with the blows of arrows and the great sovereign were highly enraged in the battlefield. —711

That demon in great rage revolved and showered a volley of arrows on the brothers of Ram; the arrow which was given by Ram for the destruction of the enemy, Shatrughan discharged it on the demon, repeating the name of Durga. —712

The enemy received a wound and while revolving, he fell down on the earth and he was killed by Shatrughan; the gods were overjoyed in the sky and began to shower flowers; with the killing of this malignant demon, all their agony ended. —713

All the saints were delighted with the destruction of the demon named Lavan; the enemies became depressed and fled away, after forsaking the city; Shatrughan stayed in the city of Mathura. —714

After destroying Lavan, Shatrughan ruled over Mathura and all the weapon-wielders gave the blessings of good wishes to him, he ended all the tyrants and ruled over Mathura like Ram ruling over Oudh. —715

On destroying the tyrant all the people of all the directions hailed Shatrughan; his fame spread in all the directions nicely and the people came to know with great zeal that the demon Lavan had been killed. —716

End of the chapter entitled "The Meeting with Mothers and Killing of Demon Lavan" in Ramavatar in Bachittar Natak.

Now begins the Description about the Exile of Sita

It happened there like this and on this side Ram said to Sita with Love, "A forest may be created, seeing which the brightness of Nanden forest (of heaven) be dimmed." —717

Listening to the orders of Ram, the abode of *dharma*, a very beautiful garden was created; that garden looked like one bedecked with gems and diamonds and before which the forest of Indra felt shy. —718

It was thus decorated with jewels, wreaths and diamonds that all the gods had considered it as a second heaven; Ramchander went to abide there with Sita and many beautiful women. —719

A beautiful palace was built there where Ram, the abode of *dharma*, used to sleep and enjoyed at different times in various ways. —720

After sometime all the women heard that Sita was pregnant, then Sita said to Ram, "I have wondered enough in this forest, O my Lord, bid me farewell." —721

Ram sent Sita alongwith Lakshman; Lakshman left her in the Vihar forest, where there were awful trees of *saal* and *tamaal*. —722

Finding herself in a desolate forest, Sita understood that Ram had exiled her; there she began to weep in a fatal sound in a land loud voice like a warrior being shot by an arrow on the secret parts. —723

The sage Valmiki heard this voice and forsaking his silence and shouting in wonder went towards Sita; he returned to his home alongwith Sita repeating the name of Durga with mind, speech and action. —724

Sita bore a son there who was just a replica of Ram, he had the same colour, make and splendour and it seemed that Ram had taken out his part and given to him. —725

The great sage brought up that boy who was moonlike and looked like the sun during the dry, One day the sage went for Sandhya worship and Sita taking the boy with her went to take a bath. —726

When the sage came out of his contemplation after the departure of Sita, he became anxious on not seeing the boy; he created another boy quickly of the same colour and form like the first boy out of the *kusha* grass holding him in his hand. —727

When Sita came back she saw another boy of the same form seated there; Sita said, "O great sage, you had been highly graceful towards me and given me the gift of two sons gracefully." —728

End of the chapter entitled "The Birth of Two Sons" in Ramavatar in Bachittar Natak.

BHUJANG PRAYAAT STANZA

On that side the boys were being brought up and in this side Ram, the king of Avadh called the Brahmins and performed a *yajna* and for this purpose he let off a horse; Shatrughan went with that horse with a huge army. —729

That horse reached in the territories of various kings, but none of them tied him; the great kings, alongwith their great forces fell at the fact of Shatrughan with presents. —730

Wandering at the four directions the horse also reached the hermitage of the sage Valmiki, when Lava and his companions read the letter written on the head of the horse, they in great fury looked like Rudra. —731

They tied the horse with a tree and the whole army of Shatrughan saw it, the warriors of the army shouted, "O boy! Where are you taking this horse? Either leave it or wage a war with us." —732

When those weapon-wielders heard the name of

war, they showered arrows extensively; all the warriors began to fight with persistence, holding their weapons and here Lava jumped into the army raising a frightening thundering sound. —733

Many warriors were killed, they fell down on the earth and the dust arose on all the four sides; the warriors began to shower blows of their weapons and the trunks and heads of the warriors began to fly hither and thither. —734

The path was filled with the corpses of the horses and the elephants and horses began to run without drivers, the warriors fell being deprived of weapons and the ghosts, fiends and the heavenly damsels began to wander smilingly. —735

The trumpets resounded violently, the warriors began to fight and the blows of weapons were showered; the arrows were discharged creating wondrous types of heating and the mighty warriors moved in the battlefield being highly infuriated. —736

CHACHARI STANZA

The sword arose, seemed, danced and was struck. —737

An illusion was created; the sword was shown again and the blow was struck tremblingly. —738

Blows were struck with various spears. —739

The swords were down, the warriors challenged and the blows were struck with spears. —740

The warriors were raised, caused to fall and run and shown the way. —741

The arrows were discharged endured and the warriors were made feerful. —742

ANKA STANZA

When the arrows struck, then all ran away; the general were killed and the warriors ran hither and thither. —743

Leaving their horses, they ran towards Ram and lamenting in various ways, they had no courage to come face to face. —744

(The soldiers said to Ram) Lava killing the enemies, has defeated your army; those two boys are fearlessly waging the war and have gained victory. —745

Ram asked Lakshman to take a huge army and sent him; he said to him, "Do not kill these boys, but catch hold of them and show them to me." —746

Hearing the words of Raghuvir, Lakshman started, decorating his forces and shaking the waters and the planes. —747

The sky was filled with dust because of the movement of the army, all the soldiers rushed forth from all the four directions and began to remember the name of the Lord. —748

The stagging soldiers began to shower arrows, the banners waved and the arms fought with one another. —749

Coming near smilingly they shouted loudly, "O boys! Forsake your persistence quickly." —750

DOHIRA

The boys said, "O Lakshman! We shell not unfasten the horse, abandoning all your doubts you come forward to fight with all your might." —751

ANKA STANZA

Catching hold of his very huge bow Lakshman thundering like clouds, showered a volley of arrows. —752

From the other side the gods are seeing the war and the sound of "bravo, bravo" is being heard, on this side the arrows are being discharged and lots of flesh are being chopped. —753

The warriors are thundering, the drums are resounding the arrows are being discharged, but still they are not retreating from the war-arena. —754

The Speech of Lakshman Addressed to the Boys

"O boys! Listen and do not wage the war, meet me while bringing the horse, because you have inadequate strength." —755

"Come after forsaking your persistence and do not confront me, have no fear, come and meet me." —756

The boys did not agree because they were proud of their strength, they caught hold of their bows and roared and did not retrace even two steps. —757

AJBA STANZA

Both the brothers were absorbed in war and showering their arrows, they tested the strength of the soldiers. —758

The warriors fell in the battlefield being chopped into bits, and the limbs of the fighting soldiers were cut. —759

The pools of blood waved with the shower of arrows; many enemies were killed and many were filled with fear. —760

The superb warriors began to fell in the battlefield which swinging the wounds in the bodies were inflicted but still there was no dearth of zeal in them. —761

APOORAV STANZA

The number of dead is unaccountable, how many of them were killed and how many of them were defeated. —762

Feeling ashamed in their mind all ran away and absorbed in fear they went away, saving their lives. —763

Those who returned, were killed, many were wounded and many fled away. —764

The boys were victorious and the warriors were frightened, they being highly infuriated waged the war. —765

Both the brothers who were specialist in swordsmanship in great fury were engrossed in great war. —766

They pulled their bows and discharged the arrows and seeing these warriors absorbed in a terrible war, the clusters of forces fled away. —767

After getting their limbs chopped, the warriors fled away and the remaining ones fought in the war. —768

The army, being confounded, fled away, then Lakshman returned with composure. —769

Lava, stretching his bow, discharged an arrow towards the enemy, which struck Lakshman on the forehead and who fell like a tree. —770

End of the chapter entitled "Killing of Lakshman" in Ramavatar in Bachittar Natak.

ANUHAA STANZA

Making a sacrifice of Lakshman in the war, his army, being frightened fled away; the warriors reached the place where Ram was standing. —771

When all the events were recited to him, he was in great anguish hearing their words the mighty sovereign remained silent like a portrait, becoming like a stone-slab. —772

Then sitting down, he held consultations and addressing Bharat, he asked him to go, saying "Do not kill the boys of the sages, but bring them and show them to me." —773

Bharat decorating his army marched to the place where the boys were standing ready (for war); they were ready to kill the warriors by strucking blows with many types of arrows. —774

Bharat went forward towards the brave boys alongwith various types of forces of Sugriva, Vibhishana, Hanuman, Angad and Jambwant. —775

When Bharat reached the battlefield, he saw both the boys of the sages; both boys looked impressive and both the gods and demons were allured on seeing them. —776

Speech of Bharat Addressed to Lava

AKRAA STANZA

O boys of the sages! Forsake your pride, come and meet me, I shell dress you and take you to (Raghava) Ram. —777

Hearing these words the boys were filled with pride and being enraged they pulled their bows; they discharged many arrows like the clouds of the month of Savan. —778

Those, whom those arrows struck, fell down and overturned; somewhere whose arrows chopped the limbs and somewhere they penetrated thighs the fly whisk and armour. —779

Somewhere they created portraits on coming out of the beautiful bows and somewhere they pierced the limbs of the warriors; somewhere the wounds of the limbs burst open and somewhere the streams of blood overflowed. —780

Somewhere the ghosts and fiends shouted and somewhere the headless trunks began to rise in the battlefield; somewhere the brave Vaitals danced and somewhere the vampires raised flames of fire. —781

The garments of warriors were saturated with blood, on being wounded in the battlefield; on one side the warriors are running away and on the other side they are coming and fighting in the war. —782

On one side, the warriors are stretching their bows and discharging arrows; on the other side they are running away and breathing their last, but not getting a place in the heaven. —783

Many elephants and horses died and not even one was saved; then Vibhishana, the lord of Lanka, fought with the boys. —784

BAHARA STANZA

The sons of Ram pulling their bow shot an arrow in the heart of the king of Lanka; that demon fell down on the earth and considering him unconscious, the boys did not kill him. —785

Then Sugriva came and stopped them and said, "O boys! Where are you going? You cannot get away and remain safe," then the boys of the sages made a target of his forehead and shot his arrow which struck his forehead and feeling the sharpness of the arrow he became actionless. —786

On seeing this the whole army was pressed and in great fury, they began to fight alongwith Nal; Neel, Hanuman and Angad; then the boys took three arrows each and shot them on the foreheads of all. —787

Those who remained in the field, they embraced death and those who survived lost their senses and ran away; then those boys tightly shot their arrows on their targets and destroyed fearlessly the forces of Ram. —788

ANOOP NARAAJ STANZA

Seeing the strength and rage of the boys (sons of Ram) and visualising their volley of arrows in that wonderful type of war, the army of demons, raising terrible sound, fled away and wandered circularly. —789

Many wounded warriors after being shot of sharp arrows began to wander and many warriors began to roar and many of them becoming helpless breathed their last; the sharp swords of white edges were struck in the battlefield, the strength or Angad, Hanuman, Sugriva etc., began to wean away. —790

The demons began to fell in the battlefield and they got this illusion that these boys were the magical demon boys, they began to leave the earth and flee away saving their lives; the headless trunks, chopping their shackles began to rise violently and being shot of the arrows began to fell again in the battlefield. —791

The warriors being shot of arrows quickly began to fell on the earth, the dust clung to their bodies and the blood oozed out from their mouths; the vultures shrieked and roamed circularly in the sky and the ghosts and fiends began to shout in the battlefield and the vampires roamed while belching. —792

The warriors on whatever side of the earth they were began to fell, the blood flowed from the bodies of the fleeing warriors and there were terrible shouts; the resonance of fifes filled the battlefield and the clusters of warriors showering the arrows and being inflicted with wounds began to wander. —793

Seeing the war of Bharat, many warriors began to run away fearfully, on this side, in great fury, Bharat began to shower arrows; the sons of the sages in great ire showered a volley of arrows and caused Bharat to fall on the earth. —794

The warriors fled leaving Bharat fallen on the earth and rising and felling over the corpses they came to Ram; when Ram came to know of the death of Bharat; then high anguished with sorrow he fell down on the earth. —795

Ram himself started for war in great fury after decorating his army of warriors in order to kill the brave fighters and punish the unpunished; hearing the voices of the elephants and the horses the gods also became fearful and in this army there were several heroes who could destroy the bedecked forces. —796

Roaming in the sky; the vultures began to move on the earth, the goddess Durga, appeared showering innumerable fires and eating the flesh, it seemed that Shiva, the Lord of Parvati was engaged in Tandava dance in the battlefield, the heinous shouts of ghosts, fiends and brave Baitals is being heard. —797

TILKA STANZA

The warriors began to fight, the arrows were

showered, the limbs were chopped and the saddles of the horses were torn. —798

The warriors began to run on being shot by arrows; the abode of *dharma* (Ram) saw all this. —799

Being enraged the warriors began to fight and said, "arrest and bend these boys quickly." —800

The soldiers rushed forth and besieged both the death like radiant boys. —801

The boys fearlessly discharged arrows with which the warriors fell and very enduring ones fled away. —802

The warriors of chopped limbs fell in the field, they were looking extremely magnificent. —803

They are running away without seeing anything; they are leaving even Ram, the abode of *dharma*. —804

The warriors disguising themselves loosening their hair and forsaking their weapons, are running away by the sides of the battlefield. —805

DOHIRA

The warriors of both sides were killed and for two *pahars* (about six hours), the war continued; all the forces of Ram were killed and now he survived alone. —806

Lava and Kusha killed the three brothers and their forces fearlessly and now they challenged Ram. —807

The boys (of the sages) said to Ram, "O, the king of Kaushal! You have got all your army killed and where are you hiding now? Now come and fight with us." —808

Seeing the children as his own replica, Ram asked smilingly "O boys! Who are your parents." —809

AKRAA STANZA

Sita, the daughter of the king Janak of Mithilapur is beautiful like a propitious song. —810

O the king of Raghu clan! She has come to the forest and given birth to us and we are two brothers. —811

When Sita heard and came to know about Ram, she then even recognising him, did not utter a word form her mouth. —812

She forbade her sons and told them, "Ram is extremely mighty, you are persistently waging a war against him," saying this even Sita did not say the whole thing. —813

Those boys did not retreat and accepted defeat and discharged their arrows with full force after stretching their bows. —814

All the limbs of Ram were pierced and his whole body eroded, the whole army came to know this that Ram had passed away. —815

When Ram passed away, then the whole army began to flee accordingly infront of these two boys. —816

They were not even turning around to see Ram, and being helpless they fled away to whichever side they could. —817

CHAUPAI

Then both the boys without any anxiety looked towards the battlefield like Rudra surveying, the forest; the banners were cut and attached to the trees and the unique ornaments of the soldiers were removed from their limbs and thrown away. —818

Those who were unconscious, the boys raised them and reached the place alongwith the horses, where Sita was sitting, seeing her dead husband Sita said, "O sons! You have made me a widow." —819

End of the chapter entitled "The Tying of Horse by Lava and the Killing of Ram" in Ramavatar in Bachittar Natak

The Description of the Revival of All by Sita

CHAUPAI

"Bring wood for me so that I may get myself reduced to ashes with my husband," hearing this, the great sage (Valmiki) lamented greatly and said, "These boys have destroyed all our comforts." —820

When Sita said this that she would forsake her body by emanating the yoga-fire from her own body, then there was heard this speech from heaven, "O Sita, why are you acting child-like." —821

AROOPA STANZA

Sita heard the speech and took water in her hand. —822

Address of Sita to Her Mind

DOHIRA

If in mind, speech and action someone else except Ram had not been there at any time, then at this time all the dead alongwith Ram may be reanimated. —823

AROOPA STANZA

All the dead were reanimated, the illusion of all was removed and all leaving their persistence fell at the feet of Sita. —824

Sita was accepted as queen of the world and a *sati*, the source of *dharma*. —825

Ram loved her and considering her a *sati*, he hugged her to his bosom. —826

DOHIRA

Instructing Sita in many ways and taking Lava and Kusha with him Raghuvir (Ram) started for Ayodhya. —827

CHAUPAI

The children were also instructed in many ways and Sita and Ram moved towards Oudh, all the three were carrying weapons in different styles and it seemed that three Rams were walking. —828

End of the chapter entitled "The Reanimation of the Three Brothers alongwith Their Forces" in Ramavatar in Bachittar Natak.

The Description of the Entry of Sita alongwith Her Two Sons in Oudhpuri

CHAUPAI

All the three mothers hugged all of them to their bosoms and Lava and Kusha came forward to touch their feet; Sita also touched their feet and it appeared that the time of suffering had ended. —829

Raghuvir (Ram) completed the Ashvamedha *yajna* (horse-sacrifice) and in his house, his two sons seemed very impressive who had come back home after conquering many countries. —830

All the rituals of *yajna* were performed according to Vedic rules, seven *yajnas* were performed at one place, seeing which Indra wondered and fled away. —831

Ten Rajsu *yajnas* and twenty-one kinds of Ashvamedh *yajnas* were performed. Gomedh, Ajmedh and Bhupmedh several types of *yajnas* were performed. —832

Six Nagmedh *yajnas* were performed which bring victory in life, to what extent I should enumerate them because there is fear of the *Granth* becoming voluminous. —833

Ram ruled in Oudhpuri for ten thousand and ten years, then according to time schedule the death beat its turn. —834

I bow before death in various ways, which has conquered the whole world and keeping it under its control, the drum of death beats on everyone's head and no king or person had been able to conquer it. —835

DOHIRA

He, who came under its refuge, it saved him, and he, who did not go under its refuge, he could not be saved whether he was Krishna or Vishnu or Ram. —836

CHAUPAI STANZA

Performing his royal duties in many ways and preaching *sama, dama, dand* and *bhed* and other methods of administration, Ram conquered other kings of many countries. —837

He caused every cast to do its duties and set in motion *varnashrama dharma* Kshatriyas began to serve the Brahmins and the Vaishyas considered the Kshatriyas as god. —838

The Shudras began to serve all and they went wherever they were sent; Ram always talked from his mouth about practising administration according to Vedas. —839

Ram ruled by killing the tyrants like Ravana, by emancipating different devotees and attendants (Ganas) and by collecting the taxes of Lanka. —840

DOHIRA

In this way Ram ruled for a long time and on one

day Kaushalya breathed her last on the bursting of her nerve *Brahmrandhras*. —841

CHAUPAI

The ritual which is performed on the death of someone, the same was performed according to the Vedas, the benign son Ram went to the home (and himself being an incarnation) he had no shortage of any type. —842

Many rituals were performed for the salvation of the mother and by that time Kaikeyi had also passed away. After her death, look at the doing of Kal (Death), Sumitra also died. —843

One day explaining to women, Sita drew the portrait of Ravana on the well, when Ram saw this, he said somewhat angrily. —844

Speech of Ram in his Mind

She (Sita) must have had some love for Ravana, that is the reason why she is looking at his portrait drawn by her, Sita became angry on hearing these words and said, "That even the Ram had been accusing her." —845

DOHIRA

"If Ram the king of Raghu clan abides ever me in my heart in my speech and action there O mother earth! You give me some place and merge me in yourself." —846

CHAUPAI

Hearing these words the earth tore asunder and Sita merged in it; seeing this Ram wondered and in this suffering he ended all hope of ruling. —847

DOHIRA

This world is the palace of smoke which had been of no value to any one; Sita could not live without Ram and it is impossible for Ram to remain alive without Sita. —848

CHAUPAI

Ram said to Lakshman, "You sit on the gate and do not let anyone to come in." Ram himself went into the palace and abandoning his body left this abode of death. —849

DOHIRA

The way in which the king Aja had accepted Yoga for Indumati and left his home, in the same manner, Ram abandoned his body on having been separated from Sita. —850

End of the chapter entitled "Forsaking the Abode of Death for Sita" in Ramavatar in Bachittar Natak.

The Description of the Death of the Three Brothers alongwith Their Wives

CHAUPAI

There was great tumult in the whole city and none of the residents was in his senses; the men and women staggered like the warriors writhing after falling during fight in battlefield. —851

There was uproar throughout the city and the elephants and horses also began to fall, being worried, what types of sport has been played by Ram? Thinking about this thing the men and women remained under depression. —852

Bharat also produced yoga fire in his body by practising yoga and with a jerk got his *Brahmrandhra* burst and definitely went towards Ram. —853

Lakshman also did this, practising all types of yoga, his *Brahmrandhra* burst and he breathed his last to be at the feet of the Lord. —854

Lava and Kusha both came forward and performed the funeral rites of Ram and Sita; they also performed the funeral rites of the brothers of their father and in this way Lava assumed the royal canopy over his head. —855

The wives of the three brothers came there and they also became *satis* and left for the heavenly abode, Lava assumed the kingship and made the three cousins the kings of three directions. —856

Kusha himself ruled over the north, the son of Bharat was given the kingship of east, the son of Lakshman the kingship of the south and the son of the Shatrughan the kingship of the west. —857

DOHIRA

The story of Ram will remain immortal throughout the ages and in this way Ram went to abide in heaven alongwith (all the residents of) the city. —858

End of the chapter entitled "Ram went to Heaven alongwith Brothers and Their Wives." He went alongwith all the residents of the city in Ramavatar in Bachittar Natak.

CHAUPAI

He, who will listen to this story and sing it, he will be free from the sufferings and sins. The reward of the devotion to Vishnu (and his incarnation Ram), that no ailment of any kind will touch him. —859

This *Granth* (Book) has been completed (and improved) in Vadi first in the month of Asarh in the year seventeen hundred and fifty-five if there has remained any error in it, then kindly correct it. —860

DOHIRA

The story of Raghuvar Ram was completed of the grace of god on the bank of Sutlej in the valley of the mountain. —861

The saint be not considered as unsaintly ever and the debate as controversial ever; this whole *Granth* (Book) his been completed by the grace of god. —862

SWAYYA

O god! the day when I caught hold of your feet, I do not being anyone else under my sight; none other is liked by me now; the Puranas and the *Quran* try to know Thee by the name of Ram and Rahim and talk about you through several stories, but I do not accept any of their opinions; the Smritis, Shastras and Vedas describe several mysteries of yours, but I do not agree with any of them. O sword-wielder god! This all has been described by Thy grace, what power can I have to write all this? —863

DOHIRA

O Lord! I have forsaken all other door and have caught hold of only Thy door. O Lord! Thou has caught hold of my army, I, Govind, am Thy self, kindly take (care of me and) protect my honour. —864

Benign end of "The Description of the Twentieth Incarnation i.e., Ram" in Bachittar Natak.

THE LORD IS ONE AND THE VICTORY IS OF THE LORD

KRISHNA, THE TWENTY-FIRST INCARNATION

CHAUPAI

Now I describe the Krishna incarnation as to how he assumed the physical form,
The earth, with unsteady gait, reached near the Lord. —1

CHAUPAI

Amidst the milk-ocean, where the immanent Lord was seated, Brahma reached there,
The Lord called Vishnu near Him and said, "You go to the earth and assume the form of Krishna incarnation." —2

DOHIRA

Vishnu took birth in Mathura area for the welfare of saints, on receiving the orders of the Lord. —3

CHAUPAI

The sportive plays exhibited by Krishna have been described in the tenth Skandh,
There were eleven thousand and ninety-two stanzas in respect of Krishna incarnation in the tenth Skandh. —4

Now begins the Description in Praise of the Goddess

SWAYYA

On receiving Thy grace, I shall assume all the virtues,
I shall destroy all the vices, ruminating on Thy attributes in my mind,
O Chandi! I cannot utter a syllable from my mouth without Thy grace,
I can ferry across the ocean of poesy, on only the boat of Thy name. —5

DOHIRA

O mind! remember the goddess Sharda of innumerable qualities,
And if she be kind, I may compose this *Granth* (based on) Bhagavata. —6

The large-eyed Chandika is the remover of all sufferings, the donor of powers and support of the helpless in ferrying across the fearful ocean of the world,

BACHITTAR NATAK

It is difficult to know her beginning and end, she emancipates and sustains him, who takes refuge in her,
She destroys the demons, finishes various types of desires and is saviour from the noose of death,
The same goddess is capable of bestowing the boon and good intellect; by Her grace this *Granth* can be composed. —7

SWAYYA

She, who is the daughter of the mountain and the destroyer of Mahishasura,
She, who is the bestower of the kingdom on Indra by killing Sumbh and Nisumbh,
He, who remembers and serves Her, he receives the reward to his heart's desire,
And in the whole world, none other is the supporter of the poor like Her. —8

End of "The Praise of the Goddess" in Krishnavatar in Bachittar Natak.

Earth's Prayer to Brahma

SWAYYA

When the earth was overburdened by the weight and fear of the demons, she assumed the form of a cow and went to the sage Brahma,
Brahma said, "We too will go the Supreme Vishnu in order to request him to listen to our supplication." —9
All the powerful people went there under the leadership of Brahma; the sages and others began to weep before the Supreme Vishnu as if someone had beaten them;
The poet mentioning the beauty of that spectacle said that those people appeared like a trader crying before a police officer having been plundered at the instance of the headman. —10
Brahma reached the milk-ocean alongwith the gods and the forces and washed the feet of the Supreme Vishnu with water;
Seeing that Supreme Immanent Lord, the four-headed Brahma fell at His feet, whereupon the Lord said, "You may leave, I shall incarnate and destroy the demons." —11

SWAYYA

Listening to the words of the Lord, all the gods were pleased and went back to their places after paying their obeisance to him,
Visualising that spectacle the poet said that they were going back like a herd of cows. —12

Speech of the Lord

DOHIRA

Then the Lord called all the gods and ordered them to incarnate before Him. —13
When the gods heard this, they bowed and assumed the new forms of cowherds alongwith their wives. —14

DOHIRA

In this way, all the gods assumed new forms on the earth and now I narrate the story of Devaki. —15

End of "The Description about the Decision of Vishnu to incarnate" in Krishnavatar in Bachittar Natak.

Now begins the Description about the Birth of Devaki

DOHIRA

The birth of the daughter of Ugrasain named Devaki took place on Monday. —16

End of the first chapter regarding "The Description about the Birth of Devaki" in Krishnavatar in Bachittar Natak.

Now begins the Description about the Search of the Match for Devaki

DOHIRA

When that beautiful girl reached the marriageable age, then the king asked his men to search for a suitable match for her. —17

DOHIRA

The consul was sent, who approved the selection of Vasudev, whose face was like Cupid and who was the abode of all comforts and master of discriminating intellect. —18

KABIT

Putting a coconut in the lap of Vasudev and blessing him, a frontal mark was put on his forehead,
He eulogised him, sweeter then the sweetmeats, which was even liked by the Lord,
Coming home, he fully appreciated him before the women of the house,
His praises were sung in the whole world, which echoed not only in this world but also penetrated into twenty-thirty other regions. —19

DOHIRA

On this side Kansa and on that side Vasudev made arrangements for the marriage,
All the people of the world were filled with joy and the musical instruments were played. —20

Description of the Marriage of Devaki
SWAYYA

The seats were presented to Brahmins respectfully, who reciting Vedic *mantras* and rubbing saffron etc., applied it on the forehead of Vasudev, they mixed also the flowers and *panchamrit* and sang songs of praise;
On this occasion the minstrels, artists and talented persons eulogised them and received awards. —21

DOHIRA

Vasudev made all the preparations for wedding and made arrangements for going to Mathura. —22
When Ugrasain came to know of the arrival of Vasudev, he sent his four types of forces to welcome him in advance. —23

SWAYYA

The forces of both sides moved for mutual union; all of them had tied red turbans and they looked very impressive, filled with joy and gaity; the poet briefly mentioning that beauty says that they seemed like the beds of saffron coming out of their abode in order to see this delightful spectacle of the wedding. —24

DOHIRA

Kansa and Vasudev hugged each other to his bosom and then began to give gifts of various types of colourful attires. —25

SORATHA

Beating their drums, they came near Mathura and all the people were pleased to see their elegance. —26

SWAYYA

Hearing the arrival of Vasudev, all the bedecked women began to sing in tune and showered satires on the coming marriage party, the poet, mentioning the women seeing from their roofs said that they appeared like the mothers of the gods seeing the marriage party from their air-vehicles. —27

KABIT

On the arrival of Vasudev, the king got the pavilion constructed, and he was very much pleased on seeing his beautiful face; the fragrances were sprinkled on all; the songs were sung and the consul who had approved the selection, he was greatly awarded; Ugrasain worshipped the match by putting his hand on his breast, joyfully bowing his head and getting pleased in his mind—at this time the king Ugrasain appeared like the heavenly cloud showering gold, he gave in charity innumerable gold coins to the beggars. —28

DOHIRA

Then Ugrasain called Kansa near him and said, "Go and open the doors of the stores for charity." —29
Bringing the materials like corn etc., and bowing down, he requested Vasudev thus: —30
Kansa said, "The marriage has been fixed for the night of Amavas (the dark night);" on this the priest of Vasudev gave his acceptance saying "As you please." —31
The coming on this side, Kansa with folded hands related all the happenings and when the Pundits came to know that the people of Vasudev had accepted the date and time of wedding, then all gave their blessings to him within their minds. —32

SWAYYA

The night passed, the day dawned and again the night fell and then during that night, the fireworks were displayed, scattering the colours of thousands of flowers;

BACHITTAR NATAK

Seeing the flying fireworks in the sky, the poet Shyam says this figuratively that it appears to him that the gods were flying the citadels of paper in the sky, seeing this miracle. —33

SWAYYA

The priests taking Vasudev with them, are going towards the home of Kansa and seeing a beautiful woman in front of them, the Pundits caused her metallic pitcher to fall, from which the sweetmeats have fallen out with a jerk; they have taken up and eaten these sweetmeats; knowing all about it, both the sides of Yadava clan have been ridiculed in various ways. —34

KABIT

The women singing and playing their musical instruments and chanting their satirical songs look very impressive, they have slim waists like lions, eyes like does and gait like elephants; within the square of gems and on the seats of diamonds and jewels, the bride and bridegroom both look splendid; within the chanting of Vedic *mantras* and giving and taking of religious gifts, the marriage ceremony was completed with seven matrimonial rounds by God's will. —35

DOHIRA

During the night Vasudev stayed at some place and getting up in the morning, he went to meet his father-in-law Ugrasain. —36

SWAYYA

Bedecked elephants and horses and threefold chariots were given (in marriage), one lakh warriors, ten lakhs of horses and many camels laden with gold were given, thirty-six crores of soldiers on foot were given, who seemed to be given for the protection of all and Kansa himself became the charioteer of Devaki and Vasudev and for the protection of all. —37

DOHIRA

When Kansa was going with all the forces, he heard, on going forward, an invisible and inauspicious voice. —38

The Heavenly Speech addressed to Kansa
KABIT

The Lord, remover of suffering, performer of austerities for great powers and bestower of prosperity, said through the heavenly speech: "O fool ! Where are you taking your death? The eighth son of this (Devaki) will be the cause of your death;" being greatly astonished Kansa ruminated in his mind whether they be killed by taking out the sword; till what time, this fact will be kept concealed? And he will be able to save himself? Therefore he will be within his right to destroy instantly this very root of fear. —39

DOHIRA

Kansa took out his sword in order to kill both of them and seeing this both husband and wife were frightened. —40

Speech of Vasudev addressed to Kansa
DOHIRA

Absorbed in fear, Vasudev said to Kansa, "Do not kill Devaki, but O king; whosoever will be born to her, you may kill him." —41

Speech of Kansa in His Mind
DOHIRA

May it not happen that under the impact of her affection for her son, she may hide her offspring from me, therefore I feel that they may be imprisoned. —42

Imprisonment of Devaki and Vasudev
SWAYYA

Putting chains in their feet Kansa brought them back to Mathura and when the people came to know about it, they greatly talked ill of Kansa, Kansa kept them imprisoned in his own house and forsaking the traditions of his elders, he engaged servants to keep a watch over them and bound them to submit to his orders, remaining fully under his control. —43

Speech of the Poet
DOHIRA

Many days passed during the tyrannical rule of Kansa and in this way, according to the fate, the story took a new turn. —44

Description of the Birth of the First son of Devaki

DOHIRA

The first son named Kiratmat was born to Devaki and Vasudev took him to the house of Kansa. —45

SWAYYA

When the father reached the gate of the palace, he asked the gatekeeper to inform Kansa about it, Seeing the baby and taking pity Kansa said, "I have forgiven you," Vasudev started back to his house, but there was no cheerfulness in his mind. —46

Speech of Vasudev in His Mind

DOHIRA

Vasudev thought in his mind that Kansa was a man of vicious intellect, with fear, he will definitely kill the infant. —47

Speech of the Sage Narada addressed to Kansa

DOHIRA

Then the sage Narada came to Kansa and drawing eight lines before him, he told him some mysterious things. —48

Speech of Kansa to His Servants

SWAYYA

When the king listened to the speech of Narada, it went deeper into his mind; he told his servants with signs to kill the infant immediately; receiving his order all (the servants) ran away and they dashed the baby against a stone like a hammer, separated the soul from the body. —49

Killing of the First Son

SWAYYA

Another son who was born to Devaki and Vasudev, who was also killed on the orders of Kansa of vicious intellect, by his servants by dashing him on the stone; the dead body was given back to the parents; hearing about this heinous crime, there was great uproar in the whole city and this tumult appeared to the poet like the cried of gods on the death of Indra. —50

Another son was born in their house who was named Jaya, but he was also dashed against the stone by the king Kansa; Devaki began to pull out the hair of his head and began to cry like the bird called Karauncha in the sky in the spring season. —51

KABIT

The fourth son was born and he was also killed by Kansa; the flames of sorrow blazed in the hearts of Devaki and Vasudev; all the beauty of Devaki was finished by the noose of great attachment around her neck and she was drowned in great anguish; she says, "O my God! What type of Lord Thou art and what type of protected people we are? We have neither received any honour nor have got any physical protection; because of the death of our son, we are also being ridiculed, O immortal Lord! Such a cruel joke by you is sharply stinging us like an arrow." —52

SWAYYA

Hearing about the birth of fifth son, Kansa also killed him by dashing him against the stone; the soul of the infant went to heaven and his body was merged in the flowing current, hearing this Devaki began to sigh and because of the attachment she experienced such a great anguish that she appeared to have given birth to the attachment itself. —53

Speech Regarding the Supplication of Devaki

KABIT

When the sixth son was also killed by Kansa, Devaki prayed thus to God, "O, master of the lowly! Either kill us or kill Kansa; Kansa is a great sinner, whom the people consider as their king and whom they remember; O Lord! Put him in the same condition as Thou hast put us; I have heard that Thou didst save the life of the elephant; do not delay now, be kind to do any one of the two for us." —54

End of "The Description regarding the Killing of the Sixth Son" in Krishnavatar in Bachittar Natak.

Now begins the Description about the Birth of Balabhadra

SWAYYA

When Balabhadra was conceived, Devaki and Vasudev sat to hold consultations and with the power of *mantras*, he was transferred from the womb of Devaki to the womb of Rohini; thinking that Kansa may also kill him, Vasudev was frightened. It seemed that Seshanaga had assumed a new form in order to see the world.—55

DOHIRA

Both Devaki and Vasudev, began to remember Vishnu, the Lord of Lakshmi, with extreme saintliness and here Vishnu entered and enlightened the body of Devaki in order to redeem the world darkened by vices. —56

Now begins the Description about the Birth of Krishna

SWAYYA

Vishnu appeared in the womb of sleeping Devaki (in the form of Krishna) in yellow dress, wearing armour on body and holding conch, mace, trident, sword and bow in his hands; Devaki was terrified, she awoke and sat down; she did not know that a son had been born to her; seeing Vishnu apparently, she bowed at his feet. —57

DOHIRA

Devaki did not consider him as a son, but saw him in the form of god, still being a mother, her attachment grew. —58

As soon as Krishna was born the gods were filled with joy and thought that then the enemies would be destroyed and then they would be overjoyed. —59

DOHIRA

Filled with delight, the gods showered flowers and believed that Vishnu, the destroyer of sorrows and tyrants had manifested himself in the world. —60

When Devaki heard the hailings with her own ears, then she with fear began to think as to who was creating noises? —61

DOHIRA

Vasudev and Devaki began to think between themselves and considering Kansa as butcher, their hearts were filled with great fear. —62

End of "The Description about the Birth of Krishna" in Krishnavatar in Bachittar Natak.

SWAYYA

Both of them thought that the king may not also kill this son, they decided to leave him in the house of Nand; Krishna said, "Do not be fearful and go without any suspicion," saying this Krishna spread his deceptive show (*yogamaya*) in all the four directions and sat himself in the form of a beautiful child. —63

DOHIRA

On the birth of Krishna, Vasudev, in his mind, gave in charity ten thousand cows for the protection of Krishna. —64

SWAYYA

When Vasudev started, the doors of the house opened, his feet began to move further and went to enter Yamuna; the water of Yamuna came forward to see Krishna and Seshanaga powerfully ran forward, he spread his hoods and waved them like fly whisk and alongwith it the waters of Yamuna and Seshanaga both conveyed to Krishna about the increasing dirt of sin in the world. —65

DOHIRA

When Vasudev began to walk taking Krishna with him, Krishna spread his deceptive show (*maya*), on account of which the demons, who were there as watchmen went to sleep. —66

SWAYYA

Because of the fear of Kansa, when Vasudev put his feet in Yamuna, it surged up to touch the feet of Krishna, recognising in its mind some old affection; the poet felt thus about the high praise of that elegance that considering Krishna her Lord, Yamuna rose up to touch his feet. —67

DOHIRA

On this side when Yashoda went to sleep and *yoga-maya* (deceptive show) appeared in her womb; putting Krishna by the side of Yashoda Vasudev picked up her daughter and started backwards. —68

SWAYYA

Taking Maya in his hands, Vasudev quickly went to his house and at that time all the people were sleeping and none had the consciousness about the happenings inside and outside; when Vasudev came near Devaki, the doors closed themselves; when the servants heard the cries of the female infant, they informed the king. —69

When that female infant wept, then all the people heard her cries, the servants ran to inform the king, they told him that his enemy had taken birth; holding fast his sword in both his hands Kansa went there; look at the vicious action of this great fool, who himself is going to drink the poison i.e., he himself is preparing for his own death. —70

Devaki had hugged the female infant to her bosom; she said, "O fool; listen to me, you have already killed my radiant sons by dashing them against the stones," hearing these words, Kansa immediately seized the infant and said, "Now, I shall also kill her by dashing her," when Kansa did all that, then this infant, who was protected by the Lord, went as lightning in the sky and flashed. —71

KABIT

Kansa said to his servants in great fury and after great considerations, "I order you to kill her;" holding her in his hand and without caring for royal discipline, she was dashed against a huge stone, but inspite of being held in such strong hands, she herself was slipping away and spattering; because of the impact of *maya*, she splashed like mercury, causing every one to listen to her voice. —72

SWAYYA

This *maya* manifested herself assuming eight arms and holding her weapons in her hands; the flames of fire were coming out of her mouth, she said, "O foolish Kansa! Your enemy has taken birth at another place," saying this much, and creating fear in the hearts of the enemies, she began to wave like lightning in the sky and all the demons became fearful, thinking that she may kill all of them. —73

Now begins the Description of the Liberation of Devaki and Vasudev

SWAYYA

When Kansa heard all this with his own ears, then he, the slanderer of gods, came to his house; he thought that he had uselessly killed the sons of his sister; thinking this, he bowed down his head on the feet of his sister; talking to them at length, he delighted both Devaki and Vasudev; having been pleased himself, he called the ironsmith, he got the chains of Devaki and Vasudev cut and freed them. —74

End of "The Description about the Liberation of Devaki and Vasudev" in Krishnavatar in Bachittar Natak.

Consultations of Kansa with His Ministers

DOHIRA

Calling all his ministers and holding consultations with them, Kansa said, "All the boys in my country be killed." —75

SWAYYA

This chaste story of *Bhagavata* has been described very aptly and now I am narrating only from that one. In Braja country Vishnu had assumed the form of Murari, seeing whom the gods as well as the men and women of the earth were filled with joy, seeing this incarnation of incarnations, there were rejoicings in every house. —76

SWAYYA

When Yashoda awoke, she became extremely happy on seeing the son, she bestowed charities in abundance on the Pundits, singers and talented persons; knowing about the birth of a son to Yashoda, the women of Braja moved out of their houses wearing red head clothes; it seemed that within the clouds, the gems are moving scattered hither and thither. —77

Speech of Nand addressed to Kansa

DOHIRA

The chieftain Nand went to meet Kansa alongwith some people and he prayed that a son had been born in his house. —78

Speech of Vasudev addressed to Nand

DOHIRA

When Vasudev heard about the return (journey) of Nand, then he said to Nand, the chief of *gopas* (milkmen), "You should be extremely fearful" (because Kansa had ordered the killing of all the boys). —79

Speech of Kansa addressed to Bakasur

SWAYYA

Kansa said to Bakasur, "Listen to me and do this work of mine; all the boys who are born in this country, you may destroy them immediately; one of these boys will be the cause of my death, therefore my heart is greatly fearful; Kansa was worried, thinking in this way; it seemed that the black serpent had stung him. —80

Speech of Putana addressed to Kansa

DOHIRA

Hearing this Putana said to Kansa, "I shall go and kill all the children and thus all your suffering will end." —81

SWAYYA

Saying this and bowing her head she got up and applied the sweet poison to her teats, so that whichever child will suck her teat, he may die in an instant. "O intelligent, wise and truthful king; we all have come in your service, rule fearlessly and remove all anxieties." —82

Speech of the Poet

DOHIRA

That sinful woman resolved to kill Krishna, the Lord of the world and completely embellishing herself and wearing a deceptive garb, she reached Gokul. —83

SWAYYA

She had put antimony in her eyes and a round mark on her forehead, her arms were beautiful, the waist was slim like a lion and there was sound of anklets from her feet; wearing a necklace of gems, she reached at the door of Nand in order to perform the task assigned by Kansa; the fragrance emanating from her body spread in all the four directions and seeing her face even the moon feel shy. —84

Speech of Yashoda addressed to Putana

DOHIRA

Yashoda gave her respect and asked about her welfare and giving her a seat, she began to talk to her. —85

Speech of Putana addressed to Yashoda

DOHIRA

"O mother! I have come to know that you have given birth to a unique child, give him to me so that I may cause him to drink my milk, because this promising child will become the emperor of all." —86

SWAYYA

Then Yashoda put Krishna in her lap and in this way Putana called her own end; that woman of vicious intellect had been very fortunate because she made the Lord to drink milk from her teats; Krishna sucked her blood (instead of milk) with his mouth alongwith his life-force like the pressing and filtering the oil from the colocynth. —87

DOHIRA

Putana committed such a great sin, which may even frighten the hell, while dying she said, "O Krishna! Leave me" and saying this much she went to heaven. —88

SWAYYA

The body of Putana grew as long as six *kos*; her belly looked like a tank and face like a gutter; her arms were like the two banks of the tank and hair like the scum spread on the tank; her head became like the top of the Sumeru mountain and there appeared great pits in place of her eyes; within the pits of her eyes, the eyeballs appeared like the cannons fixed in the fort of a king. —89

DOHIRA

Krishna went to sleep with the teat of Putana in his mouth and the residents of Braja woke him up. —90

DOHIRA

The people gathered the parts of the body of Putana and got it burnt by putting fuel on all the four sides. —91

SWAYYA

When Nand came to Gokul and knowing all that had happened, he was extremely wonder-struck; when the people told him the saga of Putana, then he also was filled with fear in his mind, he began to think about the warning given to him by Vasudev, which was true and he was seeing the same apparently; on that day Nand gave charity to Brahmins in various ways, who gave him many blessings. —92

DOHIRA

The Lord, ocean of mercy has incarnated in the form of a child and in the first place he liberated the earth from the burden of Putana. —93

End of the chapter entitled "Killing of Putana" in Krishnavatar (based on *Dasham Skandapurana*) in Bachittar Natak.

Now begins the Description of the Naming Ceremony

DOHIRA

Then Vasudev requested the family-preceptor Garg to kindly go to Gokul in the house of Nand. —94

My son is there, kindly perform the naming ceremony take care that no one else knows this secret except you and me. —95

SWAYYA

Accepting the saying of Vasudev, the Brahmin Garg quickly started for Gokul and reached the house of Nand, where he was warmly received by the wife of Nand. The Brahmin gave the name Krishna to the boy, which was accepted by all, then he, studying the date and time of the birth of the boy, he pointed out the coming mysterious events in the life of the boy. —96

DOHIRA

Garg thought out in his mind and gave the name of Krishna to the boy and when the boy raised his feet, it seemed to the Pundit that he was similar to Vishnu. —97

The black colour is the symbol of Satyuga and the yellow of Treta, but wearing the yellow clothes and having the body of dark colour, both of these are not the characteristics of ordinary men. —98

SWAYYA

When Nand presented the alms of corn to Garg, he taking all, came to the banks of Yamuna in order to cook food; after taking bath, he offered food to gods and the Lord; while he was remembering the Lord Krishna, the son of Nand reached there and taking the food from the hand of Garg, he ate it; the Brahmin, in wonder, began to see this and think that this boy with his touch had soiled his food. —99

Then the Pundit thought in his mind, how can he be a boy? This is some illusion. The creator has created this world with the unison of the mind, five elements and the soul; I had been merely remembering Nandlal and this will be my illusion; that Brahmin could not recognise and his intellect closed down just as the tailor covers the body with a cloth. —100

SWAYYA

When this thing happened thrice, the Brahmin's mind was filled with rage; the mother Yashoda cried at such saying and she hugged Krishna to her bosom; then Krishna said that he was not to be blamed for this, this Brahmin is only to be blamed, he remembered me thrice for eating food and I have gone there; hearing this, the Brahmin realised in his mind and getting up, he touched the feet of Krishna. —101

DOHIRA

The charity given by Nand to the Brahmin cannot be described; with happy mind, Garg went to his home. —102

End of "The Description of Naming Ceremony" in Krishnavatar in Bachittar Natak.

SWAYYA

Krishna is swinging in the cradle in the form of a boy and his mother is oscillating him with affection; the poet has described the simile of this beautiful scene in this way; just as the earth sustains both friends and foes equally, in the same way, the mother Yashoda, knowing fully well the possibilities of the difficulties in bringing up Krishna, is sustaining him happily. —103

When Krishna became hungry, he wanted to drink his mother Yashoda's milk; the mother got up without getting angry, when Krishna moved his foot with force and the vessels full of oil and ghee fell down from her hands on the earth; the poet Shyam visualised this scene in his imagination; on the other hand, hearing about the killing of Putana, there was great tumult in Braja country and the suffering of the earth ended. —104

All the people of Braja came running and every one of them hugged Krishna; the women of Braja country began to sing songs of joy of various types; the earth shook and the children began to relate various stories about the killing of Putana, hearing which all marvelled in their minds and hesitated to accept this true episode. —105

SWAYYA

Inviting all the people of Braja, Nand and Yashoda gave good deal of alms by touching them with the head and other limbs of Krishna; the charity of clothes etc., was given to many beggars; in this way many gifts of charity were presented in order to remove the sufferings of all. —106

Speech of Kansa addressed to Tranavrata
ARIL

When Kansa came to know that Putana had been killed in Gokul, he said to Tranavrata, "You go there and kill the son of Nand by dashing him like a stone with a jerk." —107

SWAYYA

Bowing before Kansa, Tranavrata quickly reached Gokul and transformed himself into a duststorm and began to blow with a great speed, Krishna became extremely weighty and colliding against him, Tranavrata fell down on the earth, but still when the eyes of the people were filled with dust and closed down, he flew in the sky taking Krishna with him. —108

When he reached high in the sky alongwith Krishna, because of the beating of Krishna his power began to decline; manifesting himself in a dreadful form Krishna fought a battle with that demon and wounded him; then with his own hands and with the ten nails, he chopped the head of the enemy; the trunk of Tranavrata fell on the earth like a tree and his head fell like a lemon falling down from a bough. —109

End of "The Description of the Killing of Tranavrata" in Krishnavatar in Bachittar Natak.

SWAYYA

The people of Gokul felt helpless without Krishna, they gathered together and went in search for him; during search, he was found at a distance of twelve *kos* and all the people hugged him and sang songs of joy; that scene has been described thus by the great poet. —110

Seeing the dreadful form of the demon, all the *gopas* were frightened; what to say of men, even Indra, the king of gods, seeing the body of the demon, was filled with fear; Krishna killed this terrible demon in an instant; then he returned to his home and all the inhabitants talked amongst themselves about all this event. —111

After bestowing great deal of gifts in charity to the Brahmins, the mother Yashoda plays again with her child Krishna, who keeping his finger on his lips gradually smiles mildly; the mother Yashoda feels great joy and her happiness cannot be described; this scene extremely allured the mind of the poet also. —112

Now Krishna shows the Whole Universe from His Mouth to Yashoda

SWAYYA

With the increased attachment in her mind, the mother Yashoda again began to play with her son; then Krishna ruminating in his mind quickly yawned; Yashoda was nonplussed and queer type of suspicious arose in her mind; she moved forward and with her own hand covered the mouth of her son and in this way, she saw the *maya* of Vishnu. —113

Krishna began to crawl on his knees in the house and the mother felt delight in using various similies about him; the cows of Nand walked behind the marks of the feet of the companions of Krishna; the mother Yashoda, seeing this, flashed in delight like the lightning among the clouds and why should that mother be not happy, in whose house a son like Krishna had taken birth. —114

SWAYYA

In order to give training in walking to Krishna, all the *gopas* together made a cart for children and causing Krishna to sit in that cart, they wheeled it; then Yashoda taking him in her lap, made him to suck her milk and when he slept, the poet considered it supreme bliss. —115

DOHIRA

When he awoke from sleep, Krishna quickly got up and through signs of his eyes, he insisted on playing. —116

In this way, Krishna played various types of plays in Braja and now I describe the story of his walking on feet. —117

SWAYYA

After one year, Krishna began to walk on his strengthened feet, Yashoda was greatly pleased and in order to keep his son before his eyes, she walked behind him; she told about Krishna's walking to all the *gopis* and the fame of Krishna spread throughout the world; the beautiful ladies also came to see Krishna bringing with them butter etc. —118

Krishna plays with the children of *gopas* on the banks of Yamuna and imitates the voices of birds. He imitates their gait also; then sitting on the sand, all the children clap their hands and the poet Shyam says that all of them sing songs from their beautiful mouths. —119

Krishna plays in the company of *gopa* children in the alleys on the banks of Yamuna and swimming the whole of the river, he lies down on the sand on the other side; then he jumps like a juggler with all the children; he rips the waters with his breast; then fighting like sheep among themselves and smite their head against the head of another one. —120

When Krishna comes to his home, then after taking food, he goes to play again, the mother asks him to stay at home, but inspite of saying, he does not stay within his home and gets up and runs outside; the poet Shyam says that Krishna, the Lord of Braja, loves the streets of Braja

and he is fully absorbed in the game of hide and seek with other *gopa* children. —121

Playing on the banks of Yamuna Krishna enjoys with other *gopa* children; climbing on the tree, he throws his club and then seeks it and brings it from amongst the milkmaids; the poet Shyam says while mentioning this simile that in order to see this splendour, the sages engaged in various disciplines of yoga are also getting sacrificed. —122

End of the eighth chapter entitled "Description of the Plays with Gopa Children" in Krishnavatar in Bachittar Natak.

Now begins the Description of Stealing and Eating Butter

SWAYYA

With the pretence of playing, Krishna is eating butter within the house and with the signs of his eyes, he is calling other *gopa* children asking them to eat; they are offering the remaining butter to monkeys causing them to eat; the poet Shyam says that in this way Krishna is annoying the *gopis*. —123

When Krishna ate all the butter, the *gopis* cried and said to Nand's wife Yashoda that Krishna had caused all the vessels to fall down; "Because of the fear of Krishna, we keep the butter at a higher place, but still he, with the support of mortars, gets high up and abusing us eats the butter alongwith other children. —124

O Yashoda! The person in whose house, they do not get butter, there they raising noises, call bad names; if someone gets angry with them, considering them as boys, they then beat him with their clubs; besides this if some woman comes and tries to reprimand them, then they all pull down her hair and O Yashoda! Listen to the behaviour of your son, he does not comply without conflict. —125

Hearing the words of the *gopis*, Yashoda became angry in her mind, but when Krishna came home, she was delighted to see him; Krishna said on coming, "These milkmaids annoy me very much, they are blaming me only for curd, they will not get right without beating." —126

The mother asked the son, "Alright son! Tell me, how do these *gopis* annoy you?" Then the son said to the mother, "They all run away with my cap, they close my nose, strike my head and then return my cap after getting my nose rubbed and after making mockery of me." —127

Speech of Yashoda addressed to Gopis
SWAYYA

The mother Yashoda said angrily to those *gopis*, "Why do you annoy my child? You are bragging with your mouth that the curd, cow and wealth is only in your house and none other has got them; O foolish milkmaids! You continue to speak without thinking, stay here and I shall set you right; Krishna is very simple, if you will say anything to him without any fault, you will be considered mad." —128

DOHIRA

Then Yashoda instructed both Krishna and *gopis* and caused peace for both the parties; she said to *gopis*, "If Krishna soils one *seer* of your milk, you come and take a *maund* from me." —129

Speech of Gopis addressed to Yashoda
DOHIRA

Then the *gopis* said, "O mother Yashoda! Your dear son may live for ages, we ourselves shall give him a mine of milk and shall never have an ill-thought in our mind." —130

End of "The Description about the Stealing of Butter" in Krishnavatar in Bachittar Natak.

Now fully opening His Mouth Krishna shows the Whole Universe to His Mother Yashoda

SWAYYA

When the *gopis* went to their own homes, then Krishna exhibited a new show; he took Balram with him and began to play; during the play, Balram noticed that Krishna is eating clay; when leaving the play all the children of milkmen came to their homes in order to have meal, then Balram silently told mother Yashoda about Krishna eating clay. —131

The mother angrily caught hold of Krishna and taking the stick, began to beat him; then Krishna got afraid in his mind and cried "Yashoda mother! Yashoda mother!" The mother said, "All of you may come and see in his mouth;" when the mother asked him to show his mouth, Krishna opened his mouth; the poet says that Krishna at the same time showed the whole universe to them in his mouth. —132

He showed the ocean, the earth, the nether-world and the region of Nagas; the reciters of Vedas were seen warming themselves with Brahma-fire; seeing the powers, wealth and herself, the mother Yashoda realising that Krishna was beyond all mysteries, began to touch his feet; the poet says that those who saw this spectacle with their own eyes, are very fortunate. —133

DOHIRA

The mother saw the beings of all the divisions of creation in the mouth of Krishna; forsaking the notion of sonship, she began to touch the feet of Krishna. —134

End of the description entitled "Showing the Whole Universe, to Mother Yashoda fully opening his Mouth" in Krishnavatar in Bachittar Natak.

Now begins the Description of the Salvation of Yamlarjuna on breaking off the Trees

SWAYYA

Then Yashoda got up from the feet of Krishna and she eulogised Krishna in many ways: "O Lord! Thou art the master of the world and the ocean of mercy, I had considered myself the mother in ignorance; I am of low intellect, forgive all my vices;" then Hari (Krishna) closed his mouth and concealed this fact under the impact of affection. —135

KABIT

Yashoda very kindly allowed Krishna to go and play in the forest alongwith the children of *gopas*, but on complaint of other children the mother began to beat Krishna again with sticks; then seeing the marks of sticks on the body of Krishna, the mother, in attachment, began to weep; the poet Shyam says that beating of such a saintly personality cannot be thought about, one should not even get angry before him. —136

DOHIRA

The mother Yashoda has got up to churn the curd; she is uttering a eulogy of her son from her mouth and his praise cannot be described. —137

SWAYYA

Once Yashoda was churning the curd alongwith the *gopis*; she had tied her waist and she was meditating on Krishna; there were small bells tightened over the girdle; the poet Shyam says that the charity and the glory of austerity cannot be described; the mother, in delight, is singing the songs about Krishna from her mouth. —138

When the teats of mother Yashoda were filled with milk, then Krishna awoke; she began to give him milk and Krishna was absorbed in that pleasure; on the other side the milk in the vessel turned sour, thinking about that vessels the mother went to see it, then Krishna began to weep; he, (the king of Braja) got so much angry that he ran out from the house. —139

DOHIRA

Krishna, in rage, went out of the house, taking the *gopa* children and monkeys with him, he formulated an army and then returned. —140

All of them broke the pitchers of milk by pelting stones on them and the milk flowed on all the four sides; Krishna and his companions drank the milk to their fill. —141

SWAYYA

In this way, formulating an army, Krishna began to plunder the milk of Yashoda; catching the vessels in their hands, they began to throw them hither and thither; seeing the milk and curd spread here and there, this idea has come into the mind of the poet that the spread of milk is a sign in advance of the bursting of the marrow from the cracked skull. —142

SWAYYA

When all the vessels were broken by Krishna, then Yashoda ran with rage; the monkeys ascended the trees and the army of *gopa* children was made to run away by signs by Krishna; Krishna kept running and his mother was exhausted; the poet Shyam says that when Krishna was caught, he the Lord of Braja was tied with the *ukhal* tree. —143

SWAYYA

When Yashoda ran to catch Krishna and tied him, he began to cry; the mother gathered together the ropes of Braja, but Krishna could not be bound down; ultimately, he was tied with *ukhal* and began to roll on the earth; this was being done only for the salvation of Yamlarjuna. —144

DOHIRA

Dragging the *ukhal* behind him, Krishna began to emancipate the saints, He, the unfathomable Lord went near them. —145

SWAYYA

Krishna entangled *ukhal* with another tree and uprooted it with the force of his body; there appeared Yamlarjuna from underneath the tree and after bowing before Krishna, he went to heaven; the beauty of this spectacle has attracted so much the great poet that it seemed that he has obtained the pitcher of honey, pulled down from the region of Nagas. —146

SWAYYA

Seeing this wonderful spectacle, the people of Braja came running to Yashoda and told her that Krishna had uprooted the trees with the force of his body; describing that winsome scene, the poet has said that the mother was overwhelmed and she flew like a fly to see Krishna. —147

SWAYYA

Krishna is like Shiva for the killing of demons; He is the Creator, the giver of comforts, the remover of sufferings of the people and the brother of Balram; the mother, under the impact of attachment, called his as her son and said that this is the sport of God that a son like Krishna had taken birth in her house. —148

End of the description of the "Salvation of Yamlarjuna by Uprooting the Trees" in Krishnavatar in Bachittar Natak.

SWAYYA

When the trees were uprooted, all the *gopas* decided after consultations that then they should leave Gokul and live in Braja, because it had become difficult to live in Gokul; hearing about such a decision, Yashoda and Nand also decided that there was no other suitable place except Braja for the protection of their son. —149

The grass, the shade of trees, the bank of Yamuna and the mountain are all there; there are many cataracts there and there is no other place like it in the world; there the voice of peacocks and nightingales is heard on all four sides, therefore we should leave Gokul immediately and go to Braja in order to earn the merit of thousands of virtuous actions. —150

DOHIRA

Nand said this to all the *gopas* that they should then leave Gokul for Braja, because there is no other good place like it. —151

All of them tied their goods quickly and came to Braja; there they saw the flowing waters of Yamuna. —152

SWAYYA

With the concurrence of Nand, all the *gopas* decorated their chariots, the women sat in them and they started with the resonance of their musical instruments; Yashoda looks impressive with Krishna in her lap; it seems that she has obtained this good reward after offering gold in charity; Yashoda seems like a rock in the mountain and Krishna in her lap appears like a sapphire. —153

The *gopas* forsaking Gokul came to their abodes in Braja; they sprinkled buttermilk and fragrances and burnt incenses within their houses and outside; the great poet has said about this beautiful scene that it seemed to him that after bestowing the kingdom of Lanka on Vibhishana, Ram had purified Lanka again. —154

Speech of the Poet
DOHIRA

All the *gopas* were delighted to be in Braja and now I narrate the wonderful sports of Krishna. —155

SWAYYA

After seven years Krishna began to graze cows, he produced tunes by combining the leaves of the *pipal* tree and all the boys began to sing on the tune of the flute; he used to bring the *gopa* boys in his home and also caused fear in them and threatened them at his will; the mother Yashoda on getting pleased and seeing them dancing she served milk to all of them. —156

SWAYYA

The trees of Braja began to fall and with this the demons were also redeemed; seeing this the flowers were showered from the sky; the poets gave various similes regarding this scene; the voices of "bravo, bravo" were heard in the three worlds and there were supplications: "O Lord! Lighten the burden of the earth." Listen to this story attentively, as described by the poet Shyam. —157

Seeing this wonderful sport, the boys of Braja, visiting every home, have related it; listening about the killing of demons, Yashoda was pleased in her mind and whatever description the poet has given through the flow of his composition, the same has become famous in all the four directions; there was the flowing current of joy in the mind of the mother Yashoda. —158

Now begins the Description of the Killing of the Demon Bakasura

SWAYYA

Hearing about the killing of demons, the king Kansa said to Bakasura, "Now you abandon Mathura and go to Braja." He bowed and stated on saying this: "I am going there, when you are sending me;" Kansa said smiling, "You will now kill Him (Krishna) through deception." —159

SWAYYA

As the day dawned, Krishna (Girdhari) took the cows and calves to the forest; then he went to the bank of Yamuna, where the calves drank pure (and not saltish) water; at that time there came a dreadful-looking demon named Bakasura; he transformed himself into a heron and gulped all the cattle, whom Krishna had left there. —160

DOHIRA

Then Vishnu assuming the form of fire, burnt his throat and Bakasura considering his end near, out of fear, vomitted them all. —161

SWAYYA

When Bakasura hit them, then Krishna caught his beak with force and ripped him, a stream of blood began to flow; what more should I describe this spectacle; the soul of that demon merged in God like the light of the stars merging in the light of the day. —162

KABIT

When the demon came and opened his mouth, then Krishna thought about his destruction; Krishna, who is worshipped by gods and adepts, disjoined his beak and killed the mighty demon; he fell on the earth in two halves and the poet felt inspired to relate it; it seemed that the children having gone to play in the forest cleaved the long grass through the middle. —163

End of "The Killing of the Demon Bakasura" in Krishnavatar in Bachittar Natak.

SWAYYA

Krishna returned to his home in the evening alongwith the calves and the *gopa* boys and everyone was delighted and sang songs of joy; the poet has figuratively described this spectacle saying that Krishna killed deceptively the demon who had come to kill him through deception. —164

Speech of Krishna addressed to Gopas
SWAYYA

Krishna said to *gopas* again that they would go again early next morning; they should take some eatables with them from their homes, which they would eat together in the forest; they would swim Yamuna and go to the other bank, dance and jump there and play their flutes. —165

SWAYYA

All the *gopas* agreed on this arrangement; when the night passed and the day dawned, Krishna played on his flute and all the *gopas* awoke and released the cows, some of them, twisting the leaves began to play on them like musical instruments; the poet Shyam says that seeing this wonderful spectacle, the wives of Indra felt embarrassed in heaven. —166

Krishna applied the red ochre to his body and fixed the feather of the peacock on his head; he put his green flute on his lips and his face, adored by the whole world looked splendid; he bedecked his head with the bunches of flowers and that Creator of the world, standing under a tree, is showing to the world His play, which was comprehended only by Him. —167

Speech of Kansa addressed to His Ministers
DOHIRA

When Kansa heard about the killing of Bakasura, then he called his ministers and held consultations regarding the demon to be sent next. —168

Speech of the Ministers addressed to Kansa
SWAYYA

The king Kansa, after holding consultation with his ministers asked Aghasura to go to Braja, so that he may assume the form of a dreadful snake and lie down in the way, and when Krishna comes to that side, he may chew him alongwith the *gopas*; either Aghasura should come back after chewing them or failing in this endeavour, he should be killed by Kansa. —169

Now begins the Description regarding the Arrival of the Demon Aghasura

SWAYYA

As commanded by Kansa, Aghasura assumed the form of a dreadful snake went (for his errand) and hearing about the killing of his brother Bakasura and his sister Putana, he was also highly infuriated; he sat down in the way, opening widely his dreadful mouth, keeping in his mind, his errand of killing Krishna; seeing him, all the boys of Braja, considered it a play and none could know his real objective. —170

Speech of all the Gopas amongst Themselves
SWAYYA

Someone said that it is a cave within the mountain; someone said that there was the abode of darkness; someone said that it was a demon and someone said that it was a huge snake; some of them expressed a desire to go into it and some of them refused to go and in this way, the discussion continued; then one of them said, "Go into it fearlessly, Krishna will protect us." —171

They called Krishna and all of them entered in it and that demon closed his mouth; he had already thought about it that as Krishna would enter, he would close his mouth; when Krishna went in, he closed his mouth and there was great lamentation amongst the gods; all of them began to say that he was the only support of their life and he was also chewed by Aghasura. —172

SWAYYA

Krishna prevented the full closure of the mouth of the demon by extending his body; Krishna obstructed the whole way with his force and hands and thus the breath of Aghasura began to be puffed up; Krishna tore away his head and this brother of Bakasura breathed his last; the marrow of his head came out like the breaking of the pitcher of ghee of some trader. —173

In this way, when the passage was created, Krishna came out alongwith his *gopa* friends from the head of the demon; all the gods were overjoyed to see Krishna surviving from the attack of the huge serpent; the Ganas and Gandharvas began to sing songs and Brahma began to recite Vedas; there was happiness in the minds of all; and Krishna and his companions, the conquerors of the Naga, started for their home. —174

SWAYYA

Krishna came out from the head of the demon and not from his mouth, saturated with blood, all were standing like a sage clad in red ochre clothes; the poet has also given a simile for this spectacle; it seemed that the *gopas* had become red by carrying on heads the bricks and Krishna had run and stood on the top of the citadel. —175

End of "The Killing of the Demon Aghasura" in Krishnavatar in Bachittar Natak.

Now begins the Description of the Calves and Gopas stolen by Brahma

SWAYYA

After killing the demon, all went to the bank of Yamuna and put the articles of meal together; all the boys gathered around Krishna; putting his flute in his waist, Krishna felt great delight, they immediately seasoned the food and began to eat it quickly with their left hand and put the tasty food in the mouth of Krishna. —176

Someone, being frightened, began to put the morsels in the mouth of Krishna and someone causing Krishna to eat the food, began to put the morsels in his own mouth; in this way all began to play with Krishna and at the same time, Brahma gathered together their calves closed them in a cottage; all of them went in search of their calves, but not any *gopa* and calf could be found. —177

DOHIRA

When Brahma did all this stealing, then at the same instant Krishna created the calves alongwith *gopas*. —178

SWAYYA

The same forms, the same garments and exactly the same colour of the calves, when evening fell, Krishna returned to his home; who is there to adjudge his power? Brahma thought that the parents would, seeing all this, understand the whole thing and the game of Krishna would now be finished. —179

When Krishna played on his flute, Yashoda kissed his head and none other paid attention to his boy; they all loved Krishna; whatever tumult is there in Braja, such a tumult is not there at any other place; it is not being known how the time is passing Krishna began to sing songs with *gopis* alongwith the newly married women. —180

SWAYYA

When the day dawned, Krishna again went to the forest taking the calves with him; he saw there all the *gopa* boys singing songs and twirling their clubs; continuing the play, Krishna went towards the mountain; someone said that

Krishna was angry with them and someone said that he was unwell. —181

SWAYYA

Krishna moved on with the boys and the cows; seeing them on the top of the mountain all ran towards them; *gopas* also went towards them; Yashoda also saw this spectacle; Krishna was standing there in anger without moving; and all these people told many things to Krishna. —182

Speech of Nand addressed to Krishna
SWAYYA

"O son! Why have you brought the cows here? In this way, the production of milk for us has declined; all the calves have drunk their milk and this illusion persists in our mind;" Krishna did not tell them anything and in this way, he increased their feeling of attachment; seeing the form of Krishna, the anger of all cooled down like water. —183

SWAYYA

The affection increased in the minds of all, because no one of them could abandon his son; the affection of cows and calves could be forsaken; in the way, gradually, remembering all these things all went to their homes; seeing all this Yashoda was also frightened and thought that possibly this was some miracle of Krishna. —184

After the lapse of several years, once Krishna went to the forest, Brahma also reached there in order to see his wonderful play; he was astonished to see the same *gopa* children and calves that he had stolen; seeing all this, Brahma fell at the feet of Krishna, in fear and in bliss, he began to play the musical instruments denoting rejoicings. —185

Speech of Brahma addressed to Krishna

"O Lord of the world! Treasure of mercy! Immortal Lord! Listen to my request; I have erred, kindly forgive me for this fault;" Krishna said, "I have forgiven, but abandoning the nectar, the poison should not be taken; go and bring all the men and animals without delay." —186

Brahma brought all the calves and *gopas* in an instant; when all the *gopa* boys met Krishna, all were greatly pleased; with this, all the calves made by the *maya* of Krishna, disappeared, but none could know this mystery; nobody understood this secret and all said, "Bring, whatever you have brought, we all may eat it together." —187

The boys of Braj gathered together all the food and began to eat it; Krishna said, "I have killed the Naga (serpent)," but none could know about this play; they were all pleased considering the Garuda (blue jay) as their protector; and Krishna said, "You may tell this at your home that Lord has protected our lives." —188

End of the description of "Coming of Brahma alongwith the Calves and Falling at the Feet of Krishna" in Krishnavatar in Bachittar Natak.

Now begins the Description of the Killing of the Demon named Dhenuka

SWAYYA

Krishna went to graze the cows till the age of twelve; his form was extremely beautiful and every one praised him. Seeing Krishna in the forest with *gopa* boys the poet says that the Lord has prepared the army for killing Kansa. —189

KABIT

His face is like lotus, the eyes are winsome, his waist is like lion and his arms are long like lotus-stalk; his throat is sweet like that of a nightingale, the nostrils are like that of the parrot, the eyebrows like a bow and the speech pure like Ganges; with whomsoever he talks, he remains restless; on alluring the women, he moves in the neighbouring villages like the moon, moving in the sky, exciting the love-sick ladies; the men of low intellect, not knowing this secret, call Krishna of supreme qualities as mere cow-grazer. —190

Speech of Gopis addressed to Krishna
SWAYYA

All the women of Braja, gathering together, talk among themselves that though his face is dark, his countenance is like moon, eyes are like doe, he ever abides in our heart day and night; O friend! knowing about him, the fear emanates in the heart and it appears that the god of love resides in the body of Krishna. —191

Speech of Krishna
SWAYYA

All the *gopis* went with Krishna and said to him, "You are going to manifest yourself as an incarnation; none can know your greatness;" Krishna said, "Nobody will come to know about my personality, I just exhibit all my plays only to amuse the mind." —192

SWAYYA

There were beautiful tanks at that place, which created peace in the mind and among them there was one tank gleaming with beautiful white flowers; a mound was seen bulging out within that tank and seeing the white flowers it seemed to the poet that the earth, with hundreds of eyes, has come to see the wonderful play of Krishna. —193

Krishna has an extremely beautiful form, seeing which the bliss increases; Krishna plays in the forest at those places, where there are deep tanks; the *gopa* boys look impressive with Krishna and seeing them, the suffering of grievous hearts is removed; observing the wonderful play of Krishna, the earth also became pleased and the trees, the symbols of the hair of the earth, also feel coolness on seeing his amorous sport. —194

Standing aslant under a tree Krishna plays on his flute and all are allured including Yamuna, birds, serpents, yakshas and wild animals; he, who heard the voice of the flute, whether he was a Pundit or an ordinary person, he was fascinated; the poet says that it is not the flute, it appears that it is a long path of male and female musical modes. —195

The earth, seeing the beautiful face of Krishna is enamoured of him in her mind and thinks that because of his form, his figure is extremely radiant; speaking out his mind, the poet Shyam gives this simile that the earth, clad in the garments of various colours is imagining herself becoming the chief queen of Krishna. —196

Speech of the Gopas
SWAYYA

One day the *gopas* requested Krishna saying that there is a tank, where there are planted many fruit trees; adding that the bunches of wine there are very fit to be eaten by him, but there lives a demon named Dhenuka, who kills the people; the same demon protects that tank; he catches the sons of the people at night and getting up at dawn, he devours them. —197

Speech of Krishna
SWAYYA

Krishna told all his companions that the fruit of that tank are really good; Balram also said at that time that the nectar is insipid before them; "Let us go there and kill the demon, so that the suffering of the gods in heaven (sky) be removed." In this way, all being pleased and playing on their flutes and conches proceeded to that side. —198

Krishna, being pleased, accompanying all, went towards the bank of that tank; Balram knocked off the fruit of that tree which fell like the drops on the earth; with great rage, the demon Dhenuka struck with feet together, but Krishna, catching his legs, threw him like a dog. —199

SWAYYA

Then the army of that demon, considering their general as killed, assumed the form of cows and in great fury, raising dust, attacked them; Krishna and mighty Haldhar caused that four-typed army fly away in all the ten directions like a farmer causing the chaff to fly away at the threshing floor, while separating it from the grain. —200

End of the description of "The Killing of the Demon Dhenuka" in Krishnavatar (based on *Dasham Skandapurana*) in Bachittar Natak.

SWAYYA

Hearing about the destruction of the four-typed army of demons, the gods eulogised Krishna; all the *gopa* boys started back eating fruit and raising dust; the poet has described that scene like this; that the dust raised by the hoofs of the horses reached the sun. —201

Destroying the demons alongwith the army, *gopas*, *gopis* and Krishna came back to their homes; the mothers were pleased and began to praise all in various ways; all were getting strengthened by eating rice and milk; the mothers said to the *gopis*, "In this way, the top-knots of all the people will become long and thick." —202

Krishna slept after taking meal and dreamt that after drinking good deal of water, his belly had been greatly filled; when the night advanced further, he heard a frightening sound, which asked him to go away from that place; Krishna came away from that place and reached his home and met his mother. —203

SWAYYA

Krishna went to sleep and went again to the forest early in the morning, taking away his calves; at noon, he reached a place, where there was a very big tank; there the Kali serpent stung all the cows, calves and the *gopa* boys and they all fell down dead; seeing this Balram said to Krishna, "Run away, all your army of the boys has been killed by the snake. —204

DOHIRA

Krishna looked towards all with his graceful glance, and all the cows and *gopa* boys came back to life instantly. —205

DOHIRA

All got up and touched his feet, saying, "O giver of life to us! None is greater than you." —206

Now begins the Description of the Stringing of the Serpent Kali

DOHIRA

Krishna held consultations with the *gopa* boys that the tyrant Naga (Kali) lives in that tank and it should be ejected. —207

SWAYYA

Ascending the *kadamba* tree, Krishna jumped in the tank from its height; he did not fear even a little and moved patiently; the water arose to sevenfold height of man and from that, the Naga appeared, but Krishna even then was not frightened at all; when the Naga saw a man riding upon him, he began to fight. —208

He intertwined Krishna, who in great fury, chopped its body; the grasp of the snake on Krishna loosened, but the viewers held great fear in their hearts; the ladies of the Braja village started moving towards that side pulling their hair and carding their heads, but Nand reprimanded them saying "Do not weep, O people! Krishna will return only on killing him." —209

SWAYYA

Intertwining Krishna, that huge snake began to hiss in great rage; the serpent was hissing like a moneylender sighing on the loss of his cashbox; that snake was breathing like a resounding drum or his voice was like that of a great-whirlpool in water. —210

The boys of Braja were seeing all this in wonder and catching the arms of one another, they were thinking that Krishna should kill the snake in any way; all the men and women of Braja were seeing this wonderful spectacle and on this side the black snake was biting Krishna like a person eating his food with relish. —211

When Yashoda also began to weep, her friends consoled her saying, "Do not be anxious at all, Krishna has killed the demons like Tranavrata, Bakasura etc., Krishna is extremely powerful, he will come back after killing the snake on the other side, Krishna destroyed all the hoods of that snake with his power. —212

Speech of the Poet

SWAYYA

Seeing all his people in great distress, standing on the bank, Krishna got his body released from the entanglement of the snake; seeing this that dreadful snake got furious, he again spread his hoods, came running in front of Krishna; Krishna, saving himself from the ambush jumped and stood with his feet on the forehead of the serpent. —213

SWAYYA

Ascending on the head of that snake, Krishna began to jump and the currents of hot blood began to flow from the head (of the serpent); when that serpent was to breathe his last, all the lustre of his being ended; then Krishna dragged the serpent to the bank of the river with his power; that Naga was pulled towards the bank and on tying ropes from all the four sides, he was dragged out. —214

Speech of the Wife of the Serpent Kali

Then the wives of the snake, while weeping, said, with folded hands, "O Lord! Grant us the boon of the protection of this snake; O Lord! If you give ambrosia to us, we adopt the same and if you give the poison, that also is adopted by us; there is no fault of our husband in this," saying this much they bowed their heads. —215

"We people had great fear of Garuda (blue jay) and we had concealed ourselves in this pool; our husband had definitely some pride and he has not remembered the Lord: O Lord! Our foolish husband did not know that it were you who had chopped all the ten heads of Ravana; we all had destroyed ourselves our family in vain, on being agitated." —216

Speech of Krishna addressed to the Family of the Serpent Kali

SWAYYA

Then Krishna said, "Now I release you all, you go away towards the south; do not abide ever in this pool, all of you may go away now alongwith your children. All of you taking your women with you leave immediately and remember the Name of the Lord." In this way, Krishna released Kali and being tired he lay down on the sand. —217

Speech of the Poet

SWAYYA

Krishna saw that that huge snake got up and moved back to its own place and lying on the sand wanted to sleep comfortably as though he had remained awake for several nights; his pride had been smashed and he was absorbed in the love of the Lord; he began to praise the Lord and lay down there like the unused manure left in the field by the farmer. —218

When the consciousness of the snake returned, he fell at the feet of Krishna: "O Lord! Being tired, I had slept and on waking, I have come to touch your feet," Krishna said, "Whatever I have said, you act on it and observe the *dharma* (discipline) and O women! Undoubtedly my vehicle Garuda was desirous of killing him, but still I have not killed him." —219

End of the description of "The Ejection of the Serpent Kali" in Krishnavatar in Bachittar Natak.

Now begins the Description of the Bestowal of Charity

SWAYYA

Bidding farewell to Naga, Krishna came to his family; Balram came running to him, his mother met him and the sorrow of everyone ended; at the same time, one thousand golden-horned cows, sacrificing them on Krishna, were given in charity; the poet Shyam says that in this way, extending their extreme attachment in mind, this charity was given to Brahmins. —220

Red gems, pearls, jewels and horses were given in charity; many types of brocaded garments were given to Brahmins; the bags filled with necklaces of diamonds, jewels and gems were given and giving the golden ornaments, the mother Yashoda prays that her son be protected. —221

Now begins the Description of the Forest-fire

SWAYYA

All the people of Braja, being pleased, slept in their homes at night; the fire broke out at night in all directions and all became afraid; all of them thought that they would be protected by Krishna; Krishna told them to close their eyes, so that all their sufferings may end. —222

As soon as all the people closed their eyes, Krishna drank the whole fire; he removed all their sufferings and fears; they, whose agony is removed by Krishna, how can they remain anxious for anything? The heat of all was cooled down as if they were cooled by washing in the waves of water. —223

KABIT

By getting the eyes of the people closed and expanding his body in endless pleasure, Krishna devoured all the fire; the poet Shyam says that Krishna performed a very difficult task and with this his name spread in all the ten directions and all this work was done like a juggler, who chews and digests all, keeping himself out of sight. —224

End of the description regarding "The Protection from Forest-fire" in Krishnavatar of Bachittar Natak.

Now begins the Description of playing Holi with the Gopas

SWAYYA

After the month of Magh, in the season of Phagun, all began to play Holi; all the people gathered together in couples and sang songs with the playing of musical instruments; various colours were splashed on women and the women beat the men with staffs (with affection); the poet Shyam says that Krishna and beautiful damsels are together playing this tumultuous Holi. —225

When the spring season ended, and with the beginning of the summer Krishna began to play Holi with pomp and show; the people poured in from both sides and were pleased to see Krishna as their leader; in all this tumult, a demon named Pralamb assuming the appearance of youth came and mixed with other youths; he carried Krishna on his shoulder and flew; Krishna caused the fall and death of that demon with fists. —226

Krishna became the leader and began to play with lovely boys; the demon also became the playmate of Krishna and in that play Balram won and Krishna was defeated; then Krishna asked Haldhar to mount on the body of that demon; Balram put his foot on his body and causing his fall, he threw him (on the ground) and with his fists killed him. —227

End of "The Killing of the Demon Pralamb" in Krishnavatar in Bachittar Natak.

Now begins the Description of the Play of "Hide and Seek"

SWAYYA

Haldhar killed the demon Pralamb and called Krishna; then Krishna kissed the faces of cows and calves and being pleased, the treasure of mercy (Krishna) began the play of "hide and seek;" this spectacle has been described by the poet in various ways. —228

KABIT

One *gopa* boy closes the eyes of another boy and leaving him, he closes the eyes of another one; then that boy closes the eyes of that boy who had been closing the eyes and whose body has been touched with hands; then with deception, he tries not to be touched with hand; in this way, the poet says that the praise of this cannot be described and Krishna is receiving endless pleasure in this play. —229

SWAYYA

The summer season ended and the comfort-giving rainy season came; Krishna is wandering with his cows and calves in the forest and caves and singing the songs liked by him; the poet has described this spectacle in this way. —230

All of them are causing one another to listen to the musical modes of Sorath, Sarang, Gujri, Lalit, Bhairava, Deepak, Todi, Megh Malhar, Gaund, and Shuddh Malhar; all are singing there Jaitsri, Malsri and Sri *ragas*; the poet Shyam says that Krishna, in pleasure, is playing several musical modes on his flute. —231

KABIT

Krishna is playing on his flute the musical modes named Lalit, Dhanasari, Kedara, Malwa, Bihagra, Gujri, Maru, Kanhra, Kalyan, Megh, and Bilawal; and standing under the tree, he is playing the musical modes of Bhairava, Bhim Palasi, Deepak, and Gauri; hearing the sound of these modes, leaving their homes, the doe-eyed women are running hither and thither. —232

SWAYYA

The winter has come and with the arrival of the month of Kartik, the water became less; Krishna bedecking himself with the flowers of *kaner*, is playing on his flute early in the morning; the poet Shyam remembering the simile, he is composing the Kabit stanza in his mind and describing that the god of love has awakened in the body of all women and rolling like a snake. —233

Speech of the Gopi
SWAYYA

"O mother! This flute has performed many austerities, abstinences and baths at pilgrim stations; it has received instructions from Gandharvas; it has been instructed by the god of love and Brahma has made it himself; this is the reason that Krishna has touched it with his lips." —234

Krishna, the son of Nand, is playing on his flute and the poet Shyam says that hearing the sound of the flute, the sages and the beings of the forest are getting pleased; the bodies of the *gopis* have been filled with lust and they are saying that the mouth of Krishna is like a rose and the voice of the flute seems like the essence of the rose dripping down. —235

Hearing the voice of the flute, the fish, deer and bird all are infatuated; "O people! Open your eyes and see that the water of Yamuna is flowing in the opposite direction;" the poet says that hearing the flute, the calves stopped eating grass; the wife has left her husband like a *sannyasi* leaving his home and wealth. —236

The nightingales, parrots and deer etc., all have been absorbed in the anguish of lust; all the people of the city are getting pleased and saying that the moon seems bedimmed before the face of Krishna; all the musical modes are sacrificing themselves before the tune of the flute; the sage Narad, stopping the playing of his lyre, has been listening to the flute of the black Krishna and has tired. —237

His (Krishna's) eyes are like those of the doe, the waist is like that of the lion, the nose is like that of the parrot, the neck like that of the pigeon and (*sustenance*) is like ambrosia; his speech is sweet like the nightingale and the peacock; these sweetly-speaking beings are now feeling shy of the sound of the flute and are getting jealous in their minds. —238

The rose looks insipid before his beauty and the red and elegant colour is feeling embarrassed before his comeliness; the lotus and narcissus are feeling shy before his charm; the poet appears indecisive in his mind about his beauty and says that he has not been able to find a winsome person like Krishna though he has roamed from east to west in order to see one like him. —239

SWAYYA

In the month of Maghar all the *gopis* worship Durga wishing for Krishna as their husband; early in the morning, they take bath in Yamuna and seeing them, the lotus flowers feel shy; catching the arms of one another, they sing the songs in Bilawal *raga* and relate the story of Krishna; the god of love is increasing its hold on their limbs and seeing all of them even modesty is feeling shy. —240

All the black and white *gopis* are singing songs and all the slim and heavy *gopis* are wishing for Krishna as their husband; seeing their faces, the supernatural powers of the moon seem to have lost their brightness and taking their bath in Yamuna, they appear like a splendid garden in the house. —241

SWAYYA

All the *gopis* are bathing fearlessly; they are singing songs of Krishna and playing the tunes and they are all gathered in a group; they are all saying that such comfort is even not in the palaces of Indra; the poet says that they look splendid like a tank full of lotus flowers. —242

Speech of Gopis addressed to the Goddess
SWAYYA

Taking clay in their hands and installing the image of the goddess and bowing their heads at her feet, all of them are saying, "O goddess! We worship you for bestowing the boon according to our heart's desire, so that our husband be of the moonlike face of Krishna." —243

They apply saffron *akshat* and sandal on the forehead of the god of love, then showering flowers, they fan him affectionately; they are offering garments, incense, *panchamrit*, religious gifts and circumambulation and they making effort to wed Krishna, say that there may be some friend, who may fulfil the wish of our mind. —244

Speech of the Gopis addressed to the Goddess
KABIT

"O Goddess! Thou art the power, who destroys the demons, ferries across the sinners from this world and removes the sufferings; Thou art the redeemer of the Vedas, Giver of the kingdom to Indra the shining light of Gauri; there is no other light like Thee on the earth and in the sky; Thou art in the sun, moon, stars, Indra and Shiva etc., glowing as light in all. —245

KABIT

All the *gopis* are praying with folded hands: "O Chandi; Listen to our prayer, because you have redeemed also the gods, ferried across millions of sinners and destroyed Chand, Mund, Sumbh and Nisumbh; O mother! Bestow on us the boon asked for; we are worshipping you and Shaligram, the son of Gandak river, because you had been pleased to accept his saying; therefore bestow on us the boon." —246

Speech of the Goddess addressed to the Gopis
SWAYYA

"Your husband will be Krishna," saying thus, Durga bestowed boon on them; hearing these words, all of them got up and bowed before the goddess millions of times; the poet has considered in his mind this spectacle in this way that they all have been dyed in the love of Krishna and absorbed in him. —247

SWAYYA

All the *gopis* falling at the feet of the goddess began to eulogise him in various ways: "O the mother of the world! You are the remover of the suffering of all the world; you are the mother of Ganas and Gandharvas;" the poet says that on realising Krishna as their husband, the faces of all the *gopis* were filled with happiness and shyness and became red. —248

The *gopis* returned to their homes, being pleased, on receiving the desired boon and began to congratulate one another and exhibited their joy by singing songs; they are standing in a queue in this way as if the blossoming lotus-buds are standing in the tank and viewing the moon. —249

SWAYYA

Early in the morning all the *gopis* went towards Yamuna; they were singing songs and seeing them in bliss, 'the bliss' also seemed to be in anger; then Krishna also went towards Yamuna and seeing the *gopis*, he said to them, "Why do you not speak? And why are you keeping silent." —250

Now begins the Description about the Removal of Clothes

SWAYYA

When the *gopis* began to take bath, Krishna ascended the tree taking away their clothes; the *gopis* smiled and some of them shouted and said to him, "You have fraudulently stolen our clothes, there is no other *thug* like you; you have taken away our clothes with your hands and now are capturing our beauty with your eyes." —251

Speech of the Gopis addressed to Krishna
SWAYYA

Gopis said, "O Krishna! You have learnt this good (for nothing) job; you may see towards Nand, see towards your brother Balram; when Kansa will know of it that you have stolen our clothes, then that mighty one will kill you; none will say anything to us; the king will pluck you like the lotus." —252

Speech of Krishna addressed to the Gopis

Krishna said, "I shall not return your clothes till you come out; why all of you are hiding in water and getting your bodies bitten by leeches; the king, whom you are naming, I have not an iota of fear from him; I shall dash him (on the ground) by catching him by his hair like the faggot thrown in fire." —253

SWAYYA

Saying this, Krishna ascended further on the tree

BACHITTAR NATAK

in anger, the *gopis* then, being enraged, said, "We shall tell your parents;" Krishna said, "Go and say about it to anyone whom you want to say; I know that your mind is not so bold to say anything to any one; if any one says, anything to me, I shall deal with him accordingly." —254

SWAYYA

Speech of Krishna

"O dear ones! I shall not give back the clothes without your getting out of water; you are uselessly enduring cold in the water; O white, black, slim and heavy *gopis*! Why are you coming out keeping your hands in front and at the back? You ask with folded hands, otherwise I shall not give you clothes." —255

SWAYYA

Then Krishna said in slight anger, "Listen to my words, forsake your shyness, come out of water and bow before me with folded hands; I am telling you again and again to accept whatever I say quickly, otherwise I shall go and tell everybody; I am swearing by my Lord; accept whatever I say." —256

Speech of the Gopis addressed to Krishna
SWAYYA

"If you go and say anything, we shall also say like this that Krishna had stolen our clothes, how could we come out of water? We shall tell everything to mother Yashoda and make you feel ashamed like the one having received good thrashing from women." —257

Speech of Krishna
DOHIRA

Krishna said, "You are entangling me uselessly; if you do not bow before me, then I swear against you." —258

Speech of the Gopis
SWAYYA

The *gopis* said, "O Krishna! Why are you annoying us and swearing on us? The purpose for which you are doing all this, we have also understood it; when you have the same idea in your mind (that you want to possess all of us), then why are you quarrelling with us uselessly? We swear by the Lord that we shall not say anything about it to your mother." —259

Speech of Krishna addressed to the Gopis
SWAYYA

"What the mother will say on hearing about me? But alongwith it, all the women of Braja will know about it; I know that you are greatly foolish, therefore you are talking foolishly," Krishna added, "You do not know as yet the mode of amorous pastime (*rasa-lila*), but all of you are dear to me; I have stolen your clothes for the amorous play with you." —260

Speech of the Gopis
SWAYYA

Then *gopis* talking amongst themselves, said to Krishna, "We swear by Balram and Yashoda, please do not annoy us; O Krishna! Think in your mind, you will not gain anything in this; you hand over the clothes to us in water, we all shall bless you." —261

Speech of the Gopis
SWAYYA

Then the *gopis* said to Krishna, "The love is not observed by force; the love that is created on seeing with eyes is the actual love" Krishna said smilingly, "See, do not make me understand the mode of amorous pastime; with the support of eyes, the love is then performed with hands." —262

The *gopis* said again, "O son of Nand! Give us the clothes, we are good women; we will never come to have bath here;" Krishna replied, "Alright; come out of the water immediately and bow before me;" he added smilingly, "Be quick, I shall give you the clothes just now." —263

DOHIRA

All of them decided, "Alright, let us go out of water and then request Krishna." —264

SWAYYA

All of them came out of water concealing their secret parts with their hands; they fell at the feet of Krishna and requested him in various ways to return the stolen clothes: "We have said, whatever was in our mind; give us the clothes quickly, we are shivering with cold." —265

Speech of Krishna
SWAYYA

Krishna said, "See, whatever I shall say now all of you will have to accept that; let me kiss the faces of all; I shall kiss and you count, all of you; let me touch the nipple of your breasts, otherwise I shall behave more badly with you; I am speaking truth that I shall give you the clothes only after doing all this." —266

SWAYYA

Krishna said again, "Listen to one thing of mine and bow before me with folded hands because all of you abide now in my heart like the supernatural powers of the god of love; I have said this to all of you for doing it, seeing the proper occasion and solitude for it; my heart has become satisfied on seeing you and receiving the donation of beauty from all of you." —267

Speech of the Poet
DOHIRA

When Krishna saw towards the *gopis*, causing the dance of his eyes, then all of them, being pleased, began to utter sweet words like ambrosia. —268

Speech of the Gopis addressed to Krishna
SWAYYA

"O Krishna! Already you have less understanding, you may play now in your own home; when Nand and Yashoda will listen, then you will feel more inferior with shame; the love cannot be done with force, why are you doing all that? You cannot feel pleased in such things now, because you are still a boy." —269

KABIT

The *gopis* with lotus-like faces, doe-like eyes and with lustrous bodies filled with emotions looked impressive like the green and white colours on the rising of the moon; they are standing with Krishna, while talking about dancing and amorous pastime, they are standing like the ones standing for braiding the necklace of gems in order to vest the god of love. —270

SWAYYA

"O Krishna! Why are you discharging the arrows of the god of love from the bow of your eyebrows? Why are you advancing towards us with increased love smiling? Why do you wear slanting turban and why do you walk slantingly also? Why are you bewitching us all? O captivating one! You appear to us very fine, though you had sworn about it." —271

When the women of Braja heard the words of Krishna, they got pleased in their minds and gradually they, having the gait of the elephant, came under that tree, on which Krishna was sitting, their eyes began to see Krishna constantly; they appeared like the lightnings of lust; Krishna, greatly agitated, seeing those women, fell upon them like a hungry falcon. —272

SWAYYA

Those *gopis* had the beauty of the god of love, faces like moon, noses like parrot, eyes like doe, bodies like gold, teeth like pomegranate, necks like pigeons and sweet speech like nightingales; Krishna said to them smilingly, "You people have enchanted my mind by your signs and by causing the dance of your eyebrows." —273

Krishna appeared like a man of taste to them and they clung to him, they said, "You must swear by Yashoda that you will not tell any one that you had enticed us like that," they added: "We are your slaves; kindly return our clothes; O Krishna, how should we bow before you? We are feeling very shy." —274

SWAYYA

"I have stolen your clothes and how now you are enduring more cold uselessly; I am absorbed in your love and I have found you today after a great search; bow before me with folded hands; I tell you on oath that from today you are mine," Krishna said smilingly, "Listen, everything has occurred on your coming out of water, why are you absorbed in more thoughts now uselessly." —275

"Do not feel shy from me and also do not have any doubt about me; I am your servant; accepting my request, bow before me with folded hands;" Krishna said further, "I live only on seeing your doe-like eyes; do not delay, you will not lose anything by this." —276

DOHIRA

When Krishna did not return the clothes, then accepting defeat, the *gopis* decided to do whatever Krishna said. —277

SWAYYA

All of them smiling among themselves and uttering sweet words, began to bow before Krishna: "O Krishna! Now be pleased with us, we bow before you; now there is no difference between you and us and whatever pleases you, is good for us." —278

SWAYYA

"Your eyebrows are like a bow, from which the arrows of lust are coming out and striking us like the dagger; the eyes are extremely beautiful, the face is like moon and the hair like a she-serpent; even if we see you a little, the mind gets infatuate;" Krishna said, "When the lust has arisen in my mind, therefore I had requested you all; let me kiss your faces and I swear that I shall not tell anything at home." —279

SWAYYA

The *gopis* accepted with pleasure all, that Krishna said; the current of joy increased in their mind stream of love flowed; the shyness disappeared from both sides and Krishna also said smilingly, "I have obtained today the store of happiness." —280

SWAYYA

The *gopis* said amongst themselves, "See, what Krishna has said;" hearing the words of Krishna, the stream of love gushed up further; how from their minds all the suspicious were removed and they all said smilingly, "The boon bestowed by the mother Durga, has evidently manifested in reality before us." —281

SWAYYA

Krishna performed amorous play with them and then giving them their clothes, he released all of them; all the *gopis*, adoring the mother Durga, went to their homes; the happiness grew in their hearts to the extreme like the growth of green grass on the earth after the rain. —282

Speech of the Gopis

ARIL

Bravo to Mother Durga, who bestowed this boon on us and bravo to this day today, in which Krishna has become our friend, "O Mother Durga! Now be graceful to us so that one day also we may get opportunity of meeting, Krishna." —283

Speech of the Gopis addressed to the Goddess

SWAYYA

"O Chandi! Be graceful to us so that Krishna may remain our beloved; we fall at Thy feet that Krishna may meet us as our beloved and Balram as our brother; therefore, O Mother! Thy name is sung all over the world as the destroyer of demons; we shall fall at Thy feet again, when this boon will be bestowed upon us." —284

KABIT

The poet Shyam says "O Goddess! Thou art the death of the demons and lover of the saints and the Creator of the beginning and the end; Thou art Parvati, the eight-armed goddess, extremely beautiful and the sustainer of the hungry; Thou art the red, white and yellow colour and Thou art the manifestation and Creator of the Earth." —285

SWAYYA

The lion is Thy vehicle; O eight-armed goddess! The disc, the trident and the mace are in your hands; there are dagger, arrows, shield, bow also and the quiver in the waist; all the *gopis* are worshipping the goddess, with desire for Krishna in their minds; they are offering fragrance, incense and *panchamrit* and lighting the earthen lamps, they are putting the garlands of flowers around her neck. —286

KABIT

O mother! We are causing Thee to listen, we are

repeating Thy name, and we are not remembering anyone else; we are singing Thy praises and we are offering flowers to honour Thee; the type of boon bestowed by Thee earlier on us, likewise bestow another boon regarding Krishna; if Krishna cannot be given to us, then give us ashes (for smearing our body), a *kanthi* (necklace) to be put around our neck and rings for our ear, so that we may become yogins, forsaking the world. —287

Speech of the Goddess
SWAYYA

Then Durga said smilingly, "I have bestowed the boon of Krishna on all of you; All of you may remain pleased, because I have spoken the truth and not told a lie; Krishna will be a comfort for you and seeing you in comfort, my eyes shall be filled with comfort; you may all go to your homes and Krishna will wed all of you. —288

Speech of the Poet
DOHIRA

All the young women of Braja, getting pleased and blowing their heads and touching the feet of the goddess, went to their own homes. —289

SWAYYA

All the *gopis*, catching the hands of one another, went to their homes, with happiness in their minds; they were all saying this, that Durga, having been pleased, has bestowed on all of us Krishna as our bridegroom and filled with this delight, all those beautiful ladies reached their homes; they gave abundance of charity to Brahmins, because they had obtained their Krishna, as desired by their heart. —290

DOHIRA

On one occasion, all the girls (*gopis*) talking together sweetly, began to describe various limbs of Krishna. —291

SWAYYA

Someone says that the face of Krishna is captivating; someone says that the nostril of Krishna is winsome; someone says with pleasure that the waist of Krishna is like a lion; and someone says that the body of Krishna is made of gold; someone gives the simile of doe for the eyes and the poet Shyam says that like the soul pervading the bodies of the human beings, Krishna pervades in the minds of all the *gopis*. —292

Seeing the face of Krishna like the moon, all the girls of Braja are getting pleased; on this side Krishna is allured by all the *gopis* and on the other side, because of the boon bestowed by Durga, *gopis* are feeling impatient; in order to increase the impatience of the *gopis*, Krishna stays in some other house for some time, then the hearts of all the *gopis* cracked like the easy cracking of the chords of the tube of lotus. —293

The mutual love of Krishna and *gopis* continued increasing; both sides are feeling restless and go to take bath several times; Krishna, who had defeated the forces of demons earlier, has now come under the control of *gopis*; now he is exhibiting his amorous play to the world and after a few days, he will overthrow Kansa. —294

SWAYYA

The poet Shyam says that on one side the *gopis* are keeping awake and of the other side, Krishna does not get a wink of sleep at night; they are pleased to see Krishna with their eyes; they are not satisfied merely with love and the lust is increasing in their bodies; while playing with Krishna, the day dawns and they are not conscious about it. —295

The day dawned and the sparrows began to chirp; the cows were driven to the forest; the *gopas* have awakened, Nand has awakened and the mother Yashoda has also awakened; Krishna also awoke and Balram also awoke; on that side, the *gopas* went to take bath and on this side Krishna went to *gopis*. —296

SWAYYA

The *gopis* are smilingly busy in amorous talk; alluring the agile Krishna with their eyes, *gopis* say like this: "We do not know anything about any other, but this much is surely known to us that he, who drinks the sap, only knows the worth of sap; the depth in love comes only when one falls in love and one feels pleasure in taking about the essence. —297

Speech of the Gopis addressed to Krishna

SWAYYA

"O friend! We want to listen about the essence; make us understand the mode of realising the essence; we want to see you and you love the nipples of our teats;" the *gopis* talk such like things with Krishna and such is the condition of those women that they are becoming unconscious-like in the love of Krishna. —298

End of the chapter entitled "Stealing of Clothes" in Krishnavatar (based on *Dasham Skandapurana*) in Bachittar Natak.

Now begins the Description regarding the Sending of Gopas to the House of Brahmins

DOHIRA

After voluptuous play with the *gopis* and taking bath Krishna went to the forest to graze the cows. —299

DOHIRA

Praising the beautiful women, Krishna went further and the *gopa* boys who were with him, became hungry. —300

SWAYYA

The leaves of those trees are good, their flowers, fruit and shade are all good; at the time of coming home, Krishna played on his flute under those trees; hearing the voice of his flute, the wind seemed to stop blowing for a while and Yamuna also got entangled. —301

Krishna plays on his flute the musical modes like Malshri, Jaitshri, Sarang, Gauri, Sorath, Shuddh Malhar, and the Bilawal which is sweet like nectar and hearing these *ragas*, the heavenly damsels and the wives of demons all are getting fascinated; hearing the voice of the flute, Radha, the daughter of Brishbhan is coming running like a doe. —302

Radha said with folded hands, "O Lord! I am hungry; the milk has remained back in all the houses of the *gopas* and while playing, I forget everything; I am wandering alongwith you;" when Krishna heard this, he told all to go into the houses of Brahmins in Mathura (and bring something to eat); "I am speaking truth to you there is not an iota of falsehood in it." —303

Speech of Krishna

SWAYYA

Krishna said to all the *gopas*, "Go to Mathura, the city of Kansa and ask about the Brahmins, who perform *yajnas;* request them with folded hands and falling at their feet, saying that Krishna is hungry and is asking for food. —304

Gopas accepted the saying of Krishna and bowing their heads, they all went away and reached the houses of Brahmins; the *gopas* bowed before them and in the guise of Krishna, they asked for food; now see their cleverness that they are cheating all the Brahmins in the guise of Krishna. —305

Speech of the Brahmins

SWAYYA

The Brahmins spoke in anger: "You people have come to ask us for food; Krishna and Balram are very foolish; do you consider all of us as fools? We merely fill our bellies by begging for rice you have come to beg from us," saying these words, the Brahmins expressed their anger. —306

When the Brahmins did not give anything for eating, then getting embarrassed all the *gopas* left Mathura and came back to Krishna on the bank of Yamuna; seeing them coming without food, Krishna and Balram said, "The Brahmins come to us at the time of need, but run away when we ask for something." —307

KABIT

These Brahmins are morally vicious, cruel, coward, very mean and very inferior, even sacrifice their lives for bread; they can act like imposters and plunderers on the paths; they sit down like ignorant people; they are clever from within and though they have very little knowledge, they run hither and thither with great speed like deer; they are very ugly, but call themselves beautiful and roam in the city unobstructed like animals. —308

Speech of Balram addressed to Krishna

SWAYYA

"O Krishna! If you say, then I can tear Mathura into two halves with the blow of my mace; if you say, then I will catch the Brahmins, if you say, I will kill them and if you say, I will rebuke them a little and then release them; if you say, then I will uproot the whole city of Mathura with my power and throw it away in Yamuna; I have some fear from you, otherwise, O Yadava king! I can destroy all the enemies alone." —309

Speech of Krishna

SWAYYA

"O Balram! One may be forgiven anger," saying this Krishna addressed the *gopa* boys, "The Brahmin is the *guru* of the whole world" (but it seems wonderful) that the *gopas* obeyed and went again to ask for food and reached the capital of the king, but even on naming, the proud Brahmins did not give anything. —310

KABIT

Getting angry again at the *gopa* boys of Krishna, the Brahmins replied, but did not give anything to eat; then they being displeased, came back to Krishna and said on bowing their heads, "The Brahmins, on seeing us, have kept silent and have not given anything to eat; therefore we are enraged; O the Lord of the lowly! We are extremely hungry, take some steps for us; the strength of our body has extremely declined." —311

SWAYYA

Seeing them very hungry, Krishna said, "You may do this; go to the wives of Brahmins, these Brahmins have low intellect; the reason for which they perform *yajnas* and *havans*, these fools do not know its significance and are turning the sweet into bitter one." —312

SWAYYA

Gopas bowing their heads went again and reached the homes of Brahmins; they said to the Brahmin's wives, "Krishna is very hungry," the wives were pleased to listen about Krishna and getting up, ran to meet him, in order to remove their sufferings. —313

The wives did not stop, though they were forbidden by the Brahmins and ran to meet Krishna; someone fell in the way and someone, getting up, ran again and saving her life came to Krishna; this spectacle has been described by the poet thus; that the women moved with a great speed like the stream breaking through the closure of straw. —314

SWAYYA

Very fortunate wives of Brahmins went to meet Krishna; they advanced to touch the feet of Krishna, they are moon-faced and doe-eyed; their limbs are beautiful and they are so many in numbers that even Brahma cannot count them: they have come out of their houses like the female serpents under the control of mantras. —315

DOHIRA

They all obtained comfort on seeing the face of Krishna and seeing the women nearby, the god of love also shared that comfort. —316

SWAYYA

His eyes like the delicate lotus-flower and on his head, the peacock feathers look impressive; his eyebrows have increased the splendour of his face like millions of moon; what to say about this friend Krishna, the enemy is also fascinated on seeing him. It seems that the god has himself, rinsing the whole essence, presented it before Krishna. —317

Placing his hands on the hands of the *gopa* boys, Krishna is standing under a tree; he is wearing the yellow garments, seeing which the pleasure has increased in the mind; the poet has described this spectacle in this way; it seems that the lightning is flashing from the dark clouds. —318

SWAYYA

Seeing the eyes of Krishna, the wives of Brahmins were intoxicated with his beauty; they forgot about their houses whose memory flew away like cotton before the wind; the fire of the

BACHITTAR NATAK

separation blazed in them like the fire when the oil is poured on it; their condition was like the iron on seeing the magnet or like the iron-needle which gets extremely desirous of meeting the magnet. —319

SWAYYA

Seeing Krishna, the suffering of the wives of Brahmins was cast away and their love was greatly increased, just as the agony of Bhishma was removed on touching the feet of his mother; the women, on seeing the face of Krishna, absorbed it in their mind and closed their eyes like the wealthy person closing his cash in his safe. —320

SWAYYA

When those regained some of their consciousness, then Krishna smilingly said to them, "Now you return to your homes, live with the Brahmins and remember me day and night; when you will remember me, you will not fear Yama (death) and in this way, you will attain salvation." —321

Speech of the Wives of Brahmins
SWAYYA

"We are the wives of Brahmins, but O Krishna! we will not abandon you, we shall stay with you day and night and if you go to Braja, then we all shall accompany you there; our mind has merged in you and there is no desire now of returning home; he, who becomes a yogi completely and leaves his home, he does not takes care of his home, and wealth again." —322

Speech of Krishna
SWAYYA

Seeing them with affection, Krishna asked them to go home and also told them to redeem their husbands by relating to them the story of Krishna; he asked them to remove the sufferings of sons, grandsons and husbands with this discussion and repeating the name "Krishna," the giver of the fragrance of sandalwood, fill the other trees with this fragrance. —323

Listening to the ambrosial words of Krishna the wives of Brahmins agreed and the instructions given by Krishna to them cannot be given in the same volume by any celibate; when they discussed about Krishna with their husbands, it led to this situation that their faces turned black and the faces of these ladies became red with the essence of love. —324

All the Brahmins repented on listening to the discussion of their wives and said, "We alongwith the knowledge of our Vedas be cursed that the *gopas* came to beg from us and went away; we remained immersed in the sea of pride and awoke only on losing the opportunity; now we are fortunate only that our women dyed in the love of Krishna are our wives. —325

The Brahmins cursing themselves eulogised Krishna and said, "The Vedas tell us that Krishna is the Lord of all the worlds; we did not go to him out of the fear of Kansa, who may kill us, but O women! you have recognised that Lord in His Real Form." —326

KABIT

Krishna, who killed Putana, who destroyed the body of Tranavrata, who shattered the head of Aghasura, who redeemed Ahalya in the form of Ram and ripped the beak of Bakasura as if it was cleaved by a saw, he, who as Ram destroyed the army of demons and himself donated the complete kingdom of Lanka to Vibhishana, the same Krishna incarnating and redeeming the earth, also redeemed the wives of Brahmins. —327

SWAYYA

Listening to the words of their wives, the Brahmins asked them to relate more; the story of Krishna is very interesting, repeat it after giving it more thought, so that the life-breath is instilled in us. Those women said smilingly, "Bow before that sovereign Krishna in the beginning and then listen to his interesting story." —328

SWAYYA

The meat roasted and cooked in various ways, dish of rice-soup meat and spice etc., sweet-meat in the form of drops with a coating of sugar, noodles, preparation of soaked rice parched and beaten in a mortar, *laddoo* (sweet) meat, preparation of rice, milk and sugar boiled together, curd, milk etc., after eating all these, Krishna went towards his home. —329

SWAYYA

Singing songs and greatly pleased, Krishna went towards his home, Haldhar (Balram) was with him and this couple of white and black looked impressive; then Krishna smilingly took his flute in his hand and began to play upon it; hearing its sound, even the water of Yamuna stopped and the blowing wind also in a fix. —330

SWAYYA

The musical modes like Ramkali, Sorath, Sarang, Malshri, Gauri, Jaitshri, Gaund, Malhar, Bilawal, etc., were played on the flute; leave aside men, the heavenly damsels and female demons, became mad on hearing that sound; the women, after hearing the sound of the flute are coming with speed like the does. —331

KABIT

Krishna is playing on his flute in the forest, creating a joyous atmosphere, with the musical modes like Vasant, Bhairava, Hindol, Lalit, Dhanasari, Malwa, Kalyan, Malkauns, Maru, etc.; hearing the tune, the young damsels of gods, demons and Nagas are forgetting the consciousness of their bodies; they are all saying that the flute is being in the manner as if the male and female musical modes are living on all the four sides. —332

KABIT

The sound of the flute of that treasure of Mercy (Krishna) whose elucidation is also found in the Vedas is spreading in all the three worlds; hearing its voice, the daughters of gods, leaving their abode are coming with speed; they are saying that the providence has created these musical modes for the flute itself; all the Ganas and stars have become pleased, when Krishna played on his flute in the forests and gardens. —333

SWAYYA

Being extremely pleased, Krishna comes home and plays on his flute and all the *gopas* come springing and singing in consonance with the tune; the Lord (Krishna) himself inspires them and causes them to dance in various ways; when the night falls, all of them, being highly pleased, go to their homes and sleep. —334

End of "The Description of the Allurement, of the Wives of Brahmins, Eating their Food and Redeeming Them" in Krishnavatar (based on *Dasham Skandapurana*) in Bachittar Natak.

Now begins the Description of carrying Govardhan Mountain on Hand

DOHIRA

In this way Krishna passed a long time; when the day of Indra-worship arrived, the *gopas* held consultations with one another. —335

SWAYYA

All the *gopas* said that the day of Indra-worship has arrived; we should prepare various types of foods and *panchamrit*; when Nand said all this to *gopas* then Krishna reflected something else in his mind; who is this Indra, for whose worship the women of Braja are going, equalising him with me? —336

KABIT

Krishna, the ocean of mercy said, "O dear father! For whom all these things have been prepared?" Nand said to Krishna, "He, who is the Lord of the three worlds, for that Indra all these things have been made and we do all this for rain and grass, with which our cows have always remained protected;" then Krishna said, "These people are ignorant, they do not know that if the Lord of Braja cannot protect them, how then Indra will do it?" —337

Speech of Krishna

SWAYYA

"O dear father and other people! Listen, the cloud is not in the hand of Indra; only one Lord, who is fearless, gives everything to all; why do you hold this worship for Indra with affection? Remember the Lord, getting together, He will reward you for this." —338

"Indra is under the control of *yajnas*, Brahma has also said so; in order to sustain the people, the

Lord causes rain through the medium of the sun; He himself sees the play of the beings and within this play Shiva destroys them; that Supreme essence is like a stream and all the various types of smaller streams have emanated from it." —339

That Lord (Murari and Hari) abides in stone, water, mountain, tree, earth, men, gods and demons; the same Lord, in reality, abides in birds, deer and lions; I tell you all this secret that instead of worshipping all the gods separately, worship only the Lord-God. —340

Krishna said smilingly to Nand, "Listen to a request of mine; You may worship Brahmins, cows and the mountain, because we drink the milk of cows and on mountain, we feel happy; on giving alms to the Brahmins, we get renown here and also comfort in the next world." —341

SWAYYA

Then Krishna said this also to his father, "Go and worship the mountain, Indra will not be angry; I am a good son in your house, I shall kill Indra; O dear father; I tell you this secret; worship the mountain and forsake the worship of Indra." —342

When Nand heard the words of his son, he resolved to act on it; the arrow of sharp intellect penetrated in his mind; listening to the words of Krishna, the depravity was forsaken like the flying away a caught sparrow; the clouds of attachment flew away with the storm of knowledge. —343

Agreeing with Krishna, Nand called all the *gopas* and said, "Worship the Brahmins and the cows," he said again, "I am saying this thing to you, because I have clearly understood it; I have till today worshipped all others and not meditated upon the Lord of the three worlds." —344

SWAYYA

The *gopas* went away with the permission of Nand, the Lord of Braja and prepared for the worship bringing the fragrances, incense, *panchamrit*, earthen lamps, etc., taking their families alongwith them and beating their drum, they all went towards the mountain; Nand, Yashoda, Krishna and Balram also went. —345

Nand went with his family and when they came near the mountain, they gave food to their cows and rice boiled with milk and sugar etc., to the Brahmins; when Krishna himself began to serve food, all the *gopas* were pleased; Krishna asked all the boys to ascend his chariot and began a new amorous play. —346

SWAYYA

Keeping the new amorous play in his mind, Krishna transformed the figure of one of the boys into a mountain; he created the horns (on the head) of that boy and made him a symbol of a high mountain, where none can reach; now that mountain like boy began to eat food apparently; the Lord (Krishna) Himself began to see this spectacle and whosoever was seeing this spectacle, his thoughts only concentrated on him. —347

SWAYYA

Then the Lord (Krishna) said smilingly, "All of you may see that the mountain is eating food given by me;" all the *gopas* listening to this from the mouth of Krishna wondered; when the *gopis* came to know about this amorous play of Krishna, they were also enlightened. —348

All began to bow before Krishna with folded hands; everyone forgot Indra and were dyed in the love of Krishna; those who were sleeping, having indulged in evil deeds, they all awoke and began to meditate on the Lord. They forgot all other consciousness and were absorbed in Krishna. —349

SWAYYA

Krishna, who is the destroyer of the sins of all said smilingly to all, "All of you may go home;" Yashoda, Nand, Krishna and Balbhadra, all becoming sinless, went to their homes; when they did not worship Indra, he became furious and bore his *vajra*; there is a detailed description of Indra's power and deceit in Vedas. —350

SWAYYA

Krishna, who fighting with Bhumasura, saved

sixteen thousand women, who in Satyuga had shattered the citadels like the bangles of glass, he is virtually the Creator and the Sustainer of the whole universe; Indra of low intellect, is trying to quarrel with him. —351

SWAYYA

Annoyed with the *gopas* and forsaking his peace of mind, being in great fury, Indra asked the clouds: "All of you may go shower with full force the rain on Braja; shower so much rain, that not even one *gopa* may survive and all the brothers, sisters, fathers, sons, grandsons and uncles all may perish!" —352

SWAYYA

Getting the orders of Indra, all the clouds started towards Braja for besieging and devastating Braja; they went to kill the cows and calves, having been filled with water and rage; they left their wives and children behind and quickly left for performing the duty assigned to them by Indra. —353

He, who assumed the form of *Matsya* for killing the demon Shankhasura, who seated himself as *Kachh* (Tortoise) under the Sumeru mountain at the time of churning the ocean, the same Krishna is now grazing the cows and calves of Braja and in this way, protecting the lives of all and exhibiting the amorous play to all. —354

Obeying the orders of Indra, the clouds thundered on besieging the city; the lightning was crackling like the trumpets of Ravana resounding before Ram; hearing this sound, *gopas* ran in all the ten directions and came and fell at the feet of Krishna asking for help. —355

Fearing the clouds, all the *gopas*, crying in agony before Krishna, are saying, "O treasure of mercy! It is raining heavily for the last seven days and nights, kindly protect us; the milking cows, calves and even the barren cows have not survived, all have died;" they all began to weep before Krishna like the lover Ranjha without his beloved Heer. —356

KABIT

"O enemy of the serpent Kali and the demon Keshi! O lotus-eyed! Lotus-nucleus! And husband of Lakshmi! Listen to our request; You are beautiful like the god of love, the destroyer of Kansa, the Lord doing all deeds and satisfier of all the wishes; kindly do our work also; You are the husband of Lakshmi, the killer of Kumbhasura and destroyer of the demon named Kalnemi; do such a work for us so that we may survive; O Lord! You are the terminator of desires and accomplisher of all works; kindly listen to our request. —357

SWAYYA

The drops of rain fell on the earth of Braja in fury like the arrows, which could not be endured by anyone, because they were reaching the earth, piercing through the houses; *gopas* saw this with their own eyes and conveyed this news to Krishna, "O Krishna; Indra has got angry with us, kindly protect us." —358

SWAYYA

The clouds are coming, being surrounded from all the ten directions and the sun is not visible anywhere; the clouds are thundering like lion and lightening is frightening by showing its teeth; *gopas* went to Krishna and requested, "O Krishna, whatever pleases you, you may do the same because the lion must confront the lion and in great anger should not cause the jackals to reach the abode of Yama." —359

SWAYYA

In great fury the clusters of clouds have come down on our city; they have all been sent by that Indra, who rides upon the elephant named Airavata and who has chopped the wings of the mountains, but you are the Creator of all the worlds and you had cut the heads of Ravana; the fires of ire are frightening all, but who is more well-wisher than you for *gopas*?" —360

SWAYYA

"O Krishna! You are the seniormost and the people repeat your name all the time; you have installed the sovereigns, fire, earth, mountain and trees etc., whenever there had been destruction of knowledge in the world, it were you, who gave the knowledge of the Vedas to the people; you churned the ocean and assuming the form of Mohini, you distributed ambrosia amongst the gods and demons." —361

SWAYYA

Gopas said again, "O Krishna! There is no support for us except you; we are frightened by the destruction of the clouds like the child fearing a dreadful portrait; our heart is getting very fearful on seeing the horrible form of the clouds; O Krishna! Get ready to remove the suffering of the *gopas*." —362

SWAYYA

Under the orders of Indra, the dark clouds are surrounding from all the four directions and coming over Braja and being enraged in mind are powerfully exhibiting their force; the lightning is flashing and the drops of water are raining like arrows; the *gopas* said, "We have erred in not worshipping Indra, therefore the clouds are thundering." —363

SWAYYA

A great crime has been committed today, therefore all, having been frightened and crying for Krishna, said, "Indra has become angry with us, therefore it is raining cats and dogs over Braja; you have eaten the material brought for Indra's worship, therefore, in great rage, he is destroying the people of Braja; O Lord! You are the protector of all, therefore protect us also." —364

"O Lord! Kindly save us from these clouds; Indra has become angry with us and for the last seven days, there had been heavy raining here;" then getting infuriated, Balram got up for their protection and seeing him arising, on one side, the clouds became fearful and on the other side, there was increase of joy in the mind of *gopas*. —365

SWAYYA

Hearing the request of the *gopas*, Krishna called all the *gopas* with the signs of his hand; the powerful Krishna moved for killing the clouds; the poet considering this spectacle in his mind, says, "Krishna moved like a roaring lion, seeing the deer, with his mouth wide open." —366

SWAYYA

With great ire Krishna moved to destroy the clouds; he had destroyed Ravana in Treta age as Ram; he had powerfully ruled Oudh alongwith Sita; the same Krishna moved to-day for the protection of *gopas* and cows like an intoxicated elephant. —367

SWAYYA

For the protection of *gopas*, Krishna, greatly infuriated, uprooted the mountain and placed it on his hand; while doing this, he did not use even an iota of his power; no force of Indra could work on *gopas* and he, in embarrassment and with downcast face, he went towards his home, the story of the glory of Krishna became prevalent in the whole world. —368

SWAYYA

Krishna, the son of Nand, is the giver of comfort to all, enemy of Indra, and master of true intellect; the face of the Lord, who is perfect in all arts, ever gives its mild light like the moon; the poet Shyam says that the sage Narada also remembers him, who is the destroyer of the sorrow and anguish of the saints; the same Krishna, being highly infuriated, carried the mountain and there was no effect of the clouds on the people below and in this way, repenting the clouds returned to their homes. —369

SWAYYA

Krishna uprooted the mountain and placed it on his hand and not even one drop of water fell on the earth; then Krishna said smilingly, "Who is this Indra who will confront me? I had killed Madhu and Kaitabh also and this Indra had come to kill me;" in this way, whatever words were uttered by the Lord (Krishna) amongst *gopas*, they spread throughout the world like a story. —370

When Krishna became angry on Indra for the protection of *gopas*, then he fell down and got up like the one whose foot slips away; at the end of the age, all the world of beings terminates and then a new world arises gradually; just as the mind of an ordinary man sometimes falls down and sometimes rises very high, in the same manner, all the clouds disappeared. —371

Lowering the prestige of Indra, Krishna saved the *gopas* and the animals from destruction; just as a demon devours a being at one time only in the same manner, all the clouds were destroyed in an instant; with his amorous play, Krishna routed all his enemies and all the people began to kiss Krishna and in this way, Indra folded up his *maya* for the protection of *gopas*. —372

SWAYYA

When the clouds went away and Krishna uprooted the mountain, then removing his anxiety from his mind that mountain seemed very light to him; Krishna is the destroyer of the demons, giver of the comforts and the donor of the life-force; all the people should meditate on Him, forsaking all meditations on others. —373

SWAYYA

When the clouds dwindled away, then all the *gopas* were pleased and said, "The Lord (Krishna) has given us fearlessness; Indra had attacked us in his fury, but he is invisible now and through the glory of Krishna, there is not even one cloud in the sky." —374

SWAYYA

All the *gopas* said, "Krishna is extremely powerful; He, who killed Mura by jumping in the fort and Shankhasura in water, He is the Creator of the whole world and pervades on the plains and in waters, He, who was felt imperceptible earlier, He has come now in Braja apparently. —375

He, who killed the demon Mura, by jumping in the fort, and who destroyed the army of Jarasandh, who destroyed Narakasura and who protected the elephant from octopus; he, who protected the honour of Draupadi and with whose touch, Ahalya, who had been transformed into a stone, was saved, the same Krishna protected us from extremely enraged clouds and Indra. —376

SWAYYA

He, who caused Indra to run away, who killed Putana and other demons, he is Krishna; he also is Krishna, whose name is remembered by all in the mind and whose brother is the brave Haldhar; because of that Krishna, the trouble of *gopas* was finished in an instant and this is the praise of the same Lord, who transforms ordinary buds into big lotus-flowers and raises very high an ordinary man. —377

SWAYYA

On this side, Krishna carried the Govardhan mountain, on the other side Indra, feeling ashamed in his mind, said, "He, who was Ram in Treta age, has now incarnated in Braja and in order to shower to the world his amorous play, He has assumed the short-statured form of man; He killed Putana in an instant by pulling her teat and also destroyed the demon Aghasura in an instant." —378

SWAYYA

The mighty Krishna was born in Braja, who removed all the sufferings of *gopas*; on his manifestation, the comforts of the saints increased and the sufferings being created by the demons were lessened; He is the Creator of the whole world and is the dispeller of the pride of Bali and Indra; by repeating His Name, the clusters of the sufferings are destroyed. —379

SWAYYA

The mighty Krishna killed Putana, who was sent by Kansa; He also killed the enemy named Tranavrata; all should remember Him and the *gopas* also say that He is very persistent; He fulfils the task, which he takes up in his hand; the same Krishna also cooled down the power of the clouds. —380

SWAYYA

The *gopas* say that He has established Himself in the mind of all, on removing the sufferings of the saints; He is extremely potent, and there is none who can confront Him; all repeat His name; the poet Shyam says, that the Lord (Krishna) is the greatest of all; he, who saw him slightly with his mind, he was assuredly allured by His power and beauty in an instant. —381

SWAYYA

The clouds on repenting and the *gopas* on being pleased went away to their homes; all the *gopas* gathered in a house and said to their wives, "This Krishna, in great rage, caused Indra to run away in an instant; we are telling the truth; it is only through His grace that our sufferings have been destroyed." —382

SWAYYA

The *gopas* said again, "The armies of the clouds of the infuriated Indra showered heavy rain and the Lord (Krishna) carrying the mountains on his hand, stood fearlessly; the poet Shyam has said about this spectacle that Krishna was standing like a warrior with his shield, not caring for the rain of arrows." —383

SWAYYA

The *gopas* said, "He removed the suffering of the saints and He abides in the minds of all; He has manifested Himself in an extremely mighty form and there is none to resist Him; he, whose mind is slightly absorbed in Him, he was assuredly allured by His Power and Beauty." —384

SWAYYA

The mighty Krishna caused the army of Indra to run away, just as Shiva had destroyed Jalandhar and the Goddess had annihilated the army of Chand and Mund; Indra went back to his home repenting and he lost all his self-respect; Krishna destroyed the clouds like a great celibate, quickly destroying his attachment. —385

SWAYYA

The Lord who protected the elephant in the water, the same in fury, destroyed the clouds; He, who with the touch of his foot, ferried across Durga-like Ahalya; he, who protected Draupadi; whosoever will be inimical towards that Krishna the *gopas* said, that He will not be with them and whosoever will serve Him with love and full mind, He will be on his side. —386

SWAYYA

The clouds do no harm to the army of Krishna; though Indra was highly infuriated, but whatever was in his control, he could not cast any impact; who can then have power (or use force) over Him in whose service there is the whole world; therefore, with bowed head and sorrowful mind, in great embarrassment, Indra went away to his home. —387

SWAYYA

When Krishna smashed the pride of Indra, then he, repenting went to his home; he, in great rage, showered heavy rain on Braja, but Krishna did not consider it of any significance; the poet Shyam has said regaining his going away that he went, repenting, like a serpent losing his glory after getting its jewel (*mani*) plundered. —388

SWAYYA

He, whose secret is not known to the sages and whose mystery cannot be realised through the repetition of all kinds of *mantras*, the same Krishna gave kingship to Bali and installed the earth; the *gopas* said that within a few days, this glorious Krishna will destroy all the enemies because he has incarnated only to kill the tyrants of the world. —389

SWAYYA

He, from whom Brahma had concealed the *gopas* through deception and in order to see his amorous play, he was hidden in a cave; Krishna, without getting angry with him also had astonished and puzzled him and had created the replica of those *gopas* and calves. —390

When krishna uprooted and carried the mountain, he called all the *gopas* under the same; the same Krishna had killed the brave demons like Bakasura, Gajasura, Tranavrata, etc., he, who stringed the serpent Kali his meditation be never forgotten from the mind; all the saints heard the auspicious story of Krishna; now listen to another story. —391

Speech of the Gopas addressed to Nand

SWAYYA

The *gopas* went to Nand and told him about the strength and glory of Krishna, they told him that Krishna had flown into the sky and killed the demons named Aghasura and Tranavrata; then he killed Bakasura and made *gopas* fearless; "O the Lord of *gopas*! Though great effort may be made, still such a son cannot be obtained." —392

SWAYYA

"O Nand! We are saying this that the warriors meditate on this Krishna; even the sages, Shiva, ordinary individuals, lustful persons etc., also meditate on him; all the women meditate on him; the world acknowledge him as the Creator, which is quite true, there is no flaw in it." —393

SWAYYA

This mighty Lord has destroyed Putana; he killed Ravana and gave the kingdom to Vibhishana; he protected Prahlad by bursting open the belly of Hiranayakashipu: "O Nand, the Lord of the people! Listen, He has now saved us." —394

SWAYYA

He is the creator of all the people; on this side, the whole of Braja was fearful and he was engaged in his amorous play; Krishna is the fast of the disciples and he is also the effort in the saint's body; He protected the high character of Sita and Draupadi; "O Nand! The performer of all these works is this persistent Krishna." —395

SWAYYA

Many days elapsed after the event of carrying the mountain; now Krishna began to go to the forest alongwith the calves; seeing the cows grazing there, the Lord (Krishna) remained absorbed in bliss in his mind; taking up his flute in his hand, he played on it, having filled with intensive emotion; everyone who listened to the sound of the flute, including the heavenly damsels, got allured. —396

He, who killed Bali in rage and destroyed the army of Ravana; he, who gave the kingdom (of Lanka) to Vibhishana and made him the Lord of Lanka in an instant; he, who killed the demon named Sura and killing the enemy, removed the sufferings of Sita, the same Lord, having taken birth in Braja, is playing with his cows. —397

SWAYYA

He, who plays in the waters, being seated on Seshanaga of thousands of heads, who in great ire, agonised Ravana and gave kingdom to Vibhishana; he, who mercifully gave life-breath to the movable and immovable beings and to the elephants and worms in the whole world; he is the same Lord, who is playing in Braja and who has ever seen the war between the gods and demons. —398

SWAYYA

He, from whom, Duryodhana and other great warriors fear in the battlefield; he, who, in great rage, killed Shishupala, the same mighty hero is this Krishna; the same Krishna is playing with his cows and the same Krishna is the killer of enemies and the Creator of the whole world; and the same Krishna shines like a spark of fire amidst the smoke and calls himself a *gopa*, being a Kshatriya. —399

SWAYYA

Engaged in war with him, the demons Madhu and Kaitabh were killed and it was he, who gave kingdom to Indra; Kumbhakarna also died, fighting with him and he killed Ravana in an instant; it was he, who after giving kingdom to Vibhishana and taking Sita with him, went towards Avadh and now he has incarnated in Braja in order to kill the sinners. —400

SWAYYA

The way in which the *gopas* praised Krishna, in same way, Nand, the Lord of *gopas* said, "The description, that you have given about the might of Krishna, is quite correct; *purohit* (the priest) has called him the son of Vasudev and this is his good fortune; he, who came to kill him, himself was destroyed physically. —401

Now begins the Description of Indra's coming to see Krishna and Supplicate to Him

SWAYYA

One day, when Krishna went to the forest, then casting away his pride, Indra came to him and bowed his head at the feet of Krishna for forgiveness of his sins; he prayed to Krishna and pleased him by saying, "O Lord! I have erred; I have not been able to know Thy end." —402

"O treasure of Mercy! Thou art the Creator of the world; Thou art the killer of the demon Mura and also Ravana and the saviour of the chaste Ahalya; Thou art the Lord of all gods and the remover of the sufferings of saints; O Lord! He, who defies Thee, Thou art his destroyer." —403

SWAYYA

When Krishna and Indra were engaged in talk, there came Kamadhenu, the cow; the poet Shyam says that she eulogised Krishna in various ways; she realised the Lord by praising Krishna; the poet says that her approbation allured the mind in several ways. —404

SWAYYA

All the gods left heaven and came there in order to bow at the feet of Krishna; someone is touching His feet and someone is singing songs and dancing; someone is coming for performing the service of burning saffron, incense and wick; it seems that the Lord (Krishna) had made earth, the abode for gods in order to destroy the demons from the world. —405

DOHIRA

The gods including Indra gathered together in order to eulogise Krishna, forgetting their pride. —406

KABIT

The eyes of Krishna are the ship of love and assume the elegance of all the ornaments; they are the ocean of gentleness, sea of attributes and remover of the sufferings of people; the eyes of Krishna are the killers of the enemies and the effacer of the sufferings of the saints; Krishna is the sustainer of friends and the benevolent saviour of the world, seeing whom, the tyrants are agonised in their hearts. —407

SWAYYA

All the gods, taking permission of Krishna bowed their heads and went to their abodes; in their delight, they have named Krishna as "Govind;" when the night fell, Krishna also returned to his home; early next morning prepared for the new and elegant sport for his amorous play for the world. —408

End of the description of "The Request of Indra for Forgiveness" in Krishnavatar in Bachittar Natak.

Now begins the Description of the Arrest of Nand by Varuna

SWAYYA

On the twelfth lunar night, the father of Krishna went to take a bath in Yamuna; He took off his clothes and entered the water; the attendants of Varuna got infuriated; they arrested Nand and proceeded to take him to Varuna, thundering in rage and when they presented him before Varuna, he was recognised by Varuna, the king of the rivers. —409

SWAYYA

In the absence of Nand, the whole city was deserted; all the residents went together to meet Krishna; all of them bowed before him and touched his feet and all the women and others beseeched him earnestly; they prayed before him in many ways and pleased him; they said, "We have tried to find out Nand (at many Places), but have not been able to locate him." —410

Speech of Krishna

SWAYYA

Krishna said smilingly to Yashoda, "I shall go to bring my father and bring him back, searching all the seven skies and seven nether-worlds, wherever he is; if he has passed away, then I shall fight with Yama, the god of death and bring him back; I shall cause him to meet all after coming back; he will not go away like this." —411

SWAYYA

All the *gopas* went home after bowing before him and Krishna said smilingly, "I am speaking truth; I shall cause all of you to meet Nand, the Lord of *gopas*; there is not even a little falsehood in it, I am speaking the truth; the anguish of the mind of *gopas* was removed on hearing the words of Krishna and without losing patience, they went away. —412

SWAYYA

Early in the morning Hari (Krishna) entered the water and reached before Varuna, who at the same time, clung to the feet of Krishna and said with a choked throat, "My attendants have arrested and brought your father; O Krishna! Please forgive my fault, I did not know about it." —413

He, who gave kingdom to Vibhishana and in great rage, killed Ravana in the battlefield; He who killed Mura and Aghasura and duped the king Bali; He, who tarnished the honour of the wife of Jalandhar, I am seeing today that Krishna (the incarnation of Vishnu), I am very fortunate. —414

DOHIRA

Falling at the feet of Krishna, Varuna sent Nand to him; he said, "O Krishna! I am fortunate, this story will be related in books." —415

SWAYYA

Taking his father with him and very much pleased, Krishna moved towards his city; the people of Braja met him on the outskirts, who bowed before Krishna and his feet; they all fell at his feet and they all gave many things in charity to the Brahmins; they said in gratitude, "Krishna has, in reality, has justified his words and has caused us to meet Nand, the Lord of Braja." —416

Speech of Nand

SWAYYA

When Nand came out, he said, "He is not only Krishna, but is the Creator of the whole world; it was he, who on being pleased, gave kingdom to Vibhishana and has killed millions of enemies like Ravana; the attendants of Varuna had arrested me and he is the one who has liberated me from all; do not consider him only a boy, he is the Creator of the whole world." —417

SWAYYA

All the *gopas* have understood this mystery in their mind; knowing this, Krishna asked them to visit heaven and also caused them to see it; considering this spectacle, the poet has said, "This spectacle appeared like this; that the knowledge given by Krishna was like philosopher's stone because of it the iron-like *gopas* had been transformed into gold. —418

SWAYYA

When the night fell, Krishna, the knower of the secrets of all the hearts went to sleep; all the sufferings are destroyed by the repetition of the Name of the Lord; all the men and women saw heaven in their dreams, in which they visualised Krishna seated in an unparalleled posture on all the sides. —419

SWAYYA

All the *gopas* thought and said, "O Krishna! To be in Braja in your company is much better than heaven; we see only the Lord (Krishna); In Braja, Krishna asks for milk and curd from us and eats them; he is the same Krishna, who has the power to destroy all the beings; the Lord (Krishna), whose power pervades all the heavens and nether-worlds, the same Krishna (Lord) asks for butter-milk from us and drinks it." —420

End of the chapter entitled "Getting the Release of Nand from the Imprisonment of Varuna and Showing the Heaven to All Gopas" in Krishnavatar in Bachittar Natak.

Now begins the Description of the Praise of the Goddess

BHUJANG PRAYAAT STANZA

"O Goddess! Thou art Ambika, the wielder of arms and weapons and also the destroyer of Jambhasura; Thou art Ambika, Shitala etc.; Thou art also the installer of the world, earth and sky." —421

"Thou art the smasher of heads in the battlefield; thou art also Kalka, Jalpa and giver of the kingdom to gods; Thou art the great Yogamaya and Parvati; Thou art the light of the sky and the support of the earth." —422

"Thou art Yogamaya, the sustainer of all; all the fourteen worlds are illumined by Thy light; Thou art Bhavani, the destroyer of Sumbh and Nisumbh; Thou art the brilliance of the fourteen worlds." —423

"Thou art the sustainer of all and also the wielder of weapons; Thou art the remover of the sufferings of all and also the wielder of arms; Thou art Yogamaya and the power of speech; O Goddess! Thou, as Ambika, art the destroyer of Jambhasura and the giver of the kingdom to gods." —424

"O great Yogamaya! Thou art the eternal Bhavani in the past, present and future; Thou art consciousness-incarnate, pervading as sovereign in the sky; Thy vehicle is supreme and Thou art the revealer of all the sciences." —425

"Thou art the great Bhairavi, Bhuteshvari and Bhavani; Thou art Kali, the wielder of the sword in all the three tenses; Thou art the conqueror of all, residing on Hinglaj mountain; Thou art Shiva, Shitala and stammering Mangala." —426

Thou art in the form of Syllable (*Akshara*), heavenly damsel, Buddha, Bhairavi, sovereign and an adept; Thou hast a supreme vehicle (i.e., lion); Thou art also the wielder of arms and weapons; and O Goddess! Thou art also in the form of an arrow, a sword and a dagger. —427

Thou art *rajas, tamas* and *sattva*, the three modes of *maya*; Thou art the three ages of life i.e., childhood, youth and old age; Thou art demoness, goddess and Dakshini; Thou art also Kinnar-woman, fish-girl and Kashyap woman. —428

Thou art the power of gods and the vision of the demons; Thou art the steel-striker and wielder of arms; Thou art Rajrajeshwari and Yogamaya and there is the prevalence of your *maya* in all the fourteen worlds. —429

Thou art the power of Brahmani, Vaishnavi, Bhavani, Basavi, Parvati, and Kartikeya; Thou art Ambika and the wearer of the necklace of skulls; O Goddess! Thou art the destroyer of the sufferings of all and also gracious towards all. —430

As the power of Brahma and as the lion, Thou didst overthrow Hiranayakashipu; Thou didst measure the three worlds as the power of Vaman and Thou didst establish the gods, demons and Yakshas. —431

Thou didst kill Ravana as Ram; Thou didst kill the demon Keshi as Krishna; Thou didst annihilate the demon Biraksha as Jalapa and Thou didst destroy the demons Sumbh and Nisumbh. —432

DOHIRA

Considering me as Thy slave, be gracious towards me and keep Thy hand over my head and protect me with Thy mind, action, and speech and thought. —433

CHAUPAI

I do not adore Ganesha in the beginning and also do not meditate on Krishna and Vishnu; I have heard about them with my ears and I do not recognise them; my consciousness is absorbed at the feet of the Supreme Kal (the Immanent Brahman). —434

The Supreme Kal (God) is my protector and O *Lauha-Purusha* Lord! I am Thy slave; Protect me, considering me as Thy own and do me the honour of catching my arm. —435

Sustain me ever, considering me as Thy own and destroy my enemies, pitching them up; O Lord! With Thy grace, let the free kitchen and sword (for the protection of the lowly) should ever flourish through me and none should be able to kill me except You. —436

Sustain me ever, O Lord! Thou art my master and I am Thy slave; be gracious towards me, considering me as Thy own and complete all my works. —437

O Lord! Thou art the King of all kings and gracious towards the poor; be benevolent towards me, considering me as Thy own, because, I have surrendered and fallen at Thy gate. —438

Sustain me, considering me as Thy own; Thou art my Lord and I am Thy slave; considering me as Thy slave, save me with Thy own hands and destroy all my enemies. —439

At the very outset, I meditate on Bhagavata (Lord-God) and then endeavour to compose various types of Poesy; I speak out the memoirs of Krishna according to my intellect and if there remains any shortcoming in it, then the poets may improve it. —440

End of the Eulogy of the Goddess.

Now begins the Description of the Sphere of Amorous Pastime

SWAYYA

When the winter of the month of Kartik arrived, then the aesthete Krishna thought about his amorous sport with the *gopis*; the sins of the impious people are destroyed by the touch of the feet of Krishna; hearing about the thought of Krishna regarding his amorous sport with the women, all the *gopis* gathered around him from all the four sides. —441

SWAYYA

Their faces are like moon, their delicate eyes like lotus, their eyebrows like bows and their eyelashes like arrows; seeing such beautiful women, all the sufferings of the body are effaced; the bodies of these wanton ladies are like the weapons rubbed and sharpened on the whetstone of lust for the removal of the sufferings of saints; they all appear like the lotus-leaves connected with the moon. —442

SWAYYA

With the girdle tied around his waist and having the eyelashes straightened like arrows, with a yellow cloth tied over the head, Krishna is standing in the forest; he is moving slowly as if he had been instructed by someone to walk slowly; having the yellow garment on his shoulder and having tied the waist tightly, he looks extremely impressive. —443

He, who was Ram, the husband of Sita, in Treta age, he is now standing there in the forest and in order to exhibit his play in Yamuna, he has applied the frontal mark of sandal on his forehead; seeing the signs of his eyes, the Bhils are getting terrified; the hearts of all the *gopis* are allured by Krishna; the poet Shyam says that in order to give pleasure to all, the Lord (Krishna) has assumed the garb of a *thug*. —444

SWAYYA

The beauty of the limbs of those wanton ladies, whose eyes are like the doe, the beauty of the face like the moon, the waist like the lion and the elegance of the body like the gold, cannot be described; their legs are like the trunk of the *kadli* tree and their beauty pierces like an arrow. —445

SWAYYA

The moon-faced Krishna, being pleased, began to sing songs in the forest and that tune was heard by all the women of Braja with their ears; they are all running to meet Krishna; it appears that Krishna himself was like the horn and the beautiful women allured by the horn were like deer. —446

SWAYYA

Krishna has put his flute on his lips and he is standing under a tree; the women of Braja have come there running and forgetting the consciousness of their mind and body; on seeing the face of Krishna, they have been highly enchanted by his beauty that someone swung and fell down, someone got up singing and someone is lying inactive. —447

SWAYYA

Hearing the sound (of the flute) with their ears, all the women of Braja ran towards Krishna; seeing the wanton eyes of beautiful Krishna, they have been entrapped by the god of love; they have left their houses like deer as if they got their release from *gopas* and have come to Krishna, getting impatient and meeting him like one woman with the other woman on knowing his address. —448

SWAYYA

Enchanted by the tune of Krishna, the *gopis* have reached him from all the ten directions; on seeing the face of Krishna, their mind has been emotionally charmed like the partridge on seeing the moon; again seeing the beautiful face of Krishna, the sight of *gopis* has stayed there; Krishna also is getting pleased on beholding them like the deer seeing his doe. —449

SWAYYA

Though forbidden by the *gopas*, the impetuous *gopis*, got impatient, for listening to the Krishna's flute; they have forsaken their houses and are moving in intoxication like Shiva moving, without caring for Indra; In order to see the face of Krishna and full of lust, even abandoning the head-dress, they are moving forsaking all shyness. —450

When the *gopis* reached near Krishna, their consciousness returned and they saw that their ornaments and garments had fallen down and in their impatience, the bangles of their hands had broken; seeing the countenance of Krishna, all the *gopis*, dyed in the love of Krishna, became one with him and intoxicated with this unison they all cast away their shyness of body and mind. —451

SWAYYA

Imbued with the love of Krishna, the *gopis* forgot the consciousness about their houses; their eyebrows and eyelashes were showering wine and it appeared that the god of love had himself created them; they forgot all other pleasures except their absorption in the love of Krishna and looked splendid like the select idols of gold heaped together. —452

SWAYYA

The most beautiful *gopis* of Braja are seeing the beauty of Krishna, their eyes are beautiful like doe and their creation and features are like fish; they are playful like the wandering female dancers of Braja and on the pretext of seeing Krishna, they are charming gestures. —453

SWAYYA

The poet Shyam says that; Amidst all the *gopis*, Krishna is looking impressive, with antimony in his eyes; beauty is being seen like the pure beauty of the lotus-flowers; it seems that Brahma has created him as the brother of the god of love and he is so much beautiful that he is even alluring the minds of yogis; Krishna of unique beauty besieged by the *gopis*, appears like a Gana besieged by the Yoginis. —454

SWAYYA

The same Krishna is standing amidst *gopis*, whose end could not be comprehended by the sages; millions praise him for many years, still he cannot be comprehended a little with the eyes; in order to know His limits, many warriors have fought bravely in the battlefield; and today the same Krishna is absorbed in amorous dialogue with the *gopis* in Braja. —455

SWAYYA

When all the *gopis* reached near Krishna, they on seeing the moon-face of Krishna, became one with the good of love; when Krishna took his flute in his hand and played on it, all the *gopis* became motionless like the deer listening to the sound of horn. —456

SWAYYA

Krishna then played the musical modes like Malshri, Ramkali, Sarang, Jaishri, Shuddh Malhar, Bilawal, etc., the wind also became motionless on listening to the lovely tunes from the flute of Krishna and Yamuna also seemed to stop in fascination. —457

Listening to the sound of the flute of Krishna, all the *gopis* lost their consciousness; they abandoned their house-work, having been absorbed in the tune of the flute of Krishna; the poet Shyam says that at this time Krishna appeared like the deluder-Lord of all and the duped *gopis* have completely lost their understanding; the *gopis* are moving like does and the creeper of their shyness broke down quickly on listening to the tune of Krishna. —458

SWAYYA

Gathering together the women are looking at the form of Krishna and are moving like the deer listening to the sound of horn; they are moving on all the four sides of Krishna, absorbed in lust and abandoning their shyness; their mind seems to have been abducted like the merger of sandal rubbed on the stone. —459

Very fortunate *gopis* are talking to Krishna smilingly; they are all getting enchanted on seeing Krishna; Krishna has deeply penetrated into the minds of the women of Braja; those, in whose minds Krishna abides, they have obtained the knowledge of reality and those, in whose mind, Krishna has not stabilised as yet, they are also fortunate, because they have saved themselves from the unbearable pangs of love. —460

Stealing the eyes and slightly smiling, Krishna is standing there; seeing this and with increased pleasure in their minds, the women of Braja have become allured; that Lord, who had conquered Sita by killing his horrible enemy Ravana, the same Lord at this time is creating a sound beautiful like gems and very sweet like ambrosia. —461

Speech of Krishna addressed to the Gopis
SWAYYA

Today, there are also a few clouds in the sky and my mind is getting impatient to play on the bank of Yamuna; Krishna said smilingly, "All of you may wander with me fearlessly; the most beautiful from you may come with me, the others may not come," Krishna, the smasher of the pride of the serpent Kali, uttered such like words. —462

Krishna said such words smilingly and steeped in sentiment; his eyes are like deer and gait like an intoxicated elephant; seeing his beauty the *gopis* lost all other consciousness; the garments dropped from their bodies and they abandoned all shyness. —463

He, who on being enraged killed the demons named Madhu, Kaitabh and Mura; He, gave kingdom to Vibhishana and chopped the ten heads of Ravana; the story of his victory prevails in all the three worlds; he is the same, who is absorbed in amorous play with the *gopis* at this time. —464

Krishna, smilingly talked about a play involving bet, with the *gopis* of Braja and said, "Come, let us jump into the river together; in this way, when Krishna jumped into the water of Yamuna alongwith the *gopis*, then he very quickly kissed the face of one of them after diving. —465

Speech of the Gopis addressed to Krishna
SWAYYA

All the *gopis* together smilingly said cunningly to Krishna, whose beautiful eyes are big like deer and agile like fish; whose body is like gold, who is the protector of the lowly, to him, with pleased mind, in extreme pleasure and bowed heads, the *gopis* said humbly. —466

The *gopis* said joyfully, "He, who was the Lord of monkeys in Treta age; He, who in ire, killed Ravana and was pleased to give the kingdom to Vibhishana, whose supernatural powers are discussed throughout the world;" all these women are discussing with him about his amorous play; they have remembered and repeated the name of Chandi and begged from her Krishna as their husband. —467

When the *gopis* talked about the amorous pleasure, Krishna told them plainly that they had left behind their husbands and they would not be forgiven even after death; He said, "I do not love you and why do you talk to me about the pleasures of love," saying this Krishna became silent and began to play on the flute the tune of Kafi. —468

Speech of Krishna addressed to the Gopis
SWAYYA

When Krishna smilingly gave this reply to *gopis*, even then, they did not obey Krishna and return to their homes and remained enchanted on seeing his face; then Krishna took the flute in his hand and began to play on it; the tune of the flute had this impact on the *gopis* that they felt that Krishna had applied salt to their wounds. —469

Just as a deer is seen amongst the does, in the same manner Krishna was there amongst *gopis*; seeing Krishna, even the enemies were pleased and the glory of Krishna increased in their mind; seeing whom, the deer of the forest come running and whose mind ever wants to see Krishna, the same Krishna is there in the forest and whosoever sees him, his mind becomes covetous for seeing him. —470

Speech of the Gopis addressed to Krishna
SWAYYA

That *gopi*, uttering the sweet ambrosial speech, said, "We are holding the discussion with him, who is the remover of the sufferings of all saints; we have come to Krishna after leaving our husbands because the influence of the

BACHITTAR NATAK

power of lust is formidably increasing in our body and seeing you, we could not suppress those powers. —471

Speech of the Poet
SWAYYA

Krishna thought in his mind that these *gopis* had been intoxicated with lust on seeing him; then he, without any hesitation, copulated with them like ordinary man; he absorbed himself with the *gopis* who were blazing with lust; the poet Shyam says that in this amorous play, it is beyond comprehension whether Krishna has cheated the *gopis* or *gopis* have cheated Krishna. —472

He, who incarnated in Treta age as Ram, performed many other works of gentleness, the same is the destroyer of the enemies and the protector of saints in all conditions; the same Ram, in Dvapara age, is the wearer of yellow garments as Krishna and is the killer of enemies; he is absorbed now in amorous play smilingly with the *gopis* of Braja. —473

He is causing every one to listen through the tunes of his flute the musical modes of Malshri, Ramkali, Sarang, Jaishri, Shuddh Malhar, and Bilawal; taking his flute in his hand, Krishna is playing on it and listening to its sound the wind and Yamuna have become motionless whosoever listens to his tune, gets allured. —474

SWAYYA

Krishna is playing on the flute whatever pleases the *gopis*; Ramkali, Shuddh Malhar and Bilawal are being played in an extremely charming way; hearing the sound of the flute, the wives of gods and demons are all getting pleased and the does of the forest are coming running abandoning their deer; Krishna is so much expert in playing on the flute that he is manifesting virtually the musical modes themselves. —475

Listening to the sound of the flute all the *gopis* are getting pleased and they are enduring all sorts of talks of the people gently; they are running towards Krishna like the gathering of serpents springing on red worms. —476

He, who being pleased, gave kingdom to Vibhishana and being enraged, destroyed Ravana; he who chops into bits the demon forces in an instant, humiliating them; he, who killed the demon named Mura, the same Krishna is now absorbed in amorous play with the *gopis* in Braja. —477

SWAYYA

The same Krishna is absorbed in the amorous play; he, whom the whole world appreciates, he is the Lord of all the world and is the support of the life of the whole world; he, as Ram, in extreme ire, performing his duty of a Kshatriya, had waged a war with Ravana; the same is absorbed in sporting with the *gopis*. —478

DOHIRA

When Krishna behaved with the *gopis* like men, then all the *gopis* believed in their mind that then they had subdued the Lord (Krishna). —479

SWAYYA

Then again Krishna, separating himself from the *gopis*, disappeared; he went to the sky or penetrated into the earth or remained only suspended, none has been able to comprehend this fact; whatever happened with the *gopis*, the poet Shyam tells about it saying; they seemed like fish writhing after quarrelling and separating themselves from the sea. —480

The *gopis* lost consciousness of their bodies and ran like mad men; someone is getting up and again falling down unconscious and somewhere some woman of Braja is coming running; being perturbed, they are searching Krishna with dishevelled hair; they are meditating on Krishna in their mind and they are calling for Krishna, kissing the trees. —481

SWAYYA

Then leaving the trees, they are asking the bushes of *champak, maulshri, taal, lavanglata, kachnar*, etc., for the whereabouts of Krishna, saying "We are wandering enduring the sunshine, over our heads and the pain of thorns in our feet for his sake, tell us where is that Krishna; we fall at your feet." —482

Searching for Krishna, those *gopis* are wandering there where there are trees of *bel*, bushes of *champa*, and plants of *maulashri* and red rose; the trees of *champak, maulashri, lavanglata, kachnar*, etc., look impressive and extremely peace-giving cataracts are flowing. —483

Bound in the bond of love for Krishna, the *gopis* are saying, "Is He not there near the *peepal* tree?" And saying this and enduring the sunshine over their heads, they are running hither and thither; then they hold consultations among themselves why they have left their husbands and are oscillating here and there, but alongwith it they receive this reply from their mind that they are running because they cannot live without Krishna; in this way someone is talking and someone considering the tree as Krishna, is kissing it. —484

SWAYYA

The women of Braja have become mad in his separation and are wandering in the forest like the crying and wandering crane; they are not conscious of eating and drinking; someone droops and falls down on the ground and someone gets up saying where that proud Krishna, increasing his love with us, has gone? —485

SWAYYA

Krishna causing his eyes to dance like deer, has stolen the minds of the *gopis*; their mind has been entrapped in the eyes of Krishna and does not move hither and thither for an instant; for him, with holding their breath, they are running hither and thither in the forest and saying, "O relatives of the forest! Tell us, on which side Krishna has gone?" —486

He, who killed Marich in the forest and destroyed other servants of Ravana; he is the one whom we have loved and have endured the satirical saying of many people; regarding his delicious eyes all the *gopis* are saying thus with one voice: "Because of the hurt of those eyes, the deer of our mind has become motionless at one place." —487

SWAYYA

He, who gives charity to a beggar, he receives the reward of one reading of the Vedas; He, who gives to the stranger the food to eat, he receives many rewards; He who can get us a sight of Krishna for a short while, he can undoubtedly have the gift of our life; he will not receive a more assuring reward then this. —488

SWAYYA

He, who gave Lanka to Vibhishana and in great fury, killed the demons; the poet Shyam says that it was He who protected the saints and destroyed the wicked; the same Krishna has given love to us, but has disappeared from our eyes; O forest-dwellers! We fall at your feet; tell us to which direction Krishna has gone. —489

SWAYYA

The *gopis* searched for Krishna in the forest, but they could not find him; then thought in their mind that he might have gone to that direction; they again think in their mind and associate the string of their mind with that Krishna; the poet figuratively says about their running and thinking that they are running hither like a female partridge. —490

The place where they go in search of Krishna, they do not find him there and in this way like an idol of stone, they return in astonishment; then they took another step and totally absorbed their mind in Krishna; someone sang his qualities and someone wore the impressive garb of Krishna. —491

Someone assumed the garb of Bakasura, someone of Tranavrata and someone of Aghasura and someone putting on the garb of Krishna attacked them and threw on the ground; their mind does not abandon Krishna even for an instant; it seems that someone may be endeavouring to relish the taste of meat in the taste of forest vegetables. —492

Speech of King Parikshat addressed to Shuka

DOHIRA

The king Parikshat said to Shukadev, "O great Brahmin! Tell me how the states of separation and union of Krishna and *gopis* subsist?" —493

Speech of Shukadev addressed to the King

SWAYYA

Then Shukadev related to the king the interesting

story of the states of separation and union of Krishna and *gopis* and said, The *gopis* were burning in separation and creating the fire of separation on all the four sides; seeing this state of the *gopis*, the ordinary persons became fearful; when the *gopis* thought about Krishna, the flames of separation merging their concentration began to impart suffering to them. —494

Someone has assumed the garb of Vrishbhasura and someone of Bachharasura; someone on assuming the form of Brahma, is stealing away the *gopas* and also falling at the feet of Krishna; someone has become a heron and in fury is fighting against Krishna and in this way all the women of Braja are absorbed in exhibiting a play, which was played earlier by Krishna. —495

Performing all the acts of Krishna, all the *gopis* began to sing his praises and exhibited their happiness in playing on the flute and creating various tunes; someone is saying that Krishna had sported with her at that place and saying such things, the *gopis* lost consciousness of Krishna and they endured great pangs of separation from him. —496

In this way, the wives of *gopas* were absorbed in the meditation of Krishna and those who were themselves very beautiful, they were all subdued by the beauty of Krishna; seeing them withered, the poet has said, "They are lying in the condition of a doe shot by an arrow and thrown on the ground." —497

SWAYYA

Making arrows of their eyelashes and the bows of their eyebrows, on bedecking themselves and in great rage, the *gopis* seemed to resist and stand before Krishna; showing their anger in love, they were not going back even one step and seemed all to have dropped down dead in the battlefield while fighting with the god of love. —498

Seeing the flawless love of the *gopis*, Krishna manifested himself quickly; on his manifestation, there was so much light on the earth, which is seen when the fireworks flash during the night; all the *gopis* were startled on seeing Krishna just like one startling in a dream; the mind of all of them left their bodies like a drunkard running away from his home. —499

SWAYYA

All the *gopis* seeing their proud Lord ran to meet him like the proud does meeting their deer; the poet has mentioned this spectacle figuratively saying that they were pleased like rain-bird obtaining a drop of rain or a fish seeing water jumping in it. —500

SWAYYA

There is yellow sheet on the shoulder of Krishna; his deer-like two eyes look splendid; he also appears magnificent as Lord of the rivers; he is moving amongst those *gopis*, who are unique in the whole world; seeing Krishna, the *gopis* of Braja have been pleased and wonder-struck. —501

KABIT

Just as a lotus, at dawn, being separated during night meets the sun joyfully as a singer remains pleased and absorbed in seven tunes, just as the thief feels pleased by saving his body from any harm; just as a rich man is pleased on seeing his money and the debtor is pleased on thinking about his efforts for escaping from payments in his mind; just as a warrior is pleased on getting an opportunity to fight and one who wants to escape gets an opportunity to run way is also pleased; just as a man in agony is pleased on getting relieved from it; just as a person suffering from indigestion, is pleased on getting hungry and a king is pleased on hearing the news about the killing of his enemy, in the same manner the *gopis* are pleased on listening to the utterance of Krishna. —502

Speech of Krishna

SWAYYA

Krishna said smilingly to *gopis*, "Come, let us play on the bank of Yamuna; we may splash water over one another; you may swim and I may also swim; we may absorb ourselves in amorous play, wearing beautiful garlands; we may end the anguish of separation by our sport." —503

Agreeing with Krishna, all the *gopis* moved towards that place; one is walking smilingly, the other is walking slowly and someone is running; the poet Shyam says that the *gopis* are swimming the Yamuna's water and seeing those women of the gait of the elephant acting according to the wishes of their hearts, the deer of the forest are also getting pleased. —504

All the *gopis* crossed Yamuna alongwith Krishna and went to the other side and gathering together stood in a circle; this spectacle appeared like this; that Krishna was like the Moon and the *gopis* surrounding him looked like his family of stars. —505

SWAYYA

All the *gopis*, who were moon-faced and doe-eyed, began to talk amongst themselves; the wanton damsels of Braja held discussion with Krishna about love and absorbed in this great relish, they abandoned all their shyness. —506

The mind of the *gopis* feels greatly agitated on account of the absorption in love for Krishna or because of a *mantra* or a powerful *yantra* or it is blazing in extreme dread on account of a *tantra*; Krishna, who is merciful to the lowly has stolen the mind of the *gopis* in an instant. —507

Speech of the Gopis
SWAYYA

Gopis said to Krishna, "Where had you gone after leaving us? You had loved us and were absorbed in amorous play with us on the bank of Yamuna; you were not unacquainted with us, but you left us like a traveller abandoning his companion; our faces had bloomed here like flowers, but you had gone away elsewhere like a black bee. —508

Now begins the Description of the Differentiation of Four Types of *Purushas*

SWAYYA

There are some *Purushas*, who love without being loved; there are others, who love only when loved and consider such love as beneficence; there are such others, who know differentiations in love and accept love in their mind; the fourth type of persons are such in the world who can be called fools because they do not comprehend love even a little; the *gopis* and Krishna are absorbed in such like discussion. —509

Speech of the Gopis
SWAYYA

The *gopis* are saying, "Let us see, who deceives after ending the love? Krishna is such that he is always ready for the welfare of some one even leaving the enemy standing in front of him and is deceived himself on being defrauded; he is such a one who accompanies someone in rainy season and assuming the form of a dacoit in ambush kills his companion in the way, the *gopis* said angrily that Krishna is such a person. —510

When *gopis* said this, Krishna laughed with them; he, on uttering whose Name, the sins of a sinner like Ganika were destroyed; wherever his name was not remembered, that place became deserted; he, who remembered his Name, his home prospered; that Krishna said this to *gopis*, "I have been entrapped dreadfully in your amorous enjoyment." —511

SWAYYA

Uttering these words, Krishna got up smilingly and jumped into Yamuna; he crossed Yamuna in an instant; on seeing the *gopis* and the water (of Yamuna), Krishna laughed heartily; though *gopis* are greatly restrained and are reminded of the family practice, they are enamoured of Krishna. —512

Speech of Krishna
SWAYYA

When the night fell, Lord Krishna said smilingly, "Come, let us absorb ourselves in amorous play; there is moonlike brightness on the faces of the *gopis* and they have worn garlands of white flowers around their necks; they are all playing with their hands on the necks of one another and Krishna is saying, "The sorrow that you experienced in my absence, come, let us now remove that grief, holding ourselves in unison." —513

The women said, "O hero of the Yadavas! When you are absorbed in an amorous play, then you do not feel even an iota of shyness in holding the hand of others in your hand in this assemblage; we also play and dance with you fearlessly; kindly remove our anguish and make our minds griefless." —514

SWAYYA

Then Lord Krishna said to those women, "O dear ones! Listen to my request and be of good cheer in your mind, so that you may remain attached with my body; O friends! You may do the same whatever pleases your mind and is in your welfare; remove all your sorrows by submerging yourselves in amorous enjoyment from head to feet. —515

Lord Krishna said again smilingly, "Listen to my talk about pleasure and O friends! Do whatever you like;" Krishna said again to *gopis* and also his brother Balram, "With whosoever one may fall in love, he surrenders totally to him without any selfish motive." —516

Hearing the words of Krishna, the *gopis* felt courageous and in their mind, the straws of suffering were burnt and destroyed by fire of amorous pleasure; Yashoda also said to all, "Get together for amorous play and seeing this the dwellers of the earth and the heavenly sphere are getting pleased." —517

All the women of Braja are singing and playing on instruments and in their mind they are proud of Krishna; looking at their gait, it seems that they have learnt it from the elephants and the wives of gods; the poet says, that it seems to him that they have learnt all this from Krishna. —518

SWAYYA

The peacock feather on his head and rings in the ears look splendid; there is a rosary of gems around his neck, which cannot be compared with anything; the enemy walking on his path, deviates in order to see Krishna; what to speak of other people, the gods are also getting pleased on seeing Krishna. —519

Krishna is singing in extreme love alongwith *gopis* and he is enrapturing them in such a way that on seeing him, even the birds became motionless; the Lord, whose mystery is not known to Ganas, Gandharvas, Kinnars, etc., that Lord is singing and on listening him singing, the does are coming up, abandoning their deer. —520

He is singing the musical modes of Sarang, Shuddh Malhar, Vibhas, Bilawal and Gauri and listening to his tune, the wives of gods are also coming, abandoning their head-dresses; the *gopis* also, on listening to that tasteful sound, have become mad and come running in the company of deer and does, leaving the forest. —521

SWAYYA

Some one is dancing, someone is singing and someone is exhibiting his emotions in various ways; in that amorous display all are alluring one another in captivating manner; the poet Shyam says that the *gopis* are playing with Krishna at nice places on abandoning the city in rainy season and moonlit nights. —522

The poet Shyam says that *gopis* have played with Krishna at nice places and it seems that Brahma has created the sphere of gods; seeing this spectacle, the birds are getting pleased, the deer have lost consciousness about food and water; what else should be said, the Lord Himself has been deceived. —523

On this side, Krishna was accompanied by his boyfriends and on that side the *gopis* gathered together and started a dialogue which ensued on various issues concerning pleasure according to the poet Shyam the mystery of the Lord could not be known to Brahma and also the sage Narad; just as a deer looks elegant amongst the does, in the same manner, Krishna appears amongst the *gopis*. —524

SWAYYA

On this side Krishna is singing and on that side the *gopis* are singing; they seem like the nightingales cooing on mango trees in the season in the month of Phagun; they are singing their favourite songs; the stars of the sky are gazing their splendour with wide-open eyes; wives of the gods are also coming to see them. —525

That arena of amorous play is wonderful, where Lord Krishna danced; in that arena, the gathering splendid like gold, has raised a tumult regarding the amorous play; such a wonderful arena, even Brahma cannot create with his efforts for millions of ages; the bodies of *gopis* are like gold and their minds seem splendid like pearls. —526

Just as the fish moves in the water, in the same manner, the *gopis* are roaming with Krishna; just as the people play Holi fearlessly, in the same manner the *gopis* are flirting with Krishna; they are all warbling like a nightingale and are quaffing the Krishna nectar. —527

Lord Krishna held free discussion with them regarding amorous pleasure; the poet says that Krishna said to the *gopis*, "I have just become like a play for you;" saying this, Krishna laughed and his teeth glistened like the flash of lightning in clouds in the month of Sawan. —528

SWAYYA

The lustful *gopis* call Krishna and say, "Krishna! Come and play (sex) with us without hesitation;" they are causing their eyes to dance, they are tilting they eyebrows; it seems that the noose of attachment has fallen on the neck of Krishna. —529

SWAYYA

I am a sacrifice on the beautiful spectacle of Krishna playing amongst *gopis* (the poet says); full of lust, they are playing in the manner of one under magical charms; in the land of Braja and on the bank of the river, this beautiful arena has been formed and on seeing it, the dwellers of the earth and the whole sphere of gods is getting pleased. —530

Some *gopi* is dancing, someone is singing, someone is playing on a stringed musical instrument and someone is playing on the flute; just as a deer looks elegant amongst the does, in the same manner Krishna is there amongst the *gopis*; all are dancing with great affection and are looking winsome; seeing them singing, the Ganas and Gandharvas are getting envious and seeing their dance, the wives of the gods are feeling shy. —531

Being deeply absorbed in love, Lord Krishna played his amorous play there; it seems that he has charmed all with his *mantra*; seeing them, the heavenly damsels feeling shy, hid themselves silently in caves; Krishna has stolen the mind of the *gopis* and they are all staggering with Krishna. —532

SWAYYA

The poet says that all the *gopis* are wandering with Krishna; someone is singing and dancing and someone is moving silently, someone is repeating the name of Krishna and someone, repeating his name, is falling on the earth; they are looking like needles attached to the magnet. —533

SWAYYA

At the dead of night, Krishna said to the *gopis*, "Let us, both you and me, run away, leaving our amorous play and be absorbed at home; obeying Krishna, all the *gopis*, forgetting their sufferings, left for home; all of them came and slept in their homes and began to wait for the day-dawn. —534

The poet Shyam says that in this way, the love between Krishna and the *gopis* continued, Krishna accompanied the *gopis* and leaving the amorous play came back home; describing the loveliness of this spectacle, the poet says that it seems to him that a grand total is being prepared, talking into account all the relevant sums. —535

End of "The Description (about Amorous Play)" in Krishnavatar in Bachittar Natak.

Now begins the Description about the Play with Catching of Hands—The Arena of Amorous Sport

SWAYYA

As soon as the day dawned, Krishna left his house and went to the place, where the flowers had blossomed and Yamuna was flowing; he began to play fearlessly in a nice manner; while playing, with the pretext of the cows to listen, he began to play on his flute in order to call the *gopis*. —536

SWAYYA

The poet Shyam says that on hearing the story of the amorous play, Radha, the daughter of Brishbhan came running; the face of Radha is moonlike and her body is beautiful like gold; the charm of her body cannot be described; on listening to the glory of Krishna from the mouth of *gopis*, she came running like a doe. —537

KABIT

The daughter of Brish is wearing a white sari and it seems that God has not created anyone more winsome like her; the beauty of Rambha, Urvashi, Shachi and Mandodari is insignificant before Radha; wearing the pearl-necklace around her neck and getting ready, she started moving towards Krishna in order to receive the nectar of love; she bedecked herself and looking like moonshine in moonlit night, she came towards Krishna, being absorbed in his love. —538

SWAYYA

With antimony in her eyes and wearing silken garments and ornaments she appears like the manifestation of the supernatural power of moon or a white bud; Radhika is going with her friend in order to touch the feet of Krishna; it appears that the other *gopis* are like the light of earthen lamp and she herself is like the light of the moon. —539

SWAYYA

Her love for Krishna increased and she did not retrace her step slightly; her beauty is like Shachi, the wife of Indra and like Rati (the wife of God of Love); other women are getting envious of her; she is moving like all the bedecked dancers for the amorous play; she seems like lightning amongst the clouds-like beautiful *gopis*. —540

Brahma is also getting pleased on seeing Radha and the meditation of Shiva has been disturbed; Rati is also feeling captivated on seeing her and the pride of the god of love has been shattered; the nightingale has become silent on listening to her speech and feels herself plundered; she appears very alluring like lightning amongst the clouds-like *gopis*. —541

Radha is moving, bedecked in many ways in order to worship the feet of Krishna; everyone's mind is being enchanted on seeing her and her charm is manifesting itself on her forehead; her limbs make her appear as the sovereign of women; the god of love is also allured on seeing her and the moonshine is also feeling shy. —542

SWAYYA

In her elegant decoration, Radha appears with the face of the moon folding up thick moonshine; getting impatient, discharging the arrows of lust, moved for the nectar of love and seeing her, Lord Krishna became pleased and he imagined her like the sovereign of women. —543

Speech of Radha addressed to the Gopis

SWAYYA

Seeing Krishna, Radha said to the *gopis* smilingly and while smiling her teeth looked like a pomegranate and the face like the moon: "There is a bet between me and Krishna (regarding the theme of love), therefore you may quarrel with Krishna fearlessly." —544

Radha said this smilingly to *gopis* and on seeing Krishna, all the *gopis* got pleased; they all appeared to have been created by Brahma himself; being unable to endure the weight of their youth, they seemed leaning over Krishna. —545

All the *gopis* were participating in the amorous play with love and zeal; Radha had decorated herself nicely in white garments and seeing this spectacle, it has been thoughtfully said that on that side Krishna is seated like a cloud and on this side, Radhika appears like lightning. —546

SWAYYA

On this side Krishna is absorbed with Radha in his amorous play and on that side the *gopi* named Chandrabhaga is pasting sandal on the bodies of the *gopis*; the eyes of these *gopis* are like does and they are walking like wanton gait of the elephant; it seems that on seeing them, the moon is sacrificing the youth of his moonshine. —547

Speech of Chandrabhaga addressed to Radha

SWAYYA

Chandrabhaga said this to Radha, "With whom

you are absorbed in amorous play fruitlessly? Come, let us play with Krishna; describing the beauty of that spectacle, the poet has said, that in the light of the supernatural power of Radha, the light of the earthen-lamp like *gopis* concealed itself. —548

Speech of Radha
SWAYYA

Hearing the words of Chandrabhaga, Radha said to her, "O friend! For this objective, I have endured the ridicules of the people; on listening about the amorous play, my attention is diverted to this side and seeing Krishna with my own eyes, my mind has been fascinated. —549

Then Chandrabhaga said, "O friend! Listen to me and see, Krishna is seated there and we all are alive on seeing him; the work, by doing which the friend is pleased, that work should be done, therefore O Radha! I am saying to you that now when you have adopted this path, do not have other thoughts in your mind." —550

Speech of the Poet
SWAYYA

Radha started on listening to the words of Chandrabhaga for the attainment of Krishna and she appeared like a Naga-damsel leaving the home; giving the simile of the *gopis* coming out of the temple, the poet has said that they look like the manifestation of the creepers of lighting, leaving the clouds. —551

Lord Krishna has created the arena of amorous play in a wonderful way; down below, Yamuna is flowing with currents like moonshine; the *gopis* look splendid in white garments and they appear like a flower-garden in the forest of amorous play. —552

SWAYYA

Obeying Chandrabhaga, Radha touched the feet of Krishna; she merged like a charming portrait in Krishna on seeing him; till now she had been absorbed in the sleep of shyness, but that shyness also abandoned sleep and awoke; he whose mystery has not been comprehended by the sages, the fortunate Radhika is absorbed in playing with him. —553

Speech of Krishna addressed to Radha
DOHIRA

Krishna said smilingly to Radha, "O dear of the body of gold; you keep on playing smilingly." —554

Hearing the words of Krishna, Radha, smiling in her mind, began to sing alongwith the *gopis* in the amorous play. —555

SWAYYA

Chandrabhaga and Chandramukhi began to sing alongwith Radha and raised the tunes of Sorath, Sarang, Shuddh Malhar, and Bilawal; the women of Braja were allured and whosoever listened to that tune, he was fascinated; listening to that voice, even the deer and does of the forest moved towards this side. —556

The *gopis* filled their partings of the hair on the head with vermilion and their mind was filled with pleasure; they bedecked themselves with the nose-ornaments, necklaces and wreaths of pearls; the *gopis*, adorning all their limbs with ornaments applied antimony to their eyes; the poet Shyam says that in this way, they stole the mind of Lord Krishna. —557

SWAYYA

When Krishna began to play in moonshine, the face of Radhika appeared to him like the moon; she stole the heart of Krishna; the poet has said that Radha, the daughter of Brishbhan cheated Krishna with the deception of her eyes. —558

He, seeing whom the god of love and the moon feel shy, the poet Shyam says that the same Radha, adorning herself, is playing with Krishna; it seems that Brahma has created that portrait with interest; just as jewel looks magnificent in a wreath, in the same manner Radha appears as sovereign of women. —559

Singing a lovely song and being pleased, they also clapping her hands; those *gopis* have applied antimony in their eyes and have nicely dressed themselves in garments and ornaments; the glory of that spectacle has been described by the poet like this it seems that these women had remained like fruit, flowers and orchard for the pleasure of Krishna. —560

SWAYYA

While describing that spectacle, the poet Shyam elucidates the glory of the ladies and says that their faces are like the power of the moon and their eyes are like lotus-flowers; seeing that beauty, the poet says that those eyes remove the sufferings from the mind of the people and also fascinate the minds of the sages. —561

Someone is Shachi, someone is *chandraprabha* (glory of the moon), someone is the power of the God of Love (*kama-kala*) and someone is apparently, the image of *kama* (lust); someone is like the flash of lightning, the teeth of someone are like pomegranate, and someone is quite unique; the lightning and the doe of the deer are feeling shy and shattering their own pride; narrating that story, the poet Shyam says that all the women are allured on seeing the form of Krishna. —562

Radha, the daughter of Brishbhan, said one thing to the unapproachable and unfathomable Krishna smilingly and while speaking, she dropped her garment and said that at the time of dancing, he should also accompany, otherwise there is feeling of shyness; saying this, the face of Radha seemed like the half-moon coming out of the clouds. —563

On the heads of the *gopis*, the vermilion seems splendid and the yellow round marks on the forefead look magnificent; the whole bodies of Kanchanprabha and Chandraprabha seem to have merged in beauty; someone is wearing white raiments, someone red and someone blue; the poet says that all are getting fascinated on seeing Krishna's voluptuous state. —564

SWAYYA

Adorning their limbs, all the *gopis* are playing there and in that amorous play, they are absorbed in passionate sport in extreme excitement in the company of Krishna; the poet, while describing the beauty and elegance of *gopis*, says that it seems that seeing the comeliness of Krishna, all the *gopis* have become Krishna-like. —565

SWAYYA

All the *gopis* are saturated and absorbed in passionate sport, getting pleased in their mind; Chandramukhi with her body like gold, is saying this is extreme excitement that on seeing the image of Krishna, her passionate love is not restrained and just as a doe looks at a deer, Radha is seeing Lord Krishna in the same manner. —566

Radha is getting fascinated on seeing the beautiful face of Krishna; the river is flowing near Krishna and the forests of flowers look magnificent; the signs of Radha have allured the mind of Krishna and it appears to him that her eyebrows are like bows and the signs of the eyes like the arrows of flowers. —567

The love of Radha for Krishna, instead of decreasing, increased greatly and the mind of Radha, forsaking shyness, became eager to play with Krishna; the poet Shyam says that all the women are beautiful and seeing the beauty of Krishna, all have merged in him. —568

SWAYYA

The eyes of *gopis* are like does, their bodies gold, their faces like moon and they themselves are like locksmith; the beauty of Mandodari, Rati and Shachi is not like them; by His grace, God has made their waist slim like lion; the love of Lord Krishna continues with them formidably. —569

SWAYYA

There is great assemblage of the musical modes and garbs there; all are continuously playing for a long time, absorbed in laughter and singing songs of Braja; someone is singing and someone is playing the tune and someone has come to dance there, where Krishna has performed his amorous play. —570

Obeying Krishna, the king of Yadavas, all the women performed the amorous play nicely like the dancing heavenly damsels of the court of Indra; they are just like the daughters of Kinnars and Nagas; they are all dancing in the amorous play like the fish moving in water. —571

Seeing the beauty of these *gopis*, the light of the moon is looking dim; their eyebrows have tightened like the tightened bow of the god of love; all the tunes abide in their mouths and

SWAYYA

The poet Shyam praises him, who is the enemy of demons, who is a praiseworthy warrior, who is a great ascetic among ascetics and who is a great aesthete among men of taste, whose throat is like a pigeon and the glory of gods of face like moon and who has got ready his arrows of eyebrows (eyelashes) in order to kill the doe-like women. —584

SWAYYA

Wandering with the *gopis*, Krishna is singing the musical modes of Sarang and Ramkali; on this side Radha is also singing, greatly pleased alongwith her group of friends; in the same group, Krishna is also moving with extremely beautiful Radha; the face of that Radhika is like moon and eyes like lotus-buds. —585

SWAYYA

The aesthete Krishna talked to Radhika; the glory of the face of Radha is like moon and eyes like the black eyes of a doe; Radha, whose waist is slim like lion, when Krishna said to her in this way, all the sorrows in the mind of *gopis* were destroyed. —586

SWAYYA

The Lord, who had drunk the forest-fire, talked smilingly; that Lord, who pervades all the world and all the objects of the world including the sun, man, elephant and even the insects, he talked in extremely savoury words; listening to his words all the *gopis* and Radha were allured. —587

SWAYYA

The *gopis* were extremely pleased on listening to the talk of Krishna; they bedecked themselves with necklaces and in the parting of the hair on their head; all of them have also worn the gem-like Krishna, who is the greatest of incarnations and with extreme deceit, they have stolen him and concealed in their mind. —588

Radha caused her eyes to dance, while talking smilingly to Krishna; her eyes are extremely charming like doe; while praising the beauty of that spectacle, the poet says that they are absorbed in delightful amorous play like Rati with the god of love. —589

SWAYYA

The mind of the *gopis* is studded with the body of Krishna like a gem; they are playing with that Krishna, whose temperament cannot be described; the Lord has also created this wonderful assembly for his amorous sport and in this assembly, Radha looks splendid like the moon. —590

SWAYYA

Obeying Krishna, Radha is playing with effort single-mindedly; all the women, catching their hands, are busy in roundelays in the amorous sport; describing their story, the poet says that within the clouds-like cluster of *gopis*, the extremely beautiful women of Braja are flashing like lightening. —591

DOHIRA

Seeing Radhika dancing, Krishna felt pleased in his mind and with extreme pleasure and affection, he began to play on his flute. —592

SWAYYA

The chief dancer Krishna began to sing and play on the musical modes of Shuddh Malhar, Bilawal, Sorath, Sarang, Ramkali, and Vibhas etc., he began to attract by singing the doe-like women and it seemed that on the bow of the eyebrow, he was discharging with tightness the arrows of his eyes. —593

SWAYYA

Krishna is singing and playing beautifully on the musical modes of Megh Malhar, Devagandhari, Gauri, Jaitshri, Malshri, etc., all the women of Braja and also the gods, who are listening to them, they are getting fascinated; what more should be said, even the gods of the court of Indra, forsaking their seats, are coming to hear these *ragas* (musical modes). —594

Absorbed in the amorous play, Krishna is talking to the adorned Chandrabhaga, Chandramukhi and Radha extremely passionately; in the eyes of these *gopis* there is antimony, a fixed mark on the forehead and saffron on the parting of the hair on the head; it seems that the fortune of these women has risen just now. —595 the mind of the people has been entrapped in their speech like the flies in honey. —572

SWAYYA

Then Krishna played a beautiful tune with his comely mouth and sang the musical modes of Sorath, Sarang, Shuddh Malhar, and Bilawal; listening to them, the *gopis* of Braja obtained great satisfaction; the birds and also the deer listening to the pretty sound were fascinated and whosoever heard his *ragas* (musical modes), got greatly pleased. —573

SWAYYA

Krishna looks splendid in singing beautiful songs with charming emotions at that place; playing on his flute, he seems glorious amongst *gopis* like a deer among does; he, who is praised by every one, he cannot remain unattached with the people; he has stolen the mind of the *gopis* in order to play with them. —574

SWAYYA

The poet Shyam is appreciating him, whose beauty is unique; for having whose sight, the bliss increases and listening to whose speech, all sorts of sorrows come to an end; Radha, the daughter of Brishbhan, in great joy, is conversing with Krishna and listening to her, the women are getting allured and Krishna is also getting pleased. —575

SWAYYA

The poet Shyam says that all the *gopis* are playing together with Krishna and they have no consciousness about their limbs and raiments; to what extent their glory may be mentioned; their beauty has stabilised in my mind; now I shall discuss briefly their mind's desires.—576

Speech of Krishna

DOHIRA

Smilingly within his mind, Krishna said to the *gopis*, "O friends! Sing some songs, performing the usage of the amorous pleasure." —577

SWAYYA

Hearing the words of Krishna, all the *gopis* began to sing; even Lakshmi and Ghritachi, the heavenly damsel of the court of Indra cannot and sing like them; these *gopis*, having the gait of an elephant, are playing with Krishna fearlessly in godly manner and in order to see their amorous play, the gods are coming in their air-vehicles, leaving the heaven. —578

SWAYYA

The mighty Ram, who had lived the life of character and righteousness on conquering the world in the Treta age the same is now absorbed in amorous play with the *gopis*, singing songs very nicely; the yellow garments look splendid on his beautiful body and he is being called the persistent king of Yadavas, the performer of amorous acts with the *gopis*. —579

SWAYYA

On seeing whom, the nightingale is cooing and the peacock is repeating his utterance, the body of that Krishna seems like the cloud of the god of love; seeing Krishna, the thundering clouds arose in the mind of *gopis* and amongst them, Radha is flashing like lightning. —580

SWAYYA

The eyes in which antimony has been applied and the nose is bedecked with the ornament face, whose glory has been seen by the poet like moon; who, having been adorned completely, has fixed a mark on her forehead, seeing that Radha, Krishna has been fascinated and all the sorrow of his mind ended. —581

SWAYYA

Krishna talked to Radha smilingly, asking her for the amorous play, hearing which the mind is overjoyed and the anguish is destroyed; the mind of the *gopis* wants to see this wonderful play continuously; even in heaven, the gods and Gandharvas, on seeing this are standing motionless and getting charmed. —582

SWAYYA

The poet Shyam lauds him, who is wearing yellow garments; the women are coming towards him, singing the musical modes of Sarang and Gauri; the dark-coloured attractive women are coming (slowly) towards him and some are coming running; they appear like black bees running to embrace the flower-like Krishna. —583

SWAYYA

A profound shower of pleasure was experienced, when Chandrabhaga and Krishna played together; these *gopis* in deep love for Krishna endured ridicules of many people; the necklace of pearls has fallen down from her neck and the poet says that it seems that on the manifestation of the moon-face, the darkness has concealed itself in the nether-world. —596

DOHIRA

Seeing the beauty of the *gopis*, it seems that the tank of lotus-flowers looks splendid in moon-lit night. —597

SWAYYA

They, whose eyes are like lotus and the remaining body like the god of love, their mind has been stolen by Krishna, the protector of cows, with signs; they whose waist is like that of a lion, the throat like that of a nightingale, their mind has been abducted by Krishna with signs of his eyebrows and eyes. —598

SWAYYA

Krishna is seated amongst those *gopis* who do not fear any one; they are wandering with that Ram-like Krishna, who had gone to the forest with his brother on listening to the words of his father; the locks of his hair, which even enlighten the saints with knowledge, they seem like the young ones of black serpents on the sandalwood. —599

SWAYYA

He, who is wearing the yellow raiments, he is playing with the *gopis*; he is the destroyer of enemies and bestower of boons on the saints; he pervades all, in the world, sky, sun etc., and he is never destroyed; his locks of hair on his forehead look like the young ones of serpents hanging on the sandalwood. —600

SWAYYA

He, whose nostril is like that of the parrot and the eyes like that of the doe, he is wandering with women; he, who is always there in the minds of the enemies as well as saints, I say, while describing his beauty that he is the same Ram, who pervaded also in the heart of Ravana. —601

SWAYYA

Krishna of black colour is playing with the *gopis*; he is standing in the centre and on all the four sides, the young damsels are standing; he appears like fully-blossomed flowers or like the scattered moonshine; it seems that Lord Krishna is wearing the garland of the eyes-like flowers of the *gopis*. —602

DOHIRA

The description has been given of Chandrabhaga, the lady of extremely pure intellect; her body is effulgent in pure form like the sun. —603

SWAYYA

Going near Krishna and calling him by name, she is crying in extreme shyness; on her winsome glory, many emotions are being sacrificed, seeing which, all the people are getting pleased and the meditation of the sages has been ruptured; that Radhika, on her manifestation like the sun, is looking splendid. —604

SWAYYA

That Krishna is playing with the *gopis*, whose beautiful house is in Braja; his eyes are like that of a deer, he is the son of Nand and Yashoda; *gopis* have besieged him and my mind is eager to praise him; he seems to have been surrounded by many moons to play with him as the god of love. —605

Forsaking the fear of their mothers-in-law and also abandoning their shyness, all the *gopis* have been allured by Krishna on seeing him; without saying anything at their homes and leaving their husbands also, they have come here and are roaming hither and thither smilingly, while singing and playing on various tunes; she, whom Krishna sees, she, being charmed, falls on the earth. —606

SWAYYA

He, who is the Lord of Treta age and is wearing yellow raiments; he, who deceived the mighty king Bali and in great ire, had destroyed the persistent enemies; on the same Lord, these *gopis* are being fascinated, who has put on the yellow-coloured garments; just as the does fall down on being shot by the arrows, the same impact is being made (on the *gopis*) by the voluptuous eyes of Krishna. —607

SWAYYA

The *gopis* are playing with Krishna in extreme joy and consider themselves totally free to love Krishna; they are roaming carefree in coloured clothes and this state of theirs creates this simile in the mind that appear like the bee sucking sap of flowers and playing with them in the forest becomes one with them. —608

SWAYYA

They are all playing with joy, meditating in their mind on Lord Krishna, they have no consciousness about anyone else except the sight of Krishna; their mind is neither in the netherworld, nor in this world of death nor in the abode of gods, but being charmed by their sovereign Krishna, they are losing their balance. —609

SWAYYA

Seeing the new winsome beauty of Radha, Lord Krishna talked to her; she had worn on her limbs ornaments expressing various emotions; she had applied the mark of vermilion on her forehead and was extremely delighted in her mind on causing her eyes to dance; seeing her, Krishna, the king of Yadavas smiled. —610

SWAYYA

The *gopis* are singing with the sweet tune of lyre and Krishna is listening; their faces are like the moon and the eyes are like large lotus flowers; the jingling sound of their anklets has arisen in such a way that the sounds of small drum, *tanpura* (stringed musical instrument), drum trumpet etc., are being heard in the same. —611

The *gopis*, being intoxicated in love, are playing with black Krishna; the glory of their face is like that of the moon and their eyes are like those of the large lotus-flowers, seeing which, the god of love is also getting allured and the deer etc., have surrendered their hearts. Krishna is sacrificing on them all the emotions present in lion and nightingale. —612

SWAYYA

He, who gave kingdom to Vibhishana and destroyed the enemy like Ravana, the same is playing in the country of Braja, forsaking all kinds of shyness; he, who had killed the demon named Mura and had measured half the body of Bali; the poet Shyam says that same Madhava is absorbed in amorous and passionate play with the *gopis*. —613

SWAYYA

He, who had frightened the great demon and enemy named Mura; he, who removed the sufferings of the elephant and who is the destroyer of the sufferings of the saints, the same has stolen the clothes of *gopis* on the bank of Yamuna and is roaming amongst Ahir girls entrapped in the relish of passion and pleasure. —614

Speech of Krishna addressed to the Gopis

SWAYYA

Join me in amorous and passionate play; I am speaking the truth to you and not telling falsehood; the *gopis*, hearing the words of Krishna, forsaking their shyness, they decided to join the lustful play with Krishna in their mind; they appeared moving towards Krishna like a glow-worm rising from the bank of a lake and moving towards the sky. —615

SWAYYA

Radha is singing for Krishna amongst the group of *gopis* and is dancing like the lightning flashing among the clouds; the poet, praising her singing says that she appears cooing like a nightingale in the forest in the month of Chaitra. —616

SWAYYA

All the women bedecked and in extreme love for Krishna and forsaking all the restraints, are playing with Krishna, imbued in his love; the poet says again that they appear like the lightning flashing among the clouds in the month of Sawan. —617

Those beautiful women, imbued in the love of Krishna, are absorbed in the amorous play; their beauty is like Shachi and Rati and they have true love in their heart; their amorous sport during day and night on the bank of Yamuna, has become renowned and there, forsaking the shyness, Chandrabhaga, Chandramukhi and Radha are dancing. —618

These *gopis* have begun very nicely the amorous sport; their eyes are like does and even Shachi does not equal them in beauty; their body is like gold and face like moon; it seems that they have been created from the residue of ambrosia, churned out from the sea. —619

The women have come for the amorous play after bedecking themselves in beautiful raiments; someone's garments are of yellow colour, someone's garments are of red colour and someone's garments are saturated with saffron; the poet says that the *gopis* fall down while dancing and still their mind wants the continuity of the sight of Krishna. —620

SWAYYA

Seeing such a great love for him, Krishna is laughing; his love for *gopis* has increased so much that he is entrapped in their passion of love; on seeing the body of Krishna, the virtue is increased and vice is destroyed; just as the moon looks splendid, the lightning flashes and the seeds of pomegranates appear beautiful, in the same manner, the teeth of Krishna look magnificent. —621

Krishna, the destroyer of demons, talked affectionately with the *gopis*, Krishna is the protector of the saints and the destroyer of the tyrants; in the amorous play, the same son of Yashoda and brother of Balram is playing; he has stolen the mind of *gopis* with the signs of his eyes. —622

Krishna played on his flute the tunes of the musical modes of Devagandhari, Bilawal, Shuddh Malhar, Jaitshri, Gujri, and Ramkali, which were heard by all, the immobile, mobile, the daughters of gods, etc., Krishna played on the flute like this in the company of *gopis*. —623

Krishna played the tunes of the musical modes like Deepak, Gauri, Nat Narayan, Sorath, Sarang, Ramkali, and Jaitshri very nicely; hearing them, the inhabitants of the earth and seven Indra, the king of gods, were fascinated; in such a blissful unison with the *gopis*, Krishna played on his flute on the bank of Yamuna. —624

SWAYYA

The glory of whose face is like the glory of the moon and whose body is like gold; she, who has been created uniquely by God Himself; she is the most beautiful *gopi* Radha, amongst the group of *gopis* and she has comprehended, whatever was in the mind of Krishna. —625

Speech of Krishna addressed to Radha

DOHIRA

Looking towards the body of Radha, Krishna said smilingly, "Your body is comely like the deer and the god of love." —626

SWAYYA

"O Radha! Listen, all of them have snatched the fortune of Destiny and have stolen the light of the moon; their eyes are like sharp arrows and eyebrows like the bow; their speech is like that of the nightingale and the throat like that of a pigeon; I am saying the same whatever pleases me; the most marvellous thing is this that the lightning-like women have stolen my mind." —627

Krishna is singing a beautiful song alongwith Radha and producing the tunes of the musical modes like Sarang, Devagandhari, Vibhas, Bilawal, etc., even the immobile things, listening to the tunes, have run, leaving their places; the birds which are flying in the sky, they also have become motionless on listening to the tunes. —628

Lord Krishna is playing and singing with the *gopis*; he is playing in bliss fearlessly; he is singing and playing the tunes and it seems that the male peacock is dancing lustfully with female peacocks in the month of Sawan. —629

SWAYYA

He, whose face is beautiful like the moon, he is dancing alongwith the *gopis*; he looks splendid in the moonlit night on the bank of Yamuna within the forest; there are the proud

Chandrabhaga and Radha there and Krishna looks elegant with them like emerald and other precious stones in the mine. —630

The poet Shyam says, "Saturated with the relish of music Krishna is dancing on that plane; he is wearing tightly the white cloth, dyed in saffron; there are Radha, Chandramukhi and Chandrabhaga, the three *gopis* and Krishna has stolen the mind of all the three with the signs of his eyes. —631

The heavenly damsel named Ghritachi is not so beautiful as Radha; even Rati and Shachi do not equal her in beauty; it seems that the whole light of the moon has been put in Radha by Brahma and created her queer image for the enjoyment of Krishna. —632

Radhika, Chandrabhaga and Chandramukhi are absorbed together in the amorous sport; all of them together are singing and playing tunes; seeing this spectacle even the gods are getting fascinated; the poet Shyam says that the image of flute-wielder god of love seems magnificent amongst the *gopis*. —633

SWAYYA

Even Lakshmi is not like her and seeing her waist, the lion feels shy; seeing the glory of whose body, even the gold feels shy and seeing whom, the sorrow of the mind is removed; she, whom none else equals in beauty and who is glorious like Rati, the same Radha looks splendid amongst *gopis* like lightning among clouds. —634

All the women, having been bedecked and wearing pearl-necklace, are playing; Alongwith them, Krishna, the great lover, is absorbed in amorous and passionate sport; Chandramukhi and Radha are standing there and the beauty of Chandrabhaga is spreading its brightness amongst *gopis*. —635

Chandramukhi is charmed on seeing the beauty of Krishna and while seeing, she has played the tune and begun her song; she has also begun to dance in extreme love and being hungry of the love of Krishna, she has forsaken all the attachment of her home. —636

DOHIRA

Krishna, being greatly pleased played on his flute and listening to it all the *gopis* were delighted. —637

SWAYYA

When Krishna, the son of Nand, played on his flute, all the women of Braja were fascinated; with birds and animals of the forest, whoever listened, was filled with joy; all the women, meditating on Krishna, became motionless like portrait; the water of Yamuna became immobile and listening to the tune of the flute of Krishna, the women and even the wind got entangled. —638

For one *ghari* (a short while), the wind got entangled and the water of the river did not proceed further; all the women of Braja, who came there, their heart-throbs had increased and the limbs were trembling; they lost the consciousness of their body completely; they all became mere portraits on listening to the flute. —639

Krishna taking the flute in his hand is fearlessly playing on it and listening to its voice, the birds of the forest, deserting it, are coming away; the *gopis* are also pleased on listening it and are becoming fearless; just as on listening to the voice of the horn, the doe of the black deer becomes spell-bound, in the same way, on listening to the flute, the *gopis* are standing wonder-struck, with mouths wide open. —640

SWAYYA

The tune of the flute coming from the mouth of Krishna is highly impressive and within it abide the tunes of the musical modes of Sorath, Devagandhari, Vibhas, and Bilawal; the body of Krishna is like gold and the glory of the face is like that of the moon; listening to the tune of the flute, the mind of the *gopis* has only remained entangled therein. —641

The peace-giving tune is being played in the flute concerning the musical modes of Devagandhari, Vibhas, Bilawal, Sarang, Sorath, Shuddh Malhar, and Malshri; hearing it, all gods and men, getting pleased, are running and they are bewitched by the tune with such intensity that they seem entrapped in some noose of love spread by Krishna. —642

He, whose face is extremely beautiful and who has put on yellow cloth on his shoulder; he, who destroyed the demon Aghasura and who had protected his elders from the mouth of the snake; he, who is the destroyer of the tyrants and remover of the sufferings of the saints, that Krishna, playing on his savoury flute has allured the mind of gods. —643

He, who gave kingdom to Vibhishana, killed Ravana in great rage, who cut off the head of Shishupal with disc, who is beautiful like the god of love and who is Ram, the husband of Sita, who is unequalled in beauty by anyone, that Krishna with his flute in his hands, is now fascinating the mind of charming *gopis*. —644

SWAYYA

Radha, Chandrabhaga and Chandramukhi all are singing together and absorbed in amorous sport; the gods are also seeing this wonderful play, leaving their abodes; now listen to the short story about the killing of the demon. —645

The place, where the *gopis* were dancing, the flowers had blossomed there and the black bees were humming, the river Yamuna was flowing there and Krishna and Balram were together singing a song they were playing there fearlessly and affectionately and both of them were not accepting defeat from each other in reciting poetry. —646

Now begins the Description of the Yaksha Flying with *Gopis* in the Sky

SWAYYA

A Yaksha came and he saw this wonderful play; seeing the *gopis* he became lustful and could not restrain himself a little; he flew in the sky, taking the *gopis* with him, without any opposition; Balram and Krishna obstructed him at the same time like a lion obstructing a deer. —647

SWAYYA

Highly infuriated Balram and Krishna waged a war with that Yaksha; both the brave warriors, assuming strength like Bhim, fought, taking the trees in their hands; in this way, they overpowered the Yaksha; this spectacle appeared like a hungry falcon, pouncing upon a crane and killing him. —648

End of the description of "The Abduction of *Gopi* and Killing of Yaksha" in Krishnavatar in Bachittar Natak.

SWAYYA

Krishna and Balram played on their flutes after killing the Yaksha; Krishna had killed Ravana in rage and had given the kingdom of Lanka to Vibhishana; the servant Kubja was saved by his gracious glance and the demon named Mura was destroyed by his looks; the same Krishna causing the blaring of the drum of his praise, played on his flute. —649

On hearing the sound of the flute, the sap of the trees began to drip and peace-giving currents flowed; on hearing it, the deer abandoned the grazing of grass and the birds of the forest also were fascinated; the tunes of the musical modes of Devagandhari, Bilawal and Sarang were played from the flute and seeing Krishna, the son of Nand, playing on the flute, the gods also got together to visualise the scene. —650

SWAYYA

With the desire of listening to the music, Yamuna also became motionless; the elephants, lions and rabbits of the forest are also getting allured; the gods also, abandoning the heaven, are coming under the impact of the tune of the flute; hearing the sound of the same flute, the birds of the forest, spreading their wings on the trees, are absorbed in it. —651

The *gopis*, who are playing with Krishna, have extreme love in their mind; they who have the bodies of gold, are extremely winsome; and the *gopi* named Chandramukhi, having slim waist like lion, appears splendid amongst other *gopis*; hearing the sound of the flute and being fascinated, she fell down. —652

Having performed this wonderful play, Krishna and Balram came home singing; the beautiful area and dancing theatres in the city have a magnificent look; the eyes of Balram appear to have been prepared in the mould of the god of love; they are so charming that the god of love feels shy. —653

Being pleased in the mind and killing the enemy, both have gone away to their home; they have the faces like moon, which cannot be compared with any other; seeing them, the enemies are also charmed and they appear like Ram and Lakshman returning to their home after killing the enemy. —654

Now begins the Description of Playing in the Street-chamber

SWAYYA

Krishna said to *gopis*, "Now the amorous play be performed in alcoves and streets; while dancing and playing, charming songs may be sung; the work on doing which the mind is pleased, the same work should be done; whatever you had done under my instruction on the bank of the river, enjoy yourself in the same way, also imparting the pleasure to me. —655

Obeying Krishna, the women began the performance of the amorous play in the streets and chambers of Braja, and began to sing songs which Krishna liked; they sang in the musical modes of Gandhar and Shuddh Malhar; whosoever heard it in the earth or heaven, was fascinated. —656

All the *gopis* met Krishna in alcoves; their faces are like lotus, body like gold and the whole figure is inebriated with lust; in the play, the women are running in front of Krishna and the poet says that all are extremely beautiful damsels with the gait of the elephants. —657

SWAYYA

The *gopis* are not permitting Krishna to touch that part of the body, which he wants to touch, just like doe slipping away from the deer during the sex-play; on the bank of the river, within the alcoves, Radha is moving speedily hither and thither and according to the poet, in this way, Krishna has raised a tumult about the play. —658

The bright night of six months now changed into dark night alongwith the tumult about the play; at the same time Krishna besieged all the *gopis*; someone got intoxicated on seeing the side-glances of his eyes and someone immediately became his slave; they were moving like the does in a group towards the tank. —659

Krishna got up and ran, but still the *gopis* could not be caught by him; he pursued them riding the steed of his passion; Radha was pierced by the arrows of his eyes discharged from the bow of his eyebrows and she has fallen down on the earth like doe fallen down by a hunter. —660

On regaining consciousness, Radha began to run in front of Krishna in those street-chambers; the great aesthete Krishna, then closely followed her; on seeing this amorous play, the beings were redeemed and Radha appeared like a doe moving in front of a horse-rider. —661

SWAYYA

Krishna caught Radha running after her in the alcoves like someone wearing pearls after washing them on the bank of Yamuna; it appears that Krishna as god of love is discharging the arrows of passionate love by stretching his eyebrows; the poet describing this spectacle figuratively says that Krishna caught Radha like a horse-rider in the forest catching a doe. —662

After catching Radha, Krishna spoke these nectar-like sweet words to her; "O queen of *gopis*! Why are you running away from me? O thou of the face of lotus and body of gold! I have known the secret of your mind; you are searching Krishna in the forest intoxicated with the passion of love." —663

Seeing *gopis* with her, Radha lowered down her eyes; she appeared to have lost the glory of her lotus-eyes; looking towards the eyes of Krishna, she said smilingly, "O Krishna, leave me, because all my companions are looking." —664

Listening to the words of Radha, Krishna said, "I shall not leave you, what then, if these *gopis* are looking, I do not fear them; and do the people know that this is our own arena of amorous play; you are quarrelling with me in vain and fearing them without cause." —665

SWAYYA

Listening to the talk of Krishna, Radha said, "O Krishna! Now the night is lit by the moon, let there be some darkness in the night; I have also reflected in my mind after listening to your talk in respect of not caring for these *gopis*; and consider this that shyness has been completely bidden adieu." —666

"O Krishna! You are talking to me here and there seeing the whole play, the *gopis* are smiling; O Krishna! Accede to my request and leave me and become desireless, therefore O Krishna! I love you but still you are doubtful in your mind." —667

"O Beloved! Does the monkey leave the fruit on becoming hungry? In the same manner the lover does not leave the beloved and the police officer does not leave the cheat; therefore I am not leaving you; have you ever heard about a lion leaving the doe?" —668

Krishna thus said to that damsel saturated with the passion of her youth; Radha looked splendid in the new posture amongst Chandrabhaga and other *gopis*; just as a deer catches a doe, the poet says, Krishna, catching the wrist of Radha, subdued her with his strength. —669

SWAYYA

In this way, subduing Radha, Krishna extended further the story of his passionate love and with his nectar-like words he led the tradition of passionate love to the extreme; the proud Krishna said, "O Radha! What harm will come to you in this? All the women are your servants and you are the only queen amongst them." —670

"Where there is moonshine and a bed of the flowers of jasmine; where there are white flowers and Yamuna is flowing nearby, there Krishna embraced Radha; the white-coloured Radha and the black-coloured Krishna together appear like the moonlight coming on this path." —671

Then Krishna left her in the alcove and in great delight she joined other *gopis*; describing the beauty of that spectacle, the poet says that she went to meet the other *gopis* like a doe, escaping the clutches of a lion, joins the herd of deer. —672

Krishna began to play a charming play amongst the *gopis*; he placed his hand on the hand of Chandrabhaga, by which she experienced extreme pleasure; the *gopis* began to sing their favourite song; the poet Shyam says that they were extremely pleased and all the sorrow of their mind ended. —673

SWAYYA

During his dance, Krishna saw smilingly towards Chandrabhaga; she laughed from this side and from that side Krishna began to talk smilingly with her; seeing this Radha thought that Krishna was then absorbed in love with another women and as such his love with her had ended. —674

Seeing the face of Krishna, Radha said in her own mind, "Krishna has now been subdued by other women; therefore he does not remember me now with his heart," saying this she bade farewell to bliss from her mind; she thought that the face of Chandrabhaga is like moon for Krishna and he loves her the least out of all the *gopis*. —675

Saying thus, she ruminated in her mind and thinking that Krishna then loved someone else, she started for her home; the poet Shyam says, "Now it will be talked among women that Krishna has forgotten Radha." —676

Now begins the Description of the Honouring of Radha

SWAYYA

Saying thus, Radha is leaving the alcove; Radha, the most beautiful amongst the *gopis* has the face like moon and the body like gold; having been proud, she now was separated from her friends like a doe from the herd of does; on seeing her it seemed that Rati, being angry with the god of love, was leaving him. —677

On this side, Krishna, absorbed in the amorous play, looked towards Radha, but she was nowhere to be seen; Radha, whose face is like the moon and whose body is like gold and who is extremely charming, has either gone to her home under the impact of sleep or because of some pride and thinking about it, she has left. —678

Speech of Krishna
SWAYYA

Krishna called the young damsel named Vidyuchhata; her body glistened like gold and the glory of her face was like moon; Krishna called her and said, "You go to Radha and falling at her feet request her and persuade her to come." —679

Listening to the words of Krishna, the king of Yadavas, the young damsel obeying him, started towards Radha, who is charming like the god of love and lotus, in order to persuade her; she moved like a disc slipping from the hand. —680

Speech of the Young Damsel
SWAYYA

The damsel named Vidyuchhata came to Radha and said, "O friend! Krishna, the Lord of Braja has called you." Radha said, "Who is this Lord of Braja?" Then the damsel said, "He is the same, who is also called Kanhaiya," then Radha said, "Who is this Kanhaiya?" Now Vidyuchhata said, "He is the same, with whom, you have been absorbed in amorous sport and whom all the women loved." —681

"O friend! Do not persist a little in your mind, the son of Nand is calling you; I have come to you only for this purpose; therefore comply with my saying; you go to Krishna immediately, you will not lose anything by this; therefore I am telling you to be in the state of happiness yourself and impart happiness to others." —682

"O friend! Do not be too proud and follow my advice to go to the place, where Krishna is playing on his flute and listening to the coquettish abuses of the *gopis* therefore I am saying to you, O woman of Braja! You go there fearlessly; I fall at your feet and say again to you to go to Krishna." —683

"O honourable! You go unhesitatingly, because Krishna has very great love for you; your eyes are full of passion and it seems that they are sharp like arrows of the god of love; we do not know why Krishna has extreme love for you?" —684

SWAYYA

The poet Shyam says that Krishna, standing on a beautiful spot, is playing on his flute; I have been sent to you for this that I may run and bring you there; there Chandrabhaga and other *gopis* are singing and revolving around Krishna from all the four sides; therefore, O friend! Go quickly, because all other *gopis* are enjoying except you. —685

"Therefore, O friend! I am sacrificing myself upon you, you go there quickly, the son of Nand is calling you; he is playing on his flute and the *gopis* are singing the songs of praise; Krishna is pleasing all, by playing there on the musical modes of Sorath, Shuddh Malhar and Bilawal; what to say of others, even the gods, leaving their sphere, are coming there." —686

Speech of Radhika for an Answer
SWAYYA

"O friend! I swear by the Lord of Braja, I shall not go to Krishna; Krishna has forsaken his love with me and is absorbed in the love of Chandrabhaga;" then the friend named Vidyuchhata said to Radha, "O Radha! You go there abandoning your duality; Krishna loves you more than anyone else; he does not like to play without you, because the passionate play can only be with one, whom one loves." —687

Speech of the Messenger
SWAYYA

"O friend! I fall at your feet, do not have any arrogance like this in your mind; you go to the place, where Krishna is calling you; the way in which the *gopis* are dancing and singing, you may also dance and sing; O Radha! You may talk about everything else except your oath regarding not going." —688

Speech of Radha
SWAYYA

"O friend! If Krishna sends millions of *gopis* like you, even then I shall not go; wherever he is playing on his flute and singing the songs of praise, even if Brahma comes and asks me, even then I shall not go there; I do not consider any friend of any account; you may all go and if Krishna wants, he come himself."—689

Speech of the Messenger addressed to Radha
SWYYA

"O *gopi*! Why are you absorbed in pride? Do whatever Krishna has said; do that work, which pleases Krishna; he loves you, therefore he has sent me to call you, otherwise why there is none other so beautiful *gopi* in the whole amorous play." —690

"He is in profound love with you; everyone knows it and this is not a new thing; he, whose face is glorious like the moon and whose body is beauty-incarnate, leaving his company, O friend! You have taken the path leading to your home; there are many young damsels in the company of Krishna, the Lord of Braja, but there is none so uncivilised like you." —691

Speech of the Poet
SWAYYA

Hearing these words of the *gopi*, Radha got infuriated and said, "Without being sent by Krishna, you have come in between me and Krishna; you have come to persuade me, but whatever you have talked, I have not liked," in great ire, Radha said, "You go away from this place and do not meddle in between us uselessly." —692

Speech of the Messenger addressed to Krishna
SWAYYA

The messenger said to Krishna in ire that Radha was giving her replies in anger; she seems determined on her female persistence and she with her idiotic intellect is not agreeing in any way; she has not agreed in any of the four; calmness restraint, penalty and difference; she is also not comprehending the facet of your love; what is the use of loving such an un-civilised *gopi*? —693

Speech of Maniprabha addressed to Krishna
SWAYYA

A *gopi* named Maniprabha, who was standing near Krishna, listening to the messenger, said, "O Krishna! The *gopi* who has become angry with you, I shall bring her;" in order to bring her to Krishna, that *gopi* got up; seeing her beauty, it seems that the lotus has sacrificed all its beauty on her. —694

Standing near Krishna, Maniprabha said, "I shall go myself to her and with whatever means she comes, I shall persuade and bring her; I shall get assent of that winsome *gopi*, either by falling at her feet, or by request or getting her pleased; I shall bring her to you even today, otherwise I shall not be called yours." —695

SWAYYA

Getting up from near Krishna, Maniprabha started, Mandodari does not equal her in beauty and none of the damsels of the court of Indra, has any charm before her; the glory of this woman's charming face appears like this that the moon, deer, lion and parrot have borrowed their wealth of beauty from her. —696

Speech in Answer
SWAYYA

That moon-faced *gopi*, leaving Krishna, reached near Radha; she said on coming, "Go quickly, the son of Nand has called you; why did you say that you would not go to Krishna? Leave this duality, why are you sitting at this place on stealing the heart of charming Krishna?" —697

"When the thundering clouds spread, the peacocks shout on all the four sides, the *gopis* dance and the lovesick people offer themselves as sacrifice, at that time, O friend! Listen, Krishna, playing on his flute remembers you; O friend! Go quickly so that on reaching there we may be able to see the wonderful sport." —698

SWAYYA

"Therefore, O friend! Forsaking your pride, abandon your doubts and go to Krishna; fill your mind with passion and do not involve yourself in persistence; the poet Shyam says that without seeing the amorous sport of Krishna, why do you persist in sitting here? My mind is eager to see his amorous sport." —699

Radha said, "O friend! I shall not go to Krishna and I have no desire to see his amorous sport; Krishna has forsaken his love with me and is absorbed in the love of other women; he is absorbed in love with Chandrabhaga and does not even see me with his eyes; therefore inspite of the upthrust of your mind, I shall not go to Krishna." —700

Speech of the Messenger
SWAYYA

"Why should I go to see the women? Krishna has sent me to bring you; therefore, I keeping away from all the *gopis*, have come to you; you are sitting here in vanity and do not listen to the advice of anyone; go quickly, because Krishna will be waiting for you." —701

Speech of Radhika
SWAYYA

"O friend! I shall not go to Krishna; why are you talking in vain? Krishna has not sent you to me, because I feel an element of deceit in your talk; O *gopi*! You have become a cheat and do not feel another's pain," saying this, Radha sat down with bowed head; the poet says, "I have not seen such an ego at any other place."—702

Speech of the Messenger
SWAYYA

Then she said thus, "O friend! You go with me, I have come with a promise to Krishna while coming," I have said this to Krishna, "O, the Lord of Braja! Do not feel perturbed, I shall go now and persuade and bring Radha with me, but here you are sitting in your pride; O friend! You go to Krishna, leaving the duality, I shall not be able to go without you; reflect somewhat on another's words." —703

Speech of Radhika
SWAYYA

"O *gopi*! Why have you come without thinking? You should have come after consulting some magician; you go and tell Krishna that Radha is not feeling shy of him; tell all my words to the king of Yadavas without hesitation and also say this, 'O Krishna! You love only Chandarbhaga and you have no love for me'." —704

Hearing these words of Radha, that *gopi* fell at her feet and said, "O Radha! Krishna only loves you and he has abandoned his love for Chandrabhaga;" the poet Shyam says that messenger was telling Radha that she was impatient to behold her. "O beautiful damsel; I am a sacrifice to you; now go quickly to Krishna." —705

SWAYYA

"O friend! You are ignorant and do not comprehend the secret of amorous pleasure; Krishna is calling you, please go; Krishna is searching you here and there and is not even drinking water without you; you have just said that you would not go to Krishna; it seems to me that you have become mad on the attainment of youth." —706

SWAYYA

That *gopi* (Radha) forsaking the love of Krishna has seated herself in ego; she is concentrating like a heron; she knows that the abode of love is now nearby; then Maniprabha said again, "O friend! I have said, whatever I have in my mind, but it seems to me that your youth is only a guest for four days." —707

"He who is the enjoyer of all, you are not going to him; O *gopi*! You are only persisting and Krishna will lose nothing by it, only you will be the loser; he (or she) who is egoistic about the youth, he (or she) will be in such a state that Krishna will forsake him (or her) like a yogi leaving his home, placing the lion-skin on his shoulder." —708

"Your eyes are like that of a doe and the waist is slim like that of a lioness; your face is charming like that of the moon or lotus; you are absorbed in your persistence, he will not lose anything by this; you are becoming antagonistic to your own body by not eating and drinking, because your persistence regarding Krishna will avail nothing." —709

SWAYYA

Hearing these words of the *gopi*, Radha, filled with rage, causing her eyes to dance and filling her eyebrows and mind with ire, said this to the *gopi*, who came to persuade her, "O friend! Why should I go to Krishna? What do I care for him? " —710

When Radha replied like this, the friend said again, "O Radha! You may call Krishna; you are getting enraged in vain; on this side, you are resisting in ego and go on that side even moonshine seems inimical to Krishna, undoubtedly, you do not care for Krishna, but Krishna cares fully for you." —711

SWAYYA

Saying this, that friend said, "O Radha, you go quickly and see Krishna quickly; he who is the enjoyer of the passionate love of all, his eyes are centred on this abode of yours; O friend! If you do not go to him, he will lose nothing, the loss will be only yours; both the eyes of Krishna are unhappy because of separation from you." —712

"O Radha! He does not see towards any other women and is only looking for your coming; he is focusing his attention on you and only talks about you; sometimes, he controls himself and sometimes, he swings and falls on the ground; O friend! At the time when he remembers you, it seems that he is shattering the pride of the God of Love." —713

SWAYYA

"Therefore, O friend! Do not be egoistic and forsaking your hesitation go quickly; if you ask from me regarding Krishna, then think that his mind thinks only of your mind; he is entrapped in your thoughts under several pretensions; O foolish woman! You are becoming egoistic in vain and are not recognising the interest of Krishna." —714

Listening to the words of the *gopi*, Radha replied, "Who has asked you to leave Krishna and come to persuade me? I shall not go to Krishna; what to say of you, even if the Providence wants it, I shall not go to him; O friend! The names of others abide in his mind and is not looking towards a fool like me." —715

Listening to the words of Radha, the *gopi* replied, "O *gopi*! Listen to my words; he has asked me to say something to you for your attention; you are addressing me as a fool, but think for a while in your mind that, in fact, you are a fool; I have been sent by Krishna here and you are persistent in your thoughts about him." —716

Saying thus, the *gopi* said further, "O Radha! Forsake your doubt and go, consider it as true that Krishna loves you more than others; O dear! I fall at your feet, you leave your persistence and recognising the love of Krishna go to him without hesitation." —717

SWAYYA

"O friend! Krishna was absorbed in his amorous and passionate sport with you in the alcoves and in the forest; his love with you is much more than other *gopis*; Krishna has withered without you and he does not play with other *gopis* now; therefore, remembering the amorous play in the forest, go to him without hesitation." —718

"O friend! Krishna is calling you, you go to him without any obstinacy, you are sitting here in your pride, but you should listen to the words of others; therefore, I am telling you that you will not lose anything, if you smile for a while, having a look at me and forsaking your pride." —719

Speech of Radhika addressed to the Messenger

SWAYYA

"I shall neither smile nor go even if millions of friends like you my come; even though friends like you may make many efforts and bow their heads at my feet, I shall not go there; undoubtedly one may say millions of things; I do not say any other and say that Krishna may come himself and bow his head before me." —720

Speech in Answer

SWAYYA

When Radha said thus, the *gopi* replied, "O Radha! When I asked you to go, you said this that you do not even love Krishna; O my mother, what should I say? Krishna is forcibly exhibiting his love for her and is sending us to her; is Krishna short of *gopis* like her?" —721

"He sends us to her and she is egoistic about her beauty; she also knows that all other *gopis* do not equal her in beauty, therefore she is persistent in her attitude;" the poet Shyam says that this *gopi* (Radha) does not fear even slightly from Krishna, he is a sacrifice on her boldness when she says that Krishna be brought before her. —722

SWAYYA

"Krishna loves someone else, this *gopi* has no comprehension about it; without any words from him, she continues to say this and is not submitting to his wishes; when Krishna will forget her, then she will know the reward of such persistence and in the end, feeling embarrassed, she will conciliate him; at that time, nothing can be said, whether he will accede to her request or not." —723

Hearing this, Radha replied to her, "Krishna is absorbed in love with Chandrabhaga, therefore, I have shown my disrespect for him; on this, you have said so much, therefore my anger increased; on your request, I loved Krishna and now he has abandoned his love for me."—724

SWAYYA

Saying thus to the *gopi*, Radha added, "O *gopi*! You may go, I have endured your words very much; you have talked many things about the love-passion and pleasure, which I did not like in my mind; O friend; I therefore, shall not go to Krishna, because there is no love left now between me and Krishna." —725

Hearing this reply of Radha, the *gopi* said, talking in the interest of Krishna, "It is a very great botheration to come repeatedly and persuade her at the bidding of Krishna; O Radha! My mind says that Krishna like a partridge is anxious to see your face like moon." —726

Speech of Radha
SWAYYA

"What should I do, if he is anxious? I have already said that I shall not go; for what I should endure the sarcasm? I shall remain pleased with my husband; Krishna is roaming with other women, what approbation will I attain, if I go to him? Therefore, O friend! You may go, I shall not be seen by Krishna now in my life." —727

Now begins the Description of the Return of Maniprabha to Krishna

Speech of the Messenger addressed to Krishna
SWAYYA

When Maniprabha heard all this talk, she got up and came to the son of Nand and said, "O Krishna! That fool was greatly persuaded, but still persists in not coming; now leave her and roam with these *gopis*; or you may go yourself and bring her after persuasion," hearing these words, the poet Shyam says that Krishna went himself towards her. —728

SWAYYA

Krishna did not send another *gopi* and came himself; seeing him, Radha was extremely pleased; though she was greatly satisfied in her mind but still extremely showing her pride, she said, "You keep yourself absorbed in amorous sport with Chandarbhaga; why have you come here forsaking shyness?" —729

Speech of Radha addressed to Krishna
SWAYYA

"O Krishna! Why have you come here to me, leaving Chandrabhaga in the arena of amorous sport? Why have you come yourself agreeing with these *gopis* (messengers)? I knew you as a very cheat and now it has come clear by your actions; why are you calling me? I have not called you." —730

Speech of Krishna addressed to Radha
SWAYYA

Listening to this answer, Krishna said, "All your *gopi*-friends are calling you there; my mind-deer has been wounded because of the profuse arrows of your eyes; I am burning in the fire of separation and have not been able to save myself; I have not come at your call, I was burning there, therefore I have come here." —731

Speech of Radha addressed to Krishna
SWAYYA

The poet Shyam says that Radha said, "O Krishna! I was blissfully playing and roaming with you;

I endured the ridicule of the people and did not recognise anyone else except you; I was absorbed in love with you only, but you have forsaken my love and have brought me to such a state; you have loved other women," saying thus, Radha heaved a long sigh and tears came into her eyes. —732

Speech of Krishna
SWAYYA

"O, my dear Radha; I only love you and not any other *gopi*; if you stay with me, I see you and if do not stay, I see your shadow," saying this, Krishna caught hold of the arm of Radha and said, "Let us go to the forest and abide in pleasure; I swear to you, let us go," but Radha said, "I swear to you, I shall not go." —733

Talking in this way, the enjoyer of the passionate love of all the three worlds, caught hold of the arm of Radha; the waist of Krishna is slim like that of the lion and his face is beautiful like millions of moons; Krishna who allures the minds of the *gopis*, said, "You go with me, why are you doing this? I request you to say to me all that which and made that is in your mind." —734

"O my dear Radha! Why are you getting sarcastic with me? I have love only for you; you have fallen in illusion in vain; I have nothing in my mind regarding Chandrabhaga; therefore, forsaking your pride, go with me for playing on the bank of Yamuna;" the persistent Radha is not obeying Krishna, when, Krishna, overwrought with separation, is calling her. —735

"O dear! Forsake your pride and come; let both of us go to the forest; you are angry in your mind uselessly, because there is no other woman in my mind; therefore listen to me with delight and go with me; on the bank of the river I shall say this that there is no other *gopi* so nice as you; after that let us both in unison shatter the pride of the god of love." —736

When Krishna talked to Radha in extreme perturbance, she submitted to Krishna and abandoned her pride; holding her hand, Krishna said, "Come my friend and most dear Radha! You absorb yourself in passionate play with me." —737

Speech of Radha addressed to Krishna
SWAYYA

Hearing the words of Krishna, Radha replied, "O Krishna! Talk with her, with whom you have been in love; why have you caught hold of my arm and why are you causing anguish to my heart?" Saying thus, Radha's eyes were filled with tears and she heaved a long sigh. —738

SWAYYA

Heaving a long sigh and filling her eyes with tears, Radha said, "O Krishna! You roam with those *gopis*, with whom you have been fondly attached; you may kill me taking the weapons in your hands, but I shall not go with you; O Krishna! I am telling you the truth that you may go away, leaving me here." —739

Speech of Krishna addressed to Radha
SWAYYA

"O dear! You accompany me, forsaking your pride; I have come to you, abandoning all my doubts; please recognise somewhat the mode of love; a friend on being sold is ever ready to be sold; you might have heard this sort of love definitely with your ears; therefore O dear! I am requesting you to agree to my saying." —740

Speech of Radha
SWAYYA

Hearing the words of Krishna, Radha replied thus, "O Krishna! When did the love persist between you and me?" Saying this, the eyes of Radha were filled with tears; she said again, "You are in love with Chandrabhaga and you had compelled me in anger to leave the arena of amorous play;" the poet Shyam says that on saying this much, that deceitful one heaved a long sigh. —741

SWAYYA

Filled with fury, Radha spoke out from her beautiful mouth, "O Krishna! There is no love now between you and me, perhaps the Providence wanted that;" Krishna says that he is enamoured of her, but she retorts in rage why was he enchanted of her? She (Chandrabhaga) is absorbed in amorous play with you in the forest. —742

Speech of Krishna addressed to Radha
SWAYYA

"O dear! I am madly in love with you because of your gait and eyes; I am enamoured of you by seeing your hair, therefore, I could not go to my home, abandoning it; I am allured on even seeing your limbs; therefore my love for you has increased in my mind; I have been enchanted on seeing your face like the partridge looking at the moon." —743

"Therefore, O dear! Do not remain engrossed in pride now, get up and go with me just now; I have profound love for you; forsake your ire and talk to me; it does not behove you to talk in such an uncivilised way; listen to my request and go, because no gain will accrue to you in this way." —744

SWAYYA

When Krishna requested many times, then that *gopi* (Radha) slightly agreed; she removed the illusion of her mind and recognised the love of Krishna; Radha, the queen of women in beauty replied to Krishna; she abandoned the duality of her mind and began to talk about the passionate love with Krishna. —745

Radha said, "Being allured you have asked me to go with you, but I know that through the passionate love you will deceive me; you will take me alongwith you in the arena of amorous sport, but I know that there you will engage yourself with other *gopis*; O Krishna! I do not feel defeated by me; you do not know anything about any alcove, what will you do by taking me there." —746

The poet Shyam says that Radha became absorbed in the love of Krishna; she said smilingly to the Lord of Braja and the winsome lustre of her teeth, while smiling looked like the flash of lightening amongst the clouds, according to the poet; in this way that deceitful *gopi* (Radha) deceived the cheat (Krishna). —747

Radha was completely filled with the passionate love of Krishna and remembering his words, she was filled with joy in her mind; she said, "I shall play with Krishna in the alcoves and I shall do whatever he says," saying this she unhesitatingly, abandoned all her duality of the mind. —748

SWAYYA

When both of them, talking smilingly, fell down their love and merriment increased; Krishna smilingly hugged that beloved to his bosom and with his strength he embraced her; in this act, the blouse of Radha was pulled and its string was broken; the gems of his necklace also broke and fell down; meeting her beloved, the limbs of Radha came out of the fire of separation. —749

The poet says that Krishna, being filled with bliss in his mind, took Radha with him and went towards the forest; roaming in the alcoves, he forgot the sorrow of his mind; this love-story has been sung by Shukdev and others; Krishna, whose praise has been spread throughout the whole world, whosoever listens to his story, is fascinated by it. —750

Speech of Krishna addressed to Radha
SWAYYA

Krishna said to Radha, "You swim in Yamuna and I shall catch you; we will perform acts of love in water and shall also talk to you there everything about love; when the women of Braja will see you here covetously, they will not be able to reach upto this place; we shall remain there delightfully." —751

SWAYYA

Hearing the words of Krishna, about going within the water, Radha ran and jumped in water; Krishna followed her and according to the poet it seemed that in order to catch the Radha-bird, Krishna-falcon pounced upon her. —752

Swimming in water, Krishna, caught hold of Radha; surrendering her body to Krishna, the joy of Radha was increased and the illusions of her mind flowed away like water; the bliss enhanced in her mind and according to the poet, whosoever saw her, he was allured; Yamuna was also charmed. —753

Coming out of water, Krishna again began to engross himself in the passionate and amorous play alongwith the *gopis*; Radha, with great joy in her mind, began to sing; together with the women of Braja, Krishna played upon a tune in the musical mode of Sarang, hearing which the deer came running and the *gopis* also felt pleased. —754

DOHIRA

In Samvat 1745, the story of this poem was improved and if there is any error and omission in it, then the poets may still improve it. —755

I request folding both my hands, "O the Lord of the world! Thy servant may ever have this wish that my forehead may always remain in love with Thy Feet." —756

End of the chapter entitled "The Description of the Arena of Amorous Play" (based on *Dasham Sakandapurana*) in Krishnavatar in Bachittar Natak.

Salvation of a Brahmin named Sudarshan from Snake-birth

SWAYYA

The goddess whom the *gopis* had worshipped, her day of worship arrived; she was the same goddess who had killed the demons named Sumbh and Nisumbh and who is known in the world as the undistinguishable mother; those people who have not remembered her, they were destroyed in the world; the *gopis* and *gopas* are all going out of the city in order to worship her. —757

She, who has eight arms and is the killer of Sumbh, who is the remover of the suffering of saints and is fearless, whose fame is spread in all the seven heavens and the nether-world; all the *gopas* are going today in order to worship her. —758

DOHIRA

Krishna is going alongwith Yashoda and Balram in order to worship the great Rudra and Chandi. —759

SWAYYA

The *gopas*, being pleased, left the city for the worship; they made offerings of earthen lamps, *panchamrit*, milk and rice; they were extremely delighted and all their sufferings ended; according to the poet Shyam, this time is most fortunate for all of them. —760

SWAYYA

On this side, a snake swallowed in his mouth the whole body of the father of Krishna; that snake was black like the ebonite wood; in great fury, he stung Nand inspite of pleas; all the people of city tried to rescue the elderly Nand by severe thrashing, but when all were tired and could not rescue, then they began to look towards Krishna and shouted. —761

SWAYYA

Gopas and Balram, all together began to shout for Krishna: "Thou art the remover of sufferings and the giver of comforts;" Nand also said, "O Krishna, the snake has caught hold of me, either kill him or I shall be killed; just as a doctor is called when one catches some ailment, in the same manner, in adversity, the heroes are remembered. —762

Hearing the words of his father, Krishna pierced the body of the snake, who manifested himself as beautiful man (after relinquishing the body of the snake); describing the grandeur of the spectacle, the poet says that it seems that under the impact of virtuous actions, the glory of the moon, having been snatched, has appeared in this man, ending the enemy. —763

SWAYYA

When that Brahmin was transformed into a man named Sudarshan, Krishna asked him smilingly about his real abode, he, being pleased in mind, with bowed eyes and folded hands, greeted Krishna and said, "O Lord! Thou art the Sustainer and remover of the sufferings of the people and Thou art also the Lord of all the worlds." —764

Speech of the Brahmin

SWAYYA

"I had ridiculed the son of the sage Atri, who had cursed me to become a snake; his words became true and my body was transformed into that of a black snake; O Krishna! With Thy touch, all the sins of my body have been effaced." —765

All the people returned to their homes after worshipping the goddess of the world;

everyone praised the power of Krishna; the tune of the musical modes of Sorath, Sarang, Shuddh Malhar, and Bilawal was played, hearing which all the men and women of Braja and all others who heard, were pleased. —766

DOHIRA

In this way, worshipping Chandi, both the great heroes, Krishna and Balram returned to their home and having their food and drink, they went to sleep. —767

End of the chapter entitled "Salvation of the Brahmin and the Worship of Chandi" in Krishnavatar in Bachittar Natak.

Now beings the Description of the Killing of the Demon Vrishabhasura

SWAYYA

Both the heroes went to sleep after being served dinner by their mother Yashoda; as the day dawned, they reached the forest, where the lions and rabbits wandered; there a demon named Vrishabhasura was standing, whose both horns were touching the sky; seeing him, Krishna, in fury, caught hold of his horns with great force. —768

SWAYYA

Catching hold of him Krishna threw him at a distance of eighteen steps; then he, greatly infuriated, got up and began to fight in front of Krishna; Krishna once again raised and threw him and he could not get up again; he attained salvation at the hands of Krishna and expired without a battle. —769

End of the chapter entitled "Killing of the Demon Vrishabhasura" in Krishnavatar in Bachittar Natak.

Now begins the Description of the Killing of the Demon Keshi

SWAYYA

While fighting with Vrishabhasura, when Lord Krishna killed the great enemy, then Narada went to Mathura and said to Kansa, "The husband of your sister, the daughter of Nand and Krishna all these enemies of yours are prospering in your kingdom; it was through them that Aghasura and Bakasura were defeated and killed." —770

Speech of Kansa in Reply

SWAYYA

Kansa, the king of Mathura, getting infuriated in his mind, resolved that they may be killed by any means; there is no other work of so much importance before me; "I must fulfil this task at the earliest and save myself by killing my would-be killer;" then Narada said smilingly, "O king! You must definitely perform this one task and with deceit or strength or any other means, slash the head of your enemy." —771

Speech of Kansa addressed to Narada

SWAYYA

Then bowing before him, Kansa said, "O great sage! Your saying is true; the story of these killings permeates like the shadow of night in the day of my heart; he, who has killed Agha and brave Baka and Putana, it will be appropriate to kill him through deceit, strength or any other means." —772

Speech of Kansa addressed to Keshi

SWAYYA

When the sage (Narada) went away after meeting Kansa, then Kansa called a mighty demon named Keshi and said to him, "Go and kill Krishna, the son of Yashoda;" on this side, he got his sister and her husband Vasudev enchained in his house; Kansa told some secret things to Chandur and also sent for Kuvalyapeer (the elephant). —773

Speech of Kansa addressed to Akrur

SWAYYA

Kansa told his guards to construct a stage; he asked Chandur to make Kuvalyapeer (elephant) stand at the gate of the stage; he told Akrur to go to Nandpuri (the city of Nand) on his chariot and with the pretext of the performance of a *yajna* in our home, Krishna may be brought here. —774

SWAYYA

Kansa said to Akrur in an angry tone that he may go to Braja and announce there that a *yajna* is being performed in our house; in this way, Krishna may be enticed to come here; according to the poet this spectacle appears to suggest that a deer is being sent in advance to tempt the lion before killing him. —775

Speech of the Poet
DOHIRA

Kansa sent Akrur for waiting in ambush for the killing of Krishna; now with this I relate the story of the killing of Keshi. —776

SWAYYA

Keshi started early in the morning and assuming the form of a big horse, he reached Braja; seeing him, the sun and Indra were filled with fear; the frightened *gopas* seeing him also bowed their heads at the feet of Krishna; seeing all this Krishna became resolute with composure and on this side Keshi started a dreadful fighting. —777

The enemy Keshi, in rage, attacked Krishna with his feet, but Krishna did not let him touch his body and saved himself nicely; then Krishna caught hold of the feet of Keshi and raising him threw him at a distance, just as the boys throw the wooden stick; Keshi fell down at a distance of four hundred steps. —778

SWAYYA

Again stabilising himself and spreading his mouth Keshi fell upon Krishna; being used to frighten the heavenly beings, he opened his eyes wide and began to terrorise; Krishna put his hand in his mouth and it seemed that Krishna, assuming the form of death, was ejecting the life-force from the body of Keshi. —779

He (Keshi) tried to penetrate his teeth in the arm (of Krishna), but his teeth fell; the object for which he had come, it was defeated; he could not go back to his house and while fighting fell down on the earth; he died at the hands of Krishna and all his sins were destroyed. —780

SWAYYA

The method by which Ram killed Ravana and the method with which Narakasura died, the method with which Hiranayakashipu was killed by the Lord for the protection of Prahlad; the manner in which Madhu and Kaitabh were killed and the Lord drank away Davanal, in the same manner for the protection of the saints, Krishna with his strength, overthrew Keshi. —781

SWAYYA

After killing the great enemy, Krishna went to the forest with his cows; abandoning all his griefs from his mind, he was in his happy mood; according to the poet that spectacle seemed like this that a big deer had been killed by the lion out of the herd. —782

End of the chapter entitled "The Killing of Keshi" in Krishnavatar in Bachittar Natak.

Now begins the Description of the Arrival of Narada for Meeting Krishna

ARIL

Then Narada went to meet Krishna, who served him food to his fill; the sage stood at the feet of Krishna with bowed head and after reflecting in his mind and intellect, he addressed Krishna with great reverence. —783

Speech of the Sage Narada addressed to Krishna

SWAYYA

Before the arrival of Akrur, the sage told everything to Krishna; listening to all the talk Krishna was pleased in his mind; Narada said, "O Krishna! You have vanquished many heroes in the battlefield and have attained great brilliance; I have gathered and left many of your enemies, you may now (go to Mathura and) kill them." —784

SWAYYA

"I shall sing your praises if you kill Kuvalyapeer (elephant), kill Chandur on the stage with your fists, annihilate your great enemy Kansa by catching him from his hair and throw on the ground all the demons of the city and the forest after chopping them." —785

DOHIRA

Saying thus, Narada bade farewell to Krishna and went away; he thought in his mind that now Kansa had only a few days to live and his life would end very soon. —786

End of the chapter entitled "Going away of Narad after giving the Secrets to Krishna" in Krishnavatar in Bachittar Natak.

Now begins the Description of the Fighting with the Demon Vishwasura

DOHIRA

The Primal Lord Krishna began to play with the *gopis*; someone played the part of a he-goat, someone of a thief and someone of a policeman. —787

SWAYYA

Lord Krishna's amorous play with the *gopis* became very famous in the land of Braja; the demon Vishwasura, seeing the *gopis* came to devour them, assuming the form of a thief; he abducted many *gopas* and Krishna after a good deal of search, recognised him; Krishna ran and caught hold of his neck and dashed him against the earth and killed him. —788

DOHIRA

After killing Vishwasura and doing such deeds for the sake of saints, Krishna accompanied Balram, came to his home as the night fall. —789

End of the chapter entitled "Killing of the Demon named Vishwasura" in Krishnavatar in Bachittar Natak.

Now begins the Description of taking of Krishna to Mathura by Akrur

SWAYYA

When, after killing the enemy, Krishna was about to go, Akrur arrived there; seeing Krishna and being extremely pleased, he bowed before him; whatever Kansa had asked him to do, he did accordingly and thus delighted Krishna; just as the elephant is directed according to one's wish with the aid of goad, in the same way, Akrur, with the persuasive talk, got the assent of Krishna. —790

Listening to his words, Krishna went to his father Nand and said, "I have been called by Kansa, the king of Mathura, to come in the company of Akrur;" seeing Krishna, Nand said, "Are you alright," Krishna said, "Why do you ask it?" Saying thus, Krishna also called his brother Balram. —791

Now begins the Description of the Arrival of Krishna in Mathura

SWAYYA

Listening to their talk and accompanied by the *gopas*, Krishna started for Mathura; they also took many he-goats with them, and also great quantity of milk; Krishna and Balram were in front; seeing them, extreme comfort is obtained and all the sins are destroyed; Krishna seems like a lion in the forest of *gopas*. —792

DOHIRA

When Yashoda heard about the departure of Krishna to Mathura, she began to lament, losing consciousness. —793

SWAYYA

While weeping, Yashoda said like this, "Is there anyone in Braja, who may stop the departing Krishna in Braja? Is there any courageous person, who, may present my anguish before the king," saying this, Yashoda, withered by sorrow, fell down on the ground and became silent. —794

SWAYYA

"I kept Krishna in my womb for twelve months; O Balram! Listen, I have sustained and nourished Krishna to this age; has Kansa called him for this reason, considering him as the son of Vasudeva has my fortune, in reality, dwindled away, that Krishna will now onward not live in my house?" —795

DOHIRA

Leaving his home, Krishna mounted the chariot, now, O friends! Listen to the story of the *gopis*. —796

SWAYYA

When the *gopis* heard about the departure of Krishna, their eyes were filled with tears; many doubts arose in their mind and the happiness of their mind ended; whatever passionate love and youth they had, the same was burnt to ashes in the fire of sorrow; their mind has withered so much in the love of Krishna that now it has become difficult for them to speak. —797

SWAYYA

With whom, and whose arena, they used to sing together, for whom, they endured the ridicule of the people, but still they undoubtedly roamed with him; he, who knocked down many mighty demons for our welfare; O friend! the same Krishna, forsaking the land of Braja, is going towards Mathura. —798

SWAYYA

O friend! With whom, we have been absorbed in love on the bank of Yamuna, he is now firmly established in our mind and does not go out of it; listening to the talk about his departure, extreme sorrow permeates our mind; O friend! listen, the same Krishna, is now leaving us and going towards Mathura. —799

The poet says that with whom all the beautiful women played in extreme love; he glistened in the arena of amorous play like the flash of lightning in the clouds of Sawan; leaving the women with faces like moon, bodies like gold and gait like the elephants, O friend! now see, that Krishna is going to Mathura. —800

The *gopis* with the bodies like gold and the faces like the lotus, are lamenting in the love of Krishna; their mind is absorbed in sorrow and their comfort has sped away; all of them are saying; "O friend! look, Krishna has gone leaving all of us behind; the king of Yadavas himself has gone to Mathura and is not feeling our pain i.e., another's pain. —801

We shall wear ochre-coloured garments and carry the begging bowl in our hands; we shall have matted locks on our heads feel pleasure in begging for Krishna; wherever Krishna has gone, we shall go there; we have said that we shall become yogins and leave our homes. —802

The *gopis* are saying among themselves, "O friend! we shall do this work that we shall leave our homes, and have matted hair on our heads and begging bowls in our hands; we shall eat poison and die, we shall be drowned or burn ourselves to death;" considering their separation, all of them said that they would never leave the company of Krishna. —803

He, who was absorbed in passionate love with us and who gave us great pleasure in the forest; he, who endured ridicules for us and knocked down the demons; he, who removed all the sorrows of the *gopis* in the arena of amorous play, the same Krishna has now, forsaking our love gone away to Mathura. —804

We shall wear rings in our ears and put on the ochre-coloured garments; we shall carry mendicant's pot in our hands and rub ashes on our body; we shall hang the staghorn's trumpet by our waists and shall shout the name of Gorakhnath for alms; the *gopis* said that in this way, they would become yogins. —805

SWAYYA

Either we shall eat poison or shall commit suicide by some other method; we shall die with the blows of a knife on our body and level charge of our sin on Krishna, otherwise we shall evoke Brahma so that no injustice be done to us; the *gopis* said that they would not allow Krishna to go by any means. —806

SWAYYA

We shall wear the rosary of black wood around our necks and hang a purse by our waist; we shall carry a trident in our hand and keep awake by sitting in a posture in the sunshine; we shall drink the hemp of the meditation of Krishna and become intoxicated; in this way, the *gopis* said that they would not live in their homes and become yogins. —807

We shall light a fire in front of the house of Krishna and shall not do anything else; we shall, meditate on him and shall remain intoxicated with the hemp of meditation; we shall rub the dust of his feet on our body like ashes; the *gopis* are saying that for the sake of that Krishna, they would leave their homes and become yogins. —808

Making a rosary of our mind, we shall repeat his name; in this way, we shall perform austerity and thus please Krishna, the king of Yadavas; after getting his boon, we shall beg of him to give himself to us; thinking in this way, the *gopis* are saying that they would leave their homes and become yogins. —809

Those women gathered together and stood like the herd of deer listening to the sound of horn; this spectacle of the group of *gopis* removes all the anxieties; all these *gopis* are fascinated by Krishna nearby, in illusion, they sometimes open their eyes very quickly; they are doing this like a wounded person, who sometimes closes his eyes and sometimes opens them. —810

SWAYYA

Those, whose body was like gold and beauty like moon; those, whose glory was like that of the god of love and both of whose eyebrows were like arrows; on seeing whom, there was attainment of extreme happiness and not seeing whom, the mind experienced sorrow, those *gopis* withered away like the asphodel in water without the moonbeams. —811

SWAYYA

Taking all the *gopas* with him in the chariots, Krishna left; the *gopis* remained within their homes and the sufferings of their mind increased abundantly; the place where the *gopis* had gathered together and were waiting for Krishna, both the brothers, Krishna and Balram, went there; the faces of both the brothers were beautiful like moon and the bodies like gold. —812

SWAYYA

When Akrur reached on the bank of Yamuna with all the people, then seeing the love of all, Akrur repented in his mind; he thought that he had sinned profusely in taking away Krishna from that place; thinking like this, he entered the river-water for *sandhya* prayer and got worried on reflecting that the mighty Kansa would then kill Krishna. —813

DOHIRA

While taking bath, when Akrur remembered Lord Krishna, then the Lord (Murari) manifested Himself in real form. —814

SWAYYA

Akrur saw that Krishna with thousands of heads and thousands of arms was seated on the bed of Seshanaga; he has worn the yellow garments and had the disc and sword in his hands; in the same form Krishna manifested Himself to Akrur in Yamuna; Akrur saw that Krishna, the remover of the sorrows of the saints, has under His control the whole world and He has such brilliance that the clouds of Sawan are feeling shy. —815

SWAYYA

Then Akrur, coming out of water and in great comfort, started towards Mathura; he ran to the palace of the king and he now had no fear of Krishna being killed; seeing the beauty of Krishna, all the inhabitants of Mathura gathered together in order to have a look at him; the person, who had any slight ailment in his body, the same was removed on seeing Krishna. —816

Hearing about the arrival of Krishna, all the women of Mathura ran (to have his sight); the direction in which the chariot was going all of them gathered there; they were pleased to see the winsome elegance of Krishna and kept seeing only towards that side; whatever sorrow they had in their mind, the same was removed on seeing Krishna. —817

End of "The Description of the Arrival in Mathura of Krishna alongwith Nand and *Gopas*" in Krishnavatar (based on *Dasham Skandapurana*) in Bachittar Natak.

Description of the Killing of Kansa

DOHIRA

The poet after reflection has described the beauty of the city of Mathura; its glory is such that poets cannot describe. —818

SWAYYA

The city studded with gems looks like the flash of lightning; the river Yamuna flows by its side and its parts look splendid; seeing it Shiva and Brahma are getting pleased; the houses in the city are so high, what they seem to touch the clouds. —819

When Krishna was going, he saw a washerman in the way; when Krishna took away the clothes from him, he, in anger, began to cry for the king; Krishna, getting enraged in his mind, slapped him; after this beating, he fell dead on the ground like a washerman throwing the clothes on the earth. —820

DOHIRA

After beating the washerman, Krishna said to all the *gopas* to loot all the clothes of the king. —821

SORATHA

The ignorant *gopas* of Braja did not know the wearing of those clothes; the wife of the washerman came to cause them wear the clothes. —822

Speech of King Parikshat addressed to Shuka

DOHIRA

Krishna bestowed a boon on wife of the washerman and nodding his head, he sat down; then the (king) Parikshat enquired from Shuka, "O sage! tell me why it happened that Krishna sat down nodding his head." —823

Speech of Shuka addressed to the King

SWAYYA

The four-armed Krishna blessed her with the boon of living in happiness; with the words of the Lord, the fruit of all the three worlds are obtained, but according to tradition, the great man after bestowing something, feels shy on thinking that he had bestowed nothing; Krishna also knowing this that he had bestowed less, repented by nodding his head. —824

End of "The Description of the Killing of the Washerman and Granting of Boon to His Wife" in Krishnavatar in Bachittar Natak.

Now begins the Description of the Salvation of the Gardener

DOHIRA

After killing the washerman and bestowing boon on his wife, Krishna caused the chariot to be driven and reach in front of the palace of the king. —825

SWAYYA

The first to meet Krishna was the gardener, who garlanded him; he fell at the feet of Krishna many times and taking him alongwith himself, he served meal to Krishna; Krishna was pleased with him and told him to ask for a boon; the gardener, thought in his mind about asking for the boon of the company of a saint; Krishna read this from his mind and granted him the same boon. —826

DOHIRA

Getting pleased in his mind, Krishna granted the boon to the gardener and then went towards the city for the purpose of doing good to Kubja. —827

End of "The Description of the Salvation of the Gardener" in Krishnavatar in Bachittar Natak.

Now begins the Description of the Salvation of Kubja

SWAYYA

At the time of coming, Krishna met Kubja standing in front; Kubja saw Krishna's charming form; she was taking away the balm for the king; she thought in her mind that it would be very good if she get an opportunity for applying that balm on the body of Krishna; when Krishna visualised her love, he said himself, "Bring it and apply it to me;" the poet has described that spectacle.—828

SWAYYA

Obeying the words of the king of Yadavas, that woman applied that balm on his body; seeing the beauty of Krishna, the poet Shyam has attained extreme happiness; he is the same Lord, even Brahma eulogising him could not know his mystery; this servant is very fortunate, who has touched the body of Krishna with her own hands. —829

SWAYYA

Krishna put his foot on the foot of Kubja and caught her hand in his hand; he straightened that hump-backed and the power of doing this is not with any other in the world; he, who killed Bakasura, he will now kill Kansa, the king of Mathura; the fate of this hump-backed is appreciable, who was treated as a doctor by the Lord himself. —830

Speech in Reply

SWAYYA

Kubja asked the Lord to go with her to her home; she was fascinated on seeing the face of Krishna, but she was also afraid of the king; Krishna thought that she was allured on seeing him, but keeping her in illusion, the Lord (Krishna) said, "After killing Kansa, I shall fulfil your desire." —831

SWAYYA

After finishing the task of Kubja, Krishna was absorbed in seeing the city; the place where the women were standing he went there to see them; the spies of the king forbade Krishna, but he was filled with rage; he pulled his bow with force and with its twang, the women of the king awoke with fear. —832

Getting enraged, Krishna created fear and stood on the same place; he was standing like a lion gaping wide his eyes in wrath; whosoever saw him, fell on the ground; seeing this scene even Brahma and Indra were filled with fear; breaking his bow, Krishna began to kill with its sharp bits. —833

Speech of the Poet

DOHIRA

For the sake of the story of Krishna, I have mentioned the strength of the bow; O Lord! I have greatly and extremely erred, forgive me for this. —834

SWAYYA

Taking the bit of the bow in his hand Krishna began to kill there the great heroes; there those heroes also fell upon Krishna in great rage; Krishna also absorbed in fighting also began to kill them; there was such a great noise there that on hearing the same even Shiva arose and fled. —835

KABIT

Where great warriors are standing firmly, there Krishna is fighting greatly enraged; the warriors are falling like the trees being cut by the carpenter; there is a flood of warriors and the heads and swords are flowing in the blood; Shiva and Gauri had come riding on the white bull, but here they were dyed in red. —836

KABIT

Krishna and Balram fought the battle in great ire, which caused all the warriors to run away; the warriors fell on being struck by the bits of the bow and it seemed that the whole army of king Kansa fell on the earth; many warriors got up and ran away and many were again absorbed in fighting; The Lord Krishna also began to burn with anger like the hot water in the forest; there is splash of blood from the trunks of the elephants and the whole sky is looking reddish like the red splash. —837

DOHIRA

Krishna and Balram destroyed the whole army of the enemy with the bits of the bow; hearing about the killing of his army, Kansa sent more warriors there again. —838

SWAYYA

Krishna killed the fourfold army with the bits of the bow; those who had fled were saved and those who fought again, were killed; there was a dreadful battle of the fourfold army and the streams of blood began to flow; the battlefield looked like a woman wearing her ornaments. —839

SWAYYA

Both the brothers fought in great anger and destroyed many warriors the number of warriors who were destroyed, the same number reached again with new decoration; those who came, were also killed quickly and at that place the spectacle seemed like the offering of ornaments to the battlefield. —840

SWAYYA

Killing the enemies with the bits of the bow

Krishna came to (his father) Nand; on coming, he touched the feet of Nand, who hugged him to his bosom; Krishna told that they had gone to see the city; in this way, being delighted in their mind, all of them slept as the night fell. —841

DOHIRA

On this side, Kansa saw a dreadful dream during the night and greatly agitated, he called all his servants. —842

Speech of Kansa addressed to His Servants

SWAYYA

Calling his servants, the king said, "A stage be set up for playing; keep the *gopas* together at one place and also call our whole army; do this work very quickly and do not go even one step backward; tell the wrestlers to get ready and come and keep them standing there." —843

SWAYYA

Listening to the orders of the king, the servants did accordingly; keeping the elephant standing at the gate, a new stage was set up; on that stage the mighty warriors were standing, seeing whom, the enemies would even get disheartened; the servants set up such a place that they received all kinds of praise. —844

SWAYYA

The servant of the king brought all these people (Krishna and his companions) in the palace of king Kansa; he told all of them that this is the house of the king, therefore all the *gopas* bowed their heads in veneration; they saw before them an intoxicated elephant and the mahout is asking all of them to get away; the elephant speedily fell upon Krishna in such a way just as the vice falls upon the virtue in order to destroy it. —845

The elephant angrily entrapped both beautiful warriors (Krishna and Balram) in his trunk and began to roar in a unique way; both the brothers, who are the killers of the enemies, began to swing under the belly of the elephant and appeared to be busy in playing with the enemy. —846

SWAYYA

Then, Krishna, in great rage, extirpated the tusk of the elephant; he made another attack on the trunk of the elephant and the second attack on his head; because of the dreadful blows, the elephant became lifeless and fell on the earth; the elephant died and it seemed that Krishna had entered Mathura on that day in order to kill Kansa. —847

End of the chapter entitled "Killing of the Elephant" in Krishnavatar (based on *Dasham Skandapurana*) in Bachittar Natak.

Now begins the Description of the Battle with Chandur and Mushitak

SWAYYA

After extirpating the tusk of the elephant and placing it upon the shoulder both the brothers reached at the (newly set-up) stage; the warriors saw them as mighty warriors and the wrestlers at that place considered them as very sturdy; the saints considering them unique, visualised them as the creators of the world; the father saw them as sons and king Kansa, they seemed as destroyers of his house. —848

Sitting in the assembly, the king caused Krishna, the king of Yadavas to fight with his wrestlers; Balram fought with the wrestler named Mushitak and on his side Krishna fought with Chandur; when Krishna became infuriated, all these wrestlers fell on the earth like mountains and Krishna killed them in a very short time. —849

End of the chapter entitled "Killing of the Wrestlers Chandur and Mushitak" in Krishnavatar (based on *Dasham Skandapurana*) in Bachittar Natak.

Now begins the Description about the Killing of Kansa

SWAYYA

When both the brothers killed the enemies, the king was filled with rage; he, in great tumultuousness, said to his warriors, "Kill both of them just now;" the king of the Yadavas

BACHITTAR NATAK

(Krishna) and his brother, catching hand of each other, stood there fearlessly; whosoever fell upon them in fury, was killed at that place by Krishna and Balram. —850

SWAYYA

Now, jumping from the stage, Krishna stabilised his feet at the place where king Kansa was seated; Kansa, in anger, controlling his shield, pulled out his sword and struck a blow on Krishna; Krishna jumped away and saved himself from this stratagem; he caught hold of the enemy from his hair and with force dashed him on the ground. —851

Catching hold of his hair, Krishna threw Kansa on the earth and catching his leg, he dragged him; killing the king Kansa, Krishna's mind was filled with delight and on the other side there were loud lamentations in the palace; the poet says that the glory of Lord Krishna may be visualised, who has protected the saints and destroyed the enemies; he has broken the bondages of all and in this way, he has been praised by the world. —852

SWAYYA

After killing the enemy, Krishna came on the ferry of Yamuna and when he saw there other warriors of Kansa, he was greatly enraged; he, who did not come to him, he was forgiven, but still some warriors came and began to wage war with him; He, sustaining His power, killed all of them. —853

SWAYYA

Krishna, highly infuriated, fought persistently with the elephant, in the beginning; then fighting continuously for a few hours, he killed both the wrestlers on the stage; then killing Kansa and reaching the bank of Yamuna, he fought with these warriors and killed them; there was shower of flowers from the sky, because Krishna protected the saints and killed the enemies. —854

End of the chapter entitled "The Killing of the King Kansa" in Krishnavatar (based on *Dasham Skandapurana*) in Bachittar Natak.

Now begins the Description about the Coming of the Wife of Kansa to Krishna

SWAYYA

The queen, in her extreme sorrow, left the palaces and came to Krishna; while weeping, she began to relate her sufferings to Krishna; the garment of her head had fallen down and there was dust in her head; while coming, she hugged her (dead) husband to her bosom and seeing this, Krishna bowed down his head. —855

After performing the funeral rites of the king, Krishna came to his parents; both the parents also bowed their heads on account of the attachment and reverence; they considered Krishna as God and Krishna also penetrated more attachment in their mind; Krishna, with great modesty, instructed them in various ways and liberated them from bondages. —856

End of "The Description regarding the Liberation of the Parents by Krishna after the Funeral Rites of Kansa" in Krishnavatar in Bachittar Natak.

Now begins the Speech of Krishna addressed to Nand

SWAYYA

Krishna then came to the place of Nand and humbly requested him to tell him whether he was actually the son of Vasudeva to which Nand agreed. Then Nand asked all the people present there to go to their homes; this was that Nand said, but without Krishna the land of Braja would lose all its glory. —857

SWAYYA

Bowing his head, Nand also left for Braja, with extreme sorrow in his mind; all of them are in great anguish like the bereavement on the death of the father or brother or like the seizure of the kingdom and honour of a great sovereign by an enemy; the poet says that it appears to him that a *thug* like Vasudeva has plundered the wealth of Krishna. —858

Speech of Nand addressed to the Residents of the City

DOHIRA

On coming to Braja, Nand told all the matter

regarding Krishna, hearing which all were filled with anguish and Yashoda also began to weep. —859

Speech of Yashoda

SWAYYA

He, who saved his father from the enormous snake; he, who killed the powerful demon Bakasura; he, the brother of dear Haldhar (Balram), who killed the demon named Aghasura and he, whose feet can be realised by meditating on the Lord, O friend! that Lord Krishna of mine has been snatched away from me by the residents of Mathura. —860

Lamentation of the Gopis

SWAYYA

Hearing these words all the *gopis* were filled with sorrow; the bliss of their mind had ended, all of them meditated on Krishna, the sweat flowed from their bodies and becoming dejected, they fell down upon the earth; they began to wail and their mind and body lost all happiness. —861

SWAYYA

Having been greatly worried in the love of Krishna, they sing his praises keeping in their mind the tunes of the musical modes of Sorath, Shuddh Malhar, Bilawal, Sarang, etc., they are meditating on him in their mind and getting extremely aggrieved by it; they are withering like the lotus seeing the moon during the night. —862

Now Krishna has absorbed himself with the residents of the city and has forgotten us from his mind; he has left us here and now we forsake his love; how wonderful it is that there he has come so much under the impact of women, that he has not even sent a message to us; saying thus, someone fell on the earth and someone has begun to cry and lament. —863

SWAYYA

In this way, getting highly sorrowful, the *gopis* are talking to one another; the grief is increasing in their heart, because entrapping them in love, Krishna has abandoned them and gone away; sometimes in ire they say why Krishna does not care for the ironical shafts of the people; that he has left us in Braja and there he is involved with the residents of the city. —864

SWAYYA

All the *gopis* in their lamentation are saying modestly, "Abandoning the thoughts of love and separation, Krishna has gone to Mathura from Braja;" saying this someone is falling on the earth and someone, protecting herself, is saying, "O friend! Listen to me, the Lord of Braja has forgotten all the women of Braja." —865

Speech of the Poet

SWAYYA

Krishna is always standing before my eyes, therefore I do not see anything else; they had been absorbed with him in amorous play, their dilemma is increasing now on remembering him; he has forsaken the love of the residents of Braja and has become hardhearted, because he has not sent any message; O my mother! we are seeing towards that Krishna, but he is not visible. —866

Poem based on Twelve Months

SWAYYA

In the month of Phalgun, the young damsels are roaming with Krishna in the forest, throwing dry colours on each other; taking the pumps in their hands, they are singing charming songs; removing the sorrows from their mind they are running in the alcoves and in the love of the beautiful Krishna, they have forgotten the decorum of their house. —867

SWAYYA

The *gopis* are blooming like flowers with the flowers attached to their garments; after bedecking themselves they are singing for Krishna like nightingales; now it is the spring season, therefore they have forsaken all the embellishments; seeing their glory even Brahma is wonder-struck. —868

Once the flowers of *palash* were blooming and the comfort-giving wind was blowing; the black bees were humming here and there Krishna had played on his flute; hearing his flute, the gods were getting pleased and the beauty of that spectacle is indescribable; at that time, that season was joy-giving, but now the same has become distressing. —869

In the month of Jeth, O friend! we used to be absorbed in amorous play on the bank of the river, being pleased in our mind; we plastered our bodies with sandal and sprinkled rose-water on the earth; we applied fragrance to our clothes and that glory is indescribable; that occasion was highly pleasing, but now the same occasion has become troublesome without Krishna. —870

The time, when the wind blew ferociously, the cranes arose and the sunshine was agonising, even that time appeared to us as joy-giving; all of us played with Krishna splashing water on one another; that time was extremely comfort-giving, but now the same time has become agonising. —871

SWAYYA

Look, O friend! the clouds have surrounded us and it is a beautiful spectacle created by raindrops; the sound of cuckoo, peacock and frog is resounding; in such a time, we were absorbed with Krishna in amorous play; how much comfortable was that time and now this time is greatly distressing. —872

Sometimes the clouds burst into rain and the shade of the tree appeared comfort-giving; we used to wander with Krishna, wearing the garments of flowers; while roaming, we were absorbed in amorous play; it is impossible to describe that occasion; remaining with Krishna, that season was joy-giving and now without Krishna, the same season has become distressing. —873

In the month of Ashvin, with great joy, we played with Krishna; being intoxicated Krishna used to play on (his flute) and produce tunes of charming musical modes; we sang with him and that spectacle is indescribable; we remained in his company; that season was pleasure-giving and now the same season has become distressing. —874

In the month of Kartik, we, in delight, were absorbed in amorous play with Krishna; in the current of the white river, the *gopas* also wore white clothes; the *gopis* also wore white ornaments and necklaces of pearls; they all looked fine; that time was very comfortable and now this has become extremely agonising. —875

SWAYYA

In the month of Magha, in great pleasure, we used to play with Krishna; when we felt cold, we removed the coolness by blending our limbs with the limbs of Krishna; the flowers of jasmine are not blooming and in sorrow, the water of Yamuna has also decreased; O friend! the season alongwith Krishna was very joy-giving and this season is very troublesome. —876

In winter season, we all had been happy in the company of Krishna and removing all our doubts we were absorbed in the amorous play Krishna also unhesitating considered all the *gopis* of Braja as his wives; in his company that season was pleasure-giving and now the same season has become troublesome. —877

SWAYYA

In the month of Magha, we had made the amorous play very famous in the company of Krishna; at that time, Krishna played on his flute; that occasion cannot be described; the flowers were blossoming and Indra, the king of gods, was getting pleased on seeing that spectacle; O friend! that season was comfort-giving and now the same season has become distressing. —878

SWAYYA

The poet Shyam says, "Those very fortunate *gopis* are remembering Krishna; losing their consciousness, they are absorbed in the passionate love of Krishna; someone has fallen down, someone has become unconscious and someone has been fully engrossed in his love; all the *gopis* have begun weeping after remembering their amorous play with Krishna. —879

Here ends the lamentation of the *gopis*.

Now begins the Description of Learning Gayatri *mantra* by Krishna

SWAYYA

This was the condition of *gopis* on that side, on this side now I relate the condition of Krishna; all the priests were called in after plastering the earth with cow-dung. The sage Garg was seated on the sacred spot; that sage gave him (Krishna) the Gayatri *mantra*, which is the enjoyer of the whole earth. —880

SWAYYA

Krishna was made to wear the sacred thread and the *mantra* was given to him in his ear; after listening to the *mantra*, Krishna bowed at the feet of Garg and gave him enormous wealth, etc., He was given horses, big elephants camels and beautiful garments. On touching the feet of Garg, he was, with great delight given rubies, emeralds and jewels, in charity. —881

The priest was pleased on giving *mantra* to Krishna and receiving the wealth; all his sufferings ended and he attained supreme bliss. After receiving the wealth, he came to his house; knowing all this, his friends were extremely pleased and all types of poverty of the sage were destroyed. —882

End of the chapter entitled "Teaching of Gayatri *mantra* to Krishna and Wearing of the Sacred Thread" in Krishnavatar (based on *Dasham Skandapurana*) in Bachittar Natak.

Now begins the Description of Giving the Kingdom to Uggarsain

SWAYYA

Taking the *mantra* from the priest, then Krishna set his father free from imprisonment; after attaining freedom, seeing the divine form of Krishna, he bowed before him; Krishna said, "Now you rule over the kingdom" and then seated the king Uggarsain on the throne; there were rejoicings all over the world and the sufferings of the saints were removed. —883

When Krishna killed the enemy Kansa, he gave the kingdom to the father of Kansa; the kingdom was given like giving the smallest of the coins; he himself did not accept anything, having not even the slight greed; after killing the enemies, Krishna laid bare the hypocrisy of his enemies; after this he and Balram made up their mind for learning the science of arms and made preparations for it. —884

End of the chapter entitled "Bestowal of the Kingdom on the King Uggarsain."

Now begins the Description of Learning Archery

SWAYYA

After getting the permission of their father regarding the learning of archery, both the brothers (Krishna and Balram) started (for their destination); their faces are beautiful like moon and both are great heroes; after a few days, they reached the place of the sage Sandipan; they are the same, who, in great fury, killed the demon named Mura and deceived the king Bali. —885

SWAYYA

The poet Shyam says, "They learnt all the sciences in sixty-four days; on the sixty-fifth day they went in front of their *guru* and requested him (to accept a religious gift); the *guru* after talking with his wife asked them to bestow life to the dead son, both the brothers heard the words of the sage and agreed to give the desired present." —886

SWAYYA

Both the brothers mounted on their chariot and came to the coast of the sea; seeing the sea, they bowed their heads and told the sea about the object of their arrival; the sea said, "A mighty one lives here, but I do not know whether he is the one who has kidnapped the son of your *guru*" hearing this, both the brothers, blowing their conches entered the waters. —887

Just on entering the waters, they saw a demon of dreadful form; seeing him, Krishna held his weapon in his hand and began a terrible fight;

according to the poet Shyam, this battle continued for twenty days; just as a lion kills the deer, in the same manner Krishna, the king of Yadavas, knocked down that demon. —888

End of "The Killing of the Demon."

SWAYYA

After killing the demon, Krishna took out the conch from his heart; this conch obtained by killing the enemy, resounded the Vedic *mantras*; in this way, highly pleased, Krishna entered the world of Yama, where the god of death came and fell at his feet, thus removing all his sorrows. —889

Seeing the world of Yama, Krishna made this utterance from his mouth, "Is the son of my *guru* not here?" Yama said, "No one, who has come here, can leave this world, even on the bidding of the gods;" but Krishna asked Yama to return the son of the Brahmin. —890

SWAYYA

On receiving the order of Krishna, Yama brought forth the son of Krishna's *guru* at his feet; taking him, Krishna, the king of Yadavas, being greatly pleased in his mind, started on his return journey; bringing the *guru*'s son with him, Krishna bowed his head at the feet of the *guru* and bidding him farewells, he came back to his city. —891

DOHIRA

He came to meet his family; there was increase in happiness of all; all felt comforted and the uncertainty was destroyed. —892

End of the description entitled "After learning archery, the *Guru*'s dead Son was brought back from the World of Yama and given back to His Father as Religious Gift" in Krishnavatar in Bachittar Natak.

Now begins the Description of Sending Udhava to Braja

SWAYYA

At the time of going to sleep, Krishna thought that he should do sometimes for the residents of Braja; Udhava be called early in the morning and sent to Braja, so that he may convey words of comforts to his godmother and the *gopis* and *gopas*; and then there is no other way to solve the conflict of love and knowledge. —893

SWAYYA

When the day dawned, Krishna called Udhava and sent him to Braja; he reached the house of Nand, where the grief of all was dispelled; Nand asked Udhava whether Krishna had ever remembered him; saying only this, he on remembering Krishna, became unconscious and fell down on the earth. —894

When Nand fell down on the earth, Udhava said that the hero of Yadavas had come; hearing these words, forsaking his sorrow, Nand stood up and said, "O Udhava! I know that you and Krishna have deceived us because after abandoning Braja and going to the city, Krishna had never returned." —895

"Krishna, forsaking Braja, has given extreme grief to all the people; O Udhava! without him, Braja has become poor; the Lord God gave a son in our house, but we do not know, for which sin of our He has snatched him from us?" Saying this Nand bowed his head and began to weep. —896

SWAYYA

Saying this, he fell down on the earth and getting up again, he said to Udhava, "O Udhava! tell me the reason why Krishna has left Braja and has gone to Mathura? I fall at your feet, you should give me all details; for what sin of mine, Krishna does not communicate with me?" —897

SWAYYA

Hearing these words, Udhava replies, "He was actually the son of Vasudeva, the Lord God has not snatched him from you" hearing this, Nand heaved a cold sigh and lost patience; and seeing towards Udhava, he began to weep. —898

SWAYYA

Udhava said persistently, "O Lord of Braja! Do not be sorrowful; whatever Krishna has asked me to convey to you, all of you may listen to me; he hearing whose words, the mind is pleased and seeing whose face all receive life-force, that Krishna has asked you to abandon all anxiety; you would lose nothing." —899

SWAYYA

Hearing the talk of Udhava in this way, Nand further questioned Udhava and hearing the story of Krishna, all his grief was dispelled and happiness was increased in his mind; he forsook all other talk and absorbed himself in knowing about Krishna; the way in which the yogis meditate, just like that he only concentrated on Krishna. —900

SWAYYA

After saying this, Udhava went to the village in order to apprise himself about the state of *gopis*; all the Braja appeared to him as the abode of sorrow; there the trees and plants had withered with grief; the women were sitting silently in their houses; they appeared to be entrapped in a great Krishna, but when they came to know this that he had not come, they felt anguish. —901

Speech of Udhava
SWAYYA

Udhava said to the *gopis*, "Listen to me all about Krishna; the path on which he has asked you to tread, walk on it and whatever work he has asked you to do, you may do that; tear your garments and become yogins and whatever is being said to you, you may do that; you may concentrate your attention on him, you shall not be doing anything wrong by this." —902

Speech of the Gopis
SWAYYA

Hearing these words of Udhava, they replied, "O Udhava! hearing about whom, there is feeling of separation and the happiness is decreased, that Krishna has left us; when you go you may tell this to him, 'You have forthwith forsaken love'." —903

SWAYYA

The women of Braja said to Udhava again, "On one side he has left us and on the other side, your talk is enflaming our mind," saying thus, the *gopis* added, "O Udhava! You may tell Krishna this much definitely, O Krishna! You have bidden farewell to the passion of love." —904

Getting mad again in the passionate love of Krishna, the *gopis* said to Udhava, "O Udhava! We request you that those *gopis* whose bodies were like gold, their bodies have been destroyed; O Udhava! none except you has communicated with us." —905

SWAYYA

Someone in extreme worry and someone in extreme ire is saying, "O Udhava! He, for whose sight, our love is overflowing, the same Krishna has cast off his love for us; He has forsaken us and has absorbed himself with the residents of His city; it is true the way in which Krishna has abandoned the women of Braja now you may accept this that the women of Braja have abandoned Krishna." —906

SWAYYA

Some of the *gopis* said that they had forsaken Krishna and some of them that they would do whatever Krishna has asked them to do; the guises that Krishna had asked the *gopis* to wear, they would wear them; some of them said that they would go to Krishna and others said that they sing his praises; some *gopi* says that she will die by taking poison and someone else says that she will die while meditating upon him. —907

Speech of Udhava addressed to the Gopis
SWAYYA

Seeing such a state of *gopis*, Udhava marvelled over it and said, "I know that you are immensely in love with Krishna, but you are advised not to assume the garb of yogins; I have been sent by Krishna to you to ask you not to forsake your homely duties and only meditate on Krishna." —908

Speech of Gopis addressed to Udhava
SWAYYA

Once in the alcoves of Braja, Krishna bedecked me with ear-pendants which were studded with very precious stones; their praise could not even be uttered by Brahma; just as the lightning flashes in the clouds, their beauty was just like that; O Udhava! Krishna gave all these at that time, but now he, having clad you in the garb of a yogi, has sent you to us. —909

SWAYYA

Some *gopi* said that they would become yogins according to the saying of Krishna and rub ashes and carry begging bowls; someone said that they would go to Krishna and die there on taking poison; someone said that they would produce the fire of separation and burn themselves in it. —910

Speech of Radha addressed to Udhava
SWAYYA

Being immersed in the love of Krishna, Radha said, "Now Krishna has forsaken Braja and gone to Mathura and has put us in such straitened circumstances; he has fallen in passionate love with the women of Mathura, on seeing them; Krishna has been tamed by Kubja and in such a state no pain has arisen in the heart of that butcher. —911

SWAYYA

The bed of flowers is looking splendid in the moonlight night; the current of the white Yamuna appears like a beautiful raiment and the particles of sand appear like the necklace of gems; the god of love seeing us without Krishna is attacking us with his arrows and that Krishna has been tamed by Kubja; in doing this, there was no pang in her heart and no pain arose in the heart of that butcher. —912

SWAYYA

The embellishment of the thundering night is looking splendid, the river Yamuna of black colour is flowing, and for whom there is no helper other than Krishna;" Radha said that Krishna as Cupid was creating extreme anguish and that Krishna has been tamed by Kubja; in doing so no pang arose in her heart and no pain arose in the heart of that butcher. —913

SWAYYA

In the country of Braja all the trees are loaded with flowers and the creepers are entwined with them; the tanks and within them the storks look elegant; the glory is increasing all around; the beautiful month of Chaitra has begun, in which the voice of the wanton nightingale is being heard; but all this does not seem charming without Krishna; living with his servant no pang arose in the heart of that Krishna and no pain arose in the heart of that butcher. —914

The fine odour spread upto the sky and the whole earth appeared glorious; the cold wind is blowing slowly and slowly and the nectar of flower is mixed in it; in the month of Baisakh, the dust of the pollen of flowers now appears deplorable to the people of Braja without Krishna, because there in the city, taking flowers from the female gardener, no pain arises in the heart of that indifferent Krishna and he experiences no pang. —915

SWAYYA

The water and wind appear like fire and the earth and sky are blazing; there is no traveller moving on the path and seeing the trees, the passengers are pacifying their burning sensation; the month of Jeth is extremely hot and the mind of everyone is getting perturbed; in such a season, the mind of that indifferent Krishna neither gets deviated nor there arises any pain in it. —916

SWAYYA

The wind is blowing with fierce speed and the mercurial mind being agitated is running in all the four directions; all the men and women are in their homes and all the birds are getting the protection of the trees; in this season of Asarh the loud sounds of frogs and peacock are being heard; in such an atmosphere, the persons experiencing the pangs of separation are highly worried; but that indifferent Krishna is not showing mercy and no pang has arisen in his mind. —917

SWAYYA

The tanks are filled with water and the drains of water are merging in the tank; the clouds are causing the splash of rain and the rain-bird has begun to utter its own music; O mother! the month of Sawan has arrived, but that captivating Krishna is not in my home; That Krishna is roaming with the women in the city and in doing so, the pain is not arising in the heart of that indifferent and merciless person. —918

SWAYYA

My Lord is not here and the month of Bhadon has begun; the clouds are gathering in from all the ten direction; no difference appears between day and night and in the darkness the lightning is flashing like the sun; it is raining cats and dogs from the sky and the water has spread over all the earth; in such a time that merciless Krishna has left us and no pain has arisen in his heart. —919

SWAYYA

The powerful month of Kuaar (Asuj) has begun and that comfort-giving Krishna has not met us even now; the white clouds, the brilliance of night and mansions like mountains are being seen; these clouds are moving waterless in the sky and seeing them our heart has become more impatient; we are absorbed in love, but we are removed far away from that Krishna and there is no pang of any type in the heart of that merciless butcher. —920

In the month of Kartik, there is brightness in the sky like the light of the lamp; the intoxicated groups are scattered in the play of men and women here and there; seeing the house and courtyard all are being allured like the portraits; that Krishna has not come and his mind has been absorbed somewhere therein; in doing so, there has not been even a little suffering in the mind of that merciless Krishna. —921

SWAYYA

The mass of lotus in the tank are spreading their fragrance; all other birds except the swans are playing and hearing their sound, the affliction increases in the mind still further; Krishna has not come even in the month of Magha, therefore there is no comfort during the day and during the night; there is no peace in the mind without him, but no pang arises in the heart of that indifferent Krishna and no pain emerges. —922

SWAYYA

There is atmosphere of sadness in the earth, the sky and the home and courtyard; the agonising pain like that of the thorn is rising at the bank of the river and at other places and the oil and the wedding present are all appearing painful; just as the lily withers away in the month of Poh, in the same manner our body has withered; that Krishna has exhibited his love there under some temptation and in doing so, no pang or pain has arisen in his heart. —923

My beloved is not in my home, therefore the sun, exhibiting his effulgence wants to burn me; the day passes away unknowingly, and there is more impact of the night; seeing the nightingale, the pigeon comes to her and noticing her pang of separation, he is frightened; that Krishna has extended his love to the residents of that city and in doing so, no pain has arisen in his heart. —924

SWAYYA

In the month of Phalgun, the love for playing Holi has increased in the mind of married women; they have worn the red garments and have begun to bleach others with the colours; I have not seen the beautiful spectacle of these twelve months and my mind is burning to see that spectacle; I have abandoned all hopes and have become disappointed, but in the heart of that butcher, no pang or pain has arisen. —925

End of "The Description of the Spectacle depicting Pangs of Separation in Twelve Months" in Krishnavatar in Bachittar Natak.

Now begins the Description of the Spectacle of the Pangs of Separation and the Dialogue between Udhava and *Gopis*

Speech of Gopis with One Another

SWAYYA

O friend! listen, with the same Krishna we had been absorbed in the much-publicised amorous play in the alcoves; wherever he used to sing, we also sang songs of praise with him; the mind of that Krishna has become inattentive towards these *gopis* and having relinquished Braja, he has gone to Mathura; they said all these things, looking towards Udhava and also said regretting that Krishna had not come to their homes again. —926

Speech of Gopis addressed to Udhava
SWAYYA

"O Udhava! There was a time when Krishna used to take us alongwith him and roamed in the alcoves; he gave profound love to us; our mind was under the control of that Krishna and all the women of Braja were in extreme comfort; now the same Krishna has abandoned us and has gone to Mathura; how can we survive without that Krishna?" —927

Speech of the Poet
SWAYYA

Udhava talked to the *gopis* all the things about Krishna; they did not say anything in response to his words of wisdom and only uttered their language of love; Krishna, seeing whom, they used to take their meals and did not even drink water without him, whatever Udhava said to them about him in his wisdom, the *gopis* did not accept anything. —928

Speech of the Gopis addressed to Udhava
SWAYYA

All of them collectively said to Udhava, "O Udhava! you may talk to Krishna like this that all the words of wisdom that he had sent through you, has been imbibed by us; O Udhava! taking into consideration our welfare tell it definitely to Krishna that forsaking us he had gone to Mathura, but there also he should keep in touch with us." —929

When *gopis* said all this to Udhava, he was then also filled with love; he lost his consciousness and the brilliance of wisdom ended in his mind; he also began to talk about love in the company of *gopis* and it appeared that he put off the clothes of wisdom and had plunged into the stream of love. —930

When Udhava recognised the love of *gopis*, he also began to converse with the *gopis* about love; Udhava gathered love in his mind and abandoned his wisdom; his mind was filled with love to such an extent that he also said that on forsaking Braja, Krishna had made Braja very poor; but O friend! the day when Krishna went to Mathura, his sexual instinct has deteriorated. —931

Speech of Udhava addressed to the gopis
SWAYYA

"O young damsels! On reaching Mathura, I shall cause to send an envoy through Krishna to take you to Mathura; whatever difficulties you are experiencing, I shall relate them to Krishna; I shall try to please Krishna in any possible way after conveying your request; I shall bring him again to Braja even falling at his feet." —932

SWAYYA

When Udhava said these words, all the *gopis* arose to touch his feet; the sorrow of their mind was decreased and their inner happiness increased; imploring Udhava, they said, "O Udhava! when you go there you may tell Krishna that after falling in love, no one forsakes it."—933

"O Krishna, while playing in alcoves, you allured the mind of all the *gopis*, for which you endured the ridicule of the people and for whom you fought with the enemies," the *gopis* say this, while imploring Udhava, "O Krishna! on abandoning us, you went away to Mathura, this was your very bad act." —934

"Forsaking the residents of Braja, you went away and absorbed yourself in the love of the residents of Mathura; all the love that you had with the *gopis*, the same has now been relinquished and it is now associated with the residents of Mathura; O Udhava! He has sent to us the guise of yoga; O Udhava! tell Krishna that he has no love left for us." —935

SWAYYA

"O Udhava! after leaving Braja, when you go to Mathura, then fall at his feet with love from our side; then tell him with great humility that if one falls in love, he should carry it till the end if one cannot do it, then what is the use of falling in love." —936

SWAYYA

"O Udhava! listen to us; whenever we meditate on Krishna, then the pangs of the fire of separation greatly afflict us, by which we are neither alive nor dead; we do not even have the consciousness of our body and we fall unconscious on the ground; how to describe our perplexity to him? You may tell us how we can remain patient." —937

SWAYYA

Those *gopis* who remained proud earlier, they said these things in great humility, they are the same *gopis*, whose body was like gold, the face like lotus-flower and who were like Rati in beauty; they are saying these things, getting distempered and according to the poet they appear like fish to Udhava, who can only survive in the water of Krishna. —938

SWAYYA

Getting agitated, Radha said this to Udhava, "O Udhava! we do not like the ornaments, food, houses etc., without Krishna," saying this Radha felt pangs of separation and also felt extreme hardship even in weeping; the eyes of that young damsel appeared like the lotus-flower. —939

Being deeply absorbed in the love of Krishna, Radha began to weep in great affliction and with her tears, the antimony of the eyes also came out; the poet, getting pleased in his mind, says that the black blemish of the moon, being washed, is flowing with the water of the eyes. —940

SWAYYA

Getting strength of endurance with her talk with Udhava, Radha said, "Perhaps Krishna has forsaken his love for the residents of Braja on account of some flaw; while going away, he sat silently in the chariot and did not even look towards the residents of Braja; we know that this is our misfortune that relinquishing Braja, Krishna has gone to Mathura." —941

SWAYYA

"O Udhava! when you go to Mathura, then make a supplication to him from our side; lie prostrate at the feet of Krishna for a few hours and continue shouting my name;" after this tell him this from my side, "O Krishna! you have relinquished love for us, now absorb yourself in love with us sometime again." —942

SWAYYA

Radha spoke to Udhava in this manner, "O Udhava! absorbing myself in the love of Krishna, I have forsaken everything else; remind him about my displeasure in the forest saying that I had exhibited great persistence with you; are you now showing the same persistence with me?" —943

"O hero of Yadavas! remember those occasions, when you indulged in amorous sport with me in the forest; remember the talk of love in your mind; thinking about that, please tell me the reason why you have relinquished Braja and gone to Mathura? I know that you are not at fault in doing this, but our fortune is not good." —944

SWAYYA

Hearing these words, Udhava replied, "O Radha! the love of Krishna with you is extremely profound; my mind says that he will come now;" Radha says again that Krishna did not stop at the behest of the *gopis*, what can now be his purpose of leaving Mathura and coming here? He did not stop at our bidding and if he returns to his house, then we shall not agree that our fortune is not so forceful. —945

SWAYYA

Saying thus, Radha in great grief, began to weep bitterly; forsaking the happiness of her heart, she became unconscious and fell down upon the earth; she forgot all other things and her mind was absorbed in Krishna; she again said loudly to Udhava, "Alas! Krishna has not come to my house." —946

SWAYYA

He, with whom we sported in the alcoves and together with him, we used to sing songs of praise, the same Krishna, relinquishing Braja has gone to Mathura and his mind is displeased with the *gopis*; saying thus, Radha said to

BACHITTAR NATAK

Udhava, "Alas! Krishna has not come to my house." — 947

SWAYYA

"He relinquished Braja and went to Mathura and the Lord of Braja forgot everyone; He was engrossed in the love of the residents of the city; O Udhava! listen, the women of Braja have been worrying so much, Krishna has forsaken them just as the snake abandons its slough." —948

SWAYYA

Radha said again to Udhava, "He, the glory of whose face is like the moon and who is the donor of beauty to all the three worlds, that Krishna relinquished Braja and went away; this is the reason why we are worried; the day on which Krishna abandoned Braja and went to Mathura, O Udhava! none except you has come to enquire about us." —949

Since the day on which Krishna left Braja, he has sent none other except you; whatever love he had extended to us, he has forgotten all that; according to the poet Shyam he himself had been engrossed with the people of the city of Mathura and in order to please them, he has harassed the people of Braja; O Udhava! when you go there, kindly tell him, "O Krishna! what had occurred in your mind that you did all that." —950

"Leaving Braja, he went to Mathura and from that day to this day he has not returned to Braja; being pleased, he is absorbed with the residents of Mathura; he did not increase the happiness of the inhabitants of Braja, but gave them only suffering; Krishna born in Braja was our own, but now in an instant he belongs to others." —951

SWAYYA

"You have not communicated at all with these residents of Braja; does no attachment arise in your mind? You yourself had been absorbed with the inhabitants of the city and had relinquished all the love of these people; O Krishna! do not persist now; it is right to say that you have won and we have been defeated; O Krishna, the protector of cows! now leave Mathura and come here again." —952

SWAYYA

Remembering Krishna, the poet says, that all the *gopis* are suffering; someone on becoming unconscious, is falling on the ground and someone is singing her song of separation; someone is running hither and thither shouting the name of Krishna and listening to the sound of his moving feet with her ears and when she does not see him, she says in her state of worry that she is not getting at Krishna. —953

SWAYYA

The *gopis* are greatly worried and they have no inkling of the coming of Krishna; Radha, being in great anguish, has become lifeless; whatever agony she had in her mind, she talked about that to Udhava adding that Krishna was not coming and the suffering was indescribable. —954

SWAYYA

Udhava also extremely worried, talked thus amongst the *gopis* that fearless Krishna would be meeting them within a few days: "Become like a yogi and meditate on him; he will grant you whatever boon you will ask him." —955

SWAYYA

After talking words of wisdom with the *gopis* Udhava came to meet Nand; both Yashoda and Nand bowed their heads at his feet; Udhava said to them, "Krishna has sent me to you to instruct you regarding the remembrance of the Name of the Lord" saying this Udhava mounted on his chariot and started for Mathura. —956

Speech of Udhava addressed to Krishna

SWAYYA

After reaching Mathura Udhava bowed at the feet of Krishna and Balram and said, "O Krishna! whatever you had asked me to say, I have done accordingly; I have come back after conversing on topics concerning on divine wisdom with the *gopis* and Nand and seeing your sun-like face my agony has ended." —957

SWAYYA

Touching your feet, when I started, I reached at first at the house of Nand; after talking to him on matters of divine wisdom, I came to the *gopis*; they related to me their suffering because of their separation from you, I advised them to repeat ever the Name of Krishna; after hearing your name, their love increased greatly. —958

Speech regarding the Message of Udhava

SWAYYA

The *gopis* asked me to touch your feet on their behalf; they also said, "O Krishna! now leave the residents of the city and give comfort to the inhabitants of Braja;" Yashoda also said, "Request my son on my behalf to come again and eat the butter." —959

SWAYYA

They have also requested you O Krishna! listen to that also: Yashoda said that the Lord of Braja was very dear to them and her love was incomparable, therefore her son should immediately leave Mathura and come to Braja. —960

SWAYYA

"O Krishna! the queen of Braja, the mother Yashoda has made you this request; I have also felt her great love in my mind, therefore Yashoda has asked you to leave Mathura and come to Braja;" Yashoda has also said, "O Krishna! when you were a child you acceded to everything, but now when have grown bigger, you are not acceding to even one request." —961

Leave Mathura and come to Braja; accept my saying and do not stay even for a little while in Mathura; the *gopis* also said, kindly give comfort to the residents of Braja; you have forgotten that time when you used to fall at our feet. —962

SWAYYA

O Krishna! leave Mathura and come now to Braja; the *gopis* were saying under the impact of passionate love not to delay your coming further; the *gopis* falling at my feet said, "O Udhava! go and ask Krishna to come; tell him also to come here; he himself should feel comfortable and give comfort to us." —963

SWAYYA

O Krishna! leave Mathura and now give happiness to the residents of Braja; come again to Braja and by doing this one task for us, you will not lose anything; O merciful! come and show your brilliance, we remain alive only on seeing you; O Krishna! come again and enjoy the relish of out amorous play in the alcoves. —964

O Krishna! only they are remembering you, for whom you had great love in Braja; now Krishna is living with the residents of the city and he has now not even remembered the women of Braja; our eyes are feeling tired on looking for the arrival of Krishna; O Udhava! tell Krishna that without you all the *gopis* have become helpless. —965

SWAYYA

O Krishna! Your dear Radha has said that she has not been able to control herself since the day when you left Braja; you may come, leaving Mathura immediately, we are helpless without you; I had been very egoistic with you, come to me, I accept defeat. —966

We had not harmed you in any way, why have you forsaken us? O Lord! falling at my feet Radha said this: "O Krishna! You have absorbed Yourself with the residents of the city, forgetting the women of Braja; O Krishna! we had shown persistence towards you, but now we feel defeated." —967

SWAYYA

They have further said this thing to you; O Krishna! listen to it with all your heart; we used to play with you some time; O Krishna! do remember that occasion sometime, we used to sing with you in a lengthened tune; we have asked you to remember all this; O Krishna! communicate again with the residents of Braja. —968

SWAYYA

Listen further, Radha said, "Leave Mathura and come into the alcoves of Braja and proclaim loudly about the amorous play as you had been doing earlier; O Krishna! the desire of seeing you is getting powerful; kindly come and give happiness to us." —969

SWAYYA

O Krishna, my mind is in anguish without seeing you; Radha has withered away and has become slim and she has said, "O Krishna! listen to my request; I am not satisfied only with the talk, I shall only be satisfied on seeing you; give happiness to the partridge-like *gopis* by you moon-face." —970

Speech concerning the Message of Chandrabhaga addressed to Udhava

SWAYYA

O Krishna! Chandrabhaga has said, "Show me your moon-like face; O brother Balram! she has said that without seeing Krishna, she had become greatly worried; therefore do not delay and come to listen the voice of my heart; O Krishna! the Lord of Braja! the *gopis* have said that happiness be given to them, the female partridges. —971

SWAYYA

O the Lord of Braja! the *gopis* have said, "Do not delay now; O, the Superior amongst the chiefs of Yadavas, son of Yashoda and the protector of cows! listen to our saying, O the stringer of the serpent Kali, O the killer of demons! The Lord of Gokul! And the killer of Kansa! give happiness to the partridge-like *gopis*." —972

SWAYYA

O the son of Nand! the source of comforts and the carrier of the mountain! the Lord of Gokul and the killer of Bakasura, come and let us have your sight; O the Lord of Braja and the son of Yashoda, listen, without you the women of Braja have become helpless; O Krishna! we all know that you have forgotten all of us from your mind. —973

SWAYYA

O Krishna! You had killed Kansa and had torn the face of Bakasura; O Lord of Braja! forgiving us of all our faults, give your sight to these *gopis*, because without seeing you, they do not like anything; therefore O Krishna! leave Mathura now and come to remove all their sufferings. —974

Speech of Viduchhata and Maniprabha

SWAYYA

O Krishna! Viduchhata and Maniprabha have said this to you, "When you increased so much love, why are you forsaking it? O Krishna! do not delay now soon and absorb yourself in the same amorous play with us; Radha is angry with you, O Krishna! in some manner you may call for us." —975

SWAYYA

O Udhava! tell Krishna, that as soon as we learn of your permanent stay there, we shall be in agony, forsaking all comforts; wearing the garbs of yogis we shall take poison and die and Radha shall again be egoistic with you. —976

SWAYYA

This they said, but now listen to what Radha said, "Krishna has left us; our mind is not in peace in Braja; You are there in Mathura and our mind is getting angry; O Krishna! the manner in which You have forgotten us, may Your favourite queen also forget You like this." —977

O the Lord of Braja! the *gopis* have said that either you may come yourself or send us some messenger with invitation; if a messenger is not sent, then we shall come ourselves, otherwise O Krishna! give the gift of determination of the mind to the *gopis*. —978

O Krishna! they are meditating on you and call you by your name; they have abandoned their parental shyness and in every moment they are repeating your name; they are alive only by thy name and without the name they are in great agony; seeing them in such a plight, O Krishna! the anguish has increased in my heart. —979

SWAYYA

Forsaking their parental shyness, the *gopis* are repeating the name of Krishna; they are falling down on the earth and getting up like the intoxicated persons; they are searching you in the alcoves of Braja like a person engrossed in the greed of wealth; therefore, I am requesting you; seeing them my suffering has also increased. —980

SWAYYA

If you go yourself, nothing will be more appropriate than this; if you cannot do this, then send your messenger; I request that one of these things must be done, whatever condition is experienced by fish without water, the same is happening to the *gopis*; now whether you may meet them as water or give them the boon of the determination of the mind. —981

Speech of the Poet

SWAYYA

Krishna heard from Udhava the condition of the residents of Braja; listening to that story, the happiness decreases and the agony increases; then Krishna uttered these words from his mouth and the poet feeling the crux of these words has repeated them, "O Udhava! I grant the boon of the determination of the mind to those *gopis*." —982

DOHIRA

This *Granth* (book) has been prepared after revision in Paonta city on Wednesday in Sawan Suddi Samvat 1744. —983

DOHIRA

With the grace of the sword-wielder Lord God, this *Granth* has been prepared thoughtfully; then, if there is any mistake anywhere the poets may kindly recite it after revision. —984

End of the chapter entitled "The Dialogue of *Gopis* with Udhava containing Description of the Pangs of Separation" in Krishnavatar (based on *Dasham Skandapurana*) in Bachittar Natak.

Now begins the Description of going to the House of Kubja

DOHIRA

Gracefully sustaining the *gopas*, Krishna in his pleasure absorbed himself in other sports. —985

SWAYYA

Once Krishna, taking Udhava alongwith him, came to the house of Kubja; Kubja seeing Krishna coming advanced and welcomed him, hereby getting great happiness; she bowed at the feet of Krishna and became so much pleased in her mind, just as the peacock is pleased on seeing the clouds. —986

SWAYYA

Her abode is extremely beautiful, having paintings of red colour; there the sandalwood, *aggar*, trees of *kadamb* and earthen lamps were also seen; there is a handsome sleeping couch, on which a fancy bed has been spread; Kubja greeted Krishna with folded hands and got him seated on the couch. —987

DOHIRA

Then she brought a seat studded with jewels and requested Udhava to sit on it. —988

SWAYYA

Udhava said to Kubja that he had noticed her extremely profound love; he added that he was lowly and poor and could not sit in front of Lord Krishna; feeling the great glory of Krishna, he put the seat aside and holding the feet of Krishna in his hands with affection, he sat down on the earth. —989

The feet, which could not be attained by Seshanaga, Shiva, the Sun and the Moon and whose glory has been narrated in Vedas, Puranas, etc., those feet, on which the adepts meditate in their trance, now Udhava is pressing those feet with great affection. —990

SWAYYA

The saints who develop extremely on the spiritual plane, they only endure the Glory of Lord's Feet; those Feet, which are not observed in the meditation by the impatient yogis and whose mystery has not been understood by Brahma, Indra, Seshanaga, etc., those Lotus-Feet are now being pressed by Udhava with his hands —991

On this side Udhava is pressing the Feet of Krishna, on the other side the female gardener Kubja bedecked herself; she wore the precious stones like rubies, gems etc., and applying the mark on the forehead and putting vermilion in the parting of the hair, she went and sat near Krishna; seeing her beauty and elegance,

Krishna was very much pleased in his mind. —992

SWAYYA

After bedecking herself, the female gardener Kubja went to Krishna and appeared the second manifestation of Chandrakala; feeling the distress of the mind of Kubja, Krishna pulled her towards himself; Kubja also sitting in the embrace of Krishna abandoned her shyness and all her hesitations ended. —993

SWAYYA

When Krishna caught hold of the arm of Kubja, she felt extreme delight, she said audibly, "O Krishna! You have met me after many days; I have rubbed the sandal on my limbs for thy sake, O the hero of Yadavas for your pleasure and now on meeting you, I have attained the objective of my mind." —994

End of the description of "Fulfilling the Objective of Kubja on going to Her House" in Krishnavatar in Bachittar Natak.

SWAYYA

After imparting pleasure to Kubja, then Krishna went to the house of Akrur; on hearing about his arrival, he came to fall at his feet; when he was lying at the feet of Krishna, seeing him, he said to Udhava, "The love of the saints of this type is also profound, I have felt it." —995

Krishna said to Udhava, "Seeing the love of Akrur, I have become conscious of the love of Kubja;" seeing this and reflecting on this Udhava said, "He is exhibiting so much love, before which the love of Kubja is insignificant." —996

SWAYYA

Akrur was highly pleased on seeing the face of Krishna and he absorbed himself in selfless service of Krishna; he touched the feet of Krishna and circumambulated around him; having been absorbed in great affection, whatever food and victuals etc., were there in the house, he brought them all before Krishna, whatever desire Akrur had in his mind, the son of Yashoda fulfilled it. —997

SWAYYA

Fulfilling the desire of Akrur and taking Udhava alongwith him, Krishna returned to his home; on coming home, the mendicants were called and getting pleased various types of alms were given to them in charity; by this act, there was so much approbation of Krishna, the poet Shyam says that with this praise even uptil this day, the daytime appears white, in the sphere of death. —998

Akrur came to the palace of Krishna and fell at his feet; he began to praise Krishna, the killer of Kansa and Bakasura; absorbed in such a praise he forgot his own consciousness, all his sufferings ended and the happiness was increased in his mind. —999

SWAYYA

"This Krishna is the son of Devaki, who also graciously became the son of Nand; he had killed Kansa and also had torn asunder the heart of Bakasura; he is known as the hero of Yadavas; the killer of Keshi, the destroyer of all the sins and the killer also of Tranavrata; showing your face to me, you have destroyed all my sins." —1000

SWAYYA

Krishna is said to be the mighty and powerful, the destroyer of the sufferings of the saints, the giver of peace and comforts the *thug*, who stole the garments of the *gopis* and the overthrower of the warriors of Kansa; he stays away from the sins and the saviour of the people from all types of ailments; the poet Shyam says that the same Krishna is the Supreme Pundit who describes the mysteries of the four Vedas. —1001

SWAYYA

Saying thus, Akrur fell at the Feet of Krishna; he eulogised him repeatedly and all his sufferings ended in an instant; the poet has described the beauty of this spectacle like this that Akrur became subtle by wearing the armour of the Name of the Lord in order to fight fearlessly against the evils. —1002

SWAYYA

Then he eulogised Krishna and said, "O Lord (Krishna)! You had killed the demon Mura and killed Kabandh and Ravana etc., in the dreadful war; you gave the kingdom of Lanka to Vibhishana and you yourself went to Ayodhya alongwith Sita; I accept it without hesitation that You had Yourself performed all these feats. —1003

O banner of Garuda! O sire of Lakshmi! And the Lord of the world! listen to me, Thou art the superior of the whole world; Krishna anticipated that Akrur wanted to say sometimes about his deliverance from the attachment and mineness, therefore he effaced Akrur's mineness by granting him the boon through the mind and he himself kept sitting silently. —1004

Speech of Krishna addressed to Akrur

SWAYYA

"O uncle! without comprehending me, you have seen me as the manifestation of the Lord; give me the comfort, so that my life may become comfortable; after Vasudeva, you will be considered as the seniormost; I bow before you," saying thus Krishna smiled. —1005

SWAYYA

Hearing these words, Akrur was pleased and he hugged both Krishna and Balram; he forsook the sorrow of his mind and considered the small nephews as merely nephews and not the Creator of the world. In this way, this story happened there, which has been sung by the poet Shyam in praise of Krishna. —1006

End of the description of "Going to the House of Akrur" in Krishnavatar (based on *Dasham Skandapurana*) in Bachittar Natak.

Now begins the Description of Sending Akrur to Aunt

SWAYYA

Krishna said smilingly to Akrur, "You go to Hastinapur in order to enquire about the condition of the sons of my father's sister; there a blind king is under the control of the wicked Duryodhana, bring his news also; they are all giving sufferings instead of comforts to the sons of Pandava." —1007

SWAYYA

Hearing these words, Akrur bowed and started and reached Hastinapur, what mention should I make about the way? In the morning, he went to the court of the king, where the king said, "O Akrur! Tell me in what way Krishna overthrew Kansa?" —1008

Hearing these words, Akrur told all those devices, which were used by Krishna in fighting against his enemies; he also told him how Krishna killing the elephant and overthrowing the group of wrestlers withstood against Kansa; then Kansa fought, holding his sword and shield and at the same instant Krishna, catching hold of Kansa by his hair, knocked him down on the ground. —1009

SWAYYA

Akrur saw Bhishma, Drona, Kripacharya, Ashvathama and also Bhurshrava, the son of Sun-god, who avenged Arjuna; the king Duryodhana, on seeing Akrur, his maternal uncle asked him about the whereabouts Krishna and Vasudeva; with these words, being pleased, he met Akrur. —1010

SWAYYA

After sitting for a shortwhile in the royal court, Akrur came to the aunt; on seeing Kunti, he bowed down his head; she asked about the health of Krishna and was pleased to know about the welfare of Vasudeva, Devaki and also Krishna, whose approbation has spread throughout the world. —1011

SWAYYA

In the meantime Vidura had come; on coming he had touched the feet of the mother of Arjuna; he also asked Akrur about Krishna with affection; Vidura was absorbed so much in the affectionate talk about Krishna that he forgot any other matter; knowing about the welfare of all, he blessed them; he obtained great comfort ending his anxiety. —1012

Speech of Kunti

SWAYYA

"Krishna is absorbed in his plays in Mathura and has forgotten me," Kunti said in a loud voice,

"I have been greatly aggrieved by the behaviour of the people (Kauravas) of this place; my husband has passed away and the children are still minor; therefore, O Akrur! I am in great agony and ask you whether Krishna will also communicate with us." —1013

SWAYYA

"The blind king Dhritrashtra is angry with us," this was told by Kunti to Akrur and said further, "O Akrur! please tell Krishna that all of them are agonising us; Arjuna considers all of them as brother-like, but they do not respond likewise; how should I describe my anguish?" And saying thus, the tears rolled down from the eyes of Kunti as if some straw was troubling her eye. —1014

SWAYYA

"O Akrur! tell Krishna that I have been drowned in the ocean of sorrow and am living only on your name and best wishes; the sons of the king are making great efforts to kill my sons; O Akrur! tell Krishna that without him we are all helpless." —1015

SWAYYA

Saying this, Kunti heaved a long and sorrowful sigh and said further, "Whatever anguish I had in my heart, I have disclosed that; O Akrur! The hero of the Yadavas! you may please tell all my painful story to Krishna," and again lamenting she said, "O the Lord of Braja! kindly help the poor creatures like us." —1016

Speech of Akrur
SWAYYA

Seeing the mother of Arjuna in agony, Akrur said, "Krishna has great love for you; your son will become the king and you will be in great comfort; all the good omens will be on your side and your sons will agonise the enemies; they will obtain the kingdom and send the enemies to the abode of Yama." —1017

SWAYYA

Listening to the words of Kunti, Akrur thought of going; he bowed and left; in the order to know the affection of people whether they were with the Kauravas or with the Pandavas, Akrur entered the city; when he noticed that all of the people loved Pandavas, the anxiety of his mind vanished. —1018

Speech of Akrur addressed to Dhritrashtra
SWAYYA

After seeing the city Akrur reached again, the royal court and said there, "O king! listen to the words of wisdom from me and whatever I say, consider it as true; you have the love of your sons only in your mind and you are overlooking the interest of the sons of Pandava; O Dhritrashtra! do you not know that you are spoiling the practice of your kingdom." —1019

SWAYYA

Just as Duryodhana is your son, in the same way consider the sons of Pandava; therefore, O king! I request you not to differentiate them in the matter of kingdom; keep both the sides happy, so that the world sing your praises; Akrur said all these things in such a way to the king, that everybody was pleased. —1020

Hearing these words, the king said to Akrur, the messenger of Krishna, "all the things that you have said, I do not agree with them; now the sons of Pandava will be searched and put to death; I shall do, whatever I consider right and not accept your advice at all." —1021

The messenger said to the king, "If you do not accept my saying, then Krishna will kill you in rage; you should not think of war, keeping the fear of Krishna in your mind; consider my coming as an excuse; whatever there was in my mind, I said that and you only know, whatever is in your mind." —1022

SWAYYA

Saying thus to the king, Akrur went back to the place, where Krishna, Balabhadra and other mighty heroes were seated; seeing Krishna, Akrur bowed his head at his feet and he narrated all that had happened at Hastinapur, to Krishna. —1023

SWAYYA

"O Krishna! Kunti has addressed you to listen to the request of the helpless; she had said that she was extremely miserable at that place and without him, there was none to help her; the way in which he had removed the suffering of the elephant, in that way, O Krishna, her anguish be removed; therefore O Krishna, listen to my words attentively with affection." —1024

End of the chapter entitled "Sending of Akrur to the aunt Kunti" in Krishnavatar (based on *Dasham Skandapurana*) in Bachittar Natak.

Now begins the Description of handing over the Kingdom to Uggarsain

DOHIRA

Krishna is the preceptor of the world, son of Nand and the source of Braja; he is ever full of love, residing in the hearts of the *gopis*. —1025

CHHAPPAI

Firstly he destroyed Putana, then killed Shaktasura and then destroyed Tranavrata on getting him fly in the sky; he drove out the serpent Kali from Yamuna and tore away Bakasura by catching hold of his beak; Krishna killed the demon named Aghasura, the path-obstructing serpent and also killed Keshi, Dhenukasura and the elephant in the theatre. It was also Krishna, who knocked down Chandur with his fists and Kansa by catching him from his hair. —1026

SORATHA

The flowers were showered on Krishna from heaven and with the love of the lotus-eyed Krishna, all the suffering ended in Braja. —1027

DOHIRA

Driving away all the tyrants and giving his patronage to all the society, Krishna bestowed the kingdom of the country of Mathura on Uggarsain. —1028

End of the description of "The Bestowal of the Kingdom on Uggarsain" in Krishnavatar (based on *Dasham Skandapurana*) in Bachittar Natak.

Now begins the Description of the Arrangements of War and the Description of the War with Jarasandh

SWAYYA

When the kingdom was handed here over to Uggarsain, then the queens of Kansa went to their father Jarasandh and began to weep exhibiting their great suffering and helplessness; they told the story of the killing of their husband and their brothers, hearing which the eyes of Jarasandh reddened with rage. —1029

Speech of Jarasandh

DOHIRA

Jarasandh said to his daughter, "I shall kill Krishna and Balram and saying this he gathered together his ministers and armies and left his capital. —1030

CHAUPAI

He sent his envoys to various countries, who brought the kings of all these countries; they reverently bowed before the king and gave great amount of money as present. —1031

Jarasandh called many warriors and equipped them with various kinds of weapons; the saddles were tightened on the backs of the elephants and horses and the crowns of gold were on the heads. —1032

Many warriors gathered there both on foot and on chariots and they all bowed their heads before the king; they joined their own divisions and stood in ranks. —1033

SORATHA

All the four divisions of the army of Jarasandh were ready and the king himself mounted on the chariot taking his armour, quiver, bow and arrows etc. —1034

SWAYYA

Taking alongwith him all the four divisions of his army and his ministers, the king launched the vicious war; he moved with dreadful thundering alongwith his twenty-three units of huge armies; he reached alongwith powerful Ravana-like heroes; his forces were spread like the sea at the time of dissolution. —1035

SWAYYA

Huge warriors are powerful like the mountains and Seshanaga; the army of Jarasandh on foot is like the fish in the sea; the wheels of the chariots of the army are like sharp discs and the flash of the daggers of the soldiers and their movement is like the crocodiles of the sea; the army of Jarasandh is like the sea and before this vast army, Mathura is like a small island. —1036

In the forthcoming story, I have mentioned the names of those great heroes, who in anger fought with Krishna and eulogised them; I have also mentioned the fighters with Balabhadra and pleased the people; now I will eulogise the lion-like Krishna, forsaking all types of greed. —1037

DOHIRA

When the messenger told about the attack, then all the people of the Yadava clan heard it and all of them gathering together went to the house of the king to ponder over the situation. —1038

SWAYYA

The king told that taking alongwith him the twenty-three units of his immense army Jarasandh in great fury has attacked us; who is here in this city, who can confront the enemy; if we run away, we lose our honour and they will kill all of us in anger, therefore we have to fight with the army of Jarasandh without hesitation; because if we win, it will be good for us and if we die, we shall gain honour. —1039

SWAYYA

Then Krishna stood up in the court and said; "Who is so powerful amongst us who may fight with the army and assuming power, he may remove the demons from this earth; he may offer his flesh to the ghosts, fiends and vampires etc., and may satisfy the people becoming a martyr in the battlefield. —1040

SWAYYA

When Krishna said like this, then the endurance of every one gave way; seeing Krishna, their mouths remained wide open and they all began to think of running away; the honour of all the Kshatriyas melted away like the hails in rains; none could make himself so bold as to fight with the enemy and could not boldly come forward to fulfil the desire of the king. —1041

None could preserve his endurance and every one's mind sped away from the idea of war; none could hold his bow and arrows in anger and thus dropped the idea of fighting; all of them planned to run away; seeing this Krishna thundered like a lion after killing the elephant; even the clouds of Sawan felt shy on seeing him thundering. —1042

Speech of Krishna

SWAYYA

"O king! rule without anxiety; we both the brothers will go to fight and wage a dreadful war carrying bow, arrows, mace etc., anyone who confronts us, we shall destroy him with our arms; we shall vanquish him and will not even retrace two steps backward. —1043

Saying this, both brothers stood up and came to their parents, before whom they bowed reverently; seeing them, the attachment of Vasudeva and Devaki increased and they hugged both the sons to their bosoms; they said, "You will conquer the demons and they run away just as the clouds run away before the wind." —1044

SWAYYA

Bowing before their parents, both the heroes left home and came out; on coming out they took all the weapons; called all the warriors; the Brahmins were given a number of gifts in charity and they were greatly pleased in mind; they blessed both the brothers and said, "You will kill the enemies and return safely to your homes." —1045

DOHIRA

Seeing the army of Yadavas with him, Krishna spoke loudly with his charioteer. —1046

Speech of Krishna addressed to Daruk

SWAYYA

"O Daruk! decorate my chariot very nicely and place in it the disc and mace and all the weapons and arms which can destroy the demons taking all the Yadavas with me; you should know this that I am going to remove the suffering of my king. —1047

DOHIRA

Saying this, Krishna tied his quiver around his waist and taking some Yadavas with him, Balram also carried the plough and pestle. —1048

SWAYYA

Krishna moved forward alongwith the warriors in order to kill the demons; he took also Balram with him, the measure of whose power is known only to God Himself; who is there so dreadful like them and the fulfiller of their wishes like Parashurama? Balram and Krishna moved forward proudly in order to kill the enemies. —1049

SWAYYA

Krishna moved forward taking his bow and arrows and the sword, and mounting on his chariot; he spoke sweet, nectar-like words saying that all his companions were his brothers; taking the support of the feet of Krishna, all the warriors roared dreadfully like a lion and Balram etc., fell upon the army of the enemy with their weapons. —1050

SWAYYA

Seeing the army of the enemy, Krishna was extremely infuriated; he ordered his charioteer to move forward and thereby he fell upon the general of the enemy's army; he knocked down the elephants and horses with his arrows and they fell down like the peaks of the mountain knocked down by the *vajra* of Indra. —1051

SWAYYA

Many arrows were discharged from the bow of Krishna and many warriors were killed by them; the men on foot were killed, the charioteers were deprived of their chariots and many enemies were despatched to the abode of Yama; many warriors ran away and those who felt shy while running, they again fought with Krishna, but none could escape from death at the hands of Krishna. —1052

SWAYYA

The warriors are getting enraged in the battlefield and the shouts are being heard from all the four sides; the fighters of the army of the enemy are fighting with great excitement and they are not fearing even a little from Krishna; taking his bow and arrows in his hands, Krishna is shattering their pride in an instant and whosoever confronts him, Krishna is killing him makes him lifeless. —1053

KABIT

By discharging arrows, the enemies are being chopped into bits in the battlefield and the streams of blood are flowing; the elephants and horses have been killed; the charioteers have been deprived of their chariots and the men on foot have been killed just as a lion kills the deer in the forest; Just as Shiva destroys the beings at the time of dissolution, in the same manner Krishna has destroyed the enemies; many have been killed, many are lying wounded on the ground and many are lying powerless and frightened. —1054

SWAYYA

Krishna is thundering like clouds and his arrows are being showered like the drops of water; with the flowing of the blood of all the four divisions of the army, the battlefield has become red; somewhere the skulls are lying, somewhere there are heaps of chariots and somewhere there are the trunks of the elephants; in great fury, Krishna caused the rain of arrows; somewhere the warriors have fallen and somewhere their limbs are lying scattered. —1055

SWAYYA

The warriors, having fought bravely with Krishna, are lying on the ground; holding their bows, arrows, swords maces etc., the warriors have expired fighting till the end; the vultures are sitting sadly, and silently while devouring their flesh; it seems that the pieces of the flesh of these warriors are not being digested by these vultures. —1056

SWAYYA

Balram in great rage took his weapon in his hand and penetrated into the ranks of the enemy;

without any fear of the general of the enemy's army, he killed many warriors; he made lifeless the elephants, horses, and charioteers by killing them; just as Indra wages a war, in the same manner Balram, the powerful brother of Krishna waged the war. —1057

SWAYYA

Balram, the brother of Krishna is waging the war like Duryodhana filled with anger or like Meghnad, the son of Ravana in the Ram-Ravana war; it appears that the hero is going to kill Bhishama and Balram may be equal in strength to Ram; the dreadful Balabhadra appears in his fury like Angad or Hanuman. —1058

SWAYYA

Highly infuriated, Balram fell upon the army of the enemy; many elephants, horses, charioteers, soldiers on foot etc., have come under the shade of his fury; seeing this war Narada, ghosts, fiends and Shiva etc., are getting pleased; the enemy's army appears like a deer and Balram like a lion. —1059

SWAYYA

On one side Balram is waging the war and on the other side Krishna has taken up the sword; after killing the horses, the charioteers and the lords of the elephants, he, in great fury, has challenged the army; he has chopped into bits the gathering of the enemies with his weapons including bow and arrows, mace etc., he is killing the enemies like the clouds scattered into bits by the wind in the rainy season. —1060

SWAYYA

When Krishna, the destroyer ever of the enemies, took his dreadful bow in his hand, the clusters of arrows emanated from it and the heart of the enemies got highly enraged; all the four divisions of the army fell down wounded and the bodies were steeped in blood; it seemed that the Providence has created this world in red colour. —1061

SWAYYA

Krishna, the tormentor of the demons, in great rage and pride moved forward his chariot and fell upon the enemy fearlessly, holding his bow and arrows, he moved like a lion in the battlefield and with the strength of his arms, furiously began to chop the forces of the enemy. —1062

Krishna again took his bow and arrows in his hand and destroyed the enemy's army in the battlefield; just as the carder of cotton cards it, in the same manner Krishna carded the enemy's army; the stream of blood swelled in the battlefield like the eighth ocean. —1063

On this side the army of Krishna marched forward and on the other side the king, Jarasandh moved forward alongwith his forces; the warriors fought taking bow and arrows and swords in their hands and their limbs were being chopped; somewhere the lords of elephants and horses fell and somewhere the limbs of warriors began to fall; both the armies were locked in a close combat like the merger into one by the Ganges and Yamuna. —1064

SWAYYA

In order to fulfil the task assigned to them by their masters, the warriors of both the sides are enthusiastically moving forwards from both the sides, the warriors died with ire are ferociously waging war and confronting one another are fighting unhesitatingly; the spears piercing the white bodies appear like the serpents entwining the sandalwood tree. —1065

SWAYYA

From both sides, the warriors fought bravely with great anger and none of them retraced his steps; they are fighting quite nicely with spears, bows arrows, maces, swords etc., someone seems frightened by viewing the battlefield and someone is running; the poet says that it appears that the warriors like moths are getting burnt on the battlefield like the earthen lamps. —1066

SWAYYA

Balram fought earlier with bow and arrows and then he began the fight, taking his spear in his hand; then he took sword in his hand, killed the warriors penetrating in the army, then holding his dagger, he knocked down warriors with his mace; Balram is pulling the enemy's army with his plough like the palanquin-bearer making effort to pull the water with both the hands. —1067

Any warrior who came in front of him, Krishna knocked him down, he, who getting shy of his weakness, fought with great force, he also could not survive; penetrating into enemy's forces, Krishna fought a violent battle; Balram also fought with endurance and knocked down the enemy's army. —1068

DOHIRA

Jarasandh himself saw his army of four divisions running away, he said to the warriors fighting near him. —1069

Speech of the King Jarasandh addressed to the Army

SWAYYA

"The side on which Krishna is fighting, you may go there and strike blows to him with your bows, arrows, swords and maces, no Yadava be allowed to escape from the battlefield; kill all of them;" when Jarasandh said these words, then army set itself in ranks and marched forward towards that side. —1070

SWAYYA

On receiving the command of the king, the warriors marched forward like clouds; the arrows were showered like rain-drops and the swords flashed like lightning; someone has fallen a martyr on the earth, someone is heaving along sigh and someone's limb has been chopped; someone is lying wounded on the ground, but still he is shouting repeatedly "kill, kill." —1071

SWAYYA

Krishna took his bow and arrows in his hand knocked down all the warriors present in the battlefield; he killed the intoxicated elephants and horses and deprived many charioteers of their chariots; seeing the wounded warriors, the cowards left the battlefield and ran away; they appeared like the collective sins running before the embodiment of virtues i.e., Krishna.—1072

All the heads that were chopped in the war, they are all shouting "kill, kill" from their mouths; the headless trunks are running and moving forward to that side where Krishna is fighting; the warriors who are fighting with these headless trunks, these trunks, considering them as Krishna, are striking blows on them; those who are falling down on the earth, their sword is also falling down on the earth. —1073

KABIT

Both the sides are in rage, they are not retracing their steps from the battlefield and are fighting in excitement, playing upon their small drums; the gods are seeing all this and the Yakshas are singing songs of praise; the flowers are being showered from the sky like rain-drops; many warriors are dying and many have been wedded by the heavenly damsels; many have been eaten by the vultures and many have fallen down wounded; many are standing firmly like lion, many feel frightened in the war and may feeling shy and crying painfully are running away. —1074

SWAYYA

The wounded, getting up again are marching forward in order to fight; the poet says that those who were hiding, they are now getting enraged listening to the shouts; hearing their talk, Krishna held firmly his sword and confronting them, cut off their heads; even then they did not go back and as headless trunks moved towards Balrams. —1075

SWAYYA

Shouting "kill, kill," the warriors taking up their swords, started fighting; they besieged Balram and Krishna from all the four sides like the arena of the wrestlers; when Krishna took his bow and arrow in his hand, the warriors then feeling helpless began to flee away from the battlefield; the field seemed deserted and desolate and seeing such a pageant, they began to return to their homes. —1076

Whenever any warrior taking his sword in his hand falls upon Krishna, then seeing this spectacle, the Ganas i.e., the attendants of Shiva feel pleased and begin to sing songs of joy; someone says that Krishna will win and someone says that those warriors will gain victory; they quarrel till that time, when Krishna kills and throws them on the ground. —1077

KABIT

Wearing large-sized armour alongwith the elephants, the mighty warriors, causing their horses to dance, marched forward; they stand firm in the battlefield and for the interest of their Lords they came out of their enclosures and playing on small drums, began to fight; they reached the battlefield holding firmly their fighting with Krishna, but are not shouting "kill, kill." They are fighting with Krishna, but are not receding back from their places; they are falling down on the earth, but even receiving wounds they are getting up again. —1078

SWAYYA

In anger they are crying out and are fighting fearlessly with their weapons; their bodies are full of wounds and from them the blood is flowing; even then, holding swords in their hands, they are fighting with full strength; Balram has thrashed them like rice with pestle and again struck them with his plough, on account of which they are lying on the ground. —1079

SWAYYA

All the warriors of Krishna, taking their swords in their hands fell upon the enemies; getting enraged they fought such a battle that in all the ten directions, the jackals and vultures ate the flesh of the dead to their fill; on both sides the warriors have fallen down on the earth and are lying down after being wounded by the daggers; seeing this spectacle the gods are also saying that those mothers are blessed, who have given birth to such sons. —1080

SWAYYA

All other warriors who were there, they also came in the battlefield; from this side, the army of the Yadavas marched forward and on the other side those people began a dreadful fight; the bows, arrows, swords, maces, daggers all these weapons were used; after meeting the army of the Yadavas, the enemy's army fell upon Krishna. —1081

SWAYYA

The warriors are holding the discs, tridents, maces, swords and daggers; those mighty ones, shouting "kill, kill" are not receding from their places; Krishna has destroyed the enemy's force and it seems that on entering a tank elephant has destroyed the lotus-flowers. —1082

SWAYYA

The frightened enemy by the arrows of Krishna are losing patience; all these warriors, getting shamefaced, are going to leave and none of them is desirous of continuing the war; seeing Balram with his mace and plough in his hands, the enemy's army fled and this spectacle seems like this that seeing a lion, the deer in fear are leaving the forest running away. —1083

SWAYYA

All the soldiers staggering in the path reached near Jarasandh and shouted loudly, "O Lord! Krishna and Balram have killed all your soldiers in their fury; not even one soldier has survived; all of them have fallen on the earth in the battlefield, therefore we tell you O king! That they are victorious and your army has been defeated." —1084

SWAYYA

Then in great rage, the king called the mighty warriors in order to kill the enemies; receiving the orders of the king, they moved forward for killing Krishna; catching hold of the bow, arrows, maces etc., they swelled like clouds and fell upon Krishna; they attacked Krishna on galloping their horses. —1085

SWAYYA

They began to fight with Krishna, while shouting with great ire; they held their arrows, swords and maces in their hands and struck steel with steel; they themselves were wounded, but also inflicted wounds on the body of Krishna; Balram also ran with his plough and mace and he knocked down the army of the enemies.—1086

DOHIRA

The great warriors who fought with Krishna and fell in the field, the poet now enumerates their names. —1087

SWAYYA

The heroic warriors like Nar Singh, Gaj Singh, Dhan Singh moved forward; the kings like Hari Singh, Ran Singh etc., also moved after giving alms to the Brahmins; the large army of four divisions moved and fought with Krishna and hailing themselves, they discharged many arrows on Krishna. —1088

SWAYYA

On this side all the kings gathered together and began to discharge arrows upon Krishna; moving two steps forward, they in fury, fought with Krishna; they were all absorbed in war, leaving the hope of their survival; the white garments worn by the warriors became red in an instant. —1089

SWAYYA

The warriors greatly infuriated waged such a war with Krishna, which was waged earlier by Arjuna with Karana; Balram also in anger and standing firmly in the field destroyed a great part of the army; holding their lances and swinging the warriors encircled Balram like the elephant freeing himself from the steel-chains with his strength, but is entrapped in a deep pit. —1090

SWAYYA

There was a fierce fighting in the battlefield and the king who came there, was instantly killed; on this side Krishna waged a dreadful war and on the other side, the warriors of the enemy were filled with great rage; Nar Singh discharged his arrow towards Krishna in such a way as if someone was desirous of awaking the sleeping lion. —1091

SWAYYA

An arrow struck the chest of Krishna and penetrated upto the feathers; the arrow was filled with blood and seeing his blood flowing out from his limbs, Krishna was highly enraged; this spectacle appears like Garuda, the king of birds, swallowing the son of the great serpent Takshak. —1092

SWAYYA

In great fury, Krishna tightened the arrow on the string of the bow and discharged it towards Gaj Singh; Gaj Singh fell down on the earth as if a snake had stung him; Hari Singh who was standing near him, seeing his plight, fled away like a hare seeing the figure of a lion. —1093

SWAYYA

When Hari Singh ran away from the battlefield, then Ran Singh arose again in great ire; he held up his bow and arrows using saying, "Now stop for a while, where are you going? You have fallen in the hands of death." —1094

SWAYYA

When Ran Singh said these words, then Hari Singh smiled; he also came forward in order to fight with Krishna and did not recede; he addressed Krishna in anger: "He, who fights with me, consider him fallen in the hands of death." —1095

SWAYYA

Hearing his words, Krishna took his bow in his hand; seeing his large body and aiming his arrow on his head, he discharged it; with the stroke of his arrow, the head of Hari Singh was chopped and his trunk remained standing; the redness of blood on his body seemed to suggest that the sun of his head on Sumeru mountain had set and again the redness of the early morning was spreading. —1096

SWAYYA

When Krishna killed Hari Singh, then Ran Singh fell upon him; he waged a dreadful war holding his weapons bow and arrows, sword, mace etc., seeing his limbs bedecked with his armour, the poet says that it appeared to him that an intoxicated elephant, in his fury, fell upon a lion. —1097

He came and fought with Krishna and did not even recede one step; then he took up his mace in his hand and began to strike his blows on the body of Krishna; seeing all this, Krishna was filled with great anger, he tilted his eyebrows and took his discus in his hand in order to knock him down on the ground. —1098

At the same time, taking his dagger in his hand, Ran Singh gave its blow to Krishna, the Yadava hero, in order to kill him; it suddenly struck Krishna and tearing his right arm, it penetrated to the other side; piercing the body of Krishna it appeared like a female serpent coiling a sandalwood tree in summer season. —1099

SWAYYA

Krishna extracting the same dagger from his arm, set it in motion in order to kill the enemy; it struck like lightning within the clouds of arrows and appeared like a flying swan; it hit the body of Ran Singh and his chest was seen torn down; it seemed like Durga, steeped in blood, going to kill Sumbh and Nisumbh. —1100

When Ran Singh was killed with the dagger, then Dhan Singh ran in fury and taking his spear in his hand while shouting, he inflicted a blow on Krishna; seeing him coming, Krishna took out his sword and with his blow, chopped the enemy into two halves and this spectacle appeared as if the Garuda had killed a huge serpent. —1101

SWAYYA

Saving himself from getting wounded, Krishna took up his bow and arrows and fell upon the enemy, battle was fought for four *mahurats* (span of time), in which neither the enemy was killed, nor Krishna was wounded; the enemy in his rage discharged an arrow on Krishna and from this side Krishna also shot his arrow by pulling on bow; he began to look at the face of Krishna and from this side Krishna on seeing him smiled. —1102

One of the mighty warriors of Krishna took his sword in his hand and fell upon Dhan Singh; while coming, he shouted so loudly, when it seemed that the elephant had frightened the lion; taking up his bow and arrows Dhan Singh threw his head on the earth; this spectacle seemed like this that a deer had unknowingly fallen in the mouth of a boa. —1103

A second warrior of Krishna, greatly enraged, taking bow and arrows in his hand, unhesitatingly, marched forward towards mighty Dhan Singh, Dhan Singh took his sword in his hand and chopped and threw the enemy's forehead; it appeared like some surveyor, seeing the lotus in the tank, had plucked it. —1104

Killing the two warriors, mighty Dhan Singh, taking his bow and arrows in his hand, fell upon the army and waged a dreadful war and chopped elephants, horses, charioteers and soldiers on foot; his dagger was gleaming like fork, seeing which the canopy of the king was feeling shy; he looked like Bhishma, seeing whom Krishna began to resolve his discus. —1105

SWAYYA

Then Dhan Singh taking his bow and arrows in his hand, angrily penetrated into the ranks of the enemy; he waged such a fierce battle that the broken chariots and chopped elephants and horses cannot be counted; he sent many a warrior to the abode of Yama and then in rage, he marched towards, Krishna; he shouted "kill, kill" from his mouth and seeing him, the forces of Yadavas broke into fragments. —1106

DOHIRA

Dhan Singh destroyed much of the Yadava army, then Krishna highly infuriated and gaping his eyes wide open, said. —1107

Speech of Krishna addressed to the Army
SWAYYA

"O brave warriors! why are you standing? I know that you have lost your courage; you began to recede your feet from the battlefield, when Dhan Singh discharged his arrows and becoming careless about your weapons you ran in such a way as a gathering of goats runs away before the lion; you have become cowards and have been frightened on seeing him; you have neither died yourselves nor have killed him." —1108

SWAYYA

Hearing these words of Krishna, the warriors began to gnash their teeth in great anger and without fearing Dhan Singh, even slightly, they took out their bows and arrows and fell upon him; Dhan Singh also took out his bow and arrows in his hand and from the other side, because of the attack of the Yadava army, the heads of the demons, being chopped, fell on the earth like the flowers dropping down in the garden by the blowing fierce wind. —1109

KABIT

The warriors came in great anger and being chopped began to fall in front of Dhan Singh, while fighting with him; holding their bows and arrows in their hands, they came running before him in heroic vein, considering it a decisive war; Dhan Singh also being highly infuriated, taking his bow and arrows in his hand, he separated their heads from their trunks; it seemed that seeing the power of endurance of the earth, Indra, was worshipping it, offering flowers to it. —1110

SWAYYA

Dhan Singh in extreme anger in the war killed many warriors; others who came in front of him, he destroyed them all just as the clouds are fragmented by the blow of wind instantly; he, with his great strength, reduced considerable, numerous elephants and horses of the Yadava army; those warriors had fallen on the earth like the mountains, whose wings had been chopped by the *vajra* (weapon) of Indra. —1111

SWAYYA

Catching hold of his sword in his hand, Dhan Singh in great rage killed many large elephants; all the remaining chariots with banners fled away in fear; the poet says that spectacle appeared to him like the mountains growing wings were flying away, realising the approach of god Indra. —1112

Dhan Singh waged a dreadful war and none could withstand him; whosoever came in front of him, Dhan Singh killed him in his anger; he appeared that Ravana had begun a terrible war with the forces of Ram; fighting in this way, destroying the four divisions of the army, he rushed forward again. —1113

SWAYYA

The mighty Dhan Singh shouting loudly said, "O Krishna! do not leave the field and run away now; come yourself and fight with me; and do not get your people killed uselessly; O Balram! you may also come with your bow and arrows in your hand and fight with me coming before me, because there is nothing like the war, through which one gets praise in this and the next world. —1114

SWAYYA

All this talk of the enemy went deeper into the mind of Krishna, who in great anger fell him catching of his bow, sword, mace etc. Dhan Singh also caught hold of his bow with fearless mind and turned again for battle and stood firmly against Krishna. —1115

SWAYYA

On this side Balram was filled with rage and on the other side Dhan Singh got reddened with fury; both of them fought and blood oozing out of their wounds reddened their bodies; the enemies forgetting the consciousness of their bodies and minds began to shout "kill, kill;" the poet says that they fought like an elephant with an elephant. —1116

SWAYYA

He was saving himself from the blow of Balram and there and then he was running and striking blows on him with his sword; seeing his brother in trouble, Krishna taking some Yadava warriors with him, moved to that side; he surrounded Dhan like lakhs of stars on all four sides of the moon. —1117

When Dhan Singh was surrounded, then Gaj Singh who was standing near came there; when Balram saw this, he mounted on his chariot and came to that side and he did not allow Gaj Singh to reach there and intercepted him midway; Gaj Singh stopped there as if the feet of the elephant had been enchained. —1118

SWAYYA

Krishna is fighting with Dhan Singh and none of them is being killed; now Krishna, greatly infuriated held up his discus in his hand; he threw the discus, which cut off the head of Dhan Singh in the battlefield; he writhed on the earth like a fish taken out of the tank. —1119

SWAYYA

As soon as Dhan Singh was killed, the Yadavas blew their conch on seeing it; many warriors fought with Krishna and being chopped, they left for heaven; the place where Gaj Singh was standing, he was wonder-struck on seeing this spectacle; then the fleeing soldiers came to him and said, "Now we are the only survivors and have come to you." —1120

Hearing these words from their mouth, the mighty hero Gaj Singh was greatly infuriated; the poet says that seeing towards Balram, he caused his chariot to run towards him and then fell upon him; Krishna said, "He is Dhan Singh, who fought fearlessly; bravo to him, who fought with him face to face and ferried across the world-ocean." —1121

SWAYYA

Saying thus with affection, Krishna thought about his life in this and the next world; on this side Gaj Singh, in great fury took his terrific lance in his hand and struck Balram saying this, "O Balram! where will you go now for your safety?" —1122

SWAYYA

Catching the coming lance Balram took this measure; seeing towards the horses, he spread himself there making like an umbrella; the piercing point of the hooded snake looking from the top of a mountain. —1123

SWAYYA

Pulling out the lance with his strength, Balram revolved it slantingly; it flashed and waved in the sky in this way as if the top-knot of someone was waving; Balram struck the same lance in the battlefield in great anger on Gaj Singh; the same lance being struck looked like the fatal fire sent by mighty death to kill the king Parikshat. —1124

SWAYYA

Gaj Singh took several steps, but he could not save himself; the lance peretrated in his chest; all the kings saw it and they lamented, wringing their hands; he received a dreadful wound and became unconscious, but he did not let go the arrows from his hand; Gaj Singh fell upon the horses of the chariot like the body of an elephant fallen on a mountain. —1125

When he regained consciousness, Gaj Singh pulled his terrible bow and pulling its string upto his ear discharged the arrow in great rage; many arrows emanated from this arrow and not enduring the fury of these arrows Takshak, the king of the serpents alongwith all other serpents went to take refuge with Balram. —1126

SWAYYA

Thundering in the battlefield, Gaj Singh said, "I have captured all the deities like Seshanaga, Indra, Surya (Sun-god), Kuber, Shiva, Chandra (Moon-god), Garuda etc., Listen to me clearly; I have killed in battlefield, whomsoever I wanted to kill, but I wonder why you have survived still?" —1127

SWAYYA

Saying this, he pulled and threw his lance, which was seen by Balram, who was holding his bow in his hand; with his great strength, he intercepted that lance and caused it to fall on the ground just like Garuda the king of birds catching and killing a flying serpent. —1128

SWAYYA

In great fury, Gaj Singh struck the lance on the enemy, which hit the body of Balram; on receiving the blow of the lance, Balram suffered great agony, that lance pierced through the body to the other side and its visible blade looked like tortoise protruding its head through the current of Ganges. —1129

SWAYYA

Balram pulled out the lance from his body and drooping down he fell upon the earth just as the Elysian tree, fully enlightened, falls down on the earth; when he regained his conscious, he realising the situation got highly infuriated; seeing the chariot, he jumped and mounted it like a lion jumping and ascending the mountain. —1130

He came forward again and fought with Gaj Singh and controlling the bow and arrows, swords, mace etc., he began to strike blows; he intercepted the arrows of the enemy with his own arrows; the poet says that Balram did not retrace even one step in the battlefield. —1131

SWAYYA

Taking his plough and mace, Balram fought a dreadful battle and on this side Gaj Singh also threw his lance towards Balram; seeing the coming lance, Balram intercepted it with his plough and threw its blade on the ground; and that bladeless lance came and struck the body of Balram. —1132

SWAYYA

When Gaj Singh in his rage struck a blow with his sword from which Balram saved himself with his shield; the sparkles came out from the shield, which appeared like flashing lightning during night exhibiting the stars in rainy season. —1133

SWAYYA

Enduring the wound inflicted by the enemy, Balram struck a blow with his sword; the edge of the sword struck the throat of the enemy and his head, being chopped, fell on the ground; he fell from his chariot after receiving the blow of *vajra* (the weapon) and the poet says, while describing that spectacle that it appeared to him that for the welfare of the people, Vishnu had cut off the head of Rahu and thrown it on the earth. —1134

When Gaj Singh was killed, then all the warriors, ran away from the battlefield; seeing his corpse besmeared with blood, all of them lost the power of endurance and were bewildered as if they had not slept for several nights; the warriors of the enemy's army came to their Lord Jarasandh and said, "All the chief kings have been killed in the battlefield," hearing these words, the remaining army lost their endurance and in great anger, the king experienced an unbearable sorrow. —1135

End of the chapter entitled "Killing of Gaj Singh in the Beginning of War" in Krishnavatar in Bachittar Natak.

Now begins the Description of the Killing of Amit Singh with Army

DOHIRA

The mighty warriors like Anag Singh, Achal Singh, Amit Singh, Amar Singh and Angad Singh were sitting with the king Jarasandh. —1136

SWAYYA

Seeing them with him, the king Jarasandh, looking at the weapons and these warriors, said, "See, today in the battlefield, Krishna has killed five mighty kings; now you may go and fight with him, beating your trumpets, without fear;" hearing these words of their king all marched towards the battlefield in great rage. —1137

SWAYYA

When they came, Krishna saw them in the battlefield, wandering as the manifestation of Yama; they had caught hold of their bows and arrows in their hands and were challenging Balram; they had spears in their hands and armours were tightened on their limbs; Angad Singh, taking his lance in his hand, said loudly, "O Krishna! why are you standing now? Come and have a fight with us." —1138

Krishna seeing those five warriors challenged them; from this side, Krishna moved with his arms and from the other side they also moved beating their trumpets; taking their steel-arms, they began to strike blows in great fury; the warriors from both the sides fought fiercely and getting intoxicated, they began to fall on the ground. —1139

SWAYYA

A dreadful war was fought; the gods saw it, sitting in their air-vehicles; their minds were excited to see the sport of war; on being struck by lances, the warriors fell down from their horses and writhed on the earth; the fallen warriors, getting up began to fight again and the Gandharvas and Kinnars sang their praises. —1140

KABIT

Many warriors began to run away, many of them roared, many others ran again and again to fight with Krishna; many fell down of the earth, many died fighting with the intoxicated elephants and many lay dead on the earth; on the death of the warriors many others, taking

BACHITTAR NATAK

up their weapons and do not retrace even one step; in the sea of blood the fire is blazing and the warriors discharging swift moving arrows like wind, are burning like straw. —1141

SWAYYA

Anag Singh, considering it a decisive war, was filled with anger and mounting on his chariot, he, took out his sword and also pulled up his bow; he attacked the army of Krishna and destroyed the heroic fighters; just as the darkness moves away swiftly before the sun, similarly before the king Anag Singh, the enemy's army sped away. —1142

SWAYYA

Driving forward his horse and taking up his sword and shield he moved forward and without retracing his steps, he fought with a cluster of some Yadavas; killing many heroic fighters, he came and stood firmly in front of Krishna and said, "I have vowed that I shall not return to my home; either I shall breathe my last or I shall kill you." —1143

SWAYYA

Saying this, taking his sword in his hand, he challenged the army of Krishna; the name of Krishna was hailed in the army of the Yadavas but Anag Singh, causing his horse to run, came in front of the Yadava army; this king destroyed in an instant all the warriors of the army; the heads began to fall on the ground like the stars falling from the sky. —1144

SWAYYA

Getting very angry, he fell upon the Yadava army again; on the other side Krishna also moved in his army, which increased the anger in the mind of the enemy; the king Anag Singh shot his fire arm, by which the soldiers burnt like the straw in fire; the limbs of the warriors being chopped fell like the grass burning in the sacrificial altar. —1145

SWAYYA

Pulling their bows upto the ears, the warriors are discharging the arrows and the arrow which collides with these arrows midway, it is chopped and thrown down; holding their swords, the enemies are striking the blows on the body of Krishna, but being tired, they could not obstruct the blows of Krishna. —1146

SWAYYA

The warriors who attacked Krishna, they were chopped into bits by him; taking his bow and arrow, sword and mace in his hands, he deprived the charioteers of their chariots; many warriors being wounded have started going away from the arena of war; and many others are fighting heroically in the field; the dead warriors appear like the dead snake-kings lying down, having been killed by Garuda, the king of birds. —1147

SWAYYA

Taking his sword in his hand, that warrior engaged the Yadavas in battlefield; after killing the four division of the army, the poet Shyam says that the king began to thunder with strength; hearing him roaring, the clouds fell shy and frightened; he was looking splendid amongst the enemies like a lion among the deer. —1148

SWAYYA

Striking the blows again, the forces were killed and many kings were killed; fifty thousand soldiers were killed and the charioteers were deprived of their chariots and chopped; somewhere the horses, somewhere the elephants and somewhere the kings have fallen down; the chariot of the king Anag Singh is not stable in the battlefield and it is running like a dancing actor. —1149

There was a warrior named Ajaib Khan in the army of Krishna, he came and confronted the king, Anag Singh did not retrace his steps from the battlefield and greatly infuriated, he struck a blow with his sword on Ajaib Khan; his head was chopped, but his headless trunk began to fight; then he fell down on the ground like a huge tree broken and fallen by raging storm. —1150

SWAYYA

Seeing such a condition of Ajaib Khan, the mind of Ghairat Khan was filled with rage; he caused his chariot to be driven and fearlessly fell upon the enemy; both the mighty warriors fought a dreadful battle taking their swords in their hands; they looked like two elephants fighting with each other in the forest. —1151

SWAYYA

Holding his lance in his hand, Ghairat Khan threw it on the enemy, which was intercepted and thrown on the ground by Anag Singh with his sword, moving like lightning; that lance did not strike the enemy, but he discharged a second lance like an aerial bomb shot in the sky. —1152

SWAYYA

The second lance was also intercepted and thrown on the ground by the king and threw his lance in great fury on Ghairat Khan, which hit him on his face; the blood gushed out like the fire of anger moving out of the heart. —1153

DOHIRA

He died and fell on the ground and his consciousness ended; he appeared like the sun coming from the sky on the earth out of fear. —1154

SWAYYA

Then Krishna said this in rage, "Who is this heroic fighter who has killed all the warriors and thrown them on the ground according to his heart's desire? I know that fearing him, you are not catching your bows and arrows in your hands; in my opinion you may all go to your homes, because audacity seems to have ended. —1155

SWAYYA

When Krishna uttered these words, all of them took up their bows and arrows and thinking of their courage they gathered together and marched forward for war; they killed every one who confronted them while shouting "kill, kill;" the king Jarasandh saw this terrible war being fought from both sides. —1156

SWAYYA

One of the mighty warriors, holding his sword in his hand, caused his horse to run and killing fifty soldiers, he challenged Anag Singh from this side Sujan Singh rushed and struck a blow on the king, which was obstructed by him on his shield with his left hand; with his right hand the king chopped the head of Sujan Singh with his sword —1157

DOHIRA

When Anag Singh killed Sujan Singh, the Yadava army then highly infuriated fell upon the forces of the enemy. —1158

SWAYYA

The warriors filled with the sense of shame fell upon the army and shouted in rage, "Now we shall definitely kill Anag Singh;" they challenged him taking their lances, swords, maces spears etc., in their hands; the poet Shyam says that the strings of innumerable bows were pulled. —1159

SWAYYA

On this side Anag Singh also in great fury took up his bow and arrows and his eyes became red; shouting "kill, kill" he discharged his arrows on the hearts of his enemies, with whose penetration someone was killed, someone was wounded and someone ran away from the battlefield; those who in their pride came to fight, the war became more dreadful on their arrival. —1160

Balram, Vasudeva, Satyak etc., also marched forward and Udhava and Akrur etc., also started for war-arena; besieged by all of them, the king Anag Singh appears like sun surrounded by clouds in the rainy season. —1161

SWAYYA

Balram took his plough in his hand and killed all the four horses of the enemy; Vasudeva with his bow and arrows cut down all the four wheels of the chariot; Satyak chopped the head of his charioteer and Udhava also in his fury discharged many arrows; the king Anag Singh jumped instantly out his chariot and killed many warriors with his sword. —1162

SWAYYA

The king Anag Singh saw the warriors of Krishna standing, he then speedily struck the blow of his sword on the head of the enemy; the head of the enemy fell on the ground like Rahu killing and throwing down on the earth the moon from the sky. —1163

After killing the charioteer of the enemy, the king mounted on his chariot and carried his weapons bow and arrows, sword, mace and spear in his hands; he himself began to drive his chariot within the Yadava army; with his blows someone was killed, someone fled away and someone being wonder-struck, kept standing. —1164

SWAYYA

Now he himself is driving the chariot and showering his arrows; he himself is safe from the blows of the enemy and is himself inflicting blows on the enemy; he has chopped the bow of some warrior and has shattered someone's chariot; the sword in his hand is shining like the flash of lightning amongst the clouds.—1165

SWAYYA

The king Anag Singh, after killing many warriors in the battlefield, is cutting his lips with his teeth; whosoever falls upon him, he chops and throws him down; he has fallen upon the enemy's army and is destroying it; he does not have any fear of Krishna while fighting and with great effort is driving his chariot towards Balram. —1166

DOHIRA

When the enemy waged the dreadful war, Krishna marched towards him and said to the Yadavas, "Kill him by fighting with from both sides." —1167

SWAYYA

Satyak shattered his chariot and Krishna also began killings violently; Balram chopped the head of his charioteer and struck blows on the limbs protected by armour; the arrow of Akrur hit him so fiercely that he could not control himself; he fell unconscious in the battlefield and Udhava chopped his head with his sword. —1168

DOHIRA

When the six warriors together killed Anag Singh, then four kings of the army of Jarasandh marched forward. —1169

SWAYYA

The four kings Amitesh, Achilesh, Aghnesh, and Asuresh Singh marched forward; they were holding bows, arrows, swords, spears, maces and axes; they fought furiously and fearlessly, considering every one alien to them and surrounding Krishna, they began shower of arrows upon him. —1170

SWAYYA

Enduring the anguish of his wounds Krishna, held up his bow and arrows and cutting the head of Asuresh, he slashed the body of Amitesh; Aghnesh was cut into two parts; he fell upon the ground from his chariot, but Achilesh stood there enduring the shower of arrows and did not run away. —1171

SWAYYA

He spoke to Krishna in anger, "You have killed many of our brave fighters; you killed Gaj Singh and also killed Anag Singh by deception; you know that Amitesh Singh was also a mighty warrior and killing Dhan Singh, you are calling yourself a hero, but the elephant roars only in the forest, when the lion does not turn up." —1172

SWAYYA

Saying this, he proudly held up his bow and arrows and pulling his bow upto his ear, he discharged his sharp arrow on Krishna; Krishna did not see the coming arrow, therefore it hit him in the chest, therefore he became unconscious and fell down in his chariot and his charioteer drove off his chariot. —1173

After the passing away of one *mahurat* (a short span of time), Krishna regained his consciousness in the chariot, now Achilesh laughing proudly said, "Where will you run away from me?" Taking his mace in his hand, he uttered these ironical words like some man holding his staff and challenging a lion going away. —1174

SWAYYA

Hearing these words of the enemy, Krishna getting enraged, moved forward his chariot; his yellow garment began to wave like the lightning among the clouds; with the shower of his arrows, he killed the army of the enemy and now in great fury, taking his bow and arrows in his hands, Achilesh came and stood against Krishna. —1175

DOHIRA

Seeing Krishna, he blew his horn (roaring like a lion) and seeing the warriors on all the four sides, he said to Krishna. —1176

Speech of Achal Singh

SWAYYA

"Those who will survive in the world, they will listen to our war-episode and the poets will please the kings with that poetry; but if the Pundits will narrate it and they will also receive enormous wealth; and O Krishna! Ganas and Gandharvas will sing about this war." —1177

SWAYYA

Krishna heard all this talk of the enemy, getting enraged, and said, "The sparrow only chirps in the forest when the falcon does not come there; O fool, you are absorbed in too much pride; you will know only then, when I will chop your head; therefore forsaking all illusions come and fight and do not delay any more." —1178

SWAYYA

Hearing these words, the anger arose in the mind of the brave Achal Singh and he thundered, "O Krishna! You may feel ashamed; stand there and do not run," saying this he held up his weapon in his hand and ran forward; he, getting pleased, pulled his bow and discharged his arrow, but that arrow did not hit Krishna. —1179

SWAYYA

Every arrow discharged by Achal Singh was intercepted by Krishna; when he learnt that arrow did not hit Krishna, then in anger he would shoot another arrow; Krishna would intercept that arrow also midway and instead would inflict his arrow in his enemy's chest; seeing this spectacle, the poet Shyam is eulogising the Lord God. —1180

SWAYYA

Telling his charioteer named Daruk to drive his chariot speedily, Krishna held up his dagger in his hand; in great fury, he struck it on the head of the enemy; it was flashing like lightning; he (Krishna) cut the head of that wicked person, making his trunk headless; it seemed that the great lion has killed the small lion. —1181

DOHIRA

At that time Addar Singh, Ajab Singh, Aghat Singh, Vir Singh, Amar Singh, Atal Singh, etc., the great warriors were there. —1182

Krishna saw Arjun Singh and Amit Singh and found that eight kings were together conversing with one another. —1183

SWAYYA

Those kings were saying, "O kings! He is the mighty Krishna; let us fall upon him and without fearing Krishna and Balram even a little, we may work for our Lord; they caught their bows, arrows, swords maces, axes, daggers, etc., and went to resist; they said to all, "Let us together wage a war and kill Krishna." —1184

Taking their weapons in their hands, they fell upon Krishna; they drove their chariots and brought before him their army of four extremely large units; the poet Shyam says, they had not even have the slightest fear in this dreadful war and rushed forward shouting "kill, kill;" it appeared that the clouds of doomsday were thundering. —1185

SWAYYA

Dhan Singh came with two extremely large units of army and Angesh Singh brought three such units; they said, "O Krishna! You have killed the ten kings with deceit; we have brought four such units in great anger, therefore you may leave the war-arena and run away to your home." —1186

Speech of Krishna

SWAYYA

Hearing these words, Krishna in great ire challenged them for war and said, "We, both brothers, taking up our bows and arrows, shall destroy all your army; we have not been frightened even by Surya and Shiva, therefore we shall kill all of you and sacrifice ourselves; Even if the Sumeru mountain is moved and the water of the ocean is dried up, we shall not leave the battlefield. —1187

SWAYYA

Saying thus, he discharged one arrow towards the enemies with full strength, which hit the waist of Ajab Singh, but it could not do any harm to him; that mighty warrior said angrily to Krishna, "O Krishna who is such a Pundit, from whom you have learnt the art of warfare." —1188

SWAYYA

The Yadava army, in great fury, rushed there shouting "kill, kill;" in that war, a great part of the army fell down on the earth with the blows of arrows, swords and maces in that conflict; the gods on seeing this became pleased and showered flowers. —1189

SWAYYA

On this side, the warriors are fighting in great rage and on the other side, seeing all this, Brahma and other gods are saying among themselves in the sky, "There had not been such a dreadful war earlier," the warriors are fighting to the end and the Yoginis are shrieking while filling their bowls with blood and drinking; the Ganas of Shiva, hailing the warriors, are preparing many garlands of skulls. —1190

SWAYYA

Carrying his weapons, some warrior, running in the battlefield, is been resisting; someone is fighting like a wresteler and someone seeing the dreadful war, is running away; someone is repeating the Name of the Lord God and someone is shouting loudly "kill, kill;" someone is dying and someone, being wounded, is writhing. —1191

SWAYYA

Someone is fighting with twisted fist and someone is fighting by catching the hair; someone is running away from the battlefield and someone is moving forward; someone is fighting with the girdles and someone is fighting by inflicting blows with his spear; the poet Shyam says that only those people are fighting, who think of their family traditions. —1192

SWAYYA

All the eight kings fell upon Krishna alongwith their armies in the battlefield and said, "O Krishna! Fight with us fearlessly;" pulling their bows, they discharged their arrows towards Krishna and Krishna taking up his bow intercepted their arrows. —1193

SWAYYA

The enemy's army, in great fury, surrounded Krishna from all the four sides and said, "O warriors! All of you may join together in order to kill Krishna; it is he, who has killed Dhan Singh and Achilesh Singh and other kings," saying this they surrounded Krishna like many elephants surrounding a lion. —1194

SWAYYA

When Krishna was besieged, he held up his weapons; in his fury, he killed many enemies in the battlefield; the heads of many were chopped and many were knocked down by catching their hair; some of the warriors having been chopped fell on the earth and some of them seeing all this died without fighting. —1195

SWAYYA

All the eight kings said, "O warriors! do not run away and fight till the last; do not fear Krishna as long as we are alive; we command you to confront and fight with Krishna, the king of Yadavas; none of you will have the idea of avoiding the war, even slightly; run forward and fight till the last." —1196

SWAYYA

Then the warriors taking up their weapons fought in the battle and surrounded Krishna; they did not retrace their steps even for an instant and waged a violent war in great fury; holding their swords and maces a violent war in great fury; holding their swords and maces in their hands, they broke the enemy's army into fragments; somewhere they chopped the heads of the warriors and somewhere they tore their bosoms. —1197

Krishna taking his bow in his hand, he knocked down many warriors on chariots, but again the enemies, taking up their weapons in their hands, they fell upon Krishna; Krishna killed them with his sword and in this way those who survived, they could not stay in the battlefield. —1198

DOHIRA

After a good thrashing by Krishna, all the remaining army of the kings ran away; then holding their weapons the kings collectively marched forward for war. —1199

SWAYYA

The kings with great anger held their weapons in their hands in the battlefield and struck their blows furiously, coming in front of Krishna; Krishna holding his bow intercepted the arrows of the enemies and threw them on the ground; saving himself from the blows of the enemy, Krishna chopped the heads of many of the opponents. —1200

DOHIRA

Krishna cut away the head of Ajab Singh with his weapons and wounded Addar Singh in the battlefield. —1201

CHAUPAI

When Addar Singh was wounded, he was extremely enraged; he took a lance in his hand and discharged it towards Krishna. —1202

DOHIRA

Seeing the lance coming, Krishna took his bow and arrows in his hands and intercepting the lance with his arrow, he also killed that warrior. —1203

Aghar Singh did not run away even in being such a bad plight and confronting Krishna, spoke without feeling ashamed. —1204

CHAUPAI

He said to Krishna, "You have killed Addar Singh fraudulently; you have also killed Ajab Singh dishonestly and I know this secret very well." —1205

DOHIRA

Aghar Singh spoke extremely fearlessly in front of Krishna; whatever words he spoke to Krishna, the poet now tells them. —1206

SWAYYA

He spoke to Krishna in the battlefield without any shame, "You are uselessly angry with us; what will you gain from this war? You are still a boy, therefore do not fight with me and run away; in case you persist in fighting, then you will not find the way to your home and will be killed." —1207

DOHIRA

When he spoke with pride like this, Krishna pulled his bow and the arrow hit his face; with the infliction of the arrow, he died and fell upon the earth. —1208

DOHIRA

Then the obstinate Arjun Singh said to Krishna; "I am a mighty warrior and shall knock you down immediately." —1209

Hearing this, Krishna struck a blow on his head with his dagger and he fell down like a tree in a storm. —1210

SWAYYA

Arjun Singh and the king named Amresh Singh were killed with the dagger, then Krishna held his weapons, getting furious on Atlesh; he also began to say "kill, kill," while coming in front of Krishna; before the glory of his limbs bedecked with gold ornaments, even the sun seemed bedimmed. —1211

SWAYYA

He waged a violent war for one *pahar* (about three hours), but he could not be killed; then Krishna thundering like the cloud, struck a blow on the enemy with his sword and when Krishna cut down his head, he died and fell on the earth; seeing this, the gods hailed and said, "O Krishna! you have lightened a great burden of the earth." —1212

DOHIRA

When Atal Singh, who was the king of many warriors, was killed, then Amit Singh started his efforts for waging war. —1213

SWAYYA

He said to Krishna, "I shall consider you a great warrior, if you fight with me; will you also deceive me like these kings through stratagem?

You will definitely run away from the field seeing me greatly infuriated and if you would fight with me at any time, then you will assuredly leave your body. —1214

SWAYYA

O Krishna! why are you waging war in great anger? Why are you enduring wounds on your body? On whose bidding you are killing the kings? You will remain alive only if you do not fight with me; considering you beautiful, I condone you; therefore leave the war-arena and go to your home. —1215

SWAYYA

Amit Singh spoke again in the battlefield, "Still your age is much less and it will be of no value to you, if see me fighting; O Krishna! I am telling you the truth, but you are thinking something else in your mind; you may now either fight with me fearlessly or throw away all your weapons." —1216

SWAYYA

I shall kill you and all your army today in the battlefield; if there is any heroic fighter amongst you and if someone knows the art of warfare, then he should come forward to fight with me; I swear by God that I shall not fight with you; if anyone recedes from this war, he will not be called a lion, but only a jackal. —1217

DOHIRA

Hearing the words of Amit Singh and in great anger, carrying all his weapons in his hands, Krishna reached in front of Amit Singh.—1218

SWAYYA

Seeing Krishna coming, that mighty warrior got highly enraged; he wounded all the four horses of Krishna and inflicted a sharp arrow in the bosom of Daruk; he discharged the second arrow on Krishna, seeing him in front of himself; the poet says that Amit Singh made Krishna as the target. —1219

Discharging his arrows towards Krishna, he shot a sharp arrow, which hit Krishna, who fell down in his chariot; the charioteer of Krishna, Daruk, sped alongwith him; seeing Krishna going away, the king fell upon his army; it seemed that seeing a large tank, the king of elephants was moving to crush it. —1220

SWAYYA

When Balram saw the enemy coming, he drove his horses and came in front and pulling his bow, he discharged arrows on the enemy; his arrows were intercepted by Amit Singh and in extreme anger, came to fight with Balram. —1221

SWAYYA

The banner, chariot sword, bow etc., of Balram were all cut into bits; the mace and plough were also chopped and being deprived of his weapons, Balram began to move away; seeing this, Amit Singh said, "O Balram! why are you running away now?" Saying this and holding his sword in his hand Amit Singh challenged the Yadava army. —1222

SWAYYA

The warrior who would come in front of him, Amit Singh would kill him; pulling his bow upto his ear, he was showering his arrows on the enemies; only that warrior would remain safe, who would run away to save himself; what was number of others? even the great warriors could not go alive from that place. —1223

SWAYYA

Balram mounted on his chariot came again with the other mace and on his arrival, he began to wage war of four types with the king; he, in great anger, said to all the other remaining warriors, "Do not let him go alive;" hearing these words, the forces of Krishna also became infuriated. —1224

SWAYYA

When Balram exhibited his ire in this manner, then all the Yadava warriors fell upon the enemy; whosoever now came before them, could not return alive; all those who were standing there, they started moving with their axes and lances; keeping into consideration their honour and custom, they struck blows on the enemy with full strength. —1225

DOHIRA

When Amit Singh, in great fury, discharged

innumerable arrows, then the enemy's army fled like the darkness running away in bewilderment before the sun. —1226

SWAYYA

Balram said to the running away Yadava army, "O warriors born in the clans of Kshatriyas! Why are you running away? You are dropping your weapons without killing the enemy; you should have no fear of war, till I am alive." —1227

DOHIRA

Balram in anger, caressing the warriors, said, "Kill Amit Singh by besieging him." —1228

Speech of the Poet
SWAYYA

Receiving the command of Balram, his army fell upon the enemy challenging him from all the four directions and filled with rage resisted in front of Amit Singh; there was dreadful fighting in the battlefield but the army did not even slightly retrace king Amit Singh, taking his bow in his hand, killed many warriors of the army and made the army helpless. —1229

SWAYYA

The elephants, chariots, warriors and horses were killed and destroyed; many warriors, getting wounded, are roaming and many huge trunks are lying on the earth; those who are alive, they taking their weapons in their hands are striking blows on the enemy fearlessly, the king Amit Singh has chopped into bits the bodies of such like warriors, taking his sword in his hand. —1230

SWAYYA

With the infliction of arrows the bodies of many warriors are saturated with blood; the cowards have perspired and run away from the battlefield; the ghosts and fiends are running, raising shrieks and the Yoginis have taken the bowls in their hands; Shiva is also roaming there alongwith his Ganas and the dead lying there have been reduced into half, because their flesh is being eaten. —1231

DOHIRA

Krishna regained consciousness after about three *gharis* (short span of time) of remaining unconscious and getting his chariot driven by Daruk, he reached the battlefield again. —1232

SWAYYA

When the warriors of Yadava clan saw Krishna coming for their help, the anger awoke in them; they ran to fight against Amit Singh and none of them ran away from the battlefield; the forces rushed forward taking their swords, bows, arrows, maces, etc., the warriors filled with blood were gleaming like a heap of straw burning in fire. —1233

SWAYYA

The warriors waged the war in fury, taking up their weapons; all were shouting "kill, kill" and not fearing even slightly; the poet says again that Krishna resisted numerous warriors; on the other side, the king Amit Singh, in great rage, simultaneously chopped the bodies of two warriors at a time into four parts. —1234

Seeing such a dreadful war, those warriors who were coming for fighting left and ran away from war-arena; no one could confront Amit Singh; those who called themselves great warriors, and were roaming wielding many kinds of weapons, they ran away from the battlefield like the leaves of a tree flying away before the blow of wind. —1235

SWAYYA

Some of the warriors stood firmly in war and some of them, inflicted by the arrows of Krishna, sped away from the field crying; Amit Singh killed many warriors, they cannot be enumerated; somewhere the horses somewhere the elephants and somewhere the shattered chariots were lying on the ground; O Lord! You are the Creator, Sustainer and the Destroyer; What is in your mind, no one can understand? —1236

DOHIRA

When the warriors requested Krishna in the battlefield, greatly agitated, Krishna replies to them thus. —1237

Speech of Krishna
SWAYYA

Amit Singh has persistently performed austerities and repeated the Name of the Lord for many

BACHITTAR NATAK

months in the ocean; then he forsook his parents, home etc., and resided in the forest; the god Shiva got pleased and asked him to implore for a boon and the boon that he begged for was that no enemy could confront him. —1238

SWAYYA

Even Indra, Seshanaga, Ganesh, Chandra and Surya cannot kill him; after receiving the boon from Shiva, he has killed many kings; I think that I should confront him and ask him the manner of his death. —1239

DOHIRA

When Balram heard these words of Krishna, he spoke in anger that he would kill Amit Singh immediately. —1240

SWAYYA

In great rage, the mighty Balram said to Krishna that he would kill Amit Singh, and even if Shiva comes to his help, he also strike his blows on him alongwith Amit Singh; O Krishna! I am telling you the truth that I shall kill Amit Singh and not be vanquished; You come to my help and with the fire of Your strength, burn away this forest of the enemies. —1241

Speech of Krishna addressed to Balram

DOHIRA

When he was fighting against you, why not fight with him firmly? And now you are talking to me with pride. —1242

SWAYYA

All the Yadavas have run away and you are still talking like an egoist; what are you talking like the intoxicated persons? That you would kill Amit Singh today, you will burn like a straw before his fire; Krishna said, "He is a lion and you will run before him like the children." —1243

DOHIRA

When Krishna said these words to Balram, he replied, "You may do whatever You wish." —1244

SWAYYA

Saying thus to Balram and taking hold of His weapons in great rage, Krishna moved forward and said, "O coward! where are you going? Stay a little" Amit Singh showered many arrows, which were intercepted by the arrows of Krishna; Krishna took His bow in His hand and pulling His bow discharged many arrows on the enemy. —1245

DOHIRA

After discharging many arrows, Krishna spoke again, "O Amit Singh! your false ego will be effaced." —1246

SWAYYA

Hearing these words, Amit Singh said, "When You first started for war, You are talking such things since then; I have not paid any attention to Your talk and now I have come to confront You after finding You; therefore come without any illusion and let us fight against each other; even if the Pole Star moves away from its place and the mountain also moves away, but O Krishna! I am not moving away from You." —1247

Speech of Krishna

DOHIRA

Krishna said, "You may take millions of measures, but I shall kill You;" then Amit Singh spoke in extreme anger: —1248

Speech of Amit Singh

SWAYYA

I am not Baki or Bakasura or Vrishabhasura, whom You killed with deceit; I am not Keshi, elephant, Dhenukasura and Tranavrata, whom You knocks down on the stone; I am also not Aghasura, Mushitak, Chandur, and Kansa, whom You overthrew by catching them from their hair; Your brother is Balram and You are called mighty, tell me a little, to which mighty warrior You have killed with Your own strength. —1249

SWAYYA

Does Brahma possess such strength that he may fight with me? What are the poor Garuda, Ganesh, Surya, Chandra, etc.? All these will run away silently on seeing me; if Seshanaga, Varuna, Indra, Kuber, etc., resist me for some time, they will not harm me even slightly; the gods even run away on seeing me; You are still a child, what will You gain by fighting with me. —1250

DOHIRA

O Krishna! Why are You bent upon losing Your life? Leave the battlefield and run away; I shall not kill You today with my full strength. —1251

Speech of Krishna
DOHIRA

Hearing the words of Amit Singh, Krishna was highly enraged and said, "O Amit Singh! I shall now destroy your body and make you lifeless." —1252

SWAYYA

When Krishna fought for two *pahars* (about six hours), the enemy Amit Singh got pleased and said, "O Krishna! Although You are still a child, but You are skilful in warfare; You may ask for whatever you want." Krishna said, "Tell me the manner of your death." Then Amit Singh said, "No one can kill me from the front." Then Krishna struck a blow on him from behind. —1253

SWAYYA

The head of Amit Singh was cut, but still he ran and moved forward and he struck a dreadful blow on an elephant of the army; after killing the elephant and many warriors, he rushed forward towards Krishna; his head fell down on the ground, which was given a place of Meru by Shiva in his rosary of skulls. —1254

DOHIRA

The mighty warrior Amit Singh had waged a terrible war; just as the light moves out from the sun and moon, in the same manner, his light, coming out from his body, merged in Lord God. —1255

SWAYYA

The remaining army of the enemy fought with Krishna; they even stood firmly without their king and in their fury, they strengthened their heart; the army gathered together and fell upon Krishna, just as during night, seeing the earthen lamp, the insects move towards it and fall upon it. —1256

DOHIRA

Then Krishna, taking His sword in His hand, knocked down many of his enemies; someone fought, someone stood firmly and many sped away. —1257

CHAUPAI

Krishna destroyed the army of Amit Singh and there was great lamentation in the enemy's army; on that side, the sun set and the moon arose in the east. —1258

The warriors were exhausted and weakened by the continuous fight during the whole day; both the armies started moving back and on this side, Krishna also returned home. —1259

End of the chapter entitled "Killing of Amit Singh alongwith His Army in Warfare" in Krishnavatar in Bachittar Natak.

Now begins the Description of War with Five kings

DOHIRA

Then during night, Jarasandh called all the kings, who were equal in strength to Indra and equal in beauty to the god of love. —1260

DOHIRA

Krishna has killed eighteen kings in the war; is there anyone now, who will go and wage war with him? —1261

DOHIRA

There were seated five chief kings named Dhum Singh, Dhvaj Singh, Man Singh, Dharadhar Singh, and Dhaval Singh. —1262

All the five arose and bowed in the court and said, "As soon as the day dawns, we shall, kill Balram, Krishna and his army." —1263

SWAYYA

The kings said to Jarasandh, "Do not worry, we shall go to fight; if you command, we shall tie him down and bring him here or we may kill him there; we shall not recede in the battlefield by Balram, Krishna and Yadavas, even slightly; we shall make them lifeless fearlessly with one blow of the sword." —1264

BACHITTAR NATAK

DOHIRA

After holding these consultations, Jarasandh bade adieu to the court and the kings, getting pleased, went away to their homes. —1265

DOHIRA

All the five kings came to their places and on this side one *pahar* of night had passed; they could not sleep for the remaining three *pahars* and in this way, the day dawned. —1266

KABIT

The darkness (of night) ended with day-dawn, the warriors, in anger, and bedecking their chariots, started (for war); on this side, the Lord of Braja, in a state of supreme bliss in his mind, and calling Balram went (for war); on that side also, forsaking fear and holding their weapons, the warriors moved forward shouting loudly; driving their chariots, blowing their conches and beating small drums and riding on their horses, both the armies fell upon each other. —1267

DOHIRA

Krishna, sitting in his chariot looked splendid like the mine of unlimited light; the asphodels considered him as moon and the lotus-flowers considered him as sun. —1268

SWAYYA

The peacocks, considering him as cloud, began to dance, partridges considered him as moon and danced in the forest; the women thought that he was the god of love and the servant-maids considered him as a superb human; the yogis thought that he was a Supreme Yogi and the ailments thought that he was the remedy; the children considered him as a child and the wicked people saw him as death. —1269

SWAYYA

The ducks considered him as the sun, the elephants as Ganesh and the Ganas as Shiva; he seemed to be like Indra, Earth and Vishnu, but he also looked like an innocent doe; for the deer he was like the horn and for the men sans strifes, he was like life-breath; for the friends, he was like a friend abiding in mind and for the enemies, he looked like Yama. —1270

DOHIRA

The armies of both the sides, in great anger, gathered, together and the warriors playing upon their trumpets etc., began to wage war. —1271

SWAYYA

The kings namely Dhum, Dhvaja, Man, Dhum, and Dharadhar Singh, in great fury, reached the battlefield; they ran before Krishna, forsaking all their illusions, taking their shields and swords in their hands; seeing them, Krishna said to Balram, "Now do, whatever you wish;" the mighty Balram, taking his plough in his hand, chopped the heads of all the five and threw them on the ground. —1272

DOHIRA

Two supreme divisions of army and all the five kings were killed and those one or two who survived left the war-arena and ran away. —1273

End of the chapter entitled "Killing of Five Kings alongwith Five Supreme Divisions of the Army" in Krishnavatar in Bachittar Natak.

Now begins the Description about the War with Twelve Kings

SWAYYA

When the twelve kings saw this situation, they began to grind their teeth in great anger; they trusted their arms and weapons and distributed them amongst their force; then all of them held consultations; their hearts were in great anguish; they said, "We shall fight, die and ferry across the ocean of *samsara*; because even one praiseworthy instant of our life is superb." —1274

SWAYYA

Thinking this in their mind and bringing sufficient army, they came and began to challenge Krishna, "This Balram has already killed the five kings and now O Krishna! tell your brother to fight with us, otherwise you come to fight with us or leave the war-arena and go home; if your people are weak, then what vitality of ours you will be able to see?" —1275

SWAYYA

Hearing this talk all of them, taking up their weapons, came in front of Krishna; on their arrival the head of Sahib Singh was cut and Sada Singh was knocked down after killing him; Sundar Singh was cut into two halves and then destroyed Sajan Singh; Samlesh Singh was knocked down by catching him from his hair and in this way, a dreadful war was excited. —1276

DOHIRA

Then Shakti Singh and Sain Singh were killed; then killing Saphal Singh and Ara Singh, Krishna roared like a lion. —1277

Speech of Svachh Singh

SWAYYA

On getting furious, with great strength the king Svachh Singh said to Krishna; "You have already killed fearlessly the ten kings;" from the side of Krishna, the arrows were being showered like the raining clouds of the month of Sawan, but the king Svachh Singh did not even move slightly by the swiftness of arrows and resisted in the battlefield like a mountain. —1278

DOHIRA

The king fought with the Yadavas like Indra with Jambhasura; the king stood stable in the battlefield like a column. —1279

SWAYYA

Just as the Sumeru mountain is not moved with the strength of the elephants, just as the abode of Dhruva remains firm and the portrait of Shiva does not teach anything; just as the faithful wife does not swerve from her chastity and the adepts ever remain absorbed in their meditation, in the same manner the persistent Svachh Singh is standing amidst the four divisions of the army of Krishna, standing quite steadily. —1280

KABIT

Then the mighty Svachh Singh in great fury, killed many of the mighty warriors of the army of Krishna; he killed seven great chariot-owners and fourteen supreme chariot-owners; he also killed thousands of elephants; he killed many horses and soldiers on foot; the ground was dyed with blood and the waves of blood surged there; the wounded warriors fell down there, getting intoxicated and look like those sleeping after sprinkling the pearls of blood. —1281

DOHIRA

The pride of Svachh Singh was increased very much after killing a greater part of Yadava army; he spoke egoistically with Krishna. —1282

DOHIRA

"O Krishna! what, then, even if you have killed ten of the kings; it is just like this that the deer eat the straws of the forest, but cannot confront the lion." —1283

Hearing the words of the enemy Krishna smiled and said, "O Svachh Singh! I shall kill you just as a lion kills a jackals." —1284

SWAYYA

Just as a big lion, seeing a small lion, gets infuriated; just as seeing the king of elephants, the king of deer gets angry; just as seeing the deer, the leopard falls upon them, in the same manner, Krishna fell upon Svachh Singh; on this side, Daruk in order to leave behind the speed of the wind, drove away the chariot of Krishna. —1285

SWAYYA

From that side, Svachh Singh came forward and from this side, Krishna the brother of Balram marched forward in anger; both the warriors began to fight taking their bows, arrows and swords in their hands; both were enduring, both of them shouted "kill, kill" but they kept resisting in front of each other and did not swerve even slightly; Svachh Singh was neither feared by Krishna nor Balram nor from any of the Yadavas. —1286

DOHIRA

When he waged a dreadful war, Krishna severed his head from the trunk with the blow of his spear. —1287

DOHIRA

When Svachh Singh was killed, then Samar Singh

BACHITTAR NATAK

was extremely enraged, seeing the war, he resisted Krishna with firm feet. —1288

SWAYYA

Taking his sword in his hand, that mighty warrior killed many warriors of Krishna; many warriors were wounded and many of them fled away suffering defeat in the battlefield; the warriors shouted loudly, "We are being defeated by the mighty Samar Singh because he continues to chop into halves the warriors like the chopping saw of Kashi. —1289

SWAYYA

Krishna said loudly within his army, "Who is that warrior, who will fight with the enemy? Who will endure the blows of his arms and inflict blows on him with his weapons? Krishna is holding the betel leaf in his hand, so that some warrior may take up this betel leaf (responsibility), but none of the warriors thinks of his honour and custom; the frontal mark of approbation will only be obtained by him, who will not run away while fighting with Samar Singh. —1290

DOHIRA

Many warriors have fought a great deal and the mighty Ahab Singh from amongst them asked for that betel leaf. —1291

Speech of the Poet
DOHIRA

Someone may raise a question here; why Krishna, the Lord of Braja, does not fight himself? The answer is; He is doing this only to see the sport himself. —1292

SWAYYA

Ahab Singh, the warrior of Krishna, in his fury, fell upon Samar Singh and on the other side Samar Singh was very persistent; he also gave a terrible fight; with his heavy dagger, Samar Singh chopped Ahab Singh and knocked him down on the ground; his trunk fell on the ground like a *vajra*, as a result of which the earth trembled. —1293

KABIT

The king Aniruddha Singh was standing near Krishna; seeing him, Krishna called him; giving him great respect, he asked him to go for fighting; receiving the command, he entered the war-arena; a violent war was fought there with arrows, swords and lances; just like a lion kills a deer or a falcon killed a sparrow, in the same manner, this warrior of Krishna was killed by Samar Singh. —1294

KABIT

The poet Shyam says; just as someone removes a grave ailment with the help of medicine or a good poet on listening to a poem of a poetaster does not appreciate it in the gathering, just as a lion destroys a snake and the water destroys the fire or the intoxicating objects destroy a melodious throat, in the same manner this warrior of Krishna was also killed by Samar Singh; the life-force went out from his body like the virtues speeding away on account of greed or the darkness running away at day-dawn. —1295

KABIT

The warriors named Virbhadar Singh, Vasudeva Singh, Vir Singh and Bal Singh, in their fury, confronted the enemy; on seeing Samar Singh, standing in the battlefield, they blazed like fire; holding their weapons, these skilful warriors of Krishna fell upon Samar Singh from all the four sides; at the same time, that mighty warrior pulled his bow and knocked down all the four warriors of Krishna in an instant. —1296

Speech of Krishna
SWAYYA

When all the four warriors were killed in the war, then Krishna said to the other warriors, "Who is now so powerful to confront the enemy and falling upon this extremely mighty warrior Samar Singh and kill him while fighting fearlessly with him?" Krishna said to all of them loudly, "Is there any one can make the enemy lifeless?" —1297

SWAYYA

There was one demon in the army of Krishna, who marched forward towards the enemy; his name was Karurdhvaja; he said to Samar Singh on going near him, "I am going to kill you, therefore save yourself;" saying this, he held out his bow and arrows and knocked down Samar Singh, who seemed to have lain dead for several days. —1298

DOHIRA

In this way, Karurdhvaja killed Samar Singh in his fury in the battlefield and now he stabilised himself to kill Shakti Singh. —1299

Speech of Karurdhvaja
KABIT

Karurdhvaja seems like a mountain in the battlefield; the poet Shyam says that he is ready to kill the enemies and is saying, "O Shakti Singh! the manner in which I have killed Samar Singh, I shall kill you in the same manner, because you are fighting with me," saying thus, taking his mace and sword in his hand, he is enduring the blows of the enemy like a tree; the demon Karurdhvaja is again saying loudly to the king Shakti Singh, "O king! the life-force is now within you for a very short time." —1300

DOHIRA

On listening to the words of the enemy, Shakti Singh said, "I know that the clouds of the month of Kavar thunder, but do not cause rain." —1301

SWAYYA

Fearing this, the demon got highly infuriated and on this side, Shakti, also taking up his sword stood fearlessly and firmly before him; after a great deal of fight, that demon disappeared and manifesting in the sky, said this, "O Shakti Singh! Now I am going to kill you," saying thus, he held up his bow and arrows. —1302

DOHIRA

Showering his arrows, Karurdhvaja descended from the sky and entering the battlefield again that mighty warrior fought more terribly. —1303

SWAYYA

Killing the warriors that powerful demon was extremely pleased and with a firm mind marched forward in order to kill Shakti Singh; like the flash of lightning, the bow in his hand became mercurial and its twang was audible; just as the raindrops come from the clouds, in the same manner there was shower of arrows. —1304

SORATHA

Shakti Singh did not retrace even one step in his fight with Karurdhvaja and the manner in which Angad stood firmly in the court of Ravana, in the same manner, he also remained firm. —1305

SWAYYA

The mighty warrior Shakti Singh did not run away from the battlefield and the snare of the arrows created by the enemy was intercepted by him with his fire-shafts; in his rage, he took up his bow and arrows and knocked down the head of Karurdhvaja; he killed the demon like the killing of Vritasura by Indra. —1306

DOHIRA

When Shakti Singh knocked down Karurdhvaja, the enemies began to run away for safety just like the people running hither and thither in order to save themselves from getting wet in the rain. —1307

SWAYYA

Seeing his brother dead, Karurdhvaja in great rage came forward; he lengthened his teeth for several *yojanas* (a measure of distance) and magnified his body to the size of a mountain; he grew his hair like the trees and taking his weapons in his hand, he came in the battlefield; Shakti Singh by pulling his bow, knocked him down with a single arrow only. —1308

SWAYYA

The Lord of the army of demons was standing there; he fell upon Shakti Singh in great rage; he took the supreme divisions of his army along with him and marched forward in great ire; the name of this incoming demon in the battlefield was Kurup; he moved forward to destroy the enemy like the clouds of Sawan. —1309

SWAYYA

Seeing the four divisions of the army of his enemies, Shakti Singh was filled with ire, but with endurance in the battlefield, he took the bow and arrows in his hands; he went in front of the army of the enemy and seeing him, all began to run away; in order to destroy the clouds of demons, that warrior was looking like wind. —1310

SWAYYA

Kurup disappeared and manifesting himself in the sky, he said, "O Shakti Singh! where will you go to save yourself?" Saying this he showered elephants, horses, trees, stones, rocks, chariots, lions, mountains, bears and black cobras; all of them fell on the earth, under whom all except Shakti Singh were crushed and killed. —1311

SWAYYA

The king (Shakti Singh) intercepted with his arrows all the things thrown upon him and that mighty warrior with his strength reached there, where the demons were standing; this mighty warrior, taking his sword in his hand, wounded some of them and killed many of them; the army of demons could not do anything worthwhile and it was being defeated on account of its deceptive methods. —1312

SWAYYA STANZA

The king, taking his bow and arrows in his hands made Kurup as his target, who was alive and carrying weapons in his hands, many warriors writhed; whosoever came forward to fight, became lifeless and many were seen standing and saturated with blood; they appeared having like the red *kesu* flowers in spring season. —1313

DOHIRA

In that war, holding his weapons, Shakti Singh killed many of the warriors of the army of demons. —1314

SWAYYA

Vikartanan, the brother of Kurup caught hold of his sword in his hand in great rage and he made an effort to kill the enemy; getting his chariot driven, with his zeal for war in his mind, he reached there and said, "O king! Hold up your sword, I am going to kill you." —1315

DOHIRA

Hearing those words Shakti Singh took his *shakti* (the powerful weapon) in his hand and looking at the enemy, he discharged that *shakti*, swift like the sun-rays. —1316

SWAYYA

That *shakti* piercing the heart of Vikartanan, penetrated to the other side of the body; the body on which there were golden figures, all dyed with blood; that *shakti* driven in the body looked like the sun swallowed by Rahu on remembering its enmity. —1317

DOHIRA

With the infliction of the dagger, that mighty warrior breathed his last and all the mighty warriors, having fears in their minds lamented. —1318

DOHIRA

When the heroic Shakti Singh killed Vikartanan, Kurup could not endure the sorrow of the death of his brother. —1319

SWAYYA

Seeing the killing of Vikartanan and inspired by death, Kurup went to the sky and taking the bow, sword, mace etc., in his hand he waged a dreadful war; Shakti Singh also pulled his very large bow, made the throat of his enemy as his target; the head of the enemy was chopped and fell down on the earth and the headless trunk of the enemy, catching hold of his sword in his hand, began to run in the battlefield. —1320

Speech of the Poet

DOHIRA

The king (Vikartanan), with his sword in his hand, reached in front of Shakti Singh, but he knocked him down on the earth with a single arrow. —1321

DOHIRA

When Shakti Singh killed Kurup and the king (Vikartanan) alongwith the army, then the Yadava army seeing this began to lament. —1322

Balram said to Krishna, "This warrior is fighting for a very long time," then Krishna said, "Why should he not fight? Because his name is Shakti Singh." —1323

CHAUPAI

Then Krishna said to all, "We shall not be able to kill Shakti Singh, because he has performed austerities for a boon from Chandi with extreme devotion, therefore he has destroyed all our army." —1324

DOHIRA

Therefore you should also serve Chandi single-mindedly, with which she will bestow the boon of victory and then you will be able to kill the enemy. —1325

He, whose gleaming light pervades in water, on plain and the whole world, the same is present in Brahma, Vishnu and Shiva in the form of three modes. —1326

SWAYYA

He, whose power is present in the whole world and in all forms, whose power is present in Parvati, Vishnu and Lakshmi and whose power is present in the mountain, tree, sun, moon, Indra and clouds also; you have not adored that Bhavani, therefore now meditate on her. —1327

DOHIRA

Shakti Singh has with his austerities, obtained the boon from the Lord and through His Grace, he is winning the war and he is not losing anything. —1328

DOHIRA

If any of the gods like Shiva, Sun, Moon, Indra, Brahma, Vishnu or any other wages the war with him, he will not be able to conquer him. —1229

SWAYYA

If the God Shiva fights with him, he also does not have so much strength so as to be victorious over him; Brahma, Kartikeya, Vishnu, etc., who are considered very powerful and the ghosts, fiends, gods and demons etc., are all powerless against him; Krishna said to all the Yadavas, "This king has so much power." —1330

Speech of Krishna

SWAYYA

You may go and fight with him and I myself shall repeat the name of the goddess; I shall establish the goddess with utmost devotion so that she may manifest herself and ask me for her boon and I shall ask her to bestow me the boon of victory over Shakti Singh; then mounting on the chariot I shall kill him. —1331

Speech of the Poet

SWAYYA

Krishna, on that side, sent the Yadavas for fighting and he himself, on this side, began to repeat the name of the goddess; he, forgetting all his consciousness, absorbed his mind only in the meditation of the goddess; then the goddess manifested herself and said, "You may ask for the boon that you want;" on this Krishna asked for the destruction of Shakti Singh on that day. —1332

SWAYYA

In this way, obtaining the boon, Krishna mounted on the chariot with pleased mind; the poet Shyam says that on account of his repetition of the Name, he obtained the boon of killing the enemy; taking all His weapons, Krishna went before that mighty warrior and the hope of victory, that was on the verge of its end, a new spout erupted on account of this boon. —1333

DOHIRA

Shakti Singh knocked down many warriors in the battlefield and the earth was filled with their dead bodies. —1334

SWAYYA

The place, where the powerful Shakti Singh was fighting, Krishna reached there and said, "You may stop now; where are you going? I have deliberately come here." In great fury, Krishna struck a blow with his mace on the head of the enemy and with that remembering Chandi in his mind, Shakti Singh breathed his last; the body of Shakti Singh also went to the region of Chandi —1335

SWAYYA

With the body going to the region of Chandi, his *pranas* (life-breaths) also moved; the gods like

Surya, Indra, Sanak, Snandan, etc., began to describe his praises; they all said, "We have not seen such a fighter in our life; bravo to the mighty warrior Shakti Singh who has reached the next world after fighting with Krishna. —1336

CHAUPAI

When Krishna obtained the boon from Chandi, then he knocked down Shakti Singh; many of other enemies ran away like the darkness on seeing the sun. —1337

End of the chapter entitled "Killing of Twelve Kings including Shakti Singh in Warfare" in Krishnavatar in Bachittar Natak.

Now begins the Description of the War with Five Kings

DOHIRA

There were powerful and learned warriors in the battlefield like Asam Singh, Jas Singh, Inder Singh, Abhai Singh, and Ichh Singh. —1338

DOHIRA

When these kings saw the army running away, they marched forward to fight; all the five said proudly; we shall definitely kill Krishna, the Lord of Yadavas. —1339

On that side, taking their weapons in their hands and in great rage, all of them came forward and from this side Krishna got his chariot driven and reached in front of them. —1340

SWAYYA

The mighty warrior Subhat Singh at the same time ran from the side of Krishna and taking five arrows in his hand pulled his heavy bow in great rage; he killed all the five kings, each with a single arrow; these five kings blazed like straw and it appeared that Subhat Singh was the flame of fire. —1341

DOHIRA

Subhat Singh standing firmly in the battlefield waged a violent war and he destroyed all the five kings who had come these. —1342

End of the chapter entitled "Killing of Five Kings in Warfare" of Krishnavatar in Bachittar Natak.

Now begins the Description of War with Ten Kings

DOHIRA

Other ten kings, in great fury, marched forward alongwith their warriors; they were all great charioteers and were like intoxicated elephants in war. —1343

SWAYYA

On coming, all the ten kings discharged their arrow on Subhat Singh who seeing them, intercepted them with his own arrows; the head of Uttar Singh was cut and Ujjal Singh was wounded; Uddam Singh was killed; then Shankar Singh came forward taking up his sword. —1344

DOHIRA

After killing of Ot Singh, Oj Singh was killed; Ud Singh, Ushnesh Singh and Uttar Singh were also killed. —1345

DOHIRA

When the nine kings were killed, the king who did not run away from war, his name was Uggar Singh. —1346

SWAYYA

The great warrior Uggar Singh, reciting his *mantra*, discharged one arrow towards Subhat Singh, which hit his heart and tearing his body, penetrated through it; he died and fell down on the ground and according to the poet Shyam he might have committed the sin of killing many kings, then this arrow of Yama like a cobra had stung him. —1347

DOHIRA

Then a Yadava named Manoj Singh came forward and fell upon Uggar Singh in great rage. —1348

SWAYYA

Seeing the mighty Yadava warrior coming\, the great war hero Uggar Singh became alert and catching in ire his lance of steel, he struck a blow with great strength; on receiving the blow of that lance Manoj Singh died and proceeded to the abode of Yama; after killing him, Uggar Singh challenged the mighty warrior Balram. —1349

SWAYYA

Seeing the enemy coming, Balram caught hold of his mace and fell upon him; both these warriors fought a dreadful war between them; Uggar Singh could not save himself from trick and the mace hit his head; he died and fell down on the ground; then Balram blew his conch. —1350

End of the chapter entitled "Killing of the Kings alongwith the Army" in Krishanavatar in Bachittar Natak.

Description of the War with Ten Kings including Anup Singh

DOHIRA

When the ten kings saw that the mighty warrior Uggar Singh was killed, then these kings of powerful arms marched forward for waging war. —1351

SWAYYA

Anupam Singh and Apurav Singh, in rage, started for war; one of them Kanchan Singh marched forward and on his arrival, Balram discharged an arrow; he died and fell from the chariot, but his soul, in its divine form of light, stayed there; it seemed that Hanuman, considering the sun as a fruit, had discharged an arrow and got it down below. —1352

DOHIRA

Kop Singh and Kot Singh were killed; Apurav Singh was also killed after Mohan Singh. —1353

CHAUPAI

Then Katak Singh and Krishna Singh were killed; Komal Singh was struck by an aorrow and he went to the abode of Yama. —1354

Then Kanakchal Singh was done to death and Anupam Singh got tired by fighting with Yadavas; then coming towards Balram, he began to fight, from the other side. —1355

DOHIRA

The heroic warrior Anupam Singh, in great fury, fought with Balram and he despatched many warriors from the side of Krishna to the abode of Yama. —1356

SWAYYA

Krata Singh, from the side of Krishna, getting enraged, jumped in the war-arena and taking his sword in his hand, he waged a dreadful war; he pulled his big bow and discharged an arrow towards Anupam Singh; on being struck with it, his life-force touching the sphere of the sun, went beyond it. —1357

SWAYYA

The mighty warriors like Ishwar Singh fell upon him, seeing whom Krata Singh discharged his sharp arrows towards them; they were hit by the moonlike arrows and the heads of both of them fell upon the earth; their trunks appeared to have forgotten their heads in their homes. —1358

End of the chapter entitled "Killing of Ten Kings including Anup Singh in Warfare" in Krishnavatar in Bachittar Natak.

Now begins the Description of the War with Five Kings Karam Singh etc.

CHAUPAI

Karam Singh, Jai Singh, Jalab Singh, Gaja Singh etc., came into the battlefield in increased anger; the five noteworthy warriors, Jagat Singh etc., waged a dreadful war and killed many Yadavas; Shastra Singh, Krata Singh, Shatru Singh, etc., the four kings were killed and only one Jagat Singh survived, who firmly assumed the heroic tradition of Kshatriyas. —1359

CHAUPAI

Karam Singh and Jalab Singh marched forward; Gaja Singh and Jai Singh also came; Jagat Singh was extremely egoistic, therefore the Death inspired and sent him for war. —1360

DOHIRA

Kritash Singh, Jalpa Singh, Gaja Singh and Jai Singh, all these four warriors were killed by Kritash Singh. —1361

SWAYYA

Kritash Singh killed four warriors in the war from the side of Krishna and killed and despatched many others to the abode of Yama; now he had confronted Jagtesh Singh, taking hold of his bow and arrows; all the other warriors who were standing there at that time, they began to shower arrows on Kritash Singh. —1362

SWAYYA

After killing many warriors of the army of the enemy, he caught hold of his sword and stabilising himself, he struck a blow on the head of Jagtesh Singh; having been chopped into two parts, he fell down from the chariot like a mountain falling into two parts by the fall of lightning. —1363

DOHIRA

Within this time, Kathin Singh, coming out of his army-unit fell down on him like an intoxicated elephant in great rage. —1364

SWAYYA

Seeing the enemy coming, he killed him with a single arrow and also killed the army supporting him in an instant; he, killing many Yadava warriors in his fury saw towards Krishna and said, "Why are you standing? Come and fight with me." —1365

SWAYYA

Then Krishna, in anger, caused his chariot to be driven by Daruk, went towards him. He held his sword in his hand and challenging him, struck a blow on him, but Krata Singh saved himself with his shield and taking out his sword from his scabbard, wounded Daruk, the charioteer of Krishna. —1366

SWAYYA

Both of them, highly infuriated, began to fight with their swords; when Krishna inflicted a wound on the enemy, then he also inflicted a wound on Krishna. Seeing this sport from the sky, the gods said; "O Krishna! You are delaying, because you killed the demons like Mura and Madhu Kaitabh in an instant." —1367

SWAYYA

The war continued throughout the day, then Krishna devised a method, he said, "I am not killing you" and saying this, when the enemy looked behind, he very quickly at that very instant, struck a blow on the neck of the enemy with his sharp sword and in this way, killing the enemy, removed the fear of his army. —1368

In this way, killing his enemy, Krishna was pleased and looking at his army, he blew his conch forcefully; he is the support of the saints and capable of doing everything, he the Lord of Braja; under his command, his army of our divisions, waged a terrible war in the battlefield. —1369

End of the Description of "Killing of Five Kings in the Warfare" in Krishnavatar in Bachittar Natak.

Now begins the Description of War with Kharag Singh

DOHIRA

A friend of that king named Kharag Singh was there, who was an excellent swimmer of the ocean of war and an abode of great strength. —1370

Taking four kings and innumerable forces alongwith him, he, in great ire, went for war with Krishna. —1371

CHHAPPAI

There are many warriors there including Kharag Singh, Bar Singh, Gavan Singh, Dharam Singh, Bhav Singh etc., whom he took with himself with many chariots and warriors; ten thousands of elephants moved thundering like clouds and they collectively besieged Krishna and his army; the enemy's army was thundering and roaring like the dense clouds in the rainy season. —1372

DOHIRA

From this side, from the army of Yadavas, four kings came forward whose names were Saras Singh, Vir Singh, Maha Singh, and Saar Singh. —1373

There were four intoxicated kings with Kharag Singh; they marched towards Krishna like the persons nearing their final doom. —1374

DOHIRA

Coming out from the army of Yadavas, Saras Singh, Maha Singh, Saar Singh, and Vir Singh came in their powerful form. —1375

Kharag Singh killed in his fury all the four kings from the side of Krishna. —1376

SWAYYA

Other kings came forward from the side of Krishna, whose names were Surat Singh, Sampuran Singh, Bar Singh, etc., they were wrathful and were specialists in warfare. Mat Singh also wore his armour in order to protect his body from the blows of arms and weapons and these four kings waged a dreadful war with Kharag Singh. —1377

DOHIRA

On this side all these four kings fought with Kharag Singh and on that side the four divisions of both the armies were engaged in terrible warfare. —1378

KABIT

The charioteers began to fight with charioteers, the chariot-owners with chariot-owners, the riders with riders and the soldiers on foot with soldiers on foot in rage, forsaking their attachment of their home and family; the daggers, swords, tridents, mace and arrows were struck; the elephant fought with elephant, the speaker with speaker and the minstrel with minstrel. —1379

SWAYYA

After killing Maha Singh, Saar Singh was also killed and then Surat Singh, Sampuran Singh and Sundar Singh were also killed; seeing the cutting of the head of Mat Singh, the Yadava army became deprived of the vitality, but the Ganas and Kinnars began to eulogise Kharag Singh in the sky. —1380

DOHIRA

The mighty warrior Kharag Singh killed six kings and after that three other kings came to fight with him. —1381

Kharag Singh remained stable in the battle also after killing Karan Singh, Aran Singh, Baran Singh, etc. —1382

SWAYYA

Killing many great kings and getting enraged again Kharag Singh took his bow and arrows in his hand; he chopped the heads of many enemies and struck his blows on them with his arms; the manner in which Ram had destroyed the army of Ravana, in the same way, Kharag Singh killed the enemy's army; the Ganas, ghosts, fiends, jackals, vultures and Yoginis drank the blood to their fill in the war. —1383

DOHIRA

Kharag Singh, filled with anger, taking his dagger in his hand, was fearlessly roaming in the war-arena; he seemed to be playing Holi. —1384

SWAYYA

The arrows are being discharged like the vermilion diffused in air and the blood flowing with the blows of the lances seemed like *gulal* (red colour); the shields have become like tabors and the guns look like the pumps; the clothes of the warriors filled with blood appear having been saturated with dissolved saffron. The warriors carrying the swords appear carrying the sticks of flowers and playing Holi. —1385

DOHIRA

Kharag Singh is fighting in great anger and is agile like a healthy actor showing his acting. —1386

SWAYYA

Giving instructions to his charioteer and getting his chariot driven, he is waging a violent war; making signs with his hands, he is striking blows with his weapons; musical tunes are being played with small drums, trumpets and swords and he is dancing alongwith the shouts of "kill, kill" and also singing. —1387

SWAYYA

The shouts of "kill, kill" being heard with the blow of drums and with the striking of arms on the heads of the enemies, there is jingling of tunes; the warriors while fighting and falling down appear like offering their life-force with pleasure; the warriors are jumping up in anger and it cannot be said, whether it is the battlefield or the arena of dancing. —1388

BACHITTAR NATAK

SWAYYA

The battlefield has become like an arena of dancing, where there is play of musical instruments and drums; the heads of the enemies are producing a special sound and tune with the blows of arms; the warriors falling on the earth seem to be making offering of their life-breaths; they are dancing and singing like the actors the melody of "kill, kill." —1389

DOHIRA

Seeing such a battle, Krishna uttered loudly, his words being heard by all: "Who is that worthy warrior who is going to fight with Kharag Singh?" —1390

CHAUPAI

Ghan Singh and Ghaat Singh were such warriors, whom no one could defeat, Ghansur Singh and Ghamand Singh also moved and it seemed that death had itself called all the four. —1391

Then seeing towards them, the arrows were discharged on all the four and they were made lifeless; the horses and charioteers of their chariots were all wounded and alongwith the army, they were all sent to the abode of Yama. —1392

DOHIRA

The great warriors like Chapal Singh, Chatur Singh, Chitar Singh, Chaup Singh, etc., were present there. —1393

Chhattar Singh, Man Singh, Shatru Singh, etc., were the mighty generals who were present there. —1394

SWAYYA

All the ten kings in their fury fell upon Kharag Singh; on their arrival they discharged from their bow many arrows; sixteen horses of the chariots and ten mighty fighters were killed there; the twenty charioteers and thirty chariot-owners also died then. —1395

SWAYYA

Kharag Singh again ran forward killing seven horses and many soldiers on foot in the war; the poet Shyam says that at the same instant, Kharag Singh killed fifty other great warriors; A great portion of the army of the ten kings ran away just as the deer run away on seeing the lion in the forest; but in that war, the mighty Kharag Singh, stood firmly in great rage. —1396

KABIT

All the ten kings participated in the war; they put their army in adversity and avowed that no one will fear any one; all these ten kings, getting enraged, went before that mighty warrior Kharag Singh. When Kharag Singh pulled his bow upto his ear in great rage, he killed each king with ten arrows; though the kings were large like elephants and experts in warfare. —1397

DOHIRA

Five other warrior of Krishna fell upon the enemy, whose names were Chhakat Singh, Chhatar Singh, Chhaubh Singh, and Gaur Singh, etc. —1398

SORATHA

A great warrior Chhalbal Singh went to wage war with Kharag Singh, taking his shield and sword in his hands. —1399

CHAUPAI

When these five warriors went together and fell upon Kharag Singh, Kharag Singh took hold of his weapons and made all these warriors lifeless. —1400

DOHIRA

Twelve warriors of Krishna are extremely powerful, who have conquered the whole world with their strength. —1401

SWAYYA

Balam Singh, Mahamati Singh and Jagajat Singh, fell upon him (the army) with their swords Dhanesh Singh, Kripavat Singh, Joban Singh, Jiwan Singh, Jag Singh, Sada Singh, Jas Singh etc., also marched forward; taking his *shakti* (dagger) in his hand, Viram Singh, began the war with Kharag Singh. —1402

DOHIRA

A warrior named Mohan Singh accompanied him; he was carrying his weapons in his hands and was decorated with the quiver and armour. —1403

SWAYYA

All the kings struck their blows on the mighty

warrior Kharag Singh with their arrows, but he remained firm in the battlefield like a mountain without fear; the anger seemed greatly increased on his face and in the powerful fire of his anger, these arrows worked like ghee. —1404

SWAYYA

Krishna's force of warriors that was there, some of the warriors from it were knocked down by the enemy; he stood furiously again in the field, taking his sword in his hand; by killing the enemy's army, he decreased it like the waters of the ocean dried up by the blazing sun on doomsday. —1405

In the first place, he chopped the arms of the warriors and then their heads; the chariots alongwith the horses and the charioteers were destroyed in the battlefield; those who had passed their life in comfort, their corpses were being eaten by the jackals and vultures; those warriors who had destroyed the enemy in a dreadful war, they now became lifeless in the battlefield. —1406

SWAYYA

After killing the twelve kings, the king Kharag Singh looks splendid like the sun in distant darkness; the clouds of Sawan are feeling shy on listening to the thundering of Kharag Singh; it seems that over brimming its coasts, the ocean was thundering on the doomsday. —1407

SWAYYA

The king, exhibiting his bravery, caused much of the Yadava army to run away; the warriors who came to fight with him, they lost the hope of their survival; the poet says that any one who fought, taking his sword in his hand, he entered the abode of Death and he lost his body uselessly. —1408

SWAYYA

Getting infuriated again, he killed a thousand elephants and horse-riders; he chopped two hundred chariot and killed many sword-wielding warriors; he killed twenty thousand soldiers on foot, who fell down in the battlefield like trees; this spectacle appeared like the uprooted garden of Ravana by enraged Hanuman. —1409

SWAYYA

One demon named Abhar was on the side of Krishna; he fell upon Kharag Singh with strength; holding his weapons, he took his lightning-like sword in his hand and thundering in fury he showered arrows like Indra in rage on a gathering of *gopas*. —1410

The demon-forces rushed forward like clouds, but the king was not frightened even slightly; he caught hold of his bow and arrows in his hands, being greatly enraged in his mind; pulling his bow upto his ear, he pierced the heart of the enemy like a snake entering his hole. —1411

SWAYYA

After killing the enemy with his arrows, he made killings with his sword; because of the war, the blood began to flow on the earth and making the bodies lifeless, he knocked them down on the ground; the poet describing this spectacle says that it appears that they had not been hit by the sword and instead, they had been knocked down on account of the punishment of Yama. —1412

SWAYYA

When this demon was killed, then the army of demons in their fury, fell upon him; on their arrival, he began the war with different kinds of weapons; many of the demons were wounded at that place and Kharag Singh also received many wounds; enduring the agony of the wounds, the king fought and did not expose his wounds. —1413

All demons fell upon him with increased anger; taking up their bows, arrows, maces, daggers etc., they also drew out their swords from the scabbards; in the fire of ire, their life-energy increased and their limbs got instigated; they were striking their blows on the king like a goldsmith fashioning a body of gold. —1414

SWAYYA

All those who fought with the king were killed and in order to kill the remaining enemies, he caught hold of his weapons in his hands; taking his bow and arrows in his hands, the king made their bodies headless and those who still persisted to fight with him, they were all destroyed. —1415

SWAYYA

There was one very big demon warrior, who in extreme anger discharged many arrows on the king; these arrows penetrated into the body of the king till the final end; then the king, in great rage, struck his lance on the enemy, which penetrated into his body like lightening; it appeared that on account of the fear of Garuda, the king of the serpents came to hide himself in the forest. —1416

SWAYYA

He breathed his last, when he was hit by the lance and the king struck his blows on others with his sword; the king Kharag Singh, in great fury, killed the thirty demons at the place, where they were standing in the battlefield; they were standing lifeless like the dead mountains hit by the *vajra* of Indra. —1417

KABIT

The arms of many demons were chopped and the heads of many enemies were cut; many enemies ran away, many were killed, but still this warrior was moving with the enemy's army firmly taking his sword, axe, bow, mace, trident etc., in his hands; he is fighting while moving forward and is not receding even a step backwards; the king Kharag Singh is so swift that sometimes he is visible and sometimes he is not seen. —1418

Speech of the Poet
ARIL

Kharag Singh killed many demons in anger and they all appeared intoxicated and sleeping in the battlefield; those who survived, they ran away in fear and all of them came and lamented before Krishna. —1419

Speech of Krishna
DOHIRA

Then Krishna said to the army within its hearing: "Who is that person in my army, who is capable of fighting with Kharag Singh?" —1420

SORATHA

Two warriors of Krishna came out in extreme anger; both of them were glorious, brave and mighty warriors like Indra. —1421

SWAYYA

Jharajhar Singh and Jujhan Singh, taking with them a good deal of army, went in front of him; with the voices of the hoofs of the horses all the seven a nether-worlds and the earth trembled; Kharag Singh remained stable like the Sumeru mountain hit by the blows of wind; there was no impact on him, but the strength of Yadavas began to decrease. —1422

SWAYYA

In this fury, Kharag Singh destroyed a good deal of army of both the kings; he destroyed many horses, chariots etc., the poet says that this battlefield instead of looking like a field of battle, seemed like a place of the sport of Rudra (Shiva). —1423

Getting enraged in his mind, he penetrated into the army of the enemy and from the other side the enemy's army became very violent; Kharag Singh destroyed the enemy's army which fled away just as the darkness flies away fearing the sun. —1424

SWAYYA

Then Jharajhar Singh, getting infuriated, taking his sword in his hand struck a blow on Kharag Singh, which was snatched away from his hand; he struck the same sword on the enemy's body, by which his trunk was cut down and it fell on the earth; according to the poet it appeared that Shiva in great anger had cut down and thrown the head of Ganesha. —1425

SWAYYA

When this warriors was killed, then the second (Jujhan Singh) got infuriated in his mind; he caused his chariot to be driven and immediately taking his sword in his hand, went towards him (Kharag Singh); then the king also chopped off his head with his bow and arrows and he appeared like the one going forward greedily moving his tongue, but on account of the cutting away of his tongue, his hopes of getting relish had ended. —1426

Speech of the Poet

SWAYYA

When he chopped the warrior huge like elephant with his sword, then all other warriors who were there, fell upon him; they had got enraged taking their weapons in their hands; they were the praiseworthy warriors and appeared to have gathered as other kings gathered in the ceremony of swayamvara performed by a king. —1427

SWAYYA

All the enemies who came in front of the king, he knocked them down with his arrows; there were many fought persistently, but there were also many who ran away; many kings had gathered at one place and appeared like the intoxicated elephants gathered together at one place in the event of the forest-fire. —1428

SWAYYA

Killing many warriors in the battlefield, the king Kharag Singh became somewhat furious; as soon as he caught hold of the sword he knocked down visibly many elephants, horses and chariots; seeing him the enemies gathered together and began to think of killing him; it appeared like the deer gathered together in order to kill the lion and the lion remained standing fearlessly. —1429

SWAYYA

When the mighty king, in his anger, taking his weapons in his hands, killed the warriors according to his heart's desire; the heads of the warriors are being torn with the blows of Kharag Singh like the lotus-heads of the enemy torn in the tank of blood. —1430

DOHIRA

Seeing the dagger of Jujhan Singh, Kharag Singh took his sword in his hand and like lightning, he struck it on the head of the enemy and killed him. —1431

SWAYYA

In this way in this great war, Jujhar Singh also, went to heaven while fighting and the army which was with him, the king (Kharag Singh) was torn into fragments; those who survived, without caring for their honour and custom they fled away; they saw in the king Kharag Singh Yama, carrying the death-sentence in his hand. —1432

DOHIRA

When Kharag Singh caught hold of his bow and arrows in his hands, then all of them lost patience and all the chieftains and mighty warriors left the war-arena. —1433

When Krishna saw the Yadava army running away, then calling Satyak towards him, he said, "Go with your army." —1434

SWAYYA

He sent all his great warriors including Satyak, Krat Verma, Udhava, Balram, Vasudeva, etc., to the front and they all showered so many arrows in order to destroy Kharag Singh like powerful clouds sent by Indra for bursting into rain on the Govardhan mountain. —1435

SWAYYA

The king enduring the terrible rain of arrows also discharged arrows from his side; he wounded the horses of all the kings and killed all their charioteers; after that he jumped into the forces on foot and began to send the warriors to the abode of Yama; he shattered the chariots of many and deprived of their chariots, the Yadavas ran away. —1436

SWAYYA

"Why are you running away from the battlefield? You will not have such opportunity of war again," Kharag Singh said to Satyak, "Keep the war-tradition in your mind and do not run away, because when you will visit some society, the people will say that the king of the cowards is the same; therefore consider it and fight with me, because on running away to your home, how you will show your face there?" —1437

SWAYYA

Hearing these words, none of the warriors came back; then the king, in rage, followed the enemy: "The Yadavas were running away like goats and Kharag Singh seems like a lion; the king ran and met Balram and put his bow in his neck; then laughingly he subdued Balram, but subsequently let him go." —1438

DOHIRA

When all the warriors came before Krishna after running away, then Krishna and all the other Yadavas together devised a remedy. —1439

SWAYYA

"Let all of us besiege him," thinking like this they all marched forward; they placed Krishna in front and they all followed him in rage; they pulled their bows upto their ears, they showered arrows on the king like raindrops in rainy season. —1440

He (Kharag Singh) intercepted all their arrows he inflicted several wounds on the body of Krishna; so much blood oozed out from those wounds that Krishna could not stay in the battlefield; all the other kings, seeing Kharag Singh were wonder-struck; no patience remained in the body of any one and all the Yadava warriors ran away. —1441

After the quick departure of Krishna, all the warriors lost patience and they became greatly agitated and worried seeing the wounds on their bodies; they got their chariots driven and for the fear of the shower of arrows, they ran away and considered in their mind that Krishna has not acted sagaciously in taking up war with Kharag Singh. —1442

DOHIRA

Reflecting in his mind, Krishna returned again to the battlefield alongwith the Yadava army. —1443

Speech of Krishna

DOHIRA

Krishna said to Kharag Singh, "Now you hold your sword, because I shall kill you, till one-fourth of the day still remains. —1444

SWAYYA

Taking his bow and arrows in his hands and in great fury, Krishna said to Kharag Singh, "You have fearlessly swayed the battlefield for a short while; the intoxicated elephant can only be proud till the lion in fury does not attack him; why do you want to lose your life? Run away and give weapons to us. —1445

Hearing the words of Krishna, the king replied, "Why are you raising hue and cry in the battlefield like a looted individual in the forest; you are persistently like fools, though you have run away from the field several times before me; though you are called the Lord of Braja, but inspite of losing your respect, you are keeping your position in your society." —1446

Speech of Kharag Singh

SWAYYA

"Why are you waging war in anger, O Krishna! come and live comfortably for a few days more; you are still young with a beautiful face; you are still in early youth; O Krishna! go to your home; take rest and live in peace; do not deprive your parents of your support by losing your life in the war." —1447

SWAYYA

Why are you waging war with me with persistence? O Krishna! uselessly the war is a very bad thing and you will not gain anything by getting enraged; you know that you cannot win this war over me, therefore run away instantly, otherwise ultimately you will have to go to the abode of Yama.—1448

SWAYYA

Hearing these words Krishna took his bow in his hand and pulling it, he discharged an arrow; Krishna inflicted a wound on the king and the king on Krishna; the warriors of both the sides waged a dreadful war; there was an enormous shower of arrows from both sides and it appeared that the clouds have spread over the sky. —1449

SWAYYA

The arrows discharged by the other warriors for the help of Krishna none of them hit the king, but they were themselves killed by the distant arrows; the Yadava army, mounting on the chariots, and pulling the bows, fell upon the king; according to the poet, they come in anger, but the king destroys the clusters of the army in an instant. —1450

Some of them became lifeless and fell in the battlefield and some of them fled away; some of them were wounded and some of them kept fighting in anger; the king taking the sword in his hand, chopped the soldiers into bits; it appeared that the audacity of the king was like beloved and all of them seeing him as lovers. —1451

SWAYYA

The king in fury knocked down many mighty warriors; getting enraged, he killed the great heroes in an instant; he shattered their chariots and killed many elephants and horses with his arrows; the king danced in the battlefield like Rudra and those who survived, fled away. —1452

SWAYYA

Getting the army run away and running himself again, the king came to fight with Balram and Krishna and he waged the war fearlessly, taking the lance, axe, mace, sword, etc., in his hands; after this he took bow and arrows in his hands and like the drops of rain from the clouds, he filled the tank of the body of Krishna with the arrows. —1453

DOHIRA

When the body of Krishna was pierced by arrows, then he put his arrow named Indrastra in his bow and discharged it after reciting *mantras*. —1454

SWAYYA

As soon as the arrow was discharged, many mighty warriors like Indra manifested themselves on the earth and making the king their target, they began to shoot the arrows of fire; the king, taking his bow, intercepted those arrows and with his arrows, he wounded the manifested warriors; besmeared with blood and in fear, reached before Indra, the king of gods. —1455

SWAYYA

The warriors glorious like sun, got enraged and taking lances, swords maces etc., fought with the king Kharag Singh; they all gathered together at one place like the black bees gathered to take fragrance of flower-like arrows of the king. —1456

DOHIRA

All the menifested gods besieged the king from all the four directions; I relate now the courage shown at that time by the king. —1457

Speech of the Poet

SWAYYA

He discharged twelve arrows towards Surya and ten towards Chandrama he discharged a hundred arrows towards Indra, which, piercing his body went to the other side; all the Yakshas, Devas, Kinnars, Gandharvas, etc., who were there, the king knocked them down with his arrows; many of the manifested gods ran away from battlefield, but there were many who stood there firmly. —1458

SWAYYA

When the horrible warriors waged, then Indra in ire caught hold of his dagger in his hand and with great force hurled it on the head of that king; Kharag Singh intercepted it and let it fall on the ground, the arrow of the king is like Garuda and the dagger like she-serpent which was drowned by the Garuda-arrow. —1459

SWAYYA

Afflicted by the arrows Indra etc., ran away; Surya, Chandra and others all abandoned the battlefield and were extremely frightened in their mind; after having been wounded many of them ran away and none of them stayed there; all the gods getting ashamed went back to their abodes. —1460

DOHIRA

When all the gods ran away, the king became egoistic; now he pulled his bow and showered arrows on Krishna. —1461

Then Krishna, in fury, took out his *daityastra* (the arm meant for the demons) and discharged it after reciting *mantras* over this wonderful arrow. —1462

SWAYYA

That arrow created dreadful demons, who had discs, axes, knives, swords, shields, maces and lances in their hands; they had big maces in their hands for striking blows; they even uprooted the leafless trees; they began to frighten the big king, protruding their teeth and extending their eyes. —1463

SWAYYA

They had long hair on their heads, wore dreadful garbs and had large hair on their bodies; they were crushing the human bones in their mouths and their teeth were clattering; their eyes were like the sea of blood; who could fight with them? They were the wielders of bows and arrows, roaming throughout the nights and always absorbed in vicious acts. —1464

SWAYYA

From that side the demons fell upon him and from this side the king stood firmly peacefully; then, strengthening his mind and in rage, he said this to the enemies, "Today I shall knock down all of you;" saying this, he held up his bow and arrows; seeing the endurance of the king Kharag Singh, the army of demons felt pleased. —1465

SWAYYA

Pulling his bow, that mighty warrior showered his arrows on the enemies; he chopped someone's arm and in his rage, he discharged his arrow on someone's chest; someone, having been wounded fell down in the battlefield and some coward seeing the dreadful war ran away; only one powerful demon survived there, who stabilising himself said to the king: —1466

SWAYYA

"O King! why are you fighting? We will not let you go alive; your body is long and elegant; where shall we get such food? O fool! you do not know that we shall chew you with our teeth; we shall roast the bits of your flesh with the fire of our arrows and devour them." —1467

DOHIRA

Hearing these words, the king spoke in anger, "He, who goes away safe from me, consider that he has released himself from the bondage of the milk of his mother." —1468

Hearing these words, the demon army fell upon the king and besieged him from all the four sides like the fence of the field. —1469

CHAUPAI

When the demons besieged the king, who became extremely enraged in his mind; taking his bow and arrows in his hands, he killed many enemies. —1470

There was a demon named Karurkaram, who had conquered many wars; he went before Kharag Singh and both the heroes were enraged in a terrible war. —1471

SWAYYA

When, taking his weapons, he firmly resisted the king, he fought in many ways and no one retraced his steps from the battlefield; the king taking his sword in his hand, killed the enemy and his head fell on the earth; though he had breathed his last, but his anger did not subside even then; he pressed his lip within his teeth. —1472

DOHIRA

When Karurkaram was knocked down in the battlefield by Kharag Singh, then another demon came out of the army of demons. —1473

SORATHA

This demon named Karurdaitya was extremely powerful; he had earlier fought in several battles; he confronted the king with firmness and did not fear even slightly. —1474

CHAUPAI

When he saw the killing of Karurkaram with his own eyes, he held up his sword; now Karurdaitya fell upon the king, getting enraged, and it seemed that the death like cloud had gushed out. —1475

On coming, he challenged the king, "Where are you going after killing my brother? Now I shall fight with you and shall despatch you there where my brother has gone." —1476

Saying this, he held up his sword and getting enraged, he struck a terrible blow; the king saw this and cutting his sword, he knocked him also in the field. —1477

DOHIRA

Karurdaitya, and Karurkarma both reached the abode of Yama; the king taking his weapons, besieged their army in the battlefield. —1478

SWAYYA

The demons, who had survived fell upon the king; they had arrows, swords, maces, lances and fire-arms in their hands; the king, with his bow and arrows, chopped them midway and taking the arrows out of his quiver, pierced their chests. —1479

CHAUPAI

Then all the enemies ran away and none of them stayed before him; many demons were killed and those who survived, they ran away from the war-arena. —1480

SWAYYA

When all the demons ran away, the king, in great fury, showered his arrows on Krishna, which pierced his body and came out from the other side and then piercing the bodies of other persons, they penetrated into the bodies of the others; look at the courage of the king, though he himself is alone, but he is killing many. —1481

Then Krishna discharged his *Varunastra* (arm in relation to god Varuna), which hit the king Kharag Singh; Varuna reached there, assuming the form of a lion and brought with him the army of streams. —1482

On arrival, Varuna blew the horn (roaming like a lion) and in fury fell upon the king; listening to the dreadful roar, all the three worlds trembled, but the king Kharag Singh did not become fearful. —1483

SWAYYA

With his lance-like arrows, the king slashed the body of Varuna; the king, in great fury pierced the heart of the seven oceans; wounding all the streams, he saturated their limbs with blood; the king of water (Varuna) could not stay in the battlefield and ran away towards his home. —1484

CHAUPAI

When Varuna went away to his home the king then discharged his arrows on Krishna; at that time, Krishna shot his arm of Yama and thereby Yama manifested himself and fell upon the king. —1485

SWAYYA

The demon named Vikrat, greatly infuriated, fell upon the king Kharag Singh and taking up his bow, sword, mace, lance etc., he waged a dreadful war; continuing the discharge of his arrows, he manifested himself in many figures; the poet says that in this war, the arrow of the king was hitting like Garuda and knocking down the Cobra of the arrow of the enemy. —1486

SWAYYA

After killing Vikrat, the king said to Yama, "What then, if you have killed many people till now and you are carrying a very large staff in your hand; I have taken a vow today that I shall kill you; I am going to kill you; you may do whatever you think in your mind, because all the three worlds are aware of my strength." —1487

SWAYYA

After saying these words, according to the poet Shyam, the king was engaged in war with Yama; in this war the ghosts, jackals, crows and vampires drank the blood to their heart's content; the king is not even dying with the blows of Yama; it appears that he has quaffed ambrosia; when the king took his bow and arrows in his hands, the Yama had to run away ultimately. —1488

SORATHA

When Yama was made to run away, then the king, seeing towards Krishna said, "O the great warrior of the battlefield! Why do you not come to fight with me?" —1489

SWAYYA

He, who through the repetition of *mantras* and through the performance of austerities, does not come to abide in the mind; who is not realised through the performance of *yajnas* and giving charities; who is eulogised by even Indra, Brahma, Narada, Sharda, Vyasa, Parashar and Shukadeva; to that Krishna, the Lord of Braja, today the king Kharag Singh invited him from the whole society for war by challenging him. —1490

CHAUPAI

Then Krishna took the *Yakshastra* (the arm

relating to Yakshas) in his hand and pulling his bow discharged it; now both the sons of Kuber, Nalkoober and Manigreeve came in the battlefield. —1491

They took many Yakshas, the generous bestowers of wealth, and Kinnars alongwith them, who getting enraged, reached the battlefield; all the army came with them and they waged a terrible war with the king. —1492

SWAYYA

In great rage, taking their weapons in their hands, all of them together fell upon the king, the king taking out the arrows from his quiver, discharged them, pulling his bow; the warriors and charioteers were deprived of their chariots and the king despatched them to the abode of Yama; none of them could stay at that place and all the Yakshas and Kinnars fled away. —1493

SWAYYA

Then, in his fury, Nalkoober called his warriors for fighting; Kuber also stood there, keeping his wealth in safety; all the Yakshas then came collectively; shouting "kill, kill" they gleamed their swords and it seemed that the Ganas of Yama had attacked Kharag Singh, carrying their staffs of death. —1494

CHAUPAI

When the whole army of Kuber came, the anger increased in the mind of the king; he held up the bow and arrows in his hands and killed innumerable soldiers in an instant. —1495

DOHIRA

The mighty army of the Yakshas was despatched to the abode of Yama by the king and getting enraged, wounded Nalkoober. —1496

Then the king inflicted a sharp arrow in the chest of Kuber, which made him run away and all his pride was shattered. —1497

CHAUPAI

All of them ran away alongwith the army and none of them kept standing there; Kuber was extremely frightened in his mind and his desire to fight again ended. —1498

ARIL

When all the Yakshas had run away, then the mighty Krishna discharged *Rudrastra* (the arm in relation to Rudra), which made the earth and the nether-world tremble; then Shiva holding his trident got up and ran; he reflected how the Lord Krishna had remembered him? —1499

Rudra and his other warriors started moving alongwith him; Ganesh also accompanied with all his army; all other Ganas, taking up their weapons, moved along; they were all thinking as to who was that mighty hero born in the world, for killing whom, they had been called. —1500

All of them are thinking as to who can be that mighty one born in the world; the god Shiva and his Ganas, in their fury, came out of their abodes. —1501

When the god of dissolution came himself in the battlefield, then the field itself indeed became the field of anxiety. —1502

DOHIRA

Already when Ganesh, Shiva, Dattatreya and Ganas were viewing the battlefield, there and then the king himself challenged them to fight. —1503

SWAYYA

"O Shiva! whatever strength you have today, use it in this war; O Ganesh! do you have so much strength as to fight with me? Hell Kartikeya! For what you are becoming egoistic? You will be killed with one arrow; still nothing has gone wrong, why do You want to die while fighting in the war?" —1504

Speech of Shiva addressed to Kharag Singh

SWAYYA

Shiva spoke in anger, "O king! why are you so proud? Do not indulge in strife with us; you will see just now what strength we have? If you have greater courage, then why are you delaying, why do you not take your bow and arrows in your hands? You have a very large body and by piercing it with my arrows, I shall lighten it." —1505

Speech of Kharag Singh addressed to Shiva

SWAYYA

"O Shiva! why are you so proud? Now when there will be dreadful fighting, you will run away; with the infliction of a single arrow all your army will dance like a monkey; all the army of the ghosts and fiends will be vanquished and there will be no survivor; O Shiva! listen, this earth saturated with your blood will wear the red garb today." —1506

TOTAK STANZA

Hearing these words, Shiva held up his bow and arrows and pulling his bow upto his ear, he discharged the arrow, which struck the face of the king; it appeared that Garuda had caught the king of the snakes. —1507

Then the king struck his lance, which hit the chest of Shiva; it appeared that the ray of the sun was hovering over the lotus. —1508

Then Shiva pulled it out with both his hands and threw that lance like a black she-serpent on the earth; then the king drew out his sword from the scabbard and with great force struck its blow on Shiva. —1509

Shiva became unconscious and fell on the ground like the peak of the mountain falling down with the blow of *vajra*; when the army saw this condition of Shiva, then Ganesh, the son of Shiva, took the lance in his hand. —1510

Taking the *shakti* (lance) in his hand, he came in front of the king and with the full force of his hand, he threw it towards the king in such a way that it was not a lance, but death itself. —1511

SWAYYA

On coming, the king intercepted the lance and inflicted a sharp arrow in the heart of the enemy; that arrow attacked the vehicle of Ganesh; the second arrow hit slantingly on the forehead of Ganesh and it appeared like the arrow-like goad struck in the forehead of an elephant. —1512

On this side, regaining consciousness, mounting on his vehicle Shiva discharged the arrow from his bow and he inflicted an extremely sharp arrow in the heart of the king; Shiva was pleased to think that the king had been killed, but the king was not even slightly frightened by the impact of this arrow; the king took out an arrow from his quiver and pulled his bow. —1513

DOHIRA

The king, making Shiva his target, pulled his bow upto his ear, discharged an arrow towards his heart in order to kill him certainly. —1514

CHAUPAI

When he discharged his arrow towards the heart of Shiva and at the same time, that mighty one looked towards the army of Shiva; Kartikeya was coming speedily alongwith his army and the Ganas of Ganesh were getting extremely infuriated. —1515

SWAYYA

Seeing both of them coming, the king was extremely enraged in his mind and with the strength of his arms, he struck an arrow on their vehicle; he despatched in an instant the army of Ganas to the abode of Yama; seeing the king advancing towards Kartikeya, Ganesha abandoned the battlefield and fled away. —1516

Destroying and forcing the army of Shiva to run away, the king was pleased in his mind and said loudly, "Why all of you are running away in fear?" Kharag Singh then took his conch in his hand and blew it and he appeared as Yama, carrying his weapons in the battlefield. —1517

SWAYYA

When his challenge was heard, then carrying their swords in their hands, the warriors came back to fight; though they were definitely feeling ashamed, but now they stood firmly and fearlessly and they all blew their conches together; with the shouts of "kill, kill," they challenged and said, "O king! you have killed many people; now we shall not leave you, we shall kill you," saying this, they discharged volleys of arrows. —1518

SWAYYA

When there was dreadful destruction, the king held up his weapons and carrying the dagger,

BACHITTAR NATAK

mace, lance, axe and sword in his hands, he challenged the enemy; taking his bow and arrows in his hands and looking here and there, he killed many enemies; the faces of the warriors fighting with the king became red and ultimately they were all defeated. —1519

SWAYYA

Taking his bow and arrows in his hands, Shiva was extremely enraged he got his vehicle driven towards the king with the motive of killing him; he shouted loudly to the king, "I am just now going to kill you" and saying thus, he raised the dreadful sound of his conch; it appeared that the clouds were thundering on the doomsday. —1520

SWAYYA

That terrible sound pervaded the whole universe and even Indra was wonder-struck on listening to it; the echo of this sound thundered in the seven oceans, streams, tanks, and Sumeru mountain etc., Seshanaga listening to this sound trembles; he thought that all the fourteen worlds had trembled; the beings of all the world, listening to this sound, were bewildered; but the king Kharag Singh was not frightened. —1521

Speech of Kharag Singh addressed to Shiva
SWAYYA

Seeing towards Rudra, the king said within his hearing, "O Yogi! what difference your deceit of raising the sound will make? You engage yourself in begging for the alms of rice; I do not fear your archery; only the Kshatriyas are meant to fight, this is not the task of yogis." —1522

SWAYYA

Saying this, he took out his large dagger and in anger hurled it on the body of Shiva; after striking the blow of the dagger, on the body of Shiva, the king roaring like the sea challenged him; Shiva fell down with the blow of the dagger; his necklace of skulls slipped and fell down; somewhere his Bull fell down and somewhere his trident fell down. —1523

SWAYYA

Now the army of Shiva, in fury, surrounded the king, but the king also remained stable in the battlefield and did not retrace even one step; in that garden of the battlefield, the chariots look like small tanks, the banners like trees and the warriors like birds; the Ganas of Shiva as birds appear to fly away, when the king as falcon pounces upon them. —1524

DOHIRA

Some Ganas of Shiva remained stable; these Ganas were Ganchhabi, Ganraj, Mahavir, and Malroy. —1525

SWAYYA

From the warriors came back Ganraj, Mahavir and Ganchhabi; they returned with red eyes because they were so powerful that they had made Yama only a toy; the king seeing the enemies coming did not become fearful even slightly; while killing the Ganas in the battlefield he felt these Ganas were not actually fighting, and instead they were casting spells. —1526

CHAUPAI

Then the king killed the enemy with his arrow; the army of the Ganas looked towards him with malice; the king challenged Ganesh again, who being frightened ran away from the field. —1527

Then Shiva became somewhat conscious and he fled away from the war-arena; other Ganas, ran away in fear; there seemed to be no warrior, who could confront the king. —1528

CHAUPAI

When Krishna saw Shiva running away, then he reflected in his mind that he would then fight the enemy himself; either he would kill the enemy of die himself. —1529

Then Krishna went before the king and waged a dreadful war; making him the target, the king shot an arrow and dismounted Krishna from the chariot. —1530

Speech of the Poet
SWAYYA

He, whose Name is muttered ever by Brahma, Indra, Sanak etc., He, on whom Surya,

Chandra, Narada, Sharda meditate; He, whom the adepts search in their contemplation and whose mystery is not comprehended by the great sages like Vyasa and Parashar, Kharag Singh caught him in the battlefield by his hair. —1531

SWAYYA

He, who killed Bakasura, Aghasura and Dhenkasura in an instant; He, who became famous in all the three worlds by killing Keshi, Mahkhasura, Mushiti, Chandur, etc., that Krishna, who had knocked down many enemies with skill and had killed Kansa by catching him from his hair; the same Krishna has been caught by his hair by the king Kharag Singh; it seems that he has avenged the killing of Kansa by catching his hair. —1532

SWAYYA

The king then thought that if he killed Krishna, all his army would run away; with whom then he would fight? To whom then be would inflict a wound or from whom he be wounded himself, therefore the king set Krishna free and said, "Go away, there is no other warrior like you." —1533

SWAYYA

The great bravery that the king exhibited, was incomparable; seeing this spectacle all the warriors ran away, none of them caught his bow and arrows; the great fighters, fearing in their mind, abandoned their weapons and fled away and in the battlefield the king set free Krishna with his own will. —1534

CHAUPAI

When Krishna was set free, by loosening the grasp of his hair, he forgot his power and felt ashamed; then Brahma manifested himself and ended the mental anxiety of Krishna. —1535

CHAUPAI

He (Brahma) said to Krishna, "O Lotus-eyed! do not feel ashamed; I now please you by relating the story of the bravery (of the king)." —1536

Speech of Brahma
TOTAK

When this king was born, he left his home and went to the forest; with great austerities, he pleased the Goddess Chandika from whom he obtained the boon of conquering the enemy. —1537

CHAUPAI

I relate to you the remedy for killing him; even if Vishnu comes to fight with him, he will cause him to run away without delay. —1538

CHAUPAI

Call Indra and twelve Suryas and in unison with eleven Rudras attack him; call also Chandrama, eight Yama warriors, Brahma told Krishna all such method. —1539

SORATHA

Move to the battlefield, after calling all these warriors and challenging the king, make your army fight with him. —1540

CHAUPAI

Then call all the heavenly damsels and make them dance before him; command also the god of love and make his mind infatuated. —1541

DOHIRA

Then as told by Brahma, Krishna did all that; he called Indra, Surya, Rudra and Yamas. —1542

CHAUPAI

Then all came to Krishna and getting enraged marched for war; on this side they began to wage war and on the other side, the heavenly damsels began to dance in the sky. —1543

SWAYYA

Throwing their side-glances, the beautiful young damsels began to dance and sing in melodious voices; playing on the lyres, drums and tabors etc., they exhibited various kinds of gestures; they sang in the musical modes of Sarang, Sorath, Malvi, Ramkali, Nat etc., seeing all this let us not talk of the enjoyers, even the yogis got attracted. —1544

SWAYYA

On that side, in the sky, an elegant dance is going on, on this side, the warriors are engaged in war taking their lances, swords and daggers; the poet says that these warriors have come to fight in the war-arena, fearlessly gnashing their teeth; those who die while fighting and the trunks that rise in the battlefield, the heavenly damsels are relating them. —1545

DOHIRA

The king, in fury, waged a dreadful war and all the gods had to face extreme difficulties. —1546

SWAYYA

The king shot twenty-two arrows to the eleven Rudras and twenty-four to twelve Suryas; he shot the one thousand arrows towards Indra, six to Kartikeya and twenty-five to Krishna; he shot sixty arrows to Chandrama, seventy to Ganesh and sixty-four to the eight Vasus of gods; seven arrows were shot to Kuber and nine to Yama and killed the remaining ones by one arrow each. —1547

SWAYYA

After piercing Varuna with his arrows, he also shot an arrow in the heart of Nalkoober and Yama; how to count the others? All those who were enraged in war, they all received blows from the king; all became doubtful about their own protection, none of them took courage to see towards the king; they all considered the king as Kal (Death) who manifested himself at the end of the age in order to destroy all of them. —1548

CHAUPAI

They abandoned the war and became fearful; none of them went forward to fight with the king; all of them thought that this king would not be killed by any one. —1549

Then Brahma seeing all the army of Krishna having died, he said to Krishna, "Till the time, he has the charmed amulet in his hand, the *vajra* and trident are insignificant before him. —1550

Therefore now becoming a beggar, beg this from him; the crown that he has obtained from Ram, it could not be obtained by Indra etc. —1551

When you will take away the amulet from his hand, you will then be able to kill him in an instant; if he abandons it from his hand through any method, then he can be killed at any time." —1552

CHAUPAI

Hearing this, Krishna and Brahma put on the garb of a Brahmin and went to beg the amulet from him; then on begging, he recognised Krishna and Brahma and according to the poet, he said: —1553

Speech of Kharag Singh

SWAYYA

"O Krishna (Vishnu)! You have put on the garb of a Brahmin and have come to deceive me like the king Bali; O Brahma! You also under the control of Krishna, are running and roaming, forsaking your austerity, why? Just as the fire cannot be concealed by smoke, in the same manner, seeing you, I have understood your act of deceit; when you people have come in the garb of a beggar, then beg from me according to your heart's desire." —1554

DOHIRA

When the king said like this to Brahma, then Brahma said, "O king! become praiseworthy and give me the crown that had come out of the fire of *yajna*." —1555

When Brahma had begged it, then Krishna spoke, "Give me the amulet that had been given to you by the Goddess Chandi." —1556

CHAUPAI

Then the king thought in his mind that he had not to live for four ages, therefore he should not delay in his task of *dharma* and the things that Brahma and Krishna are begging, he should give them. —1557

SWAYYA

"O mind! why are you in doubt about the body, you have not to remain stable in the world for ever; what more virtuous act you can perform? Therefore do this praiseworthy task in the war, because ultimately once, the body is to be abandoned; O mind! do not delay, because you will avail nothing except repentance, when the opportunity is lost; therefore forsaking anxiety, give away the begged articles without any hesitation, because you will never again meet such a beggar like the Lord Himself." —1558

"Whatever Krishna is asking for, O my mind! give it without any hesitation; He, from whom all the world begs, He is standing before you as a beggar, therefore do not delay further; leave all other ideas, there will remain no shortage in your comfort; on giving charity, one should not be proud and thoughtful; therefore get the profit of approbation after surrendering everything." —1559

SWAYYA

Whatever Krishna had begged in the garb of a Brahmin, the king gave the same to him; alongwith this, whatever was in the mind of Brahma the king also did that; whatever they had asked for, the king handed it over affectionately; in this way with charity and with sword, in the bravery of both kinds, the king earned great praise. —1560

SWAYYA

Brahma took away the crown and Krishna the amulet, then all the warriors roared and getting extremely enraged in their mind, they fell upon the king; the king had destroyed many warriors and they were looking so elegant, while lying on the earth as if the hermits were sleeping on the earth, after smearing their bodies with ashes and eating thorn-apples. —1561

After searching for the king, all besieged him, who became extremely angry, He, moving in the battlefield, caught hold of a firm bow in his hand and knocked down the forces of Surya, Chandra and Yama like the leaves falling on the ground by the blowing wind in the season of Phagun. —1562

SWAYYA

Taking a large bow in his hand, the king inflicted an arrow in the forehead of Rudra; he shot one arrow in the heart of Kuber, who ran away from the field, throwing away his weapons; Varuna, seeing their plight, became fearful and fled away; on this, Yama in fury fell upon the king, who knocked him down on the ground with his arrow. —1563

SWAYYA

When Yama was knocked down, then the army of Krishna ran forward, in ire, and two of its warriors began a dreadful war, taking up various types of arms; the Yadava warriors were very brave; the king, in his anger, killed them; and in this way, both the brothers, Bahubali and Vikramakrat were despatched to the abode of Yama. —1564

SWAYYA

Mahabali Singh and Tej Singh, who were with them, they were also killed by the king; then Mahajas Singh, another warrior, getting enraged, came in front of the king, who challenged him, holding out his dagger; with only one stroke of the dagger, he went to the abode of Yama. —1565

CHAUPAI

Then Uttam Singh and Pralaya Singh ran forward and Param Singh also reached taking up his sword; the king killed all the five warriors including Atipavittar Singh and Shri Singh. —1566

DOHIRA

Fateh Singh and Fauj Singh marched forward in anger, they were also challenged and killed by the king. —1567

ARIL

Bhim Singh, Bhuj Singh, Maha Singh, Man Singh, and Madan Singh, all of them in rage fell upon the king; other great warriors also came forward, taking up their weapons, but the king killed all of them in an instant. —1568

SORATHA

There was another great warrior of Krishna, named Vikat Singh, he fell upon the king, bound by the duty of his Lord. —1569

DOHIRA

Seeing Vikat Singh coming, the king spread his bow and inflicted an arrow in the chest of the enemy; on being struck by the arrow, Vikat Singh breathed his last. —1570

SORATHA

Another warrior named Rudra Singh was standing near Krishna, that great warrior also reached in front of the king. —1571

CHAUPAI

Seeing Rudra Singh, Kharag Singh held up his

bow; he discharged his arrow with such strength that the enemy was killed when it hit him. —1572

SWAYYA

Himmat Singh, furiously, struck a blow with his sword on the king; the king saved himself from this blow with his shield; the sword struck the protruded pat of the shield and the sparks came out like the fire of the third eye shown by Shiva to Indra. —1573

SWAYYA

Then Himmat Singh again gave a blow to the king with his might; when he turned towards his army after striking the blow, the king challenged him at the same time and gave a blow of his sword on his head; he fell like down lifeless on the earth; the sword struck him on the head like the lightning cutting and dividing the mountain into two halves. —1574

SWAYYA

When Himmat Singh was killed, all the warriors were highly infuriated all the mighty warriors including Maharudra etc., they all together fell upon the king and with their bows, arrows, swords maces and lances, they hurled many blows on the king; the king saved himself from their blows and seeing such bravery of the king, all the enemies became fearful. —1575

SWAYYA

All the Ganas including Rudra, all of them together fell upon the king; seeing them all coming this great warrior challenged them and discharged his arrows; some of them fell down wounded there and some of them becoming fearful fled away; some of them fearlessly fought with the king, who killed them all. —1576

SWAYYA

Conquering the ten hundred Ganas of Shiva, the king killed one lakh Yakshas; he killed twenty-three lakh demons who reached the abode of Yama; he deprived Krishna of his chariot and wounded Daruk, his charioteer; seeing this spectacle, the twelve Suryas, Chandra, Kuber, Varuna and Pashupatnath fled away. —1577

SWAYYA

Then the king knocked down many horses and elephants and also thirty thousand charioteers; he killed thirty-six lakh soldiers on foot and ten lakh horsemen; he killed one lakh kings and caused the army of Yakshas to run away; after killing the twelve Suryas and eleven Rudras, the king fell upon the army of the enemy. —1578

SWAYYA

After killing sixty thousand warriors, the knocked down one lakh Yakshas; he deprived one lakh Yadavas of their chariots and made the Yakshas his target; he scattered fifty lakh soldiers on foot in fragments on the earth; instead of them, the warriors who attacked the king with their swords, he killed them all. —1579

SWAYYA

The king, twisting his whiskers, fearlessly fell upon the army; he again killed one lakh horsemen and shattered the pride of Surya and Chandra; even with a single arrow, he knocked down Yama on the ground; he did not become fearful even slightly; those who called themselves heroes, the king chopped them into bits. —1580

SWAYYA

He killed in the war ten lakh Yakshas and about a lakh warriors of Varuna; he also killed innumerable warriors of Indra and did not suffer defeat; he made Satyaki, Balram and Vasudeva unconscious; Yama and Indra, without taking their weapons, fled away from the battlefield. —1581

DOHIRA

When the king waged the war with such fury, then Krishna taking up his bow and arrows came forward. —1582

BISHANPADA

When Krishna, in fury, fell on the enemy powerfully, taking up his bow in his hand, then getting infuriated, the king eulogised the Lord in his mind. He, whose glory is known in all the three worlds, even Seshanaga could not comprehend whose limits and even the

Vedas could not know whose mystery, His name is Krishna, the son of Nand; He, who stringed the serpent Kaliya, the manifestation of Kal (Death), He who caught Kansa by his hair and knocked him down; I have, in fury, challenged Him in the war; He, who is even meditated upon by the sages, but still they cannot perceive Him in their heart; I am very fortunate to have waged dreadful war with Him. —1583

"O the Lord of Yadavas! You have given me your Support; even the saints do not have your sight, but I have perceived You. . . . I know that there is no other mighty warrior equal to me, who has challenged Krishna in the war; He, who is eulogised by Shukadeva, Narada and Sharda and still they are not able to comprehend His mystery, I have challenged him today for war in anger." —1584

SWAYYA

Eulogising in this way, the king caught hold of his bow and arrows in his hands and discharged many arrows, while running; those warriors who came in front of him in the war, he did not allow them to go but killed them; he did not take up his weapons to kill the wounded and killing the Yadava army, the king fell upon Krishna. —1585

SWAYYA

The king caused the crown of Krishna fell down with his arrow; he killed fifteen hundred elephants and horses; he made twelve lakh Yakshas lifeless; seeing such a war, the pride of the warriors was shattered. —1586

SWAYYA

He was engaged in war with Krishna for ten days and ten nights, but did not suffer defeat; There he killed the four greatest military units of Indra; the warriors becoming unconscious fell down on the earth and many warriors were defeated while fighting; that mighty warrior raised such a challenging shout that many warriors, in fear, fled away. —1587

SWAYYA

After hearing the challenging shout all the warriors came back again, then mighty warrior (king) inflicted blows on them with his arrows; their bodies fell down midway, because the arrows penetrated through their bodies; several warriors taking up their swords and shields ran forward, but seeing the bravery of the king Kharag Singh, they hesitated. —1588

An elephant of Indra named Jagdiragh, fell upon the king, in anger; on coming, thundering like the cloud, he exhibited his bravery; seeing him, the king took his sword in his hand and chopped down the elephants, he ran away and it seemed that he had forgotten his trunk at home and was going to bring it. —1589

DOHIRA

On this side the war is continuing and on that side, the five Pandavas reached for the help of Krishna. —1590

With them there were several extremely big military units alongwith chariots, soldiers on foot, elephants and horses; they all came there for the support of Krishna. —1591

DOHIRA

There were with them two extremely large military units of Malechhas which were bedecked with armours, daggers and *shaktis* (lances). —1592

SWAYYA

Mirs, Sayyads, Sheikhs and Pathans all fell upon the king; they were greatly enraged and were wearing armours and quivers were tied around their waists, they fell upon the king with dancing eyes, gnashing teeth and pulled eyebrows; they were challenging him and (with their weapons) inflicted many wounds on him. —1593

DOHIRA

Enduring the angiush of all the wounds, in extreme anger, the king, holding his bow and arrows despatched many enemies to the abode of Yama. —1594

KABIT

After killing Sher Khan, the king chopped the head of Said Khan and waging such a war, he jumped amongst the Sayyads; after killing

Sayyad Mir and Sayyad Nahar, the king damaged the army of Sheikhs; Sheikh Sadi Farid fought nicely; after wounding the king, he himself was wounded and then fell down; in this way, he searched for warriors and destroyed them; seeing his bravery, Krishna himself began to praise him. —1595

DOHIRA

Seeing towards Yudhishtar and considering him as his devotee, Krishna told him in a nice manner the characteristics of a king. —1596

KABIT

This king Kharag Singh has killed mighty warriors and Yama's dense army like clouds; he has despatched to the world of Death all the four divisions of the army of Seshanaga, Indra, Surya, Kuber, etc., what to say of Varuna, Ganesh etc., seeing him, even Shiva went back; he did not fear any Yadava and pleasingly, fighting with all of us, he has gained victory over all of us. —1597

Speech of King Yudhishtar

DOHIRA

Yudhishtar said with humility, "O Lord of Braja! All this play has been created by you in order to see the sport." —1598

CHAUPAI

On this side Yudhishtar said this to Krishna and on that side the king Kharag Singh knocked down a large part of the army; then the Malechha army marched forward, whose names the poet relates now. —1599

SWAYYA

Nahar Khan, Jharajhar Khan, Bahadur Khan, Nihang Khan, Bharang and Jharang were such expert warriors in warfare that they neever had any fear of war; seeing whose figures even the protectors of the directions feared, such mighty warriors could never be suppressed by anyone; all those Khans, taking their bows and arrows in their hands came to fight proudly with the king. —1600

They were accompanied by the warriors like Zahid Khan, Jabbar Khan and Wahid Khan; they rushed forward from all the four directions getting angry; the Malechhas of all colours, white, black, grey etc., marched forward to fight with the king at that very instant the king, taking his bow in his hand, pulverised all these angry warriors. —1601

SWAYYA

The king, in ire, dividing the army of Malechhas into two parts, broke them up further; somewhere the warriors, somewhere the horses and somewhere the powerful huge elephants lay dead; the elephants had fallen after swinging; some of the wounded warriors are writhing and some have lost the power of speech; some are sitting silently like some fasting hermit in meditation. —1602

SWAYYA

When the king waged a dreadful war, then in great rage Nahar Khan came and stood before him; holding his weapons, with dancing horse and challenging the king, he fell upon him; Kharag Singh caught him by his hair, threw him on the ground, with a jerk; seeing him in such plight, Tahir Khan did not stay there and fled away. —1603

When Tahir Khan fled away, then, in great fury, Jharajhar Khan came forward and holding his weapons, fell upon the king looking like Yama; He discharged many arrows on the king and the king shot many arrows on him; Kinnars and Yakshas praised their battle and the group of minstrels began to sing songs of victory. —1604

DOHIRA

Kharag Singh seeing the stern warriors before him changed the signs on his forehead and with a single arrow, chopped the head of the enemy. —1605

SWAYYA

Then Nihang Khan, Jharang Khan and Bharang Khan etc., marched forward, masticating their mouths with their shields; then holding his sword in his hand, the king challenged and fell upon Krishna; the king beat and caused the army to flee and the trunks and heads began to writhe in the battlefield like fish; the warriors did not like to withdraw from the field till their death. —1606

DOHIRA

The stream of blood flowed there in flood and it appeared like Vaitarni stream of flesh and marrow. —1607

KABIT

A dreadful war began and Dilawar Khan, Dalel Khan etc., joined speedily in the war like a falcon; these fully persistent warriors are engaged in destruction and their glory seems charming to the eyes; the king also holding his sword, proudly smashed and destroyed the army; somewhere the king killed the horses and somewhere the elephants; the warriors were cut down by the king like the trees cut down and thrown in the forest. —1608

DOHIRA

Then Kharag Singh holding his sword in ire despatched the army of Malechhas to the abode of Yama. —1609

SORATHA

When the king destroyed two extremely large units of the army of Malechhas, then the remaining warriors who marched forward for war, their names are like this. —1610

SWAYYA

Bhima taking his mace and Arjuna tightening his waist with quiver marched forward; Yudhishtar carried his bow and arrows in his hands; he took with him both the brothers and the army had began the fighting like Indra with Vratasura. —1611

SORATHA

Getting infuriated in his mind, Kharag Singh went before Krishna and spoke within the hearing of all the warriors. —1612

Speech of Kharag Singh addressed to All the Warriors

SWAYYA

Even if the sun rises from the west and the Ganges flows contrary to its course; even if it snows in the month of Jyeshth and the wing of spring gives scorching heat; even if the stable pole star moves and if the waters turn into plain and plain into waters and if the Sumeru mountain flies with wings, Kharag Singh will never get back from the war-arena. —1613

SWAYYA

Saying this and getting hold of his bow, he in a delightful mood, chopped many warriors; some warriors came in front of him to fight and some ran away; some of the warriors fell down on the earth; he knocked down many warriors on the ground and seeing such a spectacle of war, many warriors retraced their steps; the poet says that the warriors who were there in that battlefield, they had received some injury at least. —1614

SWAYYA

He caused the bow of Arjuna to fall down and also the mace of Bhima; the sword of the king itself was cut and it could not be known where it fell; the innumerable warriors of Arjuna and Bhima fell upon the king, who with his loud sounding discharge of arrows, pierced the bodies of all of them. —1615

DOHIRA

The king immediately killed one large division of military unit and then, in his fury, holding his weapons, he fell upon the enemy. —1616

SWAYYA

He killed some warriors with other weapons and some, taking his sword in his hand; he tore asunder the hearts of some with his sword and knocked down many by catching them from their hair; he threw and scattered some in all the ten directions and some died merely with fear; he killed gatherings of soldiers on feet and with both hands he uprooted the tusks of the elephants. —1617

SWAYYA

Holding his bow, Arjuna discharged one arrow to the king, whose blow destroyed the pride of the king and he suffered extreme anguish; seeing the bravery of Arjuna, the heart of the king was pleased and he said within his hearing: "Bravo to the parents of Arjuna, who gave him birth." —1618

Speech of Kharag Singh addressed to Arjuna

SWAYYA

"The hair grown on your upper lip seems saturated

BACHITTAR NATAK

(because of your youth) and your eyes are lotus; your hair upto your waist are swinging like two snakes; your face is like moon, seeing which, the anguish of the partridge is effaced; seeing your elegant figure, I feel mercy arising in my mind, therefore how can I kill you?"—1619

SWAYYA

Seeing towards the king, Arjuna laughed and got enraged in his mind; he fearlessly took his bow and arrows in his hand and shouted; from the other side, coming in front of him the king began the war but leaving aside Arjuna, he fell upon Bhima. —1620

Then he shattered the chariot of Bhima and knocked down many warriors in the field; many warriors were wounded and fell down on the ground and several wounded ones fought with the wounded ones; many have run away and some are getting infuriated, taking up their arms; the swords fell down from the hands of many warriors. —1621

DOHIRA

Then Arjuna, taking up his bow, returned and he tightening it, shot a sharp arrow on Kharag Singh, in order to kill him. —1622

SWAYYA

When the arrow hit the king, he said to Arjuna, in anger, "O the warrior of bewitching face! why are you burning yourself in the fire of another person? I shall kill you alongwith your teacher of archery; you have beautiful eyes, therefore you may go home, I leave you." —1623

SWAYYA

Saying these words to Arjuna, and taking up his sharp sword in his hand, the king fell upon the army; seeing towards the army, he, the mighty one, becoming completely fearless, challenged the army; seeing him, the enemies became fearful; they could not hold their weapons; he killed many in the war and the whole army shouted, "water, water." —1624

DOHIRA

When Krishna saw the Pandava army running away, he asked Duryodhana to attack. —1625

SWAYYA

Hearing the words of Krishna, Duryodhana marched forward with his bedecked army; There were Bhishma, Dronacharya, Kripacharya, etc., with Karana and all these mighty ones waged a dreadful war with the king Kharag Singh; the king fought fearlessly advancing forward and he discharged one arrow towards each. —1626

SWAYYA

Then Bhishma got infuriated and discharged many arrows towards the king; who intercepting all these arrows ran forward with his sword; in that dreadful war, the king said within the hearing of Bhishma, "You will only know my power, when you reach the abode of Yama." —1627

DOHIRA

Kharag Singh saw that Bhishma was not running away from the war, he cut down the head of the charioteer of Bhishma with a single arrow. —1628

SWAYYA

Taking Bhishma (in the chariot), the horses ran away, then Duryodhna was filled with anger; he fell upon the king alongwith the son of Dronacharya, Kripacharya, Kratvarma and Yadavas, etc., Dronacharya himself, taking up his bow and arrows persistently and fearlessly resisted and waged a dreadful war with his sword, dagger, trident, lance, discus, etc. —1629

Speech of Krishna addressed to Kharag Singh

SWAYYA

Krishna, taking his bow in his hand, said to Kharag Singh, "O fool! what if you have waged a dreadful war; I shall now kill you powerfully; you may fight for one *ghari* (short duration of time), because I know that your death is very near and you have to die;" telling him to remain cautious, Krishna discharged his arrow. —1630

DOHIRA

Intercepting the coming arrow, Kharag Singh said

furiously, "Seshanaga, Indra and Shiva know quite nicely about my bravery." —1631

KABIT

"I shall devour the ghosts; I shall cause the gods and demons to run away and throw Krishna on the ground; such is the power in my arms; by waging a terrible war, I shall cause Bhairava to dance; O Krishna, I am telling the truth that I shall not run away from the war-arena; it will not take more than a moment to kill Dronacharya; I can kill Indra or Yama alongwith their military power, whomsoever I want to kill; O Krishna! all your Kshatriyas engaged in war, I can kill all of them, but being Kharag Singh, I cannot tolerate your said words." —1632

CHHAPPAI

Then Dronacharya came angrily before the king and he waged a dreadful war, holding his weapons and arms; the warriors getting wounded and good deal of blood out of their bodies they appear to have played the Holi with red colour and also wearing red clothes; the gods seeing this hailed Dronacharya and the king Kharag Singh and also said, "Such a war has not been fought on the earth during the four ages." —1633

DOHIRA

Then greatly infuriated, Arjuna, Bhishma, Bhima, Dronacharya, Kripacharya, and Duryodhana, etc., of the Pandava army besieged Kharag Singh. —1634

KABIT

Just as the fence surrounds the field, death surrounds the living being the beggar surrounds the donor and the bangle surrounds the hand; just as the body surrounds the vital force (*prana*) the light surrounds the spheres of sun and moon, nescience surrounds knowledge and *gopis* surround Krishna; just as the tank surrounds the water, the rosary surrounds the repetition of the Name, the virtues surround the vices and the creeper surrounds the cucumber; just as the sky surrounds the pole star, the ocean surrounds the earth, in the same way, these heroes have surrounded the mighty Kharag Singh. —1635

SWAYYA

After surrounding Kharag Singh, Duryodhana was greatly enraged; Arjuna, Bhima, Yudhishtar and Bhishma took their weapons and Balram carried his plough; Dronacharya, Kripacharya, Karana, etc., have advanced towards the enemy and the dreadful fighting began with arms, legs, fists and teeth. —1636

SWAYYA

Kharag Singh, holding his bow and arrows killed millions of enemies; somewhere horses, somewhere crowns and somewhere the black elephants like mountains have fallen down; some of them, having fallen, are writhing like young one of an elephant crushed by a lion and some of them are so powerful, who are severing the heads of the fallen corpses. —1637

SWAYYA

The king, taking up his bow and arrows pulverized the pride of Yadavas and then taking up the axe in his hand, he tore away the hearts of the enemies; the warriors, getting wounded in the war, are remembering the Lord in their mind; those who have died in the war, have attained salvation and they have ferried across the dreadful ocean of *samsara* and gone to the abode of the Lord. —1638

DOHIRA

The mighty warriors were chopped very quickly and the dreadfulness of the war cannot be described; those who are running away quickly, Arjuna said to them: —1639

SWAYYA

"O warriors! do not shirk task assigned by Krishna and do not run away from war-arena; hold your bow and arrows in your hands and fall upon the king shouting at him; holding your weapons in your hands, shout "kill, kill;" think at least something of the tradition of your clan and fight with Kharag Singh fearlessly." —1640

SWAYYA

Karana, the son of Surya, in anger, stood firmly

BACHITTAR NATAK

with persistence in front of the king; and pulling his bow and taking his arrow in his hand, he said to the king, "Do you listen, O king! now you have fallen like a deer in the mouth of a lion like me," the king took his bow and arrow in his hands and said to the son of Surya, instructing him: —1641

SWAYYA

"O Karana, the son of Surya! why do you want to die? You may go and remain alive for some days; why are you taking poison with your own hands; go to your home and quaff the nectar comfortably," saying this, the king discharged his arrow and said, "Look to the reward of coming to the war;" on being hit by the arrow he fell down unconscious and all his body was filled with blood. —1642

SWAYYA

Then Bhima ran with his mace and Arjuna with his bow; Bhishma, Drona, Kripacharya, Sahdeva, Bhurshrava, etc., also got enraged; Duryodhana, Yudhishtra and Krishna also came with their army; with the arrows of the king, the mighty warriors became fearful in their mind. —1643

SWAYYA

Till that time, Krishna, in great ire, shot an arrow in the heart of the king; now he pulling his bow discharged an arrow towards the charioteer; now the king advanced forward and his feet slipped in the battlefield; the poet says that all the warriors began to eulogise this war. —1644

SWAYYA

Seeing Krishna, the king said, "You have got very beautiful hair and the glory of your face is indescribable; your eyes are extremely charming and they cannot be compared with any thing; O Krishna! You may go away, I leave you; what will you gain by fighting?" —1645

SWAYYA

Holding his bow and arrows, the king said to Krishna, "You listen to me, why are you coming before me to fight persistently? I shall kill you now and shall not leave you, otherwise you may go away; nothing has gone wrong even now; obey me and do not uselessly put in anguish the women of the city by dying." —1646

SWAYYA

"I have killed many warriors engaged in war persistently; O Krishna; who has instigated you to fight with me? And you are not running away from the war-arena? The mercy has arisen in my heart, therefore why should I kill you? hearing about your death all your friends will also die in an instant." —1647

SWAYYA

Listening to such a talk, Krishna fell upon Kharag Singh, in ire and according to the poet he continued the war for two *gharis* (very short period); sometime Krishna and sometimes the king caused the other to fall from the chariot; seeing this spectacle the minstrel began to praise the king and Krishna. —1648

SWAYYA

On this side Krishna mounted his chariot and on the other side, the king Kharag Singh ascended his vehicle; the king, in fury, drew out his sword from the scabbard; the army of Pandavas also got blazed with anger; it appeared that the sound of the weapons and arms was the recitation of the Vedic *mantras*. —1649

SWAYYA

Seeing the army of Duryodhana, the king showered his arrows; he depriving many warriors of their chariots, despatched them to the abode of Yama; the warriors like Bhishma and Drona ran away from the battlefield and relinquishing all hope of victory, they did not come again before Kharag Singh. —1650

DOHIRA

Forsaking their endurance, the son of Drona, the son of Surya and Kripacharya ran away and seeing the dreadful fighting Bhurshrava and Duryodhana also fled. —1651

SWAYYA

Seeing all of them fleeing, Yudhishtar said to Krishna; "This king is very powerful and is not receding by anyone; we have waged a terrible war with him, taking Karana, Bhishma, Drona, Kripacharya, Arjuna, Bhima, etc., with us, but he did not even slightly get aside from war and all of us had to surrender." —1652

SWAYYA

Bhishma, Karana, Duryodhana, Bhima, etc., waged a persistent and terrible war and Balram, Kratvarma, Satyak, etc., also became extremely enraged in their mind; all the warriors are being defeated; O Lord! what is in your mind now that you want to do? Now all the warriors are running away and we have no control over them now. —1653

SWAYYA

All the Ganas of Rudra etc., who were there and all other gods who were there, they all together fell upon the king Kharag Singh; seeing them all coming, this mighty warrior challenged all of them by pulling his bow; some of them, who were wounded, fell down, and some becoming fearful ran away; the warriors who fought fearlessly, were ultimately killed by the king. —1654

SWAYYA

After gaining victory over Surya, Kuber, Garuda etc., the king wounded Ganesh and made him unconscious; seeing Ganesh fallen on the ground, Varuna, Surya and Chandrama fled away; the hero like Shiva also went away and did not come before the king; whosoever came before the king, getting enraged, the king caused him to fall down with the blow of his hand on the ground. —1655

DOHIRA

Brahma said to Krishna, "You are the master of *dharma*" and at the same time Shiva said to Brahma, smiling: —1656

SWAYYA

"Many mighty warriors like us have fought heroically with the king, but none has been able to kill him;" then Shiva said further to Brahma, "Indra, Yama and all of us have waged a dreadful war with the king; the army of the fourteen worlds has been defeated, but the power of the king has not even slightly declined." —1657

DOHIRA

In this way, Brahma and Shiva are holding consultations on this side and on the other side, the sun set, the moon arose and the night fell. —1658

CHAUPAI

Both the armies were extremely agitated and with hunger and thirst, the bodies of the warriors withered; the evening fell with continued fighting and all of them had to remain in the battlefield. —1659

CHAUPAI

In the morning all the warriors awoke and the battle-drums were played from both the sides; the warriors wearing their armours and holding weapons marched for war. —1660

SWAYYA

Vasudeva, the son of Vasudeva accompanied by Shiva, Yama and Surya went towards the battlefield and Krishna said to Brahma, "We have to kill the enemy definitely, stabilising ourselves;" many warriors rushed forward in the company of Krishna and holding their bows and arrows came to fight with Kharag Singh fearlessly. —1661

SWAYYA

The eleven Ganas of Shiva were wounded and the chariots of the twelve Suryas were shattered; Yama was wounded and all the eight Vasus were challenged and frightened; many enemies were made headless and those who survived, ran away from the battlefield; the arrows of the king were discharged with the speed of wind and all the forces were torn like clouds. —1662

SWAYYA

When all ran away from the battlefield, Shiva thought of a remedy; he created a human being of clay, in which the life-force was put by Krishna on seeing it; he was named Ajit Singh, who was also unconquerable before Shiva; he held the weapons and started away in order to kill Kharag Singh. —1663

ARIL

Many powerful warriors went forward for

fighting; holding their weapons they blew their conches; the twelve Suryas, pulled their bows and discharged their arrows like the raining clouds of doomsday. —1664

DOHIRA

They intercepted the arrows with arrows and looking furiously, the king said to Krishna: —1665

SWAYYA

"O Krishna! why are you egoistic? I shall cause you to run away from the battlefield just now; why are you resisting me? I shall again catch you by your hair; O Gujjar! are you not feeling afraid? I shall not let you go, live and kill all including Indra, Brahma, Kuber, Varuna, Chandra, Shiva, etc." —1666

SWAYYA

At that time, the mighty warrior Kata Singh, getting enraged in his mind and fearlessly taking his sword in his hand, fell upon the king; both of them waged a dreadful war and none of them retraced even one step; ultimately Kharag Singh struck a blow with his sword and making him lifeless caused him to fall on the earth. —1667

SWAYYA

Seeing him in this plight, Vichitra Singh who was standing there, came forward and waged a dreadful war with the king with his bow and arrows; the mighty warrior Kharag Singh, pulled his bow in anger and discharged his arrow in such a way that it hit his heart and his head was chopped and fell down. —1668

CHAUPAI

Then Ajit Singh himself took his bow and arrows and reached the war-arena; he said to the king, "Shiva has created me only for the purpose of killing you." —1669

Ajit Singh saying like this challenged Kharag Singh for fighting; the king was not frightened on listening this and that mighty one came forward. —1670

CHAUPAI

The eleven Rudras and Surya reached there for the protection of Ajit Singh; Indra, Krishna, Yama, Varuna, Kuber, etc., all had surrounded him. —1671

SWAYYA

When Ajit Singh waged a dreadful war with Kharag Singh, then all his accompanying mighty warriors like Shiva etc., held out their weapons in order to kill the enemy; the arrows were showered in the battlefield, but the king, in his fury, intercepted all the arrows; that mighty warrior, Ajit Singh taking his bow and arrows did not leave any one and killed all the warriors. —1672

CHAUPAI

When Ajit Singh killed the warriors, then the other warriors became fearful in their minds; the king again held out his sword, all the people were wonder-struck by this warfare, they lost their valour. —1673

Then Krishna and Brahma consulted each other and said, "This king will not even be killed by the blazing fire, therefore nor making some effort, he should be killed." —1674

Brahma said, "When he will lose his power by being allured by the heavenly damsels and in this way, when we will see him declining, then he will be despatched to the abode of Yama." —1675

CHAUPAI

"Therefore the heavenly damsels be commanded to do that with which the king feels pleased; when the king will be immersed in such a spectacle, his power will decline. —1676

DOHIRA

When Brahma said this, Indra heard all this: Brahma looking towards the sky, said to Indra; "O the king of gods! arrange the dance." —1677

SWAYYA

On that side, the heavenly damsels began to dance, and on this side, the warriors began the war; Kinnars and Gandharvas sang and the musical instruments of war were played; seeing this spectacle, the mind of the king deviated and at the same time, suddenly Krishna pulled his bow and shot an arrow into the body of the king. —1678

SWAYYA

With the infliction of the arrow, the king became enamoured, but still he killed the warriors; killing innumerable Ganas of eleven Rudras, he despatched them to the next world; twelve Suryas, Varuna, Chandra, Indra, Kuber, etc., were struck blows; the poet Shyam says that all other warriors who were standing there, they were all put to shame. —1679

He discharged sixty arrows towards Indra, two hundred to Krishna, sixty-four to Yama and twelve to Suryas and wounded them; he shot one hundred arrows to Chandrama and four to Rudra; the clothes of all these warriors were saturated with blood and it seemed that that all of them had come after playing Holi. —1680

CHAUPAI

Many other warriors were killed there and they reached the abode of Yama; then the king came to Brahma and said: —1681

"Why are you killing them in the war uselessly?; now you may do one thing and go to heavens along with your body." —1682

Do not think of war now and amend your future; do not delay now and follow my saying. —1683

SWAYYA

"O mighty one! now you may go to the world of Indra without any delay and meeting the desired damsels enjoy them; O king! you have fulfilled your objective and now you may quaff the nectar of the Name of the Lord; you may now leave the company of these kings and do not put to anguish these warriors uselessly." —1684

DOHIRA

Hearing these words of Brahma, that calamitous king for the enemies, getting extremely pleased in his mind, said to Brahma: —1685

CHAUPAI

"O Brahma! I tell you whatever I think in my mind; a hero like me, taking up his weapons, with whom shall he fight except Vishnu?" —1686

DOHIRA

"O, the Creator of the world! You know that my name is Kharag Singh; I have to justify my name; then you may tell, where should I run away?" —1687

SWAYYA

"O Brahma! listen to me and hearing with ears, adopt it in your mind; when the mind wishes to praise, then only the Lord should be praised; None other's feet should be worshipped except those of God, *Guru* and Brahmin; He, who is worshipped in all the four ages, one should fight with Him, die at His hands and ferry across the dreadful ocean of *samsara* through His grace. —1688

He, whom Sanak etc., Seshanaga etc., search and still they do not know His mystery; He, whose praises are sung by Shukadeva, Vyas etc., in all the fourteen worlds; and with the glory of whose name Dhruva and Prahlad attained eternal state, that Lord should fight with me." —1689

ARIL

Hearing these words, Brahma was wonder-struck and on this side the king absorbed his mind in the devotion of Vishnu; seeing the face of the king, Brahma shouted "*sadhu, sadhu*" and observing his love (for the Lord), he became silent. —1690

Brahma said to the king again, "O king! you have very nicely understood the elements of devotion, therefore you should go to heaven alongwith your body and getting salvation do not look towards the side of war." —1691

DOHIRA

When the king did not follow the desire of Brahma, then Brahma thought of Narada and Narada reached there. —1692

SWAYYA

On coming there, Narada said to the king, "O king! there is no other king like you in all the fourteen worlds; this has been said by the Lord; therefore you have waged your dreadful war with Krishna like heroes;" hearing the words of the sage, the king was extremely pleased in his mind. —1693

DOHIRA

Recognising Narada, the king gave a ceremonious welcome to the sage; then Narada instructed the king about waging the war. —1694

DOHIRA

On this side, the king as mine of devotion met Narada and on that side Shiva reached there, where Krishna was standing. —1695

CHAUPAI

Reflecting in his mind, Shiva said to Krishna, "Command Death now to kill the king." —1696

DOHIRA

"Make the step of getting Death seated in your arrow and pulling the bow, discharge the arrow so that this king may forget doing all acts of injustice." —1697

CHAUPAI

Krishna acted according to the suggestion of Shiva; Krishna thought of Death and the God of Death manifested himself. —1698

DOHIRA

Krishna said to the God of Death to abide in his arrow and on my discharging the arrow, you may destroy the enemy. —1699

SWAYYA

The king was allured by the side-glances of the heavenly damsels; on this side Narada and Brahma together engrossed the king in their talk; at the same time, seeing a good opportunity, Krishna discharged his death-arrow and with the force of *mantras* deceptively caused the head of the king to fall down. —1700

SWAYYA

Though the head of the king was cut, but still he remained stable and catching his head from his hair, he threw it towards Krishna; it seemed as if his *pranas* (vital force) had reached Krishna in order to bid farewell to him; that head hit Krishna and he could not keep standing; he fell down unconscious; see the bravery of the head of the king; on being hit by it, the Lord (Krishna) fell down from his chariot on the earth. —1701

SWAYYA

The king Kharag Singh exhibited extraordinary bravery, seeing which the women of Yakshas, Kinnars and Devas are allured; they descended on the earth playing on their musical instruments like lyres, drums etc., and all are showing their pleasure by dancing and singing and making others pleased. —1702

DOHIRA

The beautiful damsels came down from the sky after embellishing themselves and the poet says that the objects of their coming was to wed the king. —1703

SWAYYA

The headless king was extremely enraged in his mind and advanced towards the twelve Suryas; they all ran away from that place, but Shiva kept standing there and fell upon him; but that mighty one caused Shiva to fall on the ground with his blow. —1704

SWAYYA

Someone fell with his blow and someone with the thumping of that blow; he ripped and threw someone towards the sky; he; caused the horses to collide with horses, the chariots to collide with chariots and the elephants to collide with the elephants; in this way, according to the poet, be began to despatch the enemy to the abode of Yama. —1705

SWAYYA

When Krishna regained consciousness, he mounted on his chariot in great ire and thinking of his great strength, he drew his sword from the scabbard; getting highly enraged, he fell upon the terrible enemy like the sea; the warriors also pulled their bows and began to discharge arrows in excitement. —1706

SWAYYA

When the warriors inflicted wounds, then the headless trunk of the king controlling his strength and taking up his weapons, thought of destroying the enemy in his mind; he appeared to be like the moon amongst the stars and on the appearance of the moon, the darkness fled away. —1707

SWAYYA

The heroes like Krishna ran away, and none of the warriors stayed there to all the warriors the king seemed like Kal (Death); all the arrows emanating from the bow of the king were being showered like clouds of the doomsday; seeing all this, all ran away and none of them fought with the king. —1708

SWAYYA

When all the warriors ran away, the king then remembered the Lord and forsaking the fighting, he absorbed himself with the devotion of the Lord; in that society of the kings, the mind of the king Kharag Singh became absorbed in the Lord; he is firmly standing on the earth; who else is so fortunate like the king? —1709

SWAYYA

When the warriors of Krishna thought of getting the king fall on the ground, at the same time discharged clusters of arrows on him; all the women of the gods together lifted and put the trunk of the king on the air-vehicle, but still he jumped down from the vehicle and taking his weapons reached the battlefield. —1710

DOHIRA

Taking his bow and arrows in his hands he reached the battlefield and killing many warriors, he began to challenge death. —1711

CHAUPAI

When the messengers of Yama came to take him, he even discharged his arrows towards them; he moved here and there, feeling his death at hand, but on being killed by the Kal (Death), he was not dying. —1712

CHAUPAI

He again, in his fury, fell upon in the direction of the enemy and it seemed that Yama himself was coming in person; he began to fight with the enemies, when observing this, Krishna and Shiva were infuriated in their minds. —1713

SWAYYA

Being tired, they began to persuade the king by saying, "O king! do not fight now uselessly; there is no warrior like you in all the three worlds and your praise has spread in all these worlds; abondoning your weapons and ire, now be peaceful; we all forsake our weapons; go to heaven, mounting on the air-vehicle." —1714

ARIL

When all the gods and Krishna said these words very humbly and taking the blades of straw in their mouths, they went away from the battlefield, then listening to their words of distress, the king also abandoned his anger and put his bow and arrows on the earth. —1715

DOHIRA

The Kinnars, Yakshas and the heavenly damsels got him mounted on the air-vehicle and listening to the shouts hailing him, even Indra, king of the gods also got pleased. —1716

SWAYYA

When the king reached the abode of gods, all the warriors became pleased and said, "We are all saved from the mouth of Kal (Death) when Chandra, Surya, Kuber, Rudra, Brahma, etc., reached the abode of the Lord, the gods showered flowers from the sky and blew the horn of victory. —1717

End of the chapter entitled "Killing of Kharag Singh in Warfare" in Krishnavatar in Bachittar Natak.

Now begins the Description of Arresting and then Releasing Kharag Singh

SWAYYA

Till that time, in great fury, Balram discharged his arrows and killed many enemies; pulling his bow he made many enemies lifeless and threw on the ground; he caught some of the mighty ones with his hands and knocked them down on the earth; those who survived from amongst them with their strength, they

BACHITTAR NATAK

abandoned the war-arena and came before Jarasandh. —1718

CHAUPAI

Coming before Jarasandh, they said, "Kharag Singh has been killed in the war;" listening to their talk, his eyes became red with ire. —1719

He called all his ministers and said, "Kharag Singh has been killed in the battlefield and there is no other warrior like him." —1720

"There is no other warrior like Kharag Singh, who can fight like him; now you may tell me what should be done? and who should now be ordered to go?" —1721

Speech of the Ministers addressed to Jarasandh

DOHIRA

Now the minister Sumati by name, spoke to the king Jarasandh, "Now it is evening; who will fight at this time?" —1722

On that side, listening to the minister, the king sat down silently and on this side Balram reached there where Krishna was sitting. —1723

Speech of Balram addressed to Krishna

DOHIRA

"O the ocean of mercy! who was this king Kharag Singh? I have not seen till now such a powerful hero." —1724

CHAUPAI

"Therefore telling me his episode remove the illusion of my mind;" when Balram said this, Krishna listening to him, remained silent. —1725

Speech of Krishna

SORATHA

Then Krishna gracefully said to his brother, "O Balram! now I relate story of the birth of the king, listen to it." —1726

DOHIRA

Kartikeya (the six-faced), Rama, Ganesh, Shringi and Ghanshyam taking the first letters of these names, he was named Kharag Singh. —1727

DOHIRA

The power of the sword, the beauty of Rama, the body of an elephant, glory and roaring like lion in the war, these five qualities were adopted by the king. —1728

CHHAPPAI

Shiva gave him the sword of victory in the war; Lakshmi gave him the beauty of the body and pure intellect; Ganesh gave him, the miraculous power of *garima* (heaviness) and the sage Shringi gave him the roaring sound of the lion; Ghanshyam gave him the power to wage dreadful war; O Balram! as I have told you, the king took birth like this; then Balram said, "You are with the helpless people like us and you have destroyed today a very great enemy." —1729

SORATHA

Then Krishna gracefully said to Balram, "The Yadava forces are under the impact of bad intellect and they are proud of the strength of their arms." —1730

CHAUPAI

"Yadavas had become proud because of the patronage of Balram and Krishna; for this reason, they did not consider anyone equal to them; they have now reaped the reward of this weakness." —1731

"The Lord destroys the ego, consider this saying of mine as true; and for the sake of destroying the ego, the Providence had incarnated this king." —1732

DOHIRA

"This poor king waged such a great war; the Lord had created him to destroy the pride of the Yadavas." —1733

CHAUPAI

"The Yadava clan has still not been destroyed and for their destruction a sage has been born, who will curse them in distress and all of them will be destroyed once for all." —1734

DOHIRA

The Lotus-eyed Krishna said again, "O sagacious Balram! now you listen to the interesting episode." —1735

CHAUPAI

"Listen attentively to my words and understand who has been victorious over me in the war? There is no difference between me and Kharag Singh and my form only pervades the whole world." —1736

"O Balram! I am telling you the truth; none knows about this mystery there is no warrior amongst the warriors like him, in whose heart abides my name with such profundity." —1737

DOHIRA

"Residing in the womb of the mother for ten months, when he passed his life by relinquishing eating and drinking and subsisting only on air, then the Lord bestowed on him a boon." —1738

DOHIRA

"The powerful Kharag Singh asked for the boon of conquering the enemy and then for twelve years, he performed most stern austerities." —1739

CHAUPAI

This episode ended and the day dawned; the warriors of both the sides awoke; bedecking his army, Jarasandh came into the battlefield and from this side, the Yadava army, gathering all its warriors set itself against the enemy. —1740

SWAYYA

Balram from this side and the enemy from the other side alongwith their armies rushed forward; Balram took his plough in his hand and challenging the enemy struck his blows; someone died and fell upon the earth, someone fought and someone fled away; then Balram took his mace in his hand despatched many enemies to the abode of Yama. —1741

SWAYYA

Krishna took his bow and arrows in his hands and marched towards the same side and falling upon the enemy, he caused a stream of blood to flow; a great affliction fell upon the horses, elephants and the chariot-owners; none could stay in the war-arena; all are running away, they are in anger and anguish and also helpless. —1742

SWAYYA

When the confronting army fled, Krishna in extreme anger sustained his strength and thinking in his mind, he reached there, where the general of the army was standing; holding his weapons, Krishna reached that place, where the king Jarasandh was standing he held his bow and arrows and pulverized the ego of Jarasandh. —1743

SWAYYA

When the arrows were discharged from the bow of Krishna, who could then stand against him? Those who were hit by these arrows, they reached the abode of Yama in an instant; no such warrior has been born, who could fight in front of Krishna; the warriors of the king said to him, "Krishna is coming alongwith his army in order to kill us." —1744

SWAYYA

Many warriors on the side of the king were killed, when the arrows were discharged from the side of Krishna; those who fought with Krishna, reached the abode of Yama; seeing this spectacle, the king got agitated and told and instructed his warriors, "Let Krishna come near me, then I shall see."—1745

SWAYYA

When the king saw Krishna coming, he marched forward alongwith his army; he caused his warriors to advance and taking up his conch in his hand, he blew it; the poet says that there is no fear in the mind of any one in the war; hearing the sound of the conch, the minds of the warriors were excited. —1746

DOHIRA

The fourfold army of Jarasandh rushed forward, but Krishna taking his bow and arrows in hands destroyed all in an instant. —1747

SWAYYA

The enemies lost all courage as the arrows emanated form the bow of Krishna; the dead elephants fell on the earth like the trees falling after being sawed and cut; the dying enemies were innumerable and at that place there were heaps of the lifeless heads of Kshatriyas; the battlefield had become a tank in which the heads were flowing like leaves and flowers. —1748

SWAYYA

Someone is wounded and swinging and the blood is oozing out from the body of someone; someone is running away and frightened by the dreadfulness of war, Seshanaga has lost his presence of mind; those who are being killed in the act of running away and retracing their steps from the war-arena, their flesh is not even being eaten by the jackals and vultures; the warriors are roaring and shouting like the intoxicated elephants in the forest. —1749

SWAYYA

Taking his sword in his hand, Krishna made many warriors lifeless; he killed thousands of the riders of horses and elephants; the heads of many were chopped and the chests of many were torn; he was moving as the manifestation of Death and killing the enemies. —1750

KABIT

Being enraged again and taking his bow and arrows in his hands, Krishna is killing the enemies; he killed many, deprived the chariot-rider of their chariots and such a dreadful war is being fought that doomsday seems to have arrived; sometimes he is displaying the sword and sometimes as Glorious one, he sets in motion his discus; those wearing clothes, saturated with blood, appear like hermits playing Holi in their pleasure. —1751

The enemies do not fear Krishna and are rushing forward, challenging him to fight; the warriors remaining stable in war and performing duty for their master, are getting infuriated in their own groups; they are most sincere servants of their king Jarasandh and are moving fearlessly near Krishna; Krishna is steady like Sumeru maintained and with the infliction of his arrows, the warriors are falling down like the stars of the sky. —1752

SWAYYA

In this way, on this side, Krishna was surrounded and on the other side, getting angry, Balram killed many warriors; holding his bow, arrows and sword in his hands, Balram made the warriors lifeless and laid them on the earth; the warriors were chopped into many bits and the great warriors becoming helpless, fled away; Balram was getting victorious in the battlefield, the enemies were fleeing and the king saw all this spectacle. —1753

SWAYYA

Being wonder-struck, the king said to his army, "Warriors! the time for war has come now; where you people are running away? This challenge of the king was heard by the whole army; and all the warriors taking their weapons in their hands, in extreme rage, began to wage a dreadful war. —1754

When Krishna saw the greatly powerful warriors coming, he confronted them in great fury, he struck blows on them with his weapons; the heads of many were chopped and the trunks of many were thrown on the ground; many of them abandoned the hope of victory and throwing their weapons ran away. —1755

DOHIRA

When the army fled away, the king thought of a plan and called his minister Sumati before him. —1756

"You go now with twelve extremely large units of army for fighting" and saying thus, the king Jarasandh gave him weapons, arms, armours, quivers etc. —1757

While marching, the minister Sumati said to the king, "O king! how much great warriors are Krishna and Balram? I shall even kill Kal (Death)." —1758

CHAUPAI

Saying this, the minister marched forward with his companies and twelve extremely large military units, playing on the war-arena and other musical instruments in Maru musical mode. —1759

DOHIRA

Balram said to Krishna, "Some step may be taken,

because the minister Sumati has reached with innumerable forces in the battlefield. —1760

SORATHA

Then Krishna said, "Leave your idleness and take up your plough; be near me and do not go anywhere." —1761

SWAYYA

Balram held up his bow and arrows and in great fury, jumped into the war-arena; he killed many warriors and waged a dreadful war with the enemy; whosoever came to fight with Balram, he was wounded very badly and the warrior who confronted him, he either fell down unconscious on the ground or hissed while dying. —1762

SWAYYA

When Krishna, taking up his bow and arrows, is challenging in the war like a lion, who is then so mighty not to forsake endurance and fight with him? Who is there in all the three worlds who can be inimical Balram and Krishna, but still if anyone comes persistently to fight with them, he reaches the abode of Yama in an instant. —1763

SWAYYA

Which mighty warrior will observe endurance, seeing Balram and Krishna coming to fight; He who is the Lord of the fourteen worlds, the king considering him a child, is fighting with him; He with the Glory of whose Name, all the sins are destroyed, who can kill him in the war? All the people getting together are saying this that the enemy Jarasandh will die without cause. —1764

SORATHA

On this side in the army of the king, such like thoughts are arising in the minds of the warriors and on that side Krishna sustaining his power and weapons, fearlessly fell upon the army. —1765

SWAYYA

Balram taking his mace in his hand, killed a group of enemies in an instant; the warriors with blood-saturated bodies, are lying wounded on the earth; the poet Shyam, while describing that spectacle says that it appears to him that the anger had manifested apparently in order to see the war-scenes. —1766

SWAYYA

On this side Balram is enraged in fighting and on that side Krishna is getting with rage; taking up his weapons he is resisting the enemy's army and killing the army of the enemy, he has created a queer scene; the horse is seen lying on the horse, the chariot-rider on the chariot-rider, elephant upon the elephant and the rider on the rider. —1767

SWAYYA

Some warrior is cut into halves, the heads of many warriors have been chopped and thrown; many are lying wounded on the earth, being deprived of their chariots; many people have lost their hands and many their feet; they cannot be enumerated; the poet says that all have lost their endurance and all have run away from the war-arena. —1768

The army of the enemy, which had conquered the whole world and was never defeated; this army had not retraced its steps even if several kings like Indra had fought against it in unison; the same army has been caused to flee by Krishna in an instant and none could even take up his bow and arrows; the gods and demons both are appreciating the war of Krishna. 1769

DOHIRA

When Krishna destroyed two extremely large military units, then the minister Sumati, challenging in anger, fell upon him. —1770

SWAYYA

The warriors getting enraged taking up the swords and shields in their hands fell upon Krishna, who challenged them and they persistently came in front of him; on this side, Krishna, catching hold of his club, discus, mace, etc., in his hands struck terrible blows and the sparks emanated from the armours; it appeared that an ironsmith was fashioning according to his desire the iron by the strokes of his hammer. —1771

SWAYYA

Till that time, Kratvarma and Uddava reached for

the help of Krishna; Akrur also taking the Yadava warriors with him fell upon the enemies in order to kill them; holding their weapons and shouting "kill, kill," a dreadful war was waged from both sides with maces, lances, swords, daggers, etc. —1772

SWAYYA

Kratvarma on coming chopped down many warriors; someone has been cut into two parts, someone's head had been cut down; from the bows of several powerful warriors the arrows are being discharged in this way that it seems the birds are flying in groups towards the trees for rest in the evening before the night falls. —1773

SWAYYA

Somewhere the headless trunks are roaming in the battlefield, taking the swords in their hands and whosoever challenges in the field the warriors fall upon him; someone has fallen because his foot has been cut and for getting up, he is taking the support of the vehicle and somewhere the chopped arm is writhing like a fish out of water. —1774

The poet Shyam says that some headless trunk is running in the battlefield without the weapons and catching hold of the trunks of the elephants, is shaking them violently with force; he is also pulling the neck of dead horses lying on the ground with both his hands and is trying to break the heads of the dead horse riders with one slap. —1775

SWAYYA

The warriors are fighting while continuously jumping and swinging in the battlefield; they are not afraid even slightly from the bows, arrows and swords; many cowards are relinquishing their weapons in the battlefield in fear and running away and many feeling ashamed are coming back to the battlefield and fighting and falling dead on the ground. —1776

SWAYYA

When Krishna held up his discus, the enemy forces became fearful; Krishna while smiling deprived many mighty ones of their life-force; many were pulverised with the blows of the mace and with his power Krishna subdued all the warriors in the war-arena. —1777

SWAYYA

On this side Balram and on the other side Krishna killed many warriors; the warriors, who were the conquerors of the world and were to be very useful to the king in the days of affliction, Krishna made them lifeless and laid them on the ground like the uprooted banana trees by the violent blowing of wind. —1778

The kings who had left their homes and had come to fight with Krishna and who had been looking splendid while riding on their horses, elephants and chariots, they were destroyed by the power of Krishna like the clouds destroyed by the wind in an instant; the cowards, running away and protecting their lives were considering themselves very fortunate. —1779

SWAYYA

Seeing the arrows and discus of Krishna being discharged, the wheels of the chariots also revolved marvellously; the kings, considering the honour and tradition of their clans, are fighting with Krishna and several other kings, getting orders from Jarasandh are proudly shouting and going for war; great warriors with eagerness in their minds to have the sight of Krishna, are coming for fighting. —1780

Krishna than pulled his bow and discharged a cluster of arrows and the warriors who were hit by them, writhed in great suffering; the arrows have penetrated into the legs of the horses; these winged arrows discharged by Krishna on the bodies of the horses appear like new wings cut earlier by the sage Shalihotri. —1781

CHAUPAI

Then all the enemies were filled with rage and they fearlessly surround Krishna; shouting "kill, kill," they began to fight, taking up various kinds of weapons. —1782

SWAYYA

Taking out his sword, Karodhit Singh came in front of Krishna and said, "When Kharag Singh had caught you from your hair and then released you, then you thinking of your protection, took up your discus at a distance; you drank the milk in the houses of milkmaids; have you forgotten those days? And now you have made up your mind to fight; the poet says that Karodhit Singh appeared to be killing Krishna with arrows of his words. —1783

SWAYYA

Hearing these words, Krishna, getting enraged, held up his discus and exhibiting his anger through his eyes, discharged it on the neck of the enemy; on being hit by the discus, his head fell down on the earth like a potter taking down the pitcher from the wheel cutting it with his wire. —1784

SWAYYA

Famous by the name *shatru-hanta* (killer of the enemies), Karodhit Singh fought with Krishna, who made this warrior lifeless; this warrior had earlier been the conqueror of all the ten directions; his soul merged in the Lord like the light of the earthen lamp with the sun; touching the sphere of the sun, his soul reached the Supreme abode. —1785

SWAYYA

Killing this enemy, Krishna being highly enraged, forsaking all hesitations, jumped into the enemy's army; he fought with king Bhairav Singh and killed him also in an instant and he fell down on the ground from his chariot like something breaking and falling down from the sky. —1786

SWAYYA

The warriors are roaming in the battlefield, saturated with blood and with wounds full of pus; some have fallen on the earth and their bodies are being pulled by jackals and vultures; the crows are pulling with force the eyes and faces of many and the Yoginis are shaking in the hands the intestines of many others. —1787

SWAYYA

Taking their swords in their hands, the enemies fell upon Krishna's army proudly from all the four directions; from this side Krishna's warriors advanced and challenging the enemy began to strike blows with their arrows, swords and daggers; those who come to fight, they are conquered, but many have run away and many are being knocked down. —1788

SWAYYA

Those warriors who did not even retrace one step while fighting; those who conquered all the countries and wherever they looked, the enemies fled away; who even fought with Yama and whom not even the god of death could kill, those warriors have been killed and laid down on the earth, by the angry sword of Krishna. —1789

A mighty warrior of the enemy's army shot one arrow on the forehead of Krishna, whose hinder part remained fixed in the eyebrows, but the arrow pierced, through the head to the other side; according to the poet good deal of blood flowed out from that wound and it seemed that Shiva in anger had shown to Indra the light of his third eye. —1790

SWAYYA

Getting his chariot driven, Krishna moved away saying this, "Look, Balram! the enemy's army is marching forward enormously from the South;" listening to the words of Krishna, Balram carrying his plough in great zeal, marched towards that side and so much blood of that army flowed that the Saraswati seemed to flow on the earth. —1791

SWAYYA

Many warriors seeing the dreadfulness of war, fled away; many of them getting wounded and weak are roaming like the ones having kept awake for several nights; many great warriors masters of great strength are absorbed only on fighting with Krishna and many, abandoning their weapons have fallen at the feet of Krishna. —1792

DOHIRA

When, becoming fearful, the enemies ran away many other warriors reached there, gleaming their swords. —1793

SWAYYA

Holding their weapons, the enemies fell upon

Krishna and on this side, Krishna taking his discus in his hand, ran towards them; he killed many warriors and caused the enemy's army to flee like the violent Krishna, wind had caused enemies as clouds to fly away. —1794

SWAYYA

Krishna is chopping the head of someone with his discus and striking blows with his mace on the body of another; he is causing the third one to fall down by showing him the outrageous eyes; and the fourth is being killed with the slap of his blow; by inflicting blows on the limbs of warriors, Krishna has ripped their hearts; in any direction, wherever he goes, the power of endurance of all the warriors is lost. —1795

When the hero of Braja looks towards the enemy's army angrily, then you can tell thoughtfully as to who is the other such warrior, who can keep his power of endurance; any warrior, who tries courageously to fight with Krishna even slightly, he is killed by Krishna in an instant. —1796

SWAYYA

Any warrior, who taking up his weapons comes, proudly in front of Krishna and discharges his arrow by pulling his bow from a distance and talks contemptuously and does not come near him, Krishna seeing him with his far-off sight, is sending him to the next world with a single arrow. —1797

KABIT

Seeing them in such a plight, the great warriors on the enemy's side are getting furious; they, in fury, shouting "kill, kill," are fighting with Krishna; many of them, in fear, are not coming near and are receiving wounds smilingly from a distance; many of them are playing on their cheeks from a distance, but several of them, following the duties of Kshatriyas, are leaving for heaven. —1798

SWAYYA

Those who are capable of fighting with Krishna, they are coming before him and catching hold of bow, arrows, swords, maces, etc., they are waging a dreadful war; someone, becoming lifeless is falling on the ground and someone is roaming in the battlefield though his head has been chopped; someone catching the lying corpses, is throwing them towards the enemy. —1799

The warriors have killed horses, elephants and warriors; many powerful chariot-riders and soldiers on foot have been killed; many of them have fled away, seeing the ferocity of war; so many of the wounded are challenging the wounded ones; many are fighting fearlessly and running here and there, are striking blows with their swords. —1800

DOHIRA

The warriors holding their weapons, have surrounded Krishna from all the four sides like the fence surrounding the field, the ring surrounding the studded precious stone and the sphere (halo) of sun and moon surrounding the sun and moon. —1801

SWAYYA

When Krishna was surrounded, he caught hold of his bow and arrows in his hands; penetrating into the enemy's army, he killed innumerable army-warriors in an instant; he waged the war so skilfully that there were corpses over corpses; the enemy who came in front of him, Krishna did not let him remain alive. —1802

SWAYYA

Seeing most of the army being killed, many mighty warriors got enraged and fell upon Krishna persistently and fearlessly; all of them, holding their weapons, struck blows and did not go even one step backward; Krishna taking up his bow, killed them all with a single arrow. —1803

SWAYYA

Seeing many soldiers laid on the earth the warriors got greatly infuriated; and looking at Krishna said, "Why run away in fear from this son of a milkman? We shall kill him just now in the battlefield; but on the discharge of arrows by Krishna, the hero of Yadavas, the illusion of all was shattered and it appeared that the warriors have awakened from sleep. —1804

JHOOLNA STANZA

Krishna took the discus in his hand in anger and chopped enemy's army, the earth trembled because of the dreadfulness of war; all the ten Nagas ran away; Vishnu awoke from his sleep and the meditation of Shiva was impaired; Krishna killed the army rushing like clouds; a great part of the army was divided into fragments on seeing Krishna; the poet Shyam says that there the hope of the warriors for victory ended. —1805

JHOOLNA STANZA

A dreadful war began there; the death danced and the warriors, leaving the battle, ran away, with the infliction of the arrows of Krishna many breathed their last; many of the wounded appeared to have come after wearing red garments. —1806

JHOOLNA STANZA

When Krishna and Balram took the discus and the sword in their hands, then someone went pulling his bow and someone went holding the shield, trident, mace or dagger; there was consternation in the army of Jarasandh, because the mighty Krishna ran hither and thither to kill the army; the steel collided with steel on both sides and because of the dreadfulness of war, the meditation of Shiva was also impaired. —1807

There was terrible destruction with the swords, lances, maces, daggers, axes, etc., and the enemy's army was being killed; the flowing stream of blood was flooded; the elephants, horses, chariots, heads and the trunks of elephants were seen flowing in it; the ghosts, Vaitala and Bhairavas became thirsty and the Yoginis also ran away with overturned bowls; the poet Ram says that in this terrible battle even Shiva and Brahma leaving their concentration became fearful. —1808

SWAYYA

When Krishna exhibited so much bravery a warrior from enemy's army cried out: "Krishna is a very powerful hero and is not being defeated even slightly in the war; now leave the battlefield and run away, because all will die and none will survive; do not fall in the illusion that he is a boy; he is the same Krishna, who had knocked down Kansa by catching him from his hair. —1809

SWAYYA

Hearing these words, the suspense arose in the minds of all; the coward thought of running away from the battlefield, but the warriors were infuriated; taking up their bows, arrows swords, etc., they began to fight proudly (with their opponents); Krishna took his sword in his hand, challenged all of them and killed them. —1810

SWAYYA

Seeing the warriors running away in this calamitous situation, Krishna said to Balram, "You may control this situation and catching hold of all weapons, challenge the enemy and kill him; fall upon them unhesitatingly and all those enemies who are running away, entrap and catch without killing them." —1811

SWAYYA

Hearing these words from the mouth of Krishna, Balram took his plough and mace ran to pursue the enemy's army; reaching near the running enemies, Balram bound their hands with his noose; some of them fought and died and some were taken alive as prisoners. —1812

SWAYYA

The warriors of Krishna, holding their swords ran after the enemy's army; those who fought were killed; and whosoever surrendered, he was released; those enemies, who had never retraced their steps in the war, they had to get back before the strength of Balram; they became cowards and becoming the burden on the earth, ran away and the swords and daggers dropped from their hands. —1813

SWAYYA

Those warriors who kept standing in the battlefield, they now, getting enraged and taking discus, swords, lances, axes, etc., gathered together and rushed to the front; all of them fearlessly thundering ran to conquer Krishna; a dreadful war ensued from both sides for the attainment of heaven. —1814

SWAYYA

Then Yadavas from this side and the enemies from that side confronted the opponents; and mutually locked began to strike blows while challenging one another; many of them died and writhed on being wounded and many were laid down on the earth; it appeared that the wrestlers drinking excessive hemp were rolling in the arena. —1815

KABIT

The great warriors are enraged in fighting firmly and are not retracing their steps while confronting the enemy; taking their lances, swords, arrows, etc., in their hands they are fighting delightfully, being quite alert; they are embracing martyrdom in order to ferry across the dreadful ocean of *samsara*; and after touching the sphere of the sun, they are abiding in heaven; just as the foot thrusts further in a deep place, similarly according to the poet, the warriors are advancing forward. —1816

SWAYYA

Seeing such like fighting, the warriors, getting enraged, are looking towards the enemy; they are holding in their hands lances, arrows, bows, swords, maces, tridents, etc., they are fearlessly striking blows, going in front of the enemy and are also enduring their blows on their bodies; the bodies have been penetrated and cut into parts, still the warriors are not uttering the word "alas" from their mouths. —1817

SWAYYA

The warriors who fought fearlessly and unhesitatingly in the battlefield and forsaking the attachment for their life, taking their weapons, they clashed with their opponents; those who in great fury, fought and died in the battlefield; according to the poet all of them went to abide in heaven; they are all considering themselves fortunate because they have attained an abode in heaven. —1818

SWAYYA

Some warriors fell on the earth while fighting and someone seeing this plight of the co-warriors, began to fight in great anger; and holding his weapons and challenging fell upon Krishna; the warriors fell as martyrs unhesitatingly and began to wed the heavenly damsels. —1819

SWAYYA

Someone died, someone fell and someone got infuriated; the warriors are resisting one another, getting their chariots driven by their charioteers; they are fighting fearlessly with their swords and daggers; they are even confronting Krishna, fearlessly shouting "kill, kill." —1820

Seeing the warriors coming in front of him, Krishna held his weapons and getting enraged, he showered arrows on the enemies; he crushed some of them under his feet and knocked down some others catching them with his hands; he made many warriors lifeless in the battlefield. —1821

SWAYYA

Many warriors, getting wounded, went to the abode of Yama; the elegant limbs of many were filled with blood; having their heads chopped, many warriors are roaming as headless trunks in the field; many getting afraid of war, forsaking it, reached before the king. —1822

SWAYYA

All the warriors, abandoning the war, reached before the king and said; "O king! all the warriors whom you sent bedecked with weapons, they have been defeated and none of us had been victorious; with the discharge of his arrows, he has made all of them lifeless." —1823

SWAYYA

The warriors said like this to the king, "O king! listen to our request; return to your home, authorising the ministers for the conduct of war; and bestow comfort on all the citizens; your honour has remained there till today and you have not confronted Krishna; we cannot hope for victory even in our dream while fighting with Krishna." —1824

DOHIRA

Hearing these words, Jarasandh became angry and said, "I shall despatch all the warriors of Krishna's army to the abode of Yama." —1825

SWAYYA

"If even Indra comes today with full force I shall also fight with him; Surya considers himself very powerful, I shall also fight with him and despatch him to the abode of Yama; the powerful Shiva will also be destroyed before my fury; I have so much strength, then why should I bow before a milkman?" —1826

SWAYYA

Saying thus, the king in great anger addressed the four divisions of his army; the whole army got ready to fight with Krishna, holding the weapons; the army moved in front and the king followed it; this spectacle appeared like the thick clouds rushing forward in rainy season. —1827

Speech of the King addressed to Krishna

DOHIRA

Then looking at Krishna, the king said, "How will you fight with Kshatriyas being only a milkman?" —1828

Speech of Krishna addressed to the King

SWAYYA

"You call yourself a Kshatriya; I shall wage a war with you and you will run away; I shall test your endurance then, when you will be in trouble and will not be able to discharge even one arrow; you will just now fall unconscious on the ground and will not be able to remain firmly in your chariot; you will fly to the sky with only the blow of one of my arrows." —1829

SWAYYA

When Krishna said this, the king grew enraged in his mind and he got his chariot driven towards Krishna; pulling his bow he discharged such an arrow as if the serpent Takshak was coming to bind down Garuda. —1830

SWAYYA

Seeing that arrow coming, Krishna held his weapons; and pulling his bow upto his ear, he discharged the arrows; the king held his shield; the arrows struck it, which could not be pulled out inspite of the effort; it seemed as if the vehicle of advancing Rahu had spread its wings in order to swallow the sun. —1831

SWAYYA

The king took his bow and arrows in his hands and making Krishna as his target, he discharged his arrows; the arrows were shot by the king in such a way and were showered on Krishna like the drops of rain coming down from the clouds; it appeared that the arrows were running as moths in order to eat the fire of anger of the warriors. —1832

SWAYYA

All the arrows discharged by the king had been intercepted by Krishna; and he has been chopping the blades and middle portions of the arrows into bits in an instant like the portions of the sugarcane chopped by the farmer for sowing; the arrows of Krishna are like falcons who are destroying the enemies as birds. —1833

DOHIRA

On one side Krishna is fighting with Jarasandh and on the other side, the mighty Balram is destroying the army taking up his plough in his hand. —1834

SWAYYA

Balram taking his sword in his hand killed horses, elephants and soldiers on foot and shattered the chariots; he fell upon the group of kings and with his plough, caused all of them to run away; he deprived many chariot-riders of their chariots and wounded many of them. The poet Shyam says that in this way Balram exhibited his bravery to the warriors. —1835

SWAYYA

Balram is proudly moving in the war-arena, filled with ire and taking his sword in his hand; he is not caring for anyone else; he looks like the one intoxicated with wine and filled with ire he is killing the enemies manifesting himself like the dreadful Yama. —1836

In great fury, the heads of the enemies were cut down; the hands and feet of many have been cut and there are wounds on other parts of the body have left their places and fled and the

BACHITTAR NATAK

warriors inflicted with arrows look like porcupine. —1837

SWAYYA

On this side Balram waged war like this and on that side Krishna getting enraged knocked down any one with a single arrow, who ever confronted him; all the army of the king that was there, he despatched it to the abode of Yama in an instant; seeing such a fighting of Krishna, all the enemies, forsaking their endurance, ran away. —1838

SWAYYA

Those warriors who were feeling ashamed, they also now with the object of defeating Krishna, got infuriated and forsaking their hesitation and playing on their war-drums, came in front of him; Krishna holding his bow in his hand discharged his arrows and he knocked down a hundred with each single arrow. —1839

CHAUPAI

The army of Jarasandh was knocked down by Krishna and in this way pulverised the pride of the king; the king thought then what step should he take? And how should he die in the war on that day? —1840

Thinking thus, he caught hold of his bow in his hand and also thought of fighting with Krishna again; he wore his armour and came in front of Krishna. —1841

DOHIRA

Jarasandh then taking up his bow and arrows and wearing his crown, said thus to Krishna: —1842

Speech of Jarasandh addressed to Krishna

SWAYYA

"O Krishna! if you have any power and strength, then show it to me; what are you looking towards me, standing there? I am going to hit you with my arrow, do not run away anywhere; O foolish Yadava! surrender yourself otherwise fight with me with great caution; why do you want to end your life in the war? Go and graze your cows and calves peacefully in the forest." —1843

SWAYYA

When Krishna heard these words of the king, the anger erupted in his mind like the fire flaming up on putting ghee in it; or the lion gets infuriated on hearing the howls of the jackals or like the mind getting angry on thorns being struck into the clothes. —1844

SWAYYA

On this, side, Krishna getting infuriated discharged many arrows; on that side the king in anger, with reddened eyes, took up his bow in his hand; the arrows which were coming towards Krishna were intercepted by him and the arrows of Krishna are not even touching the king. —1845

SWAYYA

On this side the king is fighting with Krishna and on that side Balram said to the king, "We have killed your warriors, but still you do not feel ashamed; O king! go back to your home; what will you gain by fighting? O king! you are like deer and are only dreaming about your victory over the lion." —1846

DOHIRA

The warriors on whose strength you are fighting, they have all fled away; therefore O fool! either run away while fighting or fall down at the feet of Krishna. —1847

Speech of Jarasandh addressed to Balram

DOHIRA

What if the warriors of my side have been killed, the tasks of the warriors are fighting, dying or gaining victory. —1848

SWAYYA

Saying this, in great fury, the king shot an arrow towards Balram; which when hit him gave him extreme agony, he became unconscious and fell in his chariot as if the snake like arrow had stung him and he had fallen down forgetting his wealth and home. —1849

SWAYYA

When Balram regained consciousness, he became extremely enraged; he caught hold of his huge mace and got ready again in the battlefield in order to kill the enemy; leaving his chariot, he ran away even on foot and none could see him except the king. —1850

Seeing Balram coming, the king got enraged and pulling his bow with his hand, he got ready for war; he intercepted the mace coming like lighting and in this way, the hope of Balram for killing the enemy was shattered. —1851

SWAYYA

When the king intercepted the mace, then Balram took up his sword and shield; he marched forward to kill the enemy fearlessly; the king seeing him coming showered his arrows and thundered; he cut the shield of Balram into one hundred parts and the sword into three parts. —1852

SWAYYA

Krishna saw Balram with his broken shield and sword and on this side, the king Jarasandh thought of killing him at the same instant; then Krishna moved forward for fighting, holding his discus; according to the poet Ram, he began to challenge the king for fighting. —1853

SWAYYA

Hearing the challenge of Krishna, the king marched forward for waging war; he got enraged and fitted his arrow in his bow; because of the thick armour on his body, the king Jarasandh appeared like Ravana falling on Ram, being highly enraged in the war. —1854

SWAYYA

Seeing the king coming in front of him, Krishna held up his bow and came before the king fearlessly; pulling the bow upto his ear, he shot his arrow on the canopy of the enemy and in an instant, the canopy fell down and broken into bits; it seemed that Rahu had broken the moon into fragments. —1855

SWAYYA

With the chopping down of the canopy, the king got highly infuriated; and he, looking towards Krishna with evil glance, took his dreadful bow in his hand; he began to pull the bow with force, but his hand trembled and the bow could not be pulled; at the same time, Krishna with his bow and arrows intercepted with jerk the bow of Jarasandh. —1856

SWAYYA

When Krishna intercepted the bow of Jarasandh, he getting, enraged and challenging took his sword in his hand and fell upon the enemy's army; the shield collided with the shield and the sword with the sword in such a war as if straw were producing a cracking sound on burning, having been set on fire in the forest. —1857

Someone, getting wounded, was roaming, throwing away blood and someone was roaming without head, becoming only a headless trunk; seeing which the cowards are getting frightened; some of the warriors, leaving the war-fray are running away; some of them are absorbed in war, getting intoxicated; some warriors are lying lifeless like the one highly intoxicated after drinking wine. —1858

SWAYYA

In extreme fury, the Yadavas, holding their weapons, have fallen on Jarasandh; the mighty warriors, taking up their swords are challenging all; the king Jarasandh, taking his bow in his hand is proudly discharging his arrows towards the enemies and even with a single arrow, he is routing many, making them headless. —1859

SWAYYA

He cut down the arm of some one and caused the head of some one fall down after cutting it; some Yadava was deprived of his chariot; then he shot an arrow towards Krishna; he got many horses and elephants killed and fall on the ground; and the Yoginis, ghosts, fiends, jackals etc., began to bathe in the sea of blood in the battlefield. —1860

SWAYYA

After killing the warriors of Krishna the king became extremely angry and he was absorbed in fighting to such an extent that he forgot the consciousness of his body and mind; he destroyed the army of Krishna and scattered it in the earth; it appeared that the king has raised the tax of their heads from the warriors. —1861

SWAYYA

Those who wanted to be on the side of truth, they were released and those who sided with falsehood, they were knocked down; the wounded warriors are lying in the battlefield like the punished criminals; many were killed by cutting their hands and feet; every one received the reward of his actions; it appeared that the king sitting on chariot as throne was imparting justice regarding the sinner and sinless. —1862

SWAYYA

Seeing such a dreadful war of the king, Krishna was filled with rage and abandoning the fear began terrible fighting in front of the king; an arrow of Krishna struck the heart of the king and he fell down on the earth; the arrow of Krishna, penetrated in such a way in the white marrow of the king that it seemed like a snake drinking milk. —1863

SWAYYA

Enduring the arrow of Krishna, which struck his heart, he shot an arrow towards Krishna, which hit Daruk, whom it caused great agony; he was about to fall from his seat in the chariot, when the brisk horses exhibited their speed and fled. —1864

DOHIRA

Catching hold of the arm of the charioteer and controlling the chariot Krishna himself drove it while fighting. —1865

SWAYYA

When Balram did not see the charioteer on the chariot of Krishna, He said in anger, "O king! the way, in which I have conquered your army, similarly after conquering you, I shall cause the drum of victory to be beaten, "O fool! calling yourself a king, you are fighting with the Lord of all the fourteen words and appear exactly like the tiny worms and insects, getting wings who are trying to complete the falcon flying in the sky." —1866

SWAYYA

"I am leaving you today; do not fight with the Lord of all the fourteen worlds; accept the wise saying and forsake your ignorance; believe it that Krishna is the Protector of all; therefore you should abandon your weapons, fall at his feet instantly." —1867

CHAUPAI

When Balram said these words, the king got infuriated; he said, "I shall kill all and being a Kshatriya, I shall not fear the milkmen."—1868

SWAYYA

Hearing these words of the king, Krishna was filled with rage and he unhesitatingly fell upon him; the king taking his bow in his hand, chopped the soldiers and caused them to fall down on the earth in such a way as if with blowing of the violent wind, the fruit of the *bel* tree had fallen down. —1869

SWAYYA

The king, destroying the army, was nor considering any war significant; the horses of the king are saturated with blood from head to feet; he has deprived many chariot-riders of their chariot; the limbs of the warriors are lying scattered on the earth like the seed scattered by the farmer. —1870

SWAYYA

Seeing one another in this way, Krishna and Balram both became extremely filled with the fire of anger and reached before the enemy for fighting asking their charioteers to proceed; holding their weapons, and dressed in their armours and also in great fury these heroes looked like the fire; and seeing both these heroes, it appeared that two lions were causing the deer to flee in the forest. —1871

SWAYYA

At the same time, Krishna took his bow and arrow in his hands, struck a blow to the king; then with four arrows he killed the four horses of the king; in great rage, he chopped the bow of the king and also shattered his chariot; thereafter the king is advancing further with his mace in such a way, which I now describe. —1872

SWAYYA

The king, walking on foot, struck a blow on

Balram with his mace, and his whole fury became apparent to the warriors; Balram jumped and came down to stand on the earth and the king pulverised his chariot alongwith all the four horses. —1873

SWAYYA

On this side, the king advanced with his mace on that side Balram also advanced with his mace; both of them waged a terrible war in the battlefield and inspite of the continuance of the war for a long time, none of them could defeat the other; in this way, seeing their fight, the wise warriors became pleased in their mind. —1874

SWAYYA

Both the warriors used to sit, when tired and then rose again for fighting; both of them were fighting fearlessly and angrily with the shouts of "kill, kill;" both were fighting according to the manner of mace-warfare and without slightly wavering from their places, they were saving themselves from the blows of the mace with their own mace. —1875

SWAYYA

According to the poet, both Balram and Jarasandh are full of rage in the war-arena; both are challenging one another and are not afraid of the other even slightly; catching hold of huge maces both are not taking one step backward in the battlefield; they appear like lion ready for hunting. —1876

SWAYYA

Balram cut down the mace of the king and shot arrows at him; he said to him, "Did you fight with me on the strength of this thought of bravery?" Saying this and discharging his arrows, Balram put his bow around the neck of the king; Balram, the hero of Yadavas won in this war and that formidable enemy was defeated. —1877

SWAYYA

He, from whom the king of birds Garuda and the god Shiva tremble; He, from whom the sages, Seshanaga, Varuna, Surya, Chandra, Indra, etc., all of them are afraid in their mind, on the head of that king now hovered Kal (Death); all the warriors hailing said this, "By the grace of Krishna the great enemies have been conquered." —1878

SWAYYA

Balram, holding the mace in his hand, in great fury, said, "I shall kill the enemy; if even Yama comes to protect his life, then I shall also fight with him; even if Krishna asks me taking all the Yadavas alongwith him, then also I shall not let him be alive," Balram said thus, "I shall kill him just now." —1879

Hearing the words of Balram Jarasandh became extremely fearful; and he saw Balram, not as a man, but only as Yama; now the king, looking towards Krishna, abandoning his weapons clung to his feet and said while crying, "O Lord! protect me." —1880

SWAYYA

Krishna, the treasure of compassion, seeing him in such a plight, was wonder-struck and forsaking his anger, caused to flow tears from both his eyes; seeing his brother (a hero) standing there, he said this, "Leave him; to whom we had come to conquer, we have conquered him." —1881

SWAYYA

Balram said, "I have not conquered him by discharging arrows at him and then leave him; what, if I have conquered him; he is a very great and powerful enemy, who is also a great charioteer and at this time, having been deprived of his chariot, O Lord! he has fallen at your feet and saying these things; he is the master of twenty-three extremely large military units and if we had to leave him, then why we have killed his very big army?" —1882

DOHIRA

To conquer a very big army alongwith the enemy is considered a victory and this has been the practice of greatness that instead of killing the enemy, he is set free. —1883

SWAYYA

Jarasandh was set free by giving him one turban, clothes and a chariot considering the greatness of Krishna, the king was extremely ashamed; he went back to his home, repenting in affliction; in this way, the praise of Krishna spread in all the fourteen worlds. —1884

SWAYYA

Krishna destroyed the twenty-three extremely large military units in this way for twenty-three; he killed many horses and elephants and even with a single arrow, they abandoned their bodies and went to the abode of Yama; Krishna was victorious and in this way Jarasandh was defeated for twenty-three times. —1885

DOHIRA

Whatever eulogy was sung by the gods, has been described; and the way in which this story advanced, now I relate that. —1886

SWAYYA

On that side, the king on his defeat went back at his home and on this side, Krishna winning the war, came back to his home; he gave befitting respects to his parents and then caused the canopy to be swung over the head of Uggarsain; he gave gifts in chariots to the talented people, who appreciated him by saying that Krishna, the great hero of the battlefield, conquering a very great enemy has even adored approbation. —1887

SWAYYA

All the women of the city now saw Krishna in person and sacrificed their wealth and ornaments on him; all of them said smilingly; "He has conquered a very great hero in the war; his bravery is as charming as he himself," saying this all of them abandoned their sorrow. —1888

SWAYYA

Seeing Krishna all the women of the city dancing their eyes and smiling said, "Krishna has come back after winning a terrible war;" saying this, they also said unhesitatingly: "O Lord! just as you smiled on seeing Radha, you may also smile looking towards us." —1889

SWAYYA

When the citizens said this, then Krishna began to smile, looking towards all; seeing their charming thought their sorrows and sufferings ended; the women winning with the sentiments of love, fell down upon the earth; the eyebrows of Krishna were like the bow and with the speech of the eyesight, he was alluring every one. —1890

SWAYYA

On that side, the women entrapped in the illusive net of love, went to their homes, Krishna reached the gathering of warriors; seeing Krishna, the king fell at his feet and got him seated on his throne, respectfully; the king presented the extract of *varuni* to Krishna, seeing which he was extremely pleased. —1891

SWAYYA

After drinking *varuni*, Balram told every one that Krishna had killed the elephants and horses; he, who had discharged one arrow on Krishna, he was made lifeless by him; in this way Balram eulogised the way of fighting of Krishna amongst the warriors. —1892

DOHIRA

In that gathering, Balram, with red eyes due to the impact of *varuni*, said to Krishna: —1893

SWAYYA

"O warriors! drink *varuni* with pleasure and this is the duty of Kshatriyas to die while fighting; Bhrigu had spoken against this *varuni* (wine) in the episode of Kach-devyani; (though this episode is related to Shukracharya); according to the poet Ram the gods had obtained this extract (ambrosia) from Brahma. —1894

DOHIRA

The comfort that was given by Krishna, none other can give the same; because he conquered such an enemy, on whose feet, the gods like Indra kept falling. —1895

SWAYYA

Those, whom the gifts were given with delight, no desire of begging remained in them; none of them talked in ire and even if some one faltered, the same was put off smilingly; no one was punished now the wealth was seized from any one by killing him; Krishna had also vowed that none should go back after becoming victorious. —1896

SWAYYA

The comfort that was not obtained by the king Nal on becoming the sovereign of the earth; the comfort that was not obtained by the earth after killing the demon named Mura; the happiness that was not sighted on the killing of Hiranayakashipu, that comfort was obtained by the earth in her mind on the victory of Krishna. —1897

SWAYYA

Decorating their weapons on their limbs, the warriors are thundering like the clouds; the drums that are played at the door of someone on the occasion of marriage, they were being played on the doors of Krishna; there was righteousness reigning supreme within the city and the sin could not be seen anywhere. —1898

DOHIRA

I have described with affection this war of Krishna; O Lord! the temptation for which I have related it, kindly bestow on me that boon. —1899

SWAYYA

O Surya! O Chandra! O Merciful Lord! listen to a request of mine; I am not asking for anything else from you; whatever I wish in my mind, that with Thy grace; if I fall a martyr while fighting with my enemies then I shall think that I have realised truth; O Sustainer of the universe! I may always help the saints in this world and destroy the tyrants; bestow this boon on me. —1900

When I wish for the wealth, it comes to me from my country and abroad; I have no temptation for any miraculous powers; the science of Yoga is of no use to me; because spending time on that, there is no useful realisation from the physical austerities. O Lord, I beg for this boon from Thee that I may fearlessly fall a martyr in the battlefield. —1901

The praise of the Lord pervades the whole universe and this eulogy is being sung by Siddhas (adepts), the highest of sages, Shiva, Brahma, Vyas, etc., His mystery has not been comprehended even by the sage Atri, Parashar, Narada, Sharda, Seshanaga, etc. The poet Shyam has described it in poetic stanzas; O Lord! how can I then please. Thee by describing Thy glory? —1902

End of the description of "Arresting and the Releasing Jarasandh in Warfare" in Krishnavatar in Bachittar Natak.

Now begins the Description of Coming again of Jarasandh bringing Kalyavana alongwith him

SWAYYA

The king in great affection wrote a letter to his friend that Krishna had destroyed his army, had released him after arresting him. He asked him to attack from that side Kalyavana and from his side, he would gather his army. After hearing about the plight of his friend, Kalyavana started the war on Krishna. —1903

SWAYYA

He collected so much army, that it was impossible to enumerate it; when the name of one person was announced, then millions of them responded to the call; the drums of the warriors resounded and in that din, no one's voice was heard; now all were saying that none should stay behind and all should move forward for war with Krishna. —1904

DOHIRA

Kalyavana came with such a powerful and innumerable army and even if one wanted then he could count the leaves of the forest, but it was impossible to count the army. —1905

SWAYYA

Wherever their tents were pitched, there the soldiers rushed like the river-flood; on account of the speedy and thumping gait of the soldiers, the minds of the enemies were getting fearful; the Malechhas were saying in Persian language that they would not retrace even one step in the war and on seeing Krishna, they would despatch him to the abode of Yama with a singly arrow only. —1906

SWAYYA

On this side, the Malechhas advanced in great fury, and on the other side Jarasandh came with a huge army; the leaves of the trees can be counted, but this army cannot be estimated; the messengers while drinking the wine, told about the latest situation to Krishna; though all others were filled with fear and agitation, but Krishna felt pleased on listening to the news. —1907

SWAYYA

On this side, Malechhas rushed forward in great fury, and on the other side Jarasandh reached there with his huge army; all were marching like intoxicated elephants and appeared like the rushing dark clouds; Krishna and Balram were surrounded within Mathura and it seemed that considering other warriors as children, these two great were besieged. —1908

SWAYYA

Balram became highly infuriated and held up his weapons; he advanced to the side where there was the army of Malechhas; he made many warriors lifeless and knocked down many after wounding them; Krishna destroyed the enemy's army in such a manner, that none remained in senses, even slightly. —1909

SWAYYA

Someone is lying wounded and someone lifeless on the ground; somewhere there are lying chopped hands and somewhere chopped feet; many warriors in a great suspense fled away from the battlefield; in this way, Krishna became victorious and all the Malechhas were defeated. —1910

SWAYYA

Krishna killed Wahid Khan, Farzullah Khan, Nijabat Khan, Zahid Khan, Latfullah Khan, etc., and chopped them into bits; Balram struck blows on Himmat Khan, Jafar Khan, etc., with his mace and killing all the army of these Malechhas Krishna became victorious. —1911

SWAYYA

In this way, getting enraged Krishna killed the enemy's army and its kings; whosoever confronted him, he could not go away alive; getting brilliant like the noon-sun, Krishna aggravated his ire and the Malechhas ran away in this way and none could stand before Krishna. —1912

SWAYYA

Krishna waged such a war that there was no one left, who could fight with him; seeing his own plight, Kalyavana sent millions of more soldiers, who fought for a very short time and went to abide in the region of Yama; all the gods, getting pleased, said, "Krishna is waging a fine war." —1913

SWAYYA

The Yadavas holding their weapons, getting enraged in their mind, looking for the warriors equivalent to themselves, are fighting with them; they are fighting in ire and shouting "kill, kill;" the heads of the warriors on being struck with swords remaining stable for some time, are falling on the earth. —1914

SWAYYA

When Krishna waged a dreadful war in the battlefield, the clothes of the warriors became red as if Brahma had created a red world; seeing the war Shiva loosened his matted locks and began to dance and in the way none of the soldiers survived from the Malechha army. —1915

DOHIRA

None of the warriors accompanying him survived and Kalyavana came himself to fight. —1916

SWAYYA

On coming to the war-arena, Kalyavana said, "O Krishna! Come forward to fight unhesitatingly; I am the Lord of my army; I have arisen in the world like sun and I am hailed as unique; I am also the moon, the Lord of the night; O Krishna! Now do not put off the war; come with delight, so that we may be able to play the ball-game of war and win it." —1917

SWAYYA

Hearing his talk, Krishna moved towards him and

in fury discharged his firearm towards him; he knocked down his charioteer at first and then killed all his four horses, all types of weapons that he used were intercepted by Krishna. —1918

CHAUPAI

The Malechha who held up his weapon, was chopped by Krishna; when the enemy remained only on foot and he was deprived of his chariot, then Krishna said, "Had you come to fight with me relying on such strength?" —1919

SWAYYA

Krishna thought in his mind that if this Malechha Mushtaka fights with me, he will make my whole body impure; if he comes after bedecking himself with his armour and weapons, even then he would not be able to kill him and if I kill him, when he is weaponless, then his strength would decline. —1920

SWAYYA

Krishna thought in his mind that if he would run, then the Malechha would run after him, he would enter some cave, but he would not like that Malechha to touch his body; he would awaken the sleeping Muchukund (the son of Mandhata, who had been given the boon that any one who awakens him from sleep, will be reduced to ashes); he would conceal himself, but get the Malechha killed with the fire of the sight of Muchukund. —1921

SORATHA

If he killed him (Kalyavana) while fighting, he would go to heaven, therefore he would get him reduced to ashes by fire, so that his *dharma* (characteristic) as Malechha remains intact. —1922

SWAYYA

Leaving his chariot and forsaking his weapons, Krishna fled, frightening every one; Kalyavana had thought that he had run away, being fearful of him, therefore he pursued Krishna, calling him; Krishna reached there where Muchukund was sleeping and he awakened him by kicking him and then concealed himself; in this way, Krishna saved himself, but got Kalyavana reduced to ashes. —1923

SORATHA

Krishna saved himself from Muchukund, but when Muchukund awoke from sleep and saw towards Kalyavana, who was reduced to ashes. —1924

SWAYYA

When Kalyavana was burnt and reduced to ashes, then Krishna came to Muchukund; on seeing Krishna Muchukund bowed his head at his feet; the Lord Krishna consoled him with his words and instructing Muchukund and getting Kalyavana reduced to ashes, he went to his home. —1925

End of the chapter entitled "Killing of Kalyavana" in Krishnavatar in Bachittar Natak.

Now begins the Description of Arresting Jarasandh and then Releasing Him

SWAYYA

As soon as Krishna arrived in his tent, someone came to deliver the message: "O Krishna! why are you going to your home? On that side, Jarasandh is coming, bedecked with his army;" hearing these words, the minds of the warriors became fearful; but Krishna and Balram were pleased at this. —1926

DOHIRA

Absorbed in this talk, all the warriors reached in the city; the king Uggarsain then called all his wise confidants. —1927

SWAYYA

The king said, "Jarasandh is coming in fury with his huge army and we cannot save ourselves with fighting; either we should go to receive him or leaving the city, run away to some other place; this is a very serious matter; nothing will result from mere talk now." —1928

SORATHA

Ultimately it was decided to leave the city and abide at some other place, otherwise the powerful king Jarasandh would kill all. —1929

Only that decision should be taken, which is liked by all; merely the persistence of the mind should not be accepted. —1930

SWAYYA

Hearing about the coming of the enemy, the Yadavas started moving out of Mathura with their families; they felt pleased in hiding themselves on a big mountain; the king Jarasandh besieged the mountain and it appeared that in order to destroy the people waiting on the bank to cross the river, the warriors of clouds were rushing towards them from above. —1931

DOHIRA

Then Jarasandh said to his ministers, "This is a very big mountain and the army will not be able to ascend it." —1932

SORATHA

"Besiege the mountain from all the ten directions and set it on fire; and with this fire all the families of the Yadavas will be burnt." —1933

SWAYYA

The poet Shyam says that surrounding the mountain from all the ten directions, it was set on fire; with the blowing of the powerful wind, the fire burst into flames; when the straws, trees, beings etc., were all destroyed in an instant, those moments were very agonising for the Yadavas. —1934

CHAUPAI

When the beings and straws began burning, then all the Yadava warriors in great suspense came to Krishna and began to relate their sufferings while crying. —1935

Speech of all Yadavas

CHAUPAI

"O Lord! protect us and save all these beings; tell us some remedy, so that either we may die fighting or run away. —1936

SWAYYA

Hearing their talk, the Lord pressed the mountain with his feet, and the mountain could not endure his weight and sank below like water; after sinking below, the mountain rose higher and in this way, the fire could not burn any one; at the same time, Krishna and Balram jumped silently into the enemy's army. —1937

SWAYYA

Holding his mace in his hand, Krishna killed many warriors of the king, he killed many horsemen and knocked them on the ground; he destroyed the ranks of soldiers on feet and deprived the chariot-riders of their chariots; in this way, killing all the warriors, Krishna became victorious and the enemy was defeated. —1938

SWAYYA

The warriors who came to fight with Krishna, they fought with extreme zest; seeing the plight of the warriors in the war-arena, the king Uggarsain said, "The king Jarasandh is like betel, who is destroying his army like the chewing of the betel." —1939

SWAYYA

On this side, Balram taking his mace in his hand in rage, shook violently the enemy's army and the warrior who confronted him, he broke his head even with one slap; he defeated all the remaining enemy army and became completely victorious. —1940

When both the brothers Krishna and Balram together killed the whole army of the enemy, then only that person could save himself, who putting the grass-straws in his mouth, came under their refuge; when Jarasandh saw this plight with his own eyes, then abandoning the hope of victory and life, he also persistently managed to upkeep his bravery in war. —1941

SORATHA

Seeing the king, Krishna struck his mace and killing his four horses, he caused the king to fall down. —1942

DOHIRA

When the king was only on foot, Krishna struck him with his mace again and the king could not control himself. —1943

TOTAK STANZA

When the king rolled and fell down, then Krishna caught him and said, "O fool! did you come for fighting relying on this strength." —1944

Speech of the Balram addressed to Krishna

DOHIRA

Balram said, "Now I shall chop off his head, because if he is permitted to go alive, he will then return to fight again." —1945

Speech of Jarasandh

SWAYYA

Then the king controlling himself, in fear, abandoning his weapons, fell down at the feet of Krishna and said, "O Lord! do not kill me; I have not comprehended your power rightly;" in this way, coming under refuge, the king cried and seeing him in such a plight, Krishna was filled with mercy. —1946

Speech of Krishna addressed to Balram

TOTAK STANZA

"Balram! leave him now and remove the ire from our mind;" then Balram said, "Why does he fight with us?" Then Krishna replied while smiling: —1947

SORATHA

"If a greater enemy, relinquishing his weapons, falls at your feet, then forsaking all the anger from the mind, the great people do not kill him." —1948

DOHIRA

Releasing Jarasandh, the Lord said, "O king! whatever I am telling you, listen it carefully." —1949

SWAYYA

"O king! always do justice and never do any injustice with the helpless; earn praise by giving something in charity; serve the Brahmins; do not let the deceivers remain alive and never indulge in war with Kshatriyas like us." —1950

DOHIRA

Jarasandh, bowing down his head and repenting, went away to his home and on this side, Krishna, getting pleased, came to his home. —1951

End of the chapter entitled "Arresting and Releasing Jarasandh" in Krishnavatar in Bachittar Natak.

Now begins the Description of Building the City of Dwarka by Krishna

CHAUPAI

All had been puffed up on hearing the news of victory, but they had become sorrowful on knowing that king Jarasandh had been released; by this the mind of all had become fearful and all were saying that krishna had not done the right thing. —1952

SWAYYA

All of them said, "Krishna has done the child's job by releasing such a powerful one from his custody; he was released earlier and the reward that we got was that we had to abandon our city; all of them nodded negatively in affection at Krishna's child-like act; after conquering him, he has been let off now; in reality we understand that he has been sent to bring more army." —1953

SWAYYA

Someone said that it would be better to go back to Mathura; someone said that the king would come again with his army for war and then who will die in the battlefield? And even if one fought with him, he would not be able to win; therefore we may not to go back to the city immediately; whatever God Wills, will come to pass and let us see what happens. —1954

SWAYYA

The release of the king made all the Yadavas fearful; and all of them talking about various things went to reside on the seacoast; and none of them advanced his feet towards the city (Mathura); all the warriors, beaten up without weapons, were standing there, extremely frightened. —1955

SWAYYA

Krishna went and stood by the seaside and he addressed the sea to do something; when the sea was asked to vacate the earth, while fitting the arrow in the bow, he left the earth and without the desire of anybody he prepared the golden mansions; seeing this all said in their minds that Krishna has removed the sufferings of all. —1956

SWAYYA

Those who served Sanak, Sanandan etc., the Lord could not be realised by them; many sages worship Him in stones and many have determined His Form according to the Vedic instructions, but when through the Grace of Krishna, the golden mansions were raised at this place, then all the people, having sight of the Lord, began to adore Him. —1957

SWAYYA

Balram said smilingly to all the warriors, "This Krishna has improved all the fourteen worlds; you have not been able to understand His mystery till now; He is the one who has killed Ravana, Mura and Subahu and has torn the face of Bakasura; He has killed with a single blow of His mace, the powerful demon Shankhasura. —1958

SWAYYA

"He, after fighting with Madhu and Kaitabh for one thousand years, made them lifeless and when the ocean was churned, then it was he, who protected the gods and increased their happiness; it was He, who killed Ravana by discharging an arrow in his heart; and when we agonised by afflictions, then he stood firmly like a column in the battlefield." —1959

"Listen to me attentively, that He for your welfare, knocked down the king like Kansa and threw the elephants and horses after killing them like the uprooted trees; all the enemies who attacked us, He knocked down all of them and now has now bestowed on you the golden mansions removing the earthen ones." —1960

SWAYYA

When these words were uttered by Balram, then all considered them as true that the same Krishna had killed Bakasura, Aghasura Chandur, etc. Kansa could not be conquered by Indra, but Krishna, catching him his hair, knocked him down, and he has given us the golden mansions, therefore He is now the Real Lord. —1961

SWAYYA

In this way, the days passed off comfortably and no one was inflicted with sufferings; the golden mansions were made in such a way that even Shiva could have coveted for them on seeing them; Indra leaving his city alongwith the gods came to see this city and the poet Shyam says that Krishna had designed very nicely the outline of this city. —1962

End of the chapter entitled "Building of the City of Dwarka" in Krishnavatar (based on *Dasham Skandapurana*) in Bachittar Natak.

Now begins the Description of the Marriage of Balram

DOHIRA

In this way, Krishna, passed off many days in peace and comfort; after that a king named Rewat came and touched the feet of Balram. —1963

"The name of my daughter is Rewati and I request that Balram may wed her." —1964

SWAYYA

Hearing these words of the king, Balram was extremely pleased; and taking with him other members of his brotherhood, started immediately for marriage; the same was solemnised happily, and caused the Brahmins to be given the gifts in charity; in this way, after the marriage ceremony, he returned to his home delightfully. —1965

CHAUPAI

When Balram saw towards his wife and found that he himself was smaller and she was taller in size, seeing this he placed his plough on her shoulder and according to his desire fashioned her body. —1966

DOHIRA

The marriage of Balram was solemnised with Rewati and in this way according to the poet

Shyam, this episode of the marriage was completed. —1967

End of the description of "The Marriage of Balram" in Krishnavatar in Bachittar Natak.

Now begins the Description of the Marriage of Rukmani

SWAYYA

When the marriage of Balram was solemnised and all the men and women were pleased, then Krishna also coveted for marriage in his mind; the king Bhishmak arranged the marriage of his daughter and gathered together all the warriors of his army; it appeared that Krishna had prepared nicely his plan of marriage. —1968

SWAYYA

The king Bhishmak arranged the marriage of his daughter with Krishna, thinking that there could be no more suitable task than this and marrying his daughter with Krishna would bring also approbation for him; the son of Bhishmak named Rukmi then came and said to his father in rage; "What are you doing? The clan, with which we have enmity, how shall we be able to live in the world, giving our daughter in marriage to such a clan?" —1969

Speech of Rukmi addressed to the King
SWAYYA

"Shishupal, the king of Chanderi is a hero, call him for the marriage; giving the daughter in marriage to a milkman, we will die with shame, call an eminent Brahmin and send him for bringing Shishupal; whatever mode of marriage is mentioned in the Vedas, solemnise the marriage of the daughter according to that with Shishupal." —1970

SWAYYA

Hearing the words of his son, the king sent a Brahmin to bring Shishupal; bowing head, that Brahmin went towards that side; and on this side, the daughter of the king heard this talk; hearing that talk, she dashed her head in agony and the tears flowed from her eyes; her hope seemed to have been shattered and she withered like a tree. —1971

Speech of Rukmani addressed to Her Friends
SWAYYA

Rukmani said to her friends; "O friends! now I am taking a vow that I shall leave the country and become a yogini (recluse), otherwise I shall burn myself in the fire of separation; if my father is specially persistent, then I shall take poison and die; I shall marry only Krishna, otherwise I shall not be called the daughter of a king." —1972

DOHIRA

"There is another thought in my mind; an effort may be made to send a letter through someone, which may inform all this to Krishna." —1973

Keeping this thought in their mind, they called a Brahmin and giving him good deal of money they asked him to take the letter to Krishna. —1974

Letter of Rukmani to Krishna
SWAYYA

"O the one with charming eyes! do not be absorbed in more thoughts and come immediately after reading the letter; Shishupal is coming to marry me, therefore you should avoid even the slightest delay; kill him and conquering me, take me to Dwarka and earn approbation in the world; hearing this plight of mine, fixing wings on your body fly towards me." —1975

SWAYYA

"O Lord of all the fourteen worlds! Kindly listen to my message attentively; the ego and anger have increased in the souls of all except you, O the Lord and destroyer of the three worlds! I never desire that which my father and brother desire; kindly come on reading this letter, because only three days remain for the marriage." —1976

DOHIRA

"O Brahmin! kindly tell (Krishna) that only three days remain for the marriage and O Lord! kindly come without delay with this Brahmin." —1977

SWAYYA

"Tell Krishna, that without him I feel frightened throughout the night and my soul, getting extremely agitated, wants to leave the body; the moon risen in the east is burning me and without you, the red face of the god of love frightens me." —1978

SWAYYA

"O Krishna! My mind turns towards you again and inspite of restraining it, it has remained entrapped in your charming memory; it does not accept the advice although I instruct if for a lakh of times; and has become immovable from your portrait; because of shyness both eyes have become stable at their place like an acrobat." —1979

Everyone felt comfortable after sending the Brahmin, giving him the chariot, money and incentive for bringing Krishna; he also taking the letter went with greater speed than even the speed of the wind for reaching the place of Krishna at the earliest. —1980

SWAYYA

The city of Krishna's residence was extremely beautiful and on the four sides pearls, rubies and jewels were studded with glittering lights; the description of that city is beyond everybody's ken, because the regions of Seshanaga, Chandra, Varuna, and Indra looked pale before the city of Dwarka. —1981

DOHIRA

Extremely pleased on seeing the city, the Brahmin reached the palace of Krishna. —1982

SWAYYA

Seeing the Brahmin, Krishna got up and called him, "The Brahmin placed the letter before him, reading which Krishna was extremely pleased; he mounted his chariot and moved with the swift speed of wind like a hungry lion following a herd of deer." —1983

SWAYYA

On this side, Krishna went on his chariot and on the other side Shishupal reached alongwith a good deal of army; special gates were erected in the city and decorated on knowing about the arrival of Shishupal and Rukmi, and others came alongwith the army in order to welcome him; according to the poet Shyam, all the warriors were extremely pleased in their mind. —1984

SWAYYA

Many other great kings reached there alongwith their fourfold army getting pleased, reached there in order to see the wedding of Rukmani; the kettledrums, clarionets, and small drums were being played with such intensity that the ear-drums seemed to be getting torn. —1985

The marriage of both was solemnised according to Vedic rites and there were performed the matrimonial rites of moving round the sacred fire with the chanting of mantras; enormous gifts were given to the eminent Brahmins; a charming altar was erected, but nothing seemed appropriate without Krishna. —1986

SWAYYA

Then taking the priests alongwith themselves all went to worship the goddess; many warriors followed them on their chariots; seeing such an atmosphere, Rukmi, the brother of Rukmani said this, "O Lord! I am very fortunate that you have protected my honour." —1987

CHAUPAI

When Rukmani went into the temple, she became greatly agitated with affliction; she beseeched Chandi weepingly if this match was necessary for her. —1988

SWAYYA

Keeping her friends away from her, she took the small dagger in her hand and said, "I shall commit suicide; I have served Chandi greatly and for that service, I have got this reward; I shall die and this place will become polluted by my death; otherwise I shall please her now and get the boon of marrying Krishna from her." —1989

Speech of the Goddess

SWAYYA

Seeing her in such a plight, the mother of the world was pleased and said to her, "You are the wife of Krishna, you should have no duality about this, even slightly; whatever there is in the mind of Shishupal, that will never occur and whatever is in your mind, that will definitely happen." —1990

DOHIRA

After getting this boon from Chandika, and being pleased she mounted on her chariot; and went back considering Krishna as a friend in her mind. —1991

SWAYYA

Abiding Krishna in her mind, she mounted on her chariot and went back and seeing the large army of the enemies she did not utter the name of Krishna from her mouth; at the same time, Krishna reached there and he shouted the name Rukmani and catching her by her arm, he put her in his chariot with his strength. —1992

SWAYYA

Taking Rukmani in his chariot, Krishna said within the hearing of all the warriors, "I am taking her away even within the sight of Rukmi and anyone who has the audacity, he may now rescue her by fighting with me; I shall kill all today, but shall not swerve from this task." —1993

SWAYYA

Hearing these words of Krishna, all of them got infuriated and patting their arms in great anger fell upon him; all of them attacked Krishna playing their clarionets, kettledrums, small drums and war-trumpets; and Krishna taking his bow and arrows in his hands, despatched all of them to the abode of Yama in an instant. —1994

SWAYYA

The warriors fearing none and playing on their drums and chanting war-songs came before Krishna like the clouds of Sawan; when Krishna discharged his arrows, they could not stay before even for an instant; someone is groaning, while lying on the earth and someone is reaching the abode of Yama after dying. —1995

SWAYYA

Seeing such a plight of the army, Shishupal himself came forward in great fury and said to Krishna, "Do not consider me Jarasandh, whom you caused to run away;" saying this, be pulled his bow upto his ear and discharged such an arrow that it seemed that all his anger, manifesting itself in the form of an arrow had fallen on Krishna. —1996

DOHIRA

Krishna got enraged, seeing that arrow coming he intercepted the same midway with his own arrow. —1997

SWAYYA

After intercepting the arrow, he shattered the chariot, chopped the head of the charioteer; and with the blows of his arrows, and with jerks, he chopped the heads of all the four horses; then running towards him, he struck him (Shishupal), who being hurt, fell down; who is such a hero in the world, who can resist Krishna? —1998

SWAYYA

He, who meditated on the Lord, reached the abode of the Lord and whosoever, stabilising himself, fought in front of Krishna, he could not stay there even for an instant; whosoever absorbed himself in his love, he penetrating through all the worlds, realised the abode of the Lord without any abstraction; he, who opposed him, even slightly, that individual was caught and knocked down on the ground. —1999

SWAYYA

After killing innumerable army, Krishna caused Shishupal to fall down unconscious; the army that was standing there, seeing this situation fled away in fear; though efforts were made to restrain them, but none of the returned for fighting; then Rukmi came for fighting alongwith a great deal of his army. —2000

SWAYYA

From his side many warriors rushed forward, in great fury, went to kill Krishna and said, "O Krishna, where are you going? Fight with us;" they were killed by Krishna like the moths, in search of the earthen lamp fall upon it, but do not return alive. —2001

SWAYYA

When the army was killed by Krishna, then, getting infuriated Rukmi said to his army; "When Krishna, the milkman can hold the bow and arrows, then the Kshatriyas should also perform this task firmly;" when he was thus speaking, Krishna advanced forward and with his arrow made him unconscious and caught him by his top-knot and shaving his head made him look ridiculous. —2002

DOHIRA

Seeing his brother in such a plight, Rukmani caught hold of the feet of Krishna and got his brother released through several kinds of requests. —2003

SWAYYA

Those who came for his support, they were also killed as Krishna willed, the warrior who was killed, he was not killed by deception but killed after challenging him; many kings, elephants, horses and chariot riders were killed and the stream of blood flowed there; on the request of Rukmani, Krishna caught and released many warriors of the side of Rukmi. —2004

SWAYYA

Till that time, Balram also, getting enraged and carrying his mace, fell upon the army and he knocked down the running army; after killing the army, he came to Krishna and hearing about the shaving of the head of Rukmi, he said this. —2005

Speech of Balram

DOHIRA

Though Krishna conquered the brother of Rukmani, but did not perform the right type of task by shaving his head. —2006

SWAYYA

Arresting and releasing Rukmi in the city, Krishna came to Dwarka; on coming to know that Krishna has conquered and brought Rukmani, the people came to see her; several eminent Brahmins were called for performing the wedding-ceremonies; all the warriors were also invited there. —2007

SWAYYA

Hearing about the wedding of Krishna, the ladies of the city came while singing songs; they sang and danced in accompaniment with musical tunes and the damsels getting together began to laugh and play; what to speak of others, even the wives of gods came to see this spectacle. —2008

SWAYYA

He, who comes to see the beautiful damsel, Rukmani and this pageant, he, joining the dance and sport, forgets the consciousness about his home; all are getting pleased seeing the plan of wedding and seeing Krishna, all are getting charmed in their mind. —2009

SWAYYA

On the completion of the wedding-altar of Krishna, all the women sang songs of praises; the jugglers began to dance according to the musical tune of the drums; many concubines exhibited many kinds of mimicry; whosoever came to see this spectacle, obtained extreme delight. —2010

SWAYYA

Some damsel is playing the flute and someone is clapping her hands; someone is dancing according to the norms and someone is singing; someone is ringing the anklet, someone is playing on the drum and someone is showing her charms and someone is pleasing all by exhibiting her charms. —2011

SWAYYA

The place where Krishna is sitting intoxicated with wine and wearing happily his red garments, from that place, he is giving wealth in charity to the dancers and beggars; and all are getting pleased on seeing Krishna. —2012

SWAYYA

Krishna married Rukmani according to the Vedic-rites, whom he had conquered from Rukmi; the minds of all were full of the happy tidings of victory and seeing this pageant, all the Yadavas were extremely happy. —2013

SWAYYA

The mother made the offering of water and drank it; she also gave gifts in charity to the Brahmins; everyone believed that entire happiness of the universe has been attained; the mother said this; "O friend! My mind is extremely happy; I am a sacrifice to this day, when my son has been married." —2014

End of the chapter entitled "Description of the Abduction of Rukmani and Her Marriage" in Krishnavatar (based on *Dasham Skandapurana*) in Bachittar Natak.

Description of the Birth of Pradyumna

DOHIRA

The husband and wife passed many days in comfort, then Rukmani became pregnant. —2015

SORATHA

A heroic child named Pradyumna was born, whom the world know as a great warrior and conqueror of war. —2016

SWAYYA

When the child was only ten days of age, a demon named Shambar stole him and threw him in the sea, where he was swallowed by a fish; a fisherman caught that fish and brought it to Shambar, who, getting pleased, sent it to the kitchen for cooking. —2017

SWAYYA

When the belly of the fish was torn open, a beautiful child was seen there; the kitchenmaid was filled with pity; Narada came and said to her, "He is your husband;" and that woman, considering him her husband, brought him up. —2018

CHAUPAI

After being brought up for a good deal of time, he thought about a woman in his mind; the woman also, with sexual desire, said this to the son of Rukmani. —2019

Then Mainvati said this, "You are the son of Rukmani and also my husband; the demon Shambar had stolen you and thrown you into the sea." —2020

CHAUPAI

"Then a fish had swallowed you and that fish was also caught; the fisherman brought it to Shambar, where he sent it to me for cooking." —2021

"When I tore open the belly of the fish, I saw you there; my mind became pityful and at the same time Narada said to me." —2022

"That he is the incarnation of Kamadeva (the god of love), whom you seek day and night; I have served you, considering you as my husband and seeing you now I am under the impact of sexual desire." —2023

"When, because of Shiva's anger, your body was burnt to ashes, then I had meditated on Shiva, who, getting pleased, had bestowed on me this boon that the same husband would be attained by me." —2024

DOHIRA

Then I become a kitchenmaid of Shambar; now Shiva has made you the same charming one. —2025

SWAYYA

Hearing these words, the son of Krishna got extremely enraged and catching hold of bow, arrows and mace moved to kill the enemy; he began to challenge the enemy on reaching his place: "The one whom you had thrown into the sea, has now come to fight with you." —2026

SWAYYA

When the son of Krishna uttered these words, then Shambar came forward holding his weapons including the mace; he began the fight, keeping before him the norms of fighting he did not run away from the battle and began to frighten Pradyumna in order to restrain him from fighting; according; to the poet Shyam, in this way, this battle continued there. —2027

SWAYYA

When the dreadful fighting continued there, the enemy deceptively reached the sky and from there he showered stones on the son of Krishna; Pradyumna made those stones harmless with his arrows by intercepting them and pierced his body with his weapons, causing him to fall on the ground. —2028

Pradyumna struck his sword with a jerk and cutting the head of Shambar threw it down; the gods, seeing such a bravery, hailed him, making the demon unconscious, he knocked him down on the earth; bravo to the son of Krishna, who killed Shambar with one blow of his sword. —2029

End of the chapter describing "The Abduction of Pradyumna by the Demon Shambar and His Killing" in Krishnavatar in Bachittar Natak.

Now begins the Description of the Meeting of Pradyumna with Rukmani after Killing Shambar

DOHIRA

After killing him, Pradyumna came to his home, then Rati was extremely pleased to meet her husband. —2030

She transformed herself into a vulture and got her husband mounted on her and carrying him reached the palace of Rukmani. —2031

SWAYYA

She abandoned there the body of vulture and assumed her own beautiful figure of a woman; after dismounting Pradyumna from her shoulder, she caused him to wear the yellow garments; sixteen thousand women saw Pradyumna there and they thought with caution that perhaps Krishna himself had come there. —2032

SWAYYA

Seeing the likeness of Krishna in Pradyumna, the women said in their state of shyness that Krishna then wedded and brought another damsel; one woman looking towards him, said in her mind, "All other signs on his body are similar to Krishna, but there is no mark of the foot of the sage Bhrigu on his chest." —2033

SWAYYA

Seeing Pradyumna, the teats of Rukmani were filled with milk; in her attachment she did modestly, "O friend! my son was just like him; O Lord! give back to me my own son;" saying thus, she heaved a long breath and the tears rushed forth from both her eyes. —2034

Krishna came from this side and everyone began to stare at him; then Narada came and he related the whole story. He said, "O Krishna! he is your son;" hearing this the songs of joy were sung in the whole city; it appeared that Krishna had obtained an ocean of fortune. —2035

End of the description of "Pradyumna Meeting with Krishna after Killing the Demon Shambar" in Krishnavatar (based on *Dasham Skandapurana*) in Bachittar Natak.

Now begins the Description of Bringing of the Jewel by Satrajit from Surya and the Killing of Jamwant

DOHIRA

The powerful Satrajit (a Yadava) served the god Surya, and he bestowed upon him the gift of a Jewel bright like himself. —2036

SWAYYA

Satrajit after taking the Jewel from Surya came to his home; and he had pleased Surya after extremely faithful service; now he performed many austere self-mortification and sang the praises of the Lord; seeing him in such a state, the citizens gave his description to Krishna. —2037

Speech of Krishna

SWAYYA

Krishna called Satrajit and said to him, "The wealth of jewel that you have obtained from Surya, give that to the king;" there was a flash of lightning in his mind and he did not do according to the desire of Krishna; he sat silently and he also did not give any reply to Krishna's words. —2038

SWAYYA

The Lord having uttered the said words, sat silently, but his brother went away for hunting towardsthe forest; he was wearing the jewel on his head and it appeared that a second sun had risen; when he went within the forest, he saw a lion there; there he discharged several arrows one after the other towards the lion. —2039

CHAUPAI

When the arrow was shot on the head of the lion, the lion sustained his strength; he gave a slap and caused his turban to fall down alongwith the jewel. —2040

DOHIRA

After killing him and taking his turban and jewel, the lion went away to the forest, where he saw a big bear. —2041

SWAYYA

Seeing the jewel, the bear thought that the lion was bringing some fruit; he contemplated that he was hungry, therefore he would eat that fruit; when the lion was moving away, the bear suddenly attacked him and after a dreadful battle, he killed the lion with one slap. —2042

DOHIRA

Jamwant, the bear, after killing the lion, returned to his home with a happy mind and went to sleep. —2043

On this side, Satrajit, thinking about the mystery, said within the hearing of everyone, "Krishna has snatched away the jewel after killing my brother." —2044

SWAYYA

Hearing this discussion, the Lord called him; Satrajit said again, "Krishna has killed my brother for the sake of the jewel;" hearing these words, the mind of Krishna was filled with rage; he said, "You should also accompany me for searching your brother." —2045

SWAYYA

Krishna, taking the Yadavas with him, went in search of the brother of Satrajit and reached there where Ashvapati was lying dead; the people looked for the lion here and there and imagined that he had been killed by the lion; when they advanced further a little, they saw the dead lion; seeing him, all of them were wonder-struck and got agitated. —2046

DOHIRA

All of them went with bowed heads in search of that bear and wherever they found the footprints of the bear, they continued to move in that direction. —2047

Speech of the Poet

SWAYYA

The Lord, whose boon resulted in the victory over the demons, who had all run away; the Lord who made destroyed the enemies and Surya and Chandra began to perform their duties; He, who made Kubja, a most beautiful woman in an instant and incensed the atmosphere; the same Lord is going in search of the bear for his task. —2048

SWAYYA

All of them discovered him in a cave; then Krishna said, "Is there any powerful person who can enter this cave" but none of them gave a reply in the affirmative; everyone thought that the bear was in the same cave, but still some of them said that he had not entered it; Krishna said that the bear was in that cave. —2049

When none of them present heroes went into the cave, Krishna himself went therein; the bear also imagined the arrival of somebody and in great fury, rushed forward for fighting; the poet says that Krishna waged such a battle with him for twelve days, which has not been fought earlier and will not be fought afterwards in the four ages. —2050

SWAYYA

For twelve days and nights, Krishna continued fighting and did not feel afraid, even slightly; there was a dreadful battle with legs and fists, and feeling the strength of Krishna, the power of the bear declined; he abandoned the fighting and considering Krishna as the Lord, he fell down at his feet. —2051

SWAYYA

He beseeched earnestly on falling at his feet and said with utter humility, "You are the killer of

Ravana and the saviour of the honour of Draupadi; O Lord! considering Surya and Chandra as my witnesses, I request for the forgiveness of my fault;" saying this, he presented before Krishna his daughter as an offering. —2052

SWAYYA

On that side Krishna married after fighting and on this side, his companions standing outside came back to their homes; they believed that Krishna who had gone in the cave had been killed by the bear; the water flowed from the eyes of the warriors and they began to roll on the earth in affliction; several of them repented that they had not been of any use to Krishna. —2053

SWAYYA

The army accompanying Krishna came back to the king and wept, seeing which the king became extremely sorrowful; he ran towards Balram to consult him, but he also told the same thing that Krishna went into the cave, but did not turn back. —2054

Speech of Balram

SWAYYA

"Either Krishna has been killed at the hands of the enemy or this foolish Satrajit has gone to the nether-world in search of the jewel of this foolish Satrajit or he has gone to bring back the life-force (soul) of his brother from Yama or he has not returned after feeling shy of the words of this foolish man."—2055

SWAYYA

When Balram said all this to the king while weeping, then all the Yadavas together beat Satrajit with legs and fists; his turban was removed and tying his hands and feet, he was thrown in a well; no one advised for his release and contemplated to kill him. —2056

When the women heard these things regarding Krishna, they fell down weeping on the earth and some of them lamented; someone said that her husband had breathed his last, what would be her condition then; Rukmani gave gifts to the Brahmins and thoughts of becoming a *sati* (dying on the funeral pyre of the husband). —2057

DOHIRA

Vasudeva and Devaki, becoming extremely anxious, and thinking about the unapproachable Will of the Lord, restrained Rukmani from becoming a *sati*. —2058

SWAYYA

Devaki instructed her daughter-in-law in this way: "that if Krishna had died in a war, then it was appropriate for her to become a *sati*, but if he had gone far beyond in search of the jewel (of Satrajit), then it is not right to become a *sati*; therefore the search for him might still be continued." Saying this, they bowed their heads on the feet of Rukmani and with their modesty got her assent. —2059

Instructing their daughter-in-law in this way, they worshipped Chandika and serving her continuously for twenty-eight days, they pleased her; Chandika, getting pleased bestowed this boon of not getting sorrowful because Krishna would come back. —2060

Seeing Krishna with the jewel, Rukmani forgot all other things and bringing water for offering to Chandika, she reached (at the temple); all the Yadavas became pleased and there were felicitations in the city; the poet says that in this way, everyone considered the mother of the world as the right one. —2061

End of the description of "Conquering Jamwant and Bringing the Jewel alongwith His Daughter" in Krishnavatar in Bachittar Natak.

Now begins the Description of Giving the Jewel to Satrajit

SWAYYA

After finding out Satrajit, Krishna taking the jewel in his hand, threw it in front of him and said, "O fool! take away your jewel, for which you had denounced me; all the Yadavas were wonder-struck to see this anger of Krishna and the same story has been related by the poet Shyam in his stanzas." —2062

SWAYYA

He took the jewel in his hand and without seeing towards anyone and feeling ashamed, left for his home in embarrassment; now Krishna has become my enemy and this is a blemish for me, but alongwith it my brother has also been killed; I have been entrapped in a difficult situation, therefore now I should offer my daughter to Krishna. —2063

End of the description "About Giving the Jewel to Satrajit" in Krishnavatar (based on *Dasham Skandapurana*) in Bachittar Natak.

Now begins the Description of the Marriage of the Daughter of Satrajit

SWAYYA

Calling the Brahmins, Satrajit made arrangements for the marriage of his daughter according to the Vedic ceremonies; the name of his daughter was Satyabhama, whose praise had been spread amongst all the people; Even Lakshmi was not like her; Krishna was invited with respect in order to wed her. —2064

Receiving this news, Krishna went with the marriage party towards her; knowing about the impending arrival of the Lord, all the people reached to welcome him; he was taken reverently for the nuptial ceremonies; the Brahmins were given the gifts; Krishna returned to his home happily after the marriage. —2065

End of the "Completion of the Marriage Ceremonies" in Krishnavatar in Bachittar Natak.

Now begins the Description of the Episode of the House of Wax

SWAYYA

Hearing all these things till that time, the Pandavas came to the House of Wax; they all requested the Kauravas together, but the Kauravas did not have the slight element of mercy; after great reflection, they called Krishna, who, after bedecking his chariot started for that place. —2066

SWAYYA

When Krishna started going towards that place, then Kratvarma thought of something and taking Akrur with him, he asked him, "Where Krishna has gone?" Come, let us snatch away the jewel from Satrajit and thinking like this, they killed Satrajit; after killing him Kratvarma went to his home. —2067

CHAUPAI

When they killed Satrajit, Shatdhanva with them; on this side, all the three came to their homes and on that side, Krishna came to know about it. —2068

Speech of the Messenger addressed to Krishna
CHAUPAI

The messenger said to the Lord, "Kratvarma has killed Satrajit; he has snatched away the jewel from him and in this way he has inflicted great suffering on your wife Satyabhama." —2069

When Krishna heard this, he came to their side, leaving all other engagements; when Kratvarma learnt about the coming of Krishna, he said to Shatdhanva: —2070

ARIL

"O Shatdhanva! what should we do now? If you say, we shall run away or shall die fighting; advise and instruct me about one of them and tell me if there is any step, by which we can kill Krishna." —2071

After hearing the words of Kratvarma, he said, "The enemy Krishna, whom you want to kill, is a powerful and mighty warrior and I have no such strength that I can fight against him; he has, without any special effort, killed persons like Kansa in an instant." —2072

ARIL

Hearing his words, he came to Akrur and talked to him about his duality regarding Krishna. He replied, "There is only one step which can be taken now and that is to run away in order to save the life from the Lord."—2073

SWAYYA

Giving him the jewel, Kratvarma became sad and thought to which side he should run away?

Killing Satrajit for the sake of jewel, I have committed a crime towards Krishna; for that reason, Krishna has come back in great rage, in support of his strength; if I stay here, he will kill me; being frightened, he fled away towards the North. —2074

DOHIRA

Shatdhanva becoming fearful and taking the jewel with him, wherever he went running away, Krishna reached there on his chariot. —2075

The enemy fled on foot in his fear, Krishna killed him there with his sword. —2076

After killing him and searching him, the jewel was not found and he told Balram about the news of not finding the jewel. —2077

SWAYYA

Balram reflected that he had hidden the jewel from them; the whereabouts of Akrur could not be known, but it was rumoured that he had gone to Banaras taking the jewel with him: "O Krishna! I have a student of mine there, who is a king and I am going there," saying this Balram, thinking about the anxiety of Krishna, started going towards Banaras. —2078

DOHIRA

The king felt extremely pleased, when Balram reached there and welcoming him, he brought him to his home. —2079

When the people came to know that Balram is a great expert in the mace-war, then Duryodhana came to learn this science from him there. —2080

SWAYYA

When Krishna came to Dwarka after killing Shatdhanva, then he came to know that Akrur is giving great amount of gold in charity in Banaras; Krishna comprehended this in his mind that the Samantak jewel is with him; he sent someone and called him at his place. —2081

When he came to Krishna, he implored him to give the jewel; Surya had given that jewel delightfully and for this Shatdhanva had been killed; for this jewel, Balram, the brother of Krishna, had thoughts in his mind and he would come back on obtaining it; the same jewel was taken by Krishna and after showing it to all, he returned it to Akrur. —2082

SWAYYA

The jewel, which had been obtained by Satrajit after serving the god Surya jewel, for which Shatdhanva was killed by Krishna and which was taken away by Akrur and which had come again to Krishna the same was returned by Krishna to Akrur like the bestowal of a gold coin by Ram Chandra to his devotee. —2083

DOHIRA

On returning the jewel, Krishna, the chopper of the heads of the tyrants and remover of the afflictions of the saints, earned infinite approbation. —2084

End of "The Description of Killing Shatdhanva and Giving the Jewel to Akrur" in Krishnavatar (based on *Dasham Skandapurana*) in Bachittar Natak.

The Description of the Arrival of Krishna in Delhi

CHAUPAI

When the jewel was given to Akrur, then Krishna thought of going to Delhi; he reached Delhi, where all the five Pandavas fell at his feet. —2085

DOHIRA

Then he went to the home of Kunti to enquire about the welfare of the family; Kunti told him about all the sufferings experienced at the hands of Kaurvas. —2086

After staying for four months in Indraprastha, one day Krishna went a hunting alongwith Arjuna. —2087

SWAYYA

The side in which there were many animals of prey, Krishna went towards that; he killed the nilgais, pigs, bears, leopards and many rabbits, the rhinoceros, the intoxicated elephants of the forest and the lions were killed; on whosoever Krishna struck a blow, he could not endure that blow and fell unconscious. —2088

SWAYYA

Taking Arjuna with him, Krishna penetrating into the forest killed many deer; many were killed with the sword and many by hitting their bodies with arrows; causing their horses to run and releasing the dogs, the fleeing animals were killed and in this way, none could save himself from Krishna by fleeing. —2089

SWAYYA

One deer was killed by Arjuna and one by Krishna himself and those who are fleeing were got seized by releasing the dogs; Krishna sent the falcons for flying partridges in the sky and in this way, the falcons caught their prey and threw it down after killing it. —2090

SWAYYA

They took with them the falcons of the species of Shahins (Besare, Kuhi and Behri) and also the falcons of the species of hawks (Lagra, Charak and Shikra); in a similar way, they bedecked the eagles (Dhurat and Ukab) and took them alongwith them and to whichever bird, they made the target and sent these birds of prey, they did not let them escape. —2091

SWAYYA

In this way, Krishna and Arjuna together obtained the delight of hunting and they mutually increased their lover for each other; now they desired in their mind to drink water and came towards the stream; both of them left hunting and went towards the bank of Yamuna. —2092

SWAYYA

When they were coming for drinking water, they saw there a beautiful woman; Krishna asked Arjuna to enquire about that woman; Arjuna, according to the desire of Krishna, asked her, "O woman! whose daughter are you? Which is your country? Whose sister you are and whose wife you are?" —2093

Speech of Yamuna
DOHIRA

Then Yamuna said to Arjuna, "My heart desired me to wed Krishna, therefore I have performed austerities here." —2094

SWAYYA

Then Arjuna bowing down his head, requested Krishna, "O Lord! She is Yamuna, the daughter of Surya and the whole world knows her;" then Krishna said, "Why has she assumed the garb of a female ascetic and relinquished her domestic duties?" Arjuna replied, "She has done this in order to realise you." —2095

SWAYYA

Hearing the words of Arjuna, Krishna caught hold of the arm of Yamuna and caused her to mount the chariot; her face was like the moon and the brightness of her cheeks was resplendent; Krishna was much graceful to her as he had not been to any other woman and the story of bringing her in his home is world-famous. —2096

SWAYYA

Getting Yamuna mounted on his chariot, Krishna brought her home; after wedding her, he went to the court of Yudhishtar to meet him; the king Yudhistar fell at his feet; Yudhistar said, "O Lord! how have You created the Dwarka city? Kindly tell me about it;" then Krishna ordered Vishwakarma, who created another equivalent city there. —2097

End of the description "About Hunting and Marrying Yamuna" in Krishnavatar in Bachittar Natak.

Now begins the Description about the Marriage of the Daughter of the King of Ujjain

SWAYYA

After bidding farewell to Pandavas and Kunti, Krishna reached the city of Ujjain; Duryodhana desired in his mind to wed the daughter of the king of Ujjain; he also came to this side for this purpose bringing alongwith his bedecked army. —2098

SWAYYA

From that side Duryodhana came alongwith his army and from this side Krishna reached there; many other great kings came to see the wedding and caused their drums to be beaten

BACHITTAR NATAK

in felicitation of the marriage of king's daughter; then Krishna after marrying the king's daughter came to Ayodhya alongwith Arjuna. —2099

CHAUPAI

When Krishna came to Ayodhya, then the king himself went to welcome him and bring him; he got him seated on his throne and destroyed his afflictions. —2100

He caught hold of the feet of the Lord and said, "My sufferings have ended after having your sight;" he absorbed his mind in Krishna, thus increasing his love for him. —2101

Speech of Krishna addressed to the King
SWAYYA

Seeing the love of the king, Krishna said smilingly to him; "O king! you belong to the clan of Rama, who on being enraged, had killed enemies like Ravana; the Kshatriyas do not beg, but still I ask unhesitatingly and request you to marry your daughter with me according to my desire." —2102

Speech of the Krishna addressed to the King
CHAUPAI

Then the king said, "I have avowed one thing; whosoever will string these seven bulls, I shall send my daughter with him." —2103

SWAYYA

Fastening his yellow garment around his waist, Krishna made seven different guises, which looked quite similar, when observed; on tightening his turban, he caused his eyebrows to dance like the warriors; when Krishna stringed all the seven bulls, then all the spectators hailed him. —2104

SWAYYA

When Krishna was stringing the bulls, then the accompanying warriors were talking that there is no such mighty hero, who could fight with the horns of these bulls; who is such hero, who can string all the seven bulls? Then those warriors said smilingly that it was only Krishna, who could perform such a feat. —2105

SWAYYA

The saints smilingly said, "There is no hero like Krishna in the world; he chopped the head of Ravana, the conqueror of Indra and made him a headless trunk; he saved the elephant, when he was in affliction and whenever a calamity fell on the ordinary human beings, he became impatient for relieving him." —2106

SWAYYA

The marriage of Krishna was performed according to Vedic rites, and the helpless Brahmins were given new garments etc., the huge elephants and horses were given to Krishna and in this way, the praise of the king spread in the whole world. —2107

Speech of the King addressed to the Court
SWAYYA

The king said while sitting in his court, "Krishna has performed the same task which was performed by Rama while pulling the Shiva's bow" when he (Krishna) came to the city of Oudh after winning the sister of the king of Ujjain, then he was accepted as a hero at the same time. —2108

SWAYYA

Krishna did not allow any enemy king to stay long against him in the war; knowing this, the king considered him a hero; the ministers looking at Krishna, described him as the suitable match; then according to the poet Shyam, the king of Oudh felt extreme happiness. —2109

SWAYYA

The eminent Brahmins, expert in Vedic rituals, came to the court and giving their blessings to the king, they said these words, "O king! you had sent Brahmins for finding a suitable match for this daughter in different countries, but today fortunately that match has been obtained." —2110

SWAYYA

Hearing these words of the Brahmins, and getting pleased he caused the musical instruments to be played and gave various kinds of dowry;

suitable presents were given to the Brahmins and with great pleasure, he offered his daughter to Krishna. —2111

SWAYYA

When Krishna came back after winning the daughter of the king of Oudh in *swayamvara*, he made his mind to roam in the forest alongwith Arjuna; there he caused to be brought poppy plant, hemp, opium and various kinds of wines for drinking; there he also called many beggars and singers, who came in groups. —2112

SWAYYA

Many concubines, playing their anklets, lyres and drums began to dance there; someone is dancing while revolving, and some woman is spinning on all the four sides of Krishna; Krishna is giving them comfortable raiments, gems and jewels; he is giving such precious things to them, which even Indra cannot procure. —2113

The concubines after dancing and the singers after singing are receiving great gifts; someone is pleasing Krishna by reciting poetry and someone is pleasing him by reciting various stanzas; all are dancing together by revolving in all the directions; whosoever has come to the abode of Krishna, then tell us, what shortage he can have? —2114

Giving them many presents, Krishna went to dine alongwith Arjuna; they made use of poppy seeds, hemp opium and drank wine; thereby they removed all their sorrows; getting intoxicated with all these four stimulants Krishna said to Arjuna, "Brahma has not done the right thing in not creating the eighth ocean of wine." —2115

DOHIRA

Then Arjuna said to Krishna with folded hands, "What do the senseless Brahmins know about the enjoyment of these essences and pleasures?" —2116

End of the story "About the Marriage with the Daughter of the King of Oudh after Stringing the Bulls" in Krishnavatar (based on *Dasham Skandapurana*) in Bachittar Natak.

Now begins the Description of the Arrival of Indra on being agonised by the Demon Bhumasura

CHAUPAI

When Krishna came to Dwarka, then Indra came there and clung to his feet; he told about the agony caused by Bhumasura and said, "O Lord! I have been greatly distressed by him." —2117

DOHIRA

"He is very powerful; I cannot chastise him, therefore O Lord! take some step to destroy him." —2118

SWAYYA

Then Krishna giving instructions to Indra, bade farewell to him saying, "Do not have any anxiety in your mind, he will not be able to move me from my stable position; when I shall mount my chariot in anger and hold my weapon, then I shall chop your enemies into bits in an instant; therefore do not get fearful." —2119

SWAYYA

Indra bowed his head and went to his home and Krishna felt his fear from the depth; he took the Yadava army alongwith him and also called Arjuna; he also took one woman with him and absorbed in his sport, he went towards the higher regions. —2120

SWAYYA

Mounting upon Garuda, when he went towards the enemy, he first saw the citadel of stone, then the gates of steel, water, fire and fifthly he observed the wind as the protector of the citadel; seeing this Krishna challenged in great rage. —2121

Speech of Krishna

DOHIRA

"O, the Lord of Citadel! Where are you hiding yourself? You have called your death by waging war with us." —2122

SWAYYA

When Krishna said this, he saw with this that a weapon had come and with one blow it has

BACHITTAR NATAK

killed many; in that citadel surrounded by water, a demon named Mura, resided, who listening to the din, came out for fighting; on coming, he wounded the vehicle of Krishna with his trident. —2123

SWAYYA

Garuda did not feel a significant blow, but now Mur, pulling his mace, struck Krishna; Krishna saw towards the attack on his head and held in his hand his mace named Kumodki and with one blow intercepted the attack of the enemy. —2124

SWAYYA

When the blow did not hit the target, the demon began to roar in rage, he extended his body and face and advanced forward in order to kill Krishna; Krishna took out his sword named Nandak from his waist and struck the blow on the demon, removed his head like the potter chopping the pitcher from the wheel. —2125

End of "The Killing of the Demon Mura" in Krishnavatar in Bachittar Natak.

Now begins the Description of Fighting with Bhumasura

SWAYYA

Krishna killed and despatched the demon Mura to the abode of Yama; and waged a dreadful war with bow, arrows and sword; the family of Mura came know that he has been killed by Krishna; hearing this the seven sons of Mura, taking the fourfold army with them moved to kill Krishna. —2126

They surrounded Krishna from all the ten directions and showered arrows; and taking maces in their hands they all fearlessly fell upon Krishna; enduring the blows of their weapons, when Krishna in fury held up his own weapons, then as a warrior he did not let anyone go away and chopped all of them into bits. —2127

SWAYYA

Seeing the destruction of their army, the seven brothers got enraged and taking up their weapons and challenging Krishna fell upon him; they surrounded Krishna fearlessly from all the four sides and fought till the time when Krishna taking his bow in his hand chopped all of them into fragments. —2128

DOHIRA

Then Krishna in extreme rage took his bow in his hand and sent the enemies alongwith all the brothers to the abode of Yama. —2129

SWAYYA

When Bhumasura came to know that Krishna has killed the demon Mura and has also destroyed all his army in an instant, then thinking of Krishna as a brave fighter, he got infuriated in his mind and marched forward to fight with Krishna. —2130

While attacking, Bhumasura began to thunder like warriors; he held up his weapons and surrounded his enemy Krishna; he looked like the doomsday cloud and was thundering in this way as if musical instruments were being played in the region of Yama. —2131

When the enemy's army rushed forth like clouds, then Krishna thought in his mind and recognised Bhumasura, the son of the earth; it appeared that on the doomsday the ocean was surging forth, but Krishna did not fear even slightly on seeing Bhumasura. —2132

SWAYYA

Amongst the gathering of elephants of the enemy's army, Krishna looked splendid like the bow of Indra; Krishna had also destroyed Bakasura and had chopped the head of Mura in an instant; from the frontal side, the group of elephants was rushing forth like the clouds and within them, the bow of Krishna was shining like lightning among the clouds. —2133

He killed many warriors with his discus and many others by direct blows; many were killed with the mace and thrown down on the ground and they could not control themselves again; many warriors were chopped into half with the sword and were lying down like the trees chopped by the carpenter in the forest. —2134

SWAYYA

Some warriors were dead and lying down on the earth and many warriors seeing their such plight came forward; they were all completely fearless and placing their shields before their faces, and taking their swords in their hands, they fell upon Krishna; only with a single arrow Krishna despatched them all to the abode of Yama. —2135

SWAYYA

When in his fury, Krishna killed all the warriors and those who had survived, seeing such a situation, fled away; those who fell upon Krishna in order to kill him, they could not return alive; in this way, in various groups the warriors moving their heads, accompanied the king went to wage war. —2136

SWAYYA

When Krishna saw the king coming to the battlefield, he also did not stay there, but marched forward for fighting; he said, "O king! stay there, I shall kill you now;" saying this and pulling his bow, he discharged an arrow into the heart of the enemy. —2137

SWAYYA

When pulling his bow, Krishna discharged his sharp arrow, then being hit by the arrow, Bhumasura swung and fell down on the ground and went to the abode of Yama; the arrows penetrated through his body with such swiftness that even the blood could not smear it and he like the one engaged in yogic discipline, he abandoned his body and sins, and went away to heaven. —2138

End of the description of "The Killing of Bhumasura" in Krishnavatar in Bachittar Natak.

Now begins the Description of Giving Bhumasura's Kingdom to His Son and Marriage with Sixteen Thousand Princesses

SWAYYA

When Bhumasura passed through such a phase, then his mother came and paying no attention to her clothes, etc., she became unconscious and fell upon the earth; she being greatly worried, came with bare feet to Krishna and seeing him, she forgot her affliction and became pleased. —2139

DOHIRA

She praised Krishna and pleased him and her son fell on the feet of Krishna, whom he pardoned and set him free. —2140

SWAYYA

Placing his son on his throne, Krishna reached that place, where sixteen thousand princesses were imprisoned by Bhumasura; seeing the beauty of Krishna, the mind of those woman was allured and Krishna also seeing their desire, married all of them and for this received universal praise. —2141

CHAUPAI

All of them whom Bhumasura had gathered there, what about those women should I relate here; Krishna said, "According to their desire, I shall marry the sixteen thousand women together." —2142

DOHIRA

After getting enraged and killing Bhumasura in the battle, Krishna married sixteen thousand beautiful women together. —2143

SWAYYA

Getting furious in the war, Krishna killed all his enemies in an instant and giving kingdom to the son of Bhumasura, he removed his sufferings; then he after the war married sixteen thousand women and bestowing gifts on the Brahmins, Krishna returned to Dwarka. —2144

SWAYYA

He got constructed sixteen thousand houses for the sixteen thousand women and provided comfort to all; everyone of them wanted Krishna to abide with her and the description of this episode the poet has recorded after reading and listening to Puranas for the sake of saints. —2145

End of the description of "The Killing of Bhumasura, giving the Kingdom to His Son and Marrying Sixteen Thousand Princesses" in Krishnavatar in Bachittar Natak.

Now begins the Description of Conquering Indra and Bringing the Elysian tree (*Kalpavriksha*)

SWAYYA

In this way, providing comfort to those women, Krishna went to the abode of Indra; Indra gave coat of mail (*kavach*) and ringlets (*kundal*) which remove all sorrows; Krishna saw there a beautiful tree and he asked Indra to give the tree; when Indra did not give the tree, then Krishna began a war with him. —2146

SWAYYA

He also in fury, brought his army and attacked Krishna; on all the four sides were seen moving the chariots when the clouds thundered and the lightning flashed; twelve mighty warriors rushed forward, who caused damage to the hero like Ravana and getting intoxicated and without understanding any mystery, they hovered around Krishna. —2147

SWAYYA

On arrival, they all moved their elephants towards Krishna; those elephants appeared like Sumeru mountain moving wings; they were slattering their teeth in rage; Krishna chopped their trunks like the cutting of bananas, very quickly, and having been smeared with blood, he appeared like playing Holi in the month of Phalgun. —2148

SWAYYA

When, in his fury, Krishna fought the battle with the enemies, then listening to his dreadful thunder, many warriors became lifeless; Krishna was catching the elephants by their trunks and revolving them like the children playing the game of pulling one another. —2149

SWAYYA

Whosoever came in front of Krishna, he could not go alive; after conquering the twelve Suryas and Indra, he said to those people, "You may now go with me taking this tree to my home;" then taking that tree, they all went with Krishna and all this has been narrated by the poet Shyam in his poetry. —2150

Krishna, taking that beautiful tree, reached that house of Rukmani, which was studded with jewels and diamonds and even Brahma coveted for it on seeing that place; then Krishna related the whole story to his family members and the same has been described in totality by the poet Shyam in his poetry, with great pleasure. —2151

End of the description of "Conquering Indra and bringing the Elysian tree" in Krishnavatar (based on *Dasham Skandapurana*) in Bachittar Natak.

The Description of Amusement and Pleasantry of Krishna with Rukmani

SWAYYA

Krishna said to his wife, "I had taken food and drunk milk in the house of *gopis* (milk-women); and from that day I had been named as a milkman; when Jarasandh had attacked, I had forsaken patience and fled away; what should I say now about your wisdom; I do not know why you married me?" —2152

"Listen O beautiful woman! Neither you have any paraphernalia, nor I have any wealth; all this glory has been begged; I am not a warrior, because I have forsaken my country and abide on the seaside in Dwarka; my name is *chor* (thief, a butter-thief), therefore my brother Balram remains angry with me; therefore I advise you that nothing has gone wrong with you now, leave me and marry someone else." —2153

Speech of Rukmani addressed to a Friend

SWAYYA

"I have become anxious in my mind and I did not know that Krishna would act like this with me; he would say to me that I should leave him and marry someone else; it is necessary that I should die now and I shall die at this very place and if the dying is not appropriate, then with my persistence on my husband, I shall burn myself in his separation." —2154

SWAYYA

Getting angry with Krishna, Rukmani thought of only death because Krishna had spoken to her such like bitter words; in her rage, she being confounded fell down upon the earth and it appeared that with the slapping of the wind, the tree had broken and fallen down. —2155

DOHIRA

In order to remove her anger, Krishna took Rukmani in his embrace and loving her said like this: —2156

SWAYYA

"O beautiful woman! For your sake, I caught Kansa by his hair and knocked him down; I killed Jarasandh in an instant; I conquered Indra and destroyed Bhumasura; I just cut a joke with you, but you considered it a reality." —2157

Speech of Rukmani

SWAYYA

Hearing the words of the beloved, Rukmani forgot all her affliction; she said with bowed head, "O Lord! I had been mistaken; kindly forgive me;" the praises of the Lord that she uttered, cannot be described; she said, "O Lord! I did not understand your pleasantry." —2158

DOHIRA

The poet Shyam has composed this complimentary story of Rukmani absorbing himself in it and what will happen now, please listen to it with interest. —2159

Speech of the Poet

SWAYYA

All the wives that Krishna had, he was pleased to bestow on each one of them ten sons and one daughter; they wore yellow raiment on their shoulders, they were all the representations of Krishna; Krishna, the ocean of mercy had incarnated on this earth for seeing the wonderful play (of the world). —2160

End of the description of "Pleasantry with Rukmani" in Krishnavatar (based on *Dasham Skandapurana*) in Bachittar Natak.

Description of the Marriage of Aniruddha

SWAYYA

Then Krishna thought of marrying his son Aniruddha; the daughter of Rukmani was also beautiful and her marriage had also to be solemnised; the frontal mark of saffron was applied to her forehead and all the Brahmins together recited the Veda; Krishna taking all his wives with him came to see the pageant accompanied by Balram. —2161

CHAUPAI

When Krishna went to that city, many types of amusements and pleasantries occurred there; when Rukmani saw her brother Rukmi, then both the brother and sister were extremely pleased. —2162

The marriage of Aniruddh was solemnised very nicely and Krishna himself vested him with the nuptial wreath; Rukmi thought of gambling and he invited Balram for it. —2163

SWAYYA

Rukmi began to gamble with Balram and many of the kings who were standing there, placed their infinite wealth on stake; when Rukmi made use of his bet, talking from the side of Balram, all of them giggled; Krishna was pleased, but Balram got infuriated. —2164

CHAUPAI

In this way, being irritated for several times, Balram was highly enraged; he took his mace in his hand and beat all the kings. —2165

He killed many kings and they fell unconscious on the earth; being saturated with blood, they appeared roaming and intoxicated in spring. —2166

Amongst all of them Balram was roaming like a ghost like Kali on the doomsday; he appeared like Yama carrying his staff. —2167

Rukmi took his mace and stood up and became dreadfully angry; he did not run away and coming in front of Balram began to fight with him. —2168

When Balram struck a blow of his mace, on him, he also in great fury struck his mace on Balram;

both became red with the flow of blood and appeared like the manifestation of anger. —2169

DOHIRA

A warrior was laughing on seeing it, while grinning; leaving his fighting with Rukmi, Balram challenged him and fell upon him. —2170

SWAYYA

Balram, with his mace, broke all his teeth; he uprooted both of his whiskers and the blood oozed out of them; then Balram killed many warriors; he again began to fight with Rukmi, saying, "I shall kill you." —2171

SWAYYA

In great fury, and his hair standing on their ends, and taking his powerful mace in his hand, Balram fell upon Rukmi; another warrior also came forward from the other side and a dreadful fight ensued amongst them; both the warriors fell down unconscious and wounded amongst the other wounded. —2172

CHAUPAI

The battle was fought there for about half the day and none of them could kill the other one; being greatly agitated, both the warriors fell down upon the earth like the living dead. —2173

Even on becoming unconscious both of them continued fighting; and all the people saw this wonderful drama; both fought in their fury like the two lions in the forest. —2174

SWAYYA

When Rukmi got tired while fighting, then Balram struck a blow on him; Rukmi saw the coming blow and holding his mace, he intercepted the blow of the coming mace and saved himself. —2175

SWAYYA

When the enemy in this way intercepted the blow, then Balram struck another blow with his mace, getting greatly enraged; that blow fell upon the head of Rukmi and he could not control himself even slightly; his body fell upon the earth while swinging and in this way Rukmi went to the other world. —2176

All the brothers of Rukmi, seeing him killed, got infuriated and taking their lances, bows, swords, maces, etc., in their hands, fell upon Balram; they, challenging him fearlessly, surrounded him from all the ten directions, like the moths falling upon an earthen lamp after seeing it, without fear. —2177

SWAYYA

They all fought with Balram in extreme anger; Krishna also heard a battle had been fought by Balram, with the brother of his wife, he thought about it and called all his family members, but ultimately he without giving thought to all the other matters of Balram, rushed for his help. —2178

DOHIRA

When Balram, who appeared like Yama, heard about the coming of Krishna, the words of wisdom that he said to the brothers of Rukmi, I now relate them. —2179

SWAYYA

"Krishna is coming with his army, have you no fear about it? Who is so powerful on the earth, who can fight with Krishna? If any fool fights with him in persistence, is it possible that he would be able to save himself? Only he will be able to save himself today, who will run away and thus save his life." —2180

SWAYYA

Then Krishna reached the battlefield, who is the treasure of mercy; there he saw Balram, saturated with blood and also the dead Rukmi; he also saw there many other wounded kings, but he got pleased of seeing Balram and seeing the wife of Balram, he lowered down his eyes. —2181

SWAYYA

Then Krishna dismounted from the chariot and hugged him; then others carried away the dead body of Rukmi and performed his funeral rites; on other side Rukmani reached amongst her brothers and instructed them not to fight with Krishna; there is no other like him. —2182

CHAUPAI

Krishna also made them understand and came to his place taking his daughter-in-law with him; I, the poet Shyam am relating the story and pleasing the listeners. —2183

End of the chapter entitled "Solemnising the Marriage of the Son and Killing of Rukmi" in Krishnavatar in Bachittar Natak.

Now begins the Description of the Marriage of Usha and the Description of the Smashing of the Pride of Sahasarabahu

CHAUPAI

Krishna came home after the marriage of his son and Sahasarabahu became egoistic on receiving the boon from Rudra (Shiva). —2184

SWAYYA

He, appreciating himself, clapped with all his hands; the king performed austerities according to Vedic injunctions and held a *yajna* in accordance with the Vedic rites; after pleasing Rudra, he received the boon of protective power. —2185

SWAYYA

When Rudra bestowed the boon, the king established the religion in various countries; there was no sin left and the king was praised throughout the world; all the enemies came under the control of the trident of the king and no one raised his head out of fear; the poet says that the people were extremely happy during his reign. —2186

With the grace of Rudra, all the enemies came under his control and no one raised his head; all of them paid the tax and bowed at his feet; without understanding the mystery of the grace of Rudra, the king thought that this was due to his power only; thinking about the strength of his arms, he went to Shiva for the grant of the boon of the victory in war. —2187

SORATHA

Like the blazing sand heated by the sun, that foolish king, without understanding the mystery of his grace, went to Shiva for the grant of the boon of victory in war. —2188

Speech of the King addressed to Shiva
SWAYYA

Bowing down his head, the king said to Rudra (Shiva) with affection, "Wherever I go, no one raises his hand against me; my mind is eager to wage a war and I request you to bestow on me the boon some one come to fight with me." —2189

Speech of Rudra addressed to the King
CHAUPAI

Hearing this, Shiva got enraged and said, "When your banner will fall down, then someone will come to fight with you." —2190

SWAYYA

When, in anger Shiva said this to the king, he did not understand this mystery; he thought that the desired boon had been bestowed upon him; within his forest, the king got puffed up, considering the strength of his arms; and in this way, Sahasarabahu came back to his home. —2191

The king had a daughter; one day she dreamt in a dream that a very beautiful prince like the god of love had come to her home; she went to bed with him and was greatly gratified; she, being startled, awoke and became agitated. —2192

SWAYYA

On waking up, she lamented and grew greatly afflicted in her mind; she began to feel pain in her limbs and endured dilemma in her mind regarding her husband, she moved as one having been robbed; she appeared to have been possessed by some ghosts; she said to her friend, "O friend! I have seen today my beloved." —2193

SWAYYA

Saying this, she fell down unconscious on the earth as if some female serpent had stung her; it appeared that she had seen her beloved in her last hours; at that time, her friend named Chitralekha reached near her. —2194

CHAUPAI

When she described her condition to her friend, the friend became very anxious; she thought

BACHITTAR NATAK

that she would not survive then; there was then only one effort to be done. —2195

Whatever I have heard from Narada, the same measure has come to my mind; I shall make the same effort and shall not fear Banasura, even slightly. —2196

Speech of the Friend addressed to Chitralekha

DOHIRA

Getting agitated, her friend said to the other friend, "Whatever you can do, do it immediately." —2197

SWAYYA

Hearing her words, this friend created all the fourteen worlds and created all the beings, the gods and others; she made all the creation of the world; now she caught hold of the arm of Usha and showed her everything. —2198

SWAYYA

When catching her arm, she showed her all the portraits, then seeing all this she reached the Dwarka city of Krishna; the place where Shambar Kumar was written, she drooped her eyes on reaching there and said, "O friend! He is my beloved." —2199

CHAUPAI

She said, "O friend! now don't delay and cause to meet me with my beloved. O friend! If you execute this task, then consider it that my life shall be revived." —2200

SWAYYA

Hearing these words of Usha, she transformed herself into a kite and flew; she reached in Dwarka city; there she told everything to the son of Krishna, while concealing herself: "One woman is absorbed in your love and I have come to take you there for her; therefore in order to end the agitation of the mind, go with me there immediately." —2201

SWAYYA

Saying this she showed him her real form; then the prince thought that he should see that woman, who loves him; tied his bow in his waist and carrying the arrows he made up his mind to go; he accompanied the messenger to bring with him the woman in love. —2202

DOHIRA

Getting pleased, the messenger took Aniruddha with her and reached the city of Usha. —2203

SORATHA

That woman caused cleverly the meeting of both the lover and the beloved; Usha and Aniruddha then enjoyed the union with great delight. —2204

SORATHA

Getting pleased in their mind, they following the instructions of Koka Pundit about the postures of the union, they enjoyed the sexual union through four kinds of postures; Aniruddha said smilingly to Usha, causing his eyes to dance: "Just as you are mine, I have also become thine in the same manner." —2205

On this side the king saw that his pretty banner had fallen down on the ground; he came to know in his mind that the boon bestowed on him by Rudra was going to become a reality; at the same time, some one came to tell him that someone was living with his daughter in his house; hearing this and getting infuriated, the king went there. —2206

SWAYYA

On coming, and holding his weapons with great fury, he began to fight with the son of Krishna in the house of his daughter; when he fell down, then the king playing his horn and taking the son of Krishna with him, went towards his house. —2207

SWAYYA

On this side, the king bound down the son of Krishna and started and on the other side, Narada told everything to Krishna, Narada said, "O Krishna! Get up and march with all the Yadava army;" Krishna also hearing this in great rage moved; it was very difficult to see the effulgence of Krishna, when he carried his weapons. —2208

DOHIRA

Hearing the words of the sage, Krishna taking all his army alongwith him, reached there, where there was the city of the king Sahasarabahu. —2209

SWAYYA

Hearing about the coming of Krishna, the king consulted his ministers; the ministers said; "They have come to take your daughter and you do not accept this proposition; you have asked for and got the boon from Shiva without understanding (its mystery), but on that side, Krishna has also avowed, therefore it will be wise to release both Usha and Aniruddha and also pay tribute to Krishna. —2210

SWAYYA

"O king! if you agree with us, then we say, "Take both Usha and Aniruddha with you and fall at the feet of Krishna. O king! we fall at your feet; never engage in fight with Krishna; there will be no other enemy like Krishna and if this enemy is converted into a friend, then you can rule over all the world for ever." —2211

"When Krishna in his fury will take his bow and arrows in his hands, then you may tell who else is more powerful, who will stay against him? He, who will fight with him, in persistence, he will despatch him to the abode of Yama in an instant; he will chop all your arms except the two and release you alive." —2212

SWAYYA

Not accepting the advice of his minister, the king considered his power as indestructible; taking up his weapons, he began to move amongst the warriors; he called his powerful army near him and started moving for fighting with Krishna with all his strength after worshipping Shiva. —2213

On this side Krishna is discharging his arrows and from that side Sahasarabahu is doing the same; from that side Yadavas were coming and from this side, the warriors of the king fell upon them; they were mutually inflicting wounds like the warriors roaming and playing Holi in Spring Season. —2214

SWAYYA

Someone is fighting with the sword, someone with the lance, someone with the dagger and someone is getting enraged and taking his bow and arrows; from that side the king and from this side Krishna are seeing this spectacles. —2215

Those warriors who fought with Krishna, they were knocked down by Krishna and thrown on the earth with a single arrow; any powerful warrior, taking his bow and arrows in his hands and in fury, fell upon him, the poet Shyam says that he could not return alive. —2216

SWAYYA

When Krishna, the Lord of Gokul fought with his enemies, then all those enemies who were in front of him, he killed them in his anger distributed them amongst the vultures and jackals; he made many warriors on foot and on chariot lifeless and also killed many elephants and horses and did not let anyone go alive; all the gods also praised him that Krishna had destroyed even the indestructible warriors. —2217

The conquered and frightened warriors left fighting and fled away; and where Banasura was standing, they came there and rolled down at his feet; on account of fear, the endurance of all of them ended and they were saying, "No one will survive before Krishna; O king! we should run away." —2218

When the king found himself in calamitous state, he remembered Shiva and Shiva also felt that the king had come to fight with Krishna the supporter of the saints; he, taking his weapons in his hands went towards Krishna for fighting; now I relate how he waged a dreadful war. —2219

When in extreme anger, Shiva blew his war-horn, then none of the warriors could stay there even for a very short time; the enemies from both became fearful, when Shiva began his fight with Krishna. —2220

SWAYYA

Krishna saved himself from the blows of Shiva and making Shiva as target, he wounded him; both of them fought in different ways and the gods came there to see that war and ultimately, Krishna caused Shiva to fall down with the blow of his mace. —2221

CHAUPAI

In this way, when Krishna wounded Shiva and knocked him down on the earth, who also became fearful and then he did not pull his bow; he recognised Krishna in his Real Form as the Lord (God). —2222

SORATHA

Seeing the power of Krishna, Shiva forsook his anger, and fell at the feet of Krishna. —2223

SWAYYA

Seeing this condition of Shiva, the king came himself for fighting; he discharged showers of arrows with all his one thousand arms; Krishna intercepted the arrows midway, making them passive; he took his bow in his hand and wounded the enemy very badly. —2224

SWAYYA

Getting infuriated and taking his bow and arrows in his hands, Krishna recognising the indestructible effulgence of Sahasarabahu, waged a terrible war with him; he killed many powerful warriors with his strength and chopped all the arms of the king except two and then released him. —2225

Speech of the Poet
SWAYYA

"O Sahasarabahu! no one had been in such a pitiable plight as you till today; tell me, O king! why have you amassed so much wealth in your house? Being in such a state, why one keeps the Powerful Shiva as his Protector?" Though he was surely bestowed with a boon by Shiva, but only that thing happens, which is agreeable to Lord God. —2226

CHAUPAI

When the mother of the king came to know that he has been defeated, and Krishna had been victorious, then she stood naked before Krishna. —2227

CHAUPAI

Then the Lord bowed down His eyes and decided in his mind not to fight any more; during this period the king got the time to run away and he fled away, leaving the war arena. —2228

Speech of the King addressed to the Warriors
SWAYYA

Getting agonised because of his wounds, the king said to his heroic soldiers, "The direction in which I went, no warrior could stand against me; listening to my thundering, no one till today, has caught hold of his weapons; not with-standing such a position, then who has fought with me is Krishna, the real hero. —2229

SWAYYA

When Sahasarabahu fled away from Krishna, he looked at his two remaining arms; he became extremely fearful in his mind; he, who has praised Krishna, he has earned approbation in the world; the poet Shyam has related the same virtues according to his wisdom, by the grace of the saints. —2230

Getting infuriated again, Shiva reached before Krishna, taking Ganas alongwith him; they were holding the bows, swords, maces and lances and blowing their war-horn while moving forward; Krishna despatched them (the Ganas) the abode of Yama in an instant. —2231

SWAYYA

Many were killed by Krishna with his mace and many were killed by Shambar; those who fought with Balram, they did not return alive; those who came and fought again with Krishna, they were chopped into fragments and bits in such a way, that they could not be had by the vultures and jackals. —2232

Seeing such a terrible war, Shiva in anger patted his arms, raised thundering voice; the manner in which the demon Andhakasura was attacked in rage, in the same way, he fell upon Krishna in great fury and it seemed that in order to fight with a lion, the second lion had come. —2233

Waging an extremely terrible war, Shiva held his lustrous *shakti* (weapon); understanding this mystery, Krishna discharged his snow-showering shaft towards Shiva, seeing which that *shakti* became powerless; it seemed that the cloud was flying away by the blow of wine. —2234

SWAYYA

All the pride of Shiva was shattered in the war arena; the shower of arrows discharged by Shiva could not strike even one arrow to Krishna; all the Ganas with Shiva were wounded by Krishna; in this way, seeing the power of Krishna, Shiva, the Lord of Ganas fell at the feet of Krishna.—2235

Speech of Shiva
SWAYYA

"O Lord! I have executed a very mean task in thinking of fighting with you; What! if I fought with you in my fury, but you have shattered my pride at this place; Sheshanaga and Brahma have become tired of praising you; to what extent your virtues may be described? because the Vedas could not completely describe your secret." —2236

Speech of the Poet
SWAYYA

What then, if someone roamed wearing matted locks and adopting different guises; closing his eyes and singing the praises of the Lord and performing your *arati* (circumambulation) by burning the incences and blowing the conches; but the poet Shyam says that without love one cannot realise God, the hero of Braja. —2237

Brahma, Kartikeya, Sheshanaga, Narada, Indra, Shiva, Vyasa, etc., all are singing the praises of God; all the four Vedas seeking Him, have not been able to comprehend His mystery; the poet Shyam says, tell me whether without love, someone has been able to please that Lord of Braja. —2238

Speech of Shiva addressed to Krishna
SWAYYA

Shiva said, holding the feet of Krishna; "O Lord! Listen to my request; this servant of yours is asking for a boon; kindly bestow on me the same; O Lord! looking towards me, mercifully, give your consent not to kill Sahasarabahu, though his arms have been chopped. —2239

Speech of Krishna
SWAYYA

"O Shiva! listen, I shall do it now; seeing his arms cut down and his erratic behaviour, I relinquish my anger; I also think that he is the son of Prahlad, therefore I released him after punishing him and did not kill him." —2240

SWAYYA

In this way, causing the king to accept his mistakes, Shiva got him to fall at the feet of Krishna and said, "Sahasarabahu has committed a wrong act; O Lord! forsake your anger; now marry your son with his daughter without any thought and taking Usha and Aniruddha with you, go to your home." —2241

SWAYYA

He, who will listen to the praises of Krishna from others and also sing himself; he, who will read about his virtues, and cause others to read the same and sing in verse; he, who will remember him, while sleeping, waking, and moving, he will never be born again in this ocean of *samsara*. —2242

End of the description of "Conquering Banasura and Marrying Aniruddha and Usha" in Krishnavatar (based on *Dasham Skandapurana*) in Bachittar Natak.

Now begins the Description of the Salvation of the King Dig

CHAUPAI

There was a Kshatriya king named Dig, who was born as a chameleon; when all the Yadavas were playing, then being thirsty, they came to a well. —2243

Seeing a chameleon in the well, they all thought of taking it out; they made effort, but noticing their failure, they all felt amazed. —2244

Speech of the Yadavas addressed to Krishna
DOHIRA

Thinking about this, all of them came to Krishna and said, "There is a chameleon in the well; adopt some measure and take it out." —2245

KABIT

Hearing the words of Yadavas, and understanding the whole mystery, Krishna said smilingly;

"Where is that well, show it to me." The Yadavas led and Krishna followed and reaching there he saw in the well; when Krishna caught that chameleon, all its sins ended and it was transformed into a man. —2246

SWAYYA

He, who remembered Krishna for an instant, he was redeemed; instructing the parrot, Ganika obtained salvation; who is there such an individual, who has remembered the Lord (Narayana) and did not ferry across the world-ocean; then this chameleon, which was touched by Krishna, why it should not be redeemed? —2247

TOTAK STANZA

When Krishna took it up, it was transformed into a man; then Krishna asked, "What is your name? And which is your country?" —2248

Speech of the Chameleon addressed to Krishna
SORATHA

"My name is Dig and I am the king of a country; how I became a chameleon? I relate the story now." —2249

KABIT

"O Lord! I always used to give in charity one hundred cows and gold to Brahmins; one cow, which had been given in charity mixed in the cows which were to be gifted; then the Brahmins, who had got the cow earlier recognised it and said, "You are giving my own wealth to me again, he did not accept the charity and cursed me to become a chameleon and live in a well; in this way I have obtained this state." —2250

DOHIRA

"Being touched by your hand, all my sins have been destroyed and I have been thus rewarded, which is obtained by sages after recitation of the Name for many days." —2251

End of the chapter entitled "Salvation of the Chameleon after Taking it out of the Well" in Krishnavatar in Bachittar Natak.

Now begins the Description of the Arrival of Balram in Gokul

CHAUPAI

After redeeming him, the Lord came to his home and he sent Balram to Gokul; on arriving at Gokul, he touched the feet of Nand Baba, which gave him extreme comfort and no sorrow was left. —2252

SWAYYA

After touching the feet of Nand, Balram reached the place of Yashoda and seeing her, he bowed down his head at her feet; the mother hugging the son and crying said, "Krishna has at last thought of us." —2253

KABIT

When the *gopis* came to know that Balram has come, they thought that Krishna also might have come and thinking this, thought filled their parting of hair with saffron; they put the frontal mark on their foreheads and wore ornaments and used collyrium in their eyes; they flashed like lightning and forsaking the shyness of their parents and brothers, they fell at the feet of Balram saying, "O Balram! we fall at your feet; tell us something about Krishna." —2254

Speech of the Poet
SORATHA

Balram gave due respect to all *gopis* and I relate the story that advanced further. —2255

SWAYYA

Once Balram performed a play; Varuna sent wine for his drinking, drinking which he became intoxicated; Yamuna showed some pride before him, he drew the waters of Yamuna, with his plough. —2256

Speech of Yamuna addressed to Balram
SORATHA

"O Balram! take the water, I see no fault or suffering in doing so; but O conqueror of the battlefield! You listen to me, I am only the servant of Krishna. —2257

SWAYYA

Balram stayed there for two months and then went to the abode of Nand and Yashoda for bidding farewell; when he putting his head on their feet, asked for the permission to return, then both of them were filled with tears in sorrow and bidding farewell to him, said, "Ask Krishna, why he has not come himself?" —2258

SWAYYA

After saying goodbye to Nand and Yashoda, Balram left on his chariot and going through several countries and crossing rivers and mountains, he reached his own city; when Krishna came to know about his arrival, he mounted on his chariot and came to welcome him. —2259

DOHIRA

Both the brothers met one another with great delight and drinking wine and laughing they came to their home. —2260

End of the description of "Coming of Balram to Gokul and His Return" in Krishnavatar in Bachittar Natak.

Now begins the Description of This Message sent by Shragaal: "I am Krishna"

DOHIRA

Both the brothers reached their home happily and now I describe the story of Pundrik. —2261

SWAYYA

Shragaal sent a messenger to Krishna conveying that he himself was Krishna and why did he call himself (Vasudeva) Krishna? Whatever guise he had adopted, the same should be abandoned; he was only a milkman; why did he not have any fear in calling himself the Lord of Gokul? It was also conveyed by the messenger, "Either he should honour the saying or will face the attack of the army." —2262

SORATHA

Krishna did not accept the saying of the messenger and after learning it from the messenger, he sent his army for attack. —2263

SWAYYA

Taking the king of Kashi and other kings with him, Shragaal gathered his army and on this side Krishna alongwith Balram amassed their forces; taking other Yadavas alongwith him, Krishna went to fight the battle with Pundrik and in this way, the warriors of both sides confronted one another in the battlefield. —2264

SWAYYA

The amassed forces of both sides, looked like the rushing clouds on the doomsday; Krishna going away from both the forces said in a loud voice, "Let both the armies stay at their places and now we both i.e., I and Pundrik shall fight in this battlefield. —2265

SWAYYA

Krishna said this, "I call myself Ghanshyam, that is the reason why Shragaal has come to attack with his forces; why should both the forces fight with each other? Let them stand and watch; it will be appropriate for me and Pundrik to fight." —2266

DOHIRA

Agreeing to this proposal, both the forces abandoning their anger stood there and both the Vasudevas advanced forward to fight. —2267

SWAYYA

It seemed that two intoxicated elephants or two lions had come to fight with each other; it seemed that two winged mountains were flying on doomsday to fight with each other or the clouds were thundering and raining in fury on the doomsday, they appeared to be the infuriated Rudras. —2268

KABIT

Just as falsehood cannot stay against truth, the glass against the stone, the mercury against the fire and the leaf against the wave; just as attachment cannot stay against knowledge, malice against wisdom, pride against the ascetic Brahmin and the animal against the human being; just as the shame cannot stand against the lust, the cold against the heat, the sin against the Name of the Lord, temporary object before the permanent object, miserliness against the charity and the anger against the respect; in the same way these two Vasudevas consisting of opposite qualities fought against each other. —2269

SWAYYA

When the dreadful war was fought there, then ultimately Krishna holding his discus challenged Shragaal and said, "I am killing you;" he discharged his discus (*sudarshanchakra*), which chopped the head of the enemy like the potter with the aid of the thread had separated the vessel from the revolving wheel. —2270

Seeing the dead Shragaal, the king of Kashi advanced forward and he waged a dreadful war with Krishna; there was a great destruction there and here also Krishna discharged his discus and chopped the head of the king like the earlier king. —2271

Both these forces saw Krishna destroying the warrior in anger; all were pleased and the clarionets and drums were played, the warriors of the enemy's army left for their homes and there was a shower of flowers from the sky on Krishna like the rain coming from clouds. —2272

End of the chapter entitled "Killing of Shragaal alongwith the King of Kashi" in Krishnavatar in Bachittar Natak.

Now begins the Description of the Battle with Sudaksha

SWAYYA

When the enemy's forces ran away, Krishna came to his army; those gods who were there, clung to his feet; they circumambulated around Krishna, blew their conches, burnt the incences and recognised Krishna as the real hero. —2273

On that side Daksha, eulogising Krishna, went to his home and on this side Krishna came to Dwarka; on that side in Kashi, the people aggrieved on displaying the chopped head of the king; they talked like this that the behaviour that the king had adopted towards Krishna, this was its reward. —2274

Brahma, Narada and Shiva, on whom the people meditate and on burning incence and blowing the conch, they worship them on bowing their heads, they offer leaves and flowers with bowed heads, these Brahmas, Narada and Shiva etc., have not been able to comprehend the mystery of Krishna. —2275

SWAYYA

Sudaksha, the son of the king of Kashi, getting enraged, thought: "He, who has killed my father, I shall also kill him;" he served and adored Shiva with the singleness of his mind and pleasing him, he obtained the boon of killing Krishna in an instant. —2276

Speech of Shiva addressed to Sudaksha

CHAUPAI

Then Shiva again said to him, "You may perform *homa* for killing Krishna; from that *homa* (sacrifice), you will get an idol, which will seize the life of Krishna." —2277

DOHIRA

"If anyone pushes him back in the fighting and makes him inattentive then that power will come to kill you." —2278

SWAYYA

When Shiva said this to Sudaksha he was pleased; he did as directed by Shiva; he performed the *havana* by the use of fire, *ghee*, and other ingredients according to Vedic injunctions; that fool did not understand the secret of Shiva's words. —2279

An idol came out of that *homa*, seeing which all got frightened; who is that mighty one in this world, who can stay against it? That idol, gnashing its teeth in fury, stood up, taking a huge mace and everyone thought that now Krishna will not go alive. —2280

CHAUPAI

Then that idol, getting extremely enraged in its mind, started moving towards Dwarka; on the other side, Krishna came to know that some glorious entity was coming against him. —2281

Whosoever will confront it will be reduced to ashes; whosoever will fight against it, he will go to the abode of Yama. —2282

SWAYYA

"He, who comes before it, is burnt down in an instant," hearing these words Krishna mounted on his chariot and discharged his discus towards it; its strength seemed bedimmed before the discus (*sudarshanchakra*); getting extremely angry, it went back and it destroyed the king Sudaksha. —2283

Speech of the Poet
SWAYYA

He, who has not remembered Krishna; what then if he had been singing the praises of others and never eulogised Krishna; he had been adoring Shiva and Ganesha; according to the poet Shyam, he has wasted his precious birth in vain, without getting any merit for this in this and the next world. —2284

End of the description of "The Killing of the King Sudaksha by the Idol" in Krishnavatar in Bachittar Natak.

Now begins the Description of the Killing of the Monkey

SWAYYA

After conquering the kings, unavoidable in fighting, they were released; he, from whom all the fourteen worlds felt frightened, his one thousand arms were chopped; the Brahmin (Sudama), who made his both ends meet by seeking the help of others, he was given the houses of gold and then the honour of Daraupadi was saved; who else can do all this except Krishna? —2285

CHAUPAI

Balram went to the city named Rewat happily alongwith his wife; there he drank wine alongwith others and getting pleased, danced and sang. —2286

A monkey came there, who smashed the pitchers full of wine; he jumped here and there fearlessly and this enraged Balram. —2287

DOHIRA

Balram got up, holding his arms and killed the jumping monkey in an instant. —2288

End of the description of "The Killing of the Monkey by Balram" in Krishnavatar in Bachittar Natak.

The Marriage of the Daughter of the King of Gajpur

SWAYYA

Duryodhana decided to marry the daughter of the king of Gajpur and called all the kings of the world to see the spectacle of marriage; this news reached Dwarka that the son of Dhritrashtra has decided to marry (the daughter); a son of Krishna named Samb went there from the abode of his mother Jambwati. —2289

Samb caught hold of the arm of the king's daughter and put her in his chariot; he killed with a single arrow the warriors, who were there for her support; when the king challenged, then six chariot-riders together fell upon him and there a dreadful war ensued. —2290

Arjuna, Bhishma, Drona, Kripacharya, etc., were filled with anger; Karana also went wearing his very strong armour; he looked splendid among these warriors and it seemed that he was like Surya amongst gods. —2291

SWAYYA

A dreadful war was fought there; the lances and spears struck from both sides; the warriors, getting wounded were running like those going home for meals; all the warriors appeared like the intoxicated persons roamed after drinking wine; the bows and arrows were their vessels and lances their cups. —2292

Samb, taking his bow in his hand, killed many warriors; he knocked down the turbans and heads, many warriors seeing this fled away like the sin before the virtue of the saintly company. —2293

SWAYYA

Someone's arm and someone's hand were cut down; many were cut into two halves from the middle and many were deprived of their chariots by shattering them; the warriors whose heads were chopped were standing and from their trunk, the blood was flowing like the cataracts leaping in the forests. —2294

When the son of Krishna in this way killed many warriors, then many others ran away and many writhed, being wounded; many of them deprived of their weapons, catching hold of the feet, begged for protection and many warriors, holding the blades of grass in their teeth stood imploring humbly. —2295

SWAYYA

The son of Krishna waged a unique war; he was not at all inferior in strength to the six chariot-riders in any way, but they also together in their fury fell upon Samb, the son of Krishna getting infuriated and challenging and fighting with Samb, they caught him by his hair. —2296

TOTAK STANZA

When these warriors became victorious, they snatched away the daughter of the king; they brought her home again and in this way they cast off their perplexity. —2297

CHAUPAI

On this side Duryodhana was pleased and on that side Balram and Krishna heard all this; Vasudeva, in great rage, moved his hands on his whiskers. —2298

Speech of Vasudeva

CHAUPAI

"Send some messenger towards that side and get some news about the safety of my son;" Balram was sent towards that side, who reached there. —2299

SWAYYA

Obeying the orders of his father, when Balram reached Gajpur, he told Duryodhana about the objective of his coming and asked him to release Samb; hearing these words Duryodhana got angry thinking that he was being intimidated in his own home; but the fear of Balram frightened the whole city and Duryodhana came to adore him (Balram) alongwith his daughter. —2300

SWAYYA

Duryodhana became pleased by marrying the daughter with Samb; he gave innumerable gifts to the Brahmins; now Balram started for Dwarka taking his nephew alongwith him and on that side Narada reached there in order to see the whole spectacle. —2301

End of the description of "Bringing the Daughter of Duryodhana after Marrying Her with Samb" in Krishnavatar (based on *Dasham Skandapurana*) in Bachittar Natak.

The Description of the Arrival of Narada

DOHIRA

Narada reached the house of Rukmani, where Krishna was sitting; he touched the feet of the sage. —2302

SWAYYA

Krishna saw Narada entering the second house and he also went inside the house, where the sage delightfully said this, "O Krishna! I am looking at you in all the directions in the house;" Narada, in reality, considered Krishna as Lord God. —2303

SWAYYA

Somewhere Krishna is seen singing and somewhere playing on his *vina* holding it in his hand; somewhere he is drinking wine and somewhere he is seen playing affectionately with children; somewhere he is fighting with the wrestlers and somewhere he is rotating the mace with his hand; in this way, Krishna is enraged in this wondrous play; no is comprehending the mystery of this play. —2304

DOHIRA

In this way, the sage seeing the wonderful conduct of the Lord, clung to his feet and then left in order to see the spectacle of the whole world. —2205

End of the description of "The Arrival of Narada" in Krishnavatar in Bachittar Natak.

Now begins the Description of the Killing of Jarasandh

SWAYYA

Getting up at the time of meditation, Krishna concentrated on the Lord; then on sunrise, he offered water (to the sun) and performing *sandhya* etc., he recited *mantras* and as a regular routine, he read *saptashati* (a poem of seven hundred stanzas in honour of the goddess Durga); well, if Krishna does not perform the regular daily *karmas*, then who else will perform the same? —2306

SWAYYA

Krishna after taking bath, applying fragrance etc., and wearing garments comes out and sitting on his throne imparts justice etc., in a nice manner; the father of Shukadeva used to please very nicely Shri Krishna by causing him to listen to the exegesis of scriptures; one day whatever one messenger said to him on coming, the poet is telling that. —2307

Speech of the Messenger
SWAYYA

"Krishna! the king Jarasandh whom you had released, he is again demonstrating his strength; you had fought with his extremely large twenty-three military units for twenty-three times and he had ultimately caused you to run away from Mathura; that fool has now no shame left in him and has been puffed up with pride." —2308

DOHIRA

Till that time, Narada came to the court of Krishna and taking him alongwith him, he went towards Delhi. —2309

SWAYYA

Krishna said to all, "We are going towards Delhi in order to kill that Jarasandh and the idea that has cropped up in the minds of our zealous warriors, thinking about that, we are going there;" Uddhava also told this to the people that taking Arjuna and Bhima, with him, Krishna will kill the enemy. —2310

SWAYYA

Everyone agreed with Uddhava regarding the killing of the enemy; Krishna prepared his army taking with him chariot-riders, elephants and horses and also made use of opium, hemp and wine delightfully he sent Uddhava in advance to Delhi in order to keep Narada informed about the recent news. —2311

CHAUPAI

The whole army, fully embellished, reached Delhi, where the sons of Kunti clung to the feet of Krishna; they served Krishna heartily and relinquished all the afflictions of the mind. —2312

SORATHA

Yudhishtar said, "O Lord! I have to make one request; if you like, I may perform Rajsu *yajna*." —2313

CHAUPAI

Then Krishna said this, "I have come for this purpose; but we can talk about *yajna* only after killing Jarasandh." —2314

SWAYYA

The king then devised a plan of sending Bhima to the East, Sahdeva to the South and Nakul to the West; Arjuna went towards the North and he did not leave any one unattended in fighting; in this way, the most powerful Arjuna came back to Delhi to meet the Sovereign Yudhishtar. —2315

SWAYYA

Bhima came back after conquering East, Arjuna after conquering North and Sahdeva came back with pride after conquering the South; Nakul conquered the West and after returning bowed before the king; Nakul said this that they had conquered all except Jarasandh. —2316

SORATHA

Krishna said, "I want to wage a war with him in the garb of a Brahmin; now the battle will be fought between me and Jarasandh, leaving aside both the armies." —2317

SWAYYA

Krishna asked Arjuna and Bhima to assume the guise of Brahmins and said, "I shall also assume the garb of a Brahmin;" then he also, according to his desire kept a sword with him and concealed it; he himself assumed such a garb, that he may not be recognised by any one. —2318

SWAYYA

When adopting the guise of a Brahmin, all of them went to the king Jarasandh, he seeing their long arms recognised them as Kshatriyas; he also recognised that he is the same person who has fought with him from Dwarka for twenty-three times and the same Krishna has come to deceive him. —2319

Krishna himself stood and said to the king, "You have fled for twenty-three times in front of Krishna and only once you have caused him to run away;" this thought has come to my mind that on this you are calling yourself a hero; we, being Brahmins, want to fight with a Kshatriya like you. —2320

SWAYYA

The king Bali, without any other thought, gave his body to the Lord God thinking that it was the only Lord who was standing at his door like a beggar and none else; Rama gave kingdom to Vibhishana after killing Ravana and did not get it back from him; now my companions who are kings, are begging your person and you are standing there silently and hesitatingly. —2321

The god Surya gave his unique power (*kavach-kundal*-the armour-rings) and even then he was not frightened; the king Harish Chandra became a servant but his attachment with his son (and wife) could not degrade him; Krishna as Kshatriya fearlessly killed the demon Mura; now the same Brahmins want to wage a war with you; but it appears that your strength has declined. —2322

The sun can rise from the west, the Ganges can flow backwards, Harish Chandra can fall down from his truth, the mountains can flee and leave the earth, the lion can be frightened by a deer and the elephant can fly but Arjuna said, "I think, if all this happens, the king is so much frightened that he cannot wage a war." —2323

Speech of Jarasandh

SWAYYA

When Arjuna said like this to Krishna, then the king thought that they were, in fact, Krishna, Arjuna and Bhima. He said, "Krishna has fled before me, should I now fight with these children?" Saying this he stood fearlessly for waging the war. —2324

SWAYYA

There was a very huge mace in the house; the king caused to be brought for himself and gave the other to Bhima; he took his mace in his hand and other mace was given in the hand of Bhima; the fight began; they used to sleep at night and fight during the day and the story of the battle of both the warriors is related by the poet Shyam. —2325

SWAYYA

Bhima strikes the mace on the king and the king gives the blow with his mace to Bhima. Both the warriors are fighting in fury with such intensity as if two lions are fighting in the forest; they are fighting and not moving away from their determined places, It seems that the sportsmen are standing stable while playing. —2326

SWAYYA

After twenty-seven days of fighting, the king became victorious and Bhima was defeated; then Krishna gave his own strength to him and shouted in anger; he took a straw in his hand and cleaved it and saw towards Bhima with mysterious look; Bhima, likewise cleaved the king according to the saying of poet Shyam. —2327

End of the description of "The Killing of Jarasanth," in Krishnavatar (based on *Dasham Skandapurana*) in Bachittar Natak.

Now begins the Description of the Release of All the Kings after Killing Jarasandh

SWAYYA

After killing Jarasandh, they all went to that place, where he had imprisoned many kings; on seeing the Lord, their sufferings ended; but here the eyes of Krishna were filled with shyness (that he could not get them released earlier); they were liberated from their restraints in an instant and by the grace of Krishna all of them were released. —2328

SWAYYA

After freeing them from their bondages, Krishna said to them, "You may return to your own countries without any anxiety, feeling delight in your mind and take cognizance of your kingdom, society, wealth and homes." —2329

After freeing them from the bondages, when Krishna said this, then all the kings replied, "We have no royal and social connections now; we only remember you." Krishna said, "I shall make all of you kings here;" agreeing to the words of Krishna, the kings requested him, "O Lord! kindly keep us under care." —2330

End of the description of "Reaching Delhi after Killing Jarasandh and Getting all the Kings released" in Krishnavatar in Bachittar Natak.

Now begins the Description of the Rajsu yajna and the Killing of Shishupal

SWAYYA

On that side, the kings went to their homes and on this side Krishna reached Delhi; Bhima told all that he got strength from Krishna and thus killed the enemy; then calling the Brahmins respectfully, the Rajsu *yajna* was begun and this *yajna* began with the playing of the drum of Krishna. —2331

Speech of Yudhishtar addressed to the Court
SWAYYA

In the court of Kshatriyas and Brahmins, the king said; "Who should primarily be worshipped? Who is the most deserving person here, on whose forehead the saffron and other ingredients be applied? Then Sahdeva said, "Only Krishna is the most suitable; he is the real Lord and we all are a sacrifice to him."—2332

"O mind! always serve him and do not entangle yourself in other matters; abandoning all the entanglements, absorb your mind only in Krishna, his mystery is more or less, obtained by us in Vedas and Puranas and in the company of the saints; therefore primarily, the saffron and other ingredients be applied to the forehead of Krishna." —2333

This speech of Sahdeva was considered by all as true and in their minds they visualised him as Lord God; within the chanting of Vedic *mantras*, the saffron and other ingredients were applied on the forehead (of Krishna), seeing which, Shishupal sitting there, became extremely infuriated. —2334

Speech of Shishupal
SWAYYA

"Who is he, on whose forehead the frontal mark saffron has been applied, leaving aside a great warrior like me? He has living in Gokul village only among the milkmaids, eaten and drank their curd and milk; he is the same, who had escaped because of the fear of the enemy and gone to Dwarka;" all this was uttered by Shishupal in great anger. —2335

SWAYYA

In his fury, Shishupal said all this within the hearing of the whole court and got up, taking in his hand a huge mace, getting enraged; he, causing both his eyes to dance and calling bad names, said to Krishna, "Being only a *gujjar* (milkman), on what basis you call yourself as the king of Yadavas?" Krishna saw all this and kept seated silently in view of the promise made to his aunt. —2336

CHAUPAI

Remembering the promise made to his aunt, Krishna was not filled with anger after listening to one hundred bad names; upto one hundred, he was not deterred in anyway, but on reaching upto one hundred Krishna caught his discus in his hand. —2337

Speech of Krishna
SWAYYA

Krishna stood up, taking his discus in his hand and getting infuriated he said, "Remembering the words of my aunt, I have not killed you till now and kept silent; if you uttered any more bad name above one hundred, then think that you have called your death yourself; all these kings will see here that either I shall not survive or you will not survive." —2338

Speech of Shishupal

SWAYYA

When that egoist heard this, he said in anger, "O *gujjar* (milkman)! Shall I die by only your words of killing? It appears that your death has come very near in the court; this story will also continue to be told in all the four ages in Vedas and Puranas." —2339

SWAYYA

"Glistening your discus, you are threatening to kill me, shall I become afraid by this? Being called a Kshatriya, shall I become afraid in this court from a *gujjar* like you? I swear by my parents and brothers I shall not die today, but shall kill you and I shall today avenge you on account of Rukmani." —2340

When Shishupal said this, then Krishna became greatly enraged and said, "O fool! this whole court and the sun are a witness that you want death;" Krishna took the discus in his hand and jumped and advanced forward in order to kill Shishupal. —2341

On this side Krishna advanced forward and from that side Shishupal came in front of him; getting extremely angry, Krishna discharged his discus towards the enemy, which hit his throat and his head was chopped and it fell on the ground like the sun being killed had been thrown on the earth. —2342

End of the chapter entitled "Killing of Shishupal" in Krishnavatar in Bachittar Natak.

Now begins the Description of Krishna getting Infuriated and Yudhishtar asking for Forgiveness

SWAYYA

After chopping the head of Shishupal, and getting enraged, Krishna made his eyes dance and said, "Is there any one so mighty, who can fight with me;" the heroes like Arjuna and Bhima, sat silently with fear; the poet Shyam says that the poets are a sacrifice to his most charming figure. —2343

SWAYYA

Whatever power was there in Shishupal, the same got merged in the face of Krishna; many proud warriors there sat silently, Shishupal, the very powerful man of Chanderi had been killed by Krishna; everybody agreed that there was no one so mighty as Krishna in the world. —2344

Everybody said that Krishna was the most powerful hero, who had killed the mighty warrior like Shishupal, who was even unconquerable for Indra, Surya and Yama; he had killed that enemy in the winking of an eye and the same Krishna is the Creator of all the fourteen worlds. —2345

SWAYYA

Krishna is the Lord of all the fourteen worlds, all the saints accept this; the gods and others are all created by him and the Vedas also describe His attributes; Krishna, who also gets enraged on the kings was considered the mighty hero amongst the warriors and all the enemies recognised him, in reality, as the manifestation of death. —2346

SWAYYA

Krishna was standing there, holding his discus in his hand; he was extremely angry and in that state of enragement, he did not remember any other enemy; he, as manifestation of death, was thundering in the court; he was such a one, seeing whom, the enemies embraced death and the saints, on seeing him, were resuscitated. —2347

Speech of the King Yudhishtar

SWAYYA

The king Yudhishtar said with folded hands, "O Lord! forsake anger, Shishupal was a great tyrant, you have performed a noble task by killing him;" saying this, the king, caught both the feet of Krishna and the tears rolled down from his eyes; he said, "O Krishna! if you get angry, what control can have we over it?"—2348

SWAYYA

"O Lord! this servant of yours is requesting you with folded hands, kindly listen to it; if you get angry, we shall feel ourselves like dead, therefore kindly remain gracious; kindly sit in the Court blissfully and supervise the *yajna*; O Lord! I am requesting you to kindly end your anger and to forgive us." —2349

DOHIRA

The king Yudhishtar requesting most humbly caused the king of Yadavas to sit and now his eyes looked splendid like lotus and the figure elegant like that of the god of love. —2350

End of the chapter entitled "Asking the enraged Krishna for Forgiveness by Yudhishtar" in Krishnavatar in Bachittar Natak.

Now begins the Description of the Performance of the Rajsu *yajna* by the King Yudhishtar

SWAYYA

The task of serving the Brahmins was given to Arjuna; the sons of Maduri, Nakul and Sahdev, were delightfully serving the sages; Bhima became the cook and Duryodhana supervised the domestic affairs; Vyas etc., were busy in the recitation of the Vedas and Karana, the son of Surya, who frightened all the fourteen worlds, was given the task of the bestowal of charities etc. —2351

He, on whom always meditate Surya, Chandra, Ganesha and Shiva; He, whose name is repeated by Narada, Shukra and Vyas; the mighty one, who killed Shishupal and from whom all the worlds fear, the same Krishna is now washing the feet of Brahmins and who else can perform such a task except Him. —2352

SWAYYA

In the war, fighting with the enemies, the poet Shyam says, these mighty heroes realised the tax and gave gifts in charity according to the Vedic injunctions; many people were honoured and many were bestowed new kingdoms; in this way, at that time, the king Yudhishtar completed the *yajna* by all methods. —2353

Then they went to the river to take a bath and there they pleased their manes by offering the water; the beggars who were there, they were all satisfied by giving alms; they were given so much charity that their sons and grandsons never begged any more; in this way, completing the *yajna*, all of them returned to their homes. —2354

DOHIRA

When these efficient kings came to their home, then they bade farewell to all the invitees for the *yajna*. —2355

SWAYYA

Krishna stayed there for a long time with his wife; seeing his gold-like body, the god of love felt shy; wearing her ornaments on her limbs Draupadi also came and stayed there and she asked Krishna and Rukmani about their marriage. —2356

DOHIRA

When Draupadi asked all this affectionately, then every one related his/her story. —2357

SWAYYA

Seeing the *yajna* of Yudhishtar, Kauravas got angry in their mind and said, "Because of the performance of *yajna* by Pandavas, their fame has spread throughout the world; we have the mighty heroes like Bhishma and Karana with us, even then we could not perform such a *yajna* and we could not be renowned in the world." —2358

End of the description of *"Rajsu yajna"* in Krishnavatar (based on *Dasham Skandapurana*) in Bachittar Natak.

Description of the Construction of the Court-building by Yudhishtar

SWAYYA

There was a demon named Mai; he, on reaching there constructed such a Court-building, on seeing which the abode of gods feels shy; Yudhishtar was seated alongwith his four brothers and Krishna; the poet Shyam says that elegance was indescribable. —2359

SWAYYA

In that Court-construction, somewhere there were fountains of water on the roofs and somewhere the water was flowing; somewhere the wrestlers were fighting; and somewhere the intoxicated elephants were clashing among themselves; somewhere the female dancers were dancing; somewhere the horses were colliding and somewhere sturdy and shapely warriors looked splendid; Krishna was there like moon among the stars. —2360

Somewhere the splendour of stones and somewhere of jewels was seen; seeing the elegance of precious stones, the abodes of gods bowed their heads; seeing the magnificence of that Court-building, Brahma was getting pleased and Shiva was also allured in his mind; where there was earth, there was deception of water there; and somewhere where there was water, it could not be ascertained. —2361

Speech of Yudhishtar addressed to Duryodhana
SWAYYA

After the construction of this Court-building Yudhishtar invited Duryodhana; he reached there proudly alongwith Bhishma and Karana and he saw water, where there was earth and where there was water, he considered it as earth; in this way, without understanding the mystery, he fell into the water. —2362

He fell down in the tank and with all his clothes, he became drenched; when he came out after getting drowned in water, he became extremely enraged in his mind; then Krishna hinted to Bhima with his eye, who immediately said, "The sons of blind are also blind." —2363

When Bhima laughed, saying this, the king (Duryodhana) got extremely infuriated in his mind; "The sons of Pandu are laughing over me; I shall kill Bhima just now" when Bhishma and Karana also got angry, Bhima became fearful and ran away to his home and did not return. —2364

End of the chapter entitled "Duryodhana went Back to His Home after Seeing the Court-building" in Krishnavatar in Bachittar Natak.

Now begins the Description of Fighting with the Demon Bakatra

SWAYYA

On that side Duryodhana went away and on this side a demon thinking this became angry that Krishna had killed his friend Shishupal fearlessly; he thought that he could kill Krishna after obtaining a boon from Shiva and thinking about it, he started for Kedar. —2365

He went to Badri-Kedarnath, where he through great austerities, pleased the great Shiva and when he obtained the boon of killing Krishna, he mounted the air-vehicle and went; on coming to Dwarka he began the fighting with the son of Krishna; when Krishna heard this, he bade farewell to king Yudhishtar and went there. —2366

SWAYYA

When Krishna reached Dwarka, he saw the enemy and challenging him asked him to come forward for fighting with him; listening to the words of Krishna, he pulled his bow upto his ear and struck the blow with this arrow like putting *ghee* for extinguishing the fire. —2367

When the enemy was discharging his arrow, Krishna caused his chariot to be driven towards him; from that side, the enemy was coming and from this side he went to collide with him; with the strength of his chariot, he caused his enemy's chariot to fall down like a falcon knocking down the partridge with one blow. —2368

He cut down the chariot of his enemy with his dagger and then severing his neck knocked it down; he also despatched his army that was there, to the abode of Yama; Krishna stood in the battlefield filled with ire and in this way, his fame spread in all the fourteen worlds. —2369

DOHIRA

Then, getting enraged, the demon Bakatra reached there where Krishna was standing. —2370

SWAYYA

He challenged Krishna again in the war-arena and said, "The way in which you have killed the brave Shishupal, I shall not die like that." Hearing this, Krishna held his arrow in his hand and shooting it made the enemy unconscious and knocked him down on the earth. —2371

SWAYYA

When the demon Bakatra regained consciousness,

he disappeared and then, filled with anger, under the impact of *maya*, he cut the head of Krishna's father and showed it to him; Krishna was extremely infuriated and the tears flowed out of his eyes; now he took his discus in his hand and cutting the head of the enemy made it fall on the ground. —2372

End of the chapter entitled "Killing of the demon Bakatra" in Krishnavatar in Bachittar Natak.

Now begins the Description of the Killing of the Demon Vidurath

Speech of the Poet
SWAYYA

Those who have remembered in their mind the creator of Brahma, Shiva etc., that Lord, the ocean of mercy appeared before them immediately; He, who has no form, no colour and no dimension and whose mystery has been uttered by all the four Vedas; the same manifesting himself, is busy in killing in the battlefield. —2373

DOHIRA

When Krishna, in his ire, killed two enemies in the fighting and the third one who survived, he also came in the battlefield. —2374

Cutting both his lips with his teeth and dancing both his eyes, Balram said this to him: —2375

SWAYYA

"O fool! He, who killed the demons Madhu and Kaitabh; He, who finished Ravana, Hiranayakashipu, Kansa, Jarasandh and the kings of various countries, why are you fighting with Him? You are nothing, He has despatched very great enemies to the abode of Yama." —2376

Then Krishna said this to him, "I killed Bakasura and Aghasura; I knocked down Kansa by catching him from his hair; I destroyed Jarasandh alongwith his twenty-three extra-large military units; now you may tell me, whom do you think stronger then me?" —2377

Then he replied, "You are frightening me by saying this that you have killed in an instant Kansa, Bakasura and Jarasandh, the armies of Jarasandh etc.; you are asking me that who is more powerful than yourself? This is not the tradition of warriors; and O Krishna! Are you a Kshatriya or a grain-parcher?" —2378

SWAYYA

"I shall burn your answer like the blade of grass in the fire of my rage; whatever blood is in your body, I shall destroy it by boiling like water; when I shall place the vessel of my power on the fire of my rage, then the flesh of your limbs will be cooked nicely without any care." —2379

SWAYYA

In this way, disputing, both enraged themselves in dreadful fighting in the battlefield; the dust arose with the discharge of arrows, which covered all the chariots etc., in order to see the pageant of war Surya and Chandra and other gods reached singing songs of praise; the enemy ultimately could not gain victory over Krishna and reached the abode of Yama. —2380

In that dreadful fighting, Krishna killed the enemy; the body of the demon Vidurath got deformed and fell down on the earth; seeing his body smeared with blood, Krishna filled with mercy and apathy, abandoning his bow and arrows said, "Now from today, I shall not fight."—2381

End of the description of "The Killing of the Demon Vidurath" in Krishnavatar (based on *Dasham Skandapurana*) in Bachittar Natak.

Description of the Pilgrimage of Balram

CHAUPAI

Balram reached for pilgrimage at Nemisharan; on coming there he took a bath and relinquished the sorrows of his mind. —2382

TOMAR STANZA

Romharsh reached there running, where Balram was drinking wine; on coming there, he stood there with bowed head and Balram coming speedily, taking his bow and arrows in his hands, in great rage, killed him. —2383

CHAUPAI

Abandoning the peace of their mind, all the sages stood up and one of them said "O Balram! you have performed a bad act in killing a Brahmin." —2384

Then Balram said, "I was sitting here, why was he got frightened of me? Therefore, getting enraged, I killed him, by taking up my bow and arrows." —2385

SWAYYA

"I was the son of a Kshatriya and was filled with ire, therefore I destroyed him;" Balram, making this request, stood up and said, "I am telling the truth that this fool sat uselessly near me; only such a behaviour should be adopted with Kshatriyas, so that one may be able to live in the world; therefore I have killed him, but now forgive me for this lapse." —2386

Speech of the Sages addressed to Balram
CHAUPAI

All the sages, bearing testimony to the killing of the Brahmin, said to Balram, "O boy! now you removing all your anger, go to all the pilgrim stations for a bath." —2387

Speech of the Poet
SWAYYA

He (Balram) gave such a boon to the son of that Brahmin that all the four Vedas be retained in his memory; he began to recite the Puranas etc., in such a way that it appeared his father had been resuscitated; now there was no person blissful like him and in this way bowing his head and comforting him, the heroic Balram started his pilgrimage. —2388

SWAYYA

Balram, in the first place, took a bath in the Ganges; then taking a bath at Triveni, this hero reached Hardwar; taking his bath there, he went to Badri-Kedarnath comfortably; now what more should be enumerated? He reached at all the pilgrim-stations. —2389

CHAUPAI

Then again he came to Nemisharan and he bowed his head before all the sages; then he said, "Just as you had said, I have taken bath at all the pilgrim-stations according to Shastric injunction." —2390

Speech of Balram
CHAUPAI

"O sages! I fall at your feet, now I shall do whatever is desired by you; O great sage! Trust my words; whatever you will ask me to do, I shall do that." —2391

Speech of the Sage
CHAUPAI

Then the sages thought in their mind that there was a very great enemy of theirs, whose name was Balal. "O Balram! destroy him, manifesting yourself as Death." —2392

Speech of Balram
DOHIRA

"O sages! where does that enemy live? Tell me his place, so that I may kill him today." —2393

CHAUPAI

Then one of the sages showed him the place, where the enemy was living; Balram saw the enemy and challenged him for fighting. —2394

CHAUPAI

Hearing the challenge, the enemy was infuriated and on this side, these people, with signs of their hands, told Balram everything; that enemy fought the battle with Balram; there has been no mighty warrior like Balram. —2395

A dreadful battle was fought at that place, and none of both the warriors was defeated; they would sit when they felt tired and on becoming unconscious, they expressed their wish to continue fighting. —2396

CHAUPAI

Then again they thundered and continued the fight and began to strike their maces on each other; they were stable and did not recede even one step; it seemed that two mountains were fighting against each other. —2397

Both the warriors were thundering like clouds, hearing their voices, even Yama got fearful; both the warriors were fighting with each other filled with anger. —2398

In order to see this wonderful spectacle, the gods even came in their various types of air-vehicles; on that side the heavenly damsel like Rambha began to dance and on this side, these warriors were fighting on the earth. —2399

They were not caring for the blows of the maces and were uttering the shouts of "kill, kill" from their mouths; they were not receding even one step in the battlefield and both of them were fighting delightfully. —2400

SWAYYA

After the continuation of war for a long time, Balram held his huge mace and powerfully struck it with both the hands on the enemy; when the blow struck him, he died and went to the next world; in this way, killing him, Balram completed the task assigned to him by the Brahmins. —2401

SWAYYA

In this way, Shukadeva related the bravery of Balram to the king; whosoever has heard this story from the mouth of a Brahmin, he obtained happiness; he, whose creation are the sun and moon, we would listen to his words. O great Brahmin! relate the story of Him, whose secret has not even been comprehended by the Vedas. —2402

SWAYYA

"He, whom, Kartikeya and Seshanaga searched and got tired, but they could not know His end; He, who has been eulogised by Brahma in the Vedas. He, whom Shiva etc., had been searching, but could not know His mystery; O Shukadeva! relate to me the story of that Lord." —2403

When the king said this, then Shukadeva replied, "I am relating to you the mystery of that Merciful Lord, who is the support of the oppressed; now I relate this how the Lord removed the suffering of the Brahmin named Sudama; O king! now I relate that, listen attentively." —2404

End of the chapter entitled "Balram came Home after Taking Bath at Pilgrim-stations and Killing the Demon" in Krishnavatar (based on *Dasham Skandapurana*) in Bachittar Natak.

Description of the Episode of Sudama

SWAYYA

There was a married Brahmin, who had undergone great suffering; being greatly afflicted, one day he said (to his wife) that Krishna was his friend; his wife said, "You go to your friend; the Brahmin agreed; after getting his head shaved, that poor man took a small quantity of rice and started towards Dwarka." —2405

Speech of the Brahmin

"I and Krishna have been studying together with our teacher Sandipan; when I remember Krishna, then he may also be remembering me; he gives so much to the helpless people, he may also kindly give me something; but I cannot say, only the Lord knows, whether he will do such thing with me." —2406

After finishing his journey, when the Brahmin reached the residence of Krishna, Krishna recognised him that he was Brahmin Sudama; he advanced forward to receive him, affectionately, leaving his seat; he touched his feet and then hugged him. —2407

He took him to his palace and welcomed and honoured him; he caused the water to be brought with which he washed the feet of the Brahmin, he also drank the washings of his feet; on the other side, he transformed his hut into a palace; doing all this, he bade farewell to the Brahmin and apparently, he did not give him anything. —2408

DOHIRA

"When we studied at the house of our teacher, he loved me, but now the Lord has become covetous, therefore he did not give me anything." —2409

Speech of the Poet

SWAYYA

He, who served Krishna, he obtains extreme wealth, but the people do not understand this mystery and only comprehend according to their understanding; Krishna is the Sustainer of the saints, remover of their sufferings and the destroyer of their tyrant's houses; there is

SWAYYA

He, who did not care for anyone that Shishupal was killed by him in an instant; he even killed the demon Bakatra, who did not fear to go the abode of Yama; he even conquered Bhumasura, who fought like Indra and now has given the palace of gold to Sudama; then tell us, who else except him can do all this? —2411

He, who on killing Madhu and Kaitabh, full of kindness, donated the earth to Indra; he, before whom all the armies that went, he destroyed them; He, who gave kingdom to Vibhishana after killing Ravana, caused Lanka to be looted and he has given today the palace of gold to the Brahmin, then in what way it can be a significant thing for him? —2412

BISHANPADA
DHANASARI

He, whose eyes are like the eyes of the deer, the line of antimony on those charming eyes looks splendid; that line is like that trap, in which all the men and women always remain entangled; Krishna, according to his inclination, remains pleased with all. —2413

The eyes of Krishna are like lotus, which are never closed after illuminating the face; seeing them, the eyes of the mother are also absorbed in them like the bumble bees hovering over the lotus having pollen. —2414

End of the description of "Giving to Sudama the House of Gold after Removing His Poverty" in Krishnavatar (based on *Dasham Skandapurana*) in Bachittar Natak.

Description of Coming to Kurukshetra on the Day of Sun-Eclipse

SWAYYA

When the astrologers told about the sun-eclipse then the mother and brother of Krishna thought about going to Kurukshetra; forming different groups, the father of Krishna started going and this all was so mysterious and wonderful that none could understand it. —2415

From this side, Krishna was coming and from that side Nand and all other people including Chandrabhaga, Radha and *gopis* were seen coming by Krishna; they all became wonder-struck and silent on seeing the beauty of Krishna; Nand and Yashoda, feeling extreme affection, hugged him. —2416

Nand-Yashoda, affectionately, with tear flowing from their eyes said; "O Krishna! You had suddenly abandoned Braja and came here; it seems that Mathura is more dear to you; What then, if you killed Chandur and knocked down and killed Kansa by catching him from his hair; O unkind one! Did you not feel even a little of affection on seeing our condition?" —2417

SWAYYA

Then Yashoda said affectionately to Krishna, "O son! I have brought you up, but you are not at fault, all fault is mine; it appears that on tying you with the mortar, once I beat you, remembering that affliction, you are taking this revenge." —2418

"O mother! whatever I am saying unto you, consider it as true and do not conclude anything on being told anything by someone else; I feel the condition of death on being separated from you; and I can keep alive only on seeing you; O mother! during my childhood you took all my sufferings on yourself, now give me the honour of making me the ornament of Braja again." —2419

DOHIRA

Nand, Yashoda and Krishna, getting extreme happiness in their minds, reached at the place, where all the *gopis* were standing. —2420

SWAYYA

When the *gopis* saw Krishna coming and one of them got up and went forward and the delight welled up in the minds of many; the newness came on the *gopis* wearing unclean garbs as if some dead one had risen again and had got another lease of life. —2421

Speech of the Gopi
SWAYYA

One of the *gopis* said on seeing Krishna, "Since the time, when Krishna delightfully went with

Akrur, mounting on his chariot, from that time he has relinquished his kindness towards the *gopis* and thus finished the pleasure of Braja someone is taking like this and someone is standing silently. —2422

SWAYYA

"O friend! Krishna has gone to Mathura; he has never thought about us with love; he had not even the slightest attachment for us and he became unkind in his mind; Krishna has forsaken the *gopis* like the snake going away leaving behind his slough." —2423

Chandrabhaga and Radha said this to Krishna; "Krishna, relinquishing his attachment for Braja, has gone to Mathura; the way in which Radha had exhibited her pride, Krishna also thought that he should also do the same; we are seeing each other now after having been separated for a long time." —2424

SWAYYA

Saying thus, Chandrabhaga and Radha, looking charming in their red *saris* met Krishna; leaving the narration of the story of wonderful play they are seeing Krishna with wonder and the poet Shyam says that Krishna instructed the *gopis* about knowledge. —2425

BISHANPADA
DHANASARI

The damsels of Braja heard that Krishna had come to Kurukshetra; he is the same Krishna, seeing whom all the afflictions come to an end and who is called eternal (*nitya*) by the Vedas; our mind and body is absorbed in his lotus-feet and our wealth is a sacrifice to him; then Krishna called all of them in seclusion and asking them to engross themselves in the instructions of knowledge, he said, "The union and separation is the tradition of this world and the love for body is false." —2426

SWAYYA

Krishna got up after imparting to them the instructions about knowledge in this way; Nand and Yashoda were also pleased on meeting the Pandavas; on this side the Kauravas also went to their homes and Krishna again returned to Dwarka. —2427

DOHIRA

Before leaving, Krishna performed a *yajna*, because the son of Vasudeva is the god of gods in all the fourteen worlds. —2428

CHAUPAI

Krishna went away happily and on reaching his home, he worshipped the feet of his father; when his father saw him coming, he recognised him as the Creator of all the three worlds. —2429

He praised Krishna in various ways and established the figure of Krishna in his mind; considering him his Lord God, he worshipped him and Krishna also comprehended the whole mystery in his mind. —2430

End of the chapter entitled "Returning to Dwarka after Performance of *yajna* and Giving Instructions about Knowledge to *Gopis*" in Krishnavatar (based on *Dasham Skandapurana*) in Bachittar Natak.

Description about Bringing all the Six Sons of Devaki

SWAYYA

The poet Shyam says that Devaki came to Krishna and considered him as Lord in her mind and as the Creator of all the fourteen worlds and the killer of Madhu and Kaitabh; praising Krishna thus in her mind, she said, "O Lord! bring to me all our sons, who have been killed by Kansa." —2431

Hearing these words of his mother, the Lord (Krishna) brought all her sons from the netherworld; Devaki also considering them her own sons, hugged them; their consciousness about their birth also revived and they also came to know about their high lineage on seeing their parents, they all went to the abode of the Lord. —2432

Now begins the Description about the Marriage of Subhadra

CHAUPAI

Then Arjuna went on pilgrimage and he had a sight of Krishna in Dwarka; there he saw the charming Subhadra, who removed the grief of his mind. —2433

BACHITTAR NATAK

CHAUPAI

Arjuna coveted to marry Subhadra; Krishna also came to know all about that Arjuna wants to marry Subhadra. —2434

DOHIRA

Calling Arjuna towards him he instructed him to abduct Subhadra saying that he would not wage a war with him. —2435

CHAUPAI

Then Arjuna did the same and he abducted the adorable Subhadra; then all the Yadavas getting infuriated came to Krishna imploring him for help. —2436

SWAYYA

Then Krishna said to those people, "You people are known as great warriors; you may go and fight with him; if you are going to fight with Arjuna, then this means that your death has come very near; I have relinquished fighting earlier, therefore you may go and fight." —2437

CHAUPAI

Then the warriors of Krishna went and they said to Arjuna, "O Arjuna! we do not fear you, you are a great sinner, we shall kill you." —2438

DOHIRA

When Arjuna thought that the Yadavas would kill him, then he became agitated and started for Dwarka. —2439

SWAYYA

On being conquered by the people of Krishna, when Arjuna reached Dwarka, then Krishna counselled him, "O Arjuna! why are you afraid so much in your mind?" Then he explained to Balram and got the marriage of Subhadra solemnised with Arjuna. A great dowry was given to Arjuna, who on its receipt started for his home. —2440

End of the chapter entitled "Arjuna brought Subhadra after Abducting and Marrying Her" in Krishnavatar in Bachittar Natak.

Now begins the Episode of the King and Brahmin and the Description of the Killing of the Demon Bhasmasura and Getting the Release of Shiva

DOHIRA

There was a king of Mithila country, whose name was Atihulas; he used to worship and make offerings all the time to Krishna. —2441

There was a Brahmin there, who did not utter anything else except the Name of the Lord; he only used to talk about God and always remained absorbed in that in his mind. —2442

SWAYYA

The king went to that Brahmin's house and told about his intention of visiting Krishna and both of them did not talk anything else in mornings and evenings except Krishna. The Brahmin said that Krishna would come and the king also said that Krishna would come; in this way, they discussed about Krishna for hours together. —2443

SWAYYA

Krishna sensed this love of the king and the Brahmin, and he thought that these people are only absorbed in his meditation leaving other domestic tasks; he called his charioteer Daruk and caused his chariot to be driven to their side; he thought that he should gratify them by going within the sight of these helpless persons. —2444

CHAUPAI

Then Krishna manifested himself in two forms, in one form he went to the king and in the other form he went to the Brahmin; both the king and the Brahmin performed extreme service and relinquished all the afflictions of their mind. —2445

DOHIRA

Krishna stayed there for four months happily and then he went back to his home causing the resounding of his trumpets. —2446

Krishna said to the king and the Brahmin with love, "The way in which all the four Vedas repeat my name, you may also repeat and listen to my Name." —2447

The Speech of Shukadeva addressed to the King Parikshat

SWAYYA

"O king! listen, how the Vedas eulogise Him and sing the praises of the Lord causing the relinquishment of all the domestic temptations; The Vedas says that the form and colour of that Lord are invisible. O king! I have never given you such an instruction; therefore abide this instruction in your mind." —2448

That Lord, has no form, no colour, no garb and no end; His praises are sung in all the fourteen worlds day and night; His love should be kept in mind in meditation, spiritual pursuits and in the bath; O king! he, whom the Vedas remember, He should always be remembered. —2449

The Lord, whose praises are sung with love by all, my father (Vyas) also used to sing His praises which I have heard; those who are of very low intellect, they only do not remember Him. In this way Shukadeva addressed the king, "O king! that Lord should always be remembered with love." —2450

SWAYYA

He, who is not realised on enduring many sufferings and wearing matted locks; who is not realised by getting education, by performing austerities and closing the eyes; and who cannot be pleased by playing upon several types of musical instruments and by dancing; that Brahman cannot be realised by any one without love. —2451

He is being searched by Surya and Chandra, but they could not know His mystery; even the ascetic like Rudra (Shiva) and also Vedas could not know His mystery; Narada also sing His praises on his *vina* (lyre), but according to the poet Shyam without love none could realise Krishna as Lord God. —2452

DOHIRA

When Shukadeva said this to the king, the king asked Shukadeva, "How this can happen that in his birth the Lord many remain in agony and Shiva himself may remain in comfort; kindly enlighten me on this episode." —2453

CHAUPAI

When the king said this to Shukadeva, then Shukadeva while replying said this; "The same thing also occurred in the mind of Yudhishtar and he had asked Krishna the same thing and Krishna had also explained this mystery to Yudhishtar." —2454

Speech of Shukadeva

DOHIRA

"O king! listen, the saints of God live in agony in this world, but ultimately they attain salvation and realise the Lord." —2455

SORATHA

"The devotees of Rudra always pass their life in the world comfortably, but they cannot attain salvation and always remain in transmigration." —2456

SWAYYA

When the demon named Bhasmasura heard about the kindness of Rudra from Narada, he served Rudra single-mindedly and pleased him; he without any fear, cut down his flesh, performed *homa* in fire; he was bestowed this boon that on the head of whomsoever he would place his hand, he would be reduced to ashes. —2457

SWAYYA

When he obtained the boon of placing his hand and reducing the person to ashes then that fool in the first place wanted to reduce Rudra to ashes and seize Parvati; then Rudra ran and with deception, he caused the reduction of Bhasmasura; therefore O king! you may tell me now whether you are great or God is great, who protected you. —2458

End of the description of "The Episode of the King of Mithila country, the Brahmin and the Killing of the Demon Bhasmasura" in Krishnavatar (based on *Dasham Skandapurana*) in Bachittar Natak.

Now begins the Description of the Striking of Leg by Bhrigu

SWAYYA

Once the seven sages sat together; they thought

in their mind that Rudra was good, Brahma was good and Vishnu was the best of all; the play of all the three is infinite; none had been able to understand their mystery; in order to understand their tone, Bhrigu, one of the sages sitting there, went away. —2459

SWAYYA

He went to the house of Rudra; the sage said to Rudra, "You destroy the beings;" hearing this Rudra took up his trident; then that sage went to Brahma and said, "You repeat the reading of Vedas uselessly," Brahma also did not like these words; when he reached near Vishnu and seeing him sleeping, the sage struck him with his leg; Vishnu did not become angry and catching his feet, he said thus to him: —2460

Speech of Vishnu addressed to Bhrigu

SWAYYA

Enduring the blow of the leg smilingly, Vishnu said to the Brahmin, "My heart is (hard) like *vajra* and your foot might have been hurt; I ask for a boon from you; kindly forgive me for the crime and bestow on me this boon; 'Whenever I incarnate in the world, then the marks of your foot may remain imprinted on my waist'." —2461

SWAYYA

When Vishnu said this, the sage felt extreme delight; he came back to his hermitage after bowing before Him and the secret of Rudra, Brahma and Vishnu he brought home to every one and said that as incarnation of Vishnu was in reality the Lord (God); we should all remember him! —2462

SWAYYA

When Bhrigu on returning related all the episode to all of them, then all of them meditated on Krishna and found that Krishna was the ocean of infinite mercy and even the Vedas could not describe Him; Rudra keeps sitting with the rosary of skulls around his neck and making an ostentation; we shall not remember him and only remember Lord Krishna. —2463

SWAYYA

When Bhrigu, on coming back brought home this point to every one, then all of them remembered Krishna; just as the ghosts and fiends are considered unwelcome in *yajna*, in the same way, Rudra was established and it was also settled that by remembering Brahma, none will be able to realise him; therefore only meditate on Brahman and do not remember all the remaining ones. —2464

End of the chapter entitled "Description of the Episode of the Striking of Leg by Bhrigu" in Krishnavatar (based on *Dasham Skandapurana*) in Bachittar Natak.

Preparation of the Funeral Pyre by Arjuna for the Brahmin but Thinking of Burning Himself in it

CHAUPAI

One Brahmin in extreme agony said at the house of Krishna, "All my sons have been killed by Yama; O Lord! I am also alive in your kingdom." —2465

SWAYYA

Then Arjuna was filled with anger, looking at this lamentation and suffering; he thinking this, that he could not protect him, became shy and began to think of burning himself to death; at that time, Krishna reached there and making him understand, he mounted on the chariot and he started taking him alongwith him. —2466

On going, Krishna reached a place, where there was such a pitch dark, that if twelve suns could rise and then that darkness could have ended; explaining to the frightened Arjuna, Krishna said, "Do not be anxious; we shall be able to see the path in the light of the discus." —2467

CHAUPAI

They reached there where the Lord of all was sleeping on the bed of Seshanaga; seeing Krishna, He woke up and was extremely pleased. —2468

CHAUPAI

"O Krishna! how you have come here? I have been pleased on knowing this; when you go, take the Brahmin boys with you; sit down here for a while and give me the pleasure of your presence." —2469

Speech of Vishnu addressed to Krishna

CHAUPAI

When the boys came near Krishna, Vishnu said, "Go and return these boys and earn the praise in the world." —2470

Then Krishna came to Dwarka and returning the boys to the Brahmins, he obtained extreme pleasure; in this way, he saved the good men from burning fire and the saints sang the praises of the Lord. —2471

End of the chapter entitled "Preparation of the Funeral Pyre by Arjuna for the Brahmin and thinking of Burning Himself" in Krishnavatar in Bachittar Natak.

Now begins the Description of Krishna Playing with Women in Water

SWAYYA

Krishna reached the golden Dwarka, where within several places, the jewels and diamonds were studded; removing the fear of his mind, Krishna began to swim in the tank; taking the women with him and delivering the boys to the Brahmin, Krishna earned extreme approbation. —2472

SWAYYA

Krishna affectionately clung to the women in water; the women also, clinging to the limbs of the Lord, became intoxicated with lust; being absorbed in love, they became one with Krishna; the women are advancing to become one with Krishna, but they could not catch him at same time. —2473

SWAYYA

Being absorbed in the beauty of Krishna, they are all running from all the ten directions; they have applied saffron, in the parting of their hair, round mark on the forehead under he impact of lust they are running in and out their home; and shouting; "O Krishna! where have you gone after leaving us?"—2474

Someone is searching for Krishna, keeping illusion in her mind; those women are wearing several unique garbs, which cannot be described; they are repeating the name of Krishna as if they had not the slightest of shame; they are saying, "O Krishna! where have you gone after leaving us? Come within our sight." —2475

DOHIRA

Playing with Krishna for a long time, they became unconscious and in that unconscious state they saw this that they had got Krishna in their grip. —2476

The devotees of the Lord, listening to the discourse of love from the Lord, become one with him like the water being mixed with water. —2477

CHAUPAI

Then Krishna came out of water and he wore beautiful clothes; how should the poet describe his glory; seeing him even the god of love is fascinated by him. —2478

The women also wore beautiful garments and gave a great deal of charity to the Brahmins; whosoever eulogised the Lord there, they gave him there a good amount of wealth, removing his poverty. —2479

Now begins the Description of the Episode of Love

Speech of the Poet

CHAUPAI

I relate the praise of the devotees of the Lord and please the saints he, who will listen to this episode slightly, all his blemishes will be removed. —2480

SWAYYA

The war in which Tranavrata, Aghasura and Bakasura were killed and their faces were torn; the way in which chopping Shaktasura into bits and Kansa was caught and knocked down by catching him from his hair; the way in which the army of Jarasandh was churned and his pride was shattered, in the same way, Krishna wants to finish all the sins of those women. —2481

SWAYYA

Whosoever will sing the songs of Krishna with love, describe his glory in a nice way in poetry, discuss in his mind about the Lord on listening about Him from others, the poet Shyam says that he will not assume another body and transmigrate. —2482

Those who will sing the praises of Krishna and narrate him in poetry, will never burn in the fire of sin; all their anxieties will be destroyed and all their sins will end collectively; that person, who will touch the feet of Krishna, he will never assume the body again. —2483

SWAYYA

He, who will repeat the name of Krishna with love, who will give wealth etc., to the person remembering him, who will absorb his mind in the feet of Krishna, abandoning the tasks of the householder, then all the sins of the world will bid adieu to his mind. —2484

Though one was not absorbed in love, he endured, many sufferings on his body and performed austerities; though he received instructions about the recitation of the Vedas at Kashi, but did not comprehend its essence; though thinking this he gave in charity all his wealth that the Lord will be pleased, but he who has loved the Lord from the core of his heart, he only realises the Lord. —2485

What then, if some crane-like devotee had been performing heresy by closing his eyes and showing it to the people; someone might have been taking bath at all the pilgrim-stations like a fish; has he ever been able to realise the Lord? The frog croaks day and night, the birds always fly, but the poet Shyam says that inspite of repeating (the name) and running hither and thither, none has been able to please Krishna without love. —2486

He, who eulogises the Lord, coveting for wealth, and dances without loving Him, he could not realise the path leading towards the Lord; he who passed all his life in mere sporting, and did not know the essence of knowledge, he also could not realise the Lord how can one realise Lord Krishna, without loving Him? —2487

Those who meditate in the forest, they ultimately, getting tired come back to their homes; the adepts and the sages have been seeking the Lord through contemplation, but that Lord could not be realised by any one; all the Vedas, Katebs (Semitic scriptures) and the saints say this that whosoever has loved the Lord, he has realised Him. —2488

SWAYYA

I am the son of a Kshatriya and not of a Brahmin who may instruct for performing severe austerities; how can I absorb myself in the embarrassments of the world by leaving you? Whatever request I am making with my folded hands, O Lord! kindly be Graceful and bestow this boon on me that whenever my end comes, then I may die fighting in the battlefield. —2489

DOHIRA

In the year 1745 of the Vikram era in the Sudi aspect of the moon in the month of Sawan, in the town of Paonta at the auspicious hour on banks of the flowing Yamuna (this work has been completed). —2490

I have composed the discourse of the tenth part (*skandha*) of *Bhagavat* in the vernacular; O Lord! I have no other desire and have only the zeal for the war fought on the basis of righteousness. —2491

SWAYYA

Bravo to the soul of that person, who remembers the Lord through his mouth and reflects in his mind about the war of righteousness who considers this body as transient, ascends the boat of Lord's Praise and ferries across the dreadful ocean of the world; who makes this body as the abode of forbearance and enlightens it with the lamp of intellect and who taking the broom of knowledge in his hand sweeps away the rubbish of cowardice. —2492

Benign end of "The Description of the Twenty-first Incarnation i.e., Krishna" (based on *Dasham Skandapurana*) in Bachittar Natak.

NARA (ARJAN) INCARNATION

CHAUPAI

Now I enumerate the twenty-second incarnation as to how he assumed this from; Arjuna became the Nara incarnation, who conquered the warriors of all the world. —1

In the first place, he by killing all the warriors wearing unfailing coat of mail, removed the anxiety of his father Indra; then he fought a battle with Rudra (Shiva) the king of ghosts, who bestowed a boon on him. —2

Then he redeemed Duryodhana and burnt the king of Gandharvas in the fire of the Khandav forest; all these could not comprehend his secret. —3

My mind fears the enlargement of this *Granth* (Book) by relating all these stories, therefore I have said it in brief and the poets will themselves improve my mistakes. —4

He conquered all the places, where several proud Kauravas lived; he pleased Krishna and obtained the certificate of victory from him. —5

He killed Bhishma, the son of Ganga and Karana, the son of Surya after fighting a dreadful war with them; he conquered the mighty warrior Duryodhana and obtained the eternal kingdom. —6

Upto which point I should narrate this story, because I greatly fear the enlargement of this volume; what should I think of the long story? I say only this that Arjuna was the twenty-second incarnation.

End of "The Description of the Twenty-second Incarnation Nara (Arjan)" in Bachittar Natak.

BUDDHA INCARNATION

Now I describe the Buddha incarnation as to how the Lord assumed this form; Buddha incarnation is the name of that one, who has no name, no place and no village. —1

He, whose name and place are not described, he is only known as the Buddha incarnation; no one has accepted his saying in the Iron Age, which visualises the beauty only in stone (idols). —2

DOHIRA

Neither he is beautiful nor does any working; he consider the whole world like stone and calls himself the Buddha incarnation. —3

End of "The Description of Buddha, the Twenty-third Incarnation" in Bachittar Natak. —23

NIHKALANKI (KALKI) INCARNATION

CHAUPAI

Now I, purging my intellect, relate the story with full concentration of Kalki, the twenty-fourth incarnation and describe his episode, while amending it. —1

When the earth is pressed downward by the weight of sin and her suffering becomes indescribable; several types of crimes are committed and the mother sleeps for the sexual enjoyment with her son in the same bad. —2

The daughter unhesitatingly enjoys with her father and the sister embraced her brother; the brother enjoys the body of the sister and the whole world relinquishes the wife. —3

The whole subjects become hybrid and no one knows the other; the beautiful women are engrossed in adultery and forget the real love and the traditions of religion. —4

In every home, in the dark night of falsehood, the phases of the moon of truth are hidden; the crimes are committed everywhere and the son comes to the bed of his mother and enjoys her. —5

The truth is not seen even on search and the mind of everyone is absorbed in falsehood; in every home, there will be separate tenets and no one will even touch the Shastras and Smritis. —6

There will neither be a true Hindu nor a true Muslim; there will be diverse ideas in every home; no one will follow the established religious paths and will oppose the sayings of each other. —7

The earth will be pressed underneath with weight and no one will follow the religious tenets; there will be different beliefs in every home and no one will follow only one religion. —8

DOHIRA

There will be different beliefs in every home; no one will follow only one belief; there will be a great increase in the propagation of sin and there will be no *dharma* (piety) anywhere. —9

CHAUPAI

The subjects will become hybrid and no Kshatriya will be seen in the whole world; all will do such things that they will all become Shudras. —10

Hinduism and Islam will be relinquished and in every home there will be diverse beliefs; no one will listen to the ideas of another one; no one will remain with anyone. —11

All will proclaim themselves as Lord and no younger one will bow before the elder one; in every home, there will be a different belief and in every house will be born such people who will declare themselves as Ram. —12

No one will study Puranas even by mistake and will not catch the holy *Quran* in his hand; he, who will catch the Vedas and Katebs, he will be killed by burning him in the fire of cowdung. —13

The story of sin will become prevalent in the whole world and the *dharma* will flee from hearts of the people; there will be different beliefs in homes, which will cause the *dharma* and love to fly away. —14

Such notions will become prevalent that all will become Shudras; there will be no Kshatriyas and Brahmins and all the subjects will become hybrid. —15

The Brahmin-women will live with Shudras; the Vaishya-women will reside in the homes of Kshatriyas and the Kshatriya-women in the homes of Vaishyas; the Shudra-women will be in the homes of Brahmins. —16

The subjects will not follow only one religion, and there will be disobedience to both the scriptures of Hinduism and Semitic religions; various religions will be prevalent in various homes and none will follow the one and the same path. —17

GITA MALTI STANZA

When various religions will prevail in every home and all will walk in their pride and none of them will bow before any other; there will be the birth of new religions every year and the people even by mistake will not worship gods, manes and *pirs*. —18

Forgetting the gods and *pirs,* the people will call themselves God; several kinds of people will get together and spread various types of rumours; these new religions will continue for one or two months or even half a month and will ultimately end themselves like the bubbles of water. —19

Finding faults with the religions of Vedas and Katebs, they will be forsaken and the people will recite *mantras* and *yantras* according to their own interest; people will not be allowed to utter the names of Vedas and Katebs and no one will give even a cowrie in charity. —20

Forgetting the actions of *dharma*, the sinful actions will be committed and the money will be procured even by killing the son or friend; new religions will arise always and these religions will be followed without the Name of the Lord. —21

Some religions will continue for one or two days and on the third day these religions taking birth on account of power will die their own death; again on the fourth day new religions will arise, but they will all be without the idea of salvation. —22

The men and women will perform the works of deceit here and there; many *mantras*, *yantras* and *tantras* will spring up; leaving the canopies of religion, the Kshatriyas will run away from fighting, and Shudras and Vaishyas will catch hold of weapons and arms and thunder in the battlefield. —23

Leaving the functions of Kshatriyas, the kings will perform disgraceful tasks; the queens, leaving the kings, mix up with the low social orders; Shudras will be absorbed with the Brahmin girls and the Brahmins will also do likewise; seeing the daughters of the prostitutes, the great sages will lose their forbearance. —24

The honour of religion will fly away and there will be sinful acts at every step; the gurus will enjoy the wives of their disciples and the disciples will absorb themselves with the wives of their gurus; no attention will be paid to foolishness and wisdom and the head of the speaker of truth will be chopped; the falsehood will reign supreme. —25

BRIHAD NARAAJ STANZA

Forbidden works will always be performed; the saints abandoning the path of *dharma*, will look for the path of prostitutes; the friendship of a queer type will wash and destroy the sanctity of friendship; the friends and enemies will go together for their self-interest. —26

Amongst the works of the Iron Age will be the eating of the uneatables, the things worth concealing will come in the open and the *dharma* will be realised from the paths of unrighteousness, the kings of the earth will do the work of destroying *dharma*; the life of *adharma* will be considered authentic and the bad actions will be considered worth doing. —27

The people will neglect religion and the bad religious path will prevail everywhere; forsaking the *yajnas* and the repetition of the Name, people will repeat the worthless *mantras*; they will unhesitatingly consider the actions of *adharma*, as *dharma*; the saints will roam with dubious mind and the wicked people will move fearlessly. —28

The people will perform the actions of *adharma*, abandoning the actions of *dharma*; the kings will forsake the weapons of bow and arrows; making the announcement of wicked actions, the people will roam unashamedly; there will be misconduct on the earth and the people will perform useless tasks. —29

TARU NARAAJ STANZA

Castelessness will be the caste and all will forsake the refuge of the Lord. —30

All the people will forsake good actions and will absorb themselves in wicked actions. —31

All of them will abandon the remembrance of the Name of the Lord, and will remain absorbed in sexual enjoyment. —32

They will not feel shy (of the wicked acts) and will refrain from the bestowal of charity. —33

They will not meditate on the Feet of the Lord and only the tyrants will be hailed. —34

All of them will go to hell and ultimately repent. —35

All of them will ultimately repent on losing *dharma*. —36

They will abide in hell and the messengers of Yama will frighten them. —37

KUMAR LALIT STANZA

Performing wicked deeds, the people will not even by mistake remember the Name of the Lord; they will not give alms, but otherwise will loot the saints. —38

They will not return the borrowed debt-money and will not even give the promised amount in charity; they will not remember the Name of the Lord and such persons will specially be sent to hell. —39

They will not remain stable in their religion and will not do in accordance with their utterance; they will have no affection for their mother and the people will become subservient to their wives. —40

The uneatable will be eaten and people will visit the unworthy places; the people will utter the unutterable words and will not care for anybody. —41

They will perform unrighteous acts and will not have any fear of their parents or any other; they will act on ill-advice and will not seek good advice. —42

They will perform acts of unrighteousness and will loss their *dharma* in illusions; they will all be entrapped in the noose of Yama and ultimately reside in hell. —43

The people being engrossed in misconduct, will abandon good conduct and run away; they will forget all the disciplines and engross themselves in sinful actions. —44

The people intoxicated with wine and attachment will perform uncivilised acts and being absorbed in lust and anger, they will dance unashamedly. —45

BACHITTAR NATAK

NAG SAROOPI STANZA

No one will perform the rituals enjoined by religion and the people will quarrel amongst themselves in useless matters; they will engross themselves in evil actions to such an extent that they will totally forsake the religion and truth. —46

They will not study Puranas and Epics and will also not read the holy *Quran*; they will perform such acts of *adharma*, that even *dharma* will also feel frightened. —47

The whole earth will assume only one caste (of sin) and the trust in religion will be finished; there will be new sects in every home and the people will adopt only misconduct. —48

There will be new sects in every home; there will be new paths on the earth; there will be the reign of *adharma* and *dharma* will be exiled. —49

There will be no impact of knowledge on any one and *dharma* will flee in the face of *adharma*; the wicked acts will be greatly propagated and *dharma* will fly away with wings. —50

The deceit will be appointed as judge and the simplicity will fly away; the whole world will be absorbed in vicious acts and the good acts with speed away. —51

RAMAAN STANZA

The people will pay attention to wicked things forsaking the good ones. —52

They will be filled with illusions and will abandon the approbation. —53

They will do wicked deeds and quarrel uselessly amongst themselves. —54

They will recite the evil *mantras* and will establish the uncivilised notions. —55

SOMRAJI STANZA

The sages will be noticed to have performed sinful acts in various countries; they will abandon the path enjoined by the Vedas and only select the impure and false rituals. —56

The men and women will forsake *dharma* and absorb themselves in sinful deeds and the great sinners will become the administrators. —57

They will commit sins beyond their power and will perform wicked deeds in accordance with their conduct. —58

The new sects will arise always and there will be great misfortunes. —59

PRIYA STANZA

People will not worship the Lord, the remover of all sufferings. —60

The injunctions of Vedas will not be considered authentic and the people will describe various other religions. —61

No one will accept the advice of the holy *Quran* and no one will be able to see the Puranas. —62

No advice of *mantra* will be followed for more than one or two days. —63

GAHA STANZA SECOND

The performers of wicked deeds will have no fear of *adharma* and illusions and such people will never be able to enter the abode of gods. —64

The people engrossed in wrong notions will not be able to understand the reality; their desires will not even be satisfied by the rain of wealth and they will still covet for more wealth. —65

The people being intoxicated will consider it legitimate to enjoy the wives of others; both the utterance and deed will be filled with vices and there will be complete abandonment of shame. —66

People will bedeck themselves with wicked deeds and even forsake their shame; though exhibiting it; their daily routine will be full of wicked inclinations and they will abandon righteousness. —67

CHATURPADI STANZA

The people will always perform wicked deeds and abandoning good acts they will be inclined greatly towards vicious *karmas;* they will not accept Vedas, Katebs and Smritis and dance unashamedly; they will not recognise any of their gods and goddesses and even their own sayings; they will always be absorbed in evil acts; they will not accept the advice of their Guru; they will not describe any acts of goodness and will ultimately go to hell. —68

By not worshipping the goddess and being

absorbed in vicious acts, the people will perform the inexpressible task; they will not believe in God and even the sages will perform the vicious acts; being dejected with the religious rituals, the people will not recognise anyone and remain absorbed with the wives of others; not caring for any one's utterance and becoming extremely ignorant they will ultimately go to reside in hell. —69

They will always adopt new sects and without remembering the Name of the Lord, they will not have any faith in Him; forsaking the Vedas, Smritis and *Quran* etc., they will adopt new paths; being absorbed in the enjoyment of the wives of others and relinquishing the path of truth, they will not love their own wives; having no faith in the One Lord, they will worship many and ultimately go to hell. —70

Worshipping the stones, they will not meditate on the One Lord; there will be prevalent the darkness of many sects; they will desire for poison, leaving the ambrosia, they will name the evening time as early morn; absorbing themselves in all the hollow religions, they will perform evil deeds and reap the reward accordingly; they will be tied and despatched to the abode of death, where they will receive the suitable punishment. —71

BELA STANZA

The people will perform useless tasks and not the meaningful ones; they will neither remember the Name of the Lord nor ever give anything in charity; they will always leave one religion and eulogise the other one. —72

One sect will die out everyday and the other one will become prevalent; there will be no religious *karmas* and the situation of the earth will also change; the *dharma* will not be honoured and there will be the propagation of sin everywhere. —73

The people of the earth, leaving their religion, will be engrossed in very great sinful acts and when all will become defiled on account of sinful acts, even the rain will not fall on the earth, everyone will slander the other and move away after deriding. —74

Forsaking the respect and honour of others, none will accept the advice of any other; there will be the calumniation of the parents and the low people will be considered as high ones; there will be no fear of the religion and all the subjects will belong to only one category of the corrupt ones. —75

GHATTA STANZA

The people will commit many sins and will not even do one task of righteousness; the six *karmas* will be finished from all the homes and no one, on account of not doing good deeds, will enter the region of immortality and all will obtain the position of degradation. —76

Not even performing one act of righteousness, all will commit sinful acts; they will move in the world unashamedly; they will earn through sinful acts and suffer catastrophes and will remain powerless and will not be able to ferry across the sea of sin. —77

DOHIRA

New sects will arise at various places and the impact of *dharma* will end; the goodness will remain concealed and the sin will dance everywhere. —78

NAVPADI STANZA

Here and there all will leave the religious injunctions and the remembrance of the Name of the Lord and perform the sinful acts; the stone-idols will be worshipped and only on them incense, lamp-lights and sandal will be offered. —79

Here and there, forsaking the religious injunctions, people will run away; they will be absorbed in sinful acts; no religion will remain visible and the sin will become fourfold. —80

Forsaking their religious injunctions, the people will run away in such a way as if they had seen a bad dream; all the people will abandon their wives and will repeat evil notions. —81

Because of the prevalence of sin in all the four directions, no one will be able to remember the Lord; the sinful tendencies will prevail in such a way that all the religious acts will be finished in the world. —82

BACHITTAR NATAK

ARIL SECOND

Because of the birth of *adharma* here and there, the *dharma* will get wings and fly away; the bad people will roam here and there and the turn of *dharma* will never come. —83

The people will make meaningless all the meaningful things and will never let the notion of religious *karmas* enter their mind; forgetting the activities of *dharma*, they will propagate about sin here and there. —84

KULAK STANZA

They will not perform the acts of *dharma*; they will not utter the Name of the Lord; they will enter the houses of others and churning water, they will try to realise the essence. —85

Without understanding the real meaning, they will deliver useless speeches and adopting the temporary religions, they will never talk about the truth. —86

Entering the houses of others, they will roam and speak here and there and will remain absorbed with other women. —87

Coveting for wealth, they will go for theft during the night; they will be destroyed collectively and will go to hell. —88

Because of their such like sinful acts, no *dharma* will be left in the world; the parents will not enter the houses, being frightened. —89

The disciples will turn away form their Guru and the servants will leave the king; the wife, relinquishing her husband, will also forget the Lord. —90

Because of the new types of *karmas*, the illusions will increase; the whole world will become sinful and no person repeating the Name or performing austerities, will be left in the world. —91

PADMAVATI STANZA

The sinners will be seen on all sides, there will be no meditation on the Lord; even then there will be great jealousy with one another; those who go to the wives of others and commit sinful acts will have no beliefs in gods and manes; even then the sinners will remain religious leaders; none will talk on the face, but slander others at the back. —92

Without doing good work and forsaking the traditional religion of the clan, the people even then will be called good persons; the people will consider those persons good, who will always remain anxious, coveting in their mind for the sexual enjoyment; the people will follow the vicious doctrines under the impact of great greed and attachment; they will have no love for their parents and will be rebuked by their wives. —93

The pious ones will be seen performing bad acts and even then they would like to be called good ones; all of them will be under the impact of their women and remaining without intellect, will not shirk from the performance of bad *karmas*; they will roam here and there uttering uncivilised words and will also dance unashamedly. —94

KILKA STANZA

They will commit new sins and talking about the blemishes of others, they themselves will pretend to remain pure; the followers of the religions will forsake the world and run away and there will be the propagation of the sinful activities here and there. —95

All of them will roam, committing sinful acts and the activities of recitation and worship will flee from the world; they will not have any faith in gods and manes and will consider all others inferior to them. —96

MADHUBHAAR STANZA

The *dharma* will run away and there will be propagation of evil *karmas*; there will not remain any propriety of conduct in the world. —97

The powerful people will always commit bad deeds and the *dharma* will flee alongwith good acts. —98

Forsaking good character, all will be absorbed in bad conduct and wonderful activities will become apparent at several places. —99

Not absorbing themselves with the sexual enjoyment with their wives, they will have sexual relations with their unbecoming daughters. —100

The whole society will be on the run for the

abandonment of shame; *adharma* will increase and *dharma* will decrease. —101

Forsaking *dharma*, the people will have sexual enjoyment with prostitutes; the illusions will increase and the *dharma* will run away. —102

In all the countries, amongst the sinful kings, no follower of *dharma* will be left. —103

The saints, in their fear, will be seen in depression here and there the sin will reign in all the houses. —104

HARIGEETA STANZA

Somewhere there will be very great sins like the top of Dronagiri mountain; all the people will abandon *dharma* and live in the flashing lightening of illusion; somewhere the Shudras, bedecked with weapons will conquer the earth and somewhere the Kshatriyas, forsaking the weapons and arms, will be running hither and thither; there will be the prevalence of different types of activities. —105

The kings of various countries will engross themselves in sinful actions; the individuals will roam unashamedly, abandoning their shame; the religious injunction will speed away; somewhere the Brahmins will touch the feet of Shudras; somewhere the thief will be released and a pious man will be caught and his wealth will be looted. —106

TRIBHANGI STANZA

The whole world will become sinful, there will be none performing austerities; in all countries the unestablishable things will be established; the jealous persons will roams hither and thither; absorbed in sinful activities many sects, originators of vices, will come in vogue; because of the greed in their mind, the people will run here and there, but they will not realise anything. —107

Leaving the religion of the Lord, all will adopt evil ways, but without the actions related to the Lord everything will be useless; without understanding the secret, all the *mantras*, *yantras* and *tantras* will become useless; the people will not repeat the Name of the supremely heroic, unconquerable and incomprehensible goddess; they will remain absorbed in wicked deeds and morbid intellect, being devoid of the Grace of the Lord. —108

HEER STANZA

The fools will become full of qualities and the wise will lose intellect; the Kshatriyas, leaving the superb *dharma*, will consider the vices as the real *dharma*; falsehood, sin and anger will receive respect and the individuals, absorbed in *adharma* and engrossed in anger will flourish. —109

Absorbed in the love of wicked women, the people will not adopt virtues; they will honour the wicked people, leaving aside the good conduct; the groups of people, devoid of beauty, will be seen absorbed in sinful acts and will be under the impact of women devoid of *dharma*. —110

PADHISHTAKA STANZA

The sins have spread over the world and the intellect and religion have become powerless; the beings of various countries are engrossed in sinful acts. —111

The people look like the stone-images and somewhere the dialogues are held with power of intellect; there are many sects of men and women and the meaningful is always becoming meaningless. —112

MAARAH STANZA

People will love wicked and vicious women and undoubtedly the women may have taken birth in superior clans, but they will indulge in fornication; the women multi-coloured like flowers and like delicate creepers will look like the heavenly damsels coming down. —113

The men will look to their interest secretly and all will act like robbers; they will not accept the Shastras and Smritis and will only talk in an uncivilised way; their limbs will decay because of leprosy and they will be subjected to fatal diseases; these people will roam on the earth unashamedly like animals as if they had come from hell and incarnated on earth. —114

DOHIRA

All the subjects became hybrid and none of the castes had remained in tact; all of them obtained the wisdom of Shudras and whatever the Lord desires, will happen. —115

DOHIRA

There had been no remnant of *dharma* and all the subjects became hybrid; the kings became the propagators of sinful acts and the *dharma* declined. —116

SORATHA

The *dharma* was not visible in the world and the sin greatly prevailed in the world; every one forgot *dharma* and the whole world was drowned upto the throat. —117

The impossible Iron Age has come; in what way the world will be saved? Till the time they are not imbued in the love of the One Lord, up to that time there will be no safety from the impact of the Iron Age. —118

HANSA STANZA

The sinful acts increased here and there and the religious *karmas* ended in the world. —119

The sin increased to a large extent in the world and the *dharma* took wings and flew away. —120

New things began to happen always and there were misfortunes here and there. —121

The whole world began to perform the contrary *karmas* and the universal religion ended from the world. —122

MAALTI STANZA

Wherever you see, there are only people committing wicked deeds and no one who accepts religion is seen. —123

Upto the limit where we can see and listen, the whole world appears as sinner. —124

Because of vicious *karmas*, the *dharma* has fled away and no one talks about the *havana* and *yajna*. —125

All have become wicked and unrighteous; there is no meditation anywhere and only the duality resides in their minds. —126

ATMAALTI STANZA

There is no worship and offerings anywhere; there is no discussion about Vedas and Smritis anywhere; there is no *homa* and charity anywhere and nowhere the restraint and bath are seen. —127

No discussion about Vedas, no prayer, no Semitic scriptures, no rosary and no sacrificial fire are seen anywhere. —128

The contrary religious actions, feelings, secrets, rites, custom, discussions, worship and offerings are only visible. —129

The strange clothes, speech, arms, weapons, rites, customs, love, king and his justice are visible. —130

ABHIR STANZA

The king and saints etc., are engaged in evil acts and with sins in their hearts, they are doing disservice to *dharma*. —131

All the people have become cruel, characterless, sinners and hard-hearted; they do not remain stable even for half a moment and keep the desires of *adharma* in their mind. —132

They are extremely ignorant, sinners, doing disservice to *dharma* and without belief in *mantras*, *yantras* and *tantras*. —133

With the increase of *adharma*, *dharma* became fearful and fled away; new activities were introduced and the wicked intellect spread on all the four sides. —134

KUNDARIA STANZA

Several new paths were initiated and *adharma* increased in the world, the king and also his subjects performed evil acts and because of such conduct of the king and his subjects, and the character of men and women the *dharma* was destroyed and the sinful activities were extended. —135

The *dharma* disappeared from the world and the sins became prevalent apparently; the king and his subjects, the high and low all of them adopted the activities of *adharma*; the sin increased greatly and the *dharma* disappeared. —136

The earth agonised by sin trembled and began to weep while meditating on the Lord; overburdened by the weight of sin it lamented in various ways before the Lord. —137

SORATHA STANZA

The Lord instructed the earth and saw her off; He

reflected on the measure to be adopted for finishing the burden of the earth. —138

KUNDARIA STANZA

For the protection of the helpless and suffering humanity the Lord Himself will take some measure and He will manifest Himself as the Supreme *Purusha*; for the protection of the lowly and for ending the burden of the earth, the Lord will incarnate Himself. —139

At the end of the Iron Age and by the very beginning of Satyuga, the Lord will incarnate Himself for the protection of the lowly and will perform wonderful sports and in this way the incarnated *Purusha* will come for the destruction of the enemies. —140

SWAYYA STANZA

For the destruction of the sins, he will be called the Kalki incarnation and mounting on a horse and taking the sword, he will be glorious like a lion coming down from the mountain; the town of Sambhal will be very fortunate because the Lord will come there in "Hari Mandir." —141

Seeing his unique form, the gods and others will feel shy; he will kill and reform the enemies and start a new religion in the Iron Age; all the saints will be redeemed and no one will suffer any agony; the town of Sambhal will be very fortunate, because the Lord will manifest Himself there. —142

After killing the huge demons, he will cause his trumpet of victory to be sounded and killing thousands and crores of tyrant, he will spread his fame as Kalki incarnation; the place where he will manifest Himself, the condition of *dharma* will begin there and the mass of sins will fly away; the town of Sambhal will be very fortunate, because the Lord will manifest Himself there. —143

The Lord will get infuriated on seeing the pitiable plight of the talented Brahmins and taking out his sword, he will cause his horse to dance in the battlefield as a persistent warrior; he will conquer the great enemies and all will eulogise him on the earth; the town of Sambhal will be very fortunate, where the Lord will manifest Himself. —144

Seshanaga, Indra, Shiva, Ganesh, Chandra, all of them will eulogise Him; the Ganas, the ghosts, fiends, imps and fairies, all of them will hail Him; Nara, Narada, Kinnars, Yakshas, etc., will play on their lyres in order to welcome him; the town of Sambhal will be very fortunate, where the Lord will manifest Himself. —145

The sounds of drums will be heard; the tabors, the musical instruments, rababs and conches etc., will be played and hearing the sounds of large and small drums, the enemies will become unconscious; the town of Sambhal will be very fortunate, where the Lord will manifest Himself. —146

He will look splendid with bow, arrows, quiver etc., he will hold the lance and spear and his banners will wave; the Ganas, Yakshas, Nagas, Kinnars and all famous adepts will eulogise Him; the town of Sambhal will be very fortunate, where the Lord will manifest Himself. —147

He will kill in very great numbers using his sword, dagger, bow, quiver and armour; he will strike blows with his lance, mace, axe, spear, trident etc., and use his shield; in His fury, He will shower arrows in the war; the town of Sambhal will be very fortunate, where the Lord will manifest Himself. —148

Seeing his powerful beauty and glory, the tyrants will flee like the leaves flying before the strong gust of wind; wherever He will go, the *dharma* will increase and the sin will not be seen even on seeking; the town of Sambhal will be very fortunate, where the Lord will manifest Himself. —149

With the discharge of the arrows from His bow, the warriors will fall down in perplexity and there will be many powerful spirits and dreadful ghosts; the famous Ganas and adepts will eulogise Him by repeatedly raising their hands; the town of Sambhal will be very fortunate where the Lord will manifest Himself. —150

Seeing his charming form and limbs, the God of Love will feel shy and the past, present and future, seeing Him, will stay at their place; for the removal of the burden of the earth, He will be called Kalki incarnation; the town of Sambhal will be very fortunate, where the Lord will manifest Himself. —151

He will appear magnificent after removing the burden of the earth; at that time, very great warriors and persistent heroes, will thunder like cloud; Narada, ghosts, imps and fairies will sing his song of victory; the town of Sambhal will be very fortunate, where the Lord will manifest Himself. —152

He will look splendid in the battlefield after killing the great heroes with His sword; knocking down corpses upon corpses, He will thunder like clouds; Brahma, Rudra and all animate and inanimate objects will sing the declaration of His victory; the town of Sambhal will be very fortunate, where the Lord will manifest Himself. —153

Looking at His sky-reaching banner all the gods and others will become fearful; wearing His aigrette and holding his mace, lance and sword in His hands, He will move hither and thither; He will propagate His religion in the Iron Age for destroying the sins in the world; the town of Sambhal will be very fortunate, where the Lord will manifest Himself. —154

The mighty-armed Lord, taking up His sword in His hand will show His Superb Form in the battlefield and seeing His extraordinary Glory, the gods will feel shy in the sky; the ghosts, imps, fiends, fairies, Ganas, etc., will together sing the song of His victory; the town of Sambhal will be very fortunate, where the Lord will manifest Himself. —155

The trumpets will sound at the time of war and they will cause the horses to dance; the warriors will move taking with them the bows and arrows, maces, lances, spears tridents, etc., and looking at them the gods, demons, imps, fairies, etc., will become pleased; the town of Sambhal will be very fortunate where the Lord will manifest Himself. —156

KULAK STANZA

O Lord! Thou art the king of kings, most beautiful like lotus, extremely Glorious and manifestation of the desire of the mind of the sages. —157

Forsaking good actions, all will accept the enemy's *dharma* and abandoning the forbearance, there will be sinful actions in every home. —158

Wherever we shall be able to see, only sin will be visible everywhere instead of the Name of the Lord, both in water and on plain. —159

Even after searching in every home, no worship and prayer and no discussion on Vedas will be seen or heard. —160

MADHUBHAAR STANZA

The vicious conduct will be visible in all the countries and there will be meaninglessness instead of meaningfulness everywhere. —161

Evil actions were committed throughout the country and everywhere there was injustice instead of justice. —162

All the people of the earth became Shudras and all were absorbed in base acts; here was there only one Brahmin, who was full of virtues. —163

PAADHARI STANZA

A Brahmin always worshipped that goddess, who had chopped the demon named Dhumar Lochan into two parts, who had helped the gods and even saved Rudra. —164

That goddess had destroyed Shumbh and Nishumbh, who had even conquered Indra and made him poor; Indra had taken refuge with the Mother of the world, who had made him king of the gods again. —165

That Brahmin worshipped that goddess night and day, who in her fury had killed the demons of the nether-world; that Brahmin had a characterless (prostitute) wife in his home; one day she saw her husband performing the worship and presenting offerings. —166

Speech of the Wife addressed to the Husband

"O fool! why are you worshipping the goddess and for what purpose you are uttering these mysterious *mantras*? Why are you falling at her feet and deliberately making an effort for going to hell?" —167

"O fool! for what purpose you are repeating her Name? And do you not have any fear while repeating her Name? I shall tell the king about your worship and he will exile you after arresting you."—168

That vile women did not know that the Lord had incarnated Himself for the protection of *dharma*; she did not know that for the destruction the people with the wisdom of the Shudras and for making the people cautious, the Lord had incarnated Himself as Kalki. —169

He rebuked his wife, realizing her welfare and because of the fear of public discussion, the husband kept silent; on this, that women got enraged and going before the king of the town of Sambhal, she related the whole episode. —170

She showed the worshipping Brahmin to the king and the Shudra king getting infuriated, arrested him and giving him the hard punishment, the king said, "I shall kill you, therefore abandon the worship of the goddess." —171

Speech of the Shudra King

"O Brahmin! throw away this material of worship in the water, otherwise I shall kill you today; abandon the worship of the goddess, otherwise I shall chop you into two parts." —172

Speech of the Brahmin addressed to the King

"O king! I am telling you the truth; you may cut me into two parts, but I cannot leave the worship of the goddess; you may cut my body into one thousand parts without hesitation, I shall not let you have the feet of the goddess." —173

Hearing these words, the Shudra king fell upon the Brahmin like the demon Makraksha on the enemy; the blood gushed out from both the eyes of the Yama-like king. —174

That foolish king called his servants and said, "Kill this Brahmin." Those tyrants took him to the temple of the goddess. —175

Tying the bandage before his eyes and tying his hands, they took out the glistening sword; when they were about to strike the blow with sword, then that Brahmin remembered Kal (Immanent Brahmin). —176

When the Brahmin mediated on Kal (Immanent Brahmin), then he appeared before him and said, "Do not worry in your mind, I shall kill many enemies for your sake." —177

Then a dreadful sound was heard from the basement of the temple and Kalki incarnation manifested Himself; he was tall like the palm tree; He had bedecked His waist with quiver and he was riding on a beautiful horse. —178

SIRKHANDI STANZA

There was a loud sound and the heroic spirits began to dance tying small bells round the ankles; the maces, tridents, quivers and lances swung up and waved like the dark clouds of Sawan. —179

The army (with Kalki) had worn beautiful garments and that three hundred hands high Kalki drew out his double-edged sword; the horses sprung like leopards and began to rotate. —180

The trumpets were sounded and the armies confronted each other; the warriors advanced through the armies; they sprang and revolved and the swords were struck with jerks. —181

SAMANKA STANZA

Seeing him, all ran away; everyone coveted to see him. —182

Seeing his powerful form, the sun is feeling shy and his effulgence is mocking the powerful light. —183

The persistent warriors in rage are inflamed like the furnace; the powerful group of warriors is even scoffing at the sun. —184

The soldiers of the king advanced in rage and they were holding their arms and weapons in their hands. —185

TOMAR STANZA

Imbued with the idea of fighting, getting enraged, the warriors riding the horses are swinging their arms and weapons. —186

In their fury, they are grinding their teeth and talking in themselves and filled with ego these warriors are discharging their arrows. —187

Kalki, getting infuriated caught hold of His axe in his long arms and with its slightest blow four hundred warriors died and fell down. —188

BHARTHUAA STANZA

The drums sounded, the horses swung and the warriors thundered. —189

The thundering warriors discharged arrows, their shields were raised and the rhythmic sound was heard. —190

The daggers glistened, the flaming fires blazed and the flames rose high. —191

The blood oozed out from the wounds, which demonstrated the zeal of the warriors; they ran and fell in the multitude. —192

The helmets broke, the drums sounded and the heavenly damsels danced in consonance with the tune. —193

The limbs were chopped and they fell down and because of the discharged arrows, the warriors were tossed about violently. —194

The warriors fought bravely and the cowards ran away; the heroic fighters were filled with anger and malice. —195

With the discharge of the arrows, the cowards ran away and the zeal was exhibited by the oozing wounds. —196

The limbs and corpses of the warriors engaged in war fell up and down. —197

The shields gleamed and seeing the chopped heads, Shiva began to dance and wear the rosaries of skulls. —198

The horses sprang and the warriors seeing the corpses and chopped heads got pleased. —199

The swords saturated with hot blood glistened and Shiva danced and laughed. —200

The warriors, getting together, began to discharge arrows and taking their gleaming shields they began to wed the heavenly damsels. —201

The intoxicated sound is rising from all the four sides and the chopped limbs are falling down in the battlefield. —202

The warriors are fighting with each other will great zeal and the musical instruments are being played in the battlefield. —203

The tips of the arms and weapons are entering the bodies and the Kshatriyas are striking their arms and weapons in the battlefield. —204

The warriors falling on the earth and then swinging up and fighters are shouting for water. —205

The directions have disappeared by the discharge of arrows; the warriors are falling and the cowards are running away. —206

The Shiva while dancing and playing his tabor is roaming and wearing the rosaries of skulls. —207

The heavenly damsels are dancing and with the dreadful fighting by warriors and running away by the cowards, there is a break in the tune. —208

The warriors fall on being struck by the arrow and the headless trunks of the warriors are being chopped through the middle. —209

The blood-spilling warriors are fighting with double zeal and with the blows of the arms, the canopies of the warriors being cut down, are falling. —210

The tips of the striking arms are piercing the bodies; the horses are neighing and the warriors are thundering. —211

The shields and the armours are being cut; the warriors are falling on the earth and getting up while swinging. —212

The hands have fought with hands; the young soldiers being chopped and the arrows, flying numerously are being planted in the bodies. —213

ANOOP NIRAAJ STANZA

Seeing the unique beauty, the warriors are getting infuriated and wearing their weapons are reaching in the war-arena; the warriors are inflicting wounds from both the sides and are hoping to get the declaration of victory; with the breakage of weapons, their bright tips are being seen. —214

The warriors rotating while roaming, are raising dreadful sounds; seeing the glory of the warriors, the cowards are running away; Shiva is engaged in Tandava dance and the daggers are colliding with one another producing various types of sounds. —215

The sons of the demons, getting frightened are running away and the sharp arrows are being discharged on them; the Yogins are dancing in the fourteen directions and all the directions and the Sumeru mountain are trembling. —216

All the warriors of Shiva are dancing and the

heavenly damsels, after recognising the fierce fighters are wedding them; the witches in their fury are shouting and the Yakshas, Gandharvas, imps, ghosts, fiends, etc., are laughing. —217

The vultures, flying and revolving, are devouring flesh and the vampires are drinking blood, filling it in their bowls; the female ghosts and fiends are laughing while drinking blood and the lustre of the swords is being seen and the continued laughter is being heard in the battlefield. —218

AKWA STANZA

The warriors fought, the arrows were discharged, the horses died and the fighters fell down. —219

The soldiers discharging their arrows and being absorbed in the war are fighting with various limbs. —220

The swords are broken, the limbs are splitting, the warriors are bedecking themselves and the heavenly damsels are roaming for wedding them. —221

The elephants are engaged in fighting with other elephants; the camels, very high, are absorbed in fighting with other powerful camels. —222

With the discharge of arrows, the warriors being chopped are falling of the ground; they are getting up again. —223

They are shouting "kill, kill" in all the four directions and bedecking themselves, they are striking their weapons. —224

CHACHARI STANZA

There are seen there many warriors able to confront the very great power and there are also seen those in helpless condition. —225

The warriors are challenging and are consciously striking blows. —226

The warriors of Shiraz sat down after feeling shy. —227

Kalki inspires them to get up and cause them to see; he revolves the sword and strikes its edge. —228

KRAPAAN KRAT STANZA

Where the warriors are fighting and the arrows are being discharged, there the warriors get up and their armours, being shattered are falling down. —229

The warriors falling down in the war-arena are ferrying across the ocean of fear and heavenly damsels roaming in the sky, are wedding the warriors. —230

Listening to the musical instruments of the battlefield, the coward are running away and abandoning the battlefield, they are feeling shy. —231

The warriors are again rotating and embracing death by fighting; they do not retrace even one step from the battlefield and are ferrying across the dreadful ocean of *samsara* by dying. —232

In the dreadful war, the fourfold army was scattered into fragment and because of the infliction of wounds on the bodies of the warriors, their honour and respect declined. —233

Without retracing their steps even slightly, the warriors are fighting and in anger, they are besieging the army. —234

They fall down on the earth after dying and the women of gods are wedding them; the warriors getting enraged in their mind, do not retrace even one step. —235

Getting infuriated, the warriors do not run for two steps and fighting in anger, they fall on the ground. —236

Because of the sound of the musical instruments of the battlefield the clouds are feeling shy and the bedecked warriors are not retracing, even slightly. —237

The striking discus are shattering the glory and pride of the warriors; because of the dreadfulness of war, the Sumeru mountain has also trembled and the stream of the blood of the warriors is flowing. —238

The dreadful war is going on with terrible explosions and the horse-riders are fixing their columns of victory. —239

Holding their swords in fury, the warriors are fighting and fighting with the strength of their mind, they are not moving back. —240

CHACHARI STANZA

The warriors are challenging and shouting; they

are striking blows with their swords. —241

The warriors are raising their weapons and exhibiting them; they are revolving and striking them. —242

They are aiming at the target in fury and carrying their weapons, they are giving the relish of their edges to the enemies. —243

There are thousand of staunch warriors. —244

The shouting and crying warriors have gathered; they are excited and being chopped they are falling and bowing down. —245

The soldiers are hesitatingly aiming their arrows on their targets. —246

The echoes are being heard and the arrows are being shot.—247

The embellished warriors are thundering and are not running away. —248

Taking up their bows, arrows and quivers, the charming warriors are fighting. —249

With the winking of their eyelids, the warriors are getting angry and giving jolts to one another while laughing. —250

The charming warriors are discharging their arrows patiently. —251

The warriors are fighting in retaliation and are grappling one another. —252

The warriors are challenging without getting tired; and they are penetrating forward. —253

The unchoppable warriors are being killed. —254

The warriors striking blows, are bowing, challenging and getting up again. —255

BHAGAUTI STANZA

The arrows are being discharged, the warriors are fighting, the limbs are being split and the war is continuing. —256

The warriors are getting excited, the heavenly damsels are roaming and the sparks of fire are coming out of the colliding swords. —257

The limbs are being splitted, all are absorbed in the war, the horses are dancing and the warriors are thundering. —258

The blows are being endured with pleasure; the warriors are falling down while swinging and thundering. —259

Contacting the numberless spirits, the warriors are lamenting; they are getting unconscious and falling down; the ghosts are dancing. —260

The warriors are fighting catching hold of arrows; the beauty is resplendent on all the faces and the heavenly damsels are looking at the warriors. —261

The warriors are fighting with the elephants after killing the enemies; they are running away after being hit by the arrows. —262

The warriors are lying down unconscious and in their fury; their hair have been loosened and their attires have been damaged. —263

The warriors have been destroyed while fighting with the elephants; the horses are roaming openly and the warriors are thundering. —264

The heavenly damsels are roaming over the whole earth; on being hit be the arrows, the warriors are embracing martyrdom. —265

With the discharge of the arrows the directions have been hidden from view and the swords are gleaming high up in the sky. —266

The ghosts, arising from the graves, are coming towards the battlefield; the warriors are thundering and the horses are running. —267

The warriors whose limbs have been chopped, are falling in the war-arena and the intoxicated warriors are being killed. —268

There are cries of "kill, kill" are being heard in all the four directions; the warriors are closing in and are not backing out. —269

They are striking blows with their lances, while shouting; the whiskers of those egoists are also charming. —270

The drums are being played and the warriors are shouting; the trumpets are sounding and the persistent warriors are fighting with one another. —271

The warriors are thundering, the horses are jumping, the arrows are being discharged and the fighters are going astray in the multitude. —272

BHAVANI STANZA

Where the warriors are fighting in the battlefield, there is much pomp and show; when the lances are turned upside down, there appears a miracle (that all the warriors are killed). —273

Where the steel is colliding, there the warriors are thundering; the armours, are colliding with the armours, but the warriors are not retracing even two steps. —274

Somewhere the horses are running, somewhere the warriors are thundering; somewhere the heroic fighters are fighting and somewhere the warriors with the breaking of their helmets, are falling down. —275

Where the warriors have gathered, there they are striking the blows of their arms; they are fearlessly chopping with their weapons and killing the fighters. —276

Somewhere there are cries of "kill kill;" and somewhere the horses are springing; somewhere seeing the opportunity the army is being removed. —277

Somewhere the wounds are being inflicted and somewhere the army is being pushed; somewhere the bodies saturated with blood are falling on the earth. —278

DOHIRA

In this way, the dreadful war continued for a short while and two lakhs and one thousand warriors died in this war. —279

RASAAVAL STANZA

When the king of Sambhal heard this, he, getting mad with anger turned black like the dark cloud; during the night, with his magic power, he magnified his body to such an extent that his head touched the sky. —280

With helmet on his head, he seems like the sun among the clouds; powerful body is like Shiva, the Lord of Chandra, which is indescribable. —281

It seemed that the flames were rising and the king had worn the weapons like the Guru Dronacharya. —282

The warriors shouting "kill, kill" were coming near and with the blows of their arms and weapons, the wounds were being inflicted. —283

With the sound of the collision of the dagger with dagger, the fishes of water were getting agitated and on all the four sides the arrows were being showered violently. —284

Wearing beautiful garments, the warriors are falling down and on all the four sides, the warriors of charming whiskers, were absorbed in lamenting. —285

The arrows and swords of sharp edges are being struck and the warriors are moving inspite of the chopping of their limbs. —286

The flesh-eating beings are dancing and the vultures and crows in the sky are getting pleased; the rosaries of skulls are being strung for the neck of Shiva and it seems that all have got intoxicated on drinking wine. —287

The warriors being chopped by the edges of the weapons and the blow of the arms, spilling their blood are getting unconscious and falling down. —288

The warriors, flowing in the current of anger, are striking dreadfully their weapons and with the collision of the bloody daggers, they are being excited doubly. —289

The goddess, thirsty of blood, is laughing, and her laughter is pervading on all the four sides like the illumination of her light. —290

The determined warriors are fighting, taking up their shields and Shiva wearing his rosary of skulls is dancing; the blows of weapons and arms are being struck. —291

The patient warriors are discharging arrows by repeatedly pulling their bows and the swords are being struck like the flash of lightning. —292

The bloody daggers are colliding and with double excitement, the warriors are fighting; those elegant warriors are shouting "kill, kill." —293

Pressing one another, the warriors are looking magnificent and the great warriors are inflicting wounds on one another. —294

The warriors are engaged like wrestlers among themselves and striking their weapons they are desiring for their victory. —295

The warriors are imbued with war and with double excitement, they are striking their bloody dagger. —296

The heavenly damsels are moving in the sky and the warriors, greatly tired, are falling down; the sound of clapping is being heard and Shiva is dancing. —297

The sound of lamentation is rising in the battlefield and alongwith it, there is also shower of arrows; the warriors are thundering and the horses are running from this side to that side. —298

CHAUPAI

In this way, a dreadful war was waged and the ghosts, fiends and Baitals began to dance; the lances and arrows have spread in the sky and it appeared that the night had fallen during the day. —299

Somewhere the imps and fiends are dancing in the battlefield and somewhere after continued fighting the warriors have fallen in the war-arena; somewhere the Bhairavas are shouting loudly and somewhere the dreadful crows are flying. —300

The small and big drums, trumpets, flutes, etc., are all being played; the pipe and fife are also being played and the warriors, getting frightened, are running away. —301

Great warriors fell martyrs in that battlefield and there was commotion in the country of Indra; the lances and arrows spread in the world like the rushing fourth of the clouds of Sawan. —302

TOMAR STANZA

Getting infuriated in many ways, the warriors are discharging arrows by pulling their bows; whosoever is hit by these arrows, he leaves for heaven. —303

There are heaps of chopped limbs lying somewhere and somewhere there are lying arrows and swords, somewhere there are seen garments, somewhere lances and somewhere armours of steel. —304

The warriors are dyed in the colour of war like the *kinsuk* flowers; some of them are dying while fighting as if they are playing Holi. —305

Someone is coming running and is not retracing even two steps backwards; they are striking blows like playing Holi. —306

TARAK STANZA

Now Kalki will get enraged and will knock down and kill a gathering of warriors; he will strike blows with various types of weapons and will destroy the groups of enemies. —307

The arrows contacting the armours will be discharged and in this war, the gods and demons will all confront one another; there will be showers of lances and arrows and the warriors will strike shouting "kill, kill" from their mouths. —308

He will take out his axe and sword and in his fury, he will strike the gods and demons; he will cause the corpses fall over corpses in the war-arena and seeing this, the fiends and fairies will get pleased. —309

The Ganas of Shiva will roar and seeing them in affliction, all the people will run away; they will move in the war-arena discharging the arrows continuously. —310

The swords will collide with one another and seeing all this, the great warriors will thunder; the generals will march forward from both the sides and shout "kill, kill" from their mouths. —311

Ganas, Gandharvas and gods will see all this and will raise the sound of "hail, hail;" the axes and swords will be struck and the limbs, being cut into halves, will fall. —312

The intoxicated horses imbued with war, will neigh and the sound of anklets and small cymbals will be heard; the generals of both the sides will fall upon each other and will glisten their swords, while holding them in their hands. —313

The groups of elephants will roar in the war-arena and seeing them, the clouds will feel shy; all will fight in anger and the canopies of chariots etc., will drop from the hands of the warriors very quickly. —314

The war-trumpets sounded in all the directions and the warriors raising shouts turned towards the war-arena; now in their fury, they will strike blows with their swords and will quickly inflict wounds on the warriors. —315

Taking out his sword in his hand and glistening it, Kalki will increase his approbation in the Iron Age; he will scatter the corpse upon corpse and aiming the warriors as targets, he will kill them. —316

The thick clouds will rush forth in the war-arena and in the winking of the eye, the arrows will be discharged; he will hold his sword and strike it with a jerk and the crackling noise of the arrows will be heard. —317

The elephants, horses, chariots and chariot-riders will be chopped and the warriors catching each other by their hair, they will swing the swing; there will be blows of legs and fists and the heads will be shattered with teeth. —318

The kings of the earth will re-array their armies and hold their bows and arrows; there will be fought a dreadful war in anger in both the directions and the warriors will obtain a place in heaven in the dreadful war. —319

The swords will clatter and the jingling of the steel armours will be heard; the sharp-edged weapons will produce knocking sounds and the Holi of the war will be played. —320

The lances will be struck from both sides and the matted locks of the warriors will roll in dust; the spears will collide while striking blows like the thundering of the clouds of Sawan. —321

The warriors grinding their teeth in anger will cause their horses to dance from both sides; they will discharge arrows from their bows in the war-arena and will cut the saddles of horses and the armours. —322

The warriors will rush forth like clouds and will roam in all the ten directions, shouting "kill, kill;" with their utterance of "kill, kill," the heart of Sumeru mountain will all move. —323

Crores of elephants and horses and also the riders of elephants will die fighting and to what extent the poets will describe them? The Ganas, gods and demons will all see and hail. —324

Lakhs of lances and arrows will be discharged and the banners of all colours will wave in the war-arena; the superb warriors will fall on the enemies taking their shields etc., and in all the ten directions the sound of "kill, kill" will be heard. —325

The armours etc., will be seen flying in the war and the warriors will pitch their column of praise; the lance and arrows will be seen shining in the war-arena; besides the warriors, the ghosts and fiends will also be seen shouting loudly in the war. —326

Somewhere the lances and the arrows will be seen striking the targets; many will be thrown in all the ten directions by catching them from their hair. —327

The warriors of red colour will be seen and the arrows will be struck like the rays of the sun; the glory of the warriors will be of different type and seeing them, the *kinsuk* flowers will also feel shy. —328

The elephants, horses and chariot-riders will fight in such numbers that the poets will not be able to describe them; their songs of praise will be composed and they will be sung till the end of four ages. —329

The stable warriors will fall upon their opponents from both sides and will shout "kill, kill" from their mouths; the weapons will strike from both sides and the volleys of arrows will be discharged. —330

HARIBOLMANA STANZA

The warriors will shout, the clouds will be shy, the armies will fight and the arrows will be discharged.—331

The arrows will be showered, there will be the twang of the bows, the swords will collide and the war will continue, —332

The earth will thrust in and become fearful; the warriors will run away without getting shy. —333

The Ganas will see, they will hail; they will sing, praises and smile. —334

The warriors will fulfil their promises and will look beautiful; even the gods will feel shy from them in the war-arena. —335

In their fury, they will discharge arrows; during their fighting in the war, their swords will break. —336

The warriors will thunder, not run away; they will strike their blows with swords and will knock down their enemies. —337

The horses will fight, the warriors will be killed and will ferry-across the world-ocean. —338

The gods will see and hail; they will utter "bravo, bravo" and will be pleased in their mind. —339

The Lord is the cause of all victories and the remover of the enemies; He is the destroyer of the tyrants and is Full of Glory. —340

He is the giver of suffering to the tyrants and is the ornamentation of the world; the praiseworthy Lord is the punisher of the enemies. —341

He is the destroyer of the armies and is the striker of sword; He is the creator of the world and also its supporter. —342

He is bewitching and glorious; He is the affliction-giver for the enemies and the world remembers Him. —343

He is the masher of the enemy and fulfiller of the promise; He showers the arrows with His bow. —344

He is the fascinator of women, glorious and elegant; He allures the mind like the clouds of Sawan. —345

He is the ornament of the world and is the sustainer of tradition; He is cool like the moon and bright-faced like the sun. —346

He comes and gives comfort and happiness; seeing the thick clouds, He gets pleased like the peacock. —347

He is the merciful Lord of the world; He is the ornament of the universe and their remover of suffering. —348

He is the allurer of women and most beautiful; seeing his charming eyes, the dear are getting shy. —349

His eyes are like the deer's eyes and lotus; He is full of mercy and glory. —350

He is the cause of the Iron Age and the redeemer of the world; He is beauty-incarnate and even the gods become shy on seeing Him. —351

He is the worshipper of the sword and the destroyer of the enemy; He is the giver of happiness and killer of the enemy. —352

He is the Yaksha of water and the fulfiller of the promise; He is the destroyer of the enemy and the masher of his pride. —353

He is the creator and support of the earth and by pulling His bow, He showers the arrows. —354

He is glorious with the elegance of lakhs of moon; He is the fascinator of women with His glorious elegance. —355

He has red colour, He supports the earth and has Infinite glory. —356

He is the field of refuge, the killer of the enemy, most glorious and most charming. —357

His beauty captivates the mind; He is the cause of the causes of the world and is full of mercy. —358

He is of such captivating beauty as if He is the god of love; His brightness defeats the moon's glory. —359

He is the worshipper of the sword and the destroyer of the enemy; He is the Lord bestower of the boon. —360

SANGEET BHUJANG PRAYAAT STANZA

The warriors are fighting in the war and the arrows are being discharged; the horse-riders are fighting in the battlefield and in their fury, they are absorbed in fighting. —361

The dreadful fighting continues and the warriors have got enraged; the warriors are striking their lances and are dismounting the fighters from their horses. —362

The soldiers have discharged the arrows and the horses have been killled and the fast-moving horses jumped and ran away. —363

The battlefield was saturated with blood and the warriors became unconscious during their fight; the fighters arise, get enraged and strike blows in great excitement. —364

Shiva is dancing and the cowards are running away; the warriors are fighting and are being struck by the arrows. —365

The warriors are absorbed in fighting and the heavenly damsels are moving for wedding them; the warriors are looking at them and they are also fascinated by them. —366

Their beauty allures the lovers like falling in the well, wherefrom they can never come out; these heavenly damsels have also drowned themselves in the sexual love of the beautiful warriors. —367

The women are getting allured and there is brightness of their elegance; the warriors seeing them are playing on various kinds of musical instruments. —368

The women, full of beauty and lust are dancing and the warriors, getting pleased are wedding them. —369

The king, getting infuriated, manifested himself as Kal (Death) and in his anger, quickly advanced forward. —370

The warriors shouted, the horses danced, the fighters died and the ghost etc., became pleased. —371

The warriors were being killed and the cowards began to run away; the king also fell upon the opponents and the musical instrument of war were played. —372

The swords were broken and the fires blazed; with the infliction of arrows the warriors ran hither and thither. —373

Seeing the war, the goddess Kali also god pleased in the sky; the Bhairava and ghosts etc., also laughed in the battlefield. —374

DOHIRA

The swords broke and many weapons were shattered into bits; those warriors who fought, were chopped and ultimately only the king survived. —375

PANKAJ VAATIKA STANZA

On the destruction of his army, the king extremely agitated went forward and came at the front; getting extremely angry in his mind he moved forward in order to fight. —376

Taking his other forces with him, he struck blows in many ways; many trumpets sounded there and the onlookers of war, also fell down in fear. —377

CHAAMAR STANZA

All the warriors in their fury, took their arms and weapons in their hands moved forward with persistence and shouting loudly fell upon the opponents; they pulled their bows upto their ears and discharged their arrows and without moving backward even slightly they fought and fell. —378

Taking angrily their bows and arrows in their hands they moved and the warriors were killed selectively; they were all fearlessly inflicting wounds and their limbs are falling down, but still they did not run away from the battlefield. —379

NISHPAALAK STANZA

By pulling their bows, the warriors are proudly discharging their arrow and are uniting arrows with arrows discharging swiftly the later arrow; they are striking blows with great zeal and the great fighters also having been wounded are running away. —380

The Lord (Kalki) is moving forward, killing the enemies angrily and consciously and is striking his arrows on the opponents; the warriors with chopped limbs are falling down in the battlefield and all their blood is oozing out from their bodies. —381

The warriors come in rage, strike the swords and are killing the enemies while shouting; they breathe their last, but do not abandon the battlefield and seem splendid in this way; the women of gods are getting allured on seeing their beauty. —382

The warriors are coming, being bedecked with their swords and on this side the Lord in his fury is recognising the real fighters; after fighting and getting wounded, the warriors leave for the abode of gods and there they are welcomed with songs of victory. —383

NARAAJ STANZA

All the warriors getting bedecked are falling upon the enemy and after fighting in the war, they reach heaven; the persistent warriors run forward and endure the anguish of the wounds; their feet do not fall back and they are driving other warriors ahead. —384

All the warriors are moving forward in anger and they are embracing martyrdom in the battlefield; colliding their arms and weapons, they are striking blows and the stable warriors, who do no think of running away, are striking blows, persistently thundering fearlessly. —385

The small and big drums, flutes, anklets etc., are creating sounds and the warriors firmly putting their feet on the earth are thundering angrily; the persistent warriors recognising others are entangled with them and there is such a run in the battlefield that the direction are not being comprehended. —386

The lion of the Goddess Kali, in order to kill the army, is running angrily in this way and wants to destroy the army in this way just as the sage Agastya had completely drunk the ocean; after killing the forces, the warriors are thundering and in the dreadful fight, their weapons are colliding. —387

SWAYYA STANZA

On the arrival of the army of the king, the Lord (Kalki) chopped many elephants, horses and chariots; the horses bedecked by the king were roaming in the battlefield, somewhere neighing and somewhere the elephant were seen running; the warriors catching the hair of one another were engaged in fight with them; the arrows were being discharged like the wind and with them the clouds-like enemies had been chopped into bits. —388

Holding their arrows, bows and swords the great warriors fell upon (the opponents); the warriors were striking blows from all the four directions, taking their swords, axes, etc., in their hands; there were groups of elephants fallen in the war on the side and support of their faces and they appeared like the mountains uprooted and thrown by Hanuman in the Rama-Ravana war. —389

Taking the fourfold army, the Lord (Kalki) was attacked through elephant though the persistent warriors were chopped, but still they did not retrace their steps; enduring the blows of bows, swords and other weapons and dyed with blood, the Lord (Kalki) looked like one who had played Holi in the spring season. —390

When wounded, the Lord was greatly enraged and he took his weapon in his hand; he penetrated into the army of the enemy and killed all of them in an instant; he fell upon the warriors and he seemed splendidly beautiful as if he had given the ornaments of wounds to all the warriors in the battlefield. —391

The Lord Kalki, bedecking his limbs with weapons, and in great rage, went forward; many musical instrument including drums were played in the war-arena; seeing that dreadful war, the matted locks of Shiva were also loosened and both the gods and demons fled away; all this happened at that time, when Kalki thundered in rage in the battlefield. —392

The horses, elephants, and kings were killed in the battlefield; the Sumeru mountain trembled and thrust into the earth; the gods and demons both became fearful; all the seven oceans and all the rivers dried up in fear, all the people trembled; the guardians of all the directions were wonder-struck as to who had been attacked in anger by Kalki. —393

Holding his bows and arrows, Kalki, killed crores of enemies; the legs, heads and swords lay scattered at several places; the Lord (Kalki) rolled all in the dust; the elephants, horses, chariots and camels were lying dead; it seemed that the battlefield had become an arrow and Shiva was looking for it, roaming hither and thither. —394

The inimical kings, filled with shame ran in all the four directions and they again began to strike blows taking up their swords, maces, lances etc., with double zeal; he, whosoever came to fight with that most powerful Lord, he did not return alive; he died while fighting with the Lord (Kalki) and earning approbation, ferried across the ocean of fear. —395

With the currents of blood, having fallen on them, the elephants are seen dyed in beautiful colour; The Lord Kalki, in his fury, wrought such a havoc that somewhere the horses have fallen down and somewhere the superb warriors have been knocked down; though the warrior are definitely falling on the earth, but they are not retracing even two steps backwards; they all seem like the wrestlers playing Holi after drinking hemp. —396

The warriors who survived, they attacked from all the four sides with greater zeal; taking their bows, arrows, maces, lances and swords in their hands, they glistened them; whipping their horses and waving like the clouds of Sawan, they penetrated into the enemy's army, but taking his sword in his hand, the Lord (Kalki) killed many and many fled away. —397

When the dreadful war was waged in this way, the warriors fled way leaving behind their weapons; they put off their armours and throwing their weapons fled and then they did not turn aback; Kalki, catching his weapons in the battlefield looks so charming that seeing his beauty, the earth, sky and nether-world were all feeling shy. —398

Seeing the army of the enemy running away, Kalki holding his weapons, his bow and arrows, his sword, his mace etc., mashed everyone in an instant; the warriors ran away like the leaves before the blow of wind; those who took shelter, survived, the others, discharging their arrows fled away. —399

SUPRIYA STANZA

Somewhere the warriors, gathering together, are shouting "kill, kill" and somewhere, getting agitated, they are lamenting; many warriors are moving within their army and many after embracing martyrdom are wedding the heavenly damsels. —400

Somewhere the warriors, discharging their arrows, are roaming and somewhere the afflicted warriors, leaving the battlefield, are running away; many are destroying the warriors fearlessly and many in their rage are shouting repeatedly "kill, kill." —401

The daggers of many are falling; having been shattered into bits and many wielders of arms and weapons are running away in fear; many are roaming and fighting and embracing martyrdom are leaving for heaven. —402

Many are dying while fighting in the battlefield and many after going through the universe are getting separated from it; many are striking blows with their lances and the limbs of many, being chopped, are falling down. —403

VISHESH STANZA

Many warriors abandoning their shame, and leaving behind everything, are running away; and the ghosts, fiends and imps dancing in the battlefield, are ruling over it; the gods and demons all are saying this that this war is dreadful like the war of Arjuna and Karana. —404

The persistent warriors, in their fury, are striking blows and they appear like the furnaces of fire; the kings in their ire are striking their weapons and arms; and instead of running away, they are shouting "kill, kill." —405

The gods and demons both are saying "bravo!" looking at the fighting; the earth, sky, nether-world and all the four directions are rambling; the warriors are not running away, but are thundering in the war-arena; seeing the glory of those warriors the women of Yakshas and Nagas are getting shy. —406

The great warriors, getting enraged, have attacked and are waging a dreadful and frightening war; embracing martyrdom in the war, they are meeting the heavenly damsels and this war appears as a great war to all the gods, demons and Yakshas. —407

CHANCHALA STANZA

In order to kill Kalki, the warriors cautiously marched forward and began to wage war here, there and everywhere; the brave warriors like Bhima are fearlessly striking blows and after fighting and embracing martyrdom, they are getting abode in the region of gods. —408

Pulling their bows and discharging arrows, they are advancing towards the Lord (Kalki) and embracing martyrdom, they are going to the next world; they are absorbed in fighting and are falling into bits before him; these warriors are falling into bits for the sake of heavenly damsels and are embracing death. —409

TIRIKA STANZA

The arrows of the warriors are crackling and the drums are rolling. —410

The horses are neighing and the elephants are trumpeting in groups. —411

The warriors are discharging arrows forcefully. —412

The ghosts intoxicated in the hue of war, are dancing, in the battlefield. —413

The sky is filled with heavenly damsels and they are all dancing. —414

The swords are gleaming quickly and they are striking with clattering sound. —415

The warriors are fighting in anger and are dying. —416

The horses and horse-riders are lying unconscious in the battlefield. —417

The elephants are running away and in this way, the kings, because of the disgrace of defeat, are feeling ashamed. —418

The large daggers are striking blows on the limbs in the war-arena. —419

PAADHARI STANZA

In this way, innumerable army fought and the warriors, in anger, and discharging arrows and thundering, advanced forward; hearing the dreadful sound, the cowards ran away. —420

The warriors, in anger, marched forward with their contingents and taking out their swords, they began to strike blows; the heaps of the corpses looked like the mountains lying on the sea-coast for building the dam. —421

The limbs are being chopped, the wounds are oozing out and the warriors are fighting full of zeal; the adept, minstrels and ballad-singers etc., are looking at the fighting and are also singing the praises of the heroes. —422

Shiva, assuming his dreadful form, is dancing and his frightening tabor is being played; the goddess Kali is stringing the rosaries of skulls and is releasing the fire-flames, while drinking blood. —423

RASAAVAL STANZA

The dreadful war-drums sounded, hearing which the cloud felt shy; the Kshatriyas fought in the battlefield and pulling their bows, discharged the arrows. —424

The warriors, with the broken limbs, fell while dancing, being absorbed in fighting; the fighters drew out their daggers with double zeal. —425

Such a terrible war was fought, that none of the fighters remained in senses; Kalki, the manifestation of Yama, was victorious and all the kings fled away. —426

When all the kings fled away, then the king (of Sambhal) himself rotated and came in front and producing the terrible sound, he began the fighting. —427

He was discharging his arrows as if the leaves were flying in the forest or the current of water was flowing from the clouds, the stars were falling from the sky. —428

He caused great loss to the enemies with his arrows; the arrows of the great warriors were discharged from all the four sides. —429

The arrows flew like the innumerable worms and locusts and they were countless in numbers like the particles of sand and the hair of the body. —430

The arrows, with golden wings and steel tips, were discharged and in this way, the arrows with sharp tips were discharged on the Kshatriyas. —431

The warriors began to fall in the battlefield and the ghosts and fiends danced; the fighters, getting pleased, showered arrows. —432

The warriors challenging others in fury, inflicted wounds on them; with the collision of dagger with the dagger, the sparks of fire were emitted. —433

The horses danced and the ghosts roamed; the fiends, laughingly, were absorbed in war. —434

Shiva also fought, while dancing; and in this way, for ten days, this ire-full war was fought. —435

Then the king, abandoning his spirit of bravery, ran for two steps, but then he rotated like the revengeful snake. —436

Then he again began the war and showered arrows; the warriors discharged arrows and the death released them from the terror of the war. —437

All the adepts saw Kalki and repeated "bravo, bravo;" the cowards trembled on seeing him. —438

NARAAJ STANZA

The warriors aiming the targets of their arrows marched forward and embracing martyrdom in the war, they wedded the heaven damsels; the heavenly damsels, also being pleased, began to wed the warriors, catching their hands after selecting them. —439

The warriors, getting bedecked, fell on the direction of the opponents and striking sharp lances on the enemies; the persistent fighters are falling down after continued fighting and gathering their forces, are running in various directions here and there. —440

SANGEET BHUJANG PRAYAAT STANZA

The king trembled; the dreadful war-drums

sounded; the elephants went out of control and the warriors fought with one-another. —441

The trumpets sounded and the warriors were killed; the bloody fighters fell and their zeal bubbled. —442

The adepts laughed and the groups of warriors ran away; the arrows were discharged and the warriors fought among themselves. —443

There was the sound of arrows and the trumpets sounded; the kettledrums were played and the armies roamed. —444

The cowards trembled and were killed in the battlefield; many of them speedily ran away and felt shameful in their mind. —445

The king was released and he ran away alongwith his army; with the discharge of arrows all the directions were covered. —446

By discharging the arrows, the pride of all was mashed; with the infliction of arrows all the warriors were weakened; their weapons fell down from their hands. —447

The flowers were showered from the sky and in this way, the trouble ended; the Kalki incarnation in his fury, killed the king. —448

The gods came from the front and catching the feet of the Lord (Kalki) eulogised him; the adepts also composed epics in Praise of the Lord. —449

For eulogising the Lord, the epics were sung and the Praise of the Lord spread on all the four sides; the pious people began pilgrimages and the true devotees of the Lord began to dance. —450

PAADHARI STANZA

Ultimately, the king of Sambhal was killed; the small and large drums sounded; the warriors, frightened of war ran away and getting disappointed, they abandoned all the weapons. —451

The gods showered flowers and everywhere the patron-god was worshipped; the people adored the dreadful goddess and many works were finalised. —452

The beggars received charity and everywhere the poems were composed; the *yajnas*, burning of incense, lighting of lamps, the charities etc., were all done according to Vedic rites. —453

The heads of hermitages, leaving all other works, worshipped the goddess; the powerful goddess was established again and in this way, there was propagation of the perfect *dharma*. —454

End of the chapter first entitled "The Kalki Incarnation after Killing the King of Sambhal becomes Victorious—the Description of the War of Sambhal" in Bachittar Natak.

Now begins the Description of War with Various Countries

RASAAVAL STANZA

The king of Sambhal was killed and there was discussion regarding *dharma* in all the four directions; people made offerings to Kalki. —455

While the whole of the country was conquered, Kalki got infuriated and he reddening his eyes, called all his army. —456

He sounded the horn of victory and he planted the column of war again, the whole army in great zeal, marched forward and the whole earth trembled. —457

The earth trembled like the boat in water; the warriors moved with great excitement and the atmosphere was filled with dust on all the sides. —458

All those who had canopies over their heads, got infuriated; taking with them all their armies, in anger, they marched like Indra or Vritasura. —459

The glory of their armies is indescribable; all of them marched after bedecking themselves and the instruments of victory were played. —460

BHUJANG PRAYAAT STANZA

Many bloody and great sword-wielders and armour-wearers were conquered, many Kandhari warriors, wearing large steel-armours, were destroyed, many elegant warriors of Rum country were killed and those great warriors swung and fell on the earth. —461

The warriors of Kabul, Babylonia, Kandhar, Iraq, and Balkh were destroyed and they all, getting fearful, fled away. —462

The warriors, abandoning their arms and weapons, assumed the garb of women and getting ashamed, left their own country; the elephant riders, the horse-riders and chariot-riders were deprived of their kingdom and the warriors forsaking forbearance, became weak. —463

The negoroes and people of other countries fled away; and in the same way, the barbarians of Armenia also ran away; there one of the warriors taking out his sword, caused his horse to dance between both the armies. —464

The Lord, the Great Creator of the wars saw all this and the destroyer of the great canopied-king, the Lord (Kalki) became enraged; that Lord was the conqueror of the noteworthy most tyrannical armies and he got terribly infuriated. —465

He discharged arrows in great rage and the army of that king was chopped and knocked down; the corpses fell in groups; heaps of hand, waists and other broken limbs fell down. —466

The crows shouted caw caw and the flames of fires arose creating crackling noise; the ghosts and fiends laughed there and the goddess Kali ran, while stringing the rosaries of skulls. —467

RASAAVAL STANZA

The warriors, getting enraged, waged war and discharged arrows; they were shouting "kill, kill" while showering arrows. —468

Dancing in the mood of fighting, the warriors fell with broken limbs; and both the gods and demons, on seeing, them said "bravo, bravo." —469

ASTA STANZA

The Lord (Kalki) taking his sword in his hand, became filled with anger and began to roam in the battlefield in fighting mood; holding his bow and sword fearlessly and angrily, he began to move in the battlefield in a queer way. —470

Holding various weapons and challenging with anger and persistence, he fell upon the opponents in war; holding his sword in his hand, he became engrossed in fighting and did not recede. —471

Like the lightning of the rushing clouds, the swords gleamed; the army of the enemies did not even recede two steps backwards and in its fury, came to fight again in the war-arena. —472

The persistent warriors were getting angry in the war like the furnace with blazing flames; the army revolved and gathered together and was engrossed in fighting with great rage. —473

Thousands of swords were looking magnificent and it appeared that the snakes were stinging every limb; the swords seemed smiling like the flash of the dreadful lightening. —474

VIDHOPP NARAAJ STANZA

The swords are glistening like the fires or like the smiling damsels or like the flashing lightning. —475

While inflicting wounds, they are moving like the restless modifications of mind; the broken limbs are falling like meteors. —476

The Goddess Kalika is laughing in the battlefield and the frightening ghosts are shouting; just as the lightening is flashing, in the same manner, the heavenly damsels are looking at the battlefield and dancing. —477

Bhairavi is shouting and the Yoginis are laughing; the sharp swords, fulfilling the desires, are striking the blows. —478

The Goddess Kali is seriously enumerating the corpses and filling the bowl with blood, is looking magnificent; she is moving carelessly and seems like a portrait; she is repeating the Lord's Name. —479

She is stringing the rosary of skulls and putting it around her neck, she is laughing; the ghosts are also visible there and the battlefield has become an unapproachable place. —480

BHUJANG PRAYAAT STANZA

When the warriors waged a powerful war, many elegant fighters were killed; then Kalki thundered and bedecked with all the weapons, penetrated into the current of steel-weapons. —481

There was such a thundering sound that the people were absorbed in the illusion and the dust of the horse's feet arose high to touch the sky; because of the dust, the golden rays disappeared and the darkness prevailed; in that confusion, there was a shower of weapons. —482

In that dreadful war, the army, being destroyed, ran away and pressing straw between the teeth, it began to shout with humility; the king also seeing this abandoned his pride and ran away leaving behind his kingdom and all his paraphernalia. —483

Many Kashmiri and patient, persistent and enduring warriors were chopped and killed and many canopied and mighty Gurdezi fighters and fighters of other countries, who were siding that king with great foolishness, were defeated. —484

The Russians, Turkistanis, Sayyads and other persistent and angry fighters were killed; and angry and dreadful fighting soldiers of Kandhar and many other canopied and angry warriors were also made lifeless. —485

With the discharge of arrows, the firearms were discharged like the fires rising in clouds; Shiva, dancing with his pleasure, strung the rosaries of skulls; the warriors began to fight and wed the heavenly damsels after selecting them. —486

Getting truncated and having the limbs broken the riders of elephant, the horses and other warriors began to fall in groups; the heart of the warriors throbbed with each challenge and with the rising of the fighters with beautiful whiskers, the earth became filled with steel arms. —487

RASAAVAL STANZA

He, who resisted before them, was killed and he, who was defeated, he surrendered; in this way, all were delightfully adjusted. —488

So much charity was bestowed, that they can only be described by the poets; all the kings became happy and the horns of victory sounded. —489

The Khorasan country was conquered and taking everyone with him, the Lord (Kalika) gave his *mantra* and *yantra* to everyone. —490

From there, sounding trumpets and taking all the army alongwith him, he marched forward; the warriors had the swords and quivers; they were extremely angry and clashing warriors. —491

TOTAK STANZA

The earth trembled and the Seshanaga repeated Lord's names; the dreadful bells of war rang; the warriors in ire discharged arrows and shouted "kill, kill" from their mouths. —492

Enduring the anguish of wounds, they began to inflict wounds and cut the good steel-armours in the battlefield; the ghosts and the vultures moved in the sky and the vampires shrieked violently. —493

The heavenly damsels moved in the sky and they came to look for and take refuge with the warriors in the battlefield, they sang songs from their mouths and in this way, the Ganas and heavenly damsels roamed in the sky. —494

Seeing the warriors, Shiva began to string the rosary of skulls and Yoginis laughed and moved; the fighters, roaming in the armies received wounds and in this way they began to fulfil their promise of conquering the West. —495

DOHIRA

Conquering the whole of the West, Kalki thought of moving towards the South and I now relate the wars, that occurred there. —496

TOTAK STANZA

Remembering the war, the Yoginis are hailing and the trembling cowards of Iron Age also became fearless; the hags are laughing violently and Seshanaga, getting dubious, is wavering. —497

The gods are looking and saying "bravo, bravo;" and the goddess, getting glorious, is shouting; the flowing wounds inflicted by the swords are testing the warriors and the fighters alongwith their horses are enduring the cruelty of war. —498

The Goddess Chandi, riding on her lion, is shouting loudly and her glorious sword is gleaming; because of the Ganas and heavenly damsels, the battlefields has become filled with dust and all the gods and demons are looking at this war. —499

Seeing the radiant headless trunks, roaming in the war-arena, the gods are becoming pleased; the warriors are wedding the heavenly damsels in the battlefield and seeing the warriors, the Sun-god is withholding his chariot. —500

The ghosts and fiends are dancing to the tune of drums, anklets, tabors, conches, fifes, kettle-drums, etc. —501

Conquering the fearless kings of the West, in anger, Kalki marched forward towards the South; the enemies, leaving their countries, ran away and the warriors thindered in the battlefield. —502

The mighty ghosts and Baitals, danced; the elephants trumpeted and the heart-moving instruments were played; the horses neighed and the elephants roared; the swords in the hands of the warriors looked splendid. —503

BHUJANG PRAYYAT STANZA

After killing the proud demons of the West, now the trumpets sounded in the South; there the warriors of Bijapur and Golkunda were killed; the warriors fell and the goddess Kali, the wearer of the rosary of skulls, began to dance. —504

The battles were fought with the residents of Setubandh and other parts and with the persistent warriors of Madhya Pradesh; the inhabitants of Telangana and the warriors of Dravidians and Surat were destroyed. —505

The honour of the kings of Chand towns was mashed; the kings of Vidarbha country were suppressed in great ire; after conquering and chastising the South, the Lord Kalki journeyed towards the East. —506

End of the chapter second entitled "Victory over the South" in Kalki Incarnation in Bachittar Natak.

Now begins the Description of the Fighting in the East

PAADHARI STANZA

After conquering the West and devastating the South, Kalki incarnation went towards the East and his trumpets of victory sounded. —507

There he met the kings of Magadha, who were experts in eighteen sciences; on that side there were also fearless kings of Banga, Kalinga, Nepal, etc. —508

Many kings who were equal in authority like Yaksha, were killed, by adopting suitable measures and in this way, cruel warriors were killed and the land of the East was also snatched. —509

The demons of evil intellect were killed, then Kalki turned towards the North in great anger and after killing many dangerous kings, bestowed their kingdom on others. —510

End of the chapter third entitled "Victory over the East" in Kalki Incarnation in Bachittar Natak.

Now begins the Description of the Twenty-fourth Incarnation

PAADHARI STANZA

In this way, destroying the invincible warriors of the cities of the East and killing the fighters of indestructible Glory, the trumpets of Kalki incarnation sounded proudly. —511

The warriors were again absorbed in war and showered arrows while thundering; the cowards ran away in fear and their wounds burst. —512

The warriors were bedecked; the war-drums sounded, the ghosts danced in a charming manner, the Baitals shouted, the Goddess Kali laughed and the fire-showering tabor was played. —513

The cowards ran away from the battlefield; the ghosts, fiends and Baitals danced; the Shiva, engaged in sport, began to string the rosaries of skulls and the warriors looking at the heavenly damsels covetously, wedded them. —514

The warriors, inflicting wounds are falling upon the opponents and the ghosts are dancing and singing with zeal; Shiva is dancing, while playing on his tabor. —515

The famous Gandharvas, the minstrels and adepts are composing poems in appreciation of war;

the gods playing on their lyres, are pleasing the mind of sages. —516

There is sound of innumerable elephants and horses and the drums of war are being played; the sound is spreading in all the directions and the Sheshanaga is wavering on telling the loss of *dharma*. —517

The bloody swords have been drawn in the battlefield and the arrows are being discharged fearlessly; the warriors are fighting and their secret parts are touching each other; the heavenly damsels are roaming in the sky enthusiastically. —518

There are showers of lances and arrows and seeing the warriors, the heavenly damsels are getting pleased; the drums and dreadful tabors are being played and the ghosts and Bhairavas are dancing. —519

The knocking sound of the sheaths and the clattering of swords is being heard; the terrible-demons are being crushed and the Ganas and others are laughing loudly. —520

UTBHUJ STANZA

The Kalki incarnation like Shiva, giver of happiness to all, mounting on his Bull. remained stable in the battlefield like the dreadful fires. —521

He, assuming his great benign form, was destroying the afflicting agonies; he was redeeming those who had taken shelter and was removing the effect of sin of the sinners. —522

He was unfolding brilliance like the fire or the rosary of fire; his dreadful form was radiating brightness like fire. —523

The Lord of all the three worlds took his dagger in his hand and in his pleasure, he destroyed the demons. —524

ANJAN STANZA

Conquering the invincible people and causing the warriors to run away like cowards and taking all his allies with him. he reached the kingdom of China. —525

The anger and furious tone of the Kalki incarnation, who assumed royalty, is very queer; before him, the beauty of the women of Kamrup with bewitching eyes and the charm of Kamboj country is devoid of radiance. —526

His drums are his shields, his blows are severe, his musical instruments create loud sounds and his arrows raise anger and ire. —527

PAADHARI STANZA

He conquered the unconquerable, established the unestablished; He broke the unbreakable and divided the indivisible; He broke the unbreakable and he destroyed those who resisted. —528

The heavenly damsels, seeing both the brave and coward warriors, were getting pleased; they were all sprinkling roses, camphor and saffron on the head of Kalki incarnation. —529

In this way, after conquering the three directions the trumpet sounded in the North; He went towards China and Manchuria, where there were people in the garb of Rawalpanthis. —530

The war-musical-instruments were played and the warriors thundered; seeing the Lords, the heavenly damsels were filled with zeal; the gods and others, all were pleased and all of them, abandoning their pride, began to sing songs. —531

Listening to news about the arrival of the army, the king of China caused the war-horns to be sounded in all his territory; all the warriors marched for the war and in their fury, they began to discharge arrows. —532

The bloody daggers came out and the great warriors died in the war; the wounds were inflicted and the atmosphere became foggy with the dust of the feet of the warriors; the shouts of vultures were heard in all the four directions. —533

The dreadful Kali laughed and the huge Bhairavas and the ghosts shouted; the arrows were inflicted; the ghosts and fiends ate the flesh and the cowards in their anxiety began to run away. —534

RASAAVAL STANZA

The king of China attacked; he was ready in every way; the bloody daggers came out of scabbards with double zeal. —535

The warriors, getting enraged, discharged arrows and roamed in the battlefield, destroying the limbs of others. —536

Shiva also joined the armies and danced and discharged arrows in a queer way. —537

The warriors in their fury discharged arrows in the battlefield, the streams of blood were full and the heavenly damsels moved in the sky. —538

The Goddess Kali laughed and produced fire of Yoga; the tyrants were killed with the arrows of the soldiers. —539

The warriors are swinging and falling on the ground and the dust is rising from the earth; the fighters have gathered zealously in the battlefield and the ghosts and fiends are dancing. —540

The king of China met his men, whose objectives were fulfilled; he took many with himself and advanced forward. —541

CHHAPPAI STANZA

The king took all alongwith him and the drums of victory sounded; the warriors gathered in the battlefield and seeing them, the heavenly damsels were allured; the gods, demons and Gandharvas all were filled with wonder and pleased; all ghosts, fiends and superb Vidyadhar is wondered; Kalki (Lord) thundered as a manifestation of Kal (Death) and he was eulogised in various ways; the destroyer of invincible warriors like Chandika, the Lord Kalki was being hailed. —542

The armies fought with each other, the Sumeru mountain trembled, and the leaves of the forest quivered and fell; Indra and Sheshanaga writhed on becoming agitated; Ganas and others shrunk with fear; the elephants of the directions wondered; the moon was frightened and the sun ran hither and thither; the Sumeru mountain wavered; the tortoise became unsteady and all the oceans dried up in fear; the meditation of Shiva was shattered and the burden on the earth could not remain in equilibrium; the water sprang up, the wind flowed and the earth staggered and trembled. —543

With the discharge of arrows, the directions were covered and the mountains were pulverised; the oceans surged up and seeing the dreadfulness of war, the sage Dhruva trembled; Brahma abandoned the Vedas and ran away, the elephants fled and Indra also left his seat; the day on which the Kalki incarnation, thundered in rage in the battlefield, on that day, the dust of the hoofs of the horses, springing up, covered the whole of the sky; it seemed that in his rage the Lord had created the additional eight skies and six earths. —544

On all the four sides, all including Sheshanaga are wondering; the hearts of the fish also throbbed; the Ganas and others ran away from the war-arena; the crows and vultures violently hovered over the corpses and Shiva, the manifestation of Kal (Death), is shouting in the battlefield, without dropping the dead from his hands; the helmets are breaking, the armours are being torn and the armoured horses are also getting frightened, the cowards are running away and the warriors seeing the heavenly damsels are getting allured by them. —545

MADHO STANZA

When Lord Kalki became infuriated, then the war-horns sounded; and there was jingling sound; the Lord held up his bow and arrows and the sword and taking out his weapons, he penetrated amongst the warriors. —546

When the king of Manchuria was conquered, on that day, the war-drums sounded; the Lord, causing loud lamentation, snatched away the canopies of various countries and got his horse moved in all the countries. —547

When China and Manchuria were conquered, then Lord Kalki advanced further in the North; O my Lord! to what extent I should enumerate the kings of the North; the drum of victory sounded on the heads of all. —548

In this way, conquering various kings, the musical instrument of victory was played; O my Lord! they all left their countries and went here and there and the Lord Kalki destroyed the tyrants everywhere. —549

Many types of *yajnas* were performed; the kings of many countries were conquered: O Lord! the kings came from various countries, came with their offerings and you redeemed the saints and destroyed the evil ones —550

Religious discussions were held everywhere and the sinful acts were totally finished: O Lord! the Kalki incarnation came home after his conquests and the songs of felicitations were sung everywhere. —551

Then the end of the Iron Age came very near all came to know about this mystery; the Kalki incarnation comprehended this mystery and felt that Satyuga (the Age of Truth) was about to begin. —552

ANHAD STANZA

Everyone heard that Satyuga had come; the sages were pleased and Ganas etc., sang songs of praise. —553

This mysterious fact was comprehended by all; the sages believed, but did not feel it. —554

The whole world saw that mysterious Lord, whose elegance was of a special type. —555

He, the fascinator of the mind of the sages, looks splendid like a flower and who else has been created equivalent in beauty like him? —556

TILOKI STANZA

After the end of Kalyuga (the Iron Age), Satyuga came and the saints enjoyed bliss everywhere; they sang and played their musical instruments; Shiva and Parvati also laughed and danced. —557

The tabors and other musical instruments were played and the kings and the weapon-wielding warriors got pleased; the songs were sung and everywhere there was talk about the wars fought by Kalki incarnation. —558

MOHAN STANZA

After killing the enemies and taking the group of kings alongwith him, the Kalki incarnation bestowed charities here, there and everywhere; after killing the powerful enemies like Indra the Lord getting pleased and also getting approbation, came back to his home. —559

After conquering the enemies, he fearlessly performed many *homa*, *yajnas* and removed the sufferings and ailments of all the beggars in various countries; after removing the poverty of Brahmins, like the kings of Kuru clan, the Lord on conquering the world and spreading his glory of victory, marched towards the town of Sambhal. —560

Conquering the world, spreading the praise of the Vedas and thinking about the good works, the Lord subdued in fighting all the kings of various countries; on becoming the axe of Yama, the Lord conquered all the three worlds and sent his servants with honour everywhere, bestowing great gifts on them. —561

On destroying and punishing the tyrants, the Lord conquered the materials of the value of billions; subduing the warriors, he conquered their weapons and crown and the canopy of Kalki-incarnation revolved on all the four sides. —562

MATHAAN STANZA

His light shone like the sun; the whole world unhesitatingly adored him. —563

Before his great beauty, all the kings felt shy; all of them accepted defeat and made offerings to him. —564

The warriors equivalent to his glory also felt shy; his words are very sweet and his eyes are full of enjoyment and pleasure. —565

His body is so beautiful as if it was especially fashioned; the women of gods and saints are getting pleased. —566

He who saw him even slightly, his eyes kept on looking at him, the women of gods, getting allured are looking with love towards him. —567

Seeing the beauty-incarnate Lord, the god of love is feeling shy; the enemies are so much fearful in their mind as if they have been ripped by the weapons. —568

The warriors are looking at his glory covetously; his eyes are black and touched with antimony, which seem to have awakened continuously for several nights. —569

Filled with beauty and love, they look magnificent like a comedian king. —570

The black arrows are fitted in the bow and they hit the enemies. —571

SUKHDAAVRAD STANZA

He leads the life of a producer, a king, an authority, bestower of fortune and love. —572

BACHITTAR NATAK

He is a Sovereign, an arms-wielding warriors, elegance-incarnate and the Creator of the whole world. —573

He is lustful like the god of love, blooming like a flower and dyed in love like a beautiful song. —574

He is cobra for a female serpent, deer for the does, a canopied Sovereign for the kings and a devotee before the Goddess Kali. —575

SORATHA

In this way the Kalki incarnation conquered all the kings and ruled for ten lakh and twenty thousand years. —576

RAVAN-VAADAY STANZA

He caught his sword in his hand and knocked down everyone in the war and there was no delay in the change of destiny. —577

He gave his *mantra* to everyone; he abandoned all the *tantras* and sitting in solitude, he produced his *yantras*. —578

VAAN TURANGAM STANZA

Many people got allured by his various beautiful forms; in the language of the Vedas, his Glory was infinite. —579

Seeing his many garbs, charms and glories, the sins fled away. —580

Those who were special powerful people composed of various forms, the Lord killed these innumerable enemies and obtained approbation in the world. —581

The Lord is most powerful with indestructible arms and his pure light looks splendid; he is removing the sins by performing the *homa*, *yajna*. —582

TOMAR STANZA

When he conquered the whole world, his pride was extremely increased; he also forgot the Manifested Brahman and said this: —583

"There is no second except me and the same is accepted at all the places; I have conquered the whole world and made it my slave and have caused everyone to repeat my name." —584

"I have given life again to the traditions and have swung the canopy over my head; all the people consider me as their own and none other comes to their sight." —585

No one repeats the Name of the Lord God or the name of any other god or goddess; seeing this the Unmanifested Brahman created another *Purusha*. —586

Mehdi Mir was created, who was very angry and persistent one; he killed the Kalki incarnation and in this way, the Lord God merged Kalki incarnation within Himself again. —587

Those who conquered the world and made it their possession they are all under the control of Kal in the end; in this way, with complete improvement the description of twenty-four incarnations is completed. —588

End of "The Description of Kalki, the Twenty-fourth Incarnation" in Bachittar Natak.

* * *

Now begins the Description of the Killing of Mir Mehdi

TOMAR STANZA

In this way, destroying him, the Age of Truth was manifested; the whole of Iron Age had passed away and the light manifested itself everywhere consistently. —1

Then Mir Mehdi, conquering the whole world, was filled with pride; he also got the canopy swung over his head and caused the whole world to bow at his feet. —2

Except himself, he did not have faith in anyone; he, who did not comprehend One Lord God, he ultimately could not save himself from Kal. —3

There is none other in all colours and forms except One God; he, who has not recognised that One Lord, has wasted his birth. —4

Except that One Lord, there is none other in water, on plain and at all the places; he, who has not recognised the One Reality he only roamed away amongst the yogis. —5

He, who leaving the One, believed in another One, in my view, he is devoid of wisdom; he will be surrounded by suffering, hunger, thirst and anxiety throughout day and night. —6

He will never get peace and will always be

surrounded by ailments; he will always suffer death on account of suffering and hunger; he will always remain restless. —7

The leprosy will prevail in his body and all his body will rot, his body will not, remain healthy and his fondness for sons and grandsons will always afflict him. —8

His family will be destroyed and at the end, his body will not be redeemed also; he will always be engrossed in disease and sorrow; ultimately, he will die the death of a dog. —9

Reflecting over the egoistic state of Mir Mehdi, the Unmanifested Brahman thought of killing him; he created an insect, which entered the ear of Mir Mehdi. —10

Entering his ear, that insect conquered that base fellow, and giving him various types of sufferings, killed him in this way. —11

End of "The killing of Mir Mehdi in Bachittar Natak.

BRAHMA INCARNATION

TOMAR STANZA

The Age of Truth was established again and all the new creations appeared; the kings of all the countries became religious. —1

O the Lord of dreadful fury! There is none else except Thee, Who created the Iron Age and its fires burning the world; everyone should repeat Thy name. —2

Those who will remember the Name of the Lord in the Iron Age, all their tasks will be fulfilled; they will never experience suffering, hunger and anxiety and will always remain happy. —3

There is none else except the One Lord pervading all the colours and forms; He helps those who repeat His Name. —4

Those who remember His name, never run away; they do not fear the enemies and wearing their arms and weapons, they conquer all the directions. —5

Their houses are filled with wealth and all their tasks are fulfilled; those who remember the Name of One Lord, they are not entrapped in the noose of death. —6

That One Lord is pervading all the created beings and the whole should know that there is none else except Him. —7

The One Lord is the Creator as well as the Destroyer of the whole world and there is none other in all the colours and forms. —8

Many Indras are in His service, many Brahmas recite the Vedas, many Shivas sit at His gate and many Sheshanagas remain present in order to become His bed. —9

Many Kings like Surya, Chandra and Indra and many Indras, Upendras, great sages, the Fish incarnations, the Tortoise incarnations and Seshanagas remain ever present before Him. —10

Many Krishna and Ram incarnations sweep His door; many Fish and Tortoise incarnations are seen standing at His special gate. —11

There are many Shukras, Brihaspatis, Datts, Gorakhs, Rams, Krishnas, Rasuls, etc., but none is acceptable at His gate without the remembrance of His Name. —12

No other work is appropriate except the support of the One Name; those who will believe in the One Guru-Lord, they will only comprehend His mystery. —13

We should not know anyone else except Him and none other should be kept in mind; only One Lord should be worshipped, so that we may be redeemed at the end. —14

O being! you may consider that without Him you cannot be redeemed; if you adore anyone else, then you will get away from that Lord. —15

Only that Lord should be adored consistently, who is beyond attachment, colour and form; none other except the One Lord should be kept in view. —16

He, who creates this and the next world and merges them within Himself, if you want the salvation of your body, then worship only that One Lord. —17

He who has created the nine regions, all the worlds and the universe, why do you not meditate on Him and why do you fall in the well deliberately? —18

O foolish being! you should adore Him, who has

established all the fourteen worlds; with His meditation all the wishes are fulfilled. —19

All the twenty-four incarnations have been enumerated in detail and now I am going to enumerate the smaller incarnations; how the Lord assumed the other forms. —20

Those forms which Brahma assumed, I have narrated them in poetry and not after reflection, I narrate the incarnations of Rudra (Shiva). —21

When the Lord commanded, then Brahma prepared the Vedas; at that time his pride was increased and he did not consider anyone else like himself. —22

He thought that there was none other like him and there was no other poet like him; on this the Lord-God became unhappy and threw him on the ground like the *vajra* of Indra. —23

When Brahma, the ocean of four Vedas, fell upon the earth, he began to worship with the fullness of his heart the Mysterious Lord who is beyond the ken of gods. —24

He worshipped the Lord for ten lakh years and he said to the Lord of gods to redeem him in any way. —25

Speech of God

(Then Vishnu said) When you will adore Lord-God with the fullness of your heart, then the Lord, who is the Support of the helpless will fulfil your wish. —26

Hearing this Brahma began to worship and make offerings exactly in the same way, as Vishnu had suggested. —27

Vishnu also said this that the powerful Chandika, the destroyer of the tyrants should also be adored, who had killed the demons like Jawalaksha and Dhumar Lochan. —28

"When you will worship all of them, then the curse on you will terminate; worship the Unmanifested Brahman and abandoning your persistence, you may go under His shelter." —29

"Blessed are they, on the earth, who go under His refuge; they do not fear anyone and all their tasks are fulfilled." —30

For ten lakh years Brahma stood on one leg and when he served the Lord with the singleness of his heart, then the Guru-Lord was pleased. —31

When the goddess explained the mystery, then Brahma served with the fullness of his mind, and the Unmanifested Brahman was pleased with him. —32

Then there was such like voice from heaven: "I am the masher of pride and I have subjugated all." —33

"You had been puffed up with pride, therefore I did not like you; now I say this and tell you as to how you will be redeemed." —34

"You may now assume several incarnations on the earth for your redemption;" Brahma accepted all this and assumed new births in the world. —35

"Never forget from your mind my slander and praise; O Brahma! also listen to one thing more." —36

"A god named Vishnu has also meditated on me and greatly pleased me; he has also asked for a boon from me, which I have bestowed on him." —37

"There is no difference between Me and him, all the people know this; the people consider him the creator of this and the next world and also their destroyer." —38

Whenever he will assume the incarnations and whatever he will do, O Brahma! You may describe them. —39

NARAAJ STANZA

"You may assume the human form and take up the story of Ram; the enemies will run away, abandoning their arms and weapons, before the glory of Ram; whatever he will do, reform and describe them and inspite of the thousands of difficulties, present the same in poetry arranging the thoughtful words." —40

Obeying the saying of the Lord, Brahma assumed the form of Valmiki and manifested himself and he composed in poetry the actions performed by Ramchandra, the most powerful one; he composed in a reformed way the *Ramayana* of seven chapters for helpless people. —41

End of description "Containing Command for Brahma" in Bachittar Natak.

Now begins the Description about Valmiki, the first Incarnation of Brahma

NARAAJ STANZA

After assuming the incarnations, Brahma, with the fullness of his heart and in a special way, presented his thoughts; he remembered the Lord and composed the songs and prepared the epic skilfully arranging the selected words. —1

For the divine thoughts, he created the word "Brahma" and by remembering the Lord and with his Grace, he narrated whatever he wanted; he, unhesitatingly, composed in this way the fine epic *Ramayana*, which none else will be able to do. —2

All the poets are dumb before him, how will they compose poetry? he composed this *Granth* by the Grace of the Lord; the erudite scholars of language and literature read it with pleasure; and while comparing with their own works, they get angry in their minds. —3

The story of his immaculate poem which is really wonderful, accomplished and powerful; this story is even re-composed today. His poem is said to be extremely pure and each of its episode is spotless, sanctified and marvellous. —4

According to the instruction given in *Ramayana*, we should ever be in the service of the Lord; we should get up early in the morning and remember His Name; through the Glory of His Name, many enemies are killed and the charities of innumerable types are bestowed; that Lord, also, keeping His Name on our heads, protects the ignorant people like us. —5

Even after the fighting of many mighty warriors, the saints remain unharmed and before the white arrows of His Grace and tranquillity, the forces of agony and affliction fly away; that Lord, with His Grace, will save me and I shall never pass through any condition of suffering and hardship. —6

End of the description of "Valmiki, the First Incarnation of Brahma" in Bachittar Natak.

Now begins the Description about Kashyap, the Second Incarnation of Brahma

PAADHARI STANZA

Brahma, assuming the Kashyap incarnation, recited Shrutis (Vedas) and married four women; after that he created the whole world, when both gods and demons were created. —7

Those who became sages, he thought about them; he interpreted the Vedas and removed the misfortunes from the earth. —8

In this way, the second incarnation manifested himself and now I am describing the third one thoughtfully; the manner in which Brahma assumed his body, I now describe it nicely. —9

End of the description of "Kashyap, the Second Incarnation of Brahma" in Bachittar Natak.

Now begins the Description about Shukra, the Third Incarnation of Brahma

PAADHARI STANZA

The third form that Brahma assumed was this king that he became the King (*Guru*) of the demons; at that time, the clan of demons increased enormously and they ruled over the earth. —1

Considering him as his eldest son Brahama helped him in the form of a *Guru* and in this way Shukracharya became the third incarnation of Brahma; his fame spread further because of the slander of gods, seeing which the gods became weak. —2

End of the description of "Shukra, the Third Incarnation of Brahma" in Bachittar Natak.

Now begins the Description about Baches, the Fourth Incarnation of Brahma

PAADHARI STANZA

The lowly gods served the Lord for a hundred years, when He (the *Guru*-Lord) was pleased; then Brahma assumed the form of Baches, when Indra, the king of gods became the conqueror and the demons were defeated. —3

In this way, the fourth incarnation manifested himself, on account of which Indra conquered and the demons were defeated; then all the gods relinquished their pride and served him with bowed eyes. —4

End of the description of "Baches, the Fourth Incarnation of Brahma" in Bachittar Natak.

Now begins the Description of Vyas, the Fifth Incarnation of Brahma and the Description of the Rule of King Manu

PAADHARI STANZA

Treta age passed and the Dwapar age came, when Krishna manifested himself and performed various kinds of sports, then Vyas was born; he had a charming face. —5

Whatever sports Krishna performed, he described them with the help of Sarasvati, the goddess of learning; now I describe them in brief, all the works, which Vyas executed. —6

The manner in which he propagated his writings, in the same manner, I relate the same here thoughtfully; the poetry that Vyas composed, I now relate here the same type of glorious sayings. —7

The scholars describe the stories of all the great kings, who ruled over the earth; to what extent, they may be narrated, O my friend, listen to the same in brief. —8

Vyas narrated the exploits of the erstwhile kings, we gather this from the Puranas; there had been one mighty and glorious king named Manu. —9

He brought to light the human world and extended his approbation in all the fourteen worlds; who can describe his greatness? And listening to his praise one can only remain mute. —10

He was the ocean of eighteen sciences and he got his trumpets sounded after conquering his enemies; he made many persons kings and those who resisted, he killed them; the ghosts and fiends also used to dance in his battlefield. —11

He conquered many countries of opponents and destroyed many; he fragmented many invincible ones and raised many to the status of royalty; he snatched the countries of many and exiled them. —12

He killed many dreadful Kshatriyas and suppressed many corrupt and tyrannical warriors; many stable and invincible fighters fled before him and he destroyed many powerful warriors. —13

He subdued many mighty Kshatriyas and established many new kings in the countries of opposing kings; in this way, the king Manu was honoured throughout the world and there were declarations only of his bravery. —14

In this way, after conquering many kings, Manu performed many *homa*, *yajnas*; he bestowed different types of charities of gold and cows and took bath at various pilgrim stations. —15

He performed all the Vedic traditions with devotion; he also gave various types of charities concerning lands, jewels etc., —16

He promulgated his policies in all the countries, and donated gifts of various types; he donated elephants etc., and performed various types of Ashvamedha *yajnas* (horse-sacrifices). —17

He donated many decorated horses to those Brahmins, who, had the knowledge of eighteen sciences, who were the reciters of six Shastras, four Vedas and Smritis, who comprehended the secrets of Kokashastra etc., and also those who were skilful in playing various types of musical instruments. —18

At that time the sandal and roses were rubbed and the liquor of musk was prepared; during the reign of that king, the abodes of all the people gave out the fragrance of Kashmiri grass. —19

SANGEET PAADHARI STANZA

The tunes of lyre, flute, drum, etc., were heard; the pleasing sounds of tabors, clarionets, etc., were also heard. —20

Somewhere there was tune of drum, lyre, etc., and somewhere the sound of tabor, anklet, drum, musical instruments, etc., was heard; there was feeling of fragrance everywhere and with this rising odour, all the abodes seemed fragranced. —21

HARIBOLMANA STANZA

When Manu ruled, he removed the suffering of the people and he was so good that even the gods felt shy after listening to his approbation. —22

End of the description of "The Rule of King Manu" in Bachittar Natak.

Now begins the Description of the Rule of King Prithu

TOTAK STANZA

How many kings were there and how many of them were merged by the Lord in His Light? To what extent should I describe them? Then there was Prithu, the Lord of the earth, who donated enormous gifts to the Brahmins. —23

One day, in a desolate forest, seeing huge lions, he went hunting, alongwith his army, in order to attack them; there was a woman named Shakuntala, whose light bedimmed even the lustre of the sun. —24

HARIBOLMANA STANZA

After killing a deer and seeing a desolate cottage, the king reached there. —25

He went there and there was none with him; he saw a very charming woman there. —26

Her glory coveted his mind; when the king saw her, his mind was startled. —27

The king thought as to whose daughter that beautiful woman was? Seeing her beauty, the king was allured and his mind fell in love with her. —28

The king caught her arm and that woman kept silent; absorbed and dyed with love, both became lustful. —29

The king enjoyed her in various ways till night; both of them felt so much pieased with each other that it is not possible for me to narrate. —30

Being absorbed and dyed with love, they kept engrossed in sexual enjoyment through many types of postures. —31

They enjoyed the relish of various types of postures and in this way, both of them established their sexual sport. —32

After that, that woman, having enjoyed the sexual sport, came out of that cottage; the king went away and Shakuntala became pregnant. —33

Many days passed, when she gave birth to a child, who was wearing armour on his body and was also the abductor of moon's beauty. —34

His splendour was like the forest-fire; whosoever saw him, he was wonder-struck. —35

When the child grew a bit older, she (the mother) took him there, where his father was. —36

When the king saw her, he hesitated a little and asked her, "O woman! who are you and who is this boy?" —37

Speech of the Woman addressed to the King

HARIBOLMANA STANZA

"O king! I am the same woman, with whom you had sexual enjoyment in the forest-cottage." —38

"Then you had given your word and now you have forgotten; O king! remember that promise and now own me." —39

"If now you are forsaking me, then why did you own me at that time? O king! I am saying the truth that he is your son." —40

"If you will not wed me, then I shall curse you, therefore now do not forsake me and do not feel shy." —41

Speech of the King addressed to the Woman

"You may tell me some sign or saying, otherwise I shall not wed you; O woman! do not forsake your shyness." —42

Shakuntala placed a gold coin on the hand of the king and said, "you look at it and remember." —43

The king remembered all and recognised Shakuntala; then the king solemnised his wedding with her and enjoyed her in various ways. —44

She had seven charming sons born to her, who were men of infinite glory and destroyer of enemies. —45

They conquered the earth after killing the mighty kings and inviting the sages performed the *yajna*. —46

They performed good actions and destroyed the enemies and none seems equivalent in bravery to them. —47

They were lustrous like moonlight and women of gods of all the four directions were pleased to see them. —48

ROOAAL STANZA

They killed innumerable proud kings and snatching the kingdoms of invincible kings, they killed them; they went to the North, crossing many mountains and with the lines of the wheels of their chariots seven oceans were formed. —49

By striking their weapons and roaming on the whole earth and breaking the mountains, they threw their fragments in the North; after conquering various countries far and near and ruling over them, the king Prithu ultimately merged in the Supreme Light. —50

Considering his end very near, the king Prithu called for all his assets, friends, ministers and princes; he immediately distributed the seven continents among his seven sons and they all began to rule with extreme glory. —51

The canopies swung over the heads of all the seven princes and they were all considered as the seven incarnations of Indra; they established all the Shastras with commentaries according to Vedic rites and held in honour again the significance of charity. —52

Those princes fragmented the earth and distributed amongst themselves and they named the seven continents as "Nava-khand" (nine regions); the eldest son, whose name was Bharat, he named one of the regions as "Bharatkhand," after the name of the adept Bharat, who was expert in eighteen sciences. —53

Which names should be mentioned here by the poet? They all distributed the Nava-Khand continents among themselves; many kings of various names ruled over many places and with the power of intellect, whose names should be mentioned, with their description. —54

The kings ruled over seven continents and nine regions and taking up their swords, in various ways, they moved at all places powerfully; they forcefully promulgated their names and it seemed that they were the incarnations of the Lord on the earth. —55

They continued to conquer furiously the invincible warriors, swinging the canopies over the heads of one another; carrying on their behaviour of truth and falsehood, they acted in various ways and ultimately became the food of Kal (Death). —56

The powerful people perform many sinful actions and unjust deeds, for their interest, but ultimately they have to appear before the Lord; the being deliberately falls into the well and does not know the secret of the Lord; he will only save himself from death, when he will comprehend that Guru-Lord. —57

The fools do not know that ultimately we feel shy before the Lord; these fools forsaking their Supreme Father, the Lord, only recognise their own interest; they commit sins in the name of religion and they do not know even this much that this is the profound mystery of the Compassionate Lord. —58

They are ever absorbed in evil actions considering sin as virtue and virtue as sin, the holy as unholy and without knowing the remembrance of the Name of the Lord; the being does not believe in the good place and worships bad places; in such a position he falls in the well, even having the lamp in his hand. —59

Having no belief in holy places, he worships the unholy ones, but for how many days, he will be able to run such a cowardly race? How can one fly without the wings? And how can one see without the eyes? How can one go to the battlefield without weapons? And without understanding the meaning how can one understand any problem. —60

How can one indulge in trade without wealth? How can one visualise the lustful actions without eyes? How can one recite *Gita* without knowledge and reflect upon it without intellect? How can one go to the battlefield without courage? —61

How many kings were there? To what extent, they be enumerated? And how far should the continents and regions of the world be described? I have enumerated only those which have come within my sight, I am unable to enumerate more and this is also not possible without His devotion. —62

All the superb kings who had ruled over the earth, O Lord; with Thy Grace, I describe all of them; there was king Sagar after Bharat, who meditated on Rudra and performed austerities; he obtained the boon of one lakh sons. —63

They were princes of discus, banners and maces and it seemed that god of love had manifested himself in lakhs of forms; they conquered various countries and became kings of various places and all the kings considering them sovereigns became their servants. —64

They selected a fine horse from their stable and decided to perform Ashvamedha *yajna*; they invited the ministers, friends and Brahmins; after that they gave groups of their forces to their ministers, who moved here and there, swinging the canopies over their heads. —65

They obtained letters of victory from all the places and all their enemies were smashed; all such kings ran away, forsaking their weapons; these warriors, putting off their armours, assuming the guise of women and forgetting their sons and friends, ran away here and there. —66

The mace-wielders thundered and the cowards fled away; many warriors leaving their paraphernalia ran away; wherever these brave warriors thundered, activating their arms and weapons, they obtained victory and got the letter of conquest. —67

They conquered the East, West and South and now the horse reached there where the great sage Kapila was sitting; he was absorbed in meditation, he did not see the horse, which seeing him in the guise of Gorakh, stood behind him. —68

When all the warriors did not see the horse, they were wonder-struck; and in their shame, began to search for the horse in all the four directions; thinking this that the horse had gone to the nether-world, they tried to enter that world by digging a comprehensive pit. —69

The furious warriors began to dig the earth and the brightness of their faces became earth-like; in this way, when they made the whole of the South an abyss, then they conquering it, advanced towards the East. —70

After digging the South and the East, those warriors, who were experts in all the sciences, fell upon the West; when; advancing towards the North, they began to dig the earth, they were thinking something else in their minds, but the Lord had thought otherwise. —71

While digging the earth in various ways, scanned all the directions, they ultimately saw the sage Kapila in meditation, they saw the horse behind him and those princes in their pride, hit the sage with the leg. —72

The meditation of the sage was broken and from within him arose various kinds of huge fires; in that fire, one lakh sons of the king alongwith their horses, arms, weapons and forces were reduced to ashes. —73

MADHUBHAAR STANZA

All the sons of the king were reduced to ashes and all his forces were destroyed while lamenting. —74

When those princes of great glory were burnt down, then the pride of all was smashed. —75

That most powerful Lord is extremely Glorious and the warriors of all the four directions fear Him. —76

Some warriors who had been burnt, ran impatiently towards the king and they conveyed the whole thing to the king Sagar. —77

When the king Sagar saw this, he impatiently asked the news about his sons. —78

Then all of them talked about their strength and also said how the pride of those warriors was destroyed; the tears were flowing from their eyes while saying this. —79

The messengers told this that his sons, causing their horse to move on all the earth, had conquered all the kings and had taken them alongwith themselves. —80

"Your sons, thinking that the horse had gone to the nether-world, had dug the whole of the earth in this way, their pride had enormously increased." —81

There all of them saw the most glorious sage (Kapila) absorbed in meditation. —82

"Your sons, taking the warriors with them, hit that sage with their legs." —83

"Then the meditation of that great sage was shattered and a huge fire came out of his eyes." —84

The messenger told, "O king Sagar! In this way all your sons were burnt and reduced to ashes alongwith their army and not even one of them survived." —85

Hearing about the destruction of his sons, the whole city was steeped in sorrow and all the people here and there were filled with anguish. —86

All of them, remembering Shiva, withholding their tears assumed patience in their minds with the holy sayings of the sages. —87

Then the king performed the last funeral rites of all affectionately according to Vedic injunctions. —88

In his extreme sorrow on the demise of his sons, the king left for heaven and after him, there were several other kings; who can describe them? —89

End of "The Description of the Rule of King Prithu" in Bachittar Natak.

Now begins the Description about King Yayati

MADHUBHAAR STANZA

Then there was a most glorious king Yayati, whose fame had spread in the fourteen worlds. —90

His eyes were charming and his form of enormous glory was like the god of love. —91

The fourteen worlds had received brilliance from the glory of his charming elegance. —92

That generous king had innumerable qualities and had skill in fourteen sciences. —93

That beautiful king was most glorious, capable, expert in qualities and had faith in God. —94

The king had knowledge of Shastras; he was extremely furious in war; he was the fulfiller of all wishes like Kamadhenu, the wish-fulfilling cow. —95

The king with his bloody dagger was an invincible, complete, furious and powerful warrior. —96

When he drew his sword, he was like Kal (Death) for his enemies; and his magnificence was like the fires of the sun. —97

When he fought, none of his limb turned back; none of his enemies could stand before him and ran away. —98

The sun trembled before him, the directions shivered, the opponents stood with bowed heads and would run away in anxiety. —99

The warriors trembled, the cowards fled and the kings of various countries would break before him like thread. —100

The moon stood wonder-struck in his presence; the heart of Indra throbbed violently; the Ganas were destroyed and the mountains also fled away. —101

SANYUKTA STANZA

Everyone heard his praise at many places and the enemies, listening to this praises would become fearful and suffer mental agony; he removed the afflictions of the poor by performing the *yajnas* in a nice manner. —102

End of "The Description about King Yayati and His Death" in Bachittar Natak.

Now begins the Description about the Rule of King Ben

SANYUKTA STANZA

Then Ben became the king of the earth; he never charged tax from anyone; the beings were happy in various ways and none had any pride in him. —103

The beings were happy in various ways and even the trees did not seem to have any suffering; there was praise of the king everywhere on the earth. —104

In this way, keeping all his country happy, the king removed many afflictions of the lowly and seeing his splendour, all the gods also appreciated him. —105

Ruling for a very long time and getting the canopy swung over his head, the light of the soul of that mighty king Ben merged in the Supreme Light of the Lord. —106

All the immaculate kings ultimately merged in the Lord after their rule. Which poet can enumerate their names? Therefore, I have only hinted about them. —107

End of "The Description about the King Ben and His Death" in Bachittar Natak.

Now begins the Description about the Rule of Mandhata

DODHAK STANZA

All the kings who have ruled over the earth, which poet can describe their names? I fear the increase of this volume by narrating their names. —108

After the rule of Ben, Mandhata became the king; when he went to the country of Indra, Indra gave him half his seat. —109

The king Mandhata was filled with rage and challenging him, held his dagger in his hand; when, in his fury, he was about to strike Indra, then Brihaspati immediately caught his hand. —110

He said, "O king! do not strike Indra; there is reason on his part for offering you half of his seat; there is one demon named Lavanasura on earth; why have you not been able to kill him as yet? —111

When you will come after killing him, you will then have the full seat of Indra, therefore now be seated on half the seat and accepting this truth, do not exhibit your anger. —112

ASTAR STANZA

The king, taking up his weapons, reached there, where the demons lived in Mathura-mandal; he was a greatly stupid and an egoist; he was a most powerful one and dreadfully outrageous. —113

Thundring like the clouds Mandhata fell upon (the demon) in the battlefield like lightning; when the demon heard this, he also confronted him and furiously caused their horses to dance. —114

MEDAK STANZA

The king was determined to kill him and both the enemies, grinding their teeth and challenging each other began to fight violently; the king did not stop the showering of arrows, as he waited to get the news of the death of Lavanasura. —115

Both of them had the same objective and did not want to leave the battle without killing the opponent; both the warriors showered trees and stones etc., from both the sides. —116

Lavanasura held his trident in his hand in anger and chopped the head of Mandhata into two parts; the army of Mandhata ran away, being grouped together and got so much ashamed that it could not carry the head of the king. —117

The army, getting wounded, flew away like clouds and the blood flowed as if it was raining; abandoning the dead king in the battlefield, the whole army of the king saved itself by fleeing away. —118

Those who returned, their heads cracked, their hair were loosened and being wounded, the blood flowed from their heads; in this way, Lavanasura won the battle on the strength of his trident and caused the warriors of many kinds to run away. —119

End of "The Killing of Mandhata" in Bachittar Natak.

Now begins the Description of the Rule of Dileep

TOTAK STANZA

When Mandhata was killed in the war, then Dileep became the king of Delhi; he destroyed the demons in various ways and propagated religion at all places. —120

CHAUPAI

When taking the trident of Shiva, Lavanasura killed the superb king Mandhata, then the king Dileep came to the throne; he had various types of royal luxuries. —121

This king was a great warrior and sovereign; it seemed that he had been shaped in a mould of gold; like the form of the God of Love, this king was so beautiful, that he appreared to be the sovereign of beauty. —122

He performed various types of *yajnas* and executed *homa* and bestowed charities according to Vedic injunctions; his banner of the extension of *dharma* fluttered here and there and seeing his glory, the abode of Indira felt shy. —123

He got planted the columns of *yajnas* at short distances; and coused the granaries of corn to be built in every home; the hungry or naked, whosoever came, his desire was fulfilled immediately. —124

Whosoever asked for anything, he obtained it and no beggar returned without the fulfilment of his wish; the banner of *dharma* flew on every home and seeing this the abode of Dharmaraja also become unconscious. —125

No one remained ignorant and all children and old people studied intelligently; there was the worship of the Lord in every home and the Lord was adored and honoured everywhere. —126

Such was the rule of king Dileep, who himself was a great warrior and a great archer; he had complete knowledge of Kokashastra and Smritis and he was expert in fourteen sciences. —127

He was a great hero and superb intellectual; he was the store of fourteen sciences; he was extremely charming and enormously glorious; he was also very proud and alongwith it, he was greatly detached from the world. — 128

The king was expert in all Vedangas and six Shastras, he was the knower of the secret of Dhanurveda and also remained absorbed in the love of the Lord; he had many qualities and was unlimited like the virtue and strength of the Lord; he had conquered many enemies. —129

He had conquered many kings of undivided territories and there was none like him; he was extremely powerful and glorious and was very modest in the presence of the saints. —130

He conquered many countries far and near and his rule was discussed everywhere; he assumed many types of canopies and many great kings fell at his feet leaving their persistence. —131

The traditions of *dharma* became prevalent in all directions and there was no misconduct anywhere; he became famous in bestowing charities like the kings Varuna, Kuber, Ben, and Bali. —132

He ruled in various ways and his drum sounded upto the ocean; the vice and fear were nowhere observed and all performed the religious actions in his presence. —133

All the countries became sinless and all the kings observed the religious injunctions; the discussion about the rule of Dileep extended upto the ocean. —134

End of "The Description of the Rule of Dileep, and His Departure for Heaven" in Bachittar Natak.

Now begins the Description of the Rule of King Raghu

CHUAPI

The light of everyone merged in Supreme Light; and this activity continued in the world; the king Raghu ruled over the world and wore new arms, weapons and canopies. —135

He peformed several types of *yajnas* and spread the religion in all the countries; he did not allow any sinner to stay with him and never uttered falsehood, even though oversight. —136

The night considered him as moon and the day as sun; the Vedas considered him as "Brahma" and the gods visualised him as Indra. —137

All the Brahmins saw in him the god Brihaspati and the demons as Shukracharya; the ailments looked at him as medicine and the yogis visualised in him the Supreme Essence. —138

The children saw him as a child and the yogis as the Supreme Yogi; the donors saw in him the Supreme Donor and the pleasure-seeking persons considered him as a Supreme Yogi. —139

The sannyasis considered him as Dattatreya and the yogis as Guru Gorakhnath; the Bairagis considered him as Ramanand and the Muslims as Muhammad. —140

The gods cosidered him as Indra and the demons as Shumbh; the Yakshas and Kinnars thought of him as their king. —141

The lustful women considered him as the God of Love and the diseases thought of him as the incarnation of Dhanvantari; the kings considered him as the sovereign and the yogis thought of him as the Supreme Yogi. —142

The Kshatriyas considered him the great canopied king and the wielders of arms and weapons thought of him as the great and powerful warrior; the night considered him as moon and the day as sun. —143

The saints thought of him as manifastation of peace and the fire thought of him as effulgence; the earth considered him as a mountain and the does as the king of deer. —144

He appeared to the yogis as Sovereign and as Supreme Yogi; the mountains considerd him as Himalaya and the darkness thought of him as the effulgence of the sun. —145

The water thought of him as the sea and the cloud considered him as Indra; the Vedas considered him as Brahma and the Brahmins imagined him as the sage Vyas. —146

Lakshmi considered him as Vishnu and Indrani as Indra; the saints saw him as peace-personified and the enemies as the clash-personified. —147

The ailments saw him as medicine and the women as lust; the friends considered him as a great friend and the yogis as Supreme Essence. —148

The peacocks thought of him as cloud and the Chakvi (Brahmani duck) as sun; the female partridge viewed him as moon and the shell as rain-drop. —149

The nightingale saw him as spring and the rain-brid as the rain-drop; the *sadhus* (saints) viewed him as Siddha (an adept) and the kings as sovereign. —150

The beggers saw him as the donor and the enemies as Kal (Death); the Smritis considered him as the knowledge of Shastras and the saints as truth. —151

The saints viewed him as the personification of good conduct and absorbed his kindness in their mind; the peacocks thought of him as cloud and the thieves as peacocks. —152

The women considered him as the incarnation of lust and the saints saw him as an adept; the serpents considered him as Sheshanaga and the gods believed him to be ambrosia. —153

He seemed to be like jewel in the serpent and the creatures saw him as *prana* (life-force); in the whole Raghu clan, he was authenticated as Raghuraj (the king Raghu) and the Yadavas considered him like Krishna. —154

The affliction saw him as the destroyer of suffering and Bali saw him as Vaman, the devotees of Shiva considered him as Shiva and also as Vyas and Parashar. —155

The Brahmins considered him as Veda and Kshatriyas as war; the person who thought of him in any manner, he presented himself in accordance with his desire. —156

He ruled in various ways after conquering various countries far and near seizing various countries, he performed *yajnas* after short intervals. —157

He got planted the columns of *yajnas* at short distances and performed *havans* at various places by reciting *mantras*; no part of the earth was visible where no columns of *yajnas* were seen. —158

Inviting superb Brahmins, he performed many Gomedh *yajnas*; enjoying various types of the luxuries of the earth, he also performed Ashvamedh *yajnas* many times. —159

He also performed Gajmedh *yajnas* and he performed Ajaamedh *yajnas* so many times that they cannot be enumerated; performing Gomedh *yajnas* in various ways, he sacrificed many animals. —160

Performing many Rajsu *yajnas,* the king Raghu seemed like a second Indra after taking bath at various pilgrim stations, he bestowed various types of charities according to Vedic injunctions. —161

He got built places for drinking water at all the pilgrim-stations and stores of corn in every home; so that if anyone comes with any desire, he may be able to obtain the desired thing. —162

No body should remain hungry or naked, and any beggar who came, may return like a king; the king Raghu had such administration that anyone, who would see him once, he would become able to bestow charities himself on others. —163

He gave gifts of gold and silver in various ways; he gave so much to everyone that the recipient became like a king from the status of poor. —164

He would take bath according to Shastric injunctions and then give gifts of elephants, camels and cows; by bestowing gifts of various types of garments, he had fascinated the whole earth. —165

By honouring various types of the lowly, he gave horses and elephants in charity; none was afflicted with suffering and hunger and whosoever asked for anything, he obtained the same. —166

The king Raghu was the abode of charity and gentleness and an ocean of mercy on this earth; he was a great and expert archer and a glorious king, always remaining detached. —167

He always worshipped the goddess with roses, pandanus and sugar-candy and while worshipping, he touched her lotus-feet with his head. —168

He introduced the religious traditions at all places and all the people lived peacefully everywhere; there did not seem to be any hungry and naked, high and low and everyone seemed to be a self-sufficient person. —169

The religious banners fluttered everywhere and there seemed to be no thief or thug and had established one-canopy kingdom. —170

The kingdom of king Raghu was such that the differentiation of a saint and a thief did not exist there and all were saints; his discus fluttered in all the four directions, which returned only on cutting the heads of the sinners. —171

The cow caused the lion to drink milk and the lion supervised the cow while grazing; the persons considered to be thieves now protected the wealth and none committed any wrong act because of the fear of punishment. —172

The men and women slept peacefully in their beds and none begged for anything from others; the *ghee* and fire lived at the same place, and did not damage each other because of the fear of the king. —173

The thief and saints moved together and none frightened any other because of the fear of the administration; the cow and the lion moved freely in the same field and no power could harm them. —174

The king Raghu ruled in this way and the fame of his charity spread in all the four directions; the mighty and elegant warriors protected him in all the four directions. —175

That the king, skilful in fourteen sciences, ruled for twenty thousand years; he always performed the religious acts of this kind, which none other could perform. —176

PAADHARI STANZA

The king Raghu ruled in this way and gave in charity the elephants and horses to the poor; he conquered many kings and shattered many forts. —177

End of "The Rule of King Raghu" in Bachittar Natak.

Now begins the Description of the Rule of King Aja

PAADHARI STANZA

Then there ruled the great and powerful king Aja, who destroyed several clans after conquering many heroes; he also conquered the rebellious kings. —1

He conquered many invincible kings and shattered the pride of many egoistic kings; the great king Aja was the ocean of fourteen sciences. —2

That king was a powerful warrior and expert in the study of Shrutis (Vedas) and Shastras; that great king was full of self-pride and had a very charming face, seeing which all the kings felt shy. —3

That Sovereign was the king of kings and in his kingdom, all the houses were full of wealth; the women were lured on seeing his beauty and he was the knower of the mysteries of the Vedas; he was a great donor, skilful in sciences and a very gentle king. —4

If I relate the whole story, I fear the *Granth* to become voluminous; therefore, O friend! listen this story only in brief; there was a king named Subahu in Vidarbha country, the name of whose queen was Champavati. —5

She gave birth to a daughter, whose name was Indumati; when she attained the marriagable age, the king then consulted his ministers. —6

The king invited the kings of all the countries, who came to the kingdom of Subahu with their armies; the adorable goddess Sarasvati came to reside in the mouths of all of them and all of them with the desire of marrying that girl, they offered prayers alongwith their people. —7

All the kings of various countries came and bowed before that king Subahu and sat in the assembly, where their glory excelled that of the assembly of gods. —8

The small and big drums were resounding; the glory of that place is indescribable; all of them appeared to be like Indra. —9

That royal assembly was such that seeing it, Indra shrunk his nose, who should describe its glory? The Gandharvas and Yakshas kept silent on seeing it. —10

ARDH PAADHARI STANZA

The warriors looked splendid, seeing whom the heavenly damsels got allured; there were innumerable heavenly damsels. —11

They were singing fascinating songs, in which they were blessing together for their long life till the end of four ages. —12

The knocking on the instruments were being heard and many heavenly damsels were being seen. —13

The songs were being sung according to Vedic rites and the kings of unique glory looked magnificent. —14

The stirnged instruments were being played and the women, being pleased, were happily singing songs. —15

UCHHAAL STANZA

The women were singing with the clapping of their hands and the kings with the decoration of gods, were looking at them. —16

The singing of songs continued with happy mind and seeing the glory of that place, even the mind of greed was becoming greedy. —17

They were talking with the signs of their eyes and all the weapon-wielders were looking splendid. —18

The elephants were thundering and the companions were bedecked; the horses were jumping and dancing. —19

The young damsels were dancing and were singing happily while clapping their hands. —20

These women of the voice of a nightingale and having beautiful eyes, were alluring the mind by singing the song. —21

These women having beautiful hair, charming eyes and in the garb of heavenly damsels, had the voice of a nightingale.—22

These women had marvellous figures, full of desires, with bewitching smiles and long nostrils. —23

Seeing the beauty of the queens, the wife of Indra also felt shy; these heavenly maidens were like the rosary of musical modes. —24

MOHINI STANZA

These white-complexioned elegant women were fascinating the mind of gods and men; seeing them, the great kings got pleased; what more description can be given of their glory? —25

Seeing the embellishment of these women, many men of taste were getting pleased; the women were dancing in many emotional postures, seeing which all the gods and men were delighted. —26

The horses were neighing, the elephants were trumpetting and the people of the town were dancing; the gods, men and women were all getting pleased and the kings were busy in bestowing charities. —27

The heavenly damsels were dancing while singing, seeing whom, the kings got pleased and their queens were also getting angry; the pretty lyre of Narada was being played, seeing which the gods seemed radiant like fire. —28

All of them had put antimony in their eyes and had bedecked their limbs, having worn handsome garments; the heavenly damsels were dancing, the kings were getting pleased and were trying to wed them. —29

The women of gods were dancing and the jingling of the rosaries of their limbs was being heard; the kings were sitting with pomp and show at various places. —30

Whosoever saw this, he was pleased and he who did not see this, he got angry in his mind; the women were dancing, exhibiting various kinds of emotions and there was wonderful emotional play from every limb of theirs. —31

Those women also decided to do something marvellous at that place, because there were sitting there some persistent sages; the yogis, leaving their meditation came running and seeing the glory of this function, they were pleased. —32

Wherever the kings were sitting well-bedecked, the atmosphere of that place seemed extremely splendid; the kings were filled with pleasure here and there, accomplished with their qualities and servants and the sages seeing their magnificence had forgotten the consciousness of their mind and body. —33

The stringed musical instruments were being played there and hearing their pleasing musical modes, the experts of musicology were feeling shy; hearing the tunes of the musical instruments, the kings fell down here and there like the warriors lying wounded in the battlefield. —34

They seemed to have blossomed like the flowers of the forest and their bodies were exhibiting the fundamental emotion of the earthly comfort; the intoxicated kings were swinging here and there like the peacocks getting intoxicated hearing the thundering of clouds. —35

PAADHARI STANZA

Seeing the splendour here and there, the kings sat down; their glory cannot be described and seeing their figures, the eyes were getting pleased. —36

Seeing the colourful dance of this kind, the god of love was pulling his bow and discharging his arrows on the kings; the great glory of the atmosphere is indescribable and all were getting pleased on seeing. —37

It seemed that this was the first day of spring; in this way, seeing the whole assembly, all the kings sat down there in their glory as if they excelled even Indra. —38

In this way, the dancing continued there for one month and no one could save himself from drinking the wine of that dance; here, there and everywhere the beauty of the kings and princes was seen. —39

Sarasvati, the goddess worshipped by the world, said to the princess, "O princess! Look at these princes, who even excel Indra." —40

The princess looked towards the group of princes and did not even like the prince of Sindhu kingdom; leaving him, absorbing all the glory within herself, she moved further. —41

Sarasvati said to her again, "Here is a king of the West, you may see him;" the princess saw his natural features, but she did not like him also. —42

MADHUBHAAR STANZA

"O princess! look towards these elegantly dressed warrior-kings of the country. —43

The princess saw towards the natural features of many kings thoughtfully and that supremely immaculate damsel even did not like the king of the West —44

Then that girl moved forward and began to smile like the flash of lightning amongst the clouds. —45

The kings were getting allured on seeing her and the heavenly damsels were getting angry; they were enraged because they found the princess more beautiful than themselves. —46

The kings of charming forms, and apparently beauty-incarnate and of supreme glory were there. —47

The princess saw the kings standing there and also saw amongst them the sovereign of Multan. —48

BHUJANG PRAYAAT STANZA

Leaving all of them, the princess moved forward like the Pandavas, the sons of Pandu, moving away after leaving their kingdom etc., standing in the royal court, she appeared like the fascinating fire-flame. —49

Standing in the royal court she appeared like the portrait of a painter; she was wearing a golden ornament (*kinkini*) fitted with wreath of gems; the pigtail of her hair was apparently like fire for the kings. —50

Sarasvati, seeing the damsel said to her again, "O

princess! See these superb kings; O my beloved! obey my saying; wed him, whom you consider worthy in your mind." —51

"He, with whom there is a large army and the conches, kettledrums and the war-horns are being played, see this great king; whose thousand arms make the day appear as night." —52

"In whose banner, there is seated a huge lion and hearing whose voice, the great sins are eliminated; O princess! see that sun-faced great king of the East." —53

"Here the kettledrums, conches and drums are resounding and the Southern musical instruments are being played; the tones and tunes of many other instruments are being heard; also the drums, anklets etc., are being played. —54

"The warriors are wearing beautiful garments; and the canopied king is looking splendid alongwith his army; he, whose chariot and its horses destroy large and mountain-sized warriors; O princess! he is the king of the South." —55

"The king who has a great army and in which there are millions of soldiers on foot in green uniforms, and whose beautiful elephants tied with banners, are roaming, O princess! he is the king of the North." —56

"He, before whom the army on foot is moving enthusiastically, and who after conquering millions, has not turned away from the war, whose horses are like pigeons and who has such chariots which are not even with Indra." —57

"He, with whom there are warriors of the size of the peaks of the mountains and seeing whom, the damsels of the demons gets fascinated, smile and wave the hair of their heads and in whose fear the pregnant women lose their pregnancies." —58

"That mighty one is the king of Lanka (Ceylon), in whose company there are also Lokpals; he had once looted the store of Kuber and had also defeated the mighty Indra." —59

"O princess! tell me what is in your mind? The mention of the great kings has already been made; there are kings and kings on all the four sides, but you have equally abandoned them all." —60

"See that one who has a great army of demons with him; and with whom there are many canopied kings; on whose banner the vultures and crows are sitting; you may love that mighty king." —61

"He, who has charming garments and chariots and with whom there are all the Lokpals; even the king Indra conceals himself in fear because of that king's fame as a donor; O friend! he is the same Aditya Kumar." —62

"He, in whose chariot, there are seven horses and who can even destroy Sheshanaga with his glory; who has long arms and dreadful bow, recognise him as *dinkar* or Surya." —63

He is whom you see coming with his bow and arrows, he is the king of the night, the brilliant Chandra, who lightens up for all the creatures and whom thousands of people remember day and night. —64

"This one, who while going for war, seems like a mountain and who has conquered greatly tyrannical, multi-armed kings; his banner is powerfully exhibiting its glory, seeing which, the pride of many egoists is shattered." —65

"To what extent should I describe these great egoists? All of them are standing in groups and surrounding others; the comely and clever prostitutes are dancing and the voice of the musical instrument is being heard." —66

"The great wealthy kings taking their armies with themselves and taking pride in their riches, are seated here; O princess! see that king, the master of riches, from whose body the fires of beauty are arising." —67

Where there was the princess, all the kings were standing there; there was none other so beautiful on the earth; many egoistic canopied kings, taking their armies with them, came and stood there. —68

He, from whom the streams adopt the glory of their comeliness and from whom the oceans also spring up, not enduring His brilliance; He, whose body is very big and whose beauty is magnificent and seeing whom, the heavenly maidens get allured. —69

"O princess! all those different kings have come here seeing whom the pride of the kings is shattered; to what extent should I describe those kings who have come here?" That goddess showed the princess all those kings. —70

SWAYYA

All those kings who had come there, they were all shown to the princess; she saw the kings in all the four directions, but did not like anyone; the whole sphere of heroes was defeated and seeing such a situation, the kings also became dejected; the faces of all of them shrank and all the princes returned to their homes. —71

SWAYYA

At that time, the king Aja, taking alongwith him his big army, reached there; his unique silken garments were making the god of love feel shy; there were also many well-dressed other kings affording pleasure; the king Aja, wearing handsome garments reached there. —72

SWAYYA

His army made queues and his forces began to play on the small and big drums; on the bodies of all, the handsome ornaments were shining and the god of love also seeing their comeliness, was becoming unconscious; all were listening to the sounds of the musical instruments and all seeing their unique beauty, were getting pleased. —73

The beauty of king Aja that we saw, we had not seen the same beauty of anyone else before; the moon seeing hid comeliness, hid himself and his heart burnt with jealousy; the fire seeing his elegance, was irritated and he abandoned his burning activity; the kind of beauty that the king Aja has, the same beauty we have never seen before. —74

He was a winsome youth and had a shapely figure, which was considered foremost in all the four directions; he was radiant like the sun and was a great sovereign amongst kings; the gods and others were all wonder-struck to see him and the night considered him as moon; the day imagined him as the sun and the peacocks thought of him as the cloud. —75

The rain-birds raised their voice considering him as spring and the partridges thought of him as moon; the saints thought of him as peace and the warriors apparently as anger; the children considered him as a good-natured child and the enemies as Kal (Death); the gods thought of him as god, the ghosts and fiends as Shiva and the kings as the sovereign. —76

The saints saw him as a Siddha (adept) and the enemies as enemy; the thieves saw him as early morn and the peacocks as cloud; all the women considered him as god of love and all the Ganas as Shiva; the shell saw him as the rain-drop and the kings as the sovereign. —77

The king Aja looked splendid on the earth just as the clouds in the sky; seeing his comely nose, the parrot got jealous and seeing both of his eyes, the wagtail fly shy; seeing his limbs, the rose got dead-drunk and the god of love got angry seeing his handsome neck and the loins seeing his waist forgot themselves and were not able to reach their homes. —78

Seeing his lake-like eyes, it seemed that they became intoxicated after drinking a drought of ambrosia; the songs were being sung and the musical instruments were being played; the women in their pleasure were singing abusive songs and saying, "O prince! the Lord has created this princess for you, You may wed her." —79

Seeing the glory of his eye, the women were absorbed in love and were singing songs while playing on the drums; all the women who were coming from outside the town, seeing the beauty of the king, they threw away their gowns and were only looking at his charming face; seeing the king they all desired, "O king! let it be the God's Will that you may rule as long as the water flows in the Ganges and Yamuna." —80

While describing the glory of king Aja, I accept that whatever similes the poets generally give, they are all discourteous and I feel shy while uttering them; I have searched on all the earth in order to find someone so beautiful as you, but I was not successful; writing about your beauty, my pen is pulled down and how should I describe it from my mouth? —81

The king with the arrows of his eyes, wounded all the townfolk; even Sarasvati is unable to describe the charm of his beauty; the throat of the king is sweet like the nightingale and the neck like the pigeon; seeing his beauty, all are falling down on earth and getting wounded. —82

DOHIRA

The men and women are getting pleased on seeing the comeliness of form of king Aja and have not been able to decide whether he is Indra, Chandra or Surya. —83

KABIT

Either he is mercurial like the young ones of serpents or someone has seen him like the one who casts spells at the king Aja who has been specially created like the toy of the god of love; the king Aja is the breath of life for women, he is the mine of beauty and is skilful in the sexual sports; he is the apparent manifestation of wisdom and amongst the kings he is charming like the moon; it is not clear whether he is the sword or the arrow or a bedecked warrior; such a brave king Aja is being seen with great caution. —84

SWAYYA

He is impressive like a sword or an arrow; his simple beauty like the young one of a deer is worth seeing; all are getting pleased on seeing him; and his glory is indescribable; the princess is moving forward to see him and seeing him, the peacocks and partridges have fallen in confusion; the heart of that princess was fascinated, the moment she saw king Aja. —85

TOMAR STANZA

When the princess saw the king, the treasure of beauty, she held her wreath of flowers with smile. —86

The charming damsel caught the garland in her hand and put it around the neck of the king, expert in eighteen sciences. —87

The goddess said to that princess, who was expert in all sciences, "O beautiful maiden like moonlight having charming eyes; listen to what I say." —88

"O princess full of charm and shyness! The king Aja is a worthy match for you; you see him and listen to my speech." —89

The princess caught the wreath of flowers and put it around the neck of the king and at that time many musical instruments including the lyre were played. —90

The tabor, drum, kettledrum and many other musical instruments of various tunes and tones were played; the flutes were played and there were many beautiful ladies of charming eyes seated there. —91

The king Aja wedded that damsel and taking various types of dowry and causing the tabor and lyre to be played, he returned home with great happiness. —92

That king expert in eighteen sciences, was the ocean of pleasure and store of gentleness; he had conquered even Shiva in the war. —93

In this way, he ruled and caused the canopy to be swung over his head and in the whole world, the ceremonies regarding the divine kingship of that victorious king were performed. —94

The king Aja, after conquering all the four directions, he gave charities of materials as a generous king; being expert in all science, that king was extremely benevolent. —95

His eyes and body were so charming, that even the god of love felt jealous; hundreds of kings evaded him, seeing the moonlike beauty of his face. —96

In this way, the king ruled like a great Sovereign in the world doing religious and social services and performing *yajnas*; if I narrate all the things associated with him, the story will be greatly increased. —97

Therefore, I say in brief, O brothers! listen to it; the king Aja ruled in this way in various ways in religion and society. —98

He abandoned the idea of considering the whole world as his own and did not care for any one; then the Great Death, in great rage, reduced king Aja to ashes in its fire. —99

Seeing the king Aja merging in the Supreme Light all the people became fearful like the passengers of a boat with the sailor; the people became weak like the individual becoming

BACHITTAR NATAK

helpless with the loss of physical strength. —100

Just as a village becomes helpless without a headman, the earth becomes meaningless without fertility, the tresure charm without wealth and the trader becomes in low spirit without the trade. —101

Without the king, the people became like poetry without meaning, friend without love, the country without the king and as the army becomes helpless without the general. —102

That state becomes like a yogi without knowledge, a king without kingdom, the idea without the meaning and the donor without the material. —103

The people became like an elephant without a goad, the king without the army, the warrior without weapons and the ideas without wisdom. —104

They are just like the wife without husband, the woman without beloved, the poetry without wisdom and a friend without love. —105

They are just like the country becoming desolate, the women losing their husbands, the Brahmins without learning or the men without wealth. —106

In this way, the kings who ruled over this country, how can they be described? Vyas, the store of Vedic learning, composed eighteen Puranas. —107

He composed eighteen parvas (parts of *Mahabharata*), listening which the whole world was pleased; in this way Vyas was the fifth incarnation of Brahma. —108

End of "The Description of Vyas, the Fifth Incarnation of Brahma and the Rule of King Aja" in Bachittar Natak.

Now begins the Description of Six Sages, the Sixth Incarnation of Brahma

TOMAR STANZA

In this next Age, Vyas composed Puranas in the world and in doing this his pride was also increased; he also did not consider anyone equal to him. —1

Then the dreadful Kal (Death) in his rage divided him into six parts with his great fires; then they were considered lowly. —2

His life-force was not terminated and from his six parts emerged six sages, who were the supreme scholars of Shastras and they composed six Shastras in their names. —3

These six sages of the lustre of Brahma and Vyas, brought to light six Shastras and in this way, Brahma assumed the sixth incarnation made ideological improvements over the earth through six Shastras. —4

End of "The Description about Six Sages, the Sixth Incarnation of Brahma" in Bachittar Natak.

Now begins the Description of Kalidas, the Seventh Incarnation of Brahma

TOMAR STANZA

This Brahma, the ocean of Vedas, who was the authentic knower of eighteen Puranas and Shastras, began to scan the whole world in his incarnation named Kalidas in the Iron Age. —1

The king Vikramaditya, who himself was glorious, unconqerable, scholar full of virtues with auspicious brightness and charming eyes, remained pleased on seeing Kalidas. —2

After his manifestation, Kalidas composed in chastened form his poem *Raghuvansh*; to what extent I should describe the number of poems that he composed? —3

He was the seventh incarnation of Brahma and when he was redeemed, then he assumed the form of four-headed Brahma i.e. he merged himself in Brahma. —4

End of "The Description of Kalidas, the Seventh Incarnation of Brahma" in Bachittar Natak

RUDRA INCARNATION

TOMAR STANZA

Now I describe in chastened form those incarnations, which were assumed by Rudra;

performing extreme austerities Rudra became egoistic. —1

He did not consider anyone equal to him in all places and countries; then Mahakal (the Great Death) in ire said to him thus. —2

"Those who become proud, they deliberately perform the action of falling into a well; O Rudra! listen to me attentively that my name is also 'the Destroyer of Ego'." —3

"Brahma had also become egoistic in his mind and the evil notions arose there, but when he took birth for seven times, he was then redeemed." —4

"O the king of sages! listen to what I say and in the same way, you may go and take birth on the earth. Otherwise, O Rudra! You will not be redeemed in any other way." —5

Hearing this, Shiva, considering the Lord as the Destroyer of Ego, and leaving his persistence, incarnated on earth. —6

PAADHARI STANZA

The way, in which all the kings have been described, in the same way, the actions done by all the sages have been narrated as to how Rudra manifested himself in the castes of *dvijas* (twice born). —7

Whatsoever deeds they brought to light, I relate them here; in this way, Rudra became the sons of the sages, who adopted silence and attained recognition. —8

Then he incarnated himself as sage Atri, who was the store of eighteen sciences; he abandoned everything else and adopted yoga as his way of life and served Rudra, the store of all wealth. —9

He performed austerities for a long time, on which, Rudra got pleased and said, "You may ask for any boon which you like, I shall grant it to you." —10

Then the sage Atri stood up with folded hands and his love for Rudra was further increased in his mind; he became very happy; the tears flowed from his eyes and his hair showed signs of jubilation, when he said: —11

"O Rudra! if You want to grant me a boon, then give me a son like you; Rudra saying "let it be," disappeared and the sage came back to his home. —12

On returning, he married Ansuya, who had been blessed by Shiva, Brahma and Vishnu by their lustre. —13

Ansuya also, in consonance with her name, inspite of being a charming lady, performed austerities; she was the second manifestation of the Goddess of Love (Rati). —14

That pretty and married fortunate women was glorious in various ways, on seeing whom, the personification of beauty also got allured; her glory is indescribable. —15

Seeing her face, the moon was filled with jealousy and wept in affliction; seeing her hair, he bowed down her looks and even the Sumeru mountain, seeing her beauty, concealed himself. —16

Seeing her neck, the female pigeon got enraged and the parrot seeing her nostril hid himself in the forest; seeing her hair, even Yamuna was filled with anger and seeing her serenity, the ocean felt shy. —17

Seeing her arms, the lotus-stalk felt shy and the swans, seeing her gait got angry; seeing her legs, the *kadli* trees became shyful and the moon considered his beauty inferior to her. —18

In this way, the charm of her beauty is described, and no poet can utter her greatness; seeing such a beauteous lady, the sage Atri believed that he had obtained canopied kingdom of beauty. —19

That lady had vowed that she would not marry her husband for sexual enjoyment, and would wed that person, who would have the strength to endure the sacred tribulations of austerities. —20

The sage (Atri) had agreed with her vow and married her and sacrificed himself on her charm of beauty; he, the sage Atri, who was the father of Dattatreya, making her his wife, brought her home. —21

Several years passed after marriage and once an opportunity arose when Brahma and other gods went to the home of that sage; the women of the hermitage of the sage performed great service to them. —22

The incense was burnt, the lamps were lighted, there were libations and solutions; seeing Indra, Vishnu and Shiva, all the devotees eulogised them. —23

Seeing the devotion of the sage, all were pleased and all blessed him; then Brahma said, "O Kumar! you will be blessed with a son." —24

TOMAR STANZA

When Brahma said this that the sage would be blessed with a son, then listening to it, her eyes showed signs of anxiety. —25

The body of that young lady became agitated and the tears flowed from her eyes; she was filled with anxiety on hearing these words and she felt that the day had changed into night. —26

Her body was agitated with anxiety and she getting enraged, became impatient; her lips and eyes quivered and she lamented. —27

MOHAN STANZA

Hearing these words that doe-eyed and extremely beautiful lady (felt agitated). —28

Her mind, which was immaculate, was filled with extreme rage alongwith other women of the sages. —29

The wife of the sage plucked her hair at that place and her comely limbs were filled with extreme ire. —30

Breaking her necklaces, she plucked her hair and began to put dust on her head. —31

TOMAR STANZA

Seeing the wife of the sage in anger, getting fearful and forsaking his pride, and taking Shiva and other sages with him, Brahma fled. —32

Then the wife of the sage, uprooting one of the matted lock of her head in anger, struck it on her hand, at that time Dattatreya was born. —33

Considering Ansuya as his mother and keeping her on his right, he circumambulated around her and then saluted her; in this way, thinking about the experience of sexual pleasure, Dutt Kumar was born. —34

His body was charming and he was reciting seven Smritis; the great Dutt was reciting all the four Vedas. —35

Shiva, remembering the earlier curse assumed himself the body of Dutt and took birth in the home of Ansuya; this was his first incarnation. —36

PAADHARI STANZA

The loving Dutt, the store of eighteen sciences was born; he was the knower of Shastras and had a charming figure; he was a yogi king of all the Ganas. —37

He spread the cults of Sannyas and Yoga and he was totally spotless and servitor of all; he was the apparent manifestation of yoga, who abandoned the path of royal pleasures. —38

He was greatly praiseworthy, had a charming personality and also the store-house of grace; his disposition was rediant like sun and fire and had cool temperament like water; he manifested himself as the king of yogis in the world. —39

Dutt Dev was superior to all in Sannyas *ashrama* (monastic order) and was becoming incarnation of Rudra; his radiance was like fire and power of endurance like earth. —40

Dutt was a person of purity, indestructible splendour and pure intellect; even the gold felt shy before him and the waves of the Ganges seemed to surge over his head. —41

He had long arms and charming body and was a detached Supreme Yogi; when he applied the ashes to his limbs, he fragranced everyone around him and he brought to light *sannyas* and yoga in the world. —42

The praise of his limbs seemed boundless and he manifested himself as a generous king of the yogis; the brilliance of his body was infinite and from his great personality, he appeared to be a silence-observing ascetic and eminently glorious. —43

That king of the yogis spread his infinite greatness and glory and on his manifestation, the fraudulent tendencies trembled and he made them stingless in an instant. —44

Seeing his indestructible greatness and unique body, the mother remained wonder-struck; all the people in countries far and near also marvelled to see him and all of them abandoned their pride on listening to his greatness. — 45

The whole nether-world and sky had the feeling about his comeliness which made all the creatures full of joy; because of him, the whole earth became blissful. —46

Then she and the earth all quivered and the sages here and there abandoned their pride; on his manifestation, many instruments (musical) were played in the sky and for ten days, the presence of night was not felt. —47

Many musical instruments were played here and there and it appeared that the discriminating intellect had assumed a body itself; his glory is indescribable and he manifested himself as the king of Sannyas. —48

Even on taking birth, he absorbed himself in actions of yoga; and he destroying sins, propagated *dharma*; the great Sovereigns fell at his feet and getting up, they practised *sannyas* and yoga.—49

Seeing the unique king Dutt, all the kings bowed respectfully at his feet; seeing the greatness of Dutt, it appeared that he was the store of eighteen sciences. —50

On his head, there were the matted locks of his celibacy and on his hands grew the nails of observances; the white ashes on his body were indicative of his state devoid of illusions; his character like Brahm (Brahman) was his deerskin. —51

Having white ashes on his face and wearing loin-cloth, he was the possessor of *sannyas* and conduct and relinquisher of deceit; he remained absorbed in abstract meditation and his limbs were extremely charming; his radiance was indestructible. —52

In his mind there was only one desire of *sannyas* and yoga and for this desire he had abandoned all other desires; his body was unique and during day and night, he remained detached from the deceits of the world; leaving the desires of all kinds, he had adopted the character of sages; his eyes were red and were the store of *dharma*. —53

He had a pure mind, devoid of vices, and he meditated with his non-mercurial eyes; his praise was infinite; having only one desire in his mind of adopting *sannyas* from all sides; he was the greatest among the immaculate *sannyasis*. —54

He had a body of yogis, whose greatness was infinite and he was the store of the knowledge of Shrutis (Vedas) and extremely generous; amongst the sages, he was most skilful and great and was supremely learned. —55

The sin had not even touched him and he was elegant in virtues; the yogi Dutt wore loin-cloth and seeing him, his mother was wonder-struck. —56

Seeing the greatest *sannyasi* Dutt, having comely limbs, even the god of love felt shy; the sage Dutt was the king of *sannyasis* and he had practised all kinds of the activities of *sannyas*. —57

His body was immaculate, which had never been troubled by lust; on his head there was tuft of matted locks; such a form was adopted by Dutt, the incarnation of Rudra. —58

Who can describe his fine glory? And listening to his appreciation, the Yakshas and Gandharvas become silent; Brahma was also wonder-struck to see his glory; and even the god of love felt shy on seeing his beauty. —59

He was extremely learned, expert in actions, beyond the desires and obedient to the Lord; his elegance was like the crores of suns and the moon was also wonder-struck on seeing him. —60

He had manifested as the apparent form of yoga and then had been absorbed in the practice of yoga; that immaculate Dutt of pure intellect, did the first thing of leaving his home. —61

When he practised yoga for a long time, Kaldev (the Lord) was pleased with him; at that time, there was a heavenly voice: "O king of yogis! listen to what I say." —62

Voice from Heaven addressed to Dutt
PAADHARI STANZA

"O Dutt! listen to me with pure intellect; I say unto you that there can be no salvation without the *guru*; first of all, adopt a *guru*, then you will be redeemed; in this way, Kal told the method of yoga to Dutt. —63

Obedient to the Lord and abiding beyond the

desire, Dutt prostrated before the Lord in various ways; he practised yoga in different ways and spread the exaltation of yoga. —64

Then Dutt, bowing before the Lord, he eulogised the unmanifested Brahman Who is the Sovereign of sovereigns, the Supreme Yogi and with unique limbs pervades everywhere. —65

The Splendour of that Lord pervades in water and on plain and many sages sing His praise; He, whom the Vedas etc., call *neti, neti* (not this, not this), that Lord is eternal and pervades in the beginning, in the middle and at the end. —66

He, who created many beings from one and with His power of wisdom, created the earth and the sky; That fearless, birthless and beyond desires is there at all the places in water and on plain. —67

He is supremely immaculate, sacred, pure, long-armed, fearless and unconquerable; He is the supremely eminent *Purusha*, the Sovereign of sovereigns and the great enjoyer. —68

That Lord has indestructible lustre, light-incarnate, dagger-wielder and is eminently glorious; His infinite glory is indescribable; He pervades in all the religions. —69

Whom all call *neti, neti* (not this, not this), the power of all kinds abide at the feet of that blemishless and beauty-incarnate Lord and all the sins fly away with the remembrance of His Name. —70

He has the temperament, qualities and gentleness live the saints; and there is no other measure of achieving salvation without going under His shelter; He acts for the redemption of the lowly and if anyone calls Him with any motive, he accepts his saying. —71

The enemies and friends all are allured to see Him, Who is blemishless, Who is eternally glorious, Who is seated on a stable seat and Who has infinite qualities. —72

He considers enemies and friends alike, and also comprehends the praise and slander alike; He is seated on a stable seat; He is supremely beauty-incarnate and also immaculate; He is the Sovereign of sovereigns. —73

His tongue showers ambrosia; all the gods and demons are fascinated by Him; He is devoid of enmity and light-incarnate; His body is indestructible and is impartial all the time. —74

His glory remains the same in the beginning and at the end and is accomplished with all kinds of powers; all the beauties are there in his body and seeing his comeliness the Yakshas and Gandharvas are allured. —75

His limbs are indestructible; that Lord is the manifestation of cognition; because of His grave, the beings are scattered over the whole world; He has created many beings in water and on plains and He ultimately merges every one in His form. —76

The death and sin have not been able to touch Him at any time; the Lord of that indestructible lustre and body remains the same at all times. —77

In this way, Dutt recited the eulogy and by this recitation, all the sins fled away; who can describe his infinite greatness? Therefore I have said it in brief. —78

If the whole earth becomes the paper and Ganesha is the proud writer; all the oceans become the ink and all the forests become the pens and Sheshanaga makes a description of the Lord from his thousand mouths, then also the mystery of the Lord cannot be comprehended. —79

If Brahma also utters His glory, then also His effulgence cannot be comprehended; if Sheshanaga also utters His Names from his thousand mouths, then also His end cannot be known. —80

If Sanak, Sanandan etc., remember Him continuously night and day, then also His glory cannot be described; Brahma created all the four Vedas, but on reflecting about Him, he also talks of Him as *neti, neti* (not this, not this). —81

Shiva practised yoga for thousands of years; he left his home and all attachment and resided in the forest; he also practised yoga in various ways, but still he could not know His end. —82

Many worlds are manifested from His one form and the lustre of that Lord, Who remains unattached throughout night and day, cannot be described; His seat is permanent and He is praiseworthy, lustrous and glorious. —83

The enemies and friends are alike for Him and His invisible lustre and praise are supreme; He has the same form in the beginning and at the end and He is the creator of this fascinating world. —84

He has no form or line, no attachment or detachment; That guiseless Lord has no special name or place; That long-armed and omnipotent Lord is the manifestation of cognition and His comeliness and greatness are infinite. —85

Even those who practised yoga for various *kalpas* (ages) could not please His mind; many sages and virtuous people remember Him by the performance of many agonising austerities, but That Lord does noe even think of them. —86

He is the only One, and creates many and ultimately merges the many created forms in His Oneness; He is the life-force of millions of beings and ultimately He merges all within Him. —87

All the beings of the world are under His shelter and many sages meditate on His feet; That all-pervading Lord does not even scan those who meditate on Him for many *kalpas* (ages). —88

His greatness and glory are infinite; He is the greatest amongst the sages and is extremely generous; His effulgence is eternal and form most beautiful; the human intellect cannot reflect on Him. —89

He, the Lord of unique greatness and glory, remains the same in the beginning and at the end; He, who has instilled His light in all the beings, He has also smashed the pride of the egoists. —90

He, who has not left untouched even one egoist, He cannot be described in words; He kills the enemy with a single blow. —91

He never keeps away His devotees from Him and just smiles even on his erratic doings; He, who comes under His grace, his objectives are fulfilled by Him ultimately; though He has not married, even then *maya* is His spouse. —92

Millions are getting pleased with Him and some are getting pleased only by remembring His name; He is devoid of deceit and is the manifestation of cognition; He is omnipotent and ever remains without desires. —93

He is immaculate, perfect, store of eternal glory, indestructible, praiseworthy, holy, illustrious, omnipotent, fearless and unconquerable. —94

Millions of Indras, Chandras, Suryas, and Krishnas serve Him; many Vishnus, Rudras, Ramas, Muhammads, etc., meditate on Him, but He accepts none without true devotion. —95

There are many truthful persons like Dutt, many Yogis like Gorakh, Machhindar and other sages, but none has been able to comprehend His mystery; various types of *mantras* in various religions have manifested, but all get disappointed without the faith of One Lord. —96

Vedas speak of Him as *neti, neti* (not this, not this) and that creator is the Cause of all causes and unapproachable; He is casteless and without father, mother and servants. —97

His form and colour cannot be known; He is the King of kings and Sovereign of sovereings; He is the Primal cause of the world and is Infinite. —98

His colour and line are indescribable and the power of that guiseless Lord is endless; He is viceless, indivisible, God of gods and unique. —99

The praise and slander are alike for Him and the beauty of that great praiseworthy Lord is perfect; That Lord, the manifestation of cognition, is viceless, all-pervading and continuously unattached. —100

In this way, Dutt, the son of Atri eulogised the Lord and prostrated in devotion; then he touched the feet of that casteless and colourless Lord in various ways. —101

If one utters His praises for several ages, even then he cannot understand His mystery: "O Lord! my intellect is very low and I cannot describe Thy vastness." —102

"Thy attributes are great like the sky and my wisdom is very low like that of a child; how can I describe Thy glory? Therefore leaving all the measures, I have come under Thy refuge." —103

His mystery cannot be known to all the four Vedas; His glory is infinite and supreme; Brahma also got tired in praising Him and is uttering His greatness only by the words *neti, neti* (not his, not this). —104

Ganesha also gets tired in writing His praises and all of them, feeling His omnipresence get wonder-struck; Brahma also accepted defeat, while singing His praises and forsaking his persistence by describing Him only as infinite. —105

Rudra is remembering Him for millions of ages; the Ganges is flowing from the head of that Rudra; He is not bound down within the meditation of sagacious individuals, even on meditating Him for many *kalpas* (ages). —106

When Brahma, who is superb amongst the great sages, entered the lotus-stalk, he could not even know the end of that lotus-stalk, then how can our power of reflection and wisdom realise Him? —107

He, whose elegant comeliness cannot be described, His greatness and glory is infinite; He, who has manifested Himself in more than one forms, meditate only on His feet. —108

ROOAAL STANZA

Touching the feet of various sages and forsaking his pride, Dutt, the son of Atri, began to wander in various countries; when, for lakhs of years, he served the Lord single-mindedly, then suddenly, a voice came from heaven. —109

Now begins the Description of Adopting the Immortal Lord as the First Guru

Speech of Heavenly Voice addressed to Dutt

"O Dutt! I am telling you the truth that none out of the people, the king, the poor and others none gets salvation without the Guru; you may suffer millions of tribulations, but this body will not be redeemed therefore, O the son of Atri, you may adopt a Guru." —110

Speech of Dutt

When this voice of heaven was heard, then Dutt, store of good qualities and knowledge and ocean of gentleness, prostrating on the Feet of the Lord, said, "O Lord! kindly give me the crux of the matter as to whom I should adopt my Guru." —111

Speech of the Heavenly Voice

"Whomsoever you like in your mind, accept him as your Guru and forsaking deceit, serve him with the singleness of mind; when the Guru is pleased, he will grant you a boon, otherwise O wise and sagacious Dutt! you will not be able to achieve redemption." —112

He, who in the first place gave this mantra, feeling about that Lord in his mind and accepting Him as the Guru, Dutt proceeded for getting instructions in yoga; though the parents dissuaded him, he did not accept the saying of anyone; he assumed the garb of a yogi and went towards a dense forest. —113

In the forest, he performed austerities in many ways and concentrating his mind, he recited various kinds of *mantras*; when he, enduring tribulations for many years, performed great austerities, then the Lord, the treasure of wisdom, gave him the boon of "wisdom." —114

When this boon was bestowed upon him, then infinite wisdom penetrated within him and that great Dutt, reached the abode of that Supreme *Purusha* (Lord); his wisdom suddenly extended on various sides and he propagated *dharma*, which destroyed the sins. —115

In this way, he adopted the eternal unmanifested Brahman as his first Guru, who pervades in all directions; He, who has spread in the four major divisions of creation viz., *andaja* (oviparous), *jarayuja* (viviparous), *svedaja* (generated by heat and moisture) and *udbhijja* (germinating), the sage Dutt accepted that Lord as his first Guru. —116

End of the chapter entitled "The Description about the Adoption of the Unmanifested Brahman as the First Guru" in Bachittar Natak.

Now begins the Description of the Second Guru

ROOAAL STANZA

The sage Dutt, Supremely immaculate and the ocean of yoga, then meditated in his mind on the second Guru and made the Mind his Guru; when the mind becomes stable, that Supreme Lord is recognised and the heart's desires are fulfilled. —117

End of the chapter entitled "Description of the Second Guru" in *Bachittar Natak*.

Now begins the Description of Dasnaam

BHUJNAN PRAYAAT STANZA

When Dutt adopted two gurus and he always served them single-mindedly; The waves of the Ganges and the matted locks were auspiciously seated on his head and the god of love could never touch his body. —118

There were white ashes smeared on his body and he was alluring the mind of very honoured persons; the sage appeared very great with the waves of the Ganges and matted locks; he was the treasure of generous wisdom and learning. —119

He wore ochre-coloured clothes and also the loin cloth; he had forsaken all the expectations and recited only one *mantra*; he was a great silence-observer and practised all the practices and actions of yoga. —120

He was greatly glorious as the ocean of mercy, the doer of good actions and the smasher of the pride of all; he was the practiser of all the practices of Great yoga and was a *Purusha* of silence-observation and the discoverer of the great powers. —121

He used to go for a bath in the mornings and evenings and practised yoga; he could observe the past, present and future and was divinely-incarnate saint of pure intellect amongst all the *sannyasis*. —122

He did not allow his mind to become mercurial even on being afflicted by hunger and thirst; he, remaining supremely unattached, and wearing the patched cloak, practised yoga, for the realisation of the light of the Supreme Essence. —123

He was a great self-knowing, stable yogi performing austerities in upside down posture; he was the destroyer of evil actions through good actions and was ever and unattached ascetic of stable mind. —124

He used to live in the forest, studying all Shastras, destroying evil actions as a worthy traveller on the path of detachment; he had forsaken lust, anger, greed and attachment and was a supreme silence-observer and the adopter of the fire of yoga. —125

He was the practiser of various kinds, a great celebate and an authority on *dharma*; he was a great knower of Essence, the knower of the secrets of yoga and *sannyas* and a detached ascetic; he always remained in good health. —126

He was without expectations, practised austerities in upside-down posture, a great knower of Essence and an unattached *sannyasi*; he practised all kinds of yogic postures with concentration; forsaking all other desires, he meditated only on the One Lord. —127

While seated near the fire and smoke, he had raised his hand and while meditating, burning the fires in all the four directions, he was internally scorching it; he was the celebate adopting a great religion and also the perfect incarnation of Rudra. —128

He was persistent silence-observer performing austerities, a great knower of *mantras* and the treasure of generosity; while abandoning the royal enjoyment, he was practising yoga and seeing him, all the men and gods were wonderstruck. —129

Seeing him, the Gandharvas, who were the treasure of science and Chandra, Surya, the king of gods and other gods were full of astonishment; all the creatures were pleased to see his comely figure and all the kings, abandoning their pride, had fallen on his feet. —130

There were many ascetics, celebates, Dandis, hermits with matted locks, the wanderers of the night and many conjurers were there; there were also mighty warriors living on mountains and other countries; the mighty ones of Balkh, Bengal, Russia and Ruhelkhand were also there, in his shelter. —131

The saints with matted locks, the deceptors,

deceiving people through *yantras* and *mantras*, the residents of Aja Pradesh and Aabhir Desh and the yogis performing Neoli *karma* (purging of intestines) were also there; the Agnihotris, controlling the world and the perfect celebates adopting celibacy at all levels were also in his refuge. —132

All the canopied kings of far and near, they all fell at his feet, leaving their pride; they all practised *sannyas* and yoga and all of them became followers of this path. —133

The people of various countries from far and near, came and performed the tonsure ceremony from the hands of Dutt and many people wearing matted locks on their head, practised yoga and *sannyas*. —134

ROOAAL STANZA

The kings of various countries from far and near fell at the feet of the Supreme Guru Dutt at that place; they all abandoned the new sects and joined the one sect of yoga; they abandoned their royal responsibilities and came to get done their tonsure ceremony. —135

All of them, considering him as the Supreme Guru, came to bow at his feet and Dutt was also the great purusha comprehending the secret of weapons and Shastras; his body was invincible, the form indestructible and he had achieved oneness in yoga; he had manifested himself in the form of unlimited, lustrous and unconquerable power. —136

The animate and inanimate creation and the gods of heaven, were wonder-struck on seeing his figure and the kings looked splendid like the pretty portraits here and there; they all had forsaken their arms and canopies, had been initiated into *sannyas* and yoga and had come to him as ascetics from all directions and were there at his feet. —137

Indra, Upendra, Surya, Chandra, etc., all marvelled in their mind and were thinking that the great Dutt may not seize their kingdom; all were getting pleased in the sky, sitting in their vehicles and were considering Dutt as the great guru. —138

Here and there, in all the directions, the kings, forgetting their royal responsibilities, had caught the feet of the supremely generous Dutt; considering him as the treasure of *dharma* and the great *guru*, all had abandoned their ego and had dedicated themselves affectionately in his service. —139

The kings had worn the garb of *sannyas* and yoga, leaving their royal responsibilities and becoming unattached, they had begun the practice of yoga; smearing their bodies with ashes and wearing matted locks on their heads, various types of kings had gathered there. —140

All the kings, leaving their property, wealth, sons, friends and the attachment of the queens, their honours and victories, they adopted *sannyas* and yoga and had come there; they came and sat there as ascetics here and there, gathering together from all directions, leaving behind elephants and horses and their fine society. —141

PAADHARI STANZA   BY THY GRACE

In this way, all the kings of the earth immediately joined the path of *sannyas* and yoga; someone performed the Neoli *karma* (purging of intestines) and someone wearing the garments of hide, was absorbed in meditation. —142

Someone is wearing the garments of a recluse and someone is standing straight with a special notion; someone subsists only on milk and someone abides without eating and drinking. —143

Those great saints observed silence and many practised yoga without eating and drinking; many stood on one foot without any support and many resided in villages, forests and mountains. —144

Many taking in smoke endured suffering and many took baths of different kinds; many stood on their foot for ages and many great sages turned their arms upwards. —145

Someone sat down in water and many made themselves warm by burning fire; someone practised various postures and someone continued to live on the strength of one desire. —146

There are many, who do not see below and many warm themselves by burning fire on their back; some sit down and hold fasts and bestow charities and many are absorbed only in One Lord. —147

Many take bath according to Shastric injunctions in various ways; and many are busy in *yajnas*, charities and *homa*; many are standing with their hands touching the earth at their back and many forsaking crores of rupees are donating whatever they have with them. —148

Many are sitting in Supreme Light and many are roaming unattached on mountain and in the forest; many are sitting in one posture and many are reciting *mantras*. —149

Some are uttering the Name of the Lord, while sitting and some sages are reading the religious text with a generous heart; many are meditating on the Lord with devotion and many are repeating the Vedic verses and Smritis. —150

Many are standing on one hand and many are reciting *mantras* with fullness of mind; many go without food and many sages only subsist on air. —151

Many are sitting in postures, abandoning their desires and expectations and many have resigned themselves to the support of the Lord; many are subsisting on small quantity of fruit in the forest and many are only repeating the Name of the Lord. —152

Many are abiding only with the hope of meeting the Lord and many are enduring many kinds of suffering; many are busy in speaking a discourse of the Lord and many are ultimately obtaining salvation. —153

Many have come under the refuge of the Lord and their support is only the Name of the Lord; many are repeating His Name and are ultimately obtaining salvation. —154.

Many are uttering the Name of the Lord day and night and many, adopting the thought of the Lord in their mind, are performing Agnihotri (the rite of fire-offering); many are repeating for memory the Shastras and Smritis and many are continuously observing the saintly character. —155

Many are performing the acts of *homa* and charity according to Vedic injunctions and many friends sitting together are cramming the six Shastras; many are reciting the four Vedas and are describing the infinite greatness of the discussion about knowledge. —156

Many are ever calling the lowly and afflicted ones and serving them sweets and food; many are busy in reciting the religious texts in various ways and many, forsaking the corn, are just chewing the wood. —157

Many are meditating in various ways and many, while sitting, are elucidating about various works of the Lord; many are listening to the recitation of the holy religious texts while sitting and many do not look back even for many *kalpas* (ages). —158

Many, being seated, are drinking water and many are roaming on the mountains and countries far and near; many are sitting in the caves and repeating the Name of the Lord and many celebates are moving in the streams. —159

Many are sitting in water and many are warming themselves by burning the fire; many adepts observing silence, are remembering the Lord and many are absorbed in concentration on the sky in their mind. —160

Many are absorbed in meditation on that stable and viceless Lord, Who is supreme and praiseworthy, whose glory is unique, Who is cognition-incarnate and light-incarnate, whose splendour is unmanifested and Who is unattached. —161

In this way, he practised yoga in various ways, but the salvation is not attained without the *guru*; then they all fell at the feet of Dutt and requested him to instruct them in the method of yoga. —162

Those who were subjected to tonsure ceremony in water, all those boys are under your refuge; those who were initiated as disciples in the mountains, they are known by the name Giri. —163

He wandered in the cities and made Bharat, Parath, Puri, etc., as *sannyasis*. —164

Those who were made disciples on the mountains, they were named "Parvat" and in this way uttering the five names, Dutt took rest. —165

Those who were initiated as disciples in the sea, they were named as "Saagar" and those who were made disciples on the bank of river Sarasvati, they were named as "Sarasvati." —166

Those who were made disciples at pilgrim stations, those skilful disciples were named as "Tirath;" those who came and caught the feet of Dutt, they all become the treasure of learning. —167

In this way, wherever the disciples lived and wherever any disciple did anything, the hermitage was established there in his name. —168

That fearless *Purusha* Dutt made several disciples in the *aranyaks* (forests), they were named "Aranyaks." —169

End of the chapter entitled "The Ten Names of Cognition-Incarnate Disciples of the Sage Dutt" in Bachittar Natak.

Now begins the Description of Making Mind as the Second Guru

PAADHARI STANZA

The glory of that king of *sannyasis* was indescribable and the impact of his long arms was enormous; wherever the sage Dutt went, there also the effulgence glistened and the pure intellect extended. —170

The kings of the countries far and near, forsaking their pride came and fell at his feet; they abandoned all the false measures and with determination, made Dutt, the king of yogis, as their base. —171

Relinquishing all other desires, only one desire of meeting the Lord remained in their heart and the mind of all of them was supremely pure and without any vice; to whichever country Dutt went, the king of that place fell at his feet. —172

DOHIRA

To whichever direction, Dutt went, the subjects of those places left their homes and accompanied him. —173

CHAUPAI

To whichever country, the great sage Dutt went, all the elders and minors accompanied him; whereas he was a yogi, he was also extremely beautiful, then who would there be without allurement? —174

Wherever the impact of his yoga and *sannyas* reached, the people left all their paraphernalia and became unattached; no such place was visible, where there was not the impact of yoga and *sannyas*. —175

End of the chapter entitled "The Adoption of Manes (Mind) as the Second Guru" in Bachittar Natak.

Now begins the Description of Adopting Spider as the Third Guru

CHAUPAI

Listen not to the manner in which Dutt adopted twenty-four Gurus; He saw a spider and reflected in his mind. —176

Contemplating in his mind, he said this, "I consider it may third Guru; when the thread of love will extend, then only the Lord (Nath Niranjan— the Unmanifested Brahman) will be realised." —177

When the self will be visualised and within oneself the soul-Guru will be touched and the mind will not go anywhere else, leaving the One, then only the Supreme Essence will be realised. —178

When the Form of One will be considered and seen as One and no other thought will come into the mind and keeping one objective before oneself, the mind will not run anywhere else, then the Lord (Nath Niranjan—the Unmanifested Brahman) will be realised. —179

When the merger will be in only One and the mind will not be absorbed in anyone else except the One and meditate only on the Supreme Essence, then it will realise the Lord (Nath Niranjan— the Unmanifested Brahman). —180

Accepting the Spider as the third Guru, the glorious Dutt moved further; getting greatly pleased, he moved forward, adopting their connotation in his heart. —181

End of the chapter entitled "The Adoption of Spider as the Third Guru" in Bachittar Natak.

Now begins the Description of the Fourth Guru Crane

CHAUPAI

When Dutt moved forward, then after seeing the swarm of fish, he saw towards the meditating crane, his limbs were extremely white and seeing him all the silence-observing creatures felt shy. —182

The meditation that was being observed by the crane, made his name shameful because of his meditativeness for fish, he was observing meditation very nicely with his silence, he was pleasing the sages. —183

If such a meditativeness is observed for the sake of that Lord, He is realised in that way; seeing the crane, Dutt was allured towards him and he accepted, him as his fourth Guru. —184

End of "The Description of the Adoption of Crane as the Fourth Guru" in Bachittar Natak.

Now begins the Description of the Fifth Guru Tom Cat

CHAUPAI

Then Dutt, the king of sages, having matted locks on his head, moved further; there he saw a Tom Cat, whom he continued to scan attentively. —185

Seeing his meditativeness for the rats, even the great hermits felt shy; if such meditativeness is observed for the sake of the Lord, only then that Unmanifested Brahman can be realised. —186

I shall consider him my fifth Guru, such a thought came to the mind of Dutt, the king of sages; he who will meditate in such a way, he will assuredly realise the Lord. —187

End of "The Description of the Adoption of Tom Cat as the Fifth Guru" in Bachittar Natak.

Now begins the Description of the Cotton Carder as the Guru

CHAUPAI

Leaving all other desires and keeping only one thought in his mind, Dutt, the king of yogis moved further; there he saw a carter carting cotton and said thus in his mind. —188

"This man has not seen all the army passing in front of him and his neck remained bowed; the whole army went on this path, but he was not conscious of that. —189

While carding the cotton, he did not look back and this lowly person kept his neck bowed; seeing him, Dutt smiled in his mind and said, "I accept him as my sixth Guru." —190

The way in which he absorbed his mind in cotton and the army passed away and he did not raise his head, in the same way, the Lord will be realised. —191

End of "The Description of the Adoption of Carder as the Sixth Guru" in Bachittar Natak.

New begins the Description of the Fisherman as the Seventh Guru

CHAUPAI

That great ascetic Dutt, of the pure mind moved further; there he saw a Fisherman going with his net. —192

He was holding his lance in one of his hands and was carrying the net on one shoulder; he was standing there for the sake of fish in such a way as if his body had become breathless. —193

He was standing with the desire of catching one fish in such a way as if someone standing with patience and detached from all his paraphernalia; Dutt thought that if such a love was observed for the sake of the Lord, then that Perfect *Purusha* i.e., the Lord can be realised. —194

End of "The Description of the Adoption of Fisherman as the Seventh Guru" in Bachittar Natak.

BACHITTAR NATAK

Now begins the description of the adoption of maidservant as the Eighth Guru

CHAUPAI

When the sage Dutt reached the abode of Daksha Prajapati, he was greatly pleased alongwith his army; there the sage Dutt saw a maid-servant, who, being intoxicated, was rubbing the sandalwood. —195

The lady of good conduct was grinding sandalwood single-mindedly in her home; she had concentrated her mind and seeing her even the portrait was getting shy. —196

Dutt went that way alongwith the *sannyasis* in order to meet her but she did not raise her head and see whether some king or some pauper was going. —197

Seeing her impact, Dutt accepted her as the eighth Guru and said; "Blessed is this maidservant, who is absorbed in love with that Lord." —198

When such a love is observed with that Lord, then He is realised; He is not achieved without bringing humility in the mind and all the four Vedas tell this. —199

End of "The description of the adoption of the maid servant as the eighth Guru" in Bachittar Natak.

Now begins the Description of the Adoption of the Trader as the Ninth Guru

CHAUPAI

Then taking his disciples alongwith him, Dutt, the Yogi with matted locks, moved further; when, passing through the forests, cities and mountains, they went forward, there they saw a trader coming. —200

His coffers were full of money and he was moving with a good deal of merchandise, he had many bag full of cloves; no one could enumerate them. —201

He desired for more wealth day and night and he had left his home for selling his articles; he had no other desire except his trade. —202

He had no fear of sunshine and shade and he was always musing of moving forward day and night; he had no concern for virtue and vice and he was only absorbed in the relish of trade. —203

Seeing him, Dutt, the devotee of the Lord, whose person was revered throughout the world, thought in his mind that in such manner the Lord be remembered, only then that Supreme *Purusha* i.e., the Lord can be realised. —204

End of "The description of the adoption of the Trader as the Ninth Guru" in Bachittar Natak.

Now begins the Description of the Adoption of the Lady-gardener as the Tenth Guru

CHAUPAI

The sage forsaking all desires and observing great silence moved further in a state of apathy; he was a great knower of the Essence a silence-observer and a lover of the Lord. —205

He was a great sage, absorbed in the love of the Supreme *Purusha* i.e., the Lord; he was a devotee of Brahman, the knower of the philosophies of the six Shastras and the one who remained absorbed in the Name of the Lord. —206

The white body of the great sage was alluring the gods, men and sages; wherever Dutt, the sage performing good actions went, all those who resided there, achieved passivity. —207

Seeing him all the illusions, attachments etc., fled away and all were absorbed in the devotion of the Lord; the sins and ailments of all were destroyed, all remained engrossed in the meditation of One Lord. —208

The sage met a lady-gardener there, who was shouting continuously; the sage feeling the notion of her shouts in his mind, adopted her the tenth Guru. —209

He, who will serve the Lord, he will destroy the ego, which is the origin of the world; who will actually be awakened from the sleep of *maya*, he will enshrine the Lord in his heart; the sage accepted the voice of the lady-gardener as true and as the power of kindling the knowledge of yoga. —210

End of "The Description of the Adoption of the Lady-Gardener as the Tenth Guru" in Bachittar Natak.

Now begins the Description of the Adoption of Surath as the Eleventh Guru

CHAUPAI

Then the sage Dutt, practising all the arts of yoga, moved forward; his glory was infinite and he seemed to be the second God. —211

The great adept and the silence-observing *Purusha* practised all the skills of yoga; seeing his extreme glory and impact, the seat of Indra also trembled. —212

MADHUBHAAR STANZA BY THY GRACE

The generous sage, full of innumerable attributes, was absorbed in the devotion of the Lord and was under the submission of the Lord. —213

Forsaking the royal enjoyment that king of yogis had adopted *sannyas* and yoga for the devotion and desire of meeting the Lord. —214

The beauty of the face of that perfect incarnation was enormous; he was sharp like dagger and was also skilful in many prominent sciences. —215

That charming sage had unique greatness, unlimited glory and generous mind. —216

He was a god for *sannyasis* and for the virtuous people he was mysterious, unmanifested and of unparalleled greatness. —217

His temperament was auspicious, the impact marvellous and the greatness unlimited. —218

There was a king named Surath, who was attached with his assets and society; he worshipped Chandi uninterruptedly. —219

The king, who was extremely powerful and had complete control of his kingdom, was skilful in all the sciences and was under the submission of the goddess. —220

He served the Goddess Bhavani night and day and remained unattached with only one desire in his mind. —221

He used to worship Durga always in various ways and made offerings. —222

That king was enormously praiseworthy, treasure of virtues and had such a pure body that on seeing him, even the Ganges fell shy. —223

Seeing him, Dutt became extremely pure in intellect and completely lustrous. —224

Seeing his limbs, even Ganges became shy, because he was enormously praiseworthy and a treasure of virtues. —225

The sage saw that he was bright like light, ever unattached and a king of *sannyasis* with marvellous temperament. —226

Dutt saw his serving nature and he was extremely pleased in his mind. —227

SHRI BHAGVATI STANZA

He seemed to Dutt as a king of supreme intellect, bedecked with all the accomplishments. —228

That king was unconquerable, illustrious, elegant and respectful for all religions. —229

That long-armed king was virtuous and cared for all his subjects. —230

That long-armed king was a great sovereign, a great yogi and a monarch of *dharma*. —231

That king resembled the figure of Rudra; he was free from anxieties and remained absorbed in yoga. —232

Seeing him, Dutt, the king of yogis, who was in the garb of a Rawal, and who was the king of *sannyasis*, and respectable for all, he was allured towards him. —233

He saw him like pure moon and found him that his actions were immaculate and in accordance with yoga. —234

That *sannyasis* king was the destroyer of impiety, he went everywhere in his kingdom and was the abode of *dharma*. —235

His yoga was indestructible and wearing his loin,cloth, he moved everywhere in his kingdom. —236

His actions and duties were illustrious and not liable to decay; he was the commander of all and was like a stream of *sannyas*. —237

He was the destroyer of ignorance, skilful in sciences, the destroyer of impiety and a devotee of *sannyasis*. —238

He was the servitor of the Lord, he was felt everywhere by his subjects, a king in *sannyas* he was embellished with all learning. —239

BACHITTAR NATAK

He was the destroyer of impiety, a devotee of the path of *sannyas*, a *jivan-mukta* (redeemed while living) and was skilful in all learning. —240

He was absorbed in good deeds, an unattached yogi; he was like unmanifested *dharma* devoid of yoga; his limbs were healthy. —241

He was never in ire, even slightly; no vice touched him and he ever flowed like the river of *dharma*. —242

He adopted *sannyas* and was the supreme authority of yoga; he was the devotee of Brahman, the originator of the world. —243

That king wearing matted locks, had abandoned all the stores of materials; and he wore waistcloth. —244

He performed actions of *sannyas* and adopted Rawal religion; he always remained in bliss and was the destroyer of lust etc. —245

The tabors were being played, hearing which all the sins had fled away; his body had been smeared with ashes and all were getting allured towards him. —246

He wore loin-cloth and spoke occasionally; he was the adopter of piety and destroyer of sin. —247

The horn was being blown and the sins were running away; the orders were given there that the religious texts be read. —248

In that holy country, assuming the religious garb, the prayer was being held, thinking of that one wearing the loin-cloth as effulgence. —249

He was devoid of misfortune and attached to *sannyas*; he was supremely immaculate and friend of all. —250

He was absorbed in yoga, having indescribable form; he was a *sannyasi* king. —251

He was the hero of heroes and practiser of all the disciplines; he was a *sannyasi*, performing undefiled actions. —252

He was like that Lord, Who is imperishable, and just, the remover of injustice. —253

He was the destroyer of *karmas*, the servitor of all everywhere, unattached and glorious. —254

He was the goer to all the places, the remover of sins, beyond all ailments and the one who remained a pure yogi. —255

End of "The Description of the Eleventh Guru, the King Surath" in Bachittar Natak.

Now begins the Description of the Adoption of Girl as the Twelfth Guru

RASAAVAL STANZA

Then Dutt moved further; seeing him, the sins fled away; the thunderous sound of the gongs continued like the song of the peacocks in the forest. —256

The horns were sounded in the sky and the sins of the earth ran away; he made offerings to the goddess and there was the discussion about the four Vedas. —257

The recitation of all the Shrutis was performed for that *sannyas* at the suitable place; the great practices of yoga were held and there was atmosphere of detachment. —258

There was discussion of six Shastras and the recitation of the Vedas and the *sannyasis* observed great silence. —259

Then Dutt moved still further and seeing him, the sins fled away; there he saw a girl, making the three worlds blessed ones. —260

This authority of *dharma* and the great celebate saw a doll in her hand. —261

She was playing with it and she loved it so much that she drank water and continued to play with it. —262

All those silence-observing yogis went to that side and they saw her, but the girl did not see them and did not stop playing. —263

The teeth of the girl were like the garland of flowers; she was absorbed in frolic like the creeper clinging to the tree. —264

Then Dutt, seeing her, eulogised her and accepting her as his Guru, he was absorbed in his great *mantra*. —265

He accepted her as his Guru and in this way, adopted the *mantra*; in this way, Dutt adopted his twelfth Guru. —266

RUNJHUN STANZA

The beauty of that girl was unique and marvellous; she appeared to be a store of intellect; the sage saw her. —267

Then he saw her again and again in various ways and accepted her quality in his mind and body. —268

After adopting her as his Guru, he offered her approbation and then moved further like the flame of fire. —269

End of "The Description of the Adoption of a Girl playing with Her Doll as His Twelfth Guru" in Bachittar Natak.

Now begins the Description of the Adoption of an Orderly as the Thirteenth Guru

TOMAR STANZA

Then the great Dutt, who was a treasure in eighteen sciences and had a fine physique, used to remember the Name of the Lord at day-dawn. —270

Seeing his bright and blemishless limbs, the waves of Ganges felt shy; looking at his marvellous figure, the kings became shyful. —271

He saw an orderly, who had many qualities; even at midnight, he was standing at the gate and in this way, during the rainfall, he stood firmly without caring for the rain. —272

Dutt saw that Vikram-like individual full of qualities at midnight and he also saw that it was raining cats and dogs. —273

He seemed standing like a golden statue single-mindedly; seeing his concentration, Dutt was greatly pleased in his mind. —274

He thought that this man was not caring for cold or hot weather and there is no desire of some shade in his mind; he was standing on one foot without even slightly turning his limbs. —275

Dutt went near him and looked down upon him, leaning a bit; he was standing detachedly in that desolate atmosphere at midnight. —276

It was raining and the water was spreading on the earth; all the beings of the world ran away in fear. —277

This orderly was standing at the gate of the king like this and was repeating the name of the goddess Gauri-Parvati in his mind; he was standing on one foot, without even slightly turning his limbs. —278

A dreadful sword was shining in his hand like a flame of fire and he was standing solemnly without seeming to have friendliness for any one. —279

He was not even raising his foot slightly and he was in the posture of playing trick in many ways; he was a devotee of the king dyed unswervingly in the love of the Lord. —280

Because of heavy rain, all the animals and birds were going from various directions to their homes in order to take shelter. —281

He was standing detachedly on one foot and taking his sword in one of his hands, he was looking extremely lustrous. —282

There was no other idea in his mind except his master and he as standing on one foot like a column standing in the battlefield. —283

Wherever he placed his foot, he firmly fixed it there; at his place, he was not getting wet and seeing him the sage Dutt kept silent. —284

The sage saw him and he seemed to him like part of a blemishless moon; the sage abandoning his shyness and accepting him as his Guru, fell at his feet. —285

The blemishless Dutt, accepting him as his Guru, absorbed his mind in his love and in this way adopted him as the Thirteenth Guru. —286

End of "The Description of the Adoption of an Orderly as the Thirteenth Guru" in Bachittar Natak.

Now begins the Description of the Adoption of a Fully Devoted Lady as the Fourteenth Guru

RASAAVAL STANZA

Dutt moved further, seeing whom the sins ran away; whosoever saw him, he saw him as his Guru. —287

Seeing that lustrous and glorious sage, the sins ran away and if there was anyone like the great Shiva, it was only Dutt. —288

Whosoever saw him, saw the god of love in him; he considered him like Brahman and destroyed his duality. —289

All the women were allured by that great and illustrious Dutt and they were not anxious about their garments and ornaments. —290

They were running like the boat moving forward in the stream; none of the young, old and minors remained behind. —291

The sage, the authority on *dharma*, saw a woman, who looked like Parvati or Indrani. —292

SHRI BHAGVATI STANZA

She was looking like the Lakshmi of the kings; she was glorious like the beautiful damsels of Madra Desha. —293

She might be Sita, or the prowess of the kings, or the chief queen of some king or the moving figure behind Ram. —294

She might be Yamuna, united with the glory of the god of love; she was like the goddess of the goddesses and the heavenly damsel of the demons. —295

She was looking like Savitri, Gayatri, the supreme goddess amongst the goddesses and the chief queen amongst the queens. —296

She was a princess skilful in *mantras* and *tantras* and seemed like *hansni* (a female swan). —297

Looking like the heated gold in fire she seemed like Shachi, the wife of Indra; it seemed that Brahma had himself created her. —298

She was Like Lakshmi and supremely glorious; she was pure like the sun-rays. —299

She was mercurial like the sexual arts; she was looking splendid like Rajeshwari or was like a specially prepared banner. —300

She was like the beloved queen of Ram and glorious like Gauri-Parvati. —301.

She was superb amongst the arts of kingdom and looked like the youthful spring and seemed like the rosary of Raginis (the female musical modes). —302

She looked like Megh-Malhar, or Gauri Dhamar or the daughter of Hindol, descending from the sky. —303

That fortunate woman was engrossed in arts and absorbed in Shastras, she was the devotee of her Lord. —304

She was looking like Rambha, Shachi, the special creation of Brahma, Gandharva woman or the daughter of Vidyadhars.—305

She, seemed swinging like Rambha, Urvashi and Shachi. —306

She looked like a Gandharva woman, like the daughter of Vidyadhars or the queen combined with royal glory. —307

She seemed like a princess or like Parvati, the beloved of Rudra and seemed like pure-light-incarnate. —308

She was a fascinating beautiful woman; she appeared like a mercurial woman, portrait-like and glorious. —309

She was looking beautiful like the rivers, Ganges, Yamuna and Sarasvati or the city of Dwarka. —310

She was looking like Yamuna, Kankala, Kameshwari and Indrani. —311

She was the destroyer of fear, a pillar-like damsel, a spring-lady or an authoritative woman. —312

She was illustrious, pure and like enlightening effulgence; she was a glorious fairy. —313

She was glorious like the moon and the sun; she was supremely immaculate and radiant. —314

She was a Naga-girl and the destroyer of all sufferings; she was mercurial and glorious. —315

She was Sarasvati-incarnate, destroyer of anger, having long hair; she was like the flash of lightening. —316

She was a Kshatriya woman, a canopied queen and a glorious and beautiful damsel like the canopy. —317

Her doe's like eyes worked like arrows and she was pretty like the radiance of lotus or the moonbeams. —318

She was a Gandharva woman or a Vidyadhar girl or the spring-like lady or a beloved of all the peoples. —319

She was the beloved of Yadaveshwar (Krishna) and a charming woman like Draupadi; she appeared like the chief queen swinging in a swing. —320

She, being studded with gold, seemed to be descending from the sky; she was like a portrait of gold with the golden effulgence. —321

She was lotus-eyed with supreme radiance; she was a heroine with moon-like temperament spreading coolness. —322

She was radiant like the queen of Nagas; her eyes were like that of a doe or lotus. —323

She was a unique one with infinite radiance; her unblemished beauty was the king of all the kings. —324

MOHINI STANZA

There was radiant glory on the face of that youthful woman; her eyes were like a doe and the speech like a nightingale; she was mercurial, youthful and moon-faced. —325

Her laughter was like lightning amongst the clouds and her nostril was extremely glorious; she was wearing pretty necklaces and doe-eyed one had embellished her waist nicely. —326

That woman of elephant-gait was like a fascinating heavenly damsel and that sweetly smiling lady uttered very sweet words; seeing her pure diamond necklaces, the lightning was feeling shy. —327

She was firm in her religion and performed good actions; she appeared as the remover of suffering in the way as if she was a stream of piety; there was brilliance on her face and her body was completely healthy. —328

Dutt saw that beautiful and mercurial woman who according to her actions was observing *sati-dharma* (the conduct of truth); she was the remover of suffering and was loved by his beloved; she composed and uttered the poetic stanzas. —329

She was fascinating like the heavenly damsels like Rambha, Urvashi, Mohini, etc., and these heavenly damsels, seeing her, bowed their faces and feeling shy, they went back to their homes. —330

The beautiful ladies like Gandharva women, goddesses, Girija, Gayatri, Mandodari, Savitri, Shuchi, etc., seeing her glory felt shy. —331

The Naga-girls, the Yaksha women, the ghosts, fiends, and Naga women all were devoid of radiance before him. —332

That comely lady was the remover of all suffering, giver of happiness and moon-faced; even in the garb of Naga-girls, Gandharva-women, Yaksha-women and Indrani, she looked an extremely charming woman. —333

The eyes of that intoxicated youthful woman were tightened like arrows and she was glistening like the radiance of youth; she had worn a rosary around her neck and the arrows and she was glistening with the radiance of youth; she had worn a rosary around her neck and glory of her face seemed like the gleaming fire. —334

That queen of the earth was a canopied goddess and her eyes and words were pure; she was capable of alluring the demons, but she was the mine of learning and honour and lived unattached. —335

She was good, gentle and a lady of fine features; she was giver of comfort; she smiled mildly; she was the devotee of her beloved; she remembered the Name of the Lord; she was alluring and pleasing. —336

She was the devotee of her beloved and standing alone; she was dyed in only one dye; she had no desire whatsoever and she was absorbed in the memory of her husband. —337

She neither slept nor ate food; she was devotee of her beloved and a vow-observing lady; she was beautiful like Vasanti, Todi, Gauri, Bhupali, Sarang, etc. —338

She was glorious like Hindol, Megh, Malhar, Jaijavanti, Gaur, Basant, Bairagi etc., —339

She was emotional like Sorath, Sarang, Bairari, Malhar, Hindol, Tailangi, Bhairavi, and Deepak. —340

She was expert in all musical modes and the beauty itself was getting allured on seeing her; if I describe her glory of all types, then there will be an extension of another volume. —341

That great vow-observing Dutt saw vow-observing lady and touched her feet alongwith other hermits with matted locks; he accepted that lady, being absorbed in the love of her husband with her body and mind, as his fourteenth Guru. —342

End of "The Description of the Adoption of the fully devoted Lady as the Fourteenth Guru" in Bachittar Natak.

Now begins the Description of the Adoption of the Arrow-Maker as His Fifteenth Guru

TOTAK STANZA

Adopting the fourteenth Guru, the sage Dutt, blowing his conch, moved further; after wandering through the East, West and North and observing silence, he moved towards the Southern direction. —343

There he saw a city of portraits, where there were temples everywhere; the king of that place had killed many deer and lions with his dagger. —344

The king took the four divisions of his army with him; the banners of the army were fluttering and the studded garments were worn by all the warriors; the beauty of all of them was making the beauty of all other places shyful. —345

An arrow-maker was sitting there, and appeared to be lifeless; the small and big drums and the tabors etc., resounded. —346

The king was with his army and that army was rushing forth like the clouds of doomsday; the horses were neighing and the elephants were trumpetting; hearing the roaring of the elephants, the clouds were feeling shy. —347

That army was moving peacefully, while felling the trees and drinking the water from the water-currents, seeing which all were getting allured. —348

The sun and the moon were frightened from that army and seeing that king, all other kings of the earth were feeling happy; various kinds of musical instruments including the drums resounded. —349

Various kinds of colourful ornaments including *noopur* and *kinkini* looked splendid and there was the plastering of sandal on all the faces; all of them were moving and talking happily and were returning to their homes happily. —350

They were wiping the essences of rose and otto from their faces and there was comely antimony in their eyes; the pretty face of all looked fine like ivory and even Ganas and Gandharvas were pleased to see them. —351

There were pretty necklaces around the necks of all and there were frontal marks of saffron on the foreheads of all; this enormous army was moving on that path. —352

The sage Dutt, blowing his conch reached on that path, where he saw an arrow-maker with his bowed head, sitting like a portrait. —353

The great sage, seeing him, said this, "Where has the king gone with his army?" That arrow-maker replied, "I have not seen anyone with my eyes."—354

The sage, seeing his stable mind, was wonder-struck; that complete and great ascetic never swerved; that unattached person with vice-less mind was infinitely glorious.—355

Because of his complete austerity, there was great glory on his face and he was like a viceless celibate; his vow was perfect and the body distinctive; he was persistent, vow-observing and like the son of sage Atri. —356

The sage Dutt, seeing his arrows and meditation, was greatly pleased adopting him his fifteenth Guru and leaving all his persistence he accepted him as his redeemer. —357

In this way, whosoever loves the Lord, he crosses this infinite ocean of existence; removing the illusions of his body and mind, Dutt fell down at the feet of his fifteenth Guru in this way. —358

End of "The Description of the Adoption of an Arrow-maker as the Fifteenth Guru" in Bachittar Natak.

Now begins the Description of the Adopting of a Vulture as the Sixteenth Guru

TOTAK STANZA

The sage was alongwith his disciples having smeared his face with ashes and wearing the ochre-coloured clothes; he was singing the praises of the Lord with his mouth and was moving unattached with all kinds of desires. —359

Various sounds were created with the mouth and the sage Dutt's body was allied with many types of magnificences; he was moving silently in various countries far and near and was meditating on the Lord in his mind. —360

There he saw a vulture, who was holding a piece of flesh in his mouth and flying seeing it, more powerful four vultures moved forward. —361

They flew in the sky and there they began to fight with that vulture; she dropped the piece of flesh on seeing these powerful vultures and flew away. —362

Seeing those four vultures, even the earth below became stable out of fear, seeing them, the sage was startled and adopted it as the sixteenth Guru. —363

If anyone, getting unattached with all desires, forsakes all the assets, then only he can be considered an ascetic; then also he forsaking the relish of the five senses can make his understanding like these vultures. —364

End of "The Description of the Adoption of a Vulture as the Sixteenth Guru" in Bachittar Natak.

Now begins the Description of the Adopting of a Fish as the Seventeenth Guru

TOTAK STANZA

After adopting the vulture as the seventeenth Guru with unattached mind, Dutt proceeded again on his path; he was producing various types of sounds from his mouth and hearing the same, the gods, Gandharvas, men and women, all were getting pleased. —365

The persistent and ascetic sage reached near a stream, where he saw a flying bird named "Mahigir" near the jumping fish. —366

With concentrated mind, he was stable at one place in the sky and his limbs were extremely white and pretty; his mind was absorbed in the fish and he was not seeing anyone else. —367

There the Guru went and took bath and getting up meditated on the Lord, but that enemy of the fish, concentrated his attention to the fish even till sunset. —368

He remained unwavered in the sky and did not even think of the sunset; seeing him, the great sage observed silence and accepted him as the Seventeenth Guru. —369

End of "The Description of the Adoption of the Fishing Bird as the Seventeenth Guru" in Bachittar Natak.

Now begins the Description of the Adoption of a Hunter as the Eighteenth Guru

TOTAK STANZA

After taking bath and singing the praises of the Lord, the sage went into the forest, where there were the trees of the *saal* and *tamaal* and in the dense shade of those trees, the light of the sun could not reach. —370

There the sage saw a tank and also within the foliage he saw a hunter looking splendid like gold. —371

He had in his hand a bow and arrows of white colour, with which he had killed many deer; the sage came out from that side of the forest alongwith his people. —372.

Many persons of the magnificence of gold, accompanied the sage Dutt and they all saw that hunter. —373

Those sages raised thunderous sound and dreadful tumult at that place and scattering at various places they began to have their food and drink. —374

Those sages smeared their white bodies with ashes, practised various postures and performed various *karmas* like Neoli (purging of intestines), while wandering in all the four directions. —375

They absorbed themselves in various practices completely without the element of lust; their matted locks, appeared the manifestation of the matted locks of Shiva. —376

Their yogic matted locks waved like the waves of the Ganges emanating from Shiva; they performed various kinds of austerities following the practices of earlier ascetics. —377

All the various practices which have been described in Shrutis (Vedas), they were all performed by these sages; all the qualities of these sages flashed like lightning amongst the clouds. —378

The matted locks waved on the heads of the yogis like the rays coming out of the sun; those whose suffering could not be removed anywhere else, their agony ended on seeing these sages. —379

Those men and women, who had been cast in hell, they were redeemed on seeing these sages; those who had any sin within them, their sinful life ended on worshipping these sages. —380

On this side, this hunter was sitting, on seeing whom, the animals used to run away; he did not recognise the sage and considering him a deer, he aimed his arrow at him. —381

All the ascetics saw the arrow and also saw that the sage was seated like a deer; that person dropped his bow and arrows from his hand and felt ashamed on seeing the resoluteness of the sages. —382

After a long time, when his attention was broken, then he saw the great sage with matted locks; he said, "How all of you have come here after relinquishing your fear? I am seeing only the deer everywhere." —383

The sage, seeing his resoluteness, and accepting him as his Guru, praised him and said, "He, who is so much attentive towards the deer, then think that he is absorbed in the love of the Lord." —384

The sage accepted him as his eighteenth Guru with his melted heart; the sage Dutt thoughtfully adopted the qualities of that hunter in his mind. —385

He, who will love the Lord in this way, he will ferry across the ocean of existence; his dirt will be removed with the inner bath and his transmigration will end in the world. —386

Accepting him as his Guru, he fell at his feet and ferried across the dreadful ocean of existence; he adopted him as his eighteenth Guru and in this way, the poet has mentioned the same in verse-from. —387

All the disciples gathered and caught his feet, seeing which all the animate and inanimate beings were startled; all the animals, birds, Gandharvas, ghosts, fiends, etc., were wonder-struck. —388

End of "The Description of the Adoption of a Hunter as the Eighteenth Guru" in Bachittar Natak.

Now begins the Description of the Adoption of the Parrot as the Nineteenth Guru

KRAPAAN KRAT STANZA

The sage, benevolent in qualities, was a thinker about learning and always practised his learning. —389

Seeing his beauty, the god of love felt shy and seeing the purity of his limbs, the Ganges was wonder-struck. —390

Seeing his comeliness all the princes felt pleased, because he was the greatest scholar and generous and accomplished person. —391

The glory of his limbs was indescribable; he was pretty like the god of love. —392

He performed many practices detachedly night and day and had relinquished all the desires because of the enfoldment of knowledge. —393

The sage Dutt, the king of Sannyas looked very beautiful like Shiva, while enduring the sunshine on his body, allied with unique comeliness. —394

The beauty of his limbs and face was perfect and powerful; his limbs, practising yoga, did not bend. —395

Though extremely comely, he remained desireless night and day and adopting the qualities, the sage lived detachedly. —396

Being absorbed in inexpressible yoga, he was far away form all fondnesses; even on forsaking all the royal luxuries, he always remained healthy. —397

That kind sage, was allied with qualities; he was a man of good intellect, a resolute vow-observer and merciful. —398

Enduring coldness on his body, his mind never got impaired and in this way after many years, he had been victorious in yoga. —399

When that yogi talked, the leaves of the trees swerved; and knowing the attributes of the

Lord, he did not disclose anything to others. —400

He used to drink hemp, roamed here and there, blew his horn and remained absorbed in the meditation of the Lord. —401

His limbs and mind both remained stable; absorbed in meditation, he remained engrossed in the practice of yoga. —402

While performing austerities, he never felt any suffering; and being absorbed in various types of devotional, ideas, he always remained engrossed in devotion. —403

These sages, who relinquished their homes, subsisted on air and remained silent. —404

These sages, supreme amongst *sannyasis* understood the internal mysteries; they were the sages with mysterious mind. —405

They felt the inner Light and remained detached; they were full of virtues and were not prone to destruction. —406

They were adorable for Brahmins, and masters of mysterious qualities; they were gods of gods, who never begged alms etc. —407

They were masters of *sannyasis* and supremely mighty people; someone talked about their story and someone walked with them. —408

These gentle sages were masters of infinite qualities; they were persons of good intellect and stores of wisdom. —409

These sages in the garb of *sannyasis*, were without malice and remembering that Lord, were merged (absorbed) in that great, wise and unrealisable Lord. —410

KULAK STANZA

Indra, moon-god and wind-god silently remembered the Lord. —411

The Yakshas, birds and oceans were raising tumult in astonishment. —412

The sea alongwith his powers was visualising that God of gods and mysterious Lord. —413

Seeing these yogis, the pleasures and sexual enjoyments were getting illusioned in wonder. —414

Forsaking their arms, weapons and canopies, the people were falling at the feet of these sages. —415

The musical instruments were being played; there was the sound of thunderous music and the songs were being sung. —416

The god Surya and the heavenly damsels leaving their self-restraint, were getting pleased with them. —417

Seeing them the Yakshas and birds were getting pleased and there was a run amongst the kings for their sight. —418

CHHAPPAI STANZA

These yogis who had been immersed in yoga and who had withdrawn from all enjoyments, had been wearing the ochre-coloured clothes of various countries. —419

These yogis of firm conduct and sinless *karmas* had abandoned all enjoyments. —420

These vow-observing yogis of good conduct and sinless *karmas* had given up all evil actions. —421

These were the people who had destroyed attachment and deceit and performers of good actions like the waters of all the sacred rivers. —422

They were kind-hearted people, wearing ochre-coloured clothes, purifying all the countries far and near were the destroyers of evil actions. —423

Seeing their radiance even the sun was wonder-struck; and someone out of them was repeating the Name of the Lord and someone was singing the praises of the Lord. —424

While remembering and repeating the Name of the Lord, they were firmly establishing the Lord in their mind. —425

The horns were being sounded and there was the singing of *ragas* (musical modes); the Name of the Lord was being repeated, which had frightened the sins. —426

The moon was wondering and Indra, seeing their devotion, had been fearful; all the gods were looking at them. —427

The ghosts, fiends and Ganas, seeing their beauty were wonder-struck; and all were thinking about them with sincerity. —428

The yogi Dutt saw there a parrot, who was released from bondage and immediately flew away. —429

BACHITTAR NATAK

As soon as the pious Dutt saw him, he flew away and made known to Dutt this secret that the action-prone man with ten senses and nine doors was superior amongst beings. —430

He is the abode of wisdom, but falling in the attachment of his wife etc., he remains in illusion. —431

The individual entrapped in the net of wisdom and mineness, he is absorbed in pleasures and is removed far away from *dharma*. —432

His wisdom is seized by the attachment of mother, wife, sons and brothers. —433

Engrossed in lust, he is absorbed in attachment and burning in the fire of anger, he is occupied in the collection of wealth. —434

On getting an opportunity, he destroys the great warriors for his self-interest and in this way, he falls into hell. —435

If forsaking all, the Lord is adored with sincerity, then all the sufferings and malice come to an end. —436

If the being relinquishes all like the abandonment of the cage by parrot, then all his actions can bear fruit and he achieves the position of superiority. —437

End of "The Description of the Adoption of the Parrot as the Nineteenth Guru" in Bachittar Natak.

Now begins the Description of the Adoption of a Trader as the Twentieth Guru

CHAUPAI

Then Dutt, the wearer of matted locks moved further; the musical instruments were being played; seeing Dutt, the inanimate things were becoming animate and the animate were wonder-struck. —438

His great beauty was indescribable, seeing which all the world was in astonishment; the paths on which the sage went, it appeared that the cloud of love was raining. —439

CHAUPAI

There he saw a wealthy trader, who was extremely comely and treasure of money and materials; he was supremely splendid and it appeared that Brahma himself had created him. —440

He was extremely conscious about his sale and it seemed that he did not know anything else except trade; absorbed in desire his attention was solely engrossed in trade and he was looking like a great yogi. —441

The sage reached there alongwith *sannyasis* and innumerable disciples; the great sage Dutt sat at the gate of that trader alongwith many other sages. —442

The mind of the trader was so much absorbed in earning money that he did not pay attention to the sages even slightly; with closed eyes, he was immersed in the expectation of money like a detached hermit. —443

All the kings and poor people who were there, leaving all their doubts fell down at the feet of the sages, but that trader was so much immersed in his work that he did not even raise his eyes and see towards the sages. —444

Dutt looking at his position and impact, leaving his persistence, said openly, "If such a love is employed with the Lord, then that Supreme Lord can be realised." —445

End of "The Description of the Adoption of a Trader as the Twentieth Guru" in Bachittar Natak.

Now begins the Description of the Adoption of a Parrot-instructor as the Twenty-first Guru

CHAUPAI

Adopting twenty Gurus and learning all the arts of yoga, the sage moved further; his glory, impact and radiance were infinite and it seemed that he had completed all the practices and was roaming, remembering the Name of the Lord. —446

There he saw a person seated with a parrot and for him there was none like it in the world; that person was teaching the parrot the art of speaking; he was so much concentrated that he did not know anything else. —447

Dutt, taking with him the sages and a large gathering of silence-observing hermits, passed just before him, but that person did not see anyone from them. —448

That person kept on instructing the parrot and did not talk anything with these persons; seeing the absorption of that person the love welled up in the mind of the sage. —449

If such a love is applied towards the Lord, only then that Supreme Lord can be realised; surrendering before him with mind, speech and action, the sage adopted him as his twenty-first Guru. —450

End of "The Description of the Adoption of a Parrot-instructor as the Twenty-first Guru" in Bachitar Natak.

Now begins the Description of the Adoption of a Ploughman as the Twenty-second Guru

CHAUPAI

When after adopting his twenty-first Guru, Dutt moved further, then he saw a ploughmen; his wife was a great comfort-giving chaste woman. —451

Her husband had called her and she had come with food; that plough-man did not see anything else while ploughing and the attention of the wife was absorbed in her husband. —452

The king of sages was moving alongwith large gathering of sages and seeing the beauty of his face, even the god of love was feeling shy; the sages passed near him and the king of sages also sat there. —453

ANOOP NARAAJ STANZA

The bodies of the sages were marvellous and their magnificence were unique; their lustre was indestructible and they allured the innumerable minds; their clothes were beautifully dyed in ochre colour, seeing which the gods and demons, men and Gandharvas were all fascinated. —454

Seeing the matted locks of the sage, the Ganges was considering him as Shiva and the beings of all the worlds accepted him as one containing supernatural elegance; all the beings, in His fear, playing on the fiddle, were repeating His Name; the Yaksha and Kinnar women were all getting allured. —455

The beautiful Chitarni (a kind of women) women, getting pleased on that pure Lord, the women of Yakshas, Gandharvas and gods, were remembering Him; the evil Kinnar women were getting angry and other pretty ladies laughingly exhibited their teeth making the lightening shyful. —456

Seeing him, the formidable sins were destroyed and the silent remembrance of the Lord was the natural outcome; on their bodies, their garments were keeping under control the rising radiance; the beings of all the directions, wandering and coming there, were falling at his feet; all the beings forsaking their sins were following the path of *dharma* on reaching there. —457

There he saw two Kshatriya fighters absorbed in their actions of war; the warriors were abandoning their bows and cutting the armours; seeing that fighting, the chariot of the sun stopped there and there the fighters falling on the earth, were throwing out blood from their mouths. —458

The discus were being discharged and the fighters were falling; the persistent warriors were again rising in anger; having been cut into half in the form of headless trunks were wandering and those falling on the earth were shouting "kill, kill." —459

The horses of the warriors, were fighting in that dreadful war; the sharp arrows were being discharged and the gleaming of the dagger was being seen; the fighters were rising with the shouts of "kill, kill;" and they were not running away from that battlefield with persistence. —460

All were cutting one another in a strange way and the white arrows like the slab were flowing (like a stream); seeing that war the whole world was dazzled and wonder-struck and moving towards that hermitage, it was falling down upon the earth under the impact of attachment. —461

That woman, carrying her utensils on her head, was moving, remembering her husband like a sage and the sage seeing her and falling at her feet, adopted her as the twenty-second Guru; that great sage, who had performed innumerable yogi, practises and destroying many sins, moved towards his abode. —462

End of "The Description of the Adoption of the Ploughman as the Twenty-second Guru, and His Wife bringing the Food" in Bachittar Natak.

Now begins the Description of Adopting a Yaksha Woman as the Twenty-third Guru

ANOOP NARAAJ STANZA

The trumpets sounded and there was thundering voice; seeing the ochre-coloured garb, the sins were destroyed; the gold was seen being showered on the earth inhabited by human beings and the bodies of the ascetics were supernatural glory. —463

Many Yaksha, Gandharva, Naga and god's women were dancing; there was Parvati and the wife of the unique Kuber; there were seated the women of gods and demons. —464

There was a unique Yaksha woman, who was revolving in a circle as if she was struck be an arrow; abounding all kinds of desires, her mind absorbed only in music; she was moving agitated like a deer. —465

She was absorbed in singing in various male and female musical modes and playing on her fiddle, she went lovingly towards the hermitage; that beautiful damsel was decorated with the arrows of her art and the group of those beautiful women was enjoying the earthly existence. —466

TOMAR STANZA

A woman, gentle and virtuous, was singing a musical mode; she was the abode of happiness and her eyes were charming; she was thoughtfully singing her musical mode. —467

She was pretty, gentle and generous; that lady, the treasure of music, to whichever direction she viewed, she allured everyone. —468

TOMAR STANZA

That blemishless and honourable lady was an ocean of happiness; she was singing with full concentration of mind and the auspicious songs seemed to be springing out from her very interior. —469

Seeing her, the king of yogis gathered all his yogis and all of them were pleased to see that pure yogini. —470

The king of Yogis thought that if in this way, detaching oneself from all other sides, the mind is concentrated on the Lord, then the Lord can be realised without any apprehension. —471

The sage, enthusiastic, and accepted her as his Guru, fell at her feet; Getting absorbed in her love, the king of the sages, adopted her as his Twenty-third Guru. —473

End of "The Description of the Adoption of a Yaksha Woman-singer as the Twenty-third Guru" in Bachittar Natak.

Now begins the Description of the Adoption of the the Twenty-fourth Guru (Incarnation)

TOMAR STANZA

Then ascending the Sumeru mountain the sage performed great austerities for many years and felt pleased as the essence-finder. —474

Seeing the practice of the world, the sage thought as to Who is He? Who creates the world and then merges it within Himself? —475

When He is recognised through the knowledge, then the adoration will be complete; if He is comprehended through the medium of yoga, only then the body (and the mind) will be completely healthy. —476

Then the Supreme Essence will be known (when it will be realised) that He is also the Destroyer of the world; That Master of the world is Real and the same Lord is Supremely absorbed and He is also beyond all forms. —477

There will be no peace without that One Lord; the bath at all the pilgrim stations will be fruitless; when service will be rendered to him and His Name will be remembered, then all the desires will be fulfilled. —478

Without that One Lord, all the twenty-four incarnations and all others are meaningless;

he who recognises the One Lord, he will remain jubilant even on adoring all the twenty-four incarnations. —479

He, who falls in love with the One Lord, he will feel happy in knowing about the wonderful works of all the twenty-four incarnations; he, who does not recognise the One Lord, he cannot know the mysteries of the twenty-four incarnations; —480

He, who has not recognised the One Lord, the twenty-four are fruitless for him; he, who feels the presence of One and recognises Him, he can feel the happiness of the twenty-four. —481

VICHITRA PAD STANZA

The sage absorbed his mind in the One Lord and did not allow any other idea to enter his mind, then the gods showered flowers, beating their drums. —482

The sages, getting delighted, clapped their hands and began to sing; they forgot their domestic worriers and moved here and there happily. —483

TAARAK STANZA

In this way, when the sages performed austerities for many years and did all according to the bidding of their Guru; the great sage told them many methods and in this way, they obtained the wisdom of knowledge of all the ten directions. —484

In this way, the sage adopting twenty-four Gurus, went on the Sumeru mountain alongwith other sages; there he performed severe austerities and then the Guru Dutt, gave these instructions to all of them. —485

TOTAK STANZA

The sage having matted locks on his head and wearing ochre-coloured clothes, on his body went on the Sumeru mountain alongwith his disciples; there he performed severe austerities for many years and did not forget the Lord even for an instant. —486

There the sages performed austerities in various ways for ten lakh twenty thousand years; then they propagated the secret doctrines of that great sage in all the countries far and near. —487

When the final hour of that great sage arrived, the great sage came to know of it with the strength of yoga; then that sage with matted locks, considering this world like a cloud of smoke formulated a plan of another activity. —488

Controlling the wind with the strength of yoga, relinquishing his body left the earth; breaking the skull, his light of the soul merged in the Supreme Light of the Lord. —489

The Kal (Death) stretches his dreadful sword always on all categories of beings; it has dreadful sword always on all categories of beings; it has created the large net of this world, from which none has been able to escape. —490

This Kal (Death) has killed the great sovereigns of all the countries and the earth, who had eight powers, nine treasures, all kinds of accomplishments, moon-faced women and unlimited wealth; They all left this world with naked feet under the control of Yama without the remembrance of the Name of the Lord. —491

Even Ravana and Mahiravana were helpless before him; he did not even co-operate with king Bhoj, the Delhi kings of Surya clan the mighty Raghunath etc., he did not even side with the destroyer of the stores of sins; therefore O great animal-like unconscious mind; come into your senses, but consider that the Kal (Death) did not consider anyone its own. —492

The being, in many ways, speaking both truth and falsehood, absorbed himself in lust and anger; for earning and gathering wealth unashamedly lost both this and the next world; though he obtained education for twelve years, but did not follow its sayings and lotus-eyed (*rajiva-lochan*) could not realise that Lord; the unashamed being will ultimately be caught by Yama and it will have to go with naked feet from this place. —493

O sages! why do you wear ochre-coloured clothes? They will all be burnt in the fire at the end. Why do you introduce such-like rites, which will not continue for ever? No one will be able to deceive the great tradition of the dreadful Kal; O sage! your beautiful body will ultimately be mixed with dust. —494

O sage! why are you only subsisting on wind? You will not achieve anything by doing this; you cannot even attain that Supreme Lord by wearing the ochre-coloured clothes; look at the illustrations of all the Vedas, Puranas etc., then you will know that all are under the control of Kal; you can be called *anang* (limbless) by burning your lust, but even your matted locks will not accompany your head and all this will be destroyed over here. —495

Undoubtedly, the citadels of gold be reduced to dust, all the seven oceans be dried up, the sun may rise in the west, the Ganges may flow in the opposite direction, the sun may heat in the spring season, the sun may become cold like the moon, the earth supported by the tortoise may shake, but even then, O king of the sages; the destruction of the world is certain by Kal. —496

There have been many sages like Atri, Parashar, Narada, Sharda, Vyas, etc., who cannot be counted even by Brahma; there had been many sages like Agastya, Pulastya, Vashistha, etc., but it could not be known to which direction they have gone; they composed *mantras* and established many sects, but they merged in the cycle of dreadful existence, that after that nothing could be known about them. —497

Breaking the Brahmarandhra (an aperture in the crown of the head), the light of the king of sages merged in that Supreme Light; his love was absorbed in the Lord like all kinds of compositions are interlinked in the Veda; in this way, the poet Shyam has described the episode of the great sage Dutt; this chapter is now being completed hailing the Lord of the world and the mother of the world. —498

End of "The Description of the Composition regarding the Sage Dutt, the Incarnation of Rudra" in Bachittar Natak.

Now begins the Description of Parasnath, the Incarnation of Rudra by the Tenth Guru

CHAUPAI

In this way there was the Dutt incarnation of Rudra and he spread his religion; in the end, according to the Will of the Lord, his light (soul) merged in the Supreme Light of the Lord. —1

After that, the Yoga *marga* (path) continued its away for one lakh and ten years; with the passing away of the eleventh year, Parasnath was born on this earth. —2

On an auspicious day and at an auspicious place and country, he was born; he was supremely learned and glorious; there was none so illustrious like him and seeing him, his parents were wonder-struck. —3

His glory spread in all the ten directions and it seemed that the twelve suns were shining in one; the people in all the ten directions felt agitated and went to the king for their lamentation. —4

"O king! listen, we tell you an episode; a very proud person has been born and there is none so beautiful like him; it seems that the Lord (Providence) Himself has created him." —5

"Either he is a Yaksha or Gandharva; it appears that a second sun has arisen; his body is gleaming with youth and seeing him, even the god of love is feeling shy." —6

The king called him in order to see him and he (Parasnath) came on the very first day with the messengers; the king was pleased in his heart on seeing him wearing matted locks and it appeared to him that he was the second incarnation of Dutt. —7

Seeing his figure the sages wearing matted locks trembled and thought that he was some incarnation, who will finish their religion and no person with matted locks will survive. —8

The king, seeing the impact of his glory, was extremely pleased; whosoever saw him, he was pleased like one pauper obtaining nine treasures. —9

He put his net of allurement on all and all were getting succumbed; in wonder; all the people getting fascinated fell down here and there like the warriors falling in battle. —10

The man or woman, who saw him, considered him as the god of love; the hermits considered him as an adept and the yogis as a great yogi. —11

The group of queens was allured on seeing him and the king also decided to marry his daughter with him; when he became the son-in-law of the king, then he became famous as a great archer. —12

That extremely beautiful and infinitely glorious person was absorbed within himself; he was expert in the knowledge of Shastras and weapons and there was no Pundit like him in the world. —13

He was like the Yaksha in human garb, not being troubled by the outer afflictions, whosoever saw his beauty, he was wonder-struck and duped. —14

SWAYYA

He was glorious like the sword saturated with marrow; whomsoever he saw, he could not go back to his home; he, who came to see him, he fell down swinging on the earth, whomsoever he saw, he was inflicted with the arrows of the god of love, he fell down there and writhed and could not get up to go. —1-15

It seemed that the store of lust had been opened and Parasnath looked splendid like the moon; even if there were ships stored with shyness, he allured everyone only on seeing; in all the four directions, the beings like wandering birds were saying this that they had seen none so beautiful like him; he is a killer like Arjuna's arrow, he is a mine of youth; he controls all like the sword of Kal and is the dagger of lust. —2-16

On seeing him, the impact of *tantra*, *mantra* and *yantra* ends; his eyes, glistening with the light of youth appear to be extremely pretty and intoxicated; his eyes can kill crores of people like the roses and seeing his comely figure the mind gets fascinated on seeing him. —3-17

When he went to the court on chewing the beetle and fragrancing the body, then all killer Yakshas, Nagas, the animate and inanimate beings, gods and demons were wonder-struck; the human males and females were pleased on getting fascinated by him; they sacrificed their precious garments, diamonds and jewels on him impatiently. —4-18

SWAYYA

Indra also marvelled at Parasnath, the most beautiful person and expert in all the fourteen sciences; he knew all the arts of warfare and after conquering all the countries far and near, he got his flag of victory waved in all the ten directions; the gods comprehended him as Indra, the *gopis* as Krishna and the night as the moon. —5-19

Illumined like the full moon, Parasnath caused all the four directions wonder about him; he became famous everywhere on the earth and in the sky; the warriors recognised him as a warrior and the learned as learned; the day considered him as the sun and the night as the moon; the queens considered him as the king, other women as the husband and the goddesses as love. —6-20

BHUJANG PRAYAAT STANZA

Two years and eight months passed and Parasnath, the store of all learnings was known as a glorious king; he repeated the names of the goddess of Hinglaaj and the weapon-wearing Durga. —21

The worship of the goddesses like Shitala, Bhavani etc., was performed and the gleaming arms, weapons, splendour, canopy, pleasantry etc., increased his glory. —22

The beauty of his enjoyment and his hair appeared extremely comely and his sword glistened like lightening in his hands; he had worn a pure rosary on his head and the rows of his teeth looked magnificent; seeing him, the enemies fled away and the saints were pleased. —23

He appeared as a most beautiful king and there was a hideous halo of light around his face; on seeing him, the tyrants got illusioned and the saints smiled in their pleased mind; he remembered the formless and mysterious Durga. —24

On listening to her praise, Bhavani was pleased on him and she endowed him with unique beauty; she gave him two unfailing arms, which could cause the steel-armoured enemies to fall on the earth. —25

When this king, practising the armament, obtained the weapons, he kissed them, hugged them and placed them on his head; all the kings saw him as unconquerable warrior and a successful scholar of the Vedic learning. —26

After obtaining the unlimited arms and weapons, he also obtained the experience of the reflection of Vedic learning; he studied the science of all the countries and on the strength of his arms and weapons, he conquered the kings of all the countries. —27

BHUJANG PRAYAAT STANZA

He invited the scholars and sages from many countries far and near for consultations on Vedic learning; they included those with matted locks, Dandis, Mundis, ascetics, celibates, practisers and many other students and scholars of Vedic learning. —28

The kings of all the countries far and near and the silence-observing hermits were also called; wherever an ascetic with matted locks was seen, he was also invited with the permission of Parasnath. —29

The kings of all the countries were called and whosoever refused to meet the messengers, his canopy and the army were seized; the letters and persons were sent to all directions, so that if any ascetic with matted locks, Dandi, Mundi was found, he was brought. —30

Then the king performed a *yajna*, in which all the yogis, children, old-men, kings, paupers, men, women etc., came for participation. —31

Invitations were sent to all the countries and all the kings reached at the gate of Parasnath; all the ascetics with matted locks in the world, they all gathered together and reached before the king. —32

The practising yogis, smeared with ashes and wearing loin-cloth and all sages resided there peacefully; many great yogis, scholars, yogis and the ascetics with matted locks were seen there. —33

All the kings were invited by Parasnath and in all the four directions, he became famous as a donor; many ministers of the countries gathered there, the musical instruments of the practising yogis were played there. —34

All the saints who had come at that place, they were all called by Parasnath; he served them with various types of food and bestowed charities on them, seeing which the abode of the gods felt shy. —35

All sitting there held consultations in their own way regarding Vedic learning; all of them saw pointedly towards one another and whatever they had heard earliest with their ears, on that day they saw it there with their own eyes. —36

All of them opened up their Puranas and began to study their country's lore; they began to reflect fearlessly on their lore in various ways. —37

There were gathered there the residents of Bang country, Rafzi, Rohelas, Sami, Balakshi, Kashmiri, Kandhari and several Kalmukhi *sannyasis*. —38

The southern scholars of Shastras and the Dravidian and Telangi savants had also gathered there; alongwith them there were gathered warriors of Eastern and Northern countries. —39

PAADHARI STANZA

In this way, Parasnath gathered together many brave fighters and kings of various countries far and near and honoured all of them donating wealth and garments to them. —40

There were many canopied and fearless yogis there; there were seated unconquerable warriors, experts in arms and weapons, indestructible fighters, many mighty heroes, who had conquered thousands of wars. —41

Parasnath had taken various kinds of measures, had conquered the kings of various countries in wars; on the strength of *sam, dam, dand* and *bhed*, he brought all together and brought them under his control. —42

When all the kings were brought together by the great Parasnath and all of them gave him the letter of victory, then Parasnath gave unlimited wealth and garments to them and allured them. —43

One day, Parasnath went for the worship of the goddess; he adored her in various ways, whose description here I have composed in Mohani Satnza. —44

MOHANI STANZA

"Hail, O Bhairavi, Durga, You are the destroyer of fear, You ferry across the ocean of existence, the rider of the lion, the destroyer of fear and generous Creator." —45

"You are blemishless, adopter of arms, the fascinator of all the worlds, the Kshatriya goddess; You are Sati Savitri with blood-saturated limbs and the Supremely immaculate Parmeshwari." —46

"You are the youthful goddess of sweet words; you are the destroyer of worldly sufferings and redeemer of all; You are Rajeshwari full of beauty and wisdom; I hail You, O the obtainer of all powers." —47

"O Supporter of the world; You are superb for the devotees, holding the arms and weapons in your hands; You have the revolving maces in your hand and on their strength, You appear to be Supreme." —48

"You are Superb amongst Yakshas and Kinnars; the Gandharvas and Siddhas (adepts) remain present at your feet; Your figure is pure like the lightening in clouds. —49

"Holding the sword in your hand, You honour the saints, the giver of comfort and destroyer of sorrow; You are the destroyer of tyrants, redeemer of the saints; You are invincible and treasure of virtues." —50

"You are the bliss-giving Girija Kumari; You are indestructible, the destroyer of all and the redeemer of all; You are the eternal goddess Kali, but alongwith it, You are the doe-eyed most beautiful goddess." —51

"You are the wife of Rudra with blood-saturated limbs; You are the chopper of all, but You are also pure and bliss-giving goddess; You are the mistress of activity and harmony; You are the alluring deity and the sword-bearing Kali." —52

"You are the donor of gifts and the destroyer of world, the goddess Durga; You sit on the left limb of Rudra, the blood-coloured goddess; You are Parameshwari and the piety-adopting Mother." —53

"You are the killer of Mahishasura; You are Kali, the destroyer of Chachhasura and also the sustainer of the earth; You are the pride of the goddesses, the carrier of sword in the hand and Durga, the giver of victory." —54

"You are the brown-eyed immaculate Parvati, Savitri and Gayatri; You are the remover of fear, the mighty goddess Durga; hail, hail to Thee." —55

"You are the destroyer of armies in the war, the perisher of the fear of all; You are the Mother Durga, the killer of the enemies like Chand and Mund, hail, O goddess, the giver of victory." —56

"You are the one who ferries across the ocean of the world; You are the one who roams and crushes everyone; O Durga! you are the cause of the creation of all the worlds and You are the remover of the sufferings of Indrani." —57

"You are the killer and conqueror of Shumbh; You are the goddess Kali, having the colour of blood; You also utter words from Your sweet tongue and You are known as the Hinglaj and Pinglaj mother." —58

"You have the portrait-like beautiful limbs and your plays are extensive; You are the store of wisdom and the well of glory; O Mother! you are modest and blemishless." —59

"Hanuman and Bhairava jump and wander with your strength; O Mother; You are the donor of victory; You are the mistress of all the worlds and You are Durga, who ferries across the cycle of existence." —60

"O Goddess! You have engrossed all the world in sleep, hunger and thirst; O Kal! You are the goddess like Ratri and Indrani and the redeemer of the devotees." —61

"O Mother! The Vedas have also sung the praises of your victory; You are indiscriminate and indestructible; You are the remover of the fear of the saints, the giver of victory and sword-wielder." —62

ACHAKRAA STANZA

"O Goddess! You are Ambika and Shitala; being intoxicated, you may falter; You are influential like the ocean; You are also Dakini; You are the performer of Sambhavi *mudra* (a kind of posture) and the remover of suffering; you are absorbed in all, doer of good to all, greatly glorious and the destroyer of all." —63

"You manifest yourself in accordance with every one's emotion; you are the fear-remover of all the world; you are the chopper of everyone and associated with them, you are profound and serene like the sea; you are the double-edged sword and double-faced Durga; you are invincible; you are Hinglaj, the remover of the fear of all and all remember Thy Name." —64

"You are the rider of lion; you have charming eyes; you are Hinglaj, Pinglaj, a Gandharva woman and a Yaksha woman; you are the destroyer of armours; you are the sword-wielder and thundering goddess and you are the lance like a female serpent." —65

"You are renowned for your large body; You are Hinglaj and the goddess Kartikeyi; You are glorious and indestructible and the base of all deaths; your various names are Ginglaj, Hinglaj, Thinglaj, Pinglaj; You are Chamunda of tricky speed." —66

ACHAKRAA   BY THE GRACE

"O Goddess! You are invincible, indiscriminate, non-white and base of all; You are unchopable and beyond all splendours; You are also Anjani, the mother of Hunuman; You are Ambika, who holds the weapons; You are imperishable, support of all and the redeemer of the world." —67

"You are Anjani, You are Shitala, the destroyer of all; You are serene like the sea and always remain absorbed; You are alert, serene you are large and invincible like the sky; You have enwrapped all the world within Yourself and You Yourself are ineffaceable and destroyer of all." —68

"O Goddess! You are Bhairavi, the remover of fear and the mover in the world; You are the Trikuti, Yogini, Chamunda and Manavi in practice; You are youthful, the killer of the demons Jambh; You are the Goddess Kalika lisping, stuttering and stammering while being intoxicated." —69

"You are the wanderer, fulfiller of the emotions beyond the illusions and the remover of fear; You are the donor of boons and destroyer of enemies; You are indiscriminate, invincible and high like the tree; You are the wielder of arms, beyond all splendours, with lose matted locks and indistinguishable." —70

You are expert in *tantras* and *mantras* and black (Kali) like a cloud, You have a large body; you are the remover of fear and You are the emotion-manifestation of the whole world; You are Dakini, Shakini and sweet in speech; O Goddess! You are Kalika having the sound of *kinkini*; hail to Thee. —71

You have a subtle form; You are the adorable Hinglaj and Pinglaj; You are the wielder of arms and weapon and the agoniser like the thorn; O the Goddess of corn, pervading in all particles; You are the one to arise from the cloud and become renowned, hail to Thee; You are the quality of activity, power-manifestation and sustainer of the saints, hail to Thee. —72

You are the Goddess and the rules of prosody; you are also Yogini, enjoyer and Kalika, the destroyer of ailments; You are ever active in the form of Chamunda and You are charming like a portrait; You are the mistress of the Tantras; You are all-pervading and have canopy over your head. —73

You are the lightning of large teeth; You are unchoppable and far away from all illusions; You are also the movement of all including hunger, sleep and garb; You are the bow-wielder and ornament-wearer woman; You are everywhere seated in various adorable forms. —74

VISHNUPADA   SAYING BY THY GRACE
PARAJIKA (A MUSICAL MODE)

How can I describe the Glory of Thy Feet? They (Feet) are auspicious and viceless like lotus; my mind has become a bumble bee and is humming over the Lotus-feet; this being will be redeemed alongwith the fourteen generations of parents and manes (if it meditates on Thy Lotus-feet). —1-75

VISHNUPADA
KAFI

I shall accept that day fruitful and blessed, on which the Mother of the world, getting pleased, will bestow on me the boon of victory, on that day I shall fasten the arms and weapons with my waist, and plaster the place with Sandal; from Her I shall obtain the boon, whom the Vedas etc., call *neti, neti* (not this, not this). —2-76

| SORATHA | SAYING BY THY GRACE |

The Goddess Bhavani Who understands everything contained in the mind, seeing the extreme love of the king Parasnath, understood his mind-thought; considering him her devotee, the goddess showed him her fearless form; seeing it all the sages and men were wonder-struck and all of them attained the Supreme State. —3-77

In the left hand of the goddess that sword was there, with which she had destroyed all the Yakshas, demons and Kinnars etc., the same sword had killed Madhu-Kaitabh and Shumbh-Nishumbh. O Lord; the same sword may ever be on my left side i.e., I may wear it. —4-78

Biralaksh, Chakshrasura etc., were torn into bits with the same sword, the flesh of Dhumar Lochan was caused to be eaten by the vultures to their fill; Ram, Muhammad, Krishna, Vishnu etc., all were destroyed by this sword of Kal, crores of people took crores of measures, but with the devotion of One Lord, no one achieved redemption. —5-79

| SUHI | SAYING BY THY GRACE |

There is that sword in His hand, which had chopped crores of Vishnus, Indras and Shivas; the sages meditate on that sword-like Power; O Power! You created heroes like Rama and Krishna many times and destroyed them many times. —6-80

Your figure is a thing of perception; how can I sing about it? The tongue of the poet sings about your thousands of qualities and gets tired; He, who destroys the earth, sky, netherworld and the fourteen worlds, the Light of that Power is shining everywhere. —7-81

VISHNUPADA

SORATHA

His Form is Infinite and beyond dimension; even Shiva is begging and wandering for His realisation; Chandra is also lying at His Feet and for His realisation Indra had got marks of a thousand genital organs of a woman on his body. —8-82

Because of the impact of Kal, many Krishnas and Ramas have been created, but Kal himself is indestructible and blemishless: He, with the impact of whose Feet, the world is created and destroyed, O fool! why do you not pray to Him, considering Him as the Creator? —9-93

O being! why do you not comprehend the Lord and are lying unconscious in attachment under the impact of *maya*? O being! you always remember the names of Rama, Krishna and Rasul, tell me, are they alive and they have any village or abode in the world? —10-84

Why do you not pray to Him Who is there in the present and shall be there in future? You are worshipping the stones uselessly; what will you gain by that worship? Only worship Him Who will fulfil your wishes; meditate on His Name, which will fulfil your wishes. —11-85

| VISHNUPADA | BY THY GRACE |

RAMKALI

When He was eulogised in this way, then the Perfect Purusha, the Lord was pleased with the king Parasnath; in order to bestow His sight to him, He mounted on a lion; He had a canopy over His head and the Ganas, demons etc., began to dance in front of Him. —12-86

RAMKALI

The arms and weapons glistened and the thunderous tabors were played; the ghosts, fiends and Baitals danced and wandered; the crows cawed and the ghosts etc., laughed; the sky thundered and the sages in fear wandered in their air-vehicles. —13-87

Speech of the Goddess

| VISHNUPADA | BY THY GRACE |

SARANG

"O son! ask for a boon; no one has practised austerities like you in the past and there will also be none in the future; you may ask for anything, I shall grant the same; I shall bestow on you the gold, *vajra*, the fruit of salvation or anything else, I shall bestow the same on you. —14-88

Speech of Parasnath

VISHNUPADA

SARANG

"I may become the knower of all the Vedic learning and may also be able to strike successfully all the weapons; I may conquer all the countries and start my own sect;" the Goddess Chandi said, "Let it be" and disappeared after riding on her lion.—15-89

VISHNUPADA BY THY GRACE
GAURI

Parasnath came back after prostrating before the Goddess and as soon as he came back, he sent messages and called the warriors from all the countries far and near; seeing the glorious personality of the king all were wonder-struck and said, we have never seen such personality of the king before which we are seeing today; the heavenly damsels also marvelled and the Ganas etc., also wondered; the gods showered flowers like rain-drops; the king appeared like a mine of youth, having come out from the ocean of beauty after taking bath; he seemed like an incarnation of the god of love on earth. —16-90

VISHNUPADA BY THY GRACE
SARANG

When the king obtained the Supreme knowledge, he had earlier performed rigorous austerities for the realisation of the Lord, with his mind, speech and action, when he performed various kinds of difficult postures and the repetition of God's Name, then the goddess Bhavani appeared before him; She, the mistress of all the fourteen worlds instructed him regarding Supreme Knowledge; the king obtained the recognition of essence and non-essence at the same moment and he recited all the Shastras from his mouth; considering all the elements as destructible, he accepted only one Essence as indestructible; perceiving the unique Light of the Supreme Soul he blissfully blew the unstruck melody; he achieved the fearless state on conquering the kings of all the countries far and near. —17-91

VISHNUPADA
PARAJ

In this way, achieving the everlasting state, disciplining the kings of various countries, he invited them; they, getting pleased marched proudly towards Parasnath, sounding their trumpets; they all came and bowed at the feet of the sovereign, who welcomed them all and hugged them; he gave them ornaments, garments, elephants, horses etc., and in this way, honouring all of them, he allured their mind.—18-92

VISHNUPADA BY THY GRACE
KAFI

In this way, giving them gifts and honouring them, Parasnath, the store of wisdom, fascinated the mind of all; presenting various types of elephants and horses, Parasnath achieved the nearness of all of them; to every Brahmin, he gave in charity rubies, pearls, diamonds, gems, garments, gold, etc., then the king arranged a *yajna*, in which various kings participated. —19-93

VISHNUPADA
KAFI

One day, the king held his court, wherein he had invited the chief kings of the earth; other people of various countries were also called; all the hermits with matted locks and the yogis reached there; all of them had grown matted locks of various kinds and smeared ashes on their faces and they had worn the ochre-coloured clothes on their limbs; seeing their long nails, even the lions were feeling shy; they were the performers of supreme austerities by closing their eyes and raising their hands; they remembered the sage Dattatreya night and day.—20-94

Speech of Parasnath

DHANASARI BY THY GRACE

"Either all of you may give me cognizance of your yoga or shave off your matted locks; O yogis! if there had been some secret of yoga in the matted locks, then any yogi would not have gone for begging at different doors instead of absorbing in mediation on the Lord; if anyone recognise the essence, he achieves unity with the Supreme Essence; he sits at one place silently and does not go in search of Him at any other place; He, Who is without any form or figure and who is non-dual and garbless,

SARANG — BY THY GRACE

Those who were very wise amongst those hermits with matted locks, they accepted Parasnath the knower of the Supreme Essence; all of them bowed their heads and folded their hands; they said, "Whatever you said to us as our Guru, we shall do the same; O Sir! whatever you heve said, the same thing we heard from the sage Dutt and have perceived the truth; you have uttered these words from your tongue like the sweet ambrosia and whatever you have uttered from your mouth, we accept all of them."—22-96

SORATHA

"O yogis! the Yoga does not consist in the matted locks; you may reflect in your mind and not be puzzled in illusions; when the mind, comprehending the Supreme Essence, realises the Supreme knowledge, then it stabilises at one place and does not wander and run hither and thither; what will you gain in the forest on forsaking the domestic life, because the mind will always be thinking about home and will not be able to get detached form the world; you people have deceived the world through the medium of yoga on showing the special deceit; you have believed that you have forsaken *maya*, but, in reality, *maya* has not left you."—23-97

VISHNUPADA

SORATHA

"O yogis! The believers in various guises! You are only exhibiting the outer garb, but that Lord can not be realised by growing matted locks, by smearing ashes, by growing nails and by wearing the dyed clothes; if the yoga had been achieved by residing in the forest, then the birds always live in the forest; in the same way the elephant always puts the dust on his body; why do you not understand it in your mind? The frogs and fish always take bath at the pilgrim stations, the cats and cranes are always seen meditating, but still they had not recognised yoga; the manner in which you suffer agony for deceiving the people, in the same way make effort to absorb your mind in the Lord, only then you will realise the Supreme Essence and would be able to quaff the nectar. —24-98

SARANG

Hearing such wise words, all the great hermits with matted locks clung to the feet of Parasnath; those who were foolish and ignorant, they did not accept the words of Parasnath and those fools, getting up, began to make an argument with Parasnath; some of them arose and ran away towards the forest and some of them merged themselves in water; some of them prepared themselves for fighting and came in front of the king; some of them ran away from that place; many of them went away to heaven after fighting in the battlefield. —25-99

TILANG — SAYING BY THY GRACE

When the conch of war was blown, then all the warriors with matted locks caused the dancing of their horses; the heavenly damsels were wonder-struck; the gods and demons felt agitated; the sun-god stopped his chariot in order to see that war; he saw that various types of arms and weapons were being used in that fighting; the arrows were being showered like rain-drops; the arrows hitting the armours were producing the crackling sound and it seems that the sparks are bursting forth with the burning of the straw; the clothes saturated with blood gave the semblance of the playing of Holi.—26-100

KEDARA

In this way, there was a dreadful fighting and the fine warriors fell upon the earth; those persistent warriors in their fury struck their arms and weapons and sounding their drums and trumpets, and fighting bravely, they fell upon the ground; the sound of lamentation was heard on all sides and the warriors ran hither and thither; on this side they were falling on the earth and on that side the heavenly damsels getting agitated were putting wreaths around their necks and wedding them; the darkness spread on the discharge of innumerable arrows and the dead warriors were seen scattered hither and thither in bits. —27-101

DEVGANDHARI

The deadly musical instruments were played in the war-arena and all the fine warriors holding their weapons in their hand thundered; wearing their armours and striking, all the warriors were fighting in the battlefield like lions filled with pride; holding their maces, the fighters moved for fighting, these warriors looked splendid in the battlefield and even Indra on seeing them and their elegance was feeling shy; they were falling on the ground having been cut into bits, but they were not running away from the battlefield; they were embracing death and were moving into the worlds of gods alongwith their weapons. —28-102

KALYAN

The warriors ran in all the ten directions and struck blows with maces, cannon-balls and axes; the warriors fallen in the battlefield were looking like the flowers scattered in the spring; the proud kings, getting up again, were fighting and were challenging their gathering of warriors shouting and grinding their teeth; the Gandharvas while fighting with lances, arrows, swords and other arms and weapons, rolling in dust, shouted to the gods, saying "O Lord! We are under your refuge, why do you not save us?" —29-103

MARU

When the warriors rushed to fight from both the directions and confronted one another, then listening to the sound of drums and kettle-drums, the clouds of Sawan felt shy; the gods and demons ascended their air-vehicles in order to see the war; seeing the articles studded with gold and gems, the Gandharvas got enraged and in their fury began to chop the fighters in dreadful war; very few warriors survived in the battlefield and many abandoned the fighting and ran; the arrows were being showered like the rain-drops from the clouds on the doomsday; Parasnath himself reached there in order to see this wonderful war. —30-104

VISHNUPADA   BY THY GRACE
BHAIRAV

He said, "Strike on the trumpet and within the view of these heavenly damsels, I shall devastate the whole earth; this earth will throb and tremble and I shall satisfy the hunger of Baitals etc., I shall cause the ghosts, fiends, Dakinis, Yoginis and Kakinis to drink blood to their fill; I shall destroy everything up and down in all the directions and many Bhairavas will appear in this war; I shall kill even today Indra, Chandra, Surya, Varuna, etc., by picking them up; I have been blessed with boon by that Lord, who has no second to Him; I am the creator of the world and whatever I shall do, that will happen." —31-105

GAURI   SAYING BY THY GRACE

"Who is more powerful than me, who will become victorious over me? I shall conquer even Indra, Chandra, Upendra in an instant; who is there anyone else who will come to fight with me; on getting slightly angry, I can dry up all the seven oceans and can throw away by twisting crores of Yakshas, Gandharvas and Kinnars; I have conquered and enslaved all the gods and demons I have been blessed by the Divine Power and who is there, who can even touch my shadow?" —32-106

MARU

Saying thus, Parasnath was greatly infuriated and he came in front of the *sannyasis*, he struck blows of arms and weapons in various ways and pierced the armours of the warriors with his arrows like the leaves; the arrows were discharged from both sides, which caused the concealment of the sun; it appeared that the earth and the sky had become one; Indra, Chandra, the great sages, Dikpals etc., all trembled with fear; Varuna and Kuber etc., also feeling the presence of second doomsday, left their own abodes and ran away. —33-107

MARU

The heavenly damsels began to sing songs of felicitation thinking that they would be wedding the great warriors in that *swayamvara* of war; that they would stand on one foot and observe the warriors fighting and immediately take them to heaven, causing them to sit in their palanquins; the day on which they would come into contact with their beloved one, on that day they would decorate with sandal their pretty limbs; O friend! the day on which they would wed Parasnath, on that day they would consider their body as fruitful and then embellish it. —34-108

KAFI

The thundering horns were blown in all the four directions and the warriors holding their maces stood firmly and persistently in the battlefield; the arrows, bows, swords, lances etc., were used and the clusters of arrows were discharged in showers like the rain-drops from the clouds; the arrows piercing the armours and leather penetrated directly to the other side and even went to the nether-world after piercing the earth; the warriors struck the gleaming daggers and lances and these weapons looked like piercing the hearts and showing them the path to heaven. —35-109

SORATHA

Innumerable *sannyasis* were pierced with the arrows and they all became the residents of heaven, forsaking the attachment of wealth and property; the armours, banners, chariots and flags etc., were cut down and caused to fall; they all extended the glory of heaven and the abodes of Indra and Yama; their multi-coloured garments fell on the ground; they appeared like flowers dropping down in spring in Ashok Vatika; the trunks of the elephants and the pearl-necklaces were lying scattered on the earth and appeared like the splattered water-drops form the pool of ambrosia. —36-110

DEVGANDHARI   LIKE THE SECOND

The warriors fell from both the directions and taking out the sword they marched forward shouting "kill, kill;" holding their weapons in their hands the angry warriors wandered and killing the elephant-drivers and the charioteers, they ultimately fell down on the earth; pulling the bows upto their ears, they discharged the arrows and in this way, striking the blows with their weapons, they fulfilled the obligation of Kshatriyas; being pierced by the arrows, the warriors fell like the falling of Bhishma on the bed of arrows in the time of Arjuna. —37-111

VISHNUPADA
SARANG

In this way, many *sannyasis* were killed; many were tied and got drowned and many were burnt in fire; there were many whose one hand was cut and there were many others whose two hands were cut; many charioteers were torn into pieces and the heads of many were chopped; the canopies, fly whisks, chariots, horses etc., of many were chopped in the battlefield; the crowns of many were broken with staff and the knots of the matted locks of many were uprooted; many were wounded and fell on the earth; and from their limbs, the blood oozed out as if all were playing Holi in spring season. —38-112

VISHNUPADA
ADAAN

The heavily damsels gathered together in the battlefield from all the four directions after dressing their hair; they had pretty cheeks, there was antimony in their eyes and rings in their noses; they were stealing the hearts of all like the thieves and were conversing with one another regarding the application of saffron to the limbs, because the handsome princess was to be wedded on that day the enthusiastic heavenly damsels were picking up those warriors in the war-arena who were being conquered with swords, arrows, bows, lances etc., and were marrying those fine fighters. —39-113

VISHNUPADA
SORATHA

To what extent should I describe it, because I fear the book will become voluminous, therefore I am improving thoughtfully the story and describing it in brief, I hope that with the strength of your wisdom, you will assess it accordingly; when Parasanth waged war in this way, using various types of weapons, then those who were killed, but some of them saved their lives by running away in all the four directions; those who abandoned their persistence and clung to the feet of the king, they were saved; they were given ornaments, garments etc., and were greatly appreciated in many ways. —40-114

KAFI

Parasnath fought a dreadful war and removing the sect of Dutt, he propagated extensively his own sect; he killed many enemies in various ways with his arms and weapons; in the battles all the warriors of Parasnath were victorious and all those with matted locks were defeated; with the infliction of arrows, the warriors wearing many garbs fell down upon the earth; it appeared that they were preparing themselves to fly to the Supreme world attaching wings to their bodies; the supremely impressive armours were torn into fragments and caused to fall down; it appeared that the warriors were leaving the mark of blemish of their clan on the earth and moving towards heaven. —41-115

SUHI

Parasnath won the war and he appeared like Karana or Arjuna; various streams of blood flowed and in that current the chariots, horses and elephants also flowed; all the seven oceans felt shy before that current of blood (of war); having been struck by the arrows on their limbs, the *sannyasis* ran away hither and thither like the mounts flying away, getting fearful of Indra's *vajra*, attaching wings to themselves; the currents of blood was flowing on all sides and the wounded warriors were roaming here and there; they were running away in all the ten directions and were slandering the discipline of Kshatriyas. —42-116

VISHNUPADA

SORATHA

Those *sannyasis* who survived, they did not return because of fear and went to the forest, they were picked up from various countries and the forests and killed and searching for them in the sky and the nether-world, they were all destroyed; in this way, killing the *sannyasis*, Parasnath propagated his own sect; and extended his own mode of worship; the wounded ones, who were caught, their matted locks were shaved off and ending the impact of Dutt, Parasnath extended his fame. —117

VISHNUPADA

BASANT

In this way, Holi was played with the sword; the shields took the place of tabors and the blood became *gulal* red colour; the arrows were inflicted on the limbs of the warriors like the syringes; with the flowing out of blood, the beauty of the fighters increased as if they had splashed saffron on their limbs; the glory of the matted locks saturated with blood is indescribable; it appeared that with great love, the *gulal* was splashed on them; the enemies stringed with lances were lying hither and thither as if they had been sleeping after the tiring play of Holi. —118

VISHNUPADA

PARAJ

In this way, Parasnath ruled for one thousand years and ending the sect of Dutt, he extended his Rajayoga; he, who hid himself, remained a follower of Dutt and lived without recognition; ruling in various ways, the king gathered wealth by various means and wherever he came to know of it, he looted it; in this way, conquering many countries far and near, the king extended his fame and himself forgetting the Lord and began to consider himself the creator. —119

ROOAAL STANZA

In this way, getting onward, killing all the enemies, conquering the earth in various ways, the king ruled for ten thousand years; conquering any kings, the king thought of performing the Rajmedh *yajna*. —120

The king alongwith his sons and friends brought the kings of various countries to his own country in fetters and began to perform *yajna* with his wife; he also invited crores of Brahmins. —121

Gathering his various friends, the king began the Rajmedh *yajna*; people of various kinds gathered there and the king also seized the wealth and property of the superb kings. —122

Looking at his infinite wealth, feeling proud on the strength of his arms, he spoke thus, "O Brahmins! now perform such Bhoopmedh *yajna*, which was performed by Jambhasura in Satyuga." —123

Speech of the Minister

"If one lakh kings are killed, then the Rajmedh *yajna* can be performed and to each Brahmin innumerable wealth and one lakh horses are to be given immediately; in this way, O king! the *yajna* be completed." —124

"Many types of gifts of wealth and property and, one lakh elephants and two lakh horses and one lakh gold coins are to be given to each of the Brahmin and O king! by donating these to crores of Brahmins, this impossible *yajna* can be completed." —125

Speech of Parasnath

ROOAAL STANZA

There is no shortage of gold and inspite of donating if for many years, it will not go out of stock; look at the house of elephants and the stable of horses, there is no shortage of them; O minister-friend! do not have any doubt in your mind and whatever wealth is wanted take it immediately. —126

When the king said like this, then the minister closed his eyes and bowed before the king with folded hands; O king! listen to another thing, which I have heard in the form of a discourse on the basis of Puranas and Smritis. —127

Speech of the Minister

ROOAAL STANZA

"O king! listen, you are supremely immaculate and blemishless; you may conquer the kings of all the countries;" "The secret about which you are talking, O minister! you may yourself ask this from all the kings." —128

ROOAAL STANZA

When the king said this, the chief ministers then started for the purpose; they invited five lakh kings; when they were asked to tell as to who is that king in the seven worlds, whom the king (Parasnath) has not conquered in his ire? —129

ROOAAL STANZA

All of them looked with bowed heads and reflected as to who was that king on the earth whose name might be mentioned; the king called each one of them and asked him as to who was he who had remained unconquered? —130

Speech of a King

ROOAAL STANZA

One of the kings said, "If you promise the safety of my life, then I can say; there is a fish in the sea, in whose belly there is a sage; I am speaking the truth; ask him and do not ask any of the other kings." —131

ROOAAL STANZA

"O king! one day Shiva wearing matted locks persistently entered the ocean, where he saw an unparalleled fascinating woman; seeing her, his semen was discharged within the ocean and because of that the Yogi Matsyendra is seated within the belly of a fish." —132

ROOAAL STANZA

"O king! go and ask him, all these kings, who have been invited by you will not be able to tell you anything;" when the sovereign heard, this, he went in search of that fish in the ocean taking with him all the nets of the world. —133

ROOAAL STANZA

The king proudly moved sounding his drums, taking various types of nets and his army with him; he called all his ministers, friends, princes etc., and threw his nets here and there in the ocean; all the fish were frightened. —134

Various types of fish, tortoises and other beings, came out being entrapped in nets and began to die, then all the beings of water went before the god of ocean and described the cause of their worry. —135

The ocean came before the king in the guise of a Brahmin and offering gems, diamonds, pearls etc., to the king, he said, "Why are you killing the beings? Because the purpose for which you have come here, will not be fulfilled here." —136

Speech of the Ocean
ROOAAL STANZA

"O king! the Yogi Matsyendra is sitting in contemplation in the belly of the fish in milk-ocean; take him out with your net and ask him; O king! do whatever I have said, this is the real measure." —137

The king gathering together lakhs of his warriors moved away further from the ocean; where the heavenly damsels were moving here and there enthusiastically; they all reached there sounding their drums and playing instruments of various types, where there was the milk-ocean. —138

The nets of cotton were prepared and thrown into the ocean, in which many other beings were caught, but the son of Shiva (Matsyendra) was not seen; all the warriors, greatly tired came before the king and said, "Many other beings have been caught, but that sage is nowhere to be found." —139

"The yogi is sitting desireless in the belly of the fish and this net cannot entrap him; now, O king! throw another net immediately and this is the only step to catch him." —140

ROOAAL STANZA

"O king! we have heard about the name of the net of knowledge, throw the same in the ocean and catch the great sage; the sage will not be caught with any other measure even for years; O protector! listen to it, we are telling you the truth." —141

ROOAAL STANZA

You may take crores of measures except this, you will not be able to catch him; only throw the net of knowledge and catch him; when the king threw the net of knowledge into the ocean that net caught him like the second Dadhich. —142

The Yogi Matsyendra was caught alongwith the fish, having been entrapped in the net and seeing that fish all were wonder-struck; after sometime, when all the people regained some health, then all the warriors, depositing their arms and weapons reached at the gate of the king. —143

They began to rip the belly of the fish, but none of them could do it; when all of them gave in, then the king called his friends and asked them, "Now what measure be adopted, so that we may be successful in our objective and see the great sage." —144

HOHARA

All of them used their power, but the belly of the fish could not be ripped, then the king tried to ask the Knowledge-Guru. —145

TOMAR STANZA

All the warriors, forsaking their pride, came near the king and spoke, "O king! ask only the Knowledge-Guru, he will only tell us all the method." —146

TOTAK

The king reflected methodically and invoked Knowledge and said, "O chief Guru! tell me the mystery as to how the sage can be seen?" —147

Then the Knowledge-Guru uttered these ambrosial words, "O king! take the knife of Viveka (Discrimination) and tear off this fish." —148

TOTAK

Then, whatever the Guru had instructed, it was done accordingly; after adopting Viveka, that fish was ripped. —149

When the belly of the fish was ripped, then that great sage was seen; he was sitting there with closed eyes and concentration, detaching himself from all desires. —150

TOTAK

Then a sheet made of seven metal, was put under the view of the sage; when the contemplation of the sage broke, the sheet was reduced to ashes by the sight of the sage. —151

If anything else had come within his sight (at that time), it could not have been saved from being reduced to ashes; there can be no devotion without true love. —152

When that sheet was reduced to ashes like the destruction of the darkness by the sun, then the king went to that sage and told him the secret of his coming. —153

NARAAJ STANZA

"O sage! kindly tell me the name and address of the king, who is not fearful of me; who is that headstrong king, who has not been conquered by me? Which is that place, which has not come under my terror." —154

NARAAJ

"You may tell me the name of that mighty one unhestitatingly, who is still unconquerable. I have conquered all the kings of the countries far and near and have made all the kings of the earth my slaves." —155

NARAAJ

"I have employed many kings as my servants doing my jobs and have bestowed charities after taking bath at many pilgrim-stations; I am ruling after killing innumerable Kshatriyas; I am that one from whom the beings of all the three worlds run far away." —156

NARAAJ

I have abducted many multi-coloured horses and have performed special Rajsu and Ashvamedha *yajnas*; you may agree with me that any place or sacrificial column is not unacquainted with me; you may accept me as the second Lord of the world. —157

All the warriors who hold the arms and weapons are my servants; I have chopped into bits the unpunishable individuals and many of them are paying tributes to me; none is considered glorious like me and O great yogi! consider me as the Chief Administrator in all the three worlds. —158

Speech of Matsyendra addressed to Parasnath
SWAYYA

What then, if you have conquered and terrorised the whole world, what then, if you have got all the countries far and near crushed under the feet of your elephants; you have not got that mind, which conquers all the countries; you have felt shyful before it several times and in this way, you have not only lost this world, but also the next world. —159

SWAYYA

"O king! why to be egoistic for the land, which does not accompany anyone on death; this earth is a great deceiver, it has not become one's own until today, nor it will become anyone's own; your treasures and your beautiful women, none of them will accompany you at the end; leave all others, even your own body will not accompany you." —160

"What to talk of this royal paraphernalia, it will also not accompany at the end; all the palaces and treasures will become another's property in an instant; the sons, wife and friends etc., none of them will accompany you at the end; O great animal, living in unconscious state! forsake your sleep even now, because your body, which has been born with you, it will also not accompany you." —161

You cannot trust these warriors, because all of them will not endure the burden of your actions; they will all run away in front of all the dreadful afflictions; none of the measures will be useful to you and all these friends of yours will flow away like the flowing water; your sons, your wives, all of them will call you a ghost. —162

Speech of Parasnath addressed to Matsyendra
TOMAR STANZA

"O sage! tell me, who is that king, whom I should conquer? And then you will call me the greatest Sovereign of all." —163

Speech of Matsyendra addressed to Parasnath
TOMAR STANZA

"O Sovereign! you are the greatest on the earth; you have conquered all the kings, but, whatever I am telling you, you have not conquered it." —164

Its name is *aviveka* (ignorance) and it abides in your heart; regarding it victory, O king! you have not said anything, that also has a unique form." —165

CHHAPPAI STANZA

This *aviveka* had conquered mighty Bali and had to become sub-servient to Vaman; he destroyed Krishna (Vishnu) and received penalty from Raghupati Ram; he destroyed Ravana and Jambhasuru and killed Mahishasura, Madhu and Kaitabh; O beautiful king like the god of love! you have made that *aviveka* your minister, who after conquering the gods, demons, Gandharvas and sages has received tributes from them. —166

CHHAPPAI STANZA

Because of the anger of this *aviveka* Karana and Kauravas were destroyed in the battlefield; because of its anger, Ravana had to lose all his ten heads; because of it, there was war between the gods and the demons and because of it all the six clans of Yadavas fought amongst themselves; therefore O the master of the armies! O king! the day when getting enraged, your *viveka* will become out of control, on that day, it will overshadow all without influencing the one *viveka* (discriminating intellect). —167

Speech of Parasnath adressed to Matsyendra

CHHAPPAI STANZA

"O Matsyendra! listen, I tell you a distinctive thing; *viveka* and *aviveka* both the kings of distinct characteristics (of the world); both are great fighters and archers; both have the same caste and the same mother, both have the same father and the same dynasty, then how can there be enmity between them? O sage! now you tell me about their place, name, ornaments, chariots, arms, weapons etc. —168

Speech of Matsyendra addressed to Parasnath

CHHAPPAI STANZA

Avivek has black colour, black chariot and black horses; His garments are black also; seeing him, all the men and women are allured; his charioteer is also black, whose garments are also black, his chariot is also darkness; his bow and banner are all black and he considers himself a superb and superior person; O king! this is the pretty appearance of *aviveka* with which he had conquered the world; he is unconquerable and consider him as the likeness of Krishna. —169

CHHAPPAI STANZA

In the likeness of the god of love, he is an elegant *Purusha* and his banner looks glorious; on all his four sides, the pretty and sweet lyre is played and the horn is blown; all types of musical instruments continue to played with him; there is always a group of women with him and these women fascinate, the minds of gods, men and sages; on the day, when this *aviveka* will get enraged and come forward as the god of love, none will be able to stand before him except only *viveka*. —170

CHHAPPAI STANZA

The beautiful damsels played on lyres, sang songs of joy and danced; the collective sound of musical modes was heard; Bairari, Bangali female musical modes were played; the fine sound of Bhairava, Basant, Deepak, Hindol, etc., arose at such a pitch that all the men and women were allured; with the impact of all this demeanour, O king! the day on which he will attack, then who can face him, without adopting *viveka*? —171

SORATHA

Seeing and hearing the elegant tunes of sarang, Shuddh Malhar, Vibhas, Ramkali, Hindol, Gaur, Gujri, Lalit, Paraj, Gauri Malhar, Kanhra, etc., the warriors like you are buried under his dazzle; in this way, in the good season Basant, when *aviveka* will thunder in the likeness of the god of love, then without knowledge, O king! who will admonish him? —172

CHHAPPAI STANZA

When the clouds will surround from all the four directions, the lightenings will flash, in such an atmosphere, the love-sick women will allure the mind, the voice of frogs and peacocks and the jingling sound of *arbour* will be heard seeing the influence of the intoxicated eyes of the lustful women, the sages also fall from their vows and feel defeated in their mind, the day on which such a joyful atmosphere will present itself with full brilliance, then, O king! tell me, on that day, who will reject its impact except *viveka*? —173

CHHAPPAI STANZA

When in the likeness of *anand* (bliss), he will hold the weapons and fight in a queer way, then the sages will be frightened, who is there such a warrior, who will keep patience and confront him? he will abduct the glory of all in an instant; in this way, the day on which this tyrannical warrior will come to fight holding his weapons, on that day, O king! none else will stay there except the one with endurance. —174

CHHAPPAI STANZA

Studded with gems and full of pearls, the chariot will carry this mighty charioteer wearing embellished garments; seeing the gold, the hardest of beautiful lustful damsels, will be allured, forsaking their vows and he will wear ornaments and pretty garments on his body; O king! the joy-giver god of love, when he will come in front, thundering in such a handsome pose, then who will confront him except the one with endurance. —175

CHHAPPAI STANZA

All the gods, men and sages, will feel shy on seeing the black-coloured charioteer, black chariot and horses and glorious black garments; the black eyes and black ornaments will glisten on his black body and his enemies will be in agony; the day, on which this fourth son of the god of love, will move towards you in anger, then, O king! he will loot and cut down your army in an instant. —176

CHHAPPAI STANZA

The names of other warriors are fantastic also; they are all very brave and conquerors of wars; there is one woman named Kalha, whose figure is very hideous, she has not left untouched any god or man in all the fourteen worlds; the warriors skilful in arms and weapons and very influential fighters and the kings of the countries far and near are fearful of her. —177

CHHAPPAI STANZA

There is one invincible warrior named *shatruta* (inimical), who has never shown his back and has conquered many kings; his eyes and colour were red like blood and there were weapons on all the limbs, his banner was like sunshine and seeing his brilliance, even the sun felt shy; in this way, this mighty warrior named *shatruta*, will roar in anger, on that day, none else will confront him except *shanti* (peace). —178

CHHAPPAI STANZA

The black banner, black chariot and the black charioteer look splendid; seeing the black garment, even the smoke feels shy in his mind; there are black arrows for his black bow; seeing him the gods, men, serpents, Yakshas and demons feel shy; O king! this impressive beauty is of *aalas* (laziness) and O king! the day he will confront you for fighting, your army without diligence will be fragmented. —179

CHHAPPAI STANZA

Seeing the one having green banner, green bow, green horses, green chariots and wearing green clothes on the body, the gods and men are allured; his chariot moving with the speed of wind, causes the deer to feel shy; hearing his voice, the cloud feels happy in his mind; the day on which this individual named *garva* (pride) will cause his horse to dance before you, on that day none else will stay before him except *viveka*. —180

CHHAPPAI STANZA

He, who is decorated with black banner, black charioteer, black garment, black horse, black armour etc., who showers a continuous line of arrows, his colour is completely black, his eyes are black and he is the destroyer of suffering; the ornaments of black pearls increase the beauty of his limbs; the day on which that warrior named *kuvrati* (evil pledge) will enter the field holding his bow, the whole army will run away on that day except the one with endurance. —181

CHHAPPAI STANZA

Wearing the armour of leather, accomplisher of the vow of Kshatriya challenges all and considers himself unconquerable; no warrior stays against him and all the gods, demons,

Yakshas, Gandharvas, men, women all sing his praises, the day on which this egoist, getting highly enraged, will thunder and stand in front, on that day, O king! all others will be destroyed except *sheel* (gentleness). —182

CHHAPPAI STANZA

He is the one who thunders like the clouds of Bhadon, who cracks the sword like the lightening and who scatters the fragments of the corpses of the warriors lying in front of him; his anger cannot be endured by anyone in the war; the day on which the sentiment of anger becoming your comrade, becomes the cause of your dishonour, on that day who will fight with him except the warrior named *sheel* (gentleness). —183

CHHAPPAI STANZA

He, whose circular round is his bow and who is ever busy in fighting seeing whose sharp influence, the warriors go astray and flee; seeing him, the brilliance of the warrior drops endurance and becomes shy and they run away, not staying any more in the battlefield, fleeing in all the ten directions; the day on which this warrior named *anarth* (misfortune) will cause his horse to dance before you, O the superb one amongst the warriors! Who will fight against him except Endurance. —184

CHHAPPAI STANZA

That one is holding the yellow bow in his hand, wearing yellow garments on his body, having fixed the yellow banner on his chariot, he is the smasher of the pride of the god of love; his charioteer, chariot and horses all are of yellow colour; his arrows are also of yellow colour and he thunders in the battlefield O king! the day on which this type of warrior named *vairbhav* (enmity) will roar and incite his army, on that day, who will fight with him except *jnan* (knowledge). —185

CHHAPPAI STANZA

Wearing dirty clothes on the dirty body and having tied dirty ornaments with his chariot, with dirty crown on his head and the arrows fashioned for discharge and taking with him the charioteer of dirty colour and dirty ornamentation, this warrior with fragrance of sandal and the one agonising his enemies and named *ninda* (slander), the day when he will begin his fighting, on that day, who will confront him except Endurance? —186

CHHAPPAI STANZA

Wearing dreadful clothes, dreadful turban and dreadful crown, reformer of the dreadful enemies, having dreadful form and repeating the dreadful *mantra*, seeing whom ever the heaven becomes fearful, that tyrannical warrior named Hell (*narak*), the day when he, in great rage, will come for fighting, at that time; who will be able to save you except the name of the Lord? —187

CHHAPPAI STANZA

He, who catches hold his lance while getting back and throws it while coming forward, he attacks in great rage like an animal, he cannot be controlled by one at a time; he fights with one at a time and facing him receives the blows from his weapons; such an unkind warrior, O king! when he will thunder in fury, then none else except the Purity of Mind will be able to deal with him. —188

CHHAPPAI STANZA

Skilful in arms and weapons and scholar of Vedas and Shastras, having red eyes and wearing red garments, a patient archer, having formidable and proud mind, with unlimited brilliance, unconquerable and lustrous, this warrior named Hunger and Thirst, the day when he will precipitate the war, the O king! you will survive only on the strength of Persistence. —189

CHHAPPAI STANZA

The beauty of the chariot moving with the speed of wind is like lightning; the pretty damsels only on seeing him, fall on the earth; the god of love is also fascinated by him and the human beings seeing his beauty feel shy; on seeing him, the heart is overjoyed and the affections run away; this warrior *kapat* (deceit), O king! the day on which he will come forward with a jerk, then who will confront him except *shanti* (peace)? —190

CHHAPPAI STANZA

Seeing his beautiful eyes and feeling his mercurial influence, the birds named *khanjan* (wagtail) feel shy; he sings Basant *raga* and the lyre continues to be played near him; the sound of the drum and anklets etc., are heard near him; he allures the mind of all the birds, deer, yakshas, serpents, demons, gods and men; the day on which this mighty warrior *lobha* (greed) will come forward for war, then O king! all your army will be fragmented like the clouds before the wind. —191

CHHAPPAI STANZA

He, who is long like the banner and whose arm is like lightening; his chariot is extremely speedy and seeing him, the gods, men and sages run away; he is extremely pretty, an unconquerable warrior and performer of difficult tasks in the war; to his enemies he appears very powerful and their abductor; the day on which this warrior named *moha* (attachment) will come for fighting, then all the injudicious army will be segmented except the Judicious Notion. —192

CHHAPPAI STANZA

His chariot moves with the speed of wind and all the citizens are allured on seeing him; he is extremely glorious, unconquerable and beautiful; he is extremely powerful and master of all the forces; this warrior is named *karodha* (anger) and consider him the most powerful; the day on which wearing his armour and holding his discus, he will cause his horse to dance on the front, O king! consider it as true that on that day, none else will be able to repulse him except *shanti* (peace). —193

CHHAPPAI STANZA

With his drawn dreadful sword, he moves like an intoxicated elephant; his colour is black and he is ever studded with the blue jewels, he is a superb elephant entrapped and enchained in a net of gold and on all the people, the impact of this warrior is good; he is the mighty *ahamkara* and consider him extremely powerful; he has conquered the beings of all the world and he himself is unconquerable. —194

CHHAPPAI STANZA

He is mounted on a white elephant and the fly whisk is being swung over him from all the four sides; seeing his golden embellishment; all the men and women are allured; he has a lance in his hand and he is moving like the sun; the lightning seeing his lustre feels sorrowful also for its bedimmed radiance; consider this great warrior *droha* (malice) as extremely impressive and this warrior, O king! accepts subordination in water and on plain and in countries far and near. —195

CHHAPPAI STANZA

With curly hair like the tambourine player, he has two swords; the men and women are allured to see him; he is a mighty warrior with unlimited glory; he has long arms and is extremely brave, unconquerable and invincible; the day on which this indiscriminate warrior named *bhrama* (illusion) will get enraged in his mind, then O king! no one will be able to redeem you except *viveka* (reason). —196

CHHAPPAI STANZA

This warrior with naked head and with necklaces full of rubies, extremely powerful, indiscriminate and unconquerable; he has the sword and lance in his girdle and he is the one who showers the volley of arrows; seeing the impact of his laughter, the lightning feels shy; this warrior named *brahma-dosh* (finder of flaws in Divinity) is unconquerable and invincible; O king! this enemy is manifestation of *aviveka* (ignorance); he is the one who burns his enemy and is unconquerable; he is extremely comfortable and cosy (for the fools). —197

CHHAPPAI STANZA

He has a black body and wears black clothes; he is infinitely glorious; he is extremely powerful and he had conquered many warriors in the battlefield, he is invincible, imperishable and indiscriminate; his name is *anarth* (misfortune); he is extremely powerful and is capable of destroying the gatherings of enemies; he, who is the killer of tyrannical warriors, is considered extremely glorious; he is unconquerable, giver of pleasure and is known as extremely glorious warrior. —198

CHHAPPAI STANZA

He the master of peacock-coloured chariot and horses, is also peacock-coloured himself; seeing this Lord of infinite glory, the enemies tremble; this imperishable warrior has long arms and is the producer of dazzling light; seeing his beauty, even the god of love feels shy; the day on which warriors named *jhooth* (falsehood) will cause his horse to dance before you in great anger, then O king! consider it as true, no one can defeat him except Tuth. —199

CHHAPPAI STANZA

He, whose war-horse is black and white, whose banner is black and seeing whose black and white garments, the gods, men and sages feel shy; he, whose charioteer is black and white and whose quiver and chariot are also black, his hair are like the golden chords and he seems to be the second Indra; this is the impact and beauty of the warrior named *mithya* he is extremely powerful; he has conquered all the beings of the world and none has remained untouched by him. —200

He is wearing the curved discus and fine garments on his body; he is chewing the betel-leaf in his mouth and its fine odour is spreading on all the four sides; the fly whisk is swinging on all the four sides and the setting is very fine; seeing him, the glory of spring bows its head; this long-armed warrior named *chinta* (anxiety) is tyrannical; he is extremely powerful warrior with his indestructible body. —201

ROOAAL STANZA

He, who is wearing the handsome necklaces of rubies and diamonds; whose large-sized elephant is wearing very cleanly the golden chain; O king! the warriors mounting the elephant is named *daridra* (lethargy); who will be able to fight with him in the war? —202

He, who is wearing the garments of brocade and is riding on the horse, his beauty is eternal; he has the canopy of *dharma* on his head and is famous for the tradition and honour of his clan; the name of this warrior is *shanka* (doubt) and he is the chief of all the warriors. —203

This rider of the brown horse is the unfailing and complete warrior; he has assumed powerful form and his indestructible body is like doomsday; this warrior named *tushti* (gratification) us known by all people; there is no such *viveka* (knowledge), who will not be sorrowful on its dearth. —204

BHUJANG PRAYAAT STANZA

He, whose black horses and chariots are decorated, he is known as the great unconquerable warrior; this warrior is named *asantushta* (dissatisfaction), from whom all the three worlds, remain fearful. —205

Riding on a restless horse and wearing aigrette on his head, with his canopy of victory over his head, he causes the moon to feel shy, this great warrior named *anaash* (imperishable) looks splendid; he is a very great sovereign and very powerful. —206

Seeing the chariot of white horses, Indra also gets wonder-struck; the name of that persistent warrior is *hinsa* (violence) and that great warrior is known as unconquerable in all the worlds. —207

Here are pretty horses like sandal, seeing whom the horses of Indra feel shy; this great warrior is *kumantra* (bad counsel), who has conquered the warriors at all places in water and on plain. —208

The pigeon-shaped warrior, riding on a restless horse and a unique wearer of the armour of leather, with banner tied up, this is the warrior named *alajja* (shamelessness); he is a powerful one and his anger is dreadful. —209

Wearing dirty clothes like lazy persons, with torn banner, the great rioter, this great warrior is known by the name of *chori* (theft); seeing his glory, the dog feels shy. —210

Wearing all the torn clothes, having tied deceit on his head, half-burnt, sitting on a large-sized male buffalo, this large-sized one is the great hero *vyabhichar* (bad conduct)? —211

The warrior with complete black body and white head, he, with whose chariot the asses are yoked instead of horses, whose banner is black and arms are extremely powerful, he seems to be waving like the tank of blood. —212

The name of this great warrior is *daridra* (lethargy) he is wearing the armour of leather and has caught an axe in his hand; he is extremely angry warrior and the awful smoke is emanating from his nose. —213

ROOAAL STANZA

Vishwasghaat (deception) and *kritghanta* (ungratefulness) are also two horrible warriors, who are the killers of the brave enemies and the army; who is such a special individual, who does not fear them; seeing their unique form, the warriors, getting dejected, run away. —214

Mittar-dosh (blaming of friend) and *raaj-dosh* (blaming of the administration), both are brothers; both belong to the same family and both have the same mother; adopting the Kshatriya discipline, when these warriors will go for war, then which warrior will be able to keep patience before them? —215

Irsha (jealousy) and *uchchhatan* (indifference), both of them are warriors; they are pleased on seeing the heavenly damsels and flee; they conquer all the enemies and no fighter stays in front of them; no one can use his weapons in front of them and the warriors pressing straws within their teeth, run away. —216

Ghaat (ambush) and *vashikaran* (control) are also great warriors; their actions are hard-hearted; they have axes in their hands and their teeth are terrible; their brilliance is like lightning, their body is imperishable and their figures are horrible; which being or which great creature they have not conquered? —217

Vipada (adversity) and *jhooth* (falsehood) are like the axe for the warrior clan; they are pretty in form, sturdy in body and have infinite brilliance; they are long in stature, without clothes and have powerful limbs, they are tyrannical and lethargic and are ever ready to discharge their arrows from the seven sides. —218

When the warriors named *viyoga* (separation) and *aparaadh* (guilt) will get infuriated, then who will be able to stay before them? All will run away; your warriors will hold their spikes, arrows, lances etc., but before these cruel persons they will get ashamed and run away. —219

Like the blazing sun, when the war will be fought in full fury, then which warrior will keep patience? all of them will flee like a dog; all of them will run away leaving their arms, weapons and horses and your warriors breaking their armours will flee immediately. —220

O king! the name of this warrior is *aalas* (idleness) who has black body and black eyes; he is cruel and dreadful and is wearing the torn clothes with seven twists; which warrior will be able to kill him with the blows of his weapons and arms? —221

TOTAK STANZA

The warrior who will roar in fury, like the rushing clouds, holding his sword, his name is *khed* (regret), O king! consider him extremely powerful. —222

The name of that mighty warrior is *kutriya* (evil woman); she is dreadful like the flames of fire, has white sword, pure glory with rows of white teeth; and who is full of pleasure. —223

He, who is extremely ugly and has a black body, and seeing whom, the ignorance is produced, the name of that mighty warrior is *galaani* (hatred); he is a great fighter and with his persistence causes the defeat of others. —224

His limbs are of extremely pretty colour and he has the power to agonise hardest tribulations; this warrior has never become impatient and all the gods and goddesses recognise him quite nicely. —225

When all these warriors will assume their power, then they will ride their horses and wander; who is your fighter, who will be able to keep patience in front of them? these powerful ones will abduct the glory of all. —226

DOHIRA

O king! in this way, *aviveka* will assume the bodies of various warriors and no warrior of *viveka* will stay in front of him. —227

End of "The Description of the Dialogue of Parasnath and Matsyendra, Arrival of the King Aviveka and the Description of His Warriors" in Bachittar Natak.

Now begins the Description of the Army of King Viveka

CHHAPPAI STANZA

The way in which the army of the king *aviveka* has been described, we have known all his warriors with their name, place, garment, chariot etc., the way in which their arms, weapons, bows and banners have been described; in the same way, O great sage! kindly describe your views about *viveka* and present a complete narration about him; O great sage! give views your about the beauty and impact of *viveka*. —1-228

The sage made a great effort and recited many mantras; he performed practices of several kinds of *tantras* and *yantras*; becoming extremely pure, he spoke again and the way in which he had described *aviveka* alongwith his army, he also narrated in the same way about the king *viveka*; the gods, demons, Agni, Wind, Surya, and Chandra, all were wonder-struck; even Yakshas and Gandharvas were also immersed in astonishment thinking how the light of *viveka* will destroy the darkness of *aviveka*. —2-229

Seeing the one with white canopy, white chariot and white horses and holding white weapons, the gods and men flee in illusion; the god Chandra is astonished and the god Surya, seeing his glory is also wavering; O king! this beauty belongs to *viveka*, who may be considered extremely powerful; the sages and kings pray before him in all the three worlds. —3-230

He, on whom the fly whisk is swinging from all the four sides and seeing whom, the swans of Mansarovar feel shy; he is extremely pure, glorious and beautiful; he allures the mind of all the gods, men, Nagas, Indra, Yakshas, Kinnars, etc., the day on which *viveka* of such beauty will be ready to discharge his arrow, he will not discharge it on anyone else except *aviveka*. —4-231

He is extremely powerful, viceless, lustrous and incommensurably strong; he is extremely glorious warrior and his drum sounds at all the places including water and plain; his chariot moves with the speed of wind and seeing his speed, even the lightning feels shy in its mind; hearing him thundering violently, the clouds of all the four directions flee in confusion; he is considered unconquerable, fearless and a superb warrior is water and on plain; this invincible and mighty one is named "endurance" by the world. —5-232

The *dharma*-incarnate "*endurance*" is extremely powerful in most difficult times; he is like Elysian tree (*kalpavriksha*) and chops the evil modifications with his sword; he is extremely glorious, brilliant like the fire, he blazes all in the war with his speech, he does not care even for Brahmastra and Shivastra; when this warrior named *suvriti* (good modification) will strike his arms and weapons in the war, who else will be able to fight with him except *kuvriti* (evil modification). —6-233

This Glorious one of indestructible body and brilliance, completely strong like fire and driving his chariot with the speed of wind, all the beings in water and on plain know him; he is a skilful archer, but because of his fasting all his limbs are weak; all the men and women know him by the name of *sanjamveer* (disciplined warrior); when, holding his bow and arrows, he will thunder in his superb form, then none can withhold him except *kuvriti*. —7-234

He is a mighty warrior named *nem* (principle) his chariot is drawn by comely and restless horses; he is extremely skilful, soft-spoken and allures the mind like lyre; he is supremely glorious and is the destroyer of enemies of all the world; his sword is indestructible and he proves to be very strong in severe wars; He is said to be fearless, indestructible, the Lore of consciousness, viceless and unconquerable. —8-235

He is a warrior of infinite glory, fearless and eternal; his chariot is volatile and lustrous like lightening; seeing him, the enemies, getting fearful, run away from war-arena; looking at him, the warriors forsake their patience and the warriors cannot discharge arrows persistently; this powerful hero is known by the name of *vijnan* (science); in the country of *ajnan* (ignorance), the people fear him in every home. —9-236

He blazes like fires, sounds like the dreadful tabor and roars like the thundering clouds; holding his lance, he springs and strikes his blow on the enemy; seeing him, all the gods and demons hail him; the day on which this warrior named *snan* (bath) will thunder taking his bow in his hand, on that day, none else will be able to obstruct him except *malina* (uncleanliness). —10-237

The first warrior is *nivratti* (free) and the second warrior is *bhavana* (emotion), who are extremely powerful, indestructible and invincible; when these warriors, holding their weapons, will thunder in the battlefield, seeing them there the fighters will run away; those warriors will tremble like the yellow leaf and lose patience; in this way the day on which these mighty ones will begin fighting, then the fighters in the field will forsake their arms and weapons and no one will survive. —11-238

SANGEET CHHAPPAI STANZA

When the warriors will confront one another, the war-horns will be blown; the lances will break and the corpses will be scattered; the Bhairavas and ghosts will run and the adepts will see this spectacle; the Yakshas and Yoginis will hail the warriors; when the warrior named *sanjam* (restraint) will thunder in fury, then he will not be opposed by anyone else except *durmat* (evil intellect). —12-239

When this hailing warrior *yoga* (union) will shoot in fury, then the swords will create sensation and there will be loot and destruction; when he will hold the weapons and wear armour, on the same day all the enemies will flee away, without staying for a moment; with yellow faces they will run away on that day, the day on which he, the unconquerable warrior will throw his glances on all. —13-240

When the five evils, getting enraged and angry, will stand firmly in the field, then all will run away forsaking their arms and weapons like the leaves flying away before the wind; when the warriors will cause their running horses to dance, then all the good modifications, forgetting themselves, will experience their downfall. —14-241

CHHAPPAI STANZA

The pretty fly whisks are swinging and the beauty of this hero is fascinating; his white garments, white horses and white weapons look splendid; he is extremely immaculate, viceless, invariable, indivisible and invincible warrior, whose glory is infinite and who is unconquerable and never deceivable, O king! on the day, when holding his arms and weapons, he will thunder, then no one will be able to stay before him and even obstruct him. —15-242

Vidya (learning) and *lajja* (modesty) are also extremely glorious; they are large-bodied, powerful and indestructible; their glory is extremely strong and indivisible; they are mighty ones, long-armed and broad-shouldered like a bull; in this way, the day on which these two warriors, they will sound their trumpet, then all the kings, forsaking their modesty will run away and none of them will confront them. —16-243

NARAAJ STANZA

There is one warrior named *sanjog* (coherence), who is considered glorious in every home; he is called unpunishable, invincible and fearless; what description be given about him? —17-244

There is another powerful warrior seen in this sphere of stars; his name is *sukrit* (good deed) and he is considered unconquerable; when he comes out thundering bedecked with his weapons and mounted on his chariot, then he is supremely glorious like the sun. —18-245

Holding his special arrow, sword etc., when this warrior named *amoha* (detachment) will thunder, and when he will be accompanied by the second thundering warrior *alobha*, then infinite forces of the riders of chariots, elephants and horses will run away. —19-246

You may see many warriors lustrous and unpunishable like the sun, who may be persistent ones, worshippers, ascetics and truthful ones; but this unconquerable and pure-limbed warrior is *akaam* (desireless). —20-247

When this warrior named *akrodh* (peaceful) will be there in the battlefield in his fury, then all the fighters, forgetting their modesty, will run away; he is the same warrior, whose body is indivisible, whose form is powerful and who is modest. —21-248

When this ego-less warrior of the Supreme Essence will thunder, he will especially destroy the army and will oppose many fighters, many warriors getting together, taking their unfailing weapons will encounter him in great fury and many warriors, the bows and the dreadful armours will break up. —22-249

All the warrior will emotionally get enraged, will fall upon the enemy and look magnificent like many suns, the warriors will join hands to destroy the forces of the enemies; they will break up the forces constituting the tyrannical fighters. —23-250

The warriors after stepping back will strike their lances and enduring the anguish of many wounds, they will kill innumerable forces; the sword flashing like lightning will create sensation amongst warriors and will chop and throw away their limbs. —24-251

Turning like lions, the warriors will strike lances and will churn the army of the chief generals; the warriors mutually moving away at a distance, will come to fight with the enemy's forces in such a way that the gods, demons, Yakshas, Kinnars, etc., will not recognise them. —25-252

Riding enthusiastically on horses, the warriors will throw the pike immediately and will chop down the infinitely glorious warriors; O king! the warrior named *prem* (love) is a significant fighter, whose greatness is known in all the three worlds. —26-253

NARAAJ STANZA

This warrior of sun-like unique beauty, the killer of enemies, is known by the name of *sanjog* (coherence); there is also another warrior named *shanti* (peace), whom all the people recognise as glorious and powerful. —27-254

This warrior of indivisible and powerful beauty looks highly infuriated like a lion; his name is *supaath* (good religious study); both Surya and Chandra are a witness to it that he never runs away from war. —28-255

He has one disciple, who is known by the name *sukaran* (good action) and is considered a warrior of indestructible brilliance in the whole universe; when that warrior in his fury, thundering like the lion and clouds, will fall upon the enemy, then the dreadful musical instruments will be played and many weapons will strike the blows. —29-256

There is another warrior *suyaag* (good *yajna*), the second is *prabodh* (knowledge) and the third warrior is *daan* (charity), who is indivisible and persistent; there is another warrior named *suniyam* (good principle), who has conquered the whole world; the whole universe and the sun are its witnesses. —30-257

There is another warrior *susatya* (truth) and another one is *santokh* (contentment); the third one is *tapasya* (austerity), who has subjugated all the ten directions; another glorious warrior is *japa* (repetition of the name), who after conquering many wars has assumed detachment. —31-258

CHHAPPAI STANZA

An extremely powerful and potent warrior is named *niyam* (principle) the second warrior is *prem* (love), third one is *sanjam* (restraint) and the fourth one is *dhaira* (patience); the fifth one is *pranayama* (regulation of breath) and the sixth one is called *dhyan* (meditation); this great warrior is considered extremely truthful and glorious, he is also known by the name *dharma* (duty) by the gods, demons, Nagas, and Gandharvas. —32-259

Shubh acharan (good character) is considered the second warrior; the third warrior is *vikram* (the brave) and the fourth one is mighty *buddhi* (intellect); the fifth one is *anuraktata* (loving) and the sixth warrior is *samadhi* (contemplation); *uddam* (effort), *upkaar* (benevolence), etc., are also unconquerable, invincible and ineffacable; seeing them, the enemies forsake their seat and run away, while deviating from their position; the glory of these mighty warriors is spread all over the earth. —33-260

TOMAR STANZA

There is a warrior named *suvichar* (good thought), who has many qualities; there is another warrior named *sanjog* (coherence), who had even conquered Shiva. —34-261

There is one warrior named *homa* (sacrifice), who has made the enemies impatient; another one is *pooja* (worship), who is unequalled in courage by anyone. —35-262

The chief of all the warriors is *anurakt*; in the same way, there is none like *virakt* (unattached). —36-263

Seeing *satsang* (good company) and *bala* (power), the enthusiasm for fighting is increased and in the same way, the warrior named *saneh* (love) is terribly powerful. —37-264

There are also *har-bhakti* (devotion for the Lord) and *preet* (love), with whose light, the whole world is enlightened; the path of yoga of Dutt is also superb and is considered superior at all the places. —38-265

Seeing the war, *krodh* (anger) and *prabodh* (knowledge), in their fury, sounding their trumpets, marched for attack after decorating their forces. —39-266

DOHIRA

In this way, arranging their forces and sounding their trumpets, the attack was made; the way, in which the war was fought, I present its description. —40-267

SHRI-BHAGVATI STANZA

The arms arose, the warriors fought; the trumpets and other musical instruments were played. —41-268

The lances with tassels were lustrous like fire-flames; the warriors taking them began to fight with one another and there was lamentation. —42-269

The elephants trumpeted, the musical instruments were played; the warriors fought and the armours were torn. —43-270

The tabors were played; the Bhairavas wandered in the battlefield; and the warriors saturated with blood fell in the fighting. —44-271

Decorated with arms and weapons, the warriors like Chamunda came to the war-arena. —45-272

The warriors were decorated and the trumpets were sounded; the fighters were enraged like fire and they were not even slightly in senses. —46-273

The warriors were pleased in the war like the fish in water; they were striking blows with their arms and weapons, desirous of getting victorious. —47-274

The bows are infuriated; the warriors are looking splendid and they are destroying the army. —48-275

The goddess Kali is laughing, the Bhairavas are thundering and holding their vessels in the hands, the Yoginis have gathered together for drinking blood. —49-276

The goddess is resplendent and the Goddess Kali is shouting, the Bhairavas are thundering and are sounding their tabors. —50-277

There is shower of weapons and the dreadful arms are crackling; the arms of the demons are being discharged from one side and the arms of gods are being used form the other side. —51-278

The Shailastras, Pavanastras and Meghastras are being showered and the fire-arms are crackling. —52-279

The Hanastras, Kakastras and Meghastras are being showered and the Shukrastras are crackling. —53-280

The warriors are bedecked, the Vyomastras are thundering; the Yakshastras are being discharged and the Kinnarastras are getting exhausted. —54-281

The Gandharvastras are being discharged and the Narastras are also being used; the eyes of all the warriors are restless and all are uttering "I". —55-282

The warriors saturated with blood have fallen in the war-arena and with the sounds of arms and weapons, the warriors are also thundering. —56-283

The groups of the red-eyed heavenly damsels are roaming in the sky for the warriors. —57-284

The horses in flocks are roaming hither and thither and the warriors in their anger, are segmenting them. —58-285

The meditation of the great *sannyasi* Shiva has been broken and even he is listening to the thundering of Gandharvas and the playing of the musical instruments. —59-286

The voice of the shower of Papastras (the sinful arms) and the crackling of Dharmastras (the arms of *dharma*) is being heard; Arogyastras (the health arms) and Bhogyastras (the pleasure arms) are also being discharged. —60-287

Vivadastras (arms of dispute) and Virodhastras (arms of opposition), Kumantrastras (arms of bad spells) and Sumantrastras (arms of auspicious spells) were shot and then burst. —61-288

Kamastras (arms of lust), Krodhastras (the arms of anger) and Virodhastras (arms of opposition) were showered and Vimohastras (arms of detachment) crackled. —62-289

Charitrastras (arms of conduct) were shot, the Mohastras (the arms of attachment) collided, the Trasastras (the arms of fear) rained and Krodhastras (arms of anger) crackled. —63-290

CHAUPAI STANZA

In this way, many warriors of king *viveka* were given a jerk and they left their arms and weapons; then the king himself moved and many types of musical instruments were played. —64-291

The trumpets sounded from both the sides and there were thundering noises; the rain of arrows spread on the whole sky and the ghosts and fiends also got entangled. —65-292

There was steady rain of iron from the sky and there was testing of the great warriors alongwith it; the innumerable warriors gathered together and get contracted; there was dreadful mist on all the four sides. —66-293

CHAUPAI

The king *viveka*, getting enraged gave orders to his whole army; all those warriors who arrayed themselves in an army rushed forward, the poet now tells their names. —67-294

The warriors wearing helmets on their heads and armours on their bodies and bedecked with various kinds of arms and weapons, marched for fighting; the water of the streams dried up in fear. —68-295

DOHIRA

The deadly musical instruments were played from both the directions and the trumpets thundered; the warriors fighting on the strength of both their arms, rushed forward with the zeal for fighting in their mind. —69-296

BHUJANG PRAYAAT STANZA

The warriors thundered in the battlefield and the kettledrums and conches etc., sounded there; there was terrible uproar of the warriors; the arms and weapons were struck and the ghosts and fiends danced. —70-297

Holding the sword, the prominent warriors were fragmented and the high-speed horses ran before the Baitals in the battlefield; the warhorns were blown and the warriors thundered; the horses danced and the mighty warriors struck their blows, while turning over. —71-298

The horses neighed and the bodies of the mighty warriors writhed; then there was clattering of the arms and weapons and the adepts and yogis, getting intoxicated began to dance with the tune of the weapons. —72-299

The dreadful goddesses Kali and Kamakhya shrieked violently and the warriors throwing fire-arms and the Baitals and vultures raised terrible shouts; the sixty-four Yoginis wearing rosaries saturated with blood enthusiastically threw the flames of yoga. —73-300

The sharp knives were thrown in the field, which caused the galloping horses to become furious and the blood of the warriors oozed out and flowed; the horses of good races looked splendid and the Kandhari, Samundari and other types of horses also wandered. —74-301

The speedy horses of Kutch State were running and the horses of Arabia, while running looked like the mounts flying with wings, the dust which arose, covered the sky like this and there was so much mist that the night seemed to have fallen. —75-302

From one side, the followers of Dutt ran and from the second side other people; all the atmosphere became dusty and the chopped corpses fell; the vows of the great vows-observing warriors broke and they enthusiastically mounted on the horses of Tattar and began to dance. —76-303

The dust from the hoofs of the horses covered the chariot of the sun and it deviated from its path and was not seen on the earth; there was a great stampede and the arms and weapons, swords, spears, daggers, etc., were struck. —77-304

Holding his arrow, Dutt discharged it on others and without seeing, the whole army ran away; only one warrior conquered all, many warriors fled; the feet of the warriors were uprooted like the uprooting of the old *palaash* trees by the wind. —78-305

Getting enraged in the war, *lobha* (greed) caused his horse to run; whosoever ran away from him, was saved, he, who stood there, was killed with a jerk; the warrior named *alobha* (non-greed), seeing him, returned and *lobha* discharged so many arrows, which spread over the sky. —79-306

He attacked with ten arrows on the warrior named *dhairya* (patience) and discharged sixty arrows on, making *sanjam* (restraint) as his target; he pierced limbs of *nem* (principle) with his nine arrows and with twenty arrows, he attacked the mighty warrior *vijnan* (science). —80-307

He attacked *pavitrata* (purity) with twenty-five arrows and *archana* (adoration) with eighty arrows, whose limbs were chopped by him; he destroyed the complete *pooja* (worship) with eighty-five arrows; he beat *lajja* (modesty) with his big staff. —81-308

Eighty-two arrows were discharged on *vidya* and thirty-three on *tapasya*; the limbs of *keerti* were pierced with innumerable arrows; the warriors like *alobh* etc., were dealt with nicely. —82-309

He pierced *nir-ahamkara* (egolessness) with eighty arrows and also touched with his arms the waist of *Param Tattva* etc., the limbs of *karuna* (mercy) were cast down with many arrows and nearly one hundred arrows were discharged on the limbs of *shiksha* (learning). —83-310

DOHIRA

Then the warrior named *daan*, taking the arrow of *jnan* (knowledge) in his hand, performed worship and gave offerings, charming it with *dhyan* (attention), he discharged it on that youngman. —84-311

BHUJANG PRAYAAT STANZA

The warrior named *daan* (charity) sprang up in the war-arena, who was the store of arms, weapons and garments; taking ten arrows, he discharged them on the waist-area of *lobha*; he seemed to be swimming in the seven oceans of *krodh*. —85-312

With nine arrows, he pierced the warrior named *anyaya* (injustice) and the warrior named *avarat* was pierced with three arrows; with seven arrows, he wounded the warrior named *krodh* (anger); in this way *brahma-jnan* (knowledge of God) or *dharma* was patiently established. —86-313

Several arrows were discharged at *kalah* (conflict), making him the target and with many arrows the warriors of *vair* (enmity) were killed; many arrows struck the limbs of *aalas* (laziness) and all these warriors fled towards hell. —87-314

With one arrow the limb of *asheel* was pierced and the second arrow was very nicely inflicted on *kutistata*; the comely horses of *abhiman* (ego) were killed and also destroyed the fighters of *anarth*, etc. —88-315

Pipasa (thirst), *kshudha* (hunger), *aalas* (laziness), etc., ran away and knowing the enragement of *daiva* (divinity), *lobha* (greed) also ran away; the destroyer of *aniyam* (indiscipline), *niyam* (principle) also became enraged and that detached one without greed assumed Yogastras (the arms of yoga). —89-316

The head of *kapat* (deception) was broken and he was killed and the dreadful warriors like *rosh* (anger), *moha* (attachment), *kaam* (lust), etc., were also killed in great fury, he shot an arrow on *krodh* (anger) and in this way, the Lord in anger destroyed all the sufferings. —90-317

ROOAAL STANZA

Droha (malice) and *ahamkara* (ego) were also killed with a thousand arrows; no attention was paid, not even slightly, to *daridrata* (lethargy) and *mora* (*moha*); *ashoch* (impurity) and *kumantrana* (bad counsel) were destroyed with many arrows and *kalank* (blemish) was fearlessly pierced with thousands of arrows. —91-318

Kritaghnata (ungratefulness), *vishwasghat* (breach of trust) and *mittayaghaat* (unfriendliness) were also killed; *brahma-dosh* and *raaj-dosh* were finished with Brahmastra (the arm of Brahma); *uchchhatan*, *maaran* and *vashikaran* (controlled), etc., were killed with arrows; *vishaad* (hatred), though considered old one, was not let off. —92-319

The charioteers, horses and the masters of elephants ran away in fear; the great chariot-owners, forsaking their shame, fled away; how should I describe this impossible and dreadful war as to how it was fought? If the same is described hundreds or thousand of times, even then the end of its greatness cannot be known. —93-320

Kalank (blemish), *vibharam* (illusion) and *kritaghnata* (ungratefulness), etc., were killed; no attention was paid, even slightly, to *vishaad*, *vipda*, etc., after killing *mittar-dosh*, *raaj-dosh*, *irsha*, etc., *uchchhatan* (dissatisfaction) and *vishaad* (contention) were driven out of the battlefield. —94-321

Galani (hatred) was pierced with many arrows; *anarth* (injustice) was pierced with a thousand arrows with full power; *kuchaal* (wrong behaviour) was attacked with thousand of fine arrows; *kasht* (distress) and *kutriya* (crooked) were caused to run away. —95-322

CHHAPPAI STANZA

Tapasya inflicted seventy arrows of *atap*; *sheel* was inflicted with ninety arrows; *jaap* struck a thousand arrows to *ajaap* (non-recitation), *kumat* (bad advice) was pierced with twenty arrows and *kukaram* with thirty arrows; ten arrows were shot at *daridrata* (poverty) and *kaam* (lust) was pierced with many arrows; the warrior *aviveka* killed the warrior *virodh* in the war-arena; *sanjam* said, while taking up sword in his hand and getting infuriated in the battlefield. —96-323

Even if the sun rises in the west or the clouds begin to come from the North; if the Meru mountain flies and all the water of the ocean is dried up; even if the teeth of Kal are bent and the hood of Sheshanaga is overturned; even if the Ganges flows contrarily and Harishchandra may forsake the path of truth; even if the world is upturned and the earth stabilised on the back of the bull may burst while sinking, but O king *aviveka*, the heroic discipline of *viveka* will not step back even then. —97-324

I am dumb one, speak with your grace, I am a sacrifice to you and under your refuge.

BHUJANG PRAYAAT STANZA

The great warrior *sanjam* got infuriated; he was proud and viceless; taking up his innumerable arms, he attacked *anarth* and pierced the limbs of *anadat*. —98-325

I speak with your power; there was such a war, to what extent I should describe it? If I speak with thousands of tongues, even then I cannot know the end; the war continued for the years of ten lakh ages and innumerable warriors died. —99-326

I utter with your power; there was blind and rash destruction in war; the sixty-four Yoginis and the fiends danced; the dreadful Kamakhya like Kali danced and the Dakinis (vampires) belched like flames. —100-327

THY POWER

There was terrible war and no one retraced his steps; there were many great warriors and sovereigns there; this war continued in all the worlds and then warriors were not finished even in this dreadful war. —101-328

DOHIRA　　　　　　　　　THY POWER

In that fierce fight the great warriors were chopped quickly; no warrior ran and retraced his steps and this war did not end. —102-329

CHAUPAI　　　　　　　　　THY POWER

The war continued from both sides for twenty lakh ages, but no one was defeated; then the king got agitated and came to Matsyendra. —103-330

(The king said), "O superb sage! instruct me; both of them are great warriors; their opposition does not end and with the desire to get release from them, the whole world is going to end." —104-331

THY POWER

The whole world fought and fell on trying to kill them, but it could not know their end; these dreadful warriors are greatly persistent, greatly heroic and greatly terrible. —105-332

Hearing this Matsyendra remained silent and Parasnath etc., all of them said their things to him; there then occurred a miracle astonishing all and on the same day Charpatnath appeared. —106-333

End of "The Description of the Appearance of Charpatnath" in Bachittar Natak.

Now begins the Description of the Praise of Primal *Purusha*

CHAUPAI

"O king! listen, I speak to you a thing of knowledge; you should not consider both as one; these viceless persons are great archers and brave fighters. —107-334

When Primal *Purusha*, the Lord reflected within Himself and visualised His own form Himself, He uttered the word *Omkara*, because of which the earth, the sky and the whole world was created. —108-335

THY POWER

He created truth from the right side and made falsehood on the left; on taking birth both these warriors began to fight and since that time, they are opposing each other in the world. —109-336

If the span of life is increased by a thousand years, if the thousands of tongues are obtained and if the reflection is made for thousands of years, even then, O Lord! the limits of your form cannot be known. —110-337

The dumb speaks by Thy Power; many sages like Vyas, Parashar, Shringi, etc., have mentioned it; a Brahma of thousands of faces has been seen, but all of them could not know Thy limits. —111-338

DOHIRA   **THY POWER**

The mighty ocean, many heroes, sages, Gandharvas, Mahants, etc., have been feeling agitated since crores of *kalpas* (ages), but all of them could not know Thy limits. —112-339

BHUJANG PRAYAAT STANZA   **I SPEAK BY THY POWER**

"O lion-like king! whatever I am saying to you, listen to it attentively and do not oppose it; that Primal *Purusha* Lord, is without beginning, unconquerable, without secret, uncombustible and without form. —113-340

He is without Name and place; He is indestructible, without beginning, unconquerable, fearless and without hatred; He is infinite master of the universe and the most Ancient One; He is present, future and past. —114-341

He has conquered in this world all the yogis, the hermits with matted locks, performers of *yajnas*, the water-dwellers and Nishachars, celibates, yogis, the powerful warriors, wearers of fire-flames around their necks and the Chhattarpals of mountains have been kept under His subordination. — 115-342

Consider all the *yantras* and *mantras* as false and consider all those religions as hollow, which are deluded by the learning of *tantras*; without having hopes on that One Lord, you will be disappointed from all others sides; without the One Name of the Lord, nothing else will be of any use. —116-343

THY POWER

If the powers are realised through *mantras* and *yantras*, then no one will wander from door to door; remove your attention from all other sides, assuming only one hope in the mind and without the one action of the meditation on the Lord, consider all else as illusion. —117-344

When the king heard these words of the yogi, he became fearful in his mind like the oscillation of water; he forsook all the hopes and despairs from his mind and uttered these words to that great yogi. —118-345

RASAAVAL STANZA   THY POWER

"O great sage! you have been bestowed with all the powers; I request you to guide me." —119-346

The warriors of both the sides, persistent and enraged, ever remembering the Lord and destroyers of others uptil ocean. —120-347

They are the ones who resist, who fight persistently, who are severe and cruel and are the smashers of the enemies. —121-348

CHAUPAI   THY POWER

If I cannot conquer them, I shall burn myself on the funeral pyre; O sage! I could not conquer them; my strength and courage have weakened. —122-349

Thinking in this way in his mind, the king apparently addressed all; "I am a very great king and I have conquered the whole world." —123-350

He, who has told me to conquer both these warriors *viveka* and *aviveka*, he has agitated me and driven my life to deception; both of them are mighty warriors; the whole world is conquered, on conquering them. —124-351

Now they will not go away from me, O sage! describe them to me with clarity; now I prepare my own funeral pyre within your view, and sit within the fire-flames. —125-352

After preparing the funeral pure, he took bath and wore the garments of deep orange colour on his body; many people forbade him and even fell at his feet. —126-353

Giving in charity various types of ornaments and garments, the king prepared a seat within the pyre; he burnt his body with various kinds of fires, but the flames became cold instead of burning him. —127-354

TOMAR STANZA

Getting infuriated, Parasnath burnt the fire in his hand, which was dreadful in sight, but became cold there. —128-355

Then he got emerged the yoga-fire, which was burning dreadfully; he killed himself with that fire and the people of the city continued to see that great king. —129-356

Then with many grass-blades, the faggots alongwith *ghee* (clarified butter), the flames of fire arose, in which the king was burnt and his body was reduced to ashes. —130-357

That pyre continued to burn for several years, when the body of the king was reduced to ashes and he abandoned the attachment of wealth and place. —131-358

End of "The Description of the Praise of Primal *Purusha*" in Bachittar Natak.

* * *

HYMNS OF THE TENTH GURU

The Lord is one and the Victory is of the Lord

RAMKALI OF THE TENTH KING

O mind! the asceticism be practised in this way consider your house as the forest and remain unattached within yourself.

Consider continence as the matted hair, yoga as the ablution and daily observances as your nail, consider the knowledge as the preceptor giving lessons to you and apply the Name of the Lord as ashes. —1

Eat less and sleep less, cherish mercy and forgiveness, practise gentleness and contentment and remain free from three modes. —2

Keep your mind unattached from lust, anger, greed, insistence and infatuation, Then you will visualise the Supreme Essence and realise the supreme *Purusha*. —3-I

RAMKALI OF THE TENTH KING

O mind! the yoga be practised in this way; consider the Truth as the horn, sincerity the necklace and meditation as ashes to be applied to your body.

Make self-control your lyre and the prop of the Name as your alms, then the supreme Essence will be played like the main string creating savoury divine music. —1

The wave of colourful tune will arise, manifesting the song of knowledge, The gods, demons and sages would be amazed enjoying their ride in heavenly chariots. —2

While instructing the self in the garb of self-restraint and reciting God's name inwardly, the body will always remain like gold and become immortal. —3-II

RAMKALI OF THE TENTH KING

O man! fall at the feet of the supreme *Purusha;* why are you sleeping in worldly attachment, awake sometimes and be vigilant?

O animal! why do you preach to others, when you are quite ignorant? Why are you gathering the sins? Forsake sometimes the poisonous enjoyment. —1

Consider these actions as illusions and devote yourself to righteous actions, absorb yourself in the remembrance of the Name of the Lord and abandon and run away from sins. —2

So that the sorrows and sins do not afflict you and you may escape the trap of death, if you want to enjoy all the comforts, then absorb yourself in the Love of the Lord. —3-III

RAGA SORATHA OF THE TENTH KING

O Lord! You alone can protect my honour, O blue-throated Lord of men! O the Lord of forests wearing blue vests!

O supreme *Purusha*! supreme *Ishwara*! Master of all! Holiest divinity! living on air, O the Lord of Lakshmi; the greatest light! The destroyer of the demons Madhu; and the bestower of salvation. —1

O the Lord without evil, without decay, without sleep, without poison and the saviour from hell! O the ocean of mercy! The seer of all times! And the destroyer of evil actions! —2

O the wielder of bow! The patient! The prop of earth! The Lord without evil! And wielder of the sword! I am unwise, I take refuge at Thy Feet, catch hold of my hand and save me. —3-IV

RAGA KALYAN OF THE TENTH KING

Do not accept anyone else except God as the creator of the universe He, the unborn, unconquerable and immortal, was in the beginning, consider Him as supreme *Ishwara*.

What then, if on coming into the world, one killed about ten demons, and displayed several phenomena to all and caused others to call Him Brahman (God). —1

How can He be called God, the destroyer, the creator, the almighty and eternal, who could not save himself from the wound-causing sword of mighty Death. —2

O fool! listen, how can he cause you to cause the dreadful ocean of *samsara* (world), when he himself is drowned in great ocean? You can escape the trap of death only when you catch hold of the prop of the world and take refuge in Him. —3-V

KHYAL OF THE TENTH KING

Convey to the dear friend the condition of the disciple, without Thee, the taking over of quilt is like disease and living in the house is like living with serpents, the flask is like the spike, the cup is like a dagger and (the separation) is like enduring the chopper of the butchers, the pallet of the beloved friend is most pleasing and the worldly pleasures are like furnace. VI

TILANG KAFI OF THE TENTH KING

The supreme destroyer is alone the creator, He is in the beginning and in the end, He is the infinite entity, the creator and the destroyer.

The calumny and priase are equal to Him and He has no friend, no foe, of what crucial necessity He became the charioteer? —1

He, the giver of salvation, has no father, no mother, no son and no grandson, O what necessity He caused others to call Him the son of Devaki? —2

He, who has created gods, demons, directions and the whole expanse, on what analogy should He be called Murar? —3-VII

RAGA BILAWAL OF THE TENTH KING

How can He be said to come in human form? The Siddha (adept) in deep meditation became tired of the discipline on not seeing Him in any way.

Narad, Vyas, Parashar, Dhruva all meditated on Him, The Vedas and Puranas became tired and forsook insistence, since He could not be visualised. —1

By demons, gods, ghosts, spirits, He was called indescribable, He was considered the finest of the fine and the biggest of the big. —2

He, the one, created the earth, heaven and the nether-world and was called "Many," That man is saved form the noose of death, who takes refuge in the Lord. —3-VIII

RAGA DEVGANDHARI OF THE TENTH KING

Do not recognise anyone except one, He is always the destroyer, the creator and the almighty; He the creator is omniscient.

Of what use is the worship of the stones with devotion and sincerity in various ways? The hand became tired of touching the stones, because no spiritual power accrued. —1

Rice, incense and lamps are offered, but the stones do not eat anything, O fool! where is the spiritual power in them, so that they may bless you with some boon. —2

Ponder in mind, speech and action; if they had any life, they could have given you something, none can get salvation in any way without taking refuge in One Lord. —3-IX

RAGA DEVGANDHARI OF THE TENTH KING

None can be saved without the name of the Lord, He, who controls all the fourteen worlds, how can you run away from Him?

You cannot be saved by repeating the name of Ram and Rahim, Brahma, Vishnu, Shiva, Sun and Moon all are subject to the power of death. —1

Vedas, Puranas and the Holy *Quran* and all religious systems proclaim Him as Indescribable, Indra, Sheshanaga and the supreme sages meditated on Him for ages, but could not visualise Him. —2

He, whose form and colour are not known, how can be called black? You can only be liberated from the noose of death, when you cling to his feet. —3-X

* * *

THIRTY-THREE SWAYYAS

**The Lord is One and the Victory is of the Lord
The Utterance from the Holy mouth of the Tenth King**

SWAYYA

He is the true Khalsa (Sikh), who remembers the ever-awakened Light throughout night and day and does not bring anyone else in the mind; he practises his vow with whole-hearted affection and does not believe in even by oversight, the graves, Hindu monuments and monasteries; he does not recognise anyone else except One Lord, not even the bestowal of charities, performance of merciful acts, austerities and restraint on pilgrim stations; the perfect light of the Lord illuminates his heart, then consider him as the immaculate Khalsa. —1

He is ever the truth-incarnate, pledged to truth, the primal one. Beginningless, unfathomable and unconquerable; He is comprehended through His qualities of charitableness, mercifulness, austerity, restraint, observances, kindliness and generosity; He is primal, blemishless, beginingless, maliceless, limitless, indiscriminate and fearless; He is the formless, markless Lord protector of the lowly and ever compassionate. —2

That Great Lord is primal, blemishless, guiseless, truth-incarnate and ever-effulgent light; the essence in absolute meditation is the destroyer of all and pervades in every heart; O Lord! Thou are the Primal, from the beginning of the ages; Thou pervadest everywhere in everyone; Thou art the protector of the lowly, merciful, graceful, primal, unborn and eternal. —3

Thou art the primal, guiseless, invincible and eternal Lord; the Vedas and the Semitic holy texts could not know Thy mystery; O protector of the lowly, O compassionate and treasure of mercy Lord! Thou art ever truth and pervaders in all; Seshanaga, Indra, Ganesh, Shiva and also the Shrutis (Vedas) could not know Thy mystery; O my foolish mind! why have you forgotten such a Lord? —4

That Lord is described as eternal, beginningless, blemishless, limitless, invincible and truth-incarnate; He is powerful, effulgent, known throughout the world; His mention has been made in various ways at the same place; O my poor mind! why do you not recognise that blemishless Lord? —5

O Lord! Thou art indestructible, beginningless, limitless and ever truth-incarnate and creator; Thou art the sustainer of all the beings living in water and on plain; the Vedas, *Quran*, Puranas together have mentioned many thoughts about you; but O Lord! there is none else like Thee in the whole universe; Thou art the supremely chaste Lord of this universe. —6

Thou art considered primal, unfathomable, invincible, indiscriminate, accountless, unconquerable and limitless; Thou art considered pervasive in the present, past and future; the gods, demons, Nagas, Narada and Sharda have been ever thinking of Thee as truth-incarnate; O protector of the lowly and the treasure of grace! Thy mystery could not be comprehended by the *Quran* and the Puranas. —7

O Truth-Incarnate Lord! Thou hast created the true modifications of Vedas and Katebs (Semitic texts); at all times, the gods, demons and mountains, past and present have also considered Thee truth-incarnate; Thou art primal, from the beginning of the ages and limitless, Who can be realised with profound insight in these worlds; O my mind! I cannot say as to from which significant individual I have heard the description of such a Lord? —8

The gods, demons, mountains, Nagas and adepts practised severe austerities; the Vedas, the Puranas and the *Quran*, all were tired of singing His praises, even then they could not recognise His mystery; the earth, sky, nether-world, directions and anti-directions are all pervaded by that Lord; the whole earth is filled with His grandeur; and O mind! what new thing you have done for me by eulogising Him? —9

The Vedas and Katebs could not comprehend His mystery and the adepts have been defeated in practising contemplation, various thoughts have been mentioned about God in Vedas, Shastras, Puranas and Smritis; that Lord God is primal, beginningless and unfathomable; stories are current about Him that He redeemed Dhruva, Prahlad and Ajaamil; by remembering His name even Ganika was saved and the support of His name is also with us. —10

All know that Lord as beginningless, unfathomable and adept-incarnate the Gandharvas, Yakshas, men, Nagas consider him on the earth, and all the four directions; all the worlds, directions anti-directions, gods, demons all worship Him; O ignorant mind! by following whom, you have forgotten that self-existent and omniscient Lord? —11

Someone has tied the stone-idol around his neck and some one has accepted Shiva as the Lord; someone considers the Lord within the temple or the mosque; someone calls him Ram or Krishna and someone believes in His incarnations, but my mind has forsaken all useless actions and has accepted only the One Creator. —12

If we consider Ram, the Lord as Unborn, then how did he take birth from the womb of Kaushalya? He, who is said to be the Kal (destroyer) of Kal (death), then why did he not become subjugated himself before Kal? If he is called the truth- incarnate, beyond enmity and opposition, then why did he become the charioteer of Arjuna? O mind! you only consider him the Lord God, whose mystery could not be known to anyone. —13

Krishna himself is considered the treasure of grace, then why did the hunter shot his arrow at him? He has been described as redeeming the clans of others, then he caused the destruction of his own clan; he is said to be unborn and beginningless, then how did he come into the womb of Devaki? He, who is considered without any father or mother, then why did he cause Vasudeva to be called his father? —14

Why do you consider Shiva or Brahma as the Lord? There is none amongst Ram, Krishna and Vishnu, who may be considered as the Lord of the universe by you; relinquishing the one Lord, you remember many gods and goddesses; in this way you prove Shukadeva, Parashar, etc., as liars; all the so-called religions are hollow; I only accept the One Lord as the Providence. —15

Someone tells Brahma as the Lord God and someone tells the same thing about Shiva; someone considers Vishnu as the hero of the universe and says that only on remembering him, all the sins will be destroyed; O fool! think about it a thousand times, all of them will leave you at the time of death, therefore you should only meditate on Him, Who is there in the present and Who will also be there in future. —16

He, Who created crores of Indras and Upendras and then destroyed them; He, Who created innumerable gods, demons, Sheshanagas, tortoises, birds, animals, etc., and for knowing whose mystery, Shiva and Brahma are performing austerities even till today, but could not know His end; He is such a Guru, Whose mystery could not be comprehended also by Vedas and Katebs and my Guru has told me the same thing. —17

You are deceiving people by wearing matted locks on the head, extending the nails in the hands and practising false trance; smearing the ashes on your face, you are wandering, while deceiving all the gods and goddesses; O yogi! you are wandering under the impact of greed and you have forgotten all the discipline of yoga; in this way your self-respect has been lost and no work could be accomplished; the Lord is not realised without true love. —18

O foolish mind! why are you absorbed in heresy? because you will destroy your self-respect through heresy; why are you deceiving the people on becoming a cheat? And in this way you are losing the merit both in this and the next world; you will not get a place, even very small one in the abode of the Lord; therefore O foolish creature! you may became careful even now, because by wearing a garb only, you will not be able to realise that accountless Lord. —19

Why do you worship stones? Because the Lord God is not within those stones; you may only worship Him, whose adoration destroys clusters of sins; with the remembrance of the Name of the Lord, the ties of all sufferings are removed; ever meditate on that Lord because the hollow religious retuals will not be bring any fruit. —20

The hollow religion became fruitless and O being! you have lost crores of years by worshipping the stones; you will not get power with the worship of stones, the strength and glory will only decrease; in this way, the time was lost uselessly and nothing was achieved and you are not ashamed; O foolish intellect; you have not remembered the Lord and have wasted your life in vain. —21

You may even perform the austerities for an age, but these stones will not fulfil your wishes and please you; they will not raise their hands and grant you the boon; they cannot be trusted, because in the time of any difficulty, they will not reach and save you, therefore O ignorant and persistent being! you may become careful, these hollow religious rituals will destroy your honour. —22

All the beings are entrapped in the noose of death and no Ram or Rasul (Prophet) could escape from it; that Lord created demons, gods and all other beings living on the earth and also destroyed them; those who are known as incarnations in the world, they also ultimately repented and passed away; therefore O my mind! who do you not run and catch the feet of that Supreme Kal i.e., the Lord. —23

Brahma came into being under the control of Kal (Death) and taking his staff and pot in his hand, he wandered on the earth; Shiva was also under the control of Kal and wandered in various countries far and near; the world under the control of Kal was also destroyed, therefore all are aware of that Kal; therefore, abandoning the differentiation of Vedas and Katebs, accept only Kal as the Lord, the ocean of grace. —24

O fool! you have wasted your time in various desires and did not remember in your heart that most gracious Kal or Lord; O shameless! abandon your false shame, because that Lord has amended the works of all, forsaking the thoughts of good and bad; O fool! why are you thinking of riding on the ass of *maya* instead of riding on elephants and horses? You have not remembered the Lord and are damaging the task in false shame and honour. —25

You have studied Vedas and Katebs for a very long time, but still you could not comprehend His mystery; you had been wandering at many places, worshipping him, but you never adopted that One Lord; you had been wandering with bowed head in the temples of stones, but you realised nothing; O foolish mind! you were only entangled in your bad intellect abandoning that effulgent Lord. —26

The person, who goes to the hermitage of yogis and causes the yogis to remember the name of Gorakh; who, amongst the *sannyasis* tells them the *mantra* of Dattatreya as true, who going amongst the Muslims, speaks about their religious faith, consider him only showing off the greatness of his learning and does not talk about the mystery of that Creator Lord. —27

He, who on the persuasion of the Yogis gives in charity all his wealth to them; who squanders his belongings to *sannyasis* in the name of Dutt, who on the direction of the masands (the priests appointed for collection of funds) takes the wealth of Sikhs and gives it to me, then I think that these are only the methods of selfish-disciplines; I ask such a person to instruct me about the mystery of the Lord. —28

He, who serves his disciples and impresses the people and tells them to hand over the victuals to him and present before him whatever they had in their homes; he also asks them to think of him and not to remember the name of anyone else; consider that he has only a *mantra* to give, but he would not be pleased without taking back something, —29

He, who puts oil in his eyes and just shows to the people that he was weeping for the love of the Lord; he, who himself serves meals to his rich disciples, but gives nothing to the poor one even on begging and even does not want to see him, then consider that base fellow is merely looting the people and does not also sing the praises of the Lord. —30

He closes his eyes like a crane and exhibits deceit to the people; he bows his head like a hunter and the cat seeing his meditation feels shy; such a person wanders merely with the desire to collect wealth and loses the merit of this as well as the next world; O foolish creature! you have not worshipped the Lord and had been uselessly entangled in the domestic as well as outside affairs. —31

Why do you tell repeatedly to these people for performing the actions of heresy? These works will not be of any use to them; why are you running hither and thither for wealth? You may do anything, but you will not be able to escape from the noose of Yama; even your son, wife and friend will not bear witness to you and none of them will speak for you; therefore O fool! take care of yourself even now, because ultimately you will have to go alone. —32

After abandoning the body, O fool! your wife will also runs away calling you a ghost; the son, wife and friend, all will say that you should be taken out immediately and cause you to go to the cemetery; after passing away, the home, store and earth will become alien, therefore, O great animal! take care of yourself even now, because ultimately you have to go alone. —33

* * *

THE SWAYYAS IN PRAISE OF THE KHALSA

The Lord is One and the Victory is of the Lord, the Utterance from the Holy Mouth of the Tenth King

SWAYYA

O Brahmin! whatever the providence has recorded, it will surely happen, therefore forsake your sorrow; there is no fault of mine in this; I have only forgotten (to serve you earlier); do not get enraged on my error; I shall surely cause to send the quilt, bed etc., as religious gift; do not be anxious about that the Kshatriyas had been performing the jobs for the Brahmins; now be kind to them, looking towards them.—1

By the kindness of these Sikhs, I have conquered the wars and also by their kindness, I have bestowed charities; by their kindness the clusters of sins have been destroyed and by their kindness my house is full of wealth and materials; by their kindness I have received education and by their kindness all my enemies have been destroyed; by their kindness I have been greatly adorned, otherwise there are crores of humble persons like me. —2

I like to serve them and my mind is not pleased to serve others; the charities bestowed on them are really good and the charities given to others do not appear to be nice; the charities bestowed on them will bear fruit in future and the charities given to others in the world are unsavoury in front of donation given to them; in my house, my mind, my body, my wealth and even my head everything belongs to them. —3

DOHIRA

Just as the straws while burning in ire are flabbergasted, in the same way, the Brahmin got enraged in his mind and thinking about his means of sustenance, he wept. —4

Shri Shastar Naam-Maala Purana

The Rosary of the Names of Weapons composed with the
Support of the Primal Power by the Tenth King

DOHIRA

O Lord! protect us by creating *saang* (a kind of spear), *sarohi* (a kind of sword), *saif* (sword), *as* (sword), *teer* (arrow), *tupak* (gun), *talwaar* (sword), and other weapons and armours causing the destruction of the enemies. —1

O Lord! create *as* (sword), *kripaan* (sword), *dharadhari* (protector of the earth), *sel* (pike), *soop* (arrow), *jamdaadh* (dagger), *tegh* (sword), *teer* (arrow), *talwar* (sword) causing the destruction of armours and enemies. —2

As (sword), *kripaan* (sword), *khanda* (double-edged sword), *khadag* (sword), *tupak* (gun), *tabar* (battle-axe), *teer* (arrow), *saif* (sword), *sarohi* (sword), and *saihathi* (spear), all these are our adorable seniors. —3

Thou art the *teer* (arrow), Thou art *saihathi* (spear), Thou art *tabar* (battle-axe) and *talwaar* (sword); he, who remembers Thy name crosses the dreadful ocean of existence. —4

Thou art the Kal (Death), thou art the Goddess Kali, Thou art the sabre and arrow, Thou art the sign of victory today and Thou art the hero of the world. —5

Thou art the *sool* (spike), *saihathi* (spear), and *tabar* (hatchet), Thou art the *nikhang* (quiver) and *baan* (arrow), Thou art the *kataari* (dagger), *sel* (pike) all and Thou art the *kard* (symbolic sword) and *kripaan* (sword). —6

Thou art all the arms and weapons, Thou art the *nikhang* (quiver), and the *kavach* (armour); Thou art the destroyer of the armours and Thou art also all-pervading. —7

Thou art the cause of peace and prosperity and the essence of learning; Thou art the creator of all and the redeemer of all. —8

Thou art the day and night and Thou art the creator of all the *jivas* (beings), causing disputes among them; Thou doest all this in order to view Thy own sport. —9

O Lord! protect us by smashing the armours with the bows of Thy hands with the help of *as* (sword), *kripaan* (sword), *khanda* (double-edged sword), *kharag* (sword), *saif* (sword), *tegh* (sword), and *talwaar* (sword). —10

Thou art *katari* (dagger), *jamdaah* (dagger), *bichhuaa* (crooked dagger) and *baan* (arrow) power! I am a serf of Thy Lord's feet, kindly protect me. —11

Thou art *baank* (curved knife), *bajar* (pike), *bichhuaa* (crooked dagger), *tabar* (battle-axe) and *talwaar* (sword); Thou art the *kataari* (dagger) and *saihathi* (spear); protect me. —12

Thou art *gurj* (mace), *gadaa* (mace), *teer* (arrow), and *tufang* (gun), protect me ever considering me as Thy slave. —13

Thou art the *chhurri* (chopper) the enemy-killing *karad* (symbolic-sword), and the *khanjar* (sword), are Thy names; Thou are the adorable Power of the world, kindly protect me. —14

Firstly Thou createst the world, and then the paths; then Thou createst the disputes and also help them. —15

Thou are Machh (Fish incarnation), Kachh (Tortoise incarnation) and Varaha (the Boar incarnation); Thou art also the Dwarf incarnation; Thou art also Narasingh and Buddha and Thou art the Essence of the whole world. —16

Thou art Rama, Krishna and Vishnu; Thou art the subjects of the whole world and Thou art also the sovereign. —17

Thou art the Brahmin, Kshatriya, the king and the poor; Thou art also *saam* (sweet speech), *daam* (generous), *dand* (punishment), a d *bhed* (discrimination), and also other remedies. —18

Thou art the head, trunk and the life-force of all the creatures; the whole world imbibes all the learning from Thee and elucidates the Vedas. —19

Thou art the significant arrow fitted in the bow and Thou art also called the warrior Kaibar; O Thou called by various names of the arrows! You may also do my job. —20

Thy house is the quiver and Thou killest like deer the enemies by becoming the shaft-power; the reality is that Thou killest the enemies beforehand and the sword strikes later on. —21

Thou art the axe which tears away the enemies and also Thou art the noose, which binds down; Thou art supremely enduring One also; on whomsoever Thou didst bestow the boon, Thou didst make him the king of the world. —22

Thou art the sword and dagger chopping the enemies and considering Indra as Thy devotee, Thou didst bestow on him the position of the king of gods. —23

Yamdhaar and *yamdadh* and all other names of the weapons for the destruction of the warriors, Thou has folded up and bound all their power in Thyself. —24

Baank (curved knife), *bajar* (pike), *bichhuaa* (crooked dagger), and the shafts of love, on whomsoever Thou didst shower Thy grace they all became the sovereign of the world. —25

The lion is Thy weapon like the sword in the war, which destroys the enemies; he, on whom, Thou didst shower Thy grace, he was redeemed from the noose of Yama. —26

Thou art the *saif* (sword) and *sarohi* (sword) and Thy name is the destroyer of the enemies; You abide always in our heart and fulfil our tasks. —27

End of the first chapter entitled "The Praise of the Primal Power" in
Shri Shastar Naam-Maala Purana.

The Description of the Names of Discus

DOHIRA

Putting the word *kavach* in the beginning and adding the word *ar-deha* at the end, the wise people know all the other names of *kripaan*. —28

The word "Shatru" is uttered in the beginning and the word "Dusht" is spoken at the end and in this way all the names of Jagannath are adopted in the heart. —29

Saying the word "Prithvi" in the beginning and then uttering the word "Balak," all the Names of the Lord are stuffed in the mind. —30

Uttering the word "Sarishti" in the beginning and then the word "Nath," all the names of the Lord are adopted in the heart. —31

Uttering the word "Singh" in the beginning and then the word "Vahan," the poets may in this way say all the names of Durga, the Mother of the world. —32

That Lord is the destroyer of the enemies, Creator of the world and also the vanquisher of the foolish people in this world. His name should be remembered, by hearing which all the suffering come to an end. —33

Uttering the names of all the weapons, and saying the word "Pati" in the beginning and at the end, all the names of *kripaan* are adopted in the heart. —34

It plays in the limb of Kshatriyas; it is called *kharag, khanda* or the enemy of Kshatriyas; it brings the end of war; it is the destroyer of hides; these are thoughtfully spoken names of the sword. —35

It is described as the goddess bringing the end of all elements and the destroyer of all the suffering; O the sword-Bhavani (Goddess)! You are the destroyer of fear bring the happiness to all. —36

ARIL

If the word "Ar" is said after uttering the word "Bhoot," then all the names of the sword are uttered; if the word "Dhanu" is spoken after uttering all the names of "Mrig" (deer), then all these are the names of *khanda,* which is true. —37

DOHIRA

After speaking the names of "Yama" in the beginning, if the word "Radan" (tooth) is uttered, then O poets! the names of Jamdadh can be understood correctly. —38

Speaking the word "Udar" in the beginning and then uttering the word "Ar," the thoughts of all the names of Jamdadh can be manifested correctly. —39

After uttering "Mrig-Greevaa" and "Sir-Ar" and then speaking the word "As," all the names of *kharag* can be spoken. —40

Uttering correctly the words "Kar, Karantak, Kashtripu, Kalayudh, Karvaar, Karachol, etc. the names of *kripaan* can be spoken. —41

After uttering "Hast, Kari, Kar" in the beginning and then saying the word "Ar" is caused to be heard, then the names of *kripaan*, the king of weapons are formed; O *kripaan*! do help me. —42

O Sarohi, the symbol of victory! you are like a lion; there is none other like you; O creatures! if all of you remember Tegh, then all of you will be redeemed. —43

Uttering the words "Khag, Mrig, Yaksha, Bhujang, Gana, etc.," in the beginning and then speaking "Ar," the resultant words mean *talwaar* (sword). —44

In other countries, its names Halabbi, Junabbi, Magharbi, Misri, Una, Saif, Sirohi, etc. are the names of *kripaan*, the Lord of weapons, which has conquered the countries like Ram, Sham, etc. —45

Known as "Kanti" in Yemen and renowned as Bhagvati, the chief of all weapons in India, it had been assumed by Kalki incarnation himself. —46

Uttering the word "Shakit" in the beginning and then speaking the word "Shakat," all the names of *saihathi* are uttered. —47

Firstly utterings the word "Subhat" and then saying "Avdeh," the wise people understand the names of *saihathi* in their mind. —48

Speaking the word "Sannah" in the beginning and then saying the word "Ripu," all the names of *saihathi* are spoken cleverly. —49

Uttering the word "Kumbh" in the beginning, then saying the word "Ar," O wise people! you may understand in your mind all the names of *saihathi*. —50

After uttering the word "Tantraan" and then saying the word "Ar," O wise people! all the names of *saihathi* are said with interest. —51

Saying "Yashtishwar" in the beginning and then uttering "Arddhang," all the names of *saihathi* can be described. —52

Saihathi, manifesting the powerful form of the lance and war, which is also the best amongst the weapons, was used by the mighty warrior Indra, taking it in his own hand for conquering the war. —53

Chhattardhar, Mrigvijai, Karar, etc. are its names; it is the donor of all the powers and also the treasure of infinite powers. —54

Uttering Lakshman and Ghatichkachin in the beginning and then saying "Ar," many names of *shakat* (*kripaan*) are evloved. —55

She is the one which plants and frightens; she is also called *bhaala* (spear) and *neja* (lance); *barchhi*, *saihathi*, *shakat*, etc. are the names worth concentrating in respect of war in the mind. —56

Uttering the word Vishnu in the beginning and then saying Shastar, many names of Sudarshan continue to be formed. —57

Saying firstly the word "Mura" and then uttering the word "Marden," the wise people understand the name of Sudharshan Chakra. —58

Saying "Madhu" in the beginning and then uttering "Ha" the poets speak correctly the names of Sudharshan Chakra. —59

Uttering firstly the word "Narakasura" and then the word "Ripu" is pronounced, O wise people! The names of Sudharshan Chakra are comprehended. —60

Uttering the name of the demon Bakatra and then speaking the word "Shoodan," the names of Sudarshan Chakra and spoken. —61

Naming Chanderinath Shishupal in the beginning and then speaking the word "Ripu," the names of Sudarshan Chakra are formed. —62

Uttering "Narakasura" firstly and then saying the

SHRI SHASTAR NAAM-MAALA PURANA

word "Mardan," the names of Sudarshan Chakra are uttered correctly. —63

Uttering the words "Krishna, Vishnu" and then saying the words "Anuj" and "Aayudh," many names of Sudarshan Chakra continue to be evolved. —64

Speaking the words "Vajra and Anuj" in the beginning and then adding the word "Shastar." The names of Sudarshan Chakra are known. —65

Uttering the word "Virah" in the beginning and then speaking many names of weapons, the names of Sudarshan Chakra continue to be formed. —66

Uttering firstly the name of *Ishwara*, the treasure of all powers and then adding the word "Shastar," the names of Chakra continue to be formed. —67

Uttering the word "Girdhar" in the beginning and then speaking the word "Aayudh," many names of Sudarshan Chakra continue to be evolved. —68

Speaking the word "Kalinath" in the beginning and then adding the word "Shastar" at the end, innumerable names of Sudarshan Chakra continue to be formed. —69

Uttering firstly the name of the killer of Kansa-Keshi i.e., Krishna and then reflecting on the names of weapons, the poets pronounce the names of Sudarshan Chakra. —70

Saying the words "Bakasura and Baki" and then uttering the word "Shastru," the names of Sudarshan Chakra continue to be formed. —71

Uttering the Name of the Lord, the destroyer of sins, and then describing the weapons, the wise people know the names of Sudarshan Chakra. —72

Speaking various names of "Upendra" and then adding the word "Shastar," the learned people comprehend all the names of Sudarshan Chakra. —73

Speech of the Poet
DOHIRA

All the warriors and poets should understand this fact nicely that there is not even the slightest difference between Vishnu and the names of his Chakra. —74

End of the second chapter entitled "Names of Chakra" in Shri Shastar Naam-Maala Purana.

Now begins the Description of Shri *Baan* (Arrow)

DOHIRA

O significant *baan* (arrow), the son of the bow and destroyer of the armour! Ever bring victory to us and fulfil our tasks. —75

Uttering first the word "Dhanush" and then the word "Agraj," all the names of *baan* can be comprehended correctly. —76

Uttering first the word "Panch" and then the word "Agraj," all the names of *baan* continue to be evolved. —77

Uttering the names of Nikhang (quiver) and then describing "Vanshi," all the names of *baan* can be known. —78

After naming all the deer and then uttering the word "Ha," all the names of *baan* are comprehended in mind. —79

After uttering all the names of "Kavach" (armour) and then adding the word "Bhedak" with them, all the names of *baan* continue to be evolved. —80

After uttering the names of "Charam" and then adding the word "Chhedak," the wise people come to know all the names of *baan* in their mind. —81

After uttering the name "Subhat" and then adding the word "Ha," the wise people tell all the names of *baan*. —82

Uttering the names of all the birds and then adding the word "Par" with them, the wise people recognise the names of *baan*. —83

After adding the word "Antak" with the words "Pakshi, Paresh and Pankhdhar" all the names of *baan* are recognised in mind. —84

Uttering all the names of "Aakaash" and then saying the word "Char," the wise people recognise all the names of *baan*. —85

After saying the words "Khe, Aakaash, Nabh, and Gagan" then uttering the word "Char," the wise people may comprehend correctly all the names of *baan*. —86

After speaking the words "Aasmaan, Sipihir, Div,

Gardoon, etc., and then saying word "Char," the names of *baan* are known. —87

Uttering the name "Chandra" in the beginning and then adding the word "Deh" and afterwards speaking the word "Char," the names of *baan* are formed. —88

After adding the word "Char" at the end of the words "Go, Marich, Kiran, Chhattardhar, etc.," the names of *baan* are formed. —89

After uttering the words "Rajnishwar and Dinha" and adding the word "Dhurandhar" at the end, the names of *baan* are evolved. —90

Saying the word "Chardhar" alongwith the words "Ratri, Nisha and Dinghatini," all the names of *baan* are evolved. —91

After uttering the name "Raatri," then speaking "Char" and afterwards saying the word "Dhar," all the names of *baan* can be remembered. —92

The words "Raarti, Andhkaarpati, Nishpati, etc.," are known by the name Chandra-baan, which in the form of "Chandrama" (moon), kill the forms steeped in darkness. —93

Saying the names of all the rays, then uttering the word "Dhar" and afterwards repeating the word "Dhar" again, all the names of *baan* are known. —94

Saying all the names of "Samudra" (ocean), adding the word "Shatdeh" at the end and afterwards uttering the word "Dhar," all the names of *baan* come forward. —95

After saying the word "Samudra" (ocean), the Lord of water and the Lord of the streams then uttering the word "Shatdeh" and afterwards saying the word "Dhar," all the names of *baan* can be comprehended. —96

After uttering the words "Neeralya and Saritadhpati," then adding the word "Shat" and afterwards saying the word "Dhar," the names of *baan* are pronounced. —97

Naming once all the disputes and then saying the word "Shatdhar," many names of *baan* get evolved. —98

Naming the fish remaining alive in water, then adding the word "Aashraya" with them and then saying the word "Shatdhar," the names of *baan* continue to be described. —99

Naming the Nagas (serpents) found on the earth, and adding the word "Dharshat" and then saying the word "Dhar," the names of *baan* are known. —100

Uttering the word "Ar" after the word "Indra" and then adding the word "Shatdhar," all the names of *baan* are comprehended in mind. —101

Speaking the names of "Pushpdhanva and Kaamdev" and then uttering the word "Aayudh," the names of *baan* continue to be evolved. —102

Uttering all the names of fish and adding the word "Ketwayudh" at the end, the innumerable names of *baan* continue to be evolved. —103

If the weapons are described after uttering the word "Pushp" and then adding the word "Dhanush," then the names of *baan* continue to be evolved. —104

Saying the word "Bhramar" in the beginning, then adding the word "Panch" and then saying the word "Dhardhar," all the names of *baan* of known by the wise people. —105

Uttering the names of all the small lances and adding the word "Dhar" at end, the wise people recognise in their mind the names of *baan*—106

SORATHA

Whosoever described the earth in the beginning, many names of *baan* continue to be evolved, when her sons are brought under description. —107

DOHIRA

Uttering the names of "Vish" (poison) and then adding the word "Vish" again, all the names of *baan* are recognised. —108

Speaking the syllable "B" in the beginning and then adding the syllable "N," the wise people comprehend the names of *baan*. —109

Speaking the word "Kani" and then saying the word "Dhar," the wise people comprehend the names of *baan* in their mind. —110

Uttering the word "Phok" in the beginning and then adding the word "Dhar" all the names of *baan* can be comprehended in mind. —111

Saying the word "Pashupat" primarily and then adding the word "Asur," the wise people comprehend all the names of *baan* in their mind. —112

Uttering one thousand names of Shiva and then speaking the word "Asur," all the names of *baan* are known. —113

Saying primarily all the names of "Karan" and then adding "Ar," all the names of *baan* are recognised. —114

Uttering the destroyer of Karana, the son of Sun, all the names of *baan* of Known. —115

Uttering all the names of "Arjun" and then adding the word "Aayudh," all the names of *baan* are recognised. —116

Uttering "Arjuna and Krishna etc.," if the weapons are described, then all the words mean *baan*. —117

Uttering the words "Arjun, Parath, Duddakesh, Sanchi, etc.," and then adding the words "Aayudh," the names of *baan* are known. —118

Uttering the words "Kapidhvaj, Haidrathaat, Surya, Jari" and then adding the word "Aayudh," the names of *baan* are known. —119

After saying the words "Timiraari, Bal Vrat, Nishichar-Naashak, and then adding the words "Shat" and afterwards adding "Aayudh," many names of *baan* continue to be evolved. —120

Uttering one thousand names of Vishnu and then adding the words "Anuj, Tanuj and Shastar" in serial order, the names of *baan* are visualised. —121

Uttering the words "Narak-Nivaran, Agh-haran and Kripa-Sindhu" and then adding the words "Anuj, Tanuj and Shastar" in serial order, the name of *baan* is obtained. —122

Uttering the words "Vighan-Haran and Vyadhi-dalan" and then adding the words "Anuj, Tanuj and Shastar" in serial order, the names of *baan* are known. —123

Uttering the words "Makarketu and Makardhvaj" and then adding word "Aayudh," the wise people know all the names of *baan*. —124

Uttering the words "Pushpdhanva, Bhramar and Pinaak" and then adding the word "Aayudh," all the name of *baan* are known. —125

Uttering the words "Shambrari and Tripurari" and the adding the word "Aayudh," the names of *baan* are known. —126

Shri Saarang, Beerhaa, Balhaa, Bisikh, Bisi, etc. are known as the names of *baan*. —127

Uttering primarily the names of "Vish" and then adding the word "Dhar," all the names of *baan* are known. —128

Naming all the oceans and then adding the word "Tanai" and afterwards the word "Dhar," the names of *baan* are understood. —129

Uttering the words "Udadhi, Sindhu, Sariteshwar" and then adding the word "Dhar," the wise people know the names of *baan* (Vanshidhar). —130

Uttering the words "Baddh, Naashini, Beerhaa, Vish, Biskhagraj" and then adding the word "Dhar," the names of *baan* are known. —131

Uttering the names of all men and then adding the word "Ha," the wise people know all the names of *baan*. —132

Speaking the word "Kaalkoot," then uttering the words "Kashtkari, Shivkanthi and Ahi" and then adding the word "Dhar," the names of *baan* are known. —133

After saying the word "Shiva," then adding the words Kanthi and Dhar in serial order, the names of *baan* can be described. —134

After saying the words "Vyaadhi and Vidhimukh" in the beginning and then adding "Dhar," the wise people recognise all the names of *baan*. —135

Making the bow of the words "Khapra (Khaprail), Nalak, Dhanush, Satya, etc.," and pulling upto the ear, with the hands, those which are discharged, they are the weapons of the brotherhood of *baan*. —136

That which rains like the cloud and whose creation is "Yash" though it is not the cloud, yet it is like the cloud; someone may give its name and that is the cloud. —137

That whose names are "Vishdhar, Vishayee, Shok-Kaarak, Karunari, etc.," it is called *baan*; by naming it, all tasks are fulfilled. —138

Though it is known by names "Arivedhan and Arichhedan," its name is "Vednaakar" that *baan* (arrow) protects its people and rains on the villages of the tyrants. —139

The enemy of Krishna, the Lord of Yadavas, whose names are "Vishnadhipatiari and Krishnantak," O *baan*! you may ever bring victory to us and fulfil all our tasks. —140

After speaking the word "Haldhar," then adding "Anuj" and afterwards saying "Ar," the wise people know all the names of *baan*. —141

Uttering the words "Rohinay, Musli, Hali, Revteesh, Balram and Anuj," then adding the word "Ar," the names of *baan* are known. —142

Uttering the words "Taalketu, Langali," then adding Krishnagraj; also uttering the word "Anuj" and then adding the word "Ar," the names of *baan* are known. —143

Speaking the words "Neelambar, Rukmantkar and Pauranic Ari," then uttering the word "Anuj" and adding "Ar," the names of *baan* are understood. —144

Uttering all the names of "Arjun," adding the word "Satya" and then speaking "Ar," all the names of *baan* are spoken. —145

Uttering primarily the names of "Pawan" (wind), then adding the word "Sut," then speaking "Anuj and Sootari," all the names of *baan* are recognised. —146

Uttering the words "Maaroot, Pawan, and Ghanantkar" and then adding the words "Sut and Sutari," all the names of *baan* are known. —147

After describing "Shalyarjun," the All-pervading and then adding the words "Tanuj, Anuj," and speaking "Sutari" at the end, the names of *baan* are known. —148

Uttering the names of "Jal" (water), then speaking "Ar" and afterwards speaking the words "Tanuj, Anuj and Sutari," the names of *baan* are recognised. —149

Uttering primarily "Agni" (fire), then adding "Ar" and afterwards speaking the words "Tanuj, Anuj and Sutari," the names of *baan* are known. —150

Naming "Agni" primarily, then adding "Ar" and afterwards saying "Tanuj, Anuj and Ari," the names of *baan* are spoken. —151

Uttering primarily the names of "Agni," then adding "Ari-Ari" and afterwards saying "Tanuj, Anuj and Ari" the names of *baan* are spoken. —152

Saying "Paavkari and Agnant" and then uttering "Anuj, Tanuj and Sutari," the names of *baan* are recognised. —153

By adding the words "Tanuj, Anuj and Sutari" to the words "Himvari, Bakhaa, Gadi and Bheem," the names of *baan* are known. —154

By adding the word "Ari" with the name of Duryodhana and then uttering the words "Anuj and Sutari," the names of *baan* are known. —155

After uttering the names of the sons of Dhritrashtra, then adding the word "Ari" at the end and afterwards speaking "Anuj and Sutari," the names of *baan* are known. —156

After uttering the words "Duhshasan, Durmukh and Durvijay," then adding "Ari" and afterwards saying "Anuj and Sutari," the names of *baan* are recognised. —157

Saying primarily the word "Duryodhana" then uttering "Ari, Anuj, Tanuj and Sutari," the names of *baan* are known. —158

Placing primarily the names of "Bhisham" and then adding the words "Ari and Shatru," the names of *baan* are known. —159

Saying primarily "Jahnavi and Agarja" and then uttering "Tanuj, Shatru and Sutari," the names of *baan* are recognised. —160

Saying primarily "Ganga and Girija," then adding the word "Putra" and afterwards uttering "Shatru and Sutari," the names of *baan* are known. —161

Uttering primarily the word "Nakaleshwari" and then saying the words "Shatari and Sutari," all the names of *baan* are pronounced. —162

Uttering the words "Bhisham and Shantanu," then adding "Ari" and afterwards saying the word "Sutari," the names of *baan* are recognised. —163

Uttering the words "Gangay and Nadiyal," then saying "Saritaj Shatru," then uttering "Soot" and afterwards "Antari," the names of *baan* are known. —164

Adding the word "Ari" at the end of the words "Taalketu and Savita," uttering the word

"Ishraastra" at the end, innumerable names of *paash* continue to be evolved. —380

The names of *paash* are formed by firstly saying the word "Ripu" and then "Ishraastra," which O wise men! you may recognise. —381

Saying "Hardhar" primarily and "Ishraastra" at the end, innumerable names of *paash* continue to be evolved. —382

Uttering the word "Jalajtraan," then saying "Ishraastra," the names of *paash* are formed, which O skilful people! you may recognise. —383

The names of *paash* are formed by uttering "Hardhrad, Jaldhrad, Varidhrad, Vidhipati and Astra," which O wise men! you may recognise. —384

Saying firstly "Neerad" and "Ishraastra" at the end, many names of *paash* continue to be evolved. —385

Saying "Ambudjaadhar Niddhi" and then "Ishraastra," O wise men! recognise all the names of *paash*. —386

Saying "Dhaaraadhraj" and then "Niddhipati Ish" and "Shastar," the names of *paash* are known. —387

Saying "Dhaaraadhraj Ish" and then adding the word "Astra," the names of *paash* are formed, which may be recognised by the wise people. —388

Saying the word "Paya" primarily and then "Niddhi Ish" and afterwards uttering the word "Astra," recognise the names of *paash*. —389

Naming "Dugadh," then adding "Niddhi Ish" and afterwards uttering the word "Astra," O talented people! recognise the names of *paash*. —390

Uttering all the names of heroes in the beginning and then saying the word "Grastan," all the names of *paash* are correctly comprehended. —391

Saying all the names of "Jal," then adding "Niddhipati Ish" and afterwards uttering the word "Astra," O wise men! know all the names of *paash*. —392

Saying all the names of "Dhool" and then adding the words "Dhar Niddhi Ish" and "Astra," O wise men! recognise the names of *paash*. —393

Uttering the words "Vaarid Ari" in the beginning, then adding "Shraastra" at the end and afterwards saying "Niddhi," O wise men! recognise the names of *paash*. —394

Uttering the word "Tretantak" in the beginning and then saying "Niddhi Ishraastra," the names of *paash* are formed, which O wise men! you may recognise. —395

Uttering primarily the word "Jhakhitran" and "Ishraastra" at the end, all the names of *paash* continue to be evolved. —396

Saying "Matsyatran" primarily and then adding "Ishraastra," the names of *paash* are formed, which O wise men! you may recognise. —397

Saying "Mainketu" and "Tran" and then adding "Ishraastra," the names of *paash* are formed, which O wise men! you may recognise. —398

Saying all the names of "Jal" and then uttering the word's "Jaa, Traan" and then "Ishraastra," the names of *paash* are recognised. —399

Saying "Vaarijtraan" and then adding "Ishraastra," O wise people! the names of *paash* are formed. —400

The names of *paash* are formed by uttering primarily the word "Jalajtran" and then saying "Ishraastra," which are understood by the wise persons in their mind. —401

Saying "Neerajtran" in the beginning and "Ishraastra" at the end, all the names of *paash* continue to be evolved. —402

O wise men! the names of *paash* are formed by uttering "Kamaltran" in the beginning and then adding "Ishraastra." —403

The names of *paash* are formed by firstly uttering the word "Ripu" O wise men! and then adding "Antak." —404

Saying the word "Shatru" primarily and then adding the word "Antak," O wise men! all the names of *paash* are formed. —405

Saying the word "Khal," then adding "'Yaantak" at the end, O wise men! the names of *paash* are formed, which you may recognise. —406

All the names of *paash* are formed by uttering the word "Dusht" in the beginning and then adding "Antyantak." —407

Uttering primarily "Tanripu" and then adding "Antyantak," the names of *paash* are formed, which are recognised by the wise persons. —408

The names of *paash* are formed by uttering "Asu Ari" firstly and then saying "Antyantak" which are recognised by the wise persons in their mind. —409

The names of *paash* are formed by uttering "Dalhaa" in the beginning and then adding "Antyantak," which O wise men! you may recognise in your mind. —410

The names of *paash* are formed by uttering the word "Preetnantak" in the beginning and then adding "Antyantak," which O wise men! you may recognise. —411

Saying the word "Dhujniari" primarily and then adding "Antyantak," the names of *paash* are formed, which O poets! comprehend correctly. —412

Uttering the word "Vaahini" and then saying "Ripu Ari," O wise men! the names of *paash* are formed. —413

Saying "Vaahan" in the beginning and then "Ripu Ari," the names of *paash* are formed, which O wise men! you may recognise. —414

The names of *paash* are formed by uttering the word "Senaa" firstly and then adding "Ripu Ari," O wise men! you may recognise them. —415

The names of *paash* are formed by uttering "Hayani" in the beginning and then adding "Antyantak," which O wise men! you may recognise. —416

The names of *paash* are formed by uttering the word "Gayani" firstly and then adding the words "Antyantak Ari." —417

Saying "Patini" in the beginning and then uttering the word "Ari" the names of *paash* are formed, which you may comprehend clearly. —418

Saying the word "Rathni" in the beginning and then adding "Ripu Ari" at the end, O poets! know the names of *paash* correctly. —419

Saying "Nrapni" in the beginning and then adding the word "Ripu," the names of *paash* are known correctly. —420

Saying the word "Bhatni" in the beginning and then adding "Ripu Ari" O talented ones! the names of *paash* are formed. —421

Uttering the word "Veerni" in the beginning and then adding "Ripu Ari," the names of *paash* are formed, which O wise men! you may recognise. —422

Saying the word "Shatruni" in the beginning and then adding the words "Ripu Ari," the names of *paash* are formed, which O wise men! you may recognise. —423

The names of *paash* are formed by firstly uttering the word "Dhujni" in the beginning and then adding "Ripu Ari," O wise men! you may recognise —424

Keeping the word "Ripuni" in the beginning and saying "Ripukshai" at the end, O wise men! the names of *paash* to be recognised in the mind are formed. —425

Saying the word "Arini" in the beginning and then adding "Ripu Ari," the names of "Tupak" (*paash*) are formed. —426

Saying "Raajni" in the beginning and adding "Ripu Ari" at the end, O wise men! the names of *paash* are formed. —427

Saying the word "Isharni" in the beginning and then adding "Ripu Ari," O wise men! the names of *paash* are formed. —428

Saying the word "Bhoopani" in the beginning and then adding "Ripu Ari," O wise men! the names of *paash* are formed. —429

Saying "Nrapjan Aishvaryani" in the beginning and uttering "Ripu Ari" at the end, the names of *paash* are formed, which O poets! you may know correctly. —430

Saying the word "Rajni" in the beginning and then adding "Ripu Ari," the names of *paash* are formed. —431

Saying "Ishni" in the beginning and then uttering the word "Antak," the names of *paash* are formed, which O poets! you may improve. —432

Saying the word "Nareshni" in the beginning and then adding "Ripu Ari" at the end, the names of *paash* are formed correctly. —433

Saying the word "Ravani" in the beginning and

then adding "Ripu Ari" at the end, the names of *paash* are formed. —434

Saying "Raayan" in the beginning and then adding "Ripu Ari," O wise men! the names of *paash* are formed. —435

Saying "Isharni" primarily, add "Ripu Ari' at the end and recognise innumerable names of *paash*. —436

Saying the word "Dhujni" in the beginning and then adding "Ripu Ari" at the end, the names of *paash* are formed. —437

Saying the word "Daityani" in the beginning and then adding "Ripu Ari" at the end, the names of *paash* are recognised correctly. —438

Saying the word "Radni" in the beginning and then adding "Ripu Ari" at the end, innumerable names of *paash* are formed. —439

Saying the word "Vaarini" in the beginning and then adding "Ripu Ari" at the end, the names of *paash* are formed. —440

Saying "Duryodhana" in the beginning and then adding "Ripu Ari" at the end, thousands of names of *paash* continue to be evolved. —441

Saying the word "Durbani" in the beginning and then adding "Ripu Ari," the names of *paash* continue to be formed. —442

Saying the word "Saabajni" in the beginning and then adding "Ripu Ari" at the end, innumerable names of *paash* continue to be formed. —443

Saying the word "Maatagni" in the beginning and then adding "Ripu Ari" at the end, innumerable names of *paash* continue to be formed. —444

Saying the word "Turangni" in the beginning and then adding "Ripu Ari" at the end, the names of *paash* are formed. —445

Saying the word "Hastni" in the beginning and then adding "Ripu Ari" O wise men! the names of *paash* are formed. —446

Saying the word "Dantni" in the beginning and then adding "Ripu Ari" at the end, the names of *paash* are formed, which O wise men! you may recognise. —447

Saying the word "Durdani" primarily and then adding "Murdani" at the end, the names of *paash* are formed. —448

Saying the word "Padmani" in the beginning and then adding "Ripu Ari," the names of *paash* are formed. —449

Saying the word "Baalaa" in the beginning and then adding "Ripu Ari," O good poets! recognise the names of *paash*. —450

Saying the word "Kunjar" in the beginning and then adding the word "Patak" at the end, the names of *paash* are formed. —451

Saying the word "Hasitani" in the beginning and then adding "Ripu Ari," O skilful people! the names of *paash* are formed. —452

Saying the word "Kumbhani" in the beginning and then uttering "Ripu Ari," the names of *paash* are formed. —453

Saying the word "Karini" in the beginning and then adding "Ripu Ari," O wise men! the names of *paash* are formed. —454

Saying the word "Sindhuri" in the beginning and then uttering "Ripu Ari" at the end, the names of *paash* continue to be evolved. —455

Saying the word "Ankapi" primarily and then adding "Ripu Ari" at the end, the names of *paash* are known correctly. —456

Saying the word "Naagini" firstly and then adding "Ripu Ari," O wise men! the names of *paash* continue to be evolved. —457

Saying the word "Harni" in the beginning and then adding "Ripu Ari," O wise men! comprehend the names of *paash*. —458

Saying the word "Maatangani" in the beginning and then adding "Ripu Ari" at the end, O good poets! know the names of *paash* correctly. —459

Saying the word "Baajani" in the beginning and then adding "Ripu Ari" at the end, the names of *paash* are formed, which O talented persons! may be considered as true. —460

End of the fourth chapter entitled
"The Names of *Paash*" in
Shri Shastar Naam-Maala Purana.

Now begins the Description of the Names of *Tupak*

DOHIRA

Uttering the word "Vaahini" and then adding "Ripu Ari" at the end, the names of *tupak* are formed, which O poets! you may comprehend. —461

Uttering the word "Saindhvni" in the beginning and saying the word "Ripumi" at the end, the names of *tupak* are formed. —462

Uttering the word "Turangni" in the beginning and saying "Ripu Ari" at the end, the names of *tupak* are formed. —463

Adding the word "Haa" with the word "Hayani," O wise men! the names of *tupak* are formed. —464

Saying the word "Arbani" in the beginning and adding "Ripu Ari" at the end, the names of *tupak* are formed. —465

Saying "Kinkani" primarily and then uttering the word "Ripu," the names of *tupak* are formed. —466

Saying the word "Ashivani" in the beginning and then adding the word "Ari" at the end, O skilful people! the names of *tupak* may be comprehended. —467

Saying the word "Shvasni" in the beginning and then adding "Ripu Ari" at the end, the names of *tupak* are recognised. —468

Saying the word "Aadhani" in the beginning and adding the words "Ripu Ari," O wise men! the names of *tupak* are formed. —469

Saying the word "Prabhumi" in the beginning and then adding the word "Ripu" at the end, O wise men! the names of *tupak* are formed. —470

Uttering the word "Bhoopani" in the beginning and then adding "Ripu Ari" at the end, the names of *tupak* are known correctly. —471

Uttering the word "Ishani" in the beginning and then adding "Ripu Ari," the names of *tupak* are formed. —472

Uttering the word "Saudani" in the beginning and then adding "Ripu Ari," O wise people! the names of *tupak* come to the fore. —473

Uttering the word "Shatruni" in the beginning and then adding "Ripu Ari," the names of *tupak* are formed. —474

Naming all the canopies and uttering the word "Nee" and then adding the word "Ripuhi," the names of *tupak* continue to be evolved. —475

Saying the word "Chhatarni" in the beginning and then adding "Ripu Ari," at the end, the wise men recognise the names of *tupak*. —476

Uttering the word "Patrani" in the beginning and then saying "Ripuni" O wise men! recognise the names of *tupak*. —477

Saying the word "Patakani" in the beginning and then adding "Ripu Ari," O skilful persons! understand the names of *tupak*. —478

Saying firstly the word "Kshitipati" and then adding "Ripu Ari" at the end, the names of *tupak* are formed, which O good poets! you may consider. —479

Uttering the word "Ravdan" in the beginning and then adding "Ripu Ari" at the end, the names of *tupak* are formed, which O wise men! you may recognise. —480

Saying the word "Shastarni" in the beginning and then adding "Ripu Ari," the names of *tupak* are formed. —481

Saying the word "Shatruni" in the beginning and then adding "Ripu Ari," O skilful persons! the names of *tupak* are formed. —482

Saying the word "Subhatni" in the beginning and adding "Ripu Ari" at the end, the wise men may comprehend the names of *tupak*. —483

Saying the word "Rathni" in the beginning and then uttering "Mathni-mathan," the names of *tupak* are formed. —484

Saying the word "Sindhuni" in the beginning and then adding "Ripu Ari," the names of *tupak* are formed. —485

Saying the word "Shakatni" in the beginning and then adding "Ripu Ari," O wise people! understand the names of *tupak*. —486

Saying the word "Shatruni" in the beginning and then adding "Ripu Ari," the names of *tupak* are formed, which the good poets may improve. —487

Saying the word "Dushtni" in the beginning and then adding "Ripu Ari" at the end, O wise men! the names of *tupak* are formed, which you may recognise. —488

Saying the word "Ashtakvachani" in the beginning and then adding "Ripu Ari," the names of *tupak* are formed. —489

Saying the word "Barmani" in the beginning and then adding "Ripu Ari" at the end, O wise men! recognise the names of *tupak*. —490

Saying the word "Tantranani" in the beginning and then adding "Ripu Ari" at the end, the names of *tupak* are formed, which may be comprehended. —491

Saying the word "Charmani" in the beginning and then adding "Ripu Ari' at the end, the names of *tupak* are formed, which may be comprehended correctly. —492

Saying the word "Kshiprani" in the beginning and then adding "Ripu Ari" at the end, all the names of *tupak* in innumerable forms continue to be evolved. —493

Saying the word "Shalyani" in the beginning and then adding "Ripu Ari" the names of *tupak* are formed, which O talented persons! you may recognise. —494

Saying the word "Chakrani" in the beginning and then adding "Ripu Ari," the names of *tupak* are formed, which, O skilful people! you may comprehend. —495

Uttering the word "Kharagni" in the beginning and then saying "Ripu Ari" at the end, the names of *tupak* are formed. —496

Saying the word "Ashivni" in the beginning and then adding "Ripu Ari" at the end, the names of *tupak* are formed. —497

Saying the word "Nirstraini" in the beginning and then uttering "Ripu Ari" at the end, the names of *tupak* continue to be evolved in authenticated form. —498

Saying the word "Khagni" in the beginning and the adding "Ripu Ari" the names of *tupak* are formed. —499

Saying the word "Shastar-aishani" in the beginning and then adding "Ripu Ari," O skilful persons! comprehend the names of *tupak*. —500

Saying the word "Shastar-raajini" in the beginning and then uttering "Ripu Ari" at the end, the names of *tupak* are formed. —501

Saying the word "Shastar-ravani" in the beginning and then uttering "Ripu Ari," the names of *tupak* are formed. —502

Saying the word "Saiphani" in the beginning and then adding "Ripu Ari," O wise men! comprehend the names to *tupak*. —503

Saying firstly the word "Tegni" and then adding "Ripu Ari," the names of *tupak* are formed. —504

Saying the word "Krashanani" in the beginning and then adding "Ripu Ari" the names of *tupak* are formed. —505

Saying the word "Shamsherni" in the beginning and then adding "Ripu Ari" at the end, the names of *tupak* are formed which O wise men! recognise them in your mind. —506

Saying the word "Kandini" in the beginning and then adding "Ripu Ari" at the end, the names of *tupak* are formed, which O poets! you may comprehend correctly. —507

Saying the words "Khal-Khandan" in the beginning and then adding "Ripu Ari," O skilful persons! the names of *tupak* are formed. —508

Saying the word "Kavchanthani" in the beginning and then adding "Ripu Ari," the names of *tupak* are formed, which O wise men! you may recognise. —509

Saying the words "Dhaaraadharni" in the beginning and then adding "Ripu Ari," the names of *tupak* are formed. —510

Saying the word "Karachtaapini" in the beginning and then adding "Ripu Ari," the names of *tupak* are formed. —511

Saying the words "Tantraan Ari" in the beginning and then adding "Ripu Ari" at the end, the names of *tupak* are formed, which O wise men! you may comprehend. —512

Saying the word "Kavach-ghatini" in the beginning and then adding "Ripu Ari" at the end, the authentic names of *tupak* are formed. —513

Saying "Dusht-Dhani" in the beginning and then uttering "Ripu Ari" O wise men! comprehend the names of *tupak* —514

Saying "Durjan-dalni" primarily and then uttering "Ripu Ari" at the end, the names of *tupak* are formed. —515

Saying the words "Durjan-Dabakni" in the beginning and then adding "Ripu Ari," O skilful persons! the names of *tupak* are formed. —516

Saying the words "Dusht-charvani" in the beginning and then adding "Ripu Ari" at the end, the names of *tupak* are formed, which O wise men! you may comprehend. —517

Saying the words "Veer-Varjani" in the beginning and then adding "Ripu Ari" at the end, the names of *tupak* are evolved. —518

Saying firstly "Baan-Varjani" and uttering the word "Ripuni" at the end, the name of *tupak* are formed. —519

Saying primarily "Vishikh-varshini" in the beginning and then adding "Ripu Ari," O wise men! the names of *tupak* are formed. —520

Saying the words "Baar-Daayani" in the beginning and then adding "Ripu Ari," the names of *tupak* are formed. —521

Saying firstly the words "Vishikh-Vrashtni" and then uttering "Ripu Ari" at the end, the names of *tupak* are formed. —522

Saying the words "Panaj-Prahaaran" in the beginning and then uttering "Ripu Ari" at the end, the names of *tupak* are formed. —523

Saying firstly the word "Dhanani" and then uttering "Ripu Ari" at the end, the names of *tupak* are formed. —524

Saying firstly the word "Dhanushani" and then adding "Ripu Ari," the names of *tupak* are formed, which O wise men! you may recognise. —525

Saying firstly the word "Kuvandni" and then adding "Ripu Ari," the names of *tupak* are formed, which O skilful persons! you may comprehend. —526

Saying firstly "Baanaa-Grajni" and then adding "Ripu Ari," O wise persons! the names of *tupak* are formed. —527

Saying firstly the word "Baan-Praharni" and then adding "Ripu Ari," the names of *tupak* are formed. —528

Saying firstly the word "Baanani' and then adding "Ripu Ari," the names of *tupak* are formed. —529

Saying firstly the word "Bisikkh-pranani" and then adding "Ripu Ari" at the end, the names of *tupak* are formed. —530

Saying firstly the word "Bisikkhan" and then adding "Ripu Ari" at the end, the names of *tupak* are formed. —531

Saying the words "Subhat-ghayani" in the beginning and then adding "Ripu Ari," O wise men! the names of *tupak* are formed correctly. —532

Saying firstly the words "Shatru-Sanharni" and then adding "Ripu Ari" at the end the names of *tupak* are formed, which O poets! you may comprehend correctly. —533

Saying "Panach-Praharni" in the beginning and then uttering "Ripu Ari" at the end, the names of *tupak* are formed. —534

Saying "Kovandaj-dayani" in the beginning and then uttering "Ripu Ari," O wise men! the names of *tupak* are formed. —535

Saying firstly the word "Nishamgni" and then adding "Ripu Ari" at the end, the names of *tupak* are formed. —536

Saying firstly the word "Patrani" and then uttering "Ripu Ari" at the end, the names of *tupak* are formed, which O poets! you may comprehend correctly. —537

Saying firstly the word "Pankhini" and then adding "Ripu Ari," O wise men! the names of *tupak* are formed. —538

Saying firstly the word "Patrani" and then adding "Ripu Ari," at the end, the names of *tupak* are formed. —539

Saying firstly the word "Parini" and then adding "Ripu Ari," O wise men! recognise the names of *tupak*. —540

Saying firstly the word "Pabkhini" and then uttering "Ripu Ari," the names of *tupak* are formed. —541

Saying firstly the word "Patrani" and then uttering "Ripu Ari" at the name of *tupak* are formed. —542

Saying firstly the word "Nabhchari" and then uttering "Ripu Ari" at the end, O poets, the names of *tupak* are formed, which you may improve. —543

Saying firstly the word "Rathani" and then uttering "Ripu Ari" at the end, the names of *tupak* are formed. —544

Saying the word "Shaktani" in the beginning and then adding "Ripu Ari," O skilful persons, the names of *tupak* are formed. —545

Saying firstly the word "Rathni" and then uttering "Ripu Ari" at the end, the names of *tupak* are formed. —546

Saying firstly the word "Sayandni" and then adding "Ripu Ari" at the end, the names of *tupak* are formed. —547

Saying firstly the word "Patni" and then uttering "Ripu Ari" at the end, O wise men! the names of *tupak* are formed. —548

Saying firstly the word "Vastrani" and then uttering "Ripu Ari" at the end, the names of *tupak* are formed. —549

Saying firstly the word "Vayuhani" and then uttering "Ripu Ari" at the end, the names of *tupak* are formed. —550

Saying firstly the word "Vajrani" and then uttering "Ripu Ari" at the end, O good poets! the names of *tupak* are formed. —551

Saying firstly the word "Vajrani" and then adding "Ripu Ari" at the end, the names of *tupak* are formed. —552

Uttering firstly the word "Dalni" and then adding the word "Malni," the names of *tupak* are formed, which O wise men! you may comprehend in your mind. —553

Saying firstly the word "Vaaditrani" and then adding "Ari," the names of *tupak* are formed. —554

Saying primarily the word Naadini and then adding "Ripu Ari" at the end, the names of *tupak* are formed. —555

Saying firstly the words "Dudumbhi-dhanani" and then uttering "Ripu Ari" at the end, the names of *tupak* are formed. —556

Saying primarily the word "Bherini" and then uttering "Ripu Ari" at the end, O poets! the names of *tupak* are formed. —557

Saying firstly the word "Naadnaadini" and then uttering "Ripu Ari" at the end, the names of *tupak* are formed. —558

Saying firstly the words "Dudumbhi-dhanani" and then uttering "Ripu Ari" at the end, the names of *tupak* are formed. —559

Saying primarily the word "Bherini" and then adding the word "Ripu," O wise men, the names of *tupak* are formed. —560

Saying firstly the words "Dundubhi-Ghoshani" and then adding "Ripu Ari" at the end, the names of *tupak* are formed. —561

Saying firstly the word "Naadaaniksani" and then adding "Ripu Ari," the names of *tupak* are formed. —562

Saying firstly the word "Anikni" and then adding the word "Ripu," O wise men! the names of *tupak* are formed. —563

Saying firstly the word "Dhaalani" and then uttering "Ripu Ari" at the end, the names of *tupak* are formed, which may be comprehended thoughtfully. —564

Add the word "Ripu" after saying the word "Dhadhni" primarily, and in this way recognise the names of *tupak*. —565

Saying firstly word "Shankhnishoni" and then uttering "Ripu Ari," the names of *tupak* are formed. —566

Saying the word "Shankhshabadni" primarily and then uttering "Ripu Ari" at the end, the name of *tupak* are formed. —567

Saying the word "Shankhnaadni" in the beginning and then adding "Ripu Ari" at the end, the name of *tupak* are formed, which O wise men! you may comprehend. —568

Saying the word "Singhnadani" in the beginning and then adding "Ripu Ari" at the end, O good poet! the names of *tupak* are formed correctly. —569

Saying the words "Palbhaksh-nadani" in the beginning and then adding "Ripu Ari" at the end, the names of *tupak* are formed. —570

Saying firstly "Vyaghra-nadini" and then "Ripu Ari," the names of *tupak* are formed. —571

Saying the words "Haryaksh-nadini" in the beginning and then adding "Ripu Ari" at the end, the names of *tupak* are formed. —572

Saying firstly the words "Pundreek-naadini" and adding the word "Ripu" at the end, the names of *tupak* are formed, which O wise men! you may comprehend. —573

Saying the word "Harnadini" in the beginning

and then adding "Ripu Ari" at the end, the names of *tupak* are formed. —574

Saying firstly the words "Panchanan-Ghoshani" and then adding "Ripu Ari," the names of *tupak* are formed. —575

Saying firstly the words "Sher-shabadni" and then adding "Ripu Ari" at the end, the names of *tupak* are formed. —576

Saying firstly the words "Mrigaari-naadini" and then adding "Ripu Ari," O knowledgeable persons! the names of *tupak* are formed. —577

Uttering the words "Pashupataari-dhanini" and then adding "Ripu," O wise men! the names of *tupak* are formed. —578

Saying firstly "Mrigpati-naadini" and then uttering "Ripu Ari" at the end, the names of *tupak* are formed. —579

Saying the words "Pashu-ishran-naadini" and then uttering "Ripu Ari" at the end, the names of *tupak* are formed. —580

Saying firstly "Gaj-nadini" and then adding "Ripu" at the end, the names of *tupak* are formed. —581

Saying firstly the words "Saudiyar-dhanani' and then adding "Ripu Ari" at the end, the names of *tupak* are formed. —582

Saying firstly "Dantyari-naadini" and then uttering "Ripu Ari" at the end, the names of *tupak* are formed. —583

Saying the words "Anik-piyar-naadini" and then adding "Ripu Ari" at the end, the names of *tupak* are formed. —584

Saying the words "Sindhu-raari-dhanani" and then uttering "Ripu Ari" at the end, the names of *tupak* are formed, which you may comprehend. —585

Saying primarily "Maatangari-naadini" primarily and then uttering "Ripu Ari," the names of *tupak* are formed. —586

Uttering the words "Saavijaari-dhanani" and then adding "Ripu Ari" at the end, the names of *tupak* are formed. —587

Saying the words "Gaj-niari-naadini" in the beginning and then adding "Ripu Ari" at the end, the names of *tupak* are formed. —588

Saying "Naarari-dhanini" primarily and then adding "Ripu Ari," O wise men! the name of *tupak* continue to be evolved. —589

Uttering primarily the words "Hasit-ari-dhanini" and then adding "Ripu Ari," the names of *tupak* are formed, which O wise men! you may recognise. —590

Uttering the firstly "Hirani-ari" and then adding "Ripu," the names of *tupak* are formed, which O wise men! you may recognise in your mind. —591

Saying "Karimiari-dhanani" primarily and then adding "Ripu" at the end, the names of *tupak* are formed. —592

Saying firstly the words "Bariyar-dhanini" and then uttering "Ripu Ari," the names of *tupak* are formed. —593

Saying the words "Dhanti-ari-dhanini" in the beginning and then adding "Ripu Ari," the names of *tupak* are formed. —594

Saying the words "Dadhi-ripu-dhanini" primarily and then uttering "Ripu Ari," the names of *tupak* are formed. —595

Saying the words "Padam-ari" in the beginning and then uttering "Ripu Ari," the names of *tupak* are formed. —596

Saying firstly the word "Baliyar" and then adding "Ripu" the names of *tupak* are formed. —597

Saying the words "Imbh-ari-dhanini" and then adding "Ripu Ari" the names of *tupak* are formed. —598

Saying the words "Kumbhi-ari-naadini" primarily and then adding "Ripu-kshai," the names of *tupak* are formed. —599

Saying the words "Kunjar-ari-naadini" primarily and then uttering "Ripu," the names of *tupak* are formed. —600

Uttering "Patra-ari-dhanini" and then adding "Ripu", the names of *tupak* are formed. —601

Saying the words "Taru-ripu-ari-dhanini" and then adding "Ripu," O wise men! recognise the names of *tupak*. —602

Uttering the words "Saudiyantak-dhanini" and then saying "Ripu Ari," the names of *tupak* are formed. —603

Uttering "Hayani-ari" in the beginning and then adding "Ripu Ari" at the end, the names of

SHRI SHASTAR NAAM-MAALA PURANA

tupak are formed, which, O good poets! you may comprehend. —604

Saying the words "Hayani-ari-dhanani" in the beginning and then adding "Ripu," the name of *tupak* are formed, which O wise men! you may recognise. —605

Uttering the words "Hayani-yantak-dhanani" and then adding "Ripu," the name of *tupak* are formed. —606

Saying firstly "Ashvari-dharni" and then adding "Ripu Ari," the names of *tupak* are formed. —607

Saying "Tur-ari-naadini" primarily and then adding "Ripu Ari" at the end, the names of *tupak* are formed. —608

Saying "Turangari-dhanani" in the beginning and then adding "Ripu," the names of *tupak* are formed, which O skilful persons! you may comprehend. —609

Saying the word "Ghorantkani" in the beginning and then adding "Ripu" at the end, the names of *tupak* are formed correctly. —610

Saying firstly "Baajaantkani' in the beginning and then adding "Ripu Ari" at the end, the names of *tupak* are formed, which O wise men! you may comprehend. —611

Saying "Bahanantaki" and then uttering "Ripu-naadini," the names of *tupak* are formed. —612

Saying the words "Sarjaj-ari-dhanani" and then adding "Ripu," O wise men! the names of *tupak* are formed. —613

Saying firstly "Baaji-ari-dhanani" in the beginning and then adding "Antyantak," the names of *tupak* are formed, which O skilful persons! you may comprehend. —614

Saying the word "Ripu Ari" in the beginning and then uttering "Ripu" at the end, the names of *tupak* are formed. —615

Saying the words "Vaahini-naadi" in the beginning and then adding "Ripu" at the end, the names of *tupak* are comprehended correctly. —616

Saying "Turangari" in the beginning and then adding "Dhanani-ari," the names of *tupak* are formed. —617

Saying firstly "Arab Ari" and then adding "Ripu Ari," the names of *tupak* are comprehended. —618

Saying firstly "Turangari-dhanani" and then adding "Ripu Ari," the names of *tupak* are recognised. —619

Saying "Kinkan-ari-dhanani" and then adding "Ripu" at the end, the names of *tupak* are formed. —620

Saying "Dhari-ari-naadini" in the beginning and then adding "Ripu Ari" at the end, the names of *tupak* are formed. —621

Saying the words "Mrigaari-naadini" in the beginning and then adding "Ripu Ari" at the end, the names of *tupak* are formed, which O poets! you may comprehend correctly. —622

Saying the words "Shrani-ari-dhanani" in the beginning and then adding "Ripu Ari" at the end, the names of *tupak* are formed. —623

Saying the words "Mragi-ari-naadini" in the beginning and then adding "Ripu Ari" at the end, the names of *tupak* may be comprehended correctly. —624

Saying "Tran-ari-naadini" and then adding "Ripu," the names of *tupak* are recognised by the wise mind. —625

Saying the word "Bhoochari" in the beginning and then uttering "Ripu Ari" at the end, the names of *tupak* are formed. —626

Saying the word "Subhat" in the beginning and then adding the word "Shatru" at the end, the names of *tupak* are formed. —627

Uttering the word "Shatru" in the beginning and then adding the word "Antyantak," the names of *tupak* are formed. —628

Saying the word "Shatru" in the beginning and then adding "Jhoolani" at the end, the names of *tupak* are formed. —629

Saying the word "Yuddhani" in the beginning and then adding the word "Antkani," the names of *tupak* are formed. —630

Saying the word "Varam" in the beginning and then adding the word "Vedhani" at the end, the name of "Karmavedhani *tupak*" is uttered. —631

Saying the word "Charam" in the beginning and then adding the word "Ghayani," the name of "Charam-ghayani *tupak*" is recognised. —632

Saying the word "Durjan" in the beginning and then uttering the word "Ghayani" at the end, the name of "Durjan-bhakshani *tupak*" is comprehended correctly. —633

Saying the word "Khal" in the beginning and then adding the word "Haa," comprehend, the name of *tupak*. —634

Saying the word "Dushtan" in the beginning and then adding the word "Ripuni" at the end, O skilful persons! the names of *tupak* are formed. —635

Saying the word "Ripuni" in the beginning and then adding the word "Khipani," the name of *tupak* are formed. —636

Naal, Saiphani, Tuapk, Jabarjang, Hathnaal, Sutarnaal, Ghurnaal, Chooran-par-jawaal are also the names of *tupak*. —637

Saying the word "Jawaal" in the beginning and then uttering the word "Dharni," the names of *tupak* are formed. —638

Saying the word "Anil" in the beginning and then adding the word "Chhorani" at the end, the names of *tupak* are formed. —639

Saying the words "Jawaalaa-vamani" in the beginning and then after reflection in the mind, the names of *tupak* are comprehended. —640

Saying the word "Ghan" in the beginning and then uttering the word "Dhunani" at the end, O wise men! the names of *tupak* are formed. —641

Uttering the word "Ghan" in the beginning and then "Naadini" at the end, the names of *tupak* are formed. —642

Saying the word "Vaarid" in the beginning and then the word "Shabadni" at the end, the names of *tupak* continue to be formed. —643

Saying the words "Meghan-dhanani" in the beginning and then uttering "Ripu Ari," O wise men! the names of *tupak* are formed. —644

Uttering the word "Meghshabadni" in the beginning, the names of *tupak* are also formed, which may be comprehended correctly. —645

Uttering firstly the word "Golaa" and the word "Aalaya" at the end, the names of *tupak* are formed. —646

Saying firstly the word "Golaa" and then adding "Dharani' at the end, the names of *tupak* are formed. —647

Saying firstly the word "Golaa" in the beginning and then adding the word "Asayani," O wise men! recognise the names of *tupak*. —648

Uttering the word "Golaagatrani" in the beginning and the word "Shabad," the names of *tupak* are formed. —649

Saying the word "Golaa" in the beginning and then the word "Aalayani," the names of *tupak* are formed. —650

Saying the word "Golaa" in the beginning and then "Sadanani" at the end, O good poets! comprehend the names of *tupak*. —651

Uttering the word "Golaa" in the beginning and then "Ketani" at the end, innumerable names of *tupak* continue to be evolved. —652

Saying the word "Golaa" in the beginning and then adding the word "Ketani" at the end, O skilful persons! the names of *tupak* are formed. —653

Saying the word "Golaa" in the beginning and then uttering the word "Sadni" at the end, O wise men! the names of *tupak* are formed. —654

Saying the word "Golaa" in the beginning and uttering the word "Dhamini" at the end, the names of *tupak* are formed. —655

Saying the word "Golaa" in the beginning and then adding the word "Nivasani" at the end, innumerable names of *tupak* continue to be evolved. —656

Saying the word "Golaa" in the beginning and then adding the word "Garahikaa" at the end, the names of *tupak* continue to be evolved. —657

Saying the word "Golaa" in the beginning and then adding the word "Muktani" at the end, speak all the names of *tupak* thoughtfully. —658

Saying the word "Golaa" in the beginning and then the word "Daatri" at the end, the names of *tupak* are formed. —659

Saying the word "Golaa" in the beginning and then adding the word "Tajni," the names of *tupak* are formed. —660

SHRI SHASTAR NAAM-MAALA PURANA

Saying firstly the word "Jawaalaa" and then the word "Dakshini" at the end, the names of *tupak* continue to be formed. —661

Saying firstly the words "Jawaal-shakitni" and then adding the word "Bakatra" afterwards, the names of *tupak* are recognised. —662

Uttering firstly "Jawaalaa-Tajni" and then "Bakatra," the names of *tupak* are formed, which may be comprehended. —663

Uttering firstly "Jawaalaa-Chhaadan," the names of *tupak*, O wise men! may be comprehend correctly. —664

O wise men! comprehend correctly the names of *tupak* by uttering firstly the word "Jawaalaa-dayani." —665

O wise men! comprehend correctly the names of *tupak* by uttering firstly the word "Jawaalaa-bakatrani." —666

Saying firstly the word "Jawaalaa" and then adding the word "Praktaayani," O wise men! the names of *tupak* are formed. —667

Know the names of *tupak* by uttering firstly the word "Jawaalaa" and then saying the word "Dharni" at the end. —668

The names of *tupak* are comprehended by uttering firstly the word "Durjan" and then adding the word "Daahani." —669

Comprehend the names of *tupak* correctly by firstly uttering the word "Durjan" and saying the word "Dalni" at the end. —670

The names of *tupak* are formed by uttering firstly the word "Goli-dharani" and then the word "Bakatra." —671

By uttering firstly the word "Dusht" and the word "Dahani" afterwards, the names of *tupak* are formed, which O wise men! you may comprehend. —672

CHAUPAI

The names of *tupak* can be thought out by uttering the words "Kaashth-orashthani" and then adding the words "Bhoomij-Prashthani," the names of *tupak* can be recognised. —673

Uttering firstly the words "Kaashth-prashthani" and thinking about all the names of *tupak* and them adding the words "Drum-Jawaasani," recognise the name of "Naalidaar *tupak*." —674

Uttering firstly the words "Kashth-prashthani" and then saying the word "Bakatra" afterwards, O wise men! the names of *tupak* are formed. —675

The names of *tupak* are formed by uttering the words "Jalaj-prashthani," which may be comprehended correctly. —676

By uttering the words "Vaarij-prashthani" from the mouth, the names of *tupak* are formed. —677

Uttering the word "Bakatra" after the word "Neeljaltrani," the names of *tupak* are formed. —678

By uttering the words "Ambuj-prashthani" from the mouth, the names of *tupak* are formed. —679

By uttering the words "Ghanjaj-prashthani," O wise men! the names of *tupak* are formed, which may be comprehended correctly. —680

The names of *tupak* are formed by firstly uttering the word "Jaltaru" and then adding the words "Prashthani-dhar" afterwards. —681

The names of *tupak* are formed by firstly saying the word "Vaari" and then uttering the words "Taru-prashthani," which O wise men! you may recognised in your mind. —682

The names of *tupak* are formed by firstly uttering the word "Neer" and then adding the words "Taru-prashthani." —683

O wise men! the names of *tupak* are known by uttering the word "Arj-prashthani." —684

CHAUPAI

Saying the words "Vaarij-prashthani" in the beginning and thinking of the names of *tupak*, and then adding the words "Bhooruha-prashthani" comprehend the names of *tupak*. —685

Firstly utter the word "Bhoomi" and then add the words "Ruka-prashthani" and in this way all the names of *tupak* will be formed, which can be recognised by some wise men. —686

Saying "Taru-ruha-prashthani" in the beginning and thinking of the names of *tupak*, then adding the words "Kaashth-kundani," comprehend all the names of *tupak* in your mind. —687

Say firstly the word "Bhoomi" and then add the word "Ruha," and comprehend in this way all the names *tupak* unhesitatingly. —688

Utter the word "Ruha" after the word "Prathvi" and in this way, without any difference, know the names of *tupak*. —689

Putting firstly the word "Vraksh" and then adding the word "Prashthani" afterwards, many names of *tupak* are formed, there is no mystery in it. —690

Putting the word "Drumaj" in the beginning and the word "Prashthani" at the end, all the names of *tupak* are formed, if any wise men want to know. —691

Saying the word "Taru" in the beginning and thinking about the word "Prashthani" afterwards, comprehend all the names of *tupak* without any discrimination. —692

Putting the word "Rukh" in the beginning and the word "Prashthani" afterwards, all the names of *tupak* are formed without any difference. —693

Saying the word "Utbhuj" in the beginning and thinking about the word "Prashthani" in the mind, comprehend all the names of *tupak* without any difference. —694

Saying the word "Tarus" in the beginning and then adding the word "Prashthani," comprehend the names of *tupak* without any difference. —695

Comprehend all the names of *tupak* by putting the word "Patri" in the beginning and then adding the word "Prashthani" afterwards, and do not consider any mystery in it. —696

ARIL

Utter the word "Dharaadhaar" in the beginning, then add the word "Prashthani," and O wise men! comprehend all the names of *tupak* without any difference. —697

DOHIRA

The names of *tupak* are formed by placing the word "Dharaaraaj" in the beginning and then adding the word "Prashthani," which O wise men! comprehend them in your mind. —698

Saying firstly the word "Dharaa" and then adding the words "Naayak" and "Prashth" at the end, the names of *tupak* (Bandook) are comprehended correctly. —699

CHAUPAI

Say firstly the word "Dharaa," then add the word "Naayak" and then utter the word "Prashthani," comprehend all the names of *tupak*. —700

Uttering firstly the word "Dharni" and then the word "Raav" and afterwards adding the word "Prashthani," comprehend all the names of *tupak*. —701

Putting the words "Dharnipati" in the beginning and afterwards adding the word "Prashthani," comprehend all the names of *tupak* without any difference. —702

Saying the words "Dharaaraat" in the beginning and then adding the word "Prashthani," comprehend the names of *tupak*, there is not an iota of falsehood in it. —703

Saying the word "Dharaaraaj" in the beginning and then adding the word "Prashthani" with it, the names of *tupak* are comprehended, which is eulogised by all. —704

Utter the word "Dharaa" and then add the word "Prashthani" at the end, then comprehend the names of *tupak* without any difference. —705

Saying the word "Dharaa" in the beginning and then "Indra" and afterwards adding the word "Prashthani" all the name of *tupak* are comprehended. —706

Saying the firstly the word "Dharaa," then adding the word "Paalak" and then uttering the word "Prashthani," all the names of *tupak* are known. —707

Saying the word "Taruj" in the beginning and adding the word "Naath" and then uttering the word "Prashthani," comprehend the names of *tupak*. —708

Putting the word "Drumaj" in the beginning, then adding the word "Naayak" and then adding the word "Prashthani" at the end, all the names of *tupak* are comprehended. —709

Uttering firstly the word "Phal" then the word "Nayak" and then saying the word "Prashthani,"

SHRI SHASTAR NAAM-MAALA PURANA

all the names of *tupak* are comprehended. —710

Saying the word "Taruj" in the beginning and then adding the words "Raaj" and "Prashthani," the names of *tupak* (Tuphang) are known in the mind. —711

Saying the words "Dharni Jaa," then adding then word "Raat" and afterwards adding the words "Prashthani," comprehend all the names of *tupak*. —712

Saying the word "Vrakshaj" in the beginning and then adding the words "Raajaa" and "Prashthani," comprehend all the names of *tupak*. —713

Saying the words "Taru-ruha-anuj" in the beginning and then adding the words "Naayak" and "Prashthani," new names of *tupak* are evolved. —714

Saying the words "Taru-ruha-prashthani," O wise men! the names of *tupak* may be comprehended. —715

O good poet, utter the word "Kundani" from your mouth, from which the names of *tupak* are formed correctly. —716

ARIL

The names of *tupak* are recognised by uttering the words "Kaashth-kundani." Saying the words "Vraksh-jawaasini" from the mouth, the names of *tupak* are known in the heart. —717

Saying the words "Dhar-Ishwarjaa" and then adding the word "Kundani" after it, O good poets! comprehend it as true and utter the names of *tupak* unhesitatingly. —718

By uttering the word "Taru-jawaasini," all the names of *tupak* are comprehended in mind. Have no doubt about it in your heart and wherever you want, you may use this name. —719

CHAUPAI

Utter the word "Bhoomi" and then add the word "Jaa;" comprehend the names of *tupak* in this way and do not consider any difference in it. —720

Utter firstly the word "Prathvi" and then add the word "Jaa;" and knowing all the names of *tupak* (Tuphang), you may use them, wherever you want. —721

Add the word "Jaa" after the word "Basiddhaa" and know all the names of *tupak* without any discrimination. —722

Utter the word "Vasundaraa" and add the word "Jaa" to it, and knowing all the names the of *tupak*, you may use them according to your heart's desire. —723

Uttering firstly the word "Tarini" and then add the word "Jaa" to it, and you may use all the names of *tupak* to your heart's desire. —724

CHHAND

All the names of *tupak* are formed by putting firstly the word "Baleesh" and adding the word "Vaasini" to it, there is no mystery in it. —725

CHAUPAI

Comprehend all the names of *tupak* by uttering firstly the word "Singh" and then adding the word "Ari," there is no mystery in it. —726

Utter firstly the word "Pundareek" and then add "Ari" after it, then comprehend all the names of *tupak*, there is no mystery in it. —727

Put firstly the word "Hari-aksh" and then add the word "Taa" and thus comprehend the names of *tupak* according to your heart's desire. —728

CHHAND

Recognise the names of *tupak* (Tuphang) without any discrimination by firstly uttering the word "Mrigraaj" and then adding the word "Ari." —729

CHAUPAI

Comprehend all the names of *tupak* by adding the word "Ripu" with the word "Mrigraaj" and do not consider any mystery in it. —730

Comprehend all the names of *tupak* by firstly uttering "Pashupatesh" and then adding the word "Ari;" do not consider any mystery in it. —731

DOHIRA

Naming all the animals and then adding the word "Shatru" at the end, all the names of *tupak* continue to be evolved. —732

Saying the word "Mrig" in the beginning and then uttering the word "Pati" and afterwards adding the word "Ari," comprehend the names of *tupak* (Tuphang) correctly. —733

CHHAND

Saying firstly the word "Mrig" and then uttering the words "Pati" and "Ripu," all the names of *tupak* are comprehended. —734

The names of *tupak* are recognised by uttering firstly the word "Sharangi" (deer) and then adding the words "Ari" and "Ari." —735

CHHAND BARAA

Utter primarily the word "Pati" and then the word "Mrig" and afterwards adding the word "Ari," recognise the names of *tupak* O good poets! there is no mystery in it and use this word anywhere in Kabit stanza. —736

CHAUPAI

Saying firstly the word "Hiran," then the word "Pati" and afterwards uttering the word "Ari," think about all the names of *tupak*. —737

Recognise all the names of *tupak* by uttering the word "Shrangi" and then adding the words "Pati" and "Shatru" —738

After uttering the word "Krishnaajin," add the word "Pati" then recognise the names of *tupak* without any difference. —739

DOHIRA

Utter firstly from your mouth the word "Nayanotam" and then saying the words "Pati Ari," comprehend all the names of *tupak*. —740

CHAUPAI

Comprehend all the names of *tupak* by uttering the word "Sautani" and then saying the words "Pati Ripu." —741

ARIL

The names of *tupak* are comprehended by uttering the word "Mrigi" and afterwards adding the words "Nayak" and "Shatru," you may describe it according to your incarnation. —742

Comprehend all the names of *tupak* in your heart by uttering the words "Sit-asit-anjan" and then adding the words "Pati" and "Shatru." —743

Uttering firstly "Udar-shvet-charam" and then adding the words "Naath Ripu," comprehend all the names of *tupak*. —744

CHAUPAI

Utter firstly the words "Krishna-prashth-charam," then add the word "Nayak" and afterwards mention the word "Shatru;" in this way recognise all the names of *tupak*. —745

After the words "Chaaru-netra," add the words "Pati" and "Naath" and in this way recognise the names of *tupak* in your mind. —746

Saying the word "Nayanotam" add the words "Nayak" and "Shatru," then recognise the names of *tupak* in your mind. —747

Saying firstly the word "Mrigi," then add the words "Nayak" and "Shatru," then recognise the names of *tupak* in your mind. —748

Comprehend the names of *tupak* by firstly saying the word "Chakkhi" and then adding the words "Ripu" and "Shatru." —749

Saying firstly the words "Mrigi-aadhip" and then adding the words "Pati" and "Shatru," recognise thus all the names of *tupak*. —750

Utter firstly the words "Mrigi-raat" and then say "Pati Shatru," thus comprehend the name of *tupak*. —751

Utter firstly the words "Mrigi-Indra" and add the word "Nayak;" after that speaking the word "Ripu," recognise all the name of *tupak*. —752

Utter firstly the word "Mrigeshwar," speak the words "Pati Shatru;" then recognise all the names of *tupak*. —753

ARIL

Saying firstly the word "Mrigiraaj," then uttering the word "Nayak" and then adding the word "Shatru" at the end, O wise persons! recognise all the names of *tupak*. —754

Saying the word "Mrigaj" in the beginning and then uttering the words "Nayak" and "Shatru," O wise men! comprehend the names of *tupak*. —755

Putting firstly the word "Mrigi," the word "Nayak" and afterwards adding the word "Shatru," all

SHRI SHASTAR NAAM-MAALA PURANA

the names of *tupak* are comprehended in mind. —756

CHAUPAI

Putting firstly "Mrigi-anuj" and afterwards adding the words "Nayak" and "Shatru," all the names of *tupak* are known. —757

Putting firstly "Mrigi-anuj" and then "Nayak" and afterwards uttering the words "Shatru," all the names of *tupak* are comprehended. —758

Saying the word "Mrigi-anuj" in the beginning, then add the word "Nayak" and afterwards adding the word "Shatru," comprehend all the names of *tupak*. —759

Know the names of *tupak*, by saying firstly the word "Mrigi-raman" and then adding the words "Nayak" and "Shatru." —760

Saying firstly the words "Mrigi-jaayak" and then uttering the words "Nayak Shatru," comprehend the names of *tupak* (Bandook) in your mind. —761

DOHIRA

Saying firstly the words "Mrigi-jaa" and then uttering "Pati" and "Ripu," O poets, the names of *tupak* are formed. —762

The names of *tupak* are formed by uttering firstly "Tran-char" and then "Pati-ari." —763

ARIL

Utter the word "Tran-char," then add the word "Naath" and afterwards add "Shatru" at the end and in this way, recognise all the names of *tupak*. —764

Saying firstly the word "Tran-bhaksh" and then adding the words "Nayak" and "Shatru," consider all the names of *tupak*. —765

CHAUPAI

Utter firstly the words "Tran-haa" and then speak the words "Nayak Shatru" and then consider all the names of *tupak*. —766

ARIL

Utter firstly the words "Tran-haatri" and then add the words "Naath Shatru," and then comprehend all the names of *tupak* in your mind. —767

Saying firstly the words "Tran-bhakshi" and then adding the words "Nayak" and "Shatru," consider all the names of *tupak*. —768

Mentioning firstly "Tran-haa-ripu," then adding the words "Naath Shatru," recognise the names of *tupak*. —769

DOHIRA

Saying "Tran-ripu" and then adding "Pati-ripu" at the end, comprehend correctly all the names of *tupak*. —770

CHAUPAI

Utter firstly "Tran-ripu" and then add the words "Nayak" and "Shatru," and in this way consider all the names of *tupak*. —771

Saying firstly the word "Bhujantak" and then adding the words "Nayak" and "Shatru," recognise the name of *tupak* in your mind. —772

Saying firstly the words "Prathvi-jaa-ari" and then uttering the words "Nayak and Shatru," recognise all the names of *tupak*. —773

ARIL

Comprehend all the names of *tupak* by saying the words "Bhu-sut-ripu" and then adding the words "Naath Shatru." —774

CHAUPAI

Utter the word "Ud-bhid" and then add "Ripu-nayak," then speak the word "Shatru" and recognise the names of *tupak*. —775

Utter the words "Vasundraa-jaa-shatru," then add the words "Nayak" and "Shatru," know in this way the names of *tupak* (Bandook) in your mind. —776

Saying the word "Purni," add the words "Jaa," "Ripu" and "Shatru" and recognise all the names of *tupak*. —777

Saying firstly the word "Dvipni," then utter the words "Char" and "Shatru," and comprehend all the names of *tupak*. —778

Saying firstly the word "Srashtni," then add the words "Jaa" and "Shatru" and in this way recognise the names of *tupak* in your mind. —779

Saying firstly the word "Dharni," then add the words "Jaa," "Char" and "Shatru" and in this way comprehend all the names of *tupak*. —780

Say firstly the word "Dharaa," then utter the words "Jaa," "Char" and "Shatru," adopt the names of *tupak* in your mind. —781

DOHIRA

Utter the word "Bhoomij" and then saying "Char-ripu," comprehend correctly the names of *tupak*, the hero of the army. —782

CHAUPAI

Know all the names of *tupak* by firstly uttering the word "Drumni," then adding "Jaa, Char, Nayak and Shatru." —783

Comprehend the names of *tupak* by firstly uttering "Vrakshneej," then adding "Charanadik" and saying the word "Shatru." —784

Saying firstly the words "Dhar-aishvaryani" and then adding "Jaa, Char and Shatru" and comprehend all the names of *tupak*. —785

Saying firstly "Dharaa-taatani," then speak "Jaa-char-nayak" and knowing all the names of *tupak*, do not consider any discrimination in it. —786

ARIL

Utter firstly the word "Vaaridhni," after that add "Jaa-char-nayak," then utter after adding the word "Shatru" in this way adopt all the names of *tupak* in your mind. —787

Utter firstly the word "Saamudrani," after that add and speak the words "Jaa, Char and Shatru," O skilful people; consider all the names of *tupak*. —788

Utter firstly the word "Neer-raashi," then add "Jaa-char-nayak" and afterwards add "Shatru" at the end, and in this way, recognise all the names of *tupak*. —789

CHAUPAI

Uttering firstly the word "Neeraalayani," then add "Jaa-char-nayak" and afterwards add the word "Shatru" and recognise the names of *tupak* in mind. —790

ARIL

Utter the word "Neerdhani" in the beginning, then add "Jaa-char-nayak" and then saying the word "Shatru" at the end, O skilful people! in this way comprehend all the names of *tupak*. —791

DOHIRA

Saying firstly the word "Varalayani" then adding the words "Jaa-char-shatru," comprehend the names of *tupak*. —792

Utter firstly the word "Jalraashinani," then say the words" Jaa-char-nayak-shatru;" in this way consider all the names of *tupak*. —793

CHAUPAI

Utter firstly "Kalidhani" and afterwards "Jaa-char-nayak-shatru" and comprehend all the names of *tupak*. —794

Utter firstly the word "Ambujanani," then add "Jaa-char-nayak-shatru" and in this way comprehend the names of *tupak*. —795

Utter firstly the word "Jalni," then add "Jaa-char-pati" and then add the word "Shatru" and recognise all the names of *tupak*. —796

Utter the word "Paanini," then speak the words "Jaa-char-shatru" and in this way comprehend all the names of *tupak*. —797

Utter firstly the word "Ambujani" and then "Jaa-char-pati-shatru" and comprehend the names of *tupak*. —798

DOHIRA

Utter firstly the word "Vaarini" and then "Jaa-char-dhar and Shatru," and comprehend the names of *tupak* in your mind. —799

ARIL

Uttering firstly the word "Vaarijani" and then speaking "Jaa-char-pati-shatru," consider and remember all the names of *tupak*. —800

After firstly saying "Jalnidhani," utter the words "Jaa-char-nayak and Shatru," and comprehend all the names of *tupak*. —801

CHAUPAI

After firstly saying the word "Meghjani," utter the words "Jaa-char-nayak and Shatru" and know the names of *tupak*. —802

Know all the names of *tupak* after firstly saying the word "Ambujni" and then uttering "Jaa-char-nayak and Shatru." —803

Know the names of *tupak* by saying firstly the word "Hirni" and then uttering "Jaa-char-nayak and Shatru." —804

SHRI SHASTAR NAAM-MAALA PURANA

then utter the words "Jaa-char-nayak-shatru" and comprehend all the names of *tupak*. —853

ARIL

Saying firstly "Dvaarvati-naayakni," then utter the words "Jaa-char-nayak-shatru" and as skilled persons recognise all the names of *tupak*. —854

CHAUPAI

Saying firstly the words "Dvaarika-dhanani," then utter the words "Jaa-char-pati-shatru" and know the names of *tupak*. —855

Saying firstly the word "Dvaarkendrani," then "Jaa-char-pati-and Shatru" and know all the names of *tupak*. —856

Saying the words "Dvaarvatesh-varni" and then utter "Jaa-char-pati-shatru" and know all the names of *tupak*. —857

Saying firstly the word "Yaadveshni," add the words "Jaa-char-nayak-shatru" and recognise all the names of *tupak*. —858

Saying firstly the words "Dvaarvati-naayakni," then add the words "Jaa-char-pati-shatru" and in this way know all the names of *tupak*. —859

Saying firstly "Jagteshvarni," then add "Jaa-char-nayak-shatru" and know all the names of *tupak*. —860

ARIL

Saying firstly the words "Jaanak-dundubhi-jaa-vallabhni" and then uttering the words "Jaa-char-nayak-shatru," know all the names of *tupak*. —861

Uttering firstly the word "Halibhraatinani" and then saying "Jaa-char" and adding "Nayak-shatru" and know wisely all the names of *tupak*. —862

CHAUPAI

Saying the words "Bal-anu-janani" in the beginning, then add the words "Jaa-char-pati-shatru" and recognise the names of *tupak*. —863

Add the words "Jaa-char-pati-shatru" after firstly saying "Balbhaainani" and know the names of *tupak*. —864

Say the words "Jaa-char-pati-shatru" after firstly uttering the words "Rohineya-bhraatinani" and know the names of *tupak*. —865

Utter firstly the words "Balbhadar-bhraatinani," then add the words "Jaa-char-nayak and Shatru" and in this way know all the names of *tupak*. —866

ARIL

Saying firstly the words "Pralambghan-anujanani" and then adding the words "Jaa-char-nayak-shatru" and know all the names of *tupak*. —867

Saying firstly the words "Kaampaal-anujanani," then add the word "Jaa-char" and afterwards "Nayak" then utter the word "Shatru" at the end and in this way, know all the names of *tupak*. —868

Saying firstly the words "Hal-aayudh-anujanani," then add the words "Jaa-char-nayak-ari" and know all the names of *tupak*. —869

Saying firstly the words "Revati-raman-anujanani" and then adding the words "Jaa-char-nayak-shatru" at the end and know all the names of *tupak*. —870

CHAUPAI

Saying firstly the words "Raam-anujanani" and then add the words "Jaa-char-pati-shatru" and know all the names of *tupak*. —871

Saying the words "Jaa-char-nayak-shatru" after firstly uttering the words "Baldev-anujanani" and know all the names of *tupak*. —872

ARIL

Utter the words "Jaa-char-nayak-shatru" after firstly saying the words "Pralambari-anujanani" and know all the names of *tupak* in your mind. —873

Utter firstly the words "Tranaavrat-arnani" and then saying the words "Jaa-char-nayak-shatru," know all the names of *tupak*. —874

Utter the word "Keshiyaantaknin" in the beginning and then speak the words "Jaa-char-nayak-shatru" and in this way consider all the names of *tupak*. —875

Saying firstly the word "Bakiyantaknin" and then uttering the words "Jaa-char-nayak-shatru" and consider wisely all the names of *tupak*. —876

After saying "Patnaganin" (Sheshanaga), utter the words "Jaa-char-nayak-shatru" at the end, and in this way know all the names of *tupak*. —877

Saying firstly the words "Shaktasur-hananan" then add the words "Jaa-char-nayak-shatru" and recognise all the names of *tupak*. —878

CHAUPAI

Mention the words "Jaa-char-nayak-shatru" after firstly uttering the words "Mur-arinin" and know all the names of *tupak*. —879

Utter the word "Narkaantaknin" in the beginning and then say "Jaa-char-pati-shatru" and in this way all the names of *tupak* are spoken. —880

Saying firstly the words "Narak-haanin," then add the words "Jaa-char-nayak-shatru" and know the names of *tupak*. —881

Uttering firstly the words "Shatru-ghayanin," then add "Jaa-char-nayak" and afterwards add the word "Shatru" and in this way know the names of *tupak*. —882

ARIL

Saying firstly the words "Murmardanin" and then adding the words "Jaa-char-nayak-shatru," know all the names of *tupak*. —883

CHAUPAI

Saying firstly the word "Madhusudananin," then add the words "Jaa-char-nayak-shatru," know all the names of *tupak*. —884

ARIL

Saying firstly the words "Madhu-dundani," add the words "Jaa-char-shadendra and Shatru" and in this way know the names of *tupak* in your mind. —885

Saying "Madhunaashinani," add the words "Jaa-char, Shabdeshwar and Shatru" and in this way know the names of *tupak* in your mind. —886

Saying firstly "Kaalyamun-arinin," utter the words "Jaa-char-nayak-shatru" and consider all the names of *tupak*. —887

Saying the words "Narak-arinin," add the words "Jaa-char-nayak-shatru" and know all the names of *tupak*. —888

Saying firstly the words "Kans-kesh-karshani," add the words "Jaa-char-nayak-shatru" and consider the names of *tupak* thoughtfully. —889

Saying firstly the word "Vasudeveshnani," add the words "Jaa-char-nayak-shatru" and know all the names of *tupak*. —890

Saying the firstly words "Anik-dundu-bhishnan," add the words "Jaa-char-nayak-shatru" at the end, recognise all the names of *tupak* as the *mantras*. —891

Saying firstly the words "Raman-rasiknin," then utter the words "Jaa-char-nayak-shatru" and in this way adopt all the names of *tupak* in your mind. —892

Saying firstly the word "Naaraayanin," add "Jaa-char-raaj-shatru" and know all the names of *tupak*. —893

Saying firstly the word "Vaaraalayanani," utter the words "Jaa-char-naath-shatru" and know all the names of *tupak* authentically. —894

Utter the word "Naaraalayani," in the beginning, then add the words "Jaa-char-pati-shatru," O skilful people! know all the names of *tupak*. —895

Saying firstly the word "Naariketnin," add the words "Jaa-char-nayak-shatru" and consider all the names of *tupak*. —896

Saying firstly the word "Jalvasanani, add the words "Jaa-char-naath-shatru" and know thoughtfully all the names of *tupak*. —897

CHAUPAI

Saying firstly the word "Jal-ketanani," add the words "Jaa-char-nayak-shatru" and know all the names of *tupak*. —898

ARIL

Utter firstly the word "Jalvaasanani," then add "Jaa-char-naath-shatru" and in this way know all the names of *tupak*. —899

CHAUPAI

Utter firstly the word "Jaldhaamanani, then add the words "Jaa-char-pati-shatru" and know the names of *tupak*. —900

Saying firstly the word "Jalgrahananani," add the words "Jaa-char-pati-shatru" and know all the names of *tupak*. —901

Saying the word "Jalvaasananani," add the words "Jaa-char-nayak-shatru" and know all the names of *tupak*. —902

Saying the words "Jal-sanketni," and then speak the words "Jaa-char-pati-shatru" and know all the names of *tupak*. —903

Saying firstly the word "Varidhamani," then utter the words "Jaa-char-shabdesh-shatru" and know all the names of *tupak*. —904

Saying firstly the word "Vaarigrahanani," then add the words "Jaa-char-nayak-shatru" and know all the names of *tupak*. —905

ARIL

Saying firstly the word "Meghjanin," then add the words "Jaa-char-naath and Shatru" and consider all the names of *tupak*. —906

CHAUPAI

Uttering firstly the word "Sarasvati" and then speak the words "Jaa-char-nayak-shatru" and know all the names of *tupak*. —907

Saying firstly the words "Gang-bhetani" and then utter the words "Jaa-char-nayak-shatru" and in this way speak all the names of *tupak*. —908

Saying firstly the words "Arun-vaarinin," then add the words "Jaa-char-nayak-shatru" and know all the names of *tupak*. —909

Saying firstly the words "Arun-vaarini," then add the words "Jaa-char-nayak-shatru" and know all the names of *tupak*. —910

ARIL

Saying firstly the words "Arun-ambneen," add the words "Jaa-char-naath-shatru" and know the names of *tupak*. —911

CHAUPAI

aying firstly the words "Arun-turangni," add the words "Jaa-char-nayak-shatru" and know all the names of *tupak*. —912

aying firstly the words "Aarakat-jalni" (Brahma-putra), then add the words "Jaa-char-nayak-shatru" and know the names of *tupak*. —913

aying firstly the words "Arun-ambunani," then utter the words "Jaa-char-pati-shatru" and know the names of *tupak*. —914

Saying firstly the words "Arun-paanini," add the words "Jaa-char-nayak ari" and know all the names of *tupak*. —915

Saying firstly the words "Arun-jalnani," add the words "Jaa-char-pati-shatru" and know all the names of *tupak*. —916

Saying firstly the words "Arun-neernin," add the words "Jaa-char-nayak-shatru" and know all the names of *tupak*. —917

Saying firstly the words "Shatadar-vananni" (Sutlej), add the words "Jaa-char-nayak-ari" and know all the names of *tupak*. —918

Saying firstly the words "Sat-pravaahinin," add the words "Jaa-char-nayak-shatru" and know the names of *tupak*. —919

Saying firstly the words "Sahasar-narinin," add the words "Jaa-char-pati-shatru" and know all the names of *tupak*. —920

ARIL

Saying firstly the words "Satyadra-vananini," add the words "Jaa-char-naath-ripu" and recognise thoughtfully all the names of *tupak*. —921

CHAUPAI

Saying firstly the words "Shat-pravaahini," add the words "Jaa-char-pati-shatru" and know all the names of *tupak*. —922

Saying firstly the words "Shat-gaamini," add the words "Jaa-char-nayak-shatru" and know all the names of *tupak*. —923

Saying firstly the words "Shat-taragni," add the words "Jaa-char-nayak" and the word "Ari" at the end, know all the names of *tupak* in your mind. —924

Saying firstly the word "Bhoomi," add the words "Jaa-char-pati-shatru" and know all the names of *tupak*. —925

Saying firstly the word "Vyasanani," add the words "Jaa-char-nayak-shatru" and know the names of *tupak*. —926

Saying firstly the word "Vyaahanani" (Vyas), add the words "Jaa-char-nayak-shatru" and know all the names of *tupak*. —927

Saying firstly the word "Paashsakatanani" (Vipaasha), add the words "Jaa-char-nayak-ripu" and know all the names of *tupak*. —928

Saying firstly the word "Paashnaashanani," add the words "Jaa-char-nayak-shatru" and consider all the names of *tupak*. —929

Saying firstly the words "Varunayudh-naashanan," add the words "Jaa-char-nayak-shatru" and know all the names of *tupak*. —930

Saying the words "Jalsin-aauyudh" in the beginning, add the words "Jaa-char-nayak-shatru" and know all the names of *tupak*. —931

ARIL

Saying all the names of nooses (*paash*) utter the word "Naashnin" and then the words "Jaa-char-naath" and recognise all the names of *tupak*. —932

Saying firstly the word "Varuni," add the "Jaa-char, Naath and Shatru" at the end and in this way know all the names of *tupak*. —933

CHAUPAI

Saying firstly the word "Raavneen," add the words "Jaa-char-pati-shatru" and recognise all the names of *tupak*. —934

Saying firstly the word "Chandrabhaaganani," add the words "Jaa-char-pati-shatru" and know all the names of *tupak*. —935

Saying firstly the words "Shashi-aganan," add the words "Jaa-char-pati-shatru" and in this way know all the names of *tupak*. —936

Saying firstly the words "Chandar-anujnin," add the words "Jaa-char-pati-shatru" and know all the names of *tupak*. —937

ARIL

Saying firstly the words "Shashi-ani-janani" add the words "Jaa-char-naath" and then "Shatru" at the end, and in this way know all the names of *tupak*. —938

CHAUPAI

Saying firstly the words "Mayank-anujnani," add the words "Jaa-char-pati-ari" and know the name of *tupak*. —939

ARIL

Saying firstly the words "Mayank-sahodarnani," add the words "Jaa-char-naath-shatru" at the end and in this way O good poets! know all the names of *tupak*. —940

CHAUPAI

Saying firstly the words "Ar-anujananani," add the words "Jaa-char-pati-shatru" at the end, and consider all the names of *tupak*. —941

Saying firstly the words "Nishish-anujananani," add the words "Jaa-char-pati-shatru," and know all the names of *tupak*. —942

Saying firstly words "Nishi-ishvarananin," add the words "Jaa-char-pati-shatru" and recognise all the names of *tupak*. —943

Saying firstly the word "Rainaadhipni," add the words "Jaa-char-nayak-shatru," and know all the names of *tupak*. —944

Saying firstly the words "Rain-raatnani," add the words "Jaa-char-nayak-shatru" and know all the names of *tupak*. —945

Saying the words "Rain-raajani" and then utter the words "Jaa-char-pati-shatru" and know all the names of *tupak*. —946

Saying the words "Nishi-nayakni," add the words "Shunya-char-pati," then also "Ari" and know all the names of *tupak*. —947

Saying the words "Nishi-Ishani," add the words "Jaa-char-nayak-shatru" and know the names of *tupak*. —948

Saying firstly the words "Nishi-patnani," add the words "Sat-char-ari-shatru" at the end and know the names of *tupak*. —949

Saying firstly the words "Nishi-dhanani," add the words "Jaa-char, Ari and Shatru" and know the names of *tupak* in your mind. —950

Saying firstly the words "Rain-nayakni," add the words "Jaa-char-pati-shatru" and know the names of *tupak*. —951

Saying firstly the words "Nishi-charnan," add the words "Sat-char-nayak-shatru" and recognise the names of *tupak*. —952

Saying the words "Nishaa-charnan," add the words "Sat-char-nayak-shatru" and know all the names of *tupak*. —953

Saying firstly the words "Rain-raman," add the words "Sat-char-pati-shatru" and know all the names of *tupak*. —954

Saying firstly the words "Rain-raajnan," add the words "Sat-char-pati-shatru" and in this way know all the names of *tupak*. —955

Saying firstly the words "Nishaa-ramannin" utter the words "Sat-char-pati-shatru" and know all the names of *tupak*. —956

Saying firstly the words "Din-ari-ramnan," add the words "Sat-char-pati-shatru," and know the names of *tupak*. —957

Saying firstly the words "Harija-ari-ramanani" and add the words "Sat-char-pati," then add "Shatru" and know all the names of *tupak*. —958

Saying firstly the words "Nimir-ramanani," add the words "Sat-char-nayak-shatru" and know all the names of *tupak*. —959

Saying firstly the words "Harjari-ramnan" add the words "Jaa-char-nayak-shatru" and know all the names of *tupak*. —960

Saying firstly the words "Ravijari-ramnan," add the words "Jaa-char-pati-shatru" and know all the names of *tupak*. —961

Saying firstly the words "Maanuj-ari," add the word "Raman" and then add "Jaa-char-nayak-shatru" and in this way, know all the names of *tupak*. —962

Saying firstly the words "Surya-ari-raman," utter the words "Jaa-char-nayak-shatru" and know the names of *tupak* in your mind. —963

Saying firstly the words "Bhaanjari-ramnan," utter the words "Sat-char-pati-shatru" and know all the names of *tupak*. —964

ARIL

Uttering the words "Dindhvaj-ari-ramnan," speak the words "Jaa-char-naath-shatru" and know all the names of the *tupak*. —965

Saying firstly the words "Din-raaj-ari-ramanani," utter the words "Jaa-char-naath-shatru" and consider all the names of *tupak*. —966

CHAUPAI

Saying firstly the words "Dinas-ari-ramnan," utter the words "Jaa-char-nayak-shatru" and know all the names of *tupak*. —967

Saying firstly the words "Tam-arijari-ramnan" add the "Jaa-char-nayak and Shatru" at the end and know all the names of *tupak*. —968

Saying firstly the words "Chandrayonini," utter the words "Jaa-char-pati-shatru" and know the names of *tupak*. —969

Saying firstly the words "Shashi-up-bakhani," add the words "Jaa-char-pati-shatru" and know all the names of *tupak*. —970

Saying firstly the words "Nishi-ish-bhagini," add the words "Jaa-char-pati-shatru" and recognise all the names of *tupak*. —971

Saying the words "Shashi-bhagini," add the words "Jaa-char-pati-shatru" and know all the names of *tupak*. —972

Saying the words "Nishishbhagaa," add the words "Jaa-char-pati-shatru" and know all the names of *tupak*. —973

Saying "Rainraat" add the word "Bhagaa," utter the words "Jaa-char-pati-shatru" and know all the names of *tupak*. —974

ARIL

Say the word "Bhag" after "Rainraavani," then speak the words "Jaa-char-naath-shatru" and make the desired use of the names of *tupak*. —975

Saying the words "Rainraaj," speak the word "Bhagaa," then add the words "Jaa-char-naath-shatru" and in this way, know all the names of *tupak*. —976

CHAUPAI

After saying "Rainraaj," utter the words "Bhagaa-jaa-char-pati-shatru" and say the names of *tupak*. —977

Saying the words "Din-ari-bhag," utter the words "Jaa-char-nayak-shatru" then speak the names of *tupak*. —978

Saying "Tamchar," utter the word "Bhag," then speak the words "Jaa-char-nayak-shatru" and know all the names of *tupak*. —979

Saying "Rainraav," utter the word "Bhagini," then add the words "Jaa-char-nayak-shatru" and in this way consider all the names of *tupak*. —980

Saying "Jaunkaran," utter the word "Bhagan," then add the words "Jaa-char-nayak-shatru" and know the names of *tupak*. —981

Saying the word "Kirandharan," then speak the word "Bhagini," then utter the words "Sat-char-pati-shatru" and determine all the names of *tupak*. —982

Saying the word "Mayank," speak the word "Bhagini," then utter the words "Sat-char-naath-shatru" and know correctly all the names of *tupak*. —983

Saying the word "Mrig-vahan" and then "Bhagini," then utter the words "Sat-char-pati-shatru" and adopt all the names of *tupak* in your mind. —984

Saying "Hiran-raat," utter the word "Bhagini," then speak the words "Sat-char-nayak-shatru" and in this way know all the names of *tupak*. —985

Saying "Shrang-vahani-bhagaa," add the words "Jaa-char-pati-shatru" and know all the names of *tupak*. —986

Saying "Mrig-patini," then speak the word "Bhagini," then utter the words "Jaa-char-pati-shatru" and know all the names of *tupak*. —987

Saying "Prajaapati," add "Bhagini" and then mentioning the words "Sat-char-pati-shatru" and know all the names of *tupak*. —988

CHHAND

Saying the words "Mrignaath bhaginini," utter the words "Ripu-naath-char-pati-ripu" and in this way know all the names of *tupak*. —989

CHAUPAI

Saying the words "Nadi-raat-sut-bhagini," utter the words "Jaa-char-pati-shatru" and know the names of *tupak*. —990

Saying "Samudraj," add the word "Bhagini," then utter the words "Jaa-char-pati-shatru" and in this way know all the names of *tupak* in your mind. —991

Utter the words "Nadi-raat-sut-bhagni," then speak the words "Jaa-char-pati-shatru" and determine all the names of the *tupak*. —992

Saying the words "Samudraj-bhaginin," utter the words "Jaa-char-pati-shatru" and know all the names of the *tupak*. —993

Saying the words "Mrig-jaa-bhagini," utter the words "Jaa-char-pati-ripu" and know all the names of the *tupak*. —994

Saying the words "Nadishaj-bhagini," utter the words "Jaa-char-pati-shatru" and know all the names of the *tupak*. —995

Saying "Nadi-nayak" add the word "Bhaginin," then mention the words "Sat-char-nayak-shatru" and in this way all the names of the *tupak*. —996

Saying the words "Sarit-ish-bhaginin," add the words "Jaa-char-pati-shatru" and know all the names of the *tupak*. —997

Saying the words "Sarit-indra-bhaginin," add the words "Sat-char-pati-shatru" and recognise all the names of the *tupak*. —998

ARIL

Saying "Nishishni," add the word "Bhagnin," then add the words "Jaa-char-nayak-shatru" and know all the names of the *tupak*. —999

Saying "Tamchar-bhaginin," utter the words "Jaa-char-pati-shatru" and consider all the names of the *tupak*. —1000

Saying the words "Tamharbhaganin," utter the word "Sat-char-pati," then speaking "Shatru" know all the names of the *tupak*. —1001

Say firstly "Tam-ari-bhagnaanin," then add the words "Sat-char-pati-shatru" and know all the names of the *tupak*. —1002

CHAUPAI

Saying the words "Timirari-bhagnani," add the words "Sat-char-pati-shatru" and know all the names of the *tupak*. —1003

Saying the words "Timir-naashkar-bhagnani," utter the words "Sat-char-nayak-shatru" and know all the names of the *tupak*. —1004

Saying the words "Timir-radan-bhagnani," utter the words "Sat-char-nayak-shatru" and know the names of the *tupak*. —1005

Saying "Timir," add the words "Haa-bhagani," then add the words "Sat-char-pati-shatru" and in this way know all the names of the *tupak*. —1006

Saying the words "Timir-nikandan," add the words "Bhagnin-sat-char" and then uttering the word "Shatru," know the names of the *tupak*. —1007

Saying "Timir-mand-bhagnini," add the words "Sat-char-pati-shatru" and know all the names of the *tupak*. —1008

Saying the words "Timir-yaant," speak "Bhagnin," then add the words "Sat-char-nayak-shatru" at the end in this way know all the names of the *tupak*. —1009

ARIL

Saying the words "Timir-naash-bhagnin," utter the words "Sat-char-naath-ripu" and know all the names of the *tupak*. —1010

Saying the word "Urag-raaj," utter firstly the word "Bhagnin" and then "Sat-char-naath-shatru" and in this way know all the names of the *tupak*. —1011

CHAUPAI

Saying the words "Urgesh-bhagnini," add the words "Sat-char-nayak-ari" and know all the names of the *tupak* in your mind. —1012

Saying "Uragnaath," utter the word "Bhagini," then add the words "Sat-char-pati-ripu" and know all the names of the *tupak*. —1013

Saying the words "Urag-nrapati," add the words "Bhagini," then speak the words "Sat-char-nayak-shatru" and know all the names of the *tupak*. —1014

Saying "Uragnrapati," utter the words "Bhagani," then speak the words "Sat-char-nayak-shatru" and know the names of the *tupak*. —1015

ARIL

Saying the words "Urag-Ish-bhagnin," utter the words "Sat-char-naath-shatru" and know all the names of the *tupak*. —1016

Saying the words "Urpati-bhagnin," add the words "Sat-char-naath-shatru" and know all the names of the *tupak*. —1017

CHAUPAI

Saying the words "Urag-bhoopani-bhoop," add the words "Sat-char-nayak-shatru" and know the names of the *tupak*. —1018

Saying the words "Taaraapati-bhagnin," utter the words "Sat-char-nayak-shatru" and know the names of the *tupak*. —1019

Saying "Taareshwar," add the words "Bhagini," then add the words "Sat-char-nayak-shatru" and know the names of the *tupak*. —1020

Saying "Taaraalaya-Ish-bhagini," utter the words "Sat-char-pati-shatru" and know all the names of the *tupak*. —1021

ARIL

Saying the words "Taaraagrahneesh-bhagini," add the words "Sat-char-naath-shatru" and know wisely all the names of the *tupak*. —1022

Saying the words "Urag-naketeesh-bhagini," utter the words "Sat-char-naath-shatru" and know all the names of the *tupak*. —1023

Saying firstly the words "Urag-naath-bhaginin," add the words "Sat-char-naath-shatru" and recognise wisely the names of the *tupak*. —1024

Saying the words "Urgeshwar-bhaginin," add the words "Sat-char-naath-shatru" at the end, and know all the names of the *tupak*. —1025

Saying firstly the words "Urgeshwar-bhaginin," utter the words "Sat-char-naath-shatru" and know all the names of the *tupak*. —1026

CHAUPAI

Saying the words "Urgaashraya-bhaginin," utter the words "Sat-char-nayak-shatru" and know all the names of the *tupak*. —1027

Saying firstly the words "Rishan-bhagini," then utter the words "Sat-char-pati-shatru" and consider the names of the *tupak* in your mind. —1028

Saying firstly the words "Manij-bhagini," utter the words "Sat-char-pati, and then Shatru" and consider the names of the *tupak* in your mind. —1029

Saying "Vrati-utmaj-bhagini," utter the words "Sat-char-nayak-shatru" and know all the names of the *tupak*. —1030

Saying firstly the words "Tapeesh-bhagini," utter the words "Sat-char-shatru" and know the names of the *tupak*. —1031

Saying "Kashyap-sut-bhagini," utter the words "Sat-char-nayak-shatru" at the end and know all the names of the *tupak* in your mind. —1032

Saying the words "Jainkiran-bhagini," add the words "Sat-char-pati-shatru" and know all the names of the *tupak*. —1033

Saying firstly the word "Krishnan," utter the words "Sat-char-pati-ripu" and know all the names of the *tupak*. —1034

Saying the words "Shyam-muratnin" in the beginning, then add the words "Sat-char-pati-shatru" and know all the names of *tupak*. —1035

Saying firstly the word "Tapatni," add the words "Sat-char-nayak-shatru" and know the names of *tupak*. —1036

Saying firstly the words "Surya-putri," utter the words "Sat-char-nayak-shatru" and know all the names of *tupak*. —1037

Saying firstly the words "Surya-aatamjaa," utter the words "Sat-char-pati-shatru" and consider all the names of *tupak*. —1038

Saying the word "Maanani," and then the words "Sat-char-pati-ari" and know all the names of *tupak*. —1039

Saying firstly the word "Abhimaanini," utter the words "Sat-char-pati-ari" and know all the names of *tupak*. —1040

Saying firstly the word "Samyani," utter the words "Sat-char-nayak-shatru" and know all the names of *tupak*. —1041

Saying firstly the word "Garvini," add the words "Sat-char-nayak-ari" and consider all the names of *tupak*. —1042

ARIL

Saying the word "Darpanani," mention the words "Sat-char-naath" and "Shatru" at the end, recognise all the names of *tupak*. —1043

CHAUPAI

Saying firstly the word "Ahamkaarini," utter the words "Sat-char-pati-shatru" and know all the names of *tupak*. —1044

Saying firstly the word "Pee-anin," utter the words "Sat-char-pati-shatru" and know the names of *tupak*. —1045

DOHIRA

Saying firstly the word "Pikhani," put the word "Ripu" at the end, and know correctly all the names of *tupak*. —1046

Saying firstly the word "Medhani," and uttering the word "Ripu" at the end, all the names of *tupak* continue to be evolved. —1047

Say the word "Semukhani" in the beginning and the word "Ari" at the end, O wise men! know all the names of *tupak*. —1048

Saying firstly the word "Manikhan" add the word "Ripu" after that, and know correctly the names of *tupak*. —1049

Saying the word "Buddhani" in the beginning and the word "Ari" at the end, O wise men! recognise the names of *tupak*. —1050

CHAUPAI

Saying the word "Bhaani" in the beginning and the word "Ripu" at the end, know all the names of *tupak* without any discrimination. —1051

DOHIRA

Say the word "Abhaani" in the beginning and the word "Ripu" at the end, know the names of *tupak* without the slight difference. —1052

ARIL

Saying firstly the word "Shobhani," add the word "Shatru" at the end know the names of *tupak* without the slight difference. —1053

Saying the word "Prabhaadharni" from your mouth, add the word "Shatru" at the end, and know the names of *tupak* without slight difference. —1054

Say the word "Sukhmani" then add the word "Shatru" and know all the names of *tupak* without any difference. —1055

CHAUPAI

Say the word "Dharman" in the beginning and the word "Shatru" at the end and know all the names of *tupak* without the slight difference. —1056

Utter the word "Krantini" in the beginning and the word "Shatru" at the end and know the names of *tupak* without any discrimination. —1057

Say the word "Chhavini" in the beginning and "Ripu" at the end, and recognise all the names of *tupak* without any difference. —1058

Say the word "Baajhini" in the beginning and the word "Ari" at the end and announcing the names of *tupak*, use them as desired. —1059

ARIL

Say the word "Vaahini" in the beginning and "Shatru" at the end, and knowing all the names of *tupak*, use them as desired. —1060

SHRI SHASTAR NAAM-MAALA PURANA

Say firstly the word "Turangni" and add the word "Ari" at the end and know all the names of *tupak* without any discrimination. —1061

Utter the word "Hayani" from your mouth, then add the word "Antkar" and knowing the names of *tupak*, use them as desired. —1062

CHAUPAI

Saying the word "Saindhavani" in the beginning, add the words "Ari" at the end and know all the names of *tupak* without any difference. —1063

Say the word "Arbani" in the beginning and "Ari" at the end, and know all the names of *tupak* without any difference. —1064

Add the word "Ari" after speaking the word "Turangni" and use the name of *tupak* as desired. —1065

Add the word "Ari" after the word "Ghorni" and use name of *tupak* as desired. —1066

Uttering the word "Hasitni," add the word "Ripu" at the end and know all the names of *tupak* for speaking them in the desired way. —1067

ARIL

Uttering the word "Dantni," add the word "Shatru" at the end and recognise all the names of *tupak* without any discrimination. —1068

CHAUPAI

Saying the word "Durdani" in the beginning, add the word "Shatru" at the end and utter the names of *tupak* without any discrimination. —1069

Saying the word "Dayapani" add the word "Ari" at the end and know all the names of *tupak* for using them in the desired way. —1070

Saying firstly the word "Padmini," add the word "Ari" at the end know all the names of *tupak* without any discrimination. —1071

ARIL

Saying firstly the word "Vaarni," add the word "Shatru" at the end and know all the names of *tupak* without any discrimination. —1072

CHAUPAI

Saying the word "Vyaalni," add the word "Ari" at the end and know all the names of *tupak* without any discrimination. —1073

Utter the word "Imbhani" and add the word "Ari" at the end, then the comprehensible names for all the poets are formed. —1074

Saying the word "Kumbhani," add the word "Ari" at the end and in this way know the names of *tupak* for regular recitation. —1075

ARIL

Saying the word "Kunjarni," add the word "Ari" at the end and know all the names of *tupak* without any discrimination. —1076

Saying the word "Karini," add the word "Shatru" at the end and know the names of *tupak* for using them as desired. —1077

Saying the word "Madyadharnani," add the word "Hantaa" at the end and know all the names of *tupak*. —1078

Saying firstly the word "Sindhurni" add the word "Shatru" at the end and know all the names of *tupak*, without any discrimination. —1079

Utter the word "Anikpani," from your mouth, then add the word "Shatru" at the end and know all the names of *tupak* to say them as desired. —1080

Saying firstly the word "Naagini," add the word "Shatru" at the end and know all the names of *tupak* without any discrimination. —1081

Know the name of *tupak* for desired use, them saying the word "Harni" and then adding the word "Shatru" to it. —1082

Saying firstly the word "Gajni," add the word "Shatru" and in this way know the names of *tupak* for desired use. —1083

CHAUPAI

Saying the word "Saavjani," add the word "Ari" at the end and know all the names of *tupak*. —1084

Saying firstly the word "Maatangani," add the word "Ari" and know all the names of *tupak*. —1085

Saying the word "Gayandani" in the beginning, add the word "Ari" at the end and know all the names of *tupak*. —1086

Saying the word "Drumari" in the beginning and add the word "Ari" at the end and know all the names of *tupak*. —1087

CHAUPAI

Saying the word "Vrikshantakni," add the word "Ari" and know all the names of *tupak*. —1088

Saying the words "Phaldhar-arini," add the word "Ari" at the end and know all the names of *tupak*. —1089

Saying the words "Phaldayak-arini" in the beginning, add the word "Ari" at the end and know all the names of *tupak* without any discrimination. —1090

ARIL

Saying firstly the words "Dharaadharan-arini," add the word "Shatru" at the end and know all the names of *tupak* for desired use. —1091

CHAUPAI

Saying the words "Dhoor-raat-arini," add the word "Shatru" at the end and know all the names of *tupak*. —1092

After uttering the word "Phaladh," add the word "Ari" at the end and know all the names of *tupak* for desired description. —1093

Saying firstly the word "Phali," add the word "Ari" and know all the names of *tupak*. —1094

Saying firstly the words "Taru-arini," add the word "Ari" at the end and know all the names of *tupak* without any discrimination. —1095

Saying firstly the words "Dhari-Ishvarni," add the word "Ari" at the end and know all the names of *tupak* without any difficulty. —1096

Saying the word "Vriksharni" in the beginning, add the word "Ari" at the end, and in this way knowing all the names of *tupak*, use them as desired. —1097

Saying the word "Radani," add the word "Ari" at the end and know the names of *tupak*. —1098

Saying the words "Radan-Chhandani-arini," add the word "Ari" at the end and in this way and know all the names of *tupak* without any discrimination. —1099

ARIL

Saying the names of all the elephants, add the words "Arini-ari" and know all the names of *tupak*. —1100

CHAUPAI

Saying firstly the word "Nripni," add the word "Ari" at the end and know all the names of *tupak* without any discrimination. —1101

Saying firstly the word "Bhoopani," add the word "Ari" at the end and know all the names of *tupak*. —1102

ARIL

Saying firstly the word "Swanini," add the word "Shatru" at the end and know all the names of *tupak* without any discrimination. —1103

Saying the word "Adhipatni," add the word "Shatru" at the end and know all the names of *tupak* without any discrimination. —1104

Saying firstly the word "Dhardirani," add the word "Arini" at the end and know all the names of *tupak* for using then as desired. —1105

Saying firstly the word "Adhipani," add the word "Shatru" at the end and know all the names of *tupak* in your mind. —1106

Saying the word "Patni," utter the word "Shatruni" at the end and know all the names of *tupak* in your mind; there is no discrimination in it, use them wherever you desire. —1107

CHAUPAI

Add the word "Arini" after saying the word "Bhoopatani" and know all the names of *tupak* for using them as desired. —1108

Saying the word "Bhoopani," add the word "Ari" and recognise the names of *tupak*. —1109

ARIL

Uttering the word "Vadhkarni" from your mouth, add the word "Arini" at the end and know all the names of *tupak*. —1110

Saying firstly the word "Kinkarni," add the word "Arini" at the end recognising all the names of *tupak*, use them in poetry wherever you want. —1111

CHAUPAI

Saying firstly the word "Ancharni," add the word "Ari" at the end and know all the names of *tupak*. —1112

ARIL

Saying firstly the word "Anugani," add the word "Hanani" at the end and know all the names of *tupak*. —1113

Utter the word "Kinkarni" from your mouth, add the word "Mathani" at the end and know the names of *tupak* for using them as desired. —1114

DOHIRA

Saying firstly the word "Pratnaa," add the word "Ari" at the end and know correctly all the names of *tupak*. —1115

Saying firstly the word "Dhujani," add the word "Ari" at the end, whereby the names of *tupak* continue to be evolved. —1116

Saying the word "Vaahini" and adding the word "Shatru" at the end, O wise men! the names of *tupak* are formed. —1117

Saying firstly the word "Kaami" and adding the word "Ari," O wise men! the names of *tupak* are formed. —1118

Saying firstly the word "Kaami" and adding the word "Ari" at the end, O wise men! the names of *tupak* are formed. —1119

Saying firstly the word "Varikshani" and adding the word "Shatru" at the end, the names of *tupak* are formed. —1120

Saying firstly the word "Senaa" and adding the word "Ari" at the end, the names of *tupak* are formed. —1121

Saying firstly the word "Dhanani" and adding the word "Arini" at the end, O wise men! the names of *tupak* are formed. —1122

ARIL

Saying the word "Dhanushani," add the word "Shatru" and know all the names of *tupak* without any discrimination. —1123

Saying the word "Kovandani," add the word "Arini" at the end and know all the names of *tupak*. —1124

CHAUPAI

Saying the words "Ikshu (arrow) aasani" and adding the word "Arini" at the end, know all the names of *tupak* and use then according to your need. —1125

Saying firstly the word "Kaarmukani," add the word "Arini" at the end and recognise all the names of *tupak*. —1126

Saying firstly the words "Ripusantaapini," add the word "Arini" at the end know all the names of *tupak* without any discrimination. —1127

Saying the words "Ripukhandanani," add the word "Arini" at the end and know all the names of *tupak*. —1128

Saying firstly the words "Dusht-daahani," add the word "Arini" at the end and know all the names of *tupak*. —1129

Saying firstly the words "Ripu-ghayani," add the word "Arini" at the end and know all the names of *tupak* for using them as desired. —1130

ARIL

Saying firstly the word "Chaapani," add the word "Arini" at the end and know all the names of *tupak*. —1131

Saying firstly the word "Pratyanchani," add the word "Arini" at the end and know all the names of *tupak*. —1132

STANZA ROOAAL

Saying firstly the words "Shatru-manjani," add the word "Ripu" and know all the names of *tupak* without any discrimination. —1133

CHAUPAI

Saying firstly the word "Harishkitni," add the word "Arini" at the end and know all the names of *tupak* for using them as desired. —1134

ARIL

Saying firstly the words "Vishikh-varshani," add the word "Arini" at the end and know all the names of *tupak* in your mind. —1135

CHAUPAI

Saying firstly the words "Baan-varshani," add the word "Arini" at the end and know all the names of *tupak*. —1136

ARIL

Saying firstly the word "Baanani," add the word "arini" at the end and know all the names of *tupak* in your mind. —1137

CHAUPAI

Saying the word "Panchani," add the word "Mathani" at the end and know all the names of *tupak* for speaking them according to your inclination. —1138

Saying the word "Kovandjani" speak the word "Mathani" at the end and know all the names of *tupak*. —1139

Saying firstly the word "Ikshuaasjani," the word "Mathani" at the end and know all the names of *tupak* for using them as desired. —1140

ARIL

Saying firstly the word "Kaarmukjani," add the word "Arini" at the end and know all the names of *tupak*. —1141

Saying firstly the word "Riputaapini," add the word "Arini" at the end and O wise men! recognise the names of *tupak* for using the, unhesitatingly. —1142

Utter the word "Chaapani" from your mouth, add the word "Mathani" at the end the know the names of *tupak*. —1143

Saying firstly the word "Panchdharnani," add the word "Mathani" at the end and recognise all the names of *tupak*. —1144

CHAUPAI

Saying firstly the word "Suhirdayani," add the word "Mathani" at the end and know all the names of *tupak* for using them according to your inclination. —1145

ARIL

Saying the word "Vallabhni," add the word "Arini" at the end and know all the names of *tupak* in your mind. —1146

CHAUPAI

Saying firstly the word "Shaakhaainani," add the word "Dharani" at the end and know all the names of *tupak*. —1147

Saying firstly the word "Priyatamani," add the word "Mathani" at the end and know all the names of *tupak*; there is no falsehood in it. —1148

ARIL

Uttering firstly the word "Janani," add the word "Mathani" at the end and know all the names of *tupak* in your mind without any discrimination. —1149

Saying firstly the word "Suhirdyani," add the word "Arini" at the end and know all the names of *tupak* cleverly and use them in poetry according to your inclination. —1150

CHAUPAI

Saying firstly the word "Manushyani," add the word "Arini" at the end and know all the names of *tupak* and use them as desired. —1151

Saying the word "Mratyani," add the word "Arini" at the end and know all the names of *tupak*; you may mention them anywhere as desired. —1152

Saying the word "Manini," add the word "Mathani" and know all the names of *tupak* for using them as desired. —1153

Saying the word "Manushyani" in the beginning, add the word "Mathani" at the end and know all the names of *tupak*. —1154

Saying firstly the word "Narni," add the word "Arini" and know all the names of *tupak* without any discrimination. —1155

Saying firstly the word "Manavni," add the word "Shatru" at the end and know all the names of *tupak* without any doubt. —1156

ARIL

Saying firstly the words "Prithi-raatnani," add the word "Arini" at the end and know all the names of *tupak* without any doubt. —1157

CHAUPAI

Saying the words "Kshiti-neeshani," utter the word "Arini" and speak all the names of *tupak*. —1158

Saying firstly the word "Kshatriyeshani," add the word "Mathani" at the end and recognise all the names of *tupak* without any discrimination. —1159

Saying the word "Kshmeshani," add the word "Mathani" and know the names of *tupak* for causing the wise men to listen to them. —1160

ROOAAL STANZA

Saying the word "Dharneeshani," add the word "Ari" at the end and recognise the names of *tupak*. —1161

ARIL

Saying firstly the words "Dhaval-Dhareeshani," add the word "Arini" at the end and know cleverly the innumerable names of *tupak*. —1162

CHAUPAI

Saying firstly the words "Vrashabh-Dhareeshani," add the word "Ari" at the end and know all the names of *tupak*. —1163

Saying firstly the word "Dhaavleshani," add the word "Mathani" at the end and know all the names of *tupak*. —1164

ARIL

Saying firstly the words "Dhaval-ishani," add the word "Arini" at the end and know the names of *tupak* for pronouncing before the talented persons. —1165

Saying the words "Vrashabhani-ishani," add the word "Mathani" at the end and know all the names of *tupak* in your mind. —1166

Saying firstly the words "Gaavis-ishani" add the word "Arini" at the end and know the names of *tupak* for using them in poetry. —1167

Saying firstly the words "Bhoom-ishani," add the word "Mathani" at the end and know all the names of *tupak* for using as desired. —1168

CHAUPAI

Saying firstly the word "Urvishani," add the word "Mathani" at the end and know all the names of *tupak*. —1169

Saying firstly the word "Jagtaashani," add the word "Mathani" at the end and know the names of *tupak* without any discrimination. —1170

Saying firstly the word "Vasumanteshani" add the word "Arini" at the end and know all the names of *tupak*. —1171

ARIL

Uttering the word "Vasudheshani," add the word "Mathani" at the end and know all the names of *tupak*. —1172

Saying firstly the word "Vasundhreshani," add the word "Arini" at the end and know all the names of *tupak* cleverly in your mind. —1173

Saying firstly the word "Vasunteshni," add the word "Arini" at the end and know all the names of *tupak*. —1174

CHAUPAI

Saying firstly the words "Samudra-neeshani," speak the word "Arini" and O good men! know the names of *tupak* in your mind. —1175

Saying the words "Samundra-neeshani," add the word "Arini" and know all the names of *tupak*. —1176

Saying firstly the word "Achleshni," add the word "Mathani" at the end and know the names of *tupak* for using them as desired. —1177

Saying firstly the word "Vipleeshani," add the word "Arini" at the end and recognise all the names of *tupak* without any discrimination. —1178

ARIL

Saying firstly the word "Saagraa," add the word "Ish-dalanani" and know all the names of *tupak* for using them in poetry. —1179

Saying firstly the word "Mahaaranavi," add the words "Patmardanani" at the end and fearlessly know all the names of *tupak*. —1180

CHAUPAI

Saying firstly the word "Sindhuni," add the word "Ardani" afterwards and know all the names of *tupak*. —1181

Saying the word "Neeraalayani," add the word "Naasik-arini" and know all the names of *tupak* without any discrimination. —1182

Saying firstly the word "Jaalayani," utter the words "Patiarini" and recognise all the names of *tupak*. —1183

Saying firstly the word "Vaaridhini," add the words "Pati-ari" and speak the names of *tupak* for the talented people. —1184

Saying the word "Dhareshani," add the word "Mathani" at the end and know all the names of *tupak* without any doubt. —1185

Saying the word "Lorbhareshani," add the word "Mathani" and recognise all the names of *tupak*. —1186

Uttering the word "Goraa," add the words "Ish-antakni" at the end and recognise all the names of *tupak*. —1187

Saying the word "Avneeshani," add the word "Mathani" and know fearlessly all the names of *tupak*. —1188

Saying firstly the word "Diggajani," speak the word "Ishaaradni" at the end and recognise the names of *tupak* for using then according to your inclination. —1189

Saying firstly the words "Kumbhnaashini," add the word "Arini" at the end and recognise all the names of *tupak*. —1190

Saying firstly the word "Maheeshani," add the word "Arini" at the end and know all the names of *tupak*. —1191

Placing firstly the word "Medneeshani," add the word "Ghaayak" at the end and recognise all the names of *tupak*. —1192

ARIL

Saying firstly the word "Vasundhreshani," add the word "Aahani" and know all the names of *tupak* in your mind. —1193

CHAUPAI

Saying the word "Vasundhreshani" add the word "Mathani," at the end and know all the names of *tupak* for talented people. —1194

Saying firstly the word "Naraadhipani," add the word "Mathani" at the end and know all the names of *tupak*. —1195

ARIL

Saying firstly the word "Manushyeshani" utter the word "Antakani" and recognise all the names of *tupak* without any doubt. —1196

Saying firstly the word "Desh-ishani," add the word "Ardani" at the end and know all the names of *tupak* for using them in poetry. —1197

Saying firstly the word "Janpadeshani," add the word "Antyantakani" and know all the names of *tupak*. —1198

Saying firstly the word "Maanvendrani," utter the word "Antyantakani" and know the names of *tupak* for the present, past and future. —1199

Saying firstly the word "Lokendrani," add the word "Harni" at the end and know all the names of *tupak* in your mind for speaking them day and night. —1200

CHAUPAI

Saying firstly the word "Lokraajani," add the word "Arini" at the end and know all the names of *tupak* as spoken in Shastras and Smritis. —1201

Saying the words "Deseshani Ramanani" add the word "Antakani" at the end and know all the names of *tupak*. —1202

Saying the word "Sitharaa," utter the word "Ishani," then add the word "Antakani" and in this way know the names of *tupak*. —1203

ARIL

Saying the words "Kashyapi-ishani" add the word "Antyantakani" and utter all the names of *tupak* unhesitatingly. —1204

Saying the word "Naagin," add the words "Pitani Ishaniwant," then add the word "Ghatani" and know all the names of *tupak*. —1205

Saying the words "Saraptaatani-ishani," add the word "Mathani" at the end and know fearlessly all the names of *tupak* in your mind. —1206

Saying the word "Indredarni," add the word "Mathani" at the end and get the knowledge of all the names of *tupak* for using them in poetry. —1207

CHAUPAI

Saying the word "Devdevani," add the word "Ishraantakan" and know all the names of *tupak*. —1208

ARIL

Saying firstly the words "Sakartaat Arini," add the word "Mathani" at the end and recognise all the names of *tupak* in your mind and use them in discourses. —1209

Saying the words "Satkriteshani-shishani," add the word "Arini" at the end know all the names of *tupak*. —1210

CHAUPAI

Saying firstly the words "Shachi-pateeshani-ishani," add the word "Mathani," at the end and know all the names of *tupak*. —1211

ARIL

Saying the words "Sakrandan-taatani-ishani," add the word "Mathani" at the end and recognise the names of *tupak* cleverly and guilelessly. —1212

Saying the words "Kauskeshani-ishani," add the word "Mathani" at the end and know all the names of *tupak* unhesitatingly. —1213

CHAUPAI

Saying the words "Vaasav-ishani," add the word

SHRI SHASTAR NAAM-MAALA PURANA

"Arini" at the end and know all the names of *tupak* unhesitatingly. —1214

ARIL

Saying the words "Varhaarshani-arini," speak all the names of *tupak* in your mind and I say truly, use these names unhesitatingly. —1215

DOHIRA

By uttering the words "Mathveshani Ishvarni," the names of *tupak* are formed correctly. —1216

By uttering the words "Matuleshani-ishani Mathani," the names of *tupak* are formed, which the poet may improve. —1217

CHAUPAI

Saying firstly the word "Jisneshani," add the words "Ishani-Mathani" at the end and know the names of *tupak* of using them at the desired place. —1218

ARIL

Saying the words "Durandar-ishani," add the words Isani-Mathani" and know all the names of *tupak*, uttering them unhestitatingly. —1219

Saying firstly the words "Vajarbhareshani-arini," know thoughtfully the names of *tupak* in your mind, use them without caring for any poet. —1220

Saying the words "Tukhaar Pitani Ishani," add the word "Arini" at the end and recognise all the names of *tupak* in your mind. —1221

Saying firstly the words "Indreni Indraani," add the word "Arini" at the end and know fearlessly all the names of *tupak* for using them. —1222

Saying the words "Ucchshrivaaish Ishani," add the word "Ishani" and "Arini" and know the innumerable names of *tupak* for using them unhesitatingly. —1223

Saying the words "Hayani Ishani Ishani Ishani," add the words "Arini" at the end and know all the names of *tupak* in your mind. —1224

Saying the words "Gajraaj Rajanani Prabhuni," add the word "Mathani" at the end and know all the names of *tupak* without any discrimination. —1225

Saying the words "Ashav Ishani Ishani Ishani," add the word "Mathani" at the end and know all the names of *tupak* unhesitatingly. —1226

Saying the words "Waahiraaj Raajanani Raajan," add the word "Arini" at the end and know all the names of *tupak*. —1227

Saying firstly the words "Turang Ishani Ishani Prabhuni," add the word "Shatru" at the end and know all the names of *tupak* in your mind and use them before the talented persons unhesitatingly. —1228

CHAUPAI

Saying the words "Aayasupati Pitani," utter the words "Ishani Arini" and know the names of *tupak* for speaking them in stanzas of poetry. —1229

ARIL

Saying all the names of Baaji Raaj add the words "Prabhuni, Pitani, Ishani and Arini," recognise all the names of *tupak* and use them as desired. —1230

Saying the words "Hasit Ish Prabhu Pitani Garvini," add the word "Arini" at the end and know the names of *tupak* for using them in poetry. —1231

Saying the words "Dantiraat Prabhupit Sutani," add the word "Arini" at the end and know all the names of *tupak* in your mind. —1232

Saying the words "Durdraateshani Ishani," add the word "Arini" at the end and knowing all the names of *tupak*, use them in poetry. —1233

Saying the words "Dayupi-ish Ishani Mathani," add the word "Arini" at the end and know all the names of *tupak* in your mind. —1234

Saying firstly the words "Padmaaish Ishraatin," add the word "Arini" at the end and recognise all the names of *tupak*. —1235

Saying firstly the words "Vaarnendra Indrani Indrani," add the word "Arini" at the end and know all the names of *tupak* considering them as true. —1236

Saying firstly the words "Vyaalaha Pato Patani," add the word "Ardan" at the end and know the innumerable names of *tupak* for using them as desired. —1237

Saying the words "Imbhasheshani Ishani Ishani," add the word "Hantri" at the end and know all the names of *tupak*. —1238

Saying the words "Kumbhesh Ish Ishani," add the words "Ishani Arini" and know all the names of *tupak*. —1239

Saying the words "Kunjresh Ish Pitani Puabhuni," add the word "Hantri" at the end and know all the names of *tupak*. —1240

Saying the words "Kari-Indra Indrani Indrani," add the word "Pitani" at the end and know the names of *tupak* for using them in poetry. —1241

Saying the words "Taruvar Prabhu Prabhuni," add the word "Arini" at the end and know all the names of *tupak*. —1242

Saying the words "Saudis Ish Ish Ishani," add the word "Arini" at the end and know all the names of *tupak*. —1243

Saying the words "Sindhuresh Ishpati," add the word "Prabhuni" and "Arini" at the end and know all the names of *tupak* for using them in Kabits and Dohiras. —1244

Saying the words "Anikpendra Indrani Indrani," utter the word "Arini Ishani" at the end and know all the names of *tupak*. —1245

Saying the words "Naaginaahinaa Ishani," add the word "Mathani" at the end and know all the names of *tupak* for mentioning them in books. —1246

Saying firstly the words "Harpati Pati Pati Patani," add the word "Arini" and at the end and know all the names of *tupak* for cleverly using them in stanzas of poetry. —1247.

CHAUPAI

Saying the words "Gajpati Nirapni Nirapni" add the words "Nirapni Arini" and know all the names of *tupak* for using them in Dohiras and Chaupais. —1248

ARIL

Saying the words "Saavaj Nrip Nrip Nripati Nripani," add the word "Arini" at the end and knowing the innumerable names of *tupak*, use then in the stanzas of poetry. —1249

CHAUPAI

Saying firstly the word "Maatang," add the word "Nrip" four times and utter the word "Arini" at the end and know all the names of *tupak*. —1250

Saying firstly the word "Gayandan," add the word "Nrip" four times, then the word "Arini" and know all the names of *tupak*. —1251

Saying the word "Baaji" then adding the word "Nrip" four times, recognise the names of *tupak*, without any discrimination. —1252

Saying the word "Baahu," add the word "Nrip" four times and know all the names of *tupak* for using them as desired. —1253

Saying firstly the word "Turang," add the word "Nrip" four times and know all the names of *tupak* for using them as desired. —1254

Saying the word "Haya," add the word "Nrip" four times and know all the names of *tupak*. —1255

Saying firstly the word "Bari," add the word "Nrip" four times and speaking the word "Ari" at the end, know the names of *tupak*. —1256

Saying the word "Dev" and adding the word "Nrip" three times, utter the word "Shatru" and know all the names of *tupak*. —1257

Saying the word "Amar," add the word "Nrip" three times and then adding the word "Ari," know the names of *tupak*. —1258

Saying the word "Nirjar" add the word "Nrip" three times and then uttering the word "Ari," know the names of *tupak* unhesitatingly. —1259

Saying firstly the word "Vibuddh," add the word "Nrip" three times and then adding the word "Ripu," know the names of *tupak* without any hestitation. —1260

Saying firstly the word "Sur," add the word "Nrip" three times and then adding the word "Ari" at the end, know all the names of *tupak*. —1261

Saying the word "Suman," add the word "Naayak" three times and then adding the word "Ari" at the end, know all the names of *tupak*. —1262

Saying firstly the word "Tridevesh," add the word "Nrip" three times, and then uttering the word "Ari" at the end, know all the names of *tupak*. —1263

Saying the word "Vrindraarak," add the word "Naayak" three times and then adding the word

SHRI SHASTAR NAAM-MAALA PURANA

"Ari" at the end, know all the names of *tupak*. —1264

Saying firstly the word "Gatibivaan," add the word "Padihi" three times and then uttering the word "Ari" at the end, know all the names of *tupak*. —1265

ARIL

Saying firstly the word "Amartesh," add the word "Pati" three times and then uttering the word "Shatru" at the end and in this way, know all the names of *tupak* in your mind. —1266

Saying firstly the word "Madhu," add the word "Pati" three times and then the word then the word "Ari" and know the names of *tupak*. —1267

Saying firstly the word "Sudhaa," add the word "Nrip" three times at the end and then uttering the word "Ripu," know the names of *tupak* for using them unhesitatingly. —1268

Saying firstly the word "Payukh," add the word "Nrip" three times and then adding the word "Ripu," know the names of *tupak*. —1269

Saying the word "Asudaa," add the word "Nrip" three times and then the word "Ripu," know the names of *tupak* for using them in the Soratha stanza. —1270

Saying firstly the word "Praan," add the word "Nrip" four times and then uttering the word "Ari" at the end, know the names of *tupak*. —1271

Saying firstly the word "Jeevdat," add the word "Nrip" four times and considering my words as true today and adding the word "Ari" at the end, know all the names of *tupak*. —1272

CHAUPAI

Staying firstly the word "Bapudaa," add the word "Nayak" four times and then uttering the word "Shatru" at the end, know all the names of *tupak*. —1273

Saying the word "Deh," add the word "Pati" four times and then adding the word "Ari" at the end, use smilingly the names of *tupak* in Jhoolnaa stanza. —1274

Saying firstly the word "Praandat," add the word "Nrip" four times and then adding the word "Ari" at the end, know all the names of *tupak*. —1275

ARIL

Uttering the word "Jaraa" from the mouth, add the word "Ripu" and then the word "Nrip" four times, then adding the word "Shatru" at the end, know the names of *tupak*. —1276

Saying firstly the word "Vriddhataa," add the word "Shatru" after that and also add the word "Shatru" again, then know all the names of *tupak*. —1277

CHAUPAI

Uttering the word "Jaraa," add the word "Hari" to it and then uttering the word "Ari" from the mouth, know all the names of *tupak* authentically. —1278

ARIL

Saying the word "Aalasaya," add the word "Nrip" four times, then add the word "Ari" and in this way know all the names of *tupak* and use them fearlessly in Paadhari stanza. —1279

Saying the word "Tarundant" from the mouth, add the word "Ari" then uttering the word "Nrip" four times and adding the word "Ari," describe the names of *tupak* in Rooaal stanza. —1280

Saying the word "Yovnaantak," add the word "Nrip" four times and then adding the word "Ari" and recognising the names of *tupak*, use them in Chaupai stanza. —1281

Saying the word "Tarundant," add the word "Nrip" four times and in this way, use the names of *tupak* consciously in Dohira stanza. —1282

Saying the words "Yovnaari Ari," add the word "Nrip" four times and uttering the word "Shatru" at the end, know all the names of *tupak*. —1283

Saying the words "Chaturath Avasthaa Ari," add the word "Nrip" four times and then uttering the word "Shatru" at the end know all the names of *tupak*. —1284

Uttering firstly the names of the noose of Yama, add the word "Har" and then the word "Nrip" four times and in this way, O good poet! know the names of *tupak* and use them consciously in Swayyas. —1285

Saying firstly the words "Aribalaari Ari," add the word "Pati" four times and know all the names of *tupak* for using then in Kundaliyaa stanza. —1286

Saying firstly the words "Aarjaar Ari," add the word "Nrip" four times and uttering the word "Ari," recognise all the names of *tupak* for using them in Jhoolnaa stanza. —1287

Saying firstly the words "Dehvaasi ari Har" and uttering the word "Nrip" four times, add the word "Ari," know the names of *tupak* for using them fearlessly in Aril stanza. —1288

Saying firstly the words "Vapuvaasi Ari," add the word "Nrip" four times and uttering the word "Ari," know the names of *tupak* for using them in Chachariyaa stanza. —1289

Saying firstly the words "Tanvassi Ari Har," add the word "Nrip" four times and uttering the word "Ari," recognise cleverly the names of *tupak* for using them as desired. —1290

Saying firstly the word "Asur," add the word "Pitr" and then the word "Nrip" at the end and then uttering the word "Ari," recognise the names of *tupak* for using them as desired. —1291

Saying the word "Raakshsaari," add the word "Pati" four times and then uttering the word "Ari" at the end, know the names of *tupak* for conveying to all unhesitatingly. —1292

Saying firstly the word "Daanvaari," add the word "Nrip" four times and then adding the word "Ari," know the names of *tupak* for uttering them fearlessly. —1293

Saying firstly words "Asraardan Ari" and adding the word "Nrip" three times at the end, then uttering the word "Ari," know all the names of *tupak* for instructing all. —1294

Saying firstly the word "Sakar," add the word "Ari" and then uttering the word "Pati" four times, then adding the word "Shatru" at the end, know all the names of *tupak* cleverly. —1295

Saying the words "Satkrit Ari Ari," add the word "Nrip" four times, then adding the word "Shatru" at the end, know the names of *tupak*. —1296

Saying firstly the words "Shachipatir Ari," add the word "Nrip" four times and then adding "Ari," know the names of *tupak* and use them unhesitatingly in Jhoolnaa stanza. —1297

Saying the words "Sakar-radan Ari-ripu," add the word "Nrip" three times and then adding the word "Shatru," know the names of *tupak* for using them in Jhoolnaa stanza. —1298

Saying the word "Purhootari," then utter the words "Ari Pitneesh Ari" and know the names of *tupak* cleverly for using them unhesitatingly in Soratha. —1299

Saying the words "Vaasvaari Ari" add the words "Pitni Ishani Ishani Arini" and know the names of *tupak* for using them in Dohira stanza. —1300

Saying the words "Vritdaa Ari Ari," add the word "Ish" three times, then adding the word "Ripu" know the names of *tupak* and convey to the one who wants to know them. —1301

Saying firstly the words "Maghvaantak Ari," add the word "Nrip" three times and then adding the word "Ripu," know the names of *tupak* for using them in discourses and devotional singing. —1302

Saying firstly the words "Maatleshwar Ari," add the word "Nrip" three times, then uttering the word "Shatru" at the end, know the names of *tupak* wisely. —1303

Saying firstly the words "Jisnaatak Antak," add the word "Raaj" three times and then adding the word "Ari" at the end, know all the names of *tupak*. —1304

Saying firstly the words "Purandraari Ari," add the word "Nrip" three times at the end, then adding the word "Shatru," know the names of *tupak* scholarly. —1305

CHAUPAI

Saying the words "Vajardharar Ari," add the word "Ishwar" three times then add the word "Ari" at the end and know all the names of *tupak*. —1306

ARIL

Saying firstly the words "Tukhaar Ari Ari," add the word "Nrip" three times at the end, then adding further the word "Shatru" at the end, know all the names of *tupak*. —1307

Saying the words "Ripupaakar Ripu," add the word "Nayak" three times then uttering the word "Ripu" at the end, pronounce the names of *tupak*. —1308

Saying firstly the words "Indrantak Ari," add the word "Nayak" three times, then adding the word "Shatru" at the end, know all the names of *tupak* in your mind. —1309

Uttering the word "Dev" from your mouth, add the word "Ardan" at the end, after that speak the word "Pati" three times, then adding the word "Ari," know the names of *tupak* in your mind. —1310.

Saying the words "Amraa Ardan," add the word "Nayak" three times, then uttering the word "Ripu," use the names of *tupak* in poetry without any discrimination. —1311

Saying firstly the words "Nirjaraari Ardan," add the word "Nrip" three times, then uttering the word "Ari," know the names of *tupak* for using them in Aril stanza. —1312

Saying firstly the words "Vibudhantak Antak," add the word "Nrip" three times, then uttering the word "Ripu," know the names of *tupak* for using them unhesitatingly in Rooaal stanza. —1313

Saying firstly the words "Saparbaan Pari Ari," add the word "Pati" three times, then uttering the word "Ari," know the names of *tupak* and use them fearlessly in Chachariyaa stanza. —1314

Saying the word "Tridevesh," add the words "Ari Ari" and then the word "Nrip" three times, then connect the word "Shatru" at the end and know the names of *tupak*. —1315

Saying firstly the words "Brindaarak Ari Ari," add the word "Ari" three times, then uttering the word "Shatru" at end, and know the names of *tupak*. —1316

Saying the names of all-vehicles, utter the word "Gati," then speaking "Ari Ari," add the word "Nrip" four times, then add the word "Shatru" at the end and know the names of *tupak* intelligently. —1317

Saying the word "Aganjim," then uttering "Ari Ari," add the word "Nrip" four times, then speaking the word "Ripu," recognise the names of *tupak* and use them unhesitatingly in the stanzas of poetry. —1318

End of the fifth chapter entitled "The Names of *Tupak*" in Shri Shastar Naam-Maala Purana.

ZAFARNAMAH

The Epistle of Victory—The Sacred Utterance of the Tenth Sovereign

The Lord is perfect in all faculties. He is immortal and generous. He is the giver of victuals and emancipator. —1

He is the protector and helper, He is compassionate, giver of food and enticer. —2

He is the sovereign, treasure-house of qualities and guide; He is unparalleled and is without form and colour. —3

Through His generosity, He provides heavenly enjoyments to one without any wealth, falcon, army, property and authority. —4

He is transcendent as well as immanent; He is omnipresent, bestows honours. —5

He is holy, generous and preserver; He is merciful and provider of victuals. —6

The Lord is generous, the highest of the high; He, the preserver, is most beautiful. —7

The Lord is omniscient, the protector of the lowly; He, the friend of the poor, is the destroyer of the enemies. —8

He is the source of all virtues, keeper of *dharma*; He knows everything and is the source of all scriptures. —9

He is the perfect being and treasure of wisdom; He, the All-pervading Lord, is omniscient. —10

The Lord of the universe, knows all the sciences and breaks and knots of all complications. —11

He, the supreme and most high supervises the whole world; He, the sovereign of the universe, is the source of all learning. —12

STORY—HIKAYAT I (PARABLE I)

I have no faith in your oaths; the Lord Himself is the witness. —13

I have not an iota of faith in such a person, whose officers have relinquished the path of Truth. —14

Whosoever puts faith on the oath of *Quran*, he is subjected to punishment on the final reckoning. —15

He, who comes under the shade of the legendary Huma, a very brave crow cannot harm him. —16

He, who takes refuge of the fierce tiger; the goat, sheep and deer do not go near him. —17

Even if I had taken an oath on *Quran*, in concealment, I would not have budged an inch from my place. —18

How could forty famished persons fight in the battlefield, on whom ten lakh soldiers made a sudden attack. —19

Your army breaking the oath and in great haste plunged in the battlefield with arrows and guns. —20

For this reason, I had to intervene and had to come fully armed. —21

When all other methods fail, it is proper to hold the sword in hand. —22

I have no faith in your oaths on the *Quran*, otherwise I had nothing to do with this battle. —23

I do not know that your officers are deceitful, otherwise I would not have followed this path. —24

It is not appropriate to imprison and kill those, who put faith on the oaths of *Quran*. —25

The soldiers of your army, clad in black uniform, rushed like flies on my men. —26

Whosoever from them came near the wall of the

fort, with one arrow he was drenched in his blood. —27

None dared to come there near the wall, none faced then the arrows and destruction. —28

When I saw Nahar Khan in the battlefield, he was greeted with one of my arrows. —29

All those boasters who came near the wall, they were despatched in no time. —30

Another Afghan, with a bow and arrows came in the battlefield like a flood. —31

He shot arrows heroically, sometimes in senses and sometimes in madness. —32

He made several attacks and was drenched with blood; after killing two warriors, he breathed his last. —33

Khwaja Mardud hid himself behind the wall; he did not enter the field like a brave warrior. —34

If I had seen his face once, one of my arrows would have despatched him to the abode of death. —35

Many warriors wounded with arrows and bullets died in the battle on both the sides. —36

The darts were showered so violently, that the field became red like poppy flowers. —37

The heads and limbs of the dead were scattered in the field like the balls and sticks in the game of Polo. —38

When the arrows hissed and bows tinkled, there was a great hue and cry in the world. —39

There the spears and lances provided a dreadful sound and the warriors lost their senses. —40

How could bravery ultimately withstand in the filed, when only forty were surrounded by innumerable warriors. —41

When the lamp of the world veiled itself, the moon shone in brightness during the night. —42

He, who puts faith on the oaths of the *Quran*, the True Lord gives him the guidance. —43

There was neither any harm nor injury; my Lord the Vanquisher of the enemies, brought me to safety—44

I did not know that these oath-breakers were deceitful and followers of mammon. —45

They were neither men of faith, nor true followers of Isalm, they did not know the Lord, nor had faith in the Prophet. —46

He, who follows his faith with sincerity, he never budges an inch from his oaths. —47

I have no faith at all in such a person for whom the oath of the *Quran* has no significance. —48

Even if you swear a hundred times in the name of the *Quran*, I shall not trust you any more. —49

If you have even a little of faith in God, come in the battlefield fully armed. —50

It is your duty to act on these words, because for me, these words are like the orders of God. —51

If the Holy Prophet had been there himself, you would have acted on them with all your heart. —52

It is your duty and a binding on you to do as bidden in writing. —53

I have received your letter and the message, do, whatever is required to be done. —54

One should act on his words; the speech and action should correspond. —55

I agree with the words conveyed by the Qazi, but if you promise to come on the right path. —56

If you want to see the letter containing oaths, I can send you the same immediately. —57

If you come yourself in village Kangar, we can meet each other. —58

Do not bring in your mind the danger of coming there, because the Brar community acts according to my orders. —59

We can talk to each other in this way; kindly come so that we may have direct talk. —60

Your saying that I may bring for you a very fine steed of one thousand rupees and get this area as a fief (Jagir) from you, you may keep this thing in your mind. —61

I am the man of the Sovereign of sovereigns and His slave; He permits me, then I shall present myself there. —62

If he permits me, then I shall be present there in person. —63

If you worship One Lord, you will not cause any delay in this work of mine. —64

You should recognise the Lord, so that you may not talk ill or cause injury to anybody. —65

You are the sovereign of the world and you sit on the throne, but I wonder at your ill acts of injustice. —66

I wonder at your acts of piety and justice; I feel sorry at your sovereignty. —67

I wonder very much regarding your faith; anything said against truth brings downfall. —68

Do not be rash in striking your sword on helpless, otherwise the providence will shed your blood. —69

Do not be careless; recognise the Lord, who is averse to greed and flattery. —70

He, the Sovereign of sovereigns, fears none; He is the master of the earth and heavens. —71

He, the True Lord, is the master of both the worlds; He is the creator of all the creatures of the universe. —72

He is the preserver of all, from ant to elephant; He gives strength to the helpless and destroys the careless. —73

The True Lord is known as "Protector of the lowly," He is carefree and free from want. —74

He is unassailable and unparalleled; He shows the path as a guide. —75

You are strained by the oath of the *Quran*, therefore fulfil the promise made by you. —76

It is appropriate for you to become sane and do your task with severity. —77

What, if you have killed my four sons, the hooded cobra still sits coiled up. —78

What type of bravery it is to extinguish the spark of fire and fan the flames? —79

Listen to this well-said quotation of Firdausi: "The hasty action is the work of Satan." —80

I have also come from abode of your Lord, who will be witness on the day of judgement. —81

If you prepare yourself for the good action, the Lord will give you an apt reward. —82

If you forget this task of justice, the Lord will forget you. —83

The righteous has to tread the path of truth and virtue, but it is still better to recognise the Lord. —84

I do not believe that that man recognises the Lord, who injures the sentiments of others through his actions. —85

The true and merciful Lord does not love you, though you have unaccountable wealth. —86

Even if you swear a hundred times by the *Quran*, I shall never trust you. —87

I cannot come to you and am not prepared to tread your path of oaths; I shall go, wherever my Lord will ask me to go. —88

You are king of kings, O fortunate Aurangzeb; you are a clever administrator and a good horseman. —89

With the help of your intelligence and the sword, you have become the master of Degh and Tegh. —90

You are the acme of beauty and wisdom; you are the chief of chiefs and the king. —91

You are the acme of the beauty and wisdom; you are the master of the country and its wealth. —92

You are most generous and a mountain in battlefield; you are like angels wielding high splendour. —93

Though you are the king of kings, O Aurangzeb! you are far from righteousness and justice. —94

I vanquished the idol-woshipping hill chiefs, they were idol-worshippers and I am idol-breaker. —95

Look at the time-cycle, quite undependable; whosoever pursues it, it brings his decline. —96

Think of the power of the Holy Lord, which causes one person to kill lakhs of people. —97

If God is friendly, no enemy can do anything, the generous actions proceed from the Merciful Lord. —98

He is the emancipator and the guide, who causes our tongue to sing His praises. —99

In troubled times He withdraws the faculty of sight from the enemies; He releases without injury the suppressed and the lowly. —100

He, who is trutful and follows the right path, the Merciful Lord is graceful towards him. —101

He, who surrenders his mind and body to Him, the True Lord is graceful towards him. —102

No enemy can ever beguile him, on whom the Merciful Lord showers His Graces. —103

When one man is attacked by a lakh, the Generous Lord gives him protection. —104

Just as your hopes lie in your wealth, I depend upon the Grace of the Lord. —105

You are proud of your kingdom and wealth, but I take refuge in the Non-temporal Lord. —106

Do not be careless about this fact that this *sarai* (resting place) is not the permanent abode. —107

Look at the time-cycle, which is undependable; it gives a fatal blow to everything of this world. —108

Do not oppose the lowly and helpless; do not break the oaths taken on the *Quran*. —109

If God is friendly, what the enemy can do? Though he may be inimical in many ways. —110

The enemies may try to give thousand blows, but he cannot harm even one hair, (if God is friendly). —111

God is unaccountable, indestructible, devoid of form and mark, unfathomable, beyond all illusions and all accounts. —112

He is devoid of attachment, form, mark and colour; He is unborn, casteless, elementless and eternal. —113

He is impregnable, undistinguishable, inactive and devoid of emotions. He is sorrowless, indiscriminate, illusionless and emotionless. —114

He is formless, guiseless, accountless, eternal, merciful, colour of colours and graceful. —115

Here ends the first Hikayat.